Walker & Walker's
English Legal System

Walker & Walker's

English Legal System

Eighth Edition

Richard Ward LLB
Solicitor;
Professor of Public Law and Head of the Department of Law,
De Montfort University

Butterworths
London, Edinburgh, Dublin
1998

United Kingdom	Butterworths, a Division of Reed Elsevier (UK) Ltd, Halsbury House, 35 Chancery Lane, LONDON WC2A 1EL and 4 Hill Street, EDINBURGH EH2 3JZ
Australia	Butterworths, a Division of Reed International Books Australia Pty Ltd, CHATSWOOD, New South Wales
Canada	Butterworths Canada Ltd, MARKHAM, Ontario
Hong Kong	Butterworths Asia (Hong Kong), HONG KONG
India	Butterworths Asia, NEW DELHI
Ireland	Butterworth (Ireland) Ltd, DUBLIN
Malaysia	Malayan Law Journal Sdn Bhd, KUALA LUMPUR
New Zealand	Butterworths of New Zealand Ltd, WELLINGTON
Singapore	Butterworths Asia, SINGAPORE
South Africa	Butterworths Publishers (Pty) Ltd, DURBAN
USA	Lexis Law Publishing, CHARLOTTESVILLE, Virginia

A CIP Catalogue record for this book is available from the British Library.

Seventh edition   1994

ISBN 0 406 99682 2

Printed by The Bath Press, Somerset

Visit us at our website: http://www.butterworths.co.uk

Preface

Change to, and within, the English legal system continues at a furious pace. During the last four years, major developments have occurred in respect of the legal profession and provision of legal services, legal aid, judicial review, the police, magistrates' courts service and the civil justice process. The same period has seen three major pieces of criminal justice legislation, and the incorporation of the European Convention on Human Rights into domestic law. Many other changes of significance have been made to the law. Few parts of this book have remained unaffected by legislative or judicial developments.

This new edition seeks to reflect the main thrust of these changes, within the philosophy of providing a clear, and relatively concise, exposition of the main principles, rules and issues, and within a manageable length. The opportunity has been taken to continue the restructuring begun in the last edition, to provide scope to reflect this wealth of change. The book contains a new chapter on the European Convention on Human Rights, to reflect the passage of the Human Rights Bill, and a new chapter on Sentences, to reflect the incessant, and sometimes unnecessary, changes made since 1994. A new chapter on Tribunals and Inquiries, and a re-organisation of Part III to enable focus on the developments in civil justice, feature in this edition. Significant re-writing has occurred in many areas. To accommodate the wealth of additional material, the section on Evidence has had to go (albeit with regret). Evidence is now a specialist area, one where the rules relating to criminal and civil process increasingly diverge, and one where accurate treatment is increasingly difficult within the available space. Despite this, many of the key evidential principles feature strongly in the sections on civil and criminal procedure, and the chapter on police powers.

The law is stated as at 1 July 1998. References to the Treaty of Rome are to the treaty as it currently stands, and not to the renumbered articles that flow from the Amsterdam Treaty.

Richard Ward

Leicester
August 1998

Contents

PART I

Sources of English Law

CHAPTER 18

County Court Proceedings 408

CHAPTER 19

Costs   425

CHAPTER 20

Civil Appeals   439

PART IV

Criminal Proceedings

CHAPTER 21

Criminal Proceedings   455

CHAPTER 22

Trial of an Indictable Offence   484

CHAPTER 23

Sentences 531

CHAPTER 24

Appeal Following Trial on Indictment 546

CHAPTER 25

Summary Procedure and Appeals 560

Table of statutes

Table of EC legislation

List of cases

C

H

M

PAGE

T

Part I

Sources of English Law

CHAPTER 1

Introductory Issues

A   THE CONTEXT

The legal system that exists in England and Wales[1] is a product of evolution over many centuries. Of course it is, in many respects, very different from that from which it has evolved. Modern problems and needs have led to widespread changes in the court system, in the organisation and functions of the legal profession, and in the procedures followed by the courts and those who work within them. New courts have been created.[2] A whole body of administrative justice has developed, leading to the resolution of many disputes between state and individual in tribunals and inquiries rather than in the courts themselves.[3] Indeed, increasing emphasis is placed on seeking to avoid proceedings at all, with the development of arbitration and mediation procedures.[4] Old procedures have been developed and refined to meet modern needs; one example is the way the old supervisory functions of the Crown have developed into the process of judicial review, which now plays an important role in the scrutiny of executive bodies of the state.[5] Many other examples could be given.

Yet to concentrate exclusively upon these important modern developments is to acquire an incomplete picture, for many institutions, structures and procedures can only be understood in the light of an awareness of the historical background into which they fit. Although the modern courts may be different from their predecessors, both in terms of structure and jurisdiction,[6] the court system can be traced back to its quite ancient origins. Many rules of procedure owe their existence to the nature of the institutions in which they originally arose. For example, the modern criminal trial is still essentially oral in nature. This owes much to the old forms of trial of criminal

---

1   Scotland and Northern Ireland are separate jurisdictions with their own courts and laws. This book deals only with England and Wales.
2   See, e.g., the Crown Court, created by the Courts Act 1971; p 176, *post*.
3   See p 197, *post*.
4   See p 331, *post*.
5   See p 141, *post*.
6   See further p 153, *post*.

offences, particularly trial by jury. Again, the modern procedure of judicial review[7] already referred to can be traced back to the supervisory powers of the Crown, exercised from the twelfth century onwards through the prerogative writs used to control the actions of inferior bodies and courts. A further example is the modern body of principles of equity. These principles owe their origins to the development of concepts of equity originally by the King in Council, and, later, through the work of the old Court of Chancery.

Nor are the substantive rules of law themselves immune from this historical influence: the modern law of contract and tort can best be understood in the light of the historical development of those areas of the law, and in the light of the procedural advantages and limitations of the writ system through which they developed.[8] It is these rules of law, developed by the courts, that comprise the common law.

Despite the fact that the detailed study of legal history has ceased to form a part of the legal education of most students, some awareness of overall trends is therefore to be encouraged. Whilst, of course, many factors have contributed to the development of the modern legal system, two fundamental, but inter-related, issues dominate the development of our institutions and procedures. The first is the role of the monarch. The second is the development of the common law and equity.

1   The role of the monarch

Historically the sovereign is the fountain of justice in England. For this reason, the administration of justice is part of the prerogatives of the Crown, part of the residual common law powers that still exist and which are unique to the Crown.[9] The monarch is to be regarded as the head of the legal system. The superior courts[10] are "the Queen's courts". The Crown appoints the senior judiciary.[11] The Crown has a residual power, and duty, to ensure the maintenance of law and order,[12] and to ensure that justice is done. An example of this is the royal prerogative of mercy.[13] All these powers are exercisable by the monarch on the advice of her ministers, as of course is required by modern constitutional convention.

That these powers exist in the form that they do demonstrates the crucial role the monarch has played historically. The development of the common law, which, as we shall see, is at the heart of the legal system, arose through the unifying influence and effect created by the actions of those administering justice on behalf of the monarch. In the eleventh and twelfth centuries, the King assumed control of the administration of justice throughout England through his judges and justices, thus creating, over a long period of time, a centralised system of courts, and which led to the decline (and eventual demise) of the local courts and jurisdictions.[14] This performance of legal functions by the King was originally through the King's Council, through his local representatives, the sheriffs, and, more importantly, through justices travelling the country on his behalf. The jurisdiction of the King's Council gradually gave rise to

7   See p 141, *post*.
8   See, for discussion: Maitland, *The Forms of Action at Common Law* (Cambridge University Press).
9   See p 141, *post*.
10   See p 162, *post*.
11   See p 210, *post*.
12   For a modern example, see *R v Secretary of State for the Home Department, ex parte Northumbria Police Authority* [1989] QB 26; [1988] 1 All ER 556.
13   See p 145, *post*.
14   See, generally: Baker, *An Introduction to English Legal History* (Butterworths, 3rd Edn, 1990). Certain local courts survived formally until 1973: the Bristol Tolzey and Pie Poudre Courts, the Liverpool Court of Passage, the Norwich Guildhall Court, all abolished by Courts Act 1971, s 43.

the emergence of the common law courts.[15] The old common law courts of Exchequer, Common Pleas and King's Bench developed, and each owed their existence to the practice of the King in Council issuing writs commanding that justice be done. Similarly with the Court of Chancery, which had as its principal function the administration of the principles and rules of equity.[16] These principles of equity developed as a response to the petitions that were made to the King complaining of the injustices caused by the provisions of, or gaps in, the common law. Over a period of time these petitions ceased to be dealt with by the King himself, but rather by the old Court of Chancery.[17]

Together these courts were the King's courts administering justice on behalf of the Crown. This power to provide and administer justice stemmed from the inherent power of the Crown itself, under what is now known as the Royal Prerogative. This historical basis remains important, even though the vast majority of courts now exist because of, and within the jurisdiction defined by, statute. The role of the monarch in ensuring that justice is done was historically performed through the issue of writs, royal commands that certain things should be done. The writ system was the mechanism through which developed the common law causes of action in contract and tort.[18] Equally importantly, royal writs were used to supervise the actions of inferior courts or bodies. As noted above, these prerogative writs today remain an important remedy to control the misuse of executive power, on judicial review.[19]

2 Common law and equity

Common law and equity are two of the three main *historical* sources of English law, the third being legislation. The term "common law" reflects the fact that the law as administered by the King's courts became the common law of England and Wales, gradually supplanting local custom, either by consolidation of customary local rules into rules of general application, or by the gradual erosion of local rules themselves. The law evolved from a mass of local custom (administered by local courts) into one system of law common throughout the country. As already noted, the role of the monarch in this process was crucial: the development of administration of justice through the King himself and through the King's representatives locally, whether the sheriff or itinerant justices acting on behalf of the King, ensured the development of common and consistent rules of law. These in turn led to the administration of these common rules by courts that evolved from the royal institutions into separate courts, administering justice independently from, but in the name of, the King. The three principal courts were the Court of Exchequer, the Court of Common Pleas, and the Court of King's Bench. Thus each owed its origin to the monarch's role as the fountain of justice, originally exercised by the King in Council. These courts, dispensing justice on behalf of the monarch, were abolished by the Judicature Acts 1873–75,[20] and their jurisdiction transferred to the High Court, principally, though not exclusively, to the Queen's Bench Division.

By contrast equity itself developed to remedy the deficiencies of the common law. As the common law itself grew more rigid, principally through the writ system, those affected by that rigidity and who suffered injustice as a result would petition the King to exercise his prerogative in their favour. These petitions, at first dealt with by the

15 See p 154, *post*.
16 They are described in detail in the 6th edition of this work (1985), pp 47–55.
17 See p 159, *post*.
18 See: Milsom, *Historical Foundations of the Common Law* (Butterworths, 2nd Edn 1981).
19 See p 142, *post*.
20 For the main courts prior to 1875, see pp 153–160, *post*.

King in Council and then delegated to the King's chief minister, the Chancellor, later became formalised and dealt with in the courts of equity, leading to the formal development of the Court of Chancery, which was the principal forum for the administration of the principles of equity until its abolition in 1875.[1]

B   THE HISTORICAL SOURCES

1   Common law

It will be clear from what has already been said that the common law is one of the most important of the historical sources of law. In civil matters the law developed through the procedures that existed. One basic principle underpinned its growth: that a common law right only existed if there was a procedure for enforcing it *(ubi remedium ibi ius)*. For that reason substantive law became inextricably bound up with procedure, and, in particular, through the forms of action that developed in respect of various types of action, where real actions (actions involving land) or personal actions (involving claims) principally involved matters we would now categorise as contractual or tortious. The nature of the right sought to be enforced, and the nature of the procedure through which it could be enforced, would determine the court which would deal with such matters. Historically, such common law claims, enforced through what were known as the forms of actions, became highly technical, with the nature of the form of action often determining the content of the law, and whether a particular claim could succeed. This rigid "writ system" was effectively abolished by the Common Law Procedure Acts 1852 and 1854, resulting in the categorisations of claims becoming far less important. The law now strives to concentrate upon substance rather than form. However, the dangers that rigid procedural distinctions can create have not totally disappeared since the abolition of the writ system as described above. As recently as 1991 Henry J in *Doyle v Northumbria Probation Committees*[2] observed that the procedural requirements that now exist in respect of the challenge of public bodies was one area:

> "where the forms of action abolished by the Common Law Procedure Act 1854 in the 19th Century appear to be in danger of returning to rule us from their graves."

The extent to which the modern law of judicial review of the actions of public bodies has avoided this danger is an issue which is considered later.[3]

In criminal matters the common law developed the forms of trial which, in nature if not in detail, still exist today. Ancient procedures such as Appeal of Felony, involving in many cases trial by battle, may have disappeared,[4] but trial on indictment, involving trial by jury,[5] is of ancient origin, and was undertaken in the old courts of Assize. With the Assize courts can be bracketed the courts of Quarter Session, where judges sat usually with justices of the peace, an office of some antiquity. Both courts existed until the creation of the Crown Court by the Courts Act 1971.[6] In addition to these two courts,

1   Principles of equity are now administered and applied by all courts.
2   [1991] 4 All ER 294; [1991] 1 WLR 1340.
3   See p 147, *post*.
4   Trial by battle was not formally abolished until the decision in *Ashford v Thornton* (1818) 1 B & Ald 405 reminded Parliament that it still theoretically existed.
5   See p 230, *post*.
6   See p 176, *post*.

the criminal law was also enforced summarily, through trial by justices of the peace[7] without a jury. Though procedures are much changed, these forms of trial are distinctly recognisable to modern eyes, and form the basis for the development of the common law rules of criminal law and evidence that still play a significant role.

2   Equity

The nature of equity, and the reasons for its development, have already been noted. The distinction between common law and equity caused significant problems. Frequently in conflict with the common law, equity both supplemented the common law and corrected its deficiencies. In so far as the former was concerned, it was not repugnant to common lawyers; by contrast, the correction of the deficiencies of the common law created direct conflict between two systems of law, ultimately resolved,[8] though not without continued conflict, in favour of equity. The fact remained that the existence of two separate systems of law, administered by separate courts was bound to cause not only conflict, but also complex and inconvenient duality of jurisdiction, with differing procedures and remedies, and with different routes of appeal. The Judicature Acts 1873–75 undertook reform of a fundamental nature. The purpose and immediate effect of this legislation was to create a unified system of courts and procedure. It did not, however, of itself merge the substantive rules themselves: it is still correct to talk, for example, about the principles of equity, or about equitable remedies.[9] However, the fact that the rules of common law and equity had not been administered and applied side by side led in reality to a merger not simply of procedures but of the rules themselves. Modern courts can apply equally rules of common law and equity, irrespective of their origins, and indeed it may not always be wholly clear to which side of historical development, common law or equity, a rule owes its parentage. Its effect upon substantive law is beyond doubt, principally in relation to matters affecting property and trusts, the law of contract, and through the development of important remedies, principally the injunction.

3   Legislation

This is the third major historical source. Originally, scarcely distinguishable from common law, the historic emergence of Parliament as the dominant force within the United Kingdom constitution[10] led to the growth of legislation as a major source of law, transcending in its importance common law or equity. Its role today is unquestioned. Common law and equity essentially are concerned with the application and development of principles: whilst a modern lawyer would accept that even in such matters judges make law,[11] the courts often consider themselves not to be the appropriate forum for the development of wholly new principles of law, a task usually

---

7   See p 182, *post*.
8   Earl of Oxford 's case (1615) 1 Rep Ch 1.
9   Injunctions are an important example. For remedies in civil proceedings, see p 357, *post*. For discussion generally of equity and equitable remedies, see Pettit, *Equity and The Law of Trusts* (Butterworths, 7th Edn, 1993).
10   Through the development of the doctrine of the legislative supremacy of Parliament. Under this, no court can question the validity of an Act of Parliament. See *British Railways Board v Pickin* [1974] AC 765; [1974] 1 All ER 609.
11   See further, p 216, *post*.

considered best left to Parliament.[12] Legislation can also amend or repeal existing statute. For these reasons legislation, and delegated legislation made under the authority of an Act of Parliament, is now to be considered also in the light of the legislation of the European Union[13] and the principles developed by the European Court of Human Rights.[14]

4   Custom

Custom is another, though now less important, source of law. The term has various meanings. In one sense, it merely identifies the very nature of the common law itself: the early common law was not an entirely new set of legal rules developed by judges on behalf of the King, but rather a unification and development of the many customs used and applied by the local courts. The early common law was not an entirely new set of rules but rather that body of rules resulting from the welding of the law and custom of England into one system of law, through the historical developments in the eleventh to the fourteenth centuries. In 1350 counsel declared that "common usage is common law".[15] These customs, such as monogamy, parental rights, the right to use the seashore for navigation and fishing[16] and most of the early criminal law, are no longer regarded as a separate source of law since they have either become part of the common law or been incorporated in statute.

A second use of the word "custom" is to describe conventional trade or business usage. This is really a misuse of the word since trade usage is usually relevant only to imply terms into contracts, so that the court can decide what terms the parties intended to apply. These are questions of fact rather than questions of law so that custom, in this context, is not a source of law at all. Trade customs need not be ancient[17] provided that they can be proved to be certain. However they must not be illegal or unreasonable and they may always be expressly excluded. Many trade customs were originally an elaborate method of granting discount to purchasers; hence the "baker's dozen" and the fact that 1,000 rabbits mean 1,200 rabbits to rabbit-dealers.[18] Ancient mercantile custom fulfilled a wider function than modern commercial usage since it was the basis of a set of rules of law collectively described as the law merchant. The law merchant, unlike trade usage, is a source of law and is considered below.

The third common use of the word "custom" is to describe local custom; rules of law which apply only in a definite locality. Custom, in this sense of the word, is a separate source of law. Local custom as a source of law, distinct from common law, has two elementary and unvarying characteristics: first, it must be an exception to the common law and, second, it must be confined in its application to a particular locality such as a county, borough or parish. It may be further limited to a class of persons within that locality, for example fishermen, but it cannot apply to a class of persons generally throughout the kingdom, for if it did it would be part of the common law and not an exception to it.

---

12   See *Malone v Metropolitan Police Commissioner (No 2)* [1979] Ch 344; [1979] 2 All ER 620, and p 219, *post. McLoughlin v O'Brian* [1983] 1 AC 410; [1982] 2 All ER 298.
13   See p 103, *post.*
14   See p 132, *post.*
15   10 YB 30 Edw 3, ff 25, 26.
16   Though not for bathing or beachcombing; see *Alfred F Beckett Ltd v Lyons* [1967] Ch 449; [1967] 1 All ER 833. For a modern example of reliance on customary fishing rights, see *Anderson v Alnwick District Council* [1993] 3 All ER 613.
17   See *Noble v Kennoway* (1780) 2 Doug KB 510 at 513, per Lord Mansfield.
18   *Smith v Wilson* (1832) 3 B & Ad 728.

Many local customs have been abolished by statute. The type of local customary right still existing is in the nature of a right of way, or right to indulge in sports and pastimes on a village green[19] or a right to dry fishing-nets on land within the parish.[20] Such rights only exist in law when formally recognised by judicial decision. Thus any person who alleges a customary right must plead it and prove its existence. This involves showing that the alleged custom satisfies certain tests. Blackstone's classification of these tests is the generally accepted arrangement and is as follows.

a   Antiquity

Local custom must have existed "from time whereof the memory of man runneth not to the contrary" (time immemorial). This has been fixed by statute at 1189,[1] the first year of the reign of Richard I. In practice positive proof of existence in 1189 is rarely available so that the courts are willing to accept as proof evidence that the custom has existed for a long time. This is often done by calling the oldest available local inhabitant as a witness. The burden is then on the party denying the existence of the custom to prove that it did not exist in 1189 or that it could not have existed in 1189.

b   Continuance

The right must have existed uninterrupted. Any interruption of the custom since 1189 defeats its existence. On the other hand mere non-use does not defeat the custom; a customary right, once acquired, can only be abolished or extinguished by Act of Parliament.[2]

c   Peaceable enjoyment

A custom can only exist by common consent. It must not have been exercised by the use of force, nor secretly, nor under a revocable licence (since this would make the custom dependent upon the will of one individual rather than on public observance) (*nec per vim nec clam nec precario*). Thus, where the right to fish depended upon the grant of a licence by the owners of an oyster fishery, it was held that there was no customary right to fish since enjoyment had never been as of right, but only by licence.[3]

d   Obligatory force

Where the custom imposes a specific duty, that duty must be obligatory. This is true of all rules of law. Indeed it is this which distinguishes a rule of law from a social convention or a moral obligation.

e   Certainty

The custom must be certain.

---

19   *New Windsor Corporation v Mellor* [1975] Ch 380; [1975] 3 All ER 44.
20   *Mercer v Denne* [1905] 2 Ch 538.
1   Statute of Westminster I 1275.
2   *Hammerton v Honey* (1876) 24 WR 603; *New Windsor Corporation v Mellor* [1975] Ch 380; [1975] 3 All ER 44.
3   *Mills v Colchester Corporation* (1867) LR 2 CP 476; see also *Alfred F Beckett Ltd v Lyons* [1967] Ch 449; [1967] 1 All ER 833.

f   Consistency

Customs must be consistent with one another, since inconsistent local customs cannot stand together.

g   Reasonableness

The last and most important test that custom must satisfy is that of reasonableness. It is for the party refuting the custom to show that it is unreasonable. A custom which is repugnant to a fundamental principle of common law cannot be reasonable. For this reason the House of Lords rejected a custom which enabled a manorial lord to undermine his tenant's land without paying compensation for damage to buildings thereby caused.[4] Equally a customary right to commit a crime could not be reasonable.

Furthermore, if a custom must obviously have been unreasonable in 1189 (though not necessarily unreasonable at the present day) this will tend to show that the custom could not have existed in 1189 and it will be rejected on this ground rather than on the basis of its being unreasonable. In *Bryant v Foot*[5] the rector of a parish claimed thirteen shillings as a customary fee for the celebration of a marriage in the parish. It was held that, having regard to the value of money in 1189, the amount was totally unreasonable so that the custom could not have existed at that date.

5   Law merchant

The law of contract as administered in the common law courts in the thirteenth and fourteenth centuries was extremely rudimentary. Broadly speaking an action could only be brought within certain narrow circumstances. In addition the local courts had only a limited jurisdiction in contract.[6] Thus the existing courts were ill-equipped to deal with the increasing volume of litigation arising from England's growth as a trading centre. The result was that a new set of courts sprang up to deal solely with disputes between merchants.[7] Since these courts were not common law courts they were not rigidly tied to the common law, and a new set of rules originating partly in custom and partly in international law evolved in these courts as a gloss on the common law. Since their decisions were subject to review by the Court of King's Bench by way of writ of error their rules and doctrines of necessity followed the fundamental tenets of the common law. As noted above, these courts have gone, and with them the separate rules of law different from the common law. Both have been assimilated. However, the modern legal system recognises that special courts and procedures may be necessary

---

4   *Wolstanton Ltd and Duchy of Lancaster v Newcastle-under-Lyme Corporation* [1940] AC 860; [1940] 3 All ER 101.
5   (1868) LR 3 QB 497.
6   This was limited by the Statute of Gloucester 1278 to claims involving less than 40 shillings.
7   These included courts of fairs and boroughs, known as courts of "pie poudre". The name possibly derived from the Latin *pes pulvericatus* (dusty foot) or from the old French *pied pulderaux* (pedlar). Other such courts were staple courts, which sat in towns having the power to deal in certain commodities. The last of these courts, the Bristol Tolzey and Pie Poudre Courts, was abolished by s 43 of the Courts Act 1971. Some of the borough courts were abolished by the Municipal Corporations Act 1883, s 2 and the Justices of the Peace Act 1949, s 10 while as part of the reorganisation of local government whereby boroughs were abolished, 141 borough civil courts were abolished by the Local Government Act 1972, s 221 and Sch 28. Finally, the jurisdiction of most of the remaining local courts, including all courts of pie poudre, was formally abolished by the Administration of Justice Act 1977, s 23 and Sch 4. The High Court of Admiralty, which had existed since the fourteenth century, had both civil and criminal jurisdiction over matters arising on the high seas; its jurisdiction was transferred to the Probate, Divorce and Admiralty Division of the High Court in 1875.

in order to deal effectively with commercial disputes. One such court is the Commercial court.[8]

6   Canon law

The canon law, the law of the Western or Catholic Church, has influenced the growth of English law in two ways. First it was the basis of many concepts, which were formulated in the law courts, and as such is a primary source of other sources of law. Examples of common law concepts which originated in the canon law are: the nature of criminal law and its close association with moral fault, imprisonment as a punishment for crime (the purpose of which the canonists conceived to be the possibility of repentance through solitary contemplation), and, of course, the nature of Christian marriage and family rights. In addition the old common law trial by ordeal relied for its efficacy on the participation of the clergy. Canon law also influenced the nature of equity, the strong moral content of which is attributable to the fact of the early Chancellors being clerics.

The second, and more important, way in which canon law became a source of English law was by its application in the ecclesiastical courts. In this context canon law was a system of law wholly independent of the common law since the ecclesiastical courts were, during the Middle Ages, completely outside the control of the King. Through a complex series of historical developments the jurisdiction of the ecclesiastical courts became clearly defined, and separate from the common law, except in areas of probate and matrimonial jurisdiction. Since 1857 the jurisdiction of the ecclesiastical courts has been confined to matters affecting members of the Church where this jurisdiction does not conflict with the jurisdiction of the ordinary courts.[9]

7   Roman law[10]

Roman law, the basis of most continental systems of law, is, surprisingly, of very minor importance as a source of English law. It is not a direct source at all in the sense that there was never a system of English courts applying solely Roman law. Any influence that Roman law has had on the growth of English law has been indirect. The source of law that owes most to Roman law is canon law. The reason is that the Chancellors and advocates in the ecclesiastical courts were indoctrinated with the civil law through their studies at Oxford and Cambridge. Thus the formal requirements of wills in many cases have their counterpart in Roman law as have many of the rules relating to parental authority. Roman law also undoubtedly influenced maritime and mercantile law since the Venetian and Genoese mercantile customs, which these branches of the law utilised, had a civilian basis.

The common law itself has from time to time borrowed from Roman law. The principal link between Roman law and common law is Bracton's treatise *De Legibus et Consuetudinibus Angliae* written in Latin in about the year 1250. Bracton was well versed in Roman law and the civilian principles he incorporated into his treatise owed much to the writings of the Roman jurist Justinian. Thus common law judges, faced with a case of first impression with little or no assistance to be gleaned from English precedents, have looked to Bracton for assistance and in doing so have adopted

8   See p 399, *post*.
9   See p 194, *post*.
10   See Lee, *Elements of Roman Law* (Sweet & Maxwell).

Romanist principles. The leading example is the judgment of Holt C J in *Coggs v Bernard*[11] which classifies bailments in accordance with Bracton's classification, itself based on Roman law.

C   THE EUROPEAN SOURCES

The importance of the traditional sources of common law and equity has already been noted. Of equal importance to the modern legal system are the European sources. There are two such sources, of very different types.

The first is the European Union, which has an impact as a direct source of law, and the institutions of which fall to be regarded as integral parts of the law-making and law-enforcement machinery. The second is the European Convention on Human Rights, which is not a direct source of law, and the institutions of which cannot be regarded as integral to the English legal system.

I   The European Union

Since 1972 the United Kingdom has been a member of the European Community, a supra-national body with its own legal personality and capacity to make and enforce laws, and, since 1992, known as the European Union. By virtue of the European Communities Act 1972 (as amended) these laws of the European Community form part of English law. The importance of the Community cannot be underestimated, and is such as to warrant separate treatment as one of the sources of law.[12] It should not simply be regarded as a separate system of law, but rather as a fundamental and important source of English law.

2   European Convention on Human Rights

The United Kingdom is a signatory to the Convention for the Protection of Human Rights and Fundamental Freedoms (1950),[13] usually referred to as the European Convention on Human Rights. The Convention, and the principles developed by its institutions, have not, hitherto, been a separate, direct, source of English law, although they have had increasingly a clear and important influence on the interpretation of statutes, development of the common law and decision-making of the Government as to whether to legislate, and in what respect. The extent and effect of this influence is considered later.[14] However, the position is changing. The Human Rights Bill of 1997 is expected to receive Royal Assent during 1998 and will give the principles, and rules of law, of the Convention a clear and important role as a source of English law. These changes, and their likely impact, are discussed later.[15]

11   (1703) 2 Ld Raym 909.
12   See p 94, *post.*
13   Cmnd 8969. The United Kingdom is not a signatory to Protocols 4, 6 or 7.
14   See p 128, *post.*
15   See p 132, *post.*

D   THE DISTINCTION BETWEEN CIVIL AND CRIMINAL MATTERS

1   The importance of the distinction

The law distinguishes between civil and criminal matters, and sometimes courts are classified into civil and criminal courts. This latter classification is useful for the purposes of exposition, but in reality is not a valid one. Although certain courts do exercise a purely civil or criminal jurisdiction, most exercise both civil and criminal jurisdiction. Thus the House of Lords, Court of Appeal, High Court, Crown Court and magistrates' court exercise jurisdiction in both civil and criminal matters.

This distinction between civil and criminal matters is important, for several reasons. First, the terminology used is different. A plaintiff sues a defendant in civil proceedings, or makes an application for a civil order. In a criminal case a prosecutor prosecutes an accused person.

Secondly, the burden and standard of proof differs. In a civil case, the burden of proof of any matter is upon the party asserting that matter, to the civil standard of the balance of probabilities.[16] In a criminal case, by contrast, the burden of proof is usually[17] on the prosecution, to be proved beyond reasonable doubt.[18] This statement itself disguises the fact that even in a civil case the standard of proof may be a high one. In *R v Wolverhampton Coroner, ex parte McCurbin*[19] an inquest, which is a civil inquiry into the cause of death by a coroners' court,[20] had to decide whether the death of an individual whilst being arrested by the police amounted to unlawful killing by the police, or, alternatively, to death by misadventure. The Divisional Court, in upholding the direction given by the coroner to the jury, concluded that the standard of proof necessary to establish unlawful killing was the criminal standard, whilst that for establishing death by misadventure was the civil standard of the balance of probabilities. Findings by coroners' courts of suicide, and of unlawful killing, have been held to require proof beyond reasonable doubt.[1] In *Halford v Brooks*,[2] a civil case where the allegation against the defendant was, in effect, one of murder, Rougier J observed:

"No-one, whether in a criminal or a civil court, should be declared guilty of murder, certainly not such a terrible crime as this, unless the tribunal was sure that the evidence does not admit of any other sensible conclusion ...".

---

16   The standard is not an absolute one: see *infra; Hornal v Neuberger Products Ltd* [1957] 1 QB 247, [1956] 3 All ER 970; *Khawaja v Secretary of State for the Home Department* [1984] AC 74, [1983] 1 All ER 765.

17   See *Woolmington v Director of Public Prosecutions* [1935] AC 462. For exceptions, see the defence of insanity, Magistrates' Courts Act 1980, s 101, and specific statutory exceptions.

18   For the meaning of this phrase, see *Miller v Minister of Pensions* [1947] 2 All ER 372, per Lord Denning. In a case where the burden of proof is on an accused the standard is the civil standard of the balance of probabilities: *R v Carr-Briant* [1943] KB 607; [1943] 2 All ER 156.

19   [1990] 1 WLR 719; [1990] 2 All ER 759.

20   See p 189, *post*.

1   *R v West London Coroner, ex parte Gray* [1988] QB 467; [1987] 2 All ER 129. Cf *Dunbar (administrator of Dunbar, dec'd) v Plant* [1998] Ch 412; [1997] 4 All ER 289, where in civil proceedings it was held that the standard of proof to establish the fact that a party had aided and abetted a suicide was the civil standard.

2   (1991) Times 3 October. In that case the approach taken in *Bater v Bater* [1951] P 35; [1950] 2 All ER 458, where Lord Denning indicated that a civil court does not have to adopt so high a degree as a criminal court, even when it is considering a charge of a criminal nature, was unhelpful.

Whether there are in fact two standards at all, or rather different levels of proof which vary according to what has to be proved, is a moot point, but such questions should not be approached in an artificial manner.[3]

Thirdly, whether a matter is civil or criminal will determine which rules of evidence apply to the case. Rules of evidence[4] in civil cases often differ from those that apply in a criminal case. This was well illustrated in *R v Governor of Belmarsh Prison, ex parte Levin*[5] where the House of Lords held that, because extradition proceedings were to be regarded as criminal proceedings, the rules contained in s 69 of the Police and Criminal Evidence Act 1984, governing evidence produced by a computer, applied.

Finally, of course, the fact that proceedings are criminal, or are to be regarded as criminal, will affect the procedures to be followed, and process of challenge. It will also affect the standards those procedures and rules have to meet. Article 6 of the European Convention on Human Rights[6] applies to a "criminal charge" and the trial of a "criminal offence". The fact that English law might classify proceedings as civil will not be conclusive in the context of the Convention. Proceedings before magistrates following non-payment of council tax and for binding over to keep the peace have each been regarded by the Commission on Human Rights as criminal for the purpose of that Convention.[7]

2   Decision as to whether a matter is civil or criminal

This decision is not always easy to make, and cannot be made simply by asking whether the court that deals with the matter is a civil or criminal court, for this merely begs the very question to be answered. One recent example of a court having to determine such a question is *ex parte Levin*.[8] The issue before the House of Lords was whether extradition proceedings before a magistrates' court were civil or criminal in nature. As noted above, this was crucial to the question of whether a statutory rule of evidence applied. In an earlier case[9] a Divisional Court appeared to conclude that extradition proceedings were not criminal proceedings, and noted the argument of counsel that they were *sui generis* (ie of a type of their own). This was a view with which Lord Hoffman, giving the decision of the House, disagreed, pointing to a contrary body of authority[10] and also to the fact that extradition proceedings should be conducted "as near as may be" as if they were committal proceedings before magistrates.[11]

Matters may cross the boundary between civil and criminal proceedings. Contempt of court can be both civil and criminal in nature.[12] The same acts or omissions may give rise to both civil and criminal proceedings. A motorist who causes damage, injury or loss of life may well be prosecuted for a motoring offence; that same motorist will almost certainly be liable in damages when sued by the aggrieved party, although, of course, the reality will often be that it will be an insurance company that will pay the compensation awarded. Again, the relatives of a person who has been unlawfully killed,

---

3   See *ex parte McCurbin*, ante.
4   See p 394, *post*.
5   [1997] AC 741, [1997] 3 All ER 289.
6   See p 125, *post*.
7   See *Benham v United Kingdom* (1996) 22 EHRR 293; *Steel v United Kingdom* (9 April 1997, unreported) App No 24838.
8   [1997] 3 All ER 289, *ante*.
9   *R v Governor of Belmarsh Prison, ex parte Francis* [1995] 3 All ER 634, [1995] 1 WLR 1121.
10   *Amand v Secretary of State for Home Affairs* [1943] AC 147; [1942] 2 All ER 381, where Viscount Simon LC said that a matter may be "criminal" although a person is not charged with a breach of the criminal law.
11   Extradition Act 1989, s 9(2) and Sch 1, para 6(1). For committal proceedings, see p 484, *post*.
12   See p 224, *post*.

but in respect of whose death no prosecution has been brought, may sue in tort, ostensibly for compensation but in reality to provide a forum in which the culpability of the defendant can be established. Yet another example is provided by cases where the victim of a rape sues her (or his)[13] assailant. That assailant is liable irrespective of whether any prosecution has been brought, or has succeeded.

There is also a growing tendency for links between civil and criminal process to be formally established. One example is the Protection from Harassment Act 1997. That Act makes it a criminal offence to pursue a course of conduct amounting to harassment of a person, or which causes a person to fear that violence will be used against him. However, s 3 creates a civil remedy in tort for a person who is, or may be, the victim of harasssment, and, in addition, a criminal court, when sentencing a person for an offence, may make a restraining order. This is a civil order, but breach of it without reasonable excuse will constitute a criminal offence.

Another example is to be found in the Crime and Disorder Act 1988.[14] Sections 1 and 2 permit a magistrates' court to make, respectively, an anti-social behaviour order or a sex offender order. These are civil orders, and civil proceedings, yet non-compliance with such an order, without lawful excuse, will amount to a criminal offence triable in that, or another, magistrates' court.

E   THE ADMINISTRATION OF THE ENGLISH LEGAL SYSTEM

There has not been a unified system for the administration of the English legal system, in the form of a "Ministry of Justice". The reasons for this are historic, and reflect the piecemeal way in which the legal system has developed. Responsibility for the legal system is divided between a number of government ministers and departments, and, increasingly, a number of executive agencies. For example, the Prison Service became an executive agency of the Home Office on 1 April 1993. The Parole Board is an executive non-departmental public body.[15]

Prime responsibility in many areas lies with the Lord Chancellor, who is, of course, a leading Cabinet minister as well as the "speaker" of the House of Lords. This responsibility is managed by the Lord Chancellor's Department. By virtue of the Courts Act 1971[16] it is the responsibility of the Lord Chancellor to appoint such staff, and provide, equip and manage such buildings as is necessary for the purposes of carrying on the business of the Supreme Court[17] and county courts. Appointments of the judiciary are made by, or on the advice of, the Lord Chancellor, who also has responsibility for the appointment and training of justices of the peace.[18] In performance of these functions the Lord Chancellor may draw on the advice of the Lord Chancellor's Advisory Committee on Legal Education and Conduct (ACLEC). Section 19 of the Courts and Legal Services Act 1990 imposes a duty on the Lord Chancellor to appoint such a committee, comprising representatives of the two branches of the profession, academic lawyers as well as independent members. This committee has the general duty[19] to advise on the matters that fall within its remit. This involves the development of legal

---

13   The offence of rape extends to male victims: Sexual Offences Act 1956, s 1, substituted by Criminal Justice and Public Order Act 1994, s 142.

14   For discussion of relevant provisions, see p 533 *et seq*.

15   Criminal Justice and Public Order Act 1994, s 149.

16   See ss 27–28.

17   For definition, see p 168, *post*.

18   See Justice of the Peace Act 1997, s 5. All magistrates receive training, overseen by the Judicial Studies Board.

19   1990 Act, s 20.

services in England and Wales (and in particular the development of advocacy, litigation, conveyancing and probate services) by provision of new or better ways of providing such services and a wider choice of persons providing them while maintaining the proper and efficient administration of justice. For example it advises on all applications for rights of audience or for rights to conduct litigation. Examples of recent reports made by the ACLEC include the First Report on Education and Training, a report on the Continued Professional Development for Solicitors and Barristers and a report on Lawyers' Comments to the Media. Although the recommendations of ACLEC may be addressed to any professional body or group,[20] the committee will clearly provide a basis for action by the Lord Chancellor in exercising his own powers both generally and under the 1990 Act. This action, often of importance, provides the basis for detailed change in the workings of the legal system.

Given the wide-ranging responsibilities and powers vested in the Lord Chancellor it is perhaps surprising that, until recently, there has been no direct accountability to the elected House of Commons. This gap was filled in 1991, when it was announced that a Minister was to answer in the House of Commons for the work of the Lord Chancellor, and that a department was to be appointed.[1]

It should not be overlooked that the Lord Chancellor does not have exclusive responsibility in respect of matters affecting the English legal system. In particular, the Home Secretary has responsibility for the exercise of the prerogative powers relating to the administration of justice, and responsibility for matters relating to criminal justice. Legislation relating to the criminal justice system is developed, taken through Parliament and implemented by the Home Office, which also has responsibility for sentencing (although not in individual cases)[2] the prison service (although not on day-to-day matters which are the responsibility of the prison service), and for the maintenance of standards by the police and probation services. The Home Office also conducts, or sponsors, research into the criminal justice system.

Finally the role of a wide range of other persons and bodies should not be overlooked. The police,[3] Crown Prosecution Service,[4] magistrates' courts service,[5] Prison Service and local authority probation committees also play key roles in the criminal system and provisions in the Crime and Disorder Act 1998 will confer important functions on local authorities and create a new Youth Justice Board in respect of youth justice.[6] The Legal Aid Board is clearly of importance in the context of the funding of civil litigation.[7]

---

20   Ibid, Sch 2, para 5.
1   201 HC Official Report (6th series), col. 250, 19 December 1991.
2   See pp 531-548, *post.*
3   See p 291, *post.*
4   See p 270, *post.*
5   See p 182, *post.*
6   See p 577, *post.*
7   See p 276, *post.*

CHAPTER 2

Legislation

A   LEGISLATION AND LAW REFORM

The broad function of all legislation is to create, alter or revoke law to give effect to the intention of the legislative body. Subordinate legislation fulfils various specific functions, scarcely capable of classification. The functions of Acts of Parliament, by far the most important form of legislation, may be classified as follows.

I   Law reform

Although all statues are concerned with law revision in the broadest sense, relatively few statutes are concerned with altering or revising substantive rules of law or "lawyers' law" as it is sometimes called. Such statutes are frequently passed when the law, through the restrictive operation of the doctrine of judicial precedent, has become stale and incapable of adaptation. The need for reform often manifests itself in a House of Lords decision, or by public concern or outcry following controversial decisions.

Where a decision of a court, especially the House of Lords, is unpopular, the law is often altered by statute. There are many examples on the statute book of Acts passed with the apparent intention of overruling the effect of a House of Lords decision.[1] However, the process of law reform is often more erratic and haphazard. Reform of the substantive law, or of the processes and structures of the law itself, often occurs piecemeal. Sometimes the impetus comes from ad hoc committees, departmental working groups or Royal Commission. On other occasions, more permanent law reform committees may recommend change. Until 1965 the machinery for generating law reform was conspicuously erratic in its operation, consisting mainly of the Law Revision Committee and, subsequently, the Law Reform Committee which considered, on their own initiative or at the invitation of the Lord Chancellor, branches of the law

---

1   Examples are: Parliamentary Papers Act 1840; Limitation Act 1963; Trade Disputes Act 1965; War Damage Act 1965; Criminal Evidence Act 1979. The apparent intention of these Acts is to reverse House of Lords decisions immediately preceding them though Acts of Parliament do not expressly name cases which they are obviously intended to overrule.

requiring reform and then published reports containing recommendations. The Committees consisted of practising lawyers who met from time to time, when pressure of other work permitted. Their recommendations often, but by no means always, were subsequently taken up by Parliament. Where the question was of wider public importance, heads of government departments might refer the question to a special committee for report or the Crown might set up a Royal Commission. A modern example of law reform based on the recommendations of a Royal Commission is the Courts Act 1971 which followed basically the recommendations of the so-called "Beeching Commission".[2] The controversial Courts and Legal Services Act 1990 was passed, in part, to implement recommendations of the Civil Justice Review Body.[3]

A recent example of what can happen if law reform is not carefully considered and thorough is provided by the attempts to reform the committal proceedings procedure in criminal cases. Committal proceedings are the first stage of the trial of an indictable offence. In 1994, committals for trial were abolished, to be replaced by a new system of transfers for trial.[4] These provisions were never implemented, the Government recognising the force of objections put by those who would have to operate the new processes. The transfer for trial provisions were repealed in 1996, never having been introduced.[4] Another example is that of unit fines, introduced in 1991.[5] Following widespread criticism, the provisions were hastily withdrawn in 1993.[6]

2   The Law Commission

A major addition to the machinery of law reform was made by the Law Commissions Act 1965 which established the Law Commissions. Section 3(1) of the Act defines the duty of the Commissions (there is a separate Commission for Scotland) thus:

> "it shall be the duty of each of the Commissions to take and keep under review all the law with which they are respectively concerned with a view to its systematic development and reform, including in particular the codification of such law, the elimination of anomalies, the repeal of obsolete and unnecessary enactments, the reduction of the number of separate enactments and generally the simplification and modernisation of the law."

The creation of the Law Commission was an important step forward in law reform. The Commissions, by reason of the appointment of full-time Commissioners of the highest calibre and of full-time administrative staff, have been able to produce a steady flow of reports, recommendations and draft Bills, most of which are implemented by Act of Parliament within a relatively short time.[7] Of all the Law Commission's law reform reports, 112 have been implemented in full or in part, 16 have been expressly or impliedly rejected, and 19 were, as at March 1997, outstanding.[8]

The mission of the Law Commission is to make the law simpler, fairer and cheaper to use. Law reform projects may be included in a programme of work submitted by

2   Report of the Royal Commission on Assizes and Quarter Sessions, Cmnd 4153 (1969).
3   Report of the Review Body on Civil Justice, Cmnd 394 (1988).
4   For the saga of law reform in this area, and the current position, see p 485, *post*.
5   By Criminal Justice Act 1991, s 118.
6   Criminal Justice Act 1993, s 65.
7   See, for example, Landlord and Tenant Act 1988, Law of Property (Miscellaneous Provisions) Act 1989, Children Act 1989; Statute Law (Repeals) Act 1995; Civil Evidence Act 1995; Family Law Act 1996; Theft (Amendment) Act 1996.
8   Law Commission Annual Report, 1996, Law Comm No 244, HC 1996–1997 HC 305, Appx C, p 61.

the Commission to the Lord Chancellor. The current programme of work is the sixth such programme, approved in 1995. Alternatively, an issue may be referred to the Commission, usually by a government department. Whether a project is accepted by the Commission, or initiated by it, depends on its assessment of the relevant issues, the most significant of which are the importance of the issues, the availability of resources in terms both of expertise and funding and whether the issues are such as to be suitable to be dealt with by the Commission.[9] Invariably the projects chosen will be those where the law is confused, bad or out-of-date.

The Commission works through small teams, led by a Law Commissioner and usually comprising three government lawyers and three research assistants. Each team may have five or six projects. In some projects there may be an academic consultant. The process involves the publication of a Consultation Paper, following research and analysis of case law, legislation, academic and professional comment and analysis and any other relevant source material. The consultation paper will describe the existing problems with the law, describe possible solutions and propose possible law reform options.

Following a consultation period a final report is published, often including a draft Bill. The Commission often gives assistance to government Ministers and departments, "so as to ensure that best value is obtained from the effort and resources devoted to the project by the Commission and others".[10]

Not all Law Commission reports and recommendations are implemented, although the statistics quoted above show that the record of acceptance of Law Commission proposals is extremely good. One clear example of a report that attracted controversy, and has not yet been implemented, is in the area of criminal law reform. The Law Commission's draft Criminal Law Bill,[11] intended to be a first step at criminal law codification, still awaits implementation and has been described as "over technical, poor on exposition and a sore puzzle from beginning to end".[12]

To facilitate the process of law reform, Parliament has introduced special procedures for dealing with Bills of a technical nature and largely devoid of party political controversy, which have become known as the "Jellicoe procedure".[13] Bills to which the Jellicoe procedure apply go to a special public Bill committee which has the power to call for person, papers and hear evidence.[14] Although this is not an apt procedure for Bills which are controversial in the political sense, the procedure has been used to effect on law reform Bills which have excited strong debate. One such Bill was the Private International Law (Miscellaneous Provisions) Bill 1994 where lawyers who participated in procedure disagreed strongly about technical, but important, aspects of the application of the law of tort in an international law context. The strength of these committees has been described as their capacity "to reach well-informed consensus across party lines on what are often very difficult technical issues", and such procedures are particularly important for the effective, and speedy, implementation of Law Commission proposals.[15]

9   *Ibid*, Appx A, p 58.
10   Mr Justice Brooke: The Role of the Law Commission in Simplifying Statute Law (1995) 16 Stat LR, No 1, p 1 (1995); Law Commission Annual Report, 1996, *loc cit*, p 58.
11   Legislating the Criminal Code: Offences Against the Person and General Principles, Law Comm No 218, 1993.
12   Bennion (1994) 15 Stat LR 108; cf Smith: The Law Commission's Criminal Law Bill – A Good Start for the Criminal Code (1995) 16 Stat LR 105.
13   Named after Earl Jellicoe, the Minister who chaired the committee which introduced the procedure.
14   For discussion of the procedure, see Brooke: Special Public Bill Committees [1995] PL 351.
15   Parts I and II of the 1994 Bill were based on Law Commission recommendations that had waited some ten years for implementation, due to lack of parliamentary time: see Brooke, *op cit*, at p 354.

3   Consolidation of enactments

Where a branch of the law has evolved piecemeal, a consolidating statute may be passed, for the purpose of clarification, containing substantially the existing law in a consolidated form. There are three sorts of consolidating Acts: (1) "pure" consolidation (simple re-enactment); (2) consolidation under the Consolidation of Enactments (Procedure) Act 1949, which allows "corrections and minor improvements";[16] (3) consolidation with amendments recommended by the Law Commission, under a procedure adopted by Parliament since 1965. In practice most of the major consolidating legislation in recent years has incorporated Law Commission amendments in the light of the Commission's consideration of the relevant branch of the law.[17]

Consolidation Acts are not subject to parliamentary debate, but there are special procedures designed to ensure that the bill, when enacted, does not depart from the pre-existing statutory provisions which are to be consolidated.[18] Substantive changes in the law will often be made before the process of consolidation is undertaken. Thus, for example, the Crime and Disorder Act 1998 contains a provision with the side-heading "pre-consolidation amendments", the amendments themselves being contained in a Schedule to the Act. The type of consolidation effected appears from the long title of the Act in question which will, in the case of pure consolidation, be in the form "an Act to consolidate" while, in the case of consolidation with amendments under the 1949 procedure or with Law Commission amendments the long title will refer to the 1949 Act or to the Law Commission as the case may be.[19]

There are some who believe that the process of consolidation should be taken to the point of producing a consolidated statue book, similar to that which exists in many other countries, in which the whole of our statute law would be arranged under titles and kept up to date by textual amendments. However desirable this might be it is clear that it is not a reform that is likely to be implemented in the foreseeable future. In May 1973 the government set up a departmental committee (the Renton Committee) to review the form in which public Bills are drafted "with a view to achieving greater simplicity and clarity in statute law". The Committee reported in 1975[20] and concluded that it would not be practicable to consolidate the whole statute book within a limited number of years, nor to do so on the principle of "one Act, one subject". Although the Committee made some 87 separate recommendations, notably that the preparation of a comprehensive new Interpretation Act should be put in hand, little if any radical change in the law was recommended and, although there was an Interpretation Act passed in 1978, this was only a consolidating Act, with Law Commission amendments. It is difficult to envisage any sweeping reforms in the foreseeable future.

---

16   These are defined by s 2 of the 1949 Act as amendments of which the effect is confined to resolving ambiguities, removing doubts, bringing obsolete provisions into conformity with modern practice or removing unnecessary provisions or anomalies which are not of substantial importance, and amendments designed to facilitate improvement in the form or manner in which the law is stated, and includes any transitional provisions which may be necessary in consequence of such amendments.

17   Examples are Water Industry Act 1991, Water Resources Act 1991, Social Security Contributions and Benefits Act 1992, Taxation of Chargeable Gains Act 1992.

18   For an explanation of this, and of the significance of the consolidating procedures in the context of construction of statutes, see the speech of Lord Simon in *Farrell v Alexander* [1977] AC 59, at pp 82–85; [1976] 2 All ER 721, at pp 733–736.

19   See, for examples, Employment Protection (Consolidation) Act 1978 (pure consolidation) (see, now, Employment Rights Act 1996); Road Traffic Act 1988 (Law Commission amendments); Juries Act 1974 (1949 Act "corrections and improvements").

20   The Preparation of Legislation, Cmnd 6053 (1975).

4 Codification

Codification differs from consolidation in that an Act may only be said to consolidate statute law, whereas it may codify both case law and statute law. Nevertheless codification is similar in function to consolidation in that in both cases the object of the statute is to simplify and clarify the existing law rather than to effect substantial alterations to it. Notable examples of major codifying statutes were the Bills of Exchange Act 1882, the Partnership Act 1890, the Sale of Goods Act 1893 and the Marine Insurance Act 1906. Since then there has been very little codification. One notable exception is the Police and Criminal Evidence Act 1984 (PACE) which radically altered and codified the pre-existing common law and statutory rules relating to police powers of search, entry to premises, the treatment and questioning of suspects, and the admissibility of confession evidence.[1]

There is, in many areas of the law, a pressing need for codification. This is due to the manner in which Parliament has sometimes approached the task of amendment of statutes. Rather than produce a comprehensive re-enactment which would enable the relevant law on a topic to be clearly set out in a single statute, it has often been the practice simply to amend piecemeal by sections tucked away in a statute, often referring to one or more Schedules, which may deal with a large number of different topics and amend an equally large number of earlier statutes. Subsequently the amending provision may itself be repealed or re-amended with the result that, in order to discover what the law is, it is necessary to pick one's way through a maze of separate statutory provisions.

This situation, in the field of industrial relations legislation, led in one case to the following observation by Sir John Donaldson MR:[2]

"My plea is that Parliament, when legislating in respect of circumstances which directly affect the 'man or woman in the street' or the 'man or woman on the shop floor', should give as high a priority to clarity and simplicity of expression as to refinements of policy. Where possible statutes, or complete parts of statutes, should not be amended but re-enacted in an amended form so that those concerned can read the rules in a single document. When formulating policy, ministers, of whatever political persuasion, should at all times be asking themselves and asking parliamentary counsel; is this concept too refined to be capable of expression in basic English?' Having to ask such questions would no doubt be frustrating for ministers and the legislature generally, but in my judgment this is part of the price which has to be paid if the rule of law is to be maintained."

These remarks were expressly adopted by Lord Diplock when the case reached the House of Lords.[3] Increasingly, legislation which is significantly amending legislation will substitute one or more sections, or sub-sections, for the pre-existing provision. One example of this is Schedule 1 to the Criminal Procedure and Investigations Act 1996, which introduces five new sections into the Magistrates' Courts Act 1980. This does not, of course, remove the need for a greater measure of codification.

---

1 See p 312, *post*.
2 *Merkur Island Shipping Corporation v Laughton* [1983] 2 AC 570, at pp 594–595; [1983] 1 All ER 334, at p 351.
3 [1983] 2 AC 570 at p 662, [1983] 2 All ER 189, at pp 198–9.

5   Collection and disbursement of revenue

The annual Finance Act implementing the Budget proposals is concerned primarily with the collection of revenue by the Crown. Other Acts, notably the Income and Corporation Taxes Act 1988, fulfil the same function. Possibly on account of the considerable energies expended on the task of tax avoidance these statutes tend to promote rather more litigation than the average statute, including numerous "test cases" in which the Inland Revenue is concerned to discover whether the drafting of a measure has achieved the desired effect. Conversely, public expenditure is authorised by Parliament annually through Consolidated Fund Acts, which authorise payments out of the Consolidated Fund, and the Appropriation Act, which appropriates public expenditure to specific purposes.

6   Implementation of treaties

The United Kingdom, by entering into treaties, undertakes to implement the laws that form the subject matter of the treaty. For example directives and decisions of the Council and Commission of the European Union usually require implementation either by statute or statutory instrument[4] while, arising out of its subscription to the European Convention on Human Rights, the United Kingdom has a duty to legislate so as to enforce decisions of the European Court of Human Rights, and has invariably done so, where legislation was necessary.[5] The need for this may decrease with the passage of the Human Rights Bill.[6] With a view to standardising or harmonising branches of the law with an international element, the United Kingdom subscribes to specific treaties or conventions, following which they are implemented by domestic legislation. Examples of such legislation are the Civil Jurisdiction and Judgments Act 1982, the Taking of Hostages Act 1982, the Employment Act 1989, the Companies Act 1989 and the Civil Jurisdiction and Judgments Act 1991.

7   Social legislation

The law student, faced with a list of the Acts of Parliament passed in any single year, will probably feel that many of them do not concern him at all and will regard them as of secondary importance. This, of course, would be totally misconceived. These Acts are varied in their scope and functions but may be classified together as social legislation. Such Acts are concerned with regulating the day-to-day running of the social system rather then with creating criminal offences or rights and duties between individuals. There is an increasing tendency for Parliament to delegate to subordinate bodies the power to make regulations of this nature. Whatever the mode by which such provision is made, the potential for judicial review,[7] or the possibility of a statute giving rise to private law rights,[8] means that lawyers will be closely working with all such legislation.

4   See p 106, *post*.
5   See p 128, *post*.
6   See p 132, *post*.
7   See p 143, *post*.
8   See p 24, *post*.

B   FORMS OF LEGISLATION[9]

Early legislation in England took several different forms, such as charters,[10] provisions, ordinances and statutes. At the present day, however, there are only three different forms which United Kingdom legislation may take: Acts of Parliament, delegated legislation and autonomic legislation.

I   Acts of Parliament

Subject to compliance with the overriding legislation of the European Communities, Parliament is recognised as sovereign and as possessing unlimited legislative power. This has not always been so[11] but in modern times it had not been seriously contended that the courts have any power to override the intention of the legislature until in *British Railways Board v Pickin*[12] an attempt was made to impugn the validity of a private Act of Parliament, the British Railways Act 1968, on the ground that, in obtaining the enactment of part of the Act, the British Railway Board had fraudulently concealed certain matters from Parliament and thereby misled Parliament into an enactment which operated to deprive the plaintiff of his land or proprietary rights. If it was surprising that such a point should be pleaded it was, perhaps, more surprising that the Court of Appeal should have held that it raised a triable issue.[13] The House of Lords, however, allowed the Board's appeal and restored the judge's order that the pleading be struck out as being frivolous, vexatious and an abuse of the process of the court.[14] Accordingly, it is now clear that no court is entitled to go behind that which Parliament has enacted and that this rule is equally applicable to public and private Acts.

However, where there is a potential conflict between a United Kingdom Act and legislation of the European Communities the courts have power to restrain enforcement of the former. This occurred in *Factortame v Secretary of State for Transport (No 2)*.[15] In that case the applicants, who were companies controlled by Spanish nationals, sought to challenge the validity of the Merchant Shipping Act 1988 on the basis that it contravened the provisions of the EC Treaty by depriving them of their Community law rights. Since determination of this issue by the European Court of Justice was likely to take some time the applicants applied for an interim injunction to restrain the Secretary of State from enforcing the Act, in effect an order postponing the coming into force of the Act. The House of Lord's initial decision[16] was that the courts had no power to make any such order. However, they referred this issue to the Court of Justice, which decided otherwise, in consequence of which the House of Lords, in the exercise of its discretion, did grant the applicants the interim relief sought. Such relief is not,

9   This Chapter is confined to United Kingdom legislation. For EC legislation, see p 100, *post*.
10   For an attempt to rely upon Magna Carta, see *R v Secretary of State for the Home Department, ex parte Wynne* [1992] QB 406; [1992] 2 All ER 301.
11   See, for example, dicta of Coke C J in *Bonham*'s case (1609) 8 Co Rep 113 and of Holt C J in *City of London v Wood* (1701) 12 Mod Rep 669.
12   [1974] AC 765; [1974] 1 All ER 609.
13   The decision of the Court of Appeal is reported at [1973] QB 219; [1972] 3 All ER 923. For a further unsuccessful attempt to have an Act of Parliament declared *ultra vires*: see *Manuel v A-G* [1983] Ch 77; [1982] 3 All ER 822.
14   Under RSC, Ord 18, r 19; see p 362, *post*, for details of this procedure.
15   [1991] 1 AC 603; [1991] 1 All ER 70. For the subsequent litigation in this affair see *R v Secretary of State for Transport, ex parte Factortame (No 3)* [1992] QB 680; [1991] 3 All ER 769; *R v Secretary of State for Transport, ex parte Factortame (No 4)* Case 48/93 [1996] All ER (EC) 301; *R v Secretary of State for Transport (No 5)* (1997) Times, 16 May; *R v Secretary of State for Transport, ex parte Factortame* [1998] 1 All ER 736.
16   *Factortame Ltd v Secretary of State for Transport* [1990] 2 AC 85; [1989] 2 All ER 692.

however, automatic, but will be granted only where the facts of the individual case merit it.[17] The decision was taken a stage further in *Equal Opportunities Commission v Secretary of State for Employment*,[18] where the House of Lords held that it was entitled to judicially review legislation to ensure that it complied with European law. On the facts, provisions in the Employment Protection (Consolidation) Act 1978 relating to part-time workers were held to be contrary to European law. A declaration was issued to that effect.

The procedure for the passing of an Act of Parliament is, briefly, that Parliamentary draftsmen draft a Bill, generally, under supervision of a Minister of the Crown. The Bill is then introduced in either the House of Commons or the House of Lords. If it passes through all its stages within the parliamentary session it receives the Royal Assent and Becomes an Act of Parliament. Acts of Parliament are published: the official Queens' Printers' Copy is published by Her Majesty's Stationery Office and on sale there to the general public. The Stationery Office publishes these copies in annual volumes and also publishes annually an Index to the Statutes in Force, for reference purposes. In addition the Incorporated Council of Law Reporting publishes annually the texts of Acts taken from the Queen's Printer's Copies, and various other sets of statutes are published, often containing annotations. Examples of these are *Halsbury's Statutes* and *Current Law Statutes*. Bills, statutes and similar sources can also be found on the internet.

The mode of citation of statutes has undergone change. Early statues were cited by the name of the place where Parliament met.[19] Subsequently statutes were cited by reference to their regnal year and chapter. Thus, for example, the Criminal Justice Act 1948 would be cited as 11 & 12 Geo 6, c 58 indicating that the Act was the fifty-eighth passed in the Parliamentary session extending over the eleventh and twelfth years of the reign of George VI. This exceedingly cumbersome method of citation was not abolished until 1962.[20] Although Acts still have chapter numbers (a legacy of the fiction that only one Act was passed in a Parliamentary session), reference is now to the calendar year rather than to the regnal year. In practice Acts are commonly cited by reference to their short title, and this is permissible by section 2 of the Short Titles Act 1896. Many Acts passed prior to 1896 have been endowed with short titles retrospectively and Acts passed since that date contain a section conferring upon themselves a short title.

2   Enforcement of statutory duties

In consequence of the restrictive effect of the doctrine of judicial precedent, the creation of new rights, and causes of action to enforce them, is virtually the prerogative of Parliament. Where a statute imposes a duty the question often arises whether or not breach of that duty gives rise to an action for damages (for the tort of breach of statutory duty). The question in each case is whether the legislature intended to confer on the plaintiff a private law cause of action, not whether the plaintiff belongs to a class which the statutory provision was intended to protect.

It might be thought that where a statute created rules but provided no criminal penalty for their breach, the intention of Parliament must have been to create a right of civil action to a person who suffers as a result of the breach:

17   *R v HM Treasury, ex parte British Telecommunications plc* [1994] 1 CMLR 621; see subsequently Case 392/93 [1996] QB 615; [1996] All ER (EC) 411.
18   [1994] 1 All ER 910.
19   Eg, Statute of Gloucester 1278; Provisions of Oxford 1258.
20   Acts of Parliament Numbering and Citation Act 1962 (10 & 11 Eliz 2, c 34).

"for, if it were not so, the statute would be but a pious aspiration."[1]

This is not, however, invariably the case. Thus in *R v Deputy Governor of Parkhurst Prison, ex parte Hague*[2] the House of Lords held that the Prison Rules 1964 (made under the Prison Act 1952) conferred no right to sue for damages upon a convicted prisoner who had allegedly been restrained in a way not permitted by those Rules. The prisoner's remedies were to complain to the governor or board of visitors, and in the event of a complaint to the latter a report might be made to the Secretary of State under the Act. He might also challenge any administrative decision of the Secretary of State or the governor by judicial review proceedings.

The principles to be considered were discussed in *O'Rourke v Camden LBC*,[3] where the House of Lords considered whether the Housing (Homeless Persons) Act 1977 conferred private rights as well as public duties. Lord Hoffman explained the issue as follows:

"There is no doubt that, like several other provisions in Pt III, [the 1977 Act] creates a duty which is enforceable by proceedings for judicial review. But whether it gives rise to a cause of action sounding damages depends upon whether the Act shows a legislative intention to create such a remedy. In *X and ors (minors) v Bedfordshire CC, M (a minor) v Newham London BC, E (a minor) v Dorset BC*, the principles were analysed by Lord Browne-Wilkinson in a speech with which the other members of the House agreed. He said that although there was no general rule by reference to which it could be decided that statute created a private right of action, there were a number of 'indicators'. The indicator upon which [counsel] for Mr O'Rourke placed most reliance was the common sense proposition that a statute which appears intended for the protection of a limited class of people but provides no other remedy for breach should ordinarily be construed as intended to create a private right of action. ...Camden, on the other hand, says that although Pt III does not expressly enact any remedy for breach, that does not mean that it would be toothless without an action for damages or an injunction in private law. It is enforceable in public law by individual homeless persons who have locus standi to bring proceedings for judicial review. Furthermore, there are certain contra indications which make it unlikely that Parliament intended to create private law rights of action.

The first is that the Act is a scheme of social welfare, intended to confer benefits at the public expense on grounds of public policy. Public money is spent on housing the homeless not merely for the private benefit of people who find themselves homeless but on grounds of general public interest: because, for example, proper housing means that people will be less likely to suffer illness, turn to crime or require the attention of other social services. The expenditure interacts with expenditure on other public services such as education, the National Health Service and even the police. It is not simply a private matter between the claimant and the housing authority. Accordingly, the fact that Parliament has provided for the expenditure of public money on benefits in kind such as housing the homeless does not necessarily mean that it intended cash payments to be made by way of damages to persons who, in breach of the housing authority's

1   *Cutler v Wandsworth Stadium Ltd* [1949] AC 398, at p 407; [1949] 1 All ER 544, at p 548 per Lord Simonds.
2   [1992] 1 AC 58; [1991] 3 All ER 733.
3   [1998] AC 188; [1997] 3 All ER 23, overruling *Thornton v Kirklees MBC* [1979] QB 626; [1979] 2 All ER 349. The power to make delegated legislation may not necessarily include the power to create new enforceable rights: *Olutu v Home Office* [1997] 1 All ER 385.

statutory duty, have unfortunately not received the benefits which they should have done...".

Ultimately, it is a matter of construction of the particular legislation which is under consideration. If the matter is of a general administrative or regulatory nature imposed on a public authority, a right in tort is unlikely to be implied.[4]

3   Delegated legislation

"Delegated legislation" is the description given to the vast body of rules, orders, regulations and byelaws created by subordinate bodies under specific powers delegated to those bodies by Parliament. The advantage of delegated legislation is that it enables regulations to be made and altered quickly without the need, usually, for placing them before Parliament. The vital feature that distinguishes Parliament from any other person or body having legislative power is that the latter is not sovereign. Delegated legislation which is concerned solely with implementing the detail of a general policy contained in an Act of Parliament is useful and unexceptionable. However, the powers delegated are frequently defined in the widest terms with the effect of conferring a legislative function on some body almost equivalent to that of Parliament itself.[5] Sir John Donaldson MR in one case[6] drew attention to the Hallmarking Act 1973, which empowers the Secretary of State by statutory instrument to apply the Act to metals other than gold, silver and platinum and to include provisions "applying, extending, excluding or amending, or repealing or revoking, with or without savings, any provisions of this Act or an instrument under this Act." An even wider example is that of clause 10 of the Human Rights Bill 1998 which will, if enacted, empower a Minister to make such amendments to legislation, or subordinate legislation, as he considers appropriate in order to remove incompatibility with the European Convention on Human Rights.

Such powers are always, of course, subject to control by Parliament but, where the legislative power is conferred upon a Minister of the Crown, this may not be an effective control.[7]

Delegated legislation is valid only if it is within the legislative powers conferred by Parliament (*intra vires*). If it is not it is said to be *ultra vires* and is, in that event, inoperative. Thus, for example, the Rules of the Supreme Court are delegated legislation, being passed by a Rule Committee under powers conferred by the Supreme Court Act 1981. The power conferred upon the Committee is limited to creating rules of procedure. Consequently, if any Rule of the Supreme Court has the characteristic of a rule of substantive law rather than a rule of procedure it is ineffective.[8] However, unless and until declared ultra vires by a final judgment in an action in the courts, a

---

4   *Church of Jesus Christ of Latter Day Saints (GB) v West Yorkshire Fire & Civil Defence Authority* [1997] QB 1004; [1997] 2 All ER 865 (duty imposed by Fire Services Act 1947, s 13, to ensure a water supply did not confer enforceable right).
5   The powers tend to be very widely defined in time of war. See, for example, the extraordinarily wide powers to make defence regulations conferred by the Supplies and Services (Transitional Powers) Act 1945 and the Supplies and Services (Extended Purpose) Act 1947, cited in *Law in the Making* by CK Allen (7th Edn), pp 540 *et seq*.
6   *Aden Refinery Co Ltd v Ugland Management Co* [1987] QB 650; [1986] 3 All ER 737.
7   For an example, see *Liversidge v Anderson* [1942] AC 206; [1941] 3 All ER 338; see also *Kruse v Johnson* [1898] 2 QB 91; *Buck v A-G* [1965] Ch 745; [1964] 2 All ER 663.
8   See *Re Grosvenor Hotel London (No 2)* [1965] Ch 1210; [1964] 3 All ER 354; *Ward v James* [1966] 1 QB 273; [1965] 1 All ER 563.

statutory instrument must be treated as part of the law and enforced accordingly.[9] The courts treat delegated legislation differently from primary legislation. Unlike an Act of Parliament, delegated legislation can be declared invalid, because it is *ultra vires* (outside the power).[10] Challenge to delegated legislation is usually made in an application for judicial review,[11] but can sometimes be raised as a defence to an action or prosecution (known as collateral challenge).[12] In *R v Wicks*[13] the House of Lords cast doubt on a statement made in an earlier case[14] to the effect that collateral challenge of an order was only permissible on the grounds of substantive *ultra vires*, not on the grounds that the order was ultra vires on procedural grounds.[15] The doubts expressed in *Wicks* were confirmed as correct in 1998, when the House of Lords in *Boddington v British Transport Police*[16] concluded that the invalidity of subordinate legislation could usually be raised as a defence in criminal proceedings.[17]

The fact that part of delegated legislation is *ultra vires* does not necessarily invalidate the whole of that legislation. The valid part may be textually severable, alternatively upheld if it is substantially severable so that what remains after severance is essentially unchanged in its legislative purpose, operation and effect.[18]

The highest form of delegated legislation is Order in Council[19] which is nominally an order of the Privy Council consisting of the Sovereign and Privy Councillors. Many Acts are brought into operation by Order in Council, the power to make the Order being contained in the Act itself.[20] In fact, though not in theory, an Order in Council is generally made by the government and merely sanctioned by the Privy Council. The effect, therefore, is to confer wide legislative power upon government departments. One example of this is section 2(2) of the European Communities Act 1972, which confers a wide power on Her Majesty in Council, or on a Minister, to make orders in council or regulations to implement community obligations of the United Kingdom.[1] It is limited by Schedule 2 to that Act, which excludes power to make any provision imposing or increasing taxation, any retrospective provision or any criminal offence punishable with imprisonment for more than two years, or, on summary conviction with imprisonment for more than three months. Despite these limitations the power is far-reaching, although not as much as that contained in the Human Rights Bill of 1998.[2]

Orders in Council and certain other regulations are published in statutory instruments[3] (formerly statutory rules and orders) and are available at Her Majesty's

9   Cf *Hoffman-La Roche & Co AG v Secretary of State for Trade and Industry* [1975] AC 295 at p 329; [1974] 2 All ER 1128.
10 See p 142, *post*.
11 See *O'Reilly v Mackman* [1983] 2 AC 237, [1982] 3 All ER 1124; *R v Reading Crown Court, ex parte Hutchinson* [1988] QB 384.
12 *R v Reading Crown Court, ex parte Hutchinson, op cit, DPP v Bugg* [1993] QB 473; [1993] 2 All ER 815.
13 [1998] AC 92.
14 *DPP v Bugg* [1993] QB 473; [1993] 2 All ER 815.
15 For the grounds of judicial review, see p 150, *post*.
16 [1998] 2 All ER 203.
17 For a full discussion of the principles, see *Director of Public Prosecutions v Hutchinson* [1990] 2 AC 783; [1990] 2 All ER 836.
18 *Ibid*.
19 Note that Orders in Council can also amount to primary legislation pursuant to the Royal Prerogative: *Council of Civil Service Unions v Minister for the Civil Service* [1985] AC 374; [1984] 3 All ER 935.
20 An Act may be brought into force by Order in Council even though the power to make the order derives from the Act itself; Interpretation Act 1978, s 13.
1   See p 105, *post*.
2   See p 134, *post*.
3   Statutory Instruments Act 1946. Statutes conferring subordinate legislative powers frequently, though not always, provide that the statutory instrument made thereunder shall be laid before Parliament. In this event a copy of the instrument must be so laid before it comes into operation; Statutory Instruments Act 1946, s 4. The effect of laying the instrument before Parliament varies. In some cases the instrument

Stationery Office. They are cited by calendar year and number (for example, SI 1959 No 64) and, often, by a short title. Failure to publish will not affect the validity of the delegated legislation, but may provide an individual with a defence to a prosecution brought pursuant to that delegated legislation.[4]

4 Autonomic legislation

This differs from delegated legislation in that an autonomous body has an independent power to legislate for its own members and, in some cases, for members of the general public. Though this power is usually conferred by Parliament this is not always so. The power is in all cases, however, sanctioned by Parliament. Examples of autonomous legislative bodies are public undertakings such as transport authorities, bodies created by Royal charter, such as universities, whose byelaws may affect the public at large. The Church of England, the General Medical Council, The Law Society, trade unions and even limited companies are autonomous in the sense that they have power to control their own internal structure and to legislate for their members. It is arguable that such legislation does not affect the public but it does in a negative sense in that any individual who causes a breach of the regulations created by an autonomous body may commit a civil wrong.

In almost all cases autonomic legislation is confined in its extent by an Act of Parliament in which event it is subject to the doctrine of ultra vires. An important exception, however, is constituted by the prerogative jurisdiction of the Privy Council. This jurisdiction is principally concerned with legislating by Order in Council for Crown Colonies. The power is subject to the ordinary rules of English law though not to the doctrine of ultra vires.[5] It will thus be apparent that an Order in Council may be passed either under powers conferred by individual Acts or under a general prerogative power independent of statute. Both of these are subject to the power of the law to determine the existence and extent of the power to make the order.[6]

5 Codes of Practice

Before leaving the topic of forms of legislation, it is necessary to refer to Codes of Practice, which are of increasing significance in certain legislative contexts. In the context of the enforcement of the criminal law several Codes are of particular importance. Section 66 of the Police and Criminal Evidence Act 1984 (PACE) authorises the Home Secretary to make Codes of Practice. Codes dealing with the exercise of stop and search powers, execution of search powers, the treatment and questioning of suspects and the identification of suspects have been issued.[7] These Codes are of particular importance to the practitioner, and to the police. If there is a

---

does not take effect until expressly approved by resolution while in others it takes effect immediately subject to cancellation by negative resolution within forty "sitting" days.

It is permissible for "outside documents" to be referred to in the statutory instrument (but not laid before Parliament), provided the reference is to an existing document and there is no question of "sub-delegation"; see *R v Secretary of State for Social Services, ex parte Camden London Borough Council* [1987] 2 All ER 560; [1987] 1 WLR 819, where this practice was unsuccessfully challenged.

4   Statutory Instruments Act 1946, s 3; *R v Sheer Metelcraft* [1954] 1 QB 586, [1954] 1 All ER 542.
5   *The Zamora* [1916] 2 AC 77, PC.
6   See p 150, *post*.
7   See p 304, *post*.

"significant and substantial"[8] breach of the Codes, evidence obtained as a result of that breach may be excluded, and not considered by the jury or magistrates.

Another example is the Code of Practice on the preservation and disclosure of evidence, made under s 21 of the Criminal Procedure and Investigations Act 1996. This Code is intended to ensure that important material is made available to the prosecutor and, ultimately, disclosed to the defence if it may assist them.[9] It is very much intended to create a framework where miscarriages of justice become less likely.

In the context of the civil law perhaps the most important example of a Code of Practice is that issued by the Advisory Conciliation and Arbitration Service (ACAS) under the Employment Protection (Consolidation) Act. ACAS may issue Codes of Practice containing "such practical guidance as the Service thinks fit for the purpose of promoting the improvement of industrial relations".[10] Provision for codes of this type was first made by the Industrial Relations Act 1971 and the first such code, the Code of Practice on Disciplinary Practice and Procedures in Employment, has been of immense importance, particularly in unfair dismissal cases, where the tribunals and courts have developed principles of "procedural unfairness", whereby a dismissal, although not substantially unfair, may be held unfair because of failure on the part of the employer to adopt a fair procedure, in accordance with the Code of Practice, prior to dismissal, for example by failure to carry out a proper investigation of allegations against an employee or failure to give an employee an opportunity to state his case.

Whether Codes of Practice promulgated pursuant to Acts of Parliament are classifiable as "legislation" is a moot point. In one sense they have the characteristic of delegated legislation in that the power to issue the code is conferred by statute upon a specified person or body and, presumably, a Code of Practice could be declared ultra vires. On the other hand a Code of Practice does not, by its very nature, have the force of law. This is not to day that it does not have legal effect. Codes issued under the 1975 Act are admissible in any proceedings before an industrial tribunal or the Central Arbitration Committee.[11] By section 67(11) of the Police and Criminal Evidence Act any code under the Act is admissible in evidence, and if appearing to be relevant to any question arising in the proceedings, "it shall be taken into account in determining that question."

Codes of Practice approved or issued by the Health and Safety Commission under section 16 of the Health and Safety at Work etc Act 1974 have even greater force in that, in criminal proceedings under the Act, not only is the relevant Code admissible in evidence, but failure to comply with the Code amounts to prima facie proof of contravention of the provisions of the Act to which the Code relates.[12] Reference may also be made to the Highway Code, first issued pursuant to the Road Traffic Act 1930, failure to comply with the provisions of which is not, in itself, an offence but may be relied upon by any party in either civil or criminal proceedings.[13]

C THE OPERATION OF STATUTES

In defining the scope of a statute it is necessary to advert both to its geographical area of operation and to the time during which it is operative.

---

8   *R v Walsh* (1989) 91 Cr App Rep 161. See, further, p 297, *post*.
9   See p 500, *post*. For discussion of the Code of Practice, see Card and Ward: Criminal Procedure and Investigations Act 1996, (Jordan Publishing, 1996) Ch 3.
10   Trade Union and Labour Relations (Consolidation) Act 1992, s 199.
11   *Ibid*, s 207(1), (2).
12   Health and Safety at Work etc Act 1974, s 17(2).
13   Road Traffic Act 1988, s 38(6).

1   Geographical operation

There is a presumption that an Act of Parliament is operative throughout the United Kingdom [14] but not elsewhere unless in either case a contrary intention appears in the Act itself. The contrary intention may either limit or extend the geographical operation of the Act. Thus Acts frequently contain a section restricting their operation to exclude Scotland or Northern Ireland. The Limitation Act 1963 is a typical example. It was in three parts; Part I applying to England and Wales, Part II to Scotland and Part III to Northern Ireland. Many other examples exist. A similar reduction in the geographical operation of legislation occurs in the case of Acts, which are expressed to apply only to a limited locality; such Acts are described as "local Acts". An Act may be partly local and partly general. For example, sections 83 and 86 of the Fires Prevention (Metropolis) Act 1774 were held to be applicable throughout the United Kingdom although the operation of the Act as a whole was confined to the London area.

Conversely an Act may expressly or by necessary implication extend outside the United Kingdom, though there is a presumption against this.[15] For example, section 57 of the Offences Against the Person Act 1861 provides that the crime of bigamy is committed "whether the second marriage shall have taken place in England or Ireland, or elsewhere." Another example is Part II of the Sex Offenders Act 1997, which extends the jurisdiction of United Kingdom courts to allow trial in the UK of British citizens who commit certain sexual offences abroad. An Act which does have extraterritorial operation is, however, usually (but not always) limited to apply only to British subjects or persons owing allegiance to the Crown.[16]

2   Temporal operation

a   When a statute begins to be operative

Until 1793[17] a statute came into force on the first day of the parliamentary session in which it was passed. Consequently virtually all legislation was retrospective. The present law is that a statute comes into force on the day on which it receives the Royal Assent, unless some other date is specified in the Act itself. However, increasingly an Act may provide that it is to come into force on a "day to be appointed" by Order in Council, or by an Order made by a Minister. In either case the appointed day is published in a statutory instrument. The disadvantage of this practice is that it is slightly more difficult to determine when the Act is coming into force and it is necessary to

14   Since it lies within the prerogative power of the Crown to extend its sovereignty and jurisdiction to areas of land or sea over which it has not previously asserted sovereignty or jurisdiction, the words "United Kingdom" incorporate such area of land or sea as may from time to time be formally declared by the Crown to be subject to its sovereignty and jurisdiction as part of the United Kingdom; see *Post Office v Estuary Radio Ltd* [1968] 2 QB 740, at p 748; [1967] 3 All ER 663, at p 680, per Diplock LJ.

15   The presumption is particularly strong in criminal cases; see *Cox v Army Council* [1963] AC 48; [1962] 1 All ER 880; *Air-India v Wiggins* [1980] 2 All ER 593; [1980] 1 WLR 815.

16   *Joyce v Director of Public Prosecutions* [1946] AC 347; [1946] 1 All ER 186; but cf Internationally Protected Persons Act 1978, under which attacks upon the person or property of protected persons "(such as heads of state and their families) are offences justifiable in the United Kingdom, even though committed outside the United Kingdom by a person whether a citizen of the United Kingdom and Colonies or not" (s 1); there are similar provisions in the Suppression of Terrorism Act 1978, s 4 in relation to certain offences specified in Sch 1 to that Act (eg murder, manslaughter, kidnapping and various offences under the Offences Against the Person Act 1861) when committed in countries who subscribed to the European Convention on the Suppression of Terrorism 1977, in the Taking of Hostages Act 1982, and in the War Crimes Act 1991.

17   Acts of Parliament (Commencement) Act 1793.

consult the calendar of appointed days. Different parts of an Act or sections in an Act may be brought into force at different times. There are portions of Acts in existence which have never been brought into force.[18]

The problems that may arise from a failure to bring a statutory provision into force were vividly demonstrated in *R v Secretary of State for the Home Department, ex parte Fire Brigades' Union*.[19] Sections 108 to 117 of, and Schedules 6 and 7 to, the Criminal Justice Act 1988 introduced a statutory scheme of compensation for victims of crimes of violence, the scheme being intended to replace a scheme of ex gratia payments by the Criminal Injuries Compensation Board established in 1964 under the Royal Prerogative. These statutory provisions were to come into force on an appointed day. No order appointing a day was ever made, and in 1994 the Home Secretary purported to introduce a new scheme pursuant to royal prerogative. The House of Lords held, by a majority, that the Home Secretary had acted unlawfully. Although he was under no legal duty to bring the statutory scheme into effect and therefore could not be compelled to do so, he was under a duty to keep the matter under review as to whether he should in fact bring into force these provisions. It was an abuse of his power under the royal prerogative to use them in a way that was inconsistent with bringing the statute into force. Lord Browne-Wilkinson observed that, if the Home Secretary wanted to introduce a scheme inconsistent with that in the 1988 Act, he should first have gone back to Parliament and sought the repeal of the statutory provisions.

Sometimes the decision not to implement an Act, or parts of it, is taken quite soon after the passage of the Act itself. Thus, for example, sections 8 to 27 of the Crime (Sentences) Act 1997 introduced a new scheme for the early release of prisoners. Within months, and after a change of government, it was announced that the new scheme would not be implemented. Also, sometimes schemes are only implemented piecemeal. Again, the 1997 Act provides an example, with certain powers being introduced initially through a pilot study.

The effect of a statute coming into operation is that, if it is a Public Act, and every Act passed since 1850 is presumed to be a Public Act in the absence of a contrary provision, it immediately becomes effective and the courts take judicial notice of it.[20]

Delegated legislation generally comes into force when it is passed but section 3(2) of the Statutory Instruments Act 1946 provides that where a person is charged with contravening the provisions of a statutory instrument it shall be a defence to prove that the instrument had not been issued by Her Majesty's Stationery Office at the date of the alleged contravention, unless it is proved that at that date reasonable steps had been taken for the purpose of bringing the purport of the instrument to the notice of the public, or of persons likely to be affected by it, or of the person charged.[1]

b   Retrospective operation

As a general rule a statute only affects factual situations that arise during the period of its operations. There is a presumption against the statute being retroactive although the courts have been keen to point out that it is in each case a question of ascertaining the intentions of Parliament. As Staughton LJ stated in *Secretary of State for Social Security v Tunnicliffe*:[2]

---

18   *Current Law Statutes Annotated* incorporates a table "Legislation Not Yet in Force" to which reference may be made.
19   [1995] 2 AC 516, [1995] 2 All ER 244.
20   Interpretation Act 1978, s 3.
1   See *R v Sheer Metalcraft Ltd* [1954] 1 QB 586; [1954] 1 All ER 542.
2   [1991] 2 All ER 712, at 724, approved by the House of Lords in *L'Office Cherifien des Phosphates v Yamashita-Shinnihon Steamship Co Ltd* [1994] 1 AC 486; [1994] 1 All ER 20.

"the true principle is that Parliament is presumed not to have intended to alter the law applicable to past events and transactions in a manner which is unfair to those concerned in them, unless a contrary intention appears. It is not simply a question of classifying an enactment as retrospective or non-retrospective. Rather it may well be a matter of degree the greater the unfairness, the more it is expected that Parliament will make it clear if that is intended."

The presumption is particularly strong where the statute in question creates criminal penalties or tax obligations or would operate to deprive a person of a vested right in property.[3] However, Parliament is sovereign and statutes may be, and occasionally are, expressed to be retroactive even where this operates to deprive a person of a vested right in property. A modern illustration was the War Damage Act 1965 which operated to remove vested rights to compensation from the Crown and which was exceptional in that it was also expressed to apply to proceedings commenced before the Act came into force.[4] Also, statutes aimed at preventing tax avoidance, or recovering overpayments of state benefits paid in consequence of misrepresentation or failure to disclose a material fact, are sometimes expressed to be retroactive and there seems to be no presumption against retroactivity in the case of statutes of this type.[5]

An Act of indemnity, the purpose of which is to validate or legalise ex post facto that which was initially invalid or illegal, must by its nature be retroactive.[6] A statute which alters rules of evidence or procedure rather than rules of substantive law is always retroactive, in the absence of a contrary intention, since the rules of evidence and procedure that a court is bound to observe are those in existence at the time of the hearing.[7] Sentencing provisions usually apply only in respect of offences committed after the provisions were introduced. Even if the statutory provision itself does not take effect retrospectively, it may nevertheless be held to entitle a court to have regard to what has occurred prior to its passage. Thus in *L'Office Cherifien des Phosphates v Yamashita-Shinnihon Steamship Co Ltd*[8] the House of Lords held that "inordinate and inexcusable delay" which had occurred prior to section 13A of the Arbitration Act 1950 came into force entitled an arbitrator to dismiss a claim.[9]

c   When a statute ceases to be operative

No statute becomes obsolete by the passing of time. Nevertheless there are many ancient statutes more honoured in the breach than in the observance. At one time the approach

---

3   *Yew Bon Tew v Kenderaan Bas Mara* [1983] 1 AC 553; [1982] 3 All ER 833. In *R v Fisher* [1969] 1 All ER 100; [1969] 1 WLR 8 the rule against retrospective operation operated, for once, against the accused in that he was convicted of an offence which had, at the time of his trial, been abolished by statute since the conduct in question had been, at the time of commission, an offence; see also *R v West London Stipendiary Magistrate, ex parte Simeon* [1983] 1 AC 234; *sub nom Metropolitan Police Commissioner v Simeon* [1982] 2 All ER 813. But a retrospective statute may affect a pending action; *Zainal bin Hashim v Government of Malaysia* [1980] AC 734; [1979] 3 All ER 241.

4   Section 1(2). The action affected was *Burmah Oil Co Ltd v Lord Advocate* [1965] AC 75; [1964] 2 All ER 348.

5   See, for example, Finance Act 1936, s 18; Social Security Act 1986, s 53 as construed in *Secretary of State for Social Security v Tunnicliffe* [1991] 2 All ER 712.

6   Examples of Acts of indemnity are: Indemnity Act 1920; Indian Divorces (Validity) Act 1921; Charitable Trusts (Validation) Act 1954.

7   See *Blyth v Blyth* [1966] AC 643; [1966] 1 All ER 524; *R v Cruttenden* [1991] 2 QB 66; [1991] 3 All ER 242 (evidence); cf *Yew Bon Tew v Kenderaan Bas Mara* [1983] 1 AC 553; [1982] 3 All ER 833 (limitation statute in Malaysia held not to revive statute-barred cause of action).

8   [1994] 1 AC 486; [1994] 1 All ER 20.

9   Section 13A was incorporated into the 1950 Act by s 102 of Courts and Legal Services Act 1990. See p 331, *post*.

of the legislature was to do nothing until the need for repeal manifested itself. Thus the plaintiff in a nineteenth century case was no doubt disturbed to discover that his opponent had a right to claim trial by battle;[10] two cases in modern times have involved statutes of 1351 and 1381 respectively[11] while resort to such provisions as the preamble to the Charitable Uses Act 1601, the Statute of Frauds 1677, s 4 and the Bill of Rights 1688 is by no means uncommon.[12]

However, the present position is that the Law Commissions are expressly required to review "obsolete and unnecessary enactments" with a view to repeal.[13] In consequence there are now regular Statute Law (Repeals) Acts each of which repeals hundreds of obsolete enactments, following recommendations of the Law Commissions.

To the above rule that statutes do not become obsolete with the passing of time there is an exception. Certain statutes are expressed to be operative only for a limited period, usually because they are experimental or transitional though the best known statutes of this type, the Army Act and the Air Force Act, are re-enacted periodically so as to avoid the prohibition on keeping a standing army in time of peace.[14] Most of the provisions of the Prevention of Terrorism (Temporary Provisions) Act 1989 require annual renewal by order of the Home Secretary.[15]

Temporary statutes may acquire a new lease of life by the passing of an Expiring Laws Continuance Act which is effected solely for the purpose of renewing statutes which would otherwise expire. Thus Part I of the Commonwealth Immigrants Act 1962, an experimental measure expressed to last for only one year, was renewed annually until 1971 when the Immigration Act 1971 was passed to supersede it.

Unless it is one of those which are expressed to be operative for a limited period, a statute ceases to have effect only when repealed by another statute, since only Parliament is competent to repeal its own enactments.[16] Repeal may be express or implied. In modern times almost all repeal is express and it is common for a statute to include a schedule of repeals, expressly incorporated into the body of the Act, where there are several provisions repealed. Implied repeal is possible and occurs where two statutory provisions are inconsistent with one another. In this situation the later provision impliedly repeals the earlier to the extent of the inconsistency.[17] The courts, however, lean against implied repeal and will attempt to reconcile seemingly conflicting provisions wherever possible. In addition there is a rule that a public Act does not impliedly repeal a private or local Act (*generalia specialibus non derogant*).[18] Unless

10   *Ashford v Thornton* (1818) 1 & Ald 405.
11   *Hemmings v Stoke Poges Golf Club Ltd* [1920] 1 KB 720; *Joyce v Director of Public Prosecutions* [1946] AC 347, [1946] 1 All ER 186.
12   See, for example, *Rost v Edwards* [1990] 2 QB 460; [1990] 2 All ER 641.
13   Law Commissions Act 1965, s 3(1).
14   Prior to 1955 this was done by means of annual Acts. However a new procedure was established by the Army Act 1955, s 226 and the Air Force Act 1955, s 224. Under this procedure the Acts are renewable annually by Order in Council, a new Act of Parliament being required only every five years.
15   The 1989 Act was passed to replace the Prevention of Terrorism (Temporary Provisions) Act 1984, which in turn replaced a similar Act of 1976, each of which was renewable (and in fact renewed) annually.
16   Unless the enactment is impliedly repealed by legislation of the European Communities: *Amministrazione delle Finanze dello Stato v Simmenthal SpA* [1978] ECR 629; see p 103, or unless Parliament has conferred power on a Minister to amend or repeal statutory provisions: see, e.g., Human Rights Bill, p 134, *post*.
17   See, for example, *Smith v Benabo* [1937] 1 KB 518; [1937] 1 All ER 523; *Ellen Street Estates Ltd v Minister of Health* [1934] 1 KB 590; *Dryden v Dryden* [1973] Fam 217; [1973] 3 All ER 526.
18   Thus it was held in *Bishop of Gloucester v Cunnington* [1943] KB 101; [1943] 1 All ER 61, that the restrictions on the recovery of leasehold property imposed by the Rent and Mortgage Interest Restriction Acts 1920–39 did not affect the right of a bishop to recover possession of a parsonage under the Pluralities Act 1838.

the contrary intention appears repeal does not have the effect of reviving any earlier repealed rule of law, statutory or otherwise.[19]

There is no reason why a statute should not create a power to revive the effect of a statutory provision that it elsewhere repeals. Indeed the Crown Proceedings (Armed Forces) Act 1987 did just this, section 2(1) conferring upon the Secretary of State a power to revive a provision repealed by section 1 of the same Act.[20]

D   THE INTERPRETATION AND CONSTRUCTION OF STATUTES

I   The need for interpretation and construction

Where the words of a statute are clear and unambiguous, persons affected by its provisions will regulate their conduct according to the terms of the statute and the need for judicial interpretation will not arise. However, if the meaning or extent of a statute is uncertain or ambiguous litigation is inevitable and the statute will fall to be interpreted. There is a technical distinction between interpretation and construction. "Interpretation" is simply the process whereby a meaning is assigned to the words in a statute. The courts' primary task on interpretation is to ascertain and give effect to the meaning of the words used: the first inquiry of a court should be to ask: "what do the words themselves mean?" "Construction", on the other hand, is the process whereby uncertainties or ambiguities in a statute are resolved. It follows that every statute that comes before a court is interpreted whereas only uncertain or ambiguous provisions require construction. The processes are not usually distinguished by judges since, in the nature of things, litigation only arises around the wording of a statute where it is ambiguous or, at least, uncertain. However, Lawson J clearly did distinguish the process of interpretation and construction in one case:[1]

> "I approach the answer to the question in two stages. Stage one is this; whether the meaning of the Cyprus Act 1960 in this respect is clear and unambiguous, and if so, what does it mean? At this stage I look at the words of the enactment as a whole, including the Schedule, and I use no further aids, no further extrinsic aids in order to reach a conclusion as to the clear and unambiguous meaning of the words ... If I find that the answer on the first stage in my inquiry is that the meaning of the Act in this respect is ambiguous, then I have to go on to the second stage and consider two possible different meanings ... Now if I get to this second stage, then in my judgment, and then only, am I entitled to look at extrinsic aids,[2] such as the long title, the heading, the side notes, other legislation; then only am I entitled to resort to maxims of construction ...".

a   The words of the statute

The need for judicial interpretation or construction may arise from a variety of sources. One may be careless drafting, or the form and content of the Act having been the subject

---

19   Interpretation Act 1978, ss 15, 16(1).
20   The provision in question was Crown Proceedings Act 1947, s 10 (exclusions from liability in tort in cases involving the armed forces).
1   *Franklin v A-G* [1974] QB 185, at p 199; [1973] 1 All ER 879, at p 886 (one of the cases arising out of the attempt by the plaintiff to proceed against the Crown by way of the ancient remedy of "petition of right").
2   The aids then referred to by Lawson J are generally referred to as internal, or intrinsic (rather than extrinsic) aids since they appear in the text of the Queen's Printer's copy of the Act; see p 49, *post*.

of ad hoc, hasty or ill thought-out amendment during the parliamentary process. Other problems may arise through legislative style, which may have resulted in a narrow semantic approach to statutory interpretation by judges. However, many issues of construction arise simply because of the very uncertainty of words themselves. A vivid example of this is *DPP v Johnson*,[3] where the Divisional Court had, in a drink–driving case, to consider the meaning of the word "consume" in section 5 of the Road Traffic Act 1988. As Schiemann LJ put it: "It is not unusual to speak of a house being consumed by fire and it would not be strange to speak of a bottle of medical alcohol having been consumed by rubbing its contents into skin prior to administering an injection ... One can also talk of consuming snuff by sniffing". The meaning of a word depends on the context in which it is used. It was the context of section 5, together with the marginal note, that persuaded the court to reject the submission of the appellant that "consume" in section 5 meant "consume by mouth", holding that a drink–drive offence could be committed even if the alcohol had, in part, been ingested by injection.

b   Ambiguity

Ambiguity arises, often through careless drafting, when words used in a statute are found to be capable of bearing two or more literal meanings. Language is an imprecise tool and even Parliamentary draftsmen, in using words intended to convey one meaning, occasionally contrive to give rise to an alternative meaning which neither they nor the legislature ever envisaged. Thus the Restriction of Offensive Weapons Act 1959 made it an offence to "offer for sale" certain offensive weapons including "flick knives". A shopkeeper who displayed weapons of this type in his window was held, by a divisional court, to be not guilty of an offence under the Act because the exhibition of goods in a shop window does not constitute an offer.[4] Where the subject matter of a statute is a branch of the law which is intrinsically complex, such as landlord and tenant or income tax, it seems to be virtually impossible to choose language which is entirely free from ambiguity. Nevertheless the judiciary has on occasion been less than sympathetic to the draftsman's plight. Thus in *R v Royle*,[5] section 16 of the Theft Act 1968 was described as being so obscure as to have "created a judicial nightmare" while in *Central Asbestos Co Ltd v Dodd* [6] Lord Reid said of the Limitation Act 1963 that it had "a strong claim to the distinction of being the worst drafted Act on the statute book".[7]

c   Uncertainty

Uncertainty is far more common than ambiguity. Uncertainty occurs where the words of a statute are intended to apply to various factual situations and the courts are called upon to decide whether or not the set of facts before them amounts to a factual situation envisaged by the Act. For example the words "an accident arising out of and in the

3   [1995] 4 All ER 53.
4   *Fisher v Bell* [1961] 1 QB 394; [1960] 3 All ER 731; see also *Partridge v Crittenden* [1968] 2 All ER 421; [1968] 1 WLR 1204.
5   [1971] 3 All ER 1359, at p 1363; [1971] 1 WLR 1764, at p 1767, per Edmund Davies LJ; cf *Director of Public Prosecutions v Turner* [1974] AC 357; [1973] 3 All ER 124 in which the House of Lords expressed its own dim view of the same section. The offending part of the section (s 16(2)(a)) was eventually repealed and replaced by the Theft Act 1978.
6   [1973] AC 518, at p 529; [1972] 2 All ER 1135, at p 113; the Limitation Act 1975 (replacing that part of the 1963 Act) seemed to aim at similar distinction. The Acts concerned are now consolidated in the Limitation Act 1980.
7   See also *Great Western Rail Co v Bater* [1922] 2 AC 1, at p 11; *Barentz v Whiting* [1965] 1 All ER 685; [1965] 1 WLR 433; *London County Council v Lees* [1939] 1 All ER 191; *Davies v Warwick* [1943] KB 329; [1943] 1 All ER 309.

course of his employment" in the Workmen's Compensation Acts were the source of innumerable cases, not because they were in any way ambiguous but because their scope was uncertain, being adaptable to endless permutations of facts.[8] The use of general, and ostensibly clearly defined, words such as "road",[9] "park",[10] "premises",[11] and "board"[12] has created problems of construction that the legislature could not have envisaged, while, more recently, the courts have been called upon to resolve such conundrums as whether the cremation of humans is "the subjection of goods or materials to any process",[13] whether an orange squeezed by hand is a "manufactured beverage"[14] and whether video games constitute an "exhibition of moving pictures"[15]. Lord Denning once expressed the difficulty as follows:[16]

> "It must be remembered that it is not within human powers to foresee the manifold sets of facts which may arise, and, even if it were, it is not possible to provide for them in terms free from all ambiguity."

The main difficulty in such cases is that the intention of Parliament must be established primarily from the words used by Parliament, although increasingly extrinsic aids may be used. There is also the difficult question as to the time at which parliamentary intention is to be judged. For example in *O'Rourke v Camden LBC*[17] the question arose as to whether the Housing (Homeless Persons) Act 1977 should be construed against the background of public law as it stood on the date when it was passed, or whether the remedies which it conferred should be regarded as ambulatory, fashioned according to the law as it stood from time to time. The court considered that it should be considered as at the date of the passage of the Act, although Lord Hoffman conceded that in some circumstances the alternative approach was more appropriate. In each case the question is one of statutory construction like any other.

2   Judicial approaches to interpretation

The basic task of the judge is to ascertain the intention of Parliament. Nevertheless there are alternative approaches to this task. These approaches, which differ radically, are commonly known as the "literal" approach and the "purposive" approach. It is never possible to know in advance which approach any particular court will favour, and it may well be the case that a court may adopt the approach to interpretation which best enables it to reach the conclusion considered just in all the circumstances. Certain decisions have been based on one of these approaches, others on the application of

---

8   The words continue to be used in social security legislation (currently the Social Security Contributions and Benefits Act 1992, s 94) where they continue to cause trouble; see *R v National Insurance Commissioner, ex parte Michael* [1977] 2 All ER 420; [1977] 1 WLR 109.
9   *Griffin v Squires* [1958] 3 All ER 468; [1958] 1 WLR 1106.
10   *Re Ripon (Highfield) Housing Confirmation Order 1938* [1939] 2 KB 838; [1939] 3 All ER 548.
11   *Whitley v Stumbles* [1930] AC 544; *Maunsell v Olins* [1975] AC 373; [1975] 1 All ER 16.
12   *Otter v Norman* [1989] AC 129; [1988] 2 All ER 897.
13   *Bourne (Inspector of Taxes) v Norwich Crematorium Ltd* [1967] 2 All ER 576; [1967] 1 WLR 691.
14   *Customs and Excise Commissioners v Savoy Hotel Ltd* [1966] 2 All ER 299; [1966] 1 WLR 948. For a delightfully sardonic exposition of the difficulty of ascertaining the "right" meaning of words, see the judgment of Diplock LJ in *Slim v Daily Telegraph Ltd* [1968] 2 QB 157, at pp 171–172; [1968] 1 All ER 497, at p 504.
15   *British Amusement Catering Trades Association v Westminster City Council* [1989] AC 147; [1988] 1 All ER 740.
16   *Seaford Court Estates Ltd v Asher* [1949] 2 KB 481, at p 499; [1949] 2 All ER 155, at p 164 (affirmed [1951] AC 508; [1950] 1 All ER 1018).
17   [1998] AC 188; [1997] 3 All ER 23.

another. In *Re M (A Minor) (Care Order: Threshold Conditions)*[18] Lord Templeman noted: "the tyranny of language, and the ascertaining and giving effect to the intention of Parliament by construing a statute in accordance with the spirit rather than the letter of the Act." Thus s 31(2) of the Children Act 1989, which requires a court to be satisfied that "the child concerned is suffering, or is likely to suffer, significant harm ...", was to be construed as entitling a court to make an order if it was satisfied that the child was suffering, or was likely to suffer such harm at the date of application to the court by the local authority, not the date of the making of the order. The Court of Appeal, which had concluded to the contrary, had been suffering a "preoccupation with the present tense". The statute was to be construed in accordance with the spirit, not the letter, of the statute.

Each of these approaches to interpretation must be considered individually.[19]

a   The literal approach

The basic approach to statutory interpretation, as already stated, is to ascertain the intention of the legislature. The literal rule of interpretation is that this intention must be found in the ordinary and natural meaning of the words used. If these words, interpreted literally, are capable of alternative meanings the literal rule clearly cannot be applied. Hence the approach breaks down in the face of an ambiguity. However, if the words are capable of only one literal meaning the literal rule is that this meaning must be applied even if it appears unlikely. The rule may be expressed as an irrebuttable presumption that Parliament intends the ordinary and natural meaning of the words it employs. The rule will, in most cases, produce a reasonable interpretation of the statute. Difficulty arises, however, where, in consequence of incompetent drafting, literal interpretation produces either an improbable result or, in extreme cases, a manifest absurdity. Where the literal interpretation merely produces a result which seems less plausible than one which Parliament might be supposed to have intended the literal rule ought nevertheless to be applied. Thus in *Inland Revenue Commissioners v Hinchy*[20] the House of Lords was called upon to construe section 25(3) of the Income Tax Act 1952 which provided that any person delivering an incorrect tax return should forfeit "treble the tax which he ought to be charged under this Act". Although Parliament presumably intended[1] a penalty of treble the unpaid tax, the House of Lords held that the literal meaning of the words of the subsection was that the respondent was liable to pay treble the whole amount of tax payable by him for the year. *Fisher v Bell*, cited earlier,[2] is a further example of the application of the literal rule producing a result which appeared contrary to the intention of the legislature. On the other hand, where the application of the literal rule would produce a manifest absurdity it will not be applied. This is well illustrated by the unanimous decision of the House of Lords in *McMonagle v Westminster City Council*[3] The appellant was charged with using

18   [1994] 2 AC 424; [1994] 2 All ER 298.
19   As to the approach to the interpretation of legislation of the European Community, see p 119, *post*.
20   [1960] AC 748; [1960] 1 All ER 505.
1   The law was in fact changed shortly after this decision by the Finance Act 1960, s 44.
2   [1961] 1 QB 394; [1960] 3 All ER 731; see p 35, *ante*. For further instances of the application of the literal rule, see *Magor and St Mellons Rural District Council v Newport Corporation* [1952] AC 189; [1951] 2 All ER 839; *A-G v Prince Ernest of Hanover* [1957] AC 436; [1957] 1 All ER 49; *Barclays Bank Ltd v Cole* [1967] 2 QB 738; [1966] 3 All ER 948; *R v West Yorkshire Coroner, ex parte Smith* [1983] QB 335; [1982] 3 All ER 1098. The Law Commission report, *The Interpretation of Statutes* (1969) (Law Com No 21) recommended a statutory provision to the effect that a construction which would promote the general legislative purpose underlying the provision in question "is to be preferred to a construction which would not".
3   [1990] 2 AC 716; [1990] 1 All ER 993.

premises as a "sex encounter establishment" without a licence. The statutory definition of those words was "premises at which performances which are not unlawful are given, which wholly or mainly comprise the sexual stimulation of persons admitted to the premises."

The appellant's defence was that the prosecution had failed to prove that the performances were not unlawful and that, if they were, according to the plain words of the statute a licence was not required. The House of Lords regarded this interpretation as manifestly absurd and rejected it. The reasoning was expressed by Lord Bridge as follows:[4]

> "I am satisfied that the main object of paragraph 3A(c) of Schedule 3 is to require any premises, not falling within the proviso, where live nude entertainment is provided to be licensed and that in order to avoid the substantial frustration of that object it is both necessary and legitimate that the words 'which are not unlawful' should be treated as surplusage and as having been introduced by incompetent draftsmanship for no other purpose than to emphasise that a licence confers no immunity from the ordinary criminal law."

The difficulty, of course, lies in drawing the line between a literal interpretation which appears to the court to be improbable and one which produces a "manifest absurdity" so as to avoid an interpretation which appears to them to produce a result which they cannot believe to represent the legislative intention. One example is *DPP v McKeown*,[5] where the House of Lords had to consider the meaning of section 69 of the Police and Criminal Evidence Act 1984. That section provides that a document produced by a computer may be admissible in evidence in criminal proceedings if the court is satisfied that any fault in the operation of the computer was not such as to affect the production of the document or the accuracy of its contents. Because of the setting inaccurately of the computer's clock the time stated on the document produced by the computer was wrong. Thus, on a literal interpretation, the document was inadmissible: the contents were, at any rate in one respect, inaccurate. However, the House of Lords avoided this conclusion, because that would run counter to what Parliament intended. Section 69 is concerned with the accuracy of the statement in the document to prove the truth of which the document is being admitted.

Lord Bridge in another case[6] was highly critical of this inclination:

> "I would observe first that I believe there is a distinction to be drawn between what I would call a positive and a negative absurdity. It is one thing to abstain from giving to the language of a statute the full effect of its ordinary grammatical meaning in order to avoid some positively harmful or manifestly unjust consequence. This I would describe as a legitimate process of construction to avoid a positive absurdity. But it is quite another thing to read into a statute a meaning which the language used will not bear in order to remedy a supposed defect or shortcoming which, if not made good, will make the statutory machinery less effective than the court believes it ought to be in order to achieve its proper purpose. Even if the lacuna appears to the court as absurd, this is what I describe, inelegantly but in order to point the contrast, as a negative absurdity. I know of

4   [1990] 2 AC 716 at p 727; [1990] 1 All ER 993 at p 998.
5   [1997] 1 All ER 737.
6   *R v Central Criminal Court, ex parte Francis & Francis* [1989] AC 346, at p 375; *sub nom Francis & Francis v Central Criminal Court* [1988] 3 All ER 775, at p 783. The speech of Lord Bridge was in fact a dissenting one; the majority found the relevant statutory provision to be ambiguous and therefore were able to adopt the interpretation which appeared to produce the more satisfactory result.

no legitimate principle of construction which permits such a negative absurdity to be remedied by implying words which the court thinks necessary to enhance the operation of the statutory machinery."

The diversity of judicial approach is well illustrated by the speeches of the House of Lords in *Kammins Ballrooms Co Ltd v Zenith Investments (Torquay) Ltd.*[7] The case turned on the interpretation of section 29(3) of the Landlord and Tenant Act 1954 which provides that "no application [for the grant of a new tenancy] shall be entertained unless it is made not less than two nor more than four months" after (inter alia) the tenant's request for a new tenancy. On the question of whether the court had power to consider an application made less than two months after the tenant's request, the House of Lords (Viscount Dilhorne dissenting) held that the court did have such power, thereby appearing to disregard the clear words of the section for as Viscount Dilhorne observed:[8]

"the appellants' contention here is that the words 'no application shall be entertained' must be interpreted as meaning that an application shall in certain circumstances be entertained notwithstanding that it is made too early or too late. That seems to me to involve implying something wholly inconsistent with the words expressly used. True it is that English is a flexible language but that does not mean that one can disregard the natural and ordinary meaning of the words used unless it is apparent that some other meaning was intended.

If language is clear and explicit, the court must give effect to it 'for in that case the words of the statute speak the intention of the legislature' (*Warburton v Loveland* (1832) 2 Dow & Cl 480, Tindal CJ at p 489) and in so doing it must bear in mind that its function is *jus dicere*, not *jus dare*; the words of a statute must not be overruled by the judges, but reform of the law must be left to the hands of Parliament' (*Maxwell on Interpretation of Statutes*, 12th edn (1969), P 1)."

Viscount Dilhorne was, however, a lone voice in support of this traditional approach. Lord Diplock, who was in the majority, expressed his reasoning as follows:[9]

"Upon the literal approach, semantics and the rules of syntax alone could never justify the conclusion that the words 'No application shall be entertained unless' meant that some applications should be entertained notwithstanding that neither of the conditions which follow the word 'unless' was fulfilled. It can be justified only upon the assumption that the draftsman of the Act omitted to state in any words used in the subsection an exception to the absolute prohibition to which Parliament must have intended it to be subject. A conclusion that an exception was intended by Parliament, and what that exception was can only be reached by using the purposive approach."

It is, accordingly, rarely possible to predict with certainty which approach the court will adopt. In *Stock v Frank Jones (Tipton) Ltd*[10] (where the literal rule was applied by

7   [1971] AC 850; [1970] 2 All ER 871.
8   [1971] AC 850, at p 869; [1970] 2 All ER 871, at p 883.
9   [1971] AC 850, at p 880; [1970] 2 All ER 871, at p 892. This approach was enthusiastically adopted by Lord Denning MR in *Nothman v London Borough of Barnet* [1978] 1 All ER 1243; [1978] 1 WLR 220 but, although the House of Lords upheld the decision in that case, Lord Russell expressly disclaimed what he called the "sweeping comments" of the Master of the Rolls [1979] 1 All ER 142, at p 151; [1979] 1 WLR 67, at p 77.
10   [1978] 1 All ER 948; [1978] 1 WLR 231; the whole of this speech repays study.

the House of Lords) Lord Simon dealt with the rationale of the literal rule in considerable depth and, while favouring the literal approach, acknowledged that where this produced an anomaly a court would be justified in departing from the plain words, but only were it satisfied that:

"(1) there is clear and gross balance of anomaly; (2) Parliament, the legislative promoters and the draftsman could not have envisaged such anomaly and could not have been prepared to accept it in the interest of a supervening legislative objective; (3) the anomaly can be obviated without detriment to such legislative objective; (4) the language of the statute is susceptible of the modification required to obviate the anomaly."[11]

b   The purposive approach

The purposive approach to statutory interpretation, in more old-fashioned language to be found referred to as "the golden rule", is that words in a statute must be interpreted according to their natural, ordinary and grammatical meaning, so far as possible, but only to the extent that such an interpretation does not produce a manifestly absurd result. Perhaps the best known statement of the rule is to be found in the judgment of Parke B in *Becke v Smith*:[12]

"it is a very useful rule in the construction of a statute to adhere to the ordinary meaning of the words used, and to the grammatical construction, unless that is at variance with the intention of the legislature to be collected from the statute itself, or leads to any manifest absurdity or repugnance, in which case the language may be varied or modified so as to avoid such inconvenience, but no further."

Where the statute permits of two or more literal interpretations the court must adopt that interpretation which produces the least absurd or repugnant result. This application of the rule is not, of course, inconsistent with the literal rule since the latter cannot be applied in a case of ambiguity. This is the narrow aspect of the purposive approach and has been adopted in several well-known cases. Thus, for example, section 57 of the Offences Against the Person Act 1861 provides that "whosoever, being married, shall 'marry any other person during the life of the former husband or wife' shall be guilty of bigamy". The word "marry" permits of alternative meanings. It may be construed to mean "contracts a valid marriage" or "goes through a ceremony of marriage". Since the former meaning would produce an absurd result, the latter must be applied.[13]

However, where the statute is capable of only one literal meaning and the court rejects that meaning in favour of a construction which is obviously more rational the golden rule is, in effect, being applied in preference to the literal rule. It has been noted above that this approach will be readily adopted in order to avoid "manifest absurdity". There is also a residual category of cases in which public policy requires the rejection

---

11   At pp 952–954, pp 235–237.
12   (1836) 2 M & W 191 at p 195. The statement of Lord Wensleydale in *Grey v Pearson* (1857) 6 HL Cas 61, p 106, expressed in very similar terms, is also frequently cited as stating the rules; see, for example, *Lord Advocate v de Rosa* [1974] 2 All ER 849; [1974] 1 WLR 946. See, also, *Vacher & Sons Ltd v The London Society of Compositors* [1913] AC 107.
13   *R v Allen* (1872) LR 1 CCR 367; see also *Young v Clarey* [1948] Ch 191; [1948] 1 All ER 197; *Mills v Cooper* [1967] 2 QB 459; [1967] 2 All ER 100.

of a literal interpretation of the statute. Thus in *Re Sigsworth*[14] the purposive approach was applied to prevent a murderer from taking on the intestacy of his victim although he was, as her son, the "sole issue" on a literal interpretation of the Administration of Estates Act 1925.

More recently the Court of Appeal in *R v Registrar General, ex parte Smith*[15] adopted a similar approach. The appellant, a double killer with psychotic illness involving extreme hatred for his adoptive parents, applied under section 51 of the Adoption Act 1976 for a copy of his birth certificate (to which he had a right under that Act). The Registrar General refused that request, apprehending that the appellant might use the information on the certificate to commit a serious crime against his natural mother. The appellant applied for judicial review of this decision, contending that the statute conferred no discretion to refuse his application. The Court of Appeal, on the ground of public policy, upheld the refusal of his application. It might be supposed that in cases such as these the court is refusing to give effect to a statute, which it is axiomatic that no court has power to do,[16] but this is not so. The court is simply interpreting the statute in accordance with the presumed intention of Parliament, the presumption being that Parliament did not intend to procure a consequence which would involve a person benefiting from his crime, or would facilitate the commission of a crime. These cases could, in fact, be regarded as specific instances of the "manifest absurdity" principle.

One criticism that could be made of the wide application of the purposive approach in preference to the literal rule is that it is inherently subjective. The judge who decides that a literal interpretation is contrary to the intention of the legislature is, *ipso facto*, ascertaining the intention of the legislature from some source or sources other than the statute itself, and might, certainly in the past, have been regarded as going beyond his judicial function. Moreover, he may expose himself to the criticism that he is giving effect to his own views as to what the policy of Parliament ought to be.[17] However, it is beyond doubt that the particular approach adopted by the court will turn not only on the inclinations of the individual judge and the justice of the case, but also upon the context in which the matter is being decided. As will later be seen, the courts are always anxious to adopt a purposive approach to statutes in order to give effect to international obligations, and, in the context of the European Community, are under a legal obligation to do so.

Rejection of a literal interpretation on the ground of absurdity is, however, only possible where there is available a more rational interpretation of the provision under consideration. Thus, if there is no other possible interpretation or only an alternative which is equally, or even more, absurd than the literal interpretation, the court has to adopt the latter.[18]

SUPPLYING OMISSIONS

An interesting problem of construction arises when the court is faced with a factual situation for which the statute has not provided. Such a situation is termed a *casus omissus*. It can only be remedied by attributing to Parliament an intention which Parliament never had. This amounts to a legislative act on the part of the judiciary and

14   [1935] Ch 89.
15   [1991] 2 QB 393; [1991] 2 All ER 88.
16   See p 23, *ante*.
17   See *Duport Steels Ltd v Sirs* [1980] 1 All ER 529; [1980] 1 WLR 142; *Shah v Barnet London Borough Council* [1983] 2 AC 309; [1983] 1 All ER 226, in both of which cases the House of Lords warned the judiciary against this pitfall; see p 216, *post*.
18   The House of Lords found itself in this unenviable position in *Metropolitan Police Commissioner v Curran* [1976] 1 All ER 162; [1976] 1 WLR 87 and had to content itself with a unanimous and scathing attack on the draftsmanship of the provisions in question (s 9(3) of and Sch 4 to the Road Traffic Act 1972 repealed by the Road Traffic Act 1988).

is a function which the more conservative judges are slow to adopt. Thus Denning LJ, in the Court of Appeal, expressed his personal view of the judicial function in respect of omissions as follows:[19]

"We sit here to find out the intention of Parliament and of Ministers and carry it out, and we do this better by filling in the gaps and making sense of the enactment than by opening it up to destructive analysis."

On appeal Lord Simonds roundly condemned this approach and, in a now famous dictum, described it as a "naked usurpation of the legislative function under the thin disguise of interpretation".[20] "If a gap is disclosed," Lord Simonds explained, "the remedy lies in an amending Act."

Nonetheless it is a truism that hard cases make bad law and the courts have, from time to time, been prepared to assume the authority to supply omissions left by the legislature. An illustration of this is to be found in the majority decision of the House of Lords in *Edwards v Porter*[1] where it was held that, although a "husband need not be joined" in an action against his wife, he could be joined if the plaintiff so wished. The Married Women's Property Act 1882, the Act in question, was silent on this point.[2]

Whichever approach to interpretation is adopted, the court is still bound to interpret the words of the Act before it. If interpretation discloses an uncertainty or ambiguity the court will then be bound to construe the statute. The judges themselves have formulated a large body of rules for the interpretation and construction of statutes. These rules, which equate to the rules for the construction of documents generally, are exceedingly complex and only those most commonly encountered are discussed below, by way of example.

3   Rules of interpretation and construction

a   The statute must be read as a whole

Words in isolation may import meanings different from that which they bear in conjunction.[3] A statute must be read as a whole. Every section must be read in the light of every other section,[4] especially in the light of an interpretation section, and Schedules, if incorporated into the body of the Act, must be read with the Act.

---

19   *Magor and St Mellons Rural District Council v Newport Corporation* [1950] 2 All ER 1226 at p 1236.
20   [1952] AC 189, at p 191; [1951] 2 All ER 839, at p 841. In *James Buchanan & Co Ltd v Babco Forwarding and Shipping (UK) Ltd* [1977] QB 208; [1977] 1 All ER 518, Lord Denning reiterated what he had said in *Magor and St Mellons* in relation to a statute enacting an international convention (as to which, see p 54, *post*) on the basis of the more liberal approach to statutory interpretation adopted by the European Court (see p 59, *post*), but the House of Lords, once again, did not support his view ([1978] AC 141; [1977] 3 All ER 1048); see also, in this context, the observations of Lord Bridge in *R v Central Criminal Court, ex parte Francis & Francis* [1989] AC 346; *sub nom Francis & Francis v Central Criminal Court* [1988] 3 All ER 775 (quoted on p 38, *ante*).
1   [1925] AC 1.
2   See also *Astor v Perry* [1935] AC 398; *Re Radio Communications in Canada Regulation and Control* [1932] AC 304; *Chandris v Isbrandtsen-Moller Co Inc* [1951] 1 KB 240; [1950] 1 All ER 768; *Wagg v The Law Society* [1957] Ch 405; [1957] 2 All ER 274; *Williams v Williams* [1971] P 271: [1971] 2 All ER 764.
3   See observations on the words "unfair competition" in *Lee v Showmen's Guild of Great Britain* [1952] 2 QB 329, at p 338; [1952] 1 All ER 1175, at p 1178.
4   See, for example, *Owens Bank Ltd v Cauche* [1989] 1 WLR 559 where the statute under consideration had inconsistent provisions, so that one had to prevail over the literal meaning of the other.

An interesting illustration of this, and other rules of interpretation, is afforded by the decision of the House of Lords in the leading case of *Beswick v Beswick*.[5] The case raised the question of whether Parliament had by section 56 of the Law of Property Act 1925 inadvertently abrogated the common law rule that a person cannot sue on a contract to which he is not a party. Section 56(1) provides that "a person may take an interest in land or other property, or the benefit of any condition, right of entry, covenant or agreement over or respecting land or other property, although he may take an interest in land or other property, or the benefit of any condition, right of entry, covenant or agreement over or respecting land or other property, although he may not be named as a party to the conveyance or other instrument". Section 205(1) of the 1925 Act, the interpretation section, provides that "in this Act unless the context otherwise requires 'property' includes any thing in action". It was argued that the combined effect of these provisions was to enable a stranger to a contract to enforce the contract. This argument prevailed in the Court of Appeal[6] but was rejected by the House of Lords. Their Lordships pointed out that section 56 is one of 25 sections in the Act grouped under the heading "conveyances and other instruments" and in those circumstances held that the context did require the word "property" to be limited in its effect to real property.

The long title and the short title, being part of the enactment, must, strictly, be consulted in interpreting any part of the Act though, in practice, the courts will only refer to the long title to resolve an ambiguity and do not regard the short title as an aid to interpretation at all. Headings, marginal notes, punctuation and Schedules which are not expressly incorporated into the text are not part of the enactment. Their role as aids to interpretation is dealt with later.[7]

b   The mischief rule

The "mischief rule", or rule in *Heydon*'s case,[8] is that where a statute was passed to remedy a mischief the court will, if possible, adopt the interpretation of the statute which will have the effect of correcting the mischief in question. In *Heydon*'s case itself, the rule was defined thus:

> "four things are to be discussed and considered; (1) what was the common law before the making of the Act; (2) what was the mischief and defect for which the common law did not provide; (3) what remedy the Parliament hath resolved and appointed to cure the disease of the commonwealth; and (4) the true reason of the remedy."

A more modern formulation is that of Lord Diplock in *Jones v Wrotham Park Settled Estates*,[9] where he specified three conditions which must be satisfied before the rule can be applied:

(1) it must be possible to determine from consideration of the Act as a whole[10] precisely the mischief that it was the purpose of the Act to remedy;

5   [1968] AC 58; [1967] 2 All ER 1197; see also *Crook v Edmondson* [1966] 2 QB 81; [1966] 1 All ER 833.
6   [1966] Ch 538; [1966] 3 All ER 1. The Court of Appeal appears to have overlooked the vital words "unless the context otherwise requires" in s 205(1). In the event the House of Lords was able to uphold the decision of the Court of Appeal by an ingenious use of the remedy of specific performance.
7   See p 49, *post*.
8   (1584) 3 Co Rep 7a.
9   [1980] AC 74, at 105; [1979] 1 All ER 286, at 289.
10 In fact, in a case of ambiguity the court may look to extrinsic aids (*infra*).

(2) it must be apparent that the draftsman and Parliament had inadvertently overlooked, and so omitted to deal with, the mischief;

(3) it must be possible to state "with certainty"[11] what were the additional words that would have been inserted by the draftsman and approved by Parliament had the omission been drawn to their attention.

The rule is often used to resolve ambiguities in cases in which the literal rule cannot be applied. For example, a "single woman" for the purposes of affiliation proceedings was a woman with no husband to support her, not necessarily an unmarried woman, since the mischief which the Acts were passed to remedy was the possibility of a woman having an illegitimate child with no means of supporting it.[12]

In order to ascertain the mischief which the statute was passed to correct the judge may legitimately have regard to the preamble of the statute, the long title,[13] headings[14] and to extrinsic sources such as reports of Royal Commissions or Law Reform Committees which may indicate the state of the law before the passing of the Act.[15]

c   The eiusdem generis rule

This rule is but a particular aspect of the wider rule that the statute must be read as a whole. The rule is that general words which follow two or more particular words in an Act must be confined to a meaning of the same kind (*eiusdem generis*) as the particular words. It is common drafting practice, when the intention is to cover a wide range of similar circumstances, to use two or three particular examples to create a genus followed by a general expression, such as "or other place", which has the effect of extending the operation of the enactment to all particular circumstances which are within the genus created.

The operation of the rule can best be illustrated by two examples. Section 1 of the Betting Act 1853 prohibited the keeping of a "house, office, room or other place" for betting with persons resorting thereto. In *Powell v Kempton Park Racecourse Co*[16] the point at issue was whether Tattersalls' ring at a racecourse was an "other place" within the meaning of the Act. The House of Lords held that it was not since the words "house, office, room" created a genus of indoor places within which a racecourse, being outdoor, did not fall. Similarly in *Brownsea Haven Properties Ltd v Poole Corporation*[17] it was held that regulations enabling a local authority to make orders for the direction of traffic "in all times of public processions, rejoicings, or illuminations, and in any case when the streets are thronged or liable to be obstructed" did not confer power to create a one-way traffic system for the six months of the summer holiday season.

---

11   This cannot mean that the precise words that would have been used can be ascertained with total confidence, as the Court of Appeal pointed out in *Inland Revenue Commissioners v Trustees of Sir John Aird's Settlement* [1984] Ch 382; [1983] 3 All ER 481.

12   *Kruhlak v Kruhlak* [1958] 2 QB 32; [1958] 1 All ER 154.

13   *Suffolk County Council v Mason* [1979] AC 705; [1979] 2 All ER 369; see p 50, *post*.

14   *Qualter Hall & Co Ltd v Board of Trade* [1962] Ch 273; [1961] 3 All ER 389.

15   See, generally, the full discussion of this topic by the House of Lords in *Black-Clawson International Ltd v Papierwerke Waldhof-Aschaffenburgh AG* [1975] AC 591; [1975] 1 All ER 810.

16   [1899] AC 143; cf *Culley v Harrison* [1956] 2 QB 71; [1956] 2 All ER 254.

17   [1958] Ch 574; [1958] 1 All ER 205; see also *Director of Public Prosecutions v Jordan* [1977] AC 699; [1976] 3 All ER 775 (obscene publication justified as being for the public good on the ground that it is "in the interests of science, literature, art or learning, or of other objects of general concern" (Obscene Publications Act 1959, s 4(1)); the House of Lords held that "other objects of general concern", having regard to the preceding generic words, did not include the psychotherapeutic value of pornography to sexual deviants.

It should be noted that there must be at least two specific words to create a genus. Thus where an Act referred to "theatres and other places of amusement" it was held that a funfair was within the Act even though not eiusdem generis with the word "theatres".[18]

d   Penal provisions are construed narrowly

Where a statute imposes criminal liability or tax obligations (which are treated as penal) and the statute is ambiguous or uncertain, it should be construed in favour of the individual.[19] Thus it has been held that the offence of "knowingly possessing an explosive" requires knowledge on the part of the accused that the substance possessed is explosive, not merely that he possesses the substance.[20] One aspect of this general rule is the presumption against the imposition of liability without fault.

However, this rule of interpretation is not strong enough to displace the literal rule. Consequently, where a statute unambiguously creates a criminal offence or a tax the court is bound to give effect to it, and the provision will be regarded as unambiguous if, in the judgment of the court, the intention of Parliament is clear, notwithstanding that the words are as a matter of semantics capable of bearing more than one meaning.[1]

e   Interpretation Act 1978

This Act, which consolidated with amendments the Interpretation Act 1889, prescribes definitions of certain words and phrases which are commonly encountered in Acts of Parliament. Thus:

> "unless the contrary intention appears: (a) words importing the masculine gender include the feminine; (b) words importing the feminine gender include the masculine; (c) words in the singular include the plural and words in the plural include the singular."[2]

> "month' means calendar month".[3]

However these, and other, definitions are only presumptive and yield to a contrary intention, express or implied, in the Act being interpreted. Thus, although the word "person" is defined in Schedule 1 to the Interpretation Act to include a body corporate, it was held in one case that a corporation which undertook legal work was not guilty of the offence of acting as an "unqualified person" since the enactment in question could only apply to persons who could qualify as solicitors.[4]

---

18   *Allen v Emmerson* [1944] KB 362; [1944] 1 All ER 344. For a striking illustration of the operation of the rule see *Customs and Excise Commissioners v Savoy Hotel Ltd* [1966] 2 All ER 299; [1966] 1 WLR 948.

19   *Kingston-upon-Hull Dock Co v Browne* (1831) 2 B & Ad 43; *D'Avigdor-Goldsmid v Inland Revenue Commissioners* [1953] AC 347; [1953] 1 All ER 403.

20   *R v Hallam* [1957] 1 QB 569; [1957] 1 All ER 665.

1   See, for examples, *Director of Public Prosecutions v Ottewell* [1970] AC 642; [1968] 3 All ER 153; *Attorney-General's Reference (No 1 of 1988)* [1989] AC 971; [1989] 2 All ER 1; *Inland Revenue Commissioners v Hinchy* [1960] AC 748; [1960] 1 All ER 505, see p 37, *ante.*

2   Section 6. For an illustration of the application of this rule, see *Floor v Davis* [1980] AC 695; [1979] 2 All ER 677.

3   Section 5 and Sch 1.

4   *Law Society v United Service Bureau Ltd* [1934] 1 KB 343. This lacuna was filled by the Solicitors Act 1957 (now Solicitors Act 1974, s 20); see also *Penn-Texas Corporation v Murat-Anstalt (No 2)* [1964] 2 QB 647; [1964] 2 All ER 594.

4   Presumptions in construction

It is possible to express almost any rule of statutory interpretation in the form of a presumption. The rules against retrospective operation and against extraterritorial operation are often expressed as presumptions. The reasons for rules of statutory interpretation being described as presumptions is that their operation is rebutted by an express provision to the contrary in the Act itself. They thus have the quality of evidentiary presumptions. Nevertheless, although it is probably a mere matter of terminology, the following are always described as presumptions rather than as rules. However, care should be taken in their application: they are just a means to assist a court in finding the intention of Parliament.[5]

a   Presumption against alteration of the law

Parliament, like the judiciary, is presumed to know the law. Consequently if an Act does not expressly alter the law it will be presumed that Parliament did not intend it to have that effect. In the words of Devlin J:[6]

"a statute is not to be taken as effecting a fundamental alteration in the general law unless it uses words which point unmistakably to that conclusion."

The decision of the House of Lords in *Beswick*[7] is a paradigm of this presumption. Nevertheless it is important to remember that Parliament can and does make fundamental alterations to the common law and, if such a change appears from a literal interpretation of the words used, the use of any presumption to the contrary is out of place. The presumption against fundamental change also applies in relation to statute law, one aspect being the presumption that a consolidating statute does not, simply by verbal alteration in the provision re-enacted, thereby introduce a fundamental change of meaning.[8] Conversely the mere fact that a statutory provision is re-enacted (whether by way of consolidation or otherwise) does not necessarily mean that Parliament is intending to give statutory force to judicial interpretations of the earlier enactment. The court must interpret the enactment as it stands though, if the scales were equally balanced, the fact that Parliament had re-enacted a provision which had been the subject of judicial interpretation might tip the balance in favour of that interpretation.[9]

b   Presumption against the imposition of liability without fault

This may be regarded as an aspect of the general presumption against fundamental change in the common law by mere implication. At common law mens rea is an element in all crimes,[10] though not in all torts. Although the legislature can, and frequently does, create offences of strict or absolute liability the intention so to do must be clear and unambiguous. Lord Reid, in the leading case of *Sweet v Parsley*, explained the judicial approach as follows:[11]

5   *L'Office Cherifien des Phosphates v Yamashita-Shinnihon Steamship Co Ltd* [1994] 1 AC 486; [1994] 1 All ER 20.
6   *National Assistance Board v Wilkinson* [1952] 2 QB 648, at p 661; [1952] 2 All ER 255, at p 260.
7   [1968] AC 58; [1967] 2 All ER 1197 (p 43, *ante*); see also *Black-Clawson International Ltd v Papierwerke Waldhof-Aschaffenburg AG* [1975] AC 591; [1975] 1 All ER 810.
8   See *Beswick v Beswick (supra)*; *Woolley v Woolley* [1968] P 29; [1966] 3 All ER 855.
9   See p 59, *post*.
10   See *R v Tolson* (1889) 23 QBD 168, at p 181; *Younghusband v Luftig* [1949] 2 KB 354; [1949] 2 All ER 72.
11   [1970] AC 132, at p 148; [1969] 1 All ER 347, at p 349; see also *R v Gould* [1968] 2 QB 65; [1968] 1 All ER 849.

"our first duty is to consider the words of the Act; if they show a clear intention to create an absolute offence, that is an end of the matter. But such cases are very rare. Sometimes the words of the section which creates a particular offence make it clear that mens rea is required in one form or another. Such cases are quite frequent. But in a very large number of cases there is no clear indication either way. In such cases there has for centuries been a presumption that Parliament did not intend to make criminals of persons who were in no way blameworthy in what they did. That means that, whenever a section is silent as to mens rea, there is a presumption that, in order to give effect to the will of Parliament, we must read in words appropriate to require mens rea."

An analogous presumption is that Parliament does not intend to create new criminal offences. This is of very limited application since, in the nature of things, when Parliament does intend to create a new criminal offence it will make that fact clear, in particular by specifying penalties for the offence. However, there is an ancient doctrine of "contempt of statute" under which breach of a statutory prohibition was an indictable misdemeanour. An unsuccessful attempt to invoke this doctrine was made in *R v Horseferry Road Justices, ex parte Independent Broadcasting Authority*[12] the Queen's Bench divisional court holding that, "while the offence might still exist, the inference that Parliament did not intend to create an offence in the absence of an express provision to that effect is, nowadays, 'almost irresistible' ".

c   Presumption against depriving a person of a vested right

In the absence of express provision the courts will not construe a statute as having the effect of depriving a person of a right vested in him before the statute came into operation. This is linked with the presumption against retrospective operation though it is more than an illustration of the latter presumption. For example, every person has a right to the use and enjoyment of his own land. The remedy for infringement of this right is an action in trespass or nuisance, depending on the character of the interference. Consequently where a statute authorises the performance of an act, which constitutes a nuisance to the plaintiff, the statute will not be construed as having the effect of removing the plaintiff's right unless it is clearly intended to have that effect.[13] Even stronger is the presumption against removing a right to compensation.[14] Nevertheless, this can be done expressly as evidenced by the War Damage Act 1965 which removed a right to compensation from the Crown in respect of damage to or destruction of property caused by the Crown in time of war, or in contemplation of the outbreak of war.[15]

---

12   [1987] QB 54; [1986] 2 All ER 666; the application of the IBA was to quash a summons issued on behalf of Mr Norris McWhirter, who alleged that transmission of images of him in the television programme "Spitting Image" infringed section 4(3) of the Broadcasting Act 1981, whereby the IBA was in contempt of statute.

13   *Metropolitan Asylum District Managers v Hill* (1881) 6 App Cas 193.

14   *Ministry of Health v Stafford Corporation* [1952] Ch 730; [1952] 2 All ER 386. It was on this basis that the Court of Appeal held in *Allen v Thorn Electrical Industries Ltd* [1968] 1 QB 487; [1967] 2 All ER 1137 that the prohibition on pay increases introduced by the Prices and Incomes Act 1966 did not deprive the plaintiff of his right to an increase which had been agreed upon before the prohibition came into effect.

15   The right had been held to exist in *Burmah Oil Co Ltd v Lord Advocate* [1965] AC 75; [1964] 2 All ER 348.

d   Presumption against ousting the jurisdiction of the courts

Individuals cannot, by contract, exclude the jurisdiction of the courts. Although Parliament may exclude an individual's recourse to the courts, the provision purporting so to do must be absolutely clear and unambiguous since the courts are extremely wary about permitting legislative or executive interference with their jurisdiction. The principle was stated by Viscount Simmons as follows in *Pyx Granite Ltd v Ministry of Housing and Local Government*:[16]

> "it is a principle not by any means to be whittled down that the subject's recourse to Her Majesty's courts for the determination of his rights is not to be excluded except by clear words. That is, as McNair J called it in *Francis v Yiewsley and West Drayton Urban District Council*[17] a 'fundamental rule' from which I would not for my part sanction any departure."

So reluctant are the courts to see the jurisdiction to determine the legality of an action taken purportedly pursuant to statutory authority that even seemingly clear words may not suffice. Thus in *Anisminic v Foreign Compensation Commission*[18] the words of the Foreign Compensation Act 1950, which stated that any "determination" of the Commission "shall not be called into question in any court of law" were insufficient to prevent a court declaring that the Commission had made a fundamental error of law that deprived it of power to act. Because it had no power, there was no real "determination". Such legal sophistry can only be prevented by the clearest of words: an example of such words is the amended wording introduced following that case, section 3 of the Foreign Compensation Act 1969 preventing judicial review even of a "purported determination".

One application of this rule is the principle that a provision which expressly states that the decision of an inferior court, tribunal or administrative body shall be "final" does not include the prerogative jurisdiction of the High Court to review the decision:

> "if a tribunal goes wrong in law and the error appears on the face of the record, the High Court will interfere by certiorari to quash the decision. It is not to be deterred by the enactment that the decision is 'final'. The decision may be final on the facts but it is not final on the law."[19]

If by contrast statute permits challenge, but only within a limited period, the courts are more likely to regard themselves as limited to the stated period. In *R v Cornwall County Council, ex parte Huntington*[20] a divisional court held that the terms of the Wildlife and Countryside Act 1981, which excluded judicial challenge except within

---

16   [1960] AC 260, at p 286; [1959] 3 All ER 1, at p 6, cited with approval by Lord Donovan in *Ealing London Borough v Race Relations Board* [1972] AC 342, at p 353; [1972] 1 All ER 105, at p 108; the decision illustrates the application of the presumption in that the House of Lords held that the machinery established under the Race Relations Act 1968 for referring disputes to certain nominated county courts did not exclude the inherent jurisdiction of the High Court to make a declaration as to rights under the Act.

17   [1957] 2 QB 136, at p 148; the passage referred to does not appear in the report of the case in [1957] 1 All ER 825.

18   [1969] 2 AC 147, [1969] 1 All ER 208.

19   *Tehrani v Rostron* [1972] 1 QB 182, at p 187; [1971] 3 All ER 790, at p 793, per Lord Denning MR: see also *R v Medical Appeal Tribunal, ex parte Gilmore* [1957] 1 QB 574; *sub nom Re Gilmore's Application* [1957] 1 All ER 796, where the earlier authorities are reviewed; *Sagnata Investments Ltd v Norwich Corporation* [1971] 2 QB 614; [1971] 2 All ER 1441. See also p 146, *post.*

20   [1992] 3 All ER 566. The decision was upheld on appeal: see [1994] 1 All ER 694.

a limited period of 42 days, prevented the court from engaging in judicial review of an order made under the 1981 Act.

e Presumption that a statute does not bind the Crown

One of the few relics of the prerogative of the Crown is the rule that the Crown is not bound by a statute unless expressly named in it. The rule extends to the Crown and to its servants and agents though not to nationalised industries.[1] The Crown Proceedings Act 1947 placed the Crown, with certain exceptions, in the same position as a private person in the law of torts. Consequently, statutes which affect common law rights and duties are usually expressed to bind the Crown. Examples are the Limitation Act 1980 and the Occupiers' Liability Act 1957. In practice the general trend of modern legislation is towards the removal of the Crown's privileges and immunities.[2]

5 Material aids to construction

The distinction between interpretation and construction has already been noted. All statutes require interpretation but only statutes whose provisions are ambiguous or uncertain in extent require construction, though the processes of interpretation and construction are inextricably interrelated.

Judges frequently make no attempt to distinguish the processes of interpretation and construction. The distinction is, however, material since not all aids to construction are legitimate aids to interpretation. Thus the aids to construction which do not form part of the enactment may only be consulted where the process of interpretation has disclosed an uncertainty or an ambiguity.

There are two classes of aids to construction; internal aids and external aids.

a Internal aids

An internal (or intrinsic) aid is an aid that is to be found within the Queen's Printer's copy of the statute itself. Those parts of the statute which form part of the enactment must, of course, be consulted as part of the general process of interpretation in applying the general rule that the statute must be read as a whole. Other parts of the Queen's Printer's copy are not aids to interpretation though some, but not all, are aids to construction. There has not, however, been a universal judicial adherence to these basic principles and the modern tendency is to regard those parts of the statute which are not strictly part of the enactment, that is to say punctuation, headings and marginal notes, as aids to construction in cases of ambiguity. Thus in *Director of Public Prosecutions v Schildkamp* Lord Reid stated:[3]

> "it may be more realistic to accept the Act as printed as being the product of the whole legislative process, and to give due weight to everything found in the printed Act. I say more realistic because in very many cases the provision before the court was never even mentioned in debate in either House, and it may be

1   *Tamlin v Hannaford* [1950] 1 KB 18; [1949] 2 All ER 327; for an account of the history of this presumption, and a recent illustration of its operation, see *Lord Advocate v Dumbarton District Council* [1990] 2 AC 580; [1990] 1 All ER 1.
2   See *Madros Electric Supply Corporation (in liquidation) v Boarland (Inspector of Taxes)* [1955] AC 667; [1955] 1 All ER 753.
3   [1971] AC 1, at p 10; [1969] 3 All ER 1640, at p 1641; see also *Limb & Co (Stevedores) v British Transport Docks Board* [1971] 1 All ER 828; [1971] 1 WLR 311.

that its wording was never closely scrutinised by any member of either House. In such a case it is not very meaningful to say that the words of the Act represent the intention of Parliament but that punctuation, cross-headings and sidenotes do not.

So if the authorities are equivocal and one is free to deal with the whole matter I would not object to taking all these matters into account provided that we realise that they cannot have equal weight with the words of the Act. Punctuation can be of some assistance in construction. A cross heading ought to indicate the scope of the sections which follow it. But a sidenote is a poor guide to the scope of the section for it can do no more than indicate the main subject with which the section deals"

It is necessary to identify and distinguish the constituent parts of a statute.

LONG TITLE

The long title of an Act begins with the words "an Act" and goes on to describe the general effect of the Act. Thus the Act whose short title is the "Law of Property Act 1925" has the long title; "An Act to consolidate the enactment's relating to Conveyancing and the Law of Property in England and Wales". It might be supposed that the insertion of a long title would afford Parliament the opportunity of stating its general intention in passing the Act, but in fact long titles tend to be succinct rather than explanatory and generally do little more than identify the subject matter of the Act. Their insertion would appear to rest rather on tradition than on utility.

Until the nineteenth century the long title was not part of the Act itself and was therefore not regarded as a legitimate aid to interpretation. The modern long title, however, is part of the enactment and may be the subject of debate and amendment in Parliament. Consequently, it may be regarded as a legitimate aid both to interpretation and construction. A Master of the Rolls observed in 1899:[4]

"I read the title advisedly because now and for some years past the title of an Act of Parliament has been part of the Act. In the old days it used not to be so, and in the old books we are told not to regard it, but now the title is an important part of the Act and is so treated by both Houses of Parliament."

Although the long title is part of the Act, it is a minor aid to construction. There have been conspicuously few cases in which it has been consulted and it certainly cannot prevail over an express provision in the body of the Act. Thus an Act to "amend the law with respect to wills of personal estate made by British subjects" (Wills Act 1861) was held to apply to the will of an alien.[5] The long title should not be confused with the preamble though, now that preambles are rarely encountered, judges do occasionally describe the long title as the preamble.[6]

---

4   Lindley MR in *Fielding v Morley Corporation* [1899] 1 Ch 1 at p 3; see also *Vacher & Sons Ltd v London Society of Compositors* [1913] AC 107; *R v Delmayne* [1970] 2 QB 170; [1969] 2 All ER 980.

5   *Re Groos* [1904] P 269; see also *R v Bates* [1952] 2 All ER 842; on appeal *sub nom R v Russell* [1953] 1 WLR 77; *R v Galvin* [1987] QB 862; [1987] 2 All ER 851.

6   Eg Winn LJ in *Crook v Edmondson* [1966] 2 QB 81, at p 89; [1966] 1 All ER 833, at p 835; Baker J in *Limb & Co (Stevedores) v British Transport Docks Board* (*supra*). For an example of a statute with a preamble, see Parliament Act 1911, Canada Act 1982.

SHORT TITLE

This is the title by which Acts are commonly, and properly, cited. In theory the short title is a valid aid both to interpretation and to construction, but there appears to be no reported case in which the short title has been used to determine a point of construction, though reference has sometimes been made to it. The short title could certainly not be used to introduce ambiguity into the body of the Act and, indeed, the short titles of certain Acts do not reflect the content of the Act accurately. The Criminal Procedure Act 1865, for example, applies to both civil and criminal proceedings.

PREAMBLE

The preamble is that part of the statute which precedes the enacting words and sets out the reason for the statute being passed, for example the mischief which the statute is passed to remedy. In old cases great weight was attached to the preamble as an aid to construction.[7] Important Acts such as the Statute of Uses 1535, the Statute of Frauds 1677 and the Parliament Act 1911 have long and instructive preambles. Probably the best known preamble is that of the Charitable Uses Act 1601 which is still regarded as containing the criteria to be adopted when considering whether a particular object is a "charitable" one.[8] Where a statute has a preamble, it traditionally begins with the word "whereas". Modern statutes, however, rarely contain a preamble and where one is included it is generally too brief to be of assistance.[9] Consequently the preamble is of little importance as an aid to construction. Although the preamble is part of the enactment, like the long title, it cannot be introduced to create an ambiguity in the body of the Act.

HEADINGS

A section or group of sections in an Act may be preceded by a heading. Such headings are not part of the enactment and for that reason logic would suggest their exclusion. Notwithstanding, headings are often consulted as an aid to construction where the enactment is uncertain or ambiguous.[10] The modern judicial tendency appears to be to treat a heading as if it were a preamble.[11] In *Director of Public Prosecutions v Schildkamp*[12] Lord Upjohn was in favour of according greater weight to headings than were the other law lords, and accordingly observed:[13]

"In my opinion, it is wrong to confine their role to the resolution of ambiguities in the body of the Act. When the court construing the Act is reading it through to understand it, it must read the cross-headings as well as the body of the Act and that will always be a useful pointer as to the intention of Parliament in enacting the immediately following sections. Whether the cross-heading is no more than a pointer or label or is helpful in assisting to construe or even in some

7 *Belasco v Hannant* (1862) 3 B & S 13; *Sussex Peerage Case* (1844) 11 Cl & Fin 85.
8 See, for example, *Incorporated Council of Law Reporting for England and Wales v A-G* [1971] Ch 626; [1971] 1 All ER 436; *McGovern v A-G* [1982] Ch 321; [1981] 3 All ER 493.
9 Compare secondary legislation of the European Communities which invariably has a long preamble; for the reasons for this, see p 59, *post*.
10 For an instructive case see *Crook v Edmondson* [1966] 2 QB 81; [1966] 1 All ER 833 in which the words "immoral purposes" were construed in the light of the group of sections of the Sexual Offences Act 1956 in which those words occurred; see also *Beswick v Beswick* [1968] AC 58; [1967] 2 All ER 1197 (p 43, *ante*).
11 *Martins v Fowler* [1926] AC 746; *Re Carlton* [1945] Ch 372; [1945] 2 All ER 370n, CA; *Qualter, Hall & Co Ltd v Board of Trade* [1962] Ch 273; [1961] 3 All ER 389.
12 [1971] AC 1; [1969] 3 All ER 1640.
13 [1971] AC at 28; [1969] 3 All ER at 1656.

cases to control the meaning or ambit of those sections must necessarily depend on the circumstances of each case."

MARGINAL NOTES

Marginal notes are not part of an Act and are inserted by the draftsman purely for facility of reference. It has happened that a marginal note has borne no relation to the content of a section that had been considerably altered during the passage of the Bill.[14] More commonly, a marginal note may be misleading. For example the marginal note to section 143 of the Criminal Justice and Public Order Act 1994 refers to "male rape and buggery" despite the fact that the section relates to the latter, but not the former.

For this reason the old rule was that marginal notes were not regarded as a legitimate aid to construction, even in the event of ambiguity.[15] Nevertheless there have been cases in which the court has clearly adverted to the marginal note in construing a section.[16] Thus Upjohn LJ observed in one case:[17] "While the marginal note to a section cannot control the language used in the section, it is at least permissible to approach a consideration of its general purpose and the mischief at which it is aimed with the note in mind."

This approach is consistent with the speeches in the House of Lords in *Director of Public Prosecutions v Schildkamp* (supra), although care must be taken to ensure that they do not displace a meaning which appears from the body of the Act itself.[18] An example of a marginal note being of value in resolving an ambiguity is *DPP v Johnson*[19] where it was held that the sidenote to section 8 of the Road Traffic Act 1988, which read: "Driving or being in charge of a motor vehicle with alcohol consumption above the prescribed limit" provided evidence that the intent of Parliament was to reduce the number of people who drive with alcohol in their bodies. As a result, the court was required to construe the word "consuming" widely to embrace the ingestion of alcohol by any method and was not entitled to restrict consumption to the act of drinking. The appellant, who had had alcohol injected into his body as a constituent element of a pain-killing drug was therefore guilty of an offence under section 8.

PUNCTUATION

Before 1850 Acts of Parliament were not punctuated; even after that punctuation was left to the draftsman and not scrutinised by Parliament. Accordingly there was some old authority for the proposition that punctuation could not be taken into account as an aid to construction. However, the courts now take a for more realistic attitude and, following the observations of Lord Reid in *Director of Public Prosecutions v Schildkamp* (supra), the House of Lords has held[20] that punctuation can and should be taken into account by judges in interpreting statutes.

---

14   Married Women (Maintenance in Case of Desertion) Act 1886, s 1(2).
15   See *R v Bates* [1952] 2 All ER 842; on appeal *sub nom R v Russell* [1953] 1 WLR 77; *Chandler v Director of Public Prosecutions* [1964] AC 763; [1962] 3 All ER 142.
16   E.g., *Pride of Derby and Derbyshire Angling Association Ltd v British Celanese Ltd* [1953] Ch 149; [1952] 1 All ER 179; *R v Vickers* [1957] 2 QB 664; [1957] 2 All ER 741; *Tudor Grange Holdings Ltd v Citibank NA* [1992] Ch 53; [1991] 4 All ER 1.
17   *Stephens v Cuckfield Rural District Council* [1960] 2 QB 373, at p 383; *Limb & Co (Stevedores) v British Transport Docks Board* [1971] 1 All ER 828; [1971] 1 WLR 311 (*supra*); *Tudor Grange Holdings Ltd v Citibank NA* [1991] 4 All ER 1; [1992] Ch 53.
18   See *R v Kelt* [1977] 3 All ER 1099; [1977] 1 WLR 1365.
19   [1995] 4 All ER 53.
20   *Hanlon v The Law Society* [1981] AC 124; [1980] 2 All ER 199; see also *Bodden v Commissioner of Police of the Metropolis* [1990] 2 QB 397; [1989] 3 All ER 833.

INTERPRETATION SECTIONS

It is a relatively modern drafting technique to include an interpretation section in an Act, and nowadays most Acts include at least one such section. Although an interpretation section is as much a part of the Act as any other section, the interpretation of a word depends rather on its context than on the interpretation section, and, in any event, if there is an inconsistency between an interpretation section and the body of an Act the latter prevails.

This is especially so when the interpretation section uses the word "includes". In this case the interpretation section will be regarded as extending rather than restricting the normal meaning of the words in question. Thus, in *R v Fulling*[1] the court defined the term "oppression" in s 76 of the Police and Criminal Evidence Act 1984 by reference to its ordinary, natural meaning, as stated in the *Oxford English Dictionary*, not even citing the provisions of s 76(8) of that statute, which provides that oppression "includes" inhuman or degrading treatment, torture, violence or the threat of violence.

Again, where an interpretation section defined "street" by stating that it "should apply to and include any highway, not being a turnpike road", the Court of Appeal held that the word "street" could include a turnpike road since the interpretation section extended rather than restricted the ordinary and natural meaning of the word.[2]

One graphic example is *Shimizu (UK) Ltd v Westminster City Council*.[3] In that case the House of Lords had to consider the meaning of the term "listed building" in the Planning (Listed Buildings and Conservation Areas) Act 1990. Section 336 of the Town and Country Planning Act 1990 defined a "building" as including "part of a building", unless the context otherwise requires. That definition was incorporated into the Listed Buildings Act by s 91 of the Act. Despite that, Lord Hope was able to conclude that the expression "listed building" included part of a listed building for the purposes of section 1 of the Act, but did no do so in respect of virtually all other provisions of that Act.

SCHEDULES

Schedules are part of the enactment if expressly incorporated by a section in the Act itself. They are used (inter alia) for prescribing forms, furnishing illustrations, listing repeals effected by the Act and setting out transitional provisions. They cannot be regarded as altering or enlarging the ordinary meaning of words used in the Act. In *Ellerman Lines Ltd v Murray*[4] the House of Lords, in interpreting an Act passed to give effect to an international convention, steadfastly refused to look at a Schedule to the Act in which was set out the text of the convention because the words of the Act were unambiguous. It is to be presumed that the House would have considered the Schedule, had the Act been uncertain or ambiguous, in order to apply the mischief rule.[5] If the situation which arose in *Ellerman Lines Ltd v Murray* were to arise at the present day the contrary approach would be adopted, and indeed, the case itself was

1   [1987] QB 426, [1987] 2 All ER 65.
2   *Nutter v Accrington Local Board of Health* (1878) 4 QBD 375.
3   [1997] 1 All ER 481.
4   [1931] AC 126.
5   See *Salomon v Customs and Excise Commissioners* [1967] 2 QB 116; [1966] 3 All ER 871. In *Corocraft Ltd v Pan American Airways Inc* [1969] 1 QB 616; [1969] 1 All ER 82 there was no ambiguity or uncertainty in the English Act but the Court of Appeal nevertheless adopted the text of the Convention (the meaning of which differed from that of the Act, the Carriage by Air Act 1932), distinguishing *Ellerman Lines Ltd v Murray* on the basis that in that case the intention of Parliament had been to give effect to the English text of the Convention whereas in the present case the intention was to give effect to the original Convention. There is a presumption that Parliament intends to fulfil, rather than break, its international obligations; cf *The Andrea Ursula* [1973] QB 265; [1971] 1 All ER 821.

disapproved by the House of Lords in *James Buchanan & Co Ltd v Babco Forwarding and Shipping (UK) Ltd.*[6]

With the increasing number of statutes which are passed to implement international conventions a new difficulty has arisen; that is that the convention (which is part of the enactment) is sometimes in a foreign language and, indeed, is sometimes set out in more than one language. The House of Lords grappled with this difficulty, in construing the French and English texts of the Warsaw Convention contained in Schedule 1 to the Carriage by Air Act 1961, in *Fothergill v Monarch Airlines Ltd.*[7] Reversing the decision of the Court of Appeal, it held that a loss of articles from a suitcase constituted "damage" to baggage. This conclusion was reached by not applying a literal interpretation of the word "damage" but rather a purposive one and by looking at extrinsic sources so as to ascertain that the word "avarie" (used in the French text) is capable of meaning "loss" as well as "damage". The term used in the Convention will be construed so as to conform to the general acceptance of the meaning of that provision. As Lord Browne-Wilkinson put it in *Re H and others (minors) (abduction: acquiescence)*:[8]

"An international convention, expressed in different languages and intended to apply to a wide range of differing legal systems, cannot be construed differently in different jurisdictions."

The Consumer Credit Act 1974 utilised a novel concept in Parliamentary drafting – the use of examples. Section 188(1) provides that "Schedule 2 shall have effect for illustrating the use of terminology employed in this Act", and that Schedule contains 24 examples, each expressed in the form of a set of facts and an analysis of the application of the new terminology to those facts. The examples are expressed not to be exhaustive and section 188(3) provides that in the case of conflict between Schedule 2 and any other provision of the Act, the latter shall prevail.

b   External aids

An external (or extrinsic) aid to construction is an aid which is not to be found in the Queen's Printer's copy of the Act. Since the function of the courts is to ascertain the intention of the legislature, it might be thought that they would readily refer to statements made in Parliament as to the intention of the member or party introducing the Bill. In fact until recently the reverse was the case. The reports of debates on the Bill in its passage through Parliament were rigidly excluded[9] as explanatory memoranda upon the effects of the Act, where these are issued, generally still are.[10]

6   [1978] AC 141; [1977] 3 All ER 1048.
7   [1981] AC 251; [1980] 2 All ER 696. The 1961 Act, s 1(2) expressly provides that in the event of inconsistency between the English and French texts, the latter is to prevail.
8   [1997] 2 All ER 225.
9   *Assam Railways and Trading Co Ltd v Inland Revenue Commissioners* [1935] AC 445; In *Beswick v Beswick* [1968] AC 58, at p 74; [1967] 2 All ER 1197, at p 1202 reasons advanced for the rule were that it would add to the time and expense of preparing cases if counsel had to read all the debates in Hansard and that reports of debates in select committees are not available to the public. In *Davis v Johnson* [1979] AC 264; [1978] 1 All ER 1132, the House of Lords unanimously reaffirmed the rule that Hansard can never be relied upon by counsel in any court and can never be relied upon by the court in construing a statute or for any other purpose. However, in *Pickstone v Freemans plc* [1989] AC 66; [1988] 2 All ER 803, the House of Lords, in construing regulations made under s 2(2) of the European Communities Act 1972 for the purpose of implementing a Community obligation of the United Kingdom (as to which see p 105, *post*), in circumstances where the regulations had not been subject to any process of amendment by Parliament, was prepared to consider the explanations of the government and the criticisms voiced by members of Parliament (by reference to Hansard) as providing some indication of the intentions of Parliament.
10   *London County Council v Central Land Board* [1959] Ch 386; [1958] 1 All ER 806. However, in *Sagnata Investments Ltd v Norwich Corporation* [1971] 2 QB 614; [1971] 2 All ER 1441, Lord Denning

However, in 1993 the House of Lords in *Pepper v Hart*[11] reconsidered the position, and held (Lord Mackay LC dissenting) that in certain circumstances a court should be entitled to refer to parliamentary materials. The pre-conditions for the exercise of this power were stated as follows by Lord Browne-Wilkinson:

"the exclusionary rule should be relaxed so as to permit reference to parliamentary materials where: (a) legislation is ambiguous or obscure, or leads to an absurdity; (b) the material relied upon consists of one or more statements by a minister or other promoter of the Bill together if necessary with such other parliamentary material as is necessary to understand such statements, and their effect; (c) the statements relied upon are clear."

It should be noted that it is the statements made in respect of a Bill passing through Parliament that fall potentially to be considered under *Pepper v Hart*. The rule does not permit the use of statements to indicate what Ministers understood the then current state of the law to be.[12] The statement of the Minister must also be directed to the very point in issue in the litigation.[13] The objection that by so referring to parliamentary materials the courts would be in breach of Article 9 of the Bill of Rights 1688 was rejected by the House of Lords in *Pepper v Hart*. This provision, which prohibits the calling into question of anything said in proceedings in Parliament, did not prevent the courts using such materials as an aid to construction, and it was not upon this point that Lord Mackay dissented. His dissenting speech highlighted his concerns about the effect the change proposed by the majority of the House would have on the costs of litigation, and feared that these would be immensely increased by the onerous task of researching the record of parliamentary proceedings in *Hansard*. The number of reported decisions using parliamentary materials as an aid to construction, or where the court is asked to apply the *Pepper v Hart* rule, gives some support to Lord Mackay's concerns.[14]

Perhaps the most striking example of the rule excluding the use of extrinsic aids to construction is the case of *Ellerman Lines Ltd v Murray*, noted above, where the House of Lords refused to look at the text of an international convention when interpreting a statute passed to give effect to that convention. However, in the event of ambiguity, it is now clearly established that, when construing a statute passed to give effect to a treaty obligation or to enact matters agreed at an international convention, the court is entitled to look at the convention to ascertain what Parliament must have intended.[15]

MR did refer to Hansard, Parliamentary Debates when considering the mischief intended to be remedied by the Betting, Gaming and Lotteries Act 1963, Sch 6 and did so again in *R v Greater London Council, ex parte Blackburn* [1976] 3 All ER 184; [1976] 1 WLR 550 (albeit having first said "I known that we are not supposed to do this"). In *Pickstone v Freemans plc* (*supra*) Lord Oliver said that, though an explanatory note attached to the regulations was not part of the regulations, it was "of use in identifying the mischief which the regulations were attempting to remedy". See also *Michaels v Harley House (Marylebone) Ltd* [1997] 3 All ER 446.

11 [1993] AC 593; [1993] 1 All ER 42.
12 *Hillsdown Holdings plc v Pensions Ombudsman* [1997] 1 All ER 862.
13 *Pepper (Inspector of Taxes) v Hart, op cit*; *Melluish (Inspector of Taxes) v BMI (No 3) Ltd* [1996] AC 545; [1995] 4 All ER 453; *Three Rivers District Council v Bank of England (No 2)* [1996] 2 All ER 363.
14 See, e.g., *Warwickshire County Council v Johnson* [1993] 1 All ER 299 (reference made to Minister's speech in debate on a proposed amendment to Consumer Protection Act 1987, s 20); *Stubbings v Webb* [1993] AC 498; [1993] 1 All ER 322 (reference made to the speech of the chairman of the Committee upon whose report the Limitation Act 1980, s 11 was based); *Avon CC v Hooper* [1997] 1 All ER 532; *R v Wandsworth LBC, ex parte Mansoor* [1997] QB 953; [1996] 3 All ER 913; *Thomas Witter v TBP Industries* [1996] 2 All ER 573; *R v Hampshire; Prebble v Television New Zealand Ltd* [1995] 1 AC 321; [1994] 3 All ER 407.
15 *The Banco* [1971] P 137; [1971] 1 All ER 524.

Thus it probably makes no difference whether the text of the convention is scheduled to the Act or not. Where the convention is printed in more than one language (as will usually be the case) it is permissible to look at foreign texts as well as the English text, although the majority of the House of Lords in *James Buchanan & Co Ltd v Babco Forwarding and Shipping (UK) Ltd*[16] expressed the view that this was only permissible if the English text was ambiguous. This principle and the presumption that Parliament intends to fulfil its international obligations is of considerable practical importance now that the courts are so often called upon to construe legislation passed to implement the instruments of the European Community Institutions.

Nor does the rule apply with such strict criteria if an international or European element is involved, where the court is seeking to give a purposive approach to a statute to give effect to an international or European obligation.[17] *Pepper v Hart* was not a decision with such an element, unlike *Three Rivers District Council v Bank of England (No 2)*, where the court stated that it "would expect the courts to adopt a somewhat more flexible approach".[18] The court considered not only statements of Ministers but a range of materials relevant to the European directive in question.

It may be observed that most continental countries adopt the opposite approach to extrinsic materials and encourage consultation of the parliamentary and political history of the statute. These materials are known as *travaux préparatoires* and are an invaluable aid to the task of discovering the intention of continental legislatures. In *Gatoil International Inc v Arkwright-Boston Manufacturers Mutual Insurance Co*[19] the House of Lords decided that in construing an Act passed to implement an international convention, it was appropriate to consider *travaux préparatoires* relating to the convention for the purpose of resolving any ambiguity in the Act. In *Greenwich London Borough Council v Powell*[20] the House of Lords, in considering whether a caravan site provided by a local authority for the accommodation of gypsies was a "protected site" within section 5(1) of the Mobile Homes Act 1983 (thereby entitling the occupants to security of tenure), considered a Department of Environment circular as indicative of the policy underlying the legislation. However, although the general rule in relation to external aids is one of exclusion,[1] there are certain legitimate external aids to construction and these are set out below.

---

16   [1978] AC 141; [1977] 3 All ER 1048; Lord Wilberforce was in favour of consulting the foreign text for assistance, there was no ambiguity (or, at least, uncertainty) in the English text, it is difficult to see why assistance would be needed; cf *Fothergill v Monarch Airlines Ltd* [1981] AC 251; [1980] 2 All ER 696 (see p xx, *ante*), where some members of the House appear to have regarded the word "damage" as ambiguous in its context; but since the French text was the primary text, it could clearly have been relied upon by the parties whether the English text was ambiguous or not and the court would be bound to give effect to the French text. This is an important distinction between the two cases.

17   *Three Rivers District Council v Bank of England (No 2)* [1996] 2 All ER 363; *Pickstone v Freemans plc* [1989] AC 66; [1988] 2 All ER 803; *R v International Stock Exchange of the UK and the Republic of Ireland, ex parte Else (1982) Ltd* [1993] QB 534; [1993] 1 All ER 420.

18   [1996] 2 All ER 363, at 366.

19   [1985] AC 255; [1985] 1 All ER 129. Note also s 3(3) of the Civil Jurisdiction and Judgments Act 1982 which expressly provides that in interpreting the conventions implemented by that Act, the court may consider certain reports by named individuals (which are reproduced in the Official Journal of the Communities).

20   [1989] AC 995; [1989] 1 All ER 65.

1   The Law Commission report, *The Interpretation of Statutes* (1969, Law Com No 21) recommended the admission of extrinsic material, other than reports of parliamentary proceedings. Lord Simon more than once advocated reference to parliamentary proceedings and other preparatory material as an aid to judicial interpretation of statutes (cf *McMillan v Crouch* [1972] 3 All ER 61, at p 76; [1972] 1 WLR 1102, at p 1119; *Charter v Race Relations Board* [1973] AC 868, at p 900; [1973] 1 All ER 512, at p 527) but his views on this topic attracted little support.

EXPLANATORY NOTES

A Bill is published with an explanatory memorandum, prepared by the sponsoring department, and agreed with parliamentary counsel. This gives a brief survey of the Bill, and indicates its effects on public finances, on public sector manpower and on business compliance costs. Notes on clauses in the Bill are also prepared for Ministers and made available to backbench members of Parliament. In the future these will be compiled as one "Explanatory notes" document, which will include an explanation of the legislation and its purpose, and includes notes on clauses, as well as the financial material indicated above.[2]

DICTIONARIES

Words in statutes are presumed to bear their ordinary and natural meaning and it is legitimate to consult a dictionary to ascertain the meaning of words which have no particular legal meaning. Thus in *Re Rippon (Highfield) Housing Confirmation Order 1938*[3] the court adopted the *Oxford English Dictionary* definition of the word "park". Nevertheless dictionaries bear only slight weight and, in context, the dictionary meaning may not be the one which Parliament presumably intended. Thus in *Mills v Cooper*[4] a divisional court rejected the *Shorter Oxford English Dictionary* definition of a "gypsy" while in *Thornton v Fisher & Ludlow Ltd*[5] the same dictionary's definition of a "passage" was not adopted. Words and phrases which have a particular legal meaning are described as "terms of art" and do not necessarily bear the meaning which laymen would attribute to them.[6] In interpreting a foreign text of a convention, the court is entitled to consult foreign dictionaries, textbooks and articles and, indeed, to receive expert evidence.[7]

REPORTS OF COMMITTEES

Reports of the Law Commissions, Law Reform Committees and similar bodies are legitimate aids to discovering the state of the pre-existing law and the mischief which the statute was passed to remedy.[8] Once again, however, if the words of a statute are unambiguous, it is not legitimate to interpret them otherwise in order to accord with the recommendations of a Committee which preceded its passing.[9] Thus in *Letang v Cooper*[10] the Court of Appeal held that the words "negligence, nuisance or breach of

---

2   See Select Committee on Modernisation of HC: 2nd Report: Explanatory Material for Bills, 1997–1998, HC 389, at pp 1–2.
3   [1939] 2 KB 838; [1939] 3 All ER 548.
4   [1967] 2 QB 459, [1967] 2 All ER 100.
5   [1968] 2 All ER 241; [1968] 1 WLR 655; see also *A-G's Reference (No 1 of 1988)* [1989] AC 971; [1989] 2 All ER 1, where the *Oxford English Dictionary's* first meaning of the word "obtained" was rejected by the House of Lords, with the result that the appellant was guilty of insider dealing even if the confidential information came to him without any positive action on his part.
6   See *Sydall v Castings Ltd* [1967] 1 QB 302; [1966] 3 All ER 770, on the construction of the word "descendants" as a term of art; see also *Barclays Bank Ltd v Cole* [1967] 2 QB 738; [1966] 3 All ER 948, on the meaning of the word "fraud" and compare *Lloyds Bank Ltd v Marcan* [1973] 2 All ER 359; [1973] 1 WLR 339 where Pennycuick V-C gave a much wider meaning to the word "defraud" in s 172(1) of the Law of Property Act 1925 on the basis that the section was replacing a provision in an Act of 1571 in which the words "hinder, delay or defraud" were used.
7   *Fothergill v Monarch Airlines Ltd* (*supra*).
8   See, for example, *Rookes v Barnard* [1964] AC 1129; [1964] 1 All ER 367; *National Provincial Bank v Ainsworth* [1965] AC 1175; [1965] 2 All ER 472; *Black-Clawson International Ltd v Papierwerke Waldhof-Aschaffenburg AG* [1975] AC 591; [1975] 1 All ER 810. In *A-G's Reference (No 1 of 1988)* (n 5, *supra*) the House of Lords considered two White Papers for the purpose of ascertaining the mischief at which the Company Securities (Insider Dealing) Act 1985 was aimed.
9   *Black-Clawson International Ltd v Papierwerke Waldhof-Aschaffenburg AG* (*supra*).
10   [1965] 1 QB 232; [1964] 2 All ER 929.

duty" in the Law Reform (Limitation of Actions, &c) Act 1954 were wide enough to embrace the tort of trespass to the person even though the Tucker Committee report,[11] which preceded the 1954 Act, expressed an intention to exclude this form of action from the shorter limitation period recommended in that report.

OTHER STATUTES

Where the words of one statute are ambiguous or uncertain, assistance as to their meaning may sometimes be gained from consideration of the way in which similar words have been used in other statutes, provided that they are *in pari materia* (deal with the same subject matter) with the provision under consideration. Thus in *R v Wheatley*[12] the question before the Court of Appeal, Criminal Division, was whether a metal pipe bomb filled with fire-dampened sodium chlorate mixed with sugar was an "explosive" substance within the meaning of section 4 of the Explosive Substances Act 1883. The defendant's expert evidence was to the effect that the materials would produce only a pyrotechnic effect, and not an explosive one. The trial judge directed the jury that this was no defence, having regard to the definition of "explosive" in section 3(1) of the Explosives Act 1875, which included a substance used with a view to producing a "pyrotechnic effect". It was held that this direction was correct since, having regard to the long title of the 1883 Act ("An Act to amend the Law relating to Explosive Substances"), that Act was intended to amend, inter alia, the 1875 Act and both Acts were *in pari materia*. It followed that what was an explosive substance within section 4 of the 1883 Act was to be determined by applying the definition of "explosive" in section 3(1) of the 1875 Act.

c Judicial precedents

The application of the doctrine of judicial precedent to the interpretation of statutes was explained as follows by Lord Upjohn:[13]

"It is quite clear that judicial statements as to the construction and intention of an Act must never be allowed to supplant or supersede its proper construction and courts must beware of falling into the error of treating the law to be that laid down by the judge in construing the Act rather than found in the Act itself. No doubt a decision on particular words binds inferior courts on the construction of those words on similar facts, but beyond that the observations of judges on the construction of statutes may be of the greatest help and guidance but are entitled to no more than respect and cannot absolve the court from its duty in exercising an independent judgment."

Thus where a superior court has interpreted the words of an Act, an inferior court in the hierarchy is bound to adopt that interpretation if faced with the same words in the same Act. Similarly the Court of Appeal is bound to follow its own previous decision upon the interpretation of a statute to the same extent as it is bound to follow any other of its previous decisions. The position is less clear if the later court is called upon to interpret the same or similar words in another parts of the same Act or in another Act. In this event the earlier decision may be referred to if the two provisions in the Acts in

11   Cmnd 7740. In *Sagnata Investments Ltd v Norwich Corporation* (p 84, *ante*) Lord Denning MR in considering the legislative history of the Betting, Gaming and Lotteries Act 1963, took into account the recommendations of the Royal Commission on Betting, Lotteries and Gaming (Cmnd 8190 of 1951).
12   [1979] 1 All ER 954; [1979] 1 WLR 144.
13   *Ogden Industries Pty Ltd v Lucas* [1970] AC 113, at p 127; [1969] 1 All ER 121, at p 126.

question are *in pari materia*. This occurs most commonly when the later Act is a consolidating statute and the earlier Act is one of those repealed and consolidated. However, even in the case of consolidation Acts, the court is not bound by a precedent based upon an earlier Act consolidated by the Act under construction. The correct approach is for the court to interpret the Act in accordance with the usual principles of statutory interpretation. Only where there is a real or substantial difficulty or ambiguity should the court refer to the legislation which has been repealed or precedents based upon that legislation.[14]

Similarly, if the later Act employs words or phrases that have been the subject of judicial interpretation in an earlier Act dealing with the same subject matter it may be inferred that they are intended to bear the same meaning, on the basis that Parliament is presumed to know the law.[15] For example, the House of Lords, in assigning a meaning to the word "wreck" in the Merchant Shipping Act 1925, adopted the interpretation of that word which had been given in a case decided on the wording of the Merchant Shipping Act 1894.[16] It is, however, no more than a possible inference and it must not be supposed that by re-enacting a statutory provision which has been the subject of judicial interpretation Parliament is thereby, in effect, giving statutory force to that interpretation. If it is a wrong interpretation then (provided it is not binding on the court in accordance with the doctrine of precedent) a court is perfectly free to disregard it.[17] Moreover, where the earlier decision is upon similar words in a statute that is not *in pari materia* with the statute requiring interpretation, or where the words are used in a different context, that decision is of little, if any, value.[18]

6   Interpretation of European Community legislation

The rules, refinements, technicalities and artifices which English courts have developed over the centuries in their approach to the interpretation of statutes have been described above. As already noted approaches to interpretation have influenced approaches to legislative drafting, and vice versa. Community legislation is drafted in a different mould. It is expressed (as the domestic legislation of the other Community countries tends to be drafted) in terms of broad principle, leaving the courts to supply the detail by giving effect, in particular cases, to the general intention of the institution that has enacted the instrument in question. Thus regulations, directives and decisions of the Council and of the Commission have to state the reasons on which they have been based and have to refer to any proposals or opinions that were required to be obtained pursuant to the Treaties.[19] These reasons are normally set out in the preamble to the instrument in question.

14   *Farrell v Alexander* [1977] AC 59; [1976] 2 All ER 721; *R v Heron* [1982] 1 All ER 993; [1982] 1 WLR 451.
15   Cf *Maxwell on Interpretation of Statutes* (11th Edn, 1962) p 303, cited with approval in *R v Freeman* [1970] 2 All ER 413; [1970] 1 WLR 788 in which the Court of Appeal held that, since there was not relevant distinction between the definition of "firearm" in s 57(1) of the Firearms Act 1968 and the definitions in earlier Firearms Acts, Parliament must be taken to have adopted in the 1968 Act the interpretation which had been placed on the definition in the Firearms Act 1920.
16   *The Olympic* [1913] P 92; *Barras v Aberdeen Steam Trawling and Fishing Co Ltd* [1933] AC 402.
17   See *Dun v Dun* [1959] AC 272; [1959] 2 All ER 134; *Farrell v Alexander (supra)*; *R v Chard* [1984] AC 279; [1983] 3 All ER 637 (in which the House of Lords expressly disapproved dicta to the contrary in *Barras v Aberdeen Steam Trawling and Fishing Co Ltd (supra)*).
18   *London Corporation v Cusack-Smith* [1955] AC 337; [1955] 1 All ER 302; *Goodrich v Paisner* [1957] AC 65; [1956] 2 All ER 176.
19   Art 190.

Accordingly, in terms of the traditional approaches to interpretation which have been adopted in this country, the "literal rule" plays little or not part in the Community legislation, the purposive approach being the appropriate one. English judges are required to apply a European approach in the interpretation of Community law, making references of points of law to the Court of Justice when necessary or required.[20] In addition, the requirements of Community law may require a United Kingdom statute to be construed in a particular way. Both these matters are returned to later.[1]

CHAPTER 3

Law Reports and Precedents

A THE RELATIONSHIP BETWEEN LAW REPORTS AND THE DOCTRINE OF PRECEDENT

The operation of the doctrine of precedent is inextricably bound up with law reporting. The rule is that any decision may be cited to a court provided that it is vouched for by a barrister, solicitor or person with a Supreme Court qualification[1] who was present when judgment was delivered. In addition, since judges take judicial notice of the whole of English law, an individual judge may rely upon a precedent of which he is aware even though the decision is unreported. There is, thus, no rule that a case may only be cited or relied upon as a precedent if it is reported. Nevertheless personal recollection is so impermanent and haphazard that it could not possibly form the basis of a workable system.

Hence precedents are almost always contained in law reports. The close nexus between law reporting and the doctrine of judicial precedent is evidenced by the fact that the modern doctrine of binding precedent was formulated only when an integrated system of law reporting evolved in the nineteenth century.

In the face of the undoubted principle that reported and unreported cases are of equal authority some observations of Lord Diplock (with which all the other members of the House concurred) in *Roberts Petroleum Ltd v Bernard Kenny Ltd*[2] caused considerable consternation among some sections of the profession. After referring to a growing practice of citing unreported decisions of the Court of Appeal,[3] Lord Diplock went on:

"My Lords, in my opinion, the time has come when your Lordships should adopt the practice of declining to allow transcripts of unreported judgments of the Civil Division of the Court of Appeal to be cited on the hearing of appeals to this House unless leave is given to do so, and that such leave should only be granted on

1 Courts and Legal Services Act 1990, s 115. See pp 242–243, *post*.
2 [1983] 2 AC 192, at pp 200–202; [1983] 1 All ER 564, at pp 566–568.
3 Transcripts of judgments of the Court of Appeal and House of Lords are filed in the Supreme Court Library in London.

counsel's giving an assurance that the transcript contains a statement of some principle of law, relevant to an issue in the appeal to this House, that is binding on the Court of Appeal and of which the substance, as distinct from the mere choice, of phraseology, is not to be found in one of the generalised or specialised series of reports."

It is important to distinguish a law report from a court record. The court record contains, basically, the names of the parties, the pleadings and the decision or order of the court. A law report contains most of these and, in addition, the judgment of the court containing the reasoning upon which the decision has been based. It is this reasoning which is the important element in the decision for the purposes of the doctrine of precedent. For this reason court records, such as the Plea Rolls, copies of which dating from the twelfth century are preserved in the Public Record Office, are of little value as precedents.

One might suppose that, because law reports are fundamental to the doctrine of precedent which is the cornerstone of the English legal system, the courts would have created a methodical system of producing law reports. It is an extraordinary anomaly that this has never been done. Law reporting has been left entirely to private enterprise so that, even at the present day, there is an element of chance and individual preference in the matter of whether or not a case is reported. However, the growth of electronic legal databases, such as LEXIS,[4] means that few cases decided by the superior courts[5] (other than the Crown Court) escape the scrutiny of researchers, and even decisions of interest of some tribunals and rulings of trial judges in the Crown Court become known to practitioners and academics through specialist journals and encyclopaedias.

The historical evolution of the modern system of law reporting is considered below, but first the operation of the precedent system requires detailed examination.

B   THE OPERATION OF THE DOCTRINE OF PRECEDENT

1   The doctrine of binding precedent

The traditional view of the function of an English judge has been that it is not to make law but to decide cases in accordance with existing legal rules. Few would now deny that judges have a powerful law-making function,[6] but there is no doubt that this traditional declaratory view of the judicial process was the theoretical foundation of the doctrine of binding precedent whereby the judge is not merely referred to earlier decisions for guidance, but also bound to apply rules of law decided by those cases. The operation of the doctrine depends upon the hierarchy of the courts. All courts stand in a definite relationship to one another. A court is bound by decisions of a court above itself in the hierarchy and, usually, by a court of equivalent standing. Given that the doctrine of precedent has binding force within this framework, the question naturally arises of how the law may develop if cases are always to be determined according to ageless principles. In practice there are several ways in which the doctrine retains its flexibility. These are dealt with in detail below,[7] but it is sufficient to note at this juncture two basic principles; first, that superior courts have power to overrule decisions of inferior courts and, in certain cases, to overrule their own earlier decisions, and,

4   See p 86, post.
5   See p 162, post.
6   See p 216, post.
7   See p 71, post.

secondly, that any rule of law may be changed by statute. Consequently every rule of law is subject to change, either by the judges themselves or by Parliament. Although legislation is the ultimate source of law, in the sense that Parliament has within our constitution the ultimate power to make, or unmake any law, it should not in any way be regarded as a superior source of law. Although judges may well be reluctant to make major changes which involve policy better settled by Parliament,[8] judicial law-making can provide flexibility, and relative speed, because of the demands on parliamentary time.[9]

The advantages of the precedent system are said to be certainty, precision and flexibility.[10] Legal certainty is achieved, in theory at least, in that, if the legal problem raised has been solved before, the judge is bound to adopt that solution. Precision is achieved by the sheer volume of reported cases containing solutions to innumerable factual situations arising in any particular branch of the law. No code or statute, no matter how carefully drafted, could anticipate the legal problems which these variations of fact may promote. Consequently, the judge in a continental legal system must generally decide cases on the basis of broad principles. Finally, flexibility is achieved by the possibility of decisions being overruled and by the possibility of distinguishing and confining the operation of decisions which appear unsound, the latter process being of particular importance.

The obvious disadvantages of the system are its inherent rigidity, which may occasionally cause hardship, and the vast and ever-increasing bulk of reported cases to which the court must advert to determine what is the law, since an excess of case law tends to obscure basic principles.[11]

Finally, it is self-evident that there cannot be an infinite regression. Every rule of law must have its origin. If it was not created by statute, then it must have been created by a court. Thus where there is no precedent the doctrine breaks down and the judge is bound to reach a decision in accordance with general principles. Even in modern times cases arise for which there is no precedent. These cases are described as cases of first impression and require the judge to make law rather than to apply it.[12] This he will do by reference to analogous principles but even legal principles must have their origin so that the declaratory theory of the common law could never be of universal application.[13]

Before considering in detail the doctrine of binding precedent (or *stare decisis*) it is necessary to express a possible reservation as to its universal applicability in the English courts, which arises from the judgments of the majority of the Court of Appeal

8   See p 219, post.
9   See discussion of law reform, at p 17, ante.
10 See observations of Russell LJ in *Gallie v Lee* [1969] 2 Ch 17, at p 41, [1969] 1 All ER 1062, at p 1076 (affirmed *sub nom Saunders v Anglia Building Society* [1971] AC 1004; [1970] 3 All ER 961) and of Lord Hailsham in *Cassell & Co Ltd v Broome* [1972] AC 1027, at p 1054; [1972] 1 All ER 801, at p 809 ("in legal matters, some degree of certainty is at least as valuable a part of justice as perfection").
11 The current attitude of appellate courts, faced with ever-increasing demands upon court time, is to discourage extensive citation of authorities, particularly where they are merely illustrative of general principles which are adequately set out in a leading case; see observations of Lord Diplock in *Lexmead (Basingstoke) Ltd v Lewis* [1982] AC 225; *sub nom Lambert v Lewis* [1981] 1 All ER 1185.
12 Eg *Philips v Brooks Ltd* [1919] 2 KB 243; *Noble v Harrison* [1926] 2 KB 332; *Lancashire Loans Ltd v Black* [1934] 1 KB 380; *British Transport Commission v Gourley* [1956] AC 185; [1955] 3 All ER 796; *Malone v Metropolitan Police Commissioner (No 2)* [1979] Ch 344; [1979] 2 All ER 620; *Midland Bank Trust Co Ltd v Green (No 3)* [1982] Ch 529; [1981] 3 All ER 744; *Parker v British Airways Board* [1982] QB 1004; [1982] 1 All ER 834.
13 See Lord Simon's observations upon the declaratory theory of the common law in *Jones v Secretary of State for Social Services* [1972] AC 944, at p 1026; [1972] 1 All ER 145, at p 198, quoted at p 218, post.

in *Trendtex Trading Corporation Ltd v Central Bank of Nigeria*.[14] The question at issue was whether the defendant bank could claim sovereign immunity from action, on the basis that it was a department or organ of the state of Nigeria. The Court of Appeal held that it could not; firstly, because it had not established that it was a department of the state (a ground upon which the court was unanimous) and secondly (Stephenson LJ dissenting) on the ground that there was a rule of international law that the doctrine of sovereign immunity was not applicable to the ordinary commercial transactions, as distinct from the governmental acts, of a sovereign state, which rule was part of English law. The difficulty in the path of the second ground was that there was authority of the Court of Appeal against it which, according to the ordinary rules,[15] would bind the court in the instant case. However, Lord Denning MR, with whom Shaw LJ agreed, overcame this difficulty by stating, as a principle, that the rule of *stare decisis* had no application to the rules of international law and, therefore, no application to that part of English law which embodies current international law. The point does not appear to have been judicially considered since that case. Being a decision of the Court of Appeal it must, for the time being, be taken as an accurate statement of the law and to constitute an important, albeit limited, exception to the doctrine of binding precedent.

2   The binding element in precedents

a   The ratio decidendi

It is a misstatement to speak of a "decision" as being binding, just as it is not technically correct to regard a "decision" as overruled. It is not the decision which binds, any more than it is the decision which is overruled; it is the rule of law contained in the decision. This element in a decision is termed the *ratio decidendi* of the case. Not every statement of law made by a judge in the course of his judgment is part of the *ratio*. For this reason it is important to be able to analyse a decision and isolate from it the *ratio decidendi*.

Every decision contains the following basic ingredients:

(1) findings of material facts, direct and inferential. An inferential finding of fact is the inference which the judge (or jury if there is one) draws from the direct, or perceptible, facts. For example, from the direct facts of the speed of a vehicle, the length of skid marks and the state of the road the judge or jury may infer negligence. Negligence is an inferential finding of fact. Similarly, unreasonable behaviour, in matrimonial proceedings, is an inference of fact which may or may not be drawn from the direct facts of the respondent spouse's treatment of the other spouse during the marriage;

(2) statements of the principles of law applicable to the legal problems disclosed by the fact; and

(3) judgment based on the combined effect of (1) and (2).

For the purposes of the parties themselves, (3) is the material element in the decision for it determines finally their rights and liabilities in relation to the subject matter of the action. However, for the purpose of the doctrine of precedent, (2) is the vital element in the decision. This is, indeed, the *ratio decidendi*. Thus the *ratio decidendi* may be defined as the statement of law applied to the legal problems raised by the facts as found upon which the decision is based. The two other elements in the decision are

14   [1977] QB 529; [1977] 1 All ER 881. The question at issue in the case has now been resolved by the State Immunity Act 1978, s 3(1); see p 346, *post*.
15   As to which, see p 76, *post*.

not precedents. The judgment is not binding (except directly on the parties themselves); nor are the findings of fact.[16] This means that, even where the direct facts of an earlier case appear to be identical to those of the case before the court, the judge or jury is not bound to draw the same inference as that drawn in the earlier case. *Qualcast (Wolverhampton) Ltd v Haynes*[17] is a good example of this point. In that case an employee sued his employers for damages for negligence in failing to provide a safe system of work. The county court judge, at first instance, held himself bound to find the defendant liable by earlier cases in which employers, having taken similar precautions to those taken by the defendant in the instant case, had been held liable. This was wrong for, as the House of Lords explained, these cases, even though decided by a judge sitting alone rather than with a jury, were decisions based upon inferences of fact which were not to be regarded as binding. Otherwise, as Lord Somervell observed:[18]

"the precedent system will die from a surfeit of authorities".

Moreover, not every statement of law in a judgment is binding. Only those statements which are based upon the facts as found and upon which the decision is based are binding. Any other statement of law is, strictly, superfluous and is described as an *obiter dictum* (something said "by the way"), although it should not be concluded from this that *obiter dicta* are of little or no weight or importance.

b   Obiter dicta

There are two types of *obiter dicta*. First, a statement of law is regarded as *obiter* if it is based upon facts which either were not found to exist or, if found, were not found to be material. For example, the famous statement of equitable estoppel contained in the judgment of Denning J in *Central London Property Trust Ltd v High Trees House Ltd*[19] is clearly *obiter* since it applied to a set of facts which were not found to be present in the case. Similarly, in *Rondel v Worsley*[20] the House of Lords expressed opinions to the effect that a barrister might be held liable in tort when acting outside the province of litigation and that a solicitor, when acting as advocate, might enjoy immunity from action. Since the case concerned only the liability of a barrister when acting as advocate, the opinions in question were necessarily *obiter*.

A second type of *obiter dictum* is a statement of law which, although based on the facts as found, does not form the basis of the decision. An obvious example is a statement of law in support of a dissenting judgment. Similarly, where a court makes statements of law leading to one conclusion and then adopts a contrary decision on the facts for a different reason, those statements are necessarily *obiter* since they do not support the decision. This is illustrated by the seminal case of *Hedley Byrne & Co Ltd v Heller & Partners Ltd*.[1] The proposition of law in that case, that the maker of a statement owes a duty of care, in certain circumstances, to persons whom he may expect to rely upon that statement, is, strictly, *obiter* since the bank which gave the advice was protected by its disclaimer of responsibility. That being so, the further statement

16   See *R v Secretary of State for the Home Department, ex parte Ku* [1995] QB 364; [1995] 2 All ER 891.
17   [1959] AC 743; [1959] 2 All ER 38.
18   [1959] AC at p 758; [1959] 2 All ER at p 43. It should be remembered that, in the tort of negligence, only the existence of a duty of care is a question of law; whether or not the defendant has broken his duty is a question of fact.
19   [1947] KB 130; [1956] 1 All ER 256n.
20   [1969] 1 AC 191; [1967] 3 All ER 993; see p 264, *post*.
1   [1964] AC 465; [1963] 2 All ER 575.

as to what rule of law would have been applied but for the disclaimer cannot be regarded as essential to the decision. Nevertheless, *Hedley Byrne* does illustrate that the strict rules for isolating the *ratio decidendi* of a case are sometimes of limited value since, the reasoning of the House of Lords, having been expressly applied in the Court of Appeal and approved in the House of Lords,[2] undoubtedly represents the present state of the law. It seems that where the House of Lords states a rule of law and expressly overrules earlier contrary decisions, that statement will be treated as binding even though not strictly essential to the decision.

ASCERTAINING THE *RATIO DECIDENDI*

Despite the fact that a clear definition can be proferred as to how to ascertain the *ratio decidendi* of a case, drawing a distinction in any case between the *ratio* an *obiter dicta* can be fraught with difficulty. It is sometimes difficult to isolate the *ratio decidendi* of a case which is argued on more than one ground. If the court is willing to decide the case on one ground it will usually refrain from expressing an opinion on any other point of law raised. Such a point is then said to be "left open". However the court sometimes feels constrained to deal with every point of law raised and then to give its decision. Which of these statements of law is the *ratio decidendi* of the case? The problem often arises when considering the decisions of appellate courts where different members of the court have arrived at the same conclusion, but for different reasons. A reason adopted by a majority of the court is, prima facie, *ratio* whereas a reason adopted only by a minority is usually regarded as inessential to the decision and, therefore, not binding. The position is even more complicated where no one reason is favoured by a majority. Clearly, every case must have a *ratio decidendi* and the answer seems to be that it depends upon which of the alternative reasons subsequent courts are prepared to accept as *rationes*. One classic example is the decision of the House of Lords in *Sinclair v Brougham*,[3] where it was held that once the creditors of a society had been paid in full by agreement, the assets remaining were to be divided between depositors and members of the society in accordance with the proportion of new payments to the society. The reasonings for this conclusion were far from clear, with one member of the court concurring with a judgment the reasoning of which was at odds with his own.[4] The multiplicity of opinion and reasoning was sufficient to provoke Lord Steyn in *Westdeutsche Handesbank Girozentrale v Islington LBC*[5] to observe that *Sinclair v Brougham* was

> "a bewildering authority: no single *ratio* can be detected; all the reasoning is open to serious objection, it was only intended to deal with cases where there were no trade creditors in competition and the reasoning is incapable of application where there are such creditors."

The decision of the court in *Sinclair v Brougham*, so far as it was discernible, was overruled.

The picture is further complicated by the fact that what may initially be considered, by the court itself, by commentators or by subsequent courts to amount to *obiter dicta* may be viewed differently subsequently, or *obiter* adopted as *ratio*, by later courts.

2   *Arenson v Casson, Beckman, Rutley & Co* [1977] AC 405; [1975] 3 All ER 901.
3   [1914] AC 398; [1914–1915] All ER 622.
4   Lord Dunedin.
5   [1996] AC 669; [1996] 2 All ER 961.

Thus, in *Luc Thiet Thuan v R*[6] the court considered that what may have been an *obiter dictum* in *R v Ahluwalia*[7] "certainly ripened" into *ratio decidendi* in *R v Dryden.*[8]

It is certainly possible for a case to have two or more *rationes decidendi.* The case of *Fairman v Perpetual Investment Building Society*[9] is an example. The House of Lords in that case gave two reasons for its decision, both of which were accepted as binding by the House itself in *Jacobs v London County Council.*[10] On the other hand, in *Read v J Lyons & Co Ltd*[11] the House of Lords advanced two reasons for its decision that the defendants were not liable under the rule in *Rylands v Fletcher:*[12] (1) that the rule did not apply in the absence of an escape of the dangerous substance from the defendant's occupation or control; and (2) that the rule did not apply unless the plaintiff had an interest in land affected by the escape. The second reason, which is principally contained in the speech of Lord Macmillan, was, in a later case,[13] treated by the Court of Appeal as *obiter*, on the basis that it was not essential to the decision. The position is complicated in that the statement to this effect in the Court of Appeal case was, itself, *obiter* because the plaintiff's action failed for another reason. Consequently it remains undecided whether the second reason in *Read v J Lyons & Co Ltd* is *ratio* or *obiter.*[14]

A variation of the difficulty described above arises where the majority of a court favour a reason which does not support the decision which the court in the event gives. That reason cannot, by definition, be a *ratio decidendi* because it does not support the decision; on the other hand to treat the contrary reasoning of the minority as *ratio*, although theoretically defensible, is logically odd. The occasions on which such a dilemma will arise are likely to be very rare, but the hearing by the House of Lords of the appeal in *Central Asbestos Co Ltd v Dodd*[15] was such an occasion. The question before the House turned on the construction of the ill-drafted provisions of section 7(3) of the Limitation Act 1963. Lords Reid and Morris took one view of the law, Lords Simon and Salmon a different view. The fifth member of the court, Lord Pearson, was in favour of deciding the appeal in the same way as Lords Reid and Morris, but for a different reason, his view on the point of law substantially supporting that of Lords Simon and Salmon.

It was not long before the Court of Appeal was called upon to decide the point of law which had arisen in *Dodd*'s case (which was, put simply, whether time ran against a plaintiff who knew the facts upon which his action was based but did not know that these facts gave him a cause of action). The Court of Appeal held[16] that, since *Dodd*'s

6   [1997] AC 131; [1996] 2 All ER 1033. See also *St John the Evangelist, Chopwel* [1995] Fam 254;
    [1996] 1 All ER 275, where statements made in *Re St Thomas, Pennywell* [1995] Fam 50; [1995] 4
    All ER 167 "were not strictly necessary to that decision but now I adopt them as part of the *ratio
    decidendi* of the present case."
7   [1992] 1 All ER 889.
8   [1992] 4 All ER 987.
9   [1923] AC 74.
10 [1950] AC 361; [1950] 1 All ER 737. The case is particularly notable in that one of the two reasons
    given in *Fairman*'s case was clearly not essential to the decision.
11 [1947] AC 156; [1946] 2 All ER 471.
12 (1868) LR 3 HL 330.
13 *Perry v Kendricks Transport Ltd* [1956] 1 All ER 154; [1956] 1 WLR 85.
14 The Court of Appeal in *Dunne v North-Western Gas Board* [1964] 2 QB 806; [1963] 3 All ER 916,
    expressly left the point open.
15 [1973] AC 518; [1972] 2 All ER 1135.
16 *Harper v National Coal Board* [1974] QB 614; [1974] 2 All ER 441. The cases are of no more than
    academic interest, so far as the limitation point is concerned, since Parliament intervened by passing
    the Limitation Act 1975 (now the Limitation Act 1980), which supports the view that the interpretation
    of the law intended by Parliament was that favoured by the minority in *Dodd*'s case. In *Miliangos v
    George Frank (Textiles) Ltd* [1976] AC 443, at p 479; [1975] 3 All ER 801, at p 822 Lord Simon was
    critical of the Court of Appeal in *Harper* for not following the minority reasoning in *Dodd* but, since
    that reasoning did not support the decision, it is difficult to support Lord Simon's criticism and, indeed,
    difficult to see what other course was open to the Court of Appeal.

case had no discernible *ratio decidendi*, the Court of Appeal would go back to the law as contained in the earlier cases.

it would be erroneous to suppose that *obiter dicta* are of no authority. Strictly, they are not of binding authority but have only persuasive authority. Nevertheless, where the statement in question has come from a court of high authority and is a deliberate statement of law as opposed to a casual expression of opinion it will usually be followed in the absence of binding authority to the contrary. By way of example may be cited the case of *Adams v Naylor*[17] in which the House of Lords disapproved the practice of government departments setting up a nominal defendant to avoid the Crown's immunity from actions in tort. Although this disapproval was *obiter*, the Court of Appeal in *Royster v Cavey*[18] adopted it and refused to sanction this long-standing practice. There could be no more striking example, finally, than the "neighbour principle" propounded by Lord Atkin in *M'Alister (or Donoghue) v Stevenson*.[19] This statement of law, though far wider than the decision required, has become the basis of the modern tort of negligence and has been cited and applied on occasions too numerous to mention.

3   Precedents which are not binding

a   Persuasive authorities

Only the *ratio decidendi* of a decision is binding. *Obiter dicta* are of persuasive authority. It has already been noted that the dicta of an appellate court may carry great weight. However, dicta, of whatever weight, may be rejected if a later court wishes to adopt a contrary solution. Other persuasive authorities are decisions of courts inferior in the hierarchy to the court which is invited to follow their decisions. Thus, for example, Court of Appeal decisions are of persuasive authority in the House of Lords.

A third class of persuasive authorities consists of the decisions of Scottish, Irish, Commonwealth and foreign courts. There is an increasing tendency on the part of English judges to draw analogies from other legal systems but these authorities are accepted as being of persuasive authority only. Special mention must be made of "decisions" of the Judicial Committee of the Privy Council. The advice of the Privy Council to Her Majesty is not strictly binding on any English judge. Thus, in theory, even a first instance judge may legitimately decline to follow a decision of the Privy Council.[20] However, Privy Council decisions are of very great persuasive authority for the obvious reason that the Council is in practice composed, for judicial sittings, of those persons who usually sit in the House of Lords.

Nevertheless, despite the similarity in composition between the Privy Council and the House of Lords, there had not been any suggestion that Privy Council authorities were of equivalent weight to House of Lords cases until the Court of Appeal in *Doughty v Turner Manufacturing Co Ltd*[1] expressed the view (albeit *obiter*) that the Court of Appeal's own decision in *Re Polemis*[2] was no longer good law in the light of the subsequent Privy Council decision in *The Wagon Mound*.[3] Subsequently, in *Worcester*

17   [1946] AC 543; [1946] 2 All ER 241.
18   [1947] KB 204; [1946] 2 All ER 642. This decision precipitated the passing of the Crown Proceedings Act 1947 which enabled the Crown to be sued in tort.
19   [1932] AC 562.
20   Diplock J did so in *Port Line Ltd v Ben Line Steamers Ltd* [1958] 2 QB 146; [1958] 1 All ER 787; see also *Dulieu v White* [1901] 2 KB 669.
1   [1964] 1 QB 518; [1964] 1 All ER 98.
2   [1921] 3 KB 560.
3   *Overseas Tankship (UK) Ltd v Morts Dock and Engineering Co Ltd* [1961] AC 388; [1961] 1 All ER 404.

Works Finance Ltd v Cooden Engineering Co Ltd[4] the Court of Appeal, faced with a conflict of authority between previous decisions of the Court of Appeal and a later decision of the Privy Council, had no hesitation in preferring the latter, Lord Denning MR expounding the principle that when the Privy Council disapproves of a previous decision of the Court of Appeal, the latter is at liberty to depart from its previous decision. The Privy Council itself has stated that, where the applicable law is English, the Judicial Committee will follow a House of Lords decision which covers the point at issue, since it is the House of Lords and not the Judicial Committee of the Privy Council which is the final judicial authority for the determination of English law.[5]

b   Precedents which have been overruled

A precedent does not lose its authority with the passing of time. Indeed the strength of a precedent increases with age in that courts tend to be reluctant to overrule long-standing authorities, unless they are clearly wrong. Apart from the desirability of attaining certainty, the main reason for the reluctance of judges to overrule old decisions is the fact that, since overruling operates retrospectively, it might have the effect of disturbing financial arrangements, depriving persons of vested proprietary rights and even imposing criminal liability. Thus in *Re Compton*[6] the Court of Appeal would not overrule a long line of old authorities concerning charitable trusts although it considered these cases anomalous. Similarly the rule in *Pinnel's case*[7], though plainly anomalous, has never been overruled. In *Foakes v Beer*[8] the House of Lords would not overrule *Pinnel's case*; Lord Fitzgerald, though doubting that the rule was a good one, did not feel that the House would be justified in overruling it having regard simply to its longevity.[9]

On the other hand there is little hesitation felt in overruling decisions which the court considers to be clearly wrong. Thus in *Bourne v Keane*[10] the House, considering an aspect of the law of trusts, overruled by a majority a series of long-standing decisions even though this had the effect of disturbing many existing trusts and settlements. More recently in *Button v Director of Public Prosecutions*[11] the House of Lords, in holding that the common law offence of affray could be committed in a private place, overruled a line of authority to the effect that an affray could take place only in a public place, while in the leading case of *Miliangos v George Frank (Textiles) Ltd*[12] the House of Lords overruled[13] its own decision in *Re United Railways of the Havana and Regla Warehouses Ltd*[14] which embodied one of the clearest and most firmly entrenched rules of English law, namely that judgment must be given in sterling.

4   [1972] 1 QB 210; [1971] 3 All ER 708.
5   *Tai Hing Cotton Mill Ltd v Liu Chong Hing Bank Ltd* [1986] AC 80; [1985] 2 All ER 947.
6   [1945] Ch 123; [1945] 1 All ER 198.
7   (1602), 5 Co Rep 117a.
8   (1884) 9 App Cas 605.
9   *Ibid* at p 630. The rule has, of course, been undermined by the doctrine of equitable estoppel; see *D & C Builders Ltd v Rees* [1966] 2 QB 6 17; [1965] 3 All ER 837. See also *Re Selectmire*.
10   [1919] AC 815. On the other hand, in *Prudential Assurance Co Ltd v London Residuary Body*[1992] 2 AC 386; [1992] 3 All ER 504, the House of Lords felt unable to overrule ancient authorities which embodied the rule requiring the maximum duration of a term of years to be determinable at the outset, on the ground that to do so might upset long-established titles, notwithstanding that this led to a "bizarre outcome" in the instant case.
11   [1966] AC 591; [1965] 3 All ER 587.
12   [1976] AC 443; [1975] 3 All ER 801.
13   Although the majority of the House stated that it was "departing from" the decision in the *Havana* case, it amounted in effect to overruling that case.
14   [1961] AC 1007; [1960] 2 All ER 332.

The process of overruling must be carefully distinguished from the process of reversing a decision. A decision altered on appeal is said to be "reversed". Reversing differs from overruling in that the former affects the decision in the case whereas the latter only affects the rule of law upon which the decision is based. Semantically, it is not correct to speak of a decision as "overruled" since it is only the rule of law contained in the decision which is affected, not the decision itself.

A decision may be overruled either by statute or by a higher court. If it is overruled by a higher court the earlier decision is deemed to have been based on a misunderstanding of the law. On a strict application of the traditional declaratory theory, the earlier rule of law is deemed never to have existed. On this view the common law is never changed; it is merely restated correctly. However, such a rationalisation ignores the reality that judges do make law, and often change the law because of changing circumstances or attitudes. Whatever the theoretical basis, all judicial overruling operates retrospectively. It is this which distinguishes judicial overruling from overruling by statute, since the latter (in the absence of an express provision to the contrary) operates only when the statute becomes operative. Another difference between judicial overruling and overruling by statute is that statutes, unlike judges, do not expressly name any decisions which they overrule. Nevertheless it is not usually difficult to identify the cases which are overruled by a statute, particularly where the statute follows closely upon an unpopular decision of a superior court, often the House of Lords.

In the Supreme Court of the United States there is power to overrule decisions prospectively, that is to apply the earlier decision to the facts of the instant case but to overrule it in so far as it may affect future cases.[15] In the United States Supreme Court the power is held to be based on the common law, though it has never been recognised in this country. However, in *Jones v Secretary of State for Social Services*[16] a case in which the House of Lords declined to overrule one of its own previous decisions although a majority were of the opinion that the *ratio* of the earlier decision was wrong, Lord Simon advanced the opinion that the most satisfactory method of dealing with the appeal would have been to allow it on the basis that it was covered by the earlier decision but to have overruled the earlier decision prospectively. In the event, however, he simply concurred in allowing the appeal and went on to say that, although an extension of judicial power to include prospective overruling should be considered (a suggestion with which Lord Diplock agreed), it would preferably be the subject of Parliamentary enactment, adding:[17]

"In the first place, informed professional opinion is probably to the effect that your Lordships have no power to overrule decisions with prospective effect only; such opinion is itself a source of law; and your Lordships, sitting judicially, are bound by any rule of law arising extra-judicially. Secondly, to proceed by Act of Parliament would obviate any suspicion of endeavouring to upset one-sidedly the constitutional balance between executive, legislature and judiciary. Thirdly, concomitant problems could receive consideration for example whether other courts supreme within their own jurisdictions should have similar powers as regards the rule of precedent; whether machinery could and should be devised to apprise the courts of the potential repercussions of any particular decision;

---

15   *Linkletter v Walker* 381 US 618 (1965), cited in *Jones v Secretary of State for Social Services (infra)*.
16   [1972] AC 944; [1972] 1 All ER 145; see p 218, *post*.
17   [1972] AC, at pp 1026–1027; [1972] 1 All ER, at p 198; Lord Simon advanced substantially similar suggestions in *Miliangos v George Frank (Textiles) Ltd* [1976] AC 443, at p 490; [1975] 3 All ER 801, at p 832.

and whether any court (including the appellate committee of your Lordships' House) should sit *in banc* when invited to review a previous decision."

The passage above illustrates clearly the reasons why it is preferable for major changes in the law to be made by Parliament, rather than by the judiciary.

c Precedents which can be distinguished

The process of "distinguishing" is probably the major factor in enabling the doctrine of precedent to remain flexible and adaptable. Cases are distinguished on their facts. The *ratio decidendi* of a case is, by definition, based upon the material facts of that case. Consequently if the court is willing to regard as material any fact not common to the case before it and the precedent cited, the two cases can be distinguished. The law reports are full of strained distinctions where the court was evidently anxious not to follow an apparently binding precedent. In theory it is possible to distinguish virtually any precedent since factual situations will almost never precisely duplicate themselves. Nevertheless there are practical limits beyond which the court will be unlikely to go. Cases which are indistinguishable are described as being "on all fours" with one another. To illustrate how fine a distinction may be drawn between ostensibly parallel factual situations reference may be made to two well-known cases concerning the tort of conversion. In *England v Cowley*[18] the defendant refused to allow the plaintiff to remove goods from his, the defendant's, premises. This was held not to be conversion since there was no absolute denial of title. This case was distinguished by the Court of Appeal in *Oakley v Lyster*[19] in which the defendant refused to allow the plaintiff to remove material from his, the defendant's, land and, in addition, asserted his own title to the material. This was held to be an act of conversion, the assertion of title apparently making the denial of title absolute.

d Statements of law made per incuriam

The Court of Appeal in the leading case of *Young v Bristol Aeroplane Co Ltd*[20] established the principle that the Court of Appeal was not bound to follow its own earlier decision if satisfied that the decision in question was reached *per incuriam* (through lack of care). This almost always means that some relevant statutory provision or precedent, which would have affected the decision, was not brought to the attention of the court, although the principle is not necessarily confined to such cases. Where it is argued that a decision was reached *per incuriam* on the ground that relevant material was overlooked by the court, it is not sufficient that the material in question might have led the court to a different conclusion; the criterion is that it must have done so.[1] Although the principle in *Young*'s case was expressed to apply only to the Court of Appeal, it has been applied in other courts. Thus in *R v Northumberland Compensation Appeal Tribunal, ex parte Shaw*[2] a divisional court of the King's Bench Division declined to follow a Court of Appeal decision on the ground that the latter had been reached *per incuriam*, a relevant House of Lords decision not having been cited to the Court of Appeal. However, in *Cassell & Co Ltd v Broome*[3] the House of Lords rejected

18 (1873) LR 8 Exch 126.
19 [1931] 1 KB 148.
20 [1944] KB 718; [1944] 2 All ER 293 (affirmed [1946] AC 163; [1946] 1 All ER 98); see p 76, *post*.
1 *Duke v Reliance Systems Ltd* [1988] QB 108; [1987] 2 All ER 858, affirmed [1988] AC 618; [1988] 1 All ER 626.
2 [1951] 1 KB 711; [1951] 1 All ER 268.
3 [1972] AC 1027; [1972] 1 All ER 801.

in condemnatory terms the Court of Appeal's decision to the effect that the decision
of the House of Lords in *Rookes v Barnard*[4] on the issue of exemplary damages had
been reached *per incuriam* because of two previous decisions of the House. Lord
Hailsham LC, in the course of the leading speech for the majority, asserted that:[5]

> " it is not open to the Court of Appeal to give gratuitous advice to judges of first
> instance to ignore decisions of the House of Lords in this way. The course taken
> would have put judges of first instance in an embarrassing position, as driving
> them to take sides in an unedifying dispute between the Court of Appeal and
> the House of Lords."

While Lord Reid[6] took the view that it was "obvious that the Court of Appeal failed to
understand Lord Devlin's speech", the words of Lord Hailsham proved to be prophetic
because in *Miliangos v George Frank (Textiles) Ltd*[7] Bristow J (as he expressly
acknowledged) found himself in the position of embarrassment foreseen by Lord
Hailsham. That the learned judge found himself in such a position was due to the fact
that in *Schorsch Meier GmbH v Hennin*[8] the Court of Appeal had held that the rule of
law whereby money judgments could only be expressed in sterling had ceased to exist,
notwithstanding clear House of Lords authority for the existence of the rule. Bristow J
preferred to follow the House of Lords authority; the Court of Appeal (perhaps not
surprisingly) stated that he was wrong in so doing because *Schorsch Meier* was binding
upon him. On appeal[9] the House of Lords decision in question[10] was overruled, although
not on any of the grounds on which the Court of Appeal had cited either in the instant
case or in *Schorsch Meier*.

The *per incuriam* principle is of limited application. Very few decisions have
subsequently been regarded as having been reached *per incuriam* and in *Morelle Ltd
v Wakeling*[11] Sir Raymond Evershed MR reaffirmed that:

> "As a general rule the only cases in which decisions should be held to have been
> given *per incuriam* are those of decisions given in ignorance or forgetfulness of
> some inconsistent statutory provision or of some authority binding on the court
> concerned; so that in such cases some part of the decision or some step in the
> reasoning on which it is based is found, on that account, to be demonstrably
> wrong. This definition is not necessarily exhaustive, but cases not strictly within
> it which can properly be held to have been decided *per incuriam* must, in our
> judgment, consistently with the *stare decisis* rule which is an essential feature
> of our law, be, in the language of Lord Greene MR of the rarest occurrence."

4   [1964] AC 1129; [1964] 1 All ER 367. This decision had already been subjected to devastating criticism
     in the courts of the Commonwealth and had been repudiated by the Privy Council; see *Australian
     Consolidated Press Ltd v Uren* [1969] 1 AC 590; [1967] 3 All ER 523. No less devastating was the
     criticism of Lord Denning MR, culminating in the description of the doctrine laid down by Lord Devlin
     in *Rookes v Barnard* as "hopelessly illogical and inconsistent": *Broome v Cassell & Co Ltd* [1971] 2
     QB 354, at p 381; [1971] 2 All ER 187, at p 199, an approach which attracted vehement criticism
     from the majority of the House of Lords.
5   [1972] AC 1027, at p 1054; [1972] 1 All ER 801, at p 809.
6   [1972] AC at p 1084; [1972] 1 All ER at p 835.
7   [1975] QB 487; [1975] 1 All ER 1076.
8   [1975] QB 416; [1975] 1 All ER 152; [1975] 1 CMLR 20.
9   [1976] AC 443; [1975] 3 All ER 801.
10   *Tomkinson v First Pennsylvania Banking and Trust Co* [1961] AC 1007, *sub nom Re United Railways
     of the Havana and Ragla Warehouses Ltd* [1960] 2 All ER 332 (a decision to which Lord Denning
     himself had been a party).
11   [1955] 2 QB 379, at p 406; [1955] 1 All ER 708, at p 718; see also *Miliangos v George Frank (Textiles)
     Ltd* [1976] AC 443, at p 477; [1975] 3 All ER 801, at p 821, per Lord Simon.

Thus the doctrine will not be extended to cases which were merely not fully or expertly argued,[12] or were argued on one side only (as *Schorsch Meier* was), or were cases in which the court appeared to misunderstand the law or was not aware of considerations of policy underlying a statute[13] or adopted a statutory interpretation which appears to be wrong. However, if it appeared to a court that a previous court's interpretation of a statute was an impossible interpretation (as opposed merely to an incorrect one) then it would seem that the duty of the later court is to apply a correct interpretation;[14] whether this would be an example of the *per incuriam* doctrine or simply an illustration of the general rules relating to the interpretation of statutes, and the obligations of judges in relation thereto, is problematical.

4   The hierarchy of the courts

It has already been noted that the doctrine of binding precedent depends for its operation upon the underlying principle that the courts form a hierarchy with each court standing in a definite position in relation to every other court. The structure of this hierarchy must now be considered for the purposes of the doctrine of precedent.

a   European Court of Justice[15]

In matters concerning: (1) the interpretation of the Treaties; (2) the validity and interpretation of acts of the Community institutions; and (3) the interpretation of the statutes of bodies established by an act of the Council, the Court of Justice of the European Communities is the supreme tribunal. Accordingly its decisions, in these areas of jurisdiction, will be binding on all English courts. Indeed section 3(1) of the European Communities Act 1972 expressly provides that:

> "for the purpose of all legal proceedings any question as to the meaning or effect of any of the Treaties, or as to the validity, meaning or effect of any Community instrument, shall be treated as a question of law (and, if not referred to the European Court,[16] be for determination as such in accordance with the principles laid down by and any relevant decision of the European Court)."

The European Court of Justice does not observe a doctrine of binding precedent and does not regard itself as bound by its previous decisions.[17] That does not, of course, mean that its previous decisions are no influence upon it. Quite the reverse. Many

---

12   *Joscelyne v Nissen* [1970] 2 QB 86; [1970] 1 All ER 1213; *Morelle Ltd v Wakeling* (*supra*).
13   *Farrell v Alexander* [1976] QB 345; [1976] 1 All ER 129 (decision reversed [1977] AC 59; [1976] 2 All ER 721); but see *Industrial Properties (Barton Hill) Ltd v Associated Electrical Industries Ltd* [1977] QB 580; [1977] 2 All ER 293 in which the Court of Appeal declared one of its previous decisions *per incuriam* where the court had misunderstood an earlier case because of deficiencies in the law report of that case to which it had been referred, and *Dixon v British Broadcasting Corporation* [1979] QB 546; [1979] 2 All ER 112 in which one *ratio* of an earlier case was treated as *per incuriam* on the ground that the statutory provision under construction had apparently been considered in isolation rather than in context; for an illustration of the *per incuriam* principle in the Court of Appeal, Criminal Division, see *R v Martindale* [1986] 3 All ER 25; [1986] 1 WLR 1042.
14   *Ibid.*
15   See p 115, *post*.
16   See p 117, *post*.
17   Case 2830/62; *Da Costa en Schaake NV v Nederlandse Belastingadministratie* [1963] CMLR 224, cited in *HP Bulmer Ltd v J Bollinger SA* [1974] Ch 401; [1974] 2 All ER 1226.

important principles of European law have been developed by the ECJ on a case-by-case basis.[18]

b   House of Lords

The House of Lords stands at the summit of the English hierarchy of courts. Decisions of the House of Lords are binding upon all other courts trying civil or criminal cases, whether or not appeal lies to the House from those courts.

Formerly the House of Lords regarded itself as strictly bound by its own earlier decisions, which were thus immutable except by legislation.[19] However in 1966 Lord Gardiner LC, on behalf of himself and the Lords of Appeal in Ordinary, made a statement to the effect that their Lordships proposed in future to depart from their own earlier decisions "when it appears right to do so".[20]

They would, however, bear in mind the danger of disturbing retrospectively financial arrangements and rights in property and the especial need for certainty as to the criminal law. The Lord Chancellor made it clear, moreover, that this statement was not intended to apply elsewhere than in the House of Lords.

Although this statement was not made in the context of an actual decision it has the force of law, and the House does depart from its own earlier decisions, albeit rarely. The practical consequences of this change in the law were, at first, slight. In the five years following Lord Gardiner's statement the House of Lords did not overrule any of its previous decisions. Their reticence is aptly demonstrated by *Jones v Secretary of State for Social Services*.[1] In this case, involving the construction of the National Insurance (Industrial Injuries) Act 1946, a majority of the House (consisting of seven members) declined to overrule a previous decision of the House[2] although a majority of their Lordships were of opinion that the *ratio* of the earlier decision was wrong. Since there was no suggestion that the earlier authority could be distinguished it might appear that, a majority of the House being of the opinion that the decision was wrong, there would be no alternative but to overrule it. Three of the majority of four who believed the earlier authority to be wrong were in favour of overruling it and had the fourth, Lord Simon, agreed, the House would undoubtedly have overruled its own earlier decision. However Lord Simon gave several reasons why, in his opinion, it would be wrong to depart from *Dowling*'s case, notably that the power to depart from a previous decision "is one to be most sparingly exercised", and that a variation of view on a matter of statutory construction would rarely provide a suitable occasion.

However, the wait for a suitable occasion was not a long one and in *British Railways Board v Herrington*[3] the House, on the question of the extent of the duty of care owed by an occupier of land to trespassers, restated the law and refused to follow the statement of the law, which had stood for over 40 years, laid down in *Robert Addie & Sons (Collieries) Ltd v Dumbreck*.[4]

---

18   See, eg, doctrine of direct effects, see p 105, *post*.
19   This principle was established in *London Tramways Co v London County Council* [1898] AC 375.
20   Reported at [1966] 3 All ER 77; [1966] 1 WLR 1234.
1   [1972] AC 944; [1972] 1 All ER 145.
2   *Minister of Social Security v Amalgamated Engineering Union* [1967] 1 AC 725; [1967] 1 All ER 210.
3   [1972] AC 877; [1972] 1 All ER 749.
4   [1929] AC 358; see also *The Johanna Oldendorff* [1974] AC 479; [1973] 3 All ER 148; *Vestey v Inland Revenue Commissioners* [1980] AC 1148; [1979] 3 All ER 976; *Murphy v Brentwood District Council* [1991] 1 AC 398; [1990] 2 All ER 908.

As indicated above, the power is exercised sparingly. As Lord Reid observed in one case:[5] " our change of practice in no longer regarding previous decisions of this House as absolutely binding does not mean that whenever we think a previous decision was wrong we should reverse it. In the general interest of certainty in the law we must be sure that there is some very good reason before we so act."

Notwithstanding the especial need for certainty as to the criminal law, in *R v Shivpuri*[6] the House, dealing with the law relating to criminal attempts, departed from its own earlier decision.[7] The latter had been reached less than a year earlier but had meanwhile been the subject of devastating academic criticism. Lord Bridge (who had been a party to the earlier decision) gave the following reasons:[8]

"Firstly, I am undeterred by the consideration that the decision in *Anderton v Ryan* was so recent. The 1966 Practice Statement is an effective abandonment of our pretention to infallibility. If a serious error embodied in a decision of this House had distorted the law, the sooner it is corrected the better. Secondly, I cannot see how, in the very nature of the case, anyone could have acted in reliance on the law as propounded in *Anderton v Ryan* in the belief that he was acting innocently and now find that, after all, he is to be held to have committed a criminal offence."

Apart from the possibility of the House of Lords being prepared to depart from its own earlier decisions there are three basic means by which a House of Lords decision may lose its authority. Firstly, and most obviously, it may be overruled by statute or a decision of the European Court of Justice. Secondly, it may be distinguished. The process of distinguishing applies in the House of Lords as in other courts. Indeed, before the 1966 Practice Statement it was applied with more force in the House of Lords than elsewhere because there was no other judicial means of avoiding a precedent which the House felt to be wrong, although this has not been the case since then.

Finally, it is possible for a House of Lords decision to be rejected if given *per incuriam*, although in modern conditions it would be virtually inconceivable that a case could progress through the House of Lords with a crucial authority being overlooked.

Although the House of Lords may reject its own earlier decisions as being given *per incuriam* it is clear that no other court can legitimately do so. As noted earlier, the Court of Appeal in *Broome v Cassell & Co Ltd*[9] regarded a House of Lords decision as being given *per incuriam* on the basis that two House of Lords authorities were not cited to the House. Reference has already been made to the manner in which the House of Lords disapproved the Court of Appeal's application of the *per incuriam* doctrine. Lord Diplock was alone, however, in going so far as to state that the Court of Appeal had no power to treat a decision of the House of Lords in this way:[10]

"The Court of Appeal found themselves able to disregard the decision of this House in *Rookes v Barnard* by applying to it the label *per incuriam*. That label is relevant only to the right of an appellate court to decline to follow one of its

5   *Knuller (Publishing, Printing and Promotions) Ltd v Director of Public Prosecutions* [1973] AC 435, at p 455; [1972] 2 All ER 898, at p 903; see also, to similar effect, *Fitzleet Estates Ltd v Cherry* [1977] 3 All ER 996; [1977] 1 WLR 1345.
6   [1987] AC 1; [1986] 2 All ER 334.
7   In *Anderton v Ryan* [1985] AC 560; [1985] 2 All ER 355.
8   [1987] AC, at p 23; [1986] 2 All ER, at p 345.
9   [1971] 2 QB 354; [1971] 2 All ER 187; see p 71, *ante*. For House of Lords, see *Cassell & Co Ltd v Broome* [1972] AC 1027, at p 1131; [1972] 1 All ER 801, at p 874.
10   See *Baker v R* [1975] AC 774; [1975] 3 All ER 55; *Miliangos v George Frank (Textiles) Ltd* [1976] AC, at p 479; [1975] 3 All ER, at pp 822–823, per Lord Simon.

own previous decisions, not to its right to disregard a decision of a higher appellate court or to the right of a judge of the High Court to disregard a decision of the Court of Appeal."

However, this dictum has been approved[10] and may be treated as authoritative. By contrast, where two House of Lords decisions conflict, a court is entitled and bound to follow the later decision.[11]

c   Court of Appeal

CIVIL DIVISION

Decisions of the Court of Appeal are binding on all inferior courts trying civil or criminal cases, including divisional courts.[12] The Court of Appeal is bound by decisions of the European Court, the House of Lords, and by its own earlier decisions.[13] The latter principle was affirmatively established in the leading case of *Young v Bristol Aeroplane Co Ltd*[14] Lord Greene MR, who delivered the judgment of the court, cited three exceptional circumstances in which an earlier decision of the Court of Appeal would not be regarded as binding.

(1) Where there are two conflicting decisions, the court may choose which it will follow, the decision not followed being deemed to be overruled. Thus, in *Fisher v Ruislip-Northwood Urban District Council*[15] the court, of which Lord Greene was again a member, was required to choose between conflicting lines of authorities concerning the liability of local authorities to motorists who collided with unlit air-raid shelters, while in *Tiverton Estates Ltd v Wearwell Ltd*[16] the Court of Appeal was able to avoid following its own recent decision in the controversial case of *Law v Jones*[17] (to the effect that it was unnecessary for a memorandum under section 40 of the Law of Property Act 1925 to acknowledge the existence of a contract) because it was in conflict with earlier decisions of the court.

(2) The court is bound to refuse to follow a decision of its own which, though not expressly overruled, cannot stand with a later House of Lords decision.[18]

(3) The court is not bound to follow a decision of its own if that decision was given *per incuriam*.

11   *Moodie v Inland Revenue Commissioners* [1993] 2 All ER 49; [1993] 1 WLR 266.
12   *Brownsea Haven Properties Ltd v Poole Corporation* [1958] Ch 574; [1958] 1 All ER 205.
13   *Sed quaere*; is it bound by a decision of the Judicial Committee of the Privy Council? The Court of Appeal is also bound by decisions of courts which exercised equivalent jurisdiction prior to 1875: the Court of Exchequer Chamber and the Chancery Court of Appeal; see *Ex parte M'George* (1882) 20 Ch D 697.
14   [1944] KB 718; [1944] 2 All ER 293 (affirmed [1946] AC 163; [1946] 1 All ER 98).
15   [1945] KB 584; [1945] 2 All ER 458.
16   [1975] Ch 146; [1974] 1 All ER 209.
17   [1974] Ch 112; [1973] 2 All ER 437; see also *Starr v National Coal Board* [1977] 1 All ER 243; [1977] 1 WLR 63; *WA Sherratt Ltd v John Bromley (Church Stretton) Ltd* [1985] QB 1038; [1985] 1 All ER 216.
18   This exception, it will be observed, does not apply to cases in which a decision of the Court of Appeal is inconsistent with an earlier House of Lords decision. It may be that Lord Greene did not entertain this as a possibility and indeed it is clearly a situation which should not arise since the Court of Appeal, unless it was not referred to the earlier House of Lords decision (in which event its own decision would be *per incuriam*) should not reach decisions which are inconsistent with the existing authority of the House of Lords. When however that situation does arise, probably the better view is that the Court of Appeal should follow its own decision and give leave to appeal to the House of Lords; cf *Miliangos v George Frank (Textiles) Ltd* [1976] AC, at p 479; [1975] 3 All ER, at p 823, per Lord Simon. But see *Turton v Turton* [1988] Ch 542; [1987] 2 All ER 641, where the Court of Appeal disapproved its own earlier decision in *Hall v Hall* (1981) 3 FLR 379 on the ground that it was inconsistent with the House of Lords case of *Gissing v Gissing* [1971] AC 886; [1970] 2 All ER 780.

This principle, explained earlier, is not confined to the Court of Appeal. The *per incuriam* principle usually involves there having been overlooked by the previous court a relevant statutory provision or an authority binding on the court. There is, however, a residual undefined category of other cases in which the principle may be invoked, as Lord Greene had acknowledged in *Young*. During his tenure of the office of Master of the Rolls, Lord Donaldson occasionally tapped this slender stream. Thus in *Williams v Fawcett*[19] the Court of Appeal regarded a number of earlier authorities on a point as having been reached *per incuriam* on the ground that there had been a "manifest slip or error" in an area in which the liberty of the subject was involved (committal for contempt of court) and in which cases were most unlikely ever to reach the House of Lords. Again, in *Rickards v Rickards*[20] the court, again presided over by Lord Donaldson, applied the "manifest slip or error" test when refusing to follow an earlier decision which involved a wrongful rejection of jurisdiction by the court in circumstances in which there was no possibility of an appeal to the House of Lords.

While he was Master of the Rolls, Lord Denning engaged in a tireless, but ultimately unsuccessful, campaign to gain for the Court of Appeal the freedom that the House of Lords has to depart from its own previous decisions at will. In *Gallie v Lee*[1] Lord Denning evinced a desire to depart from the rule in *Young's* case in the following words:

"We are, of course, bound by the decisions of the House [of Lords], but I do not think we are bound by prior decisions of our own, or at any rate, not absolutely bound. We are not fettered as it was once thought. It was a self-imposed limitation; and we who imposed it can also remove it. The House of Lords have done it. So why should not we do likewise?"

This was, however, a minority opinion. Russell LJ saw the position of the House of Lords in quite a different light, saying of the Master of the Rolls:[2]

"I think that in one respect he has sought to wield a broom labelled 'for the use of the House of Lords only'. I do not support the suggestion that this court is free to override its own decisions ... the availability of the House of Lords to correct error in the Court of Appeal makes it in my view unnecessary for this court to depart from its existing discipline."

Again in *Barrington v Lee*, a case concerned with liability as between vendor and purchaser in respect of an estate agent's default over a deposit, Lord Denning dealing with the effect of an earlier decision on similar facts, boldly asserted:[3]

"We are not absolutely bound by *Burt's* case. We no longer look to see if the case can be brought within the exceptions stated in *Young v Bristol Aeroplane Co Ltd*."

19   [1986] QB 604; [1985] 1 All ER 787.
20   [1990] Fam 194; [1989] 3 All ER 193.
1   [1969] 2 Ch 17, at p 37; [1969] 1 All ER 1062, at p 1072 (affirmed *sub nom Saunders v Anglia Building Society* [1971] AC 1004; [1970] 3 All ER 961).
2   [1969] 2 Ch, at p 41; [1969] 1 All ER, at p 1082; the third member of the court, Salmon LJ, took a middle view and stated that a change in policy, though possibly desirable, would require a pronouncement of the whole Court of Appeal. Nevertheless, in *Davis v Johnson* [1979] AC 264; [1978] 1 All ER 1132, Lord Salmon, in common with the other members of the House of Lords, expressly reaffirmed *Young's* case.
3   [1972] 1 QB 326, at p 338; [1971] 3 All ER 1231, at p 1238; see also *Hanning v Maitland (No 2)* [1970] 1 QB 580, at p 587; [1970] 1 All ER 812, at p 815.

Once again, however, Lord Denning was expressing a minority view, for Edmund Davies and Stephenson LJJ, though concurring in the result of the appeal by distinguishing *Burt*'s case, both reaffirmed the principles of *Young*'s case and disagreed with the view of Lord Denning quoted above. Stephenson LJ's judgment epitomises the traditional approach:[4]

> " what may be thought timorous subservience to judicial precedent is, in my judgment, preferable to the uncertainty which will be introduced into the law in fields not easy to delimit by the bolder work of demolition and restoration proposed by Lord Denning MR in this case. We must take care lest in struggling to straighten out the law we bend it until it breaks."

Faced with such opposition to his views Lord Denning was constrained to resile from the statements he had made in *Gallie v Lee* and *Barrington v Lee*; indeed in *Miliangos v George Frank (Textiles) Ltd*[5] the Master of the Rolls expressly applied the principles in *Young v Bristol Aeroplane Co Ltd*. Nevertheless in *Davis v Johnson*, a controversial case dealing with the power of the courts to protect battered wives, Lord Denning led the full Court of Appeal in yet another attack on *Young*'s case, which attack was, again, repulsed when the case reached the House of Lords,[6] where the rule in *Young* was, in Lord Diplock's words, "expressly, unequivocally and unanimously" reaffirmed. It is not now to be anticipated that any further attempt will be made by the Court of Appeal to suggest that it is not bound by its own previous decisions (subject to the recognised exceptional cases referred to in *Young*).

The civil division of the Court of Appeal is certainly not bound by decisions of the now defunct Court of Criminal Appeal. It is uncertain whether the civil division will regard itself as bound by decisions of the criminal division of the Court of Appeal, which now exercises that jurisdiction formerly exercised by the Court of Criminal Appeal. The better view appears to be that the civil division will regard itself as bound by decisions of the criminal division so that an unedifying conflict such as has, in the past, existed between the civil and criminal appeal courts[7] is now unlikely to recur.

It may be noted finally that a "full court" of five or more judges of the civil division is sometimes convened to hear cases involving particularly important or difficult points of law. The full court of the civil division has, however, no greater authority than the normal court and its decisions carry no more weight as precedents.[8]

CRIMINAL DIVISION

Decisions of the criminal division of the Court of Appeal bind inferior courts trying criminal cases, including the divisional court of the Queen's Bench Division, and will probably be regarded as binding upon inferior courts trying civil cases. The division regards itself as bound by decisions of its predecessor, the Court of Criminal Appeal,

---

4   [1972] 1 QB, at p 345; [1971] 3 All ER, at p 1245. The law was, eventually, clarified by the House of Lords in *Sorrell v Finch* [1977] AC 728; [1976] 2 All ER 371. See also *Tiverton Estates Ltd v Wearwell Ltd* [1975] Ch 146; [1974] 1 All ER 209.

5   [1975] QB 487; [1975] 1 All ER 1076.

6   [1979] AC 264; [1978] 1 All ER 1132.

7   The historic conflict occurred in the cases of *R v Denyer* [1926] 2 KB 258, CA and *Hardie and Lane v Chiltern* [1928] 1 KB 663, CA in which the Court of Appeal, on the subject of the legality of trade stop-lists, declined to follow the earlier decision of the Court of Criminal Appeal and expressly disapproved it. The conflict on this point could thus be solved only by the House of Lords and this was done in *Thorne v Motor Trade Association* [1937] AC 797; [1937] 3 All ER 157.

8   This was established in *Young v Bristol Aeroplane Co Ltd* [1944] KB 718; [1944] 2 All ER 293. Likewise the authority of a two-judge court is no less than that of a three-judge court: *Langley v North West Water Authority* [1991] 3 All ER 610; [1991] 1 WLR 697.

and by decisions of the civil division of the Court of Appeal subject to the exceptions contained in *Young v Bristol Aeroplane Co Ltd*. Thus in *R v Merriman*[9] the criminal division allowed an appeal, totally lacking in merit, "with the utmost reluctance" because of the existence of a direct authority of the Court of Criminal Appeal in favour of the appellant. However, the court certified a point of law of general public importance and granted leave to appeal to the House of Lords where the appeal was allowed and the earlier authority overruled.[10]

The Court of Criminal Appeal formulated the principle that it would not be bound by its own previous decision where this would cause injustice to an appellant, the rationale of this principle being that the desire for attaining justice transcends the desirability of certainty. The rule was stated by Lord Goddard CJ in *R v Taylor*[11] in the following terms:

"This court, however, has to deal with questions involving the liberty of the subject, and if it finds, on reconsideration, that, in the opinion of a full court assembled for that purpose, the law has been either misapplied or misunderstood in a decision which it has previously given, and that, on the strength of that decision, an accused person has been sentenced and imprisoned, it is the bounden duty of the court to reconsider the earlier decision with a view to seeing whether that person had been properly convicted. The exceptions which apply in civil cases ought not to be the only ones applied in such a case as the present."

This rule was adopted by the criminal division of the Court of Appeal in *R v Gould*.[12]

In the past, decisions of the Court of Criminal Appeal have been somewhat less reliable as precedents than the decisions of other appellate courts. This is accounted for by the fact that the court rarely reserved judgment, that only one judgment was usually given and that dissents were not recorded. Although section 59 of the Supreme Court Act 1981 expressly provides that separate judgments may be pronounced on a question of law, precedents of the criminal division of the Court of Appeal are still regarded with more circumspection than decisions of the civil division.

d High Court

DIVISIONAL COURTS
In civil matters divisional courts are bound by decisions of the House of Lords and Court of Appeal (including, probably, the criminal division), subject to the exceptions

---

9   [1971] 2 QB 310; [1971] 2 All ER 1424.
10   [1973] AC 584; [1972] 3 All ER 42. A similar course was followed in *Director of Public Prosecutions v Kilbourne* [1973] AC 729; [1973] 1 All ER 440.
11   [1950] 2 KB 368; [1950] 2 All ER 170; see also observations of Lord Diplock in *Director of Public Prosecutions v Merriman* [1973] AC 584, at 605; [1972] 3 All ER 42, at 58; *R v Howe* [1986] QB 626; [1986] 1 All ER 833 (affirmed [1987] AC 417; [1987] 1 All ER 771); but cf *R v Charles* [1976] 1 All ER 659; [1976] 1 WLR 248 (affirmed *sub nom Metropolitan Police Commissioner v Charles* [1977] AC 177; [1976] 3 All ER 112).
12   [1968] 2 QB 5; [1968] 1 All ER 849; the necessity for a "full court" of five or more judges seems to have been tacitly abolished; cf *R v Newsome* [1970] 2 QB 711; [1970] 3 All ER 455 which appears to assert greater power for a court of five to depart from the earlier decision of a court of three than a court of three would possess. In *R v Jackson* [1974] QB 802; [1974] 1 All ER 640, a case in which the court had to choose between conflicting decisions on an important question of sentencing principle, a full court was convened; on occasions when the need to choose between conflicting decisions arises, this practice is sometimes adopted: see, generally, G Zellick, 'Precedent in the Court of Appeal, Criminal Division' [1974] Crim LR 222.

set out in *Young v Bristol Aeroplane Co Ltd*[13] and also by their own earlier decisions. Divisional court decisions in civil cases are binding on judges of the same division of the High Court sitting alone, and, possibly, on judges of other divisions.[14]

In criminal cases the position of the divisional court of the Queen's Bench Division is closely analogous to that of the criminal division of the Court of Appeal. Thus it is free to depart from its own decisions in the same circumstances as in that court. When exercising its supervisory jurisdiction, a divisional court is in the same position as a High Court judge sitting alone; thus it may depart from its own previous decision when convinced that such decision is wrong. The above principles appear from the judgment of the Queen's Bench divisional court, delivered by Goff LJ in *R v Greater Manchester Coroner, ex parte Tal.*[15]

JUDGES AT FIRST INSTANCE

Decisions of High Court judges sitting alone at first instance are binding on inferior courts but are not binding on other High Court judges. For this reason it is a dangerous practice to rely upon principles of law which are contained only in first instance decisions, since they are not binding in any High Court action. Naturally, they are of persuasive authority and a High Court judge will hesitate before "not following" the decision of one of his brethren, if only for reasons of comity. Nevertheless, where a first instance judge is clearly convinced that an earlier decision at first instance is wrong, he will be free to refuse to follow that decision. There have been several direct clashes between decisions of first instance judges, a notable modern example occurring in relation to the question of whether failure on the part of a driver or passenger in a motor vehicle to wear a seat belt amounted to contributory negligence in the event that injury suffered in an accident was aggravated by such failure. This question virtually divided the judges of the Queen's Bench Division in some fourteen reported cases on the topic between 1970 and 1975 until the Court of Appeal resolved the conflict in *Froom v Butcher*[16] where it was held that failure to wear a seat belt did, in the ordinary way, amount to contributory negligence.[17]

It is sometimes said that judges of the Chancery Division are less willing to depart from decisions of their brethren than are judges of other divisions. This is only true insofar as to depart from any earlier authority might have the effect of disturbing financial arrangements or depriving a person of a vested proprietary right.

High Court judges are bound by decisions of the Court of Appeal and House of Lords. Where there appears to be a conflict between previous decisions of the Court of Appeal and House of Lords, the High Court judge should give effect to the decision

---

13   See p 76, *ante*; *R v Northumberland Compensation Tribunal, ex parte Shaw* [1952] 1 KB 338; [1952] 1 All ER 122; *Huddersfield Police Authority v Watson* [1947] KB 842; [1947] 2 All ER 193.

14   *Bretherton v United Kingdom Totalisator Co Ltd* [1945] KB 555; [1945] 2 All ER 202; *Re Seaford, Seaford v Seifert* [1967] P 325; [1967] 2 All ER 458 (reversed [1968] P 53; [1968] 1 All ER 482) in which a judge of the Probate, Divorce and Admiralty Division regarded himself as bound by a decision of the divisional court of the Queen's Bench Division; cf *Elderton v United Kingdom Totalisator Co Ltd* (1945) 61 TLR 529 (affirmed [1946] Ch 57; [1945] 2 All ER 624).

15   [1985] QB 67; [1984] 3 All ER 240. Cf *C v DPP* [1994] 3 All ER 190. A "full" divisional court of five or more judges has no greater authority than the normal court of two or three: *Younghusband v Luftig* [1949] 2 KB 354; [1949] 2 All ER 72.

16   [1976] QB 286; [1975] 3 All ER 520; all of the reported cases on the subject are reviewed in the judgment of Lord Denning, MR in this case.

17   For other illustrations of clashes between judges at first instance, see *Esso Petroleum Co Ltd v Harper's Garage (Stourport) Ltd* [1966] 2 QB 514; [1965] 2 All ER 933 and *Petrofina Ltd v Martin* [1965] Ch 1073; [1965] 2 All ER 176; *Metropolitan Police District Receiver v Croydon Corporation* [1956] 2 All ER 785; [1956] 1 WLR 1113 and *Monmouthshire County Council v Smith* [1956] 2 All ER 800; [1956] 1 WLR 1132; *Wood v Luscombe* [1966] 1 QB 169; [1964] 3 All ER 972; *Wall v Radford* [1991] 2 All ER 741 and *Randolph v Tuck* [1962] 1 QB 175; [1961] 1 All ER 814.

of the immediately higher court, viz the Court of Appeal. The reasoning behind this is that the conflict could only arise if the Court of Appeal had been able to distinguish or otherwise avoid following a House of Lords decision; in those circumstances the High Court judge should assume that the Court of Appeal had correctly distinguished or otherwise avoided such decision.[18]

e   *Inferior and other courts*

Magistrates' courts, county courts and other inferior tribunals are bound by the decisions of all superior courts, not excluding first instance decisions of the High Court. The position of the Crown Court in the hierarchy, in relation to the doctrine of precedent, has not been authoritatively determined. When a High Court judge presides the court is, presumably, equivalent to a judge of the High Court sitting at first instance. However, when a circuit judge or Recorder presides it would seem reasonable to regard the court as inferior in status to a judge of the High Court and, therefore, bound by decisions of the High Court.[19] The decisions of one inferior court are not binding upon any other inferior court, chiefly because the decisions of inferior courts are not reported. The Employment Appeal Tribunal is bound by decisions of the Court of Appeal and House of Lords but does not regard itself as bound by decisions of the High Court (nor, presumably by its own decisions) or of the Tribunal's short-lived predecessor, the National Industrial Relations Court.[20]

In conclusion it would probably be optimistic to state categorically that the doctrine of binding precedent as applied in English courts achieves certainty while retaining flexibility. Its operation depends, as with the interpretation of statutes, on the conception of the particular judge or court trying a case of the judicial function. The rules for determining the *ratio decidendi* of a case and the hierarchy of the courts are sufficiently well defined to achieve legal certainty. On the other hand, the *per incuriam* doctrine, the process of distinguishing, the capacity of superior courts to overrule decisions and the absolute power of Parliament to change the law all serve to keep the doctrine flexible. In the last analysis the doctrine of precedent is usually seen to operate fairly, though how far this is attributable to the inherent qualities of the doctrine and how far to the good sense of English judges is a matter of debate.

C   THE HISTORICAL DEVELOPMENT OF LAW REPORTING

As stated at the beginning of this chapter, the doctrine of binding precedent became a part of English law only when the system of law reporting had become comprehensive. The doctrine of precedent, as such, is of far greater antiquity but it was only in the nineteenth century that precedents became binding rather than merely persuasive. As late as 1762 Lord Mansfield, a bitter opponent of mulish adherence to precedent, could state:[1] "the reason and spirit of cases make law, not the letter of particular precedents."

---

18   This was the analysis of Lord Simon in *Miliangos v George Frank (Textiles) Ltd* [1976] AC 443; [1975] 3 All ER 801; see p 72, *ante*.

19   In *R v Colyer* [1974] Crim LR 243 a circuit judge presiding over the Crown Court at Ipswich took the bold course of refusing to follow a decision of the divisional court of the Queen's Bench Division on the ground that it was not binding on him. This must surely have been incorrect. Since the divisional court is bound by its own previous decisions (supra) it would be bizarre if a circuit judge were not bound by them.

20   *Portec (UK) Ltd v Mogenson* [1976] 3 All ER 565.

1   *Fisher v Prince* (1762) 3 Burr 1363. This theme runs through many of Lord Mansfield's judgments. See, for example: *Jones v Randall* (1774) 1 Cowp 37; *R v Bembridge* (1783) 3 Doug KB 327.

Nevertheless the growth of a comprehensive system of law reporting brought with it the modern doctrine of binding precedent. If it were possible to mark the turning point, the decision of Parke in *Mirehouse v Rennell* in 1833[2] would appear to herald the evolution of the modern system.

It is, therefore, instructive to trace the evolution of law reporting and, incidentally, to note the methods of citation and reference.

The history of law reporting can be roughly divided into three periods; first, the period of the Year Books extending approximately from 1272 to 1535; secondly, the period of the private named reporters extending from 1535 to 1865 and, thirdly, the modern semi-official system of reporting which began in 1865.

I   The Year Books

The Year Books are the first available law reports. They were first compiled during the reign of Edward I. Exactly what function they were intended to and did fulfil at that time is uncertain. They were certainly not intended for use by the judges as precedents, and were probably simply notes compiled by students and junior advocates for use, by advocates, as guides to pleading and procedure. While they contain legal argument of counsel and notes of exchanges between bench and bar they are very far from being law reports in the modern sense. Since most litigation in the thirteenth and fourteenth centuries took the form of disputes over title to land it is natural to find that most Year Book cases are land law cases, generally being decisions of the Court of Common Pleas.

Although Year Book reports were in no sense official and were not, apparently, intended for use by the judges, there are indications that they may have been used by some judges as a direct source of precedent. Thus in 1310 Stanton J referred to a case decided at least ten years earlier,[3] while Bereford CJ in 1312 cited a decision some twenty-five years old.[4] Even allowing for the longevity of judicial recollection of case law, it seems likely that these judges were basing their knowledge upon some written record of the cases in question. By the fifteenth century there are many examples of Year Book cases in which the judge is reported as having relied upon a number of very old authorities. This is the origin of the doctrine of precedent in English law and there is ample evidence[5] that the judges were conscious that their decisions were being recorded for use as precedents.

With the introduction of printing in the fifteenth century many Year Book manuscripts were printed in the so-called "Black Letter" editions. The most widely used modern printed editions of the Year Books are the Rolls Series (RS) and the Selden Society Series (SS). Both series date from early in the present century and contain the original text of the Year Book manuscripts, which are in "law French", a peculiar combination of Norman French, English and Latin, together with an English translation. The Selden Society continue to edit and produce collections of Year Book reports. Citation of Year Book cases is usually by reference to one of these two editions.

Abridgements

The excellence of the printed editions of the original Year Books that are available has rather lessened the value of the Abridgements. These are merely collections of

2   (1833) 1 Cl & Fin 527.
3   *Kembeare v K* YB 4 Edw 2 (SS iv), 153. Note the method of citation by regnal year.
4   *Anon* YB 6 Edw 2 (SS xiii), 43.
5   For examples see Allen, *Law in the Making* (7th Edn), pp 190 *et seq.*

Year Book cases according to their subject matter in chronological order compiled by judges and lawyers, generally for their own use. Some of these Abridgements were published and may be compared to modern case books. The best known Abridgements are those of Fitzherbert and Brooke, published in 1516 and 1568 respectively.

2 The private reports

Compilation of printed Year Books ceased in about 1535.[6]

Almost immediately private sets of reports began to be produced, printed and published under the name of the law reporter. At first the private reports were scarcely fuller than the Year Book reports had been. Very soon, however, many sets of private reports became far more detailed, reproducing much of counsel's argument and virtually the whole of the judgment. The private reporters generally attached themselves to one court, probably the court in which they intended to practise, and took notes of the proceedings. These notes would later be revised and published as reports. The citation of precedents became progressively more common as the private reports became more comprehensive.

The private reporters proliferated in the period of 1535 to 1865. The standard of reporting varied greatly. At one end of the scale were the reporters whose reports contain what are still regarded today as classic expositions of the common law. These reporters did not, until the end of the eighteenth century, produce their reports contemporaneously with the decisions they were reporting. Consequently the reporter's invention and personality played no little part in the compilation of the reports. This is particularly true of Coke, possibly the greatest of all law reporters. Coke's Reports (Co Rep) are so well known as to be citable merely as "reports" (Rep). They contain comprehensive expositions of virtually every aspect of the common law supported by a wealth of authority assiduously gleaned from the Year Books and even the ancient Plea Rolls, which Coke had copied for his own use. Coke's great industry and scholarship have made his Reports and textbooks a primary literary source of the common law. Nowadays there is rarely any need to look beyond Coke to trace the origin of any old common law rule. His Reports, published between 1600 and 1658, contain many of the great constitutional cases of the seventeenth century, such as *Prohibitions del Roy*[7] *Proclamations*[8] and *Magdalen College*.[9]

It will be observed that Coke was a judge as well as a law reporter. This is true of many of the great reporters, notably Dyer, who was Chief Justice of the Common Pleas, and Saunders, Chief Justice of the King's Bench. To the great names of Coke, Dyer and Saunders may be added those of Plowden and, later, Burrow. Burrow's Reports are of cases in the Court of King's Bench between 1751 and 1772 and thus include many of Lord Mansfield's famous judgments. They are widely regarded as the first set of law reports produced in the modern pattern. They contain headnotes and the argument of counsel is carefully separated from the judgment. Nevertheless they were not contemporaneous reports. The first reports which attempted to be contemporaneous were the Term Reports which are of cases in the King's Bench in the period 1785–1800.

It must not be thought that every one of the private law reporters was a Plowden or a Coke. At the other end of the scale were reporters such as Barnardiston, Atkyns and Espinasse whose reports became virtually uncitable, so low were they held in judicial

6   Although manuscript Year Books continued to be produced into the seventeenth century.
7   (1607) 12 Co Rep 63.
8   (1610) 12 Co Rep 74.
9   (1615) 11 Co Rep 66b.

esteem.[10] Lord Mansfield, in particular, would not permit certain series of reports to be cited to him, while Holt CJ observed feelingly that "these scambling reports will make us appear to posterity for a parcel of blockheads".[11]

Citation of private reports

The private reports are cited by the name of the reporter (usually abbreviated) and a volume and page number. The date of the report is not part of the reference but is usually inserted in ordinary round (not square) brackets. Thus the reference to the case of *Ashford v Thornton* is (1818)1 B & Ald 405 which indicates that the case is reported in volume 1 of Barnewall and Alderson's Reports at page 405. The reference to *Pillans v Van Mierop* (1765) 3 Burr 1664 indicates that the case can be found in the third volume of Burrow's Reports at page 1663.

In practice most law libraries have the reports of the private reporters in the reprinted edition known as "the English Reports" (ER or Eng Rep). The English Reports are published in 176 volumes and contain all the available reports of the private reporters. With the English Reports is published a reference chart showing in which volume the reports of any individual reporter are contained.

3   The present system of law reporting

a   The Law Reports

In 1865 the system of private reporting gave way to the system which still exists at the present day. A Council was established to publish, as cheaply as possible, reports of decisions of superior courts. The Council was, from its inception, under professional control and contained representatives of the Inns of Court and The Law Society. The Council was incorporated in 1870 as the Incorporated Council of Law Reporting for England and Wales.[12] The Council produces the Law Reports, the Weekly Law Reports (WLR), the Industrial Cases Reports (ICR) and the Law Reports Statutes. The Law Reports are not an official publication but, by convention, they are the series of reports to which counsel should refer when citing a case which is reported in the Law Reports.[13] In addition the judges are given the opportunity of revising reports of their own judgments. The reporters, in order for the report to be receivable, must be present in court when judgment is delivered and must be barristers, solicitors or have a Supreme Court qualification.[14]

---

10   For an assessment of the relative merits of the private reporters see Allen, *Law in the Making* (7th Edn), pp 221 *et seq.*

11   *Slater v May* (1704) 2 Ld Raym 1071.

12   The Council is a charity: *Incorporated Council of Law Reporting for England and Wales v A-G* [1972] Ch 73; [1971] 3 All ER 1029.

13   *Practice Note* [1991] 1 All ER 352. The House of Lords has stated that counsel may refer to a report in Tax Cases, rather than the Law Reports, if they think it convenient to do so: *Bray v Best* [1989] 1 All ER 969; [1989] 1 WLR 167. An advantage of the Law Reports over other series is that legal argument, as well as the judgments, is published. Where the court has adjourned to take time to consider its decision judgment is said to be "reserved". This fact is indicated in reports by the insertion of the words *curia advisari vult*, *cur ad vult* or *cav*, before the judgment. Reserved judgments are generally accorded greater weight than *ex tempore* judgments.

14   Defined by the Courts and Legal Services Act 1990, s 115. See p 245, *post.*

b   The Weekly Law Reports

Up to and including 1952 the Incorporated Council of Law Reporting published "Weekly Notes" (WN). These reports were in the form of a current precis and did not enjoy the authority of the Law Reports. They were, indeed, not strictly citeable as reports.[15]

Weekly Notes were replaced in 1953 by the Weekly Law Reports. The Weekly Law Reports include a report of every decision which will ultimately appear in the Law Reports proper. The cases are reported in full, except that legal argument is omitted because of the restriction on space. In addition many cases are published in the Weekly Law Reports which it is not intended to include subsequently in the Law Reports. These cases are published in Volume 1 of the Weekly Law Reports whereas cases which are destined to reach the Law Reports are published in Volumes 2 and 3.

c   Citation of the Law Reports and the Weekly Law Reports

The citation of the Law Reports prior to 1891 was somewhat complex. Before 1875 a case was cited by reference to the court in which it was decided and a serial number dating from 1865, prefixed by the letters LR. The date, not being part of the reference, was inserted in ordinary round brackets. Thus *Irving v Askew* (1870) LR 5 QB 208 was reported in the fifth volume of Reports of cases in the Court of Queen's Bench at page 208.

Between 1875 and 1890 citation was by an abbreviation of the appropriate division of the High Court (Ch D; QBD; PD; CPD; Ex D[16]) or App Cas for an appeal case. The date was still not part of the reference and the serial number dated from 1875. The prefix LR was dropped. An example of citation during this period is *Symons v Rees* (1876) 1 Ex D 416.

In 1891 the date was, for the first time, made part of the reference in place of a serial number and the letter D (for Division) was dropped. The fact that the date is part of the reference is signified by its inclusion in square brackets. There is a separate volume of Reports for each division of the High Court (QB; Ch; Fam)[17] and a separate volume for House of Lords and Privy Council cases (AC).[18]

Court of Appeal decisions are reported in the volume for the division of the High Court from which the appeal came. County court appeals and appeals to the criminal division of the Court of Appeal are usually reported in the volume for the Queen's Bench Division. There is thus nothing in the reference to distinguish a Court of Appeal decision from a decision at first instance. This is the modern method of citation.

---

15   See *Re Loveridge* [1902] 2 Ch 859, at p 865, per Buckley J.

16   The last two were abolished in 1880 with the fusion of the Common Pleas Division and the Exchequer Division into the Queen's Bench Division; see p 5, *ante*.

17   When the Family Division was named the Probate, Divorce and Admiralty Division, this volume of Reports was cited by the letter P.

18   It may be noted that, prior to 1974, when a case reached the House of Lords (or Privy Council or divisional court on appeal) the appellant's name used to be cited first. Thus, for example, the case known in the Court of Appeal as *Lever Brothers Ltd v Bell* [1931] 1 KB 557 became *Bell v Lever Brothers Ltd* [1932] AC 161 in the House of Lords because the defendant, Bell, was the appellant in the House of Lords. However, this practice was altered, in relation to House of Lords cases, by a Procedure Direction (reported at [1974] 1 All ER 752; *sub nom Practice Direction* [1974] 1 WLR 305) whereby petitions for leave to appeal and appeals to the House of Lords carry the same title as that which obtained in the court of first instance. In criminal cases this has the effect of terminating the practice (which appears to have dated from *Director of Public Prosecutions v Beard* [1920] AC 479) whereby the Director of Public Prosecutions was substituted for *Rex* (or *Regina*). The All England Law Reports, since 1979, have adopted this method of citation.

In the case of the Weekly Law Reports the year is, as with the Law Reports, part of the reference and appears in square brackets. There is, however, no attempt to classify cases by the court in which they were decided. All cases appear in 1 WLR, 2 WLR or 3 WLR irrespective of whether they are House of Lords or first instance decisions.

d   Other series of reports

A case which is reported in the Law Reports should be cited by its Law Report reference in preference to any other reference, though only as a matter of practice. In addition to the Law Reports (and other reports published by the Council) there are series of reports published under government authority; these include Reports of Tax Cases, Reports of Patent, Design and Trade Mark Cases, Immigration Appeal Reports, Industrial Tribunal Reports and Value Added Tax Tribunal Reports.

There are also many series of reports published commercially. One such are the All England Law Reports. These are published weekly (and, periodically, on CD ROM) and their virtue lies principally in the speed with which they follow the decision. In addition many cases are reported in the All England Law Reports which do not find their way into the Law Reports. The All England Law Reports are cited by the year in square brackets followed by the abbreviation All ER and a page number. There are usually three or four volumes of All England Law Reports published each year though, unlike the Weekly Law Reports, there is no significance in the volume number.

The Law Journal Reports (LJ) and Law Times Reports (LT) have been incorporated in the All England Law Reports. The Times Law Reports (TLR) have also ceased to function independently. However, the Criminal Appeal Reports (CAR or Cr App Rep), first published shortly after the creation of the Court of Criminal Appeal, are still produced and report a number of criminal cases not reported elsewhere. Similarly Lloyd's List Law Reports (Lloyd's Rep) contain a number of commercial cases not reported elsewhere while the Road Traffic Reports (RTR) contain, as the title would suggest, reports of road traffic cases. Other specialist series in general use are Local Government Reports (LGR), Building Law Reports (BLR), Simon's Tax Cases (STC), Ryde's Rating Cases (RRC), Property and Compensation Reports (PCR), Industrial Relations Law Reports (IRLR), Housing Law Reports (HLR) and Fleet Street Patent Law Reports (FSR). European Community law decisions are to be found principally in the Common Market Law Reports (CMLR) and European Court Reports (ECR). Periodicals such as the Solicitors Journal, Justice of the Peace, Estates Gazette, Criminal Law Review, New Law Journal and Current Law include notes of cases to which reference may be made in the absence of a full report in a recognised series. Among newspapers only the reports of *The Times* are commonly cited (not to be confused with the Times Law Reports).

The chief criticism which may be advanced of the present system of law reporting in England is its informality. The selection of cases for reporting is entirely at the discretion of the law reporters. The Court of Appeal, for example, decides about 3,000 cases every year, of which only a small proportion are reported. Although there cannot be many cases of importance which escape the elaborate net of the law reporters there are undoubtedly some. The citation of unreported cases in court has been by no means unknown[19] but, as noted above, the growth of electronic databases means that, in one sense, there is now hardly ever an "unreported" case. However, the citation of cases

---

19   See, eg, *Barrington v Lee* [1972] 1 QB 326; [1971] 3 All ER 1231 from which it appears that the Court of Appeal in *Ryan v Pilkington* [1959] 1 All ER 689; [1959] 1 WLR 403 may have gone wrong because two important unreported authorities were not before the court. These cases, decided in 1948 and 1958, have since been reported (in [1971] 2 QB 439, 443; [1971] 2 All ER 628, 631).

reported only in series of reports other than the Law Reports is very common, especially in cases of a type where specialist series of reports exist. With the advent of computerised databases, such as LEXIS, unreported decisions, together with decisions of overseas courts, have become much more accessible to practitioners. It was this phenomenon, and the spectre of protraction of legal argument that it spawned, which led Lord Diplock to make the controversial statement that he did in *Roberts Petroleum Ltd v Bernard Kenny Ltd*[20] restricting counsel's right to cite unreported transcripts of the Court of Appeal in either the Court of Appeal or the House of Lords.

A second criticism of the system is the unnecessary duplication of effort. Many cases are reported more or less fully in three or four different series of reports and noted in many periodicals.

On the initiative of the then Lord Chancellor, a Committee was set up to report on the state of law reporting. Its report, published in 1940, was somewhat negative in character. It rejected the proposal to grant a monopoly to the Incorporated Council of Law Reporting, being content to state that the Law Reports should be cited in preference to any other series. The Committee also rejected, in the interest of publicity of judicial proceedings, a proposal to grant licences to reporters without which they would be incompetent to report. Most of the positive recommendations in the 1940 Report were contained in the minority report of Professor Goodhart. Professor Goodhart's main suggestion was that each court, through an official shorthand writer and the judge, should produce an authenticated transcript which would be filed with the court records. Copies of these transcripts would be available for sale to law reporters and other interested persons. This would amount to making law reports official. The majority of the Committee rejected Professor Goodhart's proposal as expensive and inconvenient. At the present day the main objection to Professor Goodhart's proposal would be the additional strain it would impose upon an already overworked judiciary.

---

20   [1983] 2 AC 192, at 200–202; [1983] 1 All ER 564, at 566–568 (see p 61, *ante*).

CHAPTER 4

Textbooks

A textbook differs from a statute or a law report in that it is not an original literary source of law. Textbooks, even if of the highest authority, contain only opinions as to the state of the law. In short they are a secondary source. Nevertheless it would be unrealistic in any consideration of the literary sources of English law to ignore textbooks for they are, in some cases, the earliest authority for the existence of a common law rule. The importance of textbooks as a source of law is, historically, in inverse proportion to the availability of law reports. Thus, in modern times textbooks are of comparatively little value since direct authority can almost always be found in a law report. Conversely, in the infancy of law reporting when such reports as existed were of a highly personalised nature the textbooks were, and are, the main source of authority. Indeed the line between a law report and a textbook opinion is often a narrow one, particularly in the case of Coke whose *Institutes* (Inst) are cited quite as often as his Reports and are generally accorded equivalent authority.

It will thus be apparent that there are two types of legal textbook. The first is the ancient textbook which is commonly used as an original source of common law. This type of book is a book of authority. The second type of textbook is the modern textbook which, however well respected and frequently cited, is not a book of authority. That is to say it is not a source of law and is only of use in that it indicates where a direct source, such as a statute or a law report, may be found. The dividing line between books of authority and modern textbooks is purely historical and depends, as stated above, on the availability of direct literary sources. Blackstone's *Commentaries on the Laws of England*, published in 1765, is probably the watershed in that, although it is often cited as a book of authority, it was also the forerunner of the modern textbook.

A SOME BOOKS OF AUTHORITY

Textbooks of English law have not become books of authority merely by reason of their antiquity. Of the many works produced as legal textbooks, only about a dozen are universally accepted by the legal profession and the judiciary alike as books of authority. It is no accident that almost all the authors of these works were judges. The academic lawyer in the modern sense did not appear until Blackstone, in the eighteenth century, and Blackstone himself was also a judge. The following are some of the major textbook writers whose works may be said to be sources of English law.

1   Glanvill and Bracton

Glanvill's treatise *De Legibus et Conseutudinibus Angliae* (concerning the laws and customs of England), written in about 1187, is the first major commentary on the common law in existence. Written in Latin, the manuscripts merely indicate that the treatise was written in the time of Glanvill who was Henry II's chief justiciar,[1] so that it is doubtful whether Glanvill was personally responsible for its composition. The subject matter of the treatise principally concerns land law, the basis of the common law. The form of the treatise set the pattern for legal writing for centuries to come in that it approached the common law from the standpoint of procedure, setting out the existing forms of action with a commentary on the scope of each. Glanvill is still cited as a book of authority[2] though not as frequently as the larger and more comprehensive treatise of Bracton.

Bracton's treatise, written in about 1250, was, like Glanvill's treatise, written in Latin and entitled *De Legibus et Consuetudinibus Angliae*. Although uncompleted it is a far more ambitious and comprehensive survey of English law than Glanvill's work. It adopted Glanvill's pattern of a summary of the forms of action glossed with a commentary but went further in that it illustrated the commentaries with case law. The cases in Bracton's treatise are set out very fully, generally including as much detail as the Year Books. In addition the treatise contains a long exposition of English law by way of introduction. Bracton appears to have been thoroughly grounded in Roman law and his treatise draws many Roman law analogies. Virtually all the principles of Roman law which have found their way into English law have done so via Bracton.[3] Perhaps the best known case in which Bracton's civilian analogies have been adopted into English law is *Coggs v Bernard*[4] in which Holt CJ developed the law of bailments in accordance with Roman law concepts gleaned from Bracton. The development of the law of easements also owes much to Bracton's exposition of Roman law.[5] Nevertheless, Bracton is first and foremost a chronicler of the common law and his treatise stands as the major academic work on the common law prior to Coke's *Institutes*.

2   Littleton

After Bracton there is no book of authority until the late fifteenth century when Littleton's treatise *Of Tenures* was published. This important work was the first comprehensive study of English land law which was, at the time, exceedingly complex. The work differs from that of Bracton in that it approaches the subject from the standpoint of substantive law rather than of procedure. Also it appears that the work was intended for use as a textbook and it was, in fact, used for this purpose for centuries after its composition. Coke's praise of Littleton was fulsome and he described the work as being of absolute perfection, the ornament of the common law, and "the most perfect

1   The justiciar was the forerunner of the Chancellor.
2   See, for example: *Ashford v Thornton* (1818) 1 B & Ald 405; *Warner v Sampson* [1959] 1 QB 297; [1959] 1 All ER 120.
3   See p 11, *ante*.
4   (1703) 2 Ld Raym 909.
5   *Dalton v Angus* (1881) 6 App Cas 740.

and absolute work that ever was written in any human science". Indeed, the first of Coke's *Institutes* is a commentary on Littleton's *Of Tenures*.

The work is also notable as being the first major legal work to be printed, rather than written.

3   Coke

Probably the greatest of textbook writers was Coke himself. This may be added to his other accomplishments as a judge, parliamentarian and law reporter. Coke's great contribution to academic literature, apart from the Reports, which undoubtedly contain much subjective exposition, are his *Institutes of the Laws of England*. Coke's *Institutes* were composed chiefly towards the end of his life after he had ceased to hold judicial office. They are so well known as to be citable merely as *Inst* without reference to the author.

There are four Institutes. The first, published in 1628, is a treatise on Littleton's *Of Tenures* and is commonly cited as *Co Litt*. The second, and perhaps least valuable, Institute is a summary of the principal medieval statutes. The third is concerned with criminal law, defining and describing all the Pleas of the Crown, and the fourth Institute deals with the jurisdiction of the courts. The reason for the exalted position of the Institutes as a direct source of the common law is Coke's acquaintance with the Year Books. Coke's mastery of the Year Books has probably never been equalled and his recollection in the Institutes is so accurate that, even shortly after his death, virtually no one would look beyond Coke as a direct source. For this reason the Year Books are cited comparatively infrequently while the Institutes have been cited to English courts probably more frequently than any other book of authority.

A modern instance of reliance upon Coke as a work of authority is to be found in the decision of the Court of Appeal in *Reid v Metropolitan Police Commissioner*.[6] The case was concerned with the meaning of the words "market overt" in section 22(1) of the Sale of Goods Act 1893 and, in particular, whether the operation of that section was confined to sales between sunrise and sunset:

> "to solve this question we have to go back to the works of Sir Edward Coke. In 1596 there was an important case about market overt;[7] Coke reported it. He afterwards expounded the law of market overt in his Institutes.[8] I think we should follow the words of Sir Edward Coke rather than those of Sir William Blackstone."[9]

The words that the Court of Appeal followed began:

> "the sale must not be in the night, but between the rising of the sun, and the going downe of the same"[10]

so that a purchaser who bought the plaintiff's goods some one hour before sunrise at the New Caledonian Market in Southwark was held not to have acquired a good title to them under the Sale of Goods Act.

6   [1973] QB 551; [1973] 2 All ER 97.
7   *Market-Overt case* (1596) 5 Co Rep 83b.
8   (1642) vol 2, pp 713, 714.
9   [1973] QB 551, at 559; [1973] 2 All ER 97, at 99, per Lord Denning MR.
10   *Market-Overt case* (1596) 5 Co Rep 83b.

The only weakness in Coke's work is his total devotion to the common law to the exclusion of every other branch of English law. His total abhorrence of equity and admiralty undoubtedly did much to maintain the separate administration of these branches of the law for so long.

4   Blackstone

After Coke a large number of legal textbooks were produced. A few of these, such as the works of Hale, Hawkins and Foster are citable as books of authority particularly in relation to the criminal law.[11] Due to the poverty of early reports of criminal cases, judges, when faced with a question of basic principles of criminal law, usually look no further than the early textbooks, particularly those of Coke, Hale, Hawkins, Foster and Blackstone. In the leading case of *Joyce v Director of Public Prosecutions*[12] the House of Lords, in deciding that a foreigner who enjoyed the protection of the Crown could be guilty of treason under the Treason Act 1351, relied almost entirely on Foster's *Crown Cases*, Hale's *Pleas of the Crown*, Hawkin's *Pleas of the Crown*, East's *Pleas of the Crown* and Coke's *Institutes*. More recently, in defining the common law offence of affray in the House of Lords, Lord Gardiner LC referred (inter alia) to Fitzherbert, Coke, Hale, Hawkins and Blackstone.[13]

Blackstone's *Commentaries on the Laws of England*, published in 1765, is probably the last book of authority to be written. It differs from works such as those of Hale and Hawkins in that it covers a far wider field. The four books comprising the Commentaries deal with constitutional law, family law, the law of real and personal property, succession, contract and tort, criminal law and civil and criminal procedure. It is, however, in the fields of tort and criminal law that Blackstone's authority is greatest. The authority of the *Commentaries* is rather less weighty than the authority of the earlier works cited in this section.[14] There are two reasons for this. First, the scope of the work is so wide that it cannot do more than state principles where works of narrower range can probe detail. Secondly, the *Commentaries* are later in point of time than Coke, Hale, Foster and the others so that in the event of an inconsistency between them the earlier work is almost bound to prevail. This is well illustrated by the case of *Button v Director of Public Prosecutions*[15] in which a statement of Blackstone[16] to the effect that a common law affray could take place only in a public place was rejected by the House of Lords as inconsistent with earlier statements in the works of Hale and Hawkins.

B   MODERN TEXTBOOKS

The growth of law reporting after Blackstone's era and the fact that the basic principles of the common law were well established and chronicled by that time have made it unnecessary to look at any more recent textbook as a direct source of a common law rule. Nineteenth-century works such as Stephen's *Commentaries on the Laws of*

11   See *Ashford v Thornton* (1818) 1 B & Ald 405; *R v Casement* [1917] 1 KB 98; *Joyce v Director of Public Prosecutions* [1946] AC 347; [1946] 1 All ER 186.

12   [1946] AC 347; [1946] 1 All ER 186.

13   *Button v Director of Public Prosecutions* [1966] AC 591; [1965] 3 All ER 587.

14   Cf *Reid v Metropolitan Police Commissioner* (*supra*) in which Blackstone's definition of market overt was rejected in favour of that of Coke.

15   *Supra*.

16   4 Comm 145.

England are sometimes consulted, but only as guides, not as sources. They are not books of authority.

There are, however, many standard textbooks widely used by the legal profession, and even by judges, which are of the highest persuasive authority. Virtually every branch of the law has its standard work and the judge will think twice before gainsaying a statement of law appearing in such a work. Nevertheless judges never lose sight of the fact that these works are not books of authority and, in the event of a statement in a standard textbook being inconsistent with a principle contained in a precedent or a statute, the latter will always prevail. For example, in *Watson v Thomas S Whitney & Co Ltd*[17] the Court of Appeal, in deciding that an appeal from the registrar of the (now defunct) Liverpool Court of Passage lay to the Court of Appeal, declined to adopt clear statements in *Halsbury's Laws of England* and the *Annual Practice 1966*, to the effect that the appeal lay to the divisional court of the Queen's Bench Division. Similarly, in *Button v Director of Public Prosecutions*[18] the House of Lords drew attention to errors in *Archbold's Pleadings, Evidence & Practice in Criminal Cases* and *Russell on Crimes and Misdemeanours*, both standard works on the criminal law. In *Shenton v Tyler*[19] the then Master of the Rolls, in considering the scope of marital privilege, referred to some dozen textbooks on evidence, including those of Best, Cockle, Phipson and Stephen, before deciding that all were wrong.

The above, however, are exceptional occurrences. On the whole the persuasive authority of a standard textbook is of considerable weight. There have been several cases in which a court has been willing to accept almost verbatim the view of a distinguished academician upon the law. Thus the description of easements contained in *Cheshire's Modern Real Property* was adopted by the Court of Appeal in *Re Ellenborough Park*[20] while the House of Lords in *A-G v De Keyser's Royal Hotel Ltd*[1] expressly accepted Dicey's definition of the royal prerogative. To go one step further, counsel for the respondents in *Rookes v Barnard*[2] postulated the rather startling proposition that the tort of intimidation had been created by Sir John Salmond in his leading work on the law of torts.

There was formerly a rule of practice that a textbook could not be cited in court during the lifetime of its author. The rule, which appears to have rested on no very logical foundation, has now been discounted and several textbook writers, and even the authors of articles in legal periodicals, have had the satisfaction of seeing their opinions judicially endorsed during their own lifetimes.[3] In *R v Shivpuri*, in which the House of Lords overruled its own previous decision of less than a year before in the face of considerable academic criticism, Lord Bridge (who had also been a party to the earlier decision) graciously ended his speech with the following tribute:[4]

"I cannot conclude this opinion without disclosing that I have had the advantage, since the conclusion of the argument in this appeal, of reading an article by Professor Glanville Williams entitled 'The Lords and Impossible Attempts, or *Quis Custodet Ipsos Custodies*?' [1986] CLJ 33. The language in which he

17   [1966] 1 All ER 122; [1966] 1 WLR 57.
18   [1966] AC 591; [1965] 3 All ER 587 (*supra*).
19   [1939] Ch 620; [1939] 1 All ER 827.
20   [1956] Ch 131; [1955] 3 All ER 667.
1   [1920] AC 508.
2   [1964] AC 1129; [1964] 1 All ER 367.
3   See, for example, *Performing Right Society Ltd v Mitchell and Booker (Palais de Danse), Ltd* [1924] 1 KB 762; *Read v J Lyons & Co Ltd* [1945] KB 216; [1945] 1 All ER 106 (affirmed [1947] AC 156; [1946] 2 All ER 471); *Director of Public Prosecutions v Humphrys* [1977] AC 1; [1976] 2 All ER 497.

criticises the decision in *Anderton v Ryan* is not conspicuous for its moderation, but it would be foolish, on that account, not to recognise the force of the criticism and churlish not to acknowledge the assistance I have derived from it."

4   [1987] AC 1, at 23; [1986] 2 All ER 334, at 345.

CHAPTER 5

The European Community and European Union

A INTRODUCTION

The United Kingdom has, since 1 January 1973 (the date specified in the Treaty of Accession), been a member state of the European Communities. Of three Communities that exist,[1] the most important is that now known as the European Community.

Created in 1957 by the Treaty of Rome, and then known as the European Economic Community, initially it comprised six members, but has expanded to its current composition of fifteen member states.[2] The Treaty reflected a post-war desire to achieve stability through European unity, and its Preamble stated an aim of "ever closer union" amongst the peoples of Europe. This was to be achieved in areas of economic activity. Article 2 speaks of the promotion throughout the Community of:

"a harmonious development of economic activities, a continuous expansion, an increase in stability, an accelerated raising of the standard of living and closer relations between the states belonging to it."

Article 3 identifies a wide range of activities permissible in order to achieve the economic and social goals of the Community. These include common policies in respect of agriculture and transport, regulation of competition policy, free movement for workers, goods and services, and the elimination of trade barriers. In addition to the specific provisions of the Treaty, Article 100 provides for:

"the approximation of such provisions laid down by law, regulation and administrative action in member states as directly affect the establishment or functioning of the common market."

---

1 The other Communities are the European Coal and Steel Community (ECSC) and the European Atomic Energy Community (Euratom). References in the text are to the Economic Community and to the Treaty of Rome (1957) (before the Amsterdam Treaty) unless otherwise stated.
2 Austria, Belgium, Denmark, Finland, France, Germany, Greece, Italy, Luxembourg, Netherlands, Portugal, Republic of Ireland, Spain, Sweden, United Kingdom.

A framework was thus created for common action in the economic field, not simply as joint and co-ordinated action by member states, but through the Community as a distinct legal entity. The Community was to have its own institutions and laws, that could regulate the powers and obligations of member states in the economic field.

The Community has developed far beyond the original aims set by the Treaty of Rome.[3] Not only has its membership increased, its role has expanded beyond the economic into social, financial and political areas of competence. In 1987 the Single European Act was adopted. In addition to strengthening the institutional position of the Parliament, it set as an objective the "making of concrete progress towards European unity", and in various areas sought to achieve this by amendment of the Treaty of Rome. This process has been continued by the Treaty on European Union (1992), more commonly known as the Maastricht Treaty. This Treaty was, after considerable political controversy, ratified by the United Kingdom in 1993, and given effect in law (as from 1 November 1993) by the European Communities (Amendment) Act 1993. The Treaty not only formally changes the name to the European Community, but also radically amends the Treaty of Rome in order to achieve its aims. These are stated in its Preamble to be a continuation of the process of "ever closer union", economic and monetary union, including the development of a single currency, common citizenship, common foreign and defence policies, and the enhancement of the democratic functions of Community institutions.

This movement towards political union, and the extension of Community competence, is controversial.[4] In particular, the United Kingdom has reserved its position in respect of the later stages of economic and monetary union. The Maastricht Treaty made significant change. A European Union was established, the development of which is entrusted to a European Council[5] which has the task of developing the political guidelines for the development of that Union. The area of legal competence of the Community is extended, building upon the changes made by the Single European Act. This now extends to common citizenship of the European Union, with expanded rights of movement and voting, greater co-ordination of general economic policy with the establishment of a Central Bank, increased rights for workers, the development of culture and heritage, public health and the environment. The European Union seeks to adopt a common foreign and security policy in line with Title V of the Maastricht Treaty. That treaty has itself been amended by the Amsterdam Treaty of 1997. One of the siginificant changes made (but not yet operative) is a change in the numbering of the articles of the Treaty.

B   THE SCOPE OF EUROPEAN LAW

It would be a mistake to regard English and European law as two separate systems of law. The latter has now reached the stage of being a significant source of English law. In *HP Bulmer Ltd v J Bollinger SA* Lord Denning MR stated:[6]

---

3   A Treaty between the signatory states, not to be confused with an Act of the United Kingdom Parliament.

4   For unsuccessful challenge to the incorporation of the Treaty, see *R v Secretary of State for Foreign Affairs, ex parte Lord Rees-Mogg* [1994] QB 552; [1994] 1 All ER 457.

5   Formerly the Council of the European Community: see OJ Nov 1993.

6   [1974] Ch 401, at 418; [1974] 2 All ER 1226, at 1231; for the points arising from this case, see p 118, *post*.

"The first and fundamental point is that the treaty concerns only those matters which have a European element, that is to say matters which affect people or property in the countries of the Common Market besides ourselves. The treaty does not touch any of the matters which concern solely the mainland of England and the people in it. These are still governed by English law. They are not affected by the treaty. But when we come to matters with a European element, the treaty is like an incoming tide. It flows into the estuaries and up the rivers. It cannot be held back. In future, in transactions which cross the frontiers we must no longer speak or think of English law as something on its own. We must speak or think of Community law, of Community rights and obligations, and we must give effect to them."

This statement significantly underestimated the extent of involvement of Community law beyond matters that "cross frontiers", and today does not at all reflect the true legal position. Transactions which concern "solely the mainland of England and the people in it" may nonetheless be affected by Community provisions. Some of the provisions of the Treaty, and of the legislation of the Community, concern and enforce obligations of an economic character imposed on the member states rather than individuals within states. However, others are directly effective,[7] and may therefore be taken to create individually enforceable rights even within litigation that appears on its face to have no European context. Thus Article 119 regulates equality of treatment of male and female employees. Article 30 affects the legality of Sunday trading in England and Wales. Article 130r provides for the regulation of environmental matters. Article 118a deals with health and safety matters. Even where implementation of Community obligations is achieved by domestic legislation the influence of European law is clear, and in no way limited to disputes with a distinct European context. The role of Directives, which require implementation, is an illustration: they can still be decisive of litigation despite the need for further action by way of implementation, either because they are directly effective or because of their impact on the interpretation of the implementing provision.

The extent to which Community law has an impact on the whole range of English law is well demonstrated by the decision of the Divisional Court in *R v Coventry City Council, ex parte Phoenix Aviation*.[8] During a campaign to prevent the export of live veal calves from the United Kingdom to mainland Europe (because of the cruel way they would be reared in Europe), public disturbances and protests occurred at ports and airports. As a consequence, one airport and one ferry port refused to accept trade from the applicant transporters, because they each feared unlawful disruption. The applicants sought an order of mandamus,[9] compelling the respondents to accept that trade. A local authority also sought a declaration that it was entitled to ban trade in veal calves. The Divisional Court granted the applications for order of mandamus, and refused to grant the declaration, holding that no statutory discretion existed to ban different types of trade, other than in circumstances of emergency. Further, it was an unlawful use of discretion to base decisions on the fact that trade would lead to unlawful disturbances and disruption. Although not deciding the point, the court doubted whether such a ban was lawful under Community Law.[10]

---

7   For the doctrine of direct effects, see p 105, *post.*
8   [1995] 3 All ER 37.
9   See p 142, *post.*
10   Exceptions to the general principle of free movement of goods and services under Article 30 exist by virtue of Article 36. See, generally, *R v Chief Constable of Sussex, ex parte International Trader's Ferry Ltd* [1998] QB 477; [1997] 2 All ER 65.

The scope of provision by the Community is subject only to the limits imposed by the Treaty and other fundamental sources. Articles 3, 3a and 3b of the Treaty of Rome are concluded in the widest possible terms. Legitimate areas for Community activity include the elimination of restriction of free movement of goods and services, a common commercial policy, the creation of an internal market, free movement of persons, common agricultural, fisheries and transport policies, competition policy, social and environmental policies, the strengthening of consumer protection and measures in the spheres of energy, civil protection and tourism. An adoption of a common economic policy is central to Article 3a. Article 100 confers on the Council the power to issue directives for the approximation of laws, regulation or administrative provision which directly affect the establishment or functioning of the Common market. The European Community may enter into treaties and international agreements, to fulfil the objectives stated by the Treaties,[11] although not if the proposed Treaty goes beyond such objectives.[12] The terms of the Treaty are sometimes broad enough to give scope for creative expansion of the Community role. To add to this range of powers, Article 235 grants power to take action necessary to attain any of the objectives of the Treaty. This has been a powerful tool in developing Community policy in areas such as environmental protection, not, until 1987, specifically within its area of competence.[13] Article 3 of the Treaty (as amended) attempts to define the relationship between Community institutions and member states through the principle of subsidiarity. It states as follows:

"The Community shall act within the limits of the powers conferred on it by this Treaty and of the objectives assigned to it therein. In areas which do not fall within its exclusive competence, the Community shall take action, in accordance with the principle of subsidiarity, only and in so far as the objectives of the proposed action cannot be sufficiently achieved by the member states and can therefore, by reason of the scale or effects of the proposed action, be better achieved by the Community.

Any action by the Community shall not go beyond what is necessary to achieve the objectives of this Treaty."

The meaning of this provision is unclear. Article 3b does not define the circumstances in which action at Community level is necessary to achieve treaty objectives, and for that reason is likely to lead to considerable dispute. Any such dispute would have to be determined by the Court of Justice and it is not clear that that court would regard the matter as a justiciable legal issue (ie one suitable for determination by the court) as opposed to a dispute to be resolved through the political processes of the Community.

It may be that a member state, or individual, considers that an institution of the Community has exceeded the powers granted to it. Challenges to the legal competence to act in a particular area, or in a particular way, can be made by the Commission or by member states under Article 173, to the Court of Justice, which can rule as to the legality of the challenged act; the courts of member states have no power to declare invalid the actions of Community institutions.[14] The capacity of individuals to challenge under Article 173 is limited both by its terms, and by restrictive interpretations of the

11   *Re ILO Convention 170 on Chemicals at Work* (Opinion 2/91) [1996] All ER 194 EC 653.
12   *Re the Accession of the Community to the European Rights Convention* (Opinion 2/94) [1996] CMLR 265.
13   Article 235 ought only to be relied upon as the basis for legislative action not specifically authorised by other provisions: see *EC Commission v EC Council* Case 45/86 [1987] ECR 1493; [1988] 2 CMLR 131.
14   *Firma Foto-Frost v Hauptzollamt Lübeck-Ost* Case 314/85 [1987] ECR 4199; [1988] 3 CMLR 57.

requirements of standing (*locus standi*) to bring such an action.[15] One example of a challenge under Article 173, demonstrating the breadth of Community powers, *is United Kingdom v EU Council.*[16] The United Kingdom sought, under Article 173, to challenge a Directive involving working hours, which was made pursuant to Article 118a of the Treaty. The United Kingdom argued that it should have been made under Article 100, which would have required unanimity of all member states which would not have been attainable because of the opposition to the measure by the United Kingdom. This argument, and the application, was rejected by the Court of Justice, which concluded that the Council had a wide discretion in making social policy changes. Judicial review of the exercise of that discretion went no further than consideration of whether there was a manifest error or misuse of power. In this case, there was not.

C   THE INSTITUTIONS[17]

The institutions of the three Communities are largely common, each operating through the Council, Commission, Court of Justice and the European Parliament. The European Union likewise operates through the Council and Commission. However, in respect of foreign and security policy, and justice and home affairs, the Court of Justice has limited jurisdiction.

I   The Council

This is the legislative body of the Communities. Under Article 145 it is responsible for the general co-ordination of the economic policies of the member states, has power to take decisions and legislate for the Communities, and has power to confer upon the Commission authority to act. It comprises a member from each member state.[18] Each member state holds the office of President of the Commission for rotating periods of six months. Its membership is not fixed in terms of personnel: attendance will be by the appropriate Minister or Head of State for the matters under consideration. For continuity a permanent committee of officials (COREPAR) conducts much of the routine work of the Council, for later ratification.

Sometimes unanimity is required by the Treaty. More usually it acts by a majority of its members, although Article 148 also provides for a qualified voting procedure to apply where specified in the Treaty. This weights the votes of the various member states.[19] A qualified majority means that 54 votes should be obtained, or, if acting other than on a proposal from the Commission, 54 votes cast by at least 8 member states.

15   Article 173 allows individual challenge in respect of Decisions addressed to themselves or against a Decision which, though in the form of a Regulation or Decision addressed to another person, is of direct and individual concern. For the meaning of "Decision", see *Cimenteries CR Cementbedrijven NV SA v EEC Commission* Cases 811/66 [1967] ECR 75 *sub nom Re Noordwijks Cement Accord* [1967] CMLR 77; *Plaumann & Co v EEC Commission* Case 25/62 [1963] ECR 95; [1964] CMLR 29. For the meaning of "direct and individual concern" see *International Fruit Company v Commission* Cases 41–44/70 [1975] 2 CMLR 515; *Calpack SpA v Commission* Cases 789–790/79 [1980] ECR 1949. See, further, p 148, *post.*
16   Case C-84/94, [1996] All ER (EC) 877.
17   See generally Wetherill & Beaumont, *EC Law* (2nd Edn, 1995); Craig & De Burca, *Text, Cases and Materials* (OUP, 1995).
18   Article 2 of the Merger Treaty, replacing Article 146 of the Treaty of Rome.
19   Austria, Germany, France, Italy, United Kingdom, Spain, Belgium, Greece, Netherlands, Norway, Sweden, Portugal, Denmark, Ireland, Luxembourg.

The purpose of these provisions is to prevent domination of the decision-making process by the largest and most dominant member states. The fact remains that occasionally the interests of the Community as a supra-national body and those of individual member states may not coincide.

Such conflicts are often resolved by political agreement and compromise. If a member state considers that a Community Act adopted by the Council is not valid, it may challenge that Act in the Court of Justice, under Article 173. Conversely, if it is considered that a member state is not fulfilling obligations under the Treaty, an action can be brought by the Commission under Article 169, or by another member state under Article 170. A continued failure by a member state to fulfil its Treaty obligations will be resolvable only by political, not legal, means.

2   The Commission

The Commission acts as the proposer and implementer of Community policy: by Article 155 it is under a duty to ensure the provisions of the Treaty are applied, to formulate recommendations or deliver opinions on matters under the Treaty, and has the power of decision-making conferred upon it by the Treaty, or by the Council. It comprises 17 members, drawn from member states but independent of them.[1] Each state provides at least one, but not more than two, Commissioners, who hold office for renewable terms of five years.[2]

3   The Parliament

The role of the Parliament was originally stated in Article 137 to be "advisory and supervisory", but now has a greater role in the legislative process, in the approval of the Community budget and in the scrutiny of the actions of the other Community institutions. Although originally comprising members nominated by member states, since 1979 it has been directly elected, although the aim of a uniform procedure of direct universal suffrage, stated in Article 138(3), has yet to be achieved. The Parliament can censure the Commission and remove it if such a motion of censure is passed by a two-thirds majority of the votes cast.[4] This drastic power makes it a more theoretical than real sanction. It can ask questions of the Commission and Council,[5] and has elements of budgetary control. The Treaty contains complex provisions relating to the passage of legislation.[6]

In some circumstances a co-operation procedure applies, which involves the Parliament in the legislative process.

Which legislative process specified by the Treaty applies will depend upon the terms of the enabling provision of the Treaty, but care has to be taken in the choice of procedure by the Council. In *EC Commission v EC Council*[7] a successful challenge was made by the Commission to a directive which had been made by the Council under Article 130s of the Treaty of Rome. The use of this provision avoided the use of the

1   Article 155 of the Treaty of Rome.
2   Article 10 of the Merger Treaty, replacing Article 157 of the Treaty of Rome.
3   Implemented in the United Kingdom by European Assembly Elections Act 1978, s 1.
4   Article 144 of the Treaty of Rome.
5   Article 148 of the Treaty of Rome.
6   Article 7 of the Single European Act, replacing Article 149 of the Treaty of Rome.
7   The *Titanium Dioxide* case, Case C-300/89, [1993] 3 CMLR 359. See also *UK v EU Council* Case C-84/94 [1996] All ER (EC) 877, p 98, *ante*.

co-operation procedure which would have given a power of amendment to the Parliament. The Court of Justice decided that this choice of enabling power was contrary to Community law because the purported reliance upon Article 130s, rather than on other provisions which would have required the use of the co-operation procedure, weakened the participatory role of the Parliament.

4   The Court of Justice

The Court of Justice is constituted by 13 judges who sit either in plenary session or in chambers of either three or five judges.[8] A Court of First Instance was created in 1996, to ease problems of workload and delay which had bedevilled the Court of Justice.[9] The Court of First Instance deals with disputes between the Community and its servants, and actions for judicial review brought by natural or other legal persons against the Community under Article 173. The role of the Court of Justice is fundamental in ensuring legal enforcement of Community obligations, and in ensuring uniform interpretations of European law throughout the Community.[10] Cases reach the court either through direct actions, most usually available to the Commission or other member states, or through references of points of Community law by national courts, under Article 177. European law has been incorporated into English law by virtue of the European Communities Act 1972. European law imposes an obligation to apply the principles of European law.

The fulfilment of this requirement is specifically achieved through section 3 of the 1972 Act. Questions of European law should be treated as questions of law and, by section 3, "if not referred to the European Court be for determination as such in accordance with the principles laid down by and any relevant decision of the European Court or any court attached thereto."

D   THE SOURCES OF COMMUNITY LAW

I   Legislation

The Treaties[11] are the primary source, creating a framework of powers, duties and, sometimes, individual rights. The Treaty provisions are framed in broad terms, requiring further legislative action, and subsequent interpretation by the Court of Justice. By Article 189 the Council and Commission are empowered to make Regulations, issue Directives, make Recommendations and deliver Opinions. These are the instruments through which the policies inherent in the Treaties, and those adopted by the Council in fulfilment of the Treaties, are achieved. Regulations, Directives and Decisions may be classed as Community legislation: since they are made

---

8   EC Treaty, Article 165.
9   See [1995] CML Rev 24.
10   *Van Gend en Loos v Nederlandse Administratie de Belastingen* Case 26/62 [1963] ECR 1; [1963] CMLR 105; *R v Secretary of State for Transport, ex parte Factortame (No 2)* [1990] 3 CMLR 1.
11   The original treaties comprise the Treaty of Paris which established the European Coal and Steel Community (the "ECSC" Treaty), the Treaty of Rome, which established the European Economic Community (the "EEC" Treaty), the Single European Act and Maastricht Treaties, both of which amended the Treaty of Rome, a second Treaty of Rome, which established the European Atomic Energy Community (the "EURATOM" Treaty), and further Treaties of Brussels and Luxembourg which merged the main institutions of the Communities. The Amsterdam Treaty 1997 changes the article numbers of and amends the Treay of Rome and the Maastricht Treaty. In addition, there are numerous ancillary treaties in the form of international agreements, protocols and annexes.

under the authority of the Treaty they are to be regarded as delegated legislation. Their legality may be challenged in the Court of Justice, but not directly in national courts, which have no power to declare Community measures invalid.[12] The legality of such measures may arise during other proceedings: in that situation it will be the duty of the national court to make a reference under Article 177, to the Court of Justice.

It is, generally, the Council in which the power to make such instruments lies. On a proposal by the Commission, and after consultation with the European Parliament, the Council may promulgate the instrument. We have already seen that in some cases a complex "co-operation procedure" gives a greater role to the Parliament, allowing its rejection of proposals to be overridden only by a unanimous vote of the Council. In addition, there is an Economic and Social Committee,[13] which comprises 189 members representative of professions, occupations and other interest groups and which has a consultative role in the legislative process.

The differences between the various types of measure are identified by Article 189:

"A Regulation shall have general application. It shall be binding in its entirety and directly applicable in all member states.

A Directive shall be binding, as to the result to be achieved, upon each member state to which it is addressed, but shall leave to the national authorities the choice of form and methods.

A Decision shall be binding in its entirety upon those to whom it is addressed.

Recommendations and Opinions shall have no binding force."

A distinction thus exists between Regulations and Decisions on the one hand and Directives, Recommendations and Opinions on the other. Only the former are immediately binding, although the doctrine of direct effects may confer on Directives a similar status in practice. Those measures that do not attract immediate binding force may, and sometimes must, be implemented by members states themselves. The nature of the measure may have other legal consequences: the rights of an individual to challenge are limited to a Decision addressed to that person, or to a Decision which, although in the form of a Regulation or Decision addressed to another individual, is of direct and individual concern to that individual.[14] In applying this provision, the Court of Justice has regard to the realities not the form: if a provision is not of general application it will be treated as a Decision even if it bears the name "Regulation".[15]

Regulations are published in the *Official Journal*. There is no requirement to publish Directives and Decisions, which are notified to those to whom they are addressed. All three types of measure shall state the reasons upon which they are based, including a statement of the facts and law which led the institution in question to adopt them.[16] This is required to facilitate the task of the Court of Justice on review, and so that member states and others affected may judge the legality of the Community measure.

2   Case law

Besides Community legislation, the case law of the Court of Justice is an important source. The doctrines that establish the supremacy of Community law over national

---

12   *Firma Foto-Frost*, p 97, *ante*.
13   Articles 193–198.
14   Article 173.
15   *Confédération Nationale des Producteurs de Fruits et Légumes v Commission* Case 16/7/62 [1962] ECR 471.
16   Article 190. See also *Germany v EEC Commission* Case 24/62 [1963] ECR 63.

law, and of direct effects, both owe their origin to the judicial creativity of the court. In addition, the Treaty is framed in broad terms: it is the duty of the court to interpret and apply it, and Community legislation, in ways that fulfil the spirit and policy of the Treaties.

Besides this interpretative role, the court has developed general principles of Community law. These can be identified as follows:

(a) *Legal certainty.* This principle applies in various ways. A measure may not be altered once it has been adopted. It will be presumed that provisions are not retrospective in their operation. In *Officier van Justitie v Kolpinghuis Nijmegen BV*[17] Dutch authorities sought to rely in criminal proceedings upon the direct effectiveness of a Directive that had not been implemented. The Court of Justice held that criminal liability could not be imposed in this way. The legitimate expectations[18] of individuals who are affected by Community measures will also be protected.

(b) *Natural justice.* Community bodies will be required to give reasons for their actions, and not to act arbitrarily.[19]

(c) *Equality of treatment in comparable situations.*[20]

(d) *Proportionality.* Obligations may not be imposed on an individual except to the extent necessary to achieve the purpose of the measure.[1] The concept will apply not only to Community measures, but also in determining the legality of action by member states in the light of the Treaty. Thus Hoffman J in *Stoke-on-Trent City Council v B & Q plc*[2] had to determine whether the restrictions on Sunday trading in the Shops Act 1950 were proportionate to the restrictions permitted by Article 36, a question ultimately decided in the affirmative by the House of Lords. The concept of proportionality may apply equally to the remedy the court is being asked to grant. In *Taittinger v Allbev*[3] the court granted an injunction to restrain the use of the expression "Elderflower Champagne", prohibited by Community Directive. The Court of Appeal rejected a submission that the grant of such a remedy was disproportionate to the infringement of the directive found to exist.

(e) *Fundamental rights.* The Community attaches importance to the protection of fundamental rights. In a Joint Declaration in 1977[4] the role of the European Convention on Human Rights was stressed, as were the rights protected by the constitutions of member states. The Court of Justice held in *Nold v Commission*[5] that these can supply

17   Case 80/86, [1987] ECR 3969; [1989] 2 CMLR 18.
18   The phrase is borrowed from English law. See Usher: "The Influence of National Concepts on Decisions of the European Court" [1976] 1 EL Rev 359. For an example, see *EC Commission v EC Council* Case 81/72 [1973] ECR 575.
19   *Transocean Marine Paint Association v EC Commission* Case 17/74 [1974] ECR 1063.
20   *Sabbatini v European Parliament* Case 20/71 [1972] ECR 345.
1   *Internationale Handelsgessellschaft mbH v Einfuhr- und Vorratsstelle für Getreide* Case 11/70 [1970] ECR 1125; [1972] CMLR 255; *Johnston v Chief Constable of the RUC* Case 222/84 [1987] QB 129; [1986] 3 All ER 135.
2   [1991] Ch 48; [1991] 4 All ER 221.
3   [1993] 2 CMLR 741.
4   Joint Declaration by the European Parliament, Council and Commission (OJ, 1977, C103/1). See also *Prais v Council* Case 130/75 [1976] ECR 1589; *Re Accession of the Community to the European Human Rights Convention (Opinion 2/94)* [1996] 2 CMLR 265.
5   Case 4/73 [1974] ECR 491. For discussion of the effect of this, see Drzemczewski "The Domestic Application of the European Human Rights Convention as European Community Law" (1981) 30 ICLQ 118.

guidelines which should be followed. It should also be noted that the Treaties themselves may confer rights. The Court cannot "uphold measures which are incompatible with fundamental rights recognised and protected by the constitution of member states".[6] There is, however, no power which entitles the court to examine the compatibility of national legislation with regard to the European Convention on Human Rights[7] unless Community law itself is directly involved.[8] Article 7 states that:

"within the scope of application of this Treaty, and without any special provisions contained therein, any discrimination on grounds of nationality shall be prohibited."

This provision has been used to protect rights which would otherwise not fall within Community law. It may also be noted that the trend is towards further Community protection of individual rights. The Social Charter[9] creates a wide range of individual rights for workers.

E THE RELATIONSHIP BETWEEN COMMUNITY AND NATIONAL LAW

I General approach of the Court of Justice

In a series of important decisions the Court of Justice has developed the doctrine of supremacy of Community over national law. In *Van den en Loos v Nederlandse Administratie der Berlastingen*[10] the Court of Justice stated that member states had:

"limited their sovereign rights, albeit within limited fields."

In *Costa v ENEL*[11] it stated:

"The transfer by the states from their domestic legal system to the Community legal system of the rights and obligations arising under the Treaty carries with it a permanent limitation of their sovereign rights, against which a subsequent unilateral act incompatible with the concept of the Community cannot prevail."

This concept of supremacy of Community law has been held to extend to the enforcement of Community rights even if national courts are required to override national legislation. In *Amministrazione delle Finanze dello Stato v Simmenthal*[12] the court ruled that the Treaty and directly applicable measures made thereunder:

"not only by their entry into force render automatically inapplicable any conflicting provision of current national law, but also preclude the valid adoption of new national legislative measures to the extent to which they would be incompatible with Community provisions."

The national court must if necessary refuse to apply any conflicting national measure, without waiting for it to be set aside by legislative or other constitutional means. A

6 See *Forcheri v Belgian State* Case 152/82 [1983] ECR 2323; [1984] 1 CMLR 334.
7 See p 122, *ante*.
8 See p 131, *post*.
9 *Cinétheque v Federation Nationale des Cinémera Francois* Case 60-61/84 [1985] ECR 2605; [1986] 1 CMLR 365.
10 Case 26/62 [1963] ECR 1.
11 Case 6/64 [1964] ECR 585.
12 Case 106/77 [1978] ECR 629.

similar approach is taken even in the case of inconsistent national constitutional provisions.[13]

Directly applicable Community law therefore prevails in any situation of conflict. In addition, member states are under a duty to take action necessary to implement Community law. Article 5 states:

> "Member States shall take all appropriate measures, whether general or particular, to ensure fulfilment of the obligations arising out of this Treaty or resulting from actions taken by the Institutions of the Community. They shall facilitate the achievement of the Community's tasks.
>
> They shall abstain from any measure which could jeopardise the attainment of the objectives of this Treaty."

The effect of this has been held by the Court of Justice in *R v Secretary of State for Transport, ex parte Factortame*[14] to require national courts to ensure the legal protection of the rights which persons derive from directly applicable Community law, ie those arising from the Treaty, Regulations, or pursuant to rulings of the Court of Justice. Where rules of national law prevent this, they must be set aside. There is also a need, in cases where the Community and national authorities share jurisdiction, for national courts to avoid reaching conclusions at variance with the Community institutions, and to avoid the adoption of national procedural rules which render the exercise of Community rights virtually impossible or extremely difficult.[15]

2   Direct applicability

Those provisions of European law which are incorporated automatically into law are said to be "directly applicable" or "self-executing", and may be relied upon in the domestic courts. Direct applicability is achieved in the United Kingdom by virtue of section 2(1) of the European Communities Act 1972, which states:

> "All such rights, powers, liabilities, obligations and restrictions from time to time created or arising by or under the Treaties, and all such remedies and procedures from time to time provided for by or under the Treaties, as in accordance with the Treaties are without further enactment to be given legal effect or used in the United Kingdom shall be recognised and available in law, and shall be enforced, allowed and followed accordingly; and the expression 'enforceable Community right' and similar expressions shall be read as referring to one to which this subsection applies."

---

13   *Internationale Handelsgesellschaft v Einfuhr- und Vorratsstelle für Gestreide* Case 11/70 [1970] ECR 1125; [1972] CMLR 255.

14   Case C-213/89, [1990] ECR I2433; [1990] 3 CMLR 1. For the *Factortame* litigation generally, see p 112, *post*.

15   *Iberian UK Ltd v BRB Industries Ltd* [1996] 2 CMLR 601; *FMC plc and other v Intervention Board for Agricultural Procedure and another* Case 212/94 [1996] CMLR 633; *SCS Peterbroeck van Compeenhout and Cie v Belgium* Case 312/93 [1996] All ER (EC) 242. In deciding this the basic principles of the domestic judicial system have to be taken into account: *Van Schijndel v Stichling Pensioenfonds* [1996] All ER (EC) 259.

3   Direct effects

If a provision is not directly applicable then although it imposes obligations upon the United Kingdom government under Article 5, which may be enforced by the Court of Justice, it does not directly affect the rights and duties of individuals within the domestic system. In this context the phrase "direct effects" is sometimes used to denote whether a specific provision creates rights upon which an individual may rely upon in the courts. A distinction of academic creation,[16] widely used for the purposes of analysis, the courts (whether European or those in the United Kingdom) have tended to use the phrases interchangeably, and without full consideration as to possible differences in meaning.[17] "Direct applicability" can usefully describe whether a provision needs further action by way of implementation. Thus, Directives and Decisions of the Council and Commission usually require implementation by specific member state action. In the United Kingdom power to implement such provisions by statutory instrument is contained in section 2(2) of the 1972 Act. Not all implementation can be by these means: some obligations can be implemented only through Act of Parliament or statutory instrument made under an enabling power other than the 1972 Act itself. This requirement arises out of section 2(1) of and Schedule 2 to the 1972 Act, since it is expressly provided in that Schedule that the power to implement Community obligations by statutory instrument does not include power:

"(a) to make any provision imposing or increasing taxation; or
(b) to make any provision taking effect from a date earlier than that of the making of the instrument containing the provision; or
(c) to confer any powers to legislate by means of orders, rules, regulations or other subordinate instrument, other than rules of procedure for any court or tribunal; or
(d) to create any new criminal offence punishable with imprisonment for more than two years or punishable on summary conviction with imprisonment for more than three months or with a fine."

A Community provision has direct effect if it may be relied upon by an individual because it creates legally enforceable rights upon which that individual may rely. Not all Treaty provisions or regulations are directly effective: much depends upon the interpretation of the provision itself. The matter will primarily be one for the court before which the issue arises, though there is a power, and sometimes a duty, to refer the question as to individual rights to the Court of Justice under Article 177. A finding of direct effectiveness not only opens the way to individual enforceability, but also has important consequences as to how conflicting domestic legislation should be construed. It will later be apparent that this distinction between direct applicability and direct effects may be theoretical rather than real, and have little significance. The crucial question in any case is simply this: can the provision be relied upon in the national court?

16   See, in particular, Winter: "Direct Applicability and Direct Effects" (1972) 9 CML Rev 425. The phrase is not that of the Court of Justice itself.
17   See, for example, *Johnston v Chief Constable of the RUC* Case 222/84 [1987] QB 129; *Van Duyn v Home Office (No 2)* Case 41/74 [1975] Ch 358; [1975] 3 All ER 190.

a   The Treaties

Treaty provisions are directly applicable, and therefore require no further implementation. Not all Treaty provisions create direct effects: a Treaty provision only creates individually enforceable rights where various conditions are satisfied:

(a) it must not relate to inter-state relations alone;
(b) it must be clear and precise;
(c) no further action by the State for implementation must be necessary;
(d) it must not be conditional at the time of enforcement.

These criteria can be satisfied even where, as in *Van Gend en Loos*,[18] the Article of the Treaty in question was addressed on its face only to member states. Whether a particular provision fulfils these criteria is a question of interpretation, to be determined as a question of European law, and where appropriate by the Court of Justice.

A number of Articles of the Treaty of Rome have been held by the Court of Justice to be directly effective, and may therefore, be taken to create rights and obligations within English law. These include Article 12, which prohibits the introduction of new customs duties, and held in the *Van Gend en Loos* case to be enforceable at the instance of an individual despite being addressed to the State. Other Treaty provisions found to be capable of conferring direct effects include Article 53[19] (which prohibits the introduction by member states of new restrictions on the establishment in their territories of nationals of other member states),[20] Article 95 (which prohibits the imposition by a member state of internal charges on the products of other member states in excess of those applied to similar domestic products), Article 119 (which states that men and women should receive equal pay for equal work)[1] and Article 48 (which requires the abolition of discrimination based on nationality between workers of the member states and the taking of steps to ensure the free movement of workers within the Community).[2]

b   Regulations

These have general application, are binding in their entirety and are directly applicable. In the United Kingdom there is no need for further legislation for implementation purposes. By their very nature regulations are likely to have the characteristics set out above as essentials for direct effect, though exceptional cases may arise when further implementation by the member state is required.

c   Directives

Unlike Regulations, Directives do not necessarily have immediate binding force. They are addressed to member states but it is left to the individual national authority to implement them. In the United Kingdom this may be done by Order in Council or statutory instrument made pursuant to section 2(2), or by means of specific legislative provision or subordinate legislation under another enabling Act.

Nevertheless, although Article 189 of the Treaty of Rome distinguishes between Regulations, which are not only binding but also directly applicable in the member

18   *Van Gend en Loos v Nederlandse Administratie der Belastingen* Case 26/62 [1963] ECR 1.
19   *Costa v ENEL, supra*, p 103.
20   *Alfons Lütticke GmbH v Hauptzollampt Saarelouis* Case 57/65 [1966] ECR 205; [1971] CMLR 674.
1   *Defrenne v Sabena* Case 43/75 [1976] ECR 455; [1976] 2 CMLR 98.
2   *Van Duyn v Home Office (No 2)* Case 41/74 [1975] Ch 358; [1975] 3 All ER 190.

states, and Directives which, whilst binding on member states as to the result to be achieved, have in principle no direct applicability, the Court of Justice has been prepared to develop legal rules in such a way as to confer, in appropriate circumstances, significant legal impact. This has occurred in two distinct ways; first, through the doctrine of direct effects, and secondly through their potential operation upon the process of statutory interpretation.

At first sight Directives would not seem capable of direct effects, because they require implementation and are not directly applicable. Despite this in *Grad v Finanzampt Traunstein*[3] the Court of Justice ruled that a Directive, in conjunction with a Decision which was likewise in issue, could create rights enforceable by an individual. Not to recognise such rights would be to weaken the effect of such measures. This ruling was developed in *SACE v Italian Ministry of Finance*[4] where direct effects were accorded to a Directive imposing a date for implementation of a Community obligation, and put beyond doubt by the Court in *Van Duyn v Home Office*[5] where the argument that a Directive should be treated differently from a Regulation was rejected. The purpose of this judicial creativity is to ensure that the fulfilment of the Community objectives and policies is not weakened by non-implementation by member states: in the absence of direct effects for Directives the sole remedy would be through the Court of Justice, with the delays that that would entail. Nor has the fact that Directives are not required to be published provided a basis for refusing direct effects to Directives against the State, since the State will be aware of the obligation of which it is in breach. Different considerations apply to proposed enforcement against other individuals. Various limits to the operation of the doctrine exist.

(i) The conditions for direct effect must be fulfilled. That therefore requires that the time-limit for implementation must have expired. In *Publico Ministero v Ratti*[6] the Court of Justice held that whilst one Directive could be directly effective, and prevent the Italian court from relying on domestic laws relating to solvents, another, dealing with other products containing dangerous substances, could not be relied upon by the individual because the date for implementation had not yet passed.

(ii) Directives only attract direct effects against the state. In *Becker v Finanzamt Münster-Innenstadt*[7] the Court of Justice appeared to accept that the state could not rely on national powers kept alive by its own failure to adopt a Community Directive which would have conferred rights on the litigant. In *Marshall v Southampton and South West Hampshire Area Health Authority*[8] Advocate-General Slynn repeated his statement in *Becker* that a Directive could not impose obligations on another individual (known as "horizontal" direct effects). These could be imposed only against the State "vertically". This submission was accepted by the Court of Justice. *Marshall* itself was a case where the Directive achieved vertical direct effects, the Health Authority being a State body. It therefore demonstrates the fact that in an employment case the availability of a remedy may depend on the incidental issue of who is the employer. If M had been employed by a private company she would have had no remedy available to her. It is for this reason that the distinction between "vertical" and "horizontal" direct effects have been attacked.[9] However, it is one that has to be maintained by the Court

3   Case 9/70 [1970] ECR 825; [1971] CMLR 1.
4   Case 33/70 [1970] ECR 1213; [1971] CMLR 123.
5   See n 2, *supra*.
6   Case 148/78 [1979] ECR 1629; [1980] 1 CMLR 96.
7   Case 8/81 [1982] ECR 53; [1982] CMLR 499.
8   Case 152/84 [1986] QB 401; [1986] 2 All ER 584. For the subsequent United Kingdom litigation, see *Marshall v Southampton and South West Hampshire Area Health Authority (No 2)* [1991] ICR 136.
9   See, eg, Lenz A-G *in Faccini Dori v Recrab Srl* Case C-91/92 [1995] All ER (EC) 1.

if the distinction between Regulation and Directives, inherent in Article 189, is to be maintained.[10] It should be carefully noted that the doctrine of "vertical direct effects" only operates to confer liability on the state. It does not operate the other way round, and so the state cannot justify the imposition of liability on an individual by claiming that a Directive has direct effect.[11] This would not fit within the philosophy which justifies the granting of direct effects to Directives, and, indeed, would infringe the principle of legal certainty.[12] Nor can a public body escape the limitations of the doctrine by claiming to be an "individual", an argument deployed but rejected in one case involving a local authority.[13]

What is a "state body" for the purpose of the doctrine of direct effects is not always easy to decide, there being no one single test that is applicable in all situations. In *Foster v British Gas* a group of female employees complained that their compulsory retirement at age 60 infringed a Community Directive. On a reference under Article 177 the Court of Justice ruled[14] that a Directive could be relied upon in a claim for damages against a body which, whatever its legal form, had been made responsible, pursuant to a measure adopted by the State, for providing a public service under the control of the State, and which exercised special powers for that purpose beyond those which resulted from the normal rules applicable in relations between individuals. In applying this the House of Lords held[15] that British Gas (at a time when it was a public corporation) was provided by statute with the duty of performing a public service, under the control of the State, which could dictate its policies and reclaim revenue. It had a monopoly power, and thus the Directive created direct effects. This test is not to be regarded as definitive. The ECJ in *Foster* used the word "included",[16] and it has been said that the *Foster* test may not be the right test in all circumstances.[17] Particular problems arise in the context of the privatised utilities. In *Griffin v South West Water Services Ltd*[18] it was decided that a privatised water company was an "emanation of the State". The right approach is to consider whether the public service was under the control of the State, not whether the body performing it was so controlled.

This distinction between vertical and horizontal direct effects causes difficulties, not only in determining what is a body under the control of the State, but also by applying rules unevenly. For example, we have already noted that rights in employment law may depend upon whether the employer is within the public or private sector. In the light of other rulings of the Court of Justice, though, the distinction may prove less important. This is because Directives have what can be called "indirect effects".

INDIRECT EFFECTS

In *von Colson v Land Nordrhein-Westfalen*[19] the Court of Justice stated:

10   See Slynn A-G in *Marshall v Southampton and South West Hampshire Area Health Authority* [1986] QB 401; *Faccini Dori v Recrab Srl, supra.*
11   *Officier van Justitie v Kolpinghuis* Case 80/86 [1987] ECR 3969; [1989] 2 CMLR 18; *Wychavon DC v Secretary of State for the Environment and Velcourt Ltd* [1994] Env LR 239.
12   See p 102, *ante.*
13   See *Wychavon DC v Secretary of State for the Environment and Velcourt Ltd, supra.*
14   Case C-188/89 [1991] 1 QB 405; [1990] 3 All ER 897.
15   [1991] 2 AC 306; [1991] 2 All ER 705.
16   ECJ judgment, para 20.
17   *Doughty v Rolls-Royce plc* (1994) unreported; see also *National Union of Teachers v Governing Body of St Mary's Church of England (Aided) Junior School* [1995] 3 CMLR 638, where the governing body of a voluntary aided school could be regarded as an emanation of the state.
18   (1994), unreported.
19   Case 14/83, [1984] ECR 1891; [1986] 2 CMLR 430.

"The member states' obligation arising from a Directive to achieve the result envisaged by the Directive and their duty under Article 5 of the treaty to take all appropriate measures, whether general or particular, to ensure the fulfilment of that obligation, is binding on all the authorities of member states including, for matters within their jurisdiction, the courts. It follows that, in applying the national law and in particular the provisions of a national law specifically introduced in order to implement [the Directive], national courts are required to interpret their national laws in the light of the wording and the purpose of the Directive in order to achieve the result referred to in the third paragraph of Article 189. It is for the national court to interpret and apply the legislation adopted for the implementation of the Directive in conformity with the requirements of Community law, *so far as it is given discretion to do so under national law.*" [Emphasis added.]

This requirement to construe implementing provisions consistent with the Directive being implemented may have been further strengthened by the Court in *Marleasing SA v La Commercial International de Alimentatión SA*[20] where the court ruled that where there is a national provision falling within the scope of a Directive, then the national court must apply national law in accordance with the Directive, irrespective of whether the Directive pre-dates or post-dates the legislation. It follows that, in terms of Community law, it is the duty of national courts to interpret legislation consistent with provisions of Directives if allowed to do so by national law. Such provisions which might hinder this would run counter to Article 5. In developing in this way European law is significantly reducing the importance of the distinction between directly and non-directly effective Directives: through an approach to interpretation the Court of Justice may therefore have rendered the doctrine of direct effects unimportant. It is by no means clear how far English courts will apply the *von Colson* and *Marleasing* principles in their interpretations of statutory provisions, but authority suggests that English courts do not regard themselves as having discretion in these circumstances to do other than apply the clear and plain words of the statute.[1]

DAMAGES

In some circumstances the failure of the member state to implement a Directive may give rise in Community law to an action for damages. In *Francovich v Italian State*[2] the Court of Justice held that an individual had a claim for financial loss suffered as a result of the non-implementation of a non-directly effective Directive, given that the amount of the claim was quantifiable from that Directive. Three pre-conditions exist for an award of damages to be made. Firstly, the Directive must be intended to confer individual rights. Secondly, it must be possible to identify the content of those rights on the basis of the provisions of that Directive. Thirdly, there has to be a causal link between the breach of the state's obligation and the damage suffered.[3] Although the right to seek damages for breach of Community obligations was not for some time

---

20   Case C-106/89, [1990] ECR I-4135; [1992] 1 CMLR 305; see also *Faccini Dori v Recreb Srl* Case C-91/92 [1995] All ER (EC) 1.

1   *Duke v GEC Reliance Ltd* [1988] AC 618; [1988] 1 All ER 626. See also *Webb v EMO Air Cargo* p 114, *post.*

2   Case C-6, 9/90, [1992] IRLR 84. Note that in *Emmott v Minister for Social Welfare* Case C-208/90 [1993] ICR 8 the Court of Justice ruled that where a State fails to implement a Directive properly the individual may sue the State in reliance on that Directive (if directly effective) until proper implementation occurs.

3   See *Francovich, supra; Faccini Dori v Recrab Srl, supra.*

generally accepted by English law,[4] the effect of the decision in *R v Secretary of State for Transport, ex parte Factortame (No 2)*[5] is to require the national courts to confer effective protection upon Community rights.

This was developed further in dicta in the speeches in the House of Lords in *Kirklees Metropolitan Borough Council v Wickes Building Supplies*.[6] The House had to consider whether an undertaking in damages was required of a local authority seeking an interim injunction to prevent breach of the Sunday trading legislation. In concluding that it was not, Lord Goff indicated that damages might be available to the respondent company if the Sunday trading laws were found to be in breach of Community law. He left open for future reconsideration the correctness of the majority ruling in *Bourgoin SA v Minister of Agriculture, Fisheries and Food*, which had decided that damages were not available. The position was put beyond doubt by the decisions in *Brasserie du Pêcheur SA v Germany* and *R v Secretary of State for Transport ex parte Factortame (No 4)*.[7] In the first of these two companion cases, it was alleged that a German law relating to the purity of beer contravened European law, whilst in the second the breach of Community law had been established.[8] In both cases the issue to be decided was when, if at all, damages were payable. The Court of Justice confirmed that liability for damages arose even if the infringement of Community law resulted from the legislative acts of the national legislature. Where an individual cannot obtain redress in the national courts, because the Directive is insufficiently precise and unconditional and thus does not achieve direct effects, the State may be liable to compensate that individual for that failure to implement the Directive fully, or at all. Likewise where, as in these cases, there is direct effect. In such circumstances, loss suffered must be compensated, provided the pre-conditions for the award of compensation are satisfied. The decisive test for finding that a breach of Community law is sufficiently serious to warrant compensation is whether the member state or the Community institution concerned manifestly and gravely disregarded the limits on its discretion. The court should take into account the clarity and precision of the rule breached, the measures of discretion left by that rule to the national or Community authorities, whether the infringement and the damage caused was intentional or involuntary, whether any error of law was excusable or inexcusable, the fact that the position taken by a Community institution may have contributed to the omission, and the adoption or retention of national measures or practices contrary to Community law. It should be borne in mind that the Court of Justice is concerned not to hinder the proper performance of the legislative function by the prospect of action for damages.[9]

Following these clear statements of principle by the Court of Justice, the House of Lords in *Factortame (No 5)* entered judgment[10] for the plaintiff, thus accepting the right, and indeed duty, of an English court to award damages for breach of Community obligations. The law is, however, at a formative stage. In *R v Secretary of State for the Home Department, ex parte Gallengher*[11] breaches of Community law by the United

4   *Bourgoin SA v Ministry of Agriculture Fisheries & Food* [1986] QB 716; [1985] 3 All ER 585. The earlier decision in *Garden Cottage Foods v Milk Marketing Board* [1984] AC 130; [1983] 2 All ER 770 was distinguished on the basis that that case involved the award of damages for the infringement of Community rights by one individual against another.

5   Case C-213/89, [1990] ECR I-2433; [1990] 3 CMLR 1.

6   [1993] AC 227; [1992] 3 All ER 717.

7   [1996] All ER (EC) 301. See also *R v HM Treasury, ex parte British Telecommunications plc* Case C-392/93 [1996] All ER (EC) 411; [1996] ECR I-1631.

8   See p 112, *ante.*

9   *R v HM Treasury, ex parte British Telecommunications plc, supra.*

10   See *The Times,* April 1998.

11   Per Lord Bingham CJ in *R v Secretary of State for the Home Department, ex parte Gallagher* [1996] 1 CMLR 557 (ECJ); [1996] 2 CMLR 951, CA.

Kingdom's failure to give effect to the provision of Directive 64/221 (by excluding G from the UK pursuant to the Prevention of Terrorism (Temporary Provisions) Act 1989) were not sufficient to justify the award of damages. The breaches were "manifest", but not "sufficiently grave", and no causal link existed between the breach of Community law and loss suffered. The loss would have been suffered even if the Directive had been complied with. By contrast, in *R v Ministry of Agriculture, Fisheries & Food, ex parte Hedley Lomas*[12] the breach was blatant. The United Kingdom had refused to grant a licence for the export of sheep for slaughter in Spain, without any legal justification for so doing. The fact that the United Kingdom believed that the Spanish abattoir was operating in breach of Community law was irrelevant.

4 Decisions

These may be made by the Council and Commission as a formal method of enunciating policies or initiating actions. They are binding upon those to whom they are addressed. Like Directives, they can have direct effect.

F IMPACT UPON ENGLISH COURTS

The insistence of Community law that it shall prevail over conflicting national law may be necessary if Community law is to develop as a coherent whole throughout Member States, but presents distinct challenges to constitutional orthodoxy in the United Kingdom. It was this potential conflict that led to the unsuccessful attempt in *Blackburn v AG*[13] to challenge Accession to the Treaty of Rome and the passage of the 1972 Act, the Court of Appeal ruling that the treaty-making power of the Crown was beyond challenge. The court also confirmed the traditional view that Parliament could in theory legislate in any way it chose, including repeal of the Act itself.

Implementation of the Treaty in English law was achieved by the passage of section 2(1) of the Act. In addition section 2(4) states that:

> "any enactment passed or to be passed, other than one contained in this part of this Act, shall be construed and have effect subject to the foregoing provisions of this section."

Therefore, in cases of Community obligations which are directly applicable by virtue of section 2(1), they take precedence over conflicting national provisions. By these means Parliament has ensured that most conflicts between English law, whether statute or case law, and European law are resolved in favour of the latter. The constitutional challenge can be avoided by relying on the will of Parliament itself. In *Macarthys Ltd v Smith*[14] the majority of the court took the view that the individual rights arising under Article 119 should prevail over what were considered the clear and unambiguous words of the Equal Pay Act 1970. By contrast Lord Denning used Article 119 as an aid to construction, concluding as a result that the terms of the 1970 Act were capable of bearing a meaning that would allow compliance with Community obligations. Alternatively he considered that if Parliament had intended to derogate from its obligations under the Treaty it would, and could, do so by express words, but in their absence an intention to comply with Treaty obligations would be presumed.

12   Case C-5/94, [1996] All ER (EC) 493.
13   [1971] 2 All ER 1380; [1971] 1 WLR 1037.
14   [1979] 3 All ER 325; [1979] 1 WLR 1189.

The authority conferred by the 1972 Act to apply European law has enabled courts both to quash executive actions and to declare invalid delegated legislation. More fundamentally, the courts have now accepted that this principle extends to declaring provisions of an Act of Parliament inoperative. In *Factortame v Secretary of State for Transport*[15] the question was the extent of interim relief available to the plaintiff company, a group of Spanish fishermen alleging that their rights in Community law to fish in United Kingdom waters were being infringed by the Merchant Shipping Act 1988. The Divisional Court had made a reference under Article 177 on the substantive issues to the Court of Justice, and the question remained as to whether an interim injunction could be issued by English courts as interim relief pending resolution of the substantive issues. The House of Lords ruled that English common law did not permit such interim injunctions to be granted. The court then referred to the Court of Justice the question as to whether Community law required such interim relief to be available. In *R v Secretary of State for Transport, ex parte Factortame*[16] the Court of Justice ruled that national courts were under a duty to give effective remedies for the protection of rights under Community law. As a result the House of Lords granted an interim injunction to suspend the operation of the Merchant Shipping Act 1988 pending a ruling of the substantive issues. Lord Bridge stated:

> "Whatever limitation of its sovereignty Parliament accepted when it enacted the European Community Act 1972 was entirely voluntary. Under the terms of the 1972 Act it has always been clear that it was the duty of a United Kingdom court, when delivering final judgment, to override any rule of national law found to be in conflict with any directly enforceable rule of Community law. Similarly, when decisions of the Court of Justice have exposed areas of United Kingdom statute law which failed to implement Council directives Parliament has always legally accepted the obligation to make appropriate and prompt amendments. Thus there is nothing in any way novel in according supremacy to rules of Community law in those areas to which they apply, and to insist that, in the protection of rights under Community law, national courts must not be inhibited by rules of national law from granting interim relief in appropriate cases is no more than a logical recognition of that supremacy."[17]

Whether such an injunction will be granted depends upon the merits of the particular case, and is not automatic.[18] The relevant principles to be applied in the exercise of such discretion were identified by the House of Lords in the *Factortame* case, and developed further in *R v Secretary of State for the National Heritage, ex parte Continental Television BV*.[19] A significant factor will be the degree of likelihood of the Court of Justice giving a ruling which favours one or other party. If a trial judge considers that such a likelihood is evenly balanced, he is entitled to decide that the applicant's interest in having an Act of Parliament struck down is outweighed by the public interest in the application of that Act of Parliament in the interim. However, it is not for the court of trial to consider the disputed point of law in depth.[20]

The supremacy of Community law has thus been achieved. Under section 3 of the 1972 Act this will extend to the application of principles of European law developed

15   [1990] 2 AC 85; [1989] 2 All ER 692.
16   See p 104, *ante*.
17   [1991] 1 All ER 70.
18   *R v HM Treasury, ex parte British Telecommunications plc* [1994] 1 CMLR 621, *supra*.
19   [1993] 3 CMLR 387.
20   See *Ex parte British Telecommunications plc, supra*, n 18.

by the Court of Justice. In *Stoke-on-Trent City Council v B & Q*[1] challenge was made to statutory prohibitions under the Shops Act 1950, on the basis of proportionality, a claim that was ultimately unsuccessful on its merits.[2] Further, the courts will, on judicial review, be able to issue a declaration to the effect that the United Kingdom is in breach of Community obligations. The courts will be prepared to disapply an Act of Parliament to the extent necessary to give effect to a directly effective Community provision, or may make a declaration. Thus in *Equal Opportunities Commission v Secretary of State for Employment*[3] the court issued a declaration that the United Kingdom was in breach of Article 119 and the Equal Pay Directive 57/117.

Direct conflicts with statutory provisions can often be avoided. The approach of Lord Denning in *Macarthys Ltd v Smith* was to use European law as an aid to construction to achieve a result in conformity with Community obligations. It is this interpretative approach that has generally found favour in English courts, avoiding as it does the problems raised by the disregard of words perceived to be clear and unambiguous. In *Garland v British Rail Engineering*[4] Lord Diplock stated:

"The instant appeal does not present an appropriate occasion to consider whether, having regard to the express direction as to the construction of 'enactments to be passed' which is contained in section 2(4), anything short of an express positive statement in an Act of Parliament passed after January 1, 1973, that a particular provision is intended to be made in breach of an obligation assumed by the United Kingdom under a Community treaty, would justify an English court in construing that provision in a manner inconsistent with a Community treaty obligation of the United Kingdom, however wide a departure from the prima facie meaning of the language of the provision might be needed in order to achieve consistency. For, in the instant case the words of section 6(4) of the Sex Discrimination Act 1975 that fall to be construed, 'provision in relation to retirement', without any undue straining of the ordinary meaning of the language used, are capable of bearing either the narrow meaning accepted by the Employment Appeal Tribunal or the wider meaning preferred by the Court of Appeal but acknowledged by that court to be largely a matter of first impression. Had the attention of the court been drawn to Article 119 of the EEC Treaty and the judgment of the European Court of Justice in *Defrenne v Sabena* I have no doubt that, consistently with statements made by Lord Denning MR in previous cases, they would have construed section 6(4) so as not to make it inconsistent with article 119."

This approach was adopted in *Pickstone v Freeman's plc*[5] where the House of Lords considered that a provision of the Equal Pay Act 1970 (inserted into the Act by regulations made in 1983 to give effect to obligations arising from a Court of Justice ruling)[6] was capable of being so construed. Although on a literal reading the regulation did not give effect to the position under European law, the House of Lords was able to read words into the regulations to give effect to the clear intention of Parliament. In

1 [1991] Ch 48; [1991] 4 All ER 221. For proportionality as a doctrine of European law, see p 102. For its different meaning in domestic law, and the problems it raises, see *R v Secretary of State for the Home Department, ex parte Brind* [1991] 1 AC 696; [1991] 1 All ER 720.
2 *Stoke-on-Trent City Council v B & Q plc* [1993] AC 900; [1993] 2 All ER 297.
3 [1994] 1 All ER 910.
4 See [1983] 2 AC 751.
5 [1989] AC 66; [1989] 3 All ER 756.
6 *Marshall v Southampton and South West Hampshire Area Health Authority* Case 152/84 [1986] QB 401; [1986] 2 All ER 584. See p 107, *ante*.

ascertaining what was the intention of Parliament in approving draft regulations it was entirely legitimate to refer to *Hansard* in order to consider the terms in which the draft regulations were presented to Parliament.[7] This purposive approach can be contrasted with that of the Court of Appeal in the same case, which found the words of the 1970 Act (as amended) clear and unambiguous, but that the obligations of Community law prevailed over them, and this approach has again been followed by the House of Lords. In *Litster v Forth Dry Dock and Engineering Co Ltd*[8] regulations were made to give effect to a Directive. The plaintiff employee could not rely on the Directive itself, because the defendant company was not an organ of the State, and thus no direct effects could arise. In these circumstances it was successfully argued that it was the duty of the court to give a meaning to the regulation which accorded with the rulings of the Court of Justice on equivalent words in the Directive, a clear illustration of an application by the House of Lords of the *von Colson* principle.

This purposive approach, giving effect to Community obligations through broad interpretation, was not adopted in *Duke v GEC Reliance Ltd*.[9] In that case the court was considering the effect of a non-directly effective Directive upon legislation not passed to give effect to the Directive. The House of Lords held that section 2(4) of the 1972 Act only entitled a court to distort the meaning of a statute to give effect to a Community provision where it was directly enforceable. The Directive in this case did not have direct effects, and therefore the court was required by English law to give the clear words of a statute their ordinary and natural meaning. This restrictive ruling maintains the approach that the ordinary and natural meaning must be given to the words of a statute in conflict with a Directive sought to be enforced horizontally, where the statutory provision was not intended to implement the Directive. The *von Colson* ruling[10] was not applicable because the court had no discretion as to the approach to interpretation. The extent to which this decision can be supported is debatable, since the duty to apply principles of European law arguably extends to a duty to apply the *von Colson* approach to interpretation: it is the House of Lords in its decision that is depriving itself of the power to interpret such legislation consistently with European Directives. Despite this, and despite the decision in the *Marleasing* case,[11] which extends the principle, English courts have shown a willingness to follow *Duke v GEC Reliance*. In *Webb v Emo Air Cargo (UK) Ltd*[12] it was held by the Court of Appeal that in these situations the English court was not permitted to apply anything other than the ordinary and natural meaning. The House of Lords,[13] in making a reference to the Court of Justice under Article 177 observed that the duty imposed by the *Marleasing* case was to construe a domestic law to accord with the terms of a Directive in the same field only if it is possible to do so. It is, of course, not open to a court to do so if it is bound by the doctrine of precedent to an interpretation which runs counter to Community law.

---

7   For the current position regarding the use of *Hansard*, see *Pepper v Hart* [1993] 1 All ER 42, and generally p 56.
8   [1990] 1 AC 546; [1989] 1 All ER 1134.
9   [1988] AC 618; [1988] 1 All ER 626.
10   See p 109, *ante*.
11   See p 109, *ante*.
12   [1992] 2 All ER 43.
13   [1992] 4 All ER 929; [1993] 1 WLR 49.

G   THE EUROPEAN COURT OF JUSTICE

I   Composition and procedure

The Court comprises thirteen judges,[14] and is assisted by six Advocates-General whose duties are to present publicly, with complete impartiality and independence, reasoned conclusions on cases submitted to the court with a view to assisting the latter in the performance of its duties.[15] The role of Advocate-General has no direct parallel within the English legal system; comparisons with counsel acting as *amicus curiae* are inexact, because the latter act as advocates. By contrast the Advocate-General gives a reasoned opinion following the submissions, both written and oral, by the parties and others entitled to be heard. A more apt comparison is that of a judgment at first instance being considered by an appellate court. The opinion of the Advocate-General is not binding on the Court, but will be treated as of persuasive value. It is reported with the judgment of the Court, and such opinions can be instrumental in assisting in the development of legal doctrine by the Court.[16]

Judges and Advocates-General are chosen "from amongst persons of indisputable independence who fulfil the conditions required for the holding of the highest judicial office in their respective countries or who are jurists of recognised competence".[17] They are appointed for a term of six years by the governments of member states acting in common agreement. They retire in rota and are eligible for re-appointment; the President of the Court is appointed, for a term of three years, by the judges from among their number. The Court appoints its own registrar and lays down rules governing his service.[18]

The Court has the power to adopt its own rules of procedure, which must be submitted to the Council for unanimous approval. The Court must sit in plenary session save that it may set up chambers, comprised of three or five judges,[19] to deal with certain categories of case. It must always sit in plenary session to hear cases submitted to it by a member state or by one of the institutions of the Community, and where in such circumstances it is requested to do so. In addition to the Court of Justice itself, a Court of First Instance was created in 1988.[20] It comprises 12 members, who sit in chambers of three or five judges, though having the power in some circumstances to sit in plenary session. It exercises the jurisdiction of the Court of Justice in relation to (a) disputes between the Communities and their servants; and (b) actions brought by natural or other legal persons against the Community under Article 173. It does not have jurisdiction to deal with Article 177 references. There is a right of appeal to the Court of Justice on a point of law. The Court is of importance, and likely to be increasingly so. Its rulings can be of far-reaching effect: in *BASF AG v EC Commission*[1] decisions of the Commission were struck down for failure to comply with formal procedures required by Community law. The purpose in the creation of the Court was to lessen the workload of the Court of Justice itself, thus facilitating more speedy resolution of cases. Whether it achieves this aim remains to be seen: initial evidence suggests that

---

14   Article 165.
15   Article 166.
16   See p 107, *ante* for the contribution of the Advocates-General in the development of the doctrine of direct effects.
17   The position generally is governed by Article 167.
18   Article 168.
19   Article 165.
20   See generally Article 168a.
1   [1992] ECR II-1591, CFI.

no reduction has occurred in the length of time cases take to be dealt with by the Court of Justice.[2] The Council has the power to extend the jurisdiction of this new court.

2   Jurisdiction

The main jurisdiction is as follows:

(a) Judicial review of the actions of the Community institutions. Under Article 173, the Court can review the legality of acts of the Council and the Commission, other than Recommendations or Opinions. Similar powers are granted in respect of failures to act.[3] Such actions may be brought by a member state, the Council or the Commission, on the ground of lack of competence, infringement of an essential procedural requirement, infringement of a provision of the Treaty or of any rule of Community law. The capacity of an individual to bring such an action is limited: only those to whom a decision has been addressed, or to whom a decision addressed to another person is of direct or individual concern, may do so, and these terms have been restrictively interpreted. Matters are not of direct concern to an individual if there is a discretion as to their implementation. In *Alcan v EC Commission*[4] a refusal by the Commission to allocate a quota for the importation into Belgium of types of aluminium was held not to be of direct concern to the applicant because whether the quota was used depended upon the actions of the Belgian government. Where no real discretion exists,[5] or where implementation is automatic,[6] then the "direct concern" test is satisfied. The second limb of the test for *locus standi* is individual concern. In *Plaumann & Co v EEC Commission*[7] the Court of Justice stated:

> "Persons other than those to whom a decision is addressed may only claim to be individually concerned if that decision affects them by reason of certain attributes which are peculiar to them or by reason of circumstances in which they are differentiated from all other persons and by virtue of these factors distinguishes them individually just as in the case of the person addressed."

Thus, even though the applicant was a German importer of clementines, which were subject to customs duty, the applicant did not have locus standi, since any person might import clementines. The ruling has been followed in subsequent cases.[8] The proper remedy of aggrieved individuals is through the Commission or the individual member states. Actions which an individual is entitled to bring are dealt with by the Court of First Instance.

(b) Actions brought by the Commission under Article 169. This states:

> "If the Commission considers that a member state has failed to fulfil an obligation under this Treaty, it shall deliver a reasoned opinion on the matter after giving the State concerned the opportunity to submit its observations.

2   See [1992] 17 CMLR 897.
3   Article 175.
4   Case 69/69 [1970] ECR 385.
5   *International Fruit Co v NV Commission* Case 41–44/70 [1971] ECR 411.
6   *Piraike-Patraiki v EC Commission* Case 11/82 [1985] ECR 207. *NTN Toyo Bearing Co v EC Council* Case 113/77 [1979] ECR 1185.
7   Case 25/62 [1963] ECR 95.
8   See eg *Calpak SpA v EC Commission* Case 789, 790/79 [1980] ECR 1949.

If the State concerned does not comply with the opinion within the period laid down by the Commission, the latter may bring the matter before the Court of Justice."

This basis of challenge is the single largest source of the work of the Court.

(c) Action brought by member states under Article 170. This has been little used.[9]

(d) The Court has power to deal with certain cases concerning disputes to which ordinary individuals (as opposed to member states or Community institutions) may be parties. Thus it has jurisdiction in disputes relating to compensation for damage caused by the institutions of the Communities or by their servants in the performance of their duties and in disputes between the Community and their servants within the limits and under the conditions laid down in staff regulations or the conditions of employment. This jurisdiction is exercised by the Court of First Instance.

(e) References under Article 177.[10] This is a major source of work for the Court, and has important consequences for the courts of member states.

3   References under Article 177

Article 177 creates a power, and in some circumstances imposes a duty, to refer questions concerning the interpretation of European law to the Court of Justice. It plays a key role in ensuring the preservation of the Community character of the law established by the Treaty, and has the object of ensuring that in all circumstances this law is the same in all states of the Community. Article 177 states:

"(1)The Court of Justice shall have jurisdiction to give preliminary rulings concerning:
  (a) the interpretation of this Treaty;
  (b) the validity and interpretation of acts of the institutions of the Community;
  (c) the interpretation of the statutes of bodies established by an act of the Council, where those statutes so provide.
  (2) Where such a question is raised before any court or tribunal of a member state, that court or tribunal may, if it considers that a decision on the question is necessary to enable it to give judgment, request the Court of Justice to give a ruling thereon.
  (3) Where any such question is raised in a case pending before a court or tribunal of a Member State, against whose decisions there is no judicial remedy under national law, that court or tribunal shall bring the matter before the Court of Justice."

a   The power to refer

This is conferred upon courts or tribunals. This will include organs of the state exercising judicial functions.[11] An arbitrator conducting an arbitration under a private

---

9   For an example see *France v United Kingdom* Case 141/78 [1979] ECR 2923.
10   See, generally Beaumont & Wetherill, *op cit*, pp 279–313.
11   *Vaassen* case, Case 61/65 [1966] ECR 261.

contract is not within the Article 177.[12] This will be something to borne in mind by a court in deciding whether or not to grant leave to appeal against that arbitration.

b   The mandatory reference requirement

Save in cases to which subsection (3) above applies the court or tribunal has a discretion as to whether or not to refer a case to the European Court. Where subsection (3) does apply, no such discretion exists and there must be a reference. This clearly applies to the House of Lords but it is an open question whether it would apply to courts below the House of Lords even where the decision of the court was not one from which an appeal would lie in the particular case in question. The proper construction of Article 177(3) makes the supremacy of the court in the judicial hierarchy rather than the finality of a particular decision the governing factor. This approach found some support from Lord Denning in *HP Bulmer Ltd v J Bollinger SA*.[13] However, Community law suggests a contrary approach,[14] and in *Chiron Corporation v Murex Diagnostics*[15] Balcombe LJ disapproved the obiter statement of Lord Denning. In that case it was held that, when considering leave to appeal, the House of Lords acts in a judicial, not administrative, capacity. Its power to grant leave to appeal is thus a judicial remedy within the meaning of Article 177. It followed from that that the Court of Appeal is not obliged to make a reference under Article 177(3) except in cases where it was a court of last resort.

Whether a court is one which falls within the mandatory reference requirements of Article 177(3) will itself raise questions of European law that may entitle, or require, a reference. It should also be noted that Article 177(3) applies only where there is an absence of judicial remedy: since inferior courts and tribunals are under the supervisory jurisdiction of the High Court it can be argued that such bodies will never be caught by the mandatory reference requirement, even if no right of appeal exists.[16]

In order for there to be a duty to refer the question must be "necessary". This is so irrespective of whether a reference is mandatory or merely discretionary, for necessity is a pre-condition to the exercise of discretion. In *HP Bulmer Ltd v J Bollinger SA* Lord Denning stated that, for reference to be necessary, the point of law must be conclusive of the case. This goes too far, and appears inconsistent with attitudes of European law. In the *CILFIT Case*[17] the Court of Justice held there was no need to refer a question if it was not relevant, if the answer to the question "regardless of what it might be can in no way affect the outcome of the case." Other English courts have interpreted the phrase more liberally, as meaning "reasonably necessary" or as "substantially determinative" of the litigation.[18]

Lord Denning in *HP Bulmer Ltd v J Bollinger SA* also stressed that a decision was not necessary if the same point, or substantially the same point, had already been decided by the Court of Justice. Moreover, it was not necessary when the point is "reasonably free from doubt". This mirrors the doctrine in European law of *acte clair*. In *CILFIT* the Court of Justice stated:

12   *Broekmeulen* Case, Case 246/80 [1981] ECR 2311; [1982] 1 CMLR 91.
13   [1974] Ch 401; [1974] 2 All ER 1226.
14   *Costa v ENEL* Case 6/64 [1964] ECR 585.
15   [1995] All ER (EC) 88.
16   In *Re a Holiday in Italy* [1975] 1 CMLR 184 judicial review was considered by a National Insurance Commissioner to be a "judicial remedy". It should be noted that leave to apply is required.
17   *CILFIT Srl v Ministro della Sanita* Case 283/81 [1982] ECR 3415; [1983] 1 CMLR 472.
18   *Customs and Excise Commissioners v Aps Samex* [1983] 1 All ER 1042.

"Finally the correct application of Community law may be so obvious as to leave no scope for any reasonable doubt as to the manner in which the question raised is to be resolved. Before it comes to the conclusion that such is the case, the national court or tribunal must be convinced that the matter was equally obvious to the courts of the other member states and to the Court of Justice."

In determining whether a point was *acte clair* regard should be had to the fact that Community law is drafted in several languages which may require comparison, that Community concepts may bear different meanings from similar concepts in domestic law, and that such points need to be considered in the context of Community law as a whole. The doctrine of *acte clair* applies equally to matters that fall within the mandatory and discretionary limbs of Article 177, though, it should be noted that since a national court has no power to declare actions of the Community invalid,[19] it will in such cases be necessary to make a reference even where the matter is clear.

The attitude of English courts in applying the *acte clair* doctrine has been uncertain. Kerr LJ in *R v Pharmaceutical Society of Great Britain, ex parte the Association of Pharmaceutical Importers*[20] observed that an English court should "hesitate long" before reaching a conclusion that a point of European law was so obvious as to leave no room for reasonable doubt. Indeed, in *R v International Stock Exchange of the United Kingdom and Republic of Ireland Ltd, ex parte Else (1982) Ltd*[1] Sir Thomas Bingham MR observed that the appropriate course is ordinarily to refer the issue to the Court of Justice unless the national court can with complete confidence resolve the issue itself. If it has any real doubt, it should ordinarily refer. As was indicated by Bingham J in the *Samex* case,[2] decisions of English courts on European law should be "*communautaire*", a prospect that has been described as "intimidating to an English judge."[3]

c   The discretion to refer

The discretion to refer is that of the national court or tribunal, and will not be reviewable by the Court of Justice, unless the reference is in effect spurious or an abuse of process.[4] It will be for the national court to formulate the question to be answered, though the Court of Justice will refine the question if it is clear exactly what the question for interpretation actually is. In one case,[5] the Court of Justice held that it was not necessary to rule on the questions posed by the national court as it had not provided the Court of Justice with sufficient information on the case to enable it to give a ruling. The national court should define the factual and legislative context of the question it is asking, and explain the reasons for the choice of Community provision the interpretation of which is being sought.[6] It is no part of the functions of the Court of Justice to deliver advisory opinions or opinions on hypothetical questions.[7] The decision to make a reference

---

19   See p 101, *ante. Firma Foto-Frost v Hauptzollampt Lübeck-Ost* Case 314/85 [1987] ECR 4199.
20   [1987] 3 CMLR 951.
1   [1993] QB 534, [1993] 1 All ER 420.
2   *Customs and Excise Commissioners v ApS Samex* [1983] 1 All ER 1042.
3   *R v Secretary of State for Transport, ex parte Factortame (No 2)* [1990] ECR I-243; [1990] 3 CMLR 1.
4   *Foglia v Novello* Case 104/79 [1980] ECR 745; *Foglia v Novello (No 2)* Case 244/80 [1981] ECR 3045.
5   *Telemarsicabruzzo SpA v Circostel, Ministero delle Poste e Telecommunicazioni e Ministero della Difera* Cases C-320-322/90 [1993] ECR I-393.
6   *Criminal Proceedings against Granu and others* Case 167/94 [1995] All ER (EC) 668; *Criminal Proceedings against Saddick* Case C-458/93 [1995] All ER (EC) 664.
7   *Pardini v Ministero del Commercio L'Estero* Case 338/85 [1988] ECR 2041; *Zabala Erasu v Instituto National de Empleo* Cases C-422-424/93 [1995] All ER (EC) 758.

cannot be removed from a court or tribunal by domestic law, though the decision not to make a reference will be a matter subject to such appeal as exists in the particular case.[8]

Guidelines for the exercise of the discretion by English courts were set out by Lord Denning in *Bulmer v Bollinger*.[9] They can, though, be no more than guidelines and have been stated not to be binding. They should be compared with the various statements on Article 177 by the Court of Justice. The following factors were considered by Lord Denning to be relevant:

(i)   the time needed to obtain a ruling;
(ii) the importance of not overloading the European Court with references;
(iii) the difficulty and importance of the point;
(iv) the expense involved;
(v)   the wishes of the parties.

He also stated that the facts should be established first, an "injunction of obvious merit".[10] The importance of deciding the facts first is that they provide the legal context for the point at issue, and indeed may determine whether or not a reference is in fact necessary. However, as the Court of Justice stated in *Irish Creamery Milk Suppliers Association v* Ireland,[11] it is the national court which has responsibility for giving judgment in the case and is therefore in the best position to judge at what stage in the proceedings a reference is required. There is nothing to prevent a reference being made at an interlocutory stage. In the *Factortame* litigation important issues were raised and resolved under references at interlocutory stages.[12] In *Lowenbrau Munchin v Gunhalle Lager Internationale*[13] Graham J identified the following points to be borne in mind: (i) interlocutory proceedings do not fully dispose of the points at issue; (ii) it is not always clear what the matter in issue will be; (iii) whether the facts have been ascertained; (iv) the requirement for speedy determination. The right approach is illustrated by Jacob J in *South Pembrokeshire DC v Wendy Fair Markets Ltd*,[14] who, in examining cases referred at the interlocutory stage, observed:

"...those cases were where the facts were not in dispute and the question of EC law would be determinative of the whole action either way. The [last] of those cases also perhaps has an implicit warning to a court at the interlocutory stage not too readily to regard a Euro-point as clear, for the Court of Appeal there thought there was a clear defence but the Court of Justice said not ... It is better in my judgment, therefore, to wait for the facts to be determined properly, and finally, before there is any reference. The Court of Justice will then have the full picture before it...".

In each case, however, it is a matter for the discretion of the trial court.

Likewise in criminal cases the appropriate response and time for a reference may vary. In *Henn and Darby v Director of Public Prosecutions*[15] Lord Diplock indicated that a reference should be dealt with if necessary after the trial, at the appellate stage.

---

8   *Rheinmühlen* case, Case 146/73 [1974] ECR 139; [1974] 1 CMLR 523.
9   See n 13, *ante*.
10 Per Bingham J in *Customs and Excise Commissioners v Samex*, n 2, *ante*.
11 Case 36, 71/80, [1981] ECR 735; [1981] 2 CMLR 455.
12 *R v Secretary of State for Transport, ex parte Factortame (No 2)* [1990] ECR I-243; [1990] 3 CMLR 1.
13 [1974] 1 CMLR 1.
14 [1994] 1 CMLR 213.
15 [1981] AC 850; [1980] 2 All ER 166.

By contrast in *R v Goldstein*[16] the court indicated that where it is apparent at the outset of the case that a point of European law may well be determinative, the appropriate course is to make application to quash the indictment. The right approach may be to determine whether the interests of justice provided compelling reason for going ahead with the trial pending determination of a reference.

In deciding whether or not to make a reference, the workload of the Court of Justice appears not to be a relevant factor despite the dicta of Lord Denning: the problems of the Court of Justice should not be resolved through the mechanisms of restricting reference. If a reference is indeed necessary, then such an approach in fact runs counter to the philosophy of the court in requiring references to be made. By contrast, expense is an important factor to be considered, to be weighed against other costs that are incurred in continuing the domestic proceedings with a possible or likely requirement to refer a later stage of the case. In *R v Pharmaceutical Society of Great Britain, ex parte Association of Pharmaceutical Importers*[17] Kerr LJ expected the case to reach the House of Lords, which would therefore lead to a mandatory reference under Article 177(3), and considered that an immediate reference would therefore save considerable time and costs. As Hodgson J stated in the *Factortame* case: "if a reference is going to be made the sooner it is done the better."

The wishes of the parties will be a relevant but not decisive factor. The concept of "reference by consent" should not creep into the practice of the English courts, for it is the judgment of the court as to the necessity for and desirability of a reference that is important. However, where only one party wishes a reference there is no inevitability: it will usually be the case that a reference will assist one party only. Reference may be appropriate even against the wishes of both parties. The court may also take into account the fact that the matter is one upon which the European Commission has strong views.

16   [1983] 1 All ER 434; [1983] 1 WLR 151.
17   See n 20, *ante*.

CHAPTER 6

European Convention on Human Rights

A INTRODUCTION

The United Kingdom is a signatory to the Convention for the Protection of Human Rights and Fundamental Freedoms (1950),[1] usually referred to as the European Convention on Human Rights. Conceived by the members of the Council of Europe as a mechanism for promoting European unity and for preventing abuse of human rights, it establishes both the European Commission of Human Rights and the European Court of Human Rights. Through this machinery the basic rights and freedoms recognised by the Convention are enforced. These include the right to life, the right not to be subjected to torture or inhuman or degrading treatment or punishment, the right not to be held in slavery or servitude, or to be required to perform forced or compulsory labour, the right to liberty and security of the person, the right to a fair trial, to respect for family life and home, to peaceful enjoyment of possessions, to education, to freedom of thought, conscience and religion, to freedom of expression, freedom of assembly, freedom of association and free elections. These rights are considered in more detail later in this Chapter.

These rights are not absolute. Limitations are usually permitted on the grounds stated in the Convention. Thus, the right of freedom of expression may be curtailed in the interests of national security, territorial integrity or public safety, for the prevention of disorder or crime, for the protection of health or morals, for the protection of the rights of others, for protection from the disclosure of information received in confidence, or to maintain the authority and impartiality of the judiciary.[2] The Court of Human Rights has therefore a broad function to perform, in determining the extent to which the aims of the Convention may be limited. Inherent in the Convention is the principle that a fair balance be struck between the general interests of the community and the requirements of the individual's fundamental rights.[3] Only in this way can the appropriate limitation on the right in question be established. One example of this is in the context of the right to freedom of expression, under art 10. Any limitation must

---

1   Cmnd 8969. The United Kingdom is not a signatory to Protocols 4, 6 or 7.
2   Article 10(2).
3   *Soering v UK* (1989) 11 EHRR 439.

go no further than is "absolutely necessary", ie conform to a "pressing social need" in which the interference was proportionate to the legitimate aim pursued.[4]

In addition, most, though not all, of the rights may be limited by measures derogating from the obligations under the Convention in times of war or other public emergency. The United Kingdom has entered a derogation in respect of art 5 following the decision of the Court of Human Rights in *Brogan v United Kingdom*[5] that the detention provisions of the Prevention of Terrorism (Temporary Provisions) Act 1984[6] were in breach of the Convention.

The machinery of the European Convention

The Convention is, for the moment, enforced through the Commission and the Court, a process that is subject to change as from 1 November 1998. The Commission considers complaints of alleged breaches of the Convention from signatory states, and may also consider complaints made by individuals where the state complained against has recognised the right of individual petition. The United Kingdom recognised that individual right in 1966.[7] The applicant must show that all effective remedies in his own country have been exhausted,[8] and the application must be lodged within six months of a final decision in his case by a national court or tribunal.[9] The admissibility of the complaint is determined by the Commission.

The complainant must be a victim, or potential victim, of a right protected by the Convention. The Convention does not permit applications to be made by persons who are not individually affected but who wish to test the legality, under the Convention, of a particular piece of legislation or rule of common law. Nor does the Convention permit a court to rule as to the status of a particular rule or piece of legislation: the question to be considered is whether the individual rights of a victim have, or will be, infringed. Whether a person is a "victim" is judged broadly. Article 25 of the Convention refers to a "person, non governmental organisation or group of individuals claiming to be the victim of a violation". A "victim" will be directly affected in some way. In *Klass v Federal Republic of Germany*,[10] it was decided by the Court of Human Rights that an individual may claim to be the victim of a violation occasioned by the mere existence of secret measures (in that case, telephone tapping),[11] or of legislation permitting secret measures, without having to allege that such measures were applied to him,[12] but that may in some circumstances be prospective rather than retrospective.

---

4   See *Sunday Times v UK* (1979) 2 EHRR 245; *Handyside v UK* (1976) 1 EHRR 737.
5   (1988) 11 EHRR 117.
6   See, now, Prevention of Terrorism (Temporary Provisions) Act 1989.
7   Recognised by Declaration on 14 January 1966.
8   Art 26. Allowance must be made for the system within which the right is being enforced, and without excessive formalism: *Sadick v Greece* (1996) 24 EHRR 323. There is no obligation to have recourse to remedies which are inadequate or ineffective: *Aksoy v Turkey* (1997) 23 EHRR 553.
9   Article 25.
10   (1978) 2 EHRR 214.
11   *Malone v UK* (1981) 4 EHRR 330; *Hewitt & Harman v UK* (1992) 14 EHRR 657 (violation of art 8 by security services); *Halford v UK* (1997) 24 EHRR 523 (interception of office telephone calls violated art 8).
12   See *Hilton v UK* (1988) 57 D&R 108 (persons subject to routine checks by the secret service, of a non notifiable type, was said to have to show that there was a reasonable likelihood that the security service had compiled and retained records. A person may be an "indirect victim" i.e. a person such as a family member who has therefore a personal link with the victim and is thus affected by the breach: *Open Door & Dublin Well-Women v Ireland* (1992) cf *Norris v Ireland* (1985).

Thus, a person who runs the risk of being prosecuted under a law may be a "victim" in the respect of that law.[13]

If the complaint is admissible and not manifestly ill-founded the Commission may seek to achieve a friendly settlement. If it is unable to do so it has a choice of action open to it. It may report in respect of its findings to the Committee of Ministers of the Council of Europe.[14] Alternatively, it may refer a complaint to the European Court of Human Rights for decision.[15] Signatory states have undertaken to be bound by the decisions of the Court in any case to which they are parties, and, by art 50, the Court can afford "just satisfaction" to the injured party, which may involve an order for the state to pay a sum of money by way of compensation and recompense for costs. Failure by a signatory state to comply with a judgment might, ultimately, lead to suspension of that state from the Council of Europe.

Changes in procedure under the Convention come into effect on 1 November 1998, following the adoption by the contracting states of Protocol 11 of the Convention. Protocol 11 sweeps away the pre-existing court and commission, replacing them with a single, full-time, court to which applicants will make application direct, without the "filter" of the Commission. Judges to that court will continue to be proposed by individual governments, but will be selected by the Council of Europe's Assembly. Applications were invited for the position of United Kingdom judge in press advertisements which were published in late 1997. By cl 18 of the Human Rights Bill, which will come into effect immediately upon Royal Assent, the holder of a judicial office in the United Kingdom may become a judge of the Court of Human Rights without being required to relinquish his office, but will not perform the duties of his judicial office whilst a judge of the Court of Human Rights.[16]

B   THE CONTENT OF THE CONVENTION[17]

The Convention protects a number of rights and freedoms. In summary these are as follows:

Article 2: the right to life.[18] No-one shall be deprived of his life intentionally save in the execution of a sentence of a court following conviction of a crime for which death is the prescribed penalty. Exceptions to the right permit force which is necessary in defence of any person from unlawful violence, in order to effect a lawful arrest or to prevent the escape of a person lawfully detained, or for lawful action taken to quell a riot or insurrection. Article 2 does not affect the right of a state to impose the death penalty, although, for the United Kingdom, this is now of theoretical importance only given the intention to totally abolish the residual classes of offence for which capital punishment may be imposed.[19] By contrast the effect of art 2 on the use of fatal force

---

13   *Times Newspapers v UK* (1990) D & R 307; cf *Leigh, Guardian Newspapers Ltd and Observer Ltd v UK* (1990) 65 D & R 307; *Dudgeon v UK* (1977) 4 EHRR 149. See *Sunday Times v UK* (1978) 2 EHRR 245; *Malone v UK* (1981) 4 EHRR 330.

14   Art 26.

15   Art 48.

16   Cl 18(2), (3).

17   See, generally, Harris, O'Boyle and Warbrick: *European Convention on Human Rights*, Butterworths.

18   See *Stewart v UK* (1984) 39 D & R 169 (use of plastic baton rounds); *Kelly v UK* (1993) 74 D & R 139 (use of fatal force by soldiers in Northern Ireland); *McCann v UK* (1996) 21 EHRR 97 (SAS shootings of terrorist suspects in Gibraltar: a strict view of necessity is to be taken, and the force must be strictly proportionate to the aims stated in art 2(2)).

19   See Crime and Disorder Act 1998, s 36.

by the security service continues to be of importance, particularly in the context of the Northern Ireland security situation.

Article 3: the right not to be subject to torture or to inhuman or degrading treatment or punishment. "Torture" describes inhuman treatment which has a purpose, or the infliction of punishment, and is generally an aggravated form of inhuman treatment. "Inhuman treatment" includes the deliberate causing of suffering, mental or physical. "Degrading treatment" is treatment which grossly humiliates a person before others or drives him to act against his own will or conscience.[20] Whatever the conduct complained of, whether it infringes art 3 depends on all the circumstances, but must go beyond the level of humiliation inherent in any punishment. In *Soering v UK*,[1] extradition to the United States to potentially face the death penalty was held to infringe art 3. More usually, art 3 will sometimes provide a standard against which the conditions of detention, and treatment, of suspects or prisoners can be judged.[2]

Article 4: the right not to be subject to slavery.

Article 5: the right to liberty and security of person. No-one shall be deprived of his liberty save in accordance with a procedure prescribed by law, and unless it amounts to lawful detention after conviction, the lawful arrest or detention of a person for a failure to comply with a court order or to fulfil an obligation prescribed by law, or unless the deprivation of liberty amounts to lawful arrest or detention for the purpose of bringing the person before the competent legal authority on reasonable suspicion of having committed an offence or fleeing after having done so. An arrested person shall be informed promptly, in a language which he understands, of the reasons for his arrest and of any charge against him. A detained person shall be brought promptly before a judge or other officer prescribed by law to exercise judicial power, and shall be entitled to trial within a reasonable time or to release pending trial. Release may be conditioned by guarantees to appear for trial. The right to take proceedings to challenge the lawfulness of a detention, and to be compensated for breach of the rights in art 5, are contained in it. Article 5 has proved to be an important provision in the United Kingdom in relation to detention under the Prevention of Terrorism legislation,[3] the detention of persons suffering from mental disorder,[4] and the law governing life sentences (in particular, the determination of the "tariff" to be served and questions of early release).[5]

Article 6: the right to a fair trial. This encompasses a fair and public hearing within a reasonable time by an independent and impartial tribunal established by law. Judgment is to be pronounced publicly, but the press and public may be excluded from all or part of the trial in the interests of morals, public order or national security in a democratic society, where the interests of juveniles or the protection of the private

---

20   See generally *Ireland v UK* (1976) 2 EHRR 25.
1   (1989) 11 EHRR 439. See also *D v UK* (1997) 24 EHRR 423 (deportation of man to country where there existed an insufficiency of AIDS treatment held to be in breach of art 3).
2   *Hilton v UK* (1978) 3 EHRR 104 (allegations of mistreatment in detention on remand not, on the facts, in breach of art 3); *McFeeley v UK* (1980) 3 EHRR 161.
3   *McVeigh, O'Neill and Evans v UK* (1982) 5 EHRR 71; *Fox, Campbell and Hartley v UK* (1990) 13 EHRR 157; *Murray v UK* (1994) 19 EHRR 193; *Brogan v UK* (1988) 11 EHRR 117; *Brannigan & McBride v UK* (1993) 17 EHRR 539.
4   *Ashingdale v UK* 17 EHRR 528.
5   *Weeks v UK* 7 EHRR 709; *Thynne, Wilson and Gunnell v UK* (1990) 13 EHRR 666; *Hussain and Singh v UK* (1996) 22 EHRR 1. See also p 544, *post*.

lives of the parties so require, or to the extent where the court judges that publicity would prejudice the interests of justice.

The provisions of art 6 provide an important yardstick against which to measure the operation of any aspects of the trial process, particularly criminal trials. The likelihood that the Court of Human Rights would decide, as it subsequently did in *Findlay v UK*,[6] where the army court-martial system was found to be in breach of art 6(1), was part of the motivation for the reform of the court martial system in the Armed Forces Act 1996.[7] Two aspects are of particular relevance in the context of recent legislation. The first is the principle of "equality of arms": it is a requirement of fairness that prosecuting authorities should disclose all material evidence for or against the accused to the defence.[8] The provisions of the Criminal Procedure and Investigations Act 1996 have to be judged in that context.[9] The second is the principle against self-incrimination. As in domestic law, the right not to be required to self-incriminate is a fundamental right. In *Saunders v UK*,[10] the Court of Human Rights had to consider the adducing of details of interviews held with S during which, pursuant to provisions of the Companies Act 1985, S was required to answer questions the answers to which tended to self-incriminate him. The Court, in holding, by a majority, that the questioning and admissibility of the evidence did infringe art 6, stressed the fundamental right which is to be regarded as part of the process of respecting the right of an accused person to remain silent.[11] Another aspect of the same principle was seen in *Murray v UK*[12] where it was held that the right to silence provisions of the Northern Ireland Order of 1987[13] on the facts did not contravene art 6 in the light of the overall evidence adduced by the prosecution in that case and the fact that the matters in question called for an explanation as a matter of common-sense.

Other aspects of legal process which might potentially be within the ambit of challenge under art 6 are the availability of legal aid,[14] the rights of unrepresented defendants,[15] the anonymity of witnesses and certain rules of evidence.[16]

Article 7: the right not to be subject to criminal liability or penalties retrospectively, unless the act alleged was criminal according to the general principles of law recognised by civilised nations. The relevant principle was well explained by the Commission on Human Rights in *Gay News v UK*:[17]

"... It is excluded ... that any acts not previously punishable should be held by the courts to entail criminal liability, or that existing offences should be extended to cover facts which previously clearly did not constitute a criminal offence. This implies that constituent elements of an offence such as, eg, the particular form of culpability required for its completion may not be essentially changed, at least not to the detriment to the accused, by the caselaw of the courts. On the other

6   (1996) 23 EHRR 313.
7   See p 193, *post.*
8   See *Edwards v UK* (1992) 15 EHRR 417.
9   *Funke v France* (1993) 16 EHRR 297; *Inbrioscia v Switzerland* (1994) 17 EHRR 441.
10   (1994) 18 EHRR CD 23
11   See p 318, *post.*
12   (1995) 19 EHRR 193.
13   Criminal Evidence (Northern Ireland) Order 1988, SI 1988/1987. See p 527, *post.*
14   *Monnell & Morris v UK* (1985) 7 EHRR 579; *Benham v UK* (1996) 22 EHRR 293; *Granger v UK* (1990) 12 EHRR 469; *Maxwell v UK* 19 EHRR 97.
15   *De Haes & Gijsels v Belgium.*
16   *Trivedi v UK* (operation of the statutory exceptions to the hearsay rule); *Hoare v UK* (availability of expert evidence); *Smith v UK* (entrapment).
17   *Gay News and Lemon v UK* (1982) 5 EHRR 123.

hand it is not objectionable that the existing elements of the offence are clarified and adapted to new circumstances which can reasonably be brought under the original content of the offence."

The application of these principles was seen in *Cr and SW v UK*[18] where the judicial creation of the offence of marital rape was held not to contravene art 7.

Article 8: the right to respect for a person's private and family life, his home and correspondence. An exception to this general right exists where an interference with such a right by a public body is in accordance with law and necessary in a democratic society in the interests of national security, public safety or the economic well-being of the country, for the prevention of disorder or crime, for the protection of health or morals or for the protection of the rights and freedoms of others. Article 8 will be relevant in determining whether intrusions into privacy through searches of the home, or interception of communications or surreptitious surveillance are in breach of the Convention, or whether the criminal law has unjustifiably strayed into an area of private regulation.[19]

Article 9: the right to freedom of thought, conscience and religion. This includes freedom to change religion or belief, and freedom, either alone or in community with others and in public or private, to manifest one's religion or belief, in worship, teaching, practice and observance. Again limitations on the right are permitted on limited grounds, if prescribed by law and necessary in a democratic society in the interests of public safety, for the protection of public order, health or morals, or for the protection of the rights and freedoms of others.

Article 10: the right to freedom of expression.[20] This right includes the right to hold opinions and to receive and impart information and ideas without interference by public authority and regardless of frontiers. Again limitations on the right are permitted on limited grounds: if prescribed by law and necessary in a democratic society for the prevention of disorder and crime, for the protection of health or morals, or for the protection of the rights and freedoms of others, to prevent the disclosure of information received in confidence or for maintaining the authority and impartiality of the judiciary.

Article 11: freedom of peaceful assembly, of association with others, including the right to form and to join trade unions for the protection of one's interests. Limitations are permitted if prescribed by law and necessary in a democratic society in the interests of national security or public safety, for the prevention of disorder or crime, for the protection of health or morals or for the protection of the rights and freedoms of others.

Article 12: the right to marry and found a family.

All the rights stated above are, by virtue of art 14, to be enjoyed free from discrimination. One important limitation exists. The rights, other than those contained in arts 3, 4(1) and 7, may be derogated from in time of war or other public emergency

---

18   See Criminal Justice and Public Order Act 1994, s 145; *R v R (Rape: Marital Exemption)* [1992] 1 AC 599; [1991] 4 All ER 481. See [1997] EHR Rev at p 600.
19   See, eg, *Laskey, Jaggard & Brown v UK* (1997) 24 EHRR 39.
20   Many examples exist. See, eg *Sunday Times v United Kingdom* (1979) 2 EHRR 245 (leading to Contempt of Court Act 1981).

threatening the life of the nation, to the extent strictly required by the exigencies of the situation.[1] One other provison of the Convention should be noted. Article 13 guarantees the availability of a remedy at national level to enforce substance of the Convention rights and freedoms in whatever form they may happen to be secured in the domestic legal order. It is to be regarded as "central to the co-operative relationship between the Convention and national legal system".[2] The characteristics of an effective remedy include recourse to a sufficiently independent process. The remedy must be such that the applicant must be capable of availing himself of it.

C   THE STATUS OF THE CONVENTION

As a Treaty the European Convention does not form part of English law unless and until incorporated into law by an Act of Parliament.[3] No such incorporation has occurred, and thus the rights created are not directly enforceable in the courts. Despite this the Convention can act as an indirect source in influencing the interpretation of statute, or the development of the common law, and through the decisions of the Court of Justice of the European Community.[4] The findings of the European Court of Human Rights may also provide the impetus for legislative action.

I   Indirect aid

The extent to which the courts are entitled to rely on the Convention or do in fact rely on it, as an indirect aid, varies greatly. In 1975 Lord Denning MR observed[5] that "the courts could and should take the Convention into account in interpreting the statute. An Act of Parliament should be construed as to conform with the Convention". This has, broadly, been reflected by subsequent judicial attitudes, although not uniformly so. The position was discussed by the House of Lords in *R v Secretary of State for Home Affairs, ex parte Brind*.[6] In that case there was a challenge by way of judicial review to the making of a directive pursuant to s 29(3) of the Broadcasting Act 1981, and to clause 12(4) of the licence of the BBC, which had the effect of prohibiting the broadcasting of statements by representatives of proscribed organisations. The applicant argued that such prohibitions contravened art 10 of the Convention. In dismissing the applications, and upholding the directive made by the Home Secretary, the House recognised that the Convention can be used for the resolution of ambiguity in primary or delegated legislation, and the presumption will be that Parliament intended to legislate in accordance with its international obligations.[7] This is, however, a "mere canon of construction"[8] and did not require an administrative body, such as the Home

---

1   Art 15.
2   Jacobs, *Euroepan Convention on Human Rights* (1996).
3   *Saloman v Customs and Excise Commission* [1967] 2 QB 116; [1966] 3 All ER 871; *R v Chief Immigration Officer, ex parte Bibi* [1976] 3 All ER 843; [1976] 1 WLR 979; *Maclaine Watson v Department of Trade* [1989] Ch 72; [1983] 3 All ER 257. The approach taken in *Garland v British Rail Engineering Ltd* [1983] 2 AC 751 in the context of the European Community (see p 113, *ante*) has no application in this context.
4   See p 100, *ante*.
5   (1975) Times, 12 February 1975. The view expressed in that case that a court might be able to hold an Act invalid if it did not comply with the requirements of the Convention went too far: see *R v Secretary of State for Home Affairs, ex p Singh* [1976] QB 198, [1975] 2 All ER 1080.
6   [1991] 1 AC 696, [1991] 1 All ER 720.
7   *Maclaine Watson & Co Ltd v Department of Trade and Industry* [1989] Ch 72; [1983] 3 All ER 257.
8   *Per* Lord Bridge of Harwich.

Office, to exercise its statutory discretion within the terms of the Convention. That would, in effect, to be to conclude that the judiciary had the means, without Parliament's aid, to incorporate the Convention into English law, and would amount to a judicial usurpation of the legislative function.

It should not be concluded from this that the Convention is to be ignored, or that it has had no effect. Many examples can be given of the use of the Convention to justify a conclusion. In *R v Chief Metropolitan Stipendiary Magistrate, ex parte Choudhury*[9] it was held that art 9 did not require the common law crime of blasphemy to be extended. Again, in *A-G v Guardian Newspapers Ltd*[10] Lord Bridge, in a dissenting speech, used the terms and likely application of the Convention as a basis for concluding that interim relief to restrain publication of the book in question in that case should not be granted. It is noteworthy that Lord Ackner, in the majority, used the tests required by the Convention under art 10 as the starting point for reaching a completely opposite conclusion on the facts.

One example of an area of law where the Convention has provided considerable influence, both on government in framing legislation, and on the courts in the interpretation of statute and common law, is in the area of the treatment of discretionary life prisoners. In one case, *Thynne Wilson and Gunnell v UK*[11] the European Court of Human Rights concluded that the law and practice relating to the release of those serving discretionary life sentences was in breach of the Convention. It was in response to that finding that section 34 of the Criminal Justice Act 1991 was passed. In *R v Home Secretary, ex parte Wilson*[12] the fact that Parliament had passed legislation to give effect to a ruling of the Court of Human Rights was an important factor in persuading the Court of Appeal that a common law rule should be changed pending the coming into force of that statute. More recently, when the meaning of section 34 came before the courts on an application for judicial review, the Convention was used as a yardstick against which the legality of the actions of the Home Secretary could be measured. Dyson J observed:[13]

"I do not consider that *ex parte Brind* required me to ignore the Convention when considering the lawfulness of the exercise of the discretion. I accept as a general rule the lawfulness of the executive discretion is not measured by asking whether it involves an infringement of Convention rights. But where it is clear that the statutory provision which creates the discretion was passed in order to bring the domestic law into line with the Convention, it would, in my judgment, be perverse to hold that, when considering the lawfulness of the exercise of discretion, the court must ignore the relevant provisions of the Convention."

In other cases the Convention may be noted, but has no decisive effect on the court's conclusion. Sometimes a judge may decline to use the Convention to extend or develop the law, often conscious of the limits of judicial law-making. Thus in *Malone v Metropolitan Police Commissioner (No 2)*[14] Sir Robert Megarry considered the legality of police interception of telephone calls. Even though not bound by authority on the

9   [1991] 1 QB 429; [1991] 1 All ER 306.
10   [1987] 3 All ER 316; [1987] 1 WLR 1248.
11   13 EHRR 666.
12   [1992] QB 740; [1991] 2 All ER 576.
13   *R v Secretary of State for the Home Department, ex parte Norney* (1995) 7 Admin LR 861. See also *R v Canons Park Mental Health Tribunal, ex parte A* [1995] QB 360, [1995] 2 All ER 659, where a similar approach to the construction of the Mental Health Act 1983 was taken, the relevant provision having been introduced to change previous law found to conflict with the Convention.
14   [1979] Ch 344; [1979] 2 All ER 620.

substantive issue, and despite considering that the practice may well be in breach of art 8 of the Convention,[15] he declined to develop the law in a way that would ensure compliance, a ruling that would amount to judicial legislation on a matter that should be dealt with by Parliament.[16] On other occasions the Convention may serve to confirm a conclusion that the court has reached in any event. In *John v Mirror Group Newspapers*[17] the Court of Appeal decided that a jury in a civil case might be referred to appropriate levels of damages awards in personal injuries cases, and might, in a defamation case, be given judicial guidance as to the level of exemplary damages it was appropriate to award. This conclusion was reached by interpreting and developing the common law, with art 10 of the Convention being used to reinforce and buttress the conclusion the court reached. Another example is *R v Secretary of State for the Home Department, ex p Leech*[18] where rule 33(3) of the Prison Rules was found to be *ultra vires* the Prison Act 1952 because the rule (which created an unrestricted right for a prison governor to intercept and read letters sent to and from prisoners) amounted to an interference with the right of a prisoner to seek legal advice and unimpeded access to the courts. This was a conclusion reached in the light of the fact that access to the courts is a "constitutional right", but the court noted that its conclusion was consistent with art 8 of the Convention.

This approach finds clear favour with the courts. As is noted below, the principles inherent in the Convention inform the law of the European Union. They also inform the English courts in establishing and developing the common law. In *R v Secretary of State for the Home Department, ex parte McQuillan*,[19] Sedley J observed as follows:

> "Once it is accepted that the standards articulated in the convention are standards which both march with those of the common law and inform the jurisprudence of the European Court, it becomes unreal and potentially unjust to continue to develop English public law without reference to them".

This conclusion led him to conclude that the legal standards against which the actions of public authorities are judged should differentiate between those rights which are recognised as fundamental and those not deserving of such pre-eminent status. The standard of justification for the infringement of rights and freedoms must vary according to the significance of the right in issue.[20] In the instant case the balancing function to determine whether an exclusion order made under section 5 of the Prevention of Terrorism (Temporary Provisions) Act 1989 was irrational was not possible because the competing interests of national security prevented the court from knowing the reasons the Secretary of State relied on in making his decision.

Another example is to be found in *DPP v Jones*,[1] where it was observed as follows:

> "Resort to the convention can only be made if the law is unclear and for the reasons given by McCowan LJ and in this judgment, I am satisfied that it is clear. However, in my judgment the law does in any event comply with the convention. The reality is that peaceful and non-obstructive assemblies on the highway are normally permitted. That is as it should be since, in the absence of any obstruction

---

15   In that it failed to be prescribed by law.
16   See now Interception of Communications Act 1985.
17   [1997] QB 586; [1996] 2 All ER 35.
18   [1994] QB 198; [1993] 4 All ER 539.
19   [1995] 4 All ER 400.
20   See *Ministry of Defence, ex parte Smith* [1995] 4 All ER 427 (DC); [1996] 1 All ER 257 (CA). Cf *R v Secretary of State for the Environment, ex parte National Association of Local Government Officers* (1993) 5 Admin LR 785.
1   [1997] 1 All ER 737.

or threat of disorder, there is no reason why anyone having the legal right to do so should take any action. A meeting held on the highway is not for that reason alone necessarily to be regarded as an unlawful meeting: see *Burden v Rigler*. Furthermore, it is to be noted that in the only case Mr Starmer has found on the points at issue, *Rassemblement Jurassien v Switzerland* (App no 8191/78), the European Commission of Human Rights stated that the subjection of meetings in public thoroughfares to an authorisation procedure did not normally encroach upon the essence of the right. The concern is that there should be an ability to hold a peaceful assembly and that exists."

Again in *R v Lord Chancellor, ex p Witham*[2] the judge observed:

"In the unwritten legal order of the British State, at a time when the common law continues to accord a legislative supremacy to Parliament, the notion of a constitutional right can in my judgment inhere only in this proposition, that the right in question cannot be abrogated by the state save by specific provision in an Act of Parliament, or by regulations whose *vires* in main legislation specifically confer the power to abrogate. General words will not suffice. And any such rights will be creatures of the common law, since their existence would not be the consequence of the democratic political process but would be logically prior to it."

2   The European Union

Care must be taken to distinguish between the European Union on the one hand and the Convention and Court of Human Rights on the other. A common mistake is to assume that they are directly related. This is not so, they having been established by different treaties and having different institutions. Indeed, until 1998 and unlike the European Union, the Convention has had no direct application in the law of the United Kingdom. That said, the law of the European Communities and Union has provided a means whereby indirect legal recognition of its provisions has been achieved.

The European Community and Union has not itself acceded to the Convention on Human Rights, and cannot legally do so. However, Community law recognises respect for fundamental rights as one of the general principles of law, and thus in considering the legality under Community law of acts taken either by Community institutions or by member states regard can, and will, be had to whether the standards set by the Convention have been observed. This approach has been noted by English courts. In two cases[3] in 1995 challenge was made to exclusion orders made under the Prevention of Terrorism (Temporary Provisions) Act 1989. In each case it was argued that the order infringed article 8a of the Treaty of Rome, and article 9 of Directive 64/221, the provisions of which governed exclusion from member states and the procedure to be followed. The Court of Justice in the second of the two cases (the first not reaching the ECJ because of the revocation of the order) held that such an exclusion order infringed article 9 of the Directive because of a failure to comply with minimum basic

2   [1998] QB 575; [1997] 2 All ER 779.
3   *R v Secretary of State for the Home Department, ex parte Adams* [1995] All ER (EC) 177; *R v Secretary of State for the Home Department, ex parte Galligher* [1996] 1 CMLR 557 (ECJ); [1996] 2 CMLR 951.

procedural safeguards in respect of the appointment and role of the "competent authority" before which an excluded person is entitled, under Community law, to argue its case. Further, as already noted, in *R v Secretary of State for the Home Department, ex parte McQuillan*[4] Sedley J observed that

> "once it is accepted that the standards articulated in the convention are standards which both match with those of the common law and inform the jurisprudence of the European Union, it becomes unreal and potentially unjust to continue to develop English public law without reference to them".

In that case the challenge was by way of judicial review to an exclusion order made under the 1989 Act. The applicant claimed that not only did the exclusion order contravene his right to life and the right not to be subjected to inhuman treatment contrary to articles 2 and 3 of the Convention, but it also infringed his right of free movement under article 48 of the Treaty of Rome. The court considered that the proportionality of the actions of the Secretary of State had to be considered but that was not possible because of the competing demands of national security which prevented the court being told the reasons for the exclusion order.

D   INCORPORATION OF THE CONVENTION INTO ENGLISH LAW

Despite the fact that the Convention has had clear influence in the law-making process there have, for many years, been calls for its incorporation into English law. The lack of incorporation has meant that a person aggrieved at an alleged breach of a Convention right could not directly enforce that right in the domestic courts, but was dependent on the processes of interpretation or development described above, or alternatively faced the daunting prospect of taking the case through the long, and slow, procedures of the Court of Human Rights at Strasbourg. The fact that the Government might choose, for the future, to amend the law to bring it into line with the rulings of the Court of Human Rights did not provide an automatic remedy for those who were aggrieved, although often *ex gratia* payments of compensation were made.

Parliament is now considering the formal incorporation of the Convention into English law. The Human Rights Bill 1998 will, if enacted, give legal effect to the Convention, although not to the extent of creating fundamental rights which entitle the court to declare invalid any Act of Parliament which infringes the rights contained in the Convention. The rights protected by the Bill (the "convention rights") are those contained in arts 2 to 12 and 14, described above, and in arts 1 to 3 of the First Protocol, and as read with arts 16 to 18 (cl 1(1)). Somewhat surprisingly, the Bill does not include in the rights to be protected those contained in art 13, although the effect of this omission is probably mitigated by the fact that the principles recognised therein are indirectly incorporated via the case law of the Court of Human Rights and cl 2 of the Bill. Nor is article 1 (the general statement that the High Contending parties shall secure the Convention rights and freedom) within the definition of "convention rights" incorporated.

The Bill does not directly incorporate the Convention into English law. Instead it achieves the same aim through the interpretative process and by making the Convention a consideration which must be taken into account in determining any matter. Clearly, the first question is as to what the Convention requires. For this reason cl 2(1) provides that a court or tribunal must have regard to the statements of the law emanating from

4   [1995] 4 All ER 400.

the court and institutions of the Convention. It provides that a court or tribunal determining a question which has arisen under the Human Rights Bill in connection with a Convention right must take into account (a) any judgment, decision, declaration or advisory opinion of the European Court of Human Rights; (b) an opinion of the Commission given in a report adopted under art 33; (c) any decision of the Commission in connection with art 26 or 27(2); or (d) any decision of the Committee of Ministers taken under art 46 of the Convention.

I   Interpretation of legislation

Any Act of Parliament or subordinate legislation, whenever enacted, must, so far as it is possible to do so, be read and given effect in a way which is compatible with the Convention rights.[5] This does not affect the validity, continuing operation or enforcement of any incompatible primary legislation, nor of any incompatible subordinate legislation if (disregarding any possibility of revocation) primary legislation prevents removal of the incompatibility.[6]

The key question remains as to what is meant by the phrase "so far as it is possible to do so". The approach that will be adopted by the court will be similar to that which has been undertaken in the context of the European Union. Where the intent and purpose of Parliament is clear, and expressed in unambiguous language, it may be possible for the court to interpret a piece of legislation in a way which results in a conclusion that does not give effect to the Convention. However, the clear intent of cl 3 of the Bill is that statutes should be read subject to the Convention. In the context of legislation passed after the commencement of the Human Rights Bill, the parliamentary intent will be easy to ascertain: cl 19(1) states that a Minister in charge of a Bill in either House of Parliament must, before Second Reading of the Bill, (a) make a statement to the effect that in his view the provisions of the Bill are compatible with the Convention rights (a "statement of compatibility") or (b) make a statement to the effect that although he is unable to make a statement of compatibility the Government nevertheless wishes the House to proceed with the Bill. Such a statement must be in writing and published in such manner as the Minister making it considers appropriate.

Unless there is a statement under (b) it will therefore be clear that the intention of parliament was to comply with the Convention, and the usual processes of construction and interpretation will be undertaken in that light. Just as, in the context of s 2(4) of the European Communities Act 1972, the courts have been prepared to read a statute subject to Community law even if the words of the Act are clear and unambiguous,[7] so, now, a similar situation will prevail with legislation passed after the Human Rights Bill.

In respect of pre-existing legislation the position is less clear. Patently, there will be no statement of compatibility to which the courts may have regard. Nevertheless a court can, and should, presume a past parliamentary intent to comply with international obligations, and unless words specifically prevent a contrary conclusion, the effect of cl 3(1) is that legislation must be construed subject to Community law.

If a court in any proceedings determines whether a provision of an Act of Parliament is incompatible with one or more of the Convention rights, it may make a declaration of incompatibility. Such a declaration may also be made in respect of subordinate legislation if the court is satisfied (a) that the provision is incompatible with one or

---

5   Cl 3(1).
6   Cl 3(2).
7   See p 113, *ante*.

more of the Convention rights, and (b) that (disregarding any possibility of revocation) the primary legislation concerned prevents removal of the incompatibility.[8] For this purpose the term "court" is defined widely to include the High Court, Court of Appeal, House of Lords, Judicial Committee of the Privy Council and the Courts-Martial Appeal Court. It does not include a magistrates court, youth court, Crown Court, county or family court. Such a declaration can be made during any proceedings in those courts: separate application procedures are not considered necessary. However, rules of court will be made governing such applications, and the Crown will be entitled to be given notice of the fact that a court is considering making such a declaration.[9] The reason for provision is that a Minister, or person nominated by him, is entitled, on application to the court, to be joined as a party to those proceedings. Even if a declaration is made, it does not affect the validity, continued operation or enforcement of the provision in respect of which it is given. Its effect will therefore be to highlight the incompatibility, thus placing a government under pressure to take legislative action to bring legislation into line with the Convention.

There is no question of a court declaring invalid an Act of Parliament, or part of an Act of Parliament. If a declaration of incompatibility is made, or if it appears to a Minister or Her Majesty in Council that, having regard to a finding of the European Court of Human Rights, a provision of legislation is incompatible with one or more of the obligations of the United Kingdom arising from the Convention, then the power conferred on a Minister by cl 10(2) applies. This permits him to amend legislation by delegated legislation made under cl 10, in order to remove the incompatibility. This is potentially a far-reaching provision. 'Amendments' include repeals and the application of provisions subject to modifications.[10] Detailed provisions in cl 11 relate to the procedure to be followed in the making of such an order.

2   Interpretation of common law

Perhaps surprisingly, the Human Rights Bill does not specifically require a court to give effect to the Convention in developing the common law. Of course, a court can if it wishes to do so, and, as noted above, in many instances in the past has had regard to the Convention in determining what the common law is and whether it should be developed and in what way. However, the duty of the court to give effect to the Convention in this regard is in fact created, more indirectly, by cl 6 of the Bill. This states that it is unlawful for a public authority to act in a way which is incompatible with one or more of the Convention rights. A "public authority" includes a court, a tribunal which exercises functions in relation to legal proceedings, and any person certain of whose functions are functions of a public nature. It does not include either House of Parliament or a person exercising functions in connection with proceedings in Parliament.[11] The Judicial Committee of the House of Lords is to be regarded as a court not, for this purpose, as part of Parliament.[12] A court will not be acting unlawfully if (a) as the result of one or more provisions of primary legislation, the authority could not have acted differently; or (b) in the case of one or more provisions of, or made under, primary legislation which cannot be read or given effect in a way which is

8   Cl 4(2).
9   Cl 5.
10   Cl 10(3).
11   Cl 6(4).
12   *Ibid.*

compatible with the Convention rights, the authority was acting so as to give effect to or enforce those provisions.[13]

The effect of a court acting unlawfully is stated by cl 7. By cl 7(1), a person who claims that a public authority has acted (or proposes to act) in a way which is contrary to any of the rights contained in the Convention may (a) bring proceedings against the authority in the appropriate court of tribunal, or (b) rely on the Convention right or rights concerned in any legal proceedings, but, in either case, only if he is (or would be) a victim of the unlawful act. It follows that a party to a case who believes a court decision ruling or order to be wrong may make application to that court if the case is still before that court. Thus if a matter of procedure and evidence is before a court, the Convention right can be relied on in any submissions made on that matter. If a case has been concluded, an appeal can be based on the fact that the court deciding the case acted unlawfully,[14] or the decision can be challenged by way of judicial review if judicial review is in fact available (ie the decision is that of an inferior court or tribunal). A person will have *locus standi* to bring such proceedings if, and only if, he is (or would be) a victim of the unlawful act. The question of who is a victim has already been discussed,[15] but one difficulty is that the test of who is a victim is rather narrower than the test for locus standi in an application for judicial review.[16] This is a difference that may cause unfortunate effects, with the ability to involve Convention rights in part depending on the accident of whether judicial review proceedings can be justified. There is no question of a court or tribunal being liable in damages or subject to proceedings of any type other than that set out above.[17] By contrast, the procedures and remedies in respect of such unlawful acts by bodies other than courts or tribunals are wider. Clause 7(1) of the Bill permits proceedings by way of challenge to be brought by judicial review or in proceedings before an appropriate court or tribunal, to be determined in due course by rules of court. In such a case the court may grant such relief or remedy, or make such an order, as is within its jurisdiction and it considers just and appropriate.[18] Damages may be awarded, but only after taking into account all the circumstances of the case, including (a) any other relief or remedy granted, or order made, in relation to the act in question (by that or any other court) and (b) the consequences of any decision (of that or any other court) in respect of that act.[19] The court must be satisfied that the award is necessary to afford just satisfaction to the person in whose favour it is made. In determining whether to award damages, or the amount of any damages to be awarded, the court must take into account the principles applied by the Court of Human Rights in relation to the award of compensation under art 41 of the Convention.[20]

3   The effects of incorporation on the English legal system

Clearly, incorporation may have a significant effect. The inconsistent way in which judges have used the Convention as an aid to construction or development of the common law has already been noted. The implementation of the Human Rights Bill will require all judges in the superior courts to have regard to, and seek to implement,

---

13   Cl 6(2).
14   Cl 17(5), 9(1).
15   See p 123, *ante*.
16   See p 150, *post*.
17   Cl 9.
18   Cl 8(1).
19   Cl 8(3).
20   Cl 8(4).

the principles and rules of the Convention. Although inferior courts are not so obligated the effect of the doctrine of binding precedent may in fact achieve the same result. The Convention will therefore affect approaches to statutory interpretation.

It will also remove the necessity for aggrieved applicants to go through what has been a long-winded process of taking their complaints to Strasbourg. The average time taken to handle the number of applications made to it (some 12,434 in 1996)[1] is between 4 and 5 years. In one case, *Robbins v UK*,[2] proceedings before the Court of Human Rights which concluded that English court proceedings were excessively lengthy in terms of time in fact took longer than the proceedings in which they were condemned. Henceforth, European Convention arguments can be put in the case before the domestic courts: that, of course, was always the case, but now such arguments should prevail and, in cases where there is a genuine breach of the Convention, should obviate the need to go beyond the domestic jurisdiction. Of course, those who are disappointed by the rulings, interpretations and applications of the Convention by the domestic courts (particularly where an exception, derogation or margin of appreciation is in issue) will continue to seek redress at Strasbourg. That court is not, and will not become, a further court of appeal or in any way be part of the hierarchy of the English courts.

The incorporation of the Convention may also have its effect on the legislative process. Parliamentary draftsmen, and proposing Ministers, will always have had an eye to the compatibility of proposed legislation to the Convention. That has not, however, always had the effect of preventing a finding that legislation was in contravention of the Convention. Thus in *Saunders v UK*[3] the Court of Human Rights held that the use of Department of Trade and Industry transcripts of interviews conducted under legislation that required the applicant to answer on pain of punishment by way of imprisonment, infringed the his right to a fair trial under art 6(1), because his right not to be required to self-incriminate was on the facts infringed.

More widely, a range of issues is raised both by the terms of the 1998 Bill and the substantive rights conferred by the Convention. In terms of the former, the capacity of a judge who is currently a sitting member of the United Kingdom judiciary to be appointed to the Court of Human Rights has already been noted,[4] as have the new procedures giving additional scope for appeal or judicial review.[5] It is not clear whether legal aid will be available for such proceedings, but logically the rules relating to legal aid should not differ from those for the same, or similar, proceedings on other grounds.

Substantively, the rules of the Convention may have a wide impact on the legal system and the legal process. Police powers are potentially the subject of challenge under art 8 (eg challenges to search powers or the interception of communications). Powers of magistrates to bind over to keep the peace are currently the subject of challenge at Strasbourg.[6] The availability of legal advice, or legal aid, has been the subject of legal challenge at Strasbourg. In *Benham v UK*[7] proceedings in a magistrates' court for non payment of council tax were held to amount, under the Convention, to "criminal proceedings", and thus attracted the protection of art 6(3)(c) ("the right to defend himself in person or through legal assistance of his own choosing or, if he has not sufficient means to pay for legal assistance, to be given it free when the interests

---

1   Ovey: "The European Convention on Human Rights and the Criminal Lawyer" [1998] Crim LR 4.
2   (1997) Times 24 October.
3   (1994) 18 EHRR CD23.
4   See p 124, *ante*.
5   See p 135, *ante*.
6   *Steel v United Kingdom* (9 April 1997, unreported).
7   18 EHRR 105.

of justice so require"). The availability of "green form" advice[8] prior to trial and the possibility of representation by a lawyers already at court was held, on the facts, insufficient. The applicant risked imprisonment, and, in such a case, the interests of justice called for legal representation. Again, art 10 (freedom of expression and right to disseminate information) may have an impact on reporting restrictions made under the Contempt of Court Act 1981.[9]

The court structure itself may be the subject of challenge. In *Findlay v UK*[10] the army court-martial system was found to be in breach of art 6(1). It lacked the actual, or apparent, impartiality and independence required by the Convention, the links between prosecuting officer and adjudication not being clearly separated. In addition, the right of a fair trial provision may affect a wide variety of procedural or evidential rules, such as the right to cross-examin a witness in person, the right of witnesses to remain anonymous, the burden of proof and the right of silence. All of these matters are dealt with, in more detail, at appropriate parts of this book.

8   See p 279, *post*.
9   See p 165, *post*.
10 Unreported, app. 2107/93.

PART II

The Administration of Justice

CHAPTER 7

The Royal Prerogative and Judicial Review

A THE ROYAL PREROGATIVE

Historically the sovereign is the fountain of justice in England. For this reason the administration of justice is, strictly speaking, a prerogative of the Crown. This prerogative has, however, been substantially whittled away. Thus it was decided by Coke CJ in the case of *Prohibitions del Roy*[1] that the King (James I) could not, in his own person, judge any case. It is customarily accepted that the Crown no longer has a general power to create new courts by prerogative although it can, apparently, create courts to administer only the common law.[2] Nevertheless this power is worthless since any court so created would be powerless to apply any rules of law other than common law rules and would, presumably, have difficulty in obtaining Parliamentary authority for the finance required to maintain such a court. With the drastic curtailment of the immunity of the Crown in respect of civil proceedings (other than in a personal capacity) the position of the Crown is effectively formal. The remaining powers and privileges, though nominally vested in the Crown, are in reality those of its Ministers.[3]

Dicey defined the prerogative as follows:

"The prerogative is the name for the remaining portion of the Crown's original authority, and is therefore, as already pointed out, the name for the residue of discretionary power left at any moment in the hands of the Crown, whether such power be in fact exercised by the King himself or by his Ministers."[4]

Most of the remaining vestiges of prerogative control over the administration of justice are formal rather than of substance. The superior courts are termed the "Queen's

---

1   (1607) 12 Co Rep 63.
2   *Re Lord Bishop of Natal* (1864) 3 Moo PCCNS 115. The creation of the Criminal Injuries Compensation Board, is, however, a modern example of a tribunal created by prerogative act; see p 202, *post*.
3   In accordance with constitutional principle, exercisable by and on the advice of Ministers.
4   *Introduction to the Study of the Law of the Constitution* (8th Edn, 1915), p 421, cited with approval in *A-G v De Keyser's Royal Hotel Ltd* [1920] AC 508. See also: *Council of Civil Service Unions v Minister for the Civil Service* (the GCHQ case) [1985] AC 374; [1984] 3 All ER 935.

Courts" and the judges of those courts styled "Her Majesty's Judges". Criminal proceedings, on indictment, are pursued in the name of the Queen and all criminal proceedings are conducted on behalf of the Crown. These so-called prerogatives are, however, illusory. Judges are appointed "on the advice of" the Lord Chancellor or, in some cases, the Prime Minister. There is no power in the Crown to intervene in civil proceedings and any private individual may usually commence criminal proceedings. The parts of the royal prerogative which have continuing influence on the administration of justice are few. Among them may be included the power of the Attorney-General to stop a prosecution on indictment by entering a *nolle prosequi,* the power to pardon a convicted person and the prerogative of mercy under which the Crown may, through the Home Secretary, suspend, commute or remit any sentence.[5] The process of judicial review, though, provides an important mechanism for judicial scrutiny and control over parts of the administration of justice.

B   JUDICIAL REVIEW

1   Historical origins of the powers of the High Court

Historically, the superior common law courts controlled the conduct of inferior courts of record, in the name of the King and under the royal prerogative.[6] The existence of the prerogative itself was a matter claimed to be within the province of the common law courts. In the *Case of Proclamations*[7] the court stated that "the King hath no prerogative, but which the law of the land allows him." The errors of these courts, whether errors as to jurisdiction or errors of law within jurisdiction, were again controlled through the use of the prerogative.[8] This supervisory function was achieved through use of the prerogative writs. These were as follows:

(1) *prohibition*: inferior courts or administrative bodies could be prohibited from acting in excess of jurisdiction or unlawfully;
(2) *mandamus*: an inferior court could be ordered to exercise jurisdiction where it was declining to do so or an official ordered to perform a function which the law required of him;
(3) *certiorari*: the record of an inferior court could be examined by the King's Bench and the proceedings quashed on the ground of error of law, excess of jurisdiction or abuse of process;
(4) *habeas corpus*: requiring a person holding another in custody to justify the confinement to the court;
(5) *quo warranto*: enabling a party to challenge the jurisdiction of a court or person in public office purporting to exercise jurisdiction over him by means of a writ ordering the sheriff to summon the claimant to show by what authority (quo warranto) he asserted jurisdiction.

Of the above, *quo warranto* fell into disuse long before its abolition in 1938.[9] The various forms of the writ of habeas corpus still exist and the writ of *habeas corpus ad*

5   See p 145, *post.*
6   See p 155, *post.*
7   See n 1, *supra.*
8   See p 155, *post.*
9   By Administration of Justice (Miscellaneous Provisions) Act 1938, s 9, which provided that the remedy would, in effect, be replaced by injunction; see now Supreme Court Act 1981, s 30.

subjiciendum is still frequently used, often as a means of testing the validity of detention effected for the purpose of extradition. The remaining three writs were abolished in 1938 but replaced by orders of prohibition, mandamus and certiorari. They constitute the supervisory jurisdiction of the High Court and the procedure whereby this jurisdiction is invoked and exercised is now termed "judicial review".[10] An application for any of the orders named above, or for an injunction or declaration,[11] must be made by way of application for judicial review.

2   The scope of judicial review

This has widened greatly in recent years. Despite occasional judicial confusions, it was always clear that judicial review lay against any inferior court or tribunal, and against any body exercising statutory functions affecting the rights of individuals. A striking recent example of this principle in action is the successful challenge to the actions of the Lord Chancellor. In *R v Lord Chancellor, ex parte Witham*[12] the applicant challenged the actions of the Lord Chancellor in making a statutory instrument that had the effect of repealing provisions contained in another order which relieved litigants in person who were in receipt of income support from the obligation to pay court fees. The applicant, who was on income support, was unable to pay the court fees. The Divisional Court upheld the challenge, holding that access to the courts was a constitutional right at common law in the sense that it could not be abrogated except by Act of Parliament or by regulations where the enabling power to do so was explicit. That was not the case in this instance and thus the regulations were ultra vires.

The scope of judicial review has developed to allow challenge to the actions of such a body affecting the legitimate expectations of an individual.[13] Doubt, though, remained about the reviewability of actions taken by or on behalf of the Crown under the royal prerogative. The traditional position was that though the court was entitled to rule as to the existence or extent of prerogative power, it was not entitled to review the exercise of such power.[14] Thus an attempt in *Hanratty v Lord Butler*[15] to challenge the exercise the prerogative power of mercy inevitably failed.[16]

Some evidence existed that this position was not absolute. In *R v Criminal Injuries Compensation Board, ex parte Lain*[17] the divisional court decided that certiorari could issue against decisions of that Board, a body established under prerogative power to administer a scheme for the provision of compensation to victims of crimes of violence. This, though, was not the review of the exercise of prerogative power, but rather the review of the actions taken by a body established under the prerogative. The issue arose more directly in *Laker Airways Ltd v Department of Trade*[18] where Lord Denning observed, obiter, that he saw no reason why the exercise of prerogative powers should not be reviewable. The matter was effectively put beyond doubt by the House of Lords in *Council of Civil Service Unions v Minister for the Civil Service.*[19] The litigation arose out of an instruction by the Minister to the effect that the conditions of

---

10   Under the Supreme Court Act 1981, s 31, and RSC Ord 53.
11   Available on judicial review since 1977: see RSC Ord 53, r 1.
12   [1998] QB 575; [1997] 2 All ER 779. For court fees, see p 274, *post*.
13   See Lord Diplock in the *GCHQ* case, *supra*, n 4. The legitimate expectation can be either as to the receipt of a benefit, or of being treated procedurally in a particular way.
14   Case of Saltpetre (1606) 12 Co Rep 12; *Blackburn v A-G* [1971] 2 All ER 1380; [1971] 1 WLR 1037.
15   (1971) 115 Sol Jo 386.
16   But now see p 145, *post*.
17   [1967] 2 QB 864; [1967] 2 All ER 770.
18   [1977] QB 643; [1977] 2 All ER 182.
19   See, n 4, *ante*.

employment of staff at Government Communications Headquarters (GCHQ) would be revised so as to prohibit membership of any trade union (other than an approved departmental staff association). This instruction was issued pursuant to power conferred upon the Minister by an order in council made under the royal prerogative.[20] The appellants applied for judicial review of the Minister's instruction. It was contended (*inter alia*) on behalf of the Minister that the instruction was not open to review by the courts because it was an emanation of the prerogative. In the event adjudication on this contention became unnecessary because the House of Lords held that the evidence disclosed the Minister's instruction to have been justified on the ground of national security. This being so, any observations by their Lordships upon the contention raised were necessarily obiter. However, the majority proceeded on the basis that the key question was not the source of the power, but rather whether it was of a nature suitable for judicial adjudication (ie justiciable). Lord Roskill identified certain prerogative powers as of a type not suitable for judicial determination. These included the making of treaties, the defence of the realm, the prerogative of mercy, the grant of honours, the dissolution of Parliament and the appointment of Ministers. More recent case law has shown, however, that even this list is not absolute, with a successful challenge being made to the exercise of the prerogative of mercy.[21]

The trend set by the GCHQ case has continued. Recent case law shows that it is now the nature of the function that matters, and which determines whether judicial review is available. In *R v Panel on Take-overs and Mergers, ex parte Datafin*[1] the court ruled that the absence of a statutory or prerogative power was not decisive: judicial review would lie in respect of any body performing a public law function.[2] In this case, the Take-Over Panel was acting "governmentally" in engaging in regulatory functions in the area of take-overs which would otherwise be performed by a statutory body on behalf of the State.[3] The application of the *Datafin* principle is far from easy. In *R v Disciplinary Committee of the Jockey Club, ex parte Aga Khan*[4] the Court of Appeal decided that the Jockey Club was not a public body for the purposes of judicial review, despite its important regulatory in respect of the sport of horseracing. The key features in reaching this decision were the lack of integration into a scheme of public regulation, the fact that the Jockey Club was not a "surrogate organ of government", the fact that its powers derived from consent, and the fact that effective private law remedies existed.

The availability of judicial review is dependent, therefore, upon the nature of the particular power sought to be challenged. Many of the prerogative powers involving the administration of justice may be beyond judicial review, because of their unsuitability for judicial determination, although recently Simon Brown LJ observed[5] that "only the rarest cases will today be ruled strictly beyond the court's purview". The exercise of the prerogative of mercy might be thought, in the light of the comments of Lord Roskill in the GCHQ case, to be one example. However, in *R v Secretary of*

---

20   This is primary legislation, to be distinguished from the use of Orders in Council as delegated legislation.

21   See *Ex parte Bentley, infra.*

1   [1987] QB 815; [1987] 1 All ER 564.

2   Which are not created simply by the body concerned being a public body: see *R v East Berkshire Area Health Authority, ex parte Walsh* [1985] QB 152; [1984] 3 All ER 425. For the relevant principles, see *McClaren v Home Office* [1990] ICR 824, and p 148, *post.*

3   The effect of the *Datafin* decision appears weakened by subsequent cases; See *R v Chief Rabbi of the United Hebrew Congregations of Great Britain, ex parte Wachmann* [1992] 1 WLR 1036. In *R v Insurance Ombudsman Bureau & the Insurance Ombudsman, ex parte Aegon Life Assurance Ltd* [1994] COD 426, the court held that if the exercise of the power was consensual or contractual then it was not a public law matter, despite being woven into a system of governmental control.

4   [1993] 2 All ER 853.

5   See *R v Ministry of Defence, ex parte Smith* [1996] QB 517, [1996] 1 All ER 257.

State for Home Affairs, ex parte Bentley[6] a divisional court held that the courts have jurisdiction to review the exercise of the royal prerogative of mercy by the Home Secretary. The Home Secretary, in considering whether or not to grant a posthumous free pardon to B, a person hanged in 1952 for murder, had failed to have regard to the fact that such a pardon might be used in a variety of circumstances and take different forms. It might constitute a full pardon, or, as might have been appropriate in this case, a conditional pardon substituting a lesser sentence for that in fact imposed. The Secretary of State thus had made an error of law by failing to have regard to all relevant considerations, and therefore his refusal was unlawful.

In so deciding the court was applying the reasoning of the House of Lords in the GCHQ case. Even the exercise of the prerogative of mercy could be judicially reviewed if the grounds of challenge do not involve the court in the decision of policy questions. Thus, whilst the policy to be adopted for the granting of pardons was not justiciable, the present decision was, because the Secretary of State had failed to recognise the extent of his powers.

Even if a statutory basis exists, judicial review may be limited. The courts have held that actions of the police may be reviewed, but the scope of that review is restricted. An example of this is judicial review of the prosecution process. In *R v Commissioner of Police for the Metropolis, ex parte Blackburn*[7] the applicant sought an order of mandamus to compel the Commissioner of Police to reverse a policy statement which appeared to limit the enforcement of the gaming laws. The Court of Appeal held that mandamus might issue in an appropriate case, if there was what amounted to a complete failure to perform a duty imposed by law, but declined to make an order in the particular case before the court because the Commissioner had in fact reversed that policy. In a subsequent case involving the obscene publications laws,[8] the court stressed that the discretion was that of the Commissioner, the court only intervening where there was what amounted to an abdication of function.

One area which has evolved in tune with modern approaches to judicial review is that in respect of decisions to institute proceedings. The decisions of the law officers appear generally to be beyond challenge. In *Gouriet v Union of Post Office Workers*[9] the power to enforce the criminal law through applications for injunctive relief was held to be for the Attorney-General alone. More recently, in *R v Solicitor-General, ex parte Taylor and Taylor*,[10] a Divisional Court decided that the decision whether to bring proceedings for contempt of court was not justiciable. However, in the context of judicial review of the decision to prosecute the courts are more willing to intervene. A distinction has, in the past, been drawn between decisions involving juveniles and those involving adults. In *R v Chief Constable of Kent, ex p L*[11] the court stated that, where a policy exists in respect of cautioning juveniles, the decision to commence or discontinue criminal proceedings was subject to judicial review, but only where it could be shown that the decision was made regardless of, or contrary to, that policy.[12] This was applied by another Divisional Court in *R v Commissioner of Police for the Metropolis, ex parte P*,[13] where the cautioning of a juvenile improperly, and in

6   [1994] QB 349, [1993] 4 All ER 442.
7   [1968] 2 QB 118; [1968] 1 All ER 763.
8   *R v Commissioner of Police for the Metropolis, ex parte Blackburn (No 3)* [1973] QB 241; [1973] 1 All ER 324.
9   [1978] AC 435, [1977] 3 All ER 70.
10   [1996] 1 FCR 206.
11   [1993] 1 All ER 756.
12   *R v Havering Justices, ex parte Gould* (1993), unreported.
13   (1996) 5 Admin LR 6, 160 JP 369.

contravention of the Code for Crown Prosecutors,[14] was judicially reviewable. The courts have also now been prepared to consider judicial review of decisions to prosecute an adult. *R v Inland Revenue Commissioners ex parte Mead*[15] failed on the facts, because the prosecuting authority (the Inland Revenue) had considered the matter fairly, appropriately and taking all relevant matters into account.

Moving to judicial review of the actions of the courts themselves, it is an effective means for the control of the inferior courts, ensuring a means of challenge where failures to comply with jurisdictional requirements, or with principles of fair procedure, have occurred. It also provides a remedy where no right of appeal against a decision exists.[16] However, where a right of appeal does exist, leave to apply for judicial review may be declined, unless the complaint raised is one of procedural impropriety, unfairness or bias, leaving the applicant to deal with other matters by way of appeal.[17] Similarly with the actions of other forms of judicial adjudication, such as tribunals or public inquiries. However, judicial review does not lie against superior courts. The Crown Court is a superior court of record. Despite this, it is amenable to judicial review when dealing with an appeal from a magistrates' court, for then it is exercising the jurisdiction of that court, an inferior court. Its actions are also subject to review in any other case, subject to the important limitation contained in section 29(3) of the Supreme Court Act 1981 in respect of judicial review "in matters relating to trial on indictment". The reason for this provision is historical: the Crown Court took over the appellate jurisdiction of the old courts of Quarter Sessions, which were inferior courts and thus subject to judicial review. However, the application of section 29(3) has proved less than easy. In *R v Crown Court at Sheffield, ex parte Brownlow*[18] Lord Denning sought to interpret the subsection as preventing judicial review of matters arising "in the course of trial on indictment". This extremely narrow construction was not adopted by the majority of the court, which concluded that section 29(3) prevented judicial review where a decision arose out of, or incidentally to, the jurisdiction to try cases on indictment. On this view, a decision by the trial judge as to information concerning the jury panel was held to be caught by section 29(3) and thus not judicially reviewable.

The approach taken by the majority has not been followed in subsequent cases. In *Smalley v Crown Court at Warwick*[19] the House of Lords considered a decision to forfeit a recognisance entered into by a witness to be judicially reviewable. Lord Bridge stressed the need to proceed on a case-by-case basis. He set out a working test: the limitation in section 29(3) applied to "any decision affecting the conduct of a trial on indictment". However, it has since been stressed that this is a guideline, and was not an attempt to re-write the words of the subsection.[20] In addition, the real difficulty is in applying the guidance given by Lord Bridge. Decisions to allow counts of an indictment effectively to remain untried, and applications to quash an indictment, are instances which have been held to be subject to the restrictions upon judicial review.[1]

The problem has recently been extensively considered by the House of Lords in two cases. The first was *R v Manchester Crown Court, ex parte Director of Public*

14   See p 461, *post*.
15   [1993] 1 All ER 772.
16   Judicial review can only be prevented by the clearest of words: *Anisminic Ltd v Foreign Compensation Commission* [1969] 2 AC 147; [1969] 1 All ER 208. It may be restricted: *R v Cornwall County Council, ex parte Huntington* [1992] 3 All ER 566.
17   *R v Hereford Magistrates' Court, ex parte Rowlands* [1998] QB 110; cf *R v Peterborough Magistrates' Court, ex parte Dowler* [1997] QB 911.
18   [1980] QB 530; [1980] 2 All ER 444.
19   [1985] AC 622; [1985] 1 All ER 769.
20   Per Lord Bridge in *Sampson v Crown Court at Croydon* [1987] 1 All ER 609; [1987] 1 WLR 194.
1   See *R v Central Criminal Court, ex parte Raymond* [1986] 2 All ER 379; [1986] 1 WLR 710.

Prosecutions[2] where the court held that an order of the Crown Court made upon an application to stay the proceedings for abuse of process[3] was an order affecting the conduct of the trial, and therefore fell within section 29(2). The second was *Director of Public Prosecutions v Crown Court at Manchester and Huckfield*,[4] where a decision by a circuit judge to quash an indictment for lack of jurisdiction was held to be a matter "relating to trial on indictment" and thus not judicially reviewable. One test is whether the decision sought to be reviewed arises in the issue between the Crown and the defendant formulated by the indictment, including issues relating to costs. If it does, then judicial review might well lead to delay in the trial, and therefore is probably caught by the restrictions imposed by section 29(3).

The House of Lords stressed that this test might not always be appropriate. In particular, the question was left open as to whether judicial review was available in respect of the procedures to be followed in cases of serious fraud.[5] However, the test formulated by the court would have the effect of permitting judicial review where an order was made affecting a person other than the defendant,[6] or where the court was acting under a different jurisdiction.[7]

3 Procedure

An application for any one of the prerogative orders, or for a declaration that a public law matter is unlawful, must be made by way of application for judicial review. This is the normal, though not exclusive, means of challenge where questions of public law arise. Matters relating to the administration of justice are likely to be public law matters.

Where in reality an action raises issues of public law, the normal procedure for determination of those questions is by an application for judicial review under Order 53 of the Rules of the Supreme Court, and a failure to use the Order 53 procedure may result subsequently in an application by the defendant to have the action struck out as an abuse of process of the court.[8] The Order 53 procedure that existed prior to 1977 had defects that often meant that proceeding by way of writ in the Queen's Bench Division was more attractive. Certain procedures such as discovery[9] and cross-examination of those who swore affidavits were not available on judicial review; nor was it open to a court dealing with such an application to make an award for damages, or issue a declaration.[10] These, and other, defects were remedied in 1977 when a revised Order 53 came into effect. As a result in 1981 the House of Lords in *O'Reilly v Mackman*[11] indicated firmly that the Order 53 procedure was to be the usual method of challenging public law actions or decisions. Lord Diplock stressed the advantages

2   [1994] AC 9; *sub nom Director of Public Prosecutions v Crown Court at Manchester and Ashton* [1993] 2 All ER 663.
3   See p 465, *post*.
4   [1993] 4 All ER 928.
5   In *R v Central Criminal Court, ex parte Serious Fraud Office* [1993] 2 All ER 399; [1993] 1 WLR 949 such proceedings were held not to be caught by the restriction in s 29(3). See also: *R v Crown Court at Southwark* [1993] 1 WLR 764. For procedures relating to serious fraud cases see p 508, *post*.
6   See *Smalley v Crown Court at Warwick*, n 19 *supra* (forfeiture of recognisance of third party); *R v Crown Court at Maidstone, ex parte Gill* [1987] 1 All ER 129 (forfeiture of property of third party).
7   See, eg *R v Crown Court at Inner London, ex parte Benjamin* (1986) 85 Cr App Rep 267 (binding over of acquitted person).
8   *O'Reilly v Mackman, infra*. See p 148, *post*.
9   See p 385, *post*.
10 See now RSC Ord 53, r 1.
11 [1983] 2 AC 237; [1982] 3 All ER 1124; see also *Cocks v Thanet District Council* [1983] 2 AC 286; [1982] 3 All ER 1135.

of the limited time for challenge under Order 53, and the safeguard that the filter of requiring leave to apply creates. To seek to avoid these safeguards by proceeding by writ would amount in most cases to an abuse of process, although Lord Diplock accepted that there were exceptions to this general rule.

This distinction between public and private law matters, and the procedures to be followed, has caused the courts considerable difficulty.[12] The position was somewhat clarified, if not entirely so, by the House of Lords in *Roy v Kensington and Chelsea and Westminster Family Practitioners Committee*.[13] In that case the plaintiff, a doctor, commenced an action by writ, seeking to obtain payments that he alleged were due to him, and being withheld by the defendant committee. The doctor's terms and conditions of employment were governed by regulation made pursuant to statute, and the committee sought to have the plaintiff's action struck out, arguing that the action raised public law matters which should be decided on an application for judicial review under Order 53. This application initially succeeded, but was rejected both by the Court of Appeal and by the House of Lords. The plaintiff was seeking to recover money allegedly owed to him. This raised private law rights, which could be enforced by private law action, even if they involved challenge to a public law decision. In his speech, Lord Lowry identified two approaches. The first, the "narrow" approach was that taken by the court in *O'Reilly v Mackman*: that the Order 53 procedure ought generally to be followed if there was a public law issue. The second, the 'broad' approach, was favoured by him: that the Order 53 procedure was only obligatory if no private law issue was involved. He preferred the broad approach to the narrow, although did not formally decide the matter, concluding that, on either basis, the case of *Roy* fell within the exception to the general rule in *O'Reilly*.

Such an approach is consistent with a series of cases where a claim for money from a party was held to be a private law matter, even if the defence involved an assertion that the claim was invalid because it was made pursuant to an ultra vires action.[14] Simply because one party to an action is a public body does not turn the matter into a public law matter.[15] The current position was conveniently summarised by Laws J in *British Steel v Customs and Excise Commissioners*:[16]

(1)   where a complaint raised in litigation touches only a public law issue, there being no private law issue involved, the complainant must generally proceed by way of judicial review;[17]
(2)   where a defendant to a private law suit has a defence which is based on arguments based on public law, he may raise those arguments in the private law action;[18]
(3)   where statute confers a private law right, but one which only exists in consequence of a public law decision by a body, any complaint as to the public law stage must be brought by way of judicial review;[19]

---

12   See the *cri de coeur* of Henry J in *Doyle v Northumbria Probation Committee* [1991] 4 All ER 294; [1991] 1 WLR 340. For discussion of the issues, see Lord Woolf, "Public Law – Private Law: Why the Divide? A Personal View" [1986] 2 PL 220.
13   [1992] 1 AC 624; [1992] 1 All ER 705.
14   See in particular: *Wandsworth London Borough Council v Winder* [1985] AC 461; [1984] 3 All ER 976; *Davy v Spelthorne Borough Council* [1984] AC 262; [1983] 3 All ER 278.
15   *R v East Berkshire AHA, ex parte Walsh* [1985] QB 152; [1984] 3 All ER 425.
16   [1996] 1 All ER 1002; for the Court of Appeal, see [1997] 2 All ER 366.
17   *O'Reilly v Mackman, supra*.
18   *Wandsworth LBC v Winder*, n 14, above.
19   *Cocks v Thanet DC* [1982] 2 AC 286, [1982] 3 All ER 1135.

(4)   where the complaint enjoys a private law right not contingent on a public law decision in his favour, that right may be asserted by private law action.[20]

Whatever the technical and analytical difficulties, increasingly the courts are looking to the practicalities. In *Trustees of the Dennis Rye Pensions Fund v Sheffield City Council*[21] the Court of Appeal stated that a court should look at the practical consequences and not merely at the technical distinctions between public and private rights and bodies. In the case before the court it was obvious that the issues, which related to claim for payment for work done, could be dealt with more conveniently in a private law action than in an application for judicial review.

Further, the authorities show that it is open to a party to proceedings to raise the invalidity of a public law action as a defence to criminal proceedings. The extent to which this is permissible has, until recently, been unclear. The right to use the invalidity of the by-law as a defence to criminal proceedings was accepted in the 19th Century,[1] and confirmed in *R v Reading Crown Court, ex parte Hutchinson*.[2] More recently in *Boddington v British Transport Police*[3] the House of Lords put beyond doubt the fact that a defendant in criminal proceedings is entitled to challenge the validity of subordinate legislation, or an administrative decision made pursuant to that subordinate legislation where the prosecution was based on the assumption that the subordinate legislation was valid. The only exception to that was where there was a clear Parliamentary intention to the contrary. The ability to challenge as part of one's defence (i.e. collateral challenge) did not depend on the grounds of challenge, nor whether they were of a substantive or procedural nature. The House overruled authority which appeared to suggest the contrary.[4]

The procedure under Order 53 requires that an application be made promptly and in any event within three months from the date when the grounds of the application first arise, unless the court considers that there is good reason for extending this period. The application is by originating motion, to a divisional court of the Queen's Bench Division in criminal matters, or to a judge sitting in open court in other cases. The applicant requires leave to apply for judicial review to be granted, and this is sought by ex parte application to a judge. The application is in a prescribed form, and must contain the relief sought and the grounds relied upon, and must be accompanied by an affidavit verifying the facts relied on. The judge may determine the application without a hearing (unless a hearing is requested in the notice of application). If the application for leave is refused the applicant may renew it by applying, in criminal cases to the divisional court or, in any other case, to a single judge sitting in open court or, if the court so directs, to the divisional court.

Applications for interlocutory orders, such as discovery, interrogatories, cross-examination of witnesses, may be made to a judge or master. However, it should be borne in mind that:

" in the ordinary way judicial review is designed to deal with matters which can be resolved without resorting to these procedures."[5]

20   *Roy v Kensington and Chelsea and Westminster Family Practitioners' Committee* [1992] 1 AC 624 [1992] 1 All ER 705.
21   [1997] 4 All ER 747. See also *R v Chief Constable of Warwickshire, ex parte Fitzpatrick* [1998] 1 All ER 65 (complainant should not challenge search warrant by judicial review, which was unsuitable for a fact-finding exercise, but should rely on his private rights).
1   See eg *Kruse v Johnson* [1898] 2 QB 91, [1895–1899] All ER Rep 105
2   [1988] QB 384, [1988] 1 All ER 333.
3   [1998] 2 All ER 203. See also *R v Wicks* [1998] AC 92; [1997] 2 All ER 801.
4   *Bugg v DPP* [1993] QB 473; [1993] 2 All ER 815.
5   *R v Derbyshire County Council, ex parte Noble* [1990] 1 CR 808; [1990] IRLR 332, per Woolf LJ.

On the hearing of the application for judicial review the court will hear any party served with the motion or summons and any other person who appears to be a proper person to be heard. An applicant must have *locus standi* (ie a sufficient interest). This principle is designed to prevent the court being troubled by "mere busybodies".[6] On the other hand, locus standi is not confined to persons who have a legal or financial interest.[7] Whether locus standi exists ultimately turns on the nature of the statutory provision and the nature of the person or organisation claiming locus standi. In *R v HM Inspectorate of Pollution and Ministry of Agriculture Fisheries and Food, ex parte Greenpeace (No 2)*,[8] the environmental organisation Greenpeace was held to have locus standi to challenge the actions of the respondents in varying an authorisation to discharge radioactive waste. The organisation was a large organisation with internationally recognised expertise in environmental matters.[9] The court has power to make orders of prohibition, mandamus or certiorari, to grant an injunction or declaration and to award damages if the applicant could have recovered damages had he proceeded by action, rather than application for judicial review.

The court has power to grant interim relief,[10] such as an interlocutory injunction. Where the relief sought is a declaration, an injunction or damages the court may, in certain circumstances, order the proceedings to continue as if they had been commenced by writ. As already observed, the essential feature of judicial review is that it applies to public law rather than private law matters. Thus it is not appropriate where the applicant's complaint is of a purely private nature, for example that he has been wrongfully dismissed by his employer, even where that employer is a public authority.[11] Conversely, if the applicant wishes to challenge a public-law decision he must proceed by way of application for judicial review and he cannot avoid the procedural requirements of Order 53 (notably the need for leave to move and the prescribed time-limit) by bringing an ordinary action seeking a declaration or an injunction.

4   Grounds for judicial review

Judicial review is not a form of appeal. The High Court will not substitute its own decision for that of the court, tribunal or body below on the ground that it appears to be wrong, and, generally, is at pains to avoid doing so. The circumstances in which the court will interfere are want or excess of jurisdiction or failure to comply with the rules of natural justice and procedural fairness. These standards of procedural fairness vary from case to case but generally include the right of each party to state his case, the prohibition on a person being judge in his own cause, the right to be informed of the reasons for a decision and, in some cases, the right to legal representation before a tribunal.[12] In respect of inferior courts or tribunals, the court can intervene by way of

---

6   See *R v Greater London Council, ex parte Blackburn* [1976] 3 All ER 184; [1976] 1 WLR 550; *R v Monopolies and Mergers Commission, ex parte Argyll Group* [1986] 2 All ER 257; [1986] 1 WLR 763.

7   *Inland Revenue Commissioners v National Federation of Self Employed and Small Businesses* [1982] AC 617; *R v Secretary of State for the Environment, ex parte Rose Theatre Trust* [1990] 1 All ER 754; [1990] 1 QB 504.

8   [1994] 4 All ER 329. Cf *Rose Theatre Trust* case, *supra*.

9   See also *R v Poole BC, ex parte Beebee* [1991] 2 PLR 27.

10   RSC Ord 53, r 3.

11   See *ex parte Walsh, supra* n 15.

12   See *R v Board of Visitors of HM Prison, The Maze, ex parte Hone* [1988] AC 379, *sub nom Hone v Maze Prison Board of Prison Visitors* [1988] 1 All ER 321; *R v Secretary of State for the Home Department, ex parte Cheblak* [1991] 2 All ER 319; [1991] 1 WLR 890.

judicial review if there is an error of law on the face of the record,[13] although this principle is of little practical importance given the wide interpretation the courts have given to the concept of excess of power or jurisdiction.[14]

In addition, in the case of an administrative person or body, the court will intervene when a discretion has been misused, because relevant matters have not been taken into account, or regard had to irrelevancies, or the discretion has been fettered improperly, or otherwise used contrary to the principles of the enabling power. These are often known as "the *Wednesbury* principles".[15] These matters are couched in legal terms but often bring the courts into a position where care has to be taken not to cross the boundaries between legitimate executive judgment and proper judicial intervention. Finally, if the body reaches a decision that no sensible authority could reach then it may be held to be invalid on the grounds of "*Wednesbury* unreasonableness".[16]

These grounds of judicial review were described by Lord Diplock in *Council of Civil Service Unions v Minister for the Civil Service*[17] as (1) illegality"; (2) "irrationality" (ie *Wednesbury* unreasonableness); and (3) "procedural impropriety". Whilst these terms have become widely accepted and used, it is important to recognise that they amount to no more than convenient labels,[18] and do not amount to the creation of new grounds of challenge. The meaning and scope of "irrationality" has been the subject of doubt, and has been described, graphically, as applying in respect of decisions which are so unreasonable as to "jump off the page at you".[19] It is a controversial ground that raises constitutional issues because, in effect, it requires the reviewing court to take a view as to the merits, or, more accurately, lack of merits of the decision under review. Lord Templeman in *Brind v Secretary of State for the Home Department*,[20] and Simon Brown LJ in *R v Ministry of Defence, ex parte Smith*[1] each appeared to suggest that the decision of a public authority was challengeable more readily on grounds of irrationality if it involved the fundamental rights of the individual. This is, however, controversial, and not firmly settled by authority. In *R v Secretary of State for the Environment, ex parte National Association of Local Government Officers*,[2] Neill LJ said:

" [With the exception of Lord Templeman's speech in *Brind*] I have not been able to extract from the other speeches any real support for the view that the latitude to be given to a Minister is to be confined within tighter limits when his decision impinges on fundamental human rights. As the law stands at present, it

---

13   *R v Northumberland Compensation Appeal Tribunal, ex parte Shaw* [1952] 1 KB 338; [1952] 1 All ER 122. This used to be confined to the record itself and excluded jurisdiction to correct errors in the reasons leading to the record but it is now held to extend to errors in reasons given in support of the recorded decision: *R v Crown Court at Knightsbridge, ex parte International Sporting Club (London) Ltd* [1982] QB 304; [1981] 3 All ER 417.

14   See *Anisminic Ltd v Foreign Compensation Commission*, p 146, *ante*, and Lord Browne-Wilkinson in *R v Lord President of the Privy Council, ex parte Page* [1993] AC 682.

15   *Associated Provincial Picture Houses Ltd v Wednesbury Corporation* [1948] 1 KB 223; [1947] 2 All ER 680. For examples see, eg, *Padfield v Minister of Agriculture, Fisheries and Food* [1968] AC 997, [1968] 1 All ER 694; *Wheeler v Leicester City Council* [1985] AC 1054, [1985] 2 All ER 1106; *R v Sefton Metropolitan Borough Council, ex parte Help the Aged* [1997] 4 All ER 532.

16   For discussion, see *R v Secretary of State for the Home Department, ex parte Brind* [1991] 1 AC 696; [1990] 1 All ER 469, CA; [1991] 1 AC 696; [1991] 1 All ER 720, HL.

17   See p 143, *ante*.

18   *Per* Lord Donaldson in *ex parte Brind, supra*.

19   *R v Lord Chancellor, ex parte Maxwell* [1996] 4 All ER 751.

20   [1991] 1 All ER 720 [1991] 2 WLR 588.

1   [1996] QB 517 [1996] 1 All ER 257.

2   (1993) 5 Admin LR 785; cf *R v Secretary of State for Home Department, ex parte McQuillan* [1995] 4 All ER 400.

seems to me to be clear that though the Minister is required to justify the restriction imposed by reference to an important and sufficient competing interest the court, when reviewing the Minister's decision, is not entitled (to use Lord Lowry's phrase) to lower the threshold of unreasonableness ... In the light of the decision in *Brind* ... I am quite satisfied that it is not open to a court below the House of Lords to depart from the traditional *Wednesbury* grounds when reviewing the decision of a Minister of the Crown who has exercised a discretion vested in him by Parliament."

It remains to be seen how far the courts are prepared to give themselves a wider role in the context of fundamental rights, particularly in the context of the effective incorporation of the European Convention on Human Rights.[3]

Further, one other possible extension of the grounds of challenge was canvassed by Lord Diplock in the GCHQ case as "proportionality", and is controversial. This doctrine is important in European Community law,[4] but in *Brind v Secretary of State for the Home Department*[5] the House of Lords concluded that no such ground existed as a general ground of challenge by judicial review, but rather formed part of the process by which allegations of breach of the *Wednesbury* principles, or of *Wednesbury* unreasonableness, would be judged. In any event, such a ground is more likely to be relevant to the review of administrative actions or discretions than to the judicial actions of inferior courts.

3　See p 135, *ante*
4　See p 102, *ante*.
5　See p 151, *supra*.

CHAPTER 8

The Courts

A   HISTORICAL INTRODUCTION

Some background as to the historical development of the courts is necessary for an understanding of what in fact now exists, and why modern jurisdiction is distributed in the way it is. As already noted[1] the underpinning basis of the development of the courts was the power of the monarch. This can in fact be traced back to exercise of regal power, in the King's Council, the Curia Regis.

I   The Curia Regis

In medieval times legislative, executive and some judicial functions were exercised by the King in Council. The King's Council is thus the predecessor not only of Parliament but also of the courts.

The medieval pattern was for courts to separate from the Council and eventually acquire a jurisdiction independent of it. However the King at all times retained a residual power deriving from his prerogative powers. Thus the three main common law courts, the Court of Exchequer, the Court of Common Pleas and the Court of King's Bench, split off from the Council and their judges exercised jurisdiction to decide civil disputes and major criminal cases in London and on assize. The King's justices assumed jurisdiction over criminal offences. Nevertheless the undefined residual jurisdiction of the King led to other courts deriving their jurisdiction from the Curia Regis, notably the Court of Chancery and the Star Chamber. Indeed it was not until the seventeenth century that the Council itself discontinued its judicial function. The functions of these courts were to remedy the procedural defects and restrictions of the common law courts and to dispense justice where the common law courts were for some reason unable to do so. The obvious results of this ad hoc method of creating courts were clashes between them and the common law courts over the extent of their respective jurisdiction.

---

1   See p 4, *ante*.

2 The Court of Exchequer

This was the first of the three central common law courts to split off from the Curia Regis. In the reign of Henry I the Exchequer became a separate department of the Council dealing with the collection and distribution of royal revenue. By the reign of Henry II it had become a court, the judges of which were Exchequer Barons presided over by the Chief Baron who was, after the fourteenth century, always a lawyer, frequently of great distinction.

Originally the jurisdiction of the court was confined to disputes between subjects and the Crown concerning revenue. Later the court acquired jurisdiction over disputes between subjects, such as writs of debt and covenant,[2] through the fiction of "*quominus*". This depended upon a fictitious allegation of a debt owed by the plaintiff to the Crown which the plaintiff was the less able (*quominus*) to pay because of the debt owing to him by the defendant. This fictitious allegation enabled the court to determine the substantive issue between the parties.[3]

In addition the court appears, at least in its early days, to have exercised an equity jurisdiction, though its procedure was that of the common law courts rather than of the Court of Chancery.

When the court was finally abolished in 1875 its jurisdiction was transferred to the newly-formed High Court, its common law jurisdiction being exercised by the Queen's Bench Division after 1880, and its revenue jurisdiction by the Chancery Division. Its equity jurisdiction had been transferred by statute to the Chancery in 1841.[4]

3 The Court of Common Pleas

While the King was determining civil disputes in Council suitors were obliged to follow the court wherever it travelled. Because of the inconvenience this caused it became the practice for judges to remain permanently in Westminster Hall to try Common Pleas[5] and the Magna Carta, c 17, provided that the common pleas should be held in a "certain place" which was fixed at Westminster.

The judges of the court were full-time lawyers appointed from the ranks of the serjeants-at-law, the senior advocates who had an exclusive right of audience in the court. The serjeants were the leaders of the legal profession and consequently the most highly paid. This fact, coupled with the excessive formality of pleading attendant upon the real actions[6] (over which the court had a monopoly), made proceedings in the Common Pleas dilatory and expensive.

The jurisdiction of the court existed over disputes between subjects where the King's interest was not involved. Hence it tried all the real actions and the personal actions of debt, convenant and *detinue*. It also tried actions of trespass where the title to land was involved. It must be remembered that only wealthy landowners could afford to litigate in the royal courts so that most civil actions in the early Middle Ages in fact involved disputes over title to land. Thus the Common Pleas in the early period of the

---

2   These were the earliest personal actions recognised by the common law. Debt was an action for a fixed sum of money in return for consideration already given. Covenant lay for breach of any obligation entered into under seal. For more detailed discussion, see the 6th edition of this work, pp 22–29.
3   See Baker, *Introduction to English Legal History* (Butterworths, 3rd Edn, 1990).
4   5 Vict, c 5.
5   As opposed to Pleas of the Crown, which were based upon breaches of the King's peace, and usually involved fine or forfeiture. In modern terms, these were essentially criminal in nature.
6   Actions relating to land.

development of the common law exercised a far wider jurisdiction than the Exchequer or the King's Bench.

The court was abolished in 1875 and its jurisdiction transferred to the High Court, being exercised by the Queen's Bench Division after 1880.

4   The Court of King's Bench

This was the last of the three central courts to break away from the Council. Consequently it had always remained closer to the King than the Exchequer and the Common Pleas. This is not to say that the King's Bench was not separate from the Curia Regis. Although they were closely associated there is ample evidence that the judges of the King's Bench acted independently of the King[7] by the reign of Edward I and attempts by James I to sit in the court were defeated by Coke. However, because of its association with the King, it acquired jurisdiction to issue the prerogative writs (now "orders")[8] of *mandamus*, *prohibition* and *certiorari*, restraining excesses and abuses of jurisdiction by inferior courts and public officials.[9] In addition the writ of *habeas corpus*, which it had power to issue, was later of great constitutional importance in curbing the personal exercise by the King of his prerogative powers. Its wide appellate jurisdiction may also be traced to the exercise of the royal duty to correct deficiencies in cases tried in other courts.

The judicial function was exercised by the judges of the court presided over by the Chief Justice of England, an office ranking above that of Chief Justice of the Common Pleas.[10] This function was both original and appellate and both civil and criminal.

The original jurisdiction of the King's Bench was exercised principally in civil matters, although the judges of the court exercised original criminal jurisdiction in courts of assize. The civil jurisdiction, which derived from the Pleas of the Crown and in particular from the writ of trespass, developed in about 1250.[11] This operated to confer upon the court jurisdiction over most actions in tort since nearly all torts are offshoots of trespass. It did not acquire jurisdiction over contract until some time later.[12] However it filched jurisdiction from the Common Pleas over writs of debt by various procedural means.[13] The King's Bench had jurisdiction over all cases[14] where the defendant was in the custody of the warden of the King's Bench prison. Consequently the Sheriff of Middlesex was directed by bill to arrest the defendant for a trespass *vi et armis* and take him into custody. Since the court had jurisdiction over trespass actions it was able to try the real cause of action ancillary to the fictitious trespass suit which was in fact dropped. Other fictional devices were adopted in order to secure and extend the jurisdiction of the court.[15] By the sixteenth century the issue of these fictions were dispensed with, but the result was that the very existence of the Court of Common Pleas was threatened. Further disagreements eventually resulted in that latter court

7   See Plucknett, *A Concise History of the Common Law* (5th Edn), p 151.
8   See p 143, *ante*.
9   This jurisdiction is now exercised by the divisional court of the Queen's Bench Division by way of "judicial review" proceedings; see p 147, *ante*.
10   Coke, for example, was promoted from the latter office to the former.
11   Trespass was the link from early forms of action and later writs which provided the historical basis for the modern law or contract and tort. For its origins, see Woodbine, "Origins of the Action of Trespass" 33 Yale LJ 799.
12   Until the late sixteenth century, upon the evolution of the writ of assumpsit.
13   For discussion, see 6th edition of this work, pp 89.
14   Excluding the real actions which remained in the exclusive jurisdiction of the Court of Common Pleas.
15   Principally the Bill of Middlesex procedure, whereby the court claimed jurisdiction where a person was taken into the custody of the Sheriff of Middlesex.

amending its procedures and jurisdiction so as to remove some of the difficulties that had prevented actions in debt being dealt with in the Court of Common Pleas.[16]

The appellate jurisdiction of the King's Bench existed in both civil and criminal cases. However the right of appeal was based on an error in procedure in the court below.[17]

5   The Courts of Exchequer Chamber

There were, at different periods of history, no less than four courts bearing the title "Exchequer Chamber". The jurisdiction of all of them was appellate.

(1) The oldest was established by statute in 1357 as a result of the refusal of the Exchequer to submit to the appellate jurisdiction of the King's Bench. The court was created to sit "in any council room nigh the exchequer" (hence the name Exchequer Chamber) and to consist of the Chancellor and the Treasurer with assistance from judges of the common law courts as assessors. Its jurisdiction was solely as a court of error from the Exchequer. Hence the business of the court was limited as it was also by the difficulty of getting the Chancellor and the Treasurer together, particularly when the latter office was vacant.

(2) There existed, even before 1357, a practice of judges reserving difficult points of law for consideration by a bench of judges drawn from all three common law courts and, later, the Chancery. These meetings were no doubt informal at first and the authority of the opinions delivered purely persuasive. They remained informal in the sense that no litigant had a right to require a judge to refer any point of law for consideration. However, the judgments were by the fifteenth century regarded as binding[18] and the informal meetings, by now usually held in the Exchequer Chamber, constituted the sitting of a court. Hence such a court was also termed a Court of Exchequer Chamber. Many of the leading cases of the common law were decided in this court before twelve judges and the court sat until the seventeenth century to determine civil cases and until the nineteenth century in criminal cases.

(3) A third Court of Exchequer Chamber was set up during the existence of the two already described by statute in 1585.[19] It was set up as a court of error from the King's Bench in cases of debt, detinue, covenant, account, action upon the case, ejectment or trespass commenced[20] in the King's Bench. It consisted of any six judges drawn from the Exchequer Barons and the justices of the Common Pleas. Thus there were at this time three courts of error; viz. the Court of Exchequer Chamber (1357) from the Court of Exchequer, the King's Bench from the Common Pleas and the Court of Exchequer Chamber (1585) from the King's Bench. In addition error still lay direct from the King's Bench to the House of Lords. This somewhat complex hierarchy prevailed until the creation of the last Court of Exchequer Chamber in 1830.

(4) The court created in 1830[1] was the court of error from all three common law courts and was composed of judges of the two courts other than the one in which the

---

16   For a fuller account of this struggle for jurisdiction between the King's Bench and the Common Pleas, see Baker, *op cit.*

17   31 Edw 3, St 1, c 12.

18   In 1483 the Chief Justice of the Common Pleas followed a decision of the Exchequer Chamber even though he thought it wrong (Y1 Ric 3, Michs, no 2).

19   31 Eliz 1, c 1.

20   This had the effect of confining it to proceedings commenced by bill since actions by writ were "commenced" in the Chancery.

1   11 Geo 4 & 1 Will 4, c 70.

trial at first instance took place. Appeal lay from the court to the House of Lords. The court existed until 1875 when its jurisdiction was transferred to the Court of Appeal.

6   Assizes

It was, during the Middle Ages, and indeed always has been, impossible to administer the criminal law on the basis of all trials taking place in London. Consequently, Norman and Plantagenet monarchs adopted the system, which appears to have existed even before the Conquest, of sending out royal justices throughout the kingdom to hold "assizes" (or sittings) of the royal courts. The jurisdiction of these assize courts, at first purely criminal, was later extended to civil proceedings.

The assize judges were generally the judges of the common law courts, but could also be serjeants-at-law or even prominent laymen. Consequently they exercised no jurisdiction by virtue of their office but only by reason of commissions issued by the sovereign. The commissions conferring criminal jurisdiction were the commission of Oyer and Terminer and the commission of Gaol Delivery. The first directed the persons named in the commission to hear and determine all offences in respect of which the accused had been "presented" by the grand jury of the county.[2] The second directed them to deliver from the gaols of the county, and to try, all persons there awaiting trial.[3]

So successful and popular was the assize system that Edward I organised the circuits on the modern basis with each circuit consisting of a group of counties visited regularly three or four times a year by royal judges. In addition the *Statute of Nisi Prius* 1285 extended the system to certain civil actions. The basic reason for this extension was the difficulty of transporting local juries to Westminster. Consequently in those personal actions, such as trespass, triable in the King's Bench and Common Pleas with a jury, the sheriff was directed to secure the attendance of a jury at Westminster "unless before" (*nisi prius*) that day the justices of assize should visit that county.

The system was extended in the fourteenth and fifteenth centuries to all types of civil action. It would, however, be incorrect to suppose that a trial at *nisi prius* was at this time a trial of the whole action. In fact only the issues of fact were tried at *nisi prius*. The pleading took place in banc (in Westminster) and the jury verdict was added to the record of the cause to be sent back to Westminster for judgment to be entered since the commissioner of assize had no power to enter judgment. Later, when the commissioners were always lawyers and advocates went on circuit, the whole trial took place at the assize so that the trial of actions might take place in London or at an assize.[4]

7   Justices of the peace

Originally the office of justice of the peace was an administrative rather than a judicial office but a judicial function was given to it in the fourteenth century as a direct result of the declining criminal jurisdiction of the local courts and the inability of the assizes to deal with the growing number of offenders.

---

2   See p 176, *post*.
3   These commissions were created by the Assizes of Clarendon 1166, and Northampton 1176 and continued to issue until their effective abolition under the provisions of the Courts Act 1971.
4   The assize system survived until 1st January 1972, the date on which the Courts Act 1971 came into operation; s 1(2) provides that "all courts of assize are hereby abolished, and Commissions, whether ordinary or special, to hold any court of assize shall not be issued."

The origin of the justices of the peace is to be found in a royal proclamation of 1195 creating the knights of the peace to assist the sheriff in enforcing the law. This function was of an administrative and police character rather than of a judicial character. With the decline of the office of sheriff in the fourteenth century the "keepers of the peace" (*custodes pacis*) as they were by now known,[5] were given a judicial function in addition to their administrative tasks. The former function has increased as the latter has diminished. In 1330 the holders of this new office had become so powerful locally that they were given statutory power to punish the sheriff, if he abused his powers of granting bail to prisoners.

As a result of the effects of the Black Death on the labour market, Statutes of Labourers were passed from 1351 in an attempt to regulate prices and wages and to reorganise labour generally. The enforcement of these statutes was placed in the hands of "justices of labourers" who were, in 1361, included in the same commissions as the keepers of the peace. It is from this date that the office of justices of the peace in its modern sense originates. The new justices of the peace were laymen and not usually legally qualified, a tradition which for the most part continues to exist.[6] Their criminal jurisdiction was at first exercised solely in the sessions which they were, by statute,[7] compelled to hold in each county four times a year. These were the "quarter sessions" and in 1590 the justices in quarter sessions were given jurisdiction over all criminal offences not excluding capital felonies. It was, indeed, not until the Quarter Sessions Act 1842 that the jurisdiction of quarter sessions was limited to exclude treason, murder and felonies punishable with life imprisonment.

Later, in Tudor times, a number of statutes conferred jurisdiction on justices to try offences out of sessions. From these statutes, the first of which was passed in 1496,[8] stems the summary jurisdiction of the justices of the peace in petty sessions. This summary jurisdiction, which is entirely statutory, is exercised without a jury and justices exercising this jurisdiction are now termed a "magistrates' court".[9]

As indicated earlier, the administrative jurisdiction of justices of the peace declined through the years as the criminal jurisdiction grew. Most of the administrative jurisdiction formerly exercised by justices is now in the hands of local authorities. However certain important functions remain. The common law power to issue warrants of arrest and summonses still exists. The important task of conducting preliminary investigations into indictable offences was conferred on justices of the peace by statutes of 1554 and 1555.[10]

8   The Star Chamber

The historical role of the Star Chamber should be noted, even though, strictly speaking it was not a common law court. It derived its jurisdiction from the King in the same way as the common law courts but it did not administer the common law and, more particularly, adopted a criminal and civil procedure repugnant to that obtaining in the common law courts. In addition, whereas the common law courts quite early in their existence became independent of the Council, the Star Chamber appears always to have retained the closest link with the Council. Hence it administered the royal

5   The nomenclature "justice of the peace" appears to date from about 1327, and to be an official title after 1361; Plucknett, *A Concise History of the Common Law* (5th Edn), p 168.
6   See p 182, *post*.
7   36 Edw 3, st 1, c 12.
8   11 Hen 7, c 3.
9   See p 182, *post*.
10   1 & 2 P & M, c 13 and 2 & 3 P & M, c 10.

prerogative rather than the common law although, by doing so, it added considerably to the scope of the criminal law.

Opinions differ as to the origins of the court. It seems to have originated from sittings of the Council in a chamber in Westminster known as the Star Chamber, possibly on account simply of its interior decor.[11] It consisted of members of the Council, the Chancellor, Treasurer and Privy Seal and common law judges, and had a miscellaneous civil jurisdiction over matters outside the common law such as mercantile and ecclesiastical disputes. It also assumed jurisdiction over matters within the scope of the common law courts and for this reason it fell into disfavour with common law judges. The growth of the Court of Chancery during the same period[12] effectively restricted the civil jurisdiction of the Star Chamber. It is the criminal jurisdiction of the Star Chamber which is of far greater interest and importance since it recognised and tried many new offences. Many of these were offences of a public nature such as riot, unlawful assembly, conspiracy, criminal libel, perjury, forgery and criminal attempts. All these crimes were created to fill gaps in the existing criminal law as administered in the assizes and quarter sessions.

Procedure in the Star Chamber differed radically from procedure in the common law courts. The civil procedure resembled more closely Chancery procedure than the dilatory formality of the common law. Criminal procedure was even more fundamentally different. Proceedings were commenced, not by presentment by the grand jury, but by information filed by the Attorney-General. An inquisitorial procedure followed whereby the defendant was examined on oath, sometimes under torture. Witnesses' evidence was frequently given by affidavit thus denying the accused any opportunity of cross-examination. Finally, there was no jury, guilt being determined by the members of the court. In a modern situation such a procedure would be unthinkable and condemned as a total denial of justice. Nevertheless, it was at that time justifiable in the light of the influence on juries which certain persons exercised, the bitterness of the state trials for treason (which took place before juries) and, following the Wars of the Roses, the anarchic situation throughout the realm which the existing criminal law and courts could not remedy. Even Coke, that most noted champion of the common law, described the court as "the most honourable Court" (our Parliament excepted) that is in the Christian world".[13] Nevertheless, in spite of its popularity in Tudor times, the accession of the Stuarts and, in particular, the Civil War resulted in the court becoming a symbol of prerogative power in the eyes of the Puritans and Parliamentarians and one of the first legislative acts of the Long Parliament was the abolition of the Star Chamber in 1641.

9 Court of Chancery

The development of principles of equity to supplement the common law, and remedy its weaknesses, has already been noted.[14] The Court of Chancery was the principal court of equity, and its most important jurisdiction was the recognition and enforcement of those principles, although it is a matter of debate whether the court developed to apply the Chancellor's jurisdiction to do equity, or, conversely, equity developed out of the jurisdiction of the Chancellor. What is clear is that the office of Chancellor and the principles of equity are, historically, inexorably linked. The nature and effectiveness

11 An alternative theory, that the court was created by a statute of 1487 (*pro camera stellata*), is now discounted.
12 See p 160, *post*.
13 4 Inst, p 65.
14 See p 5, *ante*.

of the court depended upon the characteristics of the particular Chancellor. The personal shortcomings of a Chancellor became ingrained in procedure in the court. Thus the court was brought into disrepute in the seventeenth century by the sale of offices in the court. All offices, including that of Master of the Rolls, were sold by the Chancellor.[15] Indeed so great was corruption in the court during this period that on the bursting of the South Sea Bubble in 1725 a deficiency of some £100,000 in court funds was discovered as a result of which Lord Macclesfield was impeached and fined.

A further defect in the Court of Chancery was the organisation of the court. There was an excess of court officials who attempted to extend the ambit of their duties so as to increase their revenue. Apart from the abuse which the sale of these clerkships created the proliferation of Chancery clerks naturally made litigation in the court extremely slow and expensive. The excess of court officers was equalled only by the paucity of judges. At first the Chancellor himself was the only judge. In practice he was unable to hear all cases himself and by the sixteenth century was accustomed to delegate his judicial function to the Masters in Chancery although judgment was delivered only by the Chancellor himself. However this did little to speed up the conduct of litigation since the parties had a right to apply to the Chancellor for a rehearing. Arrears of work were handed down through successive Chancellors. Matters reached a head in the nineteenth century with the elevation of Lord Eldon to the office of Chancellor. Lord Eldon (1807–1827) was a distinguished lawyer but unfortunately suffered from an excess of caution. He would not deliver any judgment or make any order without considering every available authority. There are records of judgments being reserved for months and even years. While this stabilised the court it also brought it into discredit with suitors and the backlog of cases pending became enormous. In 1813 Lord Eldon approved the appointment of a Vice-Chancellor as an additional judge of the Court but this brought little improvement since an appeal lay from his decisions to the Chancellor. Apart from this measure Lord Eldon stood fast against any reform and used the power of his office to thwart any attempt at reform of the judicial system. This obdurate conservatism contributed greatly to the welter of reform which in fact began shortly after his resignation from office in 1827. The Judicature Acts 1873–1875 finally abolished the Court of Chancery and its jurisdiction substantially transferred to the Chancery Division of the High Court.

In addition to it equitable jurisdiction the court, because of its close association with the Crown, acquired jurisdiction over other miscellaneous matters. For example the Crown, as *parens patriae*, had protective custody of all infants within the realm; this jurisdiction, which comprised such matters as the power to appoint guardians, was assigned to the Court of Chancery but is now exercised by the Family Division.[16] A similar concept existed in relation to persons of unsound mind; since they too were in need of protection the sovereign assumed responsibility for the care of lunatics and their property. This responsibility was, as with infants, delegated to the Chancellor and is today exercised, for the most part, by the Court of Protection, the judges of which are judges of the Chancery Division.[17]

Finally, note should be taken of the Court of Appeal in Chancery. This was established in 1851 to hear appeals from the Court of Chancery, but was abolished, along with that court, by the reforms in 1873–1875 made by the Judicature Acts.

15   The office of Master of the Rolls was apparently worth £6,000 in the eighteenth century. See *ex parte the Six Clerks* (1798) 3 Ves 589.
16   See p 175, *post*.
17   See p 172, *post*.

B   THE MODERN SYSTEM OF COURTS

The impact made by the Judicature Acts 1873–1875 has already been noted, sweeping away many of the courts described above. It is clear from this analysis, and the more general introduction in Chapter 1, that the jurisdiction of High Court judges stems originally from the royal prerogative. However, although the superior courts in England and Wales derive their jurisdiction, directly or indirectly, from the Crown, heavy regulation by statute now exists. In addition, many courts and tribunals of modern importance owe their origins not to the Crown, or to the historical development outlined above, but to statutory creation and intervention.

Courts can be classified in various ways. The two fundamental divisions of English courts are: (1) courts of record and courts not of record; and (2) superior and inferior courts. Before explaining further the significance of this classification it may be noted that there are other classifications, though these are not of universal application. Thus it is possible to classify courts according to their functions. The obvious classification in this respect would be into courts of civil jurisdiction and courts of criminal jurisdiction. This classification is not, however, a valid one since, although certain courts do exercise a purely civil or criminal jurisdiction, most English courts hear both civil and criminal cases. Thus the House of Lords, Court of Appeal High Court, Crown Court and magistrates' courts exercise jurisdiction in both civil and criminal matters. A second classification would be into courts of original and courts of appellate jurisdiction. Nor is this division of general application. Although certain courts, such as the Court of Appeal and the House of Lords, exercise a purely appellate jurisdiction, while other courts, such as magistrates' courts, have no appellate jurisdiction, many courts, notably the High Court and the Crown Court, exercise both original and appellate jurisdiction. Indeed, one court (the Queens Bench Divisional Court) is neither a court of first instance nor a court of appeal. Its unique function is as a court of review[18] (principally on judicial review)[19], although it does have appellate functions.[20]

The Court of Justice of the European Communities (the European Court of Justice) is, of course, *sui generis* since, although not an English court, it exercises jurisdiction within the English legal system. Its position within the system has already been seen,[1] but it should be noted here that it is not a court of appeal.

It may sometimes be a matter of dispute whether a particular tribunal is properly described as a "court" or not. This is not central to the question of whether the supervisory jurisdiction of the High Court extends to the body in question, since that jurisdiction is not limited to courts properly so called.[2] Nor does the fact that a body is a "court" determine whether a body must act judicially: many tribunals have powers to decide matters, and will be under a duty to act judicially.[3] The description is, however, important in the context of contempt of court[4] since the offence of contempt of court is, by definition, capable of commission only in relation to a "court". In *A-G v British Broadcasting Corporation*[5] the House of Lords (reversing the decision of the Court of Appeal) held that a valuation court constituted under section 88 of the General Rate Act 1967 was not "an inferior court", for the purposes of RSC Ord 52, r 1(2) since, although it was termed a court, its functions were essentially administrative and it was

18   *R v Leeds County Court, ex p. Morris* [1990] 1 QB 523; [1990] 1 All ER 550.
19   See p 142, *ante*.
20   See p 582, *post*.
1   See p 100, *ante*.
2   See p 146, *ante*.
3   See p 197, *post*.
4   See p 224, *ante*.
5   [1981] AC 303; [1980] 3 All ER 161.

not a court of law established to exercise the judicial power of the state. The House was, however, divided on the question of whether it was a court at all (*viz.*for any purpose other than contempt proceedings). This is no doubt of academic interest but it appears to be of no other practical significance whether a tribunal is properly describable as a "court" or not.

1 Superior and inferior courts

A traditional classification of English courts is their division into superior and inferior courts. The nature of superior courts is that their jurisdiction is limited neither by the value of the subject matter of an action nor geographically. The jurisdiction of inferior courts is limited both geographically and according to the value of the subject matter of the dispute.[6] The superior courts are the House of Lords, Court of Appeal, High Court, Crown Court, Judicial Committee of the Privy Council, Restrictive Practices Court and the Employment Appeal Tribunal. One of the distinctive features of inferior courts is that they are amenable to the supervisory jurisdiction of the High Court exercised by prerogative order,[7] though this applies also to the Crown Court in the exercise of its appellate jurisdiction even though the Crown Court is, as stated above, a superior court.[8] The most important of the inferior courts are county courts and magistrates' courts although all courts not listed above as superior are inferior courts. The distinction is also of importance in relation to contempt of court, because the penalties which may be imposed by inferior courts are far less than superior courts have power to inflict.[9]

2 Courts of record

An ancient division of courts is into courts of record and courts which are not courts of record. The basic historical distinction depended upon whether or not the court in question maintained a record of its proceedings. The records of courts of record are preserved in the Public Record Office. Courts of record may be inferior or superior. The essential characteristic of a court of record is no longer that it maintains a record; it is that it has power to punish for contempt. Consequently any court which has jurisdiction to punish contempt is a court of record. The powers of superior and inferior courts of record, and of magistrates' courts, to commit for contempt are now set out in the Contempt of Court Act 1981.[10] In addition the High Court has a common law jurisdiction to punish contempts committed before courts which are not courts of record.[11]

---

6   Whether a court is an inferior or a superior court can usually be ascertained by reference to the historical origins of the court or, if it was created by statute, by the terms of the statute creating it. However where the statute is silent it is necessary to look at the nature and powers of the court so as to decide whether they are analogous to those of a superior or an inferior court; see *R v Cripps, ex parte Muldoon* [1984] QB 68; [1983] 3 All ER 72 in which the Queen's Bench divisional court held an election court (under the Representation of the People Act) to be an inferior court.
7   See p 146, *ante*.
8   See p 161, *ante*. The Crown Court is only open to the supervisory jurisdiction of the Divisional Court where jurisdiction is expressly granted by Supreme Court Act 1981, s 28 and s 29 (1). Matters relating to "trial on indictment" are not within that jurisdiction: See p 146, *ante*.
9   See p 227, *post*.
10   See p 227, *post*.
11   *R v Davies* [1906] 1 KB 32; see p 227, *post*.

3 The principle of open justice

Before considering individually the constitution and jurisdiction of English courts attention may be drawn to the general principle of "open justice". One aspect of this is that courts should sit in public. Ever since the abolition of the Court of Star Chamber in 1641 English judges have rebelled against the notion of private sittings of courts. In the famous words of Lord Hewart CJ in *R v Sussex Justices, ex parte McCarthy*[12]

" a long line of cases shows that it is not merely of some importance but is of fundamental importance that justice should not only be done, but should manifestly and undoubtedly be seen to be done."

The principle, and the circumstances which would justify departure from it, were set out by the House of Lords in *Scott v Scott*[13] and, more recently, cogently explained by Lord Diplock in *A-G v Leveller Magazine Ltd*[14] as follows:

"As a general rule the English system of administering justice does require that it be done in public: *Scott v Scott*. If the way the courts behave cannot be hidden from the public ear and eye this provides a safeguard against judicial arbitrariness or idiosyncrasy and maintains the public confidence in the administration of justice."

From this it follows that proceedings should be held in open court wherever possible. Reports of proceedings should be permissible, provided they are fair and accurate, again wherever possible. These two principles should only be departed from where it is necessary to do so to protect the administration of justice itself, or where Parliament has specifically created an exception.

Several examples exist where Parliament has granted a power to sit in camera. These include wardship proceedings, proceedings involving a secret process, cases involving evidence of sexual capacity in suits for annulment of marriage, certain proceedings for injunctions,[15] youth court proceedings[16] and proceedings under the Official Secrets Acts.[17] A court may also sit in camera where the presence of the public would render the administration of justice impracticable. In deciding this question the court must take into account the effect of publicity on the parties only in so far as that affects the administration of justice. In *R v Malvern Justices, ex parte Evans*[18] magistrates sat *in camera* in order to hear a plea in mitigation in respect of a driving offence. The mental health of the defendant was such that, if the court had not sat *in camera*, the defendant would have been inhibited in making her plea in mitigation. Whilst an appeal against

---

12 [1924] 1 KB 256, at 259; see also *R v Denbigh Justices, ex parte Williams* [1974] QB 759; [1974] 2 All ER 1052; Supreme Court Act 1981, s 67.
13 [1913] AC 417.
14 [1979] AC 440; [1979] 1 All ER 745.
15 See *Practice Direction (Matrimonial Causes; Injunction)* [1974] 2 All ER 1119; [1974] 1 WLR 936; see also p 357, *post* as to hearing applications for *Anton Piller* orders.
16 Though bona fide representatives of the press may not be excluded: Children and Young Persons Act 1933, s 37. Any court may also prohibit the publication of the name of any child involved in legal proceedings: s 39. For the relevant principles, see *R v Leicester Crown Court, ex parte S* [1992] 2 All ER 659; *R v Leicester City Justices, ex parte Barrow* [1991] 2 QB 260; [1991] 3 All ER 935; cf *R v Lee* [1993] 2 All ER 170.
17 Official Secrets Act 1920, s 8.
18 [1988] QB 540; [1988] 1 All ER 371. See also *R v Evesham Justices, ex parte McDonagh* [1988] QB 553; [1988] 1 All ER 371, where a magistrates' court was held not entitled to prohibit publication of the defendant's address to save him possible harassment from his ex-wife.

the making of that order to sit *in camera* was dismissed, the divisional court observed that the occasions when it would be appropriate to make such an order would be rare, and in fact doubted whether on the facts of this particular case the magistrates had been correct to make the order they did. In this context, note should be taken of the terms of Article 6 of the European Convention on Human Rights.[19] This creates a right to a "fair and public hearing", but the exception to that right, which permits exclusion of the public:

" in the interests of morals, public order or national security in a democratic society, where the interests of juveniles or the protection of the private life of the parties so require, or … where publicity would prejudice the interests of justice …"

goes further than English law currently permits. It remains doubtful whether the passage of the Human Rights Bill[20] will broaden the scope for exclusions under English law.

The second aspect of the principle of open justice is that all the evidence should be communicated publicly and the third is that nothing should be done to discourage or prevent publication of fair and accurate reports of judicial proceedings. However, just as there are limitations on the principle that proceedings should be conducted in public, so are there circumstances which may justify a court restricting publicity of evidence, either within or outside the courtroom. To quote a common example, victims of blackmail are usually permitted to communicate their names and addresses in court by writing them down and to be referred to throughout the proceedings as "Mr X" or some such title. There are provisions in the Sexual Offences (Amendment) Act 1976 for preserving the anonymity of complainants in rape and similar offences.[1] However, anonymity of parties to proceedings will not generally be granted.

The general position was discussed by the Court of Appeal in *R v Legal Aid Board, ex parte Kaim Todner*[2] where a firm of solicitors from whom a franchise had been withdrawn[3] sought anonymity in judicial review proceedings brought by them against the Legal Aid Board. In rejecting any special rule relating to the legal profession, Lord Woolf MR stressed that exceptions to the general rule in *Scott v Scott* could only be justified if necessary in the interests of justice. That was a matter for the court, but could not be determined by agreement of parties in the case. As had been noted in *ex parte P*,[4] "When both sides agreed that information should be kept from the public that was when the court had to be the most vigilant." Public scrutiny was necessary in order to deter inappropriate behaviour by the courts, and to maintain confidence in the administration of justice. In addition, members of the public could not come forward with relevant evidence if they were unaware of the relevance of it to proceedings. A court might have regard not only to the nature of the proceedings and the length of restriction requested, but also to the nature of the person for whom anonymity was sought: it is not unreasonable for a party who initiates proceedings to be regarded as having accepted the normal incidence of public proceedings. By contrast a witness

19   See p 125, *ante*.
20   See p 132, *ante*.
1   Sexual Offences (Amendment) Act 1976, s 46, as amended by Criminal Justice Act 1988 and Sexual Offences (Amendment) Act 1992; after a person has been "accused" (as to which, see s 4(6)) of a rape offence it is an offence to publish in a written publication or broadcast any matter likely to lead members of the public to identify a woman as the complainant; in each case a judge of the Crown Court has power, on application, to remove these restrictions in certain circumstances.
2   [1998] 3 All ER 541.
3   For franchise arrangements, see *post*.
4   (1998) Times, 31 March.

who has no interest in proceedings may have a stronger claim if he or she would be prejudiced by publicity, but nevertheless does not attract automatic anonymity: both parties and witnesses have to accept that embarrassment and damage to reputation may flow from litigation, the safeguard being the court itself, which can in its judgments refute unwarranted allegations.

This area of the law was also considered by the House of Lords in *A-G v Leveller Magazine Ltd*.[5] The House accepted that, in exercising its control over the proceedings before it, a court was entitled to derogate from the principle of open justice by sitting in private or permitting a witness not to disclose his name when giving evidence if it was necessary to do so in the interests of the due administration of justice. On the particular facts, the absence of a clear order restricting publication, and the fact that the identity of the witness in question was readily ascertainable from other evidence which was freely reportable, led to convictions for contempt of court being quashed.

Any such order will now be made pursuant to section 11 of the Contempt of Court Act 1981, unless restrictions are permissible at common law.[6] This empowers the court to give such directions "as appear to the court to be necessary" for giving effect to any order which it makes. It should be noted, however, that this section does not create a power to order a name or other matter to be withheld; it simply regulates the exercise of such power as the court may inherently possess. An appeal against the making of such an order exists.[7] A section 11 order should only be made where the administration of justice justifies such a restriction. Personal embarrassment is not sufficient.[8]

A third element relates to the postponement of the reporting of proceedings. Section 4(2) of the 1981 Act departs from the normal rule that fair and accurate reporting of legal proceedings, published contemporaneously with the case, is permissible. By section 4(2) a court may order the postponement of reporting where that is necessary in the interests of justice. If, however, these can be met in less restrictive ways, then they should be so met.[9] The court has to balance the risk of substantial prejudice to the proceedings, against whether reporting restrictions are necessary and proportionate.[10]

C THE EUROPEAN COURT OF JUSTICE AND EUROPEAN COURT OF HUMAN RIGHTS

These courts play an important role in the English legal system. Their nature, functions and powers have already been discussed.[11]

---

5   See n 14, *ante*; *R v Socialist Worker Printer and Publishers Ltd, ex parte A-G* [1975] QB 637; [1975] 1 All ER 142.

6   See *A-G v Socialist Worker, supra*; *Re M (Wardship. Freedom of Publication)* [1990] 2 FLR 36.

7   Criminal Justice Act 1988, s 159; *Re Crook* [1992] 2 All ER 687. The principles governing the making of such orders were set out in *Practice Direction (Contempt: Reporting Restrictions)* [1982] 1 WLR 1475.

8   See, eg, *R v Malvern JJ, ex parte Evans, supra*; *R v Dover JJ, ex parte Dover DC* (1992) 156 JP 433 (embarrassing publicity to a restaurant); *H v Ministry of Defence* [1991] 2 QB 103; [1991] 2 All ER 834 (protection from publication of medical evidence of an embarrassing nature permitted); cf. *R v Westminster City Council, ex p Castelli* [1996] FCR 49; [1996] 1 FLR 534.

9   In *Re Central Independent Television* [1991] 1 All ER 347 an order prohibiting radio or television reporting whilst a jury was staying overnight at a hotel was held excessive.

10   *R v Beck, ex parte Daily Telegraph plc* [1993] 2 All ER 177; *Ex parte Telegraph plc* [1993] 2 All ER 971; [1993] 1 WLR 980; *MGN v Bank of America* [1995] 2 All ER 355.

11   See pp 115–121, 123–124, *ante*.

D THE HOUSE OF LORDS

1 Constitution and procedure

Parliament is the oldest court of the common law although it is not usual nowadays to refer to it as a court. Nevertheless reference is still made to the High Court of Parliament as a judicial body. Leaving aside the jurisdiction of each House to regulate its own procedure, the judicial function of Parliament is now exercised by the House of Lords.

In theory, though not in fact, an appeal to the House of Lords is an appeal to the whole House, not merely to those members who are in fact sitting to hear the appeal. Until the nineteenth century this was literally true in that any member of the House could and did vote in judicial sessions. Not unnaturally decisions of the House of Lords at that time enjoyed no very great authority, particularly since those peers who were lawyers and took the most prominent part in the exercise of the House's jurisdiction were by no means the senior and most respected judges of their day, a remark which also applies to certain Lord Chancellors of the nineteenth century. As a matter of practice puisne judges were frequently invited to advise their Lordships on the law. Indeed this is still possible though it does not appear to have been done since 1898.[12] However it was not until the Appellate Jurisdiction Act 1876 provided for the creation of salaried life peers to hear appeals that the convention against lay peers participating in judicial sittings of the House was firmly established.[13]

This Act provided that at the hearing of an appeal there should be present at least three of the following: the Lord Chancellor, the Lords of Appeal in Ordinary ("law lords") and such peers "who hold or have held high judicial office" as defined in the Act. In practice most appeals are heard solely by the Lords of Appeal in Ordinary. These are the senior members of the judiciary. They have the same rights as other peers but in practice they sit on the cross benches and take no part in political sittings of the House unless the matter concerns the administration of justice. By custom, one or two of the law lords are Scots and the Scottish members generally sit when the House is hearing appeals from the Court of Session, which is the Scottish equivalent of the Court of Appeal. The number of law lords, originally fixed at two, is now not less than seven or more than twelve.[14]

Argument in appeals no longer takes place, as it used to do, in the chamber of the House. The appeal is argued in one of the committee rooms, their lordships sitting unrobed. The opinions of their lordships are not usually read in the chamber[15] although they retire to the chamber to state whether they would allow or dismiss the appeal. These opinions are not strictly "judgments" but speeches in support of the members' votes on the motion made by the Lord Chancellor or senior lord. Where the House is equally divided the appeal is dismissed. Equal division does not in practice occur because an uneven number of members invariably sit. Nevertheless the situation has arisen on a few occasions and arose in the case of *Kennedy v Spratt*.[16] In that case the appeal would have been dismissed by a majority of three to two but for the fact that one of the majority, Lord Upjohn, died between the hearing of the appeal and the delivery of judgment having, however, recorded his opinion before his death. In the

---

12 *Allen v Flood* [1898] AC 1.
13 An earlier attempt to create life peers by prerogative had been rejected by the House: *Wensleydale Peerage case* (1856) 5 HL Cas 958.
14 Appellate Jurisdiction Act 1947; Administration of Justice Act 1968, s 1(1)(a); this number may be increased by Order in Council (*ibid*, s 1(2)). See, now, Maximum Number of Judges Order 1994, SI 1994/3217.
15 See *Practice Direction* [1963] 1 WLR 1382.
16 [1972] AC 83; [1971] 1 All ER 805.

result, the votes being equal, the appeal was dismissed in any event.[17] The House of Lords has no power to pass judgment. It may remit the case to the Court of Appeal or the trial judge with its recommendations which must then be translated by that court into a judgment. In a criminal case the House may exercise any powers of the court below, or may remit the case back to that court.[18]

2   Jurisdiction

a   Original jurisdiction

The House of Lords has very little original jurisdiction. The right of a peer to be "tried by his peers", which was thought to have been created by Magna Carta, was finally abolished by the Criminal Justice Act 1948 and now all persons, whether peer or commoner, are subject to the ordinary jurisdiction of the English criminal courts.

Impeachment is a procedure whereby persons may be prosecuted by the House of Commons before the House of Lords. It has always been confined to the prosecution of political offenders. Although impeachment has not been abolished it is in practice obsolete and the jurisdiction has not been exercised since the impeachments of Warren Hastings and Viscount Melville in 1795 and 1805 respectively.

The Committee of Privileges, which is by convention composed of lawyers in the House, makes recommendations to the whole House arising out of the Committee trying, at the instance of the sovereign, a disputed claim to a peerage.[19]

Finally both the House of Lords and the House of Commons have jurisdiction over breaches of privilege, which include contempt of the House in question and wrongs committed within the precincts of each House. Either House may imprison the offender, who has no right of appeal and may not move for habeas corpus.

b   Appellate jurisdiction

The jurisdiction of the House of Lords is almost entirely appellate. In civil cases it hears appeals from the Court of Appeal but only with leave of either the Court of Appeal or the Appeals Committee of the House itself.[20] The ground of appeal does not have to be a point of law as it does in criminal cases but most cases which reach the House of Lords do in fact involve a point of law of public importance, in nine out of ten cases being concerned with the correct construction of Acts of Parliament.[21] The Administration of Justice Act 1969 introduced a "leap-frog" procedure whereby there can be an appeal direct from the trial court to the House of Lords without the need for a prior appeal to the Court of Appeal. Such an appeal lies subject to two conditions;

---

17   See *Kennedy v Spratt (Background Note)* [1972] AC 83. Had Lord Upjohn's written opinion indicated that he was in favour of allowing the appeal an anomalous situation would have arisen whereby his death would, in effect, have deprived the appellant of success. In such an event the members of the House would surely have changed their votes so that the appeal would be allowed or, possibly, taken no vote and had the appeal reheard by a differently constituted committee.

18   Administration of Justice Act 1960, s 1(4); Criminal Appeal Act 1968, s 35(3).

19   The Committee sat, in 1976, to hear the celebrated *Ampthill Peerage* case [1977] AC 547; [1976] 2 All ER 411, when it consisted of nine peers, four of whom were law lords and delivered speeches, and again in 1985: *Annandale and Hartfell Peerage Claim* [1986] AC 319; [1985] 3 All ER 577 when, again, only the law lords delivered speeches.

20   Administration of Justice (Appeals) Act 1934. The House also hears appeals from the equivalent civil courts of Scotland (Court of Session) and Northern Ireland (Court of Appeal).

21   See observations of Lord Hailsham to this effect in *Johnson v Moreton* [1980] AC 37, at 53; [1978] 3 All ER 37, at 44.

first the trial judge must grant a certificate,[22] which he may do only if all parties consent and the case involves a point of law of general public importance which either relates wholly or mainly to the construction of an enactment or is one in respect of which the judge was bound by a previous decision of the Court of Appeal or House of Lords; secondly the House of Lords must grant leave.[1]

The appeal to the House of Lords in criminal cases is of modern origin. Although a writ of error was available before this century, there was no general right of appeal until the Criminal Appeal Act 1907, which provided for an appeal from the Court of Criminal Appeal[2] established by the Act. The right of appeal from the divisional court of the Queen's Bench Division was created by the Administration of Justice Act 1960 and the conditions for appealing to the House of Lords in a criminal matter are now contained in that Act. These conditions are discussed fully later in this book.[3] Appeal lies, subject to similar conditions, from the High Court and Court of Appeal of Northern Ireland and from the Courts-Martial Appeal Court.

E   THE COURT OF APPEAL

The Supreme Court of Judicature was the product of the complete reorganisation of the English superior courts effected by the Supreme Court of Judicature Acts 1873–1875. These Acts are now consolidated in the Supreme Court Act 1981. The Acts created the Supreme Court of Judicature to which was transferred the original and appellate jurisdiction of the then existing superior courts of first instance and appeal. The Supreme Court now consists of the Court of Appeal, the High Court and the Crown Court. The appellate jurisdiction of the superior courts of law and equity was transferred to the Court of Appeal, while the original jurisdiction was, broadly speaking, transferred to the High Court, the Crown Court having been added by the Courts Act 1971.[4]

I   Constitution

The Court of Appeal (which is split into the civil and criminal divisions) is composed of the Lord Chancellor, the Lord Chief Justice, the Master of the Rolls, the President of the Family Division of the High Court, the Vice-Chancellor,[5] former Lord Chancellors, the Lords of Appeal in Ordinary[6] (all the above being ex officio judges) and the Lords Justices of Appeal. Ordinarily, of the ex officio judges only the Master of the Rolls (in civil cases) and the Lord Chief Justice (in criminal cases) sit in the court. They are, in fact, the presidents of the civil and criminal divisions respectively. The Master of the Rolls was a first instance judge in the Court of Chancery, and, indeed,

---

22   Act of 1969, s 12(1); there is no appeal against the grant or refusal of a certificate (s 12(5)).
1   *Ibid*, s 13. The grant of leave precludes appeal to the Court of Appeal.
2   The jurisdiction of this court was transferred to the criminal division of the Court of Appeal by the Criminal Appeal Act 1966.
3   See p 585, *post*.
4   See p 176, *post*.
5   The Vice-Chancellor became a judge of the Court of Appeal upon the implementation of the Supreme Court Act 1981.
6   The court has sometimes been composed of three law lords; see, for examples, *Mallett v Restormel Borough Council* [1978] 2 All ER 1057; *Re Amirteymour* [1978] 3 All ER 637; [1979] 1 WLR 63. Furthermore, in November 1979, the criminal division of the court sat at the law courts in Cardiff, the first time the court had sat outside London.

in the Chancery Division of the High Court until 1881. In modern times some of the greatest lawyers of their day have held the office of Master of the Rolls.

In addition to the regular judges of the court the Lord Chancellor may require any High Court judge, and may request any former judge of the High Court or of the Court of Appeal, to sit in the civil division and the Lord Chief Justice may require (or request as the case may be) any such judge or former judge to sit in the criminal division;[7] indeed, the criminal division often contains a Queen's Bench Division judge and, in practice, the first court of the criminal division usually consists of the Lord Chief Justice, a Lord Justice of Appeal and one puisne judge while a second court comprises one Lord Justice of Appeal and two puisnes.

By section 3(5) of the Supreme Court Act 1981 any number of courts of either division of the Court of Appeal may sit at the same time. In the civil division the court is duly constituted if it consists of an uneven number of judges not less than three.[8] In certain circumstances (eg if the parties agree) the court may sit with only two judges.[9] The criminal division is duly constituted with either two or an uneven number of justices not less than three, save that only a court of three or more can:

(a) determine an appeal against conviction or a verdict of not guilty by reason of insanity or a finding of unfitness to plead, an application for leave to appeal to the House of Lords; or

(b) refuse an application for leave to appeal against conviction (or any such verdict or finding referred to above) other than an application which has been refused by a single judge.[10]

In addition a single judge of the criminal division (who may be, and usually is, a High Court judge but who might be a circuit judge sitting as a High Court judge)[11] has certain jurisdiction under the Criminal Appeal Act 1968, s 31 (as amended), notably to hear applications for leave to appeal. Occasionally a "full court" of five or more members is convened to hear appeals involving novel or difficult points of law in both the civil and criminal divisions, although such a court has no wider powers than the normal court.

2 Jurisdiction

Since 1 October 1966, the date upon which the Criminal Appeal Act 1966 came into operation, the Court of Appeal has consisted of a civil and a criminal division.

a *Civil division*

The civil division exercises:

(a) all jurisdiction conferred on it by the Supreme Court Act 1981 or any other Act; and

---

7   Supreme Court Act 1981, s 9.
8   *Ibid*, s 54 (2); Court of Appeal (Civil Division) Order 1982; see p 443, *post* for details of procedure on appeals.
9   See 1981 Act s 54(4).
10   Supreme Court Act 1981, s 55; for details of procedure on appeal to the criminal division, see p 557, *post*.
11   1981 Act, s 54(2)

(b) all jurisdiction exercisable by it prior to the commencement of the 1981 Act.[12]

It is sufficient to note at this stage that the civil division has no criminal jurisdiction and hardly any original jurisdiction. Its jurisdiction is entirely civil and almost entirely appellate. It hears appeals from the High Court, county courts, the Restrictive Practices Court, the Employment Appeal Tribunal and various tribunals, notably the Lands Tribunal. Appeal is by way of rehearing, except in the case of certain appeals from tribunals where it is by "case stated".[13]

b   Criminal division

The criminal division of the Court of Appeal is the successor of the Court of Criminal Appeal, the jurisdiction of the latter being transferred to the former by section 1(1) of the Criminal Appeal Act 1966.

The Court of Criminal Appeal emerged as a result of the deficient system of criminal appeals that existed prior to 1907. The court was created by the Criminal Appeal Act 1907 and superseded the Court for Crown Cases Reserved and the right of appeal by writ of error to the Queen's Bench Division.

The criminal division of the Court of Appeal has no civil jurisdiction and no original jurisdiction, its jurisdiction being solely appellate. The jurisdiction of the criminal division in criminal cases is set out fully later.[14] Briefly, it hears appeals by persons convicted and, in certain cases, considers points of law referred to the court by the Attorney-General following acquittal,[15] following trial in the Crown Court, as well as references made to it by the Attorney-General where a sentence imposed is considered to be unduly lenient.[16] It also hears appeals against sentence from the Crown Court. Up until the passage of the Criminal Appeal Act 1995,[17] the Home Secretary could refer a case to the division, under section 17 of the Criminal Appeal Act 1968, for assistance on any point or for determination as an appeal. This power has now been replaced by the power vested in the new Criminal Cases Review Commission by section 9 of the 1995 Act.[18]

F   THE HIGH COURT OF JUSTICE

The High Court was established by the Judicature Acts and to it was transferred the jurisdiction of the three superior common law courts of first instance, the Court of Chancery, the Courts of Admiralty, Probate, Divorce and Matrimonial Causes and other superior courts of civil and criminal jurisdiction (except the Chancery Courts of the Counties Palatine of Lancaster and Durham)[19]. Its constitution and jurisdiction are now contained in the Supreme Court Act 1981. Prior to 1971 the High Court sat in the Royal Courts of Justice in the Strand, London, though High Court judges constituted a court of the High Court for all purposes when they tried cases on assize. Nevertheless their jurisdiction on assize derived not from their office but from the Commissions under

12   *Ibid*, s 15(2).
13   Rules of the Supreme Court (Revision) 1965, Ord 61.
14   See p 548, *post*.
15   See p 551, *post*.
16   See p 549, *post*.
17   Criminal Appeal Act 1995, s 3.
18   See pp 550–551, *post*.
19   These courts, which were superior courts, continued to exercise a Chancery jurisdiction equivalent to that of the High Court in the County Palatine of Lancaster and the County Borough of Teesside until their abolition by the Courts Act 1971, s 41 which merged them with the High Court.

which they sat. The Courts Act 1971 abolished all courts of assize but section 71 of the Supreme Court Act now provides that sittings of the High Court may be conducted at any place in England or Wales;[20] the centres at which sittings of the High Court are, in fact, held are determined in accordance with directions of the Lord Chancellor. Although there are standing directions, it is always open to the Lord Chancellor to give an ad hoc direction to enable a particular sitting to take place at a particular place if there is sufficient reason for it. Thus in *St Edmundsbury and Ipswich Diocesan Board of Finance v Clark*[1] a case concerning a claim to a right of way over a disputed strip of land at Iken, a small village in Suffolk, a direction was given on behalf of the Lord Chancellor, at the request of the trial judge, Megarry J, authorising the court to sit at Iken.

The jurisdiction of the High Court is both civil and criminal and both original and appellate. It has virtually unlimited jurisdiction in civil actions, though this is not generally an exclusive jurisdiction. Most actions are brought in the county courts.

The High Court, when created, consisted of five divisions, but these were reduced in 1880 to the three which now exist[2] (save that the Probate, Divorce and Admiralty Division was re-named the Family Division)[3]. Although all three divisions have equal competence each division, in fact, exercises a separate jurisdiction. This is not dictated by convenience but by the Rules of the Supreme Court which govern procedure and practice throughout the Supreme Court (except in the Crown Court where there are separate rules, the Crown Court Rules).[4] These Rules specify the manner in which an action or matter may be commenced and prosecuted in the High Court. Consequently certain types of action are confined to a particular division. Thus matrimonial causes in the High Court may only be heard in the Family Division and not in either of the two other divisions. In certain cases the jurisdiction of the divisions overlaps and it is possible to start certain proceedings in one or other of them. For example, two modern cases concerning similar conditions in similar contracts were tried within a short space of time. The first[5] was tried in the Chancery Division, the second[6] in the Queen's Bench Division. It is important to bear in mind that the divisions of the High Court are not different courts, so that the jurisdiction of any one High Court judge is exercisable by any other High Court judge, irrespective of the division to which he is assigned.[7] Furthermore the fact that a cause or matter falls within a class of business assigned to

---

20   Although evidence, including a view by the judge, may be taken outside the jurisdiction; cf *Tito v Waddell* [1975] 3 All ER 997, [1975] 1 WLR 1303.

1   [1973] Ch 323; [1973] 2 All ER 1155.

2   Under s 7 of the Supreme Court Act 1981, Her Majesty may by Order in Council, on a recommendation of the Lord Chancellor, the Lord Chief Justice, the Master of the Rolls, the President of the Family Division and the Vice-Chancellor, increase or reduce the number of divisions.

3   Administration of Justice Act 1970, s 1. The same section also effected redistribution of business between the divisions as a consequence of the main purpose of the change which was to create a division which deals solely with family and domestic matters. Thus the Admiralty jurisdiction of the High Court was assigned to the Queen's Bench Division to be exercised by the new "Admiralty Court" created by s 2 of the Act, while contentious probate business was assigned to the Chancery Division, thereby eradicating the unsatisfactory duality of jurisdiction which had hitherto existed, whereby disputes concerning the validity of wills were heard in the Probate, Divorce and Admiralty Division, while questions of the construction of wills were determined in the Chancery Division.

4   See p 180, *post*; though the inherent jurisdiction of the High Court is exercisable by a judge of any Division; see *Re L* [1968] P 119; [1968] 1 All ER 20.

5   *Petrofina (Great Britain) Ltd v Martin* [1965] Ch 1073; [1965] 2 All ER 176.

6   *Esso Petroleum Co Ltd v Harper's Garage (Stourport) Ltd* [1966] 2 QB 514; [1965] 2 All ER 933. See *Re Hastings (No 3)* [1959] Ch 368; [1959] 1 All ER 698; *Re Kray* [1965] Ch 736; [1965] 1 All ER 710; *Re L* [1968] P 119; [1968] 1 All ER 20.

7   1981 Act, s 61 (5).

a particular Division does not mean that it is obligatory for that matter to be allocated to that Division.[8]

Nevertheless, as a matter of practice, the effect of statutes and rules of procedure is usually to confer upon each division jurisdiction which is independent of that exercised by the other two divisions.[9]

The jurisdiction of the High Court is both original and supervisory. The historic role of courts in supervising the actions of inferior bodies and tribunals has already been noted.[10] This function is now mainly performed by a divisional court of the Queen's Bench Division, which also has certain appellate functions. Likewise, divisional courts of the Family Division have appellate functions. These are dealt with below.[11]

a   Chancery Division

The Chancery Division consists of the Lord Chancellor, who, although nominal head of the division, never sits at first instance, a Vice-Chancellor and such of the puisne judges as the Lord Chancellor may nominate.[12] Before 1972, sittings of the Chancery Division were held only in the Royal Courts of Justice and Chancery judges did not go on assize (though a concurrent Chancery jurisdiction was exercised by the now defunct Chancery Courts of the Counties Palatine of Lancaster and Durham). Although the Supreme Court Act 1981 authorises sittings of the High Court to be held at any place in England and Wales, in practice most Chancery business continues to be taken in London, members of the Chancery bench and bar not being noticeably peripatetic.[13] However the Vice-Chancellor of the County Palatine of Lancaster (who is now a circuit judge[14]) sits as a judge of the High Court[15] at Liverpool Manchester and Preston and, time permitting, at Leeds and Newcastle-upon-Tyne for the hearing of proceedings assigned to the Chancery Division.

Original jurisdiction. Section 34 of the Judicature Act 1873 assigned to the Chancery Division jurisdiction over matters which were heard in the Court of Chancery prior to the abolition of that court in 1875. The distribution of High Court business between the divisions is now governed by section 61 of and Schedule 1 to the Supreme Court Act 1981. Under that Schedule are assigned to the Chancery Division all causes and matters relating to:

(a) the sale, exchange or partition of land, or the raising of charges on land;
(b) the redemption or foreclosure of mortgages;
(c) the execution of trusts;
(d) the administration of estates of deceased persons;
(e) bankruptcy;
(f) the dissolution of partnerships or the taking of partnership or other accounts;
(g) the rectification, setting aside or cancellation of deeds or other instruments in writing;

8   Ibid, s 61.
9   For the distribution of business between the divisions, see Supreme Court Act 1981, s 61 and Sch 1.
10   See p 146, *ante*.
11   See p 176, *post*.
12   Supreme Court Act 1981, s 5.
13   Although Megarry J (as he then was) cast doubt upon this belief, not only by conducting a sitting of his court at a village in Suffolk (*St Edmundsbury and Ipswich Diocesan Board of Finance v Clark* (*supra*)) but by visiting two islands in the western Pacific for the purpose of conducting a view (*Tito v Waddell*, p 171).
14   By virtue of the Courts Act 1971, s 16, Sch 2.
15   Pursuant to the request of the Lord Chancellor made under s 9 of the Supreme Court Act 1981 under which section circuit judges or recorders may sit as judges of the High Court.

(h)   probate business, other than non-contentious or common form business;
(i)   patents, trade marks, registered designs or copyright;
(j)   the appointment of a guardian of a minor's estate, and all causes and matters
      involving the exercise of the High Court's jurisdiction under the enactments
      relating to companies.

This jurisdiction is augmented by statutes and rules of procedure. Thus the Chancery
Division, in addition to the matters set out above, exercises jurisdiction over revenue
matters, town and country planning and landlord and tenant disputes. Judges of the
division when sitting as the Court of Protection[16] hear applications under the Mental
Health Act 1983 concerning the management of the property and affairs of mental
patients.

  Patents Court. There are three "specialist courts" within the High Court, viz. the
Patents Court, the Admiralty Court and the Commercial Court.[17] Of these the first is
part of the Chancery Division (the other two being part of the Queen's Bench Division).
It was established by the Patents Act 1977 and consists of nominated judges of the
division. It hears patent actions at first instance and on appeal from the Comptroller-
General of Patents, Designs and Trademarks, procedure being governed by RSC Order
104.

  Probate jurisdiction and procedure. Probate procedure differs according to whether
the deceased died testate, ie leaving a valid will, or intestate, ie leaving no will or leaving
a will which is invalid, generally through failure to comply with the due formalities
which are principally contained in the Wills Act 1837.

  If a person dies testate his will should appoint one or more executors. These
executors must first apply to the Principal Registry of the Family Division or to a
District Probate Registry for a grant of probate. This application must be accompanied
by the will itself, the executors' affidavit of undertaking to administer the estate, a
statement of all the deceased's property for tax purposes and various other documents.
In the overwhelming majority of cases no-one will dispute the validity of the will and
the grant of probate will be made as a formality. However any person who disputes
the validity of a will in respect of which a grant is sought may enter a caveat at the
Registry in question. In that event the proceedings become contentious and there will
have to be a trial as to the validity of the will.[18] This trial may take place in the county
court for the district where the testator resided before his death if the net value of the
estate is less than £30,000.[19]

  If a person dies intestate a person will have to apply to be appointed an administrator
of the estate. There will then be a grant of letters of administration rather than a grant
of probate. The effect is similar in that it vests the deceased's property in the
administrators who must then distribute it in accordance with the intestacy provisions.

  Appellate jurisdiction. Although the jurisdiction of the Chancery Division is
predominately original, there is some appellate jurisdiction. A single judge of the
division has jurisdiction by statute to hear certain appeals, for example income tax
appeals from the Commissioners of Inland Revenue under section 56 of the Taxes
Management Act 1970. A divisional court of the Chancery Division, comprising at
least two judges of the division, has a limited jurisdiction, comprising bankruptcy and

16   See p 196, *post.* The wardship jurisdiction of the Chancery Division was assigned to the Family Division
     by the Administration of Justice Act 1970, s 1, Sch 1.
17   Supreme Court Act 1981, s 6.
18   The procedure is governed by RSC Ord 76; a probate action must be commenced by writ (Ord 76,
     r 2).
19   County Courts Act 1984, s 32; the limit may be raised by Order in Council (*ibid*, s 145).

land registration matters.[20] The Patents Court, as stated above, hears appeals from certain decisions of the Comptroller-General of Patents, Designs and Trademarks.

b　Queen's Bench Division

The jurisdiction of the Queen's Bench Division is wider in scope than that of the other two divisions of the High Court. It is both civil and criminal and both original and appellate. In addition it exercises the supervisory jurisdiction formerly exercised by the Court of King's Bench. The jurisdiction of the division is equivalent to the jurisdiction exercised by the three superior common law courts of first instance prior to 1875, as altered by subsequent statutes and rules. Procedure in this division is dealt with in Part III of this book.

Original civil jurisdiction. By far the most important aspect of the business of the division is its first instance jurisdiction over civil matters, principally actions in contract and tort. Jurisdiction over commercial matters is exercised in the Commercial Court, which is one of the lists in the division, maintained in London, and several regional centres.[1] Admiralty jurisdiction, assigned to the division by section 20 of the Supreme Court Act 1981, is exercised by the "Admiralty Court", the judges of which are those judges nominated to be Admiralty judges by the Lord Chancellor.[2] Admiralty business includes actions to enforce a claim for damage, loss of life or personal injury arising out of collision between ships, claims to the possession or ownership of ships, claim for loss of or damage to goods carried in a ship, towage claims and other specified proceedings.[3] When trying admiralty actions the judge often sits with lay assessors.

Appellate civil jurisdiction. The appellate jurisdiction of the Queen's Bench Division in civil matters is fairly minor. Appeal lies from an interlocutory order of a Queen's Bench Division master to a judge in chambers[4] and a single judge also has jurisdiction to hear certain appeals from tribunals, for example from the Pensions Appeal Tribunal.[5] A judge of the Commercial Court hears appeals from arbitrations and determines questions of law arising in the course of arbitrations in accordance with the provisions of the Arbitration Act 1996.[6] A divisional court of the Queen's Bench Division consisting of two or more judges of the division has a limited civil jurisdiction in hearing appeals by way of case stated from magistrates' courts, other than matrimonial proceedings, and the Crown Court, from the Solicitors Disciplinary Tribunal and in certain other cases.

Criminal and supervisory jurisdiction. The criminal jurisdiction of the High Court is exercised exclusively by the Queen's Bench Division. This is entirely appellate[7] and exercised by the divisional court consisting of at least two but often three judges

---

20　The jurisdiction in respect of bankruptcy appeals was removed by Insolvency Act 1986, s 117 (appeals lie with single judge of the High Court, and House to the Court of Appeal).

1　See Supreme Court Act 1981, s 6. As well as the Commercial lists heard in London, Liverpool and Manchester, Mercantile lists, for cases of a commercial or business character, have been created in Birmingham (see *Practice Note* [1993] 4 All ER 381) and Bristol (see *Practice Note* [1993] 4 All ER 1023, *sub nom Practice Direction* [1993] 1 WLR 1522). See further p 399, *post*.

2　Supreme Court Act 1981, s 6. Procedure in the Admiralty Court is governed by RSC, Ord 75; see p 400, *post*.

3　The full jurisdiction is listed in s 20 of the Supreme Court Act 1981.

4　See p 441, *post*.

5　Pensions Appeal Tribunals Act 1943; Tribunals and Inquiries Act 1992, s 13.

6　See p 333, *post*.

7　Prior to 1972 the division exercised a limited original criminal jurisdiction in the form of a trial "at bar", a procedure adopted in the notorious case of *R v Casement* [1917] 1 KB 98; the jurisdiction was, however, virtually obsolete and was abolished by the Courts Act 1971, s 6 (see now s 46(1) of the Supreme Court Act, which provides that all proceedings on indictment must be brought before the Crown Court).

of the division. The Lord Chief Justice often sits and the hearing will then take place in his own court in the Royal Courts of Justice. The jurisdiction is exercised over appeals by way of "case stated"[8] from magistrates' courts and the Crown Court (in the exercise of that court's appellate jurisdiction).

The supervisory jurisdiction of the division is also exercised by the divisional court. This includes jurisdiction to issue the prerogative writ of habeas corpus and to make orders of mandamus, prohibition and certiorari by which inferior courts and tribunals are compelled to exercise their powers properly and restrained from exceeding their jurisdiction. This jurisdiction is invoked by "application for judicial review", the procedure being governed by RSC Order 53. Such cases are dealt with as part of the Crown Office list, and heard by a group of judges who have become increasingly specialised in administrative law matters. This, together with a large increase in the number of cases brought, has led in effect to the development of a system of administrative law.[9]

Judges of the division exercise other functions. Thus, as has been seen, they discharge the bulk of the business of the criminal division of the Court of Appeal. They also sit in the Courts-Martial Appeal Court. Disputed Parliamentary elections are determined by an election court which consists of two judges of the Queen's Bench Division.[10]

It should be noted finally that the "first-tier" jurisdiction of the Crown Court is exercised principally by the judges of the Queen's Bench Division.[11] Judges of the Queen's Bench Division on average spend approximately half their time in the Royal Courts of Justice and half "on circuit".

c   Family Division

This division (formerly named the Probate, Divorce and Admiralty Division[12]) consists of the President and such of the puisne judges as the Lord Chancellor may nominate.[13] The jurisdiction of the division is set out in the Supreme Court Act 1981, and is both original and appellate.

Schedule 1 to the Supreme Court Act assigns to the Family Division:

(a) all High Court matrimonial causes and matters (whether at first instance or on appeal);
(b) all causes and matters (whether at first instance or on appeal) relating to:
   (i)   legitimacy;
   (ii) the exercise of the inherent jurisdiction of the High Court with respect to minors, the maintenance of minors and any proceedings under the Children Act 1989, except proceedings solely for the appointment of a guardian of a minor's estate;
   (iii) adoption;
   (iv) non-contentious or common-form probate business;

8   For details of the procedure, see p 147, *post*.
9   See the dicta of Lord Diplock in *O'Reilly v Mackman* [1983] 2 AC 237 at 279; [1982] 3 All ER 1124. See generally p 147, *ante*.
10   Representation of the People Act 1983, ss 120 *et seq*. However, this is not part of the Queen's Bench Division and, indeed, is an inferior court and therefore subject to judicial review; *R v Cripps, ex parte Muldoon* [1984] QB 68; [1984] 3 All ER 72.
11   See p 178, *post*.
12   The division was re-named by the Administration of Justice Act 1970, s 1. The late Sir Alan Herbert described the jurisdiction as "wills, wives and wrecks"; of these, "wills" have gone to the Chancery Division and "wrecks" (other than the wrecks of marriages) to the Queen's Bench Division (*supra*).
13   Supreme Court Act 1981, s 5; there are at present sixteen.

(c) applications for consent to the marriage of a minor;
(d) proceedings on appeal under section 13 of the Administration of Justice Act 1960
     from an order or decision made under section 63(3) of the Magistrates' Courts
     Act 1980 to enforce an order of a magistrates' court made in matrimonial
     proceedings or with respect to the guardianship of a minor;
(e) certain proceedings under the Family Law Act 1986;
(f) proceedings under the Children Act 1989;
(g) proceedings under various statutory provisions.[14]

The general effect of these provisions is that the division has exclusive High Court
jurisdiction over matrimonial disputes and children, thus avoiding the conflicts which,
prior to 1970, arose between the Family and Chancery Divisions.[15] However, it should
be noted that, under the Children Act 1989[16] a unified system for dealing with
proceedings under that Act exists. Magistrates' courts, county courts and the Family
Division each have jurisdiction, and the distribution of work between the three courts
is governed by an order made by the Lord Chancellor,[17] which also provides for transfer
of cases between the three courts. This is discussed later.[18]
    The appellate business of the division comprises principally appeals from family
courts, in respect of proceedings concerning matrimonial causes and children.

G   THE CROWN COURT

I   Creation of the Crown Court

The Crown Court was created by the Courts Act 1971. In order to appreciate the
jurisdiction of this court and its place in the hierarchy, it is necessary to examine briefly
the system of courts that the Crown Court replaced.
    Prior to 1 January 1972, the date upon which the Courts Act came into operation,
trials on indictment took place either at quarter sessions or at assizes. The essential
characteristics of both quarter sessions and assizes was that their jurisdiction was local.
This meant not only that the courts (as a rule) tried only offences committed within
the locality of their jurisdiction but also that the administration of the courts was
organised on a local basis, so that the methods of administration and organisation varied
from area to area.
    The most serious offences were tried at assizes before a court presided over by a
judge sitting, not by virtue of his normal judicial office, but under royal commissions
of oyer and terminer and gaol delivery; the persons named in the commissions usually
included at least two High Court judges, almost invariably judges of the Queen's Bench
Division, who would sit at the assize town for the duration of the assize. The jurisdiction
of assizes was equivalent to that of the High Court since a commissioner when engaged
in the exercise of his jurisdiction constituted a court of the High Court of Justice.[19]

---

14   Family Law Act 1996; Child Abduction and Custody Act 1985; Family Law Act 1986; Human
      Fertilisation and Embryology Act 1990, s 30; Child Support Act 1991, Sch 1.
15   See, eg, *Hall v Hall* [1963] P 378; [1963] 2 All ER 140.
16   Children Act 1989, s 92.
17   Children (Allocation of Proceedings) Order 1991, SI 1991/1677.
18   See p 187, *post*.
19   In addition to the High Court judges, county court judges and Queen's Counsel were often included
      in the commissions; furthermore the Master of the Rolls, Lords Justices of Appeal and former Lords
      Justices and High Court judges might be included in the commissions but in practice were not. The
      Commissioners of Assize also tried civil cases as a court of the High Court.

All save the most serious offences tried on indictment were tried at quarter sessions of which there were almost 150 separate courts. Quarter sessions were of two kinds, county quarter sessions and borough quarter sessions. These courts, which as their name would indicate were held at least four times a year, were composed, in the case of county quarter sessions, by the justices of the peace of the county, almost invariably presided over by a legally qualified chairman, and in the case of borough quarter sessions, by a Recorder who sat alone and was a practising barrister of at least five years' standing. The jurisdiction of quarter sessions was both civil and criminal and original and appellate. The criminal jurisdiction comprised the trial of all indictable offences, save those which had, by statute, to be tried at assizes, jurisdiction to sentence persons committed for sentence following summary conviction and the hearing of appeals from the decisions of magistrates' courts. The whole of this jurisdiction has been transferred to the Crown Court together with the civil jurisdiction of quarter sessions which comprised principally matters concerned with various forms of licensing.[20]

Before leaving the pre-1972 system, mention must also be made of the Central Criminal Court and of the Crown Courts of Liverpool and Manchester. The Central Criminal Court, established by the Central Criminal Court Act 1834 and popularly known as the "Old Bailey", after the name of the street in London in which the court is situated, was the assize court exercising criminal jurisdiction in the Greater London area. The court was a court of the High Court and its jurisdiction extended over indictable offences committed in Greater London or on the high seas; the judges of the court sat under the commissions of oyer and terminer and gaol delivery and consisted of the Lord Chancellor, the Lord Mayor of the City of London, the Lord Chief Justice and the judges of the Queen's Bench Division, the Aldermen of the City of London, the Recorder and the Common Serjeant and a number of additional judges who had to be judges of at least ten years' standing; of these only the Queen's Bench Division judges, the Recorder, the Common Serjeant and the additional judges sat in practice.

The Criminal Justice Administration Act 1956 established, as something of an experimental innovation, Crown Courts in Liverpool and Manchester presided over by the Recorders of Liverpool and Manchester who were the full-time judges of the courts. The jurisdiction of these courts was solely criminal but was both original and appellate since the courts exercised the criminal jurisdiction of both assizes and quarter sessions within the area of their respective jurisdictions. These courts, which were abolished by the Courts Act 1971, must not be confused with the present Crown Court. Apart from the difference in the judiciary of the courts, the jurisdiction of the Crown Courts of Liverpool and Manchester was, as in the case of all quarter sessions and assize, local.

This plethora of courts with workloads determined by historical rather than practical reasons led to the establishment of a Royal Commission under the chairmanship of Lord Beeching. The report[1] that followed contained recommendations which formed the basis for the system introduced by the Courts Act 1971.

The Courts Act 1971 abolished all courts of assize and quarter sessions and established in their place a single court to be known as the Crown Court. The constitution and jurisdiction of the Crown Court is now contained in the Supreme Court

---

20   Although certain administrative functions were transferred to local authorities (Courts Act 1971, ss 53, 56, Sch 8).

1   Report of the Royal Commission on Assizes and Quarter Sessions Cmnd 4153 of 1969.

Act 1981. It is part of the Supreme Court and a superior court of record.[2] The Courts Act 1971 further abolished the Crown Courts of Liverpool and Manchester and the Central Criminal Court, though the latter has been retained in name since it is expressly provided that when the Crown Court sits in the City of London it shall be known as the Central Criminal Court.[3]

As already indicated the essential feature of the Crown Court is that its jurisdiction is in no sense local. Section 78 of the Supreme Court Act 1981 provides that:

"(1) Any Crown Court business may be conducted at any place in England or Wales, and the sittings of the Crown Court at any place may be continuous or intermittent or occasional.

(2) Judges of the Crown Court may sit simultaneously to take any number of different cases in the same or different places, and may adjourn cases from place to place at any time."

Thus it is important to remember that there are not various Crown Courts throughout the country. There is one Crown Court,[4] sittings of which may be held anywhere at any time as indicated above.

2   Constitution

The judges of the Crown Court are all the judges of the High Court, the circuit judges and recorders; judges of the court sit alone as a rule, though there is provision for justices of the peace to sit, but only with one of the judges of the court.[5] This is in contrast to

2   Supreme Court Act 1981, ss 1, 45(1). This, however, appears to be largely a matter of terminology since, in the exercise of its appellate jurisdiction, the Crown Court (as were Quarter Sessions) is amenable to the supervisory jurisdiction of the High Court as if it were an inferior court (*ibid*, s 29(3); see p 146, *ante*), although it is not amenable to this jurisdiction in matters relating to trial on indictment: see p 146, *ante*. In addition s 151 of the 1981 Act, the interpretation section, provides that except where the context otherwise requires a reference in the Act, or in any other Act, to a judge of the Supreme Court shall not include a reference to a judge of the Crown Court; cf *Sirros v Moore* [1975] QB 118; [1974] 3 All ER 776; see p 215, *post*.

3   Supreme Court Act 1981, s 8(3); the Lord Mayor of the City and any Alderman of the City are entitled to sit as judges of the Central Criminal Court with any High Court judge, circuit judge or recorder. The reasons behind the preservation of this obsolete tradition are not clear. There used to be a rule to the effect that an Alderman of the City had to be present in the court; although this rule has disappeared, the central seat in the No 1 court at the Old Bailey is still traditionally left vacant for the Lord Mayor. As a further concession to the City of London the 1971 Act provides that the holders of the offices of Recorder of London and Common Serjeant, although circuit judges *ex officio*, continue to be appointed and remunerated in accordance with the provisions of the City of London (Courts) Act 1964 rather than in accordance with the provisions of the 1971 Act, which govern the appointment and remuneration of all other circuit judges (s 16, Sch 2); finally judges sitting in the Central Criminal Court continue to be addressed as "my Lord" as opposed to "your Honour", which is the appropriate form of address for circuit judges, deputy circuit judges, recorders and assistant recorders (see *Practice Direction (Judge; Mode of address)* [1982] 1 All ER 320; [1982] 1 WLR 101).

4   For an example of the relevance of this fundamental principle, see *R v Slatter* [1975] 3 All ER 215; [1975] 1 WLR 1084.

5   Supreme Court Act 1981, s 8. A further unimportant exception to the rule that the judges of the court sit alone is the right of the Lord Mayor and Aldermen of the City of London to sit in the Central Criminal Court (*supra*). Where justices do sit they are themselves judges of the Crown Court and must play a full part in all decisions of the court, whether on interlocutory matters or on sentence, so that in the event of disagreement the decision of the majority of the court prevails, even if the judge alone is in the minority. The summing-up and direction to the jury must, however, be given by the judge and where there is any ruling of law to be given that ruling must be determined by the judge alone; these principles were stated by the Court of Appeal in *R v Orpin* [1975] QB 283; [1974] 2 All ER 1121.

the former county quarter sessions which were composed entirely of justices of the peace, albeit almost always sitting with a legally qualified chairman. In addition to the regular judges of the court any judge of the Court of Appeal and any former Court of Appeal or puisne judge may, on the request of the Lord Chancellor, sit and act as a judge and when so sitting and acting is regarded as a judge of the High Court.[6] There is also provision for the temporary appointment of deputy High Court and circuit judges and assistant-recorders.[7]

There are thus basically three tiers of judiciary. At the highest level are the High Court judges who, in practice, are almost invariably judges of the Queen's Bench Division and try principally the most serious or difficult cases.[8] Below High Court judges are circuit judges and recorders.[9]

Finally there are the provisions for justices of the peace to sit in the court. Their attendance is mandatory on the hearing by the Crown Court of any appeal or of proceedings on committal to the court for sentence, on the hearing of which proceedings the judge of the court sits with not less than two nor more than four justices of the peace. In addition any jurisdiction or power of the court may be exercised by a regular judge of the court sitting with not more than four justices.[10] Where justices sit the decision of the court is by majority and if the members of the court are equally divided the regular judge has a second and casting vote.[11] As a final illustration of the departure from the principle of localised jurisdiction, section 8(2) of the 1981 Act provides that a justice of the peace shall not be disqualified from acting as a judge of the Crown Court for the reason that the proceedings are not at a place within the area for which he was appointed as a justice, or because the proceedings are not related to that area in any way.

It will be noted that the judges of the Crown Court are not, as if were, full time criminal judges. The High Court judges sit, of course, in civil cases in the High Court; the circuit judges, as well as exercising the very limited civil jurisdiction which the Crown Court inherited from quarter sessions, discharge the functions of county court judges;[12] recorders sit mainly to try criminal cases though, as well as having a civil jurisdiction of the Crown Court, there is provision for recorders to sit as county court judges.

3 Jurisdiction and procedure

The Crown Court has exclusive jurisdiction over all trials on indictment for offences wherever committed, including proceedings on indictment for offences within the jurisdiction of the Admiralty in England.[13] In addition all jurisdiction formerly exercised by any court of quarter sessions was vested in the Crown Court.[14] This, as indicated above, includes the hearing of appeals by persons convicted summarily in magistrates' courts,[15] the sentencing of persons committed for sentence following summary

6   Supreme Court Act 1981, s 9.
7   Courts Act 1971, s 24.
8   As to the distribution of business, see p 490, *post*.
9   See p 211, *post*.
10 Supreme Court Act 1981, ss 74(1), 8(1)(c).
11 *Ibid*, s 73(3).
12 Courts Act 1971, s 20; see p 409, *post*.
13 Supreme Court Act 1971, s 46.
14 Courts Act 1971, s 8, Sch 1; this was subject to the provisions of Sch 8, Part I which transferred certain administrative functions of quarter sessions to local authorities.
15 See p 580, *post*.

conviction[16] and a limited civil jurisdiction, principally concerned with licensing appeals. Procedure in the court is governed by Crown Court rules.[17]

The Lord Chief Justice has power under section 75 of the Supreme Court Act 1981, with the concurrence of the Lord Chancellor, to give directions relating to the distribution of Crown Court business. The current directions[18] classify offences, for the purposes of distribution, into four classes,[19] the first of which, being the most serious, are to be tried by a High Court judge. Class 2 offences are to be tried by a High Court judge unless a particular case is released by or on the authority of a presiding judge, that is to say, a High Court judge assigned to have special responsibility for a particular circuit. All offences triable on indictment, other than those in Classes, 1, 2 and 4 form Class 3 and may be listed for trial by a High Court judge, circuit judge or recorder, while certain indictable offences and all offences triable either way constitute Class 4 and may be tried by a High Court judge, circuit judge or recorder but will normally be listed for trial by a circuit judge or recorder.[20]

H   EMPLOYMENT APPEAL TRIBUNAL

I   History

In 1971 an attempt was made to create a specialist court to deal with matters relating to industrial relations. Section 99 of the Industrial Relations Act 1971 established the National Industrial Relations Court. The Act, together with the court itself, was extremely controversial, as was its jurisdiction and exercise of power. After a stormy and short life it was abolished in 1974. However, in 1976 the Employment Appeal Tribunal was established with similar objectives, but with different powers. The jurisdiction and functions of this tribunal are now governed by the Industrial Tribunals Act 1996. Although by name a tribunal, it is a superior court of record with all the characteristics of a court. It is, for that reason, considered here.

2   Constitution

The constitution of the tribunal comprises such number of judges as may be nominated from time to time by the Lord Chancellor from the judges of the High Court and the Court of Appeal, one of whom is appointed President, at least one nominated judge of the Court of Session of Scotland and such other members as may be appointed from time to time by Her Majesty.[1] The additional members are persons having special knowledge or experience of industrial relations, either as representatives of employers or as representatives of workers, so that, although the President is a lawyer, the Tribunal

---

16   See p 572, *post.*
17   Section 86 of the 1981 Act (as amended by the Courts and Legal Services Act 1990) confers power to make Crown Court rules upon a Crown Court rule committee consisting of the Lord Chancellor together with any four or more of the following persons, namely the Lord Chief Justice, two other judges of the Supreme Court, two circuit judges, the registrar of criminal appeals, a justice of the peace, two person who have a Supreme Court qualification (see p 245, *post*) and two persons who have the right to conduct litigation (p 245, *post*). The current rules are the Crown Court Rules 1982, SI 1982/1109.
18   See *Practice Direction (Crown Court Business: Classification)* [1987] 1 WLR 1671. The directions permit presiding judges to issue directions reserving particular cases for trial by a High Court judge.
19   For further details of the classification of offences and the distribution of business, see p 468, *post.*
20   As to when Class 4 offences will be tried by a High Court judge, see p 491.
1   Industrial Tribunals Act 1996, s 22; in addition the Lord Chancellor has power to appoint temporary judges or members (*ibid*, s 23).

consists of laymen with specialised knowledge of industrial relations. The members of the Tribunal may resign by notice in writing and may be removed by the Lord Chancellor after consultation with the Secretary of State on specified grounds, notably incapacity or misbehaviour.[2] The Tribunal, which is a superior court of record, has a central office in London and may sit at any time and in any place in Great Britain in any number of divisions concurrently. It is duly constituted when sitting with a judge and either two or four other members (or a judge and one other member by consent of the parties).[3]

3 Jurisdiction

The jurisdiction of the Tribunal is limited to that which is conferred by the 1992 Act. In sharp contrast to the National Industrial Relations Court, the Tribunal does not have the original jurisdiction which that court had to deal, for example, with unfair industrial practices. Its jurisdiction is limited to hearing appeals; these lie on questions of law from employment tribunals under the Equal Pay Act 1970, the Sex Discrimination Act 1975, the Race Relations Act 1976 and the various employment protection statutes.[4] In addition the Tribunal hears appeals on questions of fact or law arising in any proceedings before, or arising from any decision of, the Certification Officer under section 7 of the Trade Union and Labour Relations (Consolidation) Act 1992.[5]

4 Procedure

The Lord Chancellor has power to make rules of procedure, subject to which the Tribunal has power to regulate its own procedure.[6] The rules of procedure[7] aim at informality. Nevertheless any person appearing before the Tribunal may be represented by counsel or by a solicitor or, indeed, may appear in person or be represented by a representative of a trade union or employers' association or by any other person whom he desires to represent him.[8]

Procedure at hearings of the Tribunal is designed to combine informality with order. No-one appears robed, there is no bench or witness box, parties and their advisers sit at tables and address the court seated. A further departure from normal court practice is that no party is to be ordered to pay costs unless, in the opinion of the Tribunal, the proceedings were unnecessary, improper or vexatious or there has been unreasonable delay or other unreasonable conduct in bringing or conducting the proceedings.[9]

The Tribunal has powers to compel the attendance and examination of witnesses, the production and inspection of documents, the enforcement of its orders and other matters incidental to its jurisdiction under the Act, save that no person can be punished for contempt except by, or with the consent of, a judge who is a member of the tribunal.[10]

---

2   *Ibid*, s 25.
3   *Ibid*, s 28.
4   See, in particular, Employment Rights Act 1996.
5   *Ibid*, s 21.
6   *Ibid*, s 30.
7   Employment Appeal Tribunal Rules 1993, SI 1993/2854. See also Practice Direction [1996] ICR 422.
8   1996 Act, s 29.
9   *Ibid*, s 33.
10   *Ibid*, s 29

5   Appeals

Any decision of the Employment Appeal Tribunal on a question of fact is final (except in the case of committal for contempt) but appeal on a point of law lies to the Court of Appeal. The court, being a superior court of record, is not subject to the supervisory jurisdiction of the High Court.[11]

I   MAGISTRATES' COURTS

1   Constitution and organisation

The historical role of justices of the peace has already been noted.[12] Despite the antiquity of the office, the use of unpaid justices of the peace provides the basis of provision of magistrates' courts, although an increasing trend to deploy stipendiary magistrates exists. A magistrates' court is defined by section 148 of the Magistrates' Courts Act 1980, as any justice or justices of the peace acting under any enactment or by virtue of his or their commission or under common law. A magistrates' court must be composed of at least two and not more than seven justices of the peace in order to try an information summarily, hear a complaint or conduct an examination into the means of a person whom it is proposed to commit to prison for non-payment of a fine. However an exception is provided by the presence of a stipendiary magistrate who has all the powers of two lay justices.[13] Stipendiary magistrates are now increasingly common, and currently the Lord Chancellor is considering the creation of a single, unified stipendiary magistracy,[14] which would enable the work and training of stipendiaries to be managed in a coherent way. A change of name is also being considered.

There are some 1000 magistrates' courts in England and Wales. Lay magistrates are appointed by the Lord Chancellor, to sit in a particular commission area. They are ineligible to serve beyond the age of 70, and are expected to commit themselves to serve for a minimum number of days per year, currently 26. They are appointed by the Lord Chancellor, names having been submitted to him by local advisory committees. Appointments are intended to reflect all sections of the community. Whether that in fact is achieved is debatable, with persistent criticism that justices tend, stereotypically, to be white, middle class, predominantly conservative in political sympathy or allegiance and old,[15] despite there being widespread awareness of the desirability of having as diverse a magistracy as possible. Accepting the above as a correct snapshot of the current lay magistracy, it is unclear as to what level of representative membership is attainable, consistent whilst ensuring the appointment of persons who are both willing and able to serve. Some would have qualms about the appointment of justices overtly to redress and perceived political leaning of the existing

---

11   See p 162, *ante*.
12   See p 157, *ante*.
13   Justices of the Peace Act 1979, s 16.
14   Lord Irvine LC, HL Deb, vol 582, col. 1057.
15   See HC Home Affairs Committee, Judicial Appointments Procedures 1995–1996, and the analysis thereof by Darbyshire, "For The New Lord Chancellor – Some Causes for Concern About Magistrates" [1997] Crim LR 861, at 862–866.
16   For the importance of ensuring the independence of the judiciary, see p 213, post.

magistracy.[16] Despite its faults, the lay magistracy has been regarded as providing a crucial lay contribution to summary justice, bringing the standards (and presumably the prejudices and weaknesses) of the community at large to the administration of justice, in the same way as does the jury in trial on indictment. In this context, the developing trend towards the appointment of professional, legally qualified magistrates (stipendiary magistrates) amounts to a diminution of the lay input into summary justice. Such a development might be regrettable, not only in terms of the additional costs, but also because the involvement of these ordinary members of the public collectively (in benches of two or three) in reflecting the attitudes of non-professionals to the process of fact-finding and sentence determination, would be reduced.[17]

A single lay justice has a limited jurisdiction and cannot order a person to pay more than one pound or impose imprisonment for more than fourteen days. It should be noted that a single justice may discharge the function of determining the mode of trial of an offence triable summarily or on indictment and of conducting a preliminary investigation.[18] Rules may be made which entitle a justices' clerk to undertake certain functions.[19] It was partly for this reason that proposals in the Police and Magistrates' Courts Bill 1994 relating to the basis of employment of justices' clerks met a hostile response. Section 48 of the Justices of the Peace Act 1997[20] now provides that when a justices' clerk is exercising such functions in an individual case, the clerk shall not be subject to the direction of the magistrates' courts committee, the justices' chief executive or any other person.

The jurisdiction of magistrates' courts is local. Every county, the London commission areas and the City of London have a separate commission of the peace, and a county is divided into petty sessional divisions, which may be amended from time to time. The jurisdiction of the justices is generally confined to matters arising in or near these commission areas.

The responsibility for running the magistrates' courts service locally rests on magistrates' courts committees. The whole structure and powers of such committees was reviewed in 1993–1994 with the passage of the controversial Police and Magistrates' Courts Act 1994. The stated objectives of these provisions were the achievement of a better fulfilment of responsibilities by magistrates' courts committees, and the achievement of a "clear line of management accountability."[21] These objectives were to stir considerable anxiety about the maintenance of independence in the performance of judicial and legal decision-making. As the Lord Chief Justice put it in debate:

> "We shall fail in our duty if we allow this Bill to pass in a way which allows the impression to be given that the advice magistrates receive or the judicial decisions taken by their clerks are no longer a matter of their own discretion, but are instead liable to influence by the executive, either through the terms under which they are employed or because they feel under pressure from a superior officer as to the way in which they exercise them".[1]

As a result of this strength of opposition the provisions of the Bill were significantly amended as it passed through Parliament, particularly in respect of the conditions of

17   See Skyrme: *The Changing Image of the Magistracy*, 2nd Edn, 1983.
18   See p 484, *post*.
19   Magistrates' Courts Act 1980, s 144.
20   Inserted therein by Police and Magistrates Courts Act 1994, s 78.
21   Lord Mackay of Clashfern, LC, Hansard, HL Deb vol 553, col. 797.
1   Lord Taylor CJ, HL Deb, vol 551, col. 478.

service and accountability of justices' clerks. Ideas originally mooted such as fixed term contracts, or performance-related pay, do not form part of the 1994 Act.

Section 28 of the 1997 Act[2] deals with the composition of magistrates' courts committees. Each committee comprises magistrates, together with not more than two non-justices co-opted by the committee or appointed by the Lord Chancellor. The latter provision is somewhat controversial, despite assurances that co-option should be primarily local. The committee is responsible for the efficient and effective administration of the magistrates' court for the area, it may allocate administrative responsibilities and may determine administrative procedures.[3] The Lord Chancellor has residual powers of direction, and can require the preparation and submission of reports and plans.[4]

Rationalisation of the magistrates' courts system is underway. It is intended[5] that the number of magistrates' courts committees be reduced, so that their boundaries match, so far as possible, police force areas and the new Crown Prosecution areas.[6] This is all part of an attempt to ensure that the management of the criminal justice process is achieved in an efficient and effective way in any given area: the fact that different agencies have hitherto had different geographical limits has had in the past the achievement of this objective.

Every magistrates' courts committee has to appoint a justices' chief executive, a position which was originally intended to be titled "justices' chief clerk". This appointment is subject to the approval of the Lord Chancellor. The Government sought to allay fears about the mixing of administrative and legal functions, and possible loss of independence, through section 48 of the 1997 Act. The effect of that provision should be to ensure that steps taken in the cause of administrative efficiency do not impact on judicial decision-making and the advice tendered. There is likely in the future to be a greater separation of administrative management functions and the performance of legal functions.[7]

Justices' clerks are appointed by the magistrates' courts committee from persons who have a five-year magistrates' court qualification,[8] and who fall within prescribed age limits.[9] The duty of the justices' clerk is well described by section 28(3) of the Justices of the Peace Act 1979:

"The functions of a justices' clerk include the giving to the justices to whom he is their clerk, at the request of the justices or justice, of advice about law, practice or procedure on questions arising in connection with the discharge of their functions, including questions arising when the clerk is not personally attending on them".

---

2   Formerly 1979 Act, s 20.
3   1997 Act, s 31.
4   *Ibid*, s 37.
5   Lord Irvine LC, HL Deb, Vol 582 col. 1957.
6   See p 270, *post*.
7   Lord Irvine LC, *op cit*, n 5.
8   Within the meaning of the Courts and Legal Services Act 1990, s 71.
9   Justices of the Peace Act 1997, s 5. When the clerk is represented in court by an assistant (as is often the case), the assistant clerk must fulfil the qualification requirements of the Justices Clerks (Qualification of Assistants) Rules 1979 (SI 1979/570). See, also, Justices' Chief Executive and Justices Clerk (Appointment) Regulations 1995, SI 1995/686.

The task of the clerk is therefore that of a legal adviser, though care must be taken to ensure that an appearance of interference with the magisterial function is avoided.[10] The fact that there is a court clerk in each court does not mean that such persons are qualified, in the strict sense, as a "justices' clerk". Many are not professionally qualified, although, of course, all will have been, or will be in the process of being, trained. As already noted the justices' clerk is also the permanent official and administrator of the court, who is responsible for the organisation of the court, the collection of fines, for dealing with applications for legal aid in criminal cases, and other administrative work. However, the fact that justices' clerks may exercise a variety of judicial and quasi-judicial powers has already been noted.[11] The extent of this power will increase. The Narey Report into the causes of delays within the criminal justice system made wide-ranging recommendations as to what functions might be performed by justices' clerks. Among the additional powers proposed were powers to extend police bail, to vary bail conditions, to dismiss an information or discharge a defendant where no evidence is offered, to make an order for payment of costs from central funds, to request a pre-sentence report, or medical report, to extend custody time-limits (by agreement), to grant legal aid in a Crown Court case and generally to give, vary or revoke directions for the conduct of the trial including the setting of a timetable, attendance of parties, and the service of documents (including summaries of legal arguments).[12] These powers have not yet been conferred on justices' clerks, but the Crime and Disorder Act 1998 extends the powers that may be exercised by single justices.[13] In due course it is intended to confer some of the powers exercisable by a single justice on justices' clerks, in accordance with the pre-existing legal power to do so.[14]

2   Jurisdiction

It is common to suppose that the jurisdiction of the magistrates' courts is entirely criminal. This is very far from being true since magistrates have a wide and varied civil jurisdiction. The feature of both the civil and the criminal matters within the jurisdiction of the magistrates' courts is that they are matters of relatively minor importance compared with the civil matters heard in the High Court and the county courts and the criminal cases tried at the Crown Court. The compensating advantage of summary procedure is its cheapness and speed. The balance between the advantages of summary trial and Crown Court trial has led to repeated discussions as to the distribution of business between the two courts. This is discussed further in due course.[15]

Before examining more closely the civil and criminal jurisdiction of justices it should be remembered that sitting magistrates' courts is not the only function of justices of the peace. They also sit in the Crown Court.[16] Furthermore such important functions as the conduct of committal proceedings, the issue of summonses and warrants and the grant of bail are exercised by justices though not sitting as "magistrates' courts". It has only in recent years been confirmed that licensing sessions are "courts".[17]

---

10   See *Practice Direction (Justices Clerks)* [1953] 2 All ER 1306n; [1953] 1 WLR 1416.
11   See p 183, *ante*.
12   Review of Delay in the Criminal Justice System (27 February 1997).
13   See p 493, *post*.
14   See Crime and Disorder Act 1998, s 49.
15   See p 495, *post*.
16   See p 179, *post*.
17   *Jeffrey v Evans* [1964] 1 All ER 536; [1964] 1 WLR 505.

a   Criminal jurisdiction

The criminal jurisdiction of the magistrates' courts exists principally over summary offences.[18] Such offences are offences triable without a jury and are all statutory offences since all summary jurisdiction derives from statute. These offences are of a minor character since the maximum penalty which can be imposed in respect of a summary offence is six months' imprisonment[19] and a fine limited in amount.[20] Nevertheless, the consequence of any conviction can often be significant, in terms of the loss of reputation, or of the consequences upon employment. In practice most summary offenders are convicted of motoring offences under the Road Traffic Acts and regulations made under those Acts. Indeed so numerous are the convictions for minor offences such as speeding and unauthorised parking that a new procedure was introduced by the Magistrates' Courts Act 1957 enabling persons to plead guilty to minor summary offences by post.[1] There are more than 2 million persons a year found guilty of summary offences in England and Wales.

In addition to their jurisdiction over summary offences magistrates' courts also have jurisdiction to try offences "triable either way"[2] and may, on conviction, impose penalties similar to those which may be imposed following conviction of summary offences.

b   Youth courts and youth justice

Until 1991, these were known as juvenile courts,[3] and are magistrates' courts which exercise jurisdiction over offences committed by, and other matters concerning, children and young persons.[4] These are dealt with separately, below.

c   Civil jurisdiction

This aspect of the magistrates' courts' jurisdiction is very varied. It extends over the recovery of certain civil debts such as income tax, national insurance contributions, electricity, gas and water charges, council tax, the grant, revocation and renewal of licences and domestic proceedings. The latter category is probably the most important aspect of the magistrates' civil jurisdiction; it is exercised principally under the Family Law Act 1996 and Children Act 1989, in "family proceedings courts".

J   YOUTH COURTS AND YOUTH JUSTICE

Until 1991, children and young persons accused of criminal offences were dealt with in juvenile courts. These courts are now known as youth courts. The aim of the procedure in these courts is to treat the juvenile suspect differently from adult accused persons. A youth court consists of justices specially selected from a juvenile panel,

---

18   The jurisdiction appears to be exclusive: *R v East Powder JJ, ex parte Lampshire* [1979] QB 616; [1979] 2 All ER 329, *post.*
19   Magistrates' Courts Act 1980, s 31(1).
20   See p 571, *post.*
1   See p 568, *post*
2   See Magistrates' Courts Act 1980, s 17, Sch 1; for details of the procedure for determining the mode of trial of such offences, see p 471, *post.*
3   Criminal Justice Act 1991, s 70.
4   For these purposes a "child" is a person under 14 years, a "young person" aged 14–17 inclusive: Children and Young Persons Act 1933, s 107.

trained for the purpose. The chair of the court remains constant, although other members serve by rotation.[5] A youth court must not sit in a room in which sittings of another court arc held if a sitting of that other court has been or will be held there within an hour.

Proceedings are not open to the public and the only persons admitted to the court are the court officers, the parties to the case and their representatives, witnesses, bona fide members of the press and other persons authorised by the court to be present. In addition, to protect the young person, the press must not publish or broadcast the identity of any person under eighteen concerned in the proceedings, unless the court so orders. This restriction includes not only the accused, but also any witness under eighteen years of age.

The appearance of a juvenile in the youth courts is, however, seen as a last resort. Strategies followed by police in the past have included cautioning of young offenders. The Crime and Disorder Act 1998 established in statutory form the fact that the basic aim of the youth justice system is to prevent offending. It also contains provisions relating to youth justices services, a new Youth Justice Board and youth offending teams, and various detailed changes. These are considered later.[6]

K   FAMILY COURTS

These courts were constituted under section 80 of the Domestic Proceedings and Magistrates' Courts Act 1978, and were known as domestic courts. Following a radical re-shaping of the law relating to children by the Children Act 1989, they were renamed "family proceedings courts".[7] They consist of justices drawn from a specially appointed panel to deal with such proceedings,[8] comprising persons who have received special training to ensure they have appropriate skills knowledge and understanding. No person may be present during the proceedings except officers of the court, the parties and their legal representatives, witnesses and other persons directly concerned in the case, newspaper representatives and any other person whom the court may permit to be present.[9] There is provision for rules of court to be made requiring the magistrates to give and record reasons for their decisions (which they do not have to, and usually do not, do in ordinary proceedings) and for making available a copy of the record to prospective appellants.[10]

Family proceedings courts have jurisdiction to deal with applications for periodic financial payments for spouses, to make various orders in respect of domestic violence and occupation of the family home (under provisions contained in the Family Law Act 1996), and to make various orders in respect of children in private law cases (cases where one spouse seeks a residence order or a contact order in respect of a child). The court also has a public law jurisdiction, dealing with care proceedings brought by a local authority under the Children Act 1989. Although the family proceedings court has concurrent jurisdiction in such matters with the county court and the Family Division of the High Court, public law actions must be commenced in the family

---

5   Youth Court (Constitution) Rules 1954, r 12 (SI 1954/1711, as amended).
6   See pp 458, 576-580, *post.*
7   Children Act 1989, s 92.
8   The formation of these panels and the composition of domestic courts is dealt with by rules of court made under s 67 of the Magistrates Courts' Act 1980; a stipendiary magistrate who is a member of a family court panel may sit alone (s 67(7)).
9   *Ibid*, s 69(2).
10   *Ibid*, s 74(1).

proceedings court,[10A] although powers of transfer from that court to the county court or to the Family Division of the High Court exist. Transfer will usually occur in cases of complexity, gravity, or importance, or where unacceptable delay would otherwise occur. In 1996, some 13,609 out of 16,351 such applications were dealt with by family proceedings courts. By contrast, the jurisdiction to hear a private law action is much more co-terminous: such an action may be commenced in either the family proceedings court or the county court, and, in 1996, some 33,419 out of 107,527 such actions were dealt with by the family proceedings courts, with the majority (73,711) being dealt with by county courts.

Appeals from these orders lie to the Family Division, where they are usually heard by a divisional court, although in some cases they may be heard by a single judge.[10B] Further appeal lies to the Court of Appeal and then to the House of Lords, in each case with leave.

L   COUNTY COURTS

The county courts are courts of exclusively civil jurisdiction dealing, in the main, with minor civil claims such as small debts. They were established by the County Courts Act 1846 to meet the need for a system of courts to deal with small claims. Historically there have been two important limitations to the extent of the county courts' jurisdiction. First, the jurisdiction is entirely statutory so that if, in any matter, statute provides no jurisdiction then none exists. Nevertheless statutes which are likely to affect a large section of the community frequently confer jurisdiction on the county courts. Modern examples are to be found in the Hire-Purchase Act 1965 and the Rent Act 1977. The general common law and equity jurisdiction of the county courts is contained in the County Courts Act 1984 and is principally limited by the value of the plaintiff's claim.[10C]

The second limitation on the jurisdiction of the courts is geographical. The jurisdiction of county courts is local in nature so that there must be some connecting factor between the action and the county court district in which it is tried. There are about four hundred county court districts in England and Wales grouped into circuits, each of which has at least one circuit judge assigned to it. The administrative business of the court is supervised by the district judge who has a seven-year general qualification[11] and frequently holds the post of district registrar of the High Court. The 1984 Act, as amended, also permits the appointment of deputy district judges. The district judge has a limited jurisdiction to try cases in which cases appeal lies to the judge. Apart from this, county courts have no appellate jurisdiction. Appeal lies from a county court to the Court of Appeal, subject to certain conditions, except in bankruptcy matters where appeal lies to a divisional court of the Chancery Division.

The reform of civil procedure and jurisdiction has become a major issue, discussed later. These changes will have a fundamental affect on the work undertaken by the

10A Children (Allocation of Proceedings) Order 1991 (SI 1991/1677).
10B RSC Ord 90, r 16.
10C Up until 1991 this was usually the determining factor. The changes implemented in 1990 give value a less determining role.
11   Ie a right of audience granted by an authorised body in relation to any class of proceedings in the Supreme Court, or all proceedings in county courts or magistrates' courts: see p 245, *post*.

county court. Details of jurisdiction and procedure in the county courts are discussed in due course.[12]

M   CORONERS' COURTS

I   The office of coroner

This ancient office dates from the twelfth century when it principally concerned the custody of the King's revenue, particularly that revenue accruing from fines and forfeiture. In addition the coroner from time to time exercised the jurisdiction of the sheriff and enquired into such matters as deodands, treasure trove and unexplained deaths. Some of these functions, together with the administrative functions once exercised by coroners, have been removed.

The modern coroner's appointment and jurisdiction are governed by statute.[13] He must be a barrister, solicitor or registered medical practitioner of not less than five years' standing. He is removable by the Lord Chancellor for misbehaviour.

2   Jurisdiction

Although the coroner has jurisdiction over such matters as treasure trove and, in London, enquiring into the outbreak of fires, his jurisdiction is principally concerned with inquests into the death of persons "whose bodies are lying within his district"[14] where there is reasonable cause for suspecting that the person has died a violent or unnatural death, or a sudden death the cause of which is unknown, or has died in prison or that the death occurred while the deceased was in police custody, or resulted from an injury caused by a police officer in the purported execution of his duty.[15] In *R v West Yorkshire Coroner, ex parte Smith*[16] the Court of Appeal held that the phrase "lying within his jurisdiction" (which was the form of words used prior to the passing of the Coroners Act 1988) applied to a body brought into the district from abroad. This would appear to remain the position.

If the case falls within the terms of section 3 of the 1988 Act the coroner's duty is mandatory; he must hold an inquest.

To hold an inquest the coroner may, and in some cases must, summon a jury of between seven and eleven members. Witnesses attend and give evidence and the coroner may compel the attendance of a witness and fine a witness for failing to attend in answer to a summons. The procedure is entirely inquisitorial in that, although interested persons may be represented and may ask questions of the witness, it is the coroner who conducts the proceedings and there are no speeches made to the jury. The jury return their verdict which need not be unanimous provided there are not more than two dissentients. This verdict is recorded in a document termed an "inquisition".

Prior to the passing of the Criminal Law Act 1977 the jury might return a verdict of murder, manslaughter or infanticide by a named person whereupon the coroner had power, without more, to commit that person for trial. In such a case the inquest took the place of a preliminary investigation by magistrates and the inquisition performed

---

12   See p 408, *post*.
13   Coroners Act 1988 (a consolidation Act).
14   This form of words was used by Coroners Act 1988, s 8, in substitution for the phrase "lying within his jurisdiction".
15   1988 Act, s 8(3).
16   [1983] QD 335; [1982] 3 All ER 1098.

the function of an indictment.[17] This procedure, although rarely adopted, was an anachronism and it was abolished by section 56 of the 1977 Act. A coroner's inquisition cannot now charge a person with any offence. Where criminal proceedings are in hand in respect of a death which is the subject of an inquest or for an offence alleged to have been committed in circumstances connected with the death, there are provisions in section 1 of the Coroners Act 1988 for the adjournment of the inquest pending the resolution of the criminal proceedings, the decision ultimately resting with the Director of Public Prosecutions. After the conclusion of the relevant criminal proceedings the coroner will be notified of the outcome by the court concerned whereupon he may resume the inquest if in his opinion there is sufficient cause to do so. If he does, then the finding of the inquest as to the cause of death must not be inconsistent with the outcome of the relevant criminal proceedings.[18]

There is no appeal from a coroner's inquisition although the proceedings are subject to judicial review by the High Court and may be quashed by order of certiorari where, for example, the verdict cannot be supported by the evidence.[19]

Proceedings before a coroner's court are absolutely privileged for the purposes of defamation.[20]

N   JUDICIAL COMMITTEE OF THE PRIVY COUNCIL

1   Constitution

Prior to the Judicial Committee Act 1833 the jurisdiction of the Privy Council was exercised principally by laymen. This Act, as amended by the Judicial Committee Act 1844, the Appellate Jurisdiction Acts 1876–1947 and other Acts, created the Judicial Committee composed of the Lord President of the Council, the Lord Chancellor, ex-Lord Presidents, the Lords of Appeal in Ordinary and those members of the Privy Council who hold or have held high judicial office within the meaning of the Appellate Jurisdiction Acts 1876 and 1887. Membership has also been extended from time to time by Order in Council to persons who have held high judicial office in Commonwealth countries. In practice the Lord Chancellor and the Lords of Appeal in Ordinary are the members of the Committee who usually sit, with the result that decisions of the Privy Council enjoy great authority although they are not strictly binding on English courts.[1]

The hearing of appeals takes place at the bar of the Privy Council before not less than three and usually five members of the Committee, although a greater number has been known.[2] The members of the Committee sit unrobed and procedure is similar to procedure in the House of Lords.

17   See p 503, post.
18   Coroners Act 1988, s 16(7).
19   See, generally, p 142, ante.
20   See p 216, post.
1   See p 68, ante.
2   See, e.g., Pratt v A-G for Jamaica [1994] 2 AC 1; [1993] 4 All ER 769, where a court of seven judges declared gross delays in the carrying out of sentences of death to amount to inhuman and degrading treatment within the meaning of the Jamaican constitution.

2   Jurisdiction

Although all English courts derive their jurisdiction directly or indirectly from the sovereign, the Judicial Committee of the Privy Council is slightly different in that its jurisdiction is that of the Sovereign in Council. Consequently the Privy Council does not pass judgment. It merely tenders advice to the sovereign in person. This is by convention followed and implemented by an Order in Council. For this reason only one opinion is usually read and dissents were until recently not recorded.[3] However it is now provided by Order in Council that dissenting opinions may be delivered in open court.[4]

The main aspects of the jurisdiction of the Privy Council are as follows:

(a) Appeals from courts outside the United Kingdom. Since the sovereign is the fountain of justice for all her Dominions, the Privy Council has jurisdiction to hear appeals from the Isle of Man, the Channel Islands, British Colonies and Protectorates and from the highest courts of independent Commonwealth countries. However, since the Statute of Westminster 1931 Commonwealth legislatures have been competent to pass legislation excluding appeal to the Privy Council and many have done so.[5] Thus the Privy Council held in 1947 that Canada could validly enact that the decision of its own Supreme Court be final and exclusive in civil and criminal matters.[6]

Leave to appeal in criminal matters is only given in exceptional cases. Misdirection will not suffice. There must be some clear departure from the "requirements of justice" or something which, in the particular case, "deprives the accused of the substance of fair trial and the protection of the law."[7]

(b) Admiralty jurisdiction. Prior to 1875 appeal lay from the High Court of Admiralty to the Privy Council. When the Judicature Acts assigned jurisdiction to hear appeals from the Probate, Divorce and Admiralty Division of the High Court to the newly formed Court of Appeal the jurisdiction of the Privy Council was virtually limited to appeals from that division when sitting as a "prize court".[8] The jurisdiction of the High Court to sit as a prize court is now exercised, as with other Admiralty jurisdiction, by the Admiralty Court of the Queen's Bench Division.[9] A prize court is a court convened to determine issues concerning the ownership of ships and cargo and the validity of their capture by enemy warships.

(c) Appeals from ecclesiastical courts. Since the jurisdiction of the ecclesiastical courts was drastically curtailed in 1857–1858[10] their jurisdiction has been confined to matters affecting members of the clergy and church buildings. The highest ecclesiastical courts are the Canterbury Court of Arches and the Chancery Court of York. Appeal from these courts lies to the Privy Council.[11] Although archbishops and bishops are not members of the Privy Council, whenever the Council is hearing an ecclesiastical

---

3   Cf judgment in the criminal division of the Court of Appeal where only one judgment is delivered as a rule, but for different reasons.

4   Judicial Committee (Dissenting Opinions) Order in Council 1966; for a particularly vigorous dissent, see *Abbot v R* [1977] AC 755; [1976] 3 All ER 140.

5   Including Aden, Australia, Botswana, Burma, Canada, Cyprus, Ghana, Guyana, India, Lesotho, Pakistan, Sierra Leone, Sri Lanka, Tanzania and Uganda.

6   *A-G for Ontario v A-G for Canada* [1947] AC 127; [1947] 1 All ER 137.

7   *Ibrahim v R* [1914] AC 599, at 614–615, per Lord Sumner; see also *Prasad v R* [1981] 1 All ER 319; [1981] 1 WLR 469.

8   Now contained in Supreme Court Act 1981, s 16(2), although jurisdiction also exists to hear appeals from the Colonial Courts of Admiralty and from the Court of Admiralty of the Cinque Ports.

9   Supreme Court Act 1981, s 20; see p 174, *ante.*

10   Court of Probate Act 1857; Matrimonial Causes Act 1857.

11   Ecclesiastical Jurisdiction Measure 1963, s 8.

appeal, summonses are sent to one archbishop or the Bishop of London and four other bishops to sit as assessors, ie in an advisory capacity.

(d) Appeals from medical tribunals. The Privy Council hears appeals by persons who have had their names erased from the medical register by the Professional Conduct Committee of the General Medical Council under the Medical Act 1983.[12]

(e) Special references. Apart from its appellate jurisdiction outlined above, the Privy Council is sometimes required to advise on matters of law at the instance of the sovereign.[13] In the exercise of this jurisdiction the Judicial Committee has advised on such diverse matters as the powers of colonial judges,[14] legislation in Jersey[15] and the eligibility of a person to sit and vote in the House of Commons.[16] The Secretary of State may recommend Her Majesty to refer to the Judicial Committee any question of whether a provision of any Measure of the Northern Ireland Assembly or Act of Parliament of Northern Ireland is void to the extent that it discriminates against any person or class of persons on the ground of religious belief or political opinion.[17]

O   COURTS OF PARTICULAR JURISDICTION

Prior to 1977 there were many courts of local jurisdiction which constituted exceptions to the normal hierarchy of courts in that their constitution and jurisdiction were controlled locally. However the judicial functions of the vast majority of such courts which actively exercised jurisdiction were abolished by the combined effect of the Courts Act 1971, the Local Government Act 1972 and the Administration of Justice Act 1977.[18] Certain courts are outside the ordinary hierarchy because their jurisdiction is concerned with matters wholly outside the scope of the ordinary civil and criminal law. Some of these courts, such as courts-martial, derive their jurisdiction from statute while others, notably the ecclesiastical courts, are autonomous although, of course, they are recognised by the Crown. The jurisdiction of these specialist courts is usually applicable only to certain members of society who have impliedly agreed to submit to their jurisdiction, though in some instances it extends to all members of the community.

I   Courts-martial[19]

Courts-martial exercise jurisdiction over members of the armed forces, and over their dependants if an alleged offence is committed overseas. Their constitution, jurisdiction and procedure are governed by various statutes, principally the Army and Air Force Acts 1955, the Naval Discipline Act 1957 and the Armed Forces Act 1981. However, the finding by the European Court of Human Rights in *Findlay v UK*[20] that the UK court-martial system was, in significant respects, contrary to Article 6 led to widespread

---

12   Similar powers exist under the Dentists Act 1984, the Opticians Act 1989 and the Veterinary Surgeons Act 1966.
13   Judicial Committee Act 1833, s 4.
14   *Re Wells* (1840) 3 Moo PCC 216.
15   *Re Jersey States* (1853) 9 Moo PCC 185.
16   *Re Macmanaway* [1951] AC 161.
17   Northern Ireland Constitution Act 1973, s 18.
18   See p 10, *ante*; the few that remain are listed in para 23 of the Law Commission report, Jurisdiction of Certain Ancient Courts (Law Com No 72).
19   See generally, Lyon, "After Findlay – A Consideration of Some Aspects of the Military Justice System" [1998] Crim LR 109.
20   (1997) Times, 27 February. See also *Coyne v United Kingdom*, (1997) Times, 24 October.

concern about the process. This had already been anticipated by the Government which, in 1996, secured the passage of the Armed Forces Act 1996.

Air Force and military courts-martial are similar in constitution and procedure.[1] The accused may be arrested for any offence against military law by a superior officer. In many instances his offence will only be a "summary" offence against Queen's Regulations in which case he will be tried by superior officers. In other cases the accused has a choice as to whether to be tried summarily or at a court-martial. Serious offences are always tried at courts-martial, except that murder, manslaughter, treason and rape committed within the United Kingdom cannot be tried at courts-martial but must be tried in the ordinary criminal courts. In all other cases the jurisdiction of civilian and military courts is concurrent. However a person who has already been convicted or acquitted by a civilian court cannot be subsequently tried at a military or Air Force court-martial, and vice versa.[2]

The trial of an offence at a court-martial is in many ways similar to a trial in the ordinary criminal courts. It is preceded by an inquiry which is similar to a preliminary investigation. The accused is sent for trial on a charge sheet which may be compared with an indictment. The trial will be before at least three (or five in the case of a general court-martial) officers who are assisted by a judge advocate from the Judge Advocate General's department[3] who is a lawyer and advises on the law. Proceedings are in open court and both counsel and solicitors have a right of audience. The prosecution case is conducted by an Army or Air Force officer either personally or through a civilian counsel. The order of proceedings and rules of evidence applicable are similar to those applicable in other criminal proceedings. The accused may appear in person or be represented by counsel, solicitor or a defending officer. There is no jury and at the conclusion of the evidence the judge advocate sums up and advises on the law, leaving the members of the court to arrive at their decision which is by majority, except that the court must be unanimous where sentence of death is to be imposed.[4] As noted earlier, this process has been the subject of adverse findings by the European Court of Human Rights. In *Findlay v UK* the court found that several features of the pre-existing scheme were in breach of the fair trial provisions of Article 6: the role of the Convening Officer, who had responsibility for selecting the president and members of the court, the role of the Confirming Officer, who (as a non-judicial body) had the role of confirming the findings and sentence of the court, and the role of the Judge-Advocate which did not provide sufficient safeguard to counteract the appearance of lack of impartiality created by the multiple roles and potential influence of the Convening Officer.

The Armed Forces Act 1996 contains changes which should overcome the appearance of potential bias and lack of perceived independence inherent in the old system. The Act, which came into force on 1 April 1997, abolishes the Convening Officer role, distributing the functions performed hitherto by that officer between the prosecuting authority, the Commanding Officer, liaising with an advisory body, court-martial administration officer and reviewing authority. The findings of a court-martial take effect immediately.

---

1   Naval courts-martial differ slightly in their composition, although their jurisdiction and procedure are similar.

2   Armed Forces Act 1996, s 25.

3   The corresponding department in naval courts-martial is the Judge Advocate of the Fleet's department. The Judge Advocate General and the Judge Advocate of the Fleet are appointed by the Queen on the advice of the Lord Chancellor.

4   Army Act 1955, s 96. The residual power to impose a death penalty is being removed by the Crime and Disorder Act 1998, s 36.

Although courts-martial cannot generally exercise jurisdiction over civilians this can be done where Her Majesty's forces are in armed occupation of hostile territory. In these circumstances a state of martial law may be declared by Her Majesty's commanders. A state of martial law may also be declared in time of insurrection although it is doubtful whether such a declaration would be valid within the United Kingdom. Furthermore civilians who are employed in the service of the forces on active service outside the United Kingdom are liable to trial in "standing civilian courts" which may be established outside the United Kingdom under section 6 of the Armed Forces Act 1976. This power was the subject of challenge in *R v Martin*,[4A] where a prosecution against a civilian, who was the son of an Army corporal serving in Germany at the time of the alleged offence, but later discharged, was held not to amount to an abuse of process. It could not be an abuse of process to use a jurisdiction that had been conferred by Parliament.

Courts-Martial Appeal Court   Until 1951 there was no appeal from conviction by a court-martial, the only remedy being a petition to the reviewing authority or, where an excess of jurisdiction was alleged, an application for *prohibition, certiorari* or *habeas corpus*.

The Courts-Martial (Appeals) Act 1951[5] created the Courts-Martial Appeal Court which is now composed of the *ex officio* and ordinary members of the Court of Appeal, judges of the Queen's Bench Division nominated by the Lord Chief Justice, certain Scottish and Irish judges and other persons of legal experience appointed by the Lord Chancellor. In practice the composition of the court resembles closely that of the criminal division of the Court of Appeal.[6] As in the latter court, there must be at least three judges. Only one judgment is delivered and procedure is similar to that in the criminal division of the Court of Appeal. The grounds of appeal to the Courts-Martial Appeal Court and the powers of that court on determining appeals are substantially similar to those of the Court of Appeal except that there is no right of appeal against sentence.

Appeal lies from the Courts-Martial Appeal Court to the House of Lords at the instance of the prosecutor or the defence subject to the conditions under which an appeal lies from the criminal division of the Court of Appeal to the House of Lords.[7]

2   Ecclesiastical courts

These courts have a history which is as old as the common law itself. Although they have been subject to control by the sovereign since the reign of Henry VIII and although their jurisdiction over laymen has by stages been abolished there remains a hierarchy of courts within the Church of England. In addition the General Synod of the Church of England has statutory powers[8] to pass measures concerning any matter affecting the Church of England and even concerning Acts of Parliament. These measures have statutory force upon receiving the Royal Assent. One such measure has been the Ecclesiastical Jurisdiction Measure 1963 which altered the hierarchy of ecclesiastical courts and abolished a large number of obsolete courts and their jurisdiction.

The ecclesiastical judicial system may now be summarised as follows. In each diocese there is a consistory court the judge of which is a chancellor appointed by the

---

4A   [1998] 1 All ER 193.
5   Now the Courts-Martial (Appeals) Act 1968.
6   See p 170, *post*.
7   See p 558, *post*; Courts-Martial (Appeals) Act 1968, s 39.
8   Under the Church of England Assembly (Powers) Act 1919 as amended by the Synodical Government Measure 1969, s 2.

bishop. He must be at least 30 years old and either be a barrister of seven years' standing or have held high judicial office. The consistory courts' jurisdiction[9] is principally concerned with investigating allegations of conduct unbecoming a clerk in Holy Orders and persistent neglect of duty. Appeal lies from the consistory courts to the Arches Court of Canterbury, presided over by the Dean of the Arches, or the Chancery Court of York, presided over by the Auditor, both officers being barristers of ten years' standing or persons who have held high judicial office. Appeal from these two courts lies to the Privy Council.[10]

Jurisdiction equivalent to that of the consistory courts is exercised over bishops and archbishops by Commissions of Convocation. Jurisdiction over all members of the clergy in matters involving "doctrine, ritual or ceremonial" is exercised by the Court of Ecclesiastical Causes Reserved composed of five judges appointed by Her Majesty including two persons who have held high judicial office and three diocesan bishops. Finally petition lies from both the Commissions of Convocation and the Court of Ecclesiastical Causes Reserved to a Commission of Review composed of three Lords of Appeal in Ordinary and two Lords Spiritual.

The penalties which ecclesiastical courts may impose range from rebuke to deprivation of Orders and disqualification from subsequent preferment. In addition such deprivation and disqualification are automatic where a priest or deacon is sentenced to imprisonment, has a decree of divorce or judicial separation pronounced against him on certain specified grounds, is found to have committed adultery in matrimonial proceedings or has had a magistrates' court order made against him in similar circumstances.[11]

Excesses of jurisdiction by the ecclesiastical courts may be controlled by the High Court by means of the prerogative orders of mandamus and prohibition. Certiorari does not, however, lie since these courts exercise and administer a different system of law.

3 Restrictive practices court

This court of record was created by the Restrictive Trade Practices Act 1956, now repealed and replaced by the consolidating Restrictive Practices Court Act 1976 and Restrictive Trade Practices Act 1976. The function of the court is to consider "restrictive agreements" and "information agreements" relating to the supply of goods or services.[12] Cases are referred to the court by the Director General of Fair Trading or by parties to such an agreement who have been ordered to furnish particulars to the court. The scope of the court's business was temporarily increased by the Resale Prices Act 1964 which restricted minimum resale price maintenance. Any supplier or trade association was able to apply to the Restrictive Practices Court for exemption for a class of goods on the grounds that this would be in the public interest.[13] The jurisdiction of the Court was extended by the Fair Trading Act 1973 in that the Director General of Fair Trading may bring proceedings in the court against any person who either does not give or does not observe a written assurance that he will refrain from a course of conduct in

9 For a reported instance of the jurisdiction of consistory courts, see *Re St George's Church, Oakdale* [1976] Fam 210; [1975] 2 All ER 870.
10 See p 190, *ante*.
11 Ecclesiastical Jurisdiction Measure 1963, s 55 (substituted by Ecclesiastical Jurisdiction (Amendment) Measure 1974).
12 Restrictive Trade Practices Act 1976, s 1; the extension to agreements relating to services was made by the Fair Trading Act 1973; for the definitions of "restrictive agreements" and "information agreements", see ss 6, 7, 11 and 12 of the 1976 Act.
13 Resale Prices Act 1964, s 5. All applications have long since been determined.

the course of his business which appears to the Director to be detrimental to the interests of consumers in the United Kingdom and, in accordance with statutory criteria, unfair to consumers.[14]

The court consists of three judges of the High Court appointed by the Lord Chancellor, a judge of the Court of Session of Scotland, a judge of the Supreme Court of Northern Ireland and not more than ten lay members appointed by the Queen on the recommendation of the Lord Chancellor. The court is duly constituted with a presiding judge and two lay members except that in the case of proceedings involving only issues of law the court may consist of a single judge.[15] Appeal lies from the court on a question of law, and in proceedings under Part III of the Fair Trading Act 1973 (consumer protection) on a question of fact or law, to the Court of Appeal, the Court of Session or the Court of Appeal of Northern Ireland, as the case may be.[16]

4   Naval courts

A naval court may be summoned by an officer in command of one of Her Majesty's ships on any foreign station on a complaint to him by any member of the crew which appears to require immediate investigation, or where any British ship is wrecked, abandoned or lost in the area, or where the interests of the owner of any British ship or its cargo so require.[17] Such a court, consisting of naval officers, must investigate the matter judicially and may impose imprisonment or fine or forfeiture of wages, suspend or cancel officers' certificates, send an offender home for trial and order a ship to undergo a survey for unseaworthiness. Appeal lies from its decision to the divisional court of the Queen's Bench Division and thence, with leave, to the Court of Appeal.

5   Court of Chivalry

The jurisdiction of an English court can only be removed by statute. Nevertheless the jurisdiction of most local courts and feudal courts has fallen into obsolescence. However a modern sitting was held of the Court of Chivalry, an ancient feudal court, to decide the entitlement of a theatre to display the coat of arms of the City of Manchester.[18] Prior to this case the court had not been convened since 1737. The court determines disputes over the right to use armorial bearings and ensigns. It is presided over by the Earl Marshal, although he appointed the Lord Chief Justice to sit as his deputy in the modern case in question. The court appears to have no power to enforce its decisions.[19]

6   Court of Protection

At common law the sovereign has always assumed care and custody of persons of unsound mind and their property. As keeper of the Queen's conscience the Lord Chancellor was detailed to exercise this authority. At the present day the Lord

14   Fair Trading Act 1973, ss 34–35.
15   Restrictive Practices Court Act 1976, s 7.
16   *Ibid*, s 10.
17   Merchant Shipping Act 1894, s 480.
18   *Manchester Corporation v Manchester Palace of Varieties Ltd* [1955] P 133; [1955] 1 All ER 387.
19   *Ibid*. Notwithstanding, the Law Commission report of 1976 did not recommend the abolition of the court and it was one of the few courts of local and ancient jurisdiction which did not have its jurisdiction removed by the Administration of Justice Act 1977.

Chancellor and the judges of the Chancery Division administer the property of persons of unsound mind within the meaning of the Mental Health Act 1983. When exercising this function the Chancery judge sits as the Court of Protection, the constitution and jurisdiction of which is now governed by the 1983 Act.[20]

The jurisdiction of the Court of Protection should not be confused with the jurisdiction of courts under various statutes to make orders for admission of persons to hospital.

20   Though the power is exercisable in the High Court if the sum involved is a small one: *Re K's Settlement Trusts* [1969] 2 Ch 1; [1969] 1 All ER 194.

Chapter 9

Tribunals and Inquiries

I Statutory tribunals

A large number of statutory tribunals has been created during the twentieth century to provide informal, relatively cheap mechanisms for the resolution of disputes, usually between the citizen and the State. These tribunals provide a means for disputes to be resolved in a way, and by a body, that is independent of the of the government department with whom the citizen is in dispute. In that sense, tribunals are similar to courts. Most tribunals have powers to decide matters, and will be under a duty to act judicially. For this reason, the name "tribunal" does not, of itself, indicate very much. In *Attorney-General v British Broadcasting Corporation*[1] the House of Lords held that although a valuation court was a "court", it was established essentially to perform administrative functions. Conversely, the Lands Tribunal has a jurisdiction and formality very much like a court, and indeed the Employment Appeal Tribunal has already been discussed in the context of it being in reality a "court".[2] For practical, as opposed to analytical, purposes the terminology is usually unimportant. Much more important are the procedures and standards that characterise such bodies.

Tribunals have been created on an ad hoc basis, almost always by statute, to meet the need for a process of dispute adjudication in an individual context. Historically, their composition, the process of appointment of members, the procedures followed and the extent of independence from government departments has varied considerably. For that reason the concept of a "system" of administrative justice is misleading. Indeed, the idea of a system of administrative justice is one that has, in the past, caused some concern. The constitutional writer, Dicey,[3] rejected notions of a separate system of justice (a "*droit administratif*") for resolving disputes between citizens and the State. Such a view may well not have been an accurate analysis of the position even when Dicey wrote. Even if it was, such a view is not tenable today. Over the last 100 years

---

1   [1981] AC 303 [1980] 3 All ER 161. *In Pickering v Liverpool Daily Post and Echo Newspapers plc* [1991] 2 AC 370 [1991] 1 All ER 622, a Mental Health Review Tribunal was held to be a "court" for the purposes of the Contempt of Court Act 1981.
2   See p 180, *ante*.
3   Macmillan, *Introduction to the Study of the Constitution* (10th Edn, 1964), at p 318.

Governments have considered there to be a need to confer jurisdiction on tribunals rather than courts, particularly in the context of social or welfare legislation. The reasons for this are discussed below, but the result has been a form of jurisdiction which, in quantity, outstrips the jurisdiction of the courts many times over. In 1996, tribunals dealt with in excess of 300,000 cases, and as far back as 1979 tribunals dealt with almost six times as many cases as did the courts.[4] Coupled with growth in the number of tribunals has come greater regulation of the composition and procedures of such tribunals, with some 80 or so categories of tribunal now falling under the scrutiny of the Council on Tribunals. The growth of a developed system of administrative law[5] with a largely unified procedure for the challenge of the actions both of administrative bodies and inferior courts and tribunals now makes the use of the expression "system of administrative justice" appropriate, even if the particular jurisdiction and characteristics of individual tribunals vary widely. They each share common characteristics, namely the performance of adjudicative functions in a way that is, and is seen to be, fair and impartial, with, generally, recourse to the courts to review decisions of law.

2   Examples of tribunals

The range of tribunals that exist is diverse. Examples include the Agricultural Land Tribunals,[6] Child Support Appeals Tribunals,[7] Conveyancing Appeals Tribunal,[8] the Criminal Injuries Compensation Board,[9] the Data Protection Tribunal,[10] Industrial Tribunals,[11] the Immigration Appeals Tribunals,[12] Social Security Appeals Tribunals,[13] Vaccine Damage Tribunals[14] Mental Health Review Tribunals[15] the Parole Board[16] and the Interception of Communications Tribunal.[17] A perusal of Schedule 1 to the Tribunals and Inquiries Act 1992 quickly gives an indication of the total diversity and number of these, mainly statutory,[18] tribunals, which have increased significantly in number as statutory intervention into all aspects of life has increased. Some deal with matters of financial compensation, others with eligibility for financial assistance or benefit, others with interferences with property, or property rights, and still others relating to the liberty of individual or individual rights. Differences can also be seen in their role.

---

4   See Royal Commission on Legal Services (Cmnd 7648, 1979).
5   In *Ridge v Baldwin* [1964] AC 40; [1963] 2 All ER 66, Lord Reid said "We do not have a developed system of administrative law – perhaps because until fairly recently we did not need it.". This view is no longer an accurate assessment: see *O'Reilly v Mackman* [1983] 2 AC 237, per Lord Diplock.
6   See Agriculture Act 1947, s 73.
7   Child Support Act 1991, s 21.
8   Courts and Legal Services Act 1990, s 39.
9   Established under Royal Prerogative: see *R v Criminal Injuries Compensation Board, ex parte Lain* [1967] 2 QB 864, [1967] 2 All ER 770; the attempt to put the Commission on a statutory footing, contained in Part VII of the Criminal Justice Act 1988, failed, the provisions thereof never being implemented by the Government: see *R v Secretary of State for Home Affairs, ex parte Fire Brigades Union* [1995] 2 AC 513; [1995] 2 All ER 244. See now Criminal Injuries Compensation Act 1995.
10   Data Protection Act 1984, s 3.
11   See, now, Industrial Tribunals Act 1996.
12   Immigration Act 1971, s 12.
13   Social Security Administration Act 1992, s 41.
14   Vaccine Damage Payments Act 1979, s 1.
15   Mental Health Act 1983, s 8.
16   Created by the Criminal Justice Act 1967. See now Part III of the Criminal Justice Act 1991, as amended.
17   Interceptions of Communications Act 1985.
18   The Criminal Injuries Compensation Board was originally a creature of the royal prerogative, not statute: see n 16, *supra*.

Some act as appellate tribunals, for example, the Social Security Appeals Tribunals and the Immigration Appeals Tribunals, act as appellate bodies to deal with appeals from adjudicators. Others have their own, original, jurisdiction, like the Parole Board or Mental Health Review Tribunal.

Some tribunals have a more "domestic" nature, often, though not always, deriving their jurisdiction from contract rather than statute. The Solicitors Disciplinary Tribunal[19] is a good example of where tribunal is established by, or under, statute to deal with allegations of misconduct against a member of a profession. Examples of tribunals created by the domestic or private body itself are the Disciplinary Tribunal of the Bar[20] and that of the Football Association.[1]

Employment Tribunals

The role of tribunals in dispute adjudication, and the interaction between courts and tribunals, is well demonstrated by the system of employment tribunals. First established in 1964, and until 1998 known as industrial tribunals[2], their at first very limited jurisdiction has been extended greatly by various statutes. The relevant powers are now to be found in the Industrial Tribunals Act 1996 and the Employment Rights (Dispute Resolution) Act 1998, and their jurisdiction extends to a wide range of matters arising under employment and discrimination legislation. In particular, the employment tribunals deal with claims of unfair dismissal.[3] The pre-existing right to sue for breach of ordinary contractual employment rights is not taken away by legislation. Thus potentially an employee, or ex-employee may have rights that exist either under statute and at common law. Such common law disputes are often within the jurisdiction of the industrial tribunals: since 1994 many (although not all) contract claims relating to termination of employment may now be taken to an employment tribunal.[4] Thus the industrial tribunals have taken, although not completely, a significant area of jurisdiction formerly exercised by the Queens Bench Division. The current jurisdiction of employment tribunals is wide, and may be extended by order.[5] It goes beyond matters relating to unfair dismissal and redundancy, to include matters such as a failure to pay maternity pay, complaints under the Sex Discrimination Act 1975 and the Race Relations Act 1976, the prevention or deterrence of the employee to join a trade union or failure to comply with the provisions of the Disability Discrimination Act 1995, and complaints concerning alleged contravention of the Equal Pay Act 1970.

The organisation of employment tribunal system is presidential: there is a President of Employment Tribunals , who is a lawyer of not less than seven years' standing, appointed for renewable periods of five years, and who has responsible for the overall administration of the employment tribunal system. Detailed regulations prescribe the composition of an employment tribunal: a tribunal will comprise three members. The Chairman will be legally qualified, and of at least seven years' standing. Each tribunal will also contain two lay members, drawn from panels of members from each side of industry compiled by the Secretary of State for Employment. One member representing

---

19   See pp 249–251, *post.*
20   See p 265, *post.*
1   Established by contract: see *R v Football Association Ltd, ex parte Football League Ltd* [1993] 2 All ER 833; see also *R v Disciplinary Committee of the Jockey Club, ex parte Aga Khan* [1993] 2 All ER 853; [1993] 1 WLR 909.
2   See now Employment Rights (Dispute Resolution) Act 1998.
3   See Employment Protection Act 1996.
4   Industrial Tribunals Extension of Jurisdiction Order 1994, SI 1994/1623. The limitations relate personal injuries, requirements to provide living accommodation, intellectual property, breach of confidence or restrictive covenants. In addition, no claim in excess of £25,000 can be entertained.
5   Industrial Tribunals Act 1996, s 9.

employers and one representing employed persons will be appointed to each tribunal. There is thus a significant lay element. Members of tribunals are appointed because of their special knowledge and experience and they are entitled to draw on this in coming to their decisions, although if their experience is contrary to the evidence before the tribunal they should, before relying on it, make this known to the parties and give witnesses the opportunity of dealing with it.[6] Decision-making is by a majority of the members of the tribunal. If the lay members agree with each other as to the appropriate conclusion, this can prevail over the conclusion of the legally qualified chairman. This lay element is an important way of ensuring that the tribunals achieve one of the key aims of any tribunal system, namely that the tribunal should be able to deploy expertise in its area of jurisdiction. Tribunals sit frequently, and as required: on average some 75 tribunals sit in Great Britain each day, with in excess of 22,000 hearings each year.

Applicants may appear in person, or be represented by solicitor, counsel, by the representative of a trade union or employers' association, or by any other person whom he desires to represent him.[7] Legal aid is not available for these proceedings, although the Green Form scheme may assist in ensuring that an applicant can be properly advised and prepared, as may assistance by way of representation.[8] The procedure followed is often stated to be informal, but is similar to that followed by a court determining a civil action.[8A] The process cannot be regarded as devoid of structure or formality. Documentation to accompany an application, sufficient to identify the grounds of the application and details of the claim, must be completed. The power is given to a legally qualified chairman to hold a pre-trial review, although the chairman who conducts the pre-trial review cannot conduct the hearing itself. At that pre-trial review, an applicant can be required to pay a deposit, if it is considered that the application is unlikely to succeed. The tribunal must take into account the ability of the applicant to pay a deposit, and the tribunal must warn the applicant that he, or she, runs the risk of having an order for costs made against them. The actual tribunal hearing will follow normal court procedure with evidence on oath and rules of evidence generally, although not always strictly, being adhered to. Restrictions on publicity and reporting can be imposed in cases of national security, where a Minister may actually direct a tribunal to sit in private.[9] Such a power of direction in the hands of a Minister would be unthinkable in the context of a court.[10] Reasons are given for a decision, and are given in writing. Costs are not normally awarded, but, as seen above, can be awarded, and are awarded where the tribunal is of the opinion that a party has acted frivolously, vexatiously or otherwise unreasonably. Appeal against decisions of industrial tribunals lies to the Employment Appeal Tribunal.[12]

6   *Dugdale v Kraft Foods Ltd* [1977] 1 All ER 454; [1976] 1 WLR 1288.
7   1996 Act, s 6.
8   See pp 281–282, *post*.
8A   Industrial Tribunals (Constitution and Rules of Procedure) Regulations 1993, SI 1993/2687, as amended.
9   1996 Act, s 10.
10   For the principle of open justice, and the powers of courts to order a private sitting, see pp 163–165, *ante*.
11   1996 Act, ss 11–12. See also Industrial Tribunals (Constitution) Regulations SI 1993/2687. In *R v London (North) Industrial Tribunal, ex parte Associated Newspapers Ltd* (1998) Times, 13 May, it was held that a blanket reporting restriction imposed where some allegations against the running of a London Borough Council involved allegations of sexual misconduct was against the public interest in the proper running of local authorities.
12   See p 180, *ante*.

Social Security Appeals Tribunals

Another example of how a tribunal structure is integral to dispute resolution is seen in the social security appeals tribunals. The history of appeals tribunals in the social security, national insurance, medical, disability and child support areas is a chequered one. In 1984, the then existing Supplementary Benefits Appeals tribunals were merged with the National Insurance local tribunals, which had existed since 1948, creating a new system of Social Security Appeals Tribunals.[13] It was intended, through that change, to achieve the clear independence from the Department of Health and Social Security and other relevant government departments which had not always been perceived to exist. Social Security Appeals Tribunals deal with appeals from decisions of adjudication officers of the Benefits Agency or Employment Service (depending on the nature of the claim), in respect of entitlement to benefits. This entitlement to an appeal does not extend to social fund payments, which being purely discretionary payments are dealt with on an administrative basis, with no independent tribunal appeal, but merely internal departmental review.

In 1987 these tribunals were subsumed into a new presidential system, legislation creating a new office, the Office of the President of Social Security Appeals Tribunals. In 1991, this was renamed the Independent Tribunal Service. The president of the new service has since then always been a county court judge, although appointment to the office of president is open to any lawyer with a 10-year general qualification.[14] The president is responsible for the appointment of lay members, the organisation of the composition and membership of tribunals, and general co-ordination of their work. This includes issuing guidance on new legislation, subordinate legislation, case law or practice issues. The composition of each tribunal is a legally qualified chairman and two lay members. Lay members are drawn from a panel of persons who appear to the president to have knowledge or experience of conditions in the area and to be representative of persons living in the area. The extent to which this has been achieved is debatable, with some evidence to suggest that persons from the ethnic minority, lone parent families and those with disability are not being represented in the form of tribunal membership.[14A] The procedure followed at proceedings in the tribunal is intended to be, and is, informal, resting very much on the preferences and approach of the individual chairman. It is inquisitorial in nature: social security tribunals are expected to be pro-active in identifying the issues in the case, eliciting the relevant facts and law and applying it. This is extremely important given the fact that a very significant proportion of applicants will be unaccompanied by a representative. In fact, almost half of all applicants will not attend the hearing personally. If they do, and are represented, it will almost always be by a non-legally qualified representative, albeit one who often has substantial expertise in the intricacies of welfare law. A striking statistic is the success rate before the tribunal for those who are not represented: only about 7% of those who do not attend and are not represented succeed in their appeal.[15] Welfare rights workers may often have a more detailed knowledge of the relevant regulations, and their application, than most lawyers. The absence of lawyers is not however simply a question of expertise: legal aid is not available for such proceedings. Appeals from their decisions lie on points of law to one of sixteen Social Security Commissioners. These are legally qualified persons of at least 10 years' standing, and are appointed

13   Now governed by the Social Security Administrations Act 1992.
14   Social Security Administrations Act 1992, s 51(1)). For a ten-year qualification, see p 245, *post*.
14A See the commentary by Harlow and Rawlings *Law and Administration, Text and Materials* (2nd Edn, 1997) Butterworths, at p 485.
15   See Ogus, Barendt and Wikeley *The Law of Social Security* (4th Edn, 1996) Butterworths, at p 669, and the sources therein cited.

by the Crown. The Lord Chancellor has responsibility for the detailed regulation of proceedings before one of them, or, in difficult cases, before a panel of three Commissioners. From decisions of the Commissioners a further appeal lies to the Court of Appeal.

Criminal Injuries Compensation Board

Tribunals are sometimes established for the purpose of determining individuals' rights to compensation from public funds. The right to compensation arises where a person has suffered loss or damage, often by reason of an act of the legislature or the executive; compulsory acquisition of land is an obvious example.

A most important addition to compensation tribunals was the Criminal Injuries Compensation Board. The scheme was established as an experimental measure in 1964 and provides ex gratia compensation to victims of crimes of violence (or if the victim dies, his dependants). As noted above,[15A] attempts were made to create a statutory regime, but the provisions of the Criminal Justice Act 1988 were never implemented. The Criminal Injuries Compensation Act 1995 was passed to put the scheme on a statutory footing. Compensation, originally assessed on the same basis as common law damages (where the application is by a dependant the principles of the Fatal Accidents Act apply), now takes the form of a payment calculated by reference to a tariff in respect of specific injuries. Claims are determined in accordance with a scheme set out by the Home Secretary: the statute itself is merely enabling, and contains little detail.

Applications are in the first instance dealt with by a case-officer, the applicant having the right, if dissatisfied with that decision, to a hearing before an adjudicator. At the hearing the applicant must prove his case on a balance of probabilities; he may call, examine and cross-examine witnesses. The procedure is informal and hearings are in private. Compensation will not be awarded unless the Board is satisfied that the injury is one for which compensation of not less than £1,000 would be awarded. The circumstances of the injury, the level of assistance and other factors are not likely to be relevant in the future, unlike under the previous *ex gratia* scheme.

There is, at present, no right of appeal, although decisions are subject to judicial review by the High Court[15B] and will be quashed if there has been an error of law, or on *Wednesbury* principles, be deemed to have done so.[15C]

Interception of Communications Tribunals

A different type of tribunal is seen in the Interception of Communications Tribunal, established by the Interception of Communications Act 1985. This was established to adjudicate on applications made by individuals to determine whether the relevant authorisation exists for the interception of communications, and displays qualities that are different from those usually associated with tribunals. The tribunal comprises five lawyers, appointed by the Crown, and who have a status of a High Court judge, in that

15A See p 196, *supra*.
15B See, generally, pp 142–152, *ante*.
15C *R v Criminal Injuries Compensation Board, ex parte Thompstone* [1984] 3 All ER 572; [1984] 1 WLR 1234.

they are removable only on an address of both Houses of Parliament.[16] They sit in private, and report to the Prime Minister. The applicant does not receive a hearing in the generally accepted sense. The tribunal may make an order quashing a warrant authorising an interception and may direct that compensation be paid to the applicant.[17] In deciding whether there has been a contravention of the Act, the tribunal applies the principles that would be applied on an application for judicial review.[18] The decisions of the tribunal attract no right of appeal, and may not be questioned in any court of law. The tribunal, unlike those discussed earlier, is not subject to the supervision of the Council on Tribunals.[19]

3   The nature of tribunals and reasons for their creation

The diversity of tribunals can be seen in the examples set out above. Clearly, the matters within their jurisdiction relate to important areas of activity of government, and many individuals are more likely to have recourse to the adjudication procedures provided by tribunals than to the more traditional court system, except with regard to family and criminal matters. They thus form a key part of the English legal system, and, as noted above, reflect the growth of the state in the twentieth century.

The growth of this system of "administrative justice", and preference often for adjudication by tribunals rather than by the courts, reflects both the perceived disadvantages of the courts, and the perceived advantages of tribunals as a means of adjudication. The disadvantages of the courts are often considered to be formality, lack of speed, lack of expertise in some specialist areas of law, and cost. By contrast tribunals are often said to have the advantage of being bodies which follow informal procedures, can hear cases relatively quickly, are cheap, and have expertise in the particular subject matter. This analysis, although often true, is not invariably so. Given the multiplicity of tribunals that exist, not all these perceived advantages or disadvantages operate in any given instance. Tribunals vary widely in terms of their composition, procedure and efficiency. Examples include the Lands Tribunal (of almost court-like formality), industrial tribunals, rent tribunals, General and Special Commissioners of Income Tax, and (of a completely different type) social security appeals tribunals. They vary enormously in their formality, the extent to which they follow legal procedures and adopt rules of evidence, and in the speed in handling and disposing of individual cases. Much depends on the nature of the matter being determined by the tribunal, and the appropriate procedures to be followed. Thus social security appeals tribunals might be regarded as far more informal than industrial tribunals, and much less so than the court-like Lands Tribunal. Regard must also be had as to whether the tribunal is appellate in role, dealing with appeals against decisions of officials, or decision-making in a original jurisdiction sense, eg granting a licence or determining whether the applicant should be at liberty.[20] It should also be noted that sometimes tribunals are established, or jurisdiction conferred, because of the need to have a decision-making

16   Compare with the criteria for the removal of judges under Supreme Court of Judicature (Consolidation) Act 1925: see p 212, *post*.
17   Interception of Communications Act 1985, s 7(5).
18   Ibid, s 7(4).
19   See p 208, *post*.
20   See, for example, the Parole Board, which determines whether a prisoner serving a determinate or discretionary life sentence is suitable for early release on licence: see Criminal Justice Act 1991, Part III, and p 504, *post*. See also the role of the Mental Health Review Tribunal, under Mental Health Act 1983.

or review process independent of the executive. One example is the Interception of Communications Tribunal, described above. This provides the minimum level of independent scrutiny that would be regarded as acceptable under European Convention on Human Rights.[1] Another is the Parole Board, whose jurisdiction has been extended several times so as to ensure that decisions as to release on licence of prisoners[2] are taken by an independent body, and not by the Home Secretary.[3] A third is the jurisdiction of Boards of Visitors to discipline prisoners for more serious offences against prison discipline.

A further reason for the establishment of a tribunal sometimes is to provide advice on sensitive issues to government ministers. A good example is the power in the Immigration Act 1971 to deport a person, other than a British citizen, on the ground that his deportation would be "conducive to the public good".[4] No appeal exists against such a decision, but the applicant is given the opportunity to make representations to an independent advisory panel. In *R v Secretary of State for the Home Department, ex parte Cheblak*,[5] Sir John Donaldson MR explained the reasons for the introduction of the review system as follows:

"The current system of independent scrutiny ... which has involved the creation of a specialist panel currently presided over by Lloyd LJ was approved by Parliament 20 years ago. It replaced a statutory appeals system under the Immigration Appeals Act 1969. The appeal tribunal created under that Act was designed for an adversarial system of general application to all appeals against decisions to deport, each party presenting its evidence subject to cross examination, with the tribunal giving a binding decision. However, where the Secretary of State certified that matters could not be disclosed to the appellant because of the interests of national security, the essential features and safeguards of the adversarial system disappeared ...".

In that case the court accepted that the procedures, and rights of the appellant, could differ from those normally expected of a tribunal because of the nature of the issues before the advisory panel. Thus the appellant was not entitled to know the details of what was alleged against him, or allowed legal representation.[6]

One clear danger is that tribunals might be viewed as part of the process of government rather than as a part of a legal system providing means of adjudication independent of the executive. In the first half of the twentieth century concerns grew[7] about the dangers of executive encroachment into the legislative and judicial areas, through the uncontrolled use of delegated legislation and through the granting of extensive powers of adjudication to tribunals not demonstrably independent of government departments, and, sometimes, the granting of adjudicative functions to departments themselves. These concerns led firstly to the report of the Donoughmore

---

1   See *Klass v Federal Public of Germany* (1979–1980) 2 EHRR 214, and pp 123–128, *ante*.
2   See p 544, *post*
3   See *Thynne, Wilson and Gunnell v United Kingdom* (1990) 13 EHRR 666; *Hussain and Singh v United Kingdom* (1996) 22 EHRR 1.
4   1971 Act, s 3(5)(b).
5   [1991] 2 All ER 319; [1991] 1 WLR 890.
6   See also *R v Secretary of State for the Home Department, ex parte Hosenball* [1977] 3 All ER 452; [1977] 1 WLR 776.
7   See, eg Lord Hewart CJ in *The New Despotism* (1929) where he referred to "administrative lawlessness".

Committee in 1932[8] and, more recently, in 1958, to the Report of the Franks Committee.[9] The Franks Committee Report described tribunals as follows:

"[They] ... are not ordinary courts, but neither are they appendages of Government Departments ... tribunals should properly be regarded as machinery provided by Parliament for adjudication rather than as part of the machinery of administration. The essential point is that in all these cases Parliament has deliberately provided for a decision outside and independent of the Department concerned ... and the intention of Parliament to provide for the independence of tribunals is clear and unmistakable."[10]

The Franks Report highlighted the need for tribunals to have the three key characteristics of openness, impartiality and fairness, qualities which underpin the judicial system in England and Wales. It also noted that tribunals have certain advantages over courts (those of cheapness, accessibility, freedom from technicality, expedition and expert knowledge of their own area of operation). It described these as follows:[11]

"Openness appears to us to require the publicity of proceedings and knowledge of the essential reasoning underlying the decisions; fairness to require the adoption of a clear procedure which enables parties to know their rights, to present their case fully and to know the case which they have to meet; and impartiality to require the freedom of tribunals from the influence, real or apparent, of departments concerned with the subject matter of their decision."

The Committee recommended the creation of a permanent statutory body to supervise tribunal composition, organisation and procedure, and to review the working of tribunals within its remit.

The Franks Report was the catalyst for the passage of the Tribunals and Inquiries Act 1958, which established the Council on Tribunals, discussed later.[11A] The 1958 Act was repealed and re-enacted by the Tribunals and Inquiries Act 1992.

The characteristics of the tribunal system outlined above bear close resemblance to those that operate in a "court", thus emphasising the fact that whether a body is characterised as a court or tribunal is less important than its composition and rules of procedure. For example, employment tribunals can claim the expertise and specialist knowledge that flows from a limited jurisdiction presided over by those with first-hand knowledge of the types of matters before the tribunal. The volume or work, however, is very substantial and militates against speedy disposal of applications. In 1995–1996, in excess of 30,000 applications were dealt with. Further, it should be noted that the standards identified by the Franks Report, of openness, impartiality and fairness (which might be regarded as "judicializing" tribunals) are in fact the key standards of procedural fairness that a court in an application for judicial review would regard as the basic standards of procedural fairness. These are to be applied, so far as possible,

8   Report of the Committee on Ministers' Powers, HMSO, 1928, Cm 4060.
9   Committee on Tribunals and Inquiries, 1958, Cmd 218, HMSO.
10   *Ibid*, at para 2.45.
11   *Ibid*, para 42.
11A See p 208, *post*.

by any person acting in a way that affects the rights or legitimate expectations of an individual.[12]

4　Domestic tribunals

As noted above, there are a number of private or professional associations which have set up their own tribunals for resolving disputes between their own members or exercising control or discipline over them. The jurisdiction of these tribunals is based primarily on contract in that, by becoming a member of the association or professional body, a person contracts to accept the jurisdiction of the governing tribunal. Nevertheless in many cases these tribunals exist on a statutory basis with a right of appeal to the courts. Examples of domestic tribunals constituted under statute are the Solicitors Disciplinary Tribunal, under the Solicitors Act 1974,[13] and the Professional Conduct Committee of the General Medical Council, under the Medical Act 1983. Where the tribunal is not constituted under a statute then there is no appeal to the ordinary courts. However, the High Court exercises a supervisory jurisdiction over tribunals, even where their jurisdiction is not based on statute, and will intervene to prevent an abuse of natural justice.[14]

5　Statutory inquiries

Several statutory provisions provide for the establishment of a local enquiry. One example is the power contained in the Police Act 1996. Section 49 of that Act provides for the Home Secretary to cause a local inquiry to be held into any matter connected with the policing of the area. One striking example of this was the inquiry established in 1997 by the Home Secretary to inquire into the death of L in a racially-motivated killing.[15] Certain individuals had been investigated by the police, but no proceedings were brought by the Crown Prosecution Service because of the lack of sufficient evidence. A private prosecution then brought by the family of L failed, the judge declining to allow the case to go to the jury, again because of lack of evidence. When an inquiry was established to examine alleged failings in the police investigation, it was sought to put certain questions to the suspected individuals to seek to demonstrate that they were, in fact, the killers of L. In Divisional Court proceedings, however, challenge was made by the five suspects to those proposed questions. In giving judgment in *R v Chairman of Stephen Lawrence Inquiry, ex parte A*[16] the Divisional Court stressed that the task of the inquiry was to examine the conduct of the police inquiry, not to conduct a trial of those five persons suspected of having committed the killing of L. A Police Act inquiry could never be the proper forum for the conduct of a murder trial.

12　See, eg, *R v Devon County Council ex parte Baker, R v Durham County Council, ex parte Curtis*, both reported at [1995] 1 All ER 73; *R v Ministry of Agriculture Fisheries and Food, ex parte Hamble Fisheries* [1995] 2 All ER 714; *R v Gough* [1993] AC 346; [1993] 2 All ER 724; *R v Secretary of State for the Environment, ex parte Kirkstall Valley Campaign Ltd* [1996] 3 All ER 304. *Doody v Secretary of State for Home Affairs* [1993] 3 All ER 92; cf *R v Higher Education Funding Council, ex parte Institute of Dental Surgery* [1994] 1 All ER 651; *R v Board of Visitors of HM Prison, The Maze, ex parte Hone* [1988] AC 379.
13　See p 249, *post*.
14　See p 146, *ante*.
15　Inquiry into the Death of Stephen Lawrence 1997–1998.
16　See (1988) Times, 19 June.

More commonly, local inquiries are held by inspectors under town and country planning, compulsory purchase and highways legislation into proposed development, compulsory purchase and highways schemes. In practice these inquiries are conducted by inspectors, who often (although not always) have powers to determine the subject of the inquiry but ultimately it is the Minister who assumes responsibility in Parliament. Inquiries of this nature often arise when objections are lodged against orders submitted by a local or public authority to a Minister for confirmation, or, sometimes, submitted by the Minister himself but subject to confirmation.

Procedure at these inquiries is governed by the statute under which they are held. The extent of rights of appeal, usually on points of law only, again is governed by the particular statutory scheme. Furthermore, if procedural fairness is not observed (by, for example, the proper statement of reasons) judicial review may be an alternative course of action open to the aggrieved party.[17] However, as noted above, the scheme may in fact be that of the Minister himself. This is often the case with major inquiries into nationally important schemes such as the construction of a power station (the inquiry into the Sizewell B nuclear power station being an example), a motorway, the construction of an airport extension (the Stansted airport development and the Heathrow Airport Terminal 5 proposal being examples) or the Channel Tunnel rail link. In such cases, special procedures may apply,[18] but whatever procedures are adopted the inquiry often has a difficult task in distinguishing objections of detail from objections to the principle of the proposed development, which is often a matter of major government policy to be decided by government, not by a judicial or quasi-judicial process in an inquiry.[19]

6 Tribunals of inquiry

When a matter of urgent public importance arises, Parliament may resolve to set up a tribunal to inquire into it. The tribunal is then set up by Her Majesty or a Secretary of State and upon the tribunal may be conferred many of the procedural powers of the High Court, such as summoning witnesses, compelling the production of documents and taking evidence on oath. If a witness refuses to answer a question put to him he may be reported to the High Court and punished for contempt of court.[20] A tribunal of inquiry must generally sit in public unless the public interest requires otherwise. The tribunal has discretion whether or not to allow representation by counsel or solicitor before it. These tribunals of inquiry should not be confused with the frequent examples of governments appointing judges to head enquiries into particular issues.[1] A good example of a statutory inquiry was the inquiry held by Sir Richard Scott into the issues raised by the export of arms to Iraq, in breach of international embargoes.[2] That inquiry was established in the light of government embarrassment following the collapse of several high-profile prosecutions of businessmen who had, allegedly, illegally exported equipment to Iraq. In an inquiry lasting many months, with its own counsel and legal team, a range of issues of legal and political interest were covered and reported in 1996 in a multi-volume report.

17 See p 143, *ante*.
18 See Land and Buildings Act 1996.
19 For an example of the difficulties, see *Bushell v Secretary of State for the Environment* [1981] AC 75; [1980] 2 All ER 608.
20 Tribunals of Inquiry (Evidence) Act 1921, s 1; Contempt of Court Act 1981, s 20; cf *Attorney-General v Clough* [1963] 1 QB 773; [1963] 1 All ER 420; *R v Mulholland* [1963] 2 QB 477; [1963] 1 All ER 767.
1 See p 223, *post*.
2 Inquiry into the Export of Defence Equipment and Dual-Use Goods to Iraq and related prosecutions.

7   Control by the courts of administrative tribunals and inquiries

Administrative justice can create dangers unless subject to effective safeguards and control. The Donoughmore Committee[3] in 1932 recommended: firstly, that the supervisory jurisdiction of the High Court over tribunals be maintained; secondly, that tribunals be compelled by the High Court to observe natural justice; thirdly, that reports of statutory inquiries be published; and finally, that there should be an appeal on a question of law. In 1957, as a result of the Franks Committee recommendations, the Tribunals and Inquiries Act 1958 was passed. That Act (now superseded by the Tribunals and Inquiries Act 1992) created a Council on Tribunals[3A] consisting of not more than fifteen nor less than ten members appointed by the Secretary of State and Lord Chancellor.[4] The members are disqualified from membership of the House of Commons. The Council keeps under review the workings of tribunals and reports on them from time to time. The tribunals subject to the scrutiny of the Council are listed in the First Schedule to the Act and include agricultural lands tribunals, the lands tribunal, mental health review tribunals, rent tribunals and the general and special Commissioners of Income Tax. In this way the Lord Chancellor (and through him, Parliament) is able to exercise direct extra-judicial control and supervision over some of the more important tribunals. The Council on Tribunals has a purely advisory function, with no independent executive authority in respect of tribunals within its remit. Its role is supervisory and consultative. For example, in 1991 it published a set of model tribunal rules. Its work is highlighted in its various Annual Reports, and includes advice and comment on the appointment and training of members, their social, gender and racial mix, the operation of tribunals and rules under which they operate. Studies are made from time to time of specific tribunals and appropriate recommendations made. Its recommendations will, at best, be persuasive, at worst anodyne. One commentator[5A] described the Council, in its Annual reports, as "do[ing] little more than recite facts and make the occasional grumble." Clearly, there are limits to the effectiveness of what is essentially an advisory watchdog.

a   Supervisory control

The supervisory jurisdiction of the High Court, exercised in practice by the Queen's Bench Division, is a common law jurisdiction and does not depend upon statute. Any provision in an Act passed before August 1958 which excludes any of the powers of the High Court does not have effect so as to prevent the High Court from making orders of mandamus or certiorari. There are two ways in which the High Court may purport to exercise its supervisory control over tribunals. The usual method is by the issue of prerogative orders in judicial review proceedings; however these orders will lie in respect of tribunals which are exercising public law functions, which will often not be the case in the case of domestic tribunals. A person aggrieved by the decision of a voluntary tribunal may, however, invoke the High Court's supervisory jurisdiction by bringing an action against the officers of the tribunal, claiming an injunction or a declaration as to his rights.[6] In addition the High Court has shown an increased

---

3   See p 205, *ante*.
3A   For detailed discussion, see Harlow and Rawlings, *op cit*, at pp 467–471.
4   1992 Act, s 1.
5   See *R v Disciplinary Committee of the Jockey Club, ex parte Aga Khan* [1993] 2 All ER 853; [1993] 1 WLR 909.
5A   See Lomas *The Twenty-Fifth Annual Report of the Council on Tribunals* (1985), p 694.
6   Under RSC Ord 15, r 16.

willingness to intervene in the affairs of trade and professional bodies which have the power to deprive individuals of their livelihood.[7] This, of course, is part of the trend towards greater willingness of the courts to intervene through the process of judicial review.[8]

b   Appeals from tribunals

An application for judicial review is not an appeal. There is no common law right of appeal from a tribunal so that an appeal only lies where statute so provides. The Tribunals and Inquiries Act 1992, section 11, provides for any party to appeal or to require the tribunal to state a case on a point of law from certain administrative tribunals to the High Court. These appeals are heard by the divisional court of the Queen's Bench Division. Other statutes provide rights of appeal to various branches of the Supreme Court and, in the case of doctors, dentists and opticians, to the Judicial Committee of the Privy Council.[9]

---

7   *Bonsor v Musicians Union* [1956] AC 104; [1955] 3 All ER 518; *Byrne v Kinematograph Renters Society* [1958] 2 All ER 579; [1958] 1 WLR 762; *Nagle v Feilden* [1966] 2 QB 633; [1966] 1 All ER 689.
8   See p 145 et seq, *ante*.
9   See p 190, *post*.

CHAPTER 10

The Judiciary

A APPOINTMENT AND CONDITIONS OF TENURE OF OFFICE

1 Appointment

The Lord Chancellor, the Lord Chief Justice, the Master of the Rolls, the President of the Family Division of the High Court, the Vice-Chancellor, the Lords of Appeal in Ordinary and the Lords Justices of Appeal are appointed by the Queen on the advice of the Prime Minister. Of these only the Lord Chancellor's appointment is made on a political basis. The puisne judges of the High Court, circuit judges and recorders are appointed by the Queen on the advice of the Lord Chancellor. Justices of the peace are appointed by the Lord Chancellor directly.

The law has generally limited judicial appointment to barristers of specified lengths of standing; solicitors were not, until recently, eligible for most judicial appointments, appointments as Crown Court recorders and as district judges in the county court being exceptions. The composition of the judiciary has mirrored that of the Bar in terms of gender and of racial or ethnic origin.[1] The Courts and Legal Services Act 1990 has removed these barriers, by relating qualification for judicial appointment to the new provisions in respect of rights of audience contained in the Act.[2]

Lords of Appeal in Ordinary are the senior members of the judiciary, and are generally appointed from the ranks of the Court of Appeal, although exceptionally a first instance judge may be elevated directly to the House of Lords. They must either have held judicial office for two years, or have a Supreme Court qualification.[3] The number of law lords, originally fixed at two, is now not less than seven nor more than twelve.

---

1 See Pannick *Judges* (1987).
2 See Courts and Legal Services Act 1990, ss 26–27.
3 Appellate Jurisdiction Act 1876, as amended by the Courts and Legal Services Act 1990. A Supreme Court qualification is defined by the 1990 Act, s 71(3) as meaning that the person has a right of audience for all proceedings in the Supreme Court. See further p 245, *post*. The requirement does not apply to the officers, except the Lord Chancellor who is a Minister of the Crown.

Lords Justice of Appeal are appointed by Her Majesty by letters patent. They must have been judges of the High Court or have a 10-year High Court qualification.[4] There must not be more than 35 Lords Justice of Appeal.[5] High Court judges are likewise appointed by the Crown. Sometimes styled "puisne judges", they must have a 10-year High Court qualification. Some 98 puisne judges may be appointed. It is now possible for a solicitor to be appointed directly to the High Court bench. In addition, a circuit judge may be appointed to the High Court bench. High Court judges are appointed to a particular division by the Lord Chancellor, depending usually on the practice which the appointee had prior to appointment.

The office of circuit judge was created by the Courts Act 1971. Circuit judges are appointed by Her Majesty on the recommendation of the Lord Chancellor, and must have a ten-year Crown Court or ten-year county court qualification.[7] Again this permits a solicitor to be appointed directly to the circuit bench. Whereas circuit judges are full-time appointments, recorders are part-time judges of the Crown Court, appointed on a temporary basis. The terms of appointment will specify the duration of the appointment, and the number of occasions upon which they will be available to undertake judicial duties. Failure to comply with these requirements is a ground for removal of office.[8]

Considerable discussion has occurred in recent years concerning the method of appointment of judges. The independence of the judiciary is a paramount consideration and many consider it odd that the appointment process of judges should, effectively, be in the hands of the government of the day.[9] In its election manifesto of 1997 the present government indicated its intention to establish a Judicial Appointments and Training Commission to advise as to the appointment and training of judges. Such a proposal has been abandoned. The Lord Chancellor did, however, announce a series of changes to existing appointment practice. Such appointments will continue to be made "strictly on merit, after the independent views of the judiciary and the legal profession have been taken into consideration."[10] The long-standing practice that full-time judicial appointments are made normally only after satisfactory service as a part-time judge (eg a recorder) is to continue. The Lord Chancellor, Lord Irvine, announced four specific changes. First, he will report annually to Parliament on the operation of the judicial appointments system. Second, the practice of appointing High Court judges only by invitation will cease. Vacancies will be filled after advertisement. Third, there is to be flexibility in the sitting arrangements for part-time judges. Finally, the upper age-limit for appointment to Assistant Recorder is to be raised from 50 to 53, to widen the pool of potential applicants.

These changes meet some, but not all, of the calls for greater openness in the appointments process. Although judicial appointments are to be advertised, the first such advertisement for a High Court judge appearing in early 1998, it is far from certain that the traditional influence exerted through invitations to apply and the taking of informal soundings will cease. The final decision remains with the Lord Chancellor,[11] and the new process does not extend to judges at the appellate levels. Further steps

---

4 Within the meaning of the 1990 Act, s 71(3): the person has a right of audience for all proceedings in the High Court. See further p 242, *post*.
5 Maximum Number of Judges Order 1996 SI 1996/1142.
6 Supreme Court Act 1981, s 4(1); SI 1993/1255.
7 Within the meaning of the 1990 Act, s 71(3): the person has rights of audience for all purposes in the county court.
8 Courts Act 1971, ss 17(4), 21(6)*e*.
9 See Griffith *The Politics of the Judiciary* (4th Edn, 1991), p 20.
10 Lord Irvine LC, HL Deb 23 June 1997, col. 145.
11 See, generally, the criticism levelled at the current system by Drewery at [1998] PL 6–7.

may need to be taken to ensure that the appearance, as well as the reality, is of appointments made through due process designed to secure appointments free from political or other bias.

2   Tenure

Until Stuart times judges held office only during the King's pleasure and could be, and were, removed at the will of the King. Their position was altered in consequence of the Revolution settlement by the Act of Settlement 1700, which provided that:

> "Judges' commissions be made *quamdiu se bene gesserint*, and their salaries ascertained and established, but upon the address of both Houses of Parliament it may be lawful to remove them."[12]

Thus, as long as they conducted themselves properly (*quamdiu se bene gesserint*) judges of the superior courts[13] could be removed only on an address by both Houses of Parliament. Presumably a judge who was guilty of serious neglect or misconduct could be removed by the Crown without the need for an address by Parliament.[14] This prohibition still applies to judges of the Supreme Court of Judicature,[15] except, however, for circuit judges and recorders who are removable by the Lord Chancellor on the ground of incapacity or misbehaviour or, in the case of a recorder, failing to comply with the conditions of his appointment.[16]

No English judge has been removed under the Act of Settlement procedure, although an Irish judge was so removed in 1830. However, judges who are guilty of incompetence, neglect, unacceptable delay or unacceptable personal behaviour may well resign, whether of their own volition or after official encouragement. Thus in 1998 one High Court judge resigned after being castigated by the Court of Appeal, which observed:

> "Conduct like this [a 20 month delay in delivering judgment] weakens public confidence in the whole judicial process. Left unchecked, it would be ultimately subversive of the rule of law. Delays on this scale cannot and will not be tolerated."[17]

Of course, the example is an extreme one: there appears to be no consistent or clear approach to issues of judicial competence.[18]

Judges of the Supreme Court (excluding circuit judges and recorders) and Lords of

---

12   This does not apply to the Lord Chancellor, because he is a Minister of the Crown, and holds office at the Queen's pleasure.

13   See p 162, *ante*.

14   See *Earl of Shrewsbury's Case* (1610) 9 Co Rep 42a, at 50.

15   It is now contained in s 11(3) of the Supreme Court Act 1981.

16   Courts Act 1971, ss 17(4), 21(6); see p 211, *ante*. Cf the Scottish position where "inability" is a ground of removal of a sheriff pursuant to the Sheriff Courts (Scotland) Act 1971. In *Stewart v Secretary of State for Scotland* [1996] SLT 1203 it was held that this was to be construed broadly as meaning "unable to perform the judicial functions expected of a sheriff". This was demonstrated by his inability to concentrate on the matter before him and to exercise self-restraint.

17   The judge concerned was Mr Justice Harman who had regularly featured at the top of the "Worst Judge" poll conducted by a professional journal: see (1998) 148 NLJ 234.

18   For the approach to issues of competence see *Judicial Appointments* (1997), HMSO, Cm 3387.

Appeal in Ordinary must, unless appointed before 1959, retire at the age of 70, subject to limited rights of extension of office until the age of 75 years.[19] Their salaries are determined by the Lord Chancellor, with the consent of the Minister for the Civil Service, and charged on the Consolidated Fund.

Justices of the peace may be removed from the commission by the Lord Chancellor without showing cause. Several justices have been so removed, generally for refusing to administer a law with which they were not in sympathy. Although there is no retiring age for justices of the peace they are put on the supplemental list at the age of 70,[20] which is *de facto* retirement, in that they cease to be entitled to exercise judicial functions. Justices may be put on the supplemental list before they have reached this age, either at their own request or on the ground of "age or infirmity or other like cause" or on the ground that the justice declines or neglects to take a proper part in the exercise of his judicial functions.[1]

3   Training

It used to be assumed that new appointees to judicial positions were sufficiently qualified, by their professional training and experience, to perform judicial functions. That is no longer accepted as inevitably true. The Judicial Studies Board[1A] exists to provide training for new judges and on-going training for those already holding such positions. Through training courses and refresher courses, the Board seeks to create an awareness of best practice, to address problems and issues that commonly arise, and to bring to the attention of the judiciary developments in procedure, substantive law, evidence and sentencing. Judges are also exposed to related disciplines, such as penology, relevant to their work. The Board issues guidance to judges, through the formulation of model directions to the jury on points of law, a fact explicitly recognised on occasion by the courts.[1B] Such guidance is not, however, always available generally to the legal profession.[1C]

B   CONSTITUTIONAL POSITION

Much has been written on the question of whether or not judges are "servants" of the Crown. The better view seems to be that they are servants for they are appointed and, in certain circumstances, removable by the Queen and are paid out of the Consolidated Fund, although they cannot be controlled in the exercise of their office by the Queen or her Ministers. Generally the question of whether judges are properly describable as servants is unimportant though the question did arise in an acute form in 1931 when the National Economy Act of that year conferred power upon the Commissioners of Inland Revenue to reduce the remuneration of "persons in His Majesty's Service". The Commissioners purported to reduce judicial salaries. The validity of this measure, though strenuously disputed, was not decided since the Inland Revenue soon abolished these reductions under pressure of public opinion.

19   Judicial Pensions and Retirement Act 1993, s 26. For the position where a judge reaches retirement age, see *R v The Lord Chancellor, ex parte Stockler* [1996] 8 Admin LR 590.
20   Justices of the Peace Act 1997, s 7. Stipendiary magistrates retire at 70 but may be retained in office up to the age of 75 (*ibid*, s 12).
1   1997 Act, s 7.
1A   An independent body with responsibility for the provision of training and refresher courses for the judiciary and magistracy.
1B   See *R v Cowan* [1996] QB 373; [1995] 4 All ER 939.
1C   Munday "The Bench Books: Can the Judiciary Keep a Secret?" [1996] Crim LR 296.

Whether judges are or are not Crown servants, there is no doubt that the judicial function is not under the control of the legislature or the executive. Judicial independence is a fundamental principle of English constitutional law. If the courts are to perform their important function of judicial scrutiny and review of executive action, it is essential that this independence is maintained. The duty of the court may, for example, extend to declaring that a government minister has acted unlawfully, or in disobedience to a binding order of the court. Thus, in *M v Home Office*[2] the Home Secretary was held to be in contempt of court for disobedience to an order of the court.

The very function of judicial review raises the question of the role of the judiciary, and its relationship with the executive and Parliament. We have already seen[3] that a court may now hold an Act of Parliament to be invalid if it contravenes Community law. The Human Rights Bill currently before Parliament will give to the courts widespread discretion to balance competing rights and interests.[4] It has been argued by one judge, extra-judicially, that the United Kingdom constitution contains a "higher order" law which it is the task of the courts to uphold and apply.[5] Although such arguments are not universally, or even generally, accepted,[6] the grounds for judicial review are wide enough to involve a wide measure of policy choices, often within a political controversial context, which may have the effect (or give the impression) of bringing the judges into the political arena.[7]

Judicial immunity

An offshoot of this principle of judicial independence is the doctrine of judicial immunity. Historically the degree of immunity has varied with the status of the judge. The old cases distinguish between judges of superior courts, who were held immune from action even if acting maliciously, and judges of inferior courts who enjoyed immunity only while acting within their jurisdiction. These principles operated somewhat capriciously; thus a Recorder of London who unlawfully imprisoned the jurors at the trial of Penn and Meade for ignoring his direction to convict was held immune from suit[8] while an unfortunate county court judge in Lancashire was held liable in damages for a mistake of law as to his jurisdiction, made quite innocently and in good faith.[9]

Such rationale as there may have been behind this dichotomy may be thought to have little relevance to modern conditions and the Court of Appeal in *Sirros v Moore*,[10] rejected the principle whereby the degree of immunity depends upon the status of the court. Lord Denning MR stated the position in straightforward terms:[11]

2   *Re M* [1994] 1 AC 377; sub nom *M v Home Office* [1993] 3 All ER 537.
3   See p 112, *ante*.
4   See p 132, *ante*.
5   Laws J in "Law and Democracy" [1995] PL 57 at 67. See also Sedley J in "Human Rights: A Twenty-First Century Agenda" [1995] PL 386.
6   See, eg, Lord Irvine of Lairg, QC (as he then was) (1996) HL Deb, Vol 572, col. 1254 *et seq*.
7   See, eg *Bromley LBC v Greater London Council* [1983] 1 AC 768; [1982] 1 All ER 153.
8   *Hamond v Howell* (1677) 2 Mod Rep 218.
9   *Houlden v Smith* (1850) 14 QB 841.
10 [1975] QB 118, at 136; [1974] 3 All ER 776, at 785. The position of justices of the peace and their clerks is now set out in Part V of the Justices of the Peace Act 1997. They cannot be held liable in respect of acts done within their jurisdiction (s 51). There is no similar protection as regards acts done in excess of jurisdiction if, but only if, it is proved that the justice or clerk acted in bad faith (s 52) but the justice is entitled to indemnity out of local funds, in respect of both damages and costs, if he acted "reasonably and in good faith" (s 54).
11 [1975] QB, at 136; [1974] 3 All ER, at 785.

"Every judge of the courts of this land from the highest to the lowest should be protected to the same degree, and liable to the same degree. If the reason underlying this immunity is to ensure 'that they may be free in thought and independent in judgment', it applies to every judge, whatever his rank. Each should be protected from liability to damages when he is acting judicially. Each should be able to do his work in complete independence and free from fear. He should not have to turn the pages of his books with trembling fingers, asking himself; 'If I do this, shall I be liable in damages?' So long as he does his work in the honest belief that it is within his jurisdiction, then he is not liable to an action. He may be mistaken in fact. He may be ignorant in law. What he does may be outside his jurisdiction in fact or in law but so long as he honestly believes it to be within his jurisdiction, he should not be liable. Nothing will make him liable except it be shown that he was not acting judicially, knowing that he had no jurisdiction to do it."

The result in the instant case was to render immune from liability a circuit judge, exercising the appellate jurisdiction of the Crown Court, who, without authority (but in good faith), ordered the arrest and detention of the plaintiff as the latter was lawfully leaving the court.

Lord Denning, immediately after the passage quoted above, added:

"This principle should cover the justices of the peace also. They should no longer be subject to 'strokes of the rodde or spur'. Aided by their clerks, they do their work with the highest degree of responsibility and competence to the satisfaction of the entire community. They should have the same protection as the other judges."

However this dictum was rejected by the House of Lords in *McC v Mullan*[12] in which it was held that justices could be sued if they acted without or in excess of jurisdiction. The latter phrase, however, requires some elaboration. If justices have jurisdiction to entertain the proceedings then the mere fact that they impose a sentence or take some other course, which is subsequently held to be wrong, does not mean that they acted in excess of jurisdiction. They will only act without their jurisdiction if they impose a sentence or take a course which they have no power to do. In such a case they may be held liable for whatever form of trespass to the person, land or goods follows.

The House of Lords also doubted the correctness of the statements in *Sirros v Moore*[13] (including that quoted above) to the effect that the distinction between superior and inferior courts, for this purpose, no longer exists although it regarded the decision itself as defensible on narrower grounds.

This immunity, although firmly established, may not inevitably survive. One Scottish court has observed[14] that the immunity "might be ripe for reconsideration". There is no evidence that it will in fact occur.

The immunity that attaches to judicial proceedings is not personal to the judge. Thus no civil action lies in respect of words spoken in the course of proceedings by parties,[15] witnesses,[16] advocates[17] or in respect of the verdict of a jury.[18] Fair and accurate

12   [1985] AC 528; [1984] 3 All ER 908.
13   See n 10, *supra*.
14   See *Lovell v Dickson*, (1997) Times, 23 June.
15   *Astley v Younge* (1759) 2 Burr 807.
16   *Hargreaves v Bretherton* [1959] 1 QB 45; [1958] 3 All ER 122.
17   *Munster v Lamb* (1883) 11 QBD 588.
18   *Bushell's Case* (1670) Vaugh 135.

contemporaneous newspaper and broadcast reports of judicial proceedings in the United Kingdom are also absolutely privileged in the law of defamation.[19] It might also be noted that although a judge cannot be compelled to give evidence of matters which he became aware of relating to, and as a result of performance of, his judicial functions, he is a competent witness to such matters.[20] He should not let the lack of compellability stand in the way of his testifying as to such matters.

C   THE JUDICIAL FUNCTION

Most of the work of the judges is judicial in the sense that they have to adjudicate upon disputes. To do this they are required, dispassionately, to find the facts upon the evidence presented to the court, to apply the law to the facts as found and then to give the "right decision". Appellate courts have repeatedly pointed out that the judicial function in the conduct of litigation goes no further than that. Thus, in relation to finding the facts, the court must act on the evidence before it; it has no duty to seek out some "independent truth" as Lord Wilberforce called it in the following interesting passage from his speech in a case concerning discovery of documents:[1]

> "In a contest purely between one litigant and another, such as the present, the task of the court is to do, and be seen to be doing, justice between the parties, a duty reflected by the word 'fairly' in the rule. There is no higher or additional duty to ascertain some independent truth. It often happens, from the imperfection of evidence, or the withholding of it, sometimes by the party in whose favour it would tell if presented, that an adjudication has to be made which is not, and is known not to be, the whole truth of the matter; yet, if the decision has been in accordance with the available evidence and with the law, justice will have been fairly done."

To this principle there is at least one important exception, namely, cases where the issue is the welfare of a child. Such cases are to be decided not on an adversarial basis, but rather upon what the court considers to be in the best interests of the child.[2] However, even in these cases a court must base its judgments upon evidence, and not infrequently such proceedings can often be highly adversarial.

Having found the facts, judges must apply the existing rules of law to those facts. There are two aspects of this function: the interpretation and construction of statutes and the application of the doctrine of precedent.

a   Statutes

It is the duty of judges to ascertain the intention of the legislature, if the rule of law in question is statutory, or to apply the existing law where the rule of law in question is a rule of common law or equity. Different approaches to the interpretation of statutes have already been identified.[3] The traditional view is that judges are not competent to interpret a statute other than in accordance with the literal meaning of the words used, or to alter any existing rule of common law or equity. Lord Diplock explained the

---

19   Defamation Act 1952, s 8.
20   *Warren v Warren* [1997] QB 488; [1996] 4 All ER 664.
1   *Air Canada v Secretary of State for Trade (No 2)* [1983] 2 AC 394, at 438; [1983] 1 All ER 910, at 919.
2   *Re (A Minor)* [1989] 1 FLR 268.
3   See p 34, *ante*.

rationale of this view, in relation to the interpretation of statutes, in a case concerning a trade dispute in the steel industry, in the following words:[4]

> "My Lords, at a time when more and more cases involve the application of legislation which gives effect to policies that are the subject of bitter public and parliamentary controversy, it cannot be too strongly emphasised that the British Constitution, though largely unwritten, is firmly based on the separation of powers; Parliament makes the laws, the judiciary interpret them. When Parliament legislates to remedy what the majority of its members at the time perceive to be a defect or a lacuna in the existing law (whether it be the written law enacted by existing statutes or the unwritten common law as it has been expounded by the judges in decided cases), the role of the judiciary is confined to ascertaining from the words that Parliament has approved as expressing its intention what that intention was, and to giving effect to it. Where the meaning of the statutory words is plain and unambiguous it is not for the judges to invent fancied ambiguities as an excuse for failing to give effect to its plain meaning because they themselves consider that the consequences of doing so would be inexpedient, or even unjust or immoral. In controversial matters such as are involved in industrial relations there is room for differences of opinion as to what is expedient, what is just and what is morally justifiable. Under our Constitution it is Parliament's opinion on these matters that is paramount."

To similar effect, but in relation to construction of a contract, are the words of Lord Bridge in a shipping case:[5]

> "The ideal at which the courts should aim, in construing such clauses, is to produce a result such that in any given situation both parties seeking legal advice as to their rights and obligations can expect the same clear and confident answer from their advisers and neither will be tempted to embark on long and expensive litigation in the belief that victory depends on winning the sympathy of the court. This ideal may never be fully attainable, but we shall certainly never even approximate to it unless we strive to follow clear and consistent principles and steadfastly refuse to be blown off course by the supposed merits of individual cases."

Nevertheless strict adherence to this rule is not always possible since there is often uncertainty or ambiguity in the area of law being considered.[6] Indeed the rule cannot be applied in interpreting an Act of Parliament, which makes no provision for the case in question, or in deciding a case of "first impression", ie, a case for which there is no precedent. In such a case the judge must create new law. In cases of judicial review[7] this problem is particularly acute. The constitutional role of the courts is to ensure that executive bodies keep within the bounds of the power granted by Parliament. Inevitably that requires the court to engage in an interpretative function. However, in cases involving the exercise of discretionary powers, the grounds of challenge may require

4   *Duport Steels Ltd v Sirs* [1980] 1 All ER 529, at 541; [1980] 1 WLR 142, at 157.
5   *AS Awilco v Fulvia SpA di Navigazione, The Chikuma* [1981] 1 All ER 652, at 659; [1981] 1 WLR 314, at 322. This decision was an appeal to the House of Lords from the Court of Appeal presided over by Lord Denning MR as were both cases cited in the preceding two footnotes.
6   For a detailed discussion of the judicial approach to statutory interpretation and to the doctrine of judicial precedent, see pp 36, 62 *et seq, ante.*
7   See p 142, *ante.*

the court to search for a sometimes elusive Parliamentary intention.[8] In such cases the court must take care to keep within its proper functions, namely, to decide questions of law and not to impinge upon the right of the executive body to make and apply policy.[9]

The general limits as to how far judges should go on matters of policy need to be considered in the light of the incorporation of the European Convention on Human Rights into English law. As already noted,[10] judges are required to have regard to the principles developed by the Court of Human Rights[11] and duty bound where permitted to do so to give effect to Convention rights. The Convention is not, however, drawn in the form that typifies ordinary statutes. Its form, of creating general rights and exceptions, will require courts to take a view as to the proportionality of the actions taken by the Government and Parliament in the context of the intended purpose of those provisions. Such judgments will inevitably require a measure of policy evaluation by the courts and bring courts inevitably closer into the political arena, despite their reluctance to get involved in such matters.

b   Common law

In relation to the development of common law principles, traditional views are changing. In *Jones v Secretary of State for Social Services*[12] Lord Simon stated:

"In this country it was long considered that judges were not makers of law but merely its discoverers and expounders. The theory was that every case was governed by a relevant rule of law, existing somewhere and discoverable somehow, provided sufficient learning and intellectual rigour were brought to bear. But once such a rule had been discovered, frequently the pretence was tacitly dropped that the rule was pre-existing, for example, cases like *Shelley's* case,[13] *Merryweather v Nixan*[14] or *Priestley v Fowler*[15] were (rightly) regarded as new departures in the law. Nevertheless the theory, however unreal, had its value in limiting the sphere of law-making by the judiciary (inevitably at some disadvantage in assessing the potential repercussions of any decision, and increasingly so in a complex modern industrial society), and thus also in emphasising that central feature of our constitution, the sovereignty of Parliament. But the true, even if limited, nature of judicial law-making has been more widely acknowledged of recent years."

Judges do sometimes create new law. For example, Denning J (as he then was) virtually did this in *Central London Property Trust Ltd v High Trees House Ltd*[16] in a judgment which created the doctrine of equitable estoppel. The important civil remedies of *Anton Piller* orders and *Mareva* injunctions[17] are both judge-made.

8   The intention of Parliament may on occasion be ascertained from the debates of proceedings in Parliament: see *Pepper v Hart* [1993] AC 593; [1993] 1 All ER 42.
9   See *R v Secretary of State for the Home Department, ex parte Brind* [1991] 1 AC 696; [1990] 1 All ER 469.
10   See p 128, *ante*.
11   See p 124, *ante*.
12   [1972] AC 944, at 1026; [1972] 1 All ER 145, at 198; see p 70, *ante*.
13   (1581) Moore KB 136.
14   (1799) 8 Term Rep 186.
15   (1837) 3 M & W 1.
16   [1947] KB 130; [1956] 1 All ER 256n.
17   See p 357, *post*.

The self-assumed power of the House of Lords to depart from its own previous decisions[18] has had the effect of bringing into sharp relief the scope of the judicial function, for the members of the House are now free, in effect, to create new law. It is fair to say that certain judges deem it to be within their function to create new principles of law while others believe that any far-reaching change should be left to Parliament, which has greater facilities for testing the possible repercussions of law reform. The latter approach is exemplified by the following passage from the vigorous dissenting speech of Lord Simon in the leading case of *Miliangos v George Frank (Textiles) Ltd*[19].

"I am sure that an expert committee, including or taking evidence from departmental officials, would apprehend a great number of not immediately apparent repercussions of the decision which my noble and learned friends propose to take. Such a committee might conclude that the repercussions make the decision unacceptable. Or they might suggest some means of mitigating any adverse effect. Or they might advise that the repercussions were on balance acceptable. But at least the crucial decision would be taken in the light of all the consequences involved.

By contrast, the training and qualification of a judge is to elucidate the problem immediately before him, so that its features stand out in stereoscopic clarity. But the beam of light which so illuminates the immediate scene seems to throw surrounding areas into greater obscurity; the whole landscape is distorted to the view. A penumbra can be apprehended, but not much beyond; so that when the searchlight shifts a quite unexpected scene may be disclosed. The very qualifications for the judicial process thus impose limitations on its use. This is why judicial advance should be gradual. I am not trained to see the distant scene; 'one step enough for me' should be the motto on the wall opposite the judge's desk. It is, I concede, a less spectacular method of progression than somersaults and cartwheels; but it is the one best suited to the capacity and resources of a judge.

We are likely to perform better the duties society imposes on us if we recognise our limitations. Within the proper limits there is more than enough to be done which is of value to society."

Lord Simon was a lone dissenting voice in the case cited above, and the House of Lords did effect a radical reform of English law in holding that English courts have power to give judgments expressed in foreign currency.

On occasion, judicial restraint may be because the nature of the issues involved is such that resolution of a problem is best left to Parliament. Thus in *Malone v Metropolitan Police Commissioner (No 2)*[20] Sir Robert Megarry considered that the practice of interception of telephone communications "cried out" for legislation, but declined to develop common law rules to fill the vacuum that existed.

An important example of judicial law-making by the House of Lords is afforded by the cases of *WT Ramsay Ltd v Inland Revenue Commissioners*[1] and *Furniss v Dawson*[2] in which the House formulated and developed the principle whereby a series of prearranged steps or transactions, some of which have no commercial purpose other than the avoidance or deferment of tax, fall to be looked at together so that liability to

18   See p 74, *ante*.
19   [1976] AC 443, at 481–482; [1975] 3 All ER 801, at 824–825.
20   [1979] Ch 344; [1979] 2 All ER 620.
1   [1982] AC 300; [1981] 1 All ER 865.
2   [1984] AC 474; [1984] 1 All ER 530.

tax is determined according to the substance of the scheme as a whole and its end result. These cases amounted to a bombshell to the tax-avoidance industry.

In the realm of criminal law judges have sometimes regarded it as within their function to enforce public morality by creating new criminal offences. The earliest criminal offences were, of course, judge-made and even until the eighteenth century the scope of the criminal law was being extended judicially.[3] However, by the middle of the nineteenth century "times had changed and the pretensions of the judges to extend the criminal law had changed with them".[4] Accordingly it is universally accepted that judges have no power to create new criminal offences.[5] This principle has not prevented the courts on occasion from declaring that the common law recognises certain conduct to be criminal. Thus in *R v Manley*[6] the defendant had alleged falsely that she had been attacked and robbed. The police were put to considerable trouble and expense in investigating her story and members of the public were put under suspicion. She was convicted of public mischief and her appeal against conviction, on the ground that no such offence was known to the law, was dismissed. Equally striking is the decision of the House of Lords in *Shaw v Director of Public Prosecutions*[7] to the effect that an agreement to publish the "Ladies Directory", containing names, addresses and photographs of persons willing to engage in prostitution and perversion, constituted a "conspiracy to corrupt public morals" which was a criminal offence. The following observation from the speech of Viscount Simonds in that case has been widely quoted:[8]

"In the sphere of criminal law I entertain no doubt that there remains in the courts of law a residual power to enforce the supreme and fundamental purpose of the law, to conserve not only the safety and order but also the moral welfare of the State. The law must be related to the changing standards of life, not yielding to every shifting impulse of the popular will but having regard to fundamental assessments of human values and the purpose of society."

In *Knuller (Publishing, Printing and Promotions) Ltd v Director of Public Prosecutions*[9] a publication of a somewhat similar kind (although this time aimed at a homosexual market) was held to give rise to the same offence. Not only was Shaw's case followed but a majority of the House (obiter) expressed the view that there were known to the criminal law further offences of outraging public decency and conspiring so to do.

In the light of these authorities such comfort as may be drawn from the principle that judges have no power to create new criminal offences would appear to be more illusory than real. However, in the later case of *Director of Public Prosecutions v Withers*[10] the House of Lords to some extent redressed the balance by holding that conspiracy to effect a public mischief, in the sense of an agreement to do an act which, although not unlawful in itself, is injurious to the public, is not as such an offence known

3   The historical alteration in the function of the judiciary in relation to the development of criminal law is illuminatingly described in the speech of Lord Diplock in *Knuller (Publishing, Printing and Promotions) Ltd v Director of Public Prosecutions* [1973] AC 435; [1972] 2 All ER 898.
4   *Knuller (Publishing, Printing and Promotions) Ltd v Director of Public Prosecutions* [1973] AC 435, at 474; [1972] 2 All ER 898, at 918, per Lord Diplock.
5   This was virtually the only point upon which all five members of the House of Lords were agreed in *Knuller (supra)*; see also *Abbott v R* [1977] AC 755; [1976] 3 All ER 140.
6   [1933] 1 KB 529; her conduct would now amount to a summary offence under the Criminal Law Act 1967, s 5(2).
7   [1962] AC 220; [1961] 2 All ER 446.
8   [1962] AC at 267–268; [1961] 2 All ER, at 452.
9   [1973] AC 435; [1972] 2 All ER 898.
10   [1975] AC 842; [1974] 3 All ER 984.

to the law; a fortiori there is no offence of public mischief as such. Conduct which has already been held to be criminal, such as that of the defendant in *R v Manley* (*supra*), remains criminal but not simply because it falls within the general rubric of "public mischief" but rather because it is a specific form of conduct which, on the authorities, constitutes an established criminal offence.

Approaches by judges to these matters are not consistent. Sometimes judicial activism and creativity comes to the fore. *R v R*[11] is an example, the House of Lords concluding that the long-established rule that a husband cannot be criminally liable for raping his wife no longer formed part of the laws of England. The development of psychological harm as an assault[12] and of the law of provocation in the context of domestic violence cases[13] are other examples. By contrast, in *C v DPP*[14] the House of Lords declined to abolish the *doli incapax* rule which creates a presumption that a child under the age of 14 does not possess criminal intent, to be rebutted by evidence that he knew what he did was seriously wrong. At first instance, Laws J[15] had said:

"...this presumption at the present time is a serious disservice to our law. It means that a child over ten who commits an act of obvious dishonesty, or even grave violence, is to be acquitted unless the prosecution specifically prove by discrete evidence that he understands the obliquity of what he is doing...".

In rejecting the decision of the Divisional Court to accept the presumption as part of the law of England, the House of Lords was mindful of the dicta of Lord Salmon in *Abbott v R*[16]:

"Judges have no power to create new criminal offences, nor ... have they the power to invent a new defence to murder which is entirely contrary to fundamental legal doctrines, accepted for hundreds of years without question. If a policy change of so fundamental a nature were to be made it could ... be made only by Parliament. Whilst their Lordships strongly uphold the right and even the duty of the judges to adapt and develop the principles of the common law in an orderly fashion, they are equally opposed to any usurpation by the courts of the functions of Parliament."

In *C*, Lord Lowery set out five principles which he believed were generally applicable:

"(1)If the solution is doubtful the judges should beware of imposing their own remedy; (2) caution should prevail if Parliament has rejected opportunities of clearing up a known difficulty or has legislated while leaving the difficulty untouched; (3) disputed matters of social policy are less suitable areas for judicial intervention than purely legal problems; (4) fundamental legal doctrines should not lightly be set aside; (5) judges should not make a change unless they can achieve finality and certainty."

---

11 [1992] 1 AC 599; [1991] 4 All ER 481
12 *R v Chan-Fook* [1994] 2 All ER 552; *R v Ireland* [1997] 1 All ER 112; *R v Constanza* [1997] Crim LR 576.
13 *R v Thornton* [1992] 1 All ER 306; *R v Ahluwalia* [1992] 4 All ER 889.
14 [1996] AC 1; [1995] 2 All ER 43.
15 [1994] 3 All ER 190 at 196–197.
16 [1976] 3 All ER 140 at 147.

The application of these principles led Lord Lowery to the conclusion that the presumption should not be abandoned. The presumption has, however, now been abolished by statute.[17]

A still further example is to be found in the context of broad policy issues of socio-legal or medico-legal nature. In *Airedale NHS v Bland*[18] the court had to consider the question of the criminal liability of doctors removing medical treatment from an individual who was in a permanent vegetative state. The court observed:

> "The effect of the declaration, upheld by your Lordships' House, would be to create, through a binding precedent, a new common law exception to the offence of murder, which in future would not only bind all courts faced with criminal proceedings arising from the termination of life for medical reasons, but would also form a point of growth for the development of the criminal law in new and at present unforeseeable directions. This approach would have the great attraction of recognising that the law has been left behind by the rapid advances of medical technology. By starting with a clean slate the law would be freed from the piecemeal expedients to which courts throughout the common law world have been driven when trying to fill the gap between old law and new medicine. It has however been rightly acknowledged by counsel that this is a step which the courts could not properly take. Any necessary changes would have to take account of the whole of this area of law and morals, including of course all the issues commonly grouped under the heading of euthanasia. The formulation of the necessary broad social and moral policy is an enterprise which the courts have neither the means nor in my opinion the right to perform. This can only be achieved by democratic process through the medium of Parliament."

Other areas in which the judicial function goes beyond the resolution of the dispute which the judge in question is determining are "guideline" authorities in which appellate courts lay down guidelines for the guidance of judges in approaching the exercise of discretionary powers. Thus the rates of interest to be awarded on damages in personal injury actions,[19] the principles to be applied in determining applications for interlocutory injunctions[20] and the circumstances in which judges should grant leave to appeal from arbitration awards[1] are all the subject of guidelines laid down by the House of Lords. Similarly in criminal cases the modern practice of the criminal division of the Court of Appeal is, on the hearing of one or more appeals against sentence relating to a particular type of offence, to give sentencing guidelines for the assistance of Crown Court judges in dealing with offences of the type.[2]

---

17   Crime and Disorder Act 1998, s 34.
18   [1993] 1 All ER 821.
19   See p 407, *post*.
20   See p 376, *post*.
1   See p 331, *post*.
2   This practice seems to have originated in *R v Turner* (1975) 61 Cr App Rep 67 in relation to sentences for robbery and has since been followed in relation to many other sentencing areas; see, for example, *R v Clarke (Linda)* [1982] 3 All ER 232; [1982] 1 WLR 1090 (partially suspended sentences); *R v Armagh* (1982) 76 Cr App Rep 190 (drugs offences); *R v Boswell* [1984] 3 All ER 353; [1984] 1 WLR 1047 (causing death by reckless driving). See, now, Crime and Disorder Act 1998, s 80 and p 532.

Judges and extra-judicial functions

In addition to their judicial functions, judges are often asked to perform extra-judicial functions. Governments often appoint judges to head committees of inquiry or similar bodies, to investigate and report upon matters of public interest or controversy. The Denning Report into the Profumo scandal in the 1960s, the Wilberforce Report into an industrial dispute in the coal-mining industry, the Popplewell Report into a fire at Bradford City Football Club, and the Scott Inquiry into sales of arms to Iraq are all examples.[3] The reason for the use of judges in this way has been described as "borrowed authority".[4] A government with a problem or issue to address, often of a politically difficult or sensitive nature, may seek a determination or report from a judge who can bring to the process judicial independence and detachment, the forensic ability to question witnesses and sift evidence, and the general authority of the judiciary. Sir Richard Scott, the chairman of the Scott inquiry,[5] observed:

> "One of the main purposes behind the setting up of so many inquiries, it was certainly so of my own, is the allaying of public disquiet. That purpose would often have no real chance of being achieved at all if the oral hearings were conducted behind closed doors. In the case of my own inquiry, public scrutiny of at least the part of the investigative process taking place at oral hearings was desirable, in my opinion, so that if, and to the extent that any allegations or suspicions of government impropriety were eventually held to be unfounded, public disquiet would be at rest."

However, judges cannot be expected to come up with non-political solutions to political problems, and there is a danger that a judge may, unwillingly, be dragged into the political arena.

Since 1989, judges may also engage in informal and public discussion of matters of public interest, which may include the writing of books or articles, or appearances upon television or radio.[6]

Administrative functions

Finally, judges exercise certain administrative functions. This is particularly true of justices of the peace who exercise many functions which are not properly termed judicial, such as licensing and the issue of summonses and warrants. Judges of the Chancery Division sitting as a Court of Protection supervise the affairs and administer the property of persons of unsound mind. The Lord Chancellor and all High Court judges are "visitors" of the Inns of Court and, as such, hear appeals from orders of the Senate of the Inns of Court and the Bar.[7] In addition much litigation in the courts is non-contentious and concerns such matters as the administration of trusts, the winding-up of companies, adoption and legitimacy. Finally sections 85 and 86 of the Supreme Court Act 1981 empower, respectively, the Supreme Court Rule Committee and the Crown Court Rule Committee to make rules of court for the purpose of regulating

---

3　See, generally, Drewery, "Judicial Inquiries and Public Reassurance" [1996] PL 368.
4　See Griffith *The Politics of the Judiciary* (4th Edn, 1991), pp 52–55.
5　See also p 207, *ante*.
6　The Kilmuir rules, which prevented judges from making public comment on judicial matters, were abolished in 1989.
7　For this general jurisdiction, see *R v Visitors to the Inns of Court, ex parte Calder and Persaud* [1994] QB 1; [1993] 2 All ER 876.

and prescribing the practice and procedure to be followed in the Supreme Court while in county courts the rule committee derives jurisdiction from section 75 of the County Courts Act 1984. All of these committees include judges. In addition the judiciary controls practice and procedure in the courts by the issue of Practice Directions, and act as presiding judges for each of the circuits.[8] Presiding judges have wide decision-making powers.[9]

D   CONTEMPT OF COURT

1   General nature of contempt

Her Majesty's judges control the due administration of justice and have an inherent jurisdiction to punish conduct which is calculated to prejudice or interfere with the process of the law. Such conduct is termed a contempt of court. Contempt may be either of a criminal nature or of a civil nature. Criminal contempt is a common law offence punishable by fine or imprisonment. It can amount to contempt in the face of the court, where judicial proceedings are actually disrupted.[10] More commonly, offences of contempt comprise conduct which interferes more generally with the administration of justice. Provided that the conduct in question was intentional, there does not need to be an intent to interfere with the administration of justice if the conduct in fact has this effect.[11] For example, it is a criminal contempt to refuse to give evidence,[12] to use a tape-recorder in court without the leave of the court,[13] to fail to comply with a requirement to attend court under a subpoena witness order or witness summons,[14] or to interfere with a juror or witness.[15]

The workings of the jury system are strongly protected by the law of contempt. Not only is interference with a juror a contempt, as well as a substantive criminal offence, by section 8 of the Contempt of Court Act 1981[16] a contempt is committed if any person obtains, discloses or solicits any particulars of statements made, opinions expressed, arguments advanced or votes cast by a member of a jury in the course of their deliberations. In *A-G v Associated Newspapers Ltd*[17] a divisional court held that the publication of the statements, opinions and arguments of jurors concerning their verdict in a high-profile fraud trial amounted to contempt of court, even though these had been obtained indirectly from transcripts of interviews conducted by a researcher, not newspaper staff. More recently, the Divisional Court[18] considered a case where the pre-trial publicity in respect of an offence against a well-known television personality was such as to cause the trial judge to abandon the trial of the alleged assailant. The court concluded that though the publication had led to the trial being stayed, there was no contempt of court: the level of publicity about the relationship

---

8   Courts and Legal Services Act 1990, s 72.
9   See *Practice Note* [1987] 3 All ER 1064.
10   See, eg, *Morris v Crown Office* [1970] 2 QB 114.
11   *A-G v News Group Newspapers plc* [1989] QB 110; [1988] 2 All ER 906.
12   *R v Phillips* (1983) 78 Cr App Rep 88.
13   Contempt of Court Act 1981, s 9; as to considerations relevant to the grant of leave, see *Practice Direction* [1981] 3 All ER 848; [1981] 1 WLR 1526.
14   Criminal Procedure (Attendance of Witnesses) Act 1965.
15   *Re A-G's Application* [1963] 1 QB 696, *sub nom A-G v Butterworth* [1962] 3 All ER 326.
16   Passed in response to the judgments of the Divisional Court in *A-G v New Statesman and Nation Publishing Co Ltd* [1981] QB 1; [1980] 1 All ER 644. See also *Pickering v Liverpool Daily Post and Echo Newspapers plc* [1991] 2 AC 370; [1991] 1 All ER 622.
17   [1993] 2 All ER 535; [1993] 3 WLR 74.
18   See *Attorney-General v MGN Ltd* [1997] 1 All ER 456.

between the accused and the alleged victim, and publicity on previous occasions about the conduct of the accused meant that the publicity on this occasion did not create a greater risk of prejudice than already existed.

Other examples of criminal contempt include the publication of the name of a party or witness where such publication is prohibited by statute, or is contrary to an order of the court.[19] Such an order may bind a third party. One good example of the scope of the law of contempt, and the balance a court often has to strike, is provided by *Attorney-General v Newspaper Publishing plc*.[20] In that case, the defendant newspaper published extracts from documents the publication of which was expressly limited by an order of the court. The Divisional Court held that, where it was intended to impose liability on a third party, it was necessary to show that there had been some significant and adverse effect on the administration of justice. Because the restraints on freedom of expression should be no wider than were truly necessary in a democratic society, a third party's conduct which was inconsistent with an order of the court in only a trivial or technical way should not expose him to conviction for contempt. In the instant case, the breaches of the order committed by the respondents were minor and did not amount to a significant interference with the administration of justice. Furthermore, the evidence showed that editor of the newspaper genuinely believed that the newspaper could properly publish extracts from documents quoted in the judgment of the court without infringing any order it had made.

It will be a contempt of court for a journalist to refuse to disclose the source of his information, or to refuse to produce documents, when required to do so by a court,[1] or to place a party to litigation under improper pressure. Press vilification of a litigant is not permitted, although the law of contempt will not protect a litigant against fair and temperate criticism.[2]

Civil contempt will occur where a party fails to comply with an order of a court. Examples include the following: failure of a solicitor to comply with an undertaking.[3] failure to swear an account, refusal to comply with an order for discovery of documents or to answer interrogatories[4] and failure to comply with an injunction. Similarly mere failure to pay a judgment debt is not contempt, although wilful refusal to do so is.[5] However, if there is a reasonable alternative method available of securing compliance with a court order, the Court of Appeal has stated that that method should be adopted rather than committing the contemnor to prison.[6] A striking, and constitutionally important, example of civil contempt is the decision of the House of Lords in *M v Home Office*[7] At the conclusion of a hearing of an application for leave to apply for judicial review brought by an individual who was claiming he was being deported illegally, a judge accepted what was understood to be a binding undertaking on behalf of the Home Secretary, and later made an order to the same effect. Under this undertaking and order,

19 *R v Socialist Worker Printers and Publishers Ltd, ex parte A-G* [1975] QB 637; [1975] 1 All ER 142; but there must be a clear direction and not merely a request: *A-G v Leveller Magazine Ltd* [1979] AC 440; [1979] 1 All ER 745.
20 [1997] 3 All ER 159.
1   In *Director of Public Prosecutions v Channel 4 Television Co Ltd* [1993] 2 All ER 517 fines totalling £75,000 were imposed on a defendant company for failure to comply with an order to produce documents.
2   *A-G v Times Newspapers Ltd* [1974] AC 273; [1973] 3 All ER 54, one of a number of actions resulting from the thalidomide tragedy which left a large group of children badly disabled.
3   *Re Kerly* [1901] 1 Ch 467.
4   See p 391, *post*.
5   Debtors Act 1869, as amended by Administration of Justice Act 1970, s 11.
6   *Danchevsky v Danchevsky* [1975] Fam 17; [1974] 3 All ER 934.
7   *Re M* [1994] 1 AC 277 sub nom *M v Home Office* [1993] 3 All ER 537.

the Home Secretary was under an obligation to ensure that the applicant was not reported, or, alternatively, returned to the jurisdiction. The evidence showed that the Home Secretary had failed to comply with this duty, and was found, in his official capacity, to be in contempt of court.[8]

2   Strict liability contempt

It is possible for contempt to be committed in certain circumstances even in the absence of an intent to interfere with the administration of justice. This arises in respect of publications which are seriously prejudicial to a fair trial. Up until 1981 the doctrine was very vague and ill-defined as to what test was to be applied, and as to the period of time during which the potential for commission of a strict liability contempt existed. The law was often criticised for its breadth, as well as uncertainty, and in 1973 the House of Lords went as far as deciding that any prejudgment of issues that were to be decided in a pending case amounted to contempt of court.[9] Following criticism of this decision, and in the light of an adverse ruling from the European Court of Human Rights,[10] the operation of the rule was radically changed by the Contempt of Court Act 1981.

This Act amends the strict liability rule. In particular the rule is: (1) limited to "publications" (as opposed to conduct); (2) applicable only to publications which create "a substantial risk that the course of justice in the proceedings in question will be seriously impeded or prejudiced"; and (3) applicable only if the proceedings in question are "active" (as determined by reference to Schedule 1 to the Act).[11] In addition the Act creates three statutory defences to the strict liability rule, viz. "innocent publication or distribution,[12] fair and accurate reports of legal proceedings held in public published contemporaneously and in good faith[13] and discussion of public affairs or other matters of general public interest if the risk of impediment or prejudice to particular legal proceedings is merely incidental to the discussion".[14]

An illustration of how the defence of incidental discussion might work is the case of *A-G v English*[15] where the House of Lords decided that an article discussing the merits of mercy killing did not amount to contempt, even though at the time of publication a doctor was on trial accused of the mercy killing of a disabled child. Lord Diplock observed:

"Such gagging of bona fides public discussion in the press of controversial matters of general public interest, merely because there are in existence

8   See also *R v City of London MC, ex parte Green* [1997] 3 All ER 551, where it was held that proceedings for contempt could be taken against the Director of the Serious Fraud Office, although, on the facts, no contempt was established.

9   See n 2, *supra*.

10   *Sunday Times v United Kingdom* (1979) 2 EHRR 245.

11   In criminal cases this will usually be from the date of the making of an arrest, the issue of a warrant for arrest or the issue of a summons. In civil proceedings, the relevant date usually will be the date of setting down for trial, or when the date for trial is fixed.

12   Contempt of Court Act 1981, s 3(1).

13   *Ibid*, s 4; but under s 4(2) the court may order publication to be postponed for the purpose of avoiding a substantial risk of prejudice to the administration of justice in those proceedings or in other proceedings pending or imminent; see *Practice Direction* [1982] 1 WLR 1475; breach of such order could be a contempt of court: *R v Horsham Justices, ex parte Farquharson* [1982] QB 762; [1982] 2 All ER 269.

14   *Ibid*, s 5.

15   [1983] 1 AC 116; [1982] 2 All ER 903. For allocation of the principles, see *A-G v Times Newspapers Ltd* (1983) Times, 12 February.

contemporaneous legal proceedings in which some instance of those controversial matters may be in issue, is what s 5 of the Contempt of Court Act 1981 was designed to prevent."

The application of the defence in section 5 will depend upon the nature of the subject matter of the discussion, and its relationship to the particular proceedings.[16] It should be noted, however, that it does not create a simple public interest discussion defence.[17]

3   Jurisdiction to punish contempt

Civil contempt was formerly punishable by writ of attachment but the Rules of the Supreme Court (Revision) 1965 abolished attachment so that civil contempt is now punishable by committal in the same way as criminal contempt.

The jurisdiction to punish for contempt, whether committed in or out of court, is inherent in superior courts of record. Such courts may commit for contempt and also punish contempt committed in the face of the court by immediate fine and imprisonment. Imprisonment must be for a fixed term not exceeding two years.[18]

Inferior courts of record have more limited powers. They can imprison for up to one month and impose a fine.[19] Although a county court is for all other purposes an inferior court it is treated as a superior court for this purpose.[20]

The powers of magistrates' courts to commit are contained in section 12 of the 1981 Act. Any person who (a) wilfully insults a justice, any witness before or officer of the court or any solicitor or counsel having business in the court, during his or their sitting or attendance in court or in going to or returning from the court; or (b) wilfully interrupts the proceedings or otherwise misbehaves in court is liable to be detained until the rising of the court and then to be committed for up to one month, or fined. Appeal lies to the Crown Court.

The Queen's Bench Division, as the successor of the Court of King's Bench, protects inferior courts against contempt by punishing contempts committed in inferior courts.[1]

Until 1960 there was no appeal against punishment for criminal contempt. The law was altered by the Administration of Justice Act 1960, section 13, which provides that the defendant shall have a right of appeal from any order or decision of a court or tribunal in the exercise of jurisdiction to punish for contempt, including criminal contempt. Appeal lies to the Court of Appeal, divisional court or House of Lords as the case may be.

---

16   *A-G v TVS Television Ltd* (1989) Times, 7 July.
17   And thus would not have assisted the defendants' newspapers in *A-G v Times Newspapers Ltd* [1974] AC 273; [1973] 3 All ER 54, because the intent in that instance was in fact to influence the conduct of particular proceedings. Cf *Re F (a minor) (publication of information)* [1977] Fam 58; [1977] 1 All ER 114.
18   Contempt of Court Act 1981, s 14(1); previously committal could be for an indefinite term. Where the contemnor is under 21 (but not less than 17) the committal is to detention: Criminal Justice Act 1982, s 9.
19   Contempt of Court Act 1981, s 14(1), (2).
20   *Ibid*, s 14(4A) (added by County Courts (Penalties for Contempt) Act 1983).
1   *R v Davies* [1906] 1 KB 32; *R v Daily Herald, ex parte Bishop of Norwich* [1932] 2 KB 402. The High Court also has statutory power under the Parliamentary Commissioner Act 1967 to deal with a person whom the Commissioner certifies as having been guilty of conduct in the nature of contempt in relation to an investigation held by the Commissioner under the Act. But this jurisdiction only extends to "courts" properly so called, and not to tribunals which are not courts; it may therefore be important to ascertain whether a particular tribunal is or is not a "court": *A-G v British Broadcasting Corporation* [1981] AC 303; [1980] 3 All ER 161; see p 161, *ante*. Note, however, that s 20 of the 1981 Act extends the jurisdiction to tribunals to which the Tribunals of Inquiry (Evidence) Act 1921 applies.

Contempt is punishable, and is often punished, summarily; that is to say by a procedure which is far removed from the ordinary processes of the law. No precise charges are put, often the accused is given no opportunity of consulting lawyers or of an adjournment to prepare his defence. There is no jury and the decision is made by a judge who may himself have been the person insulted. Therefore the Court of Appeal has indicated that the summary jurisdiction should not be used where a more orthodox procedure could be adopted. In the words of Lawton LJ:[2]

> "In my judgment this summary and draconian jurisdiction should only be used for the purpose of ensuring that a trial in progress or about to start can be brought to a proper and dignified end without disturbance and with a fair chance of a just verdict or judgment. Contempts which are not likely to disturb trial or affect the verdict or judgment can be dealt with by a motion to commit under RSC Ord 52, or even by indictment."

It should be noted, in conclusion, that punishment for contempt of court is by no means the only legal sanction for abuse of legal process. Many forms of conduct which appear to have the characteristics of criminal contempt are not punishable as contempts because they are separate criminal offences. Where they cause damage to another person they may also be torts, although contempt of court is not in itself tortious. Thus a person who intimidates a witness commits a contempt of court but may not be sued by that witness in tort.[3]

2   *Balogh v St Albans Crown Court* [1975] QB 73, at 92–93; [1974] 3 All ER 283, at 295.
3   *Chapman v Honig* [1963] 2 QB 502; [1963] 2 All ER 513.

CHAPTER 11

Juries

A   HISTORICAL GROWTH OF THE JURY SYSTEM

There is ample evidence that some forms of jury trial existed in England prior to the Norman Conquest. However, although the jury system was not the creation of the common law, it was certainly one of the cornerstones of common law procedure both in civil and criminal trials.

In criminal cases there were, until 1948, two juries. The first of these was the grand jury. The grand jury was not principally a trial jury in the modern sense. It originated in the jury of presentment of the hundred and its function was to present persons for trial before the royal judges at assizes or the justices in quarter sessions.[1] This function was later assumed by justices of the peace in the form of the modern system of preliminary investigation. For this reason the grand jury (of up to 23 members) ceased to be functional and its duties had been reduced virtually to formality long before its abolition. It was virtually abolished by the Administration of Justice (Miscellaneous Provisions) Act 1933, save for a few purposes, and entirely abolished by the Criminal Justice Act 1948.

The second jury in criminal cases was the petty jury (of 12 members). This was the equivalent of the modern trial jury. The trial of criminals by jury evolved in the thirteenth century to replace trial by ordeal, which the Church condemned in 1215.[2] Originally the grand jury of presentment also exercised the function of the trial jury but by the middle of the fourteenth century the petty jury had become distinct from its predecessor. The petty jury was originally summoned for its local knowledge and the members were really witnesses rather than judges of fact. Their function changed gradually as the practice grew of examining independent witnesses and by the fifteenth century the trial jury had assumed its modern function as judges of fact. Nevertheless not until *Bushell*'s case in 1670[3] was it established that jurors could not be punished for returning a verdict contrary to the evidence or the direction of the trial judge.

1   See p 177, *ante*.
2   Lateran Council 1215.
3   (1670) Vaugh 135.

In civil cases there was only ever one type of jury, the trial jury of 12 members, which had its origins in the Assize of Clarendon 1166.[4] By 1304 it was the rule of the common law courts that all trespass actions had to be tried with a jury. The result was that, with the decline of the real actions and the personal actions of debt and detinue,[5] virtually all actions in the common law courts came to be tried with a jury and this was the position until 1854 when the steady decline of the jury in civil cases began. The function of civil juries was, originally, that of witnesses but, as with criminal juries, a similar transition from witnesses to judges of fact took place.

B   JURY TRIAL AT THE PRESENT DAY

Before the present century the jury system was widely pronounced to be one of the chief safeguards of the individual against the abuse of prerogative and judicial power. The vast majority of cases, both civil and criminal, were tried by a jury and this right was thought to be essential and inviolable. Blackstone, writing of the jury in criminal cases, saw the jury as a barrier between the liberties of the people and the prerogative of the Crown.[6] Lord Camden, reflecting the mood of the age, observed:

"Trial by jury is indeed the foundation of our free constitution; take that away, and the whole fabric will soon moulder into dust."[7]

By the middle of the nineteenth century this concept of the sanctity of jury trial was disappearing. Consequently the jury began to decline as a factor in the administration of justice in both civil and criminal cases. The principal reasons for this decline were the eclipse of the royal prerogative in the administration of justice, the rapid growth in the volume of litigation in civil cases, the even more rapid growth of summary jurisdiction in criminal cases and a general appreciation that juries were both unpredictable and fallible.

I   Criminal cases

In criminal cases the loss of faith in the jury system has been far less marked than in civil cases, although its use is increasingly under challenge and currently again under review. The situation is still that a person aged eighteen or over[8] who has a common law right to jury trial cannot, subject to minor exceptions[9] be deprived of that right without his consent. Since all common law offences were triable by jury an accused person still has a right to claim trial by jury for any common law offence, subject to those exceptions. However many offences which were formerly indictable are now

4   See p 157, *ante*.
5   See p 6, *ante*.
6   3 Comm 379.
7   See Jackson *The Machinery of Justice in England* (8th Edn), pp 391 *et seq.*
8   There are special provisions for children and young persons; see p 576, *post*.
9   The exceptions are incitement to commit a summary offence (Magistrates' Courts Act 1980, s 45(1)) and offences of criminal damage, and associated offences, where the value involved does not exceed £200 (*ibid*, s 22(2)). The James Committee, which was established in 1973 and reported in 1975 (*The Distribution of Criminal Business between the Crown Court and Magistrates' Courts* ; Cmnd 6323) recommended (inter alia) that theft and other related offences where the value of the property concerned was less than £20 should become summary offences; in the face of considerable public opposition provisions to this effect in the original Bill were removed during the passage of the Bill through Parliament. For the current position, see p 470, *post*.

triable "either way"[10] and most trials of such offences are, in fact, summary trials. Indeed the number of trials on indictment is very small compared with the number of summary trials. Modern legislation, especially that concerned with road traffic, has created a vast number of summary offences. The fact of the matter is that the vast majority of cases, in excess of 95%, are disposed of summarily.[11] In 1995, some 1.93 million defendants were tried summarily, compared with some 89,000 in the Crown Court.[12] The process of choice of mode of trial is discussed in due course, as are changes designed to reduce the incidence of acquittals at the Crown Court on the direction of the trial judge.[13] The result is that only about 1% of accused actually have their innocence or guilt determined by the jury. The jury, though important in terms of the trial of the most serious of criminal offences, therefore plays a small role in the overall scheme of things.

2 Civil proceedings

It is in civil actions that the decline of the jury has been most marked. Until 1854 most civil actions in the common law courts had to be tried before a jury. The Common Law Procedure Act 1854 provided for trial by a judge alone but only with the consent of both parties. This trend was continued by the Judicature Acts and by 1933 only about one half of civil actions in the Queen's Bench Division were tried with a jury. The Administration of Justice (Miscellaneous Provisions) Act 1933 was a landmark in the decline of the civil jury. By section 6 of that Act the right to claim a jury in a civil action was limited to cases of libel, slander, malicious prosecution, false imprisonment, seduction or breach of promise of marriage on the application of either party or on the application of a party against whom fraud was alleged.[14] The right to claim jury trial in the Queen's Bench Division in these cases is now contained in section 69 of the Supreme Court Act 1981.[15] Even in these cases a jury may be refused if the court considers that the trial will involve a prolonged examination of documents or accounts or a scientific or local investigation. In all other cases the grant of a jury is at the discretion of the court. It was once the case that this discretion was absolute "or completely untrammelled".[16] However in the leading case of *Ward v James*[17] the full Court of Appeal established that this was not so and that the discretion had, in the same way as any other discretion, to be exercised judicially. Furthermore, the Court of Appeal stated that in actions for damages for personal injuries trial should be by a judge alone in the absence of special circumstances, such as a substantial dispute on the facts. The basic reason for this opposition to jury trial in personal injury cases is the unpredictability of jury awards of damages. Juries, no doubt swayed by the knowledge that the substantive defendant in a "running-down" case is almost always an insurance company[18] with apparently bottomless resources, have sometimes made

10 Criminal Law Act 1977, s 16; see p 469, *post*
11 See, generally the analysis of Derbyshire: "An Essay on the Importance and Neglect of the Magistracy" [1997] Crim LR 626. For the current figures relating to trials on indictment, see *Criminal Statistics*.
12 Derbyshire, *op cit*, at p 628.
13 See p 476.
14 Of these, actions for seduction and breach of promise of marriage were abolished by the Law Reform (Miscellaneous Provisions) Act 1970.
15 See p 398, *post*. The right is confined to cases in the Queen's Bench Division.
16 *Hope v Great Western Rly Co* [1937] 2 KB 130; [1937] 1 All ER 625, per Lord Wright MR.
17 [1966] 1 QB 273; [1965] 1 All ER 563.
18 Although the court should not be informed that the defendant in a personal injuries action is insured.

disproportionate awards to successful plaintiffs in this type of action. It was following two awards of £50,000 to victims in personal injury actions in 1963[19] that the courts became acutely aware of the unsuitability of juries in this type of case. Since the majority of actions in the Queen's Bench Division are actions for damages for personal injuries,[20] *Ward v James* is a further landmark in the decline of the civil jury. Immediately before this decision approximately 2% of trials in the Queen's Bench Division took place before a jury. The figure is now minimal. In *H v Ministry of Defence*[1] the court was able to identify only one personal injury case since *Ward v James* in which trial by jury had been ordered, and, if Law Commission recommendations are implemented, the use of the jury in personal injury cases will disappear entirely. In a report in 1995,[2] it observed:

"Given the difficulty of assessing damages for non pecuniary loss in personal injury cases and the judicial tariff that has been developed to ensure a measure of consistency and uniformity, we consider it unsatisfactory that juries might ever be called on to assess compensatory damages for personal injury. Juries do not have the benefit of knowledge of the scales of values that has been developed and the inevitable consequence is unacceptable inconsistency with awards in other cases."

Consequently, in little more than a century, jury trial in civil cases has been virtually superseded by trial by a judge alone, one notable exception being trials for defamation. In *Racz v Home Office*[3] the Court of Appeal held that the torts in respect of which s 69(1) of the 1981 Act gave a prima facie entitlement to a jury trial in the Queen's Bench Division, which are libel, slander, malicious prosecution and false imprisonment, were disparate torts which did not create a presumption that a jury trial ought to be ordered whenever the question of exemplary damages was likely to arise. Accordingly, the similarity of some other tort (in this case, an alleged misfeasance in a public office) to any of the torts listed in s 69(1) was not a factor which had to be taken into account by the court in determining, in the exercise of its discretion, whether it was appropriate to rebut the presumption against jury trial created by s 69(3). The position may differ where an action involves a claim for exemplary damages.[4] The general position, however, is that, except where the case falls within the terms of s 69, jury trial is unlikely to be ordered.[5] Even where it is, the jury may be often be "sheep loosed on an unfenced common with no shepherd".[6]

Even where jury trial is available in civil cases, the role of juries in them has itself proved controversial, with extremely large awards of damages made by juries attracting considerable criticism.[7] Outside the Queen's Bench Division of the High Court, juries are hardly ever encountered in civil actions. The Chancery Amendment Act 1858 provided power to summon a jury to the Court of Chancery. This power was transferred

---

19   *Warren v King* [1963] 3 All ER 521; [1964] 1 WLR 1; *Morey v Woodfield (No 2)* [1964] 1 QB 1; [1963] 3 All ER 584. The sums at the time were extremely large.
20   *Judicial Statistics*, 1992 (HMSO).
1   [1991] 2 QB 103; [1991] 2 All ER 834.
2   *Damages for Personal Injury: Non Pecuniary Loss* (HC Working Paper (1995) no 140), p 125.
3   [1994] 1 All ER 97.
4   See *John v Mirror Group Newspapers*, n 7, infra.
5   *H v Ministry of Defence* [1991] 2 QB 103; [1991] 2 All ER 834.
6   See Lord Bingham MR in *John v Mirror Group Newspapers*, n 7, *infra*.
7   See the comments of Lord Donaldson MR in *Sutcliffe v Pressdram Ltd* [1991] 1 QB 153; [1990] 1 All ER 269; *Rantzen v Mirror Group Newspapers (1986) Ltd* [1994] QB 670; [1993] 4 All ER 975. In *John v Mirror Group Newspapers* [1997] QB 586; [1996] 2 All ER 35, a jury's award of £350,000 for defamation was reduced on appeal to £75,000. For the detail of such cases, see, further, p 397, *post*.

to the Chancery Division by the Judicature Acts but has been totally ignored. A jury of eight may be summoned in the county court in the same circumstances as in the Queen's Bench Division but this is extremely unusual mainly because of the disproportionately high costs which it would entail. Juries may also be summoned in some of the courts of local jurisdiction. Finally coroners may, in certain cases, and in a few cases must,[8] summon a jury of between seven and eleven persons.

Majority verdicts were permitted in criminal cases by the Criminal Justice Act 1967.[9] In civil cases majority verdicts (save by consent of the parties) were not receivable until the Courts Act 1971[10] which in effect extended the Criminal Justice Act provisions in civil cases.

C COMPOSITION OF JURIES

One of the most frequent criticisms of juries has related to their composition. Prior to the Juries Act 1974, eligibility for jury service depended upon the existence of a property qualification, which led in 1956 to Lord Devlin describing the jury as "predominantly male, middle-aged, middle-minded and middle-class".[11] This criticism was, to some extent, met by the Criminal Justice Act 1972 which both abolished the property qualification and extended the age limits for jurors. The relevant provisions are now contained in the Juries Act 1974, a consolidating statute. Under section 1 of this Act the basic provision is that every person is qualified to serve as a juror and liable, when summoned, to attend for jury service, if:

(a) he is registered as a parliamentary or local government elector and is not less than eighteen nor more than sixty-five years of age; and
(b) he has been ordinarily resident in the United Kingdom, the Channel Islands or the Isle of Man for any period of at least five years since attaining the age of thirteen.

There are, however, provisions relating to ineligibility, disqualification and excusal.[12] Thus the judiciary, members of the legal profession, court officers, police officers, ministers of religion and the mentally ill are ineligible[13] while persons who have in the last ten years served any part of a sentence of imprisonment, youth custody or detention, being a sentence of three months or more or have received a suspended sentence or had imposed on them a community service order or who have at any time been sentenced to custody for life or to a term of imprisonment or youth custody for a term of five years or more are disqualified from jury service.[14]

8　See Coroners Act 1988, s 8(2), and p 189, *ante*.
9　The operative provisions are now contained in the Juries Act 1974, s 17; see p 529, *post* as to the procedure.
10　Courts Act 1971, s 39.
11　Devlin *Trial By Jury*, p 20.
12　The verdict of a jury is not void only because a juror was disqualified from jury service and no verdict can be challenged on the ground that a juror was not included in the relevant list of jurors or was misnamed or misdescribed or (unless objection was taken at the time) that the provisions of the Act as to the impanelling or selection of jurors has not been complied with (Juries Act 1974, s 18).
13　The full list is contained in Sch 1, Part 1 to the 1974 Act.
14　Act of 1974, Sch 1, Part II. Youth custody and detention centre orders were replaced by detention in young offenders institutions, by the Criminal Justice Act 1988, Sch 8, and, now, by detention and training orders (Crime and Disorder Act 1998).

In addition to those who are ineligible or disqualified, certain persons, notably members of Parliament, serving members of the armed forces and medical practitioners, may be excused from jury service if they so wish.[15] So too may others where there are "circumstances of personal hardship or conscientious objections to jury service".[16]

Thus the compositions of juries has radically changed; there are, for example, far more women sitting on juries nowadays as a result of the removal of the property qualification. Indeed, criticism is sometimes levelled at the youth or seeming lack of experience of some persons called to sit in judgment upon others as jurors, a position often compounded because those with good grounds for excusal will often be those who are successfully committed elsewhere, whether in a career or otherwise. The key feature of the jury is, however, the randomly selected lay element that it provides in serious criminal cases. To this extent it mirrors the office of justice of the peace, which provides a lay element in many, although not all, summary trials.[17] Whilst the oft-quoted right to "trial by peers" contained in clause 39 of Magna Carta 1215 never really related to trial by jury in the modern sense, the existence of a lay element can be regarded as an important means of ensuring that the law operates, and is applied, fairly.

Some right to regulate this randomly selected lay element has always existed. The prosecution has always had the right to request that a juror "stand by for the Crown". The effect of this is that the juror stands down, and is not called upon for the purposes of the instant case unless the jury panel, from which the jury is selected, is exhausted. In reality it provides a mechanism for challenge not open to the defence. For this reason, the right to require a juror to "stand by" is one to be used "sparingly, and in very exceptional circumstances".[18]

The prosecution are entitled to conduct checks upon potential jurors only in limited circumstances, set out in 1988 in *Attorney-General's Guidelines on Jury Checks*.[19] The permitted checks allow, broadly speaking, checks in respect of disqualified persons, and, in limited circumstances, security checks and checks upon extreme political views which might render the fair trial of a security or terrorist case virtually impossible. Such checks have to be authorised by the Attorney-General, and should be kept to an absolute minimum. The issues of principle were well described by Lord Denning MR when he observed as follows:[20]

"To my mind it is unconstitutional for the police authorities to engage in jury vetting. So long as a person is eligible for jury service, and is not disqualified, I cannot think it right that, behind his back, the police should go through his record so as to enable him to be asked to "stand by for the Crown" or to be challenged for the defence.[1] If this sort of thing is to be allowed, what comes of a man's right of privacy? he is bound to serve on a jury when summoned. Is he therefore liable to have his past record raked up against him, and presented on a plate to prosecuting and defending lawyers who may use it to keep him out of the jury and, who knows, it may become known to his neighbours and those about him."

---

15   For full details of the excusal provisions see Act of 1974, ss 89 and Sch 1, Part III.
16   See Lord Lane in *Practice Note: (Jury Service: Excusal)* [1988] 3 All ER 177, *sub nom Practice Direction* [1988] 1 WLR 1162. Excusal on religious grounds will only be granted if the religious belief will stand in the way of proper performance of the jury function: *R v Crown Court at Guildford, ex parte Siderfin* [1990] 2 QB 683; [1989] 3 All ER 7.
17   Some summary cases are tried by legally qualified stipendiary magistrates. See, further, p 182, *ante*.
18   *R v Thomas* (1989) 88 Cr App Rep 370.
19   [1988] 3 All ER 1086.
20   *R v Sheffield Crown Court, ex parte Brownlow* [1980] QB 530; [1980] 2 All ER 444.
1   Now abolished.

Challenge to the jury by the defence has in recent years been restricted. The right of the defence to challenge without being required to show cause was first reduced and then, in 1988, abolished.[2] The defence can now challenge only if it can show cause: ie good reason why the juror should not serve. The defence will usually have details of the jury panel: these will only be withheld by a court if it is thought desirable in order to prevent a jury being "nobbled", provided the right of challenge is preserved.[3] A judge has an inherent power to intervene and prevent a person serving, where it is proper to do so.[4] For example, a judge might require a person who is manifestly unsuited, because of illiteracy, to stand down.

Juries are not generally selected on the basis of gender, race or ethnic origin, for that would run counter to the principle of randomness. In *R v Ford*[5] a judge refused to ensure a multi-racial jury in a case where racial motives were to be imputed to a police officer. An appeal against conviction was dismissed. Nevertheless, a trial judge who does in fact seek to achieve a particular balance is entitled to do so.[6]

Whatever the composition of the jury, it should not be such as to give rise to a real danger of bias. In *R v Gough*[7] the appellant and his brother were charged with robbery. At the committal proceedings the brother was discharged and the appellant was indicted on a single count that he had conspired with his brother to commit robbery. At the appellant's trial the brother was frequently referred to by name, and a photograph of him and the appellant was shown to the jury and his address was contained in a statement read to the jury. One of the jurors was a next-door neighbour of the brother but she did not recognise him or connect him with the man referred to in court until he started shouting in court after the appellant had been convicted and sentenced to 15 years' imprisonment. The appellant appealed on the ground that, applying the test of whether a reasonable and fair-minded person sitting in the court and knowing all the relevant facts would have had a reasonable suspicion that a fair trial of the appellant had not been possible, the presence of the juror on the jury constituted a serious irregularity in the conduct of the trial. An appeal against conviction was dismissed, the House of Lords holding that no such danger arose on the facts of the case.

D THE MERITS OF JURY TRIAL

Jury trial has been the subject of significant criticism in recent years, particularly in respect of what some have seen as an unacceptably high acquittal rate.[8] Various research studies[9] have shown, however, that acquittal rates may reflect as much upon decisions to offer no evidence, or upon decisions by trial judges to withdraw a case from a jury as upon the nature of the jury, or upon jury trial. The proportion of accused who are actually acquitted by jury on all counts with which they are charged is low, of the order of 7%.[10] They may also reflect the fact that those who wish to plead guilty may prefer

2 Criminal Justice Act 1988, s 118.
3 *R v Comerford*, (1997) Times, 3 November.
4 *Mansell v R* (1857) 8 E & B 54.
5 [1989] QB 868; [1989] 3 All ER 445.
6 *R v Danvers* [1982] Crim LR 680; cf *R v Bansall* [1985] Crim LR 151.
7 [1993] 2 All ER 724.
8 See, eg, Sir Robert Mark in the Dimbleby Lecture, 1973. For support that this is the perception, see James Committee, *Report on the Distribution of Criminal Business between Crown Court and Magistrates' Court* (1975, Cm 6232) where a survey of defendants showed that a majority considered jury trial would raise the chances of acquittal.
9 Baldwin & McConville *Jury Trials* (1979, Clarendon Press); Vennard, "The Outcome of Contested Trials", in Managing Criminal Justice (ed Moxon, 1985, HMSO).
10 See *Judicial Statistics*, 1996.

to get the matter dealt with quickly, before a court with lesser sentencing powers, although there is some evidence to suggest that acquittal rates in magistrates' courts cases where the accused pleads not guilty are of roughly the same order as in the Crown Court.[11]

The reality is that insufficient is known about how juries in fact work. Section 8 of the Contempt of Court Act 1981 prohibits investigations as to how juries reach their verdicts, whether or not of a serious academic nature. Breach of this rule amounts to contempt of court[12] even if the breach is indirect. In *Attorney-General v Associated Newspapers*[13] the conviction of the newspaper appellant for publication of the views of jurors who had sat in a long, and abortive, fraud case[14] was upheld, even though the newspaper had obtained its information from a researcher who had gained information from the jurors, and not from the jurors themselves. What is known is through the workings of "shadow juries", where a panel of "shadow" jurors followed real cases,[15] from the anecdotal and personal accounts of real jurors, and through studies such as the Crown Court Study undertaken for the Royal Commission on Criminal Justice.[16] Despite this large gap in knowledge, or even, perhaps, because of it, the process of jury trial has come under challenge. The trial of serious offences by judges alone is not unknown in the United Kingdom: in Northern Ireland, trial of "scheduled offences"[17] has, since 1973, been by judge alone in so-called "Diplock courts".[18] More recently, the Report of the Fraud Trials Committee in 1986[19] recommended the abolition of jury trial in some serious fraud cases, and its replacement by a fraud trial tribunal comprising a judge sitting with two lay assessors. The committee, with one dissenting member, concluded that some long fraud cases were so complex that it was not reasonable to expect juries to be able to cope with multiple defendants and charges, and the arcane nature of the evidence. This recommendation, opposed by many in the legal profession, has not been implemented. It would significantly infringe the basic right to trial by jury in respect of serious offences but the Royal Commission on Criminal Justice[20] has returned to the issue, recommending a limitation on rights to elect jury trial. The failure of several high-profile fraud cases,[1] and the desire for greater efficiency inherent in the report of the Narey Committee,[2] have kept these proposals on the agenda. These issues are discussed further in due course.[3]

The merits of jury trial are sometimes stated in terms of the deficiencies of alternative modes of trial. Summary process in the magistrates' courts is relatively quick, cheap, but by no means beyond criticism. Rightly or wrongly, it is often thought that jury trial favours an accused. Other advocates of jury trial rely upon the constitutional importance of jury trial, and the safeguards it is said to provide for an accused.[4]

---

11   Softley, "A Comparison of Acquittal Rates in Magistrates Courts and Crown Court" [1976] JP 455.
12   *A-G v New Statesman and Nation Publishing Co Ltd* [1981] QB 1; [1980] 1 All ER 644.
13   [1994] 2 AC 238; [1994] 1 All ER 556.
14   The *Blue Arrow* Case. For serious fraud trials, see p 485, *post.*
15   See McCabe and Purves *The Shadow Jury at Work*, 1974.
16   Zander and Henderson, RCCJ Research Study No 19. See p 485, *post.*
17   Defined by Northern Ireland (Emergency Provisions) Act 1978, s 30 and Sch 4 to include murder, most serious offences of violence and offences related to the causing of explosions.
18   Following the recommendations of the Committee chaired by Lord Diplock (1972, Cmd 5185, HMSO).
19   See p 485, *post.*
20   See p 485, *post.*
1   See n 14, *supra*
2   See p 564, *post.*
3   See p 470, *post.*
4   On this argument, see, generally: Cornish *The Jury* (1968, Allen Lane).

Nevertheless, despite these criticisms, the jury remains a fundamental of the English legal system. Lord Denning MR in *Ward v James*[5] explained the place of the modern jury as follows:

"Let it not be supposed that this court is in any way opposed to trial by jury. It has been the bulwark of our liberties too long for any of us to seek to alter it. Whenever a man is on trial for serious crime, or when in a civil case a man's honour or integrity is at stake, or when one or other party must be deliberately lying, then trial by jury has no equal."

It was put more graphically by Lord Devlin, who described jury trial as "the lamp that shows that freedom lives".[6] Arguably, it provides some mechanism to prevent the unjust or oppressive use of the criminal law. This justification has not been regarded as convincing by all commentators.[7] One describes the approach exemplified by Devlin as "dangerous, deceptive, distracting nonsense, as all the famous miscarriages of justice exposed in the 1990's should demonstrate."[8] Others point equally to the potentially random factors that may affect a jury's deliberations. The primacy of jury trial has also been used as a justification for judicial non-interference with verdicts in alleged miscarriage of justice cases.[9]

5   [1966] 1 QB 273; [1965] 1 All ER 563.
6   Devlin, *op cit*.
7   See Darbyshire [1991] Crim LR 740.
8   *Ibid*, p 643.
9   See p 547, *post*.

CHAPTER 12

The Legal Profession

A INTRODUCTION

A distinctive feature of the English legal system is the division of the legal profession into two separate branches: solicitors and barristers. This precise division is unknown outside Britain and the Commonwealth. Elsewhere all practitioners are described as "lawyers", a word which has no particular application in England. The division of the legal profession dates back to about 1340, the time at which professional advocacy evolved.[1] The advocates with audience in the common law courts were the serjeants[2] and barristers while the preparatory stages of an action were carried through by officers of the court in question known as attorneys. There thus developed two classes of legal practitioner: serjeants and barristers on the one hand and attorneys who were, as solicitors still are, officers of the court. Solicitors, as distinct from attorneys, first appeared in the fifteenth century and practised in the Court of Chancery. They were, at first, inferior to attorneys and could not bind their clients as attorneys could. By the eighteenth century the offices of attorney and solicitor were frequently held by the same person and the distinction between them was finally abolished by the Judicature Act 1873.

The separation of barristers and solicitors was preserved by the Inns of Court. Barristers had to be members of one of the Inns of Court and these Inns, after the sixteenth century, refused to admit attorneys or solicitors to membership. As a result the latter banded together and by 1739 had formed their own professional organisation in London. This was styled "the Society of Gentlemen Practisers in the Courts of Law and Equity" and was the forerunner of The Law Society.

Thus the separation of the legal profession has an historical foundation as has the nature of the respective functions which barristers and solicitors perform. These structures, functions and divisions are, however, increasingly undergoing both challenge and change. Barristers are still primarily advocates, although many barristers

---

1   For details of the history of the emergence of both branches of the profession, see Baker *An Introduction to English Legal History* (3rd Edn), pp 177–199.
2   Serjeants (*servientes regis ad legem*) were the senior advocates and had exclusive audience in the Court of Common Pleas. The rank of serjeant was abolished by the Judicature Act 1873.

in fact spend most of their time engaged in "paper-work" such as the drafting of pleadings, divorce petitions, complex settlements and opinions on specialised matters such as taxation and company law. Solicitors deal with the preparatory stages of litigation such as the preparation of evidence, interviewing witnesses, issuing writs and, usually, conducting interlocutory proceedings, and sometimes acting as advocates. In addition solicitors deal with a large number of non-litigious matters such as the drafting of wills, the supervision of trusts and settlements, the administration of estates and conveyancing.

To regard barristers as "advocates" and solicitors as "non advocates" would be to grossly over-simplify, and be inaccurate. Solicitors have had a right of audience in most courts and tribunals; this has not in the past extended to the Court of Appeal or to most proceedings in open court (as opposed to chambers) in the High Court, and rights of audience in the Crown Court are limited to such proceedings as the Lord Chancellor may direct.[3] Non employed solicitor advocates who have achieved a higher court qualification[4] can act as advocates in the Crown Court. Only some 600 of the 83,000 or so solicitors in England and Wales have such a qualification, and the vast majority of advocacy continues to be done by barristers. This is not only because of qualification, but also because it is often easier, and cheaper, for a solicitor (who may have very substantial practice overheads which have to be reflected in fee levels) to instruct a barrister, who may be in court on other matters in any event. A solicitor advocate may find the cost of time waiting at court for a case to come on increases costs to an extent that, again, it may be more cost-effective to brief a barrister. These issues will become even more important when, as is proposed, the exclusive rights of audience of the Bar are abolished. The proposed changes in rights of audience are discussed later.[5]

There are other distinctions between the two branches of the profession. Solicitors may enter into partnerships, barristers may not. Barristers appear in court (other than magistrates' courts) in wig and gown, although a fierce debate has occurred as to whether wigs should be retained. Solicitors appear in gown in certain courts, notably the county court, but are never bewigged. It remains doubtful whether the practice of members of the Bar of wearing wigs in the higher courts can remain given the likely opening up of rights of audience to solicitors generally. Solicitors are instructed by their clients directly; barristers are generally instructed by a solicitor and not by a lay client direct.[6] Again, in an era of change it may be that barristers will increasingly seek the right to take instructions directly from clients, rather than on a referral basis, when solicitors have the right to move generally into areas of advocacy work seen hitherto as the traditional preserves of the Bar.[7]

---

3   Supreme Court Act 1981, s 83; see *Practice Direction (Crown Court; Right of Audience)* [1972] 1 All ER 608; [1972] 1 WLR 307; *Practice Direction (Solicitors: Audience in the Crown Court)* [1988] 3 All ER 717; [1988] 1 WLR 1427. This includes the hearing of appeals, and proceedings for committal for sentence where the solicitor (or his firm) represented the defendant at the magistrates' court. Full details of the courts and tribunals in which solicitors have a right of audience may be found in 44 *Halsbury's Laws* (4th Edn), paras 68-70.

4   See p 245, *post*.

5   See pp 245-246, *post*.

6   This is a custom rather than a rule of law, and of fairly recent origin for, until the eighteenth century, it was customary for counsel to be instructed directly by law clients. There are exceptions to this general rule: see 3(1) *Halsbury's Laws* (4th Edn) para 465. The Bar Council may permit barristers to act upon the instructions of other professions duly approved: Resolution of the Bar Council, 12 November 1985. See Code of Conduct 1990, paras 102, 901.

7   See, eg *Counsel*, June 1998.

B   ROYAL COMMISSION ON LEGAL SERVICES

In 1976 a Royal Commission was set up to inquire into the law and practice relating to the provision of legal services in England, Wales and Northern Ireland to consider whether, and if so what, changes were desirable in the public interest in the structure, organisation, training, regulation of and entry to the legal profession.

The Commission produced its final report in October 1979.[8] Its conclusions and recommendations were (surprisingly, to some) basically favourable to the status quo, although it found that the distribution of legal services was uneven and the quality not uniform. The Commission summarised its observations on the quality of service in the following words:[9]

"The evidence before us shows that year by year most legal work is transacted well and efficiently. Most clients are satisfied with the service they receive. The judiciary is in general able to rely on the quality of work performed in the courts. City institutions, including The Stock Exchange, the British Bankers' Association and the Committee on Invisible Exports told us that the legal services available in London are of a high standard; this attracts legal and other business from abroad which contributes to our invisible exports."

Having said that, the Commission went on to point to certain shortcomings in the service and to suggest some remedies.[10] In particular it pointed to unacceptable delays in contentious business and noted that in the Queen's Bench Division the average lapse of time between cause of action and trial was four years. It decried "repetitious cross-examination, labouring points good and bad and general prolixity" and suggested that the remedy lay in good education and training, self-discipline, adequate research and careful preparation. It recommended *inter alia* that both solicitor and barrister should advise specifically on whether a conference before the day of trial was necessary for the proper presentation of a case (it being an occasional complaint of litigants, especially defendants in criminal cases, that they do not meet their counsel until shortly before the hearing on the day of trial), that measures should be taken to prevent parties being taken by surprise by offers of settlement at the door of the court, that The Law Society should issue guidelines on methods of office administration, that practising solicitors should plan ahead to meet the increasing need for specialisation and that written professional standards should be issued by both branches of the profession, failure to observe which would involve disciplinary proceedings.

On the controversial issue of fusion of the two branches of the profession, the Commission recommended against it on the grounds that there would be an unacceptable reduction in the number and spread of smaller firms of solicitors and an increase in the proportion of large city firms, that while there might be some saving in small cases, in large ones the expense might be greater and, with regard to the administration of justice, that:

"A two-branch profession is more likely than a fused one to ensure the high quality of advocacy which is indispensable, so long as our system remains in its present form, to secure the proper quality of justice."[11]

8   *Report of the Royal Commission on Legal Services* (Cmnd 7648, HMSO).
9   Report, para 22.16.
10   Report, paras 22.17–22.75.
11   *Ibid*, paras 17.45–17.46.

As to solicitors' practising arrangements, the Royal Commission recommended that partnership between solicitors and members of other professions should not be permitted, that incorporation of a solicitor's business with limited liability should not be permitted but that incorporation with unlimited liability should, subject to certain safeguards,[12] that legal executives should continue to perform their functions as the employees of solicitors, but not as independent practitioners,[13] that The Law Society should introduce duty solicitor schemes in all magistrates' courts,[14] that a system of citizens' law centres should be established to provide legal services, particularly in relation to social welfare law (but not to undertake community work and campaigns),[15] that the so-called "conveyancing monopoly" should be retained but with a reversion to scale charges[16] and that there should be no general extension of solicitors' rights of audience.[17] Finally the Commission made detailed recommendations on the subject of disciplinary procedures,[18] in particular that The law Society should take action when cases of bad professional work are brought to its notice, that The Law Society should ensure that independent legal advice is available for those who allege negligence against solicitors, that within The Law Society the processes of investigation and adjudication of complaints should be separated and that laymen should be involved in these processes; there are also recommendations on the subject of charges.[19]

Nor were the recommendations affecting barristers any more radical. Here again the Commission recommended that, in relation to disciplinary procedure, the processes of investigation and adjudication of complaints should be separated and that the Senate should have the responsibility of taking action when cases of bad professional work are brought to its notice.[20] It recommended that all barristers should be required to have professional indemnity insurance against negligence claims,[1] should not be compelled to have a clerk,[2] that the organisation and functions of the circuits should be reviewed[3] and that the existing restriction against partnership at the Bar should be retained, as should the two-tier system of silks and juniors.[4]

C   THE ROLE AND FUNCTIONS OF SOLICITORS AND BARRISTERS

I   Introduction

Although the Royal Commission on Legal Services did not generate immediate legislation, or impetus for change, the issues which it considered were the subject of considerable discussion and debate. The late 1980s saw a period of fundamental government reconsideration of the way legal services were being provided, and by whom, and of the rules and practices governing such provision. A series of White Papers

12   *Ibid*, paras 30.15–30.28.
13   *Ibid*, para 31.26.
14   *Ibid*, para 9.9. Such schemes now exist: see Duty Solicitor Arrangements 1992, and p 281, *post*.
15   *Ibid*, paras 8.15–8.38.
16   *Ibid*, paras 21.28–21.101.
17   *Ibid*, para 18.60. See now p 224, *post*.
18   *Ibid*, paras 25.8–25.45. See now p 249, *post*.
19   *Ibid*, paras 37.14–37.68.
20   *Ibid*, paras 26.13, 26.18.
1   *Ibid*, para 24.11. The Bar gave effect to this in 1983, since when failure to be properly insured has constituted professional misconduct.
2   *Ibid*, para 34.7.
3   *Ibid*, para 32.54.
4   *Ibid*, paras 33.66, 33.84.

on civil justice,[5] upon legal services,[6] upon the organisation of the legal profession,[7] upon contingency fees,[8] and upon conveyancing services[9] were published, and generated heated and full responses from professional bodies and other interested parties.[10] The result of the debate was legislation in the form of the Courts and Legal Services Act 1990, which adopted a much more radical approach than advocated by the Royal Commission, and which introduced fundamental change in major areas of the work of the profession.

The Act has a distinct philosophy. Section 17 sets out the objectives and principles upon which the Act is based, and which it seeks to achieve. The "statutory objective" is:

"the development of legal services in England and Wales (and in particular the development of advocacy, litigation, conveyancing and probate services) by making provision of new or better ways of providing such services, and a wider choice of persons providing them, while maintaining the proper and efficient administration of justice."

The Act identifies "general principles". Rights of audience or rights to conduct litigation should be decided only on the basis of: (i) qualifications; (ii) membership of a professional body having effective and enforceable rules of conduct; (iii) whether rules satisfactorily provide requirements for ensuring that legal services are not withheld on the basis of the objectionable nature of the case, the views of the client or because of the source of finance; and (iv) generally, whether rules of conduct are appropriate in the interests of the administration of justice.

Whilst both the solicitor and barrister branches of the profession meet these criteria, and are recognised by the Act in various ways as doing so,[11] the intent of the Act is that others might in the future equally satisfy these criteria and thus be permitted to perform certain functions hitherto regarded as the exclusive preserve of the legal profession. For this reason, significant elements of the changes made by the Act were, and remain, controversial.[12] Nevertheless the combined effect of these changes, and those relating to legal aid and the funding of legal services,[13] is increasing to change the way legal services are provided, and by whom. Not only is a shift between solicitors and the Bar in prospect, but also in prospect is the increasing provision of legal services by non-lawyers.

The Act gives important powers in respect of these matters to the Lord Chancellor. In exercising powers, and performing functions under the Act, the Lord Chancellor is, currently, advised by the Advisory Committee on Legal Education and Training, created by section 19 of the 1990 Act. This committee comprises two members of the

---

5   *Report of the Review Body on Civil Justice* (Cm 394, 1988, HMSO).
6   *Legal Services: A Framework for the Future* (Cm 740, 1989, HMSO).
7   *The Workload and Organisation of the Legal Profession* (Cm 570, 1989, HMSO).
8   *Contingency Fees* (Cm 571, 1989, HMSO).
9   *Conveyancing By Authorised Practitioners* (Cm 572, 1989, HMSO).
10   See, eg, Bar Council *The Quality of Justice – The Bar's Response* (Butterworths, 1989); The Law Society *Striking the Balance; The Green Papers – The Judges' Response* (1989).
11   Thus, ss 31–33 preserve the existing rights of audience of barristers and solicitors, and each is deemed to have in force the required qualification regulations and rules of conduct required by ss 27–28 (see p 245, *post*).
12   In particular the Bar and judiciary opposed rights of audience in higher courts for solicitors and others, as potentially weakened the quality of advocacy and expertise traditionally claimed by the Bar. Other areas of particular controversy included potential loss of independence of the judiciary and the potential for multi-disciplinary practices.
13   See p 278, *post*.

judiciary (in addition to being chaired by a judge of the Supreme Court or a Lord of Appeal in Ordinary), two practising barristers, two practising solicitors, two persons experienced in the teaching of law, and nine other persons not falling within these categories. In the appointment of such persons, the Lord Chancellor is to have regard to experience or knowledge of the provision of legal services, civil or criminal proceedings or the working of the courts, of the maintenance of professional standards amongst the legal profession, of social conditions, consumer affairs or the maintenance of standards in other professional organisations.[14] A proposal made by the Government in its Consultation Paper on Rights of Audience and Rights to Conduct Litigation in England and Wales[15] would, if accepted, lead to the abolition of ACLEC, which would be replaced by a "more focused" Legal Services Consultative Panel.

The Act also created the office of Legal Services Ombudsman to supplement the arrangements for the handling of complaints against barristers and solicitors.[16] His functions relate to the investigation of allegations properly made to him about the way in which a complaint made to a professional body has been handled. In doing that, he may also investigate the original complaint, make a report and make recommendations.[17]

2   Rights to conduct litigation

The 1990 Act removed the virtual monopoly in the right to conduct litigation vested in solicitors.[18] This right is defined by section 119(1) as the right:

(a)   to exercise all or any of the functions of issuing a writ or otherwise commencing proceedings before any court; and

(b)   to perform any ancillary functions in relation to proceedings (such as entering appearances to actions).

The principle stated by section 28 of the 1990 Act is that any person should be entitled to conduct litigation where a right to do so has been conferred by an appropriate body. That body will be required to have appropriate rules, regulations and qualifications,[19] and these broadly must satisfy the general principles set out in section 17.[20] Other rights to conduct litigation may exist by virtue of specific statutory provision. Solicitors are deemed to have been granted such rights,[1] and other bodies may be granted the right to conduct litigation following the procedures set out in some detail in the Act. It should be noted that the Law Society has created specialist panels of solicitors considered to have expertise to conduct litigation in certain areas of law, such as cases involving children, and personal injury cases. This may have the effect of limiting the conduct of such cases to such practitioners.

More change may be on the way, inevitably so if rights of audience are to be extended.[2] The Government, in its Consultation Paper, has sought comments on

14   1990 Act, s 19(5).
15   See p 245, *post*.
16   *Ibid*, ss 21–22. See, further, p 267, *post*.
17   *Ibid*, s 23.
18   *Ibid*, s 28. For the previous position, see Solicitors Act 1974, s 20.
19   *Ibid*, s 28(2).
20   See p 242, *ante*.
1   *Ibid*, s 33.
2   See p 245, *post*.

proposals to grant rights to conduct litigation to the Bar Council and the Institute of Legal Executives. If implemented this would open up the management and conduct of litigation to market forces, and, presumably, will enable the Legal Aid Board to seek competitive tenders from different parts of the profession for the provision of litigation services.[3]

3   Rights of audience

Closely connected with, but separate to, the right to conduct litigation is the question of rights of audience. It has already been noted that barristers have exclusive rights of audience in some courts, and significant discussion occurred as to the extent to which the preservation of such exclusive rights was necessary or desirable for the maintenance of a strong and effective Bar, and for the maintenance of high standards of advocacy.[4]

In any court a litigant may represent himself.[5] That litigant may also be assisted by a friend. In *R v Leicester City Justices, ex parte Barrow*[6] the Court of Appeal stressed the duty of a court to permit a litigant in person to have all reasonable facilities for exercising his right to be heard in his own defence, including quiet and unobtrusive advice from another person.[7] The court could not require such a litigant to obtain the leave of the court, although it could restrain the use of such assistance if its use was not bona fide, was unreasonable, or amounted to a hindrance to the administration of justice.

Except in such situations, representation is by solicitor, counsel or magistrates' court lay prosecutor. Until recently solicitors have limited rights of audience in the Crown Court, and in certain High Court proceedings.[8] Now rights flow from a solicitor attaining a higher court qualification.[9] The advantages of such limitations upon rights of audience were identified by the Bar Council in 1989, as follows:

(1) the operation of the "cab-rank" principle at the Bar, whereby barristers are obliged to accept any brief in an area in which they practice provided they are available, and a proper fee is offered;
(2) the limited rights of audience enable the development and maintenance of specialist advocacy skills;
(3) the availability of skilled advocates working in competition with each other;
(4) the development of standards of practice and integrity through peer-group discipline. It is also argued sometimes that exclusive rights are important to ensure a viable and thriving Bar, which in turn produces a pool of potential judicial appointees.

Not all the above points were accepted by those who favour extension of rights of audience. They pointed to the undesirability of experienced solicitors having to hand over a case to possibly a less experienced advocate, that many solicitor advocates are

---

3   See p 289, *post*.
4   See the arguments marshalled by the Bar in its response, *op cit*, n 10 *ante*, particularly at pp 128–146.
5   And often will be given assistance by the court itself.
6   [1991] 2 QB 260; [1991] 3 All ER 935.
7   Generally known as a "McKenzie friend" in the light of the decision in *McKenzie v McKenzie* [1971] P 33; [1970] 3 All ER 1034.
8   See *Practice Direction* [1986] 2 All ER 226; [1986] 1 WLR 545: a solicitor may represent his client in open court in an emergency, in formal or unopposed proceedings (ie where there is unlikely to be any argument and the court is not called upon to exercise any discretion), and when judgment is delivered in open court following a hearing in chambers at which the solicitor represented his client.
9   See p 242, *ante*, 245, *post*.

highly skilled, that barristers often return briefs at the last minute, leading to cases being handled by persons unfamiliar with the case, and that principles such as the "cab-rank" principle often do not work effectively in practice given the demands upon the time of successful advocates.[10] A busy barrister can easily be committed elsewhere, and, in any event, a barrister can only be instructed through a solicitor. There is no formal "cab-rank" system for solicitors. Opinions as to whether the "cab rank" principle operates effectively, or at all in reality as opposed to rhetoric, differ, even amongst members of the Bar.[11] One glaring, if perhaps extreme, example cited as proof that the principle operates in theory, but not in practice, is the fact that in 1973 some 24 Queen's Counsel declined to accept briefs on behalf of the IRA Old Bailey bombers.[12] It is impossible, of course, to know from such examples the reasons given by those who were unable to accept the brief. In any event, the "cab rank" rule may become redundant and inappropriate in an era of conditional fees.[13]

Original proposals in the White Paper would have given considerable power to the Lord Chancellor to determine rights of audience for individual courts.[14] By section 27 of the 1990 Act, existing rights of audience for solicitors and barristers are preserved, but a framework is created for the extension of those rights to those who are suitably qualified. This may occur after fulfilment of a complex procedure involving consultation with various persons and bodies, and requires the consent not only of the Lord Chancellor, but also of the "designated judges".[15] Section 71 identifies six classes of advocacy qualification: Supreme Court, High Court, general Crown Court, county court and magistrates' court. It has been unclear how far rights of audience will be extended, but mooted changes permitting members of the Crown Prosecution Service[16] to conduct prosecutions in the Crown Court have generated fierce criticism from the Bar. The independence of the advocate prosecuting a case on behalf of the Crown Prosecution Service is regarded by the Bar, and others, as absolutely fundamental, it being in the interests of justice for there to be maintained "a pool of high quality independent prosecutors."[17] The Lord Chancellor and the four senior designated judges approved an application by The Law Society for rights of audience in the higher courts for solicitors in practice, but in 1993 deferred a decision on rights of audience for employed solicitors. Legal executives also sought increased rights of audience.[18]

The direction of future changes has become slightly clearer with the publication, in June 1998, of a Government Consultation Paper on rights of audience.[19] Under the proposals, if implemented, all qualified barristers and solicitors would have rights of audience in the higher courts. This would include employed solicitors, such as those who work for the Crown Prosecution Service, and would "promote quality, choice and value for money". All qualified lawyers would be able to act as advocates in the Crown Court, High Court, Court of Appeal and House of Lords, provided they meet relevant training requirements and comply with professional obligations. Those might include additional training requirements and rules of conduct governing the exercise of those rights. The rules of conduct might differ as between employed lawyers and

---

10   See The Law Society response, *op cit.*
11   See the survey covered by Walson, "Advocacy for the Unpopular" (1998) 162 JP 499.
12   Robertson *The Justice Game*, at p 379.
13   See p 246, and 290, *post.*
14   Leading to arguments of potential interference in the judicial process.
15   The Lord Chief Justice, the Master of the Rolls, the President of the Family Division and the Vice-Chancellor: see 1990 Act, ss 29(1)(b), 119(1).
16   See p 271, *post.*
17   See the comments of Heather Hallett, QC, Chairman of the Bar, reported at (1998) 148 NLJ 970.
18   See [1993] NLJR 1774.
19   *Rights of Audience and Rights to Conduct Litigation in England and Wales,* (1998), HMSO.

those in private practice. Once rights of audience have been acquired, they will be retained even if the individual moves between the two branches of the profession, or from employment to private practice or vice versa. All rules will need the approval of the Lord Chancellor, who will act in consultation with senior members of the judiciary.

These proposals have been welcomed by many parts of the profession in initial responses.[20] They will create the potential for a case to be handled within one firm from beginning to end, without the prospect of returned briefs from the chosen member of the Bar who has become unavailable, create the potential for members of the Bar to join firms of solicitors as specialist advocates, the potential for the Bar to become a more specialist referral profession for the more difficult cases and the potential for prosecution of serious offences in the Crown Court by employees of the Crown Prosecution Service. Conversely, the dangers of that last change have already been identified,[1] whilst some argue that the advantages of an independent Bar in terms of availability and cost may mean that relatively few solicitors take on higher court advocacy.

4   Contingency and conditional fees

English law has always regarded "contingency fees" (that is to say, fees the amount or payment of which are contingent upon the result of litigation) as unlawful on the grounds of public policy[2] although recent case law shows that view in fact to misconceived.[3] Although the White Paper published by the Government in 1989[4] did not consider the complete abolition of all restrictions on contingency fees to be in the public interest, some change was thought to be desirable, and possibly valuable in cases where difficulties in financing litigation currently exist.[5] Section 58 of the Courts and Legal Services Act 1990 introduced important changes which permit, in some circumstances, conditional fee arrangements to be made. The details of these are discussed later.[6]

5   The conveyancing monopoly

The virtual monopoly of solicitors of the conduct for profit of conveyancing business has long been under challenge, but has continued subject only to the creation of licensed conveyancers by the Administration of Justice Act 1985, which allows members of the Council for Licensed Conveyancers, who have shown compliance with the educational requirements and practice rules of that Council to engage in conveyancing for profit, even though not qualified as solicitors.[7]

The 1990 Act[8] creates a new body, the Authorised Conveyancing Practitioners Board, comprising members to be appointed by the Lord Chancellor. It has a statutory duty:

20   See , eg, (1998) 148 NLJ at 970, (1998) Times, 29 June.
1   See p 245, *ante*.
2   See *Halsbury's Laws* (4th ed).
3   See *Thai Trading Co (A Firm) v Taylor* [1998] 3 All ER 65; *Bevan Ashford (a firm) v Geoff Yeandle (Contractors) Ltd (In Liquidation)* [1998]3 All ER 238. See, further, p 256, *post*.
4   See p 242, *ante*.
5   See p 273, *post*.
6   See p 254, *post*.
7   Such Licensed Conveyancers are subject to detailed rules concerning professional indemnity, the keeping of accounts, and subject to a disciplinary process. The Council for Licensed Conveyancers has wide powers of intervention.
8   Section 34 (not yet in force).

(a)   to seek to develop competition in the provision of legal services;
(b)   to supervise the activities of authorised practitioners in connection with the provision of conveyancing services.

In the fulfilment of that duty the Board may authorise a person to be an authorised practitioner, but can refuse an application in some circumstances.[9] These will include the applicant not being a "fit and proper" person, the applicant not complying with requirements in respect of protection against risk, the treatment of complaints or the payment of compensation. An applicant must be a member of the Conveyancing Ombudsman scheme.[10] The Lord Chancellor may also make regulations in respect of the competence and conduct of authorised practitioners. There are also specific rules designed to prohibit "tying-in" arrangements, whereby a person's freedom to secure independent legal advice might be prejudiced by a property deal which contained inclusive legal services, or which required the use of certain legal services as a condition of a loan.[11] These are thought to be particular dangers if the right to offer conveyancing services is extended to include banks or building societies.

6   Probate services

These are likewise extended. Existing restrictions in section 23 of the Solicitors Act 1974, which prohibit the preparation for reward of papers for the grant of probate or letters of administration, other than by a solicitor, barrister or notary, are relaxed. Henceforth, the authorised persons will include the Public Trustee, Official Solicitor, authorised banks, building societies and insurance companies.

D   SOLICITORS

I   The Law Society

The controlling body in the case of solicitors is The Law Society, constituted under a Royal Charter of 1845 as amended by supplemental charters,[12] and being given the name "The Law Society" by the Supplemental Charter of 1903. Membership of the Society is voluntary although the vast majority of the solicitors currently in practice are, in fact, members of the Society. The Society is governed by the President, Vice-President and a Council of not more than 70 members, the latter being elected for a period of five years; at present there are 70 members, of whom 56 are elected to represent constituencies and 14 are elected by the Council itself as specialists.

The objects of the Society remain, as defined in the Charter of 1845, as "promoting professional improvement and facilitating the acquisition of legal knowledge". Notwithstanding its voluntary composition The Law Society has important regulatory powers in respect of all solicitors, deriving mainly from the Solicitors Act 1974, a consolidating statute.

By section 2 of the 1974 Act the Society may, with the concurrence of the Lord Chancellor, the Lord Chief Justice and the Master of the Rolls, make "training regulations" about education and training for persons seeking to be admitted or to

9   *Ibid*, ss 37(1), 38(1).
10   *Ibid*, s 37(7)(e). For details of the scheme, see 1990 Act, Sch 7.
11   *Ibid*, ss 104–107.
12   In 1872, 1903, 1909 and 1954.

practise as solicitors. Training regulations may relate to education and training, whether by service under articles or otherwise, to be undergone by persons seeking admission as solicitors or by persons who have already been admitted. The profession is effectively all graduate with entrants either possessing a qualifying law degree[13] or, having taken a non-qualifying degree, whether in law or some other discipline, having passed an additional one-year[14] Common Professional Examination, which covers the relevant legal curriculum. A student then must pass a practical-orientated Legal Practice Course, before entering into a training contract. A person wishing to enter into a training Comtrex must satisfy the Society as to his character and suitability[15] and no person may be admitted as a solicitor until he has obtained a certificate that the Society is satisfied that he has complied with training regulations (which will involve satisfactory completion of the training contract, legal education and examinations) and is satisfied as to his character and his suitability to be a solicitor of the Supreme Court. The Society maintains the Roll of Solicitors and, in order to practise as a solicitor, a person must have his name on the Roll and hold a current practising certificate.

Section 32 of the Act requires the Council of The Law Society to make rules[16] governing the handling by solicitors of clients' and certain trust moneys and the right to interest thereon. Section 34 requires the Council to make rules governing the annual submission by solicitors of an accountant's report.[17] Section 31 empowers the Council to make rules regulating professional practice, conduct and discipline.[18]

As well as exercising these powers and duties The Law Society also looks after the welfare of solicitors generally and attempts to maintain good relations with other bodies and with the public. To this end the Council examines the activities of unqualified persons doing the work of solicitors and, in appropriate cases, institutes proceedings. It also performs educative and public relations activities.

In addition to its control over its own members and other solicitors the Society protects the interests of the public by the maintenance of a compensation fund[19] out of which it may make a hardship grant to any person who suffers hardship through the failure of a solicitor to account for money due in connection with his practice as a solicitor or with any trust of which he is a trustee. The result is that members of the public are indemnified against loss which might be suffered as a result of any solicitor's default in the handling of their moneys. The Law Society then assumes, through the doctrine of subrogation, the rights and remedies of the person to whom the grant was made to the extent of the grant.

By way of further protection of the public, the Society has power to take over and reorganise the practice of any solicitor who cannot safely be relied upon to continue the handling of his clients' affairs,[20] while the Council may, with the concurrence of

13   One which includes the study of the core subjects; contract, tort, public law, trusts, land law, criminal law, tort, European Community law.
14   Or a longer period for part-time or distance-learning students.
15   Qualifying Regulations 1979–86.
16   The present rules are the Solicitors' Accounts Rules 1991.
17   The present rules are the Accountant's Report Rules 1991.
18   See Solicitors Practice Rules 1990.
19   Solicitors Act 1974, s 36 and Sch 2. The fund is made up of special annual contributions payable by solicitors on application for practising certificates. The Royal Commission found the present compensation arrangements satisfactory (Report, para 23.15).
20   Solicitors Act 1974, s 35 and Sch 1; this important power was introduced by the Solicitors (Amendment) Act 1974. The circumstances in which the Society can intervene are detailed in Part I of Sch 1 (as amended by Courts and Legal Services Act 1990, s 91 and by Administration of Justice Act 1985, Sch 1) but can briefly be summarised as dishonesty, undue delay on the part of the personal representatives of a deceased solicitor, failure to comply with professional rules, bankruptcy, imprisonment, removal from or striking off the roll or suspension from practice, and incapacity or abandonment of practice by a sole practitioner.

the Master of the Rolls, make "indemnity rules" providing for the indemnity of solicitors against professional liability by the establishment of a mutual fund, by commercial insurance effected by the Society, by requiring solicitors themselves to insure or by any combination of these methods.[1]

Although the combined effect of the provisions outlined above is to provide a wide measure of protection against default or neglect, it is not intended to protect against all loss suffered by a client. The Law Society does not owe a duty of care to those who may suffer loss through its performance of regulatory functions: in *Wood v The Law Society*[2] it was held that no compensation could be recovered in respect of conduct by The Law Society found by the court to be inadequate. Negligent conduct by a solicitor is actionable in the normal way, by the aggrieved party against the solicitor. However, the relationship between the supervisory functions of The Law Society and its capacity to intervene in respect of inadequate work was brought closer in 1985 when The Law Society was given a power to reduce fees, to require rectification of an error or the taking of other action.[3] These powers were re-cast and extended by the Courts and Legal Services Act 1990. The Law Society may now, in addition to the steps described above, order the payment of compensation of up to £1,000.[4] In deciding whether to take action under these provisions, the Society must have regard to the existence of any civil remedy open to the client, and whether it is reasonable to expect the client to commence legal action against the solicitor.[5]

2 Liabilities of a solicitor

a Liability to disciplinary proceedings

Solicitors are, of course, subject to the general criminal law. However, conduct on the part of a solicitor which falls short of a criminal offence may still result in sanctions. These are usually enforced by the Solicitors Disciplinary Tribunal although, since solicitors are officers of the Supreme Court, the High Court and Court of Appeal have inherent jurisdiction to strike the name of a solicitor from the roll or suspend him for misconduct.[6] In addition to this inherent jurisdiction the High Court has a limited statutory jurisdiction in disciplinary matters. The High Court must strike off the Roll the name of a solicitor who wilfully and knowingly assists an unqualified person to practise or act as a solicitor;[7] it must strike off the Roll or suspend from practice a person who, without the written permission of The Law Society, knowingly employs a person who has been struck off the Roll involuntarily or suspended from practice.[8] However the Tribunal has, in all these cases, corresponding jurisdiction and, since it also has a wider jurisdiction than the High Court, proceedings are generally instituted before the Tribunal.

---

1   *Ibid*, s 37; this was a further important innovation effected by the Solicitors (Amendment) Act 1974. The current rules are the Solicitors Indemnity Rules 1984 under which The Law Society maintains a "master policy" of indemnity insurance on behalf of all solicitors required to be insured, practising solicitors being required to make a fixed contribution annually by way of premium.
2   [1993] NLJR 1475.
3   Solicitors Act 1974, s 44A, introduced by Administration of Justice Act 1985, s 1.
4   By virtue of Solicitors Act 1974, s 37A (inserted in that Act by Courts and Legal Services Act 1990, s 93(2)) and a new Sch 1A (inserted by 1990 Act, Sch 15).
5   1974 Act, Sch 1A, para 1(3).
6   This jurisdiction is preserved by the Solicitors Act 1974, s 50(2).
7   Solicitors Act 1974, s 39(2).
8   *Ibid*, s 41(4).

The Solicitors Disciplinary Tribunal is constituted by the Master of the Rolls from "solicitor members" who must be practising solicitors of not less than ten years' standing and "lay members" who must be neither solicitors nor barristers.[9] It is, nonetheless, independent of The Law Society. The Tribunal is a judicial tribunal and proceedings before it are absolutely privileged for the purposes of the law of defamation.[10] There is a quorum of three members of whom at least one must be a lay member, although the number of solicitor members present must exceed the number of lay members present; the Tribunal may receive evidence on oath and compel the attendance of witnesses by subpoena. It may also, with the concurrence of the Master of the Rolls, make rules regulating its own procedure.

Its jurisdiction is threefold. First, it hears applications to strike the name of a solicitor off the Roll, or to require him to answer allegations contained in an affidavit, or applications by a former solicitor whose name has been struck off the Roll or suspended to have his name restored to the Roll or suspension lifted.[11] Secondly, it hears complaints by another party against a solicitor based either upon common law disciplinary offences of professional misconduct or upon specific offences under the 1974 Act, such as failure to comply with the Solicitors' Accounts Rules,[12] or making a false statement in a declaration for obtaining a practising certificate.[13]

Finally, the Tribunal hears applications by The Law Society under section 43 of the Act to restrain the employment by solicitors, without the written permission of The Law Society, of clerks who have been convicted of criminal offences of dishonesty rendering their employment in a solicitor's practice undesirable or have been parties to disciplinary offences by solicitors. The major part of the Tribunal's business is concerned with the second type of matter, complaints against solicitors in respect of professional misconduct or offences under the Solicitors Act 1974. In dealing with these applications the Tribunal may make such order as it thinks fit.[14] In particular it may strike the solicitor's name off the Roll, suspend him from practice either for a fixed period or indefinitely, order him to pay a penalty not exceeding £5,000, to be forfeit to Her Majesty, and order him to pay a reasonable contribution towards the costs of the proceedings.[15] It may also exclude the solicitor from legal aid work, where there is good reason to do so because of his conduct in connection with a legally assisted person or in relation to the giving of advice or assistance under the legal aid scheme.[16] The Tribunal also has jurisdiction to impose sanctions for inadequate professional services.[17]

---

9   *Ibid*, s 46; the Tribunal is a successor of the Solicitors Disciplinary Committee which existed until 1974. The provision for "lay members" was to allay public criticism of the system whereby complaints against solicitors were investigated exclusively by solicitors; with the same object, s 45 of the Act permits the Lord Chancellor to appoint "lay observers" to examine written allegations made by members of the public concerning the Society's treatment of complaints made about solicitors or their employees.

10   *Addis v Crocker* [1961] 1 QB 11; [1960] 2 All ER 629.

11   Solicitors Act 1974, s 47(1), as substituted by Courts and Legal Services Act 1990, s 92.

12   Solicitors Act 1974, s 32(3).

13   *Ibid*, s 9(5).

14   *Ibid*, s 47(2).

15   *Ibid*, s 47(2). The Lord Chancellor may vary the sum of £5,000 by statutory instrument, having regard to any change in the value of money (*ibid*, s 47(4), (5), added by the Administration of Justice Act 1982, s 56).

16   *Ibid*, s 47(2A), as amended by the Courts and Legal Services Act 1990, s 92(2).

17   Solicitors Act 1974, s 47A, inserted by Administration of Justice Act 1985, s 3(2).

Any party may appeal from the decision of the Solicitors Disciplinary Tribunal to a divisional court of the Queen's Bench Division[18] and thence, with leave of either that court or the Court of Appeal, to the Court of Appeal.[19] Where the application is to restrain the employment of a clerk under section 43, appeal lies only at the instance of the clerk and the decision of the High Court is final.

b   Liability as an officer of the court

As stated above, the Supreme Court has both an inherent and a limited statutory jurisdiction over solicitors since they are officers of the Supreme Court.[20] This jurisdiction is merged in the wider jurisdiction of the Disciplinary Tribunal. In addition to this jurisdiction, the sanction for which is striking off the Roll, the High Court has further powers to impose liability upon solicitors as court officers. Thus solicitors may be, and sometimes are, ordered to pay personally costs thrown away by their neglect or improperly incurred. Such a jurisdiction is today generally exercised in fact under statutory power contained in s 51 of the Courts and Legal Services Act 1990. This confers the power to make a wasted costs order against any person, including a non party. The principles to be applied in such cases were fully discussed by the Court of Appeal in *Re A Barrister (Wasted Costs Order (No 1 of 1991))*.[1] A three-stage test is to be applied: (a) has the legal representative complained against acted improperly, unreasonably or negligently?; (b) if so, did such conduct cause the applicant to incur unnecessary costs?; (c) is it just for the legal representative to compensate the applicant? This provision is both punitive and compensatory so that a solicitor may be ordered to pay costs even where the defaulting party is his partner or a clerk.[2] A significant body of case law has developed concerning the making of such orders, and is dealt with later.

A solicitor may also be liable, as an officer of the court, for loss occasioned by his negligence or breach of duty.[3] This liability may be summarily enforced by any party who has suffered loss. This may be compared with the general civil liability of a solicitor to his client, discussed below, which is enforceable by civil proceedings.

A further way in which a solicitor may incur liability as an officer of the court is by giving an undertaking to the court or in his capacity as a solicitor. The court often makes an order, or refrains from making an order, on the faith of a personal undertaking by a solicitor appearing; for example, an undertaking to stamp a document or an unconditional undertaking not to issue execution if payment of a judgment debt is expedited. The court will enforce a solicitor's undertaking summarily, not as a

---

18   *Ibid*, s 49(1), save that appeal is to the Master of the Rolls against an order restoring or refusing to restore to the Roll the name of a solicitor who has been struck off or an order revoking or refusing to revoke an order made under s 43. The Law Society is entitled to appeal to the Master of the Rolls against a decision by the Tribunal to restore to the Roll a person previously struck off: *R v Master of the Rolls, ex parte McKinnell* [1993] 1 All ER 193.

19   Supreme Court Act 1981, s 18(1)(e).

20   See *Holden & Co v Crown Prosecution Service* [1990] 2 QB 261; [1990] 1 All ER 368 (inherent jurisdiction to order defence solicitor to pay prosecution costs where serious dereliction of duty); *Langley v North West Water Authority* [1991] 3 All ER 610 (solicitor personally liable for costs resulting from failure to comply with county court Practice Direction).

1   [1993] QB 293; [1992] 3 All ER 429, dealing with the application of the Courts and Legal Services Act 1990, s 51(6). See further p 428, *post*. For further discussion of wasted costs orders see *Ridehalgh v Horsefield* [1994] Ch 205; [1994] 3 All ER 848.

2   *Myers v Elman* [1940] AC 282; [1939] 4 All ER 484 where it was made clear that the jurisdiction ought only to be exercised in cases of "serious dereliction of duty" by a solicitor or his employee; cf *R and T Thew Ltd v Reeves (No 2)* [1982] QB 1283n; [1982] 3 All ER 1086.

3   *Marsh v Joseph* [1897] 1 Ch 213.

contractual obligation but in order to secure the proper conduct of its officers. An undertaking to pay money is an obligation *sui generis* enforceable summarily by the court and is neither a contractual obligation nor a judgment debt.[4]

Finally a solicitor is liable to be committed for contempt of court. A solicitor's liability for contempt of court is basically no different from the liability of laymen. Nevertheless solicitors, because of their close association with the court, may be guilty of contempt in a wider variety of ways. Furthermore there are various statutes and rules which impose special liability to committal upon a solicitor, for example for neglecting to inform his client of a judgment against the latter or for defaulting on an order to pay costs personally for misconduct.[5] Failure to comply with an undertaking is a contempt of court, and professional misconduct, as well as rendering the solicitor liable to perform his undertaking.

c   Civil liability

The solicitor, by his position, may render himself liable to civil proceedings either at the suit of his client or of some third party, in a variety of ways. The duty which the solicitor owes to his own client is an incident of the solicitor-client relationship and is dealt with in the following section. There are, in addition, several ways in which a solicitor may incur civil liability to persons other than his own client. In contract the solicitor's liability to third parties is governed usually by the ordinary law of agency. Thus if the solicitor contracts on behalf of an undisclosed client, the other party may elect to sue either the solicitor of the client.[6] If the solicitor acts without authority on behalf of a client he may, in accordance with general principles, be sued for breach of warranty of authority.[7] An exception to the general law of agency is that the solicitor is personally responsible for certain items of expenditure even though incurred as agent for his client, such as experts' fees and the costs of a shorthand writer. A solicitor's liability in tort is governed by the general law of torts. Thus, for example, a solicitor who fraudulently induces a third party to buy an estate with a defective title commits the tort of deceit.

A solicitor may sometimes owe a duty not only to a client, or prospective client,[8] but also to a third party. An example was seen in *White v Jones*[9] where a solicitor was held liable for loss caused to a potential beneficiary under a will. Instructions for the drafting of a new will benefiting the plaintiff had been given, but not implemented, prior to the death of the testator.

---

4   *Re Hudson* [1966] Ch 209; [1966] 1 All ER 110. However the obligation will only be enforced summarily in clear cases; in cases where there is a triable issue the plaintiff must bring an action in the normal way: *Silver and Drake v Baines* [1971] 1 QB 396; [1971] 1 All ER 473.
5   Debtors Act 1869, s 4(4).
6   *Foster v Cranfield* (1911) 46 L Jo 314. A solicitor has ostensible authority to bind his client to compromise of an action (whether or not he has actual authority so to do). Consequently, if an action is compromised on terms the client is bound by those terms and the other party may enforce them; cf *Waugh v HB Clifford and Sons Ltd* [1982] Ch 374; [1982] 1 All ER 1095.
7   *Yonge v Toynbee* [1910] 1 KB 215.
8   *Ross v Caunters* [1980] Ch 297; c.f. *Robertson v Fleming* (1861) 4 Macq 167. The decision in *Ross v Caunters* survives the House of Lords decision in *Murphy v Brentwood District Council* [1991] 1 AC 398; [1990] 2 All ER 908, where it has held that, in general, no liability existed for pure economic loss: see *White v Jones* [1995] 2 AC 207; [1993] 3 All ER 481.
9   [1993] 3 All ER 481. But cf *Carr-Glynn v Frearsons (a firm)* [1997] 2 All ER 614.

3   Incidents of the solicitor-client relationship

a   Solicitor's duty of care to his client

A solicitor's authority derives from the retainer given to him by his client. The effect of this retainer is to create a contractual relationship between the solicitor and the client. In most respects this relationship is, therefore, subject to the ordinary law of contract and in particular to that part of contract law concerning agency since the relationship created is, for purposes within the scope of the retainer, a principal and agent relationship. Consequently the solicitor has a right to be indemnified by his client for acts done within the scope of his authority. The solicitor's duty subsists throughout the period of his retainer. The general rule is that when retained the solicitor undertakes to complete the transaction for which he is retained. For that reason the solicitor is not entitled to his remuneration until the transaction is completed (although he is entitled to be put in funds for disbursements) and if he wrongfully withdraws from the retainer he will not be entitled to a *quantum meruit* for the work he has done. However, it is now provided[10] that a solicitor engaged to conduct contentious business may require payment of a reasonable amount on account of costs and if the client refuses or fails to make that payment the solicitor may, upon giving reasonable notice to the client, withdraw from the retainer. The solicitor must then have his name withdrawn from the court record since until he does so he remains in the position of the party's solicitor so far as the court and the other parties to the action are concerned.

If the solicitor is negligent the client may have an action against him for damages. The action lies in contract and, almost certainly, in tort as well.[11] A solicitor owes a duty to instruct competent counsel, where instructed.[12] However, if the solicitor himself acts he is not liable in negligence for work which, if carried out by counsel, would not have attracted liability.[13]

b   Fiduciary obligations

The solicitor-client relationship is regarded in equity as a fiduciary one. Several consequences flow from this. In general the solicitor must act in good faith in all dealings with his client. This involves making a full and honest disclosure of facts within the solicitor's knowledge in any financial transaction with his client. This principle derives from the equitable doctrine of fraud and has differing consequences which depend upon the nature of the transaction.

The principle is at its strongest in the case of gifts to the solicitor by his client. There is a presumption of undue influence in the case of such a gift, the effect of which is to make the gift voidable at the instance of the client. The solicitor can retain the gift only by showing that it was made after the fiduciary relationship had ceased, or that it was ratified by the client after the relationship had ceased or that the client had independent legal advice.[14]

This presumption of undue influence, which applies to gifts *inter vivos*, does not apply to gifts by will although any person may allege and prove actual undue influence by the solicitor. Nevertheless, where a solicitor prepares a will under which he receives a large benefit the court requires affirmative proof that the testator knew and fully

10   By Solicitors Act 1974, s 65(2).
11   *Groom v Crocker* [1939] 1 KB 194; *Midland Bank Trust Co Ltd v Hett, Stubbs and Kemp* [1979] Ch 384; [1978] 3 All ER 571; *White v Jones, supra*, n 9.
12   *Re A (A Minor)* [1988] Fam Law 339.
13   See p 265, *post*.
14   *Gibson v Jeyes* (1801) 6 Ves 266; *Lancashire Loans Ltd v Black* [1934] 1 KB 380.

approved of the contents of the will.[15] Where a client intends to give a large benefit to a solicitor in his will the latter should insist on the will being prepared by another solicitor.[16] A purchase by a solicitor from his client, or a sale to his client, is not necessarily bad but the solicitor must show that the bargain is as good as the client could have obtained with due diligence elsewhere in order to rebut the presumption of undue influence. This means that the price must be fair and that the solicitor must make a full disclosure. In practice the solicitor should see that the client has independent advice. Similar conditions apply to loans between solicitor and client.[17]

c   Obligations to preserve confidence

One particular aspect of the fiduciary relationship between solicitor and client is the confidential nature of communications between them. This gives rise to two types of privilege; privilege in the tort of defamation and privilege from disclosure in evidence. This latter privilege, legal professional privilege, is regarded as a fundamental aspect of the relationship between solicitor and client.[18] Communications between solicitor and client are regarded as privileged provided they were made in confidence and for the purposes of obtaining or giving legal advice. The privilege is that of the client, so only the client can waive it, and it can only be lost if the communication was for a criminal or fraudulent purpose, for example seeking advice on the commission of a crime or fraud.[19] Privilege also attaches to communications made in pursuance of litigation which is pending or anticipated.

4   Remuneration

Solicitors are entitled to remuneration for their services. However the way in which this remuneration is assessed and recovered is not primarily governed by the ordinary law of contract even though the right to remuneration arises out of a contractual relationship. It is governed by various statutes and rules, passed generally for the benefit of clients, and is subject to the supervision of the courts. Even where solicitor and client make an agreement as to costs, the court may still examine its reasonableness. It should also be remembered that the parties have the right, in some circumstances, to enter into a conditional fee agreement.[20]

a   Conditional fee agreements

Conditional fee agreements are sometimes referred to as a "no win, no fee" arrangement. Under such an agreement, a solicitor receives no fee if he loses the case,

---

15   *Wintle v Nye* [1959] 1 All ER 552; [1959] 1 WLR 284.

16   Failure to comply with these fiduciary obligations will invariably be regarded as serious professional misconduct and the offending solicitor is liable to be struck off the Roll; see, for example, *Re A Solicitor* [1975] QB 475; [1974] 3 All ER 853.

17   See, generally, *Cordery on Solicitors* (7th Edn), pp 9-29; cf *Spector v Ageda* [1973] Ch 30; [1971] 3 All ER 417.

18   See *R v Derby Magistrates' Court, ex parte B* [1995] 4 All ER 526.

19   *R v Cox and Railton* (1884) 14 QBD 153. See *Butler v Board of Trade* [1971] Ch 680, [1970] 3 All ER 593 and *Crescent Farm (Sidcup) Sports Ltd v Sterling Offices Ltd* [1972] Ch 553; [1971] 2 All ER 1192, where the authorities are reviewed. In *Nationwide Building Society v Various Solicitors* [1998] 06 LS Gaz R 24; [1998] 148 NLJR 241 it was held that a solicitor who acted for both a purchaser and building society in a conveyancing transaction might be overridden on a claim for discovery of documents where bad faith or impropriety had been pleaded.

20   See *infra*, and also p 289, *post*.

but receives a "success" fee if he wins. The success fee is an amount which increases the fee by a given percentage. The client pays for legal insurance to cover the risk of costs of the opposing party should he lose. Such agreements should be carefully distinguished from contingency fee arrangements, which exist in the United States, whereby the successful lawyer receives a percentage of damages awarded.

As noted earlier, contingency fees have not in the past been permitted in England and Wales.[1] Historically they amounted to maintenance (the financial support of litigation by a person not a party) and champerty (the taking of a financial interest in the outcome of litigation to which one is not a party), both of which were illegal until the passage of the Criminal Justice Act 1967. The position with what are known as conditional fees is more complex. Agreements for conditional, or contingent, fees, have been regarded as contrary to public policy, deriving from policy considerations relating to champerty and maintenance.[2] That position was reconsidered by the Court of Appeal in *Thai Trading Co (a Firm) v Taylor*[3]. In that case the court held that there was nothing unlawful in a solicitor acting for a party to litigation to agree to forgo all or part of his fee if he lost, provided that he did not seek to recover more than his profit costs and disbursements if he won. There was nothing in the Solicitors Act 1974 which prohibited the charging of contingent fees, unlike the Solicitors Practice Rules of 1987 which did contain such a prohibition. The fact that a professional rule prohibited a particular practice did not, of itself, make the practice contrary to law.[4] Furthermore, those rules were based on an assumption of public policy derived from judicial decisions, the correctness was in question in the case before the court. In the light of modern conditions, the matter should be considered afresh. There was nothing improper in a solicitor acting for a client who, to his knowledge, could not afford to pay his costs if he lost.[5] If the alleged temptation to win at all costs, which was said to be the main justification for the alleged rule of public policy, was present at all, it would be present whether or not the solicitor waived his fees if he lost. It was therefore lawful for a solicitor to agree a conditional arrangement, provided he contracted for no more than his proper fee if he won. Although legislation was needed to authorise the increase in the lawyers' reward over and above his ordinary profit if he won, there was no need for legislation to legitimise the long-standing practice of solicitors to act for meritorious clients without means. It was in the public interest that they should continue to do so.

That decision was clearly influenced by the fact that the Courts and Legal Services Act 1990 had legitimised the use of conditional fees, in classes of case to be designated by order. That legislation, which was needed to legitimise conditional fees that permitted an increase in fee to compensate for the risk of non-payment if the case were lost, followed a long period of debate during which the concept of conditional fee arrangements was strongly opposed by professional organisations. The Courts and Legal Services Act 1990 in some circumstances legitimises such conditional fee arrangements. These arrangements are intended to bridge the gap between private funds and legal aid, although they will in due course largely replace legal aid. Where such arrangements apply, an agreement may be entered into. It must state:[6]

1   See *Halsbury's Laws* (4th Edn).
2   *British Waterways Boards v Norman* (1993) 26 HLR 232; *Aratra Potato Co Ltd v Taylor Jaynson Garrett (a Firm)* [1995] 4 All ER 695. Compare the dissenting judgment of Lord Denning MR in *Wallersteiner v Moir (No 2)* [1975] QB 373, 508n[1975] 1 All ER 849.
3   (1998) Times, 6 March.
4   *Picton Jones & Co v Arcadia Developments Ltd* (1989) 1 EGLR 43.
5   *Singh v Observer Ltd* [1989] 3 All ER 777n; *A Ltd v B Ltd* [1996] 1 WLR 665.
6   Courts and Legal Services Act, s 58(1), s 119 and Conditional Fee Agreements Regulations 1995, SI 1995/1675, reg 3.

(a) the proceedings to which it relates, or the relevant part of them;
(b) the circumstances in which the legal representatives' fees are payable;
(c) what payment (if any) is due on the partial failure to occur of the circumstances in which the fee is payable, or in the event of termination of the agreement.

Such an agreement must be in writing, signed by both parties. Specimen agreements are available from the Law Society. Such agreements may currently be made in personal injury, insolvency cases and cases before the European Court of Justice and Court of Human Rights. The maximum success fee permitted is 100% of the fee, despite the fact that, during the passage of the Order introducing conditional fees, many saw the appropriate "success fee" as being no more than 25%. The current average is some 43%. As will later be noted, conditional fee arrangements are to be greatly expanded and will form a key part in the dismantling of the legal aid system, with the Middleton Report[7] recommending that conditional fee arrangements should become available for all civil proceedings. Indeed, that Report even suggests that the case for contingency fees be reconsidered. It is difficult to see the rationale for a rule that entitles the lawyer to take a success fee, quantified by reference to costs, but not a fee quantified on the basis of the award achieved. The danger of lawyers being enticed into acting improperly by the potential reward is surely small.

The move to conditional fees places the risks of litigation with the lawyer. Because of the fiduciary relationship that exists between solicitor and client, it is important that the financial interests of the solicitor do not achieve precedence over those of the client. All the options should be explained to the client, particularly as to how a conditional fee arrangement differs from the more usual basis of charging. The contents of the agreement should be clearly explained, and care taken to ensure that such agreements are fair and reasonable in all the circumstances. The risk to the client must be explained to, and understood by, the client, particularly if the amount of costs may exceed recoverable amounts. In particular, a solicitor should always consider whether settlement is in the best interests of his client. Further, there is no need for any special protection for the lawyer who enters into such a fee arrangement. In *Hodgson v Imperial Tobacco Ltd*[8] it was held that the risk of a lawyer being ordered to pay the costs of an action personally were no different from the risk that applied to lawyers acting under any other fee arrangement. A lawyer acting under a conditional fee arrangement therefore did not need any special protection, such as an order debarring a defendant from seeking costs personally from them.

The statutory provisions have provided the catalyst for further development of the common law. In *Bevan Ashford v Geoff Yeandle (Contractors) Ltd (In Liquidation)*[9], the court had to consider a conditional fee arrangement between a litigant and his solicitor in respect of a matter to be determined by arbitration. Such proceedings were not within the scope of the statutory arrangements for conditional fees, but Sir Richard Scott V-C held that an agreement which substantially complied with the requirements of the statute was not contrary to public policy and champertous, but was a valid and enforceable agreement. The agreement would have been valid if the proceedings had been before a court, not in arbitration. There being no public policy argument to stand in that way, the court was prepared to reach a conclusion that, although perfectly sensible, departed from the clear words of the statute.

7   See p 288, *post*.
8   [1998] 2 All ER 673, [1998] 148 NLJR 241.
9   [1998] 3 All ER 238.

5   Assessment of remuneration

The way in which a solicitor's remuneration is assessed depends upon whether the business done on behalf of the client is contentious or non-contentious. "Contentious business" is defined by the Act[10] as:

> "Business done, whether as solicitor or advocate, in or for the purpose of proceedings begun before a court or before an arbitrator appointed under the Arbitration Act 1950, not being business which falls within the definition of non-contentious or common form probate business in the Supreme Court Act 1981, s 128."

The test is thus whether or not proceedings are begun. If they are, all business relating to these proceedings is contentious. If proceedings are not begun, as for example where a dispute is settled before a writ is issued, the proceedings are treated as non-contentious. Non-contentious business is any business which is not contentious within the above statutory definition and comprises a very wide range of matters including conveyancing, drafting wills and settlements, advice and many other matters. The basic difference between contentious and non-contentious business in relation to the assessment of remuneration is that in the former the amount is usually fixed by the court by taxation while in the latter it is not, being fixed in accordance with statutory orders.

a   Assessment of remuneration in contentious business

The Solicitors Act 1974, section 59 expressly authorises a solicitor to enter into a written agreement with his client regulating remuneration in contentious business.[11] In the absence of such an agreement the solicitor may submit either a bill containing detailed items or one charging a gross sum.[12]

The client has a right to have this bill taxed, in which case the appropriate basis of taxation is (unless the bill is to be paid out of the Legal Aid Fund) the "indemnity" basis.[13] On this basis:

> "All costs shall be allowed except in so far as they are of an unreasonable amount or have been unreasonably incurred."[14]

All costs incurred with the express or implied approval of the client are conclusively presumed to have been reasonably incurred and, where the amount has been so approved, are presumed to have been reasonable in amount.[15] However the solicitor must expressly inform his client of any costs which are of an unusual nature and might not be allowed on a "party and party" taxation; otherwise such costs are deemed to be unreasonably incurred.[16] In certain cases costs are charged on a fixed scale[17] while in

10   Solicitors Act 1974, s 87(1) (as amended).
11   See p 259, *post*.
12   Section 64.
13   See p 429, *post*.
14   RSC, Ord 62, r 12(2).
15   Ord 62, r 15(2).
16   *Ibid*.
17   Ord 62, Appendix 3.

High Court cases, the actual amounts are within the discretion of the taxing officer.[18] These amounts are calculated in the light of various criteria, which are discussed later.[19]

An exception to the above basis of taxation applies where the client is legally aided. In such a case in the High Court the solicitor receives from the Legal Aid Board only his disbursements and his costs taxed on a "standard" basis. On this basis, which is less liberal than the "indemnity" basis of taxation, there is allowed "a reasonable amount in respect of all costs reasonably incurred".[20] In fact in respect of legal aid work, family work and Crown Court work a system of standard fees has been introduced, with basic standard fees for different types of case, and task. Such strategies have been described as "cost neutral", but fears have been expressed that such arrangements will significantly diminish the income for practitioners in these areas of work.

b   Assessment of remuneration in non-contentious business

Whereas remuneration in contentious business is usually fixed by the court, remuneration in non-contentious business is controlled differently. Save in certain exceptional cases under specific enactments,[1] the mode and amount of remuneration are regulated by orders made under section 56 of the 1974 Act.[2]

As to the mode of remuneration, orders made under section 56 may provide for remuneration: (a) according to a scale of rates of commission or a scale of percentages; or (b) by a gross sum; or (c) by a fixed sum for each document prepared or perused; or (d) in any other mode; or (e) partly in one mode and partly in another.

The amount of remuneration may be regulated by order with reference to the following, among other, considerations:

(a)   the position of the party for whom the solicitor is concerned, that is, whether he is vendor or purchaser, lessor or lessee, mortgagor or mortgagee or the like;
(b)   the place where, and the circumstances in which, the business was transacted;
(c)   the amount involved;
(d)   the skill, labour and responsibility involved on the part of the solicitor;
(e)   the number or importance of the documents prepared or perused.

The basis of remuneration under this order is a lump sum which is fair and reasonable having regard to all the circumstances of the case and in particular the complexity of the matter, the skill, specialised knowledge and responsibility involved, the number of documents, the time involved, the value of any property or amount of any sum involved, whether any land was registered, and the importance of the matter to the client.

The client has no right to have a lump sum bill itemised. He has, nevertheless, two safeguards against an excessive charge. First, he has a right to have the bill taxed and secondly, without prejudice to this right, he has a right to require the solicitor to obtain a certificate from The Law Society that the sum charged is fair and reasonable (a "remuneration certificate"), or, if it is not, what is a fair and reasonable sum. It is for the solicitor to show that the charge is fair and reasonable. A solicitor can bring no

---

18   Ord 62, Appendix 2.
19   See p 428.
20   Ord 62, r 12(1).
1   Preserved by s 75 of the 1974 Act.
2   These orders are made by a committee consisting of the Lord Chancellor, the Lord Chief Justice, the Master of the Rolls, the President of The Law Society, a nominated solicitor who is president of a local law society and (for the purpose only of business under the Land Registration Act 1925) the Chief Land Registrar (s 56(1)).

proceedings on a lump sum bill until he has drawn his client's attention to the latter's rights which are set out above. The right to require the solicitor to obtain a certificate may be exercised within one month of his being informed by the solicitor of his rights as above, provided the bill has been neither taxed nor paid. If the taxing master allows less than one half the amount charged he must bring the facts of the case to the attention of The Law Society.[3] The remuneration certificate system, amended in 1994, only applies if the bill is for an amount under £50,000, and only if the client has paid 50% of the solicitors' costs plus disbursements.

c   Special agreements as to remuneration

Solicitor and client may, in both contentious and non-contentious business, agree the amount of the solicitor's remuneration. Such agreements are, however, not freely enforceable in the same way as commercial contracts since their enforceability is regulated by statute.

In contentious business solicitor and client may make an agreement in writing, providing for remuneration by a gross sum, or by a salary, or otherwise and whether at a higher or lower rate than that at which the solicitor would otherwise have been entitled to be remunerated.[4] There is no prescribed form for the agreement and it may, for example, be contained in letters passing between solicitor and client provided that the terms of the agreement can be ascertained with certainty. However there are certain other restrictions attaching to such an agreement. Any provision exempting the solicitor from liability for negligence or any other responsibility is void. The agreement itself is void if it involves any purchase by a solicitor of any part of the interest of his client in the proceedings.[5] The agreement cannot prejudice the rights of third parties although it may indirectly benefit them since the client cannot recover more costs from a third party than he has agreed to pay his solicitor.[6]

A provision relating to remuneration in contentious business cannot be enforced by action,[7] even though the agreement as a whole can be so enforced. It may, however, be enforced summarily by the High Court or a county court on application.[8] The court may, if it considers the agreement unfair or unreasonable, declare it void and order the costs covered thereby to be taxed as if the agreement had never been made.[9]

An agreement for remuneration in non-contentious business must likewise be in writing.[10] It may specify either a gross sum or an hourly rate.[11] Such an agreement is subject to the ordinary law of contract and may be sued on in the ordinary way. Nevertheless the court has an inherent jurisdiction to order taxation in order to determine whether the gross sum agreed (but not an hourly rate) is fair and reasonable, and may cancel the agreement or reduce the amount payable if the taxing officer certifies that it is unfair or unreasonable.[12] An hourly rate is not reducible by the taxing master.

3   Solicitors' Remuneration Order 1972, arts 3, 4.
4   Act of 1974, s 59(1).
5   Solicitors Act 1974, s 59(2). A solicitor is, however, justified in acting for an impoverished client on terms that he shall receive no costs or reduced costs unless the action succeeds.
6   *Ibid*, s 60(3).
7   *Ibid*, s 61(1).
8   The appropriate court is the one in which the business to which the agreement relates was done if this is the High Court or a county court, or, if not, the High Court in respect of agreements to pay more than £50 or the county court for sums of less than £50 (1974 Act, s 61(6)). Application to the High Court is usually by originating summons; application to a county court is by originating application.
9   Solicitors Act 1974, s 61(2), (4).
10   *Ibid*, s 57.
11   *Ibid*, s 57(5), as amended by the Courts and Legal Services Act 1990, s 98.
12   *Ibid*.

d   Recovery of costs

By section 69 of the Solicitors Act 1974 no action shall be brought to recover any costs due to a solicitor until one month after delivery of a bill signed by the solicitor, or by a partner in the firm if the costs are due to a firm, or accompanied by a letter so signed and referring to the bill. However, the High Court may by order dispense with this requirement if there is probable cause for believing that the party chargeable is about to quit England and Wales, to become bankrupt or compound with his creditors or do any other act which would tend to prevent or delay the solicitor obtaining payment.

Within one month of the delivery of a bill the client has a right to have it taxed and no action may be commenced on the bill until the taxation is completed.[13] After one month has elapsed the court may, upon such terms as it thinks fit, order taxation on the application of solicitor or client and may stay proceedings on the bill, or order that no action shall be taken, until taxation is completed.[14] However, except in special circumstances, the client will not obtain an order for taxation more than twelve months after the delivery of the bill or after payment, and in no event will he obtain an order more than twelve months after payment. Unless the client does not appear on the solicitor's application to have the bill taxed or the order for taxation otherwise provides the costs of the taxation depend upon its outcome. If one-fifth of the amount of the bill is taxed off the solicitor pays the costs; otherwise the client pays the costs.[15]

Subject to the above restrictions the solicitor may proceed to recover his costs as a contractual debt. He may do so by action or by proving in the client's bankruptcy or in the liquidation of a client company. As an alternative to action the solicitor may exercise his common law lien.[16] He has a general lien over all of the client's personal property in the solicitor's possession except his will. This entitles the solicitor to retain the property until payment of the full amount due. The lien is often exercised in relation to case papers. However a solicitor's lien is subordinate to the public interest that justice be achieved in the suit. Consequently a lien over a client's papers is qualified in that the solicitor is bound to hand over the client's papers to his new solicitor on the latter's undertaking to preserve the lien.[17] In addition the solicitor has a particular lien over property, other than real property,[18] recovered or preserved or the proceeds of any judgment obtained in an action, for his costs in relation to that action.

It will be appreciated that in a long and expensive piece of litigation the solicitor may be in the position of having to wait a very long time in order to recover his remuneration. To remedy this section 65 of the Act enables the solicitor, in contentious business, to request payment of a reasonable sum of money on account of costs; if the client refuses or fails within a reasonable time to make that payment the solicitor may, upon giving reasonable notice, withdraw from the retainer. The solicitor will then have to apply to the court for removal of his name from the record.

13   *Ibid*, s 70(1).
14   *Ibid*, s 70(2).
15   *Ibid*, s 70.
16   See, generally, *Halvanon Insurance Co Ltd v Central Reinsurance Corporation* [1988] 3 All ER 857; [1988] 1 WLR 1122.
17   *Gamlen Chemical Co (UK) Ltd v Rochem Ltd* [1980] 1 All ER 1049; [1980] 1 WLR 614. Cf *A v B* [1984] 1 All ER 265.
18   But note s 73 of the 1974 Act which enables the court to make a charging order in favour of the solicitor over any property including real property.

E   BARRISTERS

1   General organisation of the Bar

a   The Inns of Court

Persons may only practise as counsel in England if they have been "called to the Bar" of one of the four Inns of Court: Lincoln's Inn, the Inner Temple, the Middle Temple and Gray's Inn. These Inns are as old as professional advocacy itself in England and appear to have originated as living quarters for those legal practitioners who were not serjeants.[19] The Inns' jurisdiction is in no way statutory. It is derived from the judges (and thus indirectly from the Crown) and is subject to control by the judges.[20] One member of the Court of Appeal has explained the Inns' functions as follows:[1]

> "I would regard the Inns of Court in their disciplinary power in relation to the practising member of the Bar as equivalently established over the centuries by its practice and acceptance as if the power had been derived from statute and as unassailable. If the Inns of Court had not controlled the professional conduct of the Bar the judges themselves would have had to do so. The judges themselves, deriving their authority from the Crown, were minded in the distant past to delegate, and the undisputed view in Lord Mansfield's time was that the judges had delegated their disciplinary power over the Bar in the Inns of Court."

In the Inns of Court there are three classes of members: benchers, who are the governors of the Inn, barristers, who are called by the benchers, and students who are admitted to membership by the benchers. The benchers of an Inn, who are judges or senior members of the Bar, have absolute control over the admission of students and the call of barristers. There is an appeal from their decisions to the Lord Chancellor and the judges of the High Court sitting as "visitors", a domestic tribunal. They cannot however, be sued in respect of any act done in their official capacity nor can they be compelled by mandamus to admit a person as a student or call a student to the Bar.[2] The principal conditions which a student must satisfy before applying for call to the Bar are payment of the requisite fees, passing the Bar Final Examination and keeping eight terms.[3] No person under the age of 21 can be called to the Bar. Before a barrister can practise he must serve a pupillage under a senior member of the Bar (not a Queen's Counsel) for not less than twelve months.[4]

b   The Bar Council

In 1966 the Senate of the Inns of Court was established and, in its original or modified form,[5] existed until 1987 when the Bar Council was reconstituted. The Bar Council is

19   Serjeants had their own Inns ("Serjeants' Inns"). There were also several Chancery Inns (eg New Inn, Clifford's Inn). All these have ceased to exist.
20   *R v Gray's Inn* (1780) 1 Doug K353, per Lord Mansfield.
1   Sellers LJ in *Lincoln v Daniels* [1962] 1 QB 237, at 250; [1961] 3 All ER 740, at 745; cf *Re S (a Barrister)* [1970] 1 QB 160; [1969] 1 All ER 949. See *R v Visitor of the Inns of Court, ex parte Calder* [1994] QB 1; [1993] 2 All ER 876.
2   *R v Lincoln's Inn Benchers* (1825) 4 B & C 855.
3   The latter obligation is not imposed upon solicitors wishing to become barristers. There are four dining terms a year in the Inns of Court: Michaelmas, Hilary, Easter and Trinity. A term is kept by dining in Hall on a number of occasions (usually three) during the term.
4   For the appointment of Queen's Counsel see p 262, *post*.
5   The original body constituted in 1966 was replaced in 1974 by the Senate of the Inns of Courts and the Bar.

the governing body of the Bar. It comprises certain *ex officio* members such as the Attorney-General, Solicitor-General, the Director of Public Prosecutions and various representative barristers, together with members nominated by the Benchers of the Inns of Court and by circuits. It also comprises elected members.

Its functions include the laying down and implementation of general policy affecting the Bar, the maintenance of standards, honour and independence of the Bar and the external relations of the Bar with other organisations.

c   The Council for Legal Education

The Council for Legal Education makes recommendations to the Bar Council on matters relating to legal education, pupillage and continuing legal education. It prescribes the content of the academic stage of legal education sufficient for entry to the Bar,[6] and provides a practical skills-based vocational training course for Bar Finals, and which all those wishing to practise at the Bar must attend.

2   Practice at the Bar

Barristers in independent practice work in sets of chambers. These are associations of barristers, who share common facilities, and administrative support. The work of individual barristers is organised and arranged by the barrister's clerk, who will also play a key role in the re-allocation of work within chambers where the barrister briefed is unable to appear, because of other commitments. It is permissible for a barrister to be employed, but he cannot then, generally speaking, offer legal services to anyone other than that employer, and cannot appear in courts where barristers have had exclusive rights of audience.[7]

Barristers' chambers are not partnerships. No statutory provision exists prohibiting such partnerships: indeed, there are no statutory restrictions upon the establishment of multi-disciplinary and multi-national practices.[8] The Bar Council may, however, continue to restrict these.

Barristers are divided into junior counsel and Queen's Counsel, the latter called "silks" because they wear a silk gown as opposed to that of stuff worn by juniors. Queen's Counsel are appointed annually by the Crown on the advice of the Lord Chancellor, on the basis of ability, experience and seniority, although some disquiet has been expressed in recent years concerning the alleged secrecy of the appointments process[9] and about whether a two-tier system can in modern times possibly be justified. The significance of appointment as a silk is two-fold. First, Queen's Counsel do not usually take on the pleading and drafting work in contentious proceedings. Secondly, they are often instructed in the most difficult, complex or important of cases, thus reflecting their expertise and standing within the profession.

Until 1977 Queen's Counsel were subject to particular rules whereby they were not permitted to appear without a junior (the "two counsel" rule), nor to do drafting work nor give written opinions on evidence. As a consequence of a recommendation of the Monopolies and Mergers Commission in 1976, the Bar Council abolished the two counsel rule, although Queen's Counsel should decline to appear without a junior if he would be unable properly to conduct that case, or other cases, or to fulfil his

6   See Consolidated Regulations of the Four Inns of Court, reg 15–16.
7   See p 244, *ante*.
8   Courts and Legal Services Act 1990, s 65.
9   See de Wilde in (1993) Counsel.

professional commitments unless a junior were also instructed. In practice, it is still comparatively rare to find Queen's Counsel appearing without a junior. Furthermore, Queen's Counsel may now engage in non-contentious drafting work and may, if he has agreed to appear without a junior in a case, settle pleadings or draft other documents in that case.

The barrister's function is primarily advocacy although he deals also with such matters as drafting conveyances, pleadings and other legal documents and advising on the law. He has a right of audience in virtually all judicial proceedings and in the House of Lords, the Judicial Committee of the Privy Council, the Court of Appeal and the High Court of Justice this right is exclusive, except in interlocutory proceedings and bankruptcy proceedings where solicitors have a concurrent right. In criminal proceedings in the Crown Court, prosecutions must be conducted by barristers[10] and prosecutors cannot appear in person. All petitions of appeal to the House of Lords from the Court of Appeal must be signed by two counsel.

In addition to these rights and privileges barristers have various duties both to the court and to their clients. Their duties to the court are all based on professional etiquette. Barristers are not, in the way that solicitors are, officers of the court so that they are not strictly subject to control by the courts. It is doubtful whether the courts could exercise jurisdiction to suspend a barrister from practising, since this power is left by the judges to the Inns of Court. Nevertheless a barrister may clearly be fined or imprisoned for contempt of court to the same extent as a solicitor or, indeed, any other person. Counsel cannot, in general, be heard in court unless they are "robed", a term which includes the wearing of wig, gown and bands, a practice which continues despite some debate as to its utility.[11] A barrister may, however, appear unrobed in magistrates' courts and also when appearing as litigant in person.[12] Although counsel are not officers of the court they are officers of justice. This is particularly true in criminal proceedings so that prosecuting counsel's function is to assist the court, not to press for a conviction. Indeed, the duty of prosecuting counsel to ensure proper disclosure of unused material[13] shows that counsel owes a wider obligation to the proper administration of justice. Even in civil cases barristers are under a duty to draw to the attention of the court authorities which do not support their client's case. Furthermore, counsel must not mislead the court by actively concealing facts[14] from the court which are material to the case, nor must he set up any affirmative case or defence inconsistent with any admission or confession made to him by his client, nor should he take a point of law which he knows to be bad.

3   Relationship between counsel and client

Historically, a barrister could not enter into a contractual relationship for the provision of his services, except, of course, in respect of employed barristers. This rule was abolished in 1990,[15] although the Bar Council can restrict or prohibit the entry into such contracts.

---

10   See also Supreme Court Act 1981, s 83, which permit the Lord Chancellor to confer unlimited rights of audience upon solicitors in proceedings in the Crown Court, and further p 244, *ante*.
11   In 1993, a decision was taken to retain the traditional court dress of wig and gown. It remains to be seen whether the practice will survive.
12   *Practice Note* [1961] 1 All ER 319.
13   See p 494, *post*.
14   *Meek v Fleming* [1961] 2 QB 366; [1961] 3 All ER 148.
15   Courts and Legal Services Act 1990. See also the statement of the General Council of the Bar, reported at LS Gazette, 28 September 1988, and summarised below.

Members of the Bar may now enter into written agreements with solicitors as to the time barrister's fees will be paid. In the absence of such an agreement, fees should be paid by solicitors within three months of the delivery of a fee note. Continued failure by a solicitor to pay barrister's fees may entitle the Chairman of the Bar Council to issue a direction prohibiting the acceptance by barristers of instructions from the solicitor concerned, unless accompanied by an agreed brief fee. Clearly, if a contractual arrangement has been entered into, it can be enforced by normal legal action.

The corollary of the historic inability to sue for their fees is their immunity from being sued in contract for professional negligence. Barristers were historically immune from actions in negligence because such actions could only be based on contract and were thus not possible against a barrister, with whom the client could not enter into a contractual relationship.[16] In the leading case of *Rondel v Worsley*[17] the House of Lords, faced with the question whether a barrister might now be held liable in negligence, decided not and dismissed the plaintiff's appeal from an order that his statement of claim be struck out as disclosing no cause of action. Lord Denning MR, in the Court of Appeal, reviewed the authorities at length, and based counsel's immunity upon various grounds of public policy and upon long usage from which the public interest did not require a departure. The grounds of public policy to which Lord Denning adverted may be summarised as follows:[18]

(1) *Independence* "that he may do his duty fearlessly and independently as he ought and to prevent him being harassed by vexatious actions. If a barrister is to be able to do his duty fearlessly and independently he must not be subject to the threat of an action for negligence."

(2) *Professional obligation to act* "A barrister cannot pick or choose his clients. He is bound to accept a brief for any man who comes before the courts. No matter how great a rascal the man may be. No matter how given to complaining. No matter how undeserving or unpopular his cause. The barrister must defend him to the end."

(3) *Duty to the court* "He has a duty to the court which is paramount. It is a mistake to suppose that he is the mouthpiece of his client to say what he wants; or his tool to do what he directs. He is none of these things. He owes allegiance to a higher cause. It is the cause of truth and justice. He must disregard the most specific instructions of his client, if they conflict with his duty to the court."

(4) *Protraction of litigation* "If a barrister could be sued for negligence, it would mean a retrial of the original case. If this action were to be permitted, it would open the door to every disgruntled client. If this action is to go for trial, it will lead to dozens of like cases."

Although the appellant's claim was "clearly as devoid of merit as it was of any prospect of success"[19] the House of Lords gave leave to appeal in view of the importance of the question of law involved. In the event the House of Lords affirmed the decision of the Court of Appeal. While their lordships differed slightly as to the emphasis to be placed upon individual heads of public policy they concurred, in the result, in each of the above four heads adverted to by Lord Denning in the Court of Appeal.

16   See *supra*.
17   [1969] 1 AC 191; [1967] 3 All ER 993.
18   [1967] 1 QB at 501–504; [1966] 3 All ER, at 665–666.
19   [1967] 1 QB at 516; [1966] 3 All ER, at 674, per Salmon LJ; [1969] 1 AC, at 226; [1967] 3 All ER, at 998, per Lord Reid.

The House of Lords also considered, as the Court of Appeal had done, the question of whether barristers' immunity extended to work done in chambers in advising, settling documents and other matters which might never come before a court. Although the majority view of the Court of Appeal had been that the immunity did so extend the House of Lords, with the exception of Lord Pearce who favoured the wider immunity, expressed the opinion that, while the immunity from action extended to pleadings and other work done while litigation was pending, it did not extend to advisory work or work done on documents outside the context of litigation. These opinions were, of course, no more than obiter dicta although of great weight.

However, in *Saif Ali v Sydney Mitchell & Co*[20] the House of Lords were once again called upon to consider the scope of barristers' immunity, but this time in relation to work done in chambers in the course of litigation. The same procedure was adopted to bring the issue before the court as had been used in *Rondel v Worsley*, namely an application to strike out a pleading alleging negligence against a barrister on the ground that it disclosed no reasonable cause of action. The case went, again, to the House of Lords where the majority (Lord Wilberforce, Lord Diplock and Lord Salmon), in allowing the solicitors' appeal, limited the immunity to those matters of pre-trial work which were so intimately connected with the conduct of the cause in court that they could fairly be said to be preliminary decisions affecting the way that the cause was conducted when it came to a hearing. Since the barrister's advice and pleadings in the instant case had in fact prevented the plaintiff's cause from coming to court at all, it could not be said to be "intimately connected" with the conduct of the plaintiff's cause in court and was therefore not within the sphere of a barrister's immunity from actions for negligence.

The test approved was taken from a New Zealand Court of Appeal case[1] and is narrower than that which had been favoured obiter in *Rondel v Worsley*. The test may not, in practice, be easy to apply in subsequent cases. Thus if, for example, the negligent conduct was failure to plead a cause of action (rather than failure to join a party) the immunity would appear to apply, although it is difficult to see why the barrister should be liable in the one case and not in the other.

Other incidents of the barrister's relationship with his client which may be noted briefly are the former's obligation to preserve the latter's confidences and counsel's authority to conduct proceedings on behalf of the client. The scope of this authority is determinable in accordance with ordinary principles of the law of agency and includes the authority to compromise proceedings on behalf of the client and the authority to make admissions on the latter's behalf in civil proceedings, though not to plead guilty in a criminal prosecution.

4   Professional conduct

The duties of solicitors towards their clients is governed both by statute and by their code of professional conduct. In the case of barristers the obligations are governed solely by self-imposed standards.[2] The rules of conduct may change from time to time and may be altered by the Bar Council.[3] In no case are the rules enforceable in any way other than by complaint to the Bar Council followed by disciplinary proceedings before a Disciplinary Tribunal which may result in the barrister being fined, disbarred

---

20   [1980] AC 198; [1978] 3 All ER 1033.
1   *Rees v Sinclair* [1974] 1 NZLR 180.
2   See *Code of Conduct of the Bar of England and Wales* (1990).
3   See p 261, *ante*.

or suspended from practising by his Inn of Court, appeal lying to the Visitors. It should, however, be remembered that the power to make a wasted costs order applies to members of the Bar just as much as to solicitors.

Certain important rules of conduct should be carefully noted. Perhaps the most important rule is that, subject to a few exceptional cases, counsel may accept instructions only from solicitors or other approved professional persons,[4] and not from a client direct.[5] Touting for business among solicitors is prohibited, but limited advertising must be permissible.[6] Counsel should not normally interview witnesses before or during a trial, nor should he consult with a client except in the presence of the solicitor. Note should also be taken of the "cab-rank" principle, discussed earlier.[7] The extent to which it in fact operates is a more controversial question. The lay client firstly has to find a solicitor, and then a set of chambers which takes the type of work on offer, and then the advocate may or may not be available. Examples of difficulties are to be found, and, for the future the cab-rank principle may be in jeopardy from conditional fees arrangements. It can scarcely be argued that a barrister should have no choice but to accept a case that exposes him to significant risk.

F   COMPLAINTS AGAINST LAWYERS

The disciplinary functions of the Solicitors Disciplinary Tribunal and the Bar Council have already been noted.[8] Other bodies exist to deal with complaints against either solicitors or barristers.

I   Office for the Supervision of Solicitors

The Office for the Supervision of Solicitors was created in 1996 to replace the much criticised Solicitors Complaints Bureau, a body comprising both lawyers and lay persons under the authority of the Law Society to provide self regulation and means of adjudicating upon complaints against solicitors by clients, other than through the formal disciplinary procedure of the profession. It had the power to investigate, and order the making of redress, payment of compensation, the giving of an apology or other appropriate redress. The Solicitors Complaints Bureau was attacked both from within the profession for what some solicitors saw as an over-emphasis upon measures designed to combat fraud, and because it (in the view of some) associated solicitors directly with complaints, and also from outside organisations who criticised what was perceived to be a lack of genuine independence.

---

4   Barristers are required "to act only as consultants instructed by solicitors and other approved professional persons": 1990 Code, para 102(a)(ii). See also p 263, *ante*.

5   *Doe d Bennett v Hale* (1850) 15 QB 171. For an unsuccessful attempt to challenge this rule, see *Re T (a barrister)* [1982] QB 430; [1981] 2 All ER 1105. In criminal cases the rule was, until 1980, subject to the exception of the "dock brief" whereby the defendant, on a trial on indictment, could instruct from the dock any barrister who was robed and sitting in court for the sum of £2.10. The dock brief became obsolete by reason of the extension of legal aid in criminal proceedings, but it may be noted that the litigation in *Rondel v Worsley (supra)* arose out of a dock brief, the plaintiff having been refused legal aid.

6   Principally limited to advertising areas of practice and expertise: see 1990 Code, para 307. A barrister must not comment to or in any news or current affairs media concerning the facts or issues arising in a particular case: para 604.

7   See p 244, *ante*.

8   See pp 249 and 261, *ante*.

As a result of this criticism the Law Society replaced the SCB with the OSS, with the objective of "creating a partnership between solicitors and the public". Its members are mainly appointed by the Master of the Rolls, having consulted consumer interests. Matters which concern negligence are not within its remit, but matters concerning proper professional standards and delay are, as are matters of lack of warning about the level of costs charged. The costs themselves are matters to be dealt with in accordance with the procedures set out earlier. Some evidence exists to suggest that the SCB was on occasion over-eager to use these exceptions from jurisdiction to decline to deal with a complaint. The OSS has been urged not to be so cautious, and, indeed, to "champion the rulebook" rather more than its predecessor body.[9]

2   The Bar Complaints system

Until 1997, the Bar did not have a complaints system distinct from is formal disciplinary procedures. Such a system was introduced in April 1997. Under the new system, the Bar Council will be able to require barristers to reduce, refund or waive fees if they have provided an inadequate service, or to pay compensation up to £2,000 where actual financial loss has been caused by poor service. The power to order financial redress does not extend to those aspects of a barrister's work which attract immunity from suit.

A post of Complaints Commissioner has been created, being a lay person with wide powers to accept or reject complaints, to attempt conciliation and to determine how complaints should be dealt with. Complaints involving poor service are referred to adjudication panels chaired by the Complaints Commissioner, comprising two barristers and two lay members (including the Chairman). The Chairman has no casting vote, and the rules provide that if a panel is evenly divided the finding shall be that most favourable to the barrister, thus giving the barrister members an effective power of veto. It remains to be seen whether this is a change in substance as opposed to on paper, as suggested by the Annual report for 1997 of the Legal Services Ombudsman.

3   The Legal Services Ombudsman

The Legal Services Ombudsman deals with complaints against solicitors or barristers by dissatisfied clients.[9] The Annual Reports for the Ombudsman show an increasing number of complaints, with an increase of complaints against solicitors in 1997 of 7%.[10]

G   LAW OFFICERS

The "law officers", legal advisers to the Crown, are the Attorney-General and the Solicitor-General. The Attorney-General is the head of the English Bar, though neither he nor the Solicitor-General may engage in private practice while they hold office. They are assisted by Junior Counsel to the Treasury who, holding no political office, are practising barristers.

Apart from his political duties, which include advising government departments and answering questions in the House of Commons, the Attorney-General represents

9   Annual Report of Legal Services Ombudsman, 1997.
10   *Ibid.*

the Crown in certain civil proceedings and, as a matter of practice, in trials for treason and other important offences with a political or constitutional element. In addition he exercises the prerogative power of staying prosecutions on indictment by the entry of a *nolle prosequi* and, by statute, leave of the Attorney-General is required for the commencement of certain criminal proceedings. Mention may also be made of "relator" proceedings in which the Attorney-General appears on behalf of a section of the public, for example to restrain a public nuisance.

Thus where there is a case of public nuisance, or some other interference with the public weal (not being a criminal offence) the rule is that an ordinary member of the public cannot sue; this rule is necessary in order to avoid multiplicity of actions. In such cases the Attorney-General has power to bring proceedings. His role was in one case defined as follows:[11]

> "It is settled in our constitutional law that in matters which concern the public at large the Attorney-General is the guardian of the public interest. Although he is a member of the government of the day, it is his duty to represent the public interest with complete objectivity and detachment. He must act independently of any external pressure from whatever quarter it may come. As the guardian of the public interest, the Attorney-General has a special duty in regard to the enforcement of the law."

However, the Court of Appeal in that case suggested that there was an exception to the general rule so that, in the last resort, if the Attorney-General refused improperly or unreasonably to exercise his power to initiate proceedings, or if there was not sufficient time, a member of the public, aggrieved by non-observance of the law, could himself come to the courts and seek a declaration and, in a proper case, an injunction, joining the Attorney-General, if need be, as a defendant. This suggestion was, however, rejected firmly by the House of Lords in the important case of *Gouriet v Union of Post Office Workers*.[12] The defendant trade union had resolved to call on its members not to handle mail from this country to South Africa, in support of a political protest against apartheid policy. This action would have amounted to a criminal offence under section 58 of the Post Office Act 1953. The plaintiff applied to the Attorney-General for his consent to act as plaintiff in a relator action against the union for an injunction to restrain the union from acting as it threatened to do, and thereby breaking the law. The Attorney-General refused his consent. The plaintiff thereupon issued a writ in his own name claiming an injunction and the question at issue was whether he was entitled so to do. The Court of Appeal held that he was[13] but the House of Lords, after hearing ten days of argument, reversed the Court of Appeal's decision. The House held that it was a fundamental principle of English law that public rights could only be asserted in a civil action by the Attorney-General as an officer of the Crown representing the public and that, except where statute otherwise provided, a private person could only bring an action to restrain a threatened breach of the law if such breach would infringe his private rights or would inflict special damage on him. Moreover the refusal of the Attorney-General to give his consent to a relator action is not subject to review by the courts, any more than is the exercise by the Attorney-General of any other of the powers and duties vested in him.

11   Per Lord Denning MR in *A-G (ex rel McWhirter) v Independent Broadcasting Authority* [1973] QB 629, at 646–647; [1973] 1 All ER 689, at 697; the case involved an unsuccessful attempt by the late Mr Ross McWhirter to prevent the showing of a television film about the American artist Andy Warhol.
12   [1978] AC 435; [1977] 3 All ER 70.
13   [1977] QB 729; [1977] 1 All ER 696.

Accordingly the plaintiff's action was struck out. It may be noted, however, that had the defendant union actually committed a criminal offence, the plaintiff (or any other private person) could have instituted and pursued a private prosecution although the Attorney-General could have brought this to a halt by entering a *nolle prosequi*.

The Solicitor-General's position is basically that of the Attorney-General's deputy and he may exercise any power vested by statute in the Attorney-General (unless the statute in question otherwise provides) if the office of Attorney-General is vacant, the Attorney-General is unable to act through illness or the Attorney-General authorises the Solicitor-General to act.[14]

H   DIRECTOR OF PUBLIC PROSECUTIONS AND CROWN PROSECUTION SERVICE

The Director of Public Prosecutions is a barrister or solicitor of not less than ten years' standing appointed by the Attorney-General.[15] The Director is the head of the Crown Prosecution Service.

Up until 1985, no national system for the prosecution of offences existed, prosecutions often being handled by the police by prosecuting solicitors departments, or by solicitors acting for the police. The arrangements which existed varied considerably in each of the police force areas: some had a prosecuting solicitor's department, others relied, on whole or in part, on local authority solicitors, whilst others, again in whole or in part, made use of solicitors in private practice. By 1986, all but six of the police force areas had a prosecuting solicitors department to handle at least some of its work.

In respect of the most serious of offences, the Director of Public Prosecutions had a supervisory and advisory role,[16] assuming responsibility for the prosecution of certain cases, such as murder.

The Royal Commission on Criminal Procedure[17] in 1980 concluded that a system of public prosecutions independent of the police was fundamental for the proper and effective functioning of the prosecution process.[18] The decision whether or not to prosecute should remain with the police, but once a prosecution was launched by charge or summons its conduct should be entrusted to a new prosecuting authority. This authority was to be locally based, but with a measure of national control and accountability. The Royal Commission rejected a proposal for the establishment of a centrally directed national prosecution service as "neither necessary nor desirable".[19] This approach did not find favour with the then Government, which proposed the creation of a national prosecution service under the control of the Director of Public Prosecutions. The DPP would head this service and have responsibility for the preparation and promulgation of guidance to be given to the Attorney-General, for decisions on prosecution in cases of particular importance or difficulty, appointment and other personnel functions for the Service and financial and administrative management. To implement this approach, the Prosecution of Offences Act 1985 was passed, which created a new Crown Prosecution Service.

14   Law Officers Act 1944, s 1.
15   Prosecution of Offences Act 1979, s 1; there are also Assistant Directors, who must be barristers or solicitors of not less than seven years' standing (s 1(2)).
16   For these, see Prosecution of Offences Regulations 1978, now no longer operative.
17   (1981) (Cm 8092, HMSO).
18   See *ibid* para 7.3.
19   See *ibid* para 7.22.

Section 3 of the 1985 Act defines the duty of the Director of Public Prosecutions. It includes the following:

(a) to take over the conduct of all criminal proceedings instituted on behalf of a police force (whether by a member of that force or some other person);
(b) to institute and conduct criminal proceedings where the importance or difficulty of the case makes it appropriate that the Director should institute the proceedings;
(c) to take over binding over proceedings brought by a police force;[20]
(d) the giving of advice to police forces on all matters relating to criminal offences;
(e) to appear in certain appeals.

Thus, the Director, and the Crown Prosecution Service effectively control the prosecution process. They do not control the process of investigation. That is a matter for the police, although the Crown Prosecution Service may direct that certain enquiries be made.[1]

The Crown Prosecution Service is a national organisation, with offices in regional centres. Initially, some 31 areas were established, each with a Chief Crown Prosecutor, and with a complement of qualified and non qualified staff. Its responsibility is for the prosecution of offences. The police continue, as they did prior to the passage of the 1985 Act, to obtain evidence, and compile case files in respect of offences to be prosecuted in special units known as Administrative Support Units. It is these files that form the basis of CPS work. The evidence in the file is reviewed by the CPS in order to ensure that the charge laid by the police can be justified and sustained. If the evidence is not sufficient the charge may be downgraded, or the case discontinued.[2] The Service was, initially, significantly undermanned and its reputation suffered in terms of the speed and competence of some of its work,[3] quite apart from tensions that often arose between prosecutors and police, the latter not always used to not having direct control over the power to continue or discontinue a prosecution.[4] In the early 1990s it was thought appropriate, for management reasons, to have the CPS more centrally managed, and, coupled with a review of the executive management structure, the CPS was reorganised into 13 areas. The intention of this reorganisation was to devolve casework to CPS local branches, whilst vesting management powers in the 13 area headquarters. The result was, however, to achieve a significant increase in centralised decision-making. Branches were required to adopt a variety of standard procedures, which some considered to be over-prescriptive, and which did not allow for variation to reflect local circumstances. The Royal Commission had expressed fears about the proposed new prosecuting agency becoming over-centralised, bureaucratic and dominated by professional administrators rather than lawyers. In 1998, the Glidewell Report[5] concluded that these fears were in fact well-founded.

During the period since the establishment of the Crown Prosecution Service, the context within which it operates has significantly changed. The Glidewell Report identifies the significant rise in serious crime, public concern in respect of a failure to bring, or continue, prosecutions, or to downgrade what are perceived as serious

20   See p 303, *post.*
1   1985 Act, s 3(2)(c).
2   See p 462, *post.*
3   See p 271, *post.*
4   See p 462, *post.*
5   See n 6, *infra.*

offences, and the general higher expectations of the performance of public bodies.[6] Further, a series of cases where prosecutions were not brought, or failed, highlighted concerns about the CPS and its effectiveness. It was as a result of this loss of confidence that in 1997 the Government appointed a judge, Sir Ian Glidewell, to head a committee of investigation into the structure and work of the CPS. The Government also announced at that time that the CPS was to be reorganised into a structure of 42 areas, each to correspond with a police force area. In that context the Gildewell Committee reported in May 1998, making some 75 recommendations. It concluded that the CPS should, structurally, be reorganised. This reorganisation was to achieve devolution of responsibility and accountability, a redefinition of the role of CPS headquarters, so as to ensure that all but the most senior lawyers spend much more time prosecuting and to ensure proper and effective administrative support and services locally, with the role of CPS Headquarters being changed. To achieve these aims Glidewell proposed that each of the 42 areas should be headed by a Chief Crown Prosecutor supported by an Area Business Manager, with responsibility for efficient and effective administration, budgeting and financial control. The prosecution process would be under the direct control of the Chief Crown Prosecutor, with the role of CPS National Headquarters being the setting of a national framework for prosecution and the resourcing and monitoring of the 42 Areas. The overall management of the Service would be split between persons responsible for the legal and managerial roles, the latter entrusted to a Chief Executive answerable to the DPP. The scheme proposed was stated by the Glidewell Report to regard the 'Area' as equivalent to a very large legal firm specialising in criminal prosecution, bound by central policies and procedures but with a very large degree of autonomy in carrying out its professional functions and managing its local offices. The appointment of a new DPP, following the resignation in June 1998 of the existing postholder, is the first stage in the achievement of these aims, which were broadly accepted by the Government.

Coupled with this structural review, the Glidewell Committee also considered the operational performance of the CPS. Despite some confusion, statistics show that more than half of all acquittals in the Crown Court result from an order or direction of the judge. This statistic was viewed with some concern by the Glidewell Report, which took the view that following review of a case by the CPS a case ought to be strong enough to put to a jury. It concluded that this position reflected the fact that the performance of the CPS was not as good as it should be,[7] with improvements in effectiveness and efficiency of the prosecution process anticipated to occur following the creation of the Service not having been met. This could partly be explained by continued tensions in role and function between the police and CPS. The Report recommended that in the future the preparation of the case file should be the responsibility of the CPS, not, as now, with a police administrative support unit. The Report proposed as a model a "criminal justice unit" which would be headed by s CPS lawyers and staffed mainly, but not entirely, by CPS staff. Such a unit would have the power to call on the police to take action in obtaining more evidence, would deal with "fast-track" cases, and which could be presented by the unit in magistrates' courts. To that end, the Crime and Disorder Act 1998 amends the 1985 Act. It does so by the insertion of a new section 7A in substitution for the pre-existing provision, and grants power to the DPP to designate members of the CPS who are not Crown Prosecutors to have the powers and rights of audience of a Crown Court Prosecutor[8] in relation to

6   See generally Review of the Crown Prosecution Service, Cm 3960 (1998).
7   *Ibid.*
8   1998 Act, s 53. The decision in *R v DPP, ex parte First Division Civil Servants* (1998) 138 NLJ 158 is no longer good law.

applications for, or relating to, bail in criminal proceedings, the conduct of criminal proceedings in magistrates' courts other than trials, and powers of Crown Prosecutors in relation generally to the conduct of criminal proceedings. This power does not extend to matters in a case involving an offence triable only on indictment or to either way offences. It is intended that these changes, which also reflect the recommendations of the Narey Committee[9] in respect of reductions in delays in the criminal justice process, will "lead to a shift in the centre of gravity of the CPS towards the Crown Court." To assist in this shift, Glidewell recommended that a CPS lawyer should be present at each major Crown Court centre, and that there be more CPS case-workers or administrative staff to support counsel in the Crown Court. In respect of the Crown Court, the Glidewell Report recommended the establishment of a Trial Unit, to be responsible for all prosecutions in the Crown Court, and to be available to undertake the advocacy in trials of either-way offences in magistrates' courts.

One important power vested in the CPS which has an important bearing on the operation of the Criminal Justice system is the power to discontinue proceedings.[10] The downgrading of charges, substituting less serious charges for charges of a more serious nature, is also an issue. The Glidewell Report observed that downgrading appeared to occur most frequently in cases of serious crime, public order offences and road traffic accidents causing death. It concluded that it "suspected" that inappropriate downgrading did in fact occur, although had no evidence to firmly support a conclusion that it occurred when it should not have occurred. This was a matter on which more research was needed. The power and criteria for the discontinuance of proceedings is discussed later.[11] The Narey Report concluded that the powers be amended to prevent the discontinuance of proceedings on public interest grounds. This recommendation was not accepted by the Glidewell Report, which concluded that that power should remain, but be exercised only rarely.

The Serious Fraud Office

Mention should also be made of the Serious Fraud Office. Created by the Criminal Justice Act 1987 to assist in the investigation and prosecution of cases of serious fraud,[12] it has wide powers that go beyond those normally available to the police and prosecuting authorities. These are discussed in due course. Its work has led to a series of high-profile prosecutions, many of which have proved unsuccessful, and raised many questions as to how the law should deal with cases of this type.

---

9   See p 460, *post*.
10   See p 462, *post*.
11   See p 462, *post*.
12   Criminal Justice Act 1987, s 1.

CHAPTER 13

Legal Aid and Advice

A THE COST OF THE LAW

Access to the courts may be regarded as a fundamental right. The role of the courts in providing the main, although not exclusive, forum for dispute resolution patently presupposes that individuals have access to them to pursue or defend their own actions. Perhaps even more importantly, access to legal advice is crucial if individuals are to become aware of what law requires of them, or entitles them to. Access to legal advice is also a fundamental right under the European Convention on Human Rights, and now has direct legal status in English law.[1] The importance of this right in English constitutional law can be gauged by the importance of the courts' role of holding the executive to account in judicial review proceedings.[2]

The costs of litigation in civil cases is high. For example the average costs for medical negligence cases were found by the Woolf Report[3] to be £38,252, with those for personal injury at £20,413. In criminal cases, the vast majority of accused will be on legal aid, but, as noted below, the costs may be considerable and provide strains on the ability, or willingness, of the state to finance them. The costs of obtaining legal advice and assistance have, in modern times, always provided obstacles to access to justice. They comprise two elements. Firstly, the fees of the solicitor and, if instructed, the barrister. The basis on which costs in litigation will be assessed has already been discussed.[4] The hourly rates charged by solicitors can be high. Barristers' brief fees, and refresher fees for subsequent days of a case, can, for leading barristers, be very high. In *Re a Company (No 004081 of 1989)*[5] brief fees of £20,000 and £7,000 for leading and junior counsel respectively were approved in a case where they were only required for a short period of a two-week trial. The level of professional fees charged by members of the legal profession is from time to time the subject of continued

---

1 See art 6, p 126, *ante*, and p 132, *ante*.
2 See p 142, *ante*.
3 Woolf Interim Report, Annex III, pp 251–256.
4 See pp 257–260, *ante*.
5 [1995] 2 All ER 155. Top barristers are reported to earn hourly rates of £350–£600, with daily refreshers of £2,500.

comment. In 1998, references were made to the "fat cats" of the legal profession,[6] with the Lord Chancellor himself publishing a "name and shame" list of barristers considered to earn excessive amounts from the legal aid fund. Even more recently, four leading barristers had the level of fees charged by them challenged in the House of Lords.[7] However, mechanisms for challenging disputed legal fees exist, and have already been discussed.[8] The second aspect of the cost of justice are the costs incidental, but essential, to it – court fees and other expenses, such as the fees payable to expert witnesses for reports or investigation. For example, if an individual has suffered an instance of alleged medical negligence, very considerable work will need to be done to ascertain what actually happened in the hospital, the likely cause of the injury or suffering and the prognosis for the patient in order to establish the possible level of potential damages. In respect of fees (which are often standard fees) and in terms of costs, mechanisms exist for alleged excess to be controlled, through taxation and the award of costs.[9]

The more crucial question is how access to justice can be achieved given the level of cost that access to lawyers incurs and given the current structures and process of litigation. Clearly, reform of the civil justice system has, as one of its aims, the reduction of cost with a view to achieving greater accessibility to civil justice. These issues are discussed later.[10] In small, but important, ways many lawyers have sought to overcome the problem of cost for those unable to afford access to justice through not charging, or undercharging, for work. In the past it has been common for a solicitor to tender initial advice free. In litigation, the Bar runs schemes such as the Free Representation Unit, established in 1973, and which in 1997 fought over 1,600 cases, and the Pro Bono scheme, which enables the services of barristers to be offered free in deserving cases. Such schemes include cases across a broad spectrum of legal issues including housing, family, immigration, criminal appeals and actions against the police. Individual firms of solicitors have historically offered services at no, or reduced cost, where they have considered it appropriate to do so, and the scope for more organised pro bono work has increased, in the context of individual firms, groups of firms and by way of input to organisations such as advice centres, Citizens' Advice Bureaux and law centres.[11] Other forms of financing of legal services are support from trade unions and similar organisations, and through legal costs insurance or other appropriate insurance provision (eg household or motoring policies). It is expected that legal costs insurance will play a bigger role in financing legal actions in the future.[12]

However, it is the legal aid and advice scheme that has, since the Second World War, sought to ensure access to justice, primarily through the financing of advice and litigation. The legal profession has hitherto provided those services through its traditional organisational structures,[13] although more recent forms of professional structure such as law centres and advice centres have played an important role in ensuring the availability of legal services, albeit funded through the existing legal aid schemes. Such schemes have become increasingly limited in their scope through tighter means limits. Inevitably however pressure on resources has increased as actions become more complex and legal costs rise. These pressures have caused successive governments to undertake a fundamental review of the legal aid system, how it operates

6   See *Counsel*, June 1998, p 12.
7   (1998) Times, 27 June.
8   See p 257, *ante*.
9   See pp 257–258, *ante*, 428–430, *post*.
10   See pp 325–326, *post*.
11   See Law Society's Gazette, 25 May 1994; The Lawyer, 15 March 1995.
12   See Woolf *Access to Justice*, *op cit* at para 3.23, and further, pp 323-340, *post*.
13   *Counsel*, June 1998.

and what is funded. In 1991, the expenditure on legal aid was some £682 million. By 1997, this figure had increased to £1,477 million.[14] One government response to this financial pressure on the provision of legal services has been to try and recoup money where it is considered possible, and appropriate, to do so. One example of this was the decision in 1996 to raise court fees for litigants. Not only were levels of fees raised, but also certain exclusions and exemptions were removed. In particular, the exemption which had hitherto existed from the paying of fees by litigants in person who were on income support was removed[15] as was the power of the Lord Chancellor to reduce or remit the fee in any case on the grounds of undue financial hardship in exceptional circumstances. This was challenged in *R v Lord Chancellor, ex parte Witham*,[16] where W, who was on income support and wished to bring proceedings in person for defamation (for which legal aid is unavailable), argued that the Lord Chancellor had acted *ultra vires*[17] in making the order. In upholding the application, Laws J held there was evidence of a wide range of situations in which persons with very low incomes were in practice denied access to the courts to prosecute claims or in some circumstances to resist the effects of claims brought against them. Access to the courts was a constitutional right at common law in the sense that it could not be abrogated by the state save by specific provision in an Act of Parliament, or by regulations which were made under clear and specifically conferred authority to remove the right of access to the courts. The Lord Chancellor had claimed that the power in s 130 of the Courts and Legal Services Act 1990 was such authority. Laws J disagreed, finding that the regulations made by the Lord Chancellor were invalid.

Prior to 1949 there were various provisions to enable persons to sue or be sued *in forma pauperis* and to prosecute and defend both civil and criminal proceedings with the financial assistance of various societies and authorities. These provisions have now been almost totally replaced by statute. Schemes in respect of advice and assistance were introduced by the Legal Aid and Advice Act 1949, though never fully implemented,[18] and specific provision in respect of legal aid in criminal cases was made by the Criminal Justice Act 1967.[19] The aim of such schemes was to make the law accessible to all, despite lack of means. The nature of the means-tested schemes adopted, together with gaps in legal provision, inevitably meant that the impact of such schemes was partial, and was supplemented by a variety of mechanisms involving both the provision of legal advice by lawyers on a voluntary or nominal fee basis,[20] or the provision of advice and assistance by persons and organisations outside the legal profession.[1]

Responsibility for the statutory schemes of advice, and for representation in civil cases, was entrusted to The Law Society, which performed its statutory functions through area offices and committees, in consultation with the Bar and under the guidance of the Lord Chancellor. Administration of the scheme for legal assistance in criminal cases lay primarily with the magistrates' courts, and, in particular, with the

14   See Middleton Report, p 288, *post*.
15   Supreme Court Fees (Amendment) Order 1996, art 3, SI 1996/3191.
16   [1998] QB 575; [1997] 2 All ER 779.
17   See p 147, *ante*.
18   The schemes established by the 1949 Act were based upon the recommendations of the Report of the Committee on Legal Aid and Advice (The Rushcliffe Committee) (Cmd 6641, 1945, HMSO). In particular, the full scope of the scheme proposed was never implemented.
19   *Implementing the recommendations of the Department Committee: Legal Aid in Criminal Proceedings* (Cmnd 2934, 1966, HMSO).
20   The old "dock brief" scheme was abolished in 1980: see p 266, *ante*. For a modern example see the Free Representation Unit of the Bar.
1   Such as Trade Unions, Citizens Advice Bureaux, Welfare and Consumer Advice agencies, and Law and Legal Advice centres often funded, in whole or in part, by local authorities.

justices' clerks.[2] The extent and quality of provision was considered by the Royal Commission on Legal Services,[3] which identified certain essential principles relating to the provision of legal services. These were:

(1) that there should be equal access to the courts;
(2) equal access demanded adequate legal services;
(3) financial assistance out of public funds should be available for every individual who, without it, would suffer an undue financial burden in properly pursuing or defending his rights;
(4) the standard of legal services should be the same irrespective of whether or not provided at the public expense;
(5) a free choice of available lawyer should be available to each individual.

Despite these principles, the proportions of persons eligible for state assistance for advice or representation diminished during the 1980s,[4] and the system itself was subjected to further review by the Government in 1988, in a White Paper entitled *Legal Aid in England and Wales*[5] These proposals formed the basis for the provisions of the Legal Aid Act 1988, although not without some changes.[6] The White Paper indicated that "the purpose of legal aid is to ensure that people of small or moderate means receive access to proper legal advice and justice."

1   The Legal Aid Board

In an attempt to achieve that aim the Act establishes a Legal Aid Board, which has the general function of securing that advice, assistance and representation are available and of administering the Act. The Board took over the running of the legal aid scheme in civil matters from the Law Society, which had operated through a scheme of local officials and Area Committees. The Board comprises no fewer than 11 and no more than 17 members, appointed in the light of their experience in, or knowledge of, the provision of legal services, the work of the court and social conditions, and of management.[7] The membership of the Board must contain at least two solicitors. Members hold office for a period not exceeding five years, and may be removed if they become unable or unfit to perform their functions, or fail to attend meetings for six consecutive months.[8]

The Board has sweeping powers. By section 4 of the 1988 Act it may do anything:

(a) which it considers necessary or desirable to provide or secure the provision of advice, assistance and representation under the Act, or
(b) which is calculated to facilitate, or is incidental or conducive to, the discharge of its functions.

---

2   See p 184, *ante*.
3   Cm 7648, 1979, HMSO. *The Report of the Royal Commission on Legal Services*, paras 8.15–8.38, recommended the establishment of a system of citizens' law centres, to provide legal advice, assistance and representation to those in the locality; these recommendations have not been adopted.
4   Due to a failure to consistently upgrade the income and capital limits.
5   *Legal Aid in England and Wales – A New Framework*, Cmnd 118 (HMSO, 1987).
6   E.g. the functions and powers of the Legal Aid Board.
7   Legal Aid Act 1988, s 3(9).
8   *Ibid*, Sch 1.

Advice, assistance and representation are terms defined by the Act.[9] Each may be provided in different ways in different areas of the country, and in different ways in different fields of law.[10] Subject to the Lord Chancellor concurring, this can include the securing of advice or assistance by contracting with any body. Thus, agreements might be reached with Citizens Advice Bureaux or other information agencies, welfare rights organisations,[11] law centres, or, indeed, franchise arrangements reached with individual firms of solicitors,[12] and, as noted below, developments of this type are already far advanced. It is also open to the Board to secure legal representation in given circumstances by contract with individual firms of solicitors, a power that might be exercised in multi-party or class actions.[13] The Royal Commission on Legal Services[14] had recommended that legal advice and assistance be made available in certain circumstances to groups. Following a series of consultations the Legal Aid Board introduced proposals which permitted the entering into multi-party arrangements, with one solicitors' firm acting as a "lead firm".[15] Such actions now form an important path towards the provision of legal services in extremely large and complex cases.

The Board operates through a legal aid area office, England and Wales being sub divided into legal aid areas. The office has powers of decision in respect of applications for civil legal aid, although aspects of its work govern parts of the operation of legal aid in criminal cases. Each area also has its own area committee, which is comprised of practising solicitors and barristers, and which provides a forum to deal with appeals against refusal of applications for civil legal aid.

In the exercise of its functions the Board must have regard to such matters as the Lord Chancellor may from time to time direct, and is under a duty to publish information and reports.

2   Legal aid franchising

It has already been noted that the Legal Aid Board has the power to enter into franchising arrangements. It has done so since 1 August 1994. The objective of franchising is to increase the availability of quality assured legal services within a context of value for money. To achieve this, if a firm of solicitors is able, through monitoring an audit of a period of time, to satisfy the Board in respect of seven key elements it may be awarded a franchise in one or more of the categories of legal aid work for which franchising is available. Those categories are matrimonial and family work, personal injury, employment, debt, consumer and general contract, housing, immigration and nationality, welfare benefits and crime. The effect of the grant of a franchise is that, in the area governed by the franchise, the Legal Aid Board devolves some of the powers which are normally exercised by it.

9   *Ibid*, s 2(2)(4).
10   *Ibid*, s 4(1).
11   Section 2(6) permits advice to be given by persons other than solicitors or barristers. Section 4 authorised the contracting out of such advice services. The Legal Aid Board is currently putting into place franchise arrangements which will allow approved firms of solicitors to engage in work, and manage their work, on behalf of the Board.
12   See pp 277-278, *post*.
13   Legal Aid Act 1988, s 4(5).
14   See n 3, *supra*.
15   See *R v Legal Aid Board , ex parte Donn & Co (A Firm)* [1996] 3 All ER 1, where an unsuccessful challenge was made by the applicant solicitors on judicial review to the refusal of a tender by the applicants for a multi-party action in respect of a claim for damages for loss caused by alleged Gulf War syndrome. Such matters were justiciable as public law matters, because of the public dimensions of the matter.

To achieve a franchise arrangement a firm of solicitors makes a detailed application. The Board then seeks to satisfy itself as to whether the firm meets its mandatory requirements in the various major elements. These cover the strategic management of the practice, its financial management (including adequate financial management systems), appropriate personnel management approaches and strategies (including training, and equal opportunities policies) effective and efficient file and case management systems, selection and quality criteria in respect of suppliers of services (eg counsel, expert witnesses), client care and availability of welfare benefits advice. All these will be checked through monitoring and quality audit of the work done by the firm in the relevant areas of practice. If granted, the franchise will, during the lifetime of the franchise contract, be monitored by the Board. The firm awarded the franchise will be able to use the franchise award in its advertising and letterheads.

3   Wider provision of legal services

In addition to the main schemes which govern the provision of legal aid and advice in civil and criminal proceedings, various initiatives have been launched to make available legal advice in different ways. The first is in respect of family mediation. When section 29 of the Family Law Act 1996 is brought into effect the Legal Aid Board will require couples who have issues relating to children to be settled in divorce or separation proceedings to attend an interview with a mediator in order that their suitability for mediation is established. This has to be done prior to consideration of any application for legal aid for such proceedings. The 1996 Act amended the Legal Aid Act 1988,[16] giving the Board power to fund mediators through contractual arrangements with the Board. It is intended that this power will be used initially on a pilot basis with a view to the establishment of a network of franchised mediators.

Secondly, the Legal Aid Board has begun a pilot project with 42 non-solicitor advice agencies, under the power contained in Part II of the 1988 Act. These organisations are non-profit making advice agencies, some of whom employ solicitors.

Other changes, or pilots, are occurring in the context of advice and duty solicitor schemes, with the Board piloting a scheme whereby it will contract individually with franchise holders for the provision of duty solicitor and other, currently "green form", advice work. Pilot work is also being undertaken in respect of contracting for the provision of legal services in multi-party actions and other high cost civil cases. Contracting for the provision of legal services forms an important element of future developments for legal aid and is discussed further later.[17]

4   The future direction of legal aid and financing of proceedings

The developments in respect of franchising, contracting for the block purchase of legal services and the extension of provision of advice through funding arrangements with non-lawyers are important developments designed to secure efficiency in the use of strained resources. Expenditure on legal aid has risen from £682 million in 1990–1991 to £1,477 million in 1997, an increase of some 115%.[18] Some 90% of that expenditure goes on lawyers' fees. In civil legal aid, expenditure since 1993 has increased by 43%, but the number of people helped has gone down by 9%. As already noted, lawyers'

16   See 1996 Act, s 26.
17   See p 288, *post.*
18   *Future of Legal Aid and the Civil Justice System*, Lord Chancellor's Department, 1997.

fees, particularly those of leading barristers, are considered to be too high. It is in this context that far-reaching changes are proposed to the legal aid scheme and the means by which advice is financed and proceedings funded. The existing advice and assistance schemes are discussed in this Chapter. However, root-and-branch reform is proposed. In October 1997[19] the Lord Chancellor, Lord Irvine, announced plans for reform of the civil justice system and the legal aid systems. The changes were stated to be aiming to drive down the costs of litigation, making the civil justice system more accessible, the achievement of better value for money and reduction of the weaknesses in the civil justice system. This announcement, and the Government's subsequent White Paper on Legal Aid, drew upon the work done on reform of the civil justice process consequent upon the recommendations of the Woolf Report,[20] on the Review of Civil Justice and Legal Aid (the Middleton Report) in 1997[1] and the development of conditional fee arrangements.[2] At this stage, particular note should be taken of the principles identified by the Middleton Report as underpinning any review of legal aid provision:

(1) Legal aid should be the servant of civil justice. It should ensure that disputes are settled in the best forum, and contribute to the efficiency with which cases are handled;
(2) Legal aid should be efficient in its own right: spending should be carefully targeted and costs minimised in relation to the benefits;
(3) Legal aid should not support a level of access that goes beyond what a private paying party would consider appropriate and proportionate to the expected redress in a case.
(4) It is reasonable and legitimate for government to reach a decision on how much legal aid the country can afford and to put a legal aid system in place which enables it to adhere to that decision.

The results of that review, and the Governemt's responses to it, are considered in due course.

B   LEGAL ADVICE AND ASSISTANCE

I   Nature of advice and assistance ("green form scheme")

The Legal Advice and Assistance Act 1972 introduced a completely new scheme for the giving of legal advice and assistance in relation to both civil and criminal matters. The aim of the scheme was to introduce a simple and effective method of providing legal advice and assistance so as to make these services more readily accessible to the public. The scheme, which is generally known as the "green form scheme", is now contained in the Legal Aid Act 1988. Under the scheme a solicitor, and so far as may be necessary counsel, may give oral or written advice on any question of English law and as to any steps which the applicant might appropriately take (whether by way of settling any claim, bringing or defending any proceedings, making an agreement, or other instrument or transaction, obtaining further legal or other advice or otherwise) having regard to the application of English law to his problem.[3] The advice may extend

19   18 October 1997, Law Society Annual Conference, Cardiff.
20   See pp 341, 364, and 365, *post*.
1   See p 288, *post*.
2   See p 254, *ante*.
3   Legal Aid Act 1988, s 2(2).

to preparatory work for a tribunal hearing (eg by the preparation for that litigant of a written submission). It may even be used to enable a solicitor to attend court to advise a litigant who is representing himself,[4] although authority may well be needed from the area office because of the charging limits. If such authority is sought, regard will be had to the level of difficulty, the importance of the matter and the ability (or lack of it) of the client to represent himself.

Where a person is financially eligible, he may obtain assistance from a solicitor until the solicitors' charges reach a total of two hours' worth of work (or in matrimonial cases involving the preparation of a divorce petition, three hours). Costs in excess of this require authorisation by the area legal aid office, unless the solicitor has a franchise arrangement for such work. The normal services which are provided under the scheme comprise such matters as general advice, writing letters, negotiating settlements and the like. It does not extend to taking any step in proceedings (other than negotiating settlement) since this is a matter for legal aid proper rather than for legal advice or assistance, nor does it cover advice from a person other than a "legal representative".[5] The 1988 Act permits[6] the scope of the scheme to be limited by regulations as to what may be undertaken, or who may undertake them. In particular, conveyancing and wills are outside the scope of the scheme.[7] This is a power most likely in the future to be used to exclude types of work considered inappropriate for support under the scheme, or where advice has been provided in other ways.

2   Financial provisions

Legal advice and assistance under the scheme is available to applicants whose resources are within the limits specified in regulations made under the Act. If an applicant's disposable income and capital fall within the limits then advice, or assistance, can be given, subject where appropriate to the payment of a contribution. To calculate this, the applicant must complete a form (the "green form") which contains requirements as to details of his income and capital so that the solicitor can decide his eligibility for legal advice and assistance.[8] If he is within the financial limits the solicitor must assess the contribution (if any) to be paid by the applicant. No contribution is payable by an applicant who is in receipt of income support or family credit or has a low disposable income. Above this a contribution calculated by reference to income, but not capital, is payable. If the solicitor is properly entitled to any further charge or fee, he has a first charge upon money or property recovered (subject to exceptions) and, in relation to any further deficiency, he is entitled to be paid out of the legal aid fund, up to the cost of two hours' work,[9] in accordance with prescribed hourly rates.

The fact that the services of counsel or solicitor are given under the Act rather than under private instructions does not, of course, affect the professional relationship and duties that spring from the relationship.[10] The solicitor must exercise the same degree of care and skill in giving advice as he would normally and he must preserve the

4   The solicitor is then, effectively, in a position of a "McKenzie friend": see p 244.
5   *R v Legal Aid Board, ex p Bruce* [1992] 1 All ER 133.
6   Legal Aid Act 1988, s 8(3).
7   *Ibid*, regs 3, 4.
8   Legal Advice and Assistance Regulations 1989, reg 8(3). The current regulations specify £80 per week as the disposable income limit, and £1,000 as that for disposable capital (or £3,000 for assistance by way of representation).
9   *Ibid*, reg 4(c). The figure in divorce is three.
10   See p 253, *ante*.

applicant's confidence[11] (except that he must complete and forward to the legal aid office the appropriate forms and must give to the legal aid authority any additional information that it may require).

3   Criminal cases

Given the fact that in criminal cases a person's liberty is at stake, or has already been curtailed by police action, the importance of availability of advice and assistance in criminal cases is undoubted. Section 1 of the Legal Aid Act 1982 authorised the creation of a scheme for the provision of advice and representation by solicitors in attendance at magistrates' courts, and at police stations. The matter is now governed by the 1988 Act, and regulations made thereunder.

The relevant regulations[12] make provision for the giving of advice to suspects at police stations. Rotas are drawn up, and ensure that a solicitor will be available to attend a police station to advise a person in custody.[13] A solicitor is also available at a magistrates' court to offer assistance by way of representation for the purposes of a bail application, plea in mitigation (where the case is to be dealt with forthwith) or other immediate application to the court. The right does not extend to a person who has already received such assistance, or who has instructed a solicitor privately. Where such advice is given, the provision of advice, or assistance, is not subject to means or to the payment of a contribution.

C   ASSISTANCE BY WAY OF REPRESENTATION

The Legal Aid Act 1979 added to the "green form scheme " provisions that entitled the giving of "assistance by way of representation"[14] which means taking on a person's behalf any step in the institution or conduct of any proceedings, whether before a court or tribunal or in connection with a statutory enquiry, whether by representing him in those proceedings or otherwise. This provision is potentially of very far-reaching effect because it extends the scope of legal aid to tribunals (which were, in general, outside the scope of the scheme prior to the 1979 Act).[15] The scheme does not apply to advice or assistance given in connection with any proceedings in which there is already in existence a legal aid certificate or (in criminal proceedings) a legal aid order.[16] Regulations specify the proceedings to which the scheme applies. Under the regulations currently in operation[17] it extends to domestic proceedings in magistrates' courts, proceedings before a Mental Health Review Tribunal, Parole Board and to representation of a parent or guardian in certain matters involving the adoption of a child. It has been extended to proceedings before boards of visitors of custodial

---

11   Legal Aid Act 1988, s 31(1). Note that legal representatives may disclose to the Legal Aid Board, or a person acting on the Board's authority, information relating to the case of clients or former clients who are, or were, legally aided: Legal Aid (Disclosure of Information) Regulations 1991 (SI 1991/1753).

12   Legal Advice and Assistance (Scope) Regulations 1989 (SI 1989/340), reg 7. See Duty Solicitor Arrangements 1990.

13   See, further, p 315, *post.*.

14   Added to the scheme by Legal Aid Act 1979, s 1. See, now, Legal Aid Act 1988, ss 2(3), 8(2).

15   Legal Aid Act 1988, Sch 2, Part II, para 1.

16   1988 Act, s 8(5).

17   Legal Advice and Assistance (Scope) Regulations 1989, SI 1989/550, reg 9.

institutions[18] in consequence of public disquiet as to the safeguards available to prisoners appearing before such bodies. It is also sometimes available in the county court.[19]

D   LEGAL AID IN CIVIL PROCEEDINGS

I   Courts and proceedings in which legal aid is authorised by the Act

Legal aid is now available in connection with proceedings (unless specifically excepted) in the House of Lords, the Court of Appeal, the High Court, the Employment Appeal Tribunal, any county court, coroners' courts, proceedings in the Restrictive Practices Court under Part III of the Fair Trading Act 1973, and proceedings in the Lands Tribunal. It is also available in certain proceedings in magistrates' courts, notably proceedings under the Family Law Act 1996, the Guardianship of Minors Acts 1971 and 1973 and in certain proceedings under the Children Act 1989.

There are, however, excepted proceedings in respect of which aid is not, at present, authorised under the Act. Of these the more important are proceedings wholly or partly in respect of defamation,[20] and undefended matrimonial proceedings[1] (that is to say proceedings for divorce or judicial separation). Where a legal aid order is made for the purpose of proceedings, that order extends to the costs of a reference to the European Court of Justice[2] since the reference to that court is simply a step in the proceedings in which it is made.[3]

Legal aid is not available in proceedings before judicial and administrative tribunals, which most people[4] consider a notable omission in view of the increasing volume, and importance, of business dealt with therein, particularly in industrial tribunals. It is for this reason that the provisions described above or assistance by way of representation are potentially so important. Nor, of course, is legal aid available in arbitrations. This may seem to confer a considerable benefit upon defendants (especially where they have insurers behind them) who can invoke an arbitration clause thereby preventing an impecunious plaintiff from pursuing his rights with proper legal representation. The mere fact that the plaintiff is insolvent does not prevent the defendant from obtaining a stay,[5] although if it appears that his insolvency was caused by the defendant's breaches of contract a stay may be refused[6] (with the result that the action will proceed and the plaintiff may apply for legal aid). Legal aid is not available for representation before coroner's courts.

2   Conditions under which aid may be granted

Any person, not being a body corporate or an unincorporated body,[7] may apply for legal aid irrespective of nationality or residence. He must, however, be within the

18   *Ibid*, reg 9(1).
19   *Ibid*, reg 8.
20   1988 Act, Sch 2, Part II, para 1.
1   See Civil Legal Aid (Matrimonial Proceedings) Regulations 1989 (SI 1989/549).
2   See p 117, *ante*.
3   *R v Marlborough Street Stipendiary Magistrate, ex parte Bouchereau* [1977] 3 All ER 365; [1977] 1 WLR 414.
4   For criticism of the current position, see Farmer *Tribunals and Inquiries* (Weidenfeld & Nicholson).
5   *Smith v Pearl Assurance Co Ltd* [1939] 1 All ER 95.
6   *Fakes v Taylor Woodrow Construction Ltd* [1973] QB 436; [1973] 1 All ER 670.
7   Legal Aid Act 1988, s 2(10).

prescribed financial limits, this being the first condition precedent to the grant of legal aid. His "disposable income" must not exceed the specified limit. Disposable income and disposable capital are assessed by the assessment officer of the Benefits Agency in the light of the Legal Aid (Assessment of Resources) Regulations 1989 as amended. These regulations are complex. It is important to note that disposable income[8] is far less than gross income. Deductions are prescribed in respect of the maintenance of dependants, income tax, interest on loan, rent and other matters. A spouse's resources are, as a rule, treated as the applicant's resources for these purposes, and regard may also be had to property of which the applicant has disposed.[9] A common criticism of the disposable capital limit is that it tends to penalise those who have been prudent enough to accumulate modest savings. The Royal Commission on Legal Services, among several recommendations concerning legal aid, advice and assistance, stated that the underlying principle should be that an assisted person "should not suffer an undue financial burden in pursuing his legal rights",[10] that the eligibility limits be abolished, that the free limit of disposable income and capital should be increased, and that the contribution proportion above the free limits be reduced to one fifth. This approach has not, generally, been adopted.

The second condition precedent to a grant of legal aid is that the applicant must show that he has reasonable grounds for taking, defending or being a party to the proceedings.[11] In particular a certificate will not be granted in respect of proceedings at first instance where it appears to the Board that the proceedings are too trivial or simple to warrant the assistance of a solicitor, that the applicant would gain only a trivial advantage from the proceedings, that the applicant could finance the proceedings from another source, or the applicant is a member of an organisation which might help him.[12]

The Middleton Committee[13] considered that changes should be made to the merits test approach. In part these changes (necessary if legal aid is to be confined to available resources) would tighten up the test, by providing for on going review of the merits of a case at various stages during the life of a case, with judges having the power to refer a case back to the Legal Aid Board for a fresh assessment of merits. However, the Board relies largely on information supplied by the applicant's lawyers, and, Middleton concluded, "there is too much scope for manipulation and not enough for control". The Report considered that a change in the law was required, and suggested two options. The first was to make the availability of legal aid depend directly on the availability of contractual capacity. Legal aid would be granted on a "first come, first served" basis, albeit with some provision for urgent cases. This approach was not favoured by the report, a second option being preferred. This involves allowing the extent to which the merits criteria had to be satisfied to differ between different types of case. In lower priority cases, the chances of success would have to be higher than those in higher priority cases. The changes now proposed by the Government do not adopt either of these two approaches. The Middleton Report also considered how merits could be more objectively assessed, and recommended a greater degree of monitoring. The Lord Chancellor has decided that the law should be amended to require applicants' solicitors to give the Legal Aid Board a precise percentage prospect of the success of

8   Receipts are "income" only if they have an element of recurrence so that ad hoc gifts are not income: *R v Supplementary Benefits Commission, ex parte Singer* [1973] 2 All ER 931; [1973] 1 WLR 713.
9   Civil Legal Aid (Assessment of Resources) Regulations 1989 (SI 1989/338), reg 9.
10   Report, para 12.28.
11   Civil Legal Aid (General) Regulations 1989 (SI 1989/339), reg 15(2), (3).
12   *Ibid*, regs 29, 30.
13   See p 288, *post*.

the case, and has suggested that the threshold for legal aid should be as high as a 75% likelihood of success.

If a certificate is granted it may be marked with a contribution payable by the assisted litigant. The maximum contribution in proceedings is all the assisted person's disposable capital above a prescribed figure and one-quarter of the amount by which his annual disposable income exceeds a prescribed figure.[14]

3   Application for a certificate

An application for a legal aid certificate must be made on one of the forms approved for the purpose. It may include an application for an "emergency certificate", which may be granted where delay would cause a risk of miscarriage of justice or an unreasonable degree of hardship or other problems in the handling of the case; emergency certificates will usually authorise only the taking of immediate steps in order to protect the interests of the applicant. Some time will usually elapse between the making of an application and its determination, this time being mainly attributable to the financial assessment, usually based on interview, which is undertaken by the legal aid assessment officers of the Department of Social Security. The area legal aid director office may grant a certificate, although only the area committee can refuse an application.[15]

Assuming that the applicant's means qualify him for legal aid, he must still satisfy other criteria before a certificate will be granted.[16] In particular he must be regarded as having a reasonable case on its merits (for which purpose the opinion of counsel is often required). The certificate may be, and often is, limited to the taking of certain steps in the action. Thus, in the first instance it is frequently limited to the taking of counsel's opinion, on the basis of which the Legal Aid Board will consider whether to amend the certificate so as to extend it to enable further steps to be taken in the action or, on the contrary, to discharge it. By these powers of amendment and discharge it is possible for the Legal Aid Board to supervise the conduct of the litigation to some extent, or at least to see, as far as possible, that large amounts of costs are not expended in pursuing hopeless lost causes, but the observations of the Middleton Committee, noted above, as to the difficulties of monitoring this must be borne in mind. There is, of course, a duty on both solicitors and counsel to advise against the pursuit of cases which do not justify the support of the legal aid fund.

4   The effects on the proceedings of a party being aided

a   Relationship between the assisted litigant and his solicitor and counsel

The professional relationship of solicitor and client is not prejudiced by the fact of the client being in receipt of legal aid. The solicitor's general duties are still owed to the client and he has authority to act for the client, unless the act performed is not within the scope of the certificate. Thus it has been held[17] that a solicitor is under a duty not to instruct leading counsel, even though authorised by the legal aid authority so to do, without first obtaining the client's specific agreement and authority after informing

14   Legal Aid Act 1988, s 9(1). The figures are regularly varied by regulations under section 9, cf Civil Legal Aid (Assessment of Resources) Regulations 1989 (SI 1989/388).
15   Civil Legal Aid (General) Regulations, reg 38(1)(a), (b).
16   See p 283, *ante*.
17   *Re Solicitors* [1982] 2 All ER 683; [1982] 1 WLR 745.

him of the probable cost and the potential effect upon the client's assets having regard to the Board's charge on property recovered or preserved in the action (as to which see *infra*). The solicitor must preserve his client's confidences though he is in some cases obliged to furnish information to the legal aid committees that would normally be privileged.

The chief effect of legal aid on the solicitor-client relationship is upon costs. The solicitor has no right to any costs from the client and he must not charge or take any sum in respect of costs. It follows that any item of costs incurred by a solicitor which is not allowed under the legal aid order is irrecoverable so that a disbursement of this nature will have to be met by the solicitor personally. In most proceedings the court must order the assisted person's costs to be taxed, on a "standard" basis.[18]

After taxation the solicitor may recover from the fund the full amount allowed on taxation for disbursements and profit costs.[19] The relevant factors to be taken into account are discussed later.[20] However taxation is not necessary where an assisted litigant is successful and the costs payable by the other party are agreed with the assisted party's solicitor and counsel (if any).[1]

b   Assisted litigant's liability for costs

An assisted person has, as stated above, no liability for costs towards his own solicitor and counsel. His primary liability to the legal aid fund is limited to the amount of his contribution. However, if he loses his action he may be ordered to pay the costs of the other side. This does not mean that he must pay the full taxed costs of his opponent. His liabilities are limited to such amount (if any) which is a reasonable one for him to pay, having regard to the means of all the parties and their conduct in connection with the dispute.[2] In determining this amount, the assisted person's dwelling house, household furniture and tools and implements of his trade are not to be taken into account.[3] In addition the order may direct payment by instalments or may suspend payment *sine die*. The order may, however, be varied within six years if circumstances change.

An assisted person cannot be required by the court to pay the costs of an unsuccessful interlocutory application forthwith.[4] Also, an assisted person is not usually ordered to give security for costs although such an order can be, and has been, made.[5]

If the assisted litigant is awarded costs, these are payable by his opponent in the ordinary way. These costs are paid directly into the legal aid fund maintained by the Board. If the sums paid out by the Board to the assisted person's solicitor and counsel exceed the amount paid in, comprising the assisted person's contribution and costs recovered from the other side, the Board has a first charge for the balance on any property recovered or preserved in the proceedings, with certain exemptions, notably maintenance in matrimonial proceedings.[6] Thus if an assisted person is successful the public will not (unless the other side is also legally aided) generally be the loser, which is the reason for the public cost of the legal aid scheme being relatively so low.

---

18   See Civil Legal Aid (General) Regulations 1989 (1989/339), reg 105, and p 429, *post*.
19   See, generally, *ibid*, regs 105, 107.
20   See p 428, *post*.
1   For remuneration agreements, see p 259, *ante*.
2   Legal Aid Act 1988, ss 12, 17(1).
3   *Ibid*, s 17(3), and General Regulations (*supra*, n 18) reg 126a.
4   *Ibid*, reg 124.
5   *Wyld v Silver (No 2)* [1962] 2 All ER 809; [1962] 1 WLR 863.
6   1988 Act, s 16(6).

c   Unassisted person's rights to costs

It follows from the preceding paragraph that the unassisted litigant appearing against an assisted litigant is at a substantial disadvantage in the matter of costs. If he loses he pays full costs; if he wins he recovers only limited costs, or, as often as not, no costs at all. It was to remedy this serious abuse that the Legal Aid Act 1964 was passed. This Act (the relevant provisions of which are now contained in sections 13 and 18 of the 1988 Act) was at first interpreted and applied by the courts in a very restrictive manner,[7] so much so that over the period of three years after the passing of the Act, Parliament provided no less than £120,000 for the purposes of the Act, of which only £1,155 was used. However, in *Hanning v Maitland (No 2)*[8] the Court of Appeal laid down broader principles for the application of the Act, stating that if the legally aided party lost the action it was usually just and equitable that the unassisted party should recover his costs from public funds, unless, for example, he has done something to bring the action on himself or has been guilty of misconduct.

The 1988 Act now provides that an unassisted party appearing against an assisted party may be awarded the whole or any part of his costs out of the legal aid fund, provided that the proceedings are finally decided in favour of the unassisted party,[9] that those proceedings were instituted by the assisted party in the court of first instance and provided "the court is satisfied that the unassisted party will suffer severe financial hardship unless the order is made".[10] "Severe financial hardship" is not, however, strictly interpreted so that in *Hanning v Maitland (No 2)*, Lord Denning MR stated that the condition should not be construed so as to exclude people of modest income or modest capital who would find it hard to bear their own costs. A company may suffer "severe financial hardship".[11] Furthermore no order is to be made unless an order in favour of the unassisted party would be made apart from this Act; thus, in divorce suits a wife is not usually ordered to pay her husband's costs, unless she has sufficient separate estate. If an assisted wife would not be required to pay her unassisted husband's costs, the latter has no recourse to the fund.[12]

Apart from the above provisions, which affect costs, proceedings are not generally affected by one or more of the parties being legally aided. Indeed proceedings may be lengthened since litigants are naturally not anxious to compromise proceedings which they are fighting at the public expense. This is one of the principal criticisms of the scheme to which may be added the fact that legal aid is not available before most tribunals and the inequitable position of the unassisted litigant, particularly where he is a plaintiff (and therefore at any rate at first instance, outside the scope of the provisions for payment of his costs out of the fund). For this reason insurance companies in industrial injuries actions often make payments in settlement of unmeritorious claims by legally aided plaintiffs, simply because, in the long run, this will prove a less expensive expedient than contesting the case successfully. There is a further anomaly

---

7   See *Nowotnik v Nowotnik* [1967] P 83; [1965] 3 All ER 167; *Re Spurling's Will Trusts* [1966] 1 All ER 745; [1966] 1 WLR 920; *Re SL (infants)* [1967] 3 All ER 538; [1967] 1 WLR 1379.
8   [1970] 1 QB 580; [1970] 1 All ER 812.
9   Legal Aid Act 1988, ss 13, 18.
10   *Ibid*. The party will be entitled only to payment of that amount which would cause him hardship not to recover: see *Adams v Riley* [1988] QB 372; [1988] 1 All ER 89.
11   *R & T Thew Ltd v Reeves* [1982] QB 172; [1981] 2 All ER 964; in *Kelly v London Transport Executive* (*supra*) the Court of Appeal, with apparent reluctance, felt unable to accede to the defendants' bold contention that the loss of £8,000 in costs would amount to severe financial hardship. For the position of a local authority, see *R v Greenwich London Borough Council, ex parte Lovelace (No 2)* [1992] QB 155; [1992] 1 All ER 679 (no reason why local authority should not establish "severe hardship").
12   *Povey v Povey* [1972] Fam 40; [1970] 3 All ER 612.

in that a successful assisted litigant appearing against another assisted litigant may well find himself in a worse position than if he were unassisted since an assisted party cannot obtain an order against the fund, whereas the property he recovers will be subject to the Legal Aid Board's statutory charge.

E   LEGAL AID IN CRIMINAL PROCEEDINGS

Legal aid in criminal cases is granted by the court. In contrast to civil proceedings, the order is made by the court. Either the court of trial or the magistrates' court committing a case for trial may grant legal aid, as may either the Court of Appeal (Criminal Division) or the Crown Court in dealing with an appeal.[13]

In most cases the grant of legal aid is discretionary.[14] The test to be applied is that it should appear to the court "to be desirable to do so in the interests of justice". In deciding that question, the court will have regard to certain factors:[15]

(1)   whether, in the event of conviction, it is likely that the court would impose a sentence which would either deprive the accused of his liberty, or lead to loss of his livelihood, or seriously damage his reputation;

(2)   whether the case may involve consideration of a substantial question of law;

(3)   whether the accused may be unable to understand the proceedings or state his own case, either through lack of knowledge of English or through mental or physical disability;

(4)   whether the nature of the defence is such as to involve the tracing and interviewing of potential defence witnesses or expert cross-examination of the prosecution witnesses; and

(5)   whether it is in the interests of a person other than the accused that the accused should be represented.

Whilst any doubt should be resolved in favour of the accused,[16] it is clear that these criteria give considerable discretion to the deciding court.

Given the different time scale within which the criminal process works, any assessment of resources or contribution by the accused may take place after an order has been made. However a court, before it makes a legal aid order, must require the applicant to furnish a written statement of means and, if it appears from this statement that he will be required to make a contribution and has the means to make an immediate payment, may refuse an order unless the applicant first makes a payment on account.[17] In magistrates' courts the application is initially dealt with by the clerk to the justices. If he refuses legal aid, appeal may be to an area committee if the offence is triable on indictment or "either way"[18] or to the justices themselves in the case of summary offences. The legal aid order will be a "through" order which covers the Crown Court as well as the committal proceedings.[19] As well as hearing appeals from refusals of

13   Legal Aid Act 1988, ss 20(3), (6).
14   But a grant is compulsory if an application is made when a person has been committed for trial on a charge of murder, where the prosecution are appealing (or apply for leave to appeal) to the House of Lords, where a person is at risk of being remanded in custody for a second time and wishes representation, and where a person is kept in custody for the preparation of reports (1988 Act, s 21(3)).
15   Legal Aid Act 1988, s 22(2).
16   *Ibid*, s 21(7).
17   *Ibid*, s 24(1).
18   See p 469, *post*.
19   1988 Act, s 20(5).

legal aid by a magistrates' court, criminal legal aid committees deal with two other matters; firstly, where there is an application to a magistrates' court for the assignment of counsel in proceedings in that court under a legal aid order the court, if it does not grant the application, must refer it to the committee; secondly, applications by solicitors for prior authority to incur expenditure on obtaining an expert's or other report, bespeaking transcripts of shorthand notes or tape recordings of any proceedings or "performing an act which is either unusual in its nature or involves unusually large expenditure" must be made direct to the committee.[20]

As a rule legal aid consists of representation by a solicitor and counsel and includes advice on the preparation of the accused's case. However in magistrates' courts legal aid does not extend to representation by counsel except in the case of an unusually grave or difficult indictable offence, while in certain cases there is power to order legal aid to consist of representation by counsel only.[1]

An assisted person may be ordered by the court to pay such contribution as appears reasonable, having regard to his commitments and resources. A contribution may be ordered to be paid by instalments. If the assisted person fails to pay any contribution, or any instalment thereof, this may be recovered in a magistrates' court as a civil debt or enforced as a judgment debt in the High Court or a county court.[2]

F   REFORM OF LEGAL AID

I   The Middleton Report

The establishment of the Middleton Committee, its statement of underlying principle, and its detailed proposals relating to the merits test have already been noted.[3] It identified the rapid growth in cost of the scheme, the lack of satisfactory mechanisms for controlling that growth, the inability to target resources on priority areas and to address unmet need and poor value for money as the main problems inherent in the current system. The agenda for change is thus motivated by economic considerations, although the interrelationship between reform of the civil justice system and of the legal aid scheme should be borne in mind. The Report identified several changes that might be made to support the civil justice reform: more funding for advice agencies and law centres, funding for alternative dispute resolution, direct financial help for litigants in person (eg for expert reports, court fees and travel costs) and representation before tribunals or coroners' inquests. However, such changes were not attainable unless the total level of spending on legal aid could be controlled. Better value for money was desirable but difficult to achieve.

The Report proposed reform both in respect of the supply of legal services (the costs of each case) and the demand for legal aid (the number of cases). In relation to the supply of legal services, the Report proposed that the Legal Aid Board should use its purchasing power to contract for legal services in a pro-active way, setting requirements of quality, access and seeking the best possible price. Only those who have a contract with the Legal Aid Board should be able to do legal aid work. Contracts could cover large blocks of work, and the Legal Aid Board would be able to compare work done, the price charged and the outcomes achieved. Such contracts might be with persons other than members of the legal profession. All this could be developed as part of the

---

20   Legal Aid in Criminal and Care Proceedings (General) Regulations 1989 (SI 1989/344), reg 44(1).
1   *Ibid*, reg 44(1).
2   1988 Act, Sch 3, para 1.
3   See pp 279 and 283, *ante*.

franchising system, with the emphasis changing from the evaluation of management systems and processes to quality of work. Fixed prices might be achieved, with solicitor providers negotiating in turn with counsel expert witnesses and other persons working within the system. This approach of course mirrors that commonly adopted in many walks of life: the Legal Aid Board would, in principle, be operating in the same way as a supermarket does with its suppliers, creating competition amongst suppliers and efficiency. There is, however, a danger that only established or favoured suppliers of legal services would succeed in being granted contracts. The potential for the Legal Aid Board to provide services directly, through employing its own staff was also not ruled out by the Report.

The second aspect of the approach of the report is to concentrate on controlling demand. The approach of the Report to changes in the merits test have already been discussed.[4]

Finally, in dealing with legal aid, the report considered the financial conditions on which legal aid in civil cases should be granted. Middleton considered that people with legal aid should pay as much as they could afford to the costs of their case, that they should be required to think carefully about the commencement and pursuance of their case, and that legally aided litigants should be in a better position than other litigants as little as possible. The statutory charge should be amended to include a contribution from the value a person has in the value of his own home, all should pay a minimum contribution (even those on income support), as a sign of commitment to the case. On balance, the Report did not favour that the removal of the statutory protection against inter party costs should be abolished. Fear of debt could act as an unreasonable deterrent to the pursuit of an important and meritorious case. However, the Report conceded that costs orders could and should be made in more cases than currently occurs. The Report also supported a proposal to relax the test (from "severe financial hardship" to "financial hardship") for ordering a payment from the legal aid fund to a successful unassisted litigant.

2 The Government's Reform Proposals

Following the publication of the Middleton Report, the Government announced its plans for the reform of the civil justice and legal aid systems.[5] The two aspects are inextricably linked. Reform of the civil justice process is seen as necessary to drive down costs for the benefit of individual litigants and the taxpayer, to ensure accessibility for everybody, not just the very poor and the very rich, and to reduce the current weaknesses in the system (excessive delay, complexity and cost). The proposals for legal aid would improve access and achieve better value for money in a scheme where costs had significantly escalated.

The main proposals, following the principles set out by the Middleton Report, were as follows:

(1) Legal aid work was to be restricted to those providers who had a contract with the Legal Aid Board.
(2) The Board would purchase services, at agreed, fixed prices, in accordance with regionally agreed purchasing plans;
(3) Contracting would extend to criminal as well as civil legal aid;
(4) The merits test was to be tightened;

4   See p 283, *ante*.
5   See Consultation Paper, *op cit*, discussed further at p 279, *ante*.

(5) A special fund was to be considered for those public interest cases where it was plainly in the public interest for a particular point of law needed to be examined, or for a precedent to be established;

(6) Most claims for money would be excluded from the legal aid scheme. Legal aid would remain for the defence of criminal cases, child care cases, judicial review and social welfare cases (eg the threat of homelessness and the enforcement of statutory rights).

(7) Conditional fee agreements[6] are to be extended to all civil proceedings other than family cases. This is a major shift.

(8) The small claims procedure in the county is court to be extended by raising the limit from £3,000 to £5,000, except for personal injury claims, which will be limited to £1,000.

(9) "Fast track" and "multi track" routes through the civil justice system, with greater influence in the hands of the courts in respect of case management.

This radical approach met fierce criticism in the light of the widespread introduction of conditional fee litigation ("no win, no fee" arrangements). In the light of that criticism, a Consultation Paper was published in March 1998 with revised proposals. Under these revised proposals, which are likely to be implemented during 1998, legal aid would be abolished for personal injury cases, which amount to some 80,000 cases each years. The effect of this change is that potentially such litigants will pay up to £100 million in meeting the success fee payable to the solicitor, compared with the saving to the Legal Aid Board of approximately £30 million per annum. The scope for conditional fee agreement is to be expanded, and the "success fee" element of such arrangements would be payable by the loser, as well as the legal insurance payments made as part of the arrangements by the victor. For the immediate future, legal aid is to be retained in medical negligence cases, which would, however, be handled by specialist solicitors. Legal aid is also to be removed from disputes about wills or inheritance, trust administration or trustees, company directors and other company law matters including minority shareholder actions, Lands Tribunals cases and boundary or business disputes. The effect of these changes will be to remove legal aid from approximately 60% of cases. A "transitional" fund run by the Legal Aid Board will give assistance with public interest cases and deserving claims that lawyers might find prohibitively expensive.

This change of emphasis since the original announcements in October 1997 has been broadly welcomed, but concern clearly exists as to the capacity of the legal profession, and the insurance industry, to cope with a large expansion, in the short-term, of conditional fee arrangements. Concerns still remain that the changes may lead to injustices. Legal practice may change in nature and extent with the bigger assumption of risk by the lawyer, as opposed to the Legal Aid Fund, possibly leading to the creation of larger legal firms, with mergers increasingly commonplace.

6   *Ibid.*

CHAPTER 14

The Police and Law Enforcement[1]

A THE LAW ENFORCEMENT FUNCTION

Law enforcement is primarily, but not exclusively, in the hands of the 43 police forces of England and Wales. Whilst individuals have both rights and duties in respect of law enforcement and keeping the peace, it would be idle to pretend that a police constable is simply "a citizen in uniform". Every police officer holds the office of constable,[2] and legal authority may stem from that fact, but the reality is that police officers form part of an organisation with its own command structure, and are governed by detailed regulations dealing with conditions of employment, personal conduct and discipline.[3]

Other organisations play a role in law enforcement. Besides the police forces that exist under the Police Act 1964, there are specialist police forces such as the Ministry of Defence Police, and British Transport Police. Officers of such forces likewise hold the office of constable.[4] Nor should the role of other investigatory agencies be overlooked. The Serious Fraud Office was created by the Criminal Justice Act 1987 to "investigate any suspected offence that appears on reasonable grounds to involve serious or complex fraud." The Director of the Serious Fraud Office is given wide ranging legal powers to assist in the investigation and prosecution of such offences.[5] Likewise the Department of Trade and Industry has wide-ranging investigative powers under the Companies Acts. Other bodies such as the Inland Revenue, Customs and Excise,[6] Health and Safety Executive and local authorities have investigative powers

---

1 The literature on the police is extensive. See, in particular, *Royal Commission on Criminal Procedure*, 1981, Cmnd 8092, and the various research studies undertaken (set out at Annex D to the Report). For the current law, see Bevan and Lidstone *A Guide to Police Powers* (1996, Butterworths). For the police more generally see Lustgarten *The Governance of Police* (1986, Sweet & Maxwell).
2 Police Act 1996, s 30.
3 Police Regulations 1987 (SI 1987/851); Police (Discipline) Regulations 1985 (SI 1985/1805).
4 See *Halsbury's Laws* (4th Edn), paras 211–219.
5 The extension of these powers has been controversial. See *Smith v Director of Serious Fraud Office* [1992] 3 All ER 456. See, generally, pp 508–509, *post*.
6 For discussion of the powers of the Revenue Departments, see the Keith Report: *Enforcement Powers of the Revenue Departments* (1985, Cmnd 8822/9120/9440, HMSO).

of importance. Nevertheless it is the police who perform the bulk of investigatory and law enforcement work. On occasions that may be with the assistance of the armed forces. They are, however, acting in aid of the civil power, and have no special legal rights.[7]

1   The role of the individual

All individuals have a duty to preserve the peace, though this is a duty of "imperfect obligation"[8] in the sense that, generally, there is no sanction for breach of that duty. A citizen who without physical impossibility or lawful excuse fails to assist a constable to restore the peace when that constable has reasonable necessity for calling on that citizen for assistance is guilty of an offence at common law.[9] The duty, though, goes further. In *Albert v Lavin*[10] Lord Diplock stated:

"every citizen in whose presence a breach of the peace is being, or reasonably appears to be about to be, committed has the right to take reasonable steps to make the person who is breaking or threatening to break the peace refrain from doing so; and those reasonable steps in appropriate cases will include detaining him against his will".

An individual is not liable in law for failure to preserve the peace in this way. By contrast, a constable may be guilty of the offence of misconduct in a public office.[11] A citizen also has more limited powers of arrest than a constable in respect of arrestable offences which are in fact occurring, or where there are reasonable grounds to believe that they have occurred.[12] It is these powers that are used by so-called "store detectives", who are, in reality, no more than citizens relying on their individual rights under law.

Apart from the above, a citizen has, generally, no duty to assist the police. The law proceeds also on the basis of a "right to silence" of an individual. Generally, there is no obligation to answer police questions or to co-operate with the police, though there is certainly a duty not to mislead.[13] Occasionally, the exercise of the right to silence in an abusive way may come close to criminal conduct.[14]

2   The organisation of the police

Police structures were radically changed by the Police Act 1964,[15] by the Police and Criminal Evidence Act 1984 and by the Police and Magistrates' Courts Act 1994. The relevant provisions were consolidated by the Police Act 1996. Policing has historically been organised around local structures. Policing arrangements are, for the most part,

---

7   *Charge to the Bristol Grand Jury* (1832) 172 ER 962; *A-G for Northern Ireland's Reference (No 1 of 1975)* [1977] AC 105; [1976] 2 All ER 937; *R v Clegg* [1995] 1 AC 482; [1995] 1 All ER 334.
8   Per Lord Diplock in *Albert v Lavin*, n 10 below.
9   *R v Brown* (1841) Car & M 314; 174 ER 522.
10   [1982] AC 546; [1981] 3 All ER 878.
11   *R v Dytham* [1979] QB 722; [1979] 3 All ER 641.
12   See s 24 of the Police and Criminal Evidence Act 1984, and p 303, *post*.
13   *Rice v Connolly* [1966] 2 QB 414; [1966] 2 All ER 649.
14   *Ricketts v Cox* (1981) 74 Cr App Rep 298; *Green v Director of Public Prosecutions* (1991) 155 JP 816.
15   Passed to implement the *Report of the Royal Commission on the Police* (1962, Cmnd 1728). For discussion of this, and of the historical development, see Lustgarten, *op cit*, pp 32–52.

on a local basis. The 1996 Act authorises the creation of police authorities for each police area. There are currently 43 police areas in England and Wales, two in London. Different policing arrangements exist for the Metropolis of London from the rest of England and Wales. In the Metropolis, the Home Secretary is the police authority. Outside London, the police authority comprises members of the local authorities, justices of the peace and members nominated by the Home Secretary.[16]

There is no direct democratic element in the management of policing. Indirect democratic input is achieved through the representatives of local authorities. In addition s 96 of the Police Act 1996 states that

"arrangements shall be made in each police area for obtaining the view of people in that area about matters concerning the policing of that area and their co-operation with the police in preventing crime in that area."[17]

The duty of the police authority is "to secure the maintenance of an adequate and efficient police force for its area".[18] To achieve that the authority is required, subject to the approval of the Home Secretary, to appoint a Chief Constable.[19] The number of officers employed generally is a matter for the police authority. It may contract for the supply of goods and services in its own right,[20] although it should be noted that the Home Secretary has the power to provide and maintain, or to contribute to the provisions of, such services as he considers necessary for promoting the efficiency and effectiveness of the police. The authority must, in the performance of its functions, have regard to objectives set by itself, by the Home Secretary and to performance targets set by itself and by any local policing plan.[1] Every authority is under a duty to set out, in a policing plan, the proposed arrangements for the policing of the authority's area each year. Of course, this is in addition to any input into any other relevant plan, such as the Youth Justice Plan.[2] Before issuing any such policing plan, the authority must consult with the Chief Constable.[3] However, all this seeming local autonomy vested in police authorities is not, however, quite what it seems.

a   Police authorities and central government

The key role of the Home Secretary in approving the appointment of Chief Constables has already been seen. Approval is also required for the removal of a Chief Constable.[4] Nor are the rights of the authority in respect of information unfettered. A Chief Constable who is unwilling to disclose information in a report requested by the police authority may refer the request to the Secretary of State for decision.[5] In addition, the Home Secretary can, where it is expedient in the interests of justice, safety or public

---

16   See 1996 Act, s 4.
17   For alternative possibilities for local accountability, see Police Act (Northern Ireland) 1970, commented upon by Dickson ((1988) 39 NILQ) and Walker ((1990) 41 NILQ 105).
18   Police Act 1996, s 6.
19   *Ibid*, s 11.
20   *Ibid*, s 18.
1   *Ibid*, s 8. For challenge to the power of the Home Secretary to supply such equipment at the request of a Chief Constable, but without the agreement of or request from the police authority, see *R v Secretary of State for Home Department, ex parte Northumbria Police Authority* [1989] QB 26; [1988] 1 All ER 556. Such action was held to be lawful under s 41 of the Police Act 1964, and by virtue of the royal prerogative.
2   Crime and Disorder Act 1998, s 40.
3   1996 Act, s 6.
4   See s 11(2).
5   *Ibid*, s 22(5).

order that a police force be reinforced, direct that such reinforcement or other assistance be given to enable that force to meet special demands on its resources.[6] That can be done on the application of the Chief Constable, and does not require the agreement of the police authority.

The Home Secretary has a wide range of powers under the Police Act 1996, which are to be exercised "in such manner and to such extent as appears to him to be best calculated to promote the efficiency of the police".[7] The compulsory retirement of a Chief Constable in the interests of efficiency can be required.[8] So too can reports on policing matters, as well as the Annual Report. An inquiry into any matter connected with the policing of any area can be called for.[9] A good example of this power in action is the inquiry held into the conduct of the police investigation into the death of a teenager.[10] It is to the Home Secretary that the Inspectorate of Constabulary report. Adverse comment and report may lead to the withholding of the whole or part of central government grant. That this is no trivial threat is demonstrated by the fact that substantial elements of expenditure are met by central government. By section 46 of the 1996 Act, the Home Secretary makes a block grant to each police authority. The threat to withhold grant is a powerful one, and can be used as a lever to secure change in the way a force is run.[11]

In addition to this range of statutory powers, the existence of the royal prerogative should not be ignored. The prerogative allows all reasonably necessary steps to be taken to ensure the preservation of the Queen's peace. In *R v Secretary of State for the Home Department, ex parte Northumbria Police Authority*[12] the Court of Appeal ruled that section 41 of the Police Act 1964 (which was then the provision which authorised the Home Secretary provide and maintain central services and other services deemed expedient for promoting the efficiency of the police) authorised the Home Secretary to supply riot control equipment from central stores without the approval of the police authority. Even if section 41 were not to be construed in this way, the action of the Home Secretary would be lawful under the prerogative. Effectively, therefore, the police authority was by-passed, its approval neither forthcoming nor necessary.

It would also be wrong to view police authorities as acting always in isolation. Chief Constables can seek mutual aid from other forces.[13] Regional organisations have from time to time been created, both formally (eg the anti-terrorism squad, regional crime squads) and informally. One example of the former is the national DNA database, managed by the Forensic Science Service.[14] An instance of the latter was the existence of the National Reporting Centre during a controversial industrial dispute in the mid 1980s.[15] Since 1992 there has existed the National Criminal Intelligence Service Authority (NCIS). This is now a statutory body, created by Part I of the Police Act 1997. Its function is to provide criminal intelligence to other police forces and national law enforcement agencies. A Service Authority for NCIS was established by s 1 of the 1997 Act, which, in ss 2 and 3, defines its functions and objectives, and authorises the appointment of a Director-General. The Director-General is to be either an existing

6   *Ibid*, s 24(2).
7   *Ibid*, s 36(1).
8   *Ibid*, s 42(1).
9   *Ibid*, s 36.
10   The Stephen Lawrence Inquiry: see p 206, *ante*.
11   In 1992, adverse reports by the Inspectorate of Constabulary upon the Derbyshire Police led to significant changes in the running of that force.
12   [1989] QB 26; [1988] 1 All ER 556.
13   Police Act 1996, s 24.
14   See p 314, *post*.
15   The national coal miners' strike in 1980. See, generally, Freeman, "Law and Order in 1984" [1984] CLP 175.

Chief Constable, or a person eligible to be promoted to Chief Constable level. The Director reports to the Authority. The Chief Constables of police forces may enter into agreements with NCIS for the performance of certain functions by it,[16] and for the provision of mutual aid by it.[17]

Part II of the 1997 Act creates a new National Crime Squad. This brings together the pre-existing Regional Crime Squads into one organisation. Effectively it has the status of a police force, with a Director-General who has the status and rank of a Chief Constable.[18] A structure similar to that for NCIS is established, with a Service Authority being created. The Squad tackles major crime which crosses force boundaries, and which can better be handled on a national basis. In any debate as to the centralising nature of such arrangements, the key issue is that the policing function be seen to be independent of the political process. It is in that context that the relationship between police authority and Chief Constable is fundamental.

b Police authorities and Chief Constables

Chief Constables have a wide degree of autonomy. Despite the terms of section 6 of the 1996 Act[19] the degree of local influence on Chief Constables is limited. Police authorities have the right to require a report in writing on such matters as may be specified, being matters connected with the policing of their area.[20] That is, though, subject to the Chief Constable's right to refer the request to the Home Secretary if the Chief Constable considers that a report would contain information which ought not, in the public interest, to be disclosed. In addition, a wise Chief Constable will no doubt be at pains to create good working relations with the police authority. Nevertheless, its legal rights are limited. It sets the establishment, and the budget, but, as has been seen, it may be liable for expenditure over which it has no control.

It is sometimes said that Chief Constables cannot be challenged on operational matters. That is an over simplification. The law recognises that it is the Chief Constable who determines strategy and decision-making. The courts have regarded the scope for judicial review of the actions of a Chief Constable to be extremely limited. The deployment of police resources, and individual policing decisions, are matters not for the courts. In *R v Commissioner of Police for the Metropolis, ex parte Blackburn*,[1] the Court of Appeal was considering an application for an order of mandamus to compel the Commissioner to reverse a policy statement which directed his officers not to enforce the Gaming Acts, except in certain circumstances. Lord Denning MR stated.

"I hold it to be the duty of [the Commissioner] as it is of every Chief Constable, to enforce the law of the land. He must take steps so to post his men that crimes must be detected; and that honest citizens may go about their affairs in peace. He must decide whether or not suspected persons are to be prosecuted; and if need be bring the prosecution or see that it is brought. But in all these things he is not the servant of anyone, save of the law itself. No Minister of the Crown can tell him that he must, or must not, prosecute this man or that one. Nor can any police authority tell him to do so. The responsibility for law enforcement lies on him. He is answerable to the law and to the law alone [but] there are many

---

16 Police Act 1997, s 22.
17 *Ibid*, s 23.
18 See 1997 Act, s 52.
19 [1968] 2 QB 118; [1968] 1 All ER 763.
20 Police Act 1996, s 22.
1   [1968] 2 QB 118; [1968] 1 All ER 763.

fields in which they have a discretion with which the law will not interfere it is [for him] to decide in any particular case whether inquiries should be pursued, or whether an arrest should be made. It must be for him to decide on the disposition of his force and the concentration of his resources on any particular crime or area. No court can or should give him direction on such a matter"

The court went on to stress, however, that if what was in issue was, in effect, an abdication of duty then the court could intervene. The matter was not put to the test because the policy statement was withdrawn. Again, in *Holgate-Mohammed v Duke*[2] whilst the House of Lords accepted that police discretion could be the subject of judicial review, provided it was used for a legitimate purpose its use was for the individual officer, not the courts.

These cases, and others like them,[3] do not strictly speaking deal with the relationship between Chief Constable and police authority. Nor is the distinction between operational and non-operational matters set out in those terms. Yet both are implicit from the approach set out above. The courts will concern themselves with issues of legality. That includes not only the existence of the power itself, but also review of police discretion on normal judicial review grounds. Thus if a Chief Constable were to abdicate the exercise of a statutory function, close his mind to the genuine exercise of discretion, or use powers for irrelevant or improper purposes, or in bad faith, the courts could intervene. Within these parameters they will not, even at the instance of the police authority.

c   Chief Constables and individual officers

Police power essentially derives from the office of constable. Section 30 of the Police Act 1996 provides that a member of a police force shall have all the powers and privileges of a constable throughout England and Wales. Constables are office holders under the Crown, though not Crown servants.[4] They are not employees of the local authority[5] nor of the Chief Constable. The consequence of all this is that the powers are those of the constable, although sometimes powers can only be exercised by a police officer holding a certain rank. Thus, an intimate search of a suspect requires authorisation by an officer at least the rank of superintendent.[6] Nor can the officer legally be directed to exercise power in a particular way. Whilst the reality is that a police force will have policing policies and instructions, to which the officer is entitled to have regard, the legal powers are those of the officer. In *Lindley v Rutter*[7] a police officer was held to be acting unlawfully by removing an item of underclothing from a drunken arrested woman. Though power existed at common law to justify such conduct, the officer had, wrongly, regarded a standing instruction as depriving her of any discretion as to whether or not such garments were to be removed from a suspect. She did not therefore address her mind as to whether the legal conditions for the exercise of the power existed.

2   [1984] AC 437; [1984] 1 All ER 1054.
3   See also *R v Commissioner of Police for the Metropolis, ex parte Blackburn (No 3)* [1973] QB 241; [1973] 1 All ER 324; *R v Chief Constable for Devon & Cornwall, ex parte Central Electricity Generating Board* [1982] QB 458; [1981] 3 All ER 826.
4   *A-G for New South Wales v Perpetual Trustee Co Ltd* [1955] AC 457; [1955] 1 All ER 846.
5   *Fisher v Oldham Corporation* [1930] 2 KB 364; [1930] All ER Rep 96.
6   Police and Criminal Evidence Act 1984, s 62 .
7   [1981] QB 128; [1980] 3 WLR 660.

That is not to say that it is always improper to rely on a standing instruction.[8] The reality is different. Individual officers are members of a force hierarchical in nature, and subject to the rules, regulations and discipline of that force. The Chief Constable will set out standing orders and other force policy, compliance with which will be expected. Failure to comply with police discipline will be an offence.[9]

B POLICE ACCOUNTABILITY

The extent to which Chief Constables are accountable to either police authorities or to the Home Secretary has already been discussed. In reality accountability of the police will be through a variety of other mechanisms.

I Rules of evidence

English courts adhere to the principle that it is no part of the courts' task to exclude evidence in order to punish the police. In *R v Leatham*[10] Crompton J observed that:

"It matters not how you get it; if you steal it even, it would be admissible."

However, in criminal cases there rules of admissibility may have the effect of excluding evidence because of the way it has been obtained. Thus section 76(2) of the Police and Criminal Evidence Act 1984 provides that the prosecution must show beyond reasonable doubt that a confession[11] was not obtained (a) by oppression of the person who made it; or (b) in consequence of anything said or done which was likely, in all the circumstances existing at the time, to render unreliable any confession which might be made by him in consequence thereof. "Oppression" carries its ordinary, natural meaning, that being "the exercise of authority or power in a burdensome, harsh or wrongful manner; unjust or cruel treatment of subjects , inferiors, etc., the imposition of unreasonable or unjust burdens."[12] Deliberate or gross police misconduct, judged in the context of the individual characteristics of the suspect, will amount to oppression, and can include not only physical mistreatment but also conduct such as gross bullying.[13] Systematic schemes of deliberate police misconduct are likely to cause any confession obtained to be excluded. Alternatively, and more likely, the police misconduct (even if not deliberate) may cause a confession to be (or likely to be) unreliable and, again excluded. The conduct will have to be considered in the light of personal characteristics of the suspect.

An alternative, and extremely important, provision is the discretion to exclude confessions by section 78 of the Police and Criminal Evidence Act 1984. Section 78 gives to the court a discretion to exclude evidence on which the prosecution proposes to rely where to admit it would create unfairness to the proceedings. The use of this discretion has meant that where police impropriety has led to potential unfairness in the proceedings then evidence may well be excluded. For this reason, significant and substantial breaches of the Codes of Practice which govern the exercise of police

8   Compare *Middleweek v Chief Constable of Merseyside* [1992] 1 AC 179n; [1990] 3 All ER 662.
9   See Police (Discipline) Regulations 1985 (SI 1985/1805).
10   [1861–73] All ER Rep Ext 1646, (1861) 8 Cox CC498; 121 ER 589.
11   Defined by PACE, s 82(3) as a statement wholly or partly adverse to the by words or otherwise.
12   *R v Fulling* [1987] QB 426, [1987] 2 All ER 65.
13   See *R v Miller* (1992) 97 Cr App Rep 99; cf *R v Emmerson* (1990) 92 Cr App Rep 284.

powers, or with the provisions of the law itself, have often led to the exclusion of evidence obtained by the police improperly.[14] Section 78 applies to both confession and non confession evidence. In *R v Mason*[15] a confession was obtained after the police had represented falsely to the accused, and to his solicitor, that they had found incriminating fingerprints. In quashing the conviction the Court of Appeal laid stress upon the fact that, but for the deceit, the accused would not have made a self-incriminatory statement. In *Mason*, section 78 was being used to protect the rights of the accused, in that case the right not to self-incriminate. In other instances the section will be used to prevent the accused being placed at a disadvantage. Some examples can be given.

(a) The obtaining of a confession through trickery or deceit is likely to lead to exclusion.[16]
(b) Refusing improperly to permit the suspect to receive legal advice will often, although not always, be held to be unfair.[17]
(c) Breach of the provisions of the Code of Practice relating to the conduct and recording of interviews will often place the accused at a disadvantage and any confession may well be excluded;[18]

In other instances, police misconduct may lead to a successful application to dismiss the prosecution because of an abuse of process.[19]

2 Criminal proceedings

Certain police misconduct may amount to a criminal offence. Thus, offences of perjury, or conspiracy to pervert the administration of justice are from time to time identified and many of the cases involving miscarriages of justice have involved incidents of police misconduct.[20] More commonly the legality of police conduct may be tested in a prosecution brought under section 89 of the Police Act 1996. This section makes it an offence to assault, or to resist or wilfully obstruct, a constable acting in the execution of his duty. Whilst the duty of the police can be stated broadly,[2] the expression "execution of duty" within section 89 has a technical meaning: an officer who infringes the rights of an individual without being able to point to some legal authority justifying such infringement will have gone outside the execution of duty, and thus a prosecution under section 89 will fail. Thus a police officer who is a trespasser and against whom reasonable force is used to eject him will not succeed in a prosecution for a section 51

---

14 Even in the use of discretion under s 78 of the Police and Criminal Evidence Act the courts have disclaimed any intention of using powers to discipline the police; see: *R v Parris* (1988) 89 Cr App Rep 68. This in reality may be the effect; see Birch at [1989] Crim LR 95, and *R v Walsh* (1989) 91 Cr App Rep 161.
15 [1987] 3 All ER 481.
16 *Ibid.*
17 *R v Samuel* [1988] QB 615; [1988] 2 All ER 135; *R v Dunford* (1991) 91 Cr App Rep 150; cf *R v Alladice* (1988) 87 Cr App Rep 380.
18 *R v Keenan* [1990] 2 QB 54, [1989] 3 All ER 598; *R v Canale* [1990] 2 All ER 187.
19 *R v Horseferry Road Magistrates' Court, ex p Bennett* [1994] AC 42; *Bennett v Horseferry Road JJ* [1993] 1 All ER 1387.
20 "It is part of the obligations and duties of a police constable to take all steps which appear to him to be necessary for keeping the peace, for preventing crime or for protecting property from criminal injury [they] also further include the duty to detect crime and to bring an offender to justice." (per Parker LCJ in *Rice v Connolly* [1966] 2 QB 414; [1966] 2 All ER 649).

assault. Similarly with an officer who is unlawfully restraining an individual: physical force to secure release from that detention would not amount to a section 89 assault.[1] The key to each of these situations is the concept of unlawful interference with individual rights. If there is no interference with individual rights, or if authority in fact exists, the constable remains within the execution of duty.

3   Civil actions

A Chief Constable is liable for any torts committed by a police officer in the performance or purported performance of police functions.[2] The police authority will only be liable if a legal duty arises for the actions of its officer. Public policy may prevent that duty from in fact arising. In *Hill v Chief Constable of West Yorkshire*,[3] it was held that no general duty of care was owed to individual members of the public to identify and apprehend an unknown criminal, even if it was reasonably foreseeable that harm was likely to result if the criminal (in that case a notorious woman-killer) was not apprehended. By contrast, a special relationship may arise. In *Swinney v Chief Constable of the Northumbria Police*[4] it was held that it was at least arguable that such a relationship arose between an informant (who passed such information in confidence) and the police. In that case, it was alleged that the police had negligently allowed the informant's identity to fall into the public domain, and the court held that an arguable case arose.

The Chief Constable will be indemnified by the police authority. In addition, a police authority has a discretion to pay damages in respect of torts and other claims committed by a constable, even if committed otherwise than in the performance of public duties.[5]

What is within "the performance of police functions" was considered in *Makanjuola v Commissioner of Police for the Metropolis*[6] where an off-duty officer used his warrant card to gain admission to the property, where he then committed a serious sexual assault on the plaintiff. The Chief Constable was held not liable in damages for the sexual assault, because it was not a fraudulent performance of what the constable had authority to do honestly. Exemplary damages were awarded against the constable. The fact remains, though, that the effectiveness of the civil law remedy may depend upon the liability of the Chief Constable, since an individual officer may be of modest means and not worth suing.

The action in tort might be for assault, trespass or false imprisonment. Alternatively, the writ of *habeas corpus* will be a means of testing the legality of police detention.

---

1   *Davis v Lisle* [1936] 2 KB 434; [1936] 2 All ER 213; *Kenlin v Gardiner* [1967] 2 QB 510; [1966] 3 All ER 931; *Collins v Wilcock* [1984] 3 All ER 374; [1984] 1 WLR 1172. Cf *Mepstead v DPP* [1996] Crim LR 111 where a divisional court held that a constable who took a person by the arm for the purposes of emphasising the content of what was being said was acting within the execution of duty.
2   Police Act 1996, s 88(1).
3   [1989] AC 53; [1988] 2 All ER 238.
4   [1997] QB 464; [1996] 3 All ER 449
5   1996 Act, s 88(4).
6   [1992] 3 All ER 617.

4 Judicial review

It has already been seen[7] that police discretion is judicially reviewable. Given the restricted role of the court, however, this is not in practice a realistic way of testing the legality of police action. By contrast, the use of the writ of *habeas corpus* can be an effective means in some circumstances of testing legality.

5 Crown Prosecution Service

The Crown Prosecution Service has responsibility for the prosecution of offences.[8] If police misconduct affects admissibility of evidence this may affect the strength of the police case and lead to a prosecution not being brought.

6 Complaints against the police

The adequacy of mechanisms for dealing with complaints against the police has been a matter of considerable debate since the 1970s. The complaints system is the non-legal mechanism available to members of the public who are dissatisfied with the conduct of an individual officer. Section 49 of the Police Act 1964 introduced a scheme for the internal investigation of complaints, with the Deputy Chief Constable of a force investigating and reporting, where appropriate, to the Director of Public Prosecutions. Continued pressure for a more independent form of scrutiny led to the Police Act 1976, which established the Police Complaints Board. The creation of this body failed to satisfy critics, principally because the police essentially still investigated complaints. As Lord Scarman observed in his Report into the Disturbances at Brixton:[9]

> "The evidence has convinced me that there is a widespread and dangerous lack of public confidence in the existing system for handling complaints against the police unless there is a strengthening of the independent 'non-police' element, public confidence will continue to be lacking."

The Royal Commission on Criminal Procedure also supported proposals for change.[10]

The Police and Criminal Evidence Act 1984 established a new system, under the control of the Police Complaints Authority. That system is now to be found in the Police Act 1996. Complaints are made initially by or on behalf of a complainant to "the appropriate authority".[11] In the Metropolis, this will always be the Commissioner. Outside the Metropolis, who fulfils this role depends upon the subject of the complaint. If it is against a senior officer, the complaint is made to the police authority. For other officers it is the Chief Officer.

(a) *Senior officers above the rank of superintendent.* The police authority may deal with the complaint at its discretion, if it is satisfied that the conduct complained of, if proved, would not justify criminal or disciplinary charges. In other cases an officer, whether from the same or another force, will be appointed to investigate.

---

7   See p 145, *ante*.
8   See p 270, *ante*.
9   (1981, HMSO).
10   Cmnd 8092-I, 1981. *Op cit*, paras 4.118–4.119.
11   Police Act 1996, s 65.

(b) *Other officers* The Chief Officer considers whether the complaint is suitable for informal resolution. This will be the case if the complainant consents, and the Chief Officer is satisfied that the conduct complained of would not justify criminal or disciplinary proceedings. In other situations an officer is appointed to investigate.

The Police Complaints Authority supervises the investigation of certain categories of complaint: (i) complaints alleging that the conduct complained of resulted in death or serious injury to some other person; (ii) other complaints specified in regulations; (iii) any complaint referred to it by the police; (iv) any complaint where the authority requires reference to itself. In addition, section 71 permits the police to refer any matter where it appears to the appropriate authority that an officer may have committed any act, which amounts to a disciplinary offence. Such a reference does not have to be after the making of a complaint, but it must be considered by the appropriate authority that it ought to be referred because of the gravity of the matter or because of exceptional circumstances.

The appropriate authority receives the report of the investigation. If it discloses a criminal offence then, in the case of senior officers, a copy of the report must be referred to the Director of Public Prosecutions.[12] In relation to other officers the Assistant Chief Constable, if he considers that criminal proceedings ought to be brought, again must refer the matter to the DPP. The Police Complaints Authority has power to direct a Chief Constable to send a report to the DPP if it considers that an officer ought to be charged.[13] It can also direct that disciplinary proceedings be brought.

C POLICE POWERS

Authority to act in a particular way is conferred on the police by a wide range of authority, both common law and statutory. The detail of such powers is beyond the scope of this book. Nevertheless, the key features of the general framework of power, particularly those in respect of the treatment of suspects, are important in assessing the effectiveness of the criminal process whilst maintaining safeguards for individuals. The need to secure this balance has been emphasised by several controversial cases involving wrongful conviction and improper police behaviour.

Historically, police powers were piecemeal and ill-defined, creating problems for both the police, who were often forced to the borders of legality in order to take necessary action, and for suspects. Disquiet over certain miscarriages of justice which raised questions as to police conduct[14] led to the setting up in 1978 of the Royal Commission on Criminal Procedure. This reported in 1981,[15] having conducted a wide-ranging review into the investigative powers of the police, and the questioning and treatment of suspects. The Report's recommendations were not accepted in their entirety by government, but the Report provided a basis for other proposals, now contained in the Police and Criminal Evidence Act 1984. In addition the Report recommended a scheme dealing with the prosecution of offenders: this resulted in the Prosecution of Offences Act 1985.[16]

---

12 Police Act 1996, s 74.
13 *Ibid*, s 76.
14 See, in particular, *R v Lattimore (the Confait Case)*, leading to the Fisher Report, HMSO, 1966).
15 Cmnd 8092. For a useful summary of the pre-1986 law, see Cmnd 8092-I: *The Investigation and Prosecution of Criminal Offences in England & Wales: Law and Procedure.*
16 See p 145, *ante*.

I   General considerations

Before consideration of the framework, certain key matters merit discussion: first, the common law powers in respect of breaches of the peace; secondly, the concepts of "reasonable suspicion" and "reasonable belief"; thirdly, the use of force in the exercise of police powers; finally, the role of the Codes of Practice.

a   Breaches of the peace

A police officer is entitled to take any action necessary to prevent the continuance of a breach of the peace that is in fact occurring, or which is about to occur.[17] Arguably the officer also has a power of arrest in respect of breaches which have in fact occurred if there is a likelihood of recurrence.

Definitions of what constitutes a breach of the peace have varied. In *R v Chief Constable of Devon & Cornwall, ex parte Central Electricity Generating Board*[18] Lord Denning stated:

"There is a breach of the peace whenever a person who is lawfully carrying out his work is unlawfully and physically prevented by another from doing it."

This definition was too wide, and was not approved by Lawton and Templeman LJJ. More accurately, in *R v Howell*[19] Watkins LJ stated:

"We cannot accept that there can be a breach of the peace unless there has been an act done or threatened to be done which either actually harms a person, or in his presence his property, or is likely to cause such harm, or which puts somebody in fear of such harm being done."

The likelihood of a breach of the peace gives rise to several consequences. It gives the officer authority to take necessary action to prevent that occurrence from happening or continuing. This may involve the restraint and temporary detention of an individual.[20] It may involve the removal of an article or item of apparel from that individual.[1] It may involve requiring an individual not to go to a certain place, to travel by a certain route,[2] to undertake proposed activity elsewhere or in a different way.[3] All of this can impinge upon conduct which in itself may be perfectly lawful, and provides a wide measure of discretionary power which supplements the statutory scheme described below. A threatened breach of the peace may also provide the basis for entry upon property.[4] Finally, it may provide the basis for the arrest of an individual with a view

---

17   *Albert v Lavin* [1982] AC 546; [1981] 3 All ER 878. The power extends to acts occurring on private property: *McConnell v Chief Constable of the Greater Manchester Police* [1990] 1 All ER 423; [1990] 1 WLR 364; *R v Howell* [1982] QB 416; [1981] 3 All ER 383.
18   [1982] QB 458; [1981] 3 All ER 826.
19   [1982] QB 416; [1981] 3 All ER 383. This definition was approved in *Parkin v Norman* [1983] QB 92; [1982] 2 All ER 583.
20   See *Albert v Lavin, supra.*
1   *Humphries v Connor* (1864) 17 ICLR 1: removal of orange lily from the lapel of the plaintiff lawful, since the intent was to prevent breaches of the peace.
2   *Moss v McLachlan* (1984) 149 JP 167. There must be some proximity in terms of time and place to the apprehended breach of the peace. See also the powers of regulation in Public Order Act 1986.
3   *Duncan v Jones* [1936] 1 KB 218; [1935] All ER Rep 710. *Piddington v Bates* [1960] 3 All ER 660; [1961] 1 WLR 162.
4   CEGB case, n 18, *supra.*

to taking an individual before a magistrates' court to be bound over to be of good behaviour and to keep the peace.[5]

b   Reasonable suspicion and reasonable belief

Virtually all police powers depend for their rightful exercise upon the existence of a particular state of mind in the person exercising the power. Usually what will be required is "reasonable suspicion" of certain facts, but sometimes in relation to particularly serious powers it will be "reasonable cause to believe" that will be required. Belief essentially involves the acceptance of the suspicion in fact held.[6]

In *Shaaban B in Hussien v Chong Fook Kam*[7] Lord Devlin observed that "suspicion in its ordinary meaning is a state of conjecture or surmise where proof is lacking: 'I suspect but cannot prove'". More recently, in *Castorina v Chief Constable of Surrey*[8] the Court of Appeal stated that honest belief was not a necessary pre-condition. Whilst clearly a reasonable suspicion must in fact be held, whether or not reasonable suspicion exists is to be determined objectively by the court. The existence or non-existence of reasonable suspicion therefore is an important element of ex post facto scrutiny of police action.

Reasonable suspicion is a suspicion based upon evidence. However, that does not have to be evidence that will be acceptable in a court of law. A wide range of factors is therefore important. They must though be characteristics individual to the person whose conduct is being considered, and not amount to stereotyping. Code of Practice A, made pursuant to section 66 of the Police and Criminal Evidence Act 1984, states that whether reasonable suspicion exists will depend upon all the circumstances. There must be some objective basis for it, such as a description of an article being carried, or a person seen acting in a certain way, or carrying an article at an unusual time or in a place where there have been a number of burglaries. Reasonable suspicion can never be supported on the basis of personal factors alone. For example a person's colour, age, hairstyle or manner of dress are matters which cannot be used alone, or in combination with each other, as the sole basis upon which to justify the exercise of the stop and search powers described below. In reality it was such stereotyping that brought stringent criticism of the exercise of stop and search powers, leading to their reform in the 1984 Act.

c   Force

The law allows necessary and reasonable force to be used in the exercise of police powers. The use of force in the exercise of police powers generally is governed by section 3 of the Criminal Justice Act 1967. This states that a person may use such force as is reasonable in the circumstances in the prevention of crime, or in effecting or assisting in the lawful arrest of an offender or suspected offender or of persons unlawfully at large. In addition, section 117 of the Police and Criminal Evidence Act 1984 provides that any power under the Act may be exercised using no more force than is reasonably necessary.

The legal tests are the same no matter what type of force is used. Traditionally, force has been by police officers armed only with a truncheon. Increasingly, firearms,

5   For powers in relation to binding over, see Justices of the Peace Act 1361, discussed generally in *Hughes v Holley* (1986) 151 JP 233. For a review of the law, see Law Commission Working Paper 103.
6   *Baker v Oxford* [1980] RTR 315. See *Bailey v Birch* [1982] Crim LR 547.
7   [1970] AC 942; [1969] 3 All ER 1626.
8   [1988] NLJR 180.

or access to them, are available. The use of such weapons will have to be justified by the user in the same way as any other force, judged by its necessity and its reasonableness in the circumstances identified by the court.[9]

d   Codes of Practice

By section 66 of the Police and Criminal Evidence Act 1984 the Secretary of State is under a duty to issue various Codes of Practice. Under that power, Codes have been issued dealing with the exercise of stop and search powers, the detention, treatment, questioning and identification of suspects, and the search of premises and seizure of property.

These Codes of Practice have legal significance in two ways. First, breach of the Codes can form the basis for disciplinary action against the officer. Secondly, and in reality more importantly, breaches of the Codes of Practice are relevant in the decision of any matter in court. This generally operates to ensure compliance with the Code.

2   Stop and search powers

Stop and search powers are amongst the most controversial of police powers. On the one hand, they provide a mechanism for action claimed to be necessary to prevent crime and detect offenders. On the other, they provide the potential for misuse and harassment of minority groups, and the success rate is low.[10] The Royal Commission on Criminal Procedure investigated a wide range of powers to stop and search individuals, exercisable on different criteria, in different circumstances and by different people. In addition local powers existed. Thus, section 66 of the Metropolitan Police Act 1839 provided a power to stop, search and detain "any vessel, boat, cart or carriage in or upon which there shall be reason to suspect that anything stolen or unlawfully obtained may be found and also any person who may be reasonably suspected of having or conveying in any manner anything stolen or unlawfully obtained."

These powers were vague, and not always focused on true policing needs. More objectionably, they provided a basis for potential abuse by their use on a stereotypical basis, on the grounds of colour or race, age, hairstyle or other unconventional characteristics. The Royal Commission proposed rationalisation and repeal of many of these powers.[11]

Sections 1 to 4 of the Police and Criminal Evidence Act 1984 deal with these matters. Section 1 provides a power for a constable to detain persons or vehicles for the purpose of search. The constable must have reasonable suspicion that stolen or prohibited articles will be found. This means that the reasonable suspicion must exist prior to the detention, for that is a power to be exercised for the purposes of making the search the Act permits. Of course, there is nothing to prevent the initial contact and questioning to be by consent. The answers obtained may form part of the material upon which the reasonable suspicion can be based, but that suspicion must exist prior to the detention.

The articles that may be searched for are stolen and prohibited articles, or face masks. The nature of the former is self-evident. Prohibited articles need further definition. They include offensive weapons, which are further defined as articles made or adopted

---

9   See *R v MacNaughton* [1975] NI 203; A-G's *Reference Northern Ireland (No 1 of 1975)* [1977] AC 105 [1976] 2 All ER 937.

10   See Zander at (1989) 40 NILQ 319; for research into use of pre-PACE powers, see Willis, "The Use, Effectiveness and Impact of Police Stop & Search Powers" (Research Study 15, Home Office, 1983).

11   Cmnd 8092, 1981, p 1011.

for use for causing injury to any person, or any article intended by the person carrying it with him to cause injury. Also included are articles with a blade or point: these will often, but not always, be offensive weapons as well.[12] Prohibited articles also include articles made or adopted for use in the course of, or in connection with burglary, theft, taking a motor vehicle without authority and obtaining property by deception; or articles intended for use by the person carrying them for use in one of these ways. It will be appreciated that the range of articles potentially within these definitions is very large indeed.

The power to stop and search is exercisable in any place to which the public have access.[13] Any article found may be seized. This of course does not include items that go beyond those described above: it is not a power to seize any evidence of any crime. In reality, however, in these circumstances the officer will usually arrest, and then use the powers of search and seizure that flow from the fact of arrest.[14] Plainly, care has to be taken to ensure that such powers are not abused. The Act creates a wide range of safeguards. The constable must give certain information to the person prior to the search, certain records are to be kept, and there are limits as to what items of clothing may be required to be removed. In particular, there is no power to require a person to remove in public any clothing other than an outer coat, jacket or gloves, and, to avoid conflict with those who wear headgear for religious or ethnic reasons, there is no power to require the removal of a hat. This of course could be achieved by consent. Note also that there is a requirement for the statement of reasons for the search. The wording of the section suggests this should be so in all cases, even if obvious.

The exercise of the power is governed by Code of Practice A. A strict approach to questions of "reasonable suspicion" is essential. The Code does not affect the capacity of an officer to speak to or question a person in the normal course of his duties (and in the absence of reasonable suspicion) without detaining him or exercising any element of compulsion. Frequently it will be such normal conduct and questioning that provide the reasonable suspicion needed to justify formal detention for the purposes of search. The converse is equally true. The Act allows reasonable suspicion to be eliminated by questioning, and in these circumstances there is no obligation to search. The power is not, though, a power to detain and question.[15]

The power includes a right to detain and search vehicles for such articles. Again, the reasonable suspicion must exist at the time of detention. The bringing of the vehicle to a rest will be achieved through the power existing under section 163 of the Road Traffic Act 1988: a constable in uniform may require a vehicle to halt. This does not provide a basis for detention. Whether the vehicle is obliged to remain at rest will depend upon the extent to which that power will be implied by the courts,[16] or the extent which it is authorised by section 1.[17]

Not all stop and search powers are as precisely circumscribed. Section 60 of the Criminal Justice and Public Order Act 1994 permits a constable to stop any person or

---

12 See ss 1(7), (8), as amended by Criminal Justice Act 1988, ss 139–140 and Crime and Disorder Act 1998, s 25. The prohibition in respect of articles with a blade or point (subject to limited exceptions) obviates the necessity for the prosecution to prove the intent of the possessor of the article.

13 Section 1(1).

14 See ss 18, 32, and p 307, *post.*

15 For the general principles, see *Rice v Connolly* [1966] 2 QB 414; [1966] 2 All ER 649 (refusal to answer police questions not a wilful obstruction of a constable acting in the execution of duty, contrary to Police Act 1964, because an individual has lawful authority to do so).

16 See *Steel v Goacher* [1983] RTR 98; *Lodwick v Sanders* [1985] 1 All ER 577; *Sanders v Director of Public Prosecutions* [1988] Crim LR 605.

17 See s 1(2)(b), which confers a power to detain a person or vehicle for the purposes of the search.

vehicle to search for offensive weapons or dangerous instruments, without there being any need for reasonable suspicion of that individual being in possession of any such article. The pre-condition is that a senior police officer must have authorised the exercise of such stop and search powers within a specified locality for a period not exceeding 24 hours. For a limited period there exists a power to stop and search that is effectively unchallengeable.

3   Surveillance

The police sometimes need to use surreptitious means of investigation. One type of such action is the use of technical devices, such as eavesdropping equipment. No statutory regime existed in respect of such actions, apart from telephone tapping, now governed by the Interception of Communications Act 1985. In *R v Khan (Sultan)*[18] the House of Lords had to consider the legality of police action in attaching a listening device to the home of a man. The police had thereby obtained incriminating evidence against the appellant, who was a visitor to that home. The appellant argued, unsuccessfully, that that evidence should have been excluded from evidence by virtue of section 78 of PACE. The House of Lords, in dismissing an appeal against conviction, held that nothing in English law made unlawful a breach of privacy (if such a right in fact existed).

Lord Nolan described the lack of statutory regulation as "astonishing". Part IV of the Police Act 1997 rectifies that omission, in the context of conduct which interferes with the property rights of an individual. Section 93 of the Police Act 1997 confers on an authorising officer[19] the power to authorise the taking of such action, in respect of such property as he may specify, or the taking of such action as he may specify in respect of wireless telegraphy. The pre-conditions for the exercise of this power are that the authorising officer must believe:

(a) that it is necessary for the action specified to be taken on the ground that it is likely to be of substantial value in the prevention or detection of serious crime,[20] and

(b) that what the action seeks to achieve cannot reasonably be achieved by other means. Section 92 of the 1997 Act gives, where authorisation has been given, immunity from criminal or civil proceedings. The Act does not confer authority in respect of the use of surveillance devices in public places, or with the consent of an individual, for example, the "wiring up" of an individual, because no authority to do so is needed. Certain authorisations relating to property used mainly as a dwelling, or bedroom in a hotel, or where the authorised action is likely to lead to the acquisition of information of a legal, journalistic or confidential personal nature, can only be granted by a Commissioner appointed under statute.[1]

18   [1997] AC 558; [1996] 3 All ER 289.
19   "Authorising officer" is defined by s 93(3) of the 1997 Act.
20   "Serious crime" is defined by s 93(4) as where "(a) it involves the use of violence, results in substantial financial gain or is conduct by a large number of persons in pursuit of a common purpose, or (b) the offence or one of the offences is an offence for which a person who has attained the age of twenty-one and has no previous convictions could reasonably be expected to be sentenced to imprisonment for a term of three years or more."
1   1997 Act, s 97; for the appointment of Commissioners, see s 91.

4 Arrest

Arrest is a matter of fact, not a legal concept, though it has legal consequences. As Viscount Dilhorne put it in *Spicer v Holt*:[2] " 'Arrest' is an ordinary English word whether or not a person has been arrested depends not upon the legality of his arrest but on whether he has been deprived of his liberty to go where he pleases."

The essence of arrest is therefore the deprivation of liberty. Since it would be illogical to categorise any detention as an arrest, an arrest must therefore be the purported exercise of authority.[3] Whether or not the authority in fact exists is a different matter: it is not a contradiction in terms to speak of an "unlawful arrest".

The nature of an arrest was explained by Lord Diplock in *Holgate-Mohammed v Duke*:[4]

"First it shall be noted that arrest is a continuing act: it starts with the arrester taking a person into his custody (by action or words restraining him from moving elsewhere beyond the arrester's control) and it continues until the person so restrained is either released from custody, or, having been brought before a magistrate, is remanded in custody by the magistrate's judicial act."

In that case an officer exercised powers of arrest on reasonable suspicion of burglary in order that he could continue questioning the suspect in a police station. Given that the power to arrest existed, its use to facilitate questioning was a legitimate use of police discretion. Therefore, whilst detention for questioning is not lawful, arrest for questioning is.

For there to be a lawful use of arrest powers there must be: (a) the power to arrest, and (b) the use of that power in the procedurally correct way.

a Powers of arrest

An arrest may be either under warrant or without a warrant. In respect of the former the Magistrates' Courts Act 1980 confers a power to issue an arrest warrant. A constable is protected by law in relying on that warrant.[5] In relation to arrest without warrant, the Police and Criminal Evidence Act 1984 made radical changes. The Royal Commission on Criminal Procedure had identified a wide variety of such powers, in both general and local Acts.[6] Section 26 has the effect of repealing all statutory powers that authorise arrest without warrant by the constable, other than those preserved by Schedule 2. This identifies 21 statutory powers that are so preserved, covering a wide range of situations. The Act also leaves untouched powers of arrest without warrant that arise at common law.[7] This therefore means that the powers of the police in relation to breaches of the peace are preserved.

The Act then goes on to deal with powers of arrest for arrestable offences, and powers of arrest pursuant to the general arrest conditions. An arrestable offence is defined by section 24(1) as:

2   [1977] AC 987; [1976] 3 All ER 71.
3   See the definition of an arrest by Blackstone (in *Commentaries* 1830, p 289) as "the apprehending or restraining of one's person in order to answer an allegation or suspected crime". Note however that arrest may be made for the purposes of questioning: see *infra*.
4   [1984] AC 437; [1984] 1 All ER 1054.
5   Magistrates' Courts Act 1980.
6   Cmnd 8092, 1981, Appendix 9.
7   PACE, s 25(6).

(a) offences for which the sentence is fixed by law. Murder, with its mandatory life sentence, is an example;
(b) offences for which a person aged 21 years or over can be sentenced to a term of imprisonment of five years or more. This relates to the maximum permitted sentence, not that likely to be imposed;
(c) certain other specified offences. These are set out in section 24(2), and comprise offences that, pre-Act, were arrestable but which do not fall within the definition of arrestable offence. This list will change from time to time, as amendments are made by subsequent legislation.[8]

The Act then defines powers of arrest in respect of arrestable offences. These can be summarised as follows:

(a) any person may arrest anyone in the act of committing an arrestable offence, or who is reasonably suspected to be committing such an offence (section 24(4));
(b) any person may arrest anyone who is reasonably suspected of having committed such an offence, or who in fact has done so (section 24(5)). The Act, however, preserves the pre-1984 Act ruling in *Walters v WH Smith & Son Ltd*[9] that an arrestable offence must in fact have been committed. In *R v Self*[10] the defendant was charged with assault to escape lawful arrest. The arrest had been made by a citizen assisting a store detective, but the defendant was able to show that he had not in fact stolen the goods in question. Since in these circumstances the arrest was not lawful, the defendant was not in law guilty of the offence charged. This restriction does not apply to the power under section 24(4), and is a trap for the unwary. It suggests that a prudent citizen may prefer to ask the police to make the arrest, for no such restriction exists for police officers exercising arrest power under section 24(6);
(c) a constable may arrest without warrant anyone who is about to commit an arrestable offence, or anyone who he has reasonable grounds for suspecting to be about to commit an arrestable offence (section 24(4));
(d) a constable may arrest without warrant where there are reasonable grounds to suspect a person of having committed an arrestable offence (section 24(6)).

Alternatively, a constable can rely on the general arrest conditions contained in section 25. These apply where a constable reasonably suspects the commission of a non-arrestable offence, or its attempt, or, alternatively, if it appears to him that the service of a summons is impracticable. The arrest conditions are:

(a) the name of the person is unknown to the constable and cannot readily be ascertained;[11]
(b) reasonable grounds for doubting whether a name furnished is the person's real name;
(c) the person has failed to furnish a satisfactory address for service of a summons, or the constable reasonably doubts whether an address furnished is a satisfactory address for service;
(d) the constable has reasonable grounds for believing that arrest is necessary to prevent the relevant person causing injury to himself or another; suffering physical

---

8   See, as examples, Official Secrets Act 1989, Football (Offences) Act 1991.
9   [1914] 1 KB 595; [1911–13] All ER Rep 170.
10   [1992] 3 All ER 476; [1992] 1 WLR 657.
11   See *G v Director of Public Prosecutions* [1989] Crim LR 150.

injury; causing loss or damage to property; committing an offence against public decency; causing an unlawful obstruction of the highway;

(e) the constable has reasonable grounds for believing that an arrest is necessary to protect a child or other vulnerable person from the relevant person.

The powers at common law to arrest for a breach of the peace also should not be forgotten. A wide variety of powers thus is vested in the hands of the police.

It should be borne in mind that the existence of a power of arrest does not require its exercise. On many occasions involving minor breaches of the law a constable may choose simply to caution the suspect informally. Alternatively, details can be taken for report and possible summons. The vast majority of non-indictable offences, and a sizeable proportion of indictable offences, are proceeded with by summons as opposed to arrest and charge.[12]

b   Mechanics of arrest

The existence of a power is not enough. It must in fact be used, and in the right way. An arrest is not lawful unless the person arrested is informed that he is under arrest as soon as practicable after his arrest.[13] The person must likewise be told of the grounds for the arrest at the time of, or as soon as practicable after, the arrest. These two rules apply even if the fact of, or ground for, the arrest is obvious.[14] Section 28 makes an exception for cases where it is not practicable because the arrested person escapes before the information can be given. A failure to state the reasons when it does become practicable will invalidate the arrest, but only from that time, for the failure does not invalidate the arrest retrospectively.[15] Conversely, when the reasons are in fact stated the arrest becomes lawful. In *Lewis v Chief Constable of the South Wales Constabulary*[16] the Court of Appeal identified arrest as a continuing act. For that reason the arrest becomes lawful as soon as the reasons for the arrest are in fact stated. Thus the claim for damages, based on the fact that the initial arrest was unlawful, failed. This does not, of course, validate the period between the fact of arrest and the proper statement of reasons.

The statement of reasons does not have to specify a particular crime, or give a technical definition of the offence charged. What is needed is sufficient information to enable the arrested person to know the substance of why his liberty is being interfered with. In a pre-1984 Act case, *Christie v Leachinsky*,[17] the statement of reasons was inadequate because the officer relied on a power that he knew did not apply because the relevant factual conditions were not satisfied. However, the limits of this ruling were shown in the more recent case of *Abbassy v Commissioner of Police*.[18] The plaintiff was told that he was being arrested for "unlawful possession" of a vehicle. He had been asked four times about ownership of the vehicle, but responded in a rude and abusive fashion. Police inquiries later showed that he was in fact authorised to drive the vehicle, and the plaintiff was later charged with an offence of wilful obstruction of a constable acting in the execution of his duty, contrary to what is now section 89 of the Police Act 1996, and a charge later dropped. In an action for damages

---

12   See further p 466, *post*.
13   Section 28(2).
14   Section 28(3).
15   *Director of Public Prosecutions v Hawkins* [1988] 3 All ER 673; [1988] 1 WLR 1166.
16   [1991] 1 All ER 206.
17   [1947] AC 573; [1947] 1 All ER 567.
18   [1990] 1 All ER 193; [1990] 1 WLR 385.

for, inter alia, unlawful arrest and false imprisonment the court ruled that it had been made clear to the plaintiff that the basis of the arrest was unlawful possession of the vehicle. The fact that the officer did not specifically mention the vehicle in the statement of reasons was irrelevant. The judge had therefore misdirected the jury on a matter of law, and a re-trial was ordered.

An arrest also has certain physical requirements. It comprises compulsion and submission to that compulsion. There must either be a touching symbolic of seizure of the body, or alternatively, words of compulsion to which there is submission.[19]

c The consequences of arrest

By section 30, an arrested person must be taken to a police station as soon as practicable after the arrest. However, nothing prevents a constable delaying taking that person to a police station if his presence elsewhere is necessary in order to carry out such investigations as it is reasonable to carry out immediately.[20] By section 32 an arrested person may be searched if the constable has reasonable grounds to believe that the arrested person may present a danger to himself or others, or if he has reasonable grounds to believe he may have concealed on him an article that may assist in escape from lawful custody, or which is evidence relating to an offence. That does not have to be the same offence for which the person has been arrested.[1] There are also powers of entry conferred by section 32(2)(b) in respect of the premises where the arrested person was immediately before he was arrested, and, under section 18, of certain other premises occupied or controlled by the arrested person.

5 Detention

The 1984 Act creates a complex structure of provisions dealing with the detention of the suspect after arrest. In this, and with the treatment and questioning of the suspect, the key role is that of the custody officer. A duty to appoint such officers for each designated police station is created by the Act[2] and it is to such a designated police station that an arrested person would normally be taken. The functions of such officers are set out in section 39. It is the duty of the custody officer to ensure that the treatment of all detained persons is in accordance with the requirements of the Act and of the Codes of Practice, and that the record-keeping required by the Act in fact occurs. The Act imposes duties on the custody officer both before and after charge. If the requirements of the Act are not complied with the detention is likely to become unlawful.

The position is therefore an important one. The Act envisages and requires a separation of function between the custody officer and those investigating the offence. Only through such division of function will the interests of the suspect be protected. Whether this concept is sustainable in reality is a moot point. Quite apart from the loyalties and pressures that membership of the same force might create, the custody

---

19   *Alderson v Booth* [1969] 2 QB 216; [1969] 2 All ER 271.
20   Section 30(10).
1   This should be contrasted with the power to search premises (described below), which is confined to a search for evidence in respect of the offence for which the arrest was made. Note also the power to search premises under s 18.
2   1984 Act, s 36. This does not require a Chief Constable to appoint more than one such officer for each designated police station: *Vince v Chief Constable of the Dorset Police* [1993] 2 All ER 321; [1993] 1 WLR 415.

officer may find it difficult on occasion to cure a natural desire to assist the investigation by asking questions or using his own personal knowledge of the suspect.[3]

In determining the legality of detention, the process must be looked at various stages:

(a) The arrested person will be taken to the police station, unless his presence elsewhere can be justified.[4] If a person attends the station voluntarily, then he should be told he is free to go. If he is not he should be arrested, and will thereafter be subject to the same regime of detention.[5]

(b) At arrival at the police station, various matters relating to the arrested person will occur. First amongst these will be the creation of a custody record, which will detail all actions taken in respect of the arrested person. In particular, it will constitute the record of the various times that will govern the length of permitted detention.

(c) It is the duty of the custody officer to decide whether sufficient evidence exists to charge the person with the offence for which the arrest was made. If there is, the custody officer should do so.[6] During the period of detention various reviews of the detention will occur. These will occur as follows:[7]

- 1st review: not later than 6 hours after detention.
- 2nd review: not later than 9 hours after 1st review.
- 3rd and subsequent reviews: not later than 9 hours after previous review. In other words, there will be at least three opportunities to consider release or charge within any 24-hour period.

In addition, when during questioning the investigating officer considers that there is sufficient evidence to charge, the arrested person must be taken before the custody officer.

(d) If there is sufficient evidence to charge, whether initially or at any of the stages outlined, the custody officer must do so. Whether the arrested person can then be detained further will depend upon whether bail is granted.

(e) If there is not sufficient evidence to charge an arrested person then the periods of detention cannot exceed those permitted by the Act. The basic rule is that detention shall not last longer than 24 hours from the time of arrest, or time of arrival at the police station, whichever is earlier. This 24-hour period may be extended by a further 12 hours (ie 36 in total) by a senior officer.[8] That officer must have reasonable grounds to believe that detention is necessary to secure or preserve evidence relating to the offence for which the arrest was made, or to obtain such evidence by questioning; and, that the offence is a serious arrestable offence; and, that the offence is being investigated diligently and expeditiously.

If the police wish to detain beyond that 36-hour period under section 43 a warrant of further detention must be obtained from the magistrates' court. That court may issue such a warrant on the same grounds as stated above for the extension of detention by a senior officer. The warrant is for such period as the court thinks fit, not exceeding 36 hours. The court may extend this still further by a period of not longer than 36 hours, ending no later than 96 hours after first

3   See eg *R v Absolam* (1988) 88 Cr App Rep 332.
4   See 1984 Act, s 30(10).
5   *Ibid* , s 29, and Code C, para 3.15.
6   Code C, para 16.1.
7   1984 Act, ss 42–44.
8   Of the rank of superintendent or above: s 42(1).

detention or arrest. In short, 4 days is the maximum permitted period of detention without charge.

(f) After a person has been charged he will be released unless the grounds for detention under section 38 exist. These are: that his name or address cannot be ascertained, or is reasonably believed to be false; it is reasonably believed that detention is necessary for the protection of, or to prevent him from causing physical injury to, any other person, or damage to property; it is reasonably believed that the arrested person will fail to appear in court to answer bail, or detention is necessary to prevent him interfering with the administration of justice or with police investigations of that or other offences.

6   Treatment of suspects

The Police and Criminal Evidence Act 1984 contains provisions designed to give proper protection to a suspect in the police station. These are supplemented by Code C dealing with the detention, treatment and questioning of suspects. The objective is to ensure not only that suspects are treated in accordance with minimum standards, but also that admissions and other evidence are obtained in such a way that they can safely be relied upon in court. The courts also regard the right of silence as important, and the Code seeks to prevent improperly induced self-incrimination. The provisions apply even if a person is at the police station voluntarily, since if it is decided that the suspect will not be allowed to leave then he must be informed at once that he is under arrest.

a   Search

When a suspect is taken into custody, the custody officer may cause a search to be made of the person detained, although such a search is not obligatory. Much will depend upon how long a suspect is being detained, whether he is to be placed in the cells, and so forth. Section 54 imposes a duty to record everything a person has with him when he is brought to the police station. A search can occur, provided it is not an intimate search. A strip search (ie one involving the removal of more than outer garments) should not occur unless the custody officer considers it to be necessary to remove an article which the detained person would not be allowed to keep. A search may also be carried out at any time whilst the person is in custody to ascertain whether or not he has anything with him that could be used for the purposes set out in section 54(4).

Section 54(4) allows certain articles to be seized, if found on search. These are articles that: (a) the custody officer believes the person may use (i) to cause physical injury to himself or to another person, (ii) to damage property, (iii) to interfere with evidence, (iv) to assist in escape, or (b) the custody officer has reasonable grounds to believe may be evidence in relation to an offence.[9]

Intimate searches are governed by different rules. Section 118 defines an intimate search as "a search consisting of the physical examination of a person's body orifices other than the mouth".[10] Intimate searches can only be carried out under section 55.

---

9   Compare with the pre-1984 Act position as stated in *Lindley v Rutter* [1981] QB 128; [1980] 3 WLR 660.

10   This definition was amended by Criminal Justice and Public Order Act 1994, s 65, following difficulties that had arisen in respect of the concealment of drugs by suspects in their mouths. See *R v Hughes*, [1994] 1 WLR 876, where the holding of a suspect's nose and jaw, to cause the extrusion of articles in the mouth, was held to be a search, but not an intimate search.

An officer of at least the rank of superintendent must have reasonable grounds to believe:

(a) that the arrested person may have concealed on him anything which he could use to cause physical injury to himself or others and might so use whilst in custody, or

(b) the arrested person may have Class A drugs concealed on him, with the requisite intent.[11]

In either case an intimate search is only permitted if it is believed that it cannot be found without such a search. The search must be conducted in accordance with Annex A of Code C.

b Information about rights

The arrested person must be informed of the right to have someone informed of his arrest. Section 56 provides that a person held in custody may on request have one person known to him, or who is likely to take an interest in his welfare, notified at public expense of his whereabouts as soon as practicable. If that person is unobtainable, the arrested person may nominate two others, and the police may extend the right further if they wish. The right is an important one, to be denied only in limited circumstances where to grant it would interfere with the investigation. Even if the grounds for denying contact with an individual may exist, they are unlikely to apply to making contact with a solicitor.[12] The arrested person also has the right to consult the Codes of Practice.[13]

c Fingerprinting

In the absence of consent, fingerprints can only be taken on the authorisation of a senior officer, on suspicion of involvement in a criminal offence, and where it is believed that fingerprints will tend to prove or disprove the suspect's involvement.[14] Alternatively, if the suspect has been charged with a recordable offence and has not had fingerprints taken in the course of the investigation, they may be taken.

d Intimate samples

These are defined by section 65 as a sample of blood, semen or any other tissue fluid, urine, or pubic hair, a dental impression, or a swab taken from a person's body orifices. It no longer includes the taking of a sample of saliva, which now is to be regarded as a non-intimate sample, and was a change made in order to facilitate the creation of a DNA database.[15] Intimate samples can, of course, be taken by consent, though it is required to be in writing, and then only if section 63 applies. Again, it must be under the authorisation of a senior officer who reasonably suspects involvement in a serious arrestable offence.[16] "Serious arrestable offences" are defined by the Act in a detailed way,[17] and are the more serious of arrestable offences, which justify the creation and

---

11 Eg with intent to supply: see s 55(17).
12 *R v Samuel* [1988] QB 615; [1988] 2 All ER 135.
13 Code C, para 4; *Director of Public Prosecutions v Skinner* [1990] RTR 254.
14 See Criminal Justice and Public Order Act 1994, s 58.
15 See p 314, *post*.
16 Section 61.
17 Section 116.

use of intrusive and onerous police powers. The senior officer must believe that the sample will confirm or disprove involvement in the offence.

As noted above, changes were made in 1994 to the detailed provisions relating to intimate samples, in order to facilitate the establishment of a DNA database. One of those changes was the extension of the power to take intimate samples from persons not in police detention. A new s 62(1A) of PACE provides that, providing certain criteria are fulfilled, such a sample may be taken in such circumstances. The criteria are that, during an investigation, two or more non-intimate samples suitable for the same method of analysis must have been taken which have proved insufficient, a police officer of at least the rank of superintendent must authorise the taking of the intimate sample, and the sample must be given with consent. This requirement for consent is of general application: the Act makes it clear that no such sample shall be taken without consent. However, refusal to grant such consent can lead to adverse inferences being drawn.[18]

Once an intimate sample has been given, the information may be checked against other samples, or the information derived from other samples.[19] Thus the basis was created for the establishment of a DNA database. This has existed since April 1995, and by March 1998 contained the DNA profiles or more than 255,000 suspects and convicted persons, as well as 30,000 profiles developed from material found at the scene of crimes.[20] Through samples DNA[1] profiles can be established which may serve to identify an offender with a high degree of accuracy and reliability.

Non-intimate samples can be taken pursuant to section 63. These can be taken without consent on authorisation of a senior police officer, who reasonably suspects involvement of the suspect in a serious arrestable offence, and that the sample will tend to confirm or disprove involvement.

e   Conditions of detention

These are governed by Code C, and may in extreme cases in any event amount to breach of Article 10 of the Bill of Rights 1688 which prohibits "cruel and unusual punishments".[2] Cells must be adequately heated, cleaned and ventilated. Clean bedding should be supplied. Access to toilet and washing facilities must be granted. Adequate replacement clothing for any item taken for investigation must be provided. Adequate meals must be provided. Brief outdoor exercise, if practicable, should be permitted. Suspects should be visited every hour, or every half-hour in the case of persons who are drunk. The custody officer is under a duty to call for medical treatment if a suspect appears to be ill or suffering from mental disorder, is injured, does not show signs of sensibility and awareness, fails to respond to questions or conversation, or otherwise appears to require medical attention.

18   Section 62(10).
19   A "speculative search", pursuant to PACE s 65 (as amended by the Criminal Justice and Public Order Act 1994, s 58(4)).
20   See Redmayne, "The DNA Database: Civil Liberty and Evidentiary Issues" [1998] Crim LR 437.
1   DNA is the genetic material found in each cell of the human body, and which provides what is in effect a genetic fingerprint. For then use of DNA evidence in court see *R v Doheny and Adams* [1997] 1 Cr App R 369.
2   *Middleweek v Chief Constable of Merseyside* [1992] 1 AC 179n; [1990] 3 All ER 662; *R v Deputy Governor of Parkhurst Prison, ex parte Hague* [1992] 1 AC 58; *sub nom Hague v Deputy Governor of Parkhurst Prison* [1991] 3 All ER 733.

f   Vulnerable suspects

Special rules apply to vulnerable persons. In respect of those who appear to be deaf, or where there is doubt about their hearing or speaking ability, or ability to understand English, and the custody officer cannot establish effective communications, the custody officer must as soon as possible call an interpreter. If the arrested person is a juvenile, the identity of the person responsible for his welfare must be ascertained and informed as soon as practicable. An "appropriate adult"[3] must be asked to come to the police station. Similar rules apply to those suffering from mental handicap or suffering mental disorder.

7   Access to legal advice

The right to access to legal advice was, in *R v Samuel*,[4] described as "fundamental". Although the Judges Rules which, prior to the 1984 Act, governed such matters, recognised the importance of such access, they were frequently broken and poorly enforced by the courts.[5] The 1984 Act has greatly strengthened the right, and led to much more rigorous enforcement by the courts.

Section 58 provides that a "person who is in police detention shall be entitled, if he so requests, to consult a solicitor privately at any time". Delay in granting this right can only be authorised, in respect of a serious arrestable offence, by an officer of the rank of superintendent or above, on certain limited grounds. These are stated to be where the officer reasonably believes that the exercise of the right:

(a)   will lead to interference with or harm to evidence connected with a serious arrestable offence or interference with or physical injury to other persons; or

(b)   will lead to the alerting of other persons suspected of having committed such an offence but not yet arrested for it; or

(c)   will hinder the recovery of any property obtained as a result of such an offence.

Certain other limited exceptions relating to drug trafficking and terrorist offences exist. These powers of delay have been construed by the courts in a way that makes them extremely limited in scope. In *R v Samuel*,[6] the accused had been denied access to a solicitor on the grounds that the accused's companions were still at large and might be alerted by the solicitor, albeit unwittingly. The court stated that any decision to deny access had to be by reference to the individual features of each case. Here the police had failed to demonstrate a reasonable belief that the particular solicitor would engage in such conduct. Indeed, if a particular solicitor was shown to fall within these provisions, the appropriate response would be to request the nomination of another solicitor, or the calling of the duty solicitor. It is not a ground of delay under these provisions that the solicitor will advise silence, or make the investigation harder.[7]

The Code of Practice sets out the detailed provisions regarding these rights. A suspect under arrest at the police station must be informed clearly of his right to have someone informed, and of his right to consult privately with a solicitor free of charge. These are continuing rights which may be exercised at any time during the period in custody. The custody officer must give suspects a written notice of these rights,

3   See Code C, para 1.7.
4   [1988] QB 615; [1988] 2 All ER 135.
5   See the Fisher Report (1977, HC 90).
6   See n 4, supra.
7   *Ibid*. See also *R v Alladice* (1988) 87 Cr App Rep 380.

containing an explanation of the arrangements for obtaining legal advice. Posters advertising the right must be displayed prominently in the charging area of each police station, and at certain stages in the process the suspect must be reminded of the right to free legal advice.

The right is one to receive legal advice if the suspect so requests. There is no obligation on the police to request a solicitor, though if the suspect's family does and the solicitor attends, the suspect has the right to see him. The police must not take action to discourage the exercise of the right, and must not misrepresent the position.[8] The Code does not specify how such advice is to be given. It may be given in person, or over the telephone. Once it has been requested the police must generally wait until after such advice has been tendered before proceeding with an interview. If an interview is taking place, a solicitor may be asked to leave if his conduct is such that the investigating officer is unable properly to put questions to the suspect.

The right is the right to legal advice from a solicitor. In reality it may be a legal executive or clerk who attends at the police station. The Code permits refusal of access to such persons if an officer of the rank of inspector or above considers that such a visit would hinder the investigation of crime. In *R v Chief Constable of Avon and Somerset Constabulary, ex parte Robinson*[9] a circular setting out force policy in this respect was held lawful because it did not fetter the discretion of the individual decision-making officer. What is not permitted is for the police to make judgments based upon the quality of advice likely to be tendered, and the terms of the Code have been amended to specify clearly what is proper. What is important is that the clerk should be admitted unless identity or status have not been properly established, if the person is not of suitable character to give advice (eg because of a criminal record) and any other matters disclosed in the letter of authorisation. The quality of advice given will, however, be important: the very fact of presence of a legal representative may "cure" procedural irregularities committed by the police which were not objected to at the time.[10]

The effectiveness of the right under section 58 has been the subject of considerable research.[11] It depends in part upon adequate availability of suitably qualified legal advisers, compliance with the spirit of the rules by the police and adequate sanctions in the courts. In relation to the availability of advice, duty solicitor schemes exist, run under the auspices of the Legal Aid Board.[12] Those who do not request a named solicitor, or whose named solicitor is unavailable, may seek free advice. This may often be initially by telephone. Whilst the duty solicitor, drawn from a rota amongst local practitioners, may choose to attend, the only obligation to do so is where the suspect is to be interviewed, an identification parade is being held, or where an allegation of serious police misconduct is being made. The effectiveness of the scheme also presupposes a sufficiently large group of solicitors undertaking criminal legal aid work.

The impact of the provisions has been mixed. Research shows that take-up rates have varied greatly between police stations.[13] Whilst direct denial of rights has been rare, it has been found that a variety of ploys, whether intentional or inadvertent, by the police can dissuade suspects from taking advantage of this legal right.[14] The revision of the Code of Practice in 1991 was designed to minimise this risk. It is also the case

8   See *R v Beycan* [1990] Crim LR 185.
9   [1989] 2 All ER 15; [1989] 1 WLR 793.
10   See *R v Dunn* (1990) 91 Cr App Rep 237.
11   See, in particular, Sanders and Bridges, "Access to Legal Advice and Police Malpractice" [1990] Crim LR 494.
12   See p 281, *ante*.
13   *Ibid*.
14   The right is to be granted access on request.

that the courts have taken a strong line in cases of breach of these legal advice provisions. Though not automatic, breach is likely in most cases to lead to exclusion of a confession subsequently obtained, under s 78 of PACE.[15] Exclusion is not automatic, but a confession made whilst the police are in breach of their obligation may well be excluded on the basis that a suspect may not have confessed if the right had been accorded.

8   Interviews

One of the most serious problems identified in recent years is the possibility that confessions by suspects may not in fact be reliable. In addition allegations were frequently made against the police. The 1984 Act and Code of Practice created a detailed framework for the conduct and recording of interviews. These provisions are regarded by the courts as of the greatest importance, and breaches of them have led to confessions subsequently obtained being excluded. Their purpose was explained by Lord Lane CJ in *R v Canale*:[16]

> "The object is two-fold. not merely to ensure that the suspect's remarks are accurately recorded and that he has an opportunity when he goes through the contemporaneous record afterwards of checking each answer and initialling each answer, but likewise it is a protection for the police, to ensure, so far as possible, that it cannot be suggested that they induced the suspect to confess by improper approaches or improper promises. If the contemporaneous note is not made then each of those two laudable objects is apt to be stultified."

At the heart of these provisions is the definition of what amounts to an interview. The Act has resulted in widespread tape-recording of interviews conducted in police stations. A detailed Code of Practice[17] deals with those tape-recordings and how transcripts thereof may be used. In addition, rules governing the keeping and verification of notes of interviews exist. For that reason there was a danger on occasion that the police would seek to circumvent such provisions by conducting conversations and obtaining admissions outside the police station. Amendments to the Code have been made in an attempt to minimise this danger. The definition of interview is now stated to be: the questioning of a person regarding his involvement or suspected involvement in a criminal offence or offences.[18] Questioning a person only to obtain information or his explanation of the facts, or in the ordinary course of the officer's duties does not constitute an interview. Neither does questioning which is confined to the proper and effective conduct of a search. There are, however, difficulties in applying this in practice.[19]

a   The right of silence

A suspect has the right not to be required to self-incriminate. This means that, generally, an accused cannot be required to answer questions. Associated with this is the so-called

---

15   See p 297, *ante*.
16   [1990] 2 All ER 187.
17   Code C.
18   For interpretation of this, see *R v Cox* (1992) 96 Cr App Rep 464.
19   For the difficulties see *R v Absolam* (1988) 88 Cr App Rep 332; *R v Blackburn and Wade* (1992) Times, 1 December.

right of silence, which governs what inferences, if any, may be drawn from a failure to answer questions or supply information. A suspect cannot be required to answer questions, whether being questioned prior to, or subsequent to, arrest. Nor can he be required to testify at trial. For this reason, a suspect must be cautioned, as discussed below, on arrest and prior to be being interviewed. Prior to 1994, a judge had to direct a jury (or magistrates, direct themselves) that no inferences could be drawn from the exercise of the right. However, the Criminal Justice and Public Order Act 1994 changed the position. Section 34 of the 1994 Act entitles a court to draw such inference as it considers proper from a failure by a person to mention a fact later relied on in his defence. Section 36 permits an inference to be drawn from a failure of an arrested person to account for any object, etc and section 37 for possession of an article or object, or mark on an article or object.

b   Cautions

A caution must be administered before questions about an offence are put to a person suspected of an offence for the purpose of obtaining evidence which may be given in court. A caution must likewise be administered on arrest. The caution states:

> "You do not have to say anything unless you wish to do so, but it may harm your defence if you do not mention when questioned something you later rely on in court. Anything you do say may be given in evidence."

This will therefore be given at the commencement of each interview. If there is a break in an interview the arrested person must be reminded that he remains under caution.

c   Interviews

These must occur at a police station, unless delay would lead to interference with or harm to evidence connected with an offence or interference with or harm to other persons, would lead to the alerting of other persons suspected of committing an offence but not yet arrested for it, or hinder the recovery of property obtained in consequence of the commission of an offence. Prior to the holding of any interview the suspect should be reminded of his rights to free legal advice.

d   Records of interviews

The Code requires accurate records of interviews to be kept. The record will state time and date, location and names of those present. Breaks in the interview must be recorded. In respect of tape-recorded records, special rules apply. In relation to other interviews, the suspect should be shown the notes of the interview, and given an opportunity to sign it as requested. If the suspect declines to do so, this must itself be recorded. If the record is not kept contemporaneously, the reasons for that failure must be recorded, and the record completed as soon as practicable. The interview notes should then be shown to the suspect for verification. Any unsolicited comments by the suspect should likewise be recorded and verified.[20]

20   See Code C, paras 11.5–11.13.

e *Conduct of interviews*

The law will exclude as evidence any confession obtained by oppression or in circumstances likely to lead to unreliability. The Code specifies detailed requirements about breaks from questioning, maximum periods of questioning, the giving of proper food and refreshment as appropriate.

f *Vulnerable suspects*

The Codes recognise that certain groups need special protection. This is true in respect of those suffering mental disability,[1] and juveniles.[2] In respect of the former, those who suffer mental handicap or mental illness should not be interviewed in the absence of an appropriate adult,[3] unless the rules in Annex C governing urgent interviews apply. These only permit an interview to be held where delay would involve an immediate risk of harm to persons or serious loss or serious damage to property. If such a person is interviewed in the absence of an appropriate adult, then not only may the confession resulting be excluded on the grounds of unreliability, the provisions of section 77 of the 1984 Act, which will require any confession to be supported with other evidence will apply. Whether a person falls within these provisions will be decided by the court.

Similar rules about the presence of an appropriate adult apply to juveniles.[4] In addition, those suffering temporary disability through drink, drugs or illness should not generally be interviewed until they are fit, though the courts seem willing to leave this judgment to the police themselves.[5]

9 **Identification**

The dangers of identification evidence are well known.[6] To minimise them the Codes of Practice set out specific rules as to how suspects are to be identified, since court identifications are not generally permissible.[7] Failure to comply with the Code is likely to lead to the exclusion of evidence of that identification.[8]

Where the identity of a suspect is not known, a witness may be taken to a particular locality to observe possible suspects, or may be shown photographs, provided certain safeguards are complied with. Once the identity of a suspect is known, however, then identification should proceed in accordance with set procedures. In such cases the preferred method of identification is through an identification parade. This will be held if the suspect consents, and either the investigating officer considers it would be useful, or the suspect requests a parade. Only if it is impracticable to secure sufficient similar-looking participants can the parade be declined by the police. If a parade is held, it must be in accordance with the detailed procedures set out in the Code. Evidence of

---

1   Code C, paras 3.93.10.
2   *Ibid*, paras 3.7-3.8.
3   Code C, para 1.7. A solicitor representing the suspect may not act as an appropriate adult.
4   *Supra*, n 2.
5   *R v Lamont* [1989] Crim LR 813; *R v Moss* (1990) 91 Cr App Rep 371.
6   See *R v Turnbull* [1977] QB 224; [1976] 3 All ER 549, and the Devlin Committee report (1976, HC 338).
7   *Ibid*.
8   See p 320, *post*.

identification can be given not only by the witness, but also by officers who saw and heard the witness identify the suspect.[9]

Where no parade is held, because it is impracticable or because no consent is given, a group identification, video identification or a confrontation (in that preferred order) are the alternatives allowed by the Code.

The dangers of relying on identification evidence in court are well known. A series of wrongful convictions led to the establishment of the Devlin Committee to investigate how the law dealt with identification evidence. It recommended that a trial judge should direct a jury not to convict on eye-witness testimony alone unless the case was exceptional or the identification was supported by substantial other evidence. No legislation followed, but the Court of Appeal in *R v Turnbull*[10] laid down certain guidelines. The court rejected a rule prohibiting conviction on identification evidence alone, and focused on the nature of the identification. Identification evidence could be split into good and poor quality identification. In all cases where the case depends wholly or substantially on the correctness of an identification the judge should direct the jury to proceed with special caution. The circumstances of the identification should be carefully considered. Where the quality of the identification is good, for example, made in good conditions of light, weather and with ample opportunity to observe, the case can safely be left to the jury. Where the identification is of poor quality (because, for example, of poor visibility or a fleeting glance) the case should be withdrawn from the jury unless there is supporting evidence. The supporting evidence does not have to be evidence that fulfils any particular criteria, but simply evidence which serves to confirm the correctness of the identification. The judge should always identify for the jury the evidence capable of supporting the identification.

Certain points should be noted. Recognition may be stronger than initial identification, but even recognition cases fall within the principles in *R v Turnbull*, which was itself a recognition case. Secondly, the rule only applies to identification of humans. The identification of objects, such as motor cars, appears not to be within the rule. Lastly, there is no difference in principle between an identification resulting from a witness seeing a person or incident, and a witness seeing the same person or thing on film, videotape or closed circuit television. In each case the witness is using his particular knowledge of a person to identify him. In such cases the *Turnbull* guidelines apply.

9   *R v McCay* [1991] 1 All ER 232; [1990] 1 WLR 645.
10   *Supra*, n 6.

Part III

Civil Procedure

Chapter 15

Resolution of Civil Disputes

A INTRODUCTION

Access to justice is a fundamental right. It has even been described as a constitutional right, insofar as such rights exist.[1] For society to operate effectively, there must be means whereby disputes between individuals, and between the state and individuals, can be resolved. The civil justice process provides those means, but must be accessible to those who need such access. Procedural, financial or other restrictions defeat the whole purpose of the civil justice process.

Civil litigation is, for the most part, adversarial in nature.[2] Within a framework of substantive and procedural law established by the state for the resolution of civil disputes, the main responsibility for the initiation and conduct of proceedings rests with the parties to each individual case, and it is normally the plaintiff who sets the pace at which the litigation proceeds. The role of the judge is to adjudicate on issues selected by the parties when they choose to present them to the court. This process is, however, often said to be excessively expensive, slow and complex.[3] Such criticisms, although not always universally accepted,[4] are not new. Since the mid-nineteenth century there have been some 60 or so reports on aspects of civil procedure and the organisation of the civil courts, including the Civil Justice Review.[5] Even today, despite this on-going scrutiny, official studies can describe the supply of civil justice as "fragmented and confusing".[6] The Woolf Interim Report identified a key reason for this as the absence of effective judicial control. Without this, the adversarial process

---

1   See Laws J in *R v Lord Chancellor, ex parte Witham* [1998] QB 575; [1997] 2 All ER 779. The significance of the constitutional right is that it should only be abrogated by the clear words of an Act of Parliament. For the detail of this case, see p 275, *ante*.

2   *Access to Justice: Interim Report to the Lord Chancellor on the Civil Justice System in England and Wales*, June 1995 ("the Woolf Interim Report"), at para 3. See also the *Final Report* (the "Woolf Final Report", 1996)

3   *Ibid*, para 8.

4   See, eg Conrad Dehn QC *Reform of Civil Justice: Essays on "Access to Justice"* (OUP, 1995) at pp 149 -161.

5   *Report of the Review Body on Civil Justice*, Cm 394, 1988, HMSO.

6   *Review of Civil Justice and Legal Aid: Report to the Lord Chancellor by Sir Peter Middleton GCB* ("the Middleton Report"), Lord Chancellors' Dept, September 1997, at para 1.7.

is likely to encourage an adversarial culture and to degenerate into an environment in which the litigation process is too often seen as a battlefield where no rules apply. In this environment, questions of expense, delay, compromise and fairness may have only low priority. The consequence is that expense is often excessive, disproportionate and unpredictable; and delay is frequently unreasonable.[7]

Clearly, the court structure, and the division of jurisdiction between High Court and county court, is one factor that creates delay. It will be recalled that the procedural reforms of the Nineteenth Century were designed to increase the efficiency and effectiveness of the process.[8] Other factors are cost, rules of court and the general expense of legal services.

I   Choice of court

The question of choice of court is at the forefront of the various factors which contribute to current problems about delay, inefficiency and cost. The jurisdictions of the county court and High Court are separate, but overlapping. Each has similar, but different, regimes of procedure and rules.

Historically, determination of civil claims has been undertaken by the High Court and the county courts. In some matters, the jurisdiction of the High Court is exclusive.[9] In others, it is concurrent with the county court, in the sense that an action may be commenced in either. The jurisdiction of the county court in respect of which the Queens Bench Division has jurisdiction has been limited by the financial value of the claim. Prior to 1991, in contract or tort actions, the value of the claim had to be no greater than £5,000. In equity and property matters the figure was £30,000. If the amount of the claim exceeded the jurisdiction of the county court then the matter had to be dealt with by the High Court, subject to statutory powers of transfer between the two courts.[10] Proceedings in the county court were potentially cheaper, but the procedures followed in the county court were not always either speedy or effective. It was hardly surprising, therefore, that the Review Body on Civil Justice[11] found that much of the work tried at High Court level was not of sufficient importance, complexity and substance to justify the time and expense involved in High Court proceedings. It identified the types of cases that did in fact justify proceedings at High Court level. These included:

(a) public law matters, which should be dealt with by way of judicial review;[12]
(b) those matters dealt with in specialist jurisdictions, especially the Commercial Court;[13]
(c) ordinary cases, which were important, complex or which involved a substantial claim. The Review recommended changes to the jurisdiction of the county court, and improved mechanisms for transfer between the two jurisdictions.[14]

As a result of this Review, the Courts and Legal Services Act 1990 altered the whole basis of distribution of work between High Court and county court, although did not

7   Woolf Interim Report, *op cit*, para 4.
8   See p 160, *ante*.
9   See p 170, *ante*.
10   See p 424, *post*.
11   See Civil Justice Review, *op cit*, n 5, *supra*.
12   See p 145, *post*.
13   See p 174, *ante*.
14   Recommendation 1.

adopt in their entirety the recommendations of the Review Body. Section 1 of the 1990 Act empowers the Lord Chancellor to make provision for the allocation of business between the two courts, other than matters to be dealt with by judicial review. In 1991 the Lord Chancellor made the High Court and County Court Jurisdiction Order,[15] which adjusted fundamentally the distribution of work between the two courts. By virtue of this order, there is no longer any limit to the jurisdiction of the county court in contract or tort. The general principle is that a plaintiff is free to choose whichever court is preferred, although in deciding where in fact to commence an action a plaintiff will usually have regard to the court by which such an action will ultimately be tried.[16] The general principle of freedom of choice expressed above is subject to one important qualification: any action of a value less than £50,000[17] and which involves a claim of damages for personal injuries, must be commenced in the county court.[18] There is also a presumption that a non-personal injuries claim of the value between £25,000 and £50,000 will be started in the county court.

This process towards removing difficulties caused by a dual jurisdiction system is taken a significant step further with the recommendations of the Woolf Report, which are discussed later.[19] In essence, in the future jurisdiction will be determined through a multi-track approach whereby the court of trial, and the procedure followed, will be determined by the nature of the claim, including its financial value.

2   Cost

The expensive nature of legal services has already been noted, with the cost of legal aid being increasingly a burden on the State and less readily available to those unable to meet, or meet in full, the costs of civil litigation.[20]

The Woolf Report considered that disproportionate costs permeated many aspects of the civil justice process. In part, this flows from the cost of legal services, and the level of fees charged by lawyers. It also flows from the fact that solicitors generally charge by an hourly rate, thus compounding the effect of cumbersome rules, procedures, or structures that allow the parties to dictate the pace of, and issues to be determined in, litigation. The question of the awards of costs is also relevant.[1] As noted earlier, if no effective rules apply, priority is not always given to the taking of steps to settle the litigation, or to progress it quicker, and therefore more cheaply.[2] Woolf concluded[3] that the expense of litigation is one of the most fundamental problems confronting the civil justice system, quoting Sir Thomas Bingham, the Master of the Rolls, as describing it as "a cancer eating at the heart of the administration of justice". The problem of cost is fuelled by the combative environment in which litigation is conducted.

Excessive cost deters people from making or defending claims. A number of businesses told the Woolf Inquiry that it is often cheaper to pay up, irrespective of the merits, than to defend an action.[4] This is particularly true at the lower end of the scale

---

15   SI 1991/724.
16   See *infra*.
17   Action above this limit must be commenced in the High Court.
18   1991 Order, art 5(1).
19   See p 338, *post*.
20   See p 273, *ante*.
1   See Chapter 19, *post*.
2   Woolf Interim Report, *op cit*, para 17, ch 4.
3   *Ibid*, para 3, ch 1.
4   *Ibid*, para 13.

of litigation. Research undertaken for the Woolf Inquiry showed that in half of the cases examined by the research team, the costs for one party to litigation equalled or exceeded the value of the claim[5] disproportionately. For individual litigants the unaffordable cost of litigation constitutes a denial of access to justice.

This problem of disproportionate cost is most acute in smaller cases where the costs of litigation, for one side alone, frequently equal or exceed the value of what is at issue. The result is often that it is impossible for ordinary people to take or defend smaller cases unless they are legally aided, have insurance backing or believe they can be certain of winning their case and their costs.

3   The adversarial nature of civil litigation

A third factor is that the conduct of civil litigation has, historically, been in the hands of the parties, operating within a framework of rules of court, creating the potential for delay. In *Rastin v British Steel Plc*,[6] Sir Thomas Bingham pointed out that "delay has long been recognised as the enemy of justice". As noted earlier, an adversarial process encourages an adversarial culture, in which the rules governing preparation for trial often contribute to delay and expense. This is discussed later.[7]

The Woolf Interim Report highlighted the problem.[8] In 1994, High Court cases on average took 163 weeks in London and 189 weeks elsewhere to progress from commencement of the action to trial. The great majority of this time was between issue and setting down: 123 weeks in London and 148 weeks elsewhere. The equivalent county court figures were around 80 weeks overall from commencement to trial, with around 60 weeks elapsing before setting down. In the majority of cases the delay arose from a failure to progress the case efficiently, wasting time on peripheral issues or from procedural skirmishing to wear down an opponent or to excuse failure to get on with the case. Woolf considered that this approach was too often condoned by the courts, paradoxically for fear of disadvantaging the litigant. Excessive discovery and the use of experts in heavy demand also both contribute to delay.

4   Rules of Court

Civil litigation is conducted by the parties in accordance with rules of court. In the county court, the relevant rules are the County Court Rules.[9] In the High Court, procedure is governed by the Rules of the Supreme Court.[10] These Rules are delegated legislation, being made by a Rule Committee under powers conferred formerly by the Judicature Acts and currently contained in section 84 of the Supreme Court Act 1981. The Rules themselves together with guides to their interpretation are to be found in the current edition of the *Supreme Court Practice* (the "White Book") which, formerly

5   *Ibid*, para 19, citing research of Professor Hazel Genn.
6   [1994] 2 All ER 641; [1994] 1 WLR 732.
7   See *infra*.
8   *Op cit*, para 35.
9   See p 408, *post*.
10   The Rules of the Supreme Court have their source in the Common Law Procedure Acts 1852 and 1854 and the Court of Chancery Procedure Act 1852 (15 & 16 Vict, c 86). These were substantially reproduced in a Schedule to the Judicature Acts 1873–1875 and later embodied in the Rules of the Supreme Court 1883, a statutory instrument drawn up by the Rule Committee. The current rules were made under the Judicature Act 1925, s 99, the statutory predecessor of the Supreme Court Act 1981, s 84.

published annually, is now produced in a new edition every three years with periodical supplements. It must be stressed that the Rules are purely procedural and cannot affect substantive rules of law. In the words of a Master of the Rolls:

"The relation of the rules of practice to the work of justice is intended to be that of handmaiden rather than mistress."[11]

It should also be appreciated that the Rules are not an exhaustive code either of the jurisdiction of the Supreme Court or of the procedure to be followed. The Supreme Court has, as have all courts whose jurisdiction does not derive entirely from statute, inherent powers and jurisdiction which do not derive from statute and are not necessarily formulated in statutory enactments. Thus, by way of example, the Supreme Court has inherent power to prevent abuse of the process of the court by staying proceedings or striking out claims.[14] The power of a judge to refuse to hear persons who have no right of audience before the court, or counsel who are improperly dressed, or to sit in camera, or to abort a trial and start a new one where a procedural irregularity has occurred, or to adjourn the proceedings are all inherent powers. In recent years the important developments of *Mareva* injunctions[13] and *Anton Piller* orders[14] have derived from the inherent jurisdiction of the court and the judges have formulated their own procedural requirements ancillary to the exercise of their jurisdiction in these areas. Likewise, the court has inherent power to regulate its own procedure. In *Langley v North West Water Authority*[15] the Court of Appeal held that a Liverpool solicitor was bound to comply with a Code of Practice issued by the Liverpool County Court. This amounted to a local Practice Direction which the court was entitled to issue under its inherent jurisdiction, except to the extent that it was concurrent with statute law or rules of court.

These rules of court have the function of providing the framework within which parties work, sometimes describing or prescribing what has to be done and when, and sometimes empowering the parties by enabling a party if it is so desired to take various steps. They have been criticised as leaving the conduct, pace and extent of a case to the parties, with little control on excesses.[16] Indeed, the Woolf Interim Report concluded that the rules are "flouted on a vast scale". The approach of courts to rules governing the timetable for litigation is discussed later,[17] and the approach to the Woolf Report discussed below.[18] Suffice to say that the Woolf Report[19] recommended that, to reduce the complexity of proceedings, there should be a simplified set of rules giving effect to the principles set out in his report, applying to both High Court and county courts, and a single method of starting all claims. To achieve this, the Civil Justice Act 1997 provides the power for a unified set of rules. These are discussed later.[20]

11   Sir Richard Henn Collins MR in *Re Coles and Ravenshear* [1907] 1 KB 1, at 4.
12   See pp 365–369, *post*.
13   See p 359, *post*.
14   See p 357, *post*.
15   [1991] 3 All ER 610, [1991] 1 WLR 697.
16   Woolf Interim Report, *op cit*, Ch 3, para 5.
17   See p 338, *post*.
18   See p 364.
19   *Op cit*, Ch 4, para 17.
20   See p 340, *post*.

5 Efficiency and cost effectiveness

The growing impetus for change is also driven by the need to achieve efficiency and cost-effectiveness. As the Middleton Report put it:[1]

"The civil justice system as a whole is not managed coherently, nor do its individual parts seem to be managed with efficiency much in mind. There is indeed a view that efficiency might be incompatible with justice: that it is always desirable and necessary to take infinite pains in order to achieve the best possible result in each case. Desirable though this may seem as a principle, it inevitably comes up against the limitation of available resources ... I have therefore concentrated on efficiency. I take that to mean getting more out of a given level of resources, or the same amount at lower cost."

It is in this context that several major developments in the civil justice process have occurred. The first is that in the last few years the need for a fundamental change of approach has been recognised, both by the courts and, as already noted, by a series of official reports and research studies. The second is by a growth in forms of dispute adjudication which do not have recourse to the traditional courts (alternative dispute resolution). These include methods of dispute resolution, such as arbitration, which are well known, and others, such as mediation and negotiation, which are newer. The third is by changes in approaches to certain types of action, principally through the small claims procedures of the county court and new approaches relating to group and multi-party actions. This Chapter examines the main features of the existing system, and the broad context of change. Later chapters deal with more detailed matters of civil procedure, actual and proposed.

B ALTERNATIVE FORMS OF RESOLUTION

Increasingly, those with disputes have sought alternative means of dispute resolution. Litigation, particularly in the High Court, is both time-consuming and expensive, and suffers the disadvantage of, generally, being conducted in public.[2] Arbitration has long been an accepted alternative to court procedures, particularly in the sphere of commerce and business, and involves a binding resolution of a dispute by an arbitrator. The principle of arbitration has now been adopted in respect of small claims in the county court[3] although, of course, there is a key difference in that arbitration in the county court results in an enforceable court order. In addition, there has begun a tendency to look for other, more informal forms of mechanism for the resolution of disputes, generally known as Alternative Dispute Resolution.

Unlike arbitration, the characteristics of such mechanisms are, often, those of conciliation, mediation and negotiation, and thus by their nature will not generally involve the imposition of the verdict or conclusion. Such means of avoiding full-scale litigation are particularly helpful to parties to disputes in the commercial or business sectors. In 1994, the Commercial Court issued a Practice Direction[4] where it was stated that:

1　*Op cit*, p 163, *ante*.
2　See p 163, *ante*.
3　See pp 334–338, *post*.
4　*Practice Note (Commercial Court Alternative Dispute Resolution)* [1994] 1 All ER 34, 1 WLR 14.

"the judges of the court wish to encourage parties to consider the use of alternative dispute resolution (ADR), such as mediation and conciliation, as a possible additional means of resolving particular issues or disputes. The judges will not act as mediators or be involved in any ADR process but will in appropriate cases invite parties to consider whether their case, or certain issues in their case, could be resolved by means of ADR. By way of example only, ADR might be tried where the costs of litigation are likely to be wholly disproportionate to the amount at stake...".

Legal advisers should ensure that parties are fully informed as to the most cost-effective means of resolving the particular dispute. The impact of this approach is uncertain, given that, by the time the case has reached the stage of litigation, the parties may be in entrenched positions, and, indeed, it is possible that fruitless mediation or negotiation only increases the delay in commercial cases. More recently, in a working paper on the Civil Justice Reforms,[5] the importance of pre-action settlement work was highlighted. It stated that pre-action work which encourages settlement without litigation, or, if proceedings are issued, provides for the expeditious conduct of those proceedings, must be the norm. It drew attention to the development by practitioners of specific pre-action protocols. Future procedures will be based on the premise that where a pre-action protocol exists, the court will expect this to have been complied with. Parties who have not complied with any such protocol, and fail to satisfy the court as to their reasons for not having done so, may be subject to sanctions, which might include costs, penalties, and refusals of extensions of time for activities that should have been dealt with under the relevant protocol. Thus a protocol specific to clinical dispute resolution has been developed by the Clinical Disputes Forum, and a court in the future may well expect it to have been complied with.[6]

I Mediation and negotiation

Consideration is also being given to forms of such conciliation and mediation in divorce proceedings. Mediation involves the parties being assisted to reach for themselves conclusions about matters in respect of which they are in dispute. Parties to mediation are exposed to a process where the mediator assists in the identification of the key issues and the possible alternative ways of resolving those disputes, leaving the parties themselves to reach an agreement, or not, as the case may be. Clearly mediation will not work if a party refuses to take place in a meaningful dialogue, or where there is no genuine dispute between the parties. The trend generally is towards less court intervention in matrimonial matters. Divorce itself is basically a paper exercise, and the majority of financial matters, and matters relating to children are dealt with by consent. Three-quarters of all financial matters are dealt with by consent orders, orders made by the court on the application of one party and with the agreement of the other. The Family Law Act 1996 encourages and requires mediation to occur. The same philosophy applies in the context of cases involving children, and a range of projects aimed to complement the judicial process through alternative dispute resolution in child care cases, by identifying and exploring the issues to be determined and exploring options to the parties to agree. Pilot projects are being run in child care cases involving

5   *Access to Justice: Judicial Case Management: The Fast Track and Multi Track* (July 1997, Lord Chancellors' Department), at para 2.1.
6   *Access to Justice: Clinical Negligence Cases: Proposed New Procedures: A Consultation Paper*, Lord Chancellors' Dept, 1997.

public law issues: a joint Alternative Dispute Resolution Project is currently being run by National Family Mediation and the Tavistock Centre, funded by the Department of Health, aiming to provide mediation as an alternative to the court process in child protection, fostering, adoption or contact cases where there is a dispute between parents, carers and local authority social workers.[7] National Family Mediation has also developed policies involving mediation in domestic violence cases. Further, statutory complaints mechanisms may exist: failure to utilise them may result in leave for judicial review not being granted.[8]

Such developments are likely to continue. When section 29 of the Family Law Act 1996 is introduced, the Legal Aid Board will require divorcing or separating couples who are eligible for legal aid and who are in dispute on matters relating to children, to attend an interview with a mediator as a pre-condition to the consideration of an application for legal aid. Mediation services are available a growing number of major centres.[9] Apart from family cases, mediation is most commonly used in neighbour and housing disputes, and in the commercial sphere, with about 10,000 cases a year in the first category and about 250 per year in the second.[10] Pilot mediation schemes are also being run in London.

2   Contractual and regulatory dispute resolution

Some contracts specify a form of dispute resolution which, at any rate initially, requires disputes to be arbitrated or decided by an arbitrator or complaint resolution procedure. Examples of this are many, and include not only standard building agreements,[11] but also more consumer-orientated matters such as some disputes between holidaymaker and travel company.[12] Such agreements do not necessarily oust the jurisdiction of the courts. In addition, a range of dispute resolution mechanisms may exist. Lord Woolf in his Final Report identified the fact that applicants for judicial review should be resolved to settle their disputes without recourse to the courts, through grievance procedures and ombudsman remedies increasingly available.[13] Such complaints mechanisms exist increasingly in the sphere of public law, of example the National Health Service complaints procedure or the independent Housing Ombudsman.[14]

These mechanisms may have consequences for the availability of judicial remedies. For example, section 26 of the Children Act 1989 provides for a mechanism for dealing with complaints. In *R v Birmingham City Council, ex parte A*,[15] the applicant sought judicial review of the actions of the local authority in failing to provide suitable accommodation for a severely disturbed child. The application failed, the court holding

7   See Walsh *Working in the Family Justice System* (1997, Family Law) at pp 109–110.
8   See *infra*.
9   The main organisations providing mediation services are Mediation UK (about 2,000 mediators, of whom few are lawyers); the Centre for Dispute Resolution (about 400 mediators, over 60% of whom are lawyers); the ADR Group (56 mediators, all qualified lawyers) and the Academy of Experts (129 mediators, of whom 27 are lawyers): see Middleton Report, *op cit*, p 95.
10   *Ibid*, p 95.
11   See Gould and Cohen, ADR: "Appropriate Dispute Resolution in the UK Construction Industry" [1997] Civil Justice Quarterly, p 103.
12   In the period July 1996–July 1997, some 15,933 complaints were received by the Association of British Travel Agents, of which 1,472 went to arbitration: see Middleton Committee, *op cit*, p 96.
13   *Access to Justice: The Final Report to the Lord Chancellor on the Civil Justice System in England and Wales* ("The Woolf Final Report") 1996, at p 251.
14   For detailed analysis, see Nicol, "Available dispute resolution?" Legal Action, September 1997, p 6.
15   [1997] 2 FLR 841. See also Sir John Donaldson in *R v Secretary of State for the Home Department, ex parte Swati* [1986] 1 All ER 717; [1986] 1 WLR 477.

that the appropriate response was to utilise the statutory complaints mechanism, not to seek judicial review.

3   Arbitration

Arbitration is one, long-standing alternative form of dispute resolution used by parties to contracts, particularly contracts involving the construction industry, and favoured as a form of dispute resolution by parties to international commercial contracts. The law hitherto has been governed by statutory provision, principally the Arbitration Acts of 1950 and 1979, as explained and developed by common law. In 1996 a new Arbitration Act was passed, which repealed earlier legislation, and which was designed to provide a statutory statement of the relevant statutory and common law principles, in clear and comprehensible language, complying where appropriate with international rules and principles governing arbitration.[16] Section 1 of that Act states the general principles governing arbitration:

(a)   the object of arbitration is to obtain the fair resolution of disputes by an impartial tribunal without unnecessary delay or expense;

(b)   the parties should be free to agree how their disputes are resolved, subject only to such safeguards as are necessary in the public interest;

(c)   in matters governed by Part I of the Act (which governs arbitration under an arbitration agreement) the court should not intervene except as the Act provides. The Act applies where the "seat" of the arbitration is in England and Wales, in other words, that it is the jurisdiction designated by the parties to the arbitration agreement, or by or in accordance with that agreement.

The jurisdiction of arbitrators usually arises out of contract, though there are numerous statutory provisions which provide for the reference of disputes to arbitration. An agreement to refer disputes to arbitration is a contract and, as such, is subject to the ordinary law of contract. Such an agreement must be in writing if the provisions of the 1996 Act are to apply.[17] Any provision purporting to oust the jurisdiction of the courts is not effective to do so,[18] though there is no objection to a clause which makes reference to arbitration a condition precedent to a right of action. The effect of such a clause, traditionally known as a *Scott v Avery*[19] clause, is that if a party does institute proceedings without referring the dispute to arbitration, the clause may be pleaded as a defence in those proceedings and the other party may, after acknowledging service of the writ but before taking any other step in the proceedings, apply to the court for an order staying the proceedings.[20] The court must grant a stay unless satisfied that the arbitration agreement is null and void, inoperative, or incapable of being performed. Since legal aid is not available in arbitrations an impecunious plaintiff is at a severe disadvantage if proceedings (in which he would be eligible for legal aid) are stayed.

---

16   See *Report of the Department of Trade and Industry Departmental Advisory Committee on International Commercial Arbitration, 1985* (the Mustill Report). That Committee prepared the draft Bill in 1995.

17   1996 Act, s 5(1).

18   *Ibid*, s 87.

19   (1856) 5 HL Cas 811.

20   Arbitration Act 1996, s 9.

Unlike the position at common law which sometimes applies at common law, the poverty or insolvency of such a plaintiff is not a ground for refusing a stay.[1]

a   Procedure

Procedure on arbitrations is governed (except, in relation to statutory references, where the statute in question otherwise provides) by the Arbitration Act 1996. The issues arising must (in the absence of contrary agreement) be decided according to the rules of law considered to be applicable by the court to be decided in accordance with the principles of conflict of laws.[2] The arbitrator shall act fairly and impartially as between the parties, giving each party a reasonable opportunity of putting his case, and for dealing with his opponents' case, and must adopt procedures suitable to the circumstances of the particular case, avoiding unnecessary delay and expense.[3] The arbitrator shall decide all procedural and evidential matters, subject to the right of the parties to agree any matter. The arbitrator may thus decide when and where proceedings are to be held, in what language, what documents should be produced and disclosed, what questions should be put to and answered by the parties, whether to apply strict rules of evidence, the extent to which their should be oral or written submissions and whether the tribunal should take the initiative in ascertaining the facts and the law.[4] In other words, the arbitrator has complete discretion to depart from traditional procedures, and to act inquisitorially. The arbitrator may appoint experts, legal advisers or assessors to advise them.[5] Parties to arbitration are entitled to legal representation unless they agree otherwise.[6] Since 1990,[7] an arbitrator had no power to dismiss an arbitration for want of prosecution. Section 41 of the 1996 Act entitles an arbitrator to dismiss a claim where:

(a) there has been inordinate and inexcusable delay on the part of the claimant in pursuing the claim; and
(b) the delay
    (i)   will give rise to a substantial risk that it is not possible to have a fair resolution of the issues in that claim; or
    (ii) has caused, or is likely to cause or have caused, serious prejudice to the respondent.

In the absence of specific provision reference to arbitration connotes reference to a single arbitrator.[8] Where specific provision is made for the appointment of two arbitrators there is a requirement to appoint an additional person as chairman. Under section 18 of the 1996 Act the High Court has various powers to appoint arbitrators and umpires in default of appointment by the parties, the Act specifying in detail the various powers that arise so that disputes are resolved without recourse to the court. The High Court also has power to revoke the authority of an arbitrator or umpire on

---

1   Cf *Fakes v Taylor Woodrowe Construction Ltd* [1973] QB 436, [1973] 1 All ER 670. The 1996 Act, s 9, does not include the limited grounds accepted as just reason for a stay in this case.
2   1996 Act, s 46(3).
3   *Ibid*, s 33(1).
4   *Ibid*, s 34(1).
5   *Ibid*, s 37(1).
6   *Ibid*, s 36(1).
7   Arbitration Act 1950, s 13A, introduced by the Courts and Legal Services Act 1990, s 102.
8   1996 Act, s 15(3).

the ground of delay, bias or improper conduct[9] and has inherent jurisdiction to stay arbitration proceedings by injunction. There used to be provision whereby an arbitrator might, and, if directed by the court, had to, state in the form of a "special case" for the opinion of the High Court, either his award or any question of law arising in the reference.[10] The power to apply for a special case was sometimes exercised by a party to delay unduly the resolution of the dispute and to add needlessly to costs. This was altered in 1979, the current provision being found in s 87 of the 1996 Act. This provides that the parties may enter into an "exclusion agreement", but only if they do so after the arbitration has commenced. There will then be no power in the High Court to consider a question of law arising in the course of the arbitration; nor will there be any right of appeal (*infra*). Therefore (subject to the limited power of the High Court to set aside or remit an award for misconduct (*infra*)) the arbitrator's decision will be final. Exclusion agreements entered into before the arbitration is commenced are effective only in a limited class of cases and in particular, are invalid in the case of a "domestic arbitration agreement", that is, basically, an agreement which does not provide for arbitration outside the United Kingdom and is not one to which no United Kingdom national or resident is a party.[11] The decision of the arbitrator is in the form of an "award", dealing with all the issues on which reference was made. The award may contain provision for the payment of money, costs or an order of specific performance (except of a contract relating to land).[12] As between the parties the award gives rise to an estoppel *in personam* in relation to the issues decided, thus extinguishing any cause of action in relation thereto.

b   Intervention by the court

An arbitration award may, with leave of the High Court, be enforced in the same way as a judgment or order of that court and, where leave is granted, judgment may be entered in the terms of the award. In addition action may be brought on the award as a contractual debt.

The court's powers over arbitration proceedings were altered and extended by the 1979 Act and are now contained in s 69 of the 1996 Act. The court may hear an application challenging the award if there has been an error by the arbitrator as to a matter relating to substantive jurisdiction, or where there has been a serious irregularity.[13] A right of appeal on any question of law arising out of an award made on an arbitration agreement exists (unless excluded by a valid "exclusion agreement" (*supra*)) but only by consent of all parties or with leave of the court; the court may not grant leave unless it considers that the determination of the question of law could affect substantially the rights of the parties, that the question was one the arbitrator was asked to determine, that on the basis of the findings of fact the decision is obviously wrong or one of general public importance and the arbitrator's decision is open to serious doubt, and, finally that it is just and proper in all the circumstances for the court to determine the question. It may attach conditions to the grant of leave (for example the provision of security for the amount claimed). In addition to the right of appeal, there

---

9   *Ibid*, s 24.
10   Arbitration Act 1950, s 21.
11   1996 Act, s 85.
12   *Ibid*, s 67.
13   *Ibid*, s 68. The term "serious irregularity" is broadly defined by s 68(2) and includes one or more of the following matters which the court considers has caused or will cause substantial injustice to the applicant: failure to comply with general duties under s 33, exceeding its powers, failure to conduct proceedings in accordance with agreed procedures, uncertainty or ambiguity about its award, the award being obtained by fraud, or irregularity in the conduct of the proceedings.

is jurisdiction in the High Court (save where there is a valid exclusion agreement) to determine any question of law arising in the course of the reference,[14] but only with the consent of the arbitrator or of all the parties. There is an appeal from the High Court to the Court of Appeal, from decisions under Act, but only

(a) with leave of the High Court; and
(b) if the High Court certifies that the question of law is one of general public importance or one which for some other special reason should be considered by the Court of Appeal.[15]

Where an arbitrator has misconducted himself or the proceedings the court may remove him and may set aside the award, or may remit it for reconsideration. The parties may nominate any person they wish to act as arbitrator. Members of the Bar are not infrequently appointed. In addition, by section 93 of the Arbitration Act 1996 a judge of the Commercial Court may, if in all the circumstances he thinks fit, accept appointment as sole arbitrator or as umpire where the dispute appears to him to be of a commercial character and provided the Lord Chief Justice has informed him that, having regard to the state of business in the High Court, he can be made available to do so. Similar powers exist in respect of official referees. Where a judge has acted as arbitrator or umpire under this section appeal lies by case stated to the Court of Appeal.[16]

C   SMALL CLAIMS PROCEDURE

I   Small claims jurisdiction

Claims issued in the county courts of a value below the prevailing "small claims limit" are automatically referred into the small claims procedure when a defence is received. Before 1973 the power of county courts to refer cases to arbitration was limited to those cases in which the parties consented. Accordingly it was exercised only rarely. However, the Administration of Justice Act 1973 created powers to refer small claims of £75 or less to arbitration. That limit has grown, with five increases. The small claims limits are now £3,000, with the exception of personal injury claims where the limit remains at £1,000.[17]

The position is that either party may apply by notice for the case to be referred to arbitration, which may be ordered to take place before the judge, district judge or an outside arbitrator. In addition any proceedings in which the sum claimed or the amount involved does not exceed £3,000 (or £1,000 in personal injury cases) automatically stand referred for arbitration by the district judge[18] upon receipt by the court of a defence to the claim. However in such cases the district judge may on the application of any party rescind the reference if he is satisfied:

(a) that a difficult question of law or a question of fact of exceptional complexity is involved; or
(b) that a charge of fraud against a party is in issue; or
(c) that the parties are agreed that the dispute should be tried in court; or

---

14   *Ibid*, s 45.
15   *Ibid*, s 69(8)
16   RSC Order 61, r 2(6).
17   Ord 19, r 3.
18   But the district judge may, on the application of any party refer the proceedings for arbitration by the judge or an outside arbitrator: Ord 19, r 2(3).

(d) that it would be unreasonable for the claim to proceed to arbitration having regard to its subject matter, the circumstances of the parties or the interests of any other person likely to be affected by the award.[19]

The advantage of arbitration is that it provides a procedure for small claims which is not only expeditious but inexpensive and informal. Thus the hearing is informal and the strict rules of evidence do not apply, the arbitrator may adopt any procedure he wishes to as to afford each party a fair and equal opportunity to present his case and may, with the consent of the parties, consult any expert or call for an expert report on any matter in dispute or invite an expert to attend the hearing as assessor.[20] Furthermore, because in cases automatically referred no solicitors' charges are usually allowed as between party and party, litigants in, for example, consumer disputes can freely take their case to the county court in the knowledge that they are not at risk for substantial costs. In these ways the county court is able to exercise its original function as a "small-claims" court, readily accessible to litigants in person. An individual may be represented by a person other than a lawyer, subject to certain controls left in the hands of the court to prevent demonstrably unsuitable persons from exercising that right.[1] Rules of Court provide that the arbitrator may assist unrepresented parties where appropriate by putting questions to witnesses and the opposing party, or by explaining legal terms and expressions. Following the hearing, the costs which can be awarded to the successful party are strictly limited, unless the opposing party has been guilty of "unreasonable conduct". There is no provision for the judge to award the costs of legal representation.

2 Changes to jurisdiction

The essential feature of the small claims procedure is that many of the disputes which are brought to the court for resolution do not involve the degree of legal or factual complexity which would give rise to a need for parties to be represented by professional lawyers.[1] What is required is adjudication by an authoritative, impartial third party, with an understanding of the relevant law and both the ability and the power to decide the issues in dispute. To meet the needs of the parties, and to avoid the deterrent effect of cost and delay, the procedure should be informal and low-risk, and the case should be disposed of in a short time. In view of the volume and range of cases covered, the procedure must also have the maximum possible flexibility, commensurate with the need to safeguard the rights of the parties.

The Lord Chancellor in 1997[2] described the small claims procedure as a major success of the civil justice system. It is quick (the average time between summons and start of the hearing being 21 weeks), simple (with an informal hearing) and cheap. It is proposed that the limit for automatic reference into the procedure be raised for all cases except those for personal injury from £3,000 to £5,000. That recommendation follows the proposal of the Woolf Interim Report[3] that the small claims limit should initially be raised to £3,000, and then, after monitoring, possibly to £5,000. It is intended that the higher small claims figure will be in place by April 1999.[4] The further

---

19   Ord 19, r 2(4).
20   Ord 19, r 7.
1   Lay Representation (Rights of Audience) Order 1992, made under Courts and Legal Services Act 1990, s 11.
2   See *Small Claims Procedure*, 1997, Lord Chancellor's Dept.
3   *Op cit*, p 118.
4   Speech of Lord Irvine LC to the Solicitors' Annual Conference, Cardiff, 18 October 1997.

recommendation of the Woolf Report that the discretion given to district judges to transfer cases out of the procedure be widened is also implemented, thus perhaps meeting some of the objections of those who believe that the small claims procedure will be unsuitable for a greater number of cases as its scope is extended.[5] A protocol for the conduct of small claims arbitrations has been developed by the Judicial Studies Board and Association of District Judges and widely disseminated to the judiciary.[6]

Research commissioned by the Lord Chancellor's Department was published in 1994, which showed the popularity of the system amongst those who use it. It is this popularity, principally based on speed and cheapness, which provides justification for the extension of the small claims procedure to a greater number of cases. In its judgement in the case of *Afzal v Ford Motor Co Ltd,*[7] the Court of Appeal concluded that the small claims procedure was appropriate for the disposal of the general run of low-value personal injury claims, rejecting the argument that parties to this type of claim invariably required legal representation. Lord Woolf, in his Interim Report published in 1995, differed from the Court of Appeal in accepting some of the arguments for legal representation. He did, however, believe that lower value personal injury claims should be subject to limits on levels of cost and procedural complexity. He therefore recommended that all personal injury claims valued at less than £10,000 should be dealt with a new fast track procedure.[8] Pending introduction of the fast track, he recommended that personal injury claims valued at less than £1,000 should continue to be dealt with in the small claims procedure.[9] In the Middleton Report it was recommended that the separate, lower, limit for personal injury claims be abolished. He did not accept that exceptions of this kind were appropriate, and recommended a standard small claims limit to apply equally to all categories of claim. This recommendation was not accepted. The Lord Chancellor was concerned that claims valued at above £1,000 are likely to involve more severe injuries, and may as a result require a greater degree of investigation and, potentially, argument. By contrast, he agreed with the views of the Court of Appeal in *Afzal*, that claims relating to minor injuries do not, *per se*, require the full panoply of the courts. It is therefore proposed that personal injury cases valued at less than £1,000[10] should continue to be subject to referral into the small claims procedure after the introduction of the fast track.

It is proposed that the standard small claims limit should continue to apply to all categories of claim other than personal injury claims. The decision of the Court of Appeal in *Joyce v Liverpool City Council*[11] clarified the range of claims which should be subject to automatic reference into the small claims procedure, dealing with claims under Section 11 of the Landlord and Tenant Act 1985 (housing disrepair actions). Following publication of the Woolf Interim Report, which welcomed the judgment, the view was strongly expressed by housing law practitioners that housing disrepair claims should be excluded from reference into the small claims procedure. It was argued that disrepair cases were unsuited to the small claims forum due to complexity of the facts and law involved; inequality of means of the parties; the fact that some plaintiffs

5   See eg Zander, at [1998] MLR 538.
6   See, generally, Small Claims Procedure (1997), *op cit*, 19.
7   [1994] 4 All ER 720.
8   See p 339, *post*.
9   Interim Report, page 117.
10   Order 19 of the current County Court Rules does not specifically define which damages should be included when assessing whether a "claim for damages for personal injury" exceeds the £1,000 limit. In view of the uncertainty which this has created for some litigants it is proposed that the rules should be amended to make clear that the £1,000 limit refers only to the damages in respect of the injury itself, and not to any other damages arising from the allegedly tortious act.
11   [1996] QB 252; [1995] 3 All ER 110.

may be illiterate or otherwise incapable of conducting their case; difficulty in identifying and collecting the evidence required; and the requirement for expert evidence. These are factors that can exist in a great range of cases, and are not confined to housing disrepair actions.

There is provision for a case to be referred out of the small claims procedure where the district judge believes that it is unsuited for this method of disposal. In view of the arbitrator's responsibility to take account of the representation of the parties in his conduct of the hearing, inequality of representation is not, of itself, an appropriate reason for a case to be transferred. Excessive legal or factual complexity, on the other hand, may justify re-allocation, as may the incapacity of a party. In its judgment in *Afzal* the Court of Appeal ruled that a transfer out of the small claims procedure could be justified on the basis of "the circumstances of the parties [which] may, for example, include physical disability, poor sight, pronounced stammer or inability to read". In the light of the above, housing claims are to be retained within the scope of the small claims procedure. However, two specific amendments were made to the Rules of Court in early 1996. The first of these was an increase in amount which can be recovered for an expert's report to £200. The second was a specific new provision recognising that those bringing this type of claim or, indeed, any claim for an injunction or an order for specific performance, had a particular need for legal advice. For those eligible, such advice may be available under the Legal Aid Green Form scheme.[12] In addition, Rules of Court were amended to provide that the successful litigant in this type of claim could be awarded an additional sum of up to £260 in respect of the cost of legal advice. The Lord Chancellor believes that these new provisions will be adequate to ensure that where a case is too complex for the small claims procedure, or one of the parties is incapable of conducting their case in that procedure, it will be referred for re-allocation, and that parties in cases which remain in the small claims procedure will have access to legal advice and assistance in preparing their case.[13]

In the Woolf Interim Report, it was recommended that it should be possible for small claims to be dealt with by an arbitrator other than the district judge. This recommendation caused concern, in the light of the pivotal role of the arbitrator. Lord Woolf described this role as:

"a key safeguard of the rights of both parties ... His duty is to ascertain the main matters at issue, to elicit the evidence, to reach a view on the facts of the matter and to give a decision... he should ensure that both parties have presented the evidence and called the witnesses germane to their case and that he has identified and considered any issue of law which is pertinent to the case in hand. He must also hold the ring and ensure that each party has a fair chance to present his own case and to challenge that of his opponent".[14]

However, amendments are proposed to maintain the arbitrator's flexibility in the conduct of the hearing. Research conducted, and anecdotal evidence also, indicates that an increasing number of litigants are represented at small claims hearings by members of the legal profession, including, in some cases, representation by counsel. There is, of course, no provision for the costs of such representation to be recovered by the successful party, and the quantitative research conducted for the Lord Chancellor's Department does not indicate that an imbalance of representation between the parties has any significant impact on their chances of success. An increasing

---

12   See p 279, *ante*.
13   Small Claims Procedure, *op cit*.
14   *Op cit*, p 108.

tendency toward legal representation may be related to the increase in the small claims limit. There is no correlation between value and complexity, and it is considered that there is no reason to suppose that an increase in the limit leads to a more widespread need for legal representation.[15] However, it is possible that those with higher value claims will be more prepared to pay the costs of legal representation, as payment of these will take a smaller bite out of the moneys recovered (or saved) in a successful action.

D   THE APPROACH FOR THE FUTURE

It will be very clear from the above that key changes are underway. As already seen, the catalyst for change was provided by the Woolf Report, with its analysis and recommendations.

That analysis concentrated on the factors that make litigation expensive, slow and cumbersome. The pace, conduct and extent of litigation is left in the hands of the parties, with no effective control of excesses. Woolf considered the complexity of current rules facilitates the use of adversarial tactics.[16]

Rules of court are flouted on a vast scale. The timetables they contain are generally ignored and their other requirements are complied with when convenient to the interests of one of the parties and not otherwise. Woolf considered that the powers of the courts have fallen behind the more sophisticated and aggressive tactics of some litigators. The orders for costs which are made[17] are an ineffective sanction, applied after the damage is done. The delay in being able to obtain effective intervention by the court both encourages rule-breaking and discourages the party who would be prejudiced from applying for preventive measures. The main procedural tools for conducting litigation efficiently have each become subverted from their proper purpose. Pleadings[18] often fail to state the facts as the rules require, leading to a fundamental deficiency, namely the failure to establish the issues in the case at a reasonably early stage, from which many problems result.[19] New procedures have become bogged down in technicalities or excesses, especially in respect to expert evidence and discovery.[20]

Like the Middleton Report was later to do,[1] Woolf focused on cost.[2] The cost to society through legal aid is high and rising. In 1993/94, the net cost of civil non-matrimonial proceedings was £350 million, amounting to 34% of total legal aid expenditure in that year. This was a considerable increase from 1991/92, when the corresponding figures were £241 million or 31% of the total. For individual legally-aided litigants, the high cost of litigation impacts through the increased contributions which they now have to pay throughout the duration of the case and the statutory charge on any compensation they recover. The Report concluded the present approach to litigation usually results in total uncertainty for the parties as to what litigation will require and consequently the amount of expenditure in which they may be involved and the timescale of that involvement. This arises from a number of factors:

(a)   the rule that costs normally follow the event and the inevitable uncertainty as to the outcome of litigation;

15   Small Claims Procedure, *op cit.*
16   Woolf, Interim Report, *op cit*, para 5.
17   See Chapter 19, *post.*
18   See pp 380–385, *post.*
19   Woolf Interim Report, *op cit*, para 9.
20   *Ibid*, paras 10–11. See pp 385–390, *post.*
1   See p 323, *ante.*
2   Woolf, *op cit*, para 16.

(b) the present procedures when management of the case is primarily a matter for the parties and either side can influence not only its own costs but also its opponents';

(c) the requirement of the adversarial system that every aspect of a case be fully investigated. This encourages excessive work and cost on issues which are often recognised from an early stage as peripheral. Under the present system, this can be justified, if failure to do this might amount to professional negligence;

(d) the present charging system, on a daily or hourly basis, which means that the more that is done on a case, the more lawyers are paid;

(e) discontinuity in the handling of cases which results in the additional work necessary to refresh memories.

There is simply no effective control on costs. Woolf did not consider this situation to be inevitable. Nor, he concluded, was delay. The effect of this was explained as follows:

"Delay is an additional source of distress to parties who have already suffered damage. It postpones the compensation or other remedy to which they may be entitled. It interferes with the normal existence of both individuals and businesses. In personal injury cases, it can exacerbate or prolong the original injury. It can lead to the collapse of relationships and businesses. It makes it more difficult to establish the facts because memories fade and witnesses cannot be traced. It postpones settlement but may lead parties to settle for inadequate compensation because they are worn down by delay or cannot afford to continue."[3]

The reasons for delay may be, for example, to allow a medical condition to stabilise. Where settlement occurs, it often occurs too late.[4]

The Woolf Report analysed the whole process of civil process, particularly case management, and the procedures adopted both prior to, and at, trial. His conclusions were summarised as follows:

(a) An expanded small claims jurisdiction extended up to £3,000.[5]

(b) A new fast track for straightforward cases not exceeding £10,000. This will be a strictly limited procedure designed to take cases to trial within a short but reasonable timescale. There will be fixed costs. Discovery will be limited. The hearing will be no more than half a day and there will be no oral evidence from experts.

(c) A new multi-track, for cases above £10,000, spanning both High Court and county court cases and providing appropriate and proportionate case management. Individual hands-on case management will be concentrated on those cases which require significant attention and will most benefit from it. Other cases in the multi-track will proceed on standard or individually tailored timetables, according to standard or individual directions.

(d) Within the multi-track there will be effective consideration of the case at at least two key stages:
 (i) at a case management conference early in the case; and
 (ii) at a pre-trial review, shortly before trial.

(e) The most complex and important cases will be heard only by High Court judges and not by deputies. Other cases will be managed and heard by the appropriate level of judge and will be able to move flexibly within the system to ensure this.

---

3   *Ibid*, para 30.
4   *Ibid*, paras 34–40.
5   See p 335, *ante*.

(f) The cases will be managed by procedural judges who will generally be Masters or district judges working in teams with High Court and circuit judges. For the heavier cases, requiring full hands-on judicial control, the procedural judge may be a High Court or circuit judge. The procedural judge will: conduct the initial scrutiny of all cases to allocate them to the appropriate management track; conduct the case management conference unless it is more appropriate for the trial judge to do so; generally monitor the progress of the case and investigate if parties are failing to comply with timetables or directions; and draw the existence of Alternative Dispute Resolution (ADR) to parties' attention where this is appropriate or desirable. The trial judge will normally conduct the pre-trial review.

(g) Case management will facilitate and encourage earlier settlement through earlier identification and determination of issues and tighter timetables. Other measures to encourage settlement will include the introduction of plaintiffs' offers and a requirement to report on costs at key stages.

(h) A range of detailed procedural changes are to be introduced.

These recommendations were broadly endorsed by the Middleton Report,[6] and accepted generally by the Government. To facilitate these fundamental changes, the Government took through Parliament what is now the Civil Procedure Act 1997. That Act paves the way for detailed changes. It does so by, in s 1, providing for a new set of procedural rules, the Civil Procedure Rules, which will apply to Court of Appeal, High Court and county court proceedings. The power to make new rules is to be exercised with a view to securing that the civil justice system is accessible, fair and efficient.[7] These rules will be made by a new Civil Procedure Rule Committee.[8] In addition, a new Civil Justice Council is established by s 6 of the 1997 Act.

---

6   See p 323, *ante*.
7   1997 Act, s 1 (3).
8   *Ibid*, s 2.

Chapter 16

Commencing Proceedings

A CHOICE OF COURT

At present, but not in the future after the Woolf Civil Justice Reforms[1] are implemented and bring, in their wake, an integrated civil justice system, the choice of where to commence the action will turn on what is the appropriate court of trial. If the matter is within the exclusive jurisdiction of the High Court, or of the county court, that is where the action should be commenced, by writ or summons respectively. If small claims[2] jurisdiction is sought, clearly the county court will be the forum of the case. If judicial review[3] is sought an application will be made to the Divisional Court of the Queens Bench Division. However, it will be recalled[4] that section 1 of the Courts and Legal Services Act 1990 empowers the Lord Chancellor to make provision for the allocation of business.

Article 7 of the High Court and County Court Jurisdiction Order[5] creates a presumption that cases of a value less than £25,000 must be tried in the county court, and those of a value of £50,000 or more in the High Court. The position will be otherwise if application of certain criteria shows that a different court of trial is in fact appropriate. These criteria also apply in deciding in which court cases falling between these two financial figures should be tried, with one proviso. Cases involving personal injury claims of an estimated amount less than £50,000 must be commenced in the county court. The criteria mentioned above are set out in Article 7(5) of the order, which deals primarily with the transfer of cases between the two jurisdictions. However, they are equally relevant to the question of initial choice of jurisdiction. The factors identified are as follows:

(i)   the financial substance of the action, including that of any counter-claim;
(ii) whether the action is otherwise important, for example by raising issues of general public importance, or where the case will amount to a test case;

1   See p 339, *ante*.
2   See p 334, *ante*.
3   See p 145, *ante*.
4   See p 325, *ante*.
5   SI 1991/724.

(iii) the complexity of the facts, legal issues, remedies or procedures involved. Complex cases are more suitable for High Court trial;
(iv) whether transfer of the case will lead to more speedy trial, although this alone should not be a determining factor.

In addition certain types of case may be particularly suitable for High Court trial.[6] These include claims of professional negligence, fatal accident claims, allegations of fraud or undue influence, defamation cases, claims based on allegations of malicious prosecution or false imprisonment, and claims against the police. In such cases it is likely that High Court trial will ultimately be ordered,[7] and that may be decisive in determining where such actions should be commenced.

To facilitate the greater use of the county court jurisdiction, section 38 of the County Courts Act 1984[8] gave to the county court, generally speaking, the power to make any order which could be made by the High Court if the proceedings were in that court. That power is subject to any limitation imposed by regulations made by the Lord Chancellor,[9] and in fact regulations have been made specifically prohibiting a county court from making an *Anton Piller* order[10] or issuing a *Mareva* injunction.[11] In substantial cases where such orders may be crucial to the obtaining of information or prevention of dissipation of assets, these restrictions may conclusively influence the choice of High Court rather than county court jurisdiction. Within this framework the solicitor will choose the appropriate jurisdiction. That choice may be influenced by tactical reasons. For example, High Court proceedings may create an impression of seriousness and importance and be regarded by some as more intimidating. The solicitor may prefer the procedures of the High Court to those of the county court, or, conversely, may prefer the geographical proximity of the county court. However, where a choice of High Court jurisdiction is wrongly made, the plaintiff may be penalised by suffering a reduction in the costs that may be awarded upon taxation.[12]

The total effect of these changes is that the vast majority of actions, some 90%, commence in the county court.[13] The High Court is the forum for the more specialist and difficult cases.

B   COMMENCING A CIVIL ACTION

I   Writs and summons

A county court action is, generally, commenced by summons.[14] An action in the Queen's Bench Division is in most cases commenced by writ of summons, generally referred to as a writ. A writ notifies the defendant of the issue of the writ, and informs him that he must either satisfy the claim set out on the back of the writ or return to the court office the accompanying acknowledgement of service saying whether he intends

6   Report of the Review Body on Civil Justice (Cm 394, 1988, HMSO).
7   In some of them jury trial is available: see p 399, *post.*
8   Inserted by the Courts and Legal Services Act 1990, s 3.
9   Supreme Court Act 1981, s 38(4)
10   County Court Remedies Regulations 1991, reg 3(3)(b).
11   *Ibid.*
12   See Supreme Court Act 1981, s 51(8), inserted by the Courts and Legal Services Act 1990, s 4. For wasted costs orders, see p 428, *post.*
13   See p 325, *ante.*
14   See p 411, *post.*

to contest the proceedings. It also informs him that if he fails to satisfy the claim or return the acknowledgement, judgment may be entered against him.[15]

However there are alternative methods of proceeding, of which the most important is by originating summons.[16] The latter method is appropriate where the parties' dispute is such that it can be peremptorily determined. As the name indicates it is a summons which actually originates the action as opposed to the issue of an ordinary summons which is an interlocutory step in an action commenced by writ. The method which the plaintiff chooses is not in all cases optional. Thus the following proceedings in the Queen's Bench Division must be begun by writ:

(1) in which a claim is made by the plaintiff for any relief or remedy for any tort, other than trespass to land;

(2) in which a claim made by the plaintiff is based on an allegation of fraud;

(3) in which a claim is made by the plaintiff for damages for breach of duty where the damages claimed consist of or include damages in respect of the death of any person or in respect of personal injuries to any person or in respect of damage to any property.[17] One type of action must be commenced by originating summons; where any Act requires an application to be made to the High Court other than an application in pending proceedings and no other method is prescribed.[18] A common example is an application, made before commencing an action, for discovery of documents under section 33(2) of the Supreme Court Act 1981.[19] All other actions may be commenced either by writ or by originating summons but the following proceedings are appropriate to be commenced by originating summons:

(1) in which the sole or principal question at issue is, or is likely to be, one of the construction of an Act, or of any instrument made under an Act, or of any deed, will, contract or other document, or some other question of law, or

(2) in which there is unlikely to be any substantial dispute of fact.[20] Since these actions are not concerned with disputes as to fact it would be pedantic for the parties to have to exchange pleadings. The originating summons procedure is not, therefore, appropriate where there is a significant dispute upon the facts. Nor is it appropriate where the plaintiff intends to apply for summary judgment under Order 14, since this important order applies only to actions commenced by writ. The tort of trespass to land is excepted from those proceedings which must be begun by writ because this action frequently involves a dispute as to title which can be resolved by reference to a single deed or contract, the very type of case with which originating summons procedure is appropriate to deal. The only other methods of commencing proceedings in the High Court are by originating motion or petition, but these methods are applicable if, and only if, expressly authorised by the rules or by any Act.[1] Proceedings by petition occur in both the Chancery Division (for example for the winding-up of companies) and the Family Division (for example judicial separation proceedings), but not in the Queen's Bench Division, with the exception

---

15   RSC, App A, Form No 1 (substituted by the Rules of the Supreme Court (Writ and Appearance) 1979, with effect from 3 June 1980); the old form of writ was in the form of a royal command to the defendant to enter an appearance.

16   The extension of originating summons procedure in the Queen's Bench Division was an important innovation of the 1962 Rules. Prior to 1964 originating summonses were far more common in the Chancery Division and, in the Queen's Bench Division, were confined mainly to applications under s 17 of the Married Women's Property Act 1882 (which are now assigned to the Family Division).

17   Ord 5, r 2.

18   Ord 5, r 3.

19   See p 355, *post*.

20   Ord 5, r 4.

1   Ord 5, r 5.

of election petitions under the Representation of the People Act 1983. Having considered which is the appropriate method of proceeding the plaintiff must, before issuing his writ, consider two further preliminary matters. First he must ensure that his cause of action has accrued since, in order to succeed in his action, the plaintiff must prove a cause of action which was complete at the date of the issue of the writ. So, for example, an action for the recovery of a debt would be bound to fail if the debt had not fallen due before the issue of the writ even though, when the action came to trial, the debt was clearly overdue. It is axiomatic that English courts will not adjudicate upon hypothetical, as opposed to actual, disputes.[2]

The second matter which he must consider concerns the proper parties to the action.

2   Parties to proceedings

The names of all intended parties must appear at the head of the writ. There may be any number of plaintiffs or defendants, or both, to the action. At common law the effect of misjoinder or non-joinder of proper parties was to defeat the plaintiff's claim but nowadays "no cause or matter shall be defeated by reason of the misjoinder or non-joinder of any party".[3] However, the plaintiff must still weigh carefully his choice of parties. On the one hand he may fail to join a party from whom he is entitled to relief in which case his whole action may fail. Alternatively he may add parties whose presence is unnecessary in which event he will usually have to pay the costs occasioned by his error. Subject to the court's power to order separate trials or add or strike out parties,[4] two or more persons may be joined as plaintiffs or defendants in the following circumstances:

(1) where:
     (a) if separate actions were brought by or against each of them, as the case may be, some common question of law or fact would arise in all the actions; and
     (b) all rights to relief claimed in the action (whether they are joint, several or alternative) are in respect or arise out of the same transaction or series of transactions; and
(2) in any other case with leave of the court.[5]

The plaintiff should join all potential defendants whether relief is alleged to exist against them jointly, severally or in the alternative, for even in the latter circumstance the plaintiff, although he obviously must fail against one or more defendants, may not suffer by it. The reason is that if the court is satisfied that it was a proper course for the plaintiff to join the defendants, it may order the costs of the successful defendant to be

---

2   *Re Barnato* [1949] Ch 258; cf *Ealing London Borough v Race Relations Board* [1972] AC 342; [1972] 1 All ER 105 and authorities referred to therein. The power of the High Court to make a declaratory judgment or order (Ord 15, r 16) can be exercised in relation to future rights but is only so exercised in exceptional cases, for example where future rights affect the present situation. A declaration which relates to a purely hypothetical issue or which would serve no useful purpose will not be made; cf *Mellstrom v Garner* [1970] 2 All ER 9; [1970] 1 WLR 603. If a writ is issued prematurely the defect is incurable by amendment since amendment dates back to the issue of the writ (*Eshelby v Federated European Bank* [1932] 1 KB 254); the plaintiff's only course is to apply to discontinue the action (see p 366, *post*).
3   Ord 15, r 6(1).
4   Ord 15, rr 5(1), 6(2).
5   Ord 15, r 4.

added to the costs payable by the unsuccessful defendant.[6] Thus if a plaintiff is injured in a "running down" case he should join the drivers of all the vehicles (unless the liability of one driver, to the exclusion of the others, is prima facie obvious, in which event a wise course is to sue only one driver and then to join, by amendment, such other persons as the defendant "blames" in his defence);[7] where he seeks an injunction to abate a nuisance he should join both the landlord and the tenant of the premises from which the alleged nuisance comes; where he is uncertain whether a woman has contracted with him as agent of her husband or as a principal he should join both the husband and wife.[8] In addition, under Order 15, rule 6(2), at any stage of the proceedings the court may, of its own motion or on application

(a) strike out any party who is not a necessary or proper party; or
(b) add as a party any person whose presence is necessary to ensure that all matters in dispute may be effectively and completely determined or any person between whom and any party there may exist a question or issue connected with the action which in the opinion of the court it would be just and convenient to determine.

Thus in *Gurtner v Circuit*[9] the Motor Insurers Bureau successfully applied to be added as a defendant to an action for damages by a pedestrian against a motor cyclist, on the basis that, since neither the original defendant nor his insurers could be traced, the Bureau might, by reason of its agreement with the Minister of Transport to satisfy all unpaid damages awarded against an uninsured motorist, have to pay any damages awarded. This gave the Bureau a legal and pecuniary interest in the proceedings sufficient to justify its joinder, notwithstanding that the plaintiff had no cause of action against the Bureau. As in all branches of the law there are special rules which apply only to certain classes of person, usually by reason of a status. The prospective plaintiff must in particular determine whether a prospective defendant is the subject of any of these special rules.

Special parties

THE CROWN[10]
Until 1948, as an offshoot of the principle of Crown immunity, the Crown could not be made a party to an action in the courts, the only redress being against Crown servants in their personal capacity. However, by the Crown Proceedings Act 1947 the Crown may now, subject to minor exceptions, be sued in contract or tort. The immunity now extends only to the reigning monarch, although there is still a rule of statutory interpretation that the Crown is not bound by a statute unless expressly named in it. An action is commenced by or against the Crown through its appropriate government department as named in a list issued by the Treasury and service is on the solicitor for that department. If there is no appropriate department proceedings are carried on in the name of the Attorney-General. Although the Crown now has few relics of substantive immunity it enjoys certain procedural advantages; for example that

---

6   See p 426, *post*.
7   Counsel who fails to bear these precepts in mind may be liable in negligence; *Saif Ali v Sydney Mitchell & Co* [1980] AC 198; [1978] 3 All ER 1033; see p 265, *ante*.
8   *Morel Brothers v Earl of Westmorland* [1904] AC 11; unless, of course, prior correspondence or negotiation has disclosed that there is no issue on the point.
9   [1968] 2 QB 587; [1968] 1 All ER 328; cf *Sanders Lead Co Inc v Entores Metal Brokers Ltd* [1984] 1 All ER 857; [1984] 1 WLR 452.
10 The special rules of procedure applicable in proceedings to which the Crown is a party are contained in Ord 77.

judgment in default cannot be entered against the Crown without leave, that judgment under Order 14 cannot be entered against the Crown and that the Crown is not liable to have any judgment enforced against it. Action against the Crown pursuant to the provisions of the 1947 Act lies only in respect of liability arising in the United Kingdom.[11] In *Franklin v A-G*[12] Lawson J was faced with the difficult task of deciding what was the appropriate form of proceedings to enforce a right existing against the Bank of England in relation to the plaintiff's entitlement to interest on Southern Rhodesia stock. The method of enforcement prescribed by the Colonial Stock Act 1877, section 20 was petition of right, under the then Petitions of Right Act 1860. However, that 1860 Act had been repealed by the Crown Proceedings Act 1947 and, as noted above, no action lay under the 1947 Act since the liability of the Crown did not arise within the United Kingdom. It was held, by Lawson J, that the procedure was by petition of right but in the old form used prior to the Act of 1860. This would seem to be the only surviving instance of the ancient procedure of petition of right whereby the sovereign is petitioned to "order that right be done in this matter".[13] The sovereign then refers the petition to the Queen's Bench Division for consideration and the High Court then makes an order which appears to have the effect of a judgment against the Crown.

FOREIGN STATES

Foreign states, their sovereigns or other heads of state (in their public capacity), their governments and departments of government are immune from the jurisdiction of the courts of the United Kingdom, subject to the exceptions provided by the State Immunity Act 1978.[14] However, that does not mean that a foreign state cannot, or should not, be made a party to an action. It may submit to the jurisdiction by taking a step in the proceedings, for example acknowledging service, and a state is not immune if it intervenes or submits to the jurisdiction (unless it does so only for the purpose of claiming immunity or asserting an interest in property in circumstances in which it could have claimed immunity had it been sued, or it takes a step in ignorance of its entitlement to immunity, provided it claims immunity as soon as reasonably practicable).[15] Moreover the immunity does not extend to proceedings in respect of commercial transactions,[16] contracts requiring performance in the United Kingdom, certain contracts of employment, death, personal injury or damage to property caused in the United Kingdom and certain other proceedings described in the Act.[17] The effect of the Act has therefore been to restrict considerably the immunity from suit which foreign states formerly enjoyed at common law. Quite apart from the Act, the House of Lords has held that the immunity does not extend to activities, trading, commercial or otherwise, of a private law character in which the state in question has chosen to engage, but is limited to sovereign or public acts.[18] An international organisation created by treaty cannot sue or be sued, except in certain circumstances. In *Arab Monetary Fund v Hashim (No 3)*[19] the House of Lords held that, although such an organisation

---

11   Crown Proceedings Act 1947, s 40(2).
12   [1974] QB 185; [1973] 1 All ER 879.
13   For the full form of the petition, see *Franklin v R* [1974] QB 202n; [1973] 3 All ER 861.
14   Act of 1978, ss 1, 14.
15   *Ibid*, s 2.
16   *Ibid*, s 3(1)(a) affirming *Trendtex Trading Corporation Ltd v Central Bank of Nigeria* [1977] QB 529; [1977] 1 All ER 881; see p 64, *ante*.
17   *Ibid*, ss 2.
18   *I Congresso del Partido* [1983] 1 AC 244; [1981] 2 All ER 1064.
19   [1991] 2 AC 114; [1991] 1 All ER 871.

was not a corporate body, with capacity to sue or be sued in the English courts, the registration of the treaty in one of the sovereign states conferred legal personality on the organisation, which English courts should recognise, thus enabling it to maintain an action. This explained the earlier decision in *McClaine Watson v Department of Trade and Industry*[20] with the effect that the member states who had established the Council could not be liable in law under the International Tin Agreement. Writs and documents are served through the Foreign and Commonwealth Office to the Ministry of Foreign Affairs of the state. Foreign states enjoy certain procedural privileges under section 13 of the Act, with certain remedies not being available against them, principally injunctions and specific performance.

INCORPORATED ASSOCIATIONS

An association may be incorporated either by royal charter or under a statute, usually one of the Companies Acts. In either case the creation is a legal persona with an existence, for the purposes of the law, completely independent of its members.[1] It is this factor which distinguishes a corporation or company from an unincorporated association, which is merely a group of individuals referred to by a collective name. An incorporated association may enter into contracts and may commit torts and even crimes. As a legal personality it may sue and be sued in its corporate title or registered name. However, since it has no physical existence, it can only appear through a solicitor.[2]

UNINCORPORATED ASSOCIATIONS

An association which is not incorporated, under royal charter or statute, has no legal existence independent of the members of the association. There are for procedural purposes three classes of unincorporated association: partnerships, registered associations and unregistered associations.

Partners may sue and be sued in the firm name.[3] However if suing in the firm name they must on request disclose the name and address of every member of the firm.[4] If they are sued in the firm name, the partners must acknowledge service in their own names individually although proceedings continue in the name of the firm. Any person who denies that he is or was a partner when the cause of action arose should so state in his acknowledgement of service.[5] A judgment against a partnership may be executed against partnership property or against any person who has acknowledged service of the writ as a partner or failed to acknowledge service having been served as a partner, has admitted in his pleading that he is a partner or has been adjudged to be a partner.[6]

Certain associations are by statute registrable. This does not affect the position of the members but it does enable the association to appear in its registered name. The

---

20 [1990] 2 AC 418; [1989] 3 All ER 523.
1   *Salomon v A Salomon & Co Ltd* [1897] AC 22.
2   So that the litigant's right to appear in person (Ord 5, r 6) does not extend to corporations or companies. They may, however, acknowledge service (and give notice of intention to defend) by a duly authorised person instead of a solicitor (Ord 2, r 1(2)).
3   Ord 81, r 1
4   Ord 81, r 2
5   Ord 81, r 4; he may then apply to the court to set aside service.
6   Ord 81, r 5; such a judgment may also be executed against the private property of any other partner, but only with leave.

most common examples of such associations are trade unions[7] and friendly societies.[8] Where an association is unregistered and not a partnership it cannot appear in its group name, since that name is no more than a convenient label for the members collectively.[9] Frequently the proper parties to the action will be members of the association in their private capacity. Where, however, the right or liability is common to all the members it is inconvenient, although possible, in join them all as parties. The appropriate procedure is a "representative action". These are discussed below.[10]

PERSONS UNDER DISABILITY; INFANTS AND PATIENTS

A married woman has, since 1935, ceased to be a person under a disability[11] and that phrase now applies only to infants and patients. An infant is a person under the age of 18.[12] A patient is a person who, by reason of mental disorder within the meaning of the Mental Health Act 1983, is incapable of managing and administering his property and affairs.[13] Infants and patients cannot appear personally. They sue by their "next friend".[14] In the case of an infant this is usually the father or person *in loco parentis*; in the case of a patient, his receiver. In any case where there is no person competent or willing to appear as next friend, the Official Solicitor will do so. The next friend is not a party to the action (though he may, of course, be a co-plaintiff in his own right). Nevertheless his name must appear on the writ, viz. "AB an infant, by CD his (father and) next friend", and he is personally liable for costs with a right of indemnity from the infant or patient for costs properly incurred. Since he is not a party he cannot counterclaim in his personal capacity; nor can he be required to give security for costs.[15] The next friend cannot act in person and so must be represented by a solicitor[16] who must file two documents:

(1) the next friend's written consent to act, and
(2) a certificate that the next friend has no interest in the proceedings adverse to that of the infant or patient.[17]

They defend by a "guardian *ad litem*" who will be the same person as the next friend would have been, or the Official Solicitor. The solicitor must file the same two

---

7   Trade Union and Labour Relations Act 1974, s 2(1)(h) (replacing earlier legislation); an "employers' association" (as defined in s 28(2) of the Act of 1974) may likewise sue and be sued in its own name. In *Engineers' and Managers' Association v Advisory, Conciliation and Arbitration Service* [1979] 3 All ER 223; [1979] 1 WLR 1113 the Court of Appeal held that, in certain circumstances, a union might be permitted representation by one of its officers, so obviating the need for counsel to appear for it.
8   Friendly Societies Act 1974 (consolidating earlier legislation).
9   But see *London Association for Protection of Trade v Greenlands Ltd* [1916] 2 AC 15, where the rules of procedure appear to have been flouted.
10   See p 349, *post*.
11   Law Reform (Married Women and Tortfeasors) Act 1995, s 1; see also Law Reform (Husband and Wife) Act 1962.
12   Family Law Reform Act 1969, s 1(1); the terms "infant" and "minor" are synonymous (*ibid*, s 1(2)).
13   This definition of a " patient" in Ord 80, r 1 is narrower than the definition in s 145(1) of the Mental Health Act 1983, ie a person suffering or appearing to be suffering from mental disorder, but corresponds with the criteria under s 94 of that Act (which applies for the purpose of deciding whether a person is within the jurisdiction of the Court of Protection); where there are proceedings in the Court of Protection application for the appointment of a next friend should be made to that court: *Re S (F G) (Mental Health Patient)* [1973] 1 All ER 273; [1973] 1 WLR 178.
14   Ord 80, r 2(1).
15   Since he is not a "normal plaintiff" within Ord 23, r 1(1)(b); *Fellows v Barrett* (1836) 1 Keen 119; see p 392, *post*. Nor can he give a receipt for money recovered in settlement of an action, *Leather v Kirby* [1965] 3 All ER 927n; [1965] 1 WLR 1489.
16   Ord 80, r 2(3).
17   Ord 80, r 3.

documents as above. However the guardian ad litem is not personally liable for costs except where he has been guilty of gross misconduct, and in this respect his position differs from that of the next friend. The next friend or guardian *ad litem* must, of course, act in the best interests of the person he represents. If he does not the court has inherent power to remove him but this power will not be exercised simply because the course that a next friend is taking is opposed by a number of other litigants.[18]

Since 1971, an action has been permitted against the estate of a deceased person, rather than against the executor or administrator as was the case before. Section 87 of the Supreme Court Act 1981 (replacing the Proceedings Against Estates Act 1970) and Order 15, rule 6A enable an action to be brought against the estate of a deceased person[19] even though no grant of probate or administration has been made; the defendant should be named in the proceedings "the personal representative of AB deceased." The plaintiff must then, during the period of validity for service of the writ or originating summons, apply to the court for an order appointing a person to represent the deceased's estate or, if a grant of probate or administration has been made since the commencement of proceedings, an order that the personal representative be made a party.[20]

By section 42(1) of the Supreme Court Act 1981 (as amended) the High Court may, on the application of the Attorney-General, make a "civil proceedings order" against any person who has habitually and persistently and without any reasonable ground instituted vexatious civil proceedings or made vexatious applications in any civil proceedings. The effect of such an order is that the person against whom it has been made cannot institute or continue any civil proceedings without the leave of the High Court.[1]

3 Representative and multi-party actions

In a representative action, where numerous persons have the same interest in any proceedings, whether as plaintiffs or defendants, one or more persons may be authorised to appear on behalf of all persons so interested.[2] However a representative action is only appropriate where all the persons to be represented have a common grievance and will all benefit from the relief claimed if plaintiffs,[3] or are jointly liable if defendants.[4] Thus where the liability of defendants is several, for example in conspiracy[5] or defamation, they cannot be represented and must be sued in their own names. Nevertheless an action for negligence has been allowed to proceed against representatives of the members of a club on the ground that they were joint occupiers of the club premises.[6] A judgment against representative defendants is binding on them

---

18 *Re Taylor's Application* [1972] 2 QB 369; [1972] 2 All ER 873 one of the many actions arising out of the "thalidomide" tragedy.
19 Proceedings commenced in the name of a deceased person as plaintiff are still a nullity.
20 Ord 15, r 6A(4). Where no grant of probate or administration has been made any judgment or order binds the estate as if a personal representative of the deceased had been a party to the proceedings (Ord 15, r 6A(7)).
1 See, generally, *A-G v Jones* [1990] 2 All ER 636; [1990] 1 WLR 859
2 Ord 15, r 12.
3 *Smith v Cardiff Corporation* [1954] 1 QB 210; [1953] 2 All ER 1373; distinguished in *John v Rees* [1970] Ch 345; [1969] 2 All ER 274.
4 *Mercantile Marine Service Association v Toms* [1916] 2 KB 243.
5 *Hardie and Lane v Chiltern* [1928] 1 KB 663.
6 *Campbell v Thompson* [1953] 1 QB 445; [1953] 1 All ER 831; see also *Wallersteiner v Moir (No 2)* [1975] QB 373; [1975] 1 All ER 849 where a minority shareholder's action was likened to a representative action on behalf of the company and it was stated by the Court of Appeal that the shareholder, after issuing proceedings, should in effect apply to the court for an order sanctioning the proceedings, the effect of which would be to give the shareholder a right to have the company pay his costs.

all. However it can be executed against the actual parties but not against the persons represented without leave. An order for costs cannot be made against a person represented. The writ must define clearly the parties and the names of persons represented. Thus an order to represent "all the persons who were members of the City Livery Club on June 29, 1949" was made in one case, being a sufficient identification of the persons represented as defendants.[7] It is important to distinguish a representative action from a "test case". The latter is popular terminology for an action the function of which is to determine the legal position of numerous individuals who are not parties to the action; for example an action based on the interpretation of a Finance Act upon which depend the tax obligations of a large section of the populace. The expression "test case" has, however, no legal meaning and only the parties to a test case are bound by the judgment. However, rights are determined conclusively through the operation of the doctrine of precedent.

In recent years the form of representative action has been somewhat circumvented by group actions whereby several actions out of a large number of potential claims are litigated to establish liability and the principle for the award of damages. The types of situations suitable for multi-party actions were summarised in 1997[8] as follows:

(a)   Major one off disaster claims (such as the ferry disaster at Zeebrugge and Kings Cross tube station fire disaster) where causation is generally common to all the cases and may not be in dispute and where the class of those affected is clearly defined from the outset. In many cases the number of individuals in the class will be high.

(b)   Product liability claims (especially those involving pharmaceutical products such as Opren and benzodiazepine) where liability may be difficult to determine and common issues may be difficult to identify. Such claims are frequently complicated by a multiplicity of defendants who all manufactured similar products as well as by a multiplicity of plaintiffs. In a case involving the drug Opren there were some 1,500 plaintiffs against a drug company, which were litigated on the basis of a "master" statement of claim, and with certain "lead cases" to determine different aspects of the overall issue.

(c)   Multiple claims relating to industrial diseases deriving from the same cause, such as asbestosis claims, industrial deafness and vibration white finger claims.

(d)   Environmental cases deriving not only from specific incidents but also from damage occurring over a period of time, such a seepage from an industrial plant, or a nuclear installation, or prolonged use of chemicals in particular circumstances. These types of claim may involve both personal injury and property damage as well as, in some cases, loss of amenity.

(e)   Claims relating to use or consumption of defective goods or services causing damage to property, or personal injury and/or financial loss. Examples are claims by tenants of a block of flats or an estate for a landlord's failure to repair; shareholders against a company or its auditors for disseminating misleading information; residents of a neighbourhood against a public authority's decision to build a road or to permit development in their area; a group of package holiday customers against a tour operator; a group of customers who have bought defective goods; or for professional negligence claims. Often, but by no means always, the claims may be individually small, but together quite substantial.

7   See n 6, *supra*
8   *Multi-Party Actions, Consultation Paper from Civil Justice Working Group*, Lord Chancellor's Department, 1997.

Development of group actions in the UK has centred on "mass disasters" involving large numbers of individual claims. Instead of having to try separately a whole series of cases arising out of the same "disaster" it was more efficient for the courts to try the common questions as one action. As a result, the evolution of multi-party actions has largely occurred because of "an innovative approach by the courts and practitioners to procedure rules, in particular those relating to lead actions, or test cases, and the joining of parties to the action."[9] The impact of the actions of the Legal Aid Board in contracting representation in this type of case has already been noted.[10]

The Woolf Report[11] has identified objectives that any new system for multi-party actions should aim to achieve. Firstly, they should provide access to justice where large numbers of people have been affected by another's conduct, but individual loss is so small that it makes an individual action economically unviable. Secondly, they should provide expeditious, effective and proportionate methods of resolving cases, where individual damages are large enough to justify individual action but where the number of claimants and the nature of the issues involved mean that the cases cannot be managed satisfactorily in accordance with normal procedure. Thirdly, the rules should achieve a balance between the normal rights of claimants and defendants, to pursue and defend cases individually, and the interests of a group of parties to litigate the action as a whole in an effective manner. New rules of court will seek to achieve these objectives.

The proposed new framework for multi-party actions has been set out in a consultation paper.[12] This will involve a judge certifying an action as a multi-party action: if he does so, the judicial case management approach envisaged by Woolf will entitle the judge to make arrangements for case management generally, fix a timetable and to give directions. The action will proceed under the management and direction of the judge.

4   Issue of the writ

The writ must be issued using the prescribed form, but that form is not a writ until it has been issued. To issue his writ the plaintiff takes or sends three copies of his form to the Central Office in London or a district registry where one copy (signed by the solicitor issuing it) is stamped with the court fee and filed, and the other two are sealed and returned to the plaintiff. The action has now been commenced for the purpose of any statute of limitation. Leave is not generally required to issue a writ but to this rule there are five exceptions of which the two more important are:

(1)   where the defendant is outside the jurisdiction;[13] and
(2)   where the plaintiff has been declared a vexatious litigant.[14]

Once issued the writ is valid for four months beginning with the date of issue.[15] However it may on application be renewed for a further period not exceeding 12 months

9   *Ibid.*
10   See p 289, *ante.*
11   See pp 338–340, *ante.*
12   *Op cit*, n 7, *ante.*
13   Ord 6, r 7(1).
14   Supreme Court Act 1981, s 42. The other cases in which leave is required are under the Mental Health Act 1983, s 139(2), under the Leasehold Property (Repairs) Act 1938, s 1, under the Post Office Act 1969, s 30(3), and under Limitation Act 1980, s 32A.
15   Ord 6, r 8(1). The position differs in cases where leave to serve outside the jurisdiction has been granted, where the relevant period is 6 months.

if the court is satisfied that it has not been possible to serve it during that period. Such an application is made *ex parte* (without giving notice to the other party) on affidavit. An extension will only be granted in exceptional circumstances,[16] generally where the defendant is untraceable; it is not an exceptional circumstance that the plaintiff failed to serve the writ through accident, mistake or a delay in obtaining a legal aid certificate[17] nor that settlement negotiations were in progress.[18] While in force the writ may be served at any time of the day or night although not on Sunday except, in case of urgency, with the leave of the court.[19] A writ may be served by post. Alternatively, it may be served on the defendant's solicitor. This is an alternative to personal service. The defendant's solicitor must indorse on the writ a statement that he accepts service on behalf of the defendant.[20] The fact that a person is represented by a solicitor is insufficient, unless that solicitor in facts accepts service.

Where the plaintiff is unable to effect service as above, he may apply *ex parte* on affidavit to a master for an order for substituted service.[1] The master, if he makes such an order, will specify the form which substituted service must take, for example, service by registered or recorded delivery post to the defendant's last known address, service on the defendant's solicitor or agent or service by advertisement in the press.[2]

5   Acknowledgement of service[3]

Following service, the defendant must acknowledge service within 14 days of service (including the day of service) to avoid being in default.[4] This is done by delivering or posting[5] to the Central Office or district registry the prescribed form of acknowledgement, duly completed. This is not a defence but a formal document the

---

16   For the relevant principles, see *Kleinwort Benson Ltd v Barbrak Ltd "The Myrto"* [1987] AC 597; [1987] 2 All ER 289; *Waddon v Whitcroft-Scovill Ltd* [1988] 1 All ER 996; [1988] 1 WLR 309. A writ should be served promptly, but each case turns on its own circumstances.

17   *Baker v Bowketts Cakes Ltd* [1966] 2 All ER 290; [1966] 1 WLR 861; *Stevens v Services Window and General Cleaning Co Ltd* [1967] 1 QB 359; [1967] 1 All ER 984.

18   *Easy v Universal Anchorage Co Ltd* [1974] 2 All ER 1105; [1974] 1 WLR 899.

19   Ord 65, r 10; formerly the Sunday Observance Act 1677 (repealed by the Statute Law (Repeals) Act 1969) contained an absolute prohibition against service of process on a Sunday.

20   Ord 10, r 1(4).

1   Ord 65, r 4. An action in the Queen's Bench Division is assigned to one of the masters when the first summons in the action is issued. Masters have, with a few exceptions (set out in Ord 32, r 11), all the powers of a judge in chambers in relation to interlocutory matters. In addition masters have jurisdiction to try cases, with the consent of the parties, to assess damages and to make final orders in interpleader and garnishee disputes.

2   *Porter v Freudenberg* [1915] 1 KB 857. Where the defendant is insured against his potential liability, service may be ordered on his insurers: *Gurtner v Circuit* [1968] 2 QB 587; [1968] 1 All ER 328.

3   Prior to 3 June 1980 the defendant was required, by the writ, to "enter an appearance" and, if he did not do so, the plaintiff could enter judgment in default of appearance. The Rules of the Supreme Court (Writ and Appearance) 1979 abolished this procedure and prescribed a procedure analogous to that previously applicable under the Matrimonial Causes Rules, namely that whereby the defendant is sent a form of acknowledgment of service on which he is invited to state whether he intends to contest the proceedings.

4   Where service is out of the jurisdiction extra time is allowed. In proceedings within the State Immunity Act 1978 the period is two months (*ibid*, s 12(2)).

5   The use of registered or recorded delivery post is not required. Ordinary pre-paid post is sufficient but it must be remembered that service is acknowledged when the document actually arrives at the court office, not when it is posted. In addition there are very detailed directions as to the precise procedure to be adopted for transacting this, and other classes, of business which may now be transacted by post; these are set out in Practice Direction (Use of postal facilities; Queen's Bench Division) [1976] 2 All ER 446; [1976] 1 WLR 516.

function of which is to avoid the plaintiff obtaining judgment in default or, if liability is admitted, to obtain a stay of execution.

The form which the defendant is required to complete (on the back of which are printed notes for guidance) contains four sections. In (1) he is required to state his name; in (2) he states (by ticking the appropriate box) whether he intends to contest the proceedings; in (3) he indicates (again by ticking a box) whether, if the claim is for a debt or liquidated demand and he does not intend to contest the proceedings, he intends to apply for a stay of execution; in (4) he states (by ticking boxes) whether, if the writ was issued out of a district registry, he applies for the transfer of the action to the Royal Courts of Justice or to some other district registry.[6] Finally he (or his solicitor) must sign the form.

If any defendant fails to give "notice of intention to defend" within the time limited the plaintiff is entitled to enter judgment in default. He must either file an affidavit of service proving due service of the writ on the defendant (which, if service was effected by post (*supra*, must contain a statement to the effect that in the deponent's opinion the copy of the writ will have come to the knowledge of the defendant within seven days thereafter and that the copy writ has not been returned through the post undelivered) or produce the writ indorsed with a statement by the defendant's solicitor that he accepts service on the defendant's behalf. In some cases leave must also be obtained; examples are cases where the defendant is the Crown[7] or has served notice to reopen a credit agreement under the Consumer Credit Act 1974,[8] or the action is a mortgage action[9] or an action in tort between spouses.[10]

If the default judgment was irregularly or fraudulently obtained or is for an amount larger than is due the defendant has a right to have it set aside. In any other case, he may apply to have it set aside but he will have to show why he has failed to give notice of intention to defend, and also that he has a triable defence, which he will normally have to disclose by affidavit. In addition a third party who is affected by the judgment may apply to have it set aside even though not a party to the action. Thus an insurance company may apply to have a judgment against the insured set aside,[11] so also may a person in possession of land which the plaintiff has recovered by default.

C ALTERNATIVE MEANS OF PROCEEDING

1 Originating summons

Although most actions in the Queen's Bench Division are commenced by writ, and many must be commenced in this way, the plaintiff may in some cases proceed by originating summons.[12] An originating summons is defined as "every summons other than a summons in a pending cause or matter".[13] The procedure is aptly named since it actually raises the point at issue in the first instance, thus dispensing with the need for pleadings. It is the proper method for making applications under certain statutes;

---

6   Such application can only be made where (a) the defendant does not reside or carry on business within the district of the registry out of which the writ was issued; and (b) there is no indorsement on the writ that the plaintiff's cause of action arose wholly or in part within that district (Ord 4, r 5(3)).

7   Ord 77, r 9.

8   Ord 83, r 3.

9   Ord 88, r 6.

10   Ord 89, r 2.

11   *Windsor v Chalcraft* [1939] 1 KB 279; [1938] 2 All ER 751.

12   See p 343, *ante*.

13   Ord 1, r 4.

for example, applications to approve the compromise of an action by an infant or patient, interpleader applications where an action is not pending and summary proceedings for possession of land occupied by trespassers.[14] In addition it is a streamlined method of obtaining the court's decision on a point of law or on the construction of a document or statute.

There are now three forms of originating summons:[15]

(1)   originating summons between parties, general form;
(2)   originating summons between parties, expedited form;
(3)   *ex parte* originating summons (this form is used mainly in the Chancery Division).

The first form is the usual one in the Queen's Bench Division. The second form differs in that it makes provision for a date of hearing to be inserted (rather like an ordinary summons in a pending action) but it can only be used in a small number of cases, specified in the Rules. The summons is issued in the same way as a writ, out of the Central Office or a district registry. It remains in force and is renewable in the same way as a writ and must be served on the defendant as if it were a writ, leave being required to serve it outside the jurisdiction:

> "every originating summons must include a statement of the questions on which the plaintiff seeks the determination or direction of the High Court or, as the case may be, a concise statement of the relief or remedy claimed in the proceedings begun by the originating summons with sufficient particulars to identify the cause or causes of action in respect of which the plaintiff claims that relief or remedy."[16]

Although an originating summons is not a pleading[17] it is in many ways similar to a statement of claim and it seems that the inherent jurisdiction of the court and under Order 18, rule 19 to strike out any pleading extends to an originating summons.[18] The plaintiff must, within 14 days after any defendant has acknowledged service, file with the court the affidavit evidence on which he intends to rely (in the case of an ex parte summons he must file this not less than four clear days before the date fixed for the hearing) and must serve copies thereof on all defendants. A defendant who has acknowledged service must then within 28 days file and serve any affidavit evidence upon which he intends to rely and the plaintiff may within 14 days thereafter file and serve further affidavit evidence in reply.[19] The plaintiff will then obtain an appointment for the attendance of the parties before the court for the hearing of the summons.[20] Any defendant who has acknowledged service may raise a counterclaim whether or not that counterclaim could have been commenced by originating summons had he been the plaintiff; if the court cannot conveniently hear the counterclaim with the originating summons, it may order that it be struck out or tried separately.[1]

---

14   Ord 113.
15   Ord 7, r 2 (as amended by Rules of the Supreme Court (Writ and Appearance) Rules 1979).
16   Ord 7, r 3(1).
17   *Lewis v Packer* [1960] 1 All ER 720n, [1960] 1 WLR 452.
18   Ord 18, r 19(3); *Punton v Ministry of Pensions and National Insurance* [1963] 1 All ER 275, [[1963] 1 WLR 186.
19   Ord 28, r 1A.
20   Ord 28, r 2.
1   Ord 28, r 7.

D   PUBLIC OR PRIVATE LAW

A second preliminary factor of importance which must be considered is whether the proposed action involves questions of public law. Where in reality an action raises issues of public law, the normal procedure for determination of those questions is by an application for judicial review under Order 53 of the Rules of the Supreme Court, and a failure to use the Order 53 procedure may result subsequently in an application by the defendant to have the action struck out as an abuse of process of the court.[2] This was discussed in more detail in Chapter 7.[3]

E   PRE-COMMENCEMENT ORDERS AND PROCEDURES

Questions concerning discovery and inspection of documents and the inspection, preservation and the like of property are dealt with during the course of proceedings, usually after the close of pleadings, and these matters are dealt with below in that context.[4] However statutory provisions enable parties to obtain orders of this type prior to the commencement of proceedings. There are two distinct procedures of this type, set out below. There are also common law powers.

I   Discovery and inspection of documents

By section 33(2) of the Supreme Court Act 1981 a person who appears to the High Court to be likely to be a party to subsequent proceedings in respect of a claim of personal injuries or death may apply[5] for pre-trial discovery of documents in the possession, custody or power of a person. That person must be a likely party to the proceedings; it is not enough that that person is a potential witness. That party may be ordered to disclose whether those documents are in his custody, possession and power and, if so, to produce them to the applicant, unless they are protected from disclosure by the doctrine of privilege.[6] It is immaterial that the likelihood of the claim being made is dependent upon the outcome of the discovery, the words "likely to be made" in the section are to be construed as meaning "may or may well be made" if, on discovery, the documents in question indicate that the applicant has a good cause of action.[7] It will be noted that the above procedure is limited to personal injuries litigation. It may be utilised, for example, by a plaintiff to enable him to see his employer's accident reports or documents relating to the maintenance of a vehicle or machine which

---

2   See p 367, *post.*

3   See pp 147-150, ante.

4   See pp 385-390, *post.*

5   The application is by originating summons supported by an affidavit which must (a) state the grounds upon which it is alleged that the applicant and the person against whom the order is sought are likely to be parties to subsequent proceedings of the type specified in section 33(2); and (b) specify or describe the documents concerned and show, if practicable by reference to a draft pleading, their relevance. The summons and copy affidavit are served on the other party and require him to make an affidavit stating whether any documents specified or described are or have been in his custody, possession or power and, if not then in his custody, possession or power what has become of them: Ord 24, r 7A (1), (3) (5).

6   Ord 24, r 7A (6).

7   *Dunning v United Liverpool Hospital's Board of Governors* [1973] 2 All ER 454; [1973] 1 WLR 586. This case concerned the disclosure of medical records. Applications under the rule are frequently made in this type of case, namely actions against doctors and hospitals for damages for professional negligence because, in the nature of things, a party (and his own expert witnesses) can hardly formulate

has proved defective.[8] The object of this provision is to enable personal injuries litigation to be conducted openly and with a view to early settlement if possible, the strength or otherwise of the potential claim being identified at the outset.

2   Inspection etc of property

Section 33(1) of the Supreme Court Act 1981[9] empowers the High Court, in some circumstances, to make an order providing for the inspection, photographing, preservation, custody or detention of property (including land or chattels) which appears to the court to be property which may become the subject matter of subsequent proceedings in the court, or as to which any question may arise in such proceedings, or for the taking of samples of any such property and the carrying out of any experiment on or with any such property. This is not limited to articles in the possession of a party, a position which may be contrasted with that that exists after commencement of proceedings.[10] The relationship between the power of inspection and that of discovery was examined in *Huddleston v Control Risks Information Services Ltd.*[11] The court drew a distinction between a party wishing to examine "the medium" (ie the document itself) as opposed to being concerned with "the message" (ie with the contents of the document). Section 33(1), inspection, applied to the former, section 33(2), discovery, to the latter. Since in this case the plaintiff's concern was for the contents, which were believed to be defamatory, what was being sought was discovery, for which the relevant conditions, described above, did not apply. The power of inspection could not be used to circumvent these criteria.

3   The *Norwich Pharmacal* principle

In addition to the statutory powers described above, a court may in some circumstances order discovery against a third party who has information. Whilst this will often be during litigation,[12] it may be appropriate to obtain such discovery prior to action, in order to discover whether a basis of action exists, and against whom. The principle, which was first stated by the court in *Norwich Pharmacal Co v Commissioners of Customs and Excise*[13] does not permit discovery in all circumstances: it is only where the third party is in some way involved in the wrongdoing alleged that the court will

---

his claim properly, nor can counsel advise upon merits, without knowing what took place while the plaintiff was being treated by the defendant, and this will almost always necessitate inspecting the medical records relating to the diagnosis and treatment of the plaintiff's medical condition. The standard form of order used to limit disclosure, in the first instance, to the applicant's medical adviser, but the rules do not provide for orders in this form and the House of Lords has held that they cannot properly be made; *McIvor v Southern Health and Social Services Board* [1978] 2 All ER 625; [1978] 1 WLR 757.

8   Cf *Shaw v Vauxhall Motors Ltd* [1974] 2 All ER 1185; [1974] 1 WLR 1035 in which an order was made for the discovery of documents relating to the inspection, maintenance and repair of a fork lift truck which was alleged to have caused an accident due to a braking defect (this being the applicant's only cause of complaint against his employers). The Court of Appeal, in the case, expressly took into account the fact that the proposed plaintiff was legally aided so that there was the public interest in saving costs to be considered.

9   Replacing Administration of Justice Act 1969, s 21.

10   RSC Ord 29, r 2. *Douihech v Findlay* [1990] 3 All ER 118; [1990] 1 WLR 269.

11   [1987] 2 All ER 1035; [1987] 1 WLR 701.

12   See p 385, *post*.

13   [1974] AC 133; [1973] 2 All ER 943.

order discovery against that third party.[14] However, the rule has been extended to cases where a third party has information necessary for locating and recovering missing funds.[15]

4   Anton Piller orders

The High Court has an inherent jurisdiction to order a defendant to permit a plaintiff to enter the defendant's premises in order to inspect, remove or make copies of documents belonging to the plaintiff or relating to the plaintiff's property. Such an order is known as an *Anton Piller*[16] order, after the case in which the Court of Appeal first sanctioned this type of order.[17] An order may be obtained *ex parte* but will only be made where the plaintiff shows that there is a grave danger of property being smuggled away or vital evidence destroyed; it is usually applicable to infringement of copyright cases or cases of that sort.[18]

An *Anton Piller* order may, at first sight, appear to be in the nature of a search warrant issued to a private individual, but in fact it is not; it confers upon the plaintiff no right to enter the defendant's premises, but rather imposes a duty on a defendant to permit the plaintiff to enter his premises. Failure on the part of the defendant to comply will, however, be a contempt of court. The *Anton Piller* application has become extremely popular with plaintiffs and their advisers. By its very nature it may enable a plaintiff to strike gold in relation to wrongful acts, such as misuse of confidential information or infringement of copyright, which but for the order the plaintiff might possibly never have been in a position to prove (defendants in these matters frequently being less than frank as to voluntary discovery); all that the plaintiff risks is having to pay his opponent's costs of the application and damages if any are caused.[19]

In order to minimise speculative and oppressive applications the courts have formulated several procedural safeguards. Thus the plaintiff's solicitor should attend when the order is executed, if permission to enter premises is refused no force should be used; the defendant should have the opportunity to contact his solicitor and should be advised of his right to obtain legal advice.[20] The requirement to allow entry does not in fact operate immediately, despite the use of the word "forthwith" in an order, but operates only after there has been a reasonable period of time to obtain legal advice.[1] The applicant must make full disclosure to the court of all matters relevant to his application and if material facts are omitted the order will be discharged.[2] The nature of the *Anton Piller* procedure is exceptional, and creates potential for abuse. In *Universal Thermosensors Ltd v Hibben*[3] Sir Donald Nicholls VC identified certain key points:

---

14   *Harrington v North London Polytechnic* [1984] 3 All ER 666; [1984] 1 WLR 1293. In *Ricci v Chow* [1987] 3 All ER 534; [1987] 1 WLR 1658, the Court of Appeal decided that discovery of the identity of the publisher and printer of an alleged defamatory article would not be ordered against the defendant, a person involved in no way in the publication, but who knew the publisher's name.

15   *Arab Monetary Fund v Hashim (No 5)* [1992] 2 All ER 911; *Bankers Trust Co v Shapira* [1980] 3 All ER 353.

16   *Anton Piller KG v Manufacturing Processes Ltd* [1976] Ch 55; [1976] 1 All ER 779.

17   An example of judicial creativity in law-making: for the role of the judiciary, see pp 216–222, *ante*.

18   See, for example, *Ex parte Island Records Ltd* [1978] Ch 122; [1978] 3 All ER 824.

19   The plaintiff applying for any form of interlocutory injunction has to give an undertaking as to damages and this undertaking is always written into the court order.

20   *International Electronics Ltd v Weigh Data Ltd* [1980] FSR 423.

1   *Bhimji v Chatwani* [1991] 1 All ER 705; [1991] 1 WLR 989.

2   *Thermax Ltd v Schott Industrial Glass Ltd* [1981] FSR 289.

3   [1992] 3 All ER 257; [1992] 1 WLR 840.

(1) *Anton Piller* orders normally contain a term that, before compliance, the defendant may obtain legal advice, if this is done forthwith. If such a term is to be of use, generally such order should be executed only on working days in office hours, when a solicitor can be expected to be available.

(2) If an *Anton Piller* order is to be executed on private premises and a woman may be at the house alone, the solicitor serving the order must be, or be accompanied by, a woman.

(3) The order should expressly provide that, unless seriously impracticable, a detailed list of the items being removed should be prepared at the time of removal, with the defendant being given the opportunity to check that list.

(4) Orders sometimes contain an injunction restraining those on whom they are served from informing others of the existence of the order for a limited period, subject to an exception in respect of communication with a lawyers to gain legal advice. The length of time governed by the injunction should not be an excessively long period. In the instant case, one week was too long.

(5) An order should not be executed at business premises without a responsible officer or representative being present.

(6) Consideration should be given as to how a competitor of the business subject to the order can be prevented from having unlimited access to the documents of that business.

(7) An *Anton Piller* order should, where possible, be served by a solicitor other than a member of the firm of solicitors acting for the plaintiff. That solicitor should also have experience of the *Anton Piller* procedure. The defendant against whom an *ex parte* order has been made may apply to have the order set aside (as can any litigant against whom an *ex parte* order is made);[4] he may even refuse compliance with the order and apply urgently to have it set aside but he does so at his peril since if his application fails he will be in contempt of court and liable to severe penalties if he has in the interim breached the order, for example by destroying records.[5]

It was held by the House of Lords in *Rank Film Distributors Ltd v Video Information Centre*[6] that defendants could resist the making of an order on the ground of privilege against self-incrimination.[7] This was a serious inroad into the scope of *Anton Piller* orders since, in the nature of things, persons against whom such orders are made are frequently engaged in fraudulent activity. To remedy this, section 72 of the Supreme Court Act 1981 withdrew the privilege in relation to High Court proceedings for infringement of rights pertaining to any intellectual property or for passing-off, including proceedings brought to prevent any apprehended such infringement or passing-off and proceedings brought to obtain disclosure of information relating thereto. Other exceptions to the privilege also exist.

The extent to which *Anton Piller*, and other, orders can be resisted on the grounds of the privilege against self-incrimination was considered by the House of Lords in *AT & T Istel Ltd v Tully*.[8] The House was of the opinion that the privilege, which itself in a civil case was an "archaic and unjustifiable survival from the past", only protected the defendant if compliance with the order would provide evidence against him in a criminal trial. If the defendant could be protected against being exposed to the

---

4   Ord 8, r 2.
5   *WEA Records Ltd v Visions Channel 4 Ltd* [1983] 2 All ER 589; [1983] 1 WLR 721.
6   [1982] AC 380; [1981] 2 All ER 76.
7   See p 388, *post* and *IBM United Kingdom Ltd v Prima Data International Ltd* [1994] 4 All ER 748.
8   [1993] AC 45; [1992] 3 All ER 523.

reasonable risk of the information to be disclosed being used in a criminal prosecution by other means, then the courts were entitled to rely on those other means. In that case the Crown Prosecution Service had agreed not to seek to use in criminal proceedings the documents disclosed.

5   Mareva injunctions

a   Jurisdiction

It will be appreciated that the prospective plaintiff in an action for debt or damages faces two distinct obstacles. The first is to obtain a judgment (or settlement) in his favour; the second is to enforce that judgment. It is of little consolation to most litigants to succeed in the action and yet be unable to enforce the judgment. Regrettably, where a defendant is uninsured against his liability this is a situation which often arises. Where the defendant is simply insolvent this is a misfortune that the plaintiff must bear. However the courts can and will intervene to prevent a defendant from avoiding his liability to the plaintiff by disposing of his assets, and in particular removing them outside the jurisdiction of the English courts. An injunction to restrain a defendant from so doing is called a *Mareva* injunction, taking its name from the 1975 case in which the jurisdiction was first acknowledged by the Court of Appeal.[9]

Since 1975 the development of this area of law and practice, particularly in the Commercial Court,[10] has been rapid. The injunction was originally confined to foreign defendants and to prohibiting removal of assets from the jurisdiction but was soon extended to United Kingdom residents and to the prohibition of dispositions of assets within the jurisdiction. The jurisdiction to make such orders is now conferred by section 37(3) of the Supreme Court Act 1981 which provides:

"The power of the High Court to grant an interlocutory injunction restraining a party to any proceedings from removing from the jurisdiction of the High Court, or otherwise dealing with, assets located within that jurisdiction shall be exercisable in cases where that party is, as well as cases where he is not, domiciled, resident or present within that jurisdiction."

The words " dealing with" encompass disposing of, selling or charging assets.[11] Until recently it had been thought that one important restriction on the court's power to grant a *Mareva* injunction lay in the fact that the injunction is ancillary to a cause of action; it is not a cause of action in itself. Thus, if a plaintiff's claim is not justiciable in the English courts he could not obtain an injunction. For example, if the defendant is domiciled in a country to which section 25 of the Civil Jurisdiction and Judgments Act 1982 does not apply, leave to serve a writ outside the jurisdiction will be required. If this was not granted, there would be no basis for a successful application for a *Mareva* injunction.[12] This view was supported by the Court of Appeal in *The Veracruz I*[13] where it was stressed that the powers of the High Court to grant an injunction derived from section 37 of the Supreme Court Act 1981, and were to grant an injunction in all cases where it was just and convenient to do so. The right to obtain an interlocutory injunction

---

9   *Mareva Compania Naviera SA v International Bulkcarriers SA* [1980] 1 All ER 213n; [1975] 2 Lloyd's Rep 509.
10   As to which see p 399, *post*.
11   *CBS United Kingdom Ltd v Lambert* [1983] Ch 37; [1982] 3 All ER 237.
12   But see *infra*.
13   [1992] 1 Lloyd's Rep 353.

was not a cause of action in itself. However, this conclusion is called into doubt by the decision of the House of Lords in *Channel Tunnel Group Ltd v Balfour Beatty Construction Ltd*.[14] In that case Lord Mustill indicated that the fact that proceedings in an English court could be the subject of a stay did not prevent the court from granting interlocutory relief. Lord Browne-Wilkinson doubted whether the authority on which this restriction was based[15] remained good law.

b   Procedure

An applicant for a *Mareva* injunction is well advised to act quickly. To this end the customary practice is to apply *ex parte* in the first instance, sometimes even before issuing a writ (in which case the plaintiff will be required to undertake to issue a writ within a specified period or "forthwith") whereupon an order will be made to take effect until the return date on the summons which the plaintiff will have issued or undertaken to issue. The plaintiff must swear an affidavit in support of his application. In *Third Chandris Shipping Corporation v Unimarine SA*[16] the Court of Appeal stated guidelines that judges should follow on such applications:

(i)   the plaintiff should make full and frank disclosure of all matters in his knowledge which are material for the judge to know;
(ii)   the plaintiff should give particulars of this claim and the amount thereof and of the defendant's case against it;
(iii) the plaintiff should give some grounds for believing that the defendant has assets within the jurisdiction;
(iv)   the plaintiff should give some grounds (not merely that the defendant is abroad) for believing that there is a risk of the assets of the defendant being removed before the judgment is satisfied;
(v)   the plaintiff should give an undertaking in damages, in a suitable case to be supported by a bond or security.

In the light of the fact that the injunction is no longer limited to restraining removal of assets from the jurisdiction,[17] (iv) above is clearly modified. The court has power to order discovery of documents or to administer interrogatories as to the amount, whereabouts or other details of the defendant's assets, with a view to securing the efficacy of the injunction.[18] Copies of the injunction will generally be served upon the defendant's bank or other body having custody of his assets, so as to fix such body with knowledge of the injunction (since such body would itself be guilty of contempt of court if it assisted the defendant to act in breach of the injunction, knowing that it is probable that the asset is being disposed of in breach of the injunction). The receipt by a bank of such notice overrides its customer's instructions, eg to honour cheques.

c   Principles upon which the court acts

By section 37(1) of the Supreme Court Act 1981 the High Court may grant an injunction "in all cases in which it appears to the court to be just and convenient to do so".

14   [1993] AC 334; [1993] 1 All ER 664; as to which see p 376, *post*.
15   *The Siskina* [1979] AC 210; [1977] 3 All ER 803. See also: *South Carolina Insurance Co v Assurantie Maatschap pij, de Zeven Provincien NV* [1987] AC 24; [1986] 3 All ER 487.
16   [1979] QB 645; [1979] 2 All ER 972.
17   *A v C* [1981] QB 956n; [1980] 2 All ER 347.
18   *Bank Ellat v Kazmi* [1989] QB 541; *Yukong Line Ltd of Korea v Rendsburg Investments Corp of Liberia* [1996] 2 Lloyd's Rep 604.

However, although not subject to statutory fetters, the courts have developed principles on the basis of which to grant or refuse injunctions. The general principles affecting the discretion whether to grant or refuse an interlocutory injunction are those laid down by the House of Lords in *American Cyanamid Co v Ethicon Ltd*[19] and will be considered in due course.[20] However there are additional principles which particularly apply to *Mareva* applications. As a first step the plaintiff must satisfy the court (i) that he has at least a good arguable case; and (ii) that the refusal of an injunction would involve a real risk that a judgment or award in the plaintiff's favour would remain unsatisfied because of the defendant's removal of assets from the jurisdiction or dissipation of assets within the jurisdiction.[1] An injunction will not be granted merely for the purpose of providing a plaintiff with security for a claim, even where it appears likely to succeed and even where the granting of the injunction will not cause hardship to the defendant.[2] An injunction will not be granted so as to give the plaintiff priority over other creditors, nor to prevent the defendant from paying his debts as they fall due or carrying on his legitimate business. It is also common for the injunction to be expressed so as to exclude periodical payments of reasonable amounts to provide for the living or other expenses of the defendant,[3] including amounts to be paid to his legal advisers to contest the litigation.

d   Position of third parties

It has been noted that service of a copy of the injunction upon a third party, such as a bank, operates in effect to freeze the account. This has led to problems and the courts are vigilant to ensure that banks and other third parties do not suffer in consequence of the grant of a *Mareva* injunction. Thus, a bank is entitled to a variation of the injunction to enable it to set off against any funds which it holds any right that it has in respect of facilities granted to the client, for example bank charges, interest or the balance on another account. Similarly an injunction will not be granted, or will be discharged, where the effect would be to interfere substantially with the business of a third party.[4] In *Polly Peck International plc v Nadir (No 2)*[5] the court indicated that a *Mareva* injunction ought not to be granted against a bank, except where that bank was likely to act so as to avoid judgment. Where a bank or third party is compelled to enter the proceedings in order to obtain an order, or discharge of an order, the plaintiff will ordinarily be required to pay its cost on an indemnity basis.[6]

19   [1975] AC 396; [1975] 1 All ER 504.
20   See p 376, *post*.
1   *Ninemia Maritime Corporation v Trave Schiffahrtsgesellschaft mbH & Co KG* [1984] 1 All ER 398; [1983] 1 WLR 1412.
2   See *Polly Peck International plc v Nadir (No 2)* [1992] 4 All ER 769.
3   See, for example, *PCW (Underwriting Agencies) Ltd v Dixon* [1983] 2 All ER 158.
4   *Galaxia Maritime SA v Mineralimportexport* [1982] 1 All ER 796; [1982] 1 WLR 539.
5   See n 2, *ante*.
6   *Z Ltd v A-Z* [1982] QB 558; [1982] 1 All ER 556.

Chapter 17

High Court Actions

A INTRODUCTORY MATTERS

The context whereby the vast majority of actions are conducted in the county court has already been noted.[1] So, too, has growing dissatisfaction with the delay and cost associated with current approaches to civil litigation, particularly in the High Court, where litigation is sometimes conducted seemingly oblivious to questions of cost and the quick resolution of disputes.[2] In this Chapter, the broad features of High Court actions in Queens' Bench Division are identified, as are some of the approaches proposed for the future. The specific features and differences relating to county court actions are dealt with elsewhere.[3]

1 Current approaches to case management

Case management is basically in the hands of the parties, within a framework set out in the Rules of the Supreme Court. Increasingly, however, courts have been willing to engage in a more pro active approach, illustrated by the approaches to multi-party actions identified earlier.[4] Courts have powers to dismiss actions for want of prosecution, and are increasingly taking a firm approach.[5] The importance of cases being processed with reasonable expedition was stressed by the Court of Appeal in *Mortgage Corporation v Sandoes*.[6] Time-limits prescribed by the rules of court were not targets to be attempted, but there to be observed. Extensions of time should be granted only as a last resort, and preferably in combination with the setting of agreed new time-limits. In the context of a county court case,[7] Henry LJ observed that "[In]

---

1   See p 325, *ante*.
2   See Woolf Report, *op cit*, p 323, *ante*, and Middleton Report, *op cit*, p 323, *ante*.
3   See pp 408–424, *post*.
4   See pp 349–351, *ante*.
5   See, in particular, *Arbuthnot Latham Bank Ltd v Trafalgar Holdings Ltd* [1998] 2 All ER 181; [1998] 1 WLR 1426. See, generally, pp 367–369, *post*.
6   [1997] 03 LS Gaz R 28.
7   *Gardner v Southwark LBC (No 2)* [1996] 1 WLR 571.

personal injury cases … a new regime is in place, a regime under which the old leisurely and often rudderless way of conducting these usually simple cases will not be tolerated." That philosophy and approach is increasingly apparent in all types of litigation. The legal profession is expected to achieve high standards of diligence.[8]

2   The Woolf Report Recommendations

The broad approach of the Woolf Report has already been noted.[9] It is proposed[10] that the following categories of case will be allocated to the tracks indicated except where the procedural judge believes that particular characteristics of the individual case make it appropriate for it to be allocated to a different track:

(1) *Small claims procedure* – will normally apply to all defended claims valued at less than the small claims limit (currently £3,000), including those incorporating a claim for an injunction, order for specific performance or similar relief, but with the exception of those including a claim for damages for personal injury.

(2) *Fast track procedure* – will normally apply to all defended claims valued at more than the small claims limit but less than the fast track limit (proposed to be £10,000), including claims for professional negligence (but excluding clinical negligence claims), cases including a claim for an injunction, order for specific performance or similar relief, claims valued at less than the fast track limit which include an element of personal injury damages, including those valued at less than the small claims limit.

(3) *Multi-track procedure* – will normally apply to all defended claims valued at more than the fast track limit, all clinical negligence claims, all claims in categories over which only the High Court has jurisdiction eg judicial review, test cases, cases where there is a right to a jury trial, cases where fraud is alleged against a party.

Within this framework, effective case-management is seen as the key to achieving the wider aims of the Woolf reforms. The stated objectives of case management[11] are the achievement of early settlement, the diversion of cases to alternative methods for the resolution of disputes, the encouragement of a spirit of co-operation between the parties, the identification of the issues, and progressing a case to trial as quickly and cheaply as possible. In the "multi-track" approach "effective consideration" of the case at a case management conference early in the case is to be held; and a pre-trial review will occur, shortly before trial. The most complex and important cases will be heard only by High Court judges and not by deputies. Other cases will be managed and heard by the appropriate level of judge and will be able to move flexibly within the system to ensure this. The cases will be managed by procedural judges who will generally be Masters or district judges working in teams with High Court and Circuit judges. For the heavier cases, requiring full "hands-on" judicial control, the procedural judge may be a High Court or Circuit judge. The procedural judge will

(a) conduct the initial scrutiny of all cases to allocate them to the appropriate management track;

8   *Jackson v Slater Harrison* [1996] 1 WLR 597.
9   See pp 323, and 338, *ante*.
10   See *Access to Justice: Judicial Case Management: The Fast track and Multi Track, A Working Paper*, July 1997; Middleton Report, *op cit*, at paras 2.24-2.27.
11   See Interim Report, *op cit*, pp 26-56.

(b) conduct the case management conference unless it is more appropriate for the trial judge to do so;

(c) generally monitor the progress of the case and investigate if parties are failing to comply with timetables or directions; and

(d) draw the existence of Alternative Dispute Resolution (ADR) to parties' attention where this is appropriate or desirable.

The trial judge will normally conduct the pre-trial review. The Woolf Report also made specific recommendations in respect of litigants in person, pleadings[12] and the use of, and testimony of expert witnesses.[13]

The salient features of the "fast-track" will be a set timetable of 20–30 weeks, with a fixed date or "warned week" set at the outset for trial; limited discovery, short trials (not exceeding one half day); no oral evidence from experts, and limited evidence from non-experts, and a firm timetable for all actions.

It is against these objectives, and standards, that the workings of the existing system must be considered.

B STAY, CONTINUANCE AND DISMISSAL

I Stay

The current power of the court to stay proceedings may exist by statute, under the Rules of the Supreme Court; or under the inherent jurisdiction of the High Court. Certain Acts of Parliament contain specific provisions empowering or requiring the court to stay proceedings. Of these, the most commonly encountered, in practice, are the Arbitration Act 1996 (power to stay an action brought contrary to an arbitration agreement),[14] and in respect of certain matters under the Insolvency Act. The Rules contain some provisions empowering or requiring the court to stay proceedings, generally until a party complies with an order.[15]

The power to stay under the inherent jurisdiction is expressly acknowledged and preserved by section 49(3) of the Supreme Court Act 1981 and is exercisable in a wide range of circumstances. Thus the court may stay proceedings which are obviously frivolous, vexatious, groundless or an abuse of the process of the court. It is necessary for a stay for the applicant to show that the action could not possibly succeed. Commencing a second action while there is in being an action based on the same facts is prima facie an abuse of the process of the court.[16] Other circumstances in which the court may stay proceedings in the exercise of its inherent jurisdiction include the existence of concurrent proceedings in the courts of another country,[17] the fact that a

---

12 See p 380, *post.*

13 See p 395, *post.*

14 See p 331, *ante.*

15 See, for example, Ord 18, r 19 (p 383, *post*); Ord 6, r 5; Ord 21, r 5; Ord 81, r 2. Note also Ord 114, r 4, whereby, on an order being made referring a question to the European Court for a preliminary ruling under Article 177 of the EC Treaty, proceedings are (unless the court otherwise orders) stayed until the European Court has given a preliminary ruling on the question before it.

16 *Slough Estates Ltd v Slough Borough Council* [1968] Ch 299; [1967] 2 All ER 270.

17 *The Abidin Daver* [1984] AC 398; [1984] 1 All ER 470.

matter ought to be litigated in another country[18] or the fact that the subject matter of the action is *res judicata*.[19] In addition it appears that there is inherent jurisdiction to order a stay whenever it is just and reasonable to do so, even though no party has failed to comply with any specific obligation. This was done in *Edmeades v Thames Board Mills Ltd*.[20] The plaintiff, in an action for damages for personal injuries, refused to submit to a medical examination by the defendant's doctor for the purpose of enabling the defendant to check on the injuries which the plaintiff claimed to have sustained. The Court of Appeal ordered a stay of the action until the plaintiff submitted to such examination. The decision is a remarkable one, since there is no power in any court to order a person to submit to medical examination. It is odd that a person should be denied the use of the legal process to enforce his rights simply because he refuses to do that which he is in no way obliged to do.[1]

2   Discontinuance

The parties and their solicitors will, at every stage of the proceedings, be attempting to resolve their dispute without the expense of a trial. In fact very few actions come to trial. If the plaintiff is satisfied that his cause of action was misconceived or has ceased to exist he may at any time consent to judgment being entered against him with costs. The result will be to determine finally the issues he has raised on his writ and pleadings. However the plaintiff is better advised simply to discontinue his action since this course will not prevent him from suing again at a more convenient time. If he acts before a defence is served or within 14 days of service of a defence, the plaintiff may without leave serve a written notice on the defendant to the effect that he is discontinuing the whole or any part of his action.[2] He may serve a notice of discontinuance at a later stage of the action but only with leave (unless the defendant agrees in writing), and a condition of the grant of leave may be that the plaintiff shall take no further proceeding in the matter. Alternatively leave may be refused and judgment entered for the

---

18   See p 345, *ante*. This ground is known as *forum non conveniens* and is expressly preserved by s 49 of the Civil Jurisdiction and Judgments Act 1982. The fact that some proceedings have already commenced is relevant: *Spiliada Maritime Corporation v Cansulex Ltd* [1987] AC 460; [1986] 3 All ER 843. The authorities are unclear as to how far the allocation of jurisdiction by the 1982 Act prevents the court issuing a stay on this basis: see *Re Harrods (Buenos Aires) Ltd* [1992] Ch 72; [1991] 4 All ER 334.

19   Ie already the subject of judicial decision.

20   [1969] 2 QB 67; [1969] 2 All ER 127.

1   This view was apparently shared by Lawson J who, in holding in *Baugh v Delta Water Fittings Ltd* [1971] 3 All ER 258; [1971] 1 WLR 1295 that there was no power to require a widow to submit to medical examination by staying the action if she refused (at any rate in the absence of any reason for supposing that her medical condition was out of the ordinary), expressed the opinion that *Edmeades* was wrongly decided, an opinion which soon brought a sharp rebuke by the Court of Appeal in *Lane v Willis* [1972] 1 All ER 430; [1972] 1 WLR 326, in which case *Edmeades* was approved. Cf *Norman v Hardy* [1974] 1 All ER 1170; [1974] 1 WLR 1048 in which Goulding J declined to stay a pending action, which was registered as such under the Land Charges Act 1972, on the ground that it was not right to stay an action in circumstances not covered by the Rules of the Supreme Court for the purpose of bringing about a vacation of the register which the judge had no power to effect by direct order.

2   Ord 21, r 2(1). However a party in whose favour an interim payment has been ordered (as to which see p 378, *post*) may not discontinue except with the leave of the court or the consent of all other parties (Ord 21, r 2(2a)). This Rule was introduced to remedy the omission which was disclosed in *Castanho v Brown & Root (UK) Ltd* [1981] AC 557; [1981] 1 All ER 143 in which case the plaintiff, having obtained interim payments totalling £27,250 in his personal injuries action, together with an admission of liability, then served notice of discontinuance with a view to commencing another action in the United States based on the same accident. This was held to be an abuse of the process of the court so that the court had jurisdiction to strike out the notice.

defendant. If a defendant has served a defence, he may withdraw it in whole or in part by giving written notice to the plaintiff.[3] The plaintiff may then enter judgment in default of defence. If a subsequent action is brought in respect of a cause of action previously discontinued, the master may order the proceedings to be stayed until the costs of the discontinued action have been paid.[4]

3 Dismissal

In a case in which the court has inherent power to stay proceedings, it will sometimes make an order dismissing the action, and the courts do not usually in such cases simply stay the proceedings if, for example, they are an abuse of the process of the court or are groundless. On the other hand if, of course, the ground upon which they are stayed is one that can be removed (for example by a party complying with a court order), then it will be appropriate for the court to stay the proceedings rather than to dismiss them.

One particular occasion of the exercise of the court's power to dismiss actions under its inherent jurisdiction is encountered in cases where the plaintiff has been guilty of "want of prosecution". It is of great practical importance and covers two distinct circumstances:

(a) cases where the plaintiff has failed to comply with a peremptory ("or unless") order of the court; in such cases the action is liable to be dismissed on account of the contumelious conduct of the party in failing to comply with the court's peremptory order;

(b) cases in which the plaintiff has simply delayed getting on with the action, these are more common.

If the time-limits prescribed by the Rules were strictly observed most actions would be disposed of in a matter of months. In practice the time-limits have often not been observed. The blame for delay must, as a rule, rest with the plaintiff and the ultimate sanction is that the action may be dismissed for want of prosecution. A dismissal, not being an adjudication on the merits, does not prevent the plaintiff from issuing a fresh writ founded on the same cause of action.[5]

The approach of the courts to the exercise of this power is changing. In *Birkett v James*[6] the House of Lords held that in cases in which the limitation period had not expired (so that if the action were dismissed the plaintiff could simply issue a fresh writ), the court would not, save in rare and exceptional cases, dismiss an action for want of prosecution. The rare and exceptional cases contemplated are those in which the plaintiff's default has been contumelious or in cases, such as *Spring Grove Services Ltd v Deane*[7] where some factors other than mere delay have prejudiced the defendant. In such cases, on the basis that the court would stay a second action as between an

---

3   Ord 21, r 2(2)(a).
4   Ord 21, r 5.
5   *Pople v Evans* [1969] 2 Ch 255; [1968] 2 All ER 743. However the court has power to strike out such an action as being an abuse of the process of the court. This has been done in a few reported cases, eg *Spring Grove Services Ltd v Deane* (1972) 116 Sol Jo 844, which case was exceptional in that the defence depended essentially on the evidence of two witnesses who were no longer available to the defendant when the second action was brought; cf *Department of Health and Social Security v Ereira* [1973] 3 All ER 421. The matter is one for the discretion of the court: *Arbuthnot Latham Bank Ltd v Trafalgar Holdings Ltd* [1998] 2 All ER 181; [1998] 1 WLR 1426.
6   [1978] AC 297; [1977] 2 All ER 801.
7   See n 5, *ante*.

abuse of the process of the court, it may dismiss the first action notwithstanding the fact that the limitation period has not expired. As stated above, such cases are likely to be very rare. There have in recent years been numerous reported cases on this topic, with a growing resistance by the courts to explanations why an action should not be dismissed. Among the factors which have led, in the past, to dismissal are the following: (a) cases where the delay is intentional; and (b) where the delay is ordinate, inexcusable and prejudicial to the defence. In considering whether delay has been inordinate, the whole history of the action is considered including delay prior to the issue of the writ and delay for which the defendant has been responsible. An inordinate delay will be inexcusable unless the plaintiff has some reason for it. Even if the delay is inordinate and inexcusable the action may not be struck out if the defendant has not been prejudiced, for example where liability is admitted.[8] Moreover, in *Birkett v James*[9] the House of Lords held that prejudice occurring prior to the issue of the writ was not sufficient, since delay during this period is permitted by the Limitation Acts. Thus the plaintiff has to demonstrate new prejudice over and above that which has occurred due to permissible delay in instituting proceedings. It need not be great but it must be "more than minimal".

Nevertheless actions may be, and have been, struck out even where liability has been admitted by the defendant (thus providing an unexpected windfall for the defendant or, more often, his insurers). Thus in *Paxton v Allsopp*[10] an action for damages for personal injuries arising out of a car accident was struck out even though liability had been admitted, and, indeed, an offer of £2,050 had been made by the defendant's solicitors and rejected some years earlier. The reason for striking out was that, not only was the delay inordinate and inexcusable, but the defendant was prejudiced in that oral examination of the medical witnesses would be impossible after such a length of time. The case was, it should be pointed out, an extreme one since the application to strike out was made more than 13 years after the accident.[11] The prejudice to the defendant to be considered is not confined to prejudice affecting the actual trial. In *Department of Transport v Chris Smaller (Transport) Ltd*[12] the House of Lords observed, obiter, that prejudice to the defendant's business interests would suffice.[13] The court should, though, be cautious about going further. The mere fact of anxiety accompanying litigation would only be sufficient in an exceptional case.[14] Without prejudice to the above, RSC Order 3, rule 6 provides that where a year or more has elapsed since the last proceeding in an action, the party who desires to proceed must give to every other party not less than one month's notice of intention to proceed (whereupon the other party may, of course, apply to have the action dismissed for want of prosecution).

The rule in *Birkett v James* has received much attention from the courts. In *Grovit v Doctor*[15] the House of Lords was invited, but declined, to reconsider the principles set out in that case, preferring to wait until the more widespread reform of the civil justice system envisaged by the Woolf Report. Meanwhile, parties should be aware of the increasing willingness of court to make "unless orders", which are orders that

8   *Marlton (an infant) v Lee-Leviten* [1968] 2 All ER 874; [1968] 1 WLR 1214.
9   *Supra*, n 6.
10   [1971] 3 All ER 370; [1971] 1 WLR 1310; see also *Gloria v Sokoloff* [1969] 1 All ER 204; *Sweeney v Sir Robert McAlpine & Sons Ltd* [1974] 1 All ER 474; [1974] 1 WLR 200; *Bremer Vulkan Schiffbau und Maschinenfabrik v South India Shipping Corporation Ltd* [1981] AC 909; [1981] 1 All ER 289.
11   See also *Biss v Lambeth, Southwark and Lewisham Area Health Authority* [1978] 2 All ER 125; [1978] 1 WLR 382.
12   [1989] AC 1197; [1989] 1 All ER 897.
13   For an example, see *Antcliffe v Gloucester Health Authority* [1992] 1 WLR 1044.
14   See *Biss v Lambeth, Southwark & Lewisham Area Health Authority*, *supra*, n 11.
15   [1997] 2 All ER 417; [1997] 1 WLR 640

an action should be struck out unless certain steps are taken. Lord Woolf stressed the advantages of such orders in that they require the plaintiff to justify the action being allowed to continue.[16] In that case the court recognised that conducting litigation with no intention of bringing it to a conclusion amounted to an abuse of process. More recently still, the Court of Appeal in *Arbuthnot Latham Bank Ltd v Trafalgar Holdings Ltd*[17] stressed that wholesale failure to comply with the rules justified an action being struck out, and did not depend on prejudice to the defendant being established, or for it to be shown that a fair trial was no longer possible. Increasingly, the courts will intervene in case management, and look at the effects not only on the individual parties but also on the administration of justice generally.

C   SETTLEMENT

The parties (or their insurance companies) are likely to be in constant communication to effect a settlement of the action. This they may do with complete candour since letters which pass between them are privileged from production and any offer or admission of liability made therein is said to be made "without prejudice". The nature of a settlement is that it is a contract whereby the parties abandon their previous rights and obligations in return for the creation of new rights and obligations. Since the new obligations are contractual, they must, in accordance with general contractual principles, either be under seal or made for consideration. These releases are termed, therefore, a "release under seal" and a "release by way of accord and satisfaction"; the latter is more common and has been defined as:[18]

> "the purchase of a release from an obligation, whether arising under contract or tort, by means of any valuable consideration, not being the actual performance of the obligation itself. The accord is the agreement by which the obligation is discharged. The satisfaction is the consideration which makes the agreement operative."

The parties may effect a settlement without the consent of the court by giving notice of withdrawal before trial. Where an order of the court is required, which will usually be the case when the action is settled during the trial, the required terms will be drawn up and indorsed on counsels' briefs, or, more usually, the parties will submit to judgment on agreed terms. The settlement of any action on behalf of an infant or patient must be approved by the court.[19]

D   SUMMARY JUDGMENT UNDER ORDER 14

This procedure was introduced by the Judicature Acts 1873–75. The defendant's purpose in giving notice of intention to defend is frequently to gain time. Order 14 procedure enables the plaintiff to bring the matter to an early determination where the defendant has no triable defence to liability.[20] The rule applies to every action in the

---

16   See p 338, *ante*.
17   [1998] 2 All ER 181; [1998] 1 WLR 1426.
18   *British Russian Gazette and Trade Outlook Ltd v Associated Newspapers Ltd* [1933] 2 KB 616, at 643–644.
19   Ord 80, rr 11, 12.
20   Ord 86 provides a procedure, similar to Ord 14, in actions commenced by writ in the Chancery Division for specific performance or rescission of agreements relating to land or for the forfeiture or return of any deposit made under such an agreement.

Queen's Bench Division (or Chancery Division) begun by writ other than one which includes: (a) a claim by the plaintiff for libel, slander, malicious prosecution, false imprisonment; or, (b) an admiralty action *in rem*.[1] Provided the defendant has given notice of intention to defend and the plaintiff has served a statement of claim, the plaintiff may issue the appropriate summons. To do so he or a person duly authorised by him must first swear an affidavit setting out his cause of action, the amount claimed, if liquidated, and his belief that there is no defence to his claim except as to the amount of damages. The plaintiff should not swear to this lightly, for if he issues an Order 14 summons where the case is not a proper one, or where he must have known that the defendant had a triable defence, the master may order him forthwith to pay the whole costs of the application.[2] The plaintiff, having filed his affidavit, then takes out a summons which must be served on the defendant, together with a copy of his affidavit, not less than 10 clear days before the return day (ie the day appointed for the hearing of the summons).[3] The defendant, if he contests the summons, must attend on the return day and show that he has a triable defence. This is usually done by an affidavit, but it can be done "otherwise",[4] for example by oral testimony.

At the hearing of the summons the master[5] may make the following orders:

(1) He may give judgment for the plaintiff, final or interlocutory.[6] This must be done unless the defendant satisfies the court "that there is an issue or question in dispute which ought to be tried or that there ought for some other reason to be a trial."[7] If he has any defence on a question of law or fact then he must be given leave to defend the action, even if the master strongly doubts that the defence will succeed.

(2) He may give the defendant unconditional leave to defend the action. In this case the action will proceed to trial in the usual way.

(3) He may give the defendant conditional leave to defend. This may be done where the master is almost, but not quite, sure that there is no triable defence.[8] The effect is that the defendant may present his defence provided he makes a payment into court of the whole or part of the sum claimed. The court must not impose a condition with which it is impossible for the defendant to comply. If the defendant wishes to avoid or limit a financial condition on the ground of his own impecuniosity the onus is on him to make a full and frank disclosure of his means. Moreover he cannot complain because a financial condition is difficult for him to

---

1   Ord 14, r 1(2).
2   Ord 14, r 7(1); except where the plaintiff is an assisted person. See the remarks of Lord Goddard CJ in *BM Pocock v ADAC Ltd* [1952] 1 All ER 294n; [1952] 1 TLR 29 (*infra*).
3   Ord 14, r 2. As to the meaning of "clear days" in the Rules, see Ord 3, r 2(4).
4   Ord 14, r 4(1). The defendant must show that he has a triable defence, although he need not set out every element of that defence. A general denial of liability is not sufficient. There is no express requirement for the defendant to serve his affidavit on the plaintiff. However the summons contains a notice requiring the defendant to send a copy of his affidavit to the plaintiff to reach him not less than three days before the return day (so that the plaintiff may swear an affidavit in answer if he wishes). If the defendant sends his affidavit late or not at all, thereby necessitating an adjournment of the summons, he will usually have to pay the costs thrown away in any event; see *Practice Direction (Order 14; Return Date)* [1970] 1 All ER 343; [1970] 1 WLR 258.
5   The summons is almost always returnable before a master. However if an injunction is sought (which a master has no power to grant) the summons should be made returnable before a judge; *Shell-Mex and BP Ltd v Manchester Garages Ltd* [1971] 1 All ER 841; [1971] 1 WLR 612.
6   If the judgment is a money judgment, he may also award interest: *Gardner Steel Ltd v Sheffield Bros (Profiles) Ltd* [1978] 3 All ER 399; [1978] 1 WLR 916.
7   Ord 14, r 3(1); the latter part of this sub-rule is wide enough to enable leave to defend to be given where, even though the defendant cannot point to a specific defence, it is just that the plaintiff be put to strict proof of his case: *Miles v Bull* [1969] 1 QB 258; [1968] 3 All ER 632.
8   *Fieldrank Ltd v E Stein* [1961] 3 All ER 681n; [1961] 1 WLR 1287.

fulfil; he must prove that it will be impossible for him to fulfil.[9] The defendant may appeal to a judge in chambers against any condition imposed.

(4) He may give judgment for the plaintiff as to part and to the defendant leave to defend as to part of the claim.

(5) He may give judgment for the plaintiff with a stay of execution pending the trial of a counterclaim.

(6) If the application was not made in good faith or the case was not within the order, a libel action for example, the master may order the plaintiff to pay the costs of the application forthwith.[10] This is an extreme sanction which will rarely be invoked.

(7) If the master gives leave to defend or orders a stay of execution pending the trial of a counterclaim, he must give all directions as to the further conduct of the action as if the summons were a summons for directions; in particular he may, with the consent of all parties, order the action to be tried by himself or another master[11] or may transfer the action to a county court where it is transferable under the County Courts Act 1984.[12]

A defendant may apply for summary judgment on a counterclaim, provided it is not a claim which is outside the scope of the Order.[13] In addition any judgment under Order 14 may be set aside by the court on such terms as it thinks just.[14] This rather likens a judgment under Order 14 to a judgment on failure to give notice of intention to defend. Order 14 proceedings constitute an invaluable means of combating delaying tactics on the part of a defendant who owes money but simply wishes to postpone the evil day of payment. However, in order to obtain a judgment for part of the sum claimed, the plaintiff has to identify a part of the claim which is separately quantifiable (for example, individual invoices in a claim for the balance of an account). If the plaintiff cannot do this, then there is no power under Order 14 to give judgment for any sum at all, even though there may be no doubt whatsoever but that a substantial sum is due. Thus in a claim for the balance of an account[15] or for unliquidated damages,[16] the defendant can keep the plaintiff out of his money pending a trial (or arbitration) simply by denying that the account is accurate (if he can raise a triable issue as to its accuracy) or by putting the plaintiff to proof of his damages. However the plaintiff may in such cases obtain an interim payment and it is common for the plaintiff to apply for an interim payment as an alternative to summary judgment.

E   DISPOSAL OF A CASE ON A POINT OF LAW

By Order 14A, a district judge may determine any question of law or construction of a document summarily. In order for this power to be used, certain conditions have to be satisfied:

(a) the defendant must have given notice of intention to defend;

---

9   *M V Yorke Motors (a firm) v Edwards* [1982] 1 All ER 1024; [1982] 1 WLR 444.
10   Ord 14, r 7(1).
11   Ord 14, r 6.
12   See p 424, *post*.
13   Ord 14, r 5. 2 Ord 14, r 11.
14   Ord 14, r 11.
15   *Contract Discount Corporation Ltd v Furlong* [1948] 1 All ER 274.
16   *The Fuohsan Maru* [1978] 2 All ER 254.

(b) the question of law or construction of the document must be issuable for determination without a full trial;

(c) it must appear that such determination will finally determine the entire cause or matter or any claim or issue therein;

(d) the parties must have had an opportunity of being heard, or have consented to an order or judgment on such determination.

Any determination made will be final, subject to the usual right of appeal.

F   ACCOUNT SUMMONS

The plaintiff may indorse his writ with a claim for an account to be taken. This procedure dates back to the early days of the common law where it was available to the feudal lord against his bailiff or steward. It was extended in equity to any principal and agent relationship, such as landlord and rent-collector.[17] It is appropriate where the defendant is an accounting party, that is to say a person who has received money on the plaintiff's behalf. The plaintiff is not in possession of sufficient details to frame an action for a debt. His remedy is to ask the court to compel his agent to account for moneys received and to pay them to the plaintiff.

To do so he may, at any time after the time limited for acknowledging service of the writ, or after the defendant has acknowledged service, take out a summons. The application is usually supported by an affidavit setting out the grounds on which the plaintiff relies. Unless the defendant can show that there is some preliminary issue to be tried or that he has already accounted, the master will order an account to be taken and the amount found due to be paid to the plaintiff within a specified time. The plaintiff's rights thus become crystallised into a judgment debt in the normal way. Simple accounts may be taken by a master in the Queen's Bench Division, but the proceedings are usually transferred to the Chancery Division or to an official referee.

G   JUDGMENT ON ADMISSIONS OF FACT

Where admissions of fact are made by a party "either by his pleadings or otherwise" any other party may apply to the court for such judgment or order as upon those admissions he may be entitled to, without waiting for the determination of any other question between the parties, and the court may on the hearing of the application give such judgment or make such order as it thinks just.[18] The admissions may be made in the pleadings in which event, of course, the application will not be made at the early stages of the proceedings presently being considered. On the other hand, they may be made "otherwise", as the wording of the rule indicates; so admissions might be made in an affidavit sworn in opposition to Order 14 proceedings; or in the course of correspondence prior to the issue of proceedings, provided this was not "without prejudice".[19]

However, the power to give judgment on admissions will only be exercised in the clearest cases. So, for example, the fact that a defendant has pleaded guilty to manslaughter does not enable the widow of the deceased to obtain judgment in a Fatal

---

17   See *London, Chatham and Dover Rly Co v South Eastern Rly Co* [1892] 1 Ch 120.

18   Ord 27, r 3; the application may be made by summons or motion, but in the Queen's Bench Division is in practice made by summons.

19   See p 369, *ante*.

Accidents Act claim, because the defendant might wish to raise, for example, a plea of contributory negligence or *volenti non fit injuria*.[20] So also where, in a personal injuries action, the defendants' solicitors wrote to the plaintiff a letter saying that they were authorised to inform him that "the defendants now admit that the incident alleged in the statement of claim resulted from negligence for which they were responsible", the Court of Appeal, perhaps surprisingly, refused the plaintiff judgment on this admission since, although it amounted to an admission of negligence, it did not admit damage, which is an essential element of the tort of negligence.[1]

H PAYMENT INTO COURT

I Method of payment

In any action for debt or damages the defendant may, at any time[2] pay money into court in satisfaction of any or all of the plaintiff's claims.[3] To do so he deposits his payment at the Bank of England, Law Courts Branch, and serves a written notice to this effect on the plaintiff and on every co-defendant.[4] Where the plaintiff has included in his writ two or more claims the defendant may either: (1) make a separate payment in respect of each, or (2) make one payment in respect of any or all of those claims.[5] The latter course is usually disadvantageous to the plaintiff, since he must either continue with all of his claims or accept the payment and abandon them all. Accordingly where the payment in of a lump sum in respect of several causes of action embarrasses the plaintiff, he may apply to the court by summons for an order that the defendant apportion his payment in respect of the several causes of action.[6] However, the defendant will not be required to sever his payment in unless the causes of action are substantially different, ie where a jury might be directed to make separate awards of damages. Where the causes of action are technically different but substantially the same, for example several meanings of the same words in a defamation action, the defendant, if he makes one payment in respect of them all, will not be required to sever it.[7]

Where the defendant has a counterclaim for damages he may expressly take this into account when paying money into court;[8] thus if he values the plaintiff's claim at £1,000 and his counterclaim at £200, he will pay into court £800. It will be appreciated that where he values his counterclaim in excess of the plaintiff's claim, he should not take it into account when paying in since, as we shall see, the effect of the plaintiff accepting the payment will be that the defendant cannot proceed with his counterclaim. If the claim is for a debt or liquidated demand in foreign currency the defendant may pay into court in that currency, whereupon the currency will be held in a special

20   *Murphy v Culhane* [1977] QB 94; [1976] 3 All ER 533.
1   *Rankine v Garton Sons & Co Ltd* [1979] 2 All ER 1185. The decision seems highly technical since if the plaintiff had gone under Ord 14 it is difficult to see on what basis judgment could have been withheld.
2   Even before service of the writ.
3   Ord 22, r 1(1). This may be done after the trial of an action has begun.
4   For interest and other rules governing deposits, see Supreme Court Funds Rules 1975.
5   Ord 22, r 1(4). Until 1965 this was not possible in defamation actions.
6   Ord 22, r 1(5). This order cannot be made in relation to money paid into court after the trial or hearing of the action has begun (Ord 22, r 3(3)).
7   *Pedley v Cambridge Newspapers Ltd* [1964] 2 All ER 794; [1964] 1 WLR 988; decided under Ord 82, r 4, before that rule was amended; see n 6, *supra*.
8   Ord 22, r 2.

account.[9] The plaintiff's cause of action is deemed to include such interest as might be awarded in the judgment.[10] Consequently it is incumbent upon the defendant to make a payment which takes account of the interest which will have notionally accrued on the debt or damages up to the date of payment in.

2   Effects of a payment into court

The plaintiff must, within three days of receiving the defendant's notice of payment in, acknowledge receipt. He may then within 21 days, or later with leave, take the money out of court in respect of any cause of action for which a payment in was made.[11] If the defendant made a general payment in the plaintiff must take "all or nothing". The effect is that all the causes of action in respect of which the plaintiff accepted a payment in are stayed, as is any counterclaim which the defendant took into account under Order 22, rule 2. The plaintiff may then:

(1)   tax and sign judgment for his costs to the date of payment in (but only if his whole claim is satisfied);[12] and

(2)   in actions for defamation, malicious presentation, or false imprisonment, apply to a judge in chambers by summons for leave to make in open court a statement in terms approved by the judge.[13] This is so that he may vindicate his reputation publicly.

Alternatively the plaintiff may leave the money in court and continue with his action. In this event the court must not be told of the existence of a payment into court until all questions of liability and damages have been determined.[14] This is especially so in jury actions, notably defamation, for if the jury knew of a substantial payment into court they would obviously be likely to look upon it as an admission of liability by the defendant, rather than a genuine attempt to effect a settlement. To this rule there are two exceptions: the defences of tender before action, and apology under section 2 of the Libel Act 1843. In both these cases payment into court is an element in a defence and will therefore appear on the pleadings and be disclosed to the court.

As long as the plaintiff recovers more than the amount paid in, the payment in will have been of no avail to the defendant. However, if he recovers less or no more than

9   *The Halcyon the Great* [1975] 1 All ER 882; [1975] 1 WLR 515; see *Practice Direction (Foreign Currency)* [1976] 1 All ER 669; [1976] 1 WLR 83.

10   Ord 22, r 1(8).

11   Ord 22, r 3. He requires, under Ord 22, r 4, an order of the court in some cases; viz (a) where the payment is made by some, but not all, defendants sued jointly or in the alternative by him, (b) where the payment in was made as part of a plea of tender before action, (c) in actions by an infant or patient (Ord 80, r 12), (d) in actions under the Fatal Accidents Act and the Law Reform (Miscellaneous Provisions) Act 1934, or under the Fatal Accidents Act alone where more than one person is entitled to the money. Where the payment in was made or increased after the trial has begun the plaintiff may accept the money within two days of receiving notice but before the judge begins to deliver judgment or sum up to the jury. Save by consent, an application for leave to take out of court a sum paid in after the time for acceptance has expired should not be made to the trial judge since this would necessitate disclosing to the judge the fact (and probably the amount) of a payment in, which is specifically prohibited by Ord 22, r 7 (*infra*); *Gaskins v British Aluminium Co Ltd* [1976] QB 524; [1976] 1 All ER 208.

12   Ord 62, r 5(4).

13   Ord 82, r 5(1). There are certain limited exceptions to this right: see *Honeyford v Commission for Racial Equality* (1991) Independent, 13 May.

14   Ord 22, r 7; *Monk v Redwing Aircraft Co Ltd* [1942] 1 KB 182; [1942] 1 All ER 133; *Millensted v Grosvenor House (Park Lane) Ltd* [1937] 1 KB 717; [1937] 1 All ER 736.

the amount paid in then, although costs are discretionary, the plaintiff will usually have to pay the whole costs of the action in respect of which payment was made, from the date of payment in.[15] The modern tendency of the courts is to look at the action as a whole and not as several causes of action tried together. Thus if the plaintiff does not recover in the aggregate more than the total payment in by the defendant he may have to pay the costs of the whole action from the date of payment in.[16] To put it simply, the plaintiff is gambling to "beat the payment in".[17]

Where the plaintiff beats the payment in only by reason of interest that has accrued since the date of payment in it is to be anticipated that he would not be regarded as having beaten the payment in at all and that the trial judge would therefore order him to pay the defendant's costs from the date of payment in. In such a case it will be necessary for the judge to make a calculation of what the interest would have been at the date of payment in. Where a defendant claims an indemnity or contribution from a third party or tortfeasor liable in respect of the same damage, that third party or tortfeasor cannot make a payment into court. He can, however, obtain a similar advantage by making a written offer to the defendant to pay a specified contribution to any debt or damages recovered against the defendant. If the defendant refuses this offer it may be drawn to the attention of the trial judge, who may take it into account when making an order as to costs, as if the offer were a payment into court.[18]

Finally it should be noted that the plaintiff may make a payment into court in respect of a counterclaim against him[19] and that a party may, with leave, withdraw a payment in.[20]

I   TRIAL WITHOUT PLEADINGS

This procedure enables trial without pleadings or further pleadings as the case may be. The application may be made in any action commenced by writ other than one which includes: (a) a claim by the plaintiff for libel, slander, malicious prosecution or false imprisonment; or (b) a claim by the plaintiff based on an allegation of fraud, provided that any defendant has given notice of intention to defend.[1] The object of this procedure is to enable the parties to determine their dispute without the delay and expense of pleadings or other interlocutory applications. However it is only appropriate where there is no substantial dispute as to fact, as, for example, where the action turns on the construction of a document. In this respect, and also in the conduct of the proceedings, the procedure is very similar to originating summons procedure, except that it applies to a wider range of proceedings in the Queen's Bench Division, such as a negligence action where the sole issue is the assessment of damages. Since there are

15   Ord 62, r 5. *Findlay v Railway Executive* [1950] 2 All ER 969.
16   *Hultquist v Universal Pattern and Precision Engineering Co Ltd* [1960] 2 QB 467; [1960] 2 All ER 266.
17   Lord Denning MR in *Mason v Mason* [1965] 3 All ER 492n; [1966] 1 WLR 757 pointed out the desirability of a new rule which would have the effect of concealing the existence and amount of a payment in from the Court of Appeal so that the court would not be embarrassed by its knowledge of a payment in. With effect from 1 April 1976 such a rule was introduced (Ord 59, r 12A).
18   Ord 16, r 10; Ord 62, r 5; *Bragg v Crosville Motor Services Ltd* [1959] 1 All ER 613; [1959] 1 WLR 324. A similar course may be taken in proceedings such as matrimonial property disputes, where the Rules make no provision for payment into court; *Calderbank v Calderbank* [1976] Fam 93; [1975] 3 All ER 333 or in arbitrations where a "sealed offer" may be made.
19   Ord 22, r 6.
20   Ord 22, r 1(3); cf *W A Sherratt Ltd v John Bromley (Church Stretton) Ltd* [1985] QB 1038; [1985] 1 All ER 216.
1   Ord 18, r 21.

no pleadings the parties must agree on a statement of the issues in dispute. This may be done by letter.[2] In a commercial case application for a trial without pleadings is frequently made in conjunction with an application for transfer to the Commercial Court.[3] If the master makes an order for a trial without pleadings he must, and if he dismisses the application he may, give directions as to the further conduct of the action as if the summons were a summons for directions.

J INTERIM RELIEF

I Interlocutory injunction

The power of the High Court to grant injunctions is, of course, inherited from equity. In addition to the court's inherent power to grant an injunction by way of final remedy, section 37(1) of the Supreme Court Act 1981 empowers the court to grant an injunction by an interlocutory order "in all cases in which it appears to the court to be just or convenient so to do."[4] It may be noted that the injunction need not be directed at achieving the same relief as that which is sought by way of final relief in the proceedings. The most obvious example of this is the Mareva injunction, which has already been considered in detail.[5]

It was formerly thought that, on an application for an interlocutory injunction, the most important consideration was the relative strength of the parties' cases so that, in order to obtain an interlocutory injunction, the plaintiff had first to establish that he had a strong prima facie case.[6] The disadvantage of this approach was that it necessitated a close examination of the merits as disclosed in the affidavits sworn on behalf of each side, sometimes amounting almost to a trial of the action.[7]

In the leading case of *American Cyanamid Co v Ethicon Ltd*[8] Lord Diplock stated that the approach referred to above was incorrect and, in a speech with which the remainder of their Lordships agreed, laid down the following principles:[9]

(1) The plaintiff must first satisfy the court "that the claim is not frivolous or vexatious; in other words that there is a serious question to be tried".

(2) The court should then go on to consider the "balance of convenience".

(3) As to that, the court should first consider whether, if the plaintiff were to succeed at the trial in establishing his right to a permanent injunction, he would be adequately compensated by an award of damages for the loss he would have sustained by refusal of an interlocutory injunction.[10]

---

2   *Hill v Scott* [1895] 2 QB 371.
3   See p 399, *post*.
4   The position of the Crown was discussed in *Factortame v Secretary of State for Transport* [1990] 2 AC 85; [1989] 2 All ER 692.
5   See p 359, *ante*.
6   See *J T Stratford & Son Ltd v Lindley* [1965] AC 269; [1964] 3 All ER 102.
7   Although there was the correlative advantage that, very often, the parties would either agree to treat the hearing of the motion as the trial of the action or, in fact, compromise the action on the basis of the decision of the motion. Many "leading cases" were decided in this way; cf *Fellowes & Son v Fisher* [1976] QB 122, at p 133; [1975] 2 All ER 829, at 837.
8   [1975] AC 396; [1975] 1 All ER 504.
9   [1975] AC at 408–409; [1975] 1 All ER at 510–511.
10   *Donmar Productions Ltd v Bart* [1967] 2 All ER 338n; [1967] 1 WLR 740n; cf *Hampstead and Suburban Properties Ltd v Diomedous* [1969] 1 Ch 248; [1968] 3 All ER 545. In cases not involving monetary payment, the court should assess the relative merits of the case: *Cambridge Nutrition Ltd v British Broadcasting Corporation* [1990] 3 All ER 523; cf *A-G v Guardian Newspapers* [1987] 3 All

(4) If damages would not provide an adequate remedy (for example because the defendant may be impecunious) the court should consider whether the defendant would be adequately compensated by the plaintiff's undertaking as to damages (*infra*) in the event of an interlocutory injunction being granted but a permanent injunction being refused at the trial.

(5) Where other matters are equal, it is a "counsel of prudence to take such measures as are calculated to preserve the status quo".

(6) Finally, "if the extent of the uncompensatable disadvantage to each party would not differ widely, it may not be improper to take into account in tipping the balance the relative strength of each party's case as revealed by the affidavit evidence." By this is meant that the court should consider whether the strength of the case of one party is disproportionate to the other.[11]

Lord Diplock made it clear that there may be special factors which operate in "individual cases" in addition to the principles enumerated above. Nevertheless it is clear that the courts should not embark on anything resembling a trial of the action.

The Court of Appeal initially showed little enthusiasm for these new principles and Lord Denning MR, in particular, was apt to treat cases before him as "individual cases" taking them outside the *American Cyanamid* case.[12] In *Cayne v Global Natural Resources plc*[13] the Court of Appeal pointed out that where the grant or refusal of an interlocutory injunction will have the practical effect of putting an end to the action the task of the court is to do its best to avoid injustice, and to balance the risk of doing an injustice to either party. In such cases the *American Cyanamid* guidelines cannot apply and unless the plaintiff can show an overwhelming case he will not be granted an injunction the effect of which would be tantamount to shutting the defendant out from contesting the action. May LJ justified this departure by observing:[14]

"I think that one must be very careful to apply the relevant passages from Lord Diplock's familiar speech in the *Cyanamid* case not as rules but only as guidelines, which is what I am certain Lord Diplock intended them to be."

A master having no power to grant injunctions, application must be made to a judge. In cases of extreme urgency application can be made *ex parte* on affidavit, in which event an injunction will be granted for a very short period until an application by summons or motion can be brought before the court. Otherwise application is by summons to a judge in chambers in the Queen's Bench Division or by motion in open court in the Chancery Division.[15]

As an alternative to injunction the court will usually accept an undertaking from the defendant (which has precisely the same effect). In addition, as a condition of being granted an interlocutory injunction the plaintiff is customarily required to give his undertaking as to damages, that is an undertaking to indemnify the defendant in respect of any damages which the latter sustains by reason of the injunction in the event of the

---

ER 316; [1987] 1 WLR 1248, where the Court of Appeal appeared to adopt an "arguable case" approach. See also *Dalgety Spillers Food v Food Brokers Ltd* [1994] FSR 504.

11 See *Series 5 Software Ltd v Clarke* [1996] 1 All ER 853. A court should not grant interim relief where a new cause of action is relied on: see *Khorasandjian v Bush* [1993] QB 727.

12 *Fellowes & Son v Fisher (supra)*; *Hubbard v Pitt* [1976] QB 142; [1975] 3 All ER 1.

13 [1984] 1 All ER 225.

14 [1984] 1 All ER at 237. The *Cyanamid* principles do not apply to mandatory injunctions: *Locabail International Finance Ltd v Agroexport* [1986] 1 All ER 901; [1986] 1 WLR 657.

15 Ord 29, r 1.

action failing.[16] For this reason it is generally improvident for a plaintiff to apply for an interlocutory injunction unless he has a strong case in circumstances in which the injunction will cause the defendant heavy expense, for example by delaying building works.

2   Interim payment of damages

One long-standing criticism of civil procedure in the English courts was that wholly innocent parties, such as injured passengers in road accidents, had to wait for long periods for their damages while disputes between other parties, such as the car drivers (in fact, their insurers) were being resolved. The Report of the Committee on Personal Injuries Litigation[17] recommended that in such litigation, courts should have power to make interim payments and effect was given to this recommendation by the Administration of Justice Act 1969. This was replaced by section 32(1) of the Supreme Court Act 1981 which authorises rules of court enabling the High Court:

> "in such circumstances as may be prescribed to make an order requiring a party to the proceedings to make an interim payment of such amount as may be specified in the order, with provision for the payment to be made to such other party to the proceedings as may be so specified or, if the order so provides, by paying it into court."

The power was first exercised in personal injuries actions in 1970 and was extended in 1980 to all actions in which there is a money claim, whether by way of debt, damages, account, *quantum meruit* or whatever. The application for an interim payment may be made at any time after expiry of the time limited for acknowledgement of service and is by summons supported by an affidavit which must:

(a) verify the amount of the damages, debt or other sum to which the application relates and the grounds of the application;
(b) exhibit any documentary evidence relied on by the plaintiff in support of the application; and
(c) if the plaintiff's claim is made under the Fatal Accidents Act 1976, contain the particulars mentioned in section 2(4) of that Act.[18]

By Order 29, r 11 an interim payment in an action for damages may be ordered only in three circumstances:

(a) where the defendant has admitted liability;
(b) where the plaintiff has obtained judgment against the respondent to the application for damages to be assessed; or

---

16   Where the Crown engages in litigation for the purpose of asserting a proprietary or contractual right, the ordinary rule applies; however where the Crown has commenced proceedings for an injunction for the purpose of enforcing the law in the manner prescribed by statute, no undertaking as to damages will be required; *Hoffman-La Roche & Co AG v Secretary of State for Trade and Industry* [1975] AC 295, at 329; [1974] 2 All ER 1128. This is a rule of discretion: see also *Kirklees Metropolitan Borough Council v Wickes Building Supplies Ltd* [1993] AC 227; [1992] 3 All ER 717, where no cross-undertaking in damages was required of a local authority seeking an interim injunction to prevent stores trading illegally on Sundays.
17   Cmnd 3691 of 1968 (the Pearson Committee).
18   Ord 29, r 10.

(c)   where if the action proceeded to trial the plaintiff would obtain judgment for substantial damages. Thus the power to order a payment on account of damages is limited to clear cases.[19]

The fact of the interim payment being made must not be pleaded nor disclosed to the court at the trial until all questions of liability and damages have been decided.[20] On giving final judgment the court may make an order so as to adjust the position between the parties in relation to sums already paid by way of interim payment; such an adjustment may involve repayment by the plaintiff or compensating payments between two or more defendants.[1] Where, after making an interim payment, a defendant pays money into court under Order 22, rule 1,[2] the notice of payment must state that the defendant has taken into account the interim payment.

Power to order interim payments extends to actions for possession of land; where it appears to the court that in the event of final judgment the defendant would be held liable to pay to the plaintiff a sum in respect of the defendant's use and occupation of the land during the pendency of the action, the court may order an interim payment on account of that sum.[3] The order may be for a lump sum or for periodical payments during the pendency of the action, or both.[4] Those provisions enable, for example, a landlord to be awarded sums equivalent to rent against a tenant who is holding over at the end of his lease.

K   THIRD PARTY AND INTERPLEADER PROCEEDINGS

Irrespective of his liability to the plaintiff, the defendant may have a right to relief from a third party which relates to the original subject matter of the action or which is substantially the same as the relief or remedy claimed by the plaintiff.[5] Thus if the plaintiff is a lessor and sues the defendant lessee for breach of covenant, the defendant may be able to claim relief from a sub-lessee.[6] Usually the right claimed by the defendant is to an indemnity or a contribution. A right to indemnity may exist by contract, by statute[7] or by a rule of common law or equity. A common example is the right of an agent to be indemnified by his principal in respect of acts performed within the scope of his authority.[8] A contribution is, in effect, a partial indemnity. It arises where a person is sued and there are other persons liable in respect of the same damage. The others, who may be joint trustees, joint debtors or joint tortfeasors, for example, have a duty to contribute.[9] In any of the above cases the defendant may bring a separate action for the remedy sought against the third party. However he will save time and

---

19   It is further limited in that, in personal injuries actions, no order can be made unless the defendant is insured against his liability, a public authority or a person whose means and resources are such as to enable him to make the interim payment; Ord 29, r 11(2).
20   Ord 29, r 15; cf the rules relating to payments into court, p 373, *ante*.
1   Ord 29, r 17.
2   See p 373, *ante*.
3   Ord 29, r 12.
4   Ord 29, r 13.
5   Ord 16, r 1. Until Rules made in 1929, a third party notice could only be issued for a contribution or indemnity. It now applies to a much wider range of proceedings by virtue of the wide provisions of the present rule. Cf *Myers v N & J Sherick Ltd* [1974] 1 All ER 81; [1974] 1 WLR 31.
6   *Pontifex v Foord* (1884) 12 QBD 152.
7   Examples are: ss 76, 77 of and Sch 2 to the Law of Property Act 1925 (implied covenants); Civil Aviation Act 1982, s 76(3).
8   *Read v Anderson* (1882) 10 QBD 100; *Johnson v Kearley* [1908] 2 KB 514.
9   See Civil Liability (Contribution) Act 1978, s 1 (repealing and replacing Law Reform (Married Women and Tortfeasors) Act 1935, s 6).

costs by issuing a third party notice. He may do this without leave before serving his defence and with leave thereafter.[10] The notice must contain particulars of the nature of the claim and the relief sought and must be served on the third party together with a copy of the statement of claim and all pleadings thus far served in the action.[11] The effect of this procedure is to make the third party a defendant in relation to the original defendant. The action then proceeds between them as if the defendant had issued a writ against the third party in the ordinary way. Thus if the third party does not give notice of intention to defend, the defendant is entitled to sign judgment in default. If his claim was for an indemnity, the extent of this judgment will be the amount that the plaintiff recovers from the defendant.[12]

The third party may counterclaim against the defendant, but not against the plaintiff.[13] He can, however, interrogate the plaintiff. Alternatively the third party may join a fourth party and so on.[14] Although the third party does not, strictly speaking, stand in any relationship to the plaintiff, the court is enabled by Order 16, rules 8 and 9 to determine any issue arising between the third party and the plaintiff. Third party proceedings are independent of the main action to the extent that they may continue to trial even after the issue between the plaintiff and defendant has been disposed of by final order.[15]

L   PLEADINGS

I   The nature and function of pleadings

If the case now proceeds, the parties exchange pleadings. Pleadings are written statements served by each party on his opponent, containing the allegations of fact on which the party pleadings relies. They serve various purposes. Principally they enable each party to determine exactly which facts are alleged against him. This may save a party from preparing evidence to meet allegations which are not being made against him. Also it enables parties to establish their "common ground", that is to say facts on which they are in agreement, thus saving the expense of proving these matters at the trial. Secondly, the action is decided upon the pleadings. Thus the parties and their successors may, by reference to the pleadings, determine in the future exactly what the case decided, so that they may not have to, and indeed may not be allowed to, fight the same issues again. Similarly reference to the pleadings in an action may disclose the *ratio decidendi* of the case for the purpose of the doctrine of precedent, since any fact not pleaded will not usually be regarded as a fact upon which a judgment is based.

Whether pleadings always in fact fulfils these objectives is a matter of doubt. The Woolf Report[16] considered the use of pleadings by plaintiffs often had the effect not

10   Ord 16, rr 1, 2.
11   Ord 16, r 3. Note also Ord 15, r 10A(2) whereby a defendant to an action for wrongful interference with goods (under the Torts (Interference with Goods) Act 1977) who wishes to set up the title of a third party against the plaintiff's claim (*jus tertii*) may, at any time after giving notice of intention to defend, apply for directions as to whether any such person should be joined in the action; the application is by summons which must be served on the third party in question and if the latter does not appear on the hearing of the summons the court may by order deprive him of any right of action he might otherwise have against the defendant; Ord 15, r 10A(4).
12   Ord 16, r 5. But it cannot, without leave, be enforced until the defendant has satisfied the judgment against himself; Ord 16, r 7(2).
13   *Barclays Bank Ltd v Tom* [1923] 1 KB 221.
14   Ord 16, r 9. The procedure between a third party and a fourth party is similar to the procedure between the defendant and the third party.
15   *Stott v West Yorkshire Road Car Co Ltd* [1971] 2 QB 651; [1971] 3 All ER 534.
16   *Op cit*, paras 153.–164.

of clarifying the issues, but of merely adding to the adversarial conflict responsible for delay. For the future it is recommended that pleadings will have to spell out the facts relied on so that the parties can identify and define the matters in issue. Their content will need to be verified by the parties, so enabling the court to determine the range and scale of material required to progress the case and the necessary extent of discovery, witness statements and the use of experts.

The classic definition of what pleadings must contain is found in Order 18, rule 7(1):

"every pleading must contain, and contain only, a statement in a summary form of the material facts on which the party pleading relies for his claim or defence, as the case may be, but not the evidence by which those facts are to be proved, and the statement must be as brief as the nature of the case admits ...".

Thus pleadings must contain facts not law.[17] However, this only means that conclusions of law (such as existence of a duty of care in negligence) need not be pleaded, not that a point of law cannot be raised on the pleadings.[18] Only material facts should be pleaded. Thus immaterial facts, such as character or motive, must not be pleaded since they form no part of a cause of action or defence.[19] Evidence should not be pleaded. However, the line between facts and evidence is by no means clearly defined. It is suggested that evidence be confined to its narrow meaning, viz. the means of proof.[20] By way of exception to the rule that evidence need not be pleaded, Order 18, rule 7A provides that a party intending to adduce evidence of another party's conviction,[1] must include in his pleading a statement of his intention with particulars of the conviction and the date thereof, the court which made the conviction and the issue in the proceedings to which the conviction is relevant. If the person convicted intends to deny the conviction, allege that it was erroneous or deny its relevance, he must make the denial or allegation in his pleading.

Finally, pleadings must contain all the material facts. The reason is that at the trial a party will be confined to his pleadings and will not be allowed to raise any matter not pleaded since this would take his opponent by surprise, the very contingency which pleadings are designed to avoid.[2] Thus where, in an action based on negligence, the plaintiffs relied in their pleaded case upon vicarious liability, they were not allowed in the House of Lords to allege that the defendants were negligent personally, since this was an allegation which they had not pleaded.[3] On the other hand a variation from the pleaded case, as opposed to a complete departure, is permissible; thus where, in one case, the plaintiff in his statement of claim alleged that a large stone had struck him on the head, he was not prevented from showing at the trial that his injuries had in fact been caused by several stones.[4]

---

17 *North-Western Salt Co Ltd v Electrolytic Alkali Co Ltd* [1914] AC 461; *Gautret v Egerton* (1867) LR 2 CP 371.
18 Ord 18, r 11.
19 *Rassam v Budge* [1893] 1 QB 571; *Plato Films Ltd v Speidel* [1961] AC 1090; [1961] 1 All ER 876; but see *Goody v Odhams Press Ltd* [1967] 1 QB 333; [1966] 3 All ER 369.
20 *Davy v Garrett* (1878) 7 Ch D 473; *North-Western Salt Co Ltd v Electrolytic Alkali Co Ltd* [1914] AC 461.
1   Under Civil Evidence Act 1995, s 7.
2   Although where a party has pleaded conclusions of law he is not precluded, at the trial, from seeking to draw different conclusions of law from the facts pleaded: *Re Vandervell's Trusts (No 2)* [1974] Ch 269; [1974] 3 All ER 205.
3   *Esso Petroleum Co Ltd v Southport Corporation* [1956] AC 218; [1955] 3 All ER 864.
4   *McCarron v Cementation Co Ltd* (1964) Times, 26 October; see also *Waghorn v George Wimpey & Co Ltd* [1970] 1 All ER 474; [1969] 1 WLR 1764; *Farrell v Secretary of State for Defence* [1980] 1 All ER 166; [1980] 1 WLR 172.

Without prejudice to the generality of the above principles, the Rules prescribe certain criteria as to the contents of pleadings generally. The most important of these are as follows:

(1) Every pleading must contain the necessary particulars of any claim, defence or other matter pleaded, including particulars of any misrepresentation, fraud, breach of trust, wilful default or undue influence on which the party pleading relies.[5]

(2) A party must give particulars of any alleged condition of mind of any person other than knowledge (for example, fraudulent intention or malice).[6]

(3) A party must in any pleading subsequent to a statement of claim plead any matter, for example any relevant statute of limitation, fraud or other fact showing illegality which he alleges makes any claim or defence of the other party not maintainable or which if not specifically pleaded might take the other party by surprise or which raises issues of fact not arising out of the preceding pleading.[7] Thus, for example, if in a "running down" action the defendant driver's case is that his vehicle had a latent mechanical defect which caused it to go out of control, he cannot simply deny negligence in his defence and then raise the specific suggestion of latent defect at the trial since this would take the other party by surprise. He must plead the defence of latent mechanical defect specifically so that the plaintiff can inspect the vehicle, or have it inspected by his own expert, and join the manufacturer or person who last repaired or served the vehicle as a second defendant.

It will be observed that the above rules are of two kinds: (3) relates to matters which must be pleaded, whereas (1) and (2) relate to particulars which must be given of matters which are pleaded. It should also be noted that special rules exist that require a plaintiff in personal injury cases to serve with his statement of claim a medical report and a statement of the special damages claimed.[8]

2   The exchange of pleadings

If the writ was not endorsed with a statement of claim, but only generally indorsed, the plaintiff may serve a notice of claim at any time before the defendant gives notice of intention to defend or within 14 days thereof. The statement of claim is a document of all the facts which are alleged to constitute the plaintiff's claim, and a statement of the relief sought. It will specify whether general damages are sought, and any special damages suffered, such as loss or earnings, loss of business profits and medical expenses. A claim for interest may, in some circumstances, need to be pleaded as will any other relief sought.

---

5   Ord 18, r 12(1)(a). If these matters are not pleaded, in view of their gravity, judges are very slow to allow a party to rely upon them, directly or indirectly; see, for example, *Belmont Finance Corporation Ltd v Williams Furniture Ltd* [1979] Ch 250; [1979] 1 All ER 118.

6   Order 18, r 12(1)(b); *Fowler v Lanning* [1959] 1 QB 426; [1959] 1 All ER 290. "Condition of mind" includes the condition of mind of the party pleading, if he relies upon it; *Feeney v Rix* [1968] Ch 693; [1968] 3 All ER 22. Although the rule excludes "knowledge" it is necessary to give particulars of the facts alleged to give rise to knowledge; Ord 18, r 12(4); cf *Astrovlanis Compania Naviera SA v Linard* [1972] 2 QB 611; [1972] 2 All ER 647 where an allegation of "scuttling" (ie conniving at the loss of a vessel in order to make an insurance claim in respect thereof) was held to be wrong and inconsistent with Ord 18, r 12(1)(a).

7   Ord 18, r 8(1).

8   Ord 18, r 12(1A), (1B), (1C). For the relevant procedure where the medical condition changes, see *Owen v Grimsby & Cleethorpes Transport* [1992] PIQR Q 27.

3   Defence and counterclaim

The defendant must serve a defence on the plaintiff within 14 days of the expiration of the time-limit for acknowledging service of the writ or of receiving the statement of claim, whichever is the later.[9] If he does not, the plaintiff may enter judgment, final or interlocutory, in default of defence.[10] The procedure is similar to judgment on failure to give notice of intention to defend and the same limitations apply. The defendant must deal individually with each allegation in the statement of claim. A general denial of liability is insufficient and will result in the defendant having to give lengthy particulars, incurring extra costs. In particular it is expressly provided[11] that:

"a party must in any pleading subsequent to a statement of claim plead specifically any matter, for example, performance, release, any relevant statute of limitation, fraud or any fact showing illegality:

(a) which he alleges makes any claim or defence of the opposite party not maintainable; or

(b) which, if not specifically pleaded, might take the opposite party by surprise; or

(c) which raises issues of fact not arising out of the preceding pleadings."

In respect of each allegation in the statement of claim the defendant may: (i) admit; or, (ii) traverse; and/or, (iii) confess and avoid; and/or (iv) object in point of law. The defence may include a counterclaim. If he does, the plaintiff must serve a defence to it, or the defendant will be entitled to judgment on default on his counterclaim.

4   Amendment of writ and pleadings

A defect in a writ or pleading can almost always be cured by amendment. Nevertheless the party at fault should act quickly so as to avoid increasing the extra costs which he will have to pay. The plaintiff may amend the writ once without leave before the close of pleadings. An amended writ must be served on the defendant. The writ does not include any statement of claim indorsed upon it, since this is a pleading and not part of the writ. Amendments to the writ can be of a technical nature, for example, correction of a misspelling or an incorrect date, moreover the writ can with leave be amended under Order 20 to correct the name of a party, even if this has the effect of substituting a new party, if the court is satisfied that the mistake was a genuine one and not misleading as to the true identify of the party intended;[12] similarly an amendment may be allowed which adds or substitutes a new cause of action provided it arises out of substantially the same facts as the original cause of action. Amendments to alter the parties to the action to add or substitute a new cause of action can be made without leave only before the writ has been served.[13] Leave may be granted to make these

---

9   The effect of this is that where the statement of claim is indorsed on the writ, the defendant has 28 days in which to serve a defence.

10   The plaintiff or his solicitor must certify that the defendant is in default on the back of the court copy of the judgment which he tenders for entry; *Practice Direction (Judgment by Default)* [1979] 2 All ER 1062; [1979] 1 WLR 851.

11   Ord 18, r 8(1).

12   See *Evans Construction Co Ltd v Charrington & Co Ltd* [1983] QB 810; [1983] 1 All ER 310.

13   Ord 20, r 1(3).

amendments even after the period of limitation current at the date of issue of the writ has expired, if the courts think it just. In this way a new statute-barred cause of action may be raised, or a party may be "brought in" by amendment at a time when he could no longer be sued in a fresh action.[14] Apart from the provisions of Order 20, new parties may be added by order of the court following an application by summons[15] but a new cause of action arising since the issue of the writ, against a defendant, can never be added. The proper procedure in this case is to issue a second writ and apply to have the actions consolidated.

Any party may amend his pleadings once without leave before the close of pleadings.[16] As long as the proposed amendment does not amount to pleading a completely new cause of action and causes no injustice to an opponent it is permissible. Thus a party will be allowed to withdraw an admission mistakenly made.[17] A plaintiff may be allowed to amend his statement of claim even where the original disclosed no cause of action. To adopt any other approach would be a regression to the formalism of pleading at common law. The court's attitude is well illustrated in the judgment of Bowen LJ in *Cropper v Smith*:[18]

"I know of no kind of error or mistake which, if not fraudulent or intended to overreach, the court ought not to correct, if it can be done without injustice to the other party. Courts do not exist for the sake of discipline, but for the sake of deciding matters in controversy, and I do not regard such amendment as a matter of favour or grace. It seems to me that as soon as it appears that the way in which a party has framed his case will not lead to a decision of the real matter in controversy it is as much a matter of right on his part to have it corrected if it can be done without injustice, as anything else in the case is a matter of right."

The amended pleading must be served on the opponent who may himself serve an amended pleading to it within 14 days.[19] Alternatively he may allow his original pleading to stand, or he may apply to the master to disallow the amendment on the ground that it causes injustice.[20] The writ and pleadings may be amended after the close of pleadings but only with leave.[1] The application is by summons, usually the summons for directions. Amendment may even be allowed at the trial if the judge is satisfied that no injustice is thereby caused.[2] If amendment is allowed it is almost always on terms that the party amending pays the costs thrown away in any event and if the

---

14   See *Rodriguez v Parker* [1967] 1 QB 116; [1966] 2 All ER 349; *Mitchell v Harris Engineering Co Ltd* [1967] 2 QB 703; [1967] 2 All ER 682; *Chatsworth Investments Ltd v Cussins (Contractors) Ltd* [1969] 1 All ER 143; [1969] 1 WLR 1; *Sterman v EW and WJ Moore* [1970] 1 QB 596; [1970] 1 All ER 581; cf *Braniff v Holland and Hannen and Cubitts (Southern) Ltd* [1969] 3 All ER 959; [1969] 1 WLR 1533; *Brickfield Properties Ltd v Newton* [1971] 3 All ER 328; [1971] 1 WLR 862.

15   Under Ord 15, rr 6, 7. The court will not, however, grant an application so as to deprive the proposed defendant of a defence of limitation; therein lies the great advantage of adding a party under Ord 20 rather than under Ord 15 (where possible). By s 35 of the Limitation Act 1980 a new claim (including a new cause of action and a claim against an added or substituted party) is deemed to have been commenced on the same date as the original action.

16   Ord 20, r 1(1), subject to limits. The one amendment rule does not apply in the circumstances identified by Ord 20, r 1(3).

17   *Hollis v Burton* [1892] 3 Ch 226.

18   (1884) 26 Ch D 700, at 710–711.

19   Ord 20, r 3.

20   Ord 20, r 4. The application is by summons and is usually made on the summons for directions.

1   Ord 20, r 5. The court may even amend a pleading on its own motion: see *Nottage v Jackson* (1883) 11 QBD 627.

2   *Ives v Brown* [1919] 2 Ch 314; but see *Esso Petroleum Co Ltd v Southport Corporation* [1956] AC 218; [1955] 3 All ER 864.

amendment necessitates an adjournment of the trial he will usually be ordered to pay the costs thrown away by the adjournment.

5 Particulars

If a pleading is vague or too general the party on whom it is served may apply for particulars. The application should first be by letter, and the court will not usually make an order until there has been an application to the other side by letter. If particulars are not forthcoming, application may be made by summons for an order for further and better particulars.[3] The functions of particulars are broadly twofold. First they prevent the party giving them from framing his case too widely, since at the trial he will be confined to his particulars as if they had been incorporated in his pleading. Thus if he relies in his particulars on conduct which he alleges amounts to negligence, he cannot at the trial give evidence as to other conduct (unless he obtains leave to amend his particulars). Secondly the party who is served with particulars is thereby better acquainted with the case against him so that he will not be taken by surprise at the trial. Any particulars which ought to have been included in the pleadings may be ordered,[4] for example particulars of special damages. However particulars cannot be ordered of matters which have not been specifically pleaded, nor can particulars be required of a simple traverse.[5] Particulars are most often sought in respect of the statement of claim. Particulars cannot be required of any matter not pleaded. In this respect they differ from interrogatories which may, as we shall see, relate to any relevant matter whether pleaded or not.

M DISCOVERY AND INSPECTION OF DOCUMENTS

Discovery of documents[5A] is the procedure whereby a party discloses, to the court or to any other party, the relevant documents in the action that he has, or has had, in his possession, custody or power. Documentary evidence plays an important part in nearly all civil cases. Its purpose was explained by Sir John Donaldson as follows:[6]

"In plain language litigation is conducted 'cards face up on the table'. Some people from other lands regard this as incomprehensible. 'Why' they ask 'should I be expected to provide my opponent with the means of defeating me?' The answer, of course, is that litigation is not a war or even a game. It is designed to do real justice between opposing parties and, if the court does not have all the relevant information, it cannot achieve this object."

In an action for breach of contract, for example, the transactions between the parties may be contained entirely in letters which have passed between them. One party's letters may not be intelligible unless read in conjunction with letters in the possession of the other party. Similarly, in an industrial injuries action, the employers are likely to have internal accident reports, machine maintenance records, records of complaints and the like which it is very much in the plaintiff's interests to see, while, on the other

---

3   Ord 18, r 12(3), (6); *Millbank v Millbank* [1900] 1 Ch 376.
4   See p 381, *ante*.
5   *Weinberger v Inglis* [1918] 1 Ch 133; *Chapple v Electrical Trades Union* [1961] 3 All ER 612; [1961] 1 WLR 1290.
5A   To be renamed "discosure" in 1999, under the new Civil Justice Rules.
6   *Davies v Eli Lilly & Co* [1987] 1 All ER 801; [1987] 1 WLR 428

hand, the plaintiff may have documents relating to his medical condition, or to his earnings since the accident or state benefits which he has received, all of which may be highly relevant to the quantification of his claim by the defendants.

Accordingly a party will want to have his opponent disclose which documents the latter has, or has had, in his possession (discovery), and, secondly, to inspect and take copies of those documents in his opponent's possession (inspection).[7] Sometimes a party may have documents which are relevant to the litigation, and therefore disclosable, but which he wishes to safeguard against circulation either to third parties, or occasionally to the plaintiff himself for extraneous reasons. As to this point, the position is that on discovery each party impliedly undertakes not to use the documents which are disclosed for any ulterior or improper purpose. The use of such documents in breach of that implied undertaking will amount to a contempt of court. Thus in *Home Office v Harman*[8] a solicitor who passed documents to a journalist to assist in the preparation of an article was held to be in contempt, even though the documents had been read in open court. Nor can a party generally rely upon such documents in other proceedings. Thus where a plaintiff in proceedings against his employers obtained discovery of a memorandum about him which contained an alleged libel, the court held that he could not found a libel action on that publication since that would be an abuse of the process of the court.[9] In *Crest Homes plc v Marks*[10] the court indicated that it would release a party from that undertaking if the applicant could demonstrate "cogent and persuasive reasons" for such a release, and that the release did not cause injustice. If there is a real risk of the plaintiff using documents for an improper collateral purpose, the court may restrict inspection, for example to a party's legal advisers.[11] Discovery may take place in two ways, under the Rules.

It should be borne in mind that the greater the level of disclosure the greater burden is imposed on parties to identify and produce information. This can potentially add to the length of time litigation takes, and its cost. It is for this reason that the Woolf Report[12] recommends that discovery should be controlled by the court as part of its case-management function, it being regulated with regard to the size of the case, the cost of discovery and the likely cost. For the future it is envisaged that discovery on the scale that it now occurs will rarely take place.

I   Discovery without order

Until 1964 discovery of documents was dependent upon the order of a master, which was made in most cases on the summons for directions. While discovery by order still exists, one major alteration in procedure effected in 1962 was the introduction of "automatic" discovery. Parties must now in any action commenced by writ, with certain

7   "Inspection" is not limited to ocular inspection but includes examination by any of the senses. Thus, a tape-recording is a document, inspection of which would be effected by playing the same upon a tape-recorder to the inspecting party: *Grant v Southwestern and County Properties Ltd* [1975] Ch 185; [1974] 2 All ER 465; similar considerations apply to untransmitted television film: *Senior v Holdsworth, ex parte Independent Television News Ltd* [1976] QB 23; [1975] 2 All ER 1009.
8   [1983] 1 AC 280; [1982] 1 All ER 532.
9   *Riddick v Thames Board Mills Ltd* [1977] QB 881; [1977] 3 All ER 677.
10   [1987] AC 829; [1987] 2 All ER 1074. Order 24, r 4A now has the effect of removing the implied undertaking, once the document has been read or referred to in open court. See also *Apple Corp Ltd Apple Computer Inc* (1991, LEXIS, unreported).
11   For a discussion of this power, and some illustrations of the difficulties involved in its exercise, see *Church of Scientology of California v Department of Health and Social Security* [1979] 3 All ER 97; [1979] 1 WLR 723.
12   *Op cit*, Recommendation 23.

exceptions, make discovery by exchanging lists within 14 days of the close of pleadings.[13] The lists are in a prescribed form[14] and annexed are two schedules, as follows.

"SCHEDULE 1

Part 1

Relevant documents, listed numerically, which the party has in his possession, custody or power[15] and which he does not object to produce.

Part 2

Relevant documents as above which he objects to produce.[16]

SCHEDULE 2

Relevant documents, listed as above, which have been, but at the date of service of the list are not, in the possession, custody or power of the party in question."[17]

A party serving a list of documents must also serve on his opponent a notice to inspect the documents in the list (other than those which he objects to produce) setting out a time within 7 days and place where the documents in Part 1 of the first schedule may be inspected.[18]

The right to inspect includes the right to take copies of the documents in question, although these will, as a matter of courtesy, be supplied on payment by the solicitors for the party in question.[19] The foregoing provisions for automatic discovery do not apply to actions commenced by originating summons. There are certain other proceedings to which the procedure is not applicable; notably actions to which the Crown is a party, and actions arising out of an accident on land involving a vehicle, where the defendant must not make discovery unless ordered to do so.[20] In addition, the court may, on the application of any party, made by summons, waive discovery by all or any of the parties or restrict discovery to certain classes of documents for disposing fairly of the action or for saving costs.

13 Ord 24, r 2. If any party does not comply he may be ordered to do so and may also be ordered to file an affidavit verifying his list; Ord 24, r 3(2).
14 Ord 24, r 5(1).
15 This comprises documents of which a party has an enforceable right to obtain possession; for example a director of a company of which he is, in effect, the alter ego, would have the right to obtain possession of that company's documents (which he would, therefore, have to disclose) whereas a company director simpliciter, though he has a right to inspect the company's documents, has no right to possess them (so that he could not, in the circumstances, be required to disclose them); *B v B (Matrimonial Proceedings; Discovery)* [1978] Fam 181; [1979] 1 All ER 801.
16 The list must contain a sufficient statement of the grounds of the privilege claimed; Ord 24, r 5(2).
17 He must state what has become of them and who is presently in possession of them.
18 Ord 24, r 9. As to the court's power to restrict inspection, see *Church of Scientology of California v Department of Health and Social Security* (p 386, n 11, *supra*); there is, however, no apparent power to withhold inspection entirely (*ibid*).
19 *Ormerod, Grierson & Co v St George's Ironworks Ltd* [1905] 1 Ch 505.
20 Ord 77, r 12(1); Ord 24, r 2(2).

2 Discovery by order

There are two important circumstances in which an order for discovery will be required. The first is where the action is one of those to which the above rule relating to automatic discovery is not applicable or where any party has failed to comply with that rule. In such a case there must be an application for an order for discovery of all relevant documents, if discovery is required. The second case arises where a party is dissatisfied with his opponent's list. He may then apply for discovery of particular documents. A party who is served with a list of documents may believe that relevant documents which the maker of the list has, or has had, in his possession, custody or power are not included in his list. This may be due to a bona fide belief on the maker's part that the document in question is not relevant to the action, or to an omission, accidental or deliberate. In either case application may be made by summons to the master for an order for discovery of the documents in question. This application must be accompanied by an affidavit setting out the grounds for the deponent's belief and identifying the documents of which discovery is required. If the other party admits the existence of the documents in question but denies their relevance, the master may inspect them in order to decide whether they are in fact relevant. In addition that party may be required to make an affidavit stating whether or not any particular document is, or has at any time been, in his possession, custody or power and, if it no longer is, what has become of it.[1]

Finally, independent of the above provisions, any party may at any time require inspection of any document referred to in any other party's pleadings or affidavits.[2] If any party fails to comply with an order for discovery the master may order his statement of claim to be struck out, if he is a plaintiff, or his defence to be struck out and judgment entered against him, if a defendant. In a case of extreme and wilful disobedience the offender may be committed for contempt of court.[3] There is another issue which may be raised in connection with discovery. This arises where a party refuses to produce a document in his possession, custody or power.

The only circumstance in which a party may refuse to produce a document is where that document is one of a class which the law recognises as privileged. The privilege which attaches to documents must be carefully distinguished from privilege in the law of defamation. Thus a document which attracts qualified privilege for the purposes of defamation, the minutes of a company meeting for example, is not necessarily privileged from discovery. The former rule is a rule of law, the latter a rule of evidence or procedure,[4] which entitles a legal advisor to claim privilege for a document prepared for the purpose of litigation, or which is a communication between solicitor and client. Privilege is not granted if the document was made in the furtherance of a fraudulent or criminal purpose, and is that of the client, not the legal advisor. A party who wishes to claim privilege for a document cannot merely omit to include in it his list. He must include it in the second part of the first schedule to his list, together with a statement in the body of the list of the ground upon which he claims privilege for it. The principal classes of documents which the law recognises as being privileged from production

---

1   Ord 14, r 7; *Astra-National Productions Ltd v Neo-Art Productions Ltd* [1928] WN 218.
2   Ord 24, r 10.
3   Ord 24, r 16. The object of this rule is to secure compliance with the rules and orders of the court, relating to discovery, and not to punish a party for non-compliance; thus where a summons is taken out for a punitive order under rule 16 and the defaulting party complies before the hearing of that summons, it is wrong to make an order requiring payment into court of the balance of the claim: *Husband's of Marchwood Ltd v Drummond Walker Developments Ltd* [1975] 2 All ER 30; [1975] 1 WLR 603.
4   See *Calcraft v Guest* [1898] 1 QB 759; *R v Cox & Railton* (1884) 14 QBD 153; *R v Central Criminal Court, ex parte Francis and Francis* [1989] AC 346; *Nederlandse Reassurantie Groep Holding NV v Bacon and Woodrow* [1995] 1 All ER 976.

are: documents which relate solely to the deponent's own case, incriminating documents, documents attracting legal professional privilege and documents whose production would be injurious to the public interest.

3 Discovery and inspection against other persons

We have already examined the procedure introduced by the Administration of Justice Act 1970, whereby orders for discovery and inspection of documents against proposed parties may be made before the commencement of proceedings.[5] Under section 34 of the Supreme Court Act 1981 there is, in addition, power, in actions for damages for death or personal injuries, to order a person who is not a party to the proceedings and who appears to be likely to have or have had in his possession, custody or power any documents which are relevant to an issue arising out of the action to disclose whether these documents are in his possession, custody or power and to produce those which he has to the applicant. This power is exercisable only after the commencement of proceedings, the application being by summons (which must be served on the person against whom the order is sought and on all parties to the action) supported by affidavit.[6] As stated above, the procedure is limited in its application to personal injuries litigation where it may be used, for example, by defendants to obtain a sight of the plaintiff's hospital notes or by plaintiffs to obtain copies of manufacturers' instructions for using and maintaining machines, reports by employers to the Health and Safety at Work Executive and documents of that type. It is not clear why it is so limited, and the Civil Justice Review[7] supported its extension to all actions. It is not limited to parties to proceedings already commenced.

4 Action for discovery

Save for the limited exception, in personal injuries actions, discussed above there is, as a rule, no procedure for obtaining discovery against persons who are not parties to an action. They can, of course, be compelled to attend the trial and to produce, at that stage, documents in their possession (by means of *subpoena duces tecum*) but there is a rule, sometimes known as the "mere witness" rule, whereby discovery cannot be obtained against a person against whom no relief is sought but who might be a witness in an action. It follows that if a party wishes to inspect documents in the possession of a person against whom he has no cause of action, he cannot sue that person simply for the purpose of obtaining evidence, by way of discovery of documents, for use against the party against whom there is a cause of action. This rule appears to have little in the way of logic to commend it but it is, nevertheless, too firmly entrenched to be altered save by way of legislation.

However, it has already been seen that a limited exception to the rule was formulated by the House of Lords in the case of *Norwich Pharmacal Co v Customs and Excise Commissioners*.[8] The facts of the case were unusual. The appellants, who were the owners of a patent covering a chemical compound, learned from information published by the respondents that a number of consignments of the compound had been imported

5   See p 355, *ante*.
6   Ord 24, r 7A.
7   *Op cit*, p 323, *ante*, at p 43.
8   [1974] AC 133; [1973] 2 All ER 943, applied in *Loose v Williamson* [1978] 3 All ER 89; [1978] 1 WLR 639; [1974] AC, at 175; [1973] 2 All ER, at 948; see also, on the *Norwich Pharmacal* principle, *Arab Monetary Fund v Hashim (No 5)* [1992] 2 All ER 911.

between 1960 and 1970, none of which had been licensed by the appellants. The appellants therefore knew that others were infringing their patent but did not know their identity. The respondents refused to disclose the identity of the importers whereupon the appellants brought an action against the respondents seeking an order for discovery of documents relating to the importations. The House of Lords granted such an order; the reasoning behind the decision was expressed by Lord Reid, as follows:

"if through no fault of his own a person gets mixed up in the tortious acts of others so as to facilitate their wrong-doing he may incur no personal liability but he comes under a duty to assist the person who has been wronged by giving him full information and disclosing the identity of the wrongdoers."

N INSPECTION OF PROPERTY

I Inspection of property inter partes

The court has power, on the application of any party, to make an order for the detention, custody or preservation of any property which is the subject-matter of the action or as to which any question may arise therein or for the inspection of any such property in the possession of a party to the action and, for the purpose of enabling such an order to be carried out, may authorise any person to enter a party's land or building.[9] The application is often made on the summons for directions but may, if need be, be made by summons at any stage of the proceedings. The procedure is widely used in personal injuries actions, usually to enable an export engineer on behalf of the plaintiff to inspect the defendant's factory premises, but is not confined to such actions. As has already been noted,[10] section 33(1) of the Supreme Court Act 1981 enables an order to be made before the commencement of proceedings.

2 Orders against third persons

Analogous to the power of the court to order discovery and inspection of documents against strangers to the proceedings is the power, now contained in section 34(3) of the Supreme Court Act 1981, to make orders for the inspection, photographing, preservation, custody or detention of property[11] which is not the property of, or in the possession of, any party to the proceedings but which is the subject matter of the proceedings or as to which any question arises in the proceedings; orders[12] may also be made for the taking of samples of any such property and the carrying out of any experiment in relation thereto. Application for such an order is by summons supported by affidavit. No order will be made if it appears that compliance would result in the disclosure of information relating to a secret process, discovery or invention not in issue in the proceedings.[13] The courts will take particular care with applications to

---

9   Ord 29, r 2. There is no express power to order photographing but this is obviously an oversight since inspection will often be worthless without a right to take photographs.
10   See p 355, *ante*.
11   "Property" includes any land, chattel or other corporeal property of any description: Supreme Court Act 1981, s 35(5).
12   See also p 389, *ante*.
13   Ord 29, r 7A(6).

inspect computer databases, including ensuring that the information stored is not corrupted, and that the respondent's use of the database is not interfered with.[14]

O   INTERROGATORIES

Interrogatories are questions answerable on oath which any party may administer to his opponent.[15] The purpose of interrogatories is twofold: first to obtain admissions, and secondly to limit the scope of one's opponent's case. It may thus seem that answers to interrogatories are similar to particulars. In fact, they differ in several important respects:

(1)   The scope of particulars is limited to matters in question between the parties, and must be necessary either (a) for disposing fairly of the cause or matter, or (b) for securing costs. Thus particulars cannot be required of matters not pleaded. Interrogatories, on the other hand, may relate to any matter relevant to the action.[16] For example, in an action for defamation, a defendant cannot ask the plaintiff to give particulars of why the words complained of are untrue since it is no part of the plaintiff's case to allege or prove the falsity of the words in question. However, if the defendant pleads justification, he may administer interrogatories to the plaintiff the function of which is to elicit from the plaintiff how far the latter is prepared to admit that the words, or any part of them, are true.[17] Broadly speaking, any question which could be asked of a witness at the trial may be asked in the form of an interrogatory, with the notable exception of questions as to the witness's credit or credibility.[18]

(2)   Particulars cannot relate to evidence. Interrogatories are usually aimed at evidential matters, although they cannot extend to asking a party to disclose his means of proof or to name his witnesses.[19]

(3)   Particulars are not given on oath. Interrogatories must always be answered on affidavit (though parties often agree to accept answers by open letter, which answers can be put in at the trial in the same way as sworn answers).

(4)   A party may apply for particulars by letter on his own initiative. Indeed he should do so. A party may also apply for leave to administer interrogatories[20] on any matter in question.

The interrogatories must be answered on oath within the time prescribed, being not less than 28 days.[1] The only ground upon which a party may refuse to answer is that of privilege. The privilege must be claimed in the answer[2] and the grounds are the same as those for the privilege from production of documents. Other objections must be taken at the hearing of the summons at which the order for interrogatories is made, or the application to withdraw or vary them is made, or not at all. Answers to

---

14   *Huddleston v Control Risks Information Services Ltd* [1987] 2 All ER 1035; [1987] 1 WLR 701.
15   Ord 26, r 1. Leave is not now required. A party has an automatic right, subject only to an order of the court disallowing the interrogatories. Rules introduced in 1990 provide for service of interrogatories without order, the party on whom they are served being obliged either to answer them or apply to the court for them to be varied or disallowed.
16   Ord 26, r 1(1)(a); *Nash v Leyton* [1911] 2 Ch 71.
17   *Marriott v Chamberlain* (1886) 17 QBD 154; *Peter Walker & Son Ltd v Hodgson* [1909] 1 KB 239.
18   *Kennedy v Dodson* [1895] 1 Ch 334.
19   *Marriott v Chamberlain (supra)*; *Knapp v Harvey* [1911] 2 KB 725.
20   Ord 26, r 1(2).
1   See Ord 26, r 2.
2   Ord 26, r 5; *Dalgleish v Lowther* [1899] 2 QB 590.

interrogatories are binding and the party administering them is in a position of advantage since he may put in evidence at the trial all or any of the answers. He cannot be compelled to put in any answer which does not favour his case.[3] If a party's answers are evasive or ambiguous he may be ordered to make a further answer either on affidavit or by oral examination.[4] The final sanctions for failing to comply with an order for interrogatories are the same as for disobedience to any other interlocutory order. Thus the defaulter's statement of claim may be struck out if he is a plaintiff or his defence if a defendant. In an extreme case of wilful disobedience the offender may be committed for contempt of court.[5]

P   SECURITY FOR COSTS

As a rule no party can be required to deposit money or a bond as security for the costs of a pending action. This rule applies even if the party concerned is insolvent or even bankrupt.[6] However there are exceptions to this rule. In these exceptional cases the defendant may apply by summons, usually on the summons for directions, for an order that the plaintiff provide security for costs. These exceptions are:

(a)   where the plaintiff is ordinarily resident out of the jurisdiction.[7] However security will not be ordered on this ground if the plaintiff has substantial property within the jurisdiction out of which costs may be defrayed, since the basis of the exception is that the defendant, if successful, would not be able to enforce an order for his costs;[8]

(b)   where the plaintiff is a nominal plaintiff suing for the benefit of a third party and there is reason to believe that he would be unable to pay the defendant's costs if ordered to do so;[9] a person suing in a representative capacity is not a nominal plaintiff;

(c)   where the plaintiff has deliberately misstated his address on the writ, or has changed his address since the issue of the writ in order to evade the consequences of litigation;[10]

(d)   where a plaintiff company may not be able to pay costs awarded against it.[11]

---

3   Ord 26, r 7. The court may, however, order an answer to be put in where it is so closely connected with another answer which has been put in evidence that the court considers that one ought not to be used without the other.
4   Ord 26, r 5. The test is whether the answer is sufficient, not whether it is true; *Lyell v Kennedy (No 3)* (1884) 27 Ch D 1.
5   Ord 26, r 6.
6   *Cowell v Taylor* (1885) 31 Ch D 34; *Cook v Whellock* (1890) 24 QBD 658; *Rhodes v Dawson* (1886) 16 QBD 548.
7   Ord 23, r 1(1)(a). As to the meaning of the words "ordinarily resident", see *Levene v Inland Revenue Commissioners* [1928] AC 217 and *Inland Revenue Commissioners v Lysaght* [1928] AC 234. This rule does not conflict with the Treaty of Rome, but the court may take into account the fact that the plaintiff is an EC resident and refuse to order security: *Landi Den Hartog BV v Stopps* [1976] FSR 497. The High Court may by issue of the prerogative writ *ne exeat regno* restrain a defendant from leaving the jurisdiction, subject to the conditions contained in the Debtors Act 1869, s 6, of which the most important is that the defendant's absence will materially prejudice the plaintiff in prosecuting his action; see, generally the judgment of Megarry J *Felton v Callis* [1969] 1 QB 200; [1968] 3 All ER 673. Note also the power to grant *Mareva* injunctions (see p 359, *ante*).
8   See *Kevorkian v Burney (No 2)* [1937] 4 All ER 468.
9   Ord 23, r 1(1)(b). The next friend of a person under a disability is not a nominal plaintiff: *Fellows v Barrett* (1836) 1 Keen 119. An example of a nominal plaintiff is one who, before action, assigns to a third party any damages he may recover; see *Semler v Murphy* [1968] Ch 183; [1967] 2 All ER 185.
10   Ord 23, r 1(1)(c), (d); Ord 23, r 1(2); *Knight v Ponsonby* [1925] 1 KB 545.
11   Companies Act 1985, s 726(1).

Certain other orders may be made.

Q   DIRECTIONS

I   Automatic directions

The majority of actions in the Queen's Bench Division are personal injury actions. Since 1980 a system of automatic direction has existed in personal injury cases. This rule applies to any action for personal injuries except:

(a) any Admiralty action; and
(b) any action where the pleadings contain an allegation of negligent medical treatment.

The effect of the rule is that when the pleadings are closed the following directions take effect automatically:

(a) save where liability is admitted or where the action arises out of a road accident (in which case discovery is limited to disclosure by the plaintiff of documents relating to special damages) there must be discovery of documents within 14 days and inspection within seven days thereafter;
(b) where any party intends to rely on expert evidence he must within 10 weeks disclose the substance of that evidence to the other parties in the form of a written report, which shall be agreed if possible;[12]
(c) unless such reports are agreed, the parties shall be at liberty to call as expert witnesses those witnesses whose reports have been disclosed, limited to two medical experts and one expert of any other kind;
(d) photographs, a sketch plan and the contents of any police accident report book shall be receivable in evidence at the trial, and shall be agreed if possible;
(e) the action shall be tried at the trial centre of the place where the action is proceeding or at such other trial centre as the parties may in writing agree,[13]
(f) the action shall be tried by judge alone, as a case of substance or difficulty (Category B) and shall be set down within six months;
(g) the court shall be notified, on setting down, of the estimated length of the trial. It should be noted that there is nothing to prevent any party from applying by summons for further or different directions or orders. In addition the court may elect to transfer the action to a county court.[14]

2   Summons for directions

In cases outside the automatic directions procedure, directions are given by the master or district judge on the hearing of a summons for directions. The plaintiff must, within one month of the close of pleadings, take out a summons for directions returnable in

---

12   Where more than one party intends to rely on expert evidence, disclosure is by mutual exchange of reports (r 8(2)).
13   Except where the Crown is a party, since the Crown has a right to trial in London (Ord 77, r 13).
14   See p 424, *post*. Many such actions will in fact be commenced in the county court, by virtue of the High Court and County Courts Jurisdiction Order 1990.

not less than 14 days.[15] To do so he issues the summons, using the appropriate form, at the Central Office or a district registry, and serves it on all defendants to the action. The plaintiff must issue a summons for directions in every action commenced by writ with a few exceptions, the chief of which are: automatic directions cases, cases where directions have already been given following an application for summary judgment under Order 14 or for a trial without pleadings under Order 18, rule 21, actions for an account and actions which have been referred to an official referee or transferred to the Commercial Court.[16] The general functions of the summons for directions are summarised in Order 25, r 1(1), so that:

(a)   all matters which must or can be dealt with on interlocutory applications and have not already been dealt with may so far as possible be dealt with, and
(b)   such directions may be given as to the future course of the action as appear best adapted to secure the just, expeditious and economical disposal thereof.

The summons for directions has been described as a "stocktaking" of all the interlocutory matters in the action. It is possible for a party to issue a separate summons for each interlocutory application which he wishes to make, but to save time and expense it is generally prudent to await the summons for directions to apply for all the orders required.[17] Among the matters which are, in fact, dealt with on the summons for directions are particulars of pleading, amendment of writ and pleadings, discovery and inspection of documents, security for costs and interrogatories. Other matters will include an application to consolidate an action, matters relating to expert evidence and trial.

a   Evidence

Facts to be proved in a civil case are proved by the testimony of a witness in person and in open court.[18] To that basic rule there are exceptions. Facts can be proved by formal admissions. A party need produce no proof of any matter admitted in his favour. Admissions on the pleadings may be expressed or implied from a failure to traverse.[19] Admissions may also be made in answer to interrogatories. A useful means of compelling an opponent to admit a fact is to serve him with a "notice to admit facts", calling upon him to admit the facts listed in the notice.[20] If he will not admit these facts and they are proved at the trial, unless the court otherwise orders, he will bear the costs of proof.[1] This is, of course, a powerful weapon but it must not be abused. A party should not be asked to admit the facts in issue or any inference of fact, such as negligence. He should only, in practice, be asked to admit facts of a formal nature or facts which can easily be proved against him if he does not admit them. If admissions

---

15   Ord 25, r 1(1). In Admiralty actions the period is seven weeks and the summons will be returnable before a judge of the Admiralty Court; Ord 75, r 25; see p 400, *post*. There is a lacuna in the Rules of the Supreme Court in that if no defence is served the close of pleadings never occurs and there is no provision for applying for directions; fortunately the High Court has an inherent power to give directions on application: *Austin v Wildig* [1969] 1 All ER 99n; [1969] 1 WLR 67.
16   The full list of exceptions is embodied in Ord 25, r 1(2).
17   There is a general rule that particulars will not be ordered before the summons for directions; nevertheless in exceptional cases, for example cases where the pleading is so vague that the other party cannot properly ascertain the case against him, particulars may be ordered; *Cyril Leonard & Co v Simo Securities Trust Ltd* [1971] 3 All ER 1313; [1971] 1 WLR 80.
18   RSC Ord 38, r 1.
19   Ord 18, r 13; see p 383, *ante*.
20   Ord 27, r 2.
1   Ord 62, r 6.

are made which clearly establish one party's liability the other party may, without waiting for a trial, apply for judgment based on those admissions.[2] Similar to such a notice is a "notice to admit documents", calling upon the party served to admit the authenticity of the documents listed, though not the truth of their contents. The effect of failure to admit is, again, that the party who was served with the notice has to pay the costs of proving the documents at the trial, unless the court otherwise orders, which may involve an extra witness, such as a handwriting expert.[3]

Wide powers are conferred on the master by order 38 as to the means of proof. Thus he may order evidence to be given at the trial by affidavit or in any other specified manner.[4] For example, he may order the date on which an important event occurred to be proved by production of a newspaper containing a report of the event. In addition he may restrict the number of medical or other expert witnesses who may be called at the trial.[5] Finally, it should be noted that Ord 38, r 2A permits a court to direct that a written statement be treated as the evidence in chief of the witness.

b Disclosure of experts' reports

Many actions involve the giving of expert evidence. Thus, for example, in actions for damages for personal injuries there is invariably medical evidence concerning the extent of the plaintiff's injuries. In practice the plaintiff's advisers will obtain a medical report (upon which the pleaded case will be based); thereafter the defendants will have the plaintiff medically examined and will in consequence obtain their own medical report. These reports, coming into existence in contemplation of litigation, are privileged from disclosure[6] so that neither party can be directly compelled to disclose his expert evidence to the other side.[7] This was widely thought to be an unsatisfactory state of affairs, particularly in personal injuries actions where, not only might a party be taken by surprise at the trial, but also the ignorance of the strength or weakness of the other party's case may act as a factor inhibiting settlement of the claim or the making of a realistic payment into court. Following recommendations made by various committees,[8] changes were introduced in 1972, designed to secure the disclosure of expert evidence.

The number of medical or other expert witnesses who may be called at a trial can be limited by order, usually made on the hearing of the summons for directions.[9] Although this does not give the power to the court to order exchange of reports, no party can adduce expert evidence except:

(1) with leave of the court; or
(2) where the parties agree; or
(3) where evidence is given by affidavit; or
(4) where an application has been made to the court to determine what disclosure should be made, and such directions have been complied with; or
(5) the party has complied with automatic directions. The court will direct disclosure of experts' reports unless there exist special reasons not to.

2 Ord 27, r 3; see p 372, *ante*.
3 Ord 27, r 5.
4 Ord 38, rr 1, 2.
5 Ord 38, r 4. Note the restrictions embodied in the automatic direction (c) (*supra*).
6 See p 389, *ante*.
7 *Causton v Mann Egerton (Johnsons) Ltd* [1974] 1 All ER 453; [1974] 1 WLR 162.
8 *Report of Committee on Personal Injuries Litigation* (Cmnd. 3691, 1969); *Seventeenth Report of the Law Reform Committee on Evidence of Opinion and Expert Evidence* (Cmnd. 4489 of 1970).
9 Ord 38, r 4(1).

The court must have regard to all the circumstances but circumstances which may justify not ordering disclosure are that the evidence is or will be based upon a version of the facts which is in dispute between the parties, and where, for example, there are suspicions that disclosure will lead to dishonest claims being discovered.[10] The substance of the evidence has to be disclosed. This deals with the practice of part of the statement being edited, or evidence being in statements in two or more parts. In *Kenning v Eve Construction Ltd*[11] two unfavourable points were omitted by a consulting engineer from his report, but dealt with in an accompanying letter. The court held that both the report and letter should be disclosed. The court may also direct that "without prejudice" meetings of experts be held, for the purpose of identifying those parts of their evidence which were in issue.[12] Where such a meeting is held, they may prepare a joint statement indicating those parts of the evidence on which they are, and are not, in agreement, thus facilitating the trial of the case with as limited a degree of expert disagreement as possible.

Expert evidence is one area which potentially adds to the costs of litigation, with the trial becoming a "battle of experts", the witnesses selected for their opinions being favourable to the party calling them, and becoming "in substance, professional advocates".[13] Experts on either side can agree reports (for example, medical reports) and can reduce the partial use of experts, as could the use of court appointed experts. The Woolf Report[14] recommended a series of changes to reduce the partisan use of experts. Co-operation will be encouraged, the use of a single expert more widespread, a wider range of experts employed and more openness as to the instructions given to experts, so that the context of their reports is clear. Woolf recommended there should be greater use, at trial, of written reports. In fast-track cases, parties would be limited to one expert within a given field of expertise and two in total. Experts would not be expected to give oral testimony. The court should have the power to appoint a single expert.

One area where expert evidence is particularly crucial is medical negligence claims. This provides a useful example of how such matters will be dealt with in the future. A Working Group[15] pointed out that in such cases the preliminary investigations can be just as lengthy and expensive whatever the value of the claim, and expert evidence on liability may be just as strongly contested. Clinical negligence cases would usually entail a substantial amount of documentation, involving complex issues of law, and of expert evidence. The Working Group recommended that future changes should provide that witness statements in clinical negligence cases, and then most expert reports, will be disclosed on a simultaneous basis at the relevant points in a case, unless the procedural judge considers that sequential disclosure would be more appropriate. When sequential disclosure is ordered, the procedural judge should also direct which party should disclose first. Experts' meetings should be used as a means of narrowing issues. Meetings would usually be held in private, though parties' legal representatives might apply to attend. The procedure governing such an expert's meeting would be for the procedural judge to determine.

---

10 "Special reasons" are not defined. They may exist where there is evidence that surprise is necessary in the interests of justice. See eg, dicta in *Naylor v Preston Area Health Authority* [1987] 2 All ER 353. The fact that fraud is pleaded, or that there is not a real risk of dishonest evidence may not suffice: *Khan v Armaguard* [1994] 3 All ER 545; [1994] 1 WLR 1204.
11 [1989] 1 WLR 1189.
12 Ord 38, r 38.
13 Middleton Report, *op cit*, para 2.32.
14 See Interim Report, *op cit*, recommendation 25, and Middleton Report, *op cit*, para 2.32.
15 *Access to Justice: Clinical Negligence Cases- Proposed New Procedures, A Consultation Paper* (Lord Chancellor's Dept, 1997).

The Group considered that meetings between experts would be more productive and their discussions more focused if experts were provided with a list of issues for discussion at the meeting, the list having been agreed by the parties. A rule should require reports from all experts, when filed, to be accompanied by the oral, written and supplementary instructions: knowledge of the instructions added considerably to the value to the court of the report received and strongly promoted the aim of improved impartiality in report writing. However, the Working Group considered that it would be very onerous to introduce a rule requiring reports from all experts, when filed, to be accompanied by the oral, written and supplementary instructions. It therefore proposed that the rule of privilege regarding the instructions given to experts should be abrogated to the extent necessary to empower the court to require disclosure of the instructions in particular cases; and the rules will not require as a standard condition of filing expert evidence that they be accompanied by a copy of all the instructions. The Group felt strongly that, in clinical negligence cases in particular, any fettering of experts' privilege would be seriously detrimental to the conduct of the case. For example, an order to disclose written instructions might result in instructions being given only verbally, resulting in misunderstandings and possibly wasted reports on the wrong issue. To overcome this difficulty, the Group considered that the introduction of a certification procedure would on its own achieve the desired result of ensuring that experts' reports are properly focused, without inhibiting the relationship between an expert and the solicitor. They supported Lord Woolf's suggestion that an expert's report should end with a declaration that it includes everything which the expert regards as being relevant to the opinion which has been expressed in the report, and that the report draws to the attention of the court any matter which would affect the validity of that opinion. It is proposed that experts should be required to provide such a declaration.

c   Disclosure of non-expert evidence

Order 38, rule 2A introduced a wide power in respect of the disclosure of all evidence. In its present form it requires the High Court to direct every party to serve on other parties copies of the written statements of the testimony of the witnesses upon whom they intend to rely at trial. This disclosure is intended to streamline the trial process by reducing "trial by ambush" and reducing the element of surprise. Disclosure is also intended to promote the potential for settlement of the case, or the making of admissions on points that hitherto might have been contested or in dispute right up to the trial itself. It is also intended to assist in defining the key issues for decision at trial. The powers of the court are exercised for the purpose of disposing fairly and expeditiously of the action and saving costs.[16] Where the witness is not called at trial, the written statement may not be put in evidence by any other party. Where he is, then it may be ordered that the statement serve as the evidence-in-chief of the witnesses. The statements are required to be in a prescribed form.

d   Place of trial

The master sometimes exercises his power to transfer the action to another division of the High Court or to a county court.[17] In other cases he must direct where and in what manner the action is to be tried.[18] This must be the last matter upon which the master gives directions. The place of trial will be either London or a centre at which the Lord

16   Ord 38, r 2A(1).
17   Ord 33, r 4.
18   Ord 77, r 13(1).

Chancellor has directed sittings of the High Court to be held, pursuant to section 71 of the Supreme Court Act 1981. No party, other than the Crown,[19] has a right to trial in London, and the place of trial will be fixed where it is most convenient for all parties having regard to such matters as the availability of witnesses. This will generally be London, if service was acknowledged in London, or the centre for the district in the registry of which service was acknowledged, though the place of acknowledgement of service is not conclusive since the jurisdiction of the High Court, unlike that of county courts, is in no way local.

e   Mode of trial

The master or district judge will determine the mode of trial. Order 33, rule 2 sets out the possible modes of trial, viz trial before:

(a)   a judge alone;
(b)   a judge with a jury;
(c)   a judge with the assistance of assessors;
(d)   an official referee with or without the assistance of assessors;
(e)   a master;
(f)   a special referee.

If the master orders trial in London, he must fix the list in which the case is to be set down for trial. There are six such lists in the Queen's Bench Division, viz Crown Office List, Jury List, Non-Jury List, Short Cause List, Commercial List, Arbitration Case List and Admiralty List.[20] Cases which are to be tried without a jury and which are not likely to last more than four hours are set down in the Short Cause List. Most actions are tried in the Non-Jury List by a judge sitting alone. Provisions relating to jury trial are now contained in section 69 of the Supreme Court Act 1981 which provides that the only cases in which either party has a right[1] to a jury are actions to be tried in the Queen's Bench Division where: (a) a charge of fraud against the party; or (b) a claim for libel, slander, malicious prosecution or false imprisonment is in issue unless in either case the trial requires any prolonged examination of documents or accounts of any scientific or local investigation which cannot conveniently be made with a jury.[2] In any other case the master has a discretion whether or not to order a jury. In *Ward v James*[3] the Court of Appeal formulated the principle that, in the absence of special circumstances, it is a wrong exercise of the master's discretion to order a jury in an action based on a claim for damages for personal injuries. Thus the law is that the

---

19   See *Practice Direction* [1981] 3 All ER 61; [1981] 1 WLR 1296. For directions outside London see *Practice Direction* [1972] 1 All ER 287; [1972] 1 WLR 5.
20   See p 400, *post*.
1   The right must be claimed before the master first fixes the place and mode of trial (Ord 33, r 5). "Fraud", in this context, is limited to deceit: *Barclays Bank Ltd v Cole* [1967] 2 QB 738; [1966] 3 All ER 948.
2   See also p 232, *ante*. Even though a case does, prima facie, fall within this exception, jury trial may be ordered where a party's honour or reputation is at stake: *Rothermere v Times Newspapers Ltd* [1973] 1 All ER 1013; [1973] 1 WLR 448. Note that the right to jury trial should not be extended by analogy: *Racz v Home Office* [1994] 2 AC 45. Rules may provide for additional cases (Supreme Court Act 1981, s 69(1)(c)). It will be noted that the right to jury trial is limited to the Queen's Bench Division. If an action involving a charge of fraud is started in the Chancery Division, therefore, it will be tried by a judge alone; however an application could be made under Ord 4, r 3 to have the action transferred to the Queen's Bench Division and a transfer would be ordered if the Chancery master or judge considered the case suitable for jury trial; see *Stafford Winfield Cook & Partners Ltd v Winfield* [1980] 3 All ER 759; [1981] 1 WLR 458.
3   [1966] 1 QB 273; [1965] 1 All ER 563.

discretion as to the mode of trial is a judicial rather than an absolute one, and that, in the absence of special circumstances, it is a wrong exercise of that discretion to order a jury in a personal injuries action. In the result jury trial has virtually disappeared in personal injuries actions. However, in *H v Ministry of Defence*[4] the position was said to be different where a claim for exemplary damages was being made. Jury trial is extremely rare in any case other than those in which the right to jury trial has been preserved by statute. Thus in *Williams v Beesley*,[5] an action alleging professional negligence against a solicitor, the House of Lords refused to order trial by jury, Lord Diplock stating that:[6] "the fact that a case involves issues of credibility is not a ground for departing from the usual rule that cases, other than those in which a prima facie right to trial by jury is conferred by statute, should be tried by judge alone."

3 The Commercial Court

A separate list is kept in London, Liverpool, Manchester, Birmingham, Leeds, Newcastle and Bristol to hear "commercial actions", which are defined by Order 72, rule 1(2) to include:

> "any cause arising out of the ordinary transactions of merchants and traders and, without prejudice to the generality of the foregoing words, any cause relating to the construction of a mercantile document, the export or import of merchandise, affreightment, insurance, banking, mercantile agency and mercantile usage."

The judges of the Commercial Court are such of the puisne judges of the High Court as the Lord Chancellor may from time to time nominate[7] and are usually judges of the Queen's Bench Division with special experience in commercial matters. Except by consent their powers are no greater than those of any other judge. However, procedure in the court is more flexible than the normal procedure. Thus the pleadings must be in the form of points of claim, defence, counterclaim, defence to counterclaim or reply and must be as brief as possible. Applications for particulars are not allowed unless essential. By consent the strict rules of evidence are relaxed. Thus evidence is admitted which would generally be excluded, and witness fees may be saved by deciding the case on documentary evidence alone. Moreover the judges regard it as their duty to be available at short notice at any stage of the action on the initiative of either party, so that disputes being dealt with in the Commercial Court are dealt with as quickly as possible. However, such is the popularity of the Commercial Court that a date for a trial of any substance is currently liable to be fixed at between one and two years from the date of the application to fix. A summons for directions may be taken out before the pleadings are closed. Summonses are heard by the judges. In one case the Master of the Rolls, Sir John Donaldson (himself a sometime member of the court) paid it the following tribute:[8]

> "it may be situated in London, but, unlike the courts of Kuwait, those of Scotland or other English courts (other perhaps than the Admiralty Court), it is far more

---

4   [1991] 2 QB 103; [1991] 2 All ER 834.
5   [1973] 3 All ER 144; [1973] 1 WLR 1295, an exceptional instance of leave being granted to appeal to the House of Lords on an interlocutory appeal.
6   [1973] 3 All ER 144 at 146; [1973] 1 WLR, at 1298.
7   Supreme Court Act 1981, s 6. There are at present five at any one time.
8   *Amin Rasheed Shipping Corporation v Kuwait Insurance Co* [1983] 1 All ER 873, at 882; [1983] 1 WLR 228, at 240 (affirmed [1984] AC 50; [1983] 2 All ER 884).

than a national or domestic court; it is an international commercial court the overwhelming majority of whose judgments are concerned with the rights and obligations of foreign nationals. It is a court which has an unrivalled expertise in marine insurance where that insurance is governed by English law. This is the result of the sheer volume of work of this nature which comes to the court and to the practitioners from whom the judges of the court are appointed."

A writ or originating summons may be marked in the top left hand corner, with the words "Commercial Court" and on the issue of the writ or summons so marked, the action will be entered immediately in the commercial list.[9] Actions may be transferred to the Commercial Court apart from this rule and, indeed, actions commenced in the Commercial Court under the rule may be removed from the list. Any party who seeks the removal of an action from the Commercial Court, when it has been set down in that list, must apply within seven days of giving notice of intention to defend.[10] Any party to an action in the Commercial Court may take out a summons for directions in the action before the close of pleadings, and should do so as early as possible in the action. This is principally because the directions required may, in fact, relate to the framing of the pleadings. The summons is heard by a commercial judge rather than a master.

Finally it should be noted that special Mercantile Courts have been created in both the Midlands, North-East and the South-West of England to deal with commercial cases. These amount to new Queen's Bench lists in the district registries concerned, and have the capacity to deal with a wide variety of commercial cases. Cases follow the rules of court relating to commercial practice.[11]

4   The Admiralty Court

The Admiralty jurisdiction of the High Court, assigned to the Queen's Bench Division by the Administration of Justice Act 1970, is administered by the Admiralty Court, created by that Act as part of the Queen's Bench Division and consisting of such of the puisne judges of the High Court as the Lord Chancellor may from time to time nominate to be Admiralty judges.[12] Procedure is governed by RSC Order 75. There are special forms of writ for the commencement of proceedings and special rules of procedure, depending upon the type of Admiralty proceeding. To take but one example, in actions to enforce a claim for damage, loss of life or personal injury arising out of a collision between ships, each party must lodge a document known as a "preliminary act" which contains a statement of the material facts relating to the collision including such matters as the state of the weather, the course steered and speed of the ships, the lights on the ships, alterations in course, the angle of the ships at the moment of contact and what sound signals were given and heard. The preliminary acts are sealed and are not opened before the close of pleadings.[13]

---

9   Ord 72, r 4.
10   Ord 72, r 6.
11   See [1993] 4 All ER 381, 1023.
12   Under s 68(1) of the Supreme Court Act 1981 (as amended); the Lord Chancellor may also nominate deputy circuit judges or recorders (*ibid*).
13   Ord 75, r 18.

Official referees

The office and title of "official referee" was created by the Judicature Act 1873 and abolished by the Courts Act 1971. However the title survives and is used to describe those circuit judges who are nominated by the Lord Chancellor[14] to deal with "official referees' business" which is defined by Order 36, rule 1(2) to include a cause or matter:

"(a) which involves a prolonged examination of documents or accounts, or a technical, scientific or local investigation such as could more conveniently be conducted by an official referee; or (b) for which trial by an official referee is desirable in the interests of one or more of the parties on grounds of expedition, economy or convenience or otherwise."

In practice the bulk of the work of the official referees concerns building disputes, civil or mechanical engineering matters, actions against architects, engineers, surveyors and other professionals, for breach of duty, claims by and against local authorities relating to their statutory duties concerning building regulations and claims involving adjudication over lists of complaints or defects. In the latter type of case the pleadings often consist of or include a "Scott Schedule" (so named after a former official referee) which is a document containing a list of numbered items divided across the page into a number of columns in which there are completed by the parties, in turn, their respective contentions in respect of those items, the final column being left blank for the purpose of the judge completing his adjudication on that item. As in the Commercial Court, actions may be allocated to an official referee at the time that the writ is issued (by marking it "official referees' business") or may subsequently be transferred to an official referee. Thereafter all summonses are heard by the official referee (rather than a master or district judge) to whom the case is allocated. An application for directions (including an application to fix a date for trial) must be made by the plaintiff within 14 days of the giving of notice of intention to defend or the date of the order transferring the cause or matter, whichever is the later.[15]

Unfortunately, as in the Commercial Court, the state of the lists is such that the interval between the application and the fixed date is usually measured in years rather than months. It should be noted that the court has power to order any issue to be tried before, at or after the trial of the action and may order different issues to be tried separately.[16] Thus the master can order the assessment of damages, for example, to be postponed until after the trial on the issues of liability.[17] Under these provisions a preliminary point of law is often tried before the facts where this may effectively dispose of the action.[18] However, in *Tilling v Whiteman*[19] the House of Lords stated that this course should only be adopted where the facts are complicated and the legal issues short and easily decided, for otherwise (as happened in that case) very considerable costs may be incurred in litigating through the appellate courts a point of law based

14   Under s 68(1) of the Supreme Court Act 1981, as amended.
15   Ord 36, r 6.
16   Ord 33, rr 3, 4(2).
17   This power has been sparingly exercised; see observations of Winn LJ in *Stevens v William Nash Ltd* [1966] 3 All ER 156; [1966] 1 WLR 1550, and in *Hawkins v New Mendip Engineering Ltd* [1966] 3 All ER 228; [1966] 1 WLR 1341. Cf *Coenen v Payne* [1974] 2 All ER 1109; [1974] 1 WLR 984. One advantage of trying the issue of liability before damages is that a judgment on liability for damages to be assessed enables the plaintiff to apply for an interim payment; see p 378, *ante*.
18   See, for example *Everett v Ribbands* [1952] 2 QB 198; [1952] 1 All ER 832; *Carl Zeiss Stiftung v Herbert Smith & Co* [1969] 1 Ch 93; [1968] 2 All ER 1002.
19   [1980] AC 1; [1979] 1 All ER 737.

on hypothetical facts which might never have required determination if the facts of the case had first been found.

Having dealt with all the interlocutory matters raised on the summons for directions including, finally, the mode and place of trial, the master will give an estimate of the length of trial, together with a provisional assessment of the substance, difficulty or public importance of the case.[20] He will then fix a period within which the plaintiff must set the action down for trial. When the plaintiff has done so he must, within 24 hours, inform all the other parties.[1] The parties must then proceed to prepare their cases for trial.

R TRIAL

1 Preparation of evidence

At an early stage of the action the papers will usually have been sent to counsel.[2] Counsel will normally settle the pleadings but, in any event, he will usually be instructed before the summons for directions so as to obtain his advice on interlocutory matters. Cases are won and lost in their preparation. Counsel will therefore wish to consider which applications should be made, whether the pleadings require amendment and similar matters. The first consideration upon preparing an action for trial is on whom the burden of proof rests. The general rule is *quis affirmat debet probare*; thus where any allegation of fact is in issue the party who alleges that fact must prove it. The pleadings will disclose where the general burden lies. If an allegation in the statement of claim is admitted (expressly or impliedly) it need not be proved at all. If it is traversed then the burden rests on the plaintiff. If it is the subject of a plea in confession and avoidance, then the burden is on the defendant to prove the matters in avoidance. However, the burden may shift during the action by the effect of presumptions. If a presumption is raised in favour of a party, the effect is to shift the burden of disproving the matter presumed to his opponent.

Having decided which matters he must prove, counsel will decide how he proposed to prove them. The two principal methods of proof are by witnesses and by documents.

a Witnesses

Counsel will name the witnesses whom he requires. There is no property in a witness, so that there is no objection to interviewing or calling any witness even if he has been served with a subpoena by an opponent.[3] It is, of course, wrong to call a witness whose

---

20 The assessment is as follows: "A" cases of great substance or great difficulty or of public importance; "B" cases of substance or difficulty; "C" other cases; *Practice Direction (Summons for Directions)* [1972] 1 All ER 288; [1972] 1 WLR 3.

1 Ord 34, r 8. In addition, where the trial is set down for trial outside London, the plaintiff must, after giving to the defendant seven days' notice of his intention so to do, lodge with the district judge a certificate of readiness for trial containing certain particulars, notably whether the order made on the summons for directions has been complied with, and in particular whether medical or experts' reports have been submitted for agreement and, if so, whether they have been agreed (or if not how many medical or expert witnesses are to be called), whether plans and photographs have been agreed, an up-to-date estimate of the length of the trial and a statement that the plaintiff is ready and wishes the action to be brought on for trial: *Practice Direction (Trial out of London)* [1972] 1 All ER 287; [1972] 1 WLR 5.

2 Note that in the future a solicitor advocate may have rights of audience: see p 244, *ante*.

3 See observations of Lord Denning MR in *Fullam v Newcastle Chronicle and Journal Ltd* [1977] 3 All ER 32; [1977] 1 WLR 651; see also *Harmony Shipping Co SA v Davis* [1979] 3 All ER 177; [1979] 1 WLR 1380;

testimony is unlikely to support one's case, since a party cannot cross-examine a witness he has called, unless the court gives leave to treat the witness as hostile. Also, to intimidate or otherwise tamper with a witness amounts to a contempt of court.[4] Usually a witness will be prepared to attend voluntarily if he is tendered a reasonable fee. Where he will not, his attendance may be compelled by *subpoena ad testificandum*.[5] A witness who fails to comply may be committed for contempt of court. Where a witness will not, or may not, be able to attend the trial his testimony may, by order of the court, be taken before a special examiner.[6]

b   Documents

Documentary evidence, especially in contract cases, frequently forms the basis of a party's case. Where he is in possession of the documents himself, he is in no difficulty. However the documents which are needed by a party may be in the possession of an opponent or of a third party. If they are in the possession of a third party, the proper course is to serve him with a *subpoena duces tecum*, ie "attend and bring the document with you". If the documents are in the possession of an opponent he should be served with a "notice to produce" the documents required. This does not have the effect of a subpoena, but if he does not produce the document, he cannot use the document himself and the party who served the notice may give secondary evidence of its contents.[7] In addition, if he has served a list of documents under Order 24 he is deemed to have been served with a notice to produce all the documents in his list.[8] Formal proof of a document may be dispensed with if one's opponent is prepared to admit the authenticity of the documents in question. Accordingly, he should be served with a "notice to admit" these documents.[9] However, a party who has been served with a list of documents is deemed to admit the authenticity of every document in his list[10] unless he serves express notice of non-admission within 21 days after inspection. Since automatic discovery now takes place in nearly all actions commenced by writ, it follows that express notices to produce and notices to admit documents will rarely be necessary.

c   Notices under the Civil Evidence Act 1995

Where it is desired to put in evidence at the trial statements admissible under the provisions of the Civil Evidence Act 1995, the party desiring to do so must within 21 days after setting down serve on every other party a notice containing prescribed particulars of (if the statement is oral) the time, place and circumstances in which the statement was made, the persons by whom and to whom it was made and the substance of the statement or, if material, the words used.[11] In the case of written statements admissible by virtue of the Act, the notice must annex a copy of the document in

---

4   *Chapman v Honig* [1963] 2 QB 502; [1963] 2 All ER 513.
5   Ord 38, r 14. Where the witness is a prisoner an order may be obtained for his attendance by an application *ex parte* to a judge in chambers under the Criminal Procedure Act 1853, s 9. Where he is in custody on civil process, his attendance is secured by writ of *habeas corpus ad testificandum* upon application *ex parte* on affidavit to a judge in chambers.
6   Ord 39. Where the witness is in another country a "letter of request" is issued to the judicial authorities of that country. A deposition taken under this Order may be put in evidence at the trial either by consent of the other side or on proof that the deponent is dead, outside the jurisdiction or unable from sickness or other infirmity to attend the trial (Ord 38, r 9).
7   Ord 27, r 5(4); *Sharpe v Lamb* (1840) 11 Ad & El 805.
8   Ord 27, r 4(3).
9   Ord 27, r 5(1).
10   Ord 27, r 4(1).
11   Ord 38, r 22(1).

question as well as contain certain prescribed particulars relating to the circumstances of its compilation.[12] If the party giving the notice alleges that the maker cannot be called as a witness at the trial because he is dead, beyond the seas, unfit by reason of his bodily or mental condition to attend as a witness, cannot be found or cannot reasonably be expected to have any recollection of matters relevant to the accuracy of his statement, the notice must contain a statement to this effect[13] otherwise a party served with a notice may within 21 days serve a counter-notice requiring the maker of any statement to be called as a witness by the party who served the original notice, in which event if that person is not called as a witness, his statement is not admissible under the 1995 Act.[14]

When the evidence for each side has been prepared the parties must await trial. Neither party need serve any notice of the date of trial on his opponent. Accordingly (unless the case has been given a fixed date) all parties must watch carefully the lists. The Week's List is published on Mondays and contains the cases expected to be tried in that week. Each day there is published a Daily Cause List containing the actions to be heard that day and a Warned List consisting of actions likely to be tried in the near future. Thus neither side has any excuse if his case is not ready when the action comes on for trial. If one party fails to appeal, the trial may proceed in his absence.[15] However, if application is made within seven days, a judgment obtained in the absence of a party may be set aside, generally on condition that he pay the costs thrown away.[16] Although adjournment is possible, last minute postponements are looked upon with disfavour by the judge in charge of the list and may result in the offending firm of solicitors being penalised personally with the extra costs incurred.[17]

2   Procedure at the trial

If the action is to be tried with a jury, a jury of 12 is sworn. The trial then begins.

a   Right to begin

If damages are unliquidated or the burden of proving any single issue on the pleadings rests on the plaintiff, then the plaintiff begins. Thus the only case where the defendant has the right to begin is a case in which the plaintiff claims only liquidated damages and the defendant has not traversed any allegation in the statement of claim. The right to begin and the right to the last word are advantages which are probably exaggerated, especially in the absence of a jury.

---

12   Ord 38, rr 22(2), 23(1), 24.
13   Ord 38, rr 22(3), 23(2), 24(3), 25. Any issue as to whether these conditions are satisfied in relation to the maker of a statement may be determined conclusively before the trial on an application by summons (Ord 38, r 27). The conditions appear to be disjunctive so that if, for example, it is established that the witness is abroad, his statement is admissible and it is not necessary to prove, in addition, that he cannot be found; *Piermay Shipping Co SA v Chester* [1978] 1 All ER 1233; [1978] 1 WLR 411.
14   Ord 38, r 26. The court has, however, discretion to admit statements under the Civil Evidence Act 1995 in cases where the proper notice was not served but it will not exercise this discretion in favour of a party who, for example, has deliberately not served a notice in order to retain the possibility of surprising an opponent; cf *Ford v Lewis* [1971] 2 All ER 983; [1971] 1 WLR 623.
15   Ord 35, r 1.
16   Ord 35, r 2. There can be an appeal against such a judgment, though this is rarely appropriate: *Armour v Bate* [1891] 2 QB 233.
17   Ord 62, r 8.

b   Case for the plaintiff

Counsel for the plaintiff opens his case stating the facts on which the plaintiff relies in the order in which they appear on the pleadings, which should be chronological order. He should not rely upon any fact which he is not permitted to prove, which means, of course, that he cannot allege any fact not pleaded, although he may, even at this late stage, be allowed to amend the pleadings. Neither counsel must disclose the existence of any interim payment, nor of any payment into court, unless the defendant has raised one of the two defences in which the payment is an essential element.[18] The plaintiff's witnesses are then called and sworn. They are examined and may be cross-examined and re-examined.[19] In the course of cross-examining the plaintiff's witnesses, counsel for the defendant must "put his case" which includes making clear which part of the plaintiff's case is challenged and what positive allegations are being made in relation to the evidence of the plaintiff's witnesses, so that they may have the opportunity of dealing with those allegations. This is important to the efficient conduct of trials because if counsel for the plaintiff calls a witness whose evidence is not challenged on a particular point, then he is entitled to assume that the point is not in issue and he will not call any other witnesses to deal with it. If the defence lead evidence as to matters which should have been put but were not put to the plaintiff's witnesses, judicial rebuke is virtually inevitable and, unless counsel was responsible for the oversight (in which event he will, in the interests of his client, immediately accept responsibility for it), the judge is likely to infer, and find, that the evidence in question is a recent invention. His documents, including answers to interrogatories which he wishes to put in, are then put in evidence. Finally counsel argues the propositions of law upon which he relies, citing to the court all relevant authorities on the point whether they support his own case or that of his opponent. If they tend to support his opponent's case, he must attempt to distinguish them from the present case on their facts. He cannot, however, ignore them, since this would infringe his duty to the court.

c   Case for the defence

At the close of the plaintiff's case the defendant has the following courses open to him:

(1) he may submit "no case to answer". This is a submission that the plaintiff has failed to make out a prima facie case, or to establish the elements of a recognised cause of action. The submission is rare in a civil action since the objection will usually have been taken long before the trial. If it is made, the judge, before deciding, may require the defendant to "stand on his submission", which means that he can call no evidence if his submission fails, although this is not usual in jury actions.[20] Counsel for the plaintiff has a right to reply to the submission. If it succeeds, judgment is entered for the defendant. If it fails and the defendant has been put to his election, judgment is entered for the plaintiff.

(2) He may state that he intends to call no evidence, oral or documentary. Counsel for the plaintiff will then address the court followed by defence counsel who thus obtains the right to the last word.[1]

---

18   Ord 22, r 7; see p 373, *ante*.

19   It is a matter for the judge's discretion as to whether he allows other witnesses to remain in court while evidence is being given; *Moore v Lambeth County Court Registrar* [1969] 1 All ER 782; [1969] 1 WLR 141.

20   *Laurie v Raglan Building Co Ltd* [1942] 1 KB 152; [1941] 3 All ER 332; *Young v Rank* [1950] 2 KB 510; [1950] 2 All ER 166; *Storey v Storey* [1961] P 63; [1960] 3 All ER 279.

1   Ord 35, r 7. This rule applies expressly to jury actions, but, in the Queen's Bench Division, applies in practice to non-jury actions as well; see *Weller v O'Brien* [1962] 3 All ER 65; [1962] 1 WLR 885.

(3) In most cases the defence will be a mixture of law and fact and the defendant will want to put in some evidence. In this event defence counsel may make an opening speech outlining his defence. His witnesses give their evidence in the same way as those of the plaintiff followed by the defendant's documents and legal submissions. The plaintiff may be permitted to adduce evidence in rebuttal where the defence case has raised matters which could not reasonably have been foreseen. Defence counsel then makes a closing speech, following which counsel for the plaintiff has a right to make a closing speech in reply. Where a party in his closing speech raises any fresh point of law, the other party is entitled to reply but only in relation to that point.

d   Verdict and judgment

At the conclusion of all the evidence and the legal argument for both sides the judge sums up (if there is a jury) or either gives judgment or reserves his judgment if there is not. He must direct the jury (if there is one) as to the issues in the case, stating on whom the burden of proving the individual issues rests, and outlining the evidence in support of those issues. He must also direct upon the standard of proof required from the party on whom the burden rests. He will direct on the law applicable to the issues of fact, for example, whether the words are capable of bearing the defamatory meaning alleged or whether the defendant owes the plaintiff a duty of care in negligence. He must leave the actual issues of fact and the assessment of damages to the jury, but, now, following a series of cases involving disproportionate damages awards,[2] may give them guidance as to the appropriate level of damages that may be awarded. A modern tendency is for the judge to pose a series of questions to the jury calling for their decision on the facts and, if they find for the plaintiff on any issue, the amount of damages.[3] Where the plaintiff has sought an equitable remedy as an alternative or in addition to damages, the grant of his remedy is in the discretion of the judge.

It remains for judgment to be entered in accordance with the verdict. A judgment crystallises the rights of the parties in respect of the subject matter of the action. Thus they are estopped from litigating the same issues of fact again.[4] Even if fresh damage becomes apparent the plaintiff cannot sue because his right is extinguished.[5] Counsel for the unsuccessful party may apply for a stay of execution pending an appeal. This may be granted on terms. After judgment on the issues of liability and damages the judge may make orders as to interest and costs.

Historically damages have always been expressed in English currency. This has caused hardship in cases in which sterling has been devalued, so a party who bargained for payment in foreign currency has been awarded damages in sterling, the rate of exchange being calculated at the date upon which his entitlement to payment arose (the "breach-date" rule). Accordingly in 1975 the House of Lords changed this rule.[6] Since 1975 the English courts have shown an increasing willingness to give judgment

2   See, generally, pp 232, n 7, *ante*.
3   However where a jury delivers a general verdict, the judge is not then entitled to ask questions to ascertain the grounds for the verdict; *Arnold v Jeffreys* [1914] 1 KB 512; *Barnes v Hill* [1967] 1 QB 579; [1967] 1 All ER 347.
4   Clerical mistakes in judgments or orders, or errors arising therein from any accidental slip or omission, may at any time be corrected by the court on motion or summons without an appeal (Ord 20, r 11 the "slip rule").
5   There is an exception to this rule; if special damage is an element in a cause of action, fresh special damage arising out of the same cause of action may be the basis of a second action: *Darley Main Colliery Co v Mitchell* (1886) 11 App Cas 127; *West Leigh Colliery Co Ltd v Tunnicliffe and Hampson Ltd* [1908] AC 27.
6   *Miliangos v George Frank (Textiles) Ltd* [1976] AC 443; [1975] 3 All ER 801.

in foreign currency. At first limited to contract actions where the sum was due under the contract in a foreign currency and the proper law of the contract was the law of that country in whose currency the obligation was expressed,[7] the power is now exercised in cases where the plaintiff's loss would be most truly expressed in a foreign currency, in which case judgment will be given in that currency,[8] and in tort actions, where damages may be awarded in a currency which the plaintiff has used to make good the loss which he has suffered.[9] Nevertheless a judgment can only be enforced in terms of sterling. Accordingly if enforcement becomes necessary the judgment will be converted into its sterling equivalent at the date when leave is given to enforce the judgment.

Finally, there is, save in personal injuries actions, no procedure for successive awards of damages in the same action. Damages have to be assessed once and for all at the trial. This may cause hardship to either side, since subsequent events may demonstrate the hypotheses upon which the award of damages were based to be false with the result that the damages were too high or too low. This is particularly so in personal injury actions where, for example, an award of damages for loss of future earnings capacity must necessarily be highly speculative. To remedy this situation section 32A of the Supreme Court Act contains provision for "provisional damages" in personal injury actions. The procedure is governed by Order 37, rules 7–10. In appropriate cases the court has power to make an "award of provisional damages", which is an assessment of the plaintiff's damages on the assumption that the plaintiff will not suffer a specified disease or deterioration. If the same subsequently occurs, within the period fixed by the court, the plaintiff may apply for a further award.

Section 35A of the Supreme Court Act 1981[10] empowers the court to award simple (but not compound) interest on debts or damages "at such rate as the court thinks fit or as rules of court may provide". In commercial cases the usual rate is 1% above United Kingdom clearing banks' base rates over the relevant period.[11] Different rules exist in respect of personal injury actions, where on most awards, the court must grant interest:[12]

(1) the plaintiff is awarded interest on general damages for pain, suffering and loss of amenities from the date of service of the writ to the date of trial at a conventional rate of 2% per annum;

(2) the plaintiff is awarded interest on special damages from the date of the accident to the date of trial at half the rates which during that period were payable on money in court placed on special account;[13]

(3) no interest is awarded on future loss of earnings or other prospective financial losses.

---

7   *Miliangos v George Frank (Textiles) Ltd (supra),* not following *Tomkinson v First Pennsylvania Banking and Trust Co* [1961] AC 1007, *sub nom Re United Railways of Havana and Regla Warehouses Ltd* [1960] 2 All ER 332; for the significance of this decision in relation to the doctrine of judicial precedent, see p 72, *ante.*
8   *The Folias* [1979] AC 685; [1979] 1 All ER 421.
9   *The Despina R* [1979] AC 685; [1979] 1 All ER 421.
10 Added by Administration of Justice Act 1982, s 15, Sch 1 and replacing s 3 of the Law Reform (Miscellaneous Provisions) Act 1934.
11 See *Polish Steam Ship Co v Atlantic Maritime Co* [1985] QB 41; [1984] 3 All ER 59.
12 The principles were laid down by the Court of Appeal in *Jefford v Gee* [1970] 2 QB 130; [1970] 1 All ER 1202 and restated with modification by the House of Lords in *Wright v British Railways Board* [1983] 2 AC 773; [1983] 2 All ER 698.
13 See *Dexter v Courtaulds Ltd* [1984] 1 All ER 70; [1984] 1 WLR 372.

Chapter 18

County Court Proceedings

The major issues concerning the county court and its jurisdiction are implicit in the discussions in earlier chapters concerning the balance of work between county court and High Court, and the proposals for a unified system, which will have an enlarged small claims jurisdiction, and which will give the county court an even greater role in civil litigation. Already, the great majority of civil cases that go to hearing are determined by the county court.

The county court rules have been extensively modified in recent years, and the court now has, in many respects, similar powers to the High Court, although operating from a different set of procedural rules. This chapter concentrates on matters of detail within the current jurisdiction.

A CONSTITUTION AND JURISDICTION OF COUNTY COURTS

1 Origins and constitution

One of the principal deficiencies of the English legal system, until the reforms of the nineteenth century, was the lack of a system of courts to deal with civil actions involving only a small amount of money.[1] As a result, the modern county courts were established by the County Courts Act 1846. The upper limit of the new courts' jurisdiction was originally fixed at £20 but this figure has been progressively increased and presently stands at £50,000 in most cases. The jurisdiction of the county courts is now principally contained in the County Courts Act 1984 (as amended).

Procedure in the county courts is regulated by the County Court Rules made by a Rule Committee under powers conferred by the Act.[2] The rules presently in force are the County Court Rules 1981 (as amended). These and other rules relating to county court practice and procedure are to be found in the *County Court Practice* (the "Green

---

1 See p 153, *ante*.
2 Section 75. In any case not expressly provided for in the Act or Rules, the principles of High Court procedure apply (s 76); see *Williamson v Rider* [1963] 1 QB 89; [1962] 2 All ER 268. They also have inherent power to regulate their own procedure: see *Langley v North West Water Authority* [1991] 3 All ER 610; [1991] 1 WLR 697.

Book") which, although not an official publication, is accepted as authoritative in the same way as the White Book is accepted in the Supreme Court. England and Wales are divided into districts each having one or more county courts.[3] These courts are, for administrative convenience, grouped into circuits with one or more judges presiding over each circuit. Each court has a sitting at least once a month, and, of course, at busy centres often considerably more often.

a   Judges of county courts

The office of county court judge, as such, was abolished by the Courts Act 1971 and on the date on which that Act came into operation, 1 January 1972, all existing county court judges automatically became circuit judges.[4] Although every circuit judge is, by virtue of his office, enabled to sit in any county court the Lord Chancellor is bound to assign one or more circuit judges to each county court district.[5]

b   District judges

These are appointed by the Lord Chancellor and must be appropriately qualified.[6] The district judge exercises both an administrative and a judicial function. In his administrative capacity he maintains the court records, arranges for the issue and service of summonses, accounts for money paid into court and exercises a large number of similar functions. In practice he delegates much of this work to subordinate court officers, notably the clerks and bailiffs. The scope of his judicial function is narrower than that of the judge. He has power to hear and determine (a) any action or matter in which the defendant fails to appear at the hearing or admits the claim; (b) any action or matter in which the sum claimed or the amount involved does not exceed £5,000; (c) actions in which mortgagees of land claim possession; and (d) by leave of the judge and with the consent of the parties, any other action or matter.[7] He also deals with interlocutory matters and the taxation of costs.

2   Jurisdiction

Because county courts are the creation of statute, their jurisdiction derives entirely from statute. The general jurisdiction of the county court is to be found in the County Courts Act 1984. Nevertheless extensive jurisdiction is conferred upon the county court by other statutes. This latter jurisdiction is usually concurrent with the High Court or magistrates' court although in a few cases it is exclusive to the county court.[8]

---

3   *Ibid*, ss 1, 2; the places at which county courts are to be held and the names of those courts are specified in the Civil Courts Order 1983; they are set out in the County Court Directory in the Appendix of the Green Book.
4   Courts Act 1971, s 16, Sch 2; as to the position of circuit judges, see p 211, *ante*.
5   County Courts Act 1984, s 5. In addition every judge of the Court of Appeal, every judge of the High Court and every recorder is capable of sitting as a county court judge if he consents so to do and may be required, under s 5(3), so to act on such occasions as the Lord Chancellor considers desirable. It is difficult to envisage any judge of the Court of Appeal or High Court sitting as a county court judge.
6   *Ibid*, s 9; the Lord Chancellor may appoint assistant district judges (s 7) and deputy district judges (s 8), who must be similarly qualified.
7   CCR, Ord 21, r 5.
8   For example, under the Rent Act 1977, the Race Relations Act 1976 and the Family Law Act 1996.

a   Jurisdiction under the County Courts Act 1984

The jurisdiction of the county court under the 1984 Act may be classified as follows:

(1) Actions founded on contract or tort. The fundamental changes to the distribution of cases between High Court and county court have already been noted.[9] In particular the presumption is that cases with a value of £50,000 or more will be tried in the High Court.

(2) Actions for the recovery of land or where the title to any hereditament or right over land is in question.

(3) Equity proceedings where the sum involved does not exceed the county court limit (currently £30,000) or more by written memorandum signed by the parties or their solicitors, and then only where the proceedings fall within certain specified categories. These categories are set out in section 23 of the Act and include the administration of estates of deceased persons, the declaration and execution of trusts, the foreclosure and redemption of mortgages, the rectification or cancellation of deeds, the maintenance and advancement out of trust funds of infants and proceedings for relief against fraud or mistake.[10]

(4) Admiralty proceedings, but only in certain specified proceedings and only in county courts which have been appointed by the Lord Chancellor to exercise jurisdiction in admiralty matters.[11] All these courts, with the exception of the Mayor's and City of London Court, are on or near the coast. The admiralty proceedings in question are set out in section 27 of the Act. They include claims for damage to a ship or for damage to or loss of goods carried by sea, towage and pilotage disputes. The limit of jurisdiction is in each case £5,000 (or £15,000 in salvage claims), but this limit can be increased by memorandum of agreement, although the extent of the proceedings over which the county court has jurisdiction cannot be so increased.

(5) Contentious probate proceedings where there is an application for a grant or revocation of probate or letters of administration, where the net value of the estate at the time of death was less than the county court limit (currently £30,000). The applicant must swear an affidavit containing the value of the estate and also the place of abode of the deceased, since only the county court for that district has jurisdiction.[12]

b   Jurisdiction under other statutes.

Apart from the County Courts Act 1984, there are more than 150 statutes which confer jurisdiction in certain matters either on the county courts generally, or upon particular county courts. Of these mention may be made of the Rent Act 1977, Housing Act 1996 and the Consumer Credit Act 1974 which are fertile sources of county court litigation. Special attention should be drawn to the Matrimonial Causes Act 1973 which conferred jurisdiction upon those county courts nominated by the Lord Chancellor as "divorce county courts" to hear undefended matrimonial causes,[13] and to the Family Law Act 1996 under which a county court judge may, by injunction, exercise powers which include restraining a party from molesting the other party or a child living with the

9   See p 341, *ante*.
10 See also County Courts Act 1984, s 24 for other equity proceedings which may, by consent of the parties, be tried in a county court.
11 County Courts Act 1984, ss 26, 27.
12 *Ibid*, s 32.
13 See now: Matrimonial Causes Act 1973; Matrimonial and Family Proceedings Act 1984.

applicant, excluding one party from the "matrimonial home" or requiring him (or her) to permit the other to enter and remain in the home.[14]

B   PROCEDURE IN THE COUNTY COURT

I   Actions

a   Choice of county court

Unlike that of the High Court, the jurisdiction of county courts is local. This means that the plaintiff must usually commence proceedings:

(1) in the court for the district in which the defendant or one of the defendants resides or carries on business; or

(2) in the court for the district where the cause of action arose wholly or in part; or

(3) in the case of a default action, in any county court.[15]

If the plaintiff commences proceedings in any other county court the judge of that court may transfer the proceedings to a court which does have jurisdiction, order them to be struck out, or allow them to continue in his court.[16]

b   Parties

The County Court Rules regulating the choice and joinder of parties are parallel to the provisions of the Rules of the Supreme Court. Thus two or more persons may be joined as plaintiffs or defendants if their rights or liabilities arise out of the same transaction or series of transactions and, if separate actions were brought, any common question of law or fact would arise.[17] Parties to whom special rules of procedure apply in the High Court, such as partners, companies and persons under disability, are in a similar position in the county court. An infant must generally, as in the High Court, sue by his "next friend" who must file an undertaking to be responsible for costs.[18] However, an infant may sue in his own name for any sum not exceeding the county court limit which may be due to him for wages or piece work or for work as a servant.[19]

c   Commencement of proceedings

All proceedings, the object of which is to obtain relief against any other person, must (subject to any express provision to the contrary) be brought by action and commenced by plaint.[20] An action in which a claim is made for any relief other than the payment of money is termed a "fixed date action"; every other action is a "default action".[1] The plaintiff or his solicitor commences a default or fixed date action by filing in the court office a request for the summons (formerly called a *praecipe*) setting out the names, addresses and descriptions of all parties and the nature and amount of the claim.

---

14   See, formerly, Domestic Violence and Matrimonial Proceedings Act 1976.
15   Ord 4, r 2(1). Oddly enough the matrimonial jurisdiction of divorce county courts is not local; a petition may be filed in any divorce county court (Family Proceedings Rules 1991, SI 1991/1247, r 2.6).
16   Ord 16, r 2.
17   Ord 5, r 2.
18   Ord 10, r 2.
19   County Courts Act 1984, s 47.
20   Ord 3, r 1.
1   Ord 3, r 2.

He must also file particulars of the claim and the sum claimed with a copy for each defendant. Upon filing these documents the registrar issues to the plaintiff a plaint note containing the title of the action, the reference number of the plaint and a date and time for the return day. He also prepares, from the plaintiff's request, and issues, a summons to which are annexed the particulars of the claim. The summons and particulars are then served on every defendant at least 21 clear days before the return day.[2] The defendant is also served with forms of admission, defence and counterclaim. A county court summons may be served by the plaintiff or his agent, in which case he must file an affidavit of service,[3] but it is usually served by the county court bailiff. The summons may be served by an officer of the court sending it by first-class post to the defendant at the address stated in the request for the summons or, if the plaintiff so requests, by the plaintiff delivering the summons to the defendant personally.[4] The defendant's solicitor may accept service on the defendant's behalf, in which case he must indorse on the bailiff's copy summons a statement to this effect. Substituted service may be ordered by the district judge following application by the plaintiff on affidavit. A summons may not be served out of the jurisdiction without leave of the judge. The circumstances in which leave may be granted are similar (though not identical) to those contained in Order 11, rule 1 of the Rules of the Supreme Court.[5]

d   Defence

A defendant who is served with a summons has open to him the following courses of action:[6]

(1) In any action for debt or damages he may within 14 days of service pay into court the whole amount of the claim; the action is then stayed and if the defendant also pays in the costs stated on the summons he will not be liable for any further costs unless the court otherwise orders.[7] Alternatively he may pay into court some lesser amount, either in satisfaction of the plaintiff's claim or on account of a sum admitted by him to be due to the plaintiff. In the former case the payment in operates in the same way as a payment into court in the High Court under RSC Order 22. Thus if the payment in is accepted, the proceedings are stayed in respect of the causes of action to which the payment in relates while if the plaintiff goes on but then, at the trial, fails to "beat the payment in" he will normally be held liable for all costs subsequent to the date of payment in.

(2) Where the defendant admits the whole or any part of the claim but desires time to pay he may, within 14 days, file the form of admission attached to the summons and state how he proposes to pay the admitted sum, for example by fixed

---

2   Ord 7, r 6.
3   Ord 3, r 2.
4   Ord 7, r 10. Service by post is deemed to be effected on the seventh day after the date on which the summons was sent (Ord 7, r 10). Consequently service may be deemed to be validly effected even though the defendant never actually receives the summons. The defendant's remedy is to apply to set aside judgment, though this is a matter of discretion rather than of right: see *Cooper v Scott-Farnell* [1969] 1 All ER 178; [1969] 1 WLR 120. However where a summons sent by post has been returned undelivered, notice of non-service is sent to the plaintiff who is informed that he may request bailiff service; if he so requests the court bailiff then effects service by (a) inserting the summons through the letterbox at the address stated in the request for the summons; or (b) delivering the summons to some person, apparently not less than 16 years old, at that address; or (c) delivering the summons to the defendant personally (Ord 7, r 10).
5   Ord 8, r 2. Service on a Sunday, Christmas Day or Good Friday is prohibited except, in case of urgency, with leave of the court; Ord 7, r 3.
6   Ord 9.
7   Ord 11, rr 1, 2.

instalments. The district judge sends notice of this admission to the plaintiff who must, within 14 days, inform the court office whether or not he accepts the offer. If he does accept, the district judge will enter judgment accordingly. If he does not accept, the district judge must inform the defendant whereupon the action proceeds.[8] If the defendant admits the whole or any part of the plaintiff's claim, the plaintiff may apply to the court for such judgment as he may be entitled to on the admission; an alternative course for the plaintiff is to apply for an interim payment.[9]

(3) If the defendant denies liability or wishes to plead a set-off or counterclaim he must, within 14 days, file the forms of defence and counterclaim if appropriate. The district judge will serve copies of these upon the plaintiff.

(4) In a default action[10] if the defendant takes none of the above courses, the plaintiff may obtain judgment for the amount of the claim (if the claim is liquidated)[11] or interlocutory judgment for damages to be assessed (if the claim is for unliquidated damages) together with costs. In a fixed date action (viz an action in which there is a claim for some relief other than the payment of money) the defendant may appear on the return day without having filed a defence and dispute the plaintiff's claim. However he will be ordered to pay any extra costs incurred by his failure to file a defence.

e   *Pre-trial review and other interlocutory proceedings*

In the case of a fixed date action (other than an action for recovery of land) the return day on the summons will be, unless the court otherwise directs, a day fixed for the preliminary consideration of the action by the district judge, known as a "pre-trial review". In the case of default action, where a defence or counterclaim is delivered the court will fix either a day for the hearing of the action or a day for a pre-trial review.[12] A pre-trial review may also be held where the district judge is of the opinion that the question of giving directions ought to be considered. The pre-trial review is analogous to the summons for directions in High Court actions[13] and the district judge is enjoined to "consider the course of the proceedings and give all such directions as appear to him necessary or desirable for securing the just, expeditious and economical disposal of the action".[14]

In particular the district judge must endeavour to secure that the parties make all such admissions and agreements as ought reasonably to be made by them and may record in the order any admission or agreement so made or any refusal to make any admission or agreement. Evidence on the pre-trial review may be given by affidavit. If the defendant does not appear on the pre-trial review and has not delivered an admission or defence, the district judge may, if he thinks fit, enter judgment for the plaintiff; if the defendant does not appear on the pre-trial review and has delivered a defence, the plaintiff may proceed to prove his case (generally by affidavit) and may ask for judgment in the same way as if the defendant had not appeared at the trial.

---

8   Ord 9, r 3.
9   Ord 13, r 12; this rule applies RSC, Ord 29 (subject to minor exceptions) to county court proceedings; for details of the High Court procedure, see p 378, *ante*.
10   Ie judgment on failure to give notice of intention to defend.
11   In county courts a claim for the cost of repairs executed to a motor vehicle is treated as a liquidated claim unless the court otherwise orders (Ord 1, r 10).
12   Ord 3, r 3 (fixed date); Ord 9, r 5 (default). See generally Ord 17, r 11 (automatic directions).
13   See p 393, *ante*.
14   Ord 17, r 1.

Every party must apply on the pre-trial review for any interlocutory order which he seeks and if he does not and makes a subsequent interlocutory application, he will usually have to pay the extra costs incurred. Interlocutory orders are, in practice, required rather less frequently than in High Court actions. The interlocutory orders which the county court has power to make are similar to the orders which may be made in the High Court, the following being frequently encountered third party proceedings,[15] further and better particulars of claim,[16] discovery and inspection of documents,[17] interrogatories[18] amendment of pleadings,[19] security for costs[20] and interim payments.[1] It may also include orders as to exchange of statements.[2]

After giving all necessary directions the district judge must, if the action remains to be tried, fix a day for the trial and give notice thereof to every party.[3] The pre-trial review operates, therefore, both as a summons for directions in actions which are destined to proceed to trial and as a means of the plaintiff obtaining judgment (either by default or by proving his case, as above) in other cases, without the need of a proper trial in open court. In other cases, a system of automatic directions operates.[4] This provides a timetable for service of lists of documents, inspection of documents, disclosure of expert reports, for the making of requests for a hearing, and for the preparation of documentation prior to trial.

f   Premature determination of proceedings

A high proportion of actions never come to trial, being prematurely determined by agreement, by the defendant admitting liability, by the plaintiff discontinuing his claim, or by a judgment or order given or made on a pre-trial review. In addition Order 9, rule 14 now, in effect, applies High Court Order 14 procedure to most actions.[5] If the parties arrive at a settlement, the plaintiff must give notice of this to the district judge who notes it in the minute book. The action is thus determined. However the consent of the court is required to a settlement of an action by or on behalf of a person under disability.[6]

Some actions are brought solely for obtaining the court's sanction for a settlement which has already been reached. The particulars of claim in such an action contain only an outline of the claim, the terms of the proposed settlement and a request for the court's approval, which will be given in chambers by the judge or district judge. The judge or district judge will direct how the money is to be dealt with; in the case of an infant the money is usually paid into court and invested or applied for his benefit until he attains his majority, when he can demand payment of the capital. As has already been noted the defendant may pay money into court at any time before judgment. If the plaintiff takes the money out of court proceedings are stayed and the plaintiff may

---

15   Ord 12.
16   Ord 6, r 7.
17   Ord 14, rr 1–10; the automatic discovery provisions in the High Court do not apply in county courts.
18   Ord 14, r 11.
19   Ord 15.
20   Ord 1, r 8.
1   Ord 13, r 12.
2   Ord 20, r 12A.
3   Ord 17, r 10.
4   Ord 17, r 11.
5   For details of Ord 14 procedure in the High Court; the rule does not apply to (a) actions which stand referred to arbitration, (b) actions for the possession of land, or involving title to land, or (c) claims for libel, slander, malicious prosecution or false imprisonment.
6   Ord 10, r 10.

tax and sign judgment for his costs. The plaintiff may, at any time before trial, discontinue his action by giving notice in the prescribed form to the district judge and to the defendant, who will be entitled to his costs incurred before receiving notice of discontinuance.[7]

g References to arbitration or for inquiry and report or to the European Court

(1) ARBITRATION

This jurisdiction and procedure was discussed in Chapter 15.[8]

(2) INQUIRY AND REPORT

Section 65 of the Act empowers the court to refer to the district judge or a referee for inquiry and report proceedings which require any prolonged examination of documents or any scientific or local investigation,[9] proceedings concerning matters of account, other proceedings with the consent of the parties and any question arising in any proceedings. Such an order may be made either on application or by the court of its own motion and, as will be apparent from the terms of the section, is usually appropriate in complex cases, such as building disputes, where there is a great deal of detailed or expert evidence to be heard; the reference may be to the district judge or to an independent referee who will conduct the inquiry and make a report to the court. The procedure differs from arbitration in that it does not, as arbitration does, involve the adjudication being made by the person to whom the reference is made. Judgment will still be given by the judge (or district judge) trying the case.

(3) REFERENCE TO EUROPEAN COURT

County courts, like the High Court and the Court of Appeal, have power to refer questions for a preliminary ruling under Article 177 of the Treaty of Rome. The circumstances in which such a reference may be made and the principles which govern the court's discretion whether or not to refer have been considered elsewhere;[10] the rules applicable in county courts are substantially similar to those which apply in the High Court. In view of the costs involved there are few references to the European Court from county courts, although the terms of Article 177 have compelled the enactment of rules to deal with such a contingency.

h Trial

Unless it is settled or discontinued or disposed of at the pre-trial review the action comes on for trial on the day fixed. If the plaintiff does not appear when the case is called his action will be struck out and he will have to apply to have it reinstated at another time. If the defendant does not appear the trial may proceed in his absence and judgment may be entered against him. The trial will be before the district judge, the judge or, very rarely, the judge and a jury. The county court jury is obsolescent. No party has a right to claim trial with a jury unless there is in issue a charge of fraud against him or a claim in respect of libel, slander, malicious prosecution or false imprisonment unless the trial requires any prolonged examination of documents or accounts or any scientific or local investigation which cannot conveniently be made with a jury.[11] In any other

---

7 Ord 18, rr 1, 2.
8 See p 332, *ante.*
9 See p 389, *ante* for position in High Court.
10 See p 117, *ante.*
11 County Courts Act 1984, s 66. The application for an order for trial by jury must be made not less than 10 clear days before the return day; Ord 13, r 10.

case he may be granted a jury, eight in number. In fact actions which would be heard by a jury are usually heard in the High Court.[12] The conduct of the trial is similar to that in the High Court. Solicitors, however, have a right of audience in the county court.[13] Also, if the action is not determined in one day, the district judge must fix another date to continue the hearing which will not necessarily be the next day. If the defendant admits the plaintiff's claim or does not appear, judgment will be entered for the plaintiff. Where this judgment is for the payment of money the court may order the sum to be paid forthwith or within a specified time, or may order payment by fixed instalments.[14]

If the plaintiff does not succeed in proving his case the court may either give judgment for the defendant or non-suit the plaintiff. The non-suit has long been abolished in the High Court but still exists in the county court. It differs from a judgment for the defendant in that it does not decide the case affirmatively against the plaintiff, so that he is not estopped from bringing a subsequent action on the same facts. However a second action may be stayed until the plaintiff has complied with an order for costs made against him in the former action.[15]

2   Proceedings other than actions

Where, subject to any Act or rule, the object of proceedings is to obtain relief against any person or to compel any person to do or abstain from doing any act, the proper method of proceeding is by action, the procedure for which has been described above. Proceedings in the county court which do not fall into this category are commenced by originating application unless any Act or rule requires that they be commenced otherwise.[16]

An originating application may be likened to an originating summons in the High Court. It is appropriate where the applicant seeks an order of the court which does not amount to a claim for relief from another person. Thus the person who seeks an adoption order, a declaration of legitimacy, or an order under the Landlord and Tenant Acts will commence proceedings by originating application. Notice of the application must be served on the proper respondent; for example, an application for a declaration of legitimacy must be served on the Attorney-General and all persons whose interests might be affected by the declaration. If the respondent wishes to resist the application he must file an answer, following which there will be a hearing before the judge or district judge. Since there is no plaint, but only an application, the parties are described not as "plaintiff" and "defendant" but as "applicant" and "respondent".[17]

3   Costs in the county court

The position as to costs between a party and his own solicitor has already been considered in connection with High Court litigation. As between the parties, the court

---

12   See p 398, *ante*.
13   See also the Lay Representative (Rights of Audience) Order 1992, and generally as to the Lord Chancellor's powers, the Courts and Legal Services Act 1990, s 27, p 244, *ante*.
14   County Courts Act 1984, s 71.
15   Ord 21, r 2. For judicial discretion, see *Clack v Arthur's Engineering Ltd* [1959] 2 QB 211; [1959] 2 All ER 503.
16   Ord 3, r 4. Proceedings may also be by petition where any Act or rule so provides.
17   Ord 38, r 1.

has a judicial discretion over costs, but as a rule the successful party will recover his costs from his opponent, as in the High Court.

a Scales of costs

The essential distinction between High Court and county court costs is that the latter are fixed in amount by reference to scales[18] according to the sum claimed or recovered in the action or, where the claim is not only a money claim, according to the discretion of the court.

For the regulation of solicitors' charges and disbursements, other than court fees, there are three scales of costs. If the plaintiff succeeds the scale is determined by the amount for which he recovers judgment. If the plaintiff fails the scale is determined by the amount of the plaintiff's claim. The court has a discretion to award costs on a higher or lower scale than the one applicable in certain cases, notably if the judge certifies that a difficult question of law or fact is involved.[19] Where the claim is less than £25 the court cannot allow any solicitors' charges unless the judge certifies that a "difficult question of law or a question of fact of exceptional complexity" is involved.[20] No fee for counsel can be awarded where the defendant, in an action for money alone, delivers no defence and does not appear at the hearing, unless the judge or district judge at the hearing otherwise orders.[1] The judge also has a power to award a fixed sum by way of costs.[2]

b Assessment of costs

Certain items are fixed in amount. For example, when a summons is issued in an action where the only relief claimed is a sum of money liquidated or unliquidated, the court fee and the charges of the plaintiff's solicitor for the issue of the summons are fixed and are entered on the summons. Accordingly, if the defendant within 14 days of service pays the sum claimed and costs into court, or pays in a lesser sum with an admission of liability which the plaintiff accepts in satisfaction, the defendant is generally liable for no further costs beyond those stated on the summons. This may, of course, cause hardship to a plaintiff who has already incurred expense, for example by obtaining a medical report or by having particulars of claim settled by counsel. Where costs are on the lower scale they must be assessed as a lump sum.[3] In other cases the costs will be taxed according to the appropriate scale; the basis of taxation within the scale is similar to that applicable in the High Court so that taxation will almost always be on a "standard" basis.[4] The district judge may fix and allow costs without taxation if the successful party so requests. Otherwise they must be taxed unless the parties agree an amount of costs in lieu of taxation.[5]

---

18 These scales do not apply to bankruptcy, divorce or Companies Act proceedings (where special scales apply).
19 Ord 38, r 9.
20 Ord 38, r 4(6).
1 Ord 38, r 8(2).
2 Ord 38, r 3D.
3 Ord 38, r 19, App C. Because of the lower scale limit (£100), costs on this basis are rarely encountered.
4 See p 429, *post*.
5 Ord 38, r 19.

c   *Taxation of costs*

The district judge is the taxing officer of the court. The successful party must, within three months of the order for costs, lodge a bill of costs with the registrar and obtain an appointment for taxation. He must serve a copy of this bill on his opponent and give him not less than 14 days' notice of the appointment.[6]

On taxation the district judge will allow, in accordance with the scale, a reasonable amount for each item incurred. The judge may, at the trial, expressly authorise the district judge to allow an amount in respect of certain items, such as counsel's fee, in excess of the scale maximum. In this event the district judge may allow such sum as he considers reasonable in respect of these items. Where an item is not provided for in the scales the district judge may or may not in his discretion make an allowance in respect of it. The district judge certifies the total amount due on taxation in his *allocatur* which is endorsed on the bill.

d   *Review of taxation*[7]

Any party not satisfied with a taxation may apply to the district judge to review his taxation; the application must set out the disputed items and the grounds of objection. The district judge will then certify in writing his reasons for allowing or disallowing the disputed items. If dissatisfied with this review, any party may apply to the judge for a review. The judge then has the equivalent powers of the district judge in his review. He cannot upset the discretion of the district judge unless the exercise of this discretion was based upon a wrong principle of law.[8] There is a further appeal to the Court of Appeal, with leave of the judge, if a question of legal principle is involved.[9]

4   Execution and enforcement of judgments

a   *Judgments for the payment of money*

Where the judgment or order directs the payment of money, the methods of enforcing the judgment are similar to those available in the High Court, ie execution against the debtor's personal property, garnishee proceedings, appointment of a receiver, creation of a charge over the debtor's land, or partnership interest or other assets,[10] and bankruptcy proceedings. County court judgments used not to carry interest. This was an anomalous and unjust state of affairs since High Court judgments have carried interest since the Judgments Act 1838. It has now been remedied by order made under section 74 of the Act.[11] Furthermore the important jurisdiction to make attachment of earnings orders under the Attachment of Earnings Act 1971, which in the High Court is limited to the enforcement of maintenance orders, is, in county courts, exercisable in respect of maintenance orders, judgment debts of £15 or more and administration orders.[12]

---

6   Ord 38, r 20.
7   Ord 38, r 24
8   *White v Altringham UDC* [1936] 2 KB 138, [1936] 1 All ER 923.
9   *Goodman v Blake* (1887) 19 QBD 77; Supreme Court Act 1981, s 18(1)(f).
10   See p 436, *post*.
11   Introduced by Supreme Court Act 1981; see County Courts (Interest on Judgment Debts) Order 1991 (SI 1991/1184).
12   Attachment of Earnings Act 1971, s 1(2); see p 419, *post*. Under the same section, magistrates' courts have power to make attachment of earnings orders in respect of maintenance orders, fines and analogous impositions and legal aid contributions; Accordingly the use of attachment of earnings orders to enforce ordinary judgment debts is confined to county courts.

Finally mention may be made of the judgment summons. This was, until relatively recently, a widely used procedure to enforce both county court and High Court judgments. However, as noted below, the drastic curtailment on the power to commit to prison for default in paying civil debts in favour of the power to make attachment of earnings orders has rendered judgment summonses inappropriate in all but a very few cases.

b Execution

Execution is effected by warrant of execution issued to the county court bailiff which is in the nature of a writ of *fieri facias*.[13] The warrant directs the bailiff to execute upon the debtor's personal property for the judgment debt, costs and interest. The rules relating to property which is exempt from execution, method of execution and interpleader proceedings are similar to those in the High Court. A judgment creditor seeking the issue of a warrant of execution must file the appropriate request in the court office. A notice is usually sent to the defendant telling him that a warrant has been issued and that if he pays the debt there will be no need to execute the warrant. This often results in the warrant being paid out. As an alternative the plaintiff may agree to suspend the warrant on condition that the debt and costs are paid within a specified time or by instalments.[14] In fact most warrants are paid out or suspended in this way and only in a small proportion of cases does the warrant have to be executed.

The warrant, once issued, remains in force for one year from the date of issue unless renewed. The bailiff seizes sufficient goods to satisfy the warrant and either deposits them in a proper place, such as a warehouse or auction room, or takes "walking possession" of them. There will then be a sale of such goods as are sufficient to satisfy the judgment debt including costs. In order that the bailiff does not sell too much, he will have the goods "appraised", usually by a local auctioneer who also deals with the storage and sale of the goods. The sale is usually by public auction following advertisement and, where the execution is for a sum exceeding £20, this must be by public auction unless the court directs otherwise.[15] The jurisdiction of the county courts is local. This rule applies to the county courts' jurisdiction over the execution of warrants. Thus where the debtor has property outside the jurisdiction of the county court from which the warrant against him was issued (called the "home court"), the warrant must be sent to the district judge of the county court for that district for execution.[16]

c Attachment of earnings

Prior to 1970, attachment of earnings orders could only be made in matrimonial causes under the provisions of the Maintenance Orders Act 1958. Following recommendations of the Payne Committee[17] the procedure was extended by the Administration of Justice Act 1970 to judgment debts generally in virtual substitution for the powers of committal to prison under the Debtors Act 1869, though, as noted below, the power of committal was retained in a few cases. The relevant provisions of the 1970 Act were repealed and consolidated by the Attachment of Earnings Act 1971.

---

13 County Courts Act 1984, s 85.
14 If a suspended warrant has taken effect, there is no power to suspend it further: *Moore v Lambeth County Court Registrar* [1969] 1 All ER 782; [1969] 1 WLR 141; cf, however, *R v Bloomsbury and Marylebone County Court, ex parte Villerwest Ltd* [1976] 1 All ER 897; [1976] 1 WLR 362.
15 County Courts Act 1984, s 97.
16 *Ibid*, s 103.
17 Cmnd 3909 of 1969.

An application for an attachment of earnings order may be made by the person entitled to the benefit of the judgment or order, where the relevant order is an administration order[18] by any of the creditors scheduled to the order or (where the application is for an order to secure maintenance payments) by the judgment debtor himself.[19] The application is generally to the court for the district in which the debtor resides and must be served, in the same manner as a fixed date summons, not less than 21 clear days before the return day. The debtor must then, within eight days of service, complete and return a form containing full details of his employment, pay and income, financial liabilities and proposals for payment of the debt,[20] which proposals are notified to the applicant. The district judge may by notice require any person appearing to have the debtor in his employment to supply particulars of the debtor's earnings.

The application is heard by the district judge who may hear it in chambers, evidence being given by affidavit. If the debtor does not attend, the district judge may adjourn the hearing and notify the debtor of the date of the adjourned hearing; if the debtor then fails to attend or attends but refuses to give evidence, he may be imprisoned by the judge for up to 14 days. An attachment of earnings order may be made in respect of any sums payable by way of wages or salary or by way of pension.[1] The order requires the debtor's employer to make periodical deductions from the debtor's earnings and to pay them to the collecting officer of the court; the order specifies the "normal deduction rate" and the "protected earnings rate", the latter being the amount which the court decides the debtor must retain out of his earnings in any event.[2] It is the duty of both debtor and employer to notify the court of changes in the debtor's employment. As long as an attachment of earnings order is in force, no execution for the recovery of the judgment debt may issue without the leave of the court.[3]

d Judgment summons

This is a method of enforcing a judgment for the payment of money in that it enables the court to ascertain the debtor's means, to order payment of the debt by instalments (where the debt is a High Court debt it is not likely that the debtor will have had an opportunity to pay by instalments) and, as a final sanction, to imprison the debtor.

Imprisonment for civil debt as such was abolished by the Debtors Act 1869, section 4. However there remained a few cases under that Act in which a defaulting judgment debtor might be committed to prison. These are contained in section 5 of the Act which empowers any court to commit to prison for a term not exceeding six weeks or until payment of the sum due any person who defaults in paying a debt, or instalment of a debt, due from him under any order of that or any other competent court. This power can only be exercised by a judge who must be satisfied that the defaulter has, or has had, since the date of the judgment against him, the means to pay. It does not, therefore, render a defaulter liable to imprisonment where he simply has not the means of pay. His conduct must be in the nature of a contempt.[4]

However the power to commit under section 5 of the Debtors Act was severely curtailed by the Administration of Justice Act 1970, and the power is now exercisable by county courts only in respect of High Court or county court maintenance orders

---

18   *Infra.*
19   Attachment of Earnings Act 1971, s 3(1).
20   *Ibid*, s 14; Ord 25, r 81; Form N56. Failure to comply with this or other requirements under the Act is an offence punishable as a contempt of court with imprisonment for not more than 14 days (*ibid*, s 23).
1   Attachment of Earnings Act 1971, s 24.
2   *Ibid*, s 6. There is provision for variation and discharge of orders in ss 9–11 of the Act.
3   *Ibid*, s 8.
4   *Re Edgcome* [1902] 2 KB 403.

and orders for the payment of certain debts of a public nature such as income tax and national insurance contributions.[5]

Imprisonment does not extinguish the debt, although the debtor cannot be committed twice in respect of the same debt (though he can be committed separately in respect of separate instalments of the same debt). Since the 1970 Act, imprisonment in respect of civil debt is extremely rare and the judgment summons is of far less practical importance than formerly. Furthermore on a judgment summons the court has power, instead of making a committal order, to make an attachment of earnings order.[6] The plaintiff must file the appropriate request in the office of the county court for the district where the debtor resides or carries on business. Where the judgment in question is not a county court judgment he must also produce an office copy of the judgment or order, an affidavit verifying the amount due and a copy of the sheriff's return to any writ of execution issued in the High Court.[7] The county court will then issue a judgment summons which is served on the defendant not less than 14 days before the day fixed for the hearing.[8]

At the hearing there will be an enquiry into the debtor's means. The judgment creditor may give evidence, orally or by affidavit, as to the debtor's means and the debtor will also be required to undergo a sworn examination as to his means. If he does not appear at the hearing the judge may adjourn the hearing and order the defendant to attend the adjourned hearing. This order must be served personally on the defendant not less than five clear days before the date fixed for the adjourned hearing.[9] If he does not attend then the judge may commit him to prison for not more than 14 days.[10]

If the judge is satisfied that the debtor has had the means to pay the debt but has not done so he may commit the defendant to prison for a term not exceeding six weeks. In fact the judge usually makes an order for payment by instalments if this has not already been done. If the judgment summons was issued in respect of a default on an instalment the judge will more readily make a committal order but even then it will usually be suspended provided the debt is paid within a specified time.

e Administration orders

The great advantage of attachment of earnings orders is that they provide a means of intercepting the earnings of judgment debtors and thereby ensuring, so far as possible, that the debtor with insufficient assets to justify execution process pays his debts, albeit slowly. By the nature of things it is often the case that a judgment debtor has outstanding against him not one but several judgment debts. In such a case there is provision in the Attachment of Earnings Act 1971[11] for the making of a "consolidated attachment order" which is an attachment of earnings order for the payment of two or more judgment debts.

An alternative procedure in the case of insolvent debtors lies in the power of county courts to make administration orders. An administration order is an order providing for the administration of the debtor's estate by the court. The court may make such an

---

5   Administration of Justice Act 1970, s 11, Sch 4.
6   Attachment of Earnings Act 1971, s 3(4), (6).
7   Ord 25, r 11.
8   Ord 28, r 3.
9   Ord 27, r 8; Ord 28, r 4.
10 County Courts Act 1984, s 110.
11 Section 17. Application for a consolidated attachment order may be made by the debtor or by any person who has obtained or is entitled to apply for an attachment of earnings order or, in certain circumstances, the court may make such an order of its own motion. Payments made under the order are divided pro rata among the creditors (Ord 41, r 18).

order, under section 112 of the County Courts Act 1984[12] on the application of a debtor, creditor who has obtained a judgment against the debtor or on the motion of the court itself. The court also has an independent power under section 4 of the Attachment of Earnings Act 1971 to make an administration order on an application for an attachment of earnings order to secure payment of a judgment debt if it is of the opinion that the case is one in which all the debtor's liabilities should be dealt with together; if of the opinion that it may be such a case the court may order the debtor to furnish to the court a list of all his creditors and the amounts which he owes to them and if it appears that his total indebtedness does not exceed the county court limit the court may make an administration order.

Where an administration order has been made, any creditor, on proof of his debt before the district judge, is entitled to be scheduled as a creditor of the debtor for the amount of his proof.[13] Where the debtor applies for an order, he must file a request, verified on oath.[14] Any person who becomes a creditor after the date of the order may be scheduled as a creditor but payment to him is deferred until those who were creditors before the making of the order have been paid. The effect of an administration order is that no creditor has any remedy against the person or property of the debtor in respect of any debt which the debtor has notified to the court or which has been scheduled to the order except with leave of the court.[15] The court will, under the order, administer the debtor's estate and distribute his assets and instalments paid by him pro rata among his creditors. As has been noted, an administration order may itself be enforced by an attachment of earnings order. Further, if the debtor fails to make any payment which he is required to make by an administration order, the court may, if it thinks fit, revoke the administration order and make an order under section 429 of the Insolvency Act 1986.[16]

C   MATRIMONIAL CAUSES PROCEDURE

Both the county court and High Court have jurisdiction in matrimonial causes but generally divorce and other such proceedings should be commenced in one of the divorce county courts[17] unless by reason of their complexity, difficulty or gravity they ought to be commenced in the High Court.[18] A matrimonial cause is commenced by filing a petition in any divorce county court.[19] The form of petition is prescribed by the Matrimonial Causes Rules 1977; in addition to various formal matters the petition must contain the names of the parties, details of the marriage, the names of all children of the family, particulars of previous proceedings between the parties and details of grounds upon which relief is sought. In a divorce suit the petition must state that "the said marriage has broken down irretrievably" and must then allege which of the five facts set out in section 1(2) of the Matrimonial Causes Act 1973 the petitioner relies

12   As amended by Courts and Legal Services Act 1990, s 13(5). These amendments are not yet in force.
13   County Courts Act 1984, s 113.
14   Ord 39, rr 1, 3.
15   County Courts Act 1984, s 114(1).
16   The effect of such an order is to restrict a person's entitlement to obtain credit or enter into business transactions (see s 429(3)).
17   As nominated by Family Proceedings Rules 1991, r 2.2 (SI 1991/1247).
18   See *Practice Direction (Family Division: Distribution of Business)* [1992] 3 All ER 151; [1992] 1 WLR 586.
19   Family Proceedings Rules contain various provisions for transfer of matrimonial causes to the High Court. The Matrimonial and Family Proceedings Act 1984, s 39 confers an unrestricted power on county courts to transfer family proceedings to the High Court, either of the court's own motion or on the application of any part to the proceedings.

upon as proof of breakdown. The petition concludes with a prayer for the relief sought, which, in the case of divorce, is "that the said marriage may be dissolved", including any claim for a financial provision, costs or custody of children of the family.

The petitioner must file copies of the petition for each person to be served and their names and addresses are annexed to the petition. With the petition the petitioner must file a written statement containing details of the present and proposed arrangements for the residence, education, financial provision and contact with all children of the family under 16.[20] In addition, where a solicitor is acting for a petitioner for divorce or judicial separation a certificate as to whether or not he has discussed with the petitioner the possibility of a reconciliation must be filed with the petition. Unless the petitioner otherwise requests, the petition, together with forms of notice of proceedings and acknowledgement of service, is served by post through the court. There is no entry of appearance although a party may, within eight days of service, give "notice of intention to defend". Within 21 days of the time-limit for giving notice of intention to defend the respondent may file an answer. If an answer to the petition is filed the proceedings become defended.[1] The answer contains the respondent's defence to the allegations in the petition, together with any claim for relief which the respondent wishes to make. If an answer is filed the petitioner has 14 days in which to file a reply. The following interlocutory proceedings are similar to those in the Queen's Bench Division and may include such matters as particulars of pleading, discovery of documents and interrogatories. These are closed by the district judge giving "directions for trial"[2] whereupon the case is set down. The trial is similar to the trial of any other civil action and takes place before a judge who deals with the relief sought and ancillary matters such as custody and costs. Financial matters are usually dealt with by district judges, with a right of appeal to a judge, the appeal taking the form of a complete rehearing.[3]

In 1973 a new procedure was introduced[4] for the granting of *decree nisi* of divorce or decrees of judicial separation, virtually without a hearing. Originally limited to cases of two years' separation and consent, it now extends to undefended petitions for divorce or judicial separation on any ground. In cases to which these rules apply there is a special form of application for directions for trial which must be lodged together with an affidavit of evidence by the petitioner (and by any corroborative witness) in the prescribed form. If the district judge is satisfied that the petitioner has sufficiently proved the contents of the petition and is entitled to a decree he files a certificate to this effect whereupon a day will be fixed for the pronouncement of a decree by a judge in open court, notification of the day and place fixed being given to the parties. Where there are children of the family to whom section 41 of the 1973 Act applies (in relation to whose welfare the court has certain duties of enquiry under that section) and the respondent has neither applied for custody of or access to the children, nor returned an acknowledgement of service stating that he objects to the petitioner's claim for custody or wishes to apply on his own account, nor filed a statement as to arrangements for children proposing arrangements which differ materially from the petitioner's proposals, the district judge will fix an appointment for a judge in chambers to consider the arrangements for the children and notify the parties of that appointment. On the

---

20   And those minor children over 16 who are receiving instruction at an educational establishment or undergoing training for a trade, profession or vocation: Family Proceedings Rules, r 8(2); Form 4.
1   Until the implementation of the Matrimonial and Family Proceedings Act 1984, this required the case to be transferred to the Family Division of the High Court. This is no longer the case.
2   Family Proceedings Rules, r 33.
3   *G (formerly P) v P (ancillary relief: appeal)* [1978] 1 All ER 1099; [1978] 1 WLR 1376; cf appeals from masters (and district judges) to judges in the Queen's Bench Division (p 441, *post*).
4   Matrimonial Causes (Amendment No 2) Rules 1973.

day fixed it is unnecessary for the petitioner to appear at court or be represented; the cases are called on in a group, and, if no cause is shown to the contrary, decrees are automatically pronounced.[5]

D   TRANSFER OF PROCEEDINGS

1   From one county court to another

It must be remembered that the jurisdiction of the county courts is local, so that the plaintiff is restricted in his choice of venue. This must generally be in the court for the district in which the defendant or one of the defendants resides or carries on business, or where the cause of action wholly or in part arose. Where proceedings are commenced in the wrong county court, the judge of that court may transfer them to the court in which they ought to have been commenced.[6]

Where an action is commenced in the proper court it may still be transferred to another county court. The judge or district judge may transfer the proceedings to another court if he is satisfied that they can more conveniently or fairly be tried in that court. Secondly, where an action has been commenced in a county court against a defendant who does not reside or carry on business within the district of that court, the latter may after delivering a defence apply *ex parte* in writing for an order transferring the proceedings to the county court for the district in which he does reside or carry on business.[7]

Finally, a judgment summons can only be issued in the county court for the district in which the defendant resides or carries on business, and certain other proceedings for enforcement are confined to the debtor's local court. Thus where the action in which the judgment was obtained took place in some other court, proceedings must be transferred to the court having jurisdiction over the enforcement proceedings. The action is then transferred for all purposes to the latter court, so that money paid by the defendant must be paid to the court to which the proceedings are transferred.[8]

2   Transfer between county court and the High Court

It was noted earlier[9] that the jurisdiction of county and High Court is now largely concurrent. The criteria determining the appropriate court of trial were noted, and these apply equally to issues of transfer as to the commencement of the action.

---

5   See *Practice Direction (Matrimonial Causes; Special Procedure)* [1977] 1 All ER 845; [1977] 1 WLR 320.
6   See p 411, *ante*.
7   Ord 16, r 4(1).
8   Ord 25, r 2. The proceedings in question are judgment summonses, applications for charging orders under s 1 of the Charging Orders Act 1979, for attachment of earnings orders and for orders for the oral examination of a debtor under Ord 25, r 3.
9   See p 341, *ante*.

Chapter 19

Costs

A GENERAL PRINCIPLES

I Who must pay costs?

There are two sets of costs. First there are the costs which each party will have to pay to his own solicitor. These must be paid irrespective of the outcome of the action and, subject to the Rules, depend upon the contract between solicitor and client. Secondly there are the costs which one side may be ordered to pay to his opponent. These must be assessed or "taxed" by the court and will very rarely cover the full amount that a party has to pay to his own solicitor. It follows that even a litigant who is completely successful will often have to pay some costs himself. These represent the difference between the amount he pays his solicitor and the amount he recovers from his opponent, and are sometimes described as "irrecoverable costs". If the judge makes no order as to costs each party pays his own costs. In most cases, however, the judge will order one side to pay all or a proportion of the costs of his opponent. At common law a successful litigant had a right to costs but this right has been virtually removed by legislation so that at the present day the award of costs is discretionary. It is not, of course, an absolute discretion and it is a wrong exercise of the discretion to deprive a party of his costs if he has been completely successful and guilty of no misconduct.[1] In addition there are statutory matters on the exercise of this discretion, of which the following should be specially noted.[2]

a Costs should follow the event

Unless there are special factors present, a successful party may expect his costs from an unsuccessful opponent. Nevertheless there is clearly a power to deprive a successful party of his costs on the ground that he has conducted the litigation dishonestly or

---

1 *Donald Campbell & Co Ltd v Pollak* [1927] AC 732. See remarks of Viscount Cave LC at 811–812.
2 Though mention may also be made of the Slander of Women Act 1891, s 1 and the Rent Act 1977, s 141(4).

recovered only a small part of his claim.[3] In an extreme case a successful plaintiff may have to pay the costs of the defendant.[4] There is jurisdiction to order a successful defendant to pay costs but this jurisdiction is only exercisable in the most exceptional circumstances.[5]

There has been a considerable volume of litigation as to what is "the event" in an action.[6] In a simple action involving one plaintiff, one defendant and a single issue, no difficulty arises; the event is judgment on that issue. However, where there are several parties or several issues the situation is more complex. It must be noted, however, that costs are completely within the discretion of the court. In *Aiden Shipping Co Ltd v Interbulk Ltd*[7] the House of Lords stressed that section 51 of the Supreme Court Act 1981 permitted the ordering of costs against non-parties, and that:

> "Courts of first instance are ... well capable of exercising their discretion under the statute in accordance with reason and justice."[8]

It should, however, be noted that this was a case where a close relationship existed between the third party (who was in fact a party to a related action) and the parties to the cause in respect of which the costs were awarded.[9] Guidance as to how the power to award costs in such cases should be used was given by the Court of Appeal in *Symphony Group plc v Hodgson*[10]: it was exceptional for a non-party to be ordered to pay such costs, particularly if the party had a cause of action against the non-party. Fair procedures should be followed to ensure that the non-party had the opportunity to make representations, and to ensure that cross-examination of a non-party is not simply being directed to the issue as to whether the court should make a costs order against that non-party.

SEVERAL PARTIES

Where a plaintiff properly joins several defendants and succeeds against some but fails against others, the court may, in its discretion, order the costs of a successful defendant[11] to be paid directly or indirectly by an unsuccessful defendant. Conversely, where one defendant is sued by several plaintiffs, some of whom succeed and some of whom fail, the defendant should make a special application for the extra costs he has incurred through the presence of an unsuccessful plaintiff.[12] It may also be that a "costs sharing order" is made pre-trial. This may require a plaintiff in a multi-party action to contribute to costs incurred either personally or through the legal aid fund whilst conducting lead actions.[13]

3   *Barnes v Maltby* (1889) 5 TLR 207; *O'Connor v Star Newspaper Co Ltd* (1893) 68 LT 146.
4   See *Alltrans Express Ltd v CVA Holdings Ltd* [1984] 1 All ER 685; [1984] 1 WLR 394.
5   *Knight v Clifton* [1971] Ch 700; [1971] 2 All ER 378. There was no such power prior to the Judicature Act 1890 (now Supreme Court Act 1981, s 51(1)). An order against a successful defendant was made in *Ottway v Jones* [1955] 2 All ER 585; [1955] 1 WLR 706.
6   See *Reid, Hewitt & Co v Joseph* [1918] AC 717.
7   [1986] AC 965; [1986] 2 All ER 409.
8   Per Lord Goff [1986] AC at 981; [1986] 2 All ER at 416.
9   See [1986] 2 All ER at 416; *Steele Ford & Newton v Crown Prosecution Service* [1994] 1 AC 22; [1993] 2 All ER 769; *Shah v Karanjia* [1993] 4 All ER 792.
10   [1994] QB 179; [1993] 4 All ER 143.
11   *Bullock v London General Omnibus Co* [1907] 1 KB 264; *Sanderson v Blyth Theatre Co* [1903] 2 KB 533.
12   *Keen v Towler* (1924) 41 TLR 86.
13   See *Davies v Eli Lilly & Co* [1987] 3 All ER 94; [1987] 1 WLR 1136. In that case the plaintiff was one of some 1,500 plaintiffs, of whom about 1,000 were legally aided, bringing actions arising out of their treatment with the drug Opren. Certain "lead actions" were nominated to decide common issues. Such an order is probably not made under Ord 62 r 3(3).

SEVERAL CAUSES OF ACTION

Where several causes of action are tried together the court will, if the issues are severable, order the costs of them to be taxed separately.[14] The effect is that the plaintiff will recover the costs of the causes of action upon which he succeeds, and the defendant will be awarded the costs of the others. However this method of taxation is not possible where the several causes of action arise out of the same transaction. In such cases the judge may order that the whole of the successful plaintiff's costs be taxed, but that he shall recover only a fixed proportion of the taxed costs from the defendant.[15]

COSTS OF INTERLOCUTORY PROCEEDINGS

There will be various interlocutory applications made by each party throughout the action. There are two forms of order with respect to the costs of these applications. The court may make a special order as to the costs of these applications. The court may make a special order as to the costs of the individual application upon making or refusing an interlocutory order, that is to say that the costs be awarded to the plaintiff or defendant "in any event".[16] Alternatively the court may order that the costs of the application be "costs in the cause" which means that the party who is eventually successful will recover the costs of the application. A modification of the latter order is "plaintiff's costs in cause" or "defendant's costs in cause", the effect of which is that if the plaintiff, in the former case, or the defendant, in the latter, is eventually successful, he will be awarded his costs of the interlocutory application in question, whereas if he is ultimately unsuccessful, each party pays his own costs of the interlocutory application. A third possibility is "costs reserved", ie to be dealt with at some later stage, usually following the trial. On summons for directions the normal order is "costs in cause", on the basis that there has to be a summons, irrespective of what orders are made on the summons.

b   Payment into court

It has been noted that a payment into court (unless it is an element in a substantive defence) can affect only costs and not liability or damages. The effect is that if the successful plaintiff recovers no more than the amount paid in, in respect of one or more causes of action, he will be ordered to pay the defendant's costs of those causes of action from the date of payment in. He will still be entitled to his costs to the date of payment in, though these are often small consolation by comparison.[17]

c   Supreme Court Act 1981, section 51

Where an action is commenced in the High Court which should, in the opinion of the trial court, have been commenced in a county court, the costs awarded to the party may be reduced by up to 25%.[18] This will chiefly be relevant to personal injuries

---

14   As to what is an "issue", see *Howell v Dering* [1915] 1 KB 54, at 63; *Reid, Hewitt & Co v Joseph* [1918] AC 717. Any item of costs attributable to more than one issue will be divided between the issues.

15   *Cinema Press Ltd v Pictures and Pleasures Ltd* [1945] KB 356; [1945] 1 All ER 440; cf *Cassell & Co Ltd v Broome* [1972] AC 1027; [1972] 1 All ER 801.

16   Ord 62, r 3.

17   Ord 62, r 5; where a payment in is accepted, with other claims being abandoned, the plaintiff is entitled to his full costs: *Hudson v Elmbridge Borough Council* [1991] 4 All ER 55; [1991] 1 WLR 880.

18   Supreme Court Act 1981, s 51(8), (9), as substituted by the Courts and Legal Services Act 1990, s 4.

claims,[19] which are required to be commenced in the county court unless the amount expected to be recovered is £50,000 or more.[20]

Section 51(6) of the 1981 Act (as substituted) also permits the court to make a "wasted costs" order against a legal or other representative.[1] It permits the court to disallow costs incurred, or to make an order requiring personal payment, as a result of improper, unreasonable or negligent acts or omissions by such representatives, or in respect of costs which, in the light of such an act or omission, it would be unreasonable to expect the party on whose behalf they were incurred to pay.

This provision was the subject of judicial scrutiny and comment in *Re a Barrister (Wasted Costs Order) (No 1 of 1991)*.[2] The court identified a three-stage test:

(a) Had the legal representative of whom complaint was made acted improperly, unreasonably or negligently?
(b) If so, did such conduct cause the applicant to incur unnecessary costs?
(c) If so, was it in all the circumstances just to order the legal representative to compensate the applicant for the whole or part of the relevant costs?

However, in *Ridehalgh v Horsefield*[3] the court stressed that care should be taken not to create a new and costly form of satellite litigation. "Improper conduct" was conduct which would justify disciplinary action; "unreasonable", means not permitting of reasonable explanation; "negligent" bears the meaning of a failure to act with the competence to be reasonably expected of ordinary members of the profession. It is not improper to pursue a hopeless case, unless that amounts to an abuse of process. Nor is any distinction to be drawn between legally aided and self-financing litigants.[4] A wasted costs order may well be justified where an advocate's conduct of court proceedings is quite plainly unjustifiable. Above all, such applications should not be used as a means of intimidation, and should normally be dealt with at the conclusion of the trial.

Having considered the question of which side must pay costs, the judge must decide what is to be the basis of taxation, for this will determine how much of an opponent's costs the loser will have to pay.

2 The taxation of costs

a Bases of taxation

It was stated at the beginning of this chapter that there are two sets of costs; costs as between a solicitor and his own client, and costs as between the parties. The bases upon which these bills are taxed differ.

Regarding costs between a solicitor and his own client, each party must pay his own solicitor's costs as a contractual debt.[5] Very often the client will simply pay the

---

19   See p 341, *ante*.
20   See p 342, *ante*.
1   See p 251, *ante*.
2   [1993] QB 293; [1992] 3 All ER 429.
3   [1994]Ch 205; [1994] 3 All ER 848.
4   See also *Symphony Group plc v Hodgson* [1994] QB 179; [1993] 4 All ER 143.
5   A lay litigant appearing in person used not to be entitled to remuneration for the time and labour expended in preparation of his case, though a solicitor is entitled to have his bill taxed as if acting independently: *Eastwood Lloyds Bank Ltd v Eastwood* [1975] Ch 112; [1974] 3 All ER 603.

bill presented to him without knowing or wishing to know of his right to have it taxed.[6] He has, however, a right to have the bill taxed. In this case the bill will be taxed on the indemnity basis. This means that "all costs shall be allowed except in so far as they are unreasonable in amount or have been unreasonably incurred."[7] All costs incurred with the express or implied approval of the client are deemed to be reasonable.[8] The result is that the client must pay his solicitor all costs unless they are both unauthorised and certified by the taxing master to be unreasonable, in which case the solicitor will have to pay them personally.

There is one exception to this principle. Where a litigant is legally aided, his solicitor recovers from the fund his disbursements which may well be far less than the complete indemnity which a "solicitor and own client" taxation provides, which will be conducted on the standard basis (*infra*).[9] There is allowed, on this basis, a reasonable sum in respect of all costs reasonably incurred. Any doubts are resolved in favour of the Legal Aid Board. Reasonableness, both as to items and as to amount, depends upon all the circumstances of the case, such as its length, the sum involved and the complexity and novelty of the issues raised.

As to the costs between the parties, the court has jurisdiction to award a fixed sum by way of costs to be paid by a party to his opponent.[10] In any other case the costs must be taxed. There are now two possible bases of taxation which may be ordered:

(1) standard basis;
(2) indemnity basis.

(1) "Standard basis" is the usual basis of taxation between the parties[11] and it is also the least generous to the party in whose favour the order is made. On this basis are allowed "all such costs as were reasonably incurred". Any doubts about whether costs were reasonably incurred are resolved in favour of the paying party.[12] The taxing master must decide not only which items are reasonable, but also what is a reasonable amount in respect of each item. As to items allowable the master will not allow costs which may be termed luxuries, or costs thrown away by neglect of excessive caution.[13] As to scale the taxing master will have regard to Order 62, Appendix 2, which lists factors to which the master must have regard. These include the complexity and novelty of the questions involved, the skill, specialised knowledge and responsibility required by the solicitor or counsel, the amount involved and similar considerations.

(2) Where a party has acted improperly or unreasonably, that party may have disallowed all or part of the costs that would otherwise have been awarded.[14]

(3) As regards costs between solicitor and client, the application of the indemnity basis has already been noted.[15] The party in whose favour an order on the standard

---

6   Note also that there may be a contentious business agreement: Solicitors Act 1974, s 59, as amended by the Courts and Legal Services Act 1990, s 98. See further, p 259, *ante*.
7   Ord 62, r 12(2).
8   And be deemed to be reasonable in amount if that amount was agreed. Costs will be deemed to be unreasonably incurred if they are of an unusual nature, unless the client was informed that they might not be allowed on taxation.
9   In accordance with the Civil Legal Aid (General) Regulations 1989, r 107.
10 Ord 62, Appendix 3.
11 *Billson v Residential Apartments Ltd* [1992] 1 AC 494; [1992] 1 All ER 141. Where the paying party's conduct has been without merit (*House of Spring Gardens Ltd v Waite* [1991] 1 QB 241; [1990] 2 All ER 990) or oppressive (*Singh v Observer Ltd* [1989] 3 All ER 777n.) the indemnity basis may be ordered.
12 Ord 62, r 12(1).
13 *Smith v Buller* (1875) LR 19 Eq 473, at 475.
14 Ord 62, r 28.
15 See p 428, *ante*.

basis is made has to prove that the costs were reasonable in amount and reasonably incurred and the fact that they were incurred with his approval is not conclusive (as it is between a litigant and his own solicitor (*supra*)). Accordingly a party who is awarded costs on the standard basis must still pay the difference between indemnity costs, which is the basis of his personal liability, and standard basis taxation, which he receives from his opponent. The extent of this liability for extra costs will depend upon the degree of extravagance which he has authorised in the conduct of his case.

b   Review of taxation

Any party who is dissatisfied with a taxation of a bill of costs may apply in writing to the same taxing master for a review of his decision. The application must be made within 21 days and must set out the disputed items and a summary of the grounds of objection.[16] The taxing master will then review his taxation of those items and certify his grounds and reasons for allowing, disallowing or altering the amount of disputed items.[17] If still dissatisfied either party may apply within 14 days by summons to a judge in chambers for an order for a further review. The judge may review the taxation himself or refer it to another taxing master.[18]

B   ENFORCEMENT OF JUDGMENTS

I   Judgments for the payment of money

a   Enforcement in the High Court

The judgment creditor's rights in respect of which he brought the action are extinguished by the judgment. In their place he has a judgment debt. He will wish to enforce this debt which may consist of an award of damages and taxed costs, in addition to which may be included interest at a statutory rate from the date of judgment.[19] The judgment creditor may proceed to enforce the judgment[20] by any of the following five methods prescribed by Order 45, rule 1:

(i)   writ of *fieri facias*;
(ii)   garnishee proceedings;
(iii) a charging order;
(iv)   the appointment of a receiver;
(v)   writ of sequestration.

---

16   Ord 62, r 33.
17   Ord 62, r 34; see *Re Fraser, Leach v Public Trustee* [1958] 1 All ER 26; [1958] 1 WLR 6.
18   Ord 62, r 35.
19   Under the Judgments Act 1838, ss 17, 18 as amended by the Judgments Act 1838 (Judgments Debts (Rate of Interest)) Order 1985, made under the Administration of Justice Act 1970, s 44. This means the date upon which judgment is pronounced, not the date when it is perfected by entry in the appropriate record book: *Parsons v Mather and Platt Ltd* [1977] 2 All ER 715; [1977] 1 WLR 855.
20   A stay of execution, for example pending trial of a counterclaim or appeal, is often ordered by the court. However, although this operates to stay execution by fi-fa (*infra*) it does not prevent the judgment creditor proceeding by one or more of the other methods of enforcement since these do not constitute "execution"; they are alternatives to execution: *Berliner Industriebank Aktiengesellschaft v Jost* [1971] 2 QB 463; [1971] 2 All ER 1513. The Court of Appeal pointed out the need for some modification of the normal form of order.

WRIT OF *FIERI FACIAS* ("FI FA")[1]

This is directed to the sheriff of the county in which is situated the property which it is proposed to seize. Where the debtor has property in more than one county concurrent writs may be issued.[2] The writ commands the sheriff to cause to be made (*fieri facias*) in the name of Her Majesty and out of the debtor's chattels a sum sufficient to satisfy the judgment debt and interest together with the costs of execution. The sheriff may enter the judgment debtor's land (although he may not effect a forcible entry)[3] or the land of a third party if the debtor's goods are to be found thereon. He may seize and sell chattels, chooses in action such as banknotes or cheques, promissory notes and a lease belonging to the judgment debtor, which he may assign. He cannot, however, seize property which is exempt from execution. This comprises freehold interests in land, equitable interests in land, equitable interests in land or chattels, fixtures attached to land, wearing apparel, bedding and tools and implements of trade[4] and goods belonging to a third party. The latter provision operates to exempt property which is subject to a hire purchase agreement.

A writ of execution may be issued within the six years following the judgment or order, or later with leave.[5] It may be executed within 12 months of issue on any day not excepting Sunday.[6] There are several other cases in which leave is required, notably where the writ is to be executed against the property of a partner in a firm where the judgment is against the firm,[7] against any person not a party to the original proceedings such as an assignee and against persons represented in a representative action.[8]

It is not unusual for a sheriff to find that goods which he has seized or is about to seize in execution are claimed by a third party such as a hire purchase finance company. His proper course of action in such a situation is to interplead. To do this he issues an interpleader summons serving it on the execution creditor and the claimant.[9] All three parties attend before the master on the return day. The master may try the issue himself, direct an issue to be stated and tried or otherwise deal with the summons as he might deal with a stakeholder's interpleader summons.[10]

The sheriff must make arrangements for the sale of the property seized in execution. Such sale should normally be by public auction and should not take place on the judgment debtor's premises.[11] In practice the sheriff himself takes no part in enforcement and a local auctioneer, acting as a sheriff's officer, usually takes possession of the goods and arranges the auction, or they are left in the possession of the judgment debtor subject to periodic inspection by the sheriff's officers. This arrangement is termed "walking possession" of the goods. In practice the judgment debtor will invariably pay the debt if he can to avoid a sale of his property. Comparatively few

1 High Court enforcement by this means, of judgments less than £2,000 in value, can only occur in respect of High Court judgments. The High Court may enforce by this means county court judgments between £2,000–£5,000, and all claims over that must be enforced in the High Court: High Court and County Courts Jurisdiction Order 1991, art 8.
2 Ord 47, r 2.
3 *Semayne 's case* (1604) 5 Co Rep 91a.
4 There is no longer a prescribed value above which such goods are unprotected.
5 Ord 46, r 2(1)(a).
6 The Sunday Observance Act 1677 having been repealed by the Statute Law (Repeals) Act 1969.
7 Ord 81, r 5(4).
8 Ord 15, r 12(3).
9 Ord 17, r 1(1)(b).
10 See p 379, *ante*.
11 Ord 47, r 6; *Watson v Murray & Co* [1955] 2 QB 1; [1955] 1 All ER 350.

sales take place because the court may stay execution on application if the applicant is unable from any cause to pay the money.[12]

GARNISHEE PROCEEDINGS

The purpose of these proceedings is to enable the judgment creditor to have assigned to him the benefit of any debt owed by a third party (the garnishee) to the judgment debtor. A garnishee order will only issue in respect of a legal debt presently owing to the judgment debtor. A common object of garnishee proceedings is a credit balance at the judgment debtor's bank.[13] Earnings may be garnished but only where the right to them has accrued, so that future earnings cannot be garnished. There is, in fact, no way of seizing or intercepting the judgment debtor's future earnings in the Queens' Bench Division.[14]

The judgment debtor may be required to attend before a master to submit to an oral examination as to what debts are owing to him and as to what property or means, if any, he has of satisfying the judgment.[15] When these matters have been ascertained, by examination or otherwise, the judgment creditor may apply *ex parte* on affidavit for an order *nisi* which is served on the garnishee personally and, unless the court otherwise directs, on the judgment debtor.[16] This order calls upon the garnishee either to pay the debt, or so much of it as may be sufficient to satisfy the balance of the judgment debt, to the judgment creditor or show cause for not so doing. If the garnishee fails to comply or show cause the order is made absolute and execution may issue against the garnishee to the extent of his obligation, which is, in effect, assigned to the execution creditor.[17] If the garnishee disputes liability to pay the debt claimed to be due from him[18] the master may determine the question at issue summarily or determine the manner in which it shall be tried, no consent being required to trial before a master.[19]

---

12   Ord 47, r 1(1)(b). It may also do so if there are special circumstances which render it inexpedient to enforce the judgment or order (Ord 47, r 1(a)); under this rule execution may be suspended where a debtor company has entered into an informal scheme of arrangement with the majority of its creditors and where not to stay execution would bring down the company and compel it into a winding up or, at least, a statutory scheme of arrangement: *Prestige Publications Ltd v Chelsea Football and Athletic Co Ltd* (1978) 122 Sol Jo 436. The case is a good illustration of the modern tendency of the courts not to permit one creditor to steal a march over other creditors of an insolvent debtor; see also *Rainbow v Moorgate Properties Ltd* [1975] 2 All ER 821; [1975] 1 WLR 788 (see p 434, *post*); *D Wilson (Birmingham) Ltd v Metropolitan Property Developments Ltd* [1975] 2 All ER 814; *Roberts Petroleum Ltd v Bernard Kenny Ltd* [1983] 2 AC 192; [1983] 1 All ER 564. In these cases similar principles were applied to prevent creditors obtaining and enforcing garnishee orders and charging orders (as to which see *infra*) so as to obtain preference over other creditors.
13   *Rogers v Whitely* [1892] AC 118. The Supreme Court Act 1981, s 40 brought within the scope of garnishee orders "any deposit account with a bank or other deposit-taking institution"; this includes, for example, the National Savings Bank and the Post Office. A debt which is not assignable, such as state pension, maintenance or the pay of a member of the armed forces, cannot be attached.
14   *Mapleson v Sears* (1911) 105 LT 639. Future earnings may be attached in respect of a maintenance order under the Attachment of Earnings Act 1971, s 1. Attachment of earnings orders may be obtained in respect of judgment debts only by transferring the judgment to a county court; see p 436, *post*.
15   Ord 48, r 1.
16   Ord 49, r 3(1). The immediate effect of the order is to bind the debt specified in the order from the moment of service of the order.
17   Ord 49, r 4. The order absolute may be enforced in the same manner as any other order for the payment of money.
18   He may, for example, allege a counterclaim against the judgment debtor: *Hale v Victoria Plumbing Co Ltd* [1966] 2 QB 746; [1966] 2 All ER 672.
19   Ord 49, r 5.

Where money is standing to the credit of the judgment debtor in court, garnishee proceedings cannot be taken in respect of that money but the judgment creditor can apply by summons for an order for the payment out of all or any part of such money. This summons must be served on the judgment debtor at least seven days before the return day.[20]

CHARGING ORDER

The judgment creditor may apply *ex parte* on affidavit for an order imposing a charge on property of the kind specified in section 2 of the Charging Orders Act 1979. This comprises any interest held by the debtor beneficially in:

(1) land;
(2) securities of various kinds;
(3) funds in court; and
(4) any interest under a trust.

In addition where the debtor is a trustee of property his interest may be the subject of a charging order if the judgment or order was made against him in his capacity as trustee or the whole beneficial interest under the trust is his alone or shared with others who are all jointly liable to the creditor for the same debt. Thus, for example, if the property in question is a house in the joint names of husband and wife, the legal estate may be charged if both the husband and wife are liable to the judgment creditor, whereas if only one is liable, then all that can be charged is the beneficial interest of that one. An order may also be made charging a partnership interest.

(1) *Land*   If he discovers that the judgment debtor has land or an interest in land within the jurisdiction, the judgment creditor may apply for an order creating a charge over the land or over the interest in the land.[1] An order *nisi* is made in the first instance specifying the time and place for further consideration of the matter and imposing the charge until that time. Unless the judgment debtor pays the debt or shows cause at that time the order will be made absolute. The charge so created is a general equitable charge and the judgment creditor should register it in the Land Charges Registry under the provisions of the Land Charges Act 1925. There are two important advantages of registration: a purchaser takes the land subject to the charge (registration amounting to notice) and priority is obtained over subsequent chargees. A land charge may be enforced by an order for sale in the Chancery Division.[2]

(2) *Securities*   If the judgment debtor has government stock or stock or shares in any registered company these cannot be seized in execution of a writ of *fi-fa* because a share certificate is not a negotiable instrument. It is simply evidence of obligations owed by the company which has issued it to the person named in the certificate. The judgment creditor's proper course is to apply for an order *nisi* creating a charge over

---

20   Ord 49, r 9.
1   Ord 50, r 1. This was introduced by the Administration of Justice Act 1956, s 35(1) to replace the old writ of *elegit*.
2   Ord 31, r 1. However, it seems that a charging order on an undivided share in land is not registrable; *Perry v Phoenix Assurance plc* [1988] 3 All ER 60; [1988] 1 WLR 940.

the shares.[3] The effect of such an order is that no subsequent disposition by the judgment debtor is valid as against the judgment creditor. Unless the judgment debtor shows cause the charging order is made absolute. There is no provision for registering a charge on securities corresponding to the registration of land charges. The judgment creditor, to prevent a disposition of the securities by the judgment debtor, must serve on the company in which the shares are held a "stop notice". The effect is that the company on whom the notice is served must not register a transfer of the shares without serving notice on the judgment creditor, who may apply to the Chancery Division for an order prohibiting the transfer.[4] After the expiration of six months from the charging order *nisi* the judgment creditor may proceed to realise his charge by an order for sale obtainable in the Chancery Division.

(3) *Funds in court*   The judgment debtor may have an interest in funds or securities in court. This might occur, for example, where the judgment debtor has made a payment into court as security for costs. The court may make a "stop order" prohibiting any dealing with the whole or any part of the funds in question. Application for such an order is by summons in the cause or matter relating to the funds in court or, if there is no such cause or matter, by originating summons.[5] The summons must be served on every person whose interest may be affected by the order and on the Accountant General. The judgment creditor may enforce his charge by applying by summons for an order for payment out of the money or so much of it as is sufficient to satisfy his charge.[6]

(4) *Interest under a trust*   In relation to partnership property the sheriff cannot levy execution upon property belonging to a partnership in which the debtor is a partner (unless the judgment is against the firm). Nonetheless the judgment creditor may apply by summons to the master for an order charging the partner's interest in the partnership property.[7] The jurisdiction to create such a charge derives from section 23 of the Partnership Act 1890. The creation of a charge on a partnership interest gives the other partners the option of purchasing the interest charged.[8] Failing this the judgment creditor may apply by summons for the appointment of a receiver who will receive on behalf of the judgment creditor money accruing from the debtor's interest in the partnership.[9]

The power of the court to make charging orders, and indeed garnishee orders, is a discretionary one. It will be appreciated that the effect of such orders is to give the plaintiff priority over unsecured creditors of the defendant. Accordingly such orders should not be made against an insolvent defendant so as to place the plaintiff at an advantage over other creditors if it would be inequitable so to do.[10]

---

3   Charging Orders Act 1979, s 2(2)(b); the order may extend to any dividend or interest payable (*ibid*, s 2(3)).
4   Ord 50, r 15.
5   Ord 50, r 10.
6   Ord 49, r 9. If the judgment debtor is insolvent the judgment creditor is in the position of a secured creditor to the extent of the sum in court; *WA Sherratt Ltd v John Bromley (Church Stretton) Ltd* [1985] QB 1038; [1985] 1 All ER 216.
7   Ord 81, r 10.
8   Partnership Act 1890, s 23(3).
9   Ord 51, r 3; Ord 30, *infra.*
10   *Rainbow v Moorgate Properties Ltd* [1975] 2 All ER 821; [1975] 1 WLR 788; *Roberts Petroleum Ltd v Bernard Kenny Ltd* [1983] 2 AC 192; [1983] 1 All ER 564 (p 61, n 2, *supra*); see also, to similar effect, Charging Orders Act 1979, s 1(5).

APPOINTMENT OF A RECEIVER BY WAY OF EQUITABLE EXECUTION[11]

This is a method of enforcement directed at the interception of certain classes of income and profits before they reach the debtor so that he does not have the opportunity of disposing of them to the detriment of the judgment creditor. The judgment creditor may apply by summons or motion to the court to appoint some person as a receiver to receive income such as rents or profits in respect of any interest in land, legal or equitable, or of any interest in chattels which could not be reached by a writ of *fi-fa.*[12] It should be stressed, however, that a receiver cannot be appointed to receive the judgment debtor's future earnings of employment for, as stated earlier, there is no direct means of attaching earnings in the Queen's Bench Division.

Before appointing a receiver the court will consider whether the probable costs of the appointment are justified by the amount claimed and the amount likely to be recovered by the receiver, and may direct an enquiry on these matters before making an appointment.[13] The general powers and duties of receivers appointed by the court are contained in Order 30. The receiver is usually required to provide a guarantee as security for what he receives as receiver.[14] The receiver is allowed a proper remuneration which is fixed by court. His obligation is to submit accounts to the court for approval as and when ordered to do so and to pay into court the amounts shown by his accounts to be due.[15]

Prior to 1971, committal for contempt of court was an indirect means of enforcing a judgment debt. However section 11 of the Administration of Justice Act 1970 limited the jurisdiction of the High Court to commit to prison in respect of non-payment of a debt due under a judgment or order to cases of default in respect of maintenance orders. Since these orders are invariably made in the Family Division, committal in the Queen's Bench Division for non-payment of a debt is effectively abolished (though, as will be seen, it remains a sanction for failure to comply with orders other than orders for the payment of money). There remains, however, one process of contempt in respect of failure to pay judgment debts, the procedure by writ of sequestration.

WRIT OF SEQUESTRATION[16]

In cases of contempt of court a committal order is sometimes accompanied by a writ of sequestration. The two have much in common in that they are both indirect methods of enforcement being in the nature of punitive measures. As indicated above, although committal to prison in respect of a judgment debt (other than a maintenance order) has been abolished, a writ of sequestration may still issue in respect of continuous failure to comply with an order for the payment of money, although the procedure is very rarely used in such cases, save occasionally against corporate bodies. A writ of sequestration may issue in any case in which a person refuses or neglects to do an act within a specified time or disobeys an order requiring him to abstain from doing some act. The writ commissions not less than four persons[17] to enter upon and take possession of all the real and personal estate of the judgment debtor and to keep the same under sequestration until the debtor complies with the judgment. If a fine has been imposed

---

11   Ord 51, r 3. The expression "equitable execution" is explained by the fact that this method of enforcement originated in the Court of Chancery. It is, however, misleading since it is not confined to equitable interests, nor is it a method of execution. It is a method of enforcement alternative to execution; see *Re Shephard* (1889) 43 Ch D 131, at 137.

12   The power is now contained in Supreme Court Act 1981, s 37.

13   Ord 51, r 1.

14   Ord 30, r 2.

15   Ord 30, rr 3–6.

16   Ord 45, r 5.

17   As to the position of sequestrators and their potential liability for negligence, see *Inland Revenue Commissioners v Hoogstraten* [1985] QB 1077; [1984] 3 All ER 25.

for contempt of court and remains unpaid, a writ of sequestration may issue to enforce payment of the fine. The procedure on application is by notice of motion for leave to issue the writ stating the grounds of the application and accompanied by an affidavit in support.[18] The application must be heard in open court.[19]

A writ of sequestration is a practical alternative to committal where the judgment debtor is a corporation and the writ may issue, with leave, against the property of any director or other officer of the body. In relation to a writ of sequestration, the position of third parties is similar to that of third parties in relation to injunctions; although they are not directly bound by the order, they must not knowingly take any step which would obstruct enforcement of the order. Thus, for example, a bank is under a duty to disclose to sequestrators balances which are held to the credit of the contemner and to pay over such sums on demand (unless a third party, such as the bank itself, has a prior charge on the balance).[20]

2   Other methods of enforcing judgments for the payment of money

a   County court enforcement

A judgment of the High Court for the payment of money may be enforced in a county court as if it were a judgment of the county court only by transferring the action to a county court. However, even without such transfer, High Court judgments may be the subject of (1) judgment summons procedure; or (2) attachment of earnings in a county court.[1] The primary advantage of the judgment summons, as opposed to the power of the High Court to require a debtor to attend an examination as to his means under Order 48, rule 1, is that the county court has power to make an order for payment by instalments in the first instance. Secondly, an attachment of earnings order may now be obtained, under the provisions of the Attachment of Earnings Act 1971, in a county court in respect of a High Court judgment debt. Both of these methods of enforcement are extremely practical in relation to debtors who have insufficient assets to satisfy the judgment but who have earnings out of which the debt, or at least part of it, might be recoverable.

b   Bankruptcy

Where the debtor's total debts exceed the "bankruptcy level" and he is unable to pay his debts, the judgment creditor may issue a bankruptcy petition.[2] Bankruptcy proceedings are, in general, an unsatisfactory method of enforcement though the mere threat of bankruptcy proceedings may be a sufficient sanction where the judgment debtor is a person, such as a solicitor, whose livelihood cannot survive bankruptcy.[3]

---

18   Ord 46, r 5.
19   Except in the special cases set out in Ord 52, r 6 where the application may be heard in private, notably where the case involves the wardship, adoption, guardianship, custody or maintenance of infants, proceedings relating to mental patients, cases where a secret process, discovery or invention is involved or where it appears to the court that in the interests of the administration of justice or for reasons of national security the application should be heard in private.
20   *Eckman v Midland Bank Ltd* [1973] QB 519; [1973] 1 All ER 609, a decision of the now defunct National Industrial Relations Court, arising out of the refusal of the Amalgamated Union of Engineering Workers to recognise or comply with orders of that court.
1   County Court Rules 1981, Ord 25, r 11, Ord 27, Ord 28, r 1.
2   For details of procedure see p 419, *post.*
3   Insolvency Act 1986, s 267.

3 Judgments and orders other than for the payment of money

a Judgments for possession of land[4]

A judgment or order for the giving of possession of land may be enforced by any one or more of the following three methods:

(1) writ of possession. This is the direct method of enforcement. It directs the sheriff to enter the land and cause the plaintiff to have possession of it. The writ cannot be issued without leave,[5] application for which is *ex parte* on affidavit, and leave cannot be granted unless it is shown that every person in actual possession of the whole or any part of the land has received sufficient notice of the proceedings to enable him to apply to the court for any relief to which he may be entitled, such as relief against forfeiture.[6] In practice judgments or orders for the possession of land are always enforced in this way;
(2) order of committal; and
(3) writ of sequestration, in theory at least, is an indirect method of enforcement but is almost never employed in this context. The procedure on application for leave to issue a writ of sequestration has already been noted; committal procedure is considered below.

b Judgments for delivery of goods[7]

The appropriate writ of execution for a judgment for the delivery of goods depends upon whether or not the judgment contains an alternative provision for payment of the assessed value of the goods.

WRIT OF SPECIFIC DELIVERY
This is the appropriate writ where the judgment orders the delivery of specific goods without an alternative provision for the payment of their assessed value. It directs the sheriff to seize the goods described in the writ and deliver them to the plaintiff.

WRIT OF DELIVERY
This is appropriate where the judgment orders the delivery of goods with an alternative provision for payment of their assessed value. The writ directs the sheriff to seize the goods described and deliver them to the plaintiff and, if he cannot obtain the goods, to levy execution upon the goods and chattels of the defendant to an extent sufficient to realise the assessed value of the goods. If the alternative course is adopted the writ has the same effect as a writ of *fi-fa*. Whether a writ of delivery or a writ of specific delivery is issued the sheriff is authorised to enforce by execution the payment of any money ordered to be paid by way of damages or costs by the judgment or order which is to be enforced by the writ together with the costs of execution and interest.

Orders of committal and writs of sequestration are theoretically available as indirect methods of enforcement but, as in the case of orders for the possession of land, their use is generally inappropriate in this context.

4　Ord 45, r 3.
5　Except where the judgment or order was given or made in a mortgage action (Ord 45, r 3(2)) or where the order was made in summary proceedings for possession of land against trespassers following the issue of an originating summons under Order 113 (Ord 113, r 7); as to this procedure, see p 343, *ante*.
6　Ord 45, r 3(3).
7　Ord 45, r 4.

c   Judgments to do or abstain from doing any act

Where the judgment or order requires the defendant to perform any act other than the payment of money or the delivery of goods or land or requires him to abstain from doing any act, it is enforceable only by: (1) order of committal; and (2) writ of sequestration.

The order to which these rules apply may have been, for example, an injunction[8] (mandatory or prohibitory), an order to deliver an account, an order to produce a document or an order to answer an interrogatory. Procedure by writ of sequestration has already been noted. In cases of contempt a writ of sequestration is an appropriate method of enforcement against a corporate body and is often joined with a committal order in respect of the officers of the corporate body.[9]

COMMITTAL ORDERS

A committal order is an order committing a person to prison for contempt of court. An order may be made where a person required by a judgment or order to do an act within a time specified in the judgment or order refuses or neglects to do it within that time,[10] or a person disobeys a judgment or order requiring him to abstain from doing an act. A master or registrar has no power to make a committal order. The order is made by a judge following a motion in open court.[11] Notice of motion must have been served on the person sought to be committed together with a copy of the affidavit which must support the application. Personal service is generally required.[12] Committal must be for a fixed period although earlier discharge may be ordered if the court deems that the contemner has "purged his contempt" and releases him, generally on his undertaking to perform (or abstain from repeating, as the case may be) the act in respect of which he was committed. As an alternative to imprisonment there is jurisdiction to impose a fine for contempt.

It was formerly held that a person might not be committed for a mere neglect as opposed to a "wilful and contumacious disobedience of a court order".[13] However in *Knight v Clifton*[14] the Court of Appeal rejected this principle and asserted that in proceedings for committal for breach of an order of the court there is no need to prove that the conduct in question was wilful or contumacious; when an injunction prohibits an act, the performance of that act is a contempt irrespective of questions of intention unless otherwise stated on the face of the order. This authority was cited with apparent approval by the House of Lords in *Heaton's Transport (St Helens) Ltd v Transport and General Workers' Union*[15] inasmuch as the House of Lords accepted that wilfulness was not an element in contempt of court; however it appeared also to accept that conduct which was "casual or accidental and unintentional" would not amount to contempt. To this extent the assertion in *Knight v Clifton* that questions of intention are irrelevant is probably too wide.

8   An undertaking given to the court is equivalent to an injunction against the person giving the undertaking so that breach of the undertaking is contempt of court: cf *Biba Ltd v Stratford Investments Ltd* [1973] Ch 281; [1972] 3 All ER 1041.
9   See, for example, *Worthington v Ad-Lib Club Ltd* [1965] Ch 236; [1964] 3 All ER 674.
10   Save where the act is the payment of money, in which case (except in the case of maintenance orders) there is no power of committal (Administration of Justice Act 1970, s 11); see p 435, *ante*.
11   Except in the cases set out in Ord 52, r 6 in which the court may sit in private.
12   Ord 52, r 4.
13   See for example, *Worthington v Ad-Lib Club Ltd* [1965] Ch 236; [1964] 3 All ER 674.
14   [1971] Ch 700; [1971] 2 All ER 378, disapproving *Worthington v Ad-Lib Club Ltd, supra*); see also *Re Mileage Conference of the Tyre Manufacturers' Conference Ltd's Agreement* [1966] 2 All ER 849; [1966] 1 WLR 1137 in which breach of an undertaking was held to be contempt where the persons concerned had taken all reasonable care to avoid a breach.
15   [1973] AC 15; [1972] 3 All ER 101.

Chapter 20

Civil Appeals

A RIGHTS OF APPEAL

There is no common law right of appeal from a superior court. It was established in *Darlow v Shuttleworth*[1] that the common law jurisdiction of the Court of King's Bench to hear proceedings in error from the inferior courts of local jurisdiction was transferred by the Judicature Acts to the divisional court of the Queen's Bench Division. However since this right of appeal is confined to situations in which proceedings in error might have been brought at common law and since the local courts have ceased to function,[2] common law rights of appeal are virtually obsolete.

Apart from this all rights of appeal are statutory. The basic rights of appeal in the Supreme Court are now contained in the Supreme Court Act 1981 although numerous statutes create particular rights of appeal in special cases.

I Appeal to the Court of Appeal; civil division

The fulcrum of the system of civil appeals is the civil division of the Court of Appeal. In a number of cases the Court of Appeal hears appeals directly from the decision of the court below. In other cases the appeal lies to the High Court in the first instance and then to the Court of Appeal. Section 16(1) of the Supreme Court Act 1981 provides: "subject as otherwise provided by this or any other Act the Court of Appeal shall have jurisdiction to hear and determine appeals from any judgment or order of the High Court."[3] Appeals from county courts lie, subject to the conditions set out in section 77 of the County Courts Act 1984, to the Court of Appeal with the single exception of appeals from orders in bankruptcy matters which lie in the first instance to a divisional court of the Chancery Division and thence with special leave to the Court of Appeal. The Court of Appeal also has jurisdiction to hear appeals from the Employment Appeal

---

1   [1902] 1 KB 721.
2   See p 41, *ante*
3   Where the House of Lords grants leave to appeal direct from the High Court to the House, appeal to the Court of Appeal is excluded (Administration of Justice Act 1969, s 13(2)).

Tribunal,[4] the Restrictive Practices Court,[5] the Lands Tribunal[6] and certain other statutory tribunals[7] and from commercial judges sitting as arbitrators or umpires under section 4 of the Administration of Justice Act 1970.

a   Leave to appeal

As a general rule appeal lies to the Court of Appeal as of right but in certain cases leave is required. The more important cases in which leave is required are:

(1)   from the determination of an appeal by a divisional court of the High Court;[8] leave may be given either by the divisional court or by the Court of Appeal;

(2)   from a consent order or an order which is solely an order as to costs which by law are left to the discretion of the court; leave can only be granted by the court below;[9]

(3)   from an interlocutory order or judgment made or given by a judge (with certain exceptions, notably where the liberty of the subject or the custody of infants is involved or where an injunction or the appointment of a receiver has been granted or refused);[10]

(4)   from the decision of a county court judge, where the value of the claim in contract, tort or certain other monetary claims does not exceed £5,000, or in other cases within the equity and probate jurisdiction, does not exceed £15,000.[11] Leave is not required where the determination sought to be appealed from includes or preserves an injunction or relates to upbringing of a child;

(5)   from the decision of a commercial judge on an arbitration appeal.[12]

b   Right of appeal excluded

Although section 16 of the Supreme Court Act 1981 confers a general right of appeal from the High Court to the Court of Appeal there are certain cases specified in the Act

4   Industrial Tribunals Act 1996, s 37; appeal lies only on a point of law.

5   Restrictive Practices Court Act 1976, s 10.

6   Lands Tribunal Act 1949, s 3(4). Appeal from tribunals is by case stated on a point of law. The procedure is governed by Ord 61.

7   Transport Tribunal, Commons Commissioners, Foreign Compensation Commission.

8   Supreme Court Act 1981, s 18(1)(e). Leave may be granted by the House of Lords for an appeal direct to the House from the divisional court (Administration of Justice Act 1969, s 12(2)(c)). See also Tribunals and Inquiries Act 1992, s 13(4) as to appeals under that Act.

9   Supreme Court Act 1981, s 18(1)(f). Although the Court of Appeal will, despite this statutory restriction, entertain on appeal where it adjudges that the court below has in effect failed to exercise its discretion at all: see *Alltrans Express Ltd v CVA Holdings Ltd* [1984] 1 All ER 685; [1984] 1 WLR 394 and the cases cited therein. Where there are genuine grounds of appeal in addition to an appeal against an order as to costs the appeal is not as to costs only even if all the other grounds of appeal are unsuccessful: *Wheeler v Somerfield* [1966] 2 QB 94; [1966] 2 All ER 305.

10   Supreme Court Act 1981, s 18(1)(h). Whether an order is final or interlocutory depends on the nature of the application to the court rather than the nature of the order made. Thus, for example, the refusal of a county court judge to order a new trial is an interlocutory order as is an order dismissing an action for want of prosecution (see p 367, *ante*), even though the practical effect may be final in that the action is at an end; the test stated above was laid down by the Court of Appeal in *Salter Rex & Co v Ghosh* [1971] 2 QB 597; [1971] 2 All ER 865 and applied in *Moran v Lloyd's* [1983] QB 542; [1983] 2 All ER 200 and *White v Brunton* [1984] QB 570; [1984] 2 All ER 606. Order 59, r 1A (made under power conferred by s 60 of the Supreme Court Act 1981) lists orders which, for this purpose, are to be treated as final or interlocutory, as the case may be.

11   For the complete list, see County Court Appeals Order 1981.

12   Arbitration Act 1996, s 69; in this case a second prerequisite is that the judge certify that the question of law to which his decision relates either is of general public importance or is one which for some other special reason should be considered by the Court of Appeal. Note also Ord 58, r 7 under which appeal of the summary determination by a judge of a stakeholder's interpleader lies only with leave.

and in the Rules in which the right of appeal is excluded. Of these the most important are:

(1) from any judgment of the High Court in any criminal cause or matter.[13] In fact it is not true to say that these appeals do not lie to the Court of Appeal; they do not lie to the civil division of the Court of Appeal but they generally do lie to the criminal division with the notable exceptions of appeals from the divisional court of the Queen's Bench Division which lie, under the Administration of Justice Act 1960, direct to the House of Lords;[14]
(2) from a decision which is provided by any statute to be final;[15]
(3) from a decree absolute for dissolution or nullity of marriage provided that the party wishing to appeal had time and opportunity to appeal from the decree *nisi*;[16]
(4) from any judgment order or decision of a circuit judge in the course of official referees' business except as provided in Order 58, rule 4.[17]

c   Appeals from the registrar and the single judge

An application for leave to appeal to the Court of Appeal is determined by a single judge and there is no appeal from his decision.[18] Other applications are, according to their nature, heard either by the full court, or by a single judge or by the registrar of civil appeals. An appeal lies from the registrar to a single judge.[19] Appeal from decisions of a single judge (other than the determination of an application for leave to appeal) lies to the full court.[20]

2   Appeals from masters and district registrars

The general rule is that an appeal lies as of right from any order of a Queen's Bench Division master to a judge in chambers.[1] In certain exceptional cases, set out in Order 58, rule 2, appeal lies from a master direct to the Court of Appeal. These are appeals from any judgment, order or decision (other than an interlocutory judgment, order or decision) given or made:

---

13   Supreme Court Act 1981, s 18(1)(a). An appeal from, or application for leave for, an application for judicial review of a decision not to refer a conviction to the Court of Appeal (Criminal Division) under Criminal Appeal Act 1968, s 17 is a "criminal cause or matter": *R v Secretary of State for the Home Department, ex p Garner* ((1991) 3 Admin LR 33). The key issue is the nature of the matter being reviewed in the judicial review proceedings: *Carr v Atkins* [1987] QB 963; [1987] 3 All ER 684.
14   See p 442, *post.*
15   Supreme Court Act 1981, s 18(1)(c); *Lane v Esdaile* [1891] AC 210. Statutes under which an appeal to the High Court is final are listed in Ord 94, r 6.
16   *Ibid*, s 18(1)(d).
17   Under Ord 58, r 4(1) an appeal lies from a decision of an official referee on a point of law or as to costs or, with the leave of the official referee or the Court of Appeal on any question of fact. There is, in addition, a right to appeal against a committal order made by an official referee under the Administration of Justice Act 1960, s 13.
18   Supreme Court Act 1981, s 54(6).
19   Ord 59, r 14(11); the appeal is by way of fresh application made within 10 days of the district judge's determination (*ibid*) and the single judge approaches the matter *de novo* unfettered by the registrar's decision: *Van Stillevoldt (CM) BV v El Carriers Inc* [1983] 1 All ER 699; [1983] 1 WLR 207.
20   Ord 59, r 14(12); the appeal is by way of fresh application made within 10 days of the single judge's determination.
1   Ord 58, r 1. Likewise, appeal from any order of a district judge (Ord 58, r 3).

(a) on the hearing or determination of any cause, matter, question or issue tried before
     or referred to him under Order 36, rule 11 (power to order trial by or reference of
     issues of fact to a master);
(b) on an assessment of damages or the value of goods.[2]

Appeals from masters and district registrars take the form of a complete rehearing;
that is to say the issue which was argued below is argued out again *de novo* before the
judge. Since it is a complete rehearing, the parties are not confined to the points which
were taken before the master. Nor are they confined to the evidence which was before
the master and it is quite common for further evidence, in the form of affidavits, to be
put in before the judge.

3   Appeal to the House of Lords

In civil matters appeal lies from the civil division of the Court of Appeal to the House
of Lords only with leave of the Court of Appeal or of the House of Lords.[3] There is no
requirement that the appeal be based on a point of law, though almost always appeal
to the House of Lords is based upon a point of law rather than on an issue of fact or an
award of damages. Although leave is the only prerequisite for appealing, no appeal
lies from the decision of the Court of Appeal where any statute expresses the decision
of the Court of Appeal to be final. Thus, for example, the decision of the court is final
on any appeal from a county court in probate proceedings[4] and from the determination
by a divisional court of the Chancery Division of a bankruptcy appeal from a county
court.[5] The Administration of Justice Act 1969, Part II provides for a "leapfrog" appeal
direct from the High Court to the House of Lords subject to the grant of a certificate
by the trial judge and of leave by the House of Lords in any case in which appeal lies
to the Court of Appeal (with or without leave).[6] For the purpose of European
Community law the House of Lords is clearly "a court or tribunal of a Member State,
against whose decision there is no judicial remedy under national law" within the
meaning of Article 177(3) of the EC Treaty, so that where a question arises concerning

(a) the interpretation of the Treaty;
(b) the validity and interpretation of acts of the institutions of the Community; or
(c) the interpretation of the statutes of bodies established by an Act of the Council,
     where those statutes so provide,

the House of Lords is bound to refer that question to the European Court for a
preliminary ruling (unless, of course, the High Court or Court of Appeal has already
referred the question in the same case) and, having obtained the ruling, is bound to
follow it.[7]

---

2   An appeal lies in respect of any other matter that requires determination in order to assess the damages
    or value: RSC (Amendment) 1992/638.
3   Administration of Justice (Appeals) Act 1934, s 1.
4   County Courts Act 1984, s 82.
5   Insolvency Act 1986, s 375.
6   See p 439, *ante*; the principal conditions precedent to the grant of a certificate are (1) the consent of
    all parties, and (2) that the case involves a point of law of general public importance either relating to
    the construction of an enactment or being a point on which the judge was bound by precedent: *American
    Cyanamid Co v Upjohn Co* [1970] 3 All ER 785; [1970] 1 WLR 1507, a case concerning a petition
    for revocation of a patent, was the first "leap-frog" appeal heard by the House of Lords.
7   See, generally, *HP Bulmer Ltd v J Bollinger, SA* [1974] Ch 401; [1974] 2 All ER 1226, and p 117,
    ante.

B   PROCEDURE IN THE COURT OF APPEAL

Substantial amendments to procedure in the Court of Appeal were made by the Supreme Court Act 1981 and, more particularly, by a revision of Order 59 in 1982. These changes, and the reasons for them, were fully explained at the time by the Master of the Rolls, Sir John Donaldson.[8] The most important changes were the creation of a new office of registrar of civil appeals,[9] much wider use of two-judge courts, allocation of interlocutory applications to the registrar or to a single judge, standardisation of the time for appealing, alteration of the listing arrangements and the introduction of a practice of handing down written judgments.

An appeal is initiated by serving notice of motion in respect of the whole or any part of the judgment or order in respect of which the appeal is brought. This notice must set out the grounds of appeal shortly but with sufficient particularity to enable the respondent to ascertain exactly what issues are being raised against him. Thus, merely to complain that the trial judge misdirected the jury would be inadequate; the particular nature of the misdirection must be specified. The notice must also contain a statement of the order for which the appellant is applying to the court, and the list in which he proposes to set down the appeal. The notice must be served on all parties interested in the appeal.[10] Notice of appeal must be served within four weeks[11] of the date upon which judgment in the court below was signed or entered, though this time may be extended either by the Court of Appeal or, if application is made before the time expires, by the court below. Having served the notice of appeal, the appellant must within seven days apply to set down the appeal. To do so he produces an office copy of the judgment or order appealed from, together with two copies of his notice of appeal, one of which must bear the appropriate judicature fee stamp and an office copy of any list of exhibits made at the hearing.[12] The appeal is then set down in the appropriate list to await hearing. The next stage in the procedure is that the appeal will appear in the List of Forthcoming Appeals. Then, within 14 days, the appellant must lodge with the registrar bundles of the copy documents which are going to be required for the use of the court on the hearing; these include the notice of appeal, any respondent's notice, the judgment or order of the court below, the pleadings, a transcript of the official shorthand note of the judge's reasons (or a note of them if there is no official shorthand note), such part of the transcript of the official shorthand note of the evidence (or the judge's note if there is no official shorthand note) as is relevant to the appeal and such affidavits and exhibits used below as are relevant to the appeal.[13] After the documents have been lodged the registrar may give such directions "as appear best adapted to secure the just, expeditious and economical disposal of the appeal" and may summon the parties to appear before him for this purpose.[14]

8   The statement is reported as *Practice Note* [1982] 3 All ER 376; [1982] 1 WLR 1312 and repays study.
9   Supreme Court Act 1981, s 89(1), Sch 2. His functions include supervising the listing of appeals, giving directions as to the conduct of pending appeals (under Ord 59, r 9(3), (4)) and hearing interlocutory applications such as applications for extension of time, leave to amend a notice of appeal, security for costs, leave to adduce further evidence, expedition and vacating a hearing date.
10   Ord 59, r 3. Appeals from tribunals to the Court of Appeal are by case stated, the procedure being governed by Ord 61.
11   Ord 59, r 4. The only exceptions to the standard four-week period are: (1) six weeks in the case of appeals under s 14 of the Social Security Act 1980 (Ord 59, r 21) (see now Social Security Administration Act 1992, s 24); and (2) 14 days in the case of appeal from an order referring a question to the European Court (Ord 114, r 6).
12   Ord 59, r 5.
13   Ord 59, r 9; see also *Practice Note* [1976] 3 All ER 416, and now [1997] 2 All ER 927.
14   Ord 59, r 9(3), (4).

Thereafter the appeal will appear in the list of forthcoming appeals and will be listed for hearing. In order to save the time of the court in recording counsel's arguments, and in order to enable the court to examine those arguments in advance of the hearing, counsel submit in advance of the hearing "skeleton arguments" containing a numbered list of the points which each counsel proposes to argue and the references to the material to which counsel will refer in support of these points.[15] Counsel is not expected, or permitted, to go through lengthy recitals of fact, and citation from authority. The purpose of the skeleton argument is to focus the attention of the court, and advocates, on the issues to be argued orally. Bundles of documents relevant to the case are also prepared, although the court has become increasingly concerned about the volume of documentation lodged for the purposes of appeals and applications which is unnecessary and never referred to.[16] Henceforth, core bundles of documents must contain only those documents which the Lords Justices will need to pre-read or to which it will necessary to refer at the hearing, either in support of, or in opposition to, the appeal or application.

Appeals may be heard by two or three judges of the court.[17] Except in the case of applications for a new trial or to set aside a verdict, appeal is "by way of rehearing". That is to say the court hears full legal argument from both sides and may substitute its own judgment for that of the court below. However it is not a complete rehearing, as it is before the judge in chambers or in the Crown Court in criminal cases, since the court does not, in practice, hear again the testimony of the trial witnesses, but merely sees transcripts of their evidence.[18] In addition the appellant is normally confined to the points of law which he raised in the court below. He may in certain circumstances, discussed below, be allowed to take new points on appeal but he cannot, except with leave of the Court of Appeal, rely on any grounds of appeal or apply for any relief not specified in his notice of appeal.[19]

A respondent who, not having appealed from the decision of the court below, seeks to have the judgment or order of the court below either varied or affirmed on other grounds need not enter a separate notice of appeal. His proper course is to serve on the appellant, and on any other party directly affected, a "respondent's notice" specifying the grounds of his contention and any alteration in the judgment or order which he requests. Thus, for example, if the appellant is appealing against a finding as to his liability the respondent may, by his notice, appeal against his award of damages. A respondent's notice must be served within 21 days of service of the notice of appeal, and the respondent must, within two days after service of the notice, file two copies of the notice.[20]

C   POWERS OF THE COURT OF APPEAL

The Court of Appeal has all the powers, authority and jurisdiction of the court or tribunal from which the appeal was brought in any matter before it.[1] The court has power to

---

15   *Practice Note* (n 13, *supra*).

16   See *Practice Notes* at [1997] 2 All ER 927; [1995] 2 All ER 451.

17   Supreme Court Act 1981, s 54; if they are equally divided the case must, on the application of any party, be re-argued before another court containing an uneven number of judges (*ibid*, s 54(5)). The Court of Appeal has indicated that in complex cases, where a difference of judicial opinion may be anticipated, counsel should apply for a hearing before an uneven number: *Wandsworth London Borough Council v Winder* [1985] AC 461; [1984] 3 All ER 83.

18   Ord 59, r 12.

19   Ord 59, r 3(3).

20   Ord 59, r 6.

1   Supreme Court Act 1981, s 15. These powers are both statutory and inherent. Thus the Court of Appeal may strike out a notice of appeal in the same way as the High Court may strike out a statement of

examine trial witnesses though it rarely does so, being content in most cases to rely upon the judge's note or a transcript of the official shorthand note. It has power to receive further evidence orally, by affidavit or by deposition taken before an examiner but, where there was a trial or hearing on the merits, the Court of Appeal will not admit further evidence (other than evidence as to matters which have occurred since the trial) except on special grounds.[2] In *Ladd v Marshall*,[3] Denning LJ prescribed the following three conditions for the reception of fresh evidence in the Court of Appeal:[4]

"first, it must be shown that the evidence could not have been obtained with reasonable diligence for use at the trial; secondly, the evidence must be such that, if given, it would probably have an important influence on the result of the case, though it need not be decisive; thirdly, the evidence must be such as is presumably to be believed, or, in other words, it must be apparently credible though it need not be incontrovertible."[5]

This statement was approved by the House of Lords in *Skone v Skone*[6] where the evidence consisted of a bundle of love letters written by the co-respondent in a divorce suit to the wife which tended to prove adultery between them. The trial judge had dismissed the husband's petition and accepted the co-respondent's evidence to the effect that adultery had not taken place. It was argued that these letters (which were in the possession of the wife) could have been obtained by seeking discovery of documents from the wife. The House of Lords rejected this argument on the basis that the husband had no reason to suspect the existence of such letters, that the letters, if genuine, falsified the judge's finding to such an extent that it would be unjust to leave matters where they were and, furthermore, that there was a strong prima facie case of deception of the court. It must be emphasised that these rigorous conditions need not be satisfied in respect of evidence of matters occurring after the trial. Evidence will be admitted of matters occurring after the trial where the basis on which the trial judge gave his decision has been clearly falsified by subsequent events.[7]

Since appeal to the Court of Appeal is "by way of rehearing" the Court of Appeal has full power to make any order which should have been made in the court below[8] and to substitute its own order as to liability, quantum or costs for that of the court below. In addition the Court of Appeal is not confined to the points raised in the notice of appeal or respondent's notice. It may, though it rarely does, take any point of law or fact so far as is necessary to ensure the determination on the merits of the real question in issue between the parties. Should the Court of Appeal wish to decide an issue of fact which has not been pleaded, an extremely infrequent contingency, it may allow

claim either under Ord 18, r 19 or in exercise of its inherent power: *Aviagents Ltd v Balstravest Investments Ltd* [1966] 1 All ER 450; [1966] 1 WLR 150.

2   Ord 59, r 10(2). A hearing under Ord 14 is a "hearing on the merits" for this purpose; *Langdale v Danby* [1982] 3 All ER 129; [1982] 1 WLR 1123.

3   [1954] 3 All ER 745; [1954] 1 WLR 1489; applied in *Roe v Robert McGregor & Sons Ltd* [1968] 2 All ER 636; [1968] 1 WLR 925.

4   [1954] 3 All ER 745, at 748; [1954] 1 WLR 1489, at 1491.

5   Compare the somewhat wider provisions for the reception of fresh evidence in the criminal division of the Court of Appeal; see *post*.

6   [1971] 2 All ER 582; [1971] 1 WLR 812.

7   *Mulholland v Mitchell* [1971] AC 666; [1971] 1 All ER 307 (in which the plaintiff's condition had unexpectedly deteriorated between the trial and the hearing of the appeal) and *McCann v Sheppard* [1973] 2 All ER 881; [1973] 1 WLR 540 (in which the plaintiff had died while his appeal was pending). Where the fresh evidence becomes available to a party during the trial he must adduce it then and there, even though this may necessitate an adjournment. He must not disregard it and thereafter found an application for a new trial upon the fresh evidence: *Cowling v Matbro Ltd* [1969] 2 All ER 664; [1969] 1 WLR 598.

8   Ord 59, r 10(3).

the pleading to be amended.[9] The court has power to order an appellant to give security for the costs of an appeal in any case in which he could be required to give security for costs under Order 23[10] and, in addition, in "special circumstances"[11] generally where the appellant would be unable to pay the costs of the appeal if unsuccessful. Although an appeal does not operate as a stay of execution the Court of Appeal has power to order a stay of execution though it will only do so if there is some good reason, since it inclines against depriving a person of the fruits of his litigation. If a stay of execution is ordered on an appeal from the High Court, interest is allowed on the judgment debt unless there is an express order to the contrary.[12] Special note should be taken of the power, which the High Court also possesses, to refer a question to the European Court for a preliminary ruling. The procedure is governed by Order 114 and the principles upon which the Court of Appeal act have already been examined.[13] In addition to the powers of the Court of Appeal listed above there is an extremely important power which the High Court does not possess.[14] This is the power to order a new trial, the exercise of which is considered in detail below.

D   THE APPROACH OF THE COURT OF APPEAL TO THE DETERMINATION OF APPEALS

I   Appeal on a point of law

Most appeals to the Court of Appeal are based on a point of law. It has already been stated that, notwithstanding the general power of the Court of Appeal to take a point not raised therein, the court usually confines itself to the points raised in the notice of appeal or respondent's notice. Furthermore there is a general rule that a party cannot take on appeal a point which he did not take in the court below.[15]

To this rule there are two important exceptions. The first occurs where the point of law was expressly reserved in the court below. This might occur where the court below was not free to consider the point because it was bound by precedent on that point, whereas the Court of Appeal might be free to reconsider the precedent in question. Secondly, the Court of Appeal will allow a point to be taken, and indeed will take the point itself, where not to do so would result in an abuse of the court's process. Thus the illegality of a contract may be raised on appeal even though the point was overlooked in the court below.[16]

---

9   See *Bell v Lever Brothers Ltd* [1932] AC 161, at 216.
10   See p 392, *ante*.
11   Ord 59, r 10(5).
12   Ord 59, r 13.
13   See p 118, *ante*.
14   Although s 17(2) of the Supreme Court Act 1981 enables rules of court to provide for an application for a new trial to be determined by the High Court where the trial was by a judge alone and no error of the court at the trial is alleged.
15   The rule is not, however, invariable so that where all the findings of fact upon which the application of the point of law depends were made by the trial judge, the Court of Appeal may allow the point to be taken: *Donaghey v P O'Brien & Co* [1966] 2 All ER 822; [1966] 1 WLR 1170 (affirmed on this point, though reversed on another ground, *sub nom Donaghey v Boulton and Paul Ltd* [1968] AC 1; [1967] 2 All ER 1014); cf *Wilson v Liverpool City Council* [1971] 1 All ER 628; [1971] 1 WLR 302.
16   See *Snell v Unity Finance Ltd* [1964] 2 QB 203; [1963] 3 All ER 50; cf *Oscroft v Benabo* [1967] 2 All ER 548; [1967] 1 WLR 1087; *Brady v Brady* [1989] AC 755; [1988] 2 All ER 617.

2   Appeal against a finding of fact

Since the appeal is by way of rehearing the Court of Appeal has power to substitute its own finding of fact, direct or inferential, for that of the trial judge or jury. There are, however, three restrictions upon this general power to upset findings of fact made at the trial. First, the Court of Appeal in practice confines itself to issues of fact raised in the notice of appeal or respondent's notice. Secondly, the Court of Appeal cannot make a finding in relation to a fact not pleaded, although it can give leave to amend the pleadings.[17] Finally, the court does not as a rule upset direct findings of fact, whether they were made by a judge or by a jury. The reason for this is that, as stated earlier, the Court of Appeal does not have the advantage, which the judge and jury had, of seeing the trial witnesses and observing their demeanour.[18] Consequently the jurisdiction exercised by the Court of Appeal in relation to findings of fact is confined to inferential findings of fact. The court has power to substitute its own inference from the facts as found for that of the trial judge or jury and will not hesitate to do so. Thus, for example, in one case the Court of Appeal reduced a plaintiff's award of damages by half on the basis of his contributory negligence even though there had been no finding of contributory negligence at the trial.[19] Contributory negligence, like negligence, is an inference of fact to be drawn from the facts as found. In another medical negligence action, where the crucial issue of fact was whether a hospital registrar had pulled "too long and too hard" on the head of the infant plaintiff in the course of his birth, Lord Bridge explained his willingness to uphold an appeal from the trial judge's finding in the plaintiff's favour in the following words:[20]

> "My Lords, I recognise that this is a question of pure fact and that in the realm of fact, as the authorities repeatedly emphasise, the advantages which the judge derives from seeing and hearing the witnesses must always be respected by an appellate court. At the same time the importance of the part played by those advantages in assisting the judge to any particular conclusion of fact varies through a wide spectrum from, at one end, a straight conflict of primary fact between witnesses, where credibility is crucial and the appellate court can hardly ever interfere, to, at the other end, an inference from undisputed primary facts, where the appellate court is in just as good a position as the trial judge to make the decision."

Where a jury has returned a general verdict it is impossible to distinguish direct findings of fact from inferential findings and, indeed, the jury cannot be asked, after they have returned a general verdict, to state what their direct findings of fact were.[1] The Court of Appeal, therefore, can only upset the general verdict of a jury if it cannot be supported by the evidence or is a verdict which no reasonable men could have reached.[2]

---

17   See *Bell v Lever Brothers Ltd* [1932] AC 161.
18   The Court of Appeal feels no such inhibition when the evidence at the trial was given by written statement or deposition; see *Gallie v Lee* [1969] 1 All ER 1062, at 1079; [1969] 2 WLR 901, at 921 (affirmed *sub nom Saunders (Executrix of Will of Gallie) v Anglia Building Society* [1971] AC 1004; [1970] 3 All ER 961).
19   *Hicks v British Transport Commission* [1958] 2 All ER 39; [1958] 1 WLR 493; see also *Benmax v Austin Motor Co Ltd* [1955] AC 370; [1955] 1 All ER 326; *Qualcast (Wolverhampton) Ltd v Haynes* [1959] AC 743; [1959] 2 All ER 38.
20   *Whitehouse v Jordan* [1981] 1 All ER 267, at 286; [1981] 1 WLR 246, at 269.
1   *Barnes v Hill* [1967] 1 QB 579; [1967] 1 All ER 347.
2   *Mechanical and General Inventions Co Ltd v Austin* [1935] AC 346.

3   Appeal against the exercise of a discretion

In many circumstances the judge has a discretion as to whether, and in what manner, to exercise his powers. Commonly encountered instances of judicial discretion are the discretion as to costs, the discretion whether to grant or refuse an injunction and the discretion as to the mode of trial, in particular in relation to the question of whether or not to order jury trial. However, no discretion is absolute[3] and there may be a successful appeal to the Court of Appeal in relation to the exercise of a judicial discretion if the appellant can show that the judge exercised his discretion under a mistake of law,[4] or under a misapprehension as to the facts, or that he took into account irrelevant matters or gave insufficient weight, or too much weight, to certain factors[5] or that he failed to exercise his discretion at all.[6] If the judge gives no reasons, or insufficient reasons for the exercise of his discretion, the court may infer that he has gone wrong in one respect or another.[7] The burden of proof is on the party who alleges that the discretion was wrongly exercised and, in any event, the Court of Appeal will only allow the appeal if satisfied that the judge's conclusion is one which involves injustice or was clearly wrong.[8] In *Hadmor Productions Ltd v Hamilton* Lord Diplock explained the extent of the appellate court's powers as follows.[9]

"Before adverting to the evidence that was before the judge and the additional evidence that was before the Court of Appeal, it is I think appropriate to remind your Lordships of the limited function of an appellate court in an appeal of this kind. An interlocutory injunction is a discretionary relief and the discretion whether or not to grant it is vested in the High Court judge by whom the application for it is heard. On an appeal from the judge's grant or refusal of an interlocutory injunction the function of an appellate court, whether it be the Court of Appeal or your Lordships' House, is not to exercise an independent discretion of its own. It must defer to the judge's exercise of his discretion and must not interfere with it merely on the ground that the members of the appellate court would have exercised the discretion differently. The function of the appellate court is initially one of review only. It may set aside the judge's exercise of his discretion on the ground that it was based on a misunderstanding of the law or of the evidence before him or on an inference that particular facts existed or did not exist, which, although it was one that might legitimately have been drawn on the evidence that was before the judge, can be demonstrated to be wrong by further evidence that has become available by the time of the appeal, or on the ground that there has been a change of circumstances after the judge made his

---

3   RSC (Revision) 1962, Ord 36, r 1 described the discretion as to the mode of trial as an "absolute one" but the Court of Appeal in *Ward v James* [1966] 1 QB 273, at 293; [1965] 1 All ER 563, at 568 stated that the word "absolute" either added nothing or, if it did, was ultra vires. The current Ord 33 omits the reference to an "absolute" discretion.

4   *Evans v Bartlam* [1937] AC 473; [1937] 2 All ER 646.

5   *Re F (a minor) (wardship; appeal)* [1976] Fam 238; [1976] 1 All ER 417; *Birkett v James* [1978] AC 297; [1977] 2 All ER 801.

6   *Evans v Bartlam, supra.*

7   *Ward v James* [1966] 1 QB 273; [1965] 1 All ER 563; *Re a Debtor (No 12 of 1970)* [1971] 1 All ER 504; [1971] 1 WLR 261 (affirmed [1971] 2 All ER 1494; [1971] 1 WLR 1212).

8   *Beck v Value Capital Ltd (No 2)* [1976] 2 All ER 102; [1976] 1 WLR 572n.

9   [1983] 1 AC 191, at 220; [1982] 1 All ER 1042, at 1046. The appeal was from a decision of the Court of Appeal, presided over by the then Master of the Rolls, Lord Denning, who was thought by some to be inclined to substitute his own discretion for that of the judge below rather more freely than precedent would allow. Lord Diplock had occasion to repeat, almost verbatim, the passage quoted above, in *Garden Cottage Foods Ltd v Milk Marketing Board* [1984] AC 130; [1983] 2 All ER 770, once again in reversing the decision of the Court of Appeal presided over by Lord Denning.

order that would have justified his acceding to an application to vary it. Since reasons given by judges for granting or refusing interlocutory injunctions may sometimes be sketchy, there may also be occasional cases where even though no erroneous assumption of law or fact can be identified the judge's decision to grant or refuse the injunction is so aberrant that it must be set aside on the ground that no reasonable judge regardful of his duty to act judicially could have reached it. It is only if and after the appellate court has reached the conclusion that the judge's exercise of his discretion must be set aside for one or other of these reasons that it becomes entitled to exercise an original discretion of its own."

4   Appeal against an award of damages

The approach adopted by the Court of Appeal when determining an appeal against an award of damages differs according to whether the award was made by a jury or by a judge sitting alone. Where unliquidated damages are claimed, historically the court has not interfered with the award of a jury unless the damages awarded were so large or, more rarely, so small that no jury could reasonably have given them.[10] The reason for this is that the assessment of damages is historically the province of the jury in any case. Thus juries know of no fixed scale of damages comparable to that applied by judges, and the law has not considered it desirable that they should be made aware of any such scale.[11] In the matter of damages: "the views of the juries may form a valuable corrective to the views of judges".[12]

However a new trial may be ordered if it appears to the court either that the jury took into account irrelevant factors or failed to consider matters which it ought to have considered and in consequence awarded damages which were excessive or inadequate. The case of *Lewis v Daily Telegraph Ltd*[13] provides a good example. In that case two national newspapers published on the same day paragraphs alleged to be defamatory of the plaintiffs. The jury in the first action awarded the plaintiffs a total of £100,000; in the second action two days later in which there were factors which a jury might be entitled to take into account as aggravating damages, a different jury awarded the plaintiffs a further £117,000. New trials of both actions were ordered on the ground (inter alia) that the damages in each case were excessive. The House of Lords, affirming the decision of the Court of Appeal, stated that in such a case, pursuant to section 12 of the Defamation Act 1952, each jury should be directed to consider how far the damage suffered can reasonably be attributed solely to the libel with which they are concerned, and how far it ought to be regarded as the joint result of the two libels, bearing in mind that the plaintiff ought not to be compensated twice for the same loss. In *Rantzen v Mirror Group Newspapers (1986) Ltd*[14] the plaintiff, a well-known television presenter, had been awarded £250,000 damages for defamation. The defendant appealed, on the basis that the award was excessive, and sought an order under section 8 of the Courts and Legal Services At 1990, which now provides that

---

10   *Johnston v Great Western Rly Co* [1904] 2 KB 250. The award must be an "entirely erroneous" estimate; *Banbury v Bank of Montreal* [1918] AC 626, at 694. The principle was reaffirmed by the House of Lords in *Cassell & Co Ltd v Broome* [1972] AC 1027; [1972] 1 All ER 801 where the House, by a bare majority, upheld an award of £40,000 for libel although unanimous in regarding the sum as excessive.

11   The desirability of not informing juries of awards of damages in comparable cases was reiterated by Lord Denning MR in *Ward v James* (*supra*).

12   Per Morris LJ in *Scott v Musial* [1959] 2 QB 429; [1959] 3 All ER 193.

13   [1964] AC 234; [1963] 2 All ER 151.

14   [1994] 2 QB 670; [1993] 4 All ER 975.

where the court has the power to order a new trial on the basis of excessive or inadequate damages, it may be given the power[15] to substitute the proper sum instead of ordering that new trial. The Court of Appeal concluded that this power had to be exercised in the context of Article 10 of the European Convention on Human Rights,[16] which permitted restrictions on freedom of expression only where they were necessary in a democratic society to meet a pressing social need. On this basis large awards of damages were to be subjected to very close scrutiny. The question now to be asked is whether a reasonable jury could have thought the award necessary to compensate the plaintiff. On the facts the award was excessive by any objective standard of reasonable compensation, and an award of £110,000 was substituted for that of the jury. Where the award of damages appealed against was made by a judge sitting alone the Court of Appeal will not hesitate to interfere with the assessment, not only on the ground that the judge applied a wrong principle of law in making the assessment, but also on the ground that the award is out of scale with awards in similar cases.

The matter was considered again by the Court of Appeal in *John v MGN Ltd*,[17] where the court held that when assessing compensatory damages in a defamation case a jury could in future properly be referred by way of comparison to the conventional compensation scales in personal injury cases as well as to previous libel awards made or approved by the Court of Appeal, and there was no reason why the judge, in his directions, or counsel, should not indicate to the jury the level of award which they considered appropriate. Those changes of practice would not undermine but rather buttress the constitutional role of the libel jury by rendering their proceedings more rational and so more acceptable to public opinion. The same principle also applies in actions against the police for unlawful conduct.[18]

There is, of course, no prescribed scale of damages in any type of action but, nevertheless, there is a certain degree of parity in awards in respect of similar types of damage particularly in actions for damages for personal injuries.[19] In such cases the Court of Appeal will not make small adjustments to the sum awarded though it will make a substantial adjustment if that is found necessary. In practice the court will rarely interfere unless an adjustment of at least 20% or 25% is envisaged. It is this diversity of approach to awards of damages made by judges and juries respectively that has led to the virtual disappearance of jury trial in personal injuries actions.[20]

5   Exercise of the power to order a new trial

The Court of Appeal has power under section 17 of the Supreme Court Act 1981 and Order 59, rule 11 to order a new trial. It may exercise this power on an appeal from a judge and jury or from a judge alone just as it can on a motion for a new trial following a trial with a jury.[1] A new trial may be ordered on any one issue without disturbing the finding of the court below on any other issue. Thus the Court of Appeal may order a new trial on the issue of damages while affirming the decision on the question of

15   Ord 59, r 11(4).
16   See p 127, *ante*.
17   [1996] 2 All ER 35.
18   See *Thompson v Commissioner of Police for the Metropolis* [1998] QB 498; [1997] 2 All ER 762.
19   See observations of Lord Denning MR on scales of damages in personal injuries actions in *Ward v James* [1966] 1 QB 273, at 296 *et seq*; [1965] 1 All ER 563, at 572 *et seq*. For an illustration of the tendency to standardise damages see *Bastow v Bagley & Co Ltd* [1961] 3 All ER 1101; [1961] 1 WLR 1494. See also *Brown v Thompson* [1968] 2 All ER 708; [1968] 1 WLR 1003.
20   See p 232, *ante*.
1   Compare the more limited power of the Criminal Division of the Court of Appeal to order a new trial; see p 555, *post*.

liability. Indeed if the only ground of application is the amount of damages the court should limit the new trial to that issue and leave the findings as to liability undisturbed.[2] If there is a new trial, that trial is completely independent of the first trial. The mode of trial need not be the same, no estoppel arises as a result of the first trial and the parties may raise new points and may contest issues left uncontested at the first trial. The costs of the first trial are sometimes ordered to await the outcome of the new trial though, as a rule, the successful applicant ought to be allowed the costs of his application.[3] There are several grounds upon which a new trial may be ordered of which the more important are set out below.

a Misdirection

The judge has a duty to provide the jury with an adequate direction as to what are the issues to be decided, what is the law applicable to those issues and what is the effect in law of the evidence received. If this is not done there is a misdirection. The expression "misdirection" includes a failure to direct at all.[4]

b Improper admission or rejection of evidence

c Wrongful withdrawal of a question from the jury

It is expressly provided by order 59, rule 11(2) that the court is not bound to order a new trial on any of the above three grounds "unless in the opinion of the Court of Appeal some substantial wrong or miscarriage has been thereby occasioned".[5] There will not have been an operative miscarriage of justice unless the appellant has lost a chance of success which was fairly open to him. The burden is on the party supporting the verdict to show that, on the evidence, there has been no miscarriage of justice.

d Perverse jury verdict

The Court of Appeal is slow to order a new trial on this ground and there is a heavy burden on the applicant. He must show not merely that the verdict is one which reasonable men ought not to have reached but that it is one which no jury of reasonable men, properly directed, could have found upon the evidence. This may occur either because there was no evidence at all in support of a material fact or because such evidence as there was could not reasonably be believed.

e Jury verdict as to damages

The circumstances in which the Court of Appeal is prepared to upset a jury verdict as to damages have already been noted.[6] Where the Court of Appeal does decide that damages awarded by a jury are excessive or inadequate it now has the power to substitute its own award without the consent of all parties concerned, and may also increase or reduce an award in respect of any distinct head of damages erroneously

---

2 *Tolley v JS Fry & Sons Ltd* [1931] AC 333, at 341.
3 *Hamilton v Seal* [1904] 2 KB 262; cf *Bray v Ford* [1896] AC 44.
4 *Hobbs v CT Tinling & Co Ltd* [1929] 2 KB 1.
5 Compare the wording of s 2(1) of the Criminal Appeal Act 1968; see p 552, *post*.
6 See p 450, *ante*.

included in or excluded from the sum awarded, with consent of the party who will be adversely affected by the increase or reduction.[7]

f   Discovery of fresh evidence

The principles upon which the Court of Appeal acts when considering applications for a new trial on the ground of the discovery of fresh evidence are similar to those applicable where the court is asked to receive fresh evidence on the hearing of an appeal.[8] A common example of fresh evidence which will justify a new trial is the discovery that one of the trial witnesses gave false evidence.[9]

g   Misconduct or other irregularity at the trial

A new trial may be ordered on the ground of misconduct on the part of the judge, the jury, counsel, court officers or other persons, provided that the misconduct in question prevented either party from having a fair trial. It is not sufficient that either judge or jury expressed a strong opinion in favour of one party during the trial. However new trials have been ordered where the verdict of the jury was reached by drawing lots,[10] where the jury expressed a strong opinion in favour of the plaintiff before hearing the defendant's evidence,[11] where the court was misled by counsel[12] and where the judge's constant interruptions prevented one side from conducting an effective cross-examination.[13]

h   Surprise

The applicant for a new trial on the ground of surprise must swear an affidavit setting out the facts on which he relies. He may allege, for example, that the action came on for trial unexpectedly when his witnesses were not available or that his opponent was allowed to present his case in a way for which the applicant was not prepared. Thus where, in a personal injuries action, the plaintiff at the end of the trial confronted the defendants with, and succeeded on, a case based on allegations which had not been pleaded and which the defendants had not come to the trial prepared to meet, a new trial was ordered.[14] The application will only succeed if the surprise has occasioned a substantial miscarriage of justice.

i   Judgment obtained by fraud

There are alternative methods of challenging a judgment obtained by fraud. The first is by a motion for a new trial. Alternatively the party affected may bring an action to have the judgment set aside. In either case the party has the burden of particularising and proving the fraud alleged.[15]

---

7   Ord 59, r 11(4).
8   See p 445, *post.*
9   *Piotrowska v Piotrowski* [1958] 2 All ER 729n; [1958] 1 WLR 797. A new trial was ordered in *Skone v Skone* [1971] 2 All ER 582; [1971] 1 WLR 812; see p 445, *ante.*
10   *Harvey v Hewitt* (1840) 8 Dowl 598.
11   *Allum v Boultbee* (1854) 9 Exch 738.
12   *Meek v Fleming* [1961] 2 QB 366; [1961] 3 All ER 148.
13   *Jones v National Coal Board* [1957] 2 QB 55; [1957] 2 All ER 155.
14   *Lloyde v West Midlands Gas Board* [1971] 2 All ER 1240; [1971] 1 WLR 749.
15   *Hip Foong Hong v H Neotia & Co* [1918] AC 888.

Part IV

Criminal Proceedings

CHAPTER 21

Criminal Proceedings

A INTRODUCTION

The English criminal process is, essentially, adversarial in nature.[1] The process of investigation and evidence-gathering is conducted by the police or other investigating body, with limited powers of supervision in the hands of the Crown Prosecution Service.[2] The court plays no significant part in the preparation of the case. The trial itself is not an investigation into events or allegations, but rather a hearing to decide, within a complex set of rules,[3] whether the defendant is proved to be guilty of the particular offences which the prosecution have charged him with.[4] By contrast, in many civil law jurisdictions the process is inquisitorial in nature. This term is used to describe systems where judges or magistrates supervise the pre trial investigations and preparation of the case, to a greater or lesser extent, and play a significant part in the questioning of the witness at trial, and in the decisions as to what evidence should be considered by the court. Simply put, the trial is much more of an investigation than a contest.

This adversarial characteristic has often been viewed as a strength of the English system. These strengths were identified by the Court of Appeal in *R v Mcllkenny*:[5]

"Another feature of our law, which goes hand in hand with trial by jury, is the adversarial nature of criminal proceedings. Clearly a jury cannot embark on a judicial investigation. So the material must be placed before the jury. It is sometimes said that the adversarial system leaves too much power in the hands of the police. But that criticism has been met, at least in part, by the creation of

---

1   For assessment generally of the adversarial system, see the various submissions of evidence to the Royal Commission on Criminal Justice (1993, Cm 2263, HMSO).
2   See p 251, *ante*.
3   Detailed consideration of rules of evidence is beyond the scope of this book. See, generally, Keane *The Modern Law of Evidence* (3rd Edn, Butterworths, 1996).
4   Whilst a judge has a discretion to call a witness not called by the prosecution or defence, this power should be sparingly used, and only where necessary in the interests of justice: *R v Roberts* (1984) 80 Cr App Rep 89.
5   [1992] 2 All ER 417 at 425-6.

the Crown Prosecution Service. The great advantage of the adversarial system is that it enables the defendant to test the prosecution case in open court. Once there is sufficient evidence to commit a defendant for trial, the prosecution has to prove the case against him by calling witnesses to give oral testimony in the presence of the jury. We doubt whether there is a better way of exposing the weaknesses in the prosecution case, whether the witness be a policeman, a scientist or a bystander, than by cross-examination."

Yet, despite these perceived advantages, a series of *causes célèbres*[6] focused attention on the very nature of the criminal process. The court in *R v McIlkenny* itself identified some of the weaknesses of the system, such as the imbalance in resources as between prosecution and defence, and the need for proper disclosure of prosecution evidence to the defence. Above all, the effectiveness of any system depends upon it not being abused by those who work within it.

Criticisms and concerns as to the way in which the adversarial system works go beyond the trial process itself, and include criticisms as to how criminal investigations are conducted and supervised. Many, though not all, of the difficulties encountered in a series of well-publicised miscarriages of justice stemmed not from the trial itself, but rather from the manner of investigation by the police, and from a failure to apply properly pre-trial procedures designed to ensure the fairness of the trial itself.[7] The situation was of such public concern that in 1991 the Home Secretary established a Royal Commission on Criminal Justice. Its terms of reference required it to:

"examine the criminal justice system from the stage at which the police are investigating an alleged or reported criminal offence right through to the stage at which a defendant who has been found guilty of an offence has exhausted his or her rights of appeal."

Police powers were not within its terms of reference,[8] nor were rules relating to bail or sentencing. The Commission reported in June 1993,[9] making some 352 separate recommendations. It did not recommend a fundamental change of approach, doubting whether a general move away from an adversarial approach would be desirable. It believed that a system which kept separate roles of police, prosecutor and judge offers a better protection for the innocent defendant, including protection against the risk of "unnecessarily prolonged detention prior to trial".[10] Instead, its recommendations are intended to make the existing system "more capable of serving the interests of justice and efficiency", and to deal with matters that seemed to the Commission at present to turn what ought to be a search for the truth into "a contest played between opposing lawyers according to a set of rules which the jury does not necessarily accept or even understand".[11]

---

6   *R v McIlkenny, supra; R v Maguire* [1992] QB 936; [1992] 2 All ER 433; *R v Silcott, Braithwaite and Raghip* (1991) Times, 9 December; *R v Kisco* (1992) unreported. See generally Walker and Starmer: *Justice in Error*, Blackstone Press, 1994.

7   Many of the cases in question involved alleged police malpractice. See, eg, *R v Maguire, supra.*

8   They had been the subject of consideration by the Royal Commission on Criminal Procedure, 1981, Cmn 8292, and subsequent legislation in Police and Criminal Evidence Act 1984.

9   1993, Cmn 2263. The various Research Studies published by the Royal Commission are a valuable source of data and analysis of the trial system and the operation of the criminal justice system.

10   Ch 1, para 14.

11   Ch 1, para 11.

B   THE DECISION TO COMMENCE PROCEEDINGS

1   Discretion and cautioning

The fact that an offence is believed to have been committed does not mean that the commencement of a prosecution is inevitable. Discretion exists at various stages in the criminal process as to whether a prosecution should be commenced, or the suspect cautioned formally or informally. The police and the Crown Prosecution Service or other prosecuting authority each have discretion at appropriate times.[12]

At the policing level, an individual officer has a discretion as to what action should be taken. An officer may informally caution, make an arrest[13] or formally report a suspect for prosecution. These judgments will often be reached in the light of the overall policies adopted by the police force of which the officer is a member. At a later stage, the police may have to decide whether an offender should be charged, and if so with what offence, or, alternatively, whether a formal caution should be administered.

The practice of formally cautioning, rather than prosecuting, offenders can be traced back to 1929, but has never had a statutory basis, and was first regularised by the Home Office Circular of 1978.[14] Studies showed that cautioning practices varied widely between individual police forces, despite attempts by the Home Office to achieve greater consistency.[15] Despite this, the use of cautioning powers was unsatisfactory, inconsistent and confined, in the main, to elderly offenders, those suffering mental stress and young first offenders who have committed minor offences. In 1991, some 279,000 offenders were dealt with by way of caution. Of these, 179,000 related to indictable or either way offences.[16] The Royal Commission on Criminal Justice recommended an extension of the practice to more petty offenders. However, it also identified the need for a consistent approach nationwide, cautioning to operate within national guidelines and with information being available as to cautioning practices nationwide.[17] It recommended that consideration be given to combining cautions with other support, through social services or the probation service, but recognised that a failure to prosecute an individual can itself damage confidence in the criminal justice system.

Further guidance was issued by the Home Office in 1994; the circular issued then currently governs the use of the cautioning power. Sweeping changes are now proposed in respect of children and young persons. The circular encourages the police to caution formally rather than prosecute in some circumstances. In respect of juveniles and young adults, this can be seen as an attempt to keep them out of the criminal justice system for as long as possible. For a person to be cautioned, there must be evidence of the suspect's guilt sufficient to give a reasonable prospect of a conviction, the suspect must admit guilt, and be willing to be cautioned. The circular deals with how the cautioning power should be used. It states as follows:

---

12   The discretion may be reviewable in limited circumstances on normal judicial review principles: see p 143, *ante*.

13   Arrest for the purpose of cautioning will only be lawful if the grounds for arrest in fact exists, and an arrest is in fact made. There is no power to detain for cautioning: see *Collins v Wilcock* [1984] 3 All ER 374; [1984] 1 WLR 1172.

14   Home Office Circular 70/1978, replaced by Circular 14/1985.

15   See: Wilkinson & Evans, "Police Cautioning of Juveniles The Impact of Home Office Circular 14/1985" [1990] Crim LR 165; Westwood, "The Effects of Home Office Guidelines on the Cautioning of Offenders" [1991] Crim LR 591; Evans, "Police Cautioning and the Young Adult Offender" [1991] Crim LR 598.

16   RCCJ: Ch 5, para 57.

17   *Ibid.*

(a) in deciding whether to charge or summons an offender, no account will be taken of any previous convictions, or of any earlier caution;
(b) the seriousness of the accused's action will determine whether a prosecution should take place. The police will take into account aggravating features, such as the age of the victim, and whether violence was used;
(c) the views of the victim may be important;
(d) there is a presumption in favour of a caution for juveniles, and a high probability of a caution for young adults, aged between 17 and 20 years;
(e) if a caution is appropriate, regard will then be had to the previous cautions or pending prosecutions of the offender.

There will also need to be taken in to account criteria relating to the public interest. These will include the nature of the offence, the likely penalty, the offender's age and state of health, previous criminal history, and the offender's attitude towards the offence. The circular discouraged the use of repeat cautions, except where a second offence was trivial, or a significant period of time had elapsed since the first caution.

The total effect of these provisions is that the prosecution of a juvenile is a course of action of last resort. This power to caution juveniles is now being replaced by a scheme of reprimand and warning.

2   Reprimands and warnings

Evidence shows that the great majority of young offenders commit offences only once or twice. Some 68% of juveniles who are cautioned are not cautioned again or convicted of another offence within two years.[18] The effect of the 1994 circular was to reduce the incidence of repeat cautioning, but inconsistency of practice has continued.[19] For this reason, cautioning for juveniles is abolished by the Crime and Disorder Act 1998, to be replaced by a scheme of reprimands and warnings.

In future, a constable may use the power to administer either a reprimand or a warning where he has evidence that a child or young person has committed an offence, and he considers that the evidence is such that, if that offender were prosecuted for the offence, there would be a realistic prospect of his being convicted.[20] The power only arises if the offender admits to the constable that he committed the offence, has not previously been convicted of an offence and the constable is satisfied that it would not be in the public interest for the offender to be prosecuted.

The constable may reprimand the offender if the offender has not previously been reprimanded or warned.[1] He must warn rather than reprimand if he considers the offence to be so serious as to require a warning, but an offender may not be warned more than once. It is intended that the Home Secretary will publish guidance indicating the circumstances in which it is appropriate to give reprimands or warnings, including criteria as to levels of seriousness for the purposes of deciding whether a charge, or a warning, is appropriate, the category of constables by whom reprimands and warnings may be given, and the form of a reprimand or warning.[2]

18   See *No More Excuses – A New Approach to Tackling Youth Crime in England and Wales*, Home Office, Cm 3809, 1997, at 5.9–5.10.
19   *No More Excuses*, *op cit*, at para 5.10; Evans and Ellis: *Police Cautioning in the 1990's*, Home Office, 1997.
20   Section 65(1).
1   Section 65(2).
2   Section 65(6).

The intention is that a first offence might be met with a police reprimand, provided it was not serious. Any further offence should be met with a warning: no offender should receive two reprimands, and any offence after a warning should result in prosecution except where minor in nature and at least two years have elapsed since the administration of the warning. The reprimand or warning will be given at the police station by the constable in the presence of an appropriate adult, who will be a parent, guardian, representative of local authority if in care, local authority social worker, or other responsible adult other than a police employee. The effect will be the same as a conviction for that offence, although no provisions yet exist to deal with such reprimands and warnings becoming "spent" under the provisions of the Rehabilitation of Offenders Act 1974.[3] Where a warning is given, the constable will refer the person to a youth offending team,[4] which will assess the person referred and, unless it is considered inappropriate to do so, that team shall arrange for that person to participate in a rehabilitation programme. The nature of that programme will conform to guidance issued by the Home Secretary, but might, for example, include meeting the victim, apologising for the crime and hearing about its effects, a programme of work or the payment of compensation.[5]

The decision to caution, or to prosecute instead of cautioning, is not beyond judicial scrutiny.[6] In *R v Chief Constable of Kent County Constabulary, ex parte L*[7] the Divisional Court considered that a decision to prosecute a 12-year-old girl, which was claimed to be in breach of the policy for cautioning of juveniles, was susceptible to judicial review, although on the facts found to be a proper exercise of discretion. Watkins LJ considered that the policy of cautioning, instead of prosecuting, was well settled and played a prominent part in the process of decision-making in an individual case. Care should be taken, however, to avoid "the danger of opening too wide the door of review of the discretion to continue a prosecution", and the court appeared to draw a distinction between decisions involving adults and those involving juveniles. More recently, another Divisional Court in *R v Inland Revenue Commissioners, ex parte Mead*[8] has stressed that decisions relating to adults are not beyond judicial review, although the situations in which the courts would in fact intervene will be rare.[9] Clearly, the criteria for the administration of reprimands and warnings are now to be set out in statutory form, and will be supplemented by guidance. An individual will have a legitimate expectation that that guidance will be adhered to.[10] If no reprimand, warning or (in the case of an adult) caution is administered, prosecution is the only alternative, unless the offence attracts a fixed penalty.[11]

---

3   Which treats certain convictions as "spent" after the periods specified in the Act.
4   Section 66(1). For youth offending teams, see p 576, *post*.
5   See the examples given in the Consultation Paper, op cit, instancing local initiatives on which the legislation builds.
6   There are strictly defined limits to judicial review of the decisions of a prosecution authority: see Watkins LJ in *R v General Council of the Bar, ex parte Percival* [1991] 1 QB 212; [1990] 3 All ER 137.
7   [1993] 1 All ER 756.
8   [1993] 1 All ER 772.
9   The fact that there are alternative remedies, for example to challenge for abuse of process, does not prevent the exercise of discretion itself from being challenged by way of judicial review.
10   See p 147, *ante*.
11   The Royal Commission recommended the extension of the fixed penalty system: see ch 5, para 62, and *Keeping Offenders Out of Court: Further Alternatives to Prosecution* (HMSO, 1983, Cmnd 8958). Such a scheme successfully operates in Scotland.

3   The decision to prosecute

a   Who institutes?

The commencement of criminal proceedings is theoretically in the hands of the police, although many other organisations have law enforcement powers as well.[12] It is in most cases the police who will charge individuals, take them into custody, or provide the information sufficient for the issue of a summons or a warrant for arrest. However, it is the duty of the Director of Public Prosecutions to take over the conduct of all criminal proceedings instituted on behalf of a police force.[13] The reality is, therefore, that the DPP and Crown Prosecution Service play a central role as does, in cases of serious or complex fraud, the Serious Fraud Office. The Crown Prosecution Service, which is independent of the police, does not have responsibility for the police investigation, but may be consulted on occasion by the police at the investigation stage.[14] The decision when the prosecution should be continued, and on what basis, is that of the Crown Prosecution Service, not the police. That said, concern has arisen as to delays that occur within the criminal justice system. In 1997 a report, the Review of Delay in the Criminal Justice System,[15] was published. Its recommendations included a proposal that the CPS staff should have a permanent presence within police administrative support units, and work with the police on the speedy preparation of the prosecution file. These recommendations have been accepted by the Government.[16] Although independent of the police, the CPS will work ever more closely with them. The wider organisational issues in respect of the CPS, brought to the fore by the publication in 1998 of the Gildewell Report, are dealt with elsewhere.[17]

In respect of prosecutions by persons or bodies other than the police, the Royal Commission on Criminal Procedure in 1981 concluded it would be both impracticable and undesirable to bring all prosecutions within the ambit of the Crown prosecutions arrangements.[18] Section 6 of the Prosecution of Offences Act 1985 therefore states that nothing in that Act shall preclude any person from instituting any criminal proceedings to which the Director's duty under the Act does not apply. Private prosecutions can be brought. However, some controls are needed. By section 42 of the Supreme Court Act 1981,[19] if on the application of the Attorney-General the High Court is satisfied that any person has habitually and persistently and without any reasonable ground instituted vexatious prosecution (whether against the same or different persons) the court may make a criminal proceedings order. This has the effect that no information shall be laid before a justice of the peace, and no application for leave to prefer a bill of indictment shall be made, by that person without the leave of the court. Leave is not to be granted unless the High Court is satisfied that the institution of proceedings does not amount to an abuse of process. In addition, in some cases the consent of the Attorney-General or DPP is needed.[20]

---

12   In respect of private prosecutions, see Lidstone, Hogg & Sutcliffe: *Prosecution by Private Individuals & Non Police Agencies* (Royal Commission on Criminal Procedure Research Study No 10, HMSO, 1980).

13   Prosecution of Offences Act 1985, s 3(2)(a). In important, difficult or otherwise appropriate cases the DPP may institute proceedings: s 3(2)(b). For discussion of the office of DPP, see p 251, *ante*.

14   The Royal Commission recommends greater use of this practice: see ch 5, para 17.

15   The Narey Report, published 27 February 1997. See, generally, p 493, *post*.

16   *Government's Response to the Recommendations of the Review of Delay in the Criminal Justice System.*

17   See pp 251–254, *ante*.

18   Royal Commission on Criminal Procedure, paras 7.40–7.52 (Cmnd 8092-I, 1981).

19   Inserted by Prosecution of Offences Act 1985, s 24.

20   See, eg, offences of incitement to racial hatred (Public Order Act 1986, s 27); offences under the Prevention of Terrorism (Temporary Provisions) Act 1989.

b   The criteria

By section 10 of the 1985 Act the Director of Public Prosecutions is under a duty to issue a Code for Crown Prosecutors, giving guidance on the general principles to be applied by them in determining, in any case, whether proceedings should be instituted, discontinued, or what charges should be made. This Code is to be found set out in the Annual Reports of the DPP, and in practitioners' works such as *Archbold* or *Blackstone's Criminal Practice*. The latest edition of the Code was issued in June 1994.

The first question to be decided is whether there is sufficient evidence. There must be admissible, substantial and reliable evidence that a criminal offence has been committed by an identifiable individual. In deciding this, a prima facie case is not enough: the test is whether there is a realistic prospect of conviction. This is an objective test. It means that a jury or bench of magistrates, properly directed in law, is more likely than not to convict the defendant of the charge alleged.[1] In deciding that, a careful study will be undertaken of the available evidence. The possibility that evidence might be inadmissible either in law, or excluded because of failure to comply with relevant rules, the possibility that admissions might be unreliable, the possibility that a witness may be hostile or likely to be unreliable or not likely to tell the truth, the impression a witness will make in court, the availability of all necessary witnesses, and the competence of young children are all relevant factors. The prosecutor will look at the overall weight of the case, whether dangers of concoction of evidence exist, whether a case can be sustained against more than one accused (if there is more than one), and whether the public might consider a prosecution to be oppressive. The prosecutor will also consider what the defence case may be.

Having decided whether prosecution can be justified on the evidence, the prosecutor is then required to consider the wider public interest, although the interests of the victim should also be borne in mind. The graver the offence the less likelihood there will be that the public interest will permit the case to be dealt with by anything other than prosecution, although the Code does urge prosecutors to strive to ensure that the spirit of the cautioning guidelines is observed, where the seriousness of the offence allows. In particular the following factors may provide an indication that prosecution may not be required:

(a)   where a court is likely to impose a small or nominal penalty only;

(b)   where the offence was committed as a result of a genuine mistake or misunderstanding (balanced against the seriousness of the offence);

(c)   where the loss or harm is minor, and results from a single incident (and particularly if caused by misjudgment);

(d)   where the offences are stale. However, the staleness may have been caused by the offender himself, the offences may only just have come to light, there may have been the need for a long complex investigation, or the offences may be serious;

(e)   prosecution may have a very bad effect on the health of the victim, again bearing in mind the seriousness of the offence;

(f)   old age or infirmity;

(g)   mental disorder at the time of commission of the offence. Where the effect of proceedings upon the health of the accused is not outweighed by wider public interest in favour of prosecution, proceedings may not be commenced, or may be discontinued. In this type of case, other relevant factors will be the nature of the mental condition, and the likelihood of further offending;

---

1   The so-called "51 per cent" rule.

(h) changes in attitude by the complainant, including the making of reparation or putting right loss. However, prosecution cannot be avoided simply by an ability to pay compensation.

In addition to the Code of Practice, the CPS and police have developed charging standards for certain types of offence. These include certain assaults and other offences against the person, driving offences and public order offences. The intention is to ensure fairness and consistency in the approach to certain types of offence. Certain principles are stated in all of the charging standards. Charges should accurately reflect the extent of the defendant's involvement and responsibility, the choice of charges should ensure the clear and simple presentation of the case; it is wrong to encourage a defendant to plead guilty to a few charges by selecting more charges than are necessary, and it is wrong to select a more serious charge not supported by the evidence in order to encourage a plea of guilty to a lesser allegation.

c Discontinuance

Under section 23 of the Prosecution of Offences Act 1985 notice of discontinuance can be issued, provided this is done in summary cases before the beginning of the hearing of the evidence, or in cases to be tried on indictment, before committal for trial. This can be done by correspondence, and without the expense and inconvenience of a court hearing. It does not replace the power of a prosecutor to go before a court and offer no evidence or to withdraw a charge, both of which remain options.[2] Nor does it interfere with the power of the Attorney-General to prevent proceedings from continuing by the issue of a writ of *nolle prosequi*.[3]

In deciding the use of these various powers it is the duty of prosecutors to keep a case under review. In the case of juveniles it may become clear that caution is the more appropriate way of dealing with the matter. In respect of those suffering illness the effect on health may make it appropriate for the case to be withdrawn.[4] In any event this power of review has been shown to be important. Since the creation of the Crown Prosecution Service in 1985, the proportion of prosecutions for indictable offences that have been discontinued or withdrawn has risen rapidly, from 7 per cent in 1985 to 22 per cent in 1991,[5] emphasising the role of the Crown Prosecution Service in deciding whether a case is sufficient, and whether it is in the public interest to proceed.

The Royal Commission on Criminal Justice considered the exercise of this duty in the light of the research it received concerning ordered or directed acquittals in the Crown Court.[6] It concluded that weak cases should be identified at an early a stage as possible, before the defendant, victim and other witnesses are put to the trouble and expense of a court appearance. To that end, it recommended that the Crown Prosecution Service should have power to discontinue a case without obtaining the consent of the court at any time prior to the hearing itself.[7] More recently, it has been proposed[8] that the CPS should no longer be able to discontinue cases on public interest grounds

---

2   *R v Director of Public Prosecutions, ex parte Cooke* (1991) 95 Cr App Rep 233.
3   For the powers of the Attorney-General, see Edwards, *The Law Officers of the Crown.*
4   This power to discontinue remains throughout the trial itself. In *R v Seelig* (1993) the accused was discharged because he was medically unable to cope with the strains of a long trial in which he was defending himself: see The Times, 15 February.
5   Criminal Statistics in England & Wales, 1991, para 6(2).
6   See Block, Corbett & Peay *Ordered & Directed Acquittals in the Crown Court* (Royal Commission Research Study No 15, 1993).
7   Ch 5, para 37.
8   See Narey Report, *op cit*, p 460.

because they consider the offence is not serious. This recommendation is intended to resolve differences between the police and CPS as to whether a particular offence is worth prosecuting, by leaving that decision with the police. The fact that the offence was minor or the likely penalty trivial would no longer constitute grounds for discontinuance. This is an issue currently being considered as part of a more general review of the role and powers of the CPS.[9]

d   Time-limits for prosecution and abuse of process

It was noted above that increasing concern has arisen about delays in the criminal justice system.[10] In general there is no time-limit on the prosecution of an indictable offence, although, by contrast, summary proceedings must be brought within a specified period.[11] Even in some cases triable on indictment Parliament has for reasons of policy imposed a time limit, thus a prosecution for unlawful sexual intercourse with a girl under sixteen may not be commenced more than twelve months after the commission of the offence.[12] However, even when no specific time-limit exists the court is not powerless, and can intervene to prevent abuse of process occasioned by delay. A court can, as part of its inherent power, order a stay to prevent abuse of process.[13] Thus if the prosecution has manipulated or misused the process of the court:

> "so as to deprive the defendant of a protection provided by the law or if there has been such delay so that prejudice or unfairness to the defendant arises"[14]

then the court can order that the prosecution does not proceed. This doctrine of abuse of process has even been extended to cases where, though the fairness of the trial is not in question, nevertheless it would be unfair to try the accused because of the abuse that has occurred. In *R v Croydon Justices, ex parte Dean*[15] this was applied and a conviction quashed, the accused having been assured that he would not be prosecuted. Again, in *R v Horseferry Road MC, ex parte Bennett*[16] the House of Lords held that the doctrine of abuse of process applied to prevent the trial of an accused who had been brought to the United Kingdom through collusion of the UK and South African authorities, in breach of extradition procedures. Despite the fact that the fairness of the trial itself was not in issue, the court considered that the judiciary had a responsibility for the maintenance of the rule of law.

Dealing with a case involving delay Viscount Dilhorne in *Director of Public Prosecutions v Humphrys*[17] warned that use of this power should occur only "in the most exceptional circumstances". This was an approach echoed by Lord Lane CJ in

9   See p 251, *post*.
10   See p 456, *ante*.
11   Six months from the date of commission or when matter of complaint arose: Magistrates Courts Act 1980, s 127.
12   Sexual Offences Act 1956, s 37 and Sch 2.
13   *Connolly v Director of Public Prosecutions* [1964] AC 1254; (1964) 48 Cr App Rep 183.
14   *R v Derby Magistrates' Court, ex parte Brooks* (1984) 80 Cr App Rep 164.
15   [1993] QB 769; [1993] 3 All ER 129; see also *R v Bow Street Stipendiary Magistrate, ex parte Director of Public Prosecutions* (1989) 91 Cr App Rep 283; *R v Crown Court at Norwich, ex parte Belsham* [1992] 1 All ER 394; [1992] 1 WLR 54.
16   [1994] 1 AC 42. See also *R v Beckford* (1996) 1 Cr App Rep 94.
17   [1977] AC 1; [1976] 2 All ER 497.

A-G's Reference (No 1 of 1990)[19] where he stated that even if delay was unjustifiable the imposition of a stay:

"should be the exception rather than the rule. Still more rare should be cases where a stay can properly be imposed in the absence of any fault on the part of the complainant or prosecution."

The defendant must show on the balance of probabilities that, owing to the delay, he will suffer serious prejudice to the extent that no fair trial can be held. In deciding this, the ability of the court through the rules of evidence to regulate what is placed before it, and the ability of the judge to warn and to give appropriate directions to the jury, should both be borne in mind. The reasons for delay may also be relevant. Prosecution inefficiency is one factor,[20] as is the nature of the case. A longer period of preparation for the prosecution is only to be expected in complex cases, particularly fraud cases.[1] Delay may also arise because of the nature of the offence alleged, and the reluctance of a victim to come forward.[2] Whatever the reason, long delay is not inevitably a justification for a stay. In *R v Central Criminal Court, ex parte Randle and Pottle*,[3] a delay of 20 years in a case of assisting the Soviet spy, George Blake, from, escaping from lawful custody was held, on the facts, not to justify a stay.

Statute has created a framework within which prosecutors must work. By section 2 of the Prosecution of Offences Act 1985, and the regulations that have been made under that Act, there are time-limits regulating how long a defendant may be kept in custody pending the start of summary trial, between first appearance at court and committal for trial, and between committal for trial and the start of the trial.[4] Application can be made for extension of these limits, and a right of appeal exists in respect of a decision of a magistrates' court to extend, or a refusal to extend, these time limits. By contrast, no power exists in respect of such an order made by the Crown Court, but since this is not a matter "relating to trial on indictment" the power of judicial review arises.

Of course, delay may arise not only in respect of the commencement of proceedings but also in their conduct. The reduction of delays in the criminal justice system is regarded by the Government as a matter of high priority.[5] Despite a significant reduction in the number of cases coming to the criminal courts, delays in cases coming before the court are increasing, and the custody time-limits discussed earlier are not always met.[6] The detailed measures proposed to deal with this are discussed later.[7]

C   BRINGING THE SUSPECT BEFORE THE COURT

A person accused or suspected of having committed an offence may be brought before the court in one of three ways:

18   [1992] QB 630, [1992] 3 All ER 169.
19   The standard of proof applicable when a burden of proof is placed on an accused.
20   *R v West London Magistrates, ex parte Anderson* (1984) 80 Cr App Rep 143.
1   See Narey Report, *op cit*, p 460.
2   *R v LPB* (1990) 91 Cr App Rep 359.
3   (1992) 92 Cr App Rep 323.
4   Prosecution of Offences (Custody Time Limits) Regulations 1987, SI 1987/91.
5   See, eg, *Reducing Remand Delays – A Consultation Paper*, Home Office, 1997.
6   See Narey Report, *op cit*, n 5, *supra*.
7   See p 493 *et seq*.

(i)   by summons, this is a document, sent to or served on the defendant, ordering him to appear in court;
(ii) by warrant for his arrest; this is an order to the police, or in certain circumstances to private persons, to arrest the defendant and bring him before the court; (a summons and a warrant are generally known as "process")
(iii) by arrest without warrant, where permitted by law.

Although these three methods exist, their use varies widely. Although summary offences will most often be prosecuted by summons, research studies[8] show that in respect of offences that can be tried on indictment there is a strong tendency for the police to rely on arrest rather than summons. In one such study,[9] 76 per cent of those proceeded against for indictable offences had been arrested and charged, and a majority of those brought to court by way of summons for such offences had also at some point been arrested. It should be remembered in this context that arrest for the purposes of questioning is perfectly proper if the grounds for arrest on the facts exist.[10]

I   Information

Both a summons and a warrant are obtained by the laying of information before a magistrate:

> "an information is nothing more than what the word imports, namely the statement by which the magistrate is informed of the offence for which the summons or warrant is required."[11]

An information may be laid either by the person requiring issue of process, or by somebody authorised by that person to do so, usually that person's solicitor or barrister. The application may be made either orally or in writing: if, however, a warrant is sought the information must be in writing and substantiated on oath.[12] Where consent or authority is required for the issue of process, the magistrate before whom the information is laid should see that the consent or authority is produced before issuing process. In addition, every court may decline to hear proceedings if they amount to an abuse of the process of the court.[13]

The information should describe in ordinary language the specific offence, avoiding technical terms as far as possible, and should not charge more than one offence.[14] If it does so, it must be amended before the commencement of trial.[15] It is not necessary to set out in the information all the elements of the offence, and in particular it is not necessary to "specify or negative" any exemption or general defence;[16] however the

---

8   See McConville *Corroboration & Confessions* (Royal Commission Research Study No 13, HMSO, 1992).
9   Gemmill & Morgan Giles *Arrest, Charge & Summons* (Royal Commission on Criminal Procedure Research Study No 9, HMSO 1980).
10   *Holgate-Mohammed v Duke* [1984] AC 437; [1984] 1 All ER 1054.
11   Huddleston B, in *R v Hughes* (1879) 4 QBD 614, at 633; cited with approval by the House of Lords in *R v Manchester Stipendiary Magistrate, ex parte Hill* [1983] 1 AC 328; *sub nom Hill v Anderton* [1982] 2 All ER 963, in which it was held that the information was "laid" when received at the office of the clerk to the justices for the relevant area, and that it was not necessary for it to be personally received by the clerk or any justice; it was sufficient that it was received by a member of staff expressly or impliedly authorised to receive it for onward transmission to a justice or the justices' clerk.
12   Magistrates' Courts Act 1980, s 1(1), (3).
13   *Price v Humphries* [1958] 2 QB 353, at 357; [1958] 2 All ER 725, at 727.
14   See p 505, *post.*
15   See p 563, *post.*
16   Magistrates Court Rules, r 4(3). See p 563, *post.*

information should give such particulars as may be necessary for explaining the nature of the charge and where the offence charged is statutory there should be a reference to the relevant section of the Act.[17]

Failure to comply with these rules will not necessarily mean that the issue of process is invalid. Technical objections to informations are not to prevail, even though they touch the substance of the charge.[18] There have been, however, many decisions under the Magistrates' Courts Act 1980 that show that the Act does not operate to prevent an objection being effective where the error alleged is "fundamental."[19] It is a question of fact and degree in each case whether the error is indeed fundamental. If an information charges an offence under a statute which has been repealed,[20] if it does not charge an offence at all,[1] or if it is bad for duplicity[2] then there is a fundamental defect which cannot be cured except by amendment or dismissal of the summons.

2   Conditions for issue of process

Before issuing process, a magistrate must be satisfied as to two matters:

(a)   that jurisdiction to do so exists. It will do so if the person accused resides in that petty sessions area, or is believed to do so; if the alleged offence was committed in that area; or if it is necessary or expedient for a person to be tried in the same area as another person.[3] This may be because the offences should be tried together, perhaps because the offences are so closely connected that the same witnesses are involved.[4]

(b)   the evidence is sufficient to do so. The issue of process is discretionary, subject to challenge in the normal way by means of judicial review.

If process is to be issued, the decision remains as to whether to issue a summons or a warrant, a decision which is a judicial one to be exercised personally by the magistrate. No defect in the summons or warrant issued will invalidate any trial that follows, provided it is based upon a valid information.[5]

3   Summons

"A summons is a citation proceeding upon an information laid before the magistrate who issues the summons, and conveying to the person cited the fact that the magistrate is satisfied that there is a prima facie case against him."[6]

---

17   *Ibid*, r 4(3).
18   Magistrates' Courts Act 1980, s 123(1).
19   See Humphreys J in *Atterton v Browne* [1945] KB 122, at 127, dealing with a section of the Summary Jurisdiction Act 1848 in similar terms to s 123(1); cf Magistrates' Courts Rules 1981, r 4(1).
20   *Meek v Powell* [1952] 1 KB 164; [1952] 1 All ER 347. *Hunter v Coombs* [1962] 1 All ER 904; [1962] 1 WLR 573. *Quaere*, whether the defendant could waive the irregularity.
1   *Garman v Plaice* [1969] 1 All ER 62, at 64; [1969] 1 WLR 19, at 23.
2   For the meaning of this, see p 564, *post*.
3   Magistrates' Courts Act 1980, s 1(2).
4   See eg *R v Blandford, R v Freestone* [1955] 1 All ER 681; [1955] 1 WLR 331.
5   *R v Manchester Stipendiary Magistrates, ex parte Hill* [1983] 1 AC 328; *sub nom Hill v Anderton* [1982] 2 All ER 963.
6   Mathew J in *Dixon v Wells* (1890) 25 QBD 249, at 257.

A summons must state shortly the matter of the information and then set out the time and place at which the defendant is required by the summons to appear. A single summons may be issued in respect of several informations, but must state the matter of each information separately and has effect as several summonses, one for each information. In all cases the summons must either be signed by the magistrate issuing it or must state his name, with the signature of the clerk of the court to authenticate it in either event.[7]

The summons must then be served on the defendant. Rules exist governing how this should be effected, and how it should be proved. A summons remains in force even though the magistrate who issued it ceases for any reason to be a magistrate and with certain exceptions it may be served at any time after issue.

4 Warrant[8]

A warrant, unlike a summons, is an order for the arrest of the defendant. It contains a statement of the offence charged, is (like a summons) signed by the issuing magistrate or justices' clerk, but (unlike a summons) is an order for arrest. It is addressed to the officers of the police area in which the warrant is issued and such other persons as are named in the warrant, and directs them to arrest a particular person. That person must be mentioned by name or otherwise described; general warrants, ie warrants which do not name the person to be arrested, have been held to be illegal at common law ever since a series of famous cases[9] in the eighteenth century.

A warrant may be executed (ie the arrest effected) anywhere in the United Kingdom, at any time,[10] by any person to whom the warrant is directed or by any police officer acting within his police area;[11] an officer making the arrest need not have the warrant in his possession at the time but must show it to the defendant as soon as is practicable, if the defendant demands to see it.[12] This duty is equivalent to the duty imposed on a person making an arrest without warrant to inform the defendant of the reason for his arrest.

When a magistrate issues a warrant he may at the same time endorse it with a direction that the person named in the warrant shall, on arrest, be released on bail, on such terms as may be specified in the endorsement. The warrant is then said to be "backed for bail", and the officer in charge of the police station to which the defendant is taken after arrest must release him (subject to approving any surety tendered in compliance with the endorsement).[13]

A magistrate's discretion as to whether to issue a summons or a warrant is limited, by section 1(4) of the Magistrates' Courts Act 1980. No warrant may be issued against

---

7   In *R v Fairford Justices, ex parte Brewster* [1976] QB 600; [1975] 2 All ER 757 the court indicated that no challenge can be made to the hearing of a valid information, even if followed by an invalid summons.
8   Strictly called "a warrant of arrest", there being various other types of warrant, such as a search warrant.
9   Notably *Money v Leach* (1765) 3 Burr 1742; *Entick v Carrington* (1765) 19 State Tr 1029.
10   Until withdrawn; Magistrates' Courts Act 1980, s 125(1).
11   *Ibid*, s 125(2).
12   *Ibid*, s 125(3). This is reasonable from the point of view of the police (since there may be many police seeking to make the arrest, but only one warrant) and also for the purpose of protecting the liberty of the subject.
13   *Ibid*, s 117. Special provisions relate to the execution of warrants in the Republic of Ireland: see the Backing of Warrants (Republic of Ireland) Act 1965 which resolved the difficulties revealed by the decision of the House of Lords in *Metropolitan Police Commissioner v Hammond* [1965] AC 810; [1964] 2 All ER 722.

a person who is seventeen or over, unless the offence is indictable or punishable with imprisonment, or unless the defendant's address is not "sufficiently established" for a summons to be served on him.

5   Arrest without warrant

Finally, the defendant may be arrested without warrant, under the powers earlier discussed.[14] The purpose of an arrest in such circumstances is to commence the criminal process, but the motive may in fact be to secure the lawful detention of the arrested person, so that the questioning may occur in the police station[15] and the arrested person must be brought before a court within the relevant statutory period, or released on bail.

D   CLASSIFICATION OF OFFENCES

Prior to the implementation of Part III of the Criminal Law Act 1977 the law relating to the classification of criminal offences and the determination of the appropriate Mode of Trial, summary or on indictment, was complex. Thus there were provisions for summary offences to be tried on indictment and for indictable offences to be tried summarily, while there was a third class of offences, colloquially (though not by statute) called "hybrid" offences which might take on the character of either summary offences or indictable offences according to the election of the parties. These classifications were reviewed by the James Committee in 1975,[16] which had as its twin aims a simplification of the procedure and possible reduction in the case loads of the Crown Court. Its recommendations were in part controversial, but the majority of them were adopted, and implemented by Part III of the Criminal Law Act 1977.

As regards Mode of Trial there are now three classes of offence[17] namely:

(a)   offences triable only on indictment;[18]
(b)   offences triable only summarily;[19] and
(c)   offences triable either way.[20]

I   Offences triable only on indictment

Because offences can only fall within one of the other two categories if statute so provides, it follows that where there is no express statutory provision an offence is triable only on indictment. This involves a trial by judge and jury in the Crown Court. When the provisions in the Crime and Disorder Act 1998 are implemented, there will be no committal proceedings.[1]

---

14   See p 291, *ante*.
15   *Holgate-Mohammed v Duke* [1984] AC 437; [1984] 1 All ER 1054.
16   The Distribution of Criminal Business between the Crown Court and Magistrates' Courts, Cmnd 6323, HMSO.
17   Criminal Law Act 1977, s 14.
18   This should be distinguished from the phrase "indictable offences", which means offences which, if committed by an adult, are triable on indictment, either exclusively or because they are "either way" offences: Interpretation Act 1978, s 5, Sch 1.
19   A "summary offence" means an offence which, if committed by an adult, is triable only summarily.
20   An "offence triable either way" means an offence which, if committed by an adult, is triable either on indictment or summarily.
1   See p 486, *post*.

In practice only the gravest indictable offences are triable only on indictment; these include murder, genocide, manslaughter, infanticide, child destruction, abortion, rape, sexual intercourse with a girl under thirteen, sedition, mutiny, piracy, offences under section 1 of the Official Secrets Act 1911, robbery, wounding or causing grievous bodily harm "with intent", blackmail, assault with intent to rob, aggravated burglary and burglary comprising the commission of, or an intention to commit, an offence triable only on indictment. It will, however, be recalled that these are triable only on indictment if committed by an adult; as we shall see, in the case of children and young persons, all indictable offences (other than homicide) may, and in most cases must, be tried summarily.[2]

2   Offences triable only summarily

The expressions "summary offence" and "offence triable only summarily" may be taken as synonymous. A statute creating a summary offence will first define the offence and then state that it is punishable "on summary conviction" with a particular penalty, thereby indicating that the offence is a summary one. In addition a number of offences which, prior to the Criminal Law Act 1977, were not summary offences according to the statute creating them, became so.[3]

Special rules apply to some offences under the Criminal Damage Act 1971: offences under section 1 of this Act (excluding arson) are triable only summarily if the "value involved" does not exceed £5,000.[4] Section 22 of the Magistrates' Courts Act 1980 prescribes a procedure for determining whether such offences are to be regarded as summary or as triable either way (if the value involved exceeds £2,000). The court begins by hearing any representations made by the prosecutor or the accused as to the value involved; if it appears to the court clear that the value involved does not exceed the prescribed sum, it will proceed to summary trial. If it is clear that it does exceed that sum, then it will treat the offence as triable either way (which, of course, it then is).[5] If it is not clear whether or not the value involved does exceed the prescribed sum, then the accused is given the choice and told that if he consents to summary trial, his liability to imprisonment or to a fine will be limited to the maximum that magistrates have power to impose; the nature of the offence will then be determined in accordance with the accused's decision. If a person is convicted, either by a magistrates' court or by the Crown Court, he cannot appeal on the ground that the magistrates were mistaken as to the value involved.[6]

3   Offences triable either way

The third class of offence is offences triable either way. Those made so triable under the 1977 Act are now listed in Schedule 1 to the Magistrates' Courts Act 1980, which

2   See p 474, *post*.
3   See Criminal Law Act 1977, s 15. These comprise offences mentioned in Sch 1 to that Act, and which were formerly hybrid offences.
4   The "relevant sum" was fixed at this amount by the 1980 Act.
5   The court must hear "representations", meaning submissions, assertions of fact and sometimes production of documents; however the court is not bound to hear evidence of the value involved: *R v Canterbury and St Augustine Justices, ex parte Klisiak* [1982] QB 398; [1981] 2 All ER 129; moreover it is permissible in cases of doubt for the prosecution to limit the charge to certain items clearly below the prescribed value, even though in fact other damaged items would take the value above the prescribed value (so as to ensure summary trial) (*ibid*).
6   Criminal Law Act 1977, s 22(8).

consists of 35 paragraphs incorporating some 66 separate offences; these include unlawful wounding or inflicting grievous bodily harm, with or without a weapon, assault occasioning actual bodily harm, common assault, bigamy, certain forms of perjury and forgery, unlawful sexual intercourse with a girl under 16, all indictable offences under the Theft Act 1968 (except robbery, blackmail, assault with intent to rob and certain burglaries), arson, offences under section 1 of the Criminal Damage Act 1971 where the value exceeds £5,000 (*supra*) and indecent assault. In addition many other statutes expressly provide for an offence to be triable either summarily or on indictment (the former "hybrid" offences) and these are now triable either way.[7]

4   Possible reform

This division of functions between Crown Court and magistrates court has been the subject of continued discussion over some 20 years. The James Committee[8] considered that it was appropriate to reclassify offences of low value theft as summary offences, thus restricting the right to jury trial. This proposal met considerable resistance, in the light of the impact any conviction for theft might have on a person's reputation and career. More recently, the Royal Commission on Criminal Justice[9] concluded that the distribution of work between magistrates' court and Crown Court was neither rational, nor always amounted to an efficient use of resources. This emphasis on the resource implications of the choice of mode of trial was reiterated more recently in 1995 in a Government consultation paper.[10] This identified a large increase in the proportion of cases involving either way offences being committed to the Crown Court for trial.[11] In relation to accused persons aged 17 or over, the proportion of such cases rose from 15% in 1980 to 23% in 1987, before falling to 17% in 1992. A significant proportion of these cases were committed to the Crown Court because the magistrates themselves declined jurisdiction. In 1987 the relevant percentage was 47%, rising to 64% in 1991 and then falling to 63% in 1992. This increase in committals had an affect not only on the workload of the Court itself, but upon the size of the prison population, on the police, the Crown Prosecution Service and the Legal Aid Fund.

The Consultation Paper considered one option to be a reclassification of the mode of trial of minor thefts and certain other offences. In doing so it mirrored the approach taken by the James Committee. Two other options related not so much to the classifications themselves, but rather to the decision-making process as to where 'either way' offences should be tried. The first emanated from the Royal Commission on Criminal Justice. It recommended that a person accused of an either way offence should no longer be entitled to insist on trial in the Crown Court, but that the mode of trial should be a matter of agreement between the accused and the Crown Prosecution Service, and, in the absence of such agreement, be determined by magistrates. The other option considered was a change in the law relating to the mechanics of the decision-making process, so that magistrates could be aware, at the time of making the choice of mode of trial, of how the accused intends to plead at trial. The Consultation Paper estimated that a significant number of cases (38,000 in the year ending June 1993) were sent for trial in the Crown Court only for the accused to plead guilty on arraignment, and be given a sentence which the magistrates themselves could have

7   *Ibid*, s 17(2).
8   Cmnd 6323.
9   *Op cit*, Ch 6, para 13–19.
10   *Mode of Trial: A Consultation Paper*, 1995, Cm 2908.
11   *Ibid*, para 2.

imposed. It identified the fact that a "significant proportion" of accused falling into that category would in fact be prepared to plead guilty in a magistrates' court to an either way charge and be dealt with by the magistrates. Such cases were often committed because magistrates declined jurisdiction. It was this last option that found favour. Amended procedures have been introduced by the Criminal Procedure and Investigations Act 1996, and are dealt with below. The more fundamental questions as to the categories themselves, and the extent to which trial on indictment should, in principle, be limited, therefore remain unanswered, but, again, are under review by the Government.

E   PROCEDURE FOR DETERMINING MODE OF TRIAL

The procedure for determining the Mode of Trial differs according to whether or not the accused is an adult. If he is, then, as has been noted, he will always be tried on indictment for an offence triable only on indictment and will always be tried summarily for a summary offence; only in the case of an "either way" offence are there alternative possibilities. In the case of children and young persons the position is quite different. Before considering these procedures it should be noted that if magistrates mistakenly adopt a procedure which is not permitted, for example by "trying" a case which is triable only on indictment or by committing for trial in the case of an offence triable only summarily, then their "trial" or "committal" will be a complete nullity. Even if the defendant has been "sentenced" he may later be committed for trial and properly tried, if the offence was triable only on indictment.[12]

The choice of charge is that of the prosecution. If the charge preferred is appropriate on the facts given their seriousness, then the defence cannot challenge that charge on the basis that the preferment of another, different charge would have permitted trial on indictment.[13] Problems may also arise where fresh charges are levelled by the prosecutor, which, in reality, amount to attempts to deprive the justices of jurisdiction to try the case themselves. In *R v Brooks (Christopher)*[14] the appellant appeared before magistrates on a charge under section 20 of the Offences against the Person Act 1861. The appellant was content to be tried summarily, and the justices so ordered. The chief prosecuting solicitor then advised the bringing of a new charge under section 18 of the 1861 Act. In quashing the conviction obtained on such a charge O'Connor LJ observed that the prosecutor was seeking :

"to act as an appellate tribunal from the justices. There is no other explanation for it, and he said as much".

However, in *R v Redbridge Justices, ex parte Whitehouse*[15] it was made clear that it was the abuse of power that led to the irregularity in *Brooks*. If the facts are capable of supporting a fresh charge, the justices must decide whether it is both proper and appropriate. If they have already decided on summary trial, any further charge which would have the effect of making summary trial impossible should be scrutinised with care, but is not totally prohibited. The operation of this principle was seen in *R v Sheffield Justices, ex parte Director of Public Prosecutions*[16] where the defendant elected trial on a charge of assault occasioning actual bodily harm. The Crown then

12   See eg *R v West* [1964] 1 QB 15; [1962] 2 All ER 624.
13   *R v Canterbury & St Augustine Justices, ex parte Klisiak*, n 5, *supra*.
14   [1985] Crim LR 385.
15   (1991) 94 Cr App Rep 332.
16   [1993] Crim LR 136.

substituted a charge of common assault. Upon the magistrates staying the proceedings, the prosecutor successfully applied for judicial review. The substitution was a proper one, despite the fact that it deprived the accused of his right to trial by jury. There was no evidence of manipulation, and the defence had been notified of the proposal at an earlier stage. It was an appropriate charge on the facts.

I   Adults charged with "either way" offences

Before any evidence is called, a magistrates' court before whom a person aged seventeen or over appears charged with an offence triable either way must adopt the following procedure:

(1) If the prosecution is being carried on by the Attorney-General, the Solicitor-General or the Director of Public Prosecutions and he applies for the offence to be tried on indictment, then it must be tried in that way and the court must proceed as examining justices.[17] In any other case the following steps apply.

(2) The court must first cause the charge to be written down, if this has not already been done, and read to the accused.

(3) The court must explain to the accused in ordinary language that he may indicate whether (if the offence were to proceed to trial) he would plead guilty or not guilty (1980 Act, s 17A).

(4) The accused must also be warned that if he indicates that he intends to plead guilty the Court may proceed to summary trial, and that if appropriate he may be committed for sentence.

(5) If the accused does indicate he would plead guilty then the Court proceeds to summary trial with, of course, the power to commit for sentence which exists under section 38(2) of the 1980 Act. This indication of plea does not indicate the formal taking of a plea (1980 Act, s 17A(9)). Thus, if the accused indicates that he intends to plead not guilty, then, if the case is committed for trial, it is necessary for a formal plea to be taken in the Crown Court. If the accused indicates that his intention is to plead not guilty, then the magistrates' court proceeds to determine Mode of Trial, in accordance with the procedure set out below (s 18 of the 1980 Act, as amended).

(6) The prosecutor and then the accused are given an opportunity to make representations as to which Mode of Trial would be more suitable.

(7) The court then considers whether the offence appears more suitable for summary trial or for trial on indictment, having regard to the representations referred to in (3) above, to the nature of the case, whether the circumstances make the offence one of serious character, whether the punishment which a magistrates' court would have power to inflict for it would be adequate and

> "any other circumstances which appear to the court to make it more suitable for the offence to be tried in one way rather than the other."[18]

Although the Act is silent on the point, it is clear on principle that the "circumstances" to be taken into account by the justices in reaching their decision cannot include the accused's past record, unless, presumably, the accused himself

---

17   A single justice may discharge this function, but could not (unless a stipendiary) go on to conduct a summary trial; Magistrates' Courts Act 1980, s 18(5).

18   *Ibid*, s 19(4).

relies upon this. It would be invidious to permit the prosecution to make representations concerning the accused's past record because the justices would then (improperly) know of it when conducting the ensuing trial or committal proceedings as the case may be. This was recognised by the National Mode of Trial Guidelines,[19] and by authority.[20] Despite the amendment of the Mode of Trial Guidelines, in 1995,[1] which omits the relevant provision, this arguably remains true and sound in principle.[2]

(8) If, following consideration as above, it appears to the court that the offence is more suitable for trial on indictment, then it must tell the accused that it has so decided and will then proceed to committal for trial, the accused having no power to prevent this course even if neither he nor the prosecution has requested it.[3]

(9) If, on the other hand, it appears to the court that the offence is "more suitable for summary trial", then the court must explain to the accused in ordinary language that he can either consent to summary trial or, if he wishes, be tried by a jury and that if he is tried summarily and convicted he may be committed for sentence to the Crown Court under section 38 of the Magistrates' Courts Act 1980.[4]

(10) After explaining to the accused, as provided under (6) above, his options, the court asks him whether he consents to be tried summarily or wishes to be tried by a jury. If he consents to summary trial, the magistrates proceed to try him; if he does not consent, they proceed as examining justices.[5]

(11) There are provisions in section 25 of the Act whereby the magistrates may change from summary trial to committal proceedings and vice versa. Where the court has begun to try an either way offence summarily it may, at any time before the conclusion of the evidence for the prosecution, discontinue the summary trial and proceed to committal for trial.[6] This will necessitate starting all over again and the court must adjourn the hearing, and is not required to remand the accused. Conversely, if the court has already begun committal proceedings it may at any time, if it appears to the court having regard to any representations made by prosecutor or accused with consent of the accused (and with the consent of the Attorney-General, the Solicitor-General or the Director of Public Prosecutions if any of them is the prosecutor) proceed to try the information summarily.[7] As indicated, this can only be done with the accused's consent and, before asking him whether he consents, the court must in ordinary language explain to him what is proposed, that it can only be done with his consent and (unless it has already done so) must explain the court's power to commit to the Crown Court for sentence.[8] If the magistrates do change from committal for trial to a summary trial the prosecutor will not be able to rely on evidence contained in a written statement of deposition which has already been tendered as part of the committal proceedings. That would amount to hearsay evidence and the prosecutor will have

19   See *infra*.
20   *R v Doncaster MC, ex parte Goulding* [1993] 1 All ER 435; *R v South Hackney Juvenile Court, ex parte RB and C* (1983) 77 Cr App R 294.
1   See [1996] Crim LR 471.
2   Cf *R v Flax Vilouton MC, ex parte Commissioners of Customs and Excise*.
3   Magistrates' Courts Act 1980, s 19(3).
4   As amended by Criminal Justice Act 1991, s 25. See further, p 572, *post*. A failure to warn an accused person of the liability to committal for sentence renders the conviction and committal bad, as from the moment of that failure. A fresh charge may still be brought: Magistrates' Courts Act 1980, s 20.
5   Magistrates' Courts Act 1980, s 20(3).
6   *Ibid*, s 25(2). This cannot be done following a plea of guilty: *Re Gillard* [1986] AC 442.
7   *Ibid*, s 25(3).
8   *Ibid*, s 25(4).

to call the maker of the statement as a witness, unless the document is admissible in evidence in its own right.

The accused must usually be present in court in person during the proceedings at which the Mode of Trial is determined.[9] However, the court may proceed in the absence of the accused if they consider that by reason of his disorderly conduct before them it is not practicable for the proceedings to be conducted in his presence. In addition, where the accused is represented by counsel or a solicitor who in his absence signifies to the court the accused's consent to the proceedings for determining how he is to be tried for the offence being conducted in his absence, and the court is satisfied that there is good reason for proceeding in the absence of the accused, then the court may proceed in the accused's absence.[10] In either case the consents required either to summary trial under (6) above (in this case there is no need for the court to explain its power to commit for sentence) or to summary trial of an offence under section 1 of the Criminal Damage Act 1971 (where it is not clear whether the value involved exceeds the prescribed limit)[11] may be given by the accused's counsel or solicitor.[12]

2   Children and young persons

The law has given significant protection to children and young persons. An attempt was made by the Children and Young Persons Act 1969 to prohibit the prosecution of children[13] for all crimes except murder, and severely limit the prosecution of young persons. However, these provisions were never brought into force, and were repealed in 1991,[14] leaving children and young persons open to prosecution, but with restrictions as to how proceedings shall be heard.

Whenever a child or young person appears before a magistrates' court charged with any indictable offence except "homicide" he must, subject to certain exceptions, be tried summarily.[15] This rule does not apply to an offence of homicide. Nor does it apply:

(a) in the case of a young person charged with an offence for which the penalty is in the case of an adult fourteen years' imprisonment or more,[16] not being an offence for which the sentence is fixed by law, and the court considers that if he is found guilty it ought to be possible to sentence him to detention under section 53(2) of the Children and Young Persons Act 1933; or

(b) in the case of a child or young person charged jointly with an adult (eighteen or over) if the court considers it necessary in the interests of justice to commit them both for trial.[17] In this case the court may also commit the child or young person

9   Magistrates' Courts Act 1980, s 18(2).
10   *Ibid*, ss 18(3), 23(1).
11   See p 470.
12   Magistrates' Courts Act 1980, ss 23(3), (4).
13   A "child" is a person aged 10–13 inclusive. A "young person" is a person aged 14–17.
14   Criminal Justice Act 1991, Sch 13.
15   Magistrates' Courts Act 1980, s 24(1); "appears" means appears or is brought before the court when the court makes its decision as to the Mode of Trial so that an accused who attains the age of eighteen before this occasion is treated as an adult notwithstanding that he was a young person when he appeared at an earlier remand hearing; *R v Islington North Juvenile Court, ex parte Daley* [1983] 1 AC 347; *sub nom Re Daley* [1982] 2 All ER 974. Further, under the Crime and Disorder Act 1998, s 47, where a person attains the age of 18 before the start of the trial it may remit the person to the Crown Court for trial.
16   See p 541, *post*.
17   Magistrates' Courts Act 1980, s 24.

for any other indictable offence with which he is charged at the same time (whether jointly with an adult or not) if that other offence arises out of circumstances which are the same as or connected with those giving rise to the first offence.[18]

A child or young person not accused jointly with an adult will be tried in a youth court.[19] However, if charged jointly with an adult he will be tried in an ordinary magistrates' court unless the adult pleads guilty or is not tried summarily (so that they are no longer jointly charged) in which event the court may before any evidence is called in the case of the child or young person remit him to a youth court for trial.[20]

3 Factors that influence Mode of Trial

It has been noted that, in respect of "either way" offences, the Mode of Trial is determined both by the magistrates' court and by the accused. Magistrates were given specific guidance as to how these powers should be used by the National Mode of Trial Guidelines set out in a Practice Note.[1] A revised version of the Guidelines was issued by the Criminal Justice Consultative Committee in early 1995, but not as a Practice Direction. This revision contained significant changes, especially in the context of the relevance of antecedent history of accused persons. Surprisingly, the revised versions have not been published in any series of law reports.[2] The Practice Note, having identified the requirements of section 19 of the Magistrates Courts' Act 1980, states:

(a) the court should never make a decision on the ground of convenience or expedition;
(b) the court should assume that the prosecution version of the facts is correct;
(c) the defendant's antecedents and personal mitigating circumstances are irrelevant;
(d) the fact that the offences are specimen charges is relevant. By contrast, the fact that the defendant will be asking for other offences to be taken into consideration is not;
(e) where complex questions of fact, or difficult points of law, arise, the court should consider committal for trial;
(f) a juvenile should only be committed with a co accused aged 18 or over if it is necessary in the interests of justice. In addition the guidelines suggested that where there is more than one defendant, and one elects trial on indictment the court should proceed to deal with all the defendants as examining magistrates. However, this can no longer be regarded as sound in the light of the decision of the House of Lords in *R v Brentwood Justices, ex parte Nicholls*.[3] The House there was of the opinion that where there is more than one defendant, each has the individual right to elect the Mode of Trial, irrespective of the election made by the co-defendants;
(g) either way offences should be tried summarily unless the particular case has one of the specified features, and the court considers that its sentencing powers are insufficient.

The Note then goes into considerable detail, and in respect of each offence identifies relevant factors that may indicate that it ought to be tried on indictment. Thus, for example, burglary is made more serious if it is at night, or if during a daytime burglary

---

18   *Ibid*, s 24(2).
19   Chapter 7.
20   Magistrates' Courts Act 1980, s 29.
1   [1990] 3 All ER 979; [1990] 1 WLR 1439.
2   See Waite, "The Antecedents of the Mode of Trial Guidelines" [1996] Crim LR 471.
3   [1992] 1 AC 1; *sub nom Nicholls v Brentwood Justices* [1991] 3 All ER 539.

persons are present on the property, if soiling or vandalism occurs, if the burglary displays professional hallmarks or is one of a series of similar offences.

Statistics show that the proportion of cases involving persons aged 17 years or over being committed for trial in 1991 was 23 per cent.[4] Only about one in five of cases dealt with in the Crown Court are in fact triable only on indictment, the rest being triable either way, and some evidence exists to show that the key decisions are made by the magistrates rather than defendants. In one study[5] the research team found that about 64 per cent of cases at Crown Court had been sent there because magistrates had declined jurisdiction.[6] The research period in question was prior to the introduction of the National Mode of Trial Guidelines, and it is not clear what impact they have had on these decisions. In terms of those who elect trial, the same research study identified as important factors a belief in the better prospect of acquittal at Crown Court than on summary trial, and the possibility of receiving a lighter sentence especially in the light of the negotiations between prosecution and defence as to the charges proceeded with.[7] Yet some 70 per cent of defendants electing trial at the Crown Court ended up pleading guilty.[8]

This was not regarded as a satisfactory state of affairs by the Royal Commission on Criminal Justice. It believed that there should be a more rational division of either way cases, to be achieved by modification of the procedures for determining Mode of Trial.[9] The decision should not be left to the defendant, but ultimately should be that of the court unless both prosecution and defence were able to reach agreement.[10] In cases where that was not possible the court itself should decide, bearing in mind the gravity of the offence, the past record of the defendant, the complexity of the case, and its likely effect on the defendant were he to be convicted.[11]

These proposals have proved controversial.[12] The Royal Commission believes that the fact that a defendant anticipates a fairer trial on indictment, or a better chance of acquittal, does not provide a rational basis for determining the court of trial. By contrast, loss of reputation is regarded as an important, though not decisive, factor. The Commission also regarded the reductions of the work-load pressures on the Crown Court as a desirable objective.[13] By contrast, critics have attacked the principle of limiting jury trial further, and have pointed in particular to the unfair impact the Royal Commission's proposals will have upon those who have previous convictions, and, as a result, are more likely to be deprived of jury trial.

4   Criminal Statistics for England & Wales, 1991, para 6.4.
5   Hedderman and Moxon, *Magistrates' Court or Crown Court – Mode of Trial Decisions and Sentencing* (Home Office Research Study No 125, 1992). The Royal Commission on Criminal Justice quotes figures of 52 per cent of cases being tried on indictment by magistrates' direction, with a further 30 per cent by way of election by the defendant: Ch 6, para 5.
6   The same study found that in 62 per cent of these cases, the sentence imposed was within the power of the magistrates' court to impose.
7   *Ibid*, Table 3.1. This perception is confirmed by Zander and Henderson, *The Crown Court Study* (Royal Commission Research Study No 19, HMSO, 1993). For other research, see Bottoms and McClean, *Defendants in the Criminal Process* (Routledge & Kegan, 1976); Vennard, *The Outcome of Contested Trials' in Managing Criminal Justice* (ed Moxon, HMSO, 1985).
8   *Ibid*.
9   Ch 6, para 13.
10   *Ibid*
11   *Ibid*, para 13.
12   See in particular, Ashworth, "Plea, Venue and Discontinuance" [1993] Crim LR 830, and the sources therein cited.
13   *Op cit*, Ch 6, para 15.

F BAIL

I Nature of bail

A person is "granted bail" when he is released from the custody of the law subject to a duty to surrender to custody at some future time. The "custody" is the custody of a court unless bail was granted by a police officer, in which event it is the custody of the officer. Considerable changes in the law were effected by the Bail Act 1976, which gave effect to many, though not all, of the recommendations of a Home Office Working Party Report[14] which identified the deficiencies of the old law. Previously bail involved entering into a "recognisance" which is an acknowledgement of a debt to the Queen payable on default of compliance with the conditions of the recognisance. The 1976 Act abolished personal recognisances from the accused but preserved them for sureties (where these are required). If granted bail the accused is under a duty to surrender to custody when required; if he fails without reasonable cause to do so he commits an offence under section 6(1) of the 1976 Act, punishable either on summary conviction or as a contempt of court.[16]

Bail may be granted either unconditionally or, in some circumstances, subject to conditions. Before any conditions can be imposed it must appear to the court that such conditions are necessary to prevent a failure to surrender to custody, to prevent the commission of an offence while on bail, to prevent interference with witnesses or an obstruction of the course of justice, or to allow inquiries or reports to be made to assist the court in dealing with him for the offence.[17] These are, in fact, similar to the factors a court may rely upon in refusing bail where the court believes that "substantial grounds" to believe that any of them apply exist,[18] and in *R v Mansfield Justices, ex parte Sharkey*[19] it was argued that "substantial grounds" likewise had to exist before a court could impose conditions. This argument was rejected by the Court of Appeal. It was enough that a court considered that there was a real and not fanciful risk of an offence being committed whilst the accused was on bail. In this case, the justices were entitled to impose conditions preventing the defendants from picketing or demonstrating at places other than their own places of work, during a major industrial dispute in the coal industry and where the court knew that disturbances at coal pits had occurred.

Where conditions can be imposed, they may cover a wide variety of matters. They may comprise the provision of a surety or sureties to secure the person's surrender to custody; the provision of security (if it appears that he is unlikely to remain in Great Britain until the time appointed for him to surrender to custody); requirements to secure that he surrenders to custody, does not commit any offence while on bail, does not interfere with witnesses or otherwise obstruct the course of justice or make himself available for the purpose of enabling inquiries or a report to be made to assist the court in dealing with him for the offence.[20] It is also intended that, in future, a court will be

---

14 Bail Procedures in Magistrates' Courts (1974).
15 Bail Act 1976, s 3(2).
16 *Ibid*, s 3(4).
17 *Ibid*, s 3(6). The reports referred to will almost always be into his physical or mental state.
18 *Ibid*, Sch 1, para 1.
19 [1985] QB 613; [1985] 1 All ER 193.
20 Bail Act 1976, s 3(6); these conditions may now be imposed not only by a court but also by a police officer. In murder cases, unless satisfactory reports on the accused's mental condition have already been obtained, the court must impose as conditions of bail (a) a requirement that the accused shall undergo examination by two medical practitioners for the purpose of enabling such reports to be prepared; and (b) a requirement that he shall for that purpose attend such an institution or place as the court directs (*ibid*, s 3(6A)).

able to impose a condition requiring a defendant to attend an interview with a legal representative.[1] Failure to obtain legal advice or representation is one of the most common reasons for delay, because the necessary steps to enable the case to proceed have not been taken. Conditions commonly imposed include conditions of residence, as to surrender of passport, reporting to a police station at prescribed times, not visiting specified premises and not approaching specified persons. Conditions imposed by a court may be varied by that court on the application of the person bailed, the prosecutor or a constable.[2]

2   Occasions for the grant of bail

The question of when bail may be granted to a person may arise at various stages of his case, from the moment that he is arrested to the final determination of any appeal arising out of his conviction. Bail in cases of treason can only be granted by order of a High Court judge or the Home Secretary.[3] In other cases, bail may be granted as follows.

a   By the police

When a person is arrested, a custody officer must order his release from police detention, either on bail or without bail (unless an arrest warrant was backed for bail). This power is subject to certain limitations, designed to apply where the name and address of the arrested person is unknown, if detention is necessary for his protection or for the protection of other persons or property, if the accused is likely not to appear or to interfere with the administration of justice or, in the case of an imprisonable offence, detention is necessary to prevent his committing further offences.[4] Conditions may now be imposed on police bail.

b   By magistrates

Magistrates have power to grant bail at various stages of proceedings, subject to certain restrictions. When an accused person is first brought before a magistrates' court charged with an offence it quite often happens that the prosecution is not ready to proceed in which event the proceedings are adjourned and the accused is remanded, either in custody or on bail. This may arise in the course of summary proceedings or where the offence is triable only on indictment (in which event the magistrates will eventually conduct committal proceedings) or where it is triable "either way".[5]

Secondly, if magistrates decide to commit the accused to the Crown Court for trial, that committal may be in custody or on bail.[6]

Thirdly, following summary conviction, the magistrates have power if they commit the defendant to the Crown Court for sentence (where this is open to them)[7] to commit in custody or on bail.[8]

---

1   Crime and Disorder Act, s 54(2).
2   *Ibid*, s 3(8).
3   Magistrates' Courts Act 1980, s 41.
4   Police and Criminal Evidence Act 1984, s 38(1).
5   Magistrates' Courts Act 1980, s 18(4); see p 469, *ante*.
6   *Ibid*, s 6(3).
7   See pp 572–573, *post* for the cases in which they may do this.
8   Magistrates' Courts Act 1980, s 38 and the other provisions permitting committal, except Mental Health Act 1983, s 43.

Finally, following conviction, if the magistrates adjourn for the purpose of considering sentence they may remand the defendant on bail or in custody[9] and, having imposed a custodial sentence, they may, if a person has given notice of appeal or applied to the magistrates to state a case,[10] grant bail.[11]

If bail is refused on a remand, the maximum period of remand is eight clear days[12] unless the accused is already serving a custodial sentence, in which event it is 28 clear days.[13] There may, of course, be further remands thereafter.[14]

Where magistrates adjourn a summary trial, committal proceedings or the determination of the method of trial of any either way offence and remand the accused in custody, they may, if the accused is an adult, order that he be brought up for any subsequent remands before an alternative magistrates' court nearer to the prison where he is to be confined on remand.[15] In the future, if the accused's presence is required, this may be achievable through live TV link.[16] This is another change designed to reduce delays, in this instance delays which arise where escorted prisoners arrive late at court.

Although successive applications for bail may be made to a magistrates' court (or to any court having power to grant bail), the Bail Act 1976 restricts the scope for continued applications.[17] If bail has been refused a second application for bail can be supported with any argument that is desired, whether or not put before the court before. At any subsequent hearings the court need not hear arguments as to fact or law that it has heard previously.[18]

Concern has arisen about offences being committed whilst on bail. As a result, the Bail (Amendment) Act 1993 gives a limited right of appeal to the prosecution, in cases where the accused is charged with an offence with a maximum punishment of at least five years' imprisonment, with taking a conveyance without consent, or with aggravated vehicle-taking.[19] Further, section 5B of the Bail Act 1976[20] gives a court power, on the application of the prosecutor, to reconsider a decision to grant bail made by a magistrates' court or by a custody officer before the person's scheduled appearance in court, if new information comes to light.

9   Magistrates' Courts Act 1980, s 128(1); if the remand is for medical examination and report, it must not be for more than three weeks, if in custody, for four weeks, if on bail and, if on bail, conditions as to undergoing medical examination must be imposed (*ibid*, s 30).
10   As to this procedure, see p 582, *post*.
11   Magistrates' Courts Act 1980, s 113.
12   *Ibid*, s 128(6); "clear days" means omitting the day of the remand and the day fixed for appearance. But in certain circumstances this may be exceeded: see Magistrates' Courts Act 1980, s 128A (inserted by Criminal Justice Act 1988, s 155). The key condition is that a previous remand must have been made.
13   *Ibid*, s 131(1).
14   *Ibid*, s 129(1).
15   *Ibid*, s 130; this is a security measure introduced by the Criminal Law Act 1977 to minimise the risks inherent in transporting dangerous prisoners over long distances. There are provisions for remands to be made in the absence of the accused (ss 128, 129).
16   See Crime and Disorder Act 1998, s 57.
17   Sch 1, Part IIA to the Bail Act 1976, inserted by Criminal Justice Act 1988, s 154. These provisions are designed to implement in statutory form the decision of the court in *R v Nottingham Justices, ex parte Davies* [1981] QB 38; [1980] 2 All ER 775.
18   Even if refused bail on remand, an accused is entitled to have his right to bail fully reviewed at the stage of committal for trial: *R v Reading Crown Court, ex parte Malik* [1981] QB 451; [1981] 1 All ER 249.
19   Under the Theft Act 1968, s 12, as amended by Aggravated Vehicle-Taking Act 1992.
20   Inserted by Criminal Justice and Public Order Act 1994, s 50.

c By the Crown Court

The Crown Court may grant bail to any person:[1]

(a) who has been committed in custody for appearance (trial or sentence) before the Crown Court; or

(b) who is in custody pursuant to a sentence imposed by a magistrates' court and has appealed against conviction or sentence; or

(c) who is in the custody of the Crown Court pending the disposal of his case by the Crown Court; or

(d) who, after the decision of the Crown Court in his case, has applied to the Crown Court to state a case for the High Court;[2] or

(e) who has applied to the High Court for an order of certiorari, or for leave to apply, in respect of proceedings in the Crown Court;[3] or

(f) to whom the Crown Court has granted a certificate under the Criminal Appeal Act 1968 (case fit for appeal); or

(g) who has been remanded in custody by a magistrates' court, where he has been refused bail by that court after hearing full argument.[4]

The prosecution also has a limited right of appeal against the grant of bail.[5] For this right to exist the prosecution must have objected to bail at the hearing before the magistrates' court. The prosecution have to show that there is a risk to the public of serious harm if the accused is bailed. The appeal is by way of rehearing.[6] The Crown Court may remand the defendant in custody or on bail subject to such conditions as it thinks fit.

d By the High Court

Whenever a magistrates' court withholds bail in criminal proceedings or imposes conditions in granting bail, the High Court may grant bail or vary the conditions.[7] The High Court may also grant bail pending any application for certiorari or for the statement of a case by the Crown Court or a magistrates' court, or pending appeal from the Queen's Bench divisional court to the House of Lords.[8]

The application for bail in the High Court is by summons to the prosecutor before a judge in chambers in the Queen's Bench Division to show cause why bail should not be granted, or why the variation in conditions of bail proposed by the applicant should not be made. If an applicant for bail in the High Court is refused bail by a judge in chambers, he cannot make fresh applications to any other judge or to the divisional court[9] and there is no appeal against the judge's decision.

---

1 Supreme Court Act 1981, s 81 (as amended).
2 See p 581, *post*.
3 This only applies to appellate proceedings in the Crown Court, because while it is sitting as a court of trial it is not amenable to prerogative order; see p 143, *ante*.
4 Cases (f) and (g) were added by the Criminal Justice Act 1982. Previously the Crown Court had no power to grant bail pending appeal to the Court of Appeal, nor prior to committal for trial (in the former case application had to be made to the Court of Appeal, in the latter to a High Court judge in chambers).
5 See n 4, *supra*.
6 For the relevant procedure, see s 81(2) of the Supreme Court Act 1981. Where notice of appeal is given orally, the magistrates must remand the defendant in custody pending hearing of the appeal.
7 Criminal Justice Act 1967, s 22 (as amended by Bail Act 1976, Sch 2).
8 Administration of Justice Act 1960, s 4.
9 RSC, Ord 79, r 9(11); cf *Re Kray* [1965] Ch 736; [1965] 1 All ER 710.

e *By the Court of Appeal*

The Court of Appeal has power to grant bail pending appeal to that court or pending a retrial ordered by that court following such an appeal[10] or pending appeal from that court to the House of Lords.[11] It is rare for the Court of Appeal to grant bail, but it occasionally does so, for example where the sentence appealed against is a short one so that it might be served by the time the appeal comes on for hearing, or where there is a strong prima facie likelihood of success.[12]

3 The right to bail

The marginal note to section 4 of the Bail Act 1976 is "General right to bail of accused persons and others" (the "others" being persons who are brought up for breach of the requirements of certain community orders,[13] or persons who have been remanded following conviction for reports). The section created a statutory presumption in favour of granting bail and provides that, except as provided in Schedule 1 to the Act, bail shall be granted to a person who appears before a magistrates' court or the Crown Court in the course of or in connection with proceedings or who applies for bail in connection with proceedings. It does not apply (save in the case of remand for reports) after conviction.

The right to bail was restricted by section 25 of the Criminal Justice and Public Order Act 1994, which originally provided that a person charged with, or convicted of, murder, attempted murder, manslaughter, rape or attempted rape must not be granted bail. This provision, intended to prevent repeat offences being committed by a person whilst on bail, was introduced despite the lack of clear empirical evidence that it was needed. It is now being modified, to restore an element of discretion in the hands of the court. Section 56 of the Crime and Disorder Act 1998 will permit bail to be granted where "exceptional circumstances" exist. The Act carefully avoids defining what might be regarded as exceptional circumstances.

Schedule 1 contains detailed provisions relating to circumstances in which bail may justifiably be withheld. These vary according to whether the accused is charged with an "imprisonable offence" or a "non-imprisonable offence", that is to say whether or not the offence is punishable with imprisonment (even if the accused himself, for example by reason of his age, would not be liable to be imprisoned for it).

If the offence is non-imprisonable the only circumstances in which bail may be withheld are:

(1) if the defendant having previously been granted bail, has failed to comply with his obligation to surrender to custody and the court believes that he would so fail again;
(2) if the court is satisfied that the defendant should be kept in custody for his own protection or, if he is a child or young person, for his own welfare;

---

10 Criminal Appeal Act 1968, ss 8(2), 19; the power may be exercised by the single judge (*ibid*, ss 31, 45(2)).

11 *Ibid*, s 36. By s 37, if the prosecutor is appealing to the House of Lords and, but for the decision of the Court of Appeal, the appellant would be liable to be detained, the Court of Appeal may make an order providing for his detention or directing that he shall not be released except on bail; there is similar provision on prosecution appeals from the Queen's Bench divisional court (Administration of Justice Act 1960, s 5).

12 *R v Watton* (1978) 68 Cr App Rep 293.

13 Section 4(3), as amended by the Criminal Justice Act 1991. For these orders, see p 541, *post*.

(3) if he is already in custody pursuant to a court sentence;[14]
(4) if, having been granted bail in the instant proceedings, he has been arrested for absconding or breaking the conditions of his bail.[15]

If the offence is imprisonable, there is a much wider range of circumstances in which bail may be justifiably withheld, in addition to those listed above. These are as follows:

(5) if the court is satisfied that there are substantial grounds for believing that the defendant, if released on bail (whether subject to conditions or not) would:
     (a) fail to surrender to custody; or
     (b) commit an offence while on bail; or
     (c) interfere with witnesses or otherwise obstruct the course of justice;
(6) where it has not been practicable for want of time to obtain sufficient information to enable the court to make its decision;
(7) where a case is adjourned for inquiries or report and it appears that it would be impracticable to complete the inquiries or make the report without keeping the defendant in custody.[16]

In considering the grounds referred to under (5) above the court must have regard to the nature and seriousness of the offence or default, the character, antecedents, associations and community ties of the defendant, the defendant's record in relation to fulfilling his obligations under previous grants of bail in criminal proceedings, the strength of the evidence against him and any other considerations which appear to be relevant.[17]

A further restriction was introduced into Schedule 1 in 1994[18] in an attempt to reduce the incidence of offending by persons on bail. In 1993, a study conducted by the Metropolitan Police showed that some 40% of suspects arrested in one week were already on bail.[19] An accused need not be granted bail if the offence is an indictable-only or either-way offence, and it appears to the court that he was on bail in criminal proceedings in respect of another offence at the date of the offence. This provision supplements the other provisions of Schedule 1, and makes it unnecessary for the court to be satisfied that there is a likelihood of commission of further offences. It is the fact of offending, not the likelihood of so doing, that matters.

The Act[20] contains detailed provisions for recording the decisions of both courts and police officers in relation to bail and entitling defendants to copies of records of such decisions. Where a court withholds bail or imposes or varies conditions of bail in the case of a person who has a "right to bail" in criminal proceedings, it must give reasons and these are recorded with the record of the decision.[1]

Where a magistrates' court withholds bail from a person who is not represented by counsel or solicitor, the court must inform him of his right to apply to the High Court (and, on committal for trial, to the Crown Court) for bail.[2]

---

14   Or a sentence of an authority acting under the Army, Air Force or Naval Discipline Acts.
15   Bail Act 1976, Sch 1, Part II.
16   *Ibid*, Sch 1, Part I.
17   *Ibid*, Sch 1, Part I, para 9.
18   Criminal Justice and Public Order Act 1994, s 26.
19   See Mr Robert MacLennan MP, HC Committee.
20   Section 5.
1   Bail Act 1976, s 5(3), (4).
2   *Ibid*, s 5(6).

4 Sureties

As already noted, the 1976 Act abolished personal recognisances from defendants (although a person may be required to provide security[3]). Recognisances still exist, however, in relation to sureties; these are persons who are sometimes colloquially said to "stand bail" for the accused. If a person is granted bail subject to the provision of sureties, the court must fix the amounts of the sureties and must also be satisfied that the proposed sureties are suitable having regard to their financial resources, character and any previous convictions and proximity (whether in point of kinship, place of residence or otherwise) to the defendant.[4] In practice courts are usually guided by the police in matters relating to the suitability of proposed sureties.

Before sureties are taken it is the practice to explain the nature of the obligations being undertaken so as to ensure that the proposed surety understands them and to warn of the consequences of the defendant failing to answer to his bail. These are, prima facie, forfeiture of the amount of the recognisance and possible imprisonment in default. The court has power to order the surety, in the event of default by the defendant, to forfeit the whole of the amount of the recognisance or part thereof.[5] Before exercising its discretion the court must, in some circumstances,[6] give the surety the opportunity to be heard and must take into account circumstances relating either to means or to the surety's culpability for the non-appearance of the defendant which might make it fair and just for the surety not to be ordered to forfeit the whole amount of the recognisance. Although not decisive, the conduct of the surety will be an important factor in the decision of the court as to whether or not to order forfeiture, either in whole or in part. In *R v Southampton Justices, ex parte Green*[7] Lord Denning MR stated that if the surety was guilty of no want of diligence and used every effort to secure the appearance of the accused it might be proper to remit the sum entirely. Imprisonment may be ordered in default of payment, of up to twelve months.

It is an offence, punishable on summary conviction or as a contempt of court, to agree to indemnify a surety in criminal proceedings (or, in the case of the surety himself, to be indemnified).[8]

An order of the Crown Court entreating the recognisance of a surety for a defendant who has failed to surrender to his bail to stand trial is not a "matter relating to trial on indictment" (within section 29(3) of the Supreme Court Act 1981) so that the order is subject to judicial review.[9]

3   Hitherto limited to persons unlikely to remain in the UK, but see now Crime and Disorder Act 1998, s 54.
4   *Ibid*, s 8(2).
5   Magistrates' Courts Act 1980, s 120(3); Powers of Criminal Courts Act 1973, s 31.
6   See Crime and Disorder Act 1998 where recognisances not conditioned for the appearance of the accused, the court is not bound to secure a hearing.
7   [1976] QB 11; [1975] 2 All ER 1073.
8   Bail Act 1976, s 9; for powers of committal to the Crown Court for sentence, see p 572, *post*.
9   *Re Smalley* [1985] AC 622; *sub nom Smalley v Crown Court at Warwick* [1985] 1 All ER 769.

CHAPTER 22

Trial of an Indictable Offence

Trial of an indictable offence involves trial by judge and jury in the Crown Court, with the significant expenditure of both time and money. The nature of the jury system,[1] and the reasons for election of trial on indictment of "either way" offences[2] have already been discussed. In this Chapter we examine the procedures themselves that are involved in trial on indictment. These were the subject of significant discussion by the Royal Commission on Criminal Justice,[3] which reported in 1993, and which sought to strike a balance between changes necessary to ensure a fair trial, and those necessary to make the system of trial of indictable offences more efficient.

A COMMITTAL PROCEEDINGS

I Introduction

The first stage of the trial of an indictable offence has, until now, been the committal for trial, or, as it is sometimes known, the preliminary inquiry before justices. Increasingly this is of a formal nature and, as noted below,[4] in future will only occur in cases involving either way offences. Its purpose, where it occurs, is to provide a mechanism for initial scrutiny by a court of the prosecution case against the accused, so as to ensure that sufficient evidence exists to justify requiring the accused to stand trial on indictment, with the expense and personal suffering that inevitably follows. Fundamental changes were made to law governing committal proceedings by the Criminal Justice Act 1967. Prior to that Act committal proceedings were always oral in nature: prosecution witnesses had to give evidence orally, their evidence was recorded in the form of a document known as a deposition, and the court had to decide whether or not sufficient evidence existed to justify sending the accused for trial on indictment. This procedure had to be followed even where the sufficiency of the

1   See Chapter 11, *ante*.
2   See p 469, *ante*.
3   Cm 2263, HMSO, 1993.
4   See p 486, *post*

prosecution evidence was not being questioned, even by the accused. Furthermore, since the magistrates often sat in open court, the resulting publicity in notorious cases sometimes gave rise to the creation of a real risk of prejudice to the trial itself. The 1967 Act therefore introduced new procedures, permitting committal for trial without the consideration of the evidence, thus saving much time and expense. It also introduced changes limiting the publicity that can be given to the evidence or the details of the offence.[5]

All committals for trial now follow this procedure, following a series of changes which have occurred since 1987. As long ago as 1981 the Royal Commission on Criminal Procedure[6] concluded that committal proceedings did not operate as an effective filter to prevent weak cases from reaching court. It proposed their abolition and replacement by a new procedure, to be known as an "application for discharge". This procedure would have given the defence the option of a hearing before magistrates at which to make a submission of no case to answer, after the prosecution had disclosed its case in writing. These proposals were not implemented at that time.

In 1986 the matter was considered further by the Fraud Trials Committee,[7] which identified a whole series of objections to committal proceedings. These included the length of time taken by full committals, with the consequent delays, the potential for abuse, whereby proceedings were undertaken in the hope of acquiring material to use as a defence, in the hope that advantage could be gained if witnesses die, go abroad or suffer from fading memories. In addition, the difficulties magistrates had in dealing with serious fraud cases, the cost of such proceedings, and the small number of defendants discharged in fraud cases were all noted. The committee recommended an interim procedural reform, until action might be taken by government on the Royal Commission recommendations in respect of serious fraud cases. The resulting changes were introduced in the Criminal Justice Act 1987,[8] which introduced a notice of transfer procedure. Four years later, in 1991, a similar procedure was introduced in some cases involving children.[9] Where these provisions apply, a notice of transfer can be served which effectively deprives the magistrates of jurisdiction and leads to automatic transfer to the Crown Court. These cases are discussed later.

This approach commended itself to the Royal Commission on Criminal Justice,[10] which, in its research, found that full committal proceedings involving a hearing occurred in only about eight per cent of cases tried on indictment. It also found evidence to support a conclusion that the committal process does not act as an effective filter to weed out weak cases: a significant number of cases fail at the Crown Court because of a direction by the judge to the jury to acquit. It recommended the abolition of the full committal procedure, but with the defence being able to make oral submissions of no case to answer, to be considered on the evidence contained in the case papers. In respect of either way offences, submissions would have been to a magistrates' court, and be dealt with by a stipendiary magistrate, but in respect of offences triable only on indictment such submissions would be to the Crown Court.[11]

The principle of limiting committal proceedings was accepted by the Government, who, however, took a different view on the detail. The Criminal Justice and Public

---

5   See p 489, *post*
6   Cmnd 8092 (HMSO, 1981).
7   See *ante*.
8   Criminal Justice Act 1987, s 4. See p 491, *post*.
9   Criminal Justice Act 1991, s 53.
10 Report, Ch 6, paras 26–32, hereinafter referred to a "RCCJ".
11 The Royal Commission makes consequential recommendations about the appropriate court for an application for bail, and in respect of the time-limits for making such applications of no case to answer: paras 31 and 29.

Order Act 1994 introduced a new scheme of transfers for trial.[12] Under that scheme, a person charged before a magistrates' court with an indictable offence, in relation to whom the prosecution had served a notice of the prosecution case on the magistrates court, would have been transferred by the magistrates to the Crown Court for trial unless he had made a successful application for dismissal. It was intended that that application, if it occurred, should be made only in writing. However, these provisions were never implemented. The Government found it difficult to create a scheme that would work effectively, and met strong criticism from professional bodies. It sought to remedy some of these difficulties by further provisions in the Criminal Procedure and Investigations Act 1996. The provisions initially contained in that Act had themselves to be abandoned, in the light of practical difficulties and of representations by professional bodies. There followed the extraordinary spectacle of the Government then abandoning the original proposals of the 1994 Act, and abandoning its proposals to amend the 1994 Act in the 1996 Act, and, instead, introducing revised provisions into the 1996 Act.[13] These revised provisions, ultimately enacted, kept committal proceedings in place, but modified the rules under which they are conducted.

The result is that committal proceedings remain, subject to the changes in the 1996 Act. These have the effect of limiting the evidence to be considered at such proceedings to documentary evidence and exhibits tendered by the prosecutions. However, the right to a hearing remains, and magistrates continue to be able to consider any representations made by either the defence or the prosecution, to assist the court in reaching its decision as to whether the case should be committed for trial.

The saga is not yet complete. The Crime and Disorder Act 1998 now abolishes committal proceedings in cases where an adult is charged with an indictable only offence.[14] Instead a scheme is introduced which basically requires service of the prosecution case in writing, followed by an opportunity for the defendant to make an application to the Crown Court for the case to be dismissed. Such an application may in some circumstances be an oral application. The new procedure will govern cases of serious or complex fraud, or which involve children, which hitherto have been within the notice of transfer procedures. The effect of these proposed changes, which are quite similar to the recommendations of the Royal Commission on Criminal Justice, is that we shall now have three distinct systems:

(a)   the automatic transfer to the Crown Court of cases of an adult which include an indictable only offence, under the 1998 Act;

(b)   committal proceedings in respect of most either way offences, subject to the limitations as to evidence introduced in the 1996 Act;

(c)   the notice of transfer procedures contained in the 1987 and 1991 Acts, when they apply, in cases other than indictable-only offences.

2   Procedure

a   Indictable only offences

Under the provisions contained in the Crime and Disorder Act 1998, where an adult is charged with an indictable only offence he shall be sent forthwith to the Crown Court.[15]

---

12   1994 Act, s 44 and Sch 4.
13   1996 Act, s 47 and Sch 1.
14   1998 Act, ss 51–52 and Sch 3.
15   *Ibid.*

The person committed will be committed also in respect of any either way offences or summary offences with which he is also charged which

(a) appear to the court to be related to the indictable only offence and
(b) in the case of summary offences, are punishable with imprisonment or involve obligatory or discretionary disqualification from driving.[16] A summary offence is related to an indictable only offence if it arises out of circumstances which are the same as, or connected with, those giving rise to the indictable only offence.[17] In cases where an adult is jointly charged with an either way offence that appears to be related to the indictable only offence he also must be committed by the court. By contrast if a child or young person is jointly charged with that same indictable only offence the court may commit for trial, but is not required to do so.

A person who has been committed for trial under the 1998 Act will be entitled to receive copies of the documents containing the evidence on which the charge or charges are based.[18] When he has received that evidence, and before arraignment, he may apply either orally (provided he has given notice of intention to so) or in writing to the Crown Court sitting in the place specified, for the charge, or any of them, to be dismissed.[19] An accused will only be entitled to adduce oral evidence at such a hearing if he is granted leave to do so, and that will only be granted if it appears to the judge, having regard to any matters stated in the application for leave, that the interests of justice require him to do so. The new Act introduces detailed provisions that govern the power of the Crown Court to deal with any summary offence.[20] A Crown Court will have the power to take a plea of guilty, but not to try such an offence if a plea of not guilty is entered. The Crown Court can dismiss such a charge if the CPS does not propose to offer evidence on that charge. A complex procedure will apply also where, for whatever reason, there ceases to be an indictable only offence before the court, but an either way offence remains.[1] In such a case, following an inquiry as to the intended plea, the court has to decide whether trial on indictment or summary trial is more suitable.

b   Either-way offences

The Criminal Procedure and Investigations Act 1996 introduced significant modifications to the relevant provisions of the Magistrates Courts Act 1980. Under these provisions, as amended,[2] it is open for a magistrates' court (which comprises for this purpose a single justice, or in some circumstances a justices' clerk or member of his staff)[3] to commit the accused for trial without consideration of the evidence, where the parties agree. Where, however, committal for trial is contested, the magistrates will have to consider the evidence. That evidence to be considered is now confined to documentary evidence and exhibits tendered by the prosecution, provided these meet the conditions set out in the 1980 Act.[4] These documents, will, generally speaking, amount to the witness statements of the witnesses to be relied on by the prosecution,

---

16   *Ibid*, s 51(2),(4),(6),(11).
17   *Ibid*, s 51(11).
18   *Ibid*, Sch 3, para 1.
19   *Ibid*, Sch 3, para 2.
20   *Ibid*, paras 5–6.
1   *Ibid*, para 6.
2   See Magistrates' Courts Act 1980, s 6.
3   See p 565, *post*.
4   See 1980 Act, ss 5A–5F, introduced by 1996 Act, s 47 and Sch 1.

irrespective of whether the statement contains inadmissible evidence.[5] However it may also include depositions taken by a justice of the peace pursuant to s 97A(2) of the 1980 Act.[6] Under s 97A, a justice of the peace may, where satisfied certain conditions are fulfilled, issue a summons requiring a person to attend to have his evidence taken as a deposition or to produce a document or other exhibit. This can only occur where, inter alia, a person will not voluntarily make the statement or produce the document. Finally, in certain circumstances documents may be produced under these provisions.[7]

The effect of these provisions is to create a series of pre-conditions which apply both in respect of committals for trial without the consideration of evidence, and committals for trial where evidence has, in fact, been considered. In relation to the former, the position relating to uncontested committals is essentially unchanged. By s 6(2) of the 1980 Act the accused may be committed for trial without consideration of the contents of any statements, depositions or other documents, and without the consideration of any exhibits which are not documents, provided certain conditions are fulfilled. Such a committal without consideration of the evidence can only occur where the accused is legally represented (which does not have to be by solicitor or counsel) and there is no submission by that legal representative or by a co-accused that there is no case to answer.

In cases where the conditions for committal without consideration of the evidence are not satisfied, clearly the court will have to consider the evidence. By that one means evidence is tendered by or on behalf of the prosecutor, in the sense described above, and the magistrates may so commit if they are of the opinion that there is sufficient evidence to put the accused on trial by jury for any indictable offence. If they are not so satisfied they must discharge him. Such a committal can only be in the presence of the accused himself. The evidence relied upon, and contained in any statement admitted, must, unless the court directs otherwise, be read aloud at that hearing, and the court may direct that an account be given of any part not read aloud. As was the case under the pre-existing law, the defence may submit there is no case to answer, either on the charge brought against the accused (assuming that a specific charge has been formulated) or generally. In other words, it may be submitted that either the charge brought should be reduced to a lesser charge (for example murder to manslaughter) or that the accused should be discharged altogether as being completely innocent of any crime. Such a submission is only likely to succeed in the clearest of cases, because the magistrates are not concerned at this stage with the actual guilt or innocence of the defendant; their only duty is to decide whether or not sufficient evidence exists to justify putting the accused on trial for any indictable offence.

c   Notices of transfer

In certain cases involving serious or complex fraud, the notice of transfer provisions contained in the Criminal Justice Act 1987 apply. Similar provisions relate to certain offences involving children. These provisions are dealt with later.[8]

d   Time limits

Committal proceedings will often need to occur within a certain period because of the custody time limits contained in regulations made under s 22 of the Prosecution of

---

5   1980 Act, s 5B.
6   1980 Act, s 5C.
7   1980 Act, s 5E.
8   See p 491, *post.*

Offences Act 1985. The law and practice governing time limits and reduction of delay is undergoing change and goes far beyond committal proceedings. The issue is dealt with below.[9]

e   Publicity

Following a well-publicised murder trial where pre-trial publicity created a severe risk of prejudice to the trial itself,[10] restrictions on the reporting of committal proceedings were introduced in 1967,[11] and are now contained in the Magistrates' Courts Act 1980. Similar rules apply to cases of indictable only offences which go directly to the Crown Court.[12]

By section 8 of the 1980 Act, it is generally unlawful to publish any report of committal proceedings, apart from various formal matters such as the court, the names of the justices, defendants and advocates, a summary of the charges and the decision as to whether or not to commit. The evidence may not be published until the end of the trial,[13] if the defendant is committed, or the end of committal proceedings, if he is not. It is open to the defendants or any one of them to apply, and the court must then order that the restriction is not to apply if all defendants so require; if one or more objects to such an order the court will make an order only if it is in the interests of justice to do so.[14] The restrictions on publicity apply equally to proceedings in the magistrates' court before the court proceeds to inquire as to whether the accused should be committed for trial. This will apply where there are mode of trial proceedings leading to committal proceedings.[15]

In addition to the general restrictions imposed by the Act, it is open to the court to use its powers to postpone or limit reporting that exist under the Contempt of Court Act 1981.[16] Further, there are specific restrictions in rape cases imposed by the Sexual Offences (Amendment) Act 1976. Under that Act it is an offence to publish matters likely to lead members of the public to identify a woman as the complainant or the defendant as the person accused.[17] In relation to committal proceedings the accused can apply to the court to remove the restriction relating to publicising his identity (but not that of the complainant).[18]

All the above applies to publicity in the press, and on radio and television. As regards admission of the public to committal proceedings, the Act expressly states that examining justices must sit in public unless:

---

9   See p 493, *post*.
10   The trial of Doctor John Bodkin Adams, in 1957. Devlin J stated that it would have been far better if the preliminary proceedings had been held in private.
11   Criminal Justice Act 1967, implementing the recommendations of the Tucker Report (Cmnd 479, HMSO, 1958).
12   See 1998 Act, Sch 3, para 3.
13   By which time it will have been superseded by evidence given at the trial and will be of no general interest. See also the court's powers under s 4 of the Contempt of Court Act 1981, *post*, p 518.
14   Magistrates' Courts Act 1980, s 8(2A), inserted by Criminal Justice (Amendment) Act 1981. All co-accused must be given a fair opportunity to make such representations: see *R v Wirral District Magistrates' Court, ex parte Meikle* (1990) 154 JP 1035.
15   *Ibid*, s 25; see p 471, ante.
16   Contempt of Court Act 1981, ss 4, 11.
17   Sexual Offences (Amendment) Act 1976, s 4. The Act applies to "rape offences", and not to cases of indecent assault or other sexual offences. See *R v Funderburk* [1990] 2 All ER 482, [1990] 1 WLR 587. The restrictions on publicity apply equally to the trial and subsequent proceedings.
18   In addition he can apply to the Crown Court for a direction removing the restriction in relation to his own or the complainant's identity, but such a direction may only be given if required for the purpose of inducing likely witnesses to come forward and if the conduct of the applicant's defence at the trial is likely to be substantially prejudiced if the direction is not given (*ibid*, ss 4(2), 6(2)).

(a) statute directs to the contrary or
(b) the magistrates consider that the ends of justice would not be served by them sitting in open court, as regards the whole or any part of the committal proceedings.[19]

Thus publicity is encouraged as regards the attendance of members of the public in court, but not as regards reports to a wider public in the press and on television. Further, where the defendant is committed, or discharged after decision not to commit, there must be published on that day or the next, in a part of the magistrates' court to which the public have access, certain details such as the defendant's name and address, the charge or charges and (if there is a committal) the court of trial.[20]

3 Committal for trial

If committal for trial occurs, several questions arise:

(a) what should the charge be?
(b) to which location of the Crown Court should the defendant be committed?
(c) should the defendant be committed in custody or on bail?

a Charges

It is for the justices to consider, on all the evidence, what charge is appropriate, the only limitation being that it must be properly founded on evidence appearing in the evidence put before it. There is no power to reduce the charge on a section 6(2) committal; therefore, if such a committal is to be used, the prosecution may be wise to bring charges in the alternative. As already seen, so long as the section 6(2) procedure is used, no question of dismissing the charge arises.

b Court of trial

The structure of the Crown Court has already been dealt with.[1] It is not a single court but sits in a number of different locations. These are described as first-tier, second-tier and third-tier centres. First-tier centres deal with both civil and criminal cases and are visited by High Court and circuit judges; second-tier centres deal with criminal cases only but are visited by both High Court and circuit judges, while third-tier centres deal with criminal cases only and are visited only by circuit judges. Each circuit contains a number of each type of centre. Offences in turn are divided into four classes,[2] each containing a number of offences. Offences in Class 1 must normally be tried by a High Court judge although cases of murder may be realised by the presiding judge, for trial by a circuit judge approved for that purpose by the Lord Chief Justice; examples are murder and the rare offences for which a person may be sentenced to death. Offences in Class 2 must be tried by a High Court judge unless a presiding judge of the circuit releases any particular case for trial by a circuit judge or recorder; examples are

---

19   Magistrates' Courts Act 1980, s 4(2).
20   *Ibid*, s 6(5). It is not stated how long the notice must be displayed. But this has effect subject to the restrictions imposed by the Sexual Offences (Amendment) Act 1976 (*supra*) so that the name of the defendant will not be included, nor will any matter likely to lead members of the public to identify him or the complainant.
1   See p 176, *ante*.
2   By the directions set out in *Practice Note* [1987] 3 All ER 1064; *sub nom Practice Direction* [1987] 1 WLR 1671.

manslaughter, abortion and rape. Offences in Class 3 may be tried by a High Court judge, or by a circuit judge or recorder; these are all offences triable only on indictment not falling within any other class.

Offences in Class 4 will normally be tried by a circuit judge or recorder, although they may also be tried by a High Court judge; examples are wounding or causing grievous bodily harm with intent, conspiracy and all offences triable either way.

Therefore, when a magistrates' court commits for trial a person charged with any offence within Classes 1 or 2,[3] it must specify, as the place of trial, the location of the Crown Court where a High Court judge regularly sits.[4] In the case of an offence in Class 4 the magistrates' court must simply specify the most convenient location of the Crown Court. In selecting the most convenient location, the justices must have regard to the location of the Crown Court designated by the presiding judge as the location to which cases should normally be committed from their petty sessions area.[5] The magistrates will also need to have regard to whether live TV link facilities exist, if one of the witnesses is a child who is permitted to give evidence through such a link.[6]

c   Bail

The magistrates must consider whether to release the defendant on bail, or to commit in custody. Factors which must be considered, including the imposition of conditions, have already been explained.[7]

B   NOTICES OF TRANSFER AND VOLUNTARY BILLS

The abolition of committal proceedings in serious fraud cases has already been noted.[8] Section 46 of the Criminal Justice Act 1987 provides for cases to be automatically transferred to the Crown Court, but will not apply in the future to indictable only offences.[9] Where a person has been charged with an either way offence, and in the opinion of an appropriate officer[10] there is sufficient evidence for the accused to be committed for trial and the evidence reveals a case of fraud of such seriousness or complexity that it is appropriate that the management of the case should without delay be taken over by the Crown Court, then a notice of transfer can be served.[11] This must be done before the magistrates' court begins committal proceedings, and when served the magistrates' court loses all jurisdiction. The decision to serve the notice of transfer appears to be beyond judicial challenge;[12] however, the Act creates a procedure whereby a person may make an application for dismissal of the transferred charge.[13] Oral

---

3   See n 2, *infra*.
4   *Practice Direction*, para 2.
5   *Ibid*, para 3, and Magistrates' Courts Act 1980, s 7.
6   See p 525, *post*.
7   See p 481, *ante*.
8   See p 485, *ante*.
9   See p 486, *ante*.
10   This is given a wide meaning by s 4(2) and includes the DPP, Director of the Serious Fraud Office, Commissioners of Inland Revenue, Commissioners of Customs and Excise, and the Secretary of State.
11   The Royal Commission on Criminal Justice recommended that this be reworded to read "seriousness or complexity", bringing within the transfer provisions cases that are suitable for such treatment but which currently go through the committal process: RCCJ, Ch 7, para 60. The change was made by the Criminal Justice and Public Order Act 1994, Sch 9.
12   See Criminal Justice Act 1987, s 4(3); Criminal Justice Act 1991, s 53(4).
13   See Criminal Justice Act 1987, s 6(2); Criminal Justice Act 1987 (Dismissal Of Transferred Charges) Rules 1988 (SI 1988/1695).

evidence can be adduced only with leave of the judge, and there is no opportunity for a submission of no case to answer. The grounds of the application are that the evidence that has been disclosed would not be sufficient for a jury properly to convict the person charged.

The Criminal Justice Act 1991 introduced similar provisions in cases where a child was the victim of, or witnessed, certain offences of violence or of a sexual nature, and where the case should be taken over and proceeded with by the Crown Court to avoid prejudice to the welfare of the child.[14] Again, these provisions will, for the future apply only to either way offences.[15] Where they apply, the Director of Public Prosecutions can serve a notice of transfer. The evidence must be sufficient for the person charged to be committed for trial. Similar safeguards to those earlier described in the context of serious fraud cases apply. Similar provisions did exist in respect of war crimes, but have now been repealed.[16]

By a procedure known as the voluntary bill procedure, the prosecution can apply to a High Court judge[17] for leave to prefer a bill of indictment against the accused. The judge in his discretion grants or refuses leave,[18] with the result that if leave is granted the bill is preferred forthwith and there is no need for any committal proceedings. At the same time the defendant loses the advantage of knowing in advance the substance of the case against him. The applicant himself cannot attend unless permitted by the judge to do so, whilst the defendant is not entitled to attend at all. Even where there is a hearing it is not in open court.[19] Regular use of the voluntary bill procedure could therefore lead to hardship.

For these reasons, the voluntary bill procedure is to be regarded as exceptional. In a *Practice Direction* in 1990[20] it was stated as follows:

> "The usual means of bringing a defendant to trial on indictment is by committal for trial in the magistrates' court. A voluntary bill should only be granted where good reason to depart from the normal procedure is clearly shown and only where the interests of justice, rather than considerations of administrative convenience, require it."

It is impossible to define precisely when the voluntary bill procedure should be used, and, given the abolition of committal proceedings for indictable only offences, its future use may in the main be restricted to either way offences. To use it to circumvent the procedures set out in Schedule 3 to the Crime and Disorder Act 1998 might well amount to an abuse of process, although it will be an appropriate way of reviving proceedings struck out by the Crown Court for a failure by the prosecution to comply with relevant time-limits.[1] Hitherto, its use has been confined to situations where committal

---

14   Criminal Justice Act 1991, s 53.
15   See 1998 Act, Sch 8, para 72.
16   War Crimes Act 1991, Sch 1, para 4, repealed by the Criminal Procedure and Investigations Act 1996, s 47 and Sch 5.
17   A circuit judge has no power to give leave to prefer a bill of indictment: *R v Thompson* [1975] 2 All ER 1028; [1975] 1 WLR 1425.
18   See, eg, *Re Roberts* [1967] 1 WLR 474. The issue of a voluntary bill is not susceptible to judicial review: *R v Manchester Crown Court, ex parte Williams* (1990) 154 JP 589.
19   See, generally, *R v Raymond* [1981] QB 910; [1981] 2 All ER 246, where an attempt to challenge the validity of the voluntary bill procedure (on the grounds that it was inconsistent with the *audi alteram partem* principle) was rejected by the Court of Appeal.
20   *Practice Note* [1991] 1 All ER 288; sub nom *Practice Direction* [1990] 1 WLR 1633.
1   See p 494, *post*.

proceedings have been disrupted[2] or have failed[3] and where the public interest justifies prosecution.

C   DELAY AND TIME-LIMITS

It has already been seen that the Prosecution of Offences Act 1985 imposes time-limits upon the length of time an accused person may be held in custody.[4] The potential for delay to lead to application to stay the proceedings because of abuse of process also exists.[5] Delay is a particular matter of concern in criminal proceedings, leading to the potential for an unfair trial, because of the time between the event in question and the determination of guilt. It also prolongs the effect of the alleged crime on the victim, witnesses and, indeed, the accused. It was because of increasing, and unacceptable, delays that the Government in 1996 established the Narey Committee to review delays within the criminal justice system. The Narey Report was published in February 1997,[6] and contained some 33 different recommendations. These recommendations, discussed at the appropriate parts of this book,[7] ranged over a wide area, including the operation and powers of the CPS, the role of justices' clerks, limitations on trial by jury, abolition of committal proceedings in respect of indictable only offences, changes to the pleas-and-direction hearing and major changes to the youth justice system. Many of them, although not all, have been accepted and are the subject of implementation through legislative and administrative changes.[8]

One area undergoing change is the question of time-limits under the 1985 Act. The effect of the custody time-limits is that, if an accused is in custody, committal proceedings need to be commenced within the prescribed limits. If, for whatever reason, delay occurs, the prosecution has to obtain an extension of time from the court under section 22(3) of the 1985 Act. New provisions go further. The power to make regulations under s 22 of that Act permits time-limits generally to be set and to provide sanctions for non-compliance. It is the intention of the Government to extend the regulations beyond custody time-limits, and the Crime and Disorder Act 1998[9] confers a wider power to make regulations which govern different types of offence, of accused or different areas of the country. Statutory time-limits will be set for all non-custodial cases, both in relation to adults and to juveniles, although with tougher time-limits in cases involving persistent young offenders,[10] and young offenders on bail.[11] This latter proposal is part of the general reform of the youth justice system, with the objective of halving the time from arrest to sentence.[12] For adults, it is proposed that statutory time-limits be set for the pre-trial stage of all proceedings, both indictable and summary, broken down into three stages: the first listing of the case to start of summary trial; first appearance to committal or transfer; committal or transfer to start of Crown Court trial. It is not intended to set time-limits for the period between trial and conviction. To do so would, of course, place the fairness of proceedings in individual cases at risk.

---

2   *R v Raymond,* n 19, *supra.*
3   *R v Horsham Justices, ex parte Reeves* (1980) 75 Cr App Rep 236n.
4   See p 463, *ante.*
5   See p 462, *ante.*
6   *Review of Delay in the Criminal Justice System,* 27 February 1997 (HMSO).
7   See pp 460, 464, 486, 564.
8   See in particular, Crime and Disorder Act 1998, ss 43-57.
9   Section 40.
10   *Ibid,* s 41.
11   *Ibid,* s 41.
12   See p 575, *post.*

Accompanying this extension of time-limit provision are changes in the rules governing enforcement, contained in the Crime and Disorder Act 1988. Section 22(3) of the 1985 Act[13] now provides that an extension of the time-limit may be granted by a court, before the expiration of the time-limit, provided the court is satisfied that the need for the extension is due to:

(i)   the illness or absence of the accused, a necessary witness, a judge or magistrate; or

(ii)   a postponement which is occasioned by the ordering by the court of separate trials in the case of two or more accused; or

(iii) what is some other good and sufficient cause. In addition the court will have to be satisfied that the prosecution has acted with all due diligence and expedition, which will be a question of fact for the court to consider in the context of the individual application and its effects. No extension of time-limits will be needed in respect of periods during which the accused is unlawfully at large.[14] If, because of prosecution delay, proceedings are stayed, fresh proceedings may in some circumstances be commenced, in cases where the stay is by a Crown Court, by the preferment of a voluntary bill or indictment,[15] and in other cases by the laying of a new information.[16]

D   DISCLOSURE OF EVIDENCE

I   The common law

The effective working of the adversarial system depends, in part, upon proper disclosure.[17] Unlike in civil proceedings where discovery generally is available,[18] the duties of pre-trial disclosure in criminal cases have in the past been limited. The prosecution has always been under a duty to disclose at committal the evidence upon which it proposes to rely, subject only to the right to call additional evidence in some circumstances and subject to certain conditions.[19] Generally, there has been no obligation on an accused to disclose his defence. An accused person, or a suspect, in criminal proceedings has a "right of silence". This "right of silence"[20] has permitted the defence at any stage to adduce evidence without notice, and without adverse inferences being drawn in law from that non-disclosure. That rule was modified in 1967 in respect of evidence of alibi,[1] and, more recently, in respect of the adducing of expert evidence.[2] The general right to silence remains, although the practical effect of recent changes in the law may well be to limit or reduce reliance on the right.

---

13   See 1998 Act, s 43.
14   *Ibid*, s 40(5).
15   See p 493, *ante*.
16   1998 Act, s 40.
17   See p 455, *ante*. Note in particular *R v McIlkenny* [1992] 2 All ER 417.
18   See p 385, *ante*.
19   Service of the witness statements must occur. See p 455, *ante*.
20   For the various meanings of this term, see Lord Mustill in *R v Director of Serious Fraud Office, ex parte Smith* [1993] AC 1, *sub nom Smith v Director of Serious Fraud Office* [1992] 3 All ER 456.
1   Criminal Justice Act 1967, s 12.
2   Crown Court (Advance Disclosure of Expert Evidence) Rules 1987. See p 496, *post*.

a   Disclosure of "unused material" by the prosecution

A common law duty of disclosure on the prosecution in respect of unused material was recognised in *R v Bryant and Dickson*,[3] although the precise extent and nature of that duty remained uncertain.[4] The Royal Commission on Criminal Procedure in 1981[5] found the practices of police forces in respect of disclosure of unused material to be both inconsistent and variable. It was to deal with these uncertainties that in 1981 the Attorney-General issued the *Attorney-General's Guidelines*[6] dealing with disclosure of unused materials. These guidelines sought to define what was meant by "unused material", to identify when material should be disclosed, and when a discretion existed to refuse disclosure. In addition, they dealt with the right of the prosecution to resist disclosure on the grounds of public interest immunity. The Royal Commission on Criminal Justice in 1991 regarded these guidelines as "to all intents and purposes" as having the force of law.[7] However, it became clear later that they amounted to nothing more than "a set of instructions to Crown Prosecution Service lawyers and prosecuting counsel",[8] and indeed instructions that did not reflect the development of the common law in respect of prosecution duties of disclosure.[9] For these reasons, Steyn LJ considered the value of the guidelines to have been largely eroded. It was to the common law, not the guidelines, that one should look in determining duties of disclosure.

In *R v Saunders*,[10] the term "unused material" had been given an extremely wide definition. Henry J stated that it was clear that the term "unused material" might apply to virtually all material collected during the investigation of a case. This led to a significant extension of the duty of disclosure, with the potential for disclosure arising in respect of virtually all material collected during a prosecution investigation a position which had the potential, and sometimes the effect, of imposing unreasonable burdens on prosecutors. It also raised issues as to the extent to which the prosecution might be inhibited, or forced to change tack, by claims for disclosure of "sensitive material" which might be of marginal relevance to the actual case before the court. It was in an attempt to somewhat narrow the test, and reduce these problems, that the Court of Appeal in *R v Keane*[11] adopted the dictum of Jowitt J in *R v Melvin and Dingle*.[12] Jowitt J said:

> "I would judge to material in the realm of disclosure that which can be seen on a sensible appraisal by the prosecution: (1) to be relevant or possibly relevant to an issue in the case; (2) to raise or possibly raise a new issue whose existence is not apparent from the evidence the prosecution proposes to use; (3) to hold out a real (as opposed to fanciful) prospect of providing a lead on evidence which goes to (1) or (2)".

3   (1946) 31 Cr App Rep 146.
4   Cf Lord Denning MR in *Dallison v Caffrey* [1965] 1 QB 348; [1964] 2 All ER 610, approved in *R v Lawson* (1989) 90 Cr App Rep 107.
5   Cmnd 8092 (HMSO, 1981)
6   (1981) 74 Cr App Rep 302.
7   *Op cit*, p 91, n 20. See also Henry J in *R v Saunders* (29 September 1989, unreported).
8   See O'Connor, "Prosecution Disclosure – Principle, Practice and Justice" [1992] Crim LR 464 at 468. The guidelines only applied to lawyers, not forensic scientists or other experts.
9   *R v Brown* [1995] 1 Cr App R 191, per Steyn LJ.
10 (1991, unreported). The phrase was interpreted broadly to include a mass of notes, tape-recordings and drafts of statements. See RCCJ, *op cit*, Ch 6, paras 38–41. The Royal Commission was informed that the police were in some cases incapable of complying with the duty of disclosure, given the complexity of some cases.
11 (1994) 99 Cr App R 1.
12 20 December 1993, unreported.

The effect of this change of approach was to meet some of the concerns of the Royal Commission on Criminal Justice, which, in 1993, stated[13] that:

> "the defence can require the police and prosecution to comb through large masses of material in the hope either of causing delay or chancing upon something which will induce the prosecution to drop the case rather than to have to disclose the material concerned. The defence may do this by successive requests for more material, far beyond the stage at which it could be reasonably claimed that the information was likely to cast a doubt upon the prosecution case. Although it may be time consuming and wasteful of the sources for the police to check all the materials requested they may have to do so if they are to be sure that it can properly be released".

This duty of prosecution disclosure was in addition to that which existed in respect of expert evidence, which is discussed below. Despite the development by the common law of a modified approach, in 1995 a government consultation paper[14] proposed the introduction of a statutory scheme of disclosure, governing both prosecution and defence. This scheme was implemented by Parts I and II of the Criminal Procedure and Investigations Act 1996.

b   Expert evidence

Section 81 of the Police and Criminal Evidence Act 1984 authorises the making of rules regarding the disclosure of expert evidence. The Crown Court (Advance Notice of Expert Evidence) Rules 1987 have been made under that power, and apply to trials on indictment.[15] Following committal for trial the party who is seeking to rely on expert evidence, whether of fact or opinion, must furnish to the other party a statement in writing of any finding or opinion upon which he proposes to rely, and, on request in writing, provide a copy of (or access to, if that is more practicable) the records of any observation, test, calculation, or other procedure in respect of which the finding or opinion is based. A failure to disclose means that the evidence cannot be adduced without the leave of the court.

This obligation of disclosure under the 1987 rules is not the only obligation. In *R v Ward*[16] the Court of Appeal stressed that there is a common law obligation upon a government forensic scientist to act impartially, and to disclose any scientific evidence that might arguably assist the defence. Failure to comply with this obligation was one of the principal reasons for quashing the convictions of the defendant in that case.

It was failure to disclose fully in this way that caused problems in *R v Ward* and other cases.[17] Such obligation to disclose does not, however, meet the criticism of those who argue that the trial process is unfairly tilted in favour of the prosecution because of its command of forensic science and other scientific facilities,[18] and generally the imbalance of resources. Some argue that the court itself should appoint its own expert

13   *Op cit*, Ch 6, para 42.
14   Cm 2262, (HMSO, 1993).
15   The power to make rules in respect of expert evidence in summary cases has been conferred by the Criminal Procedure and Investigations Act 1996, s 19.
16   [1993] 2 All ER 577; [1993] 1 WLR 619.
17   See eg *R v Maguire* [1992] QB 936; [1992] 2 All ER 433.
18   For a description of the organisation of forensic science facilities, see the RCCJ, *op cit*, Ch 7, para 6–36.

witnesses, to report impartially to the court.[19] The whole question was examined extensively by the Royal Commission on Criminal Justice.[20]

The Commission considered, but rejected, a proposal to create an independent forensic science agency, as opposed to one being part of a government department or police authority. Instead, it proposed[1] the establishment of a Forensic Science Advisory Council to report to the Home Secretary on the performance, achievements and efficiency of the forensic science laboratories, in both the private and public sectors. Subject to a rule that the same laboratory should not take on work for both prosecution and defence in the same case, public sector laboratories should look on themselves as equally available to defence and prosecution. This is important in the light of research findings[2] that defence solicitors sometimes encounter difficulty in finding suitable independent experts to interpret prosecution findings.[3] In respect of the general duty of disclosure, the Royal Commission welcomed the approach taken in *R v Ward*.[4] It also recommended streamlining legal aid provision to assist in this respect.

Of significance is the approach taken by the majority of the Commission towards a more inquisitorial system in respect of forensic science evidence. The Royal Commission found[5] that a sizeable minority of contested Crown Court cases involve scientific evidence. In approximately 25% of such cases there was a defence challenge to such evidence, and in some 800 cases a year not only was such a challenge made but also expert evidence was called on behalf of the defence. In these cases the duty of disclosure applies equally to the defence as to the prosecution. The defence, however, is under no duty to disclose the evidence it has obtained from experts whom it does not intend to call, perhaps because it is unfavourable. Nor is there a duty to disclose expert evidence acquired by the defence for the purposes of discrediting prosecution evidence through cross-examination. To overcome this adversarial approach the Commission recommended as follows:

(1) The defence should not be required to disclose evidence it does not intend to call, since it must be for the defendant to decide what evidence to give.[6]

(2) When the defence is calling expert evidence, the expert witnesses on both sides should be required to meet, to draw up a report for the court setting out scientific facts and their interpretation by both sides. In cases of substantial disagreement a preparatory hearing[7] should be held to decide how such disputes could be clarified, possibly by additional tests.[8]

(3) Where the defence do not dispute scientific evidence counsel should certify this.[9]

(4) Where the defence do intend to dispute scientific evidence but do not intend to call expert evidence themselves, they should, after disclosure, indicate which matters are and are not admitted. This will enable the prosecution to see which

19 See Spencer [1992] Crim LR.
20 Report, Ch 9.
1   Ch 7, para 3.2.
2   Roberts and Willmore *The Role of Forensic Science Evidence in Criminal Proceedings* (Royal Commission on Criminal Justice Research Study No 11 (HMSO, 1992)); Stevenson *The Ability to Challenge DNA Evidence* (Royal Commission on Criminal Justice Research Study No 9 (HMSO, 1992)).
3   See RCCJ, Ch 9, paras 50–53.
4   *Ibid*, para 47.
5   Crown Court Survey: see RCCJ, para 57. The estimates ranged from 30%–40% of cases, in quantity some 10,000 cases per year.
6   *Ibid*, para 62.
7   See p 511, *post*.
8   *Ibid*, para 63.
9   *Ibid*, para 64.

areas of expert evidence are in dispute, and the matters that need further clarification at a preparatory hearing.[10]

(5) A minority of the Commission also favoured requiring defence experts to participate in pre-trial discussions.[11]

The Commission also made recommendations as to the handling of expert evidence at the trial.[12] It emphatically rejected the appointment of a court expert, or an assessor, whose views would not be susceptible to examination or cross-examination.

c   Witholding of sensitive prosecution material

Where the material in question is sensitive material the prosecution may seek to withhold it from the defence on the grounds of public interest. The rule of evidence known as public interest immunity permits the withholding of otherwise relevant material from a party to proceedings on the grounds that its disclosure, or production, is not in the public interest.[13] For example, it may deal with matters relating to national security, or reveal the identity of a member of the security services thus rendering that person operationally ineffective. One general class of case where the courts have been prepared to uphold claims of public interest immunity is that relating to information concerning law enforcement. The right of the police to withhold information concerning police informers was recognised in *Marks v Beyfus*,[14] and has been extended to the location, and identity of the occupants, of police observation posts.[15] Other successful claims of public interest immunity have related to records relating to the welfare of children.[16]

After some confusion the court in *R v Ward*[17] made it clear that the decision whether or not to permit the withholding of relevant evidence was for the court, not the prosecution. The court is entitled to inspect documents that are the subject of a claim for immunity. If the prosecution wished to withhold relevant material, it should notify the defence that it intended to make an application to the court, unless details of the application, or, exceptionally, the fact even that such an application was being made, would be contrary to the public interest.[18] The decision as to the withholding of the evidence was the court's, and an order would not be granted simply because the evidence was of a confidential nature. On the other hand, an accused will not be allowed to go on a "fishing expedition": the relevance of the document or information in question is a precondition, and a court will not order the production of material which is insufficiently relevant.[19] If material is relevant, a court is likely to order its production,[20] a position confirmed by Sir Richard Scott in his report into the "arms

---

10   *Ibid.*
11   RCCJ, Appendix.
12   *Ibid*, Ch 9, para 4.
13   See, generally, *Conway v Rimmer* [1968] AC 910; *Air Canada v Secretary of State for Trade* [1983] 1 All ER 96; *Makanjuola v Commissioner of Police for the Metropolis* [1992] 3 All ER 617.
14   (1890) 25 QBD 494.
15   See *R v Hallett* [1986] Crim LR 462; *R v Hennessy* (1979) 68 Cr App R 419; *R v Agar* [1990] Crim LR 183; *R v Rankine* [1986] 2 All ER 566.
16   *R v K (Trevor Douglas)* (1993) 97 Cr App R 342; *Re D (An Infant)* [1970] 1 All ER 1088.
17   [1993] 2 All ER 577.
18   See *R v Davis, Johnson and Rowe* [1993] 2 All ER 643.
19   *R v Chief Constable of the West Midlands Police, ex parte Wiley* [1995] 1 AC 274; [1994] 3 All ER 420.
20   See Woolf LJ in ex parte Wiley, *op cit.*

for Iraq" affair.[1] One result of this was that prosecutions were sometimes abandoned rather than the prosecution having to disclose such material.[2]

d Disclosure by defence

The law has, since 1967, required an accused to give seven days' notice of his intention to adduce evidence in support of an alibi.[3] A failure to do so meant that the evidence could not be adduced without the leave of the court.[4] The purpose of the rule is to enable checks to be made by the prosecution as to the truth or otherwise of the claims of the accused that he was elsewhere at the time of the commission of the offence. Further, in cases of serious or complex fraud where a preparatory hearing is held,[5] the defence may be required to disclose the general nature of its defence (though not the names of the witnesses it proposes to call), and the principal areas of disagreement.

Apart from these cases, and the obligation to disclose expert evidence, discussed above, there was no general duty on the defence to disclose in advance the nature and content of the defence upon which it is proposed to rely. This so-called "right to silence" meant that it was not open to a court to invite a jury to draw adverse inferences from a failure to disclose pre-trial the facts relied upon by the defence.[6]

Various calls for change were made. In 1972, the 11th Report of the Criminal Law Revision Committee recommended that a court should be permitted to draw inferences from silence in court, or from a failure to disclose facts subsequently relied upon by the defence.[7] The report was highly controversial,[8] and not acted upon. More recently, the Court of Appeal in *R v Alladice*[9] considered that it was "high time" that some change in the law was made. This was indeed recommended in 1988 by the Working Group on the Right to Silence,[10] established by the Home Secretary. It made various recommendations:

(1) that the proposals of the 11th Report be implemented, subject to modifications which place greater emphasis on the safeguards provided for the suspect;
(2) that the prosecution and trial judge should have the right to comment about a defendant's failure to mention to the police a fact later relied upon by the defence;
(3) that a new set of measures be drawn up to compel greater pre trial disclosure of both prosecution and defence cases, with greater powers of comment for both prosecution and judge;
(4) that a revised caution be implemented.

The question of defence disclosure was one of the most controversial issues considered by the Royal Commission. It took the view that no change should be made in respect of the "right to silence", except in respect of disclosure of the defence proposed to be relied upon. The majority[11] believed that those who intended to contest the charges

---

1   See, generally, Chapter 9.
2   *R v Langford* [1990] Crim LR 653.
3   An "alibi" is an assertion that the accused person was elsewhere at the time of the commission of the offence.
4   Criminal Justice Act 1967, s 11.
5   See p 511, *post*.
6   *R v Gilbert* (1977) 66 Cr App Rep 237.
7   Cmnd 4991 (HMSO, 1972).
8   See eg MacKenna at [1972] Crim LR 605.
9   (1988) 87 Cr App Rep 380.
10   See Zuckerman, "Trial By Unfair Means – The Report of the Working Group on the Right to Silence" [1989] Crim LR 855.
11   With one dissentient: see RCCJ, pp 221–235.

against them should be obliged to disclose the substance of their defence in advance of trial, or indicate that they would not be calling any evidence but simply argue that the prosecution has failed to prove its case.[12] A failure to do so, or an explanation at trial different from the one given in advance, or the advancing of mutually exclusive alternative defences, should be a matter from which the jury could draw adverse inferences, subject to the discretion of the court to prevent this where good reasons existed. A defendant who did not disclose would not generally be entitled to further disclosure of material from the prosecution.

The rationale for such proposals was a desire to reduce "trial by ambush" involving springing a defence upon the prosecution without warning. The Royal Commission did not consider the proposals to infringe the right of defendants not to incriminate themselves, but accepted that a problem existed only in a minority of cases.[13] By contrast, the dissenting opinion in essence questioned whether the fundamental right of the defence not to respond until trial, and to require the prosecution to prove its case, should be changed where no real problem exists. It also pointed to the ineffectiveness of the advance disclosure powers in serious fraud cases.[14] These recommendations have, broadly, been implemented by the "right to silence" provisions contained in the Criminal Justice and Public Order Act 1994.

2   The New Law

The Criminal Procedure and Investigations Act 1996 introduced a new and complex scheme of disclosure, applicable to both prosecution and defence. It is supplemented by a Code of Practice made by the Home Secretary,[15] which governs how material acquired during an investigation is recorded, preserved and produced to the prosecutor by the investigator. This Code is important, because, self-evidently, only if the prosecutor is in possession, or has access to, all the potentially relevant material can he make a judgment as to what, if anything, should be disclosed.

The 1996 Act creates a scheme of disclosure which is basically constructed in three stages. The first is primary prosecution disclosure. By section 3(1), the prosecutor must disclose to the accused any prosecution material which has not been previously disclosed to the accused, and which, in the prosecutor's opinion might undermine the case for the prosecution against the accused. Alternatively, he must give to the accused a written statement that there is no such material. At the same time, the prosecutor gives to the accused a schedule of non-sensitive material which he has received from the disclosure officer. By these means, the accused should be provided with relevant unused material, together with a schedule of material which is relevant and which has been acquired by the prosecutor, and, through these documents, judge what further documents may, or should, be disclosable in the light of the needs of the defence.

This scheme of prosecution disclosure is not without difficulty. Firstly, the test is subjective. The prosecutor forms an opinion as to the effect of material held by him, or the investigator, and has to form that opinion without knowledge, at that stage, as to what the precise defence case is, although in many cases that may be obvious or can be deduced easily. The subjectivity of the test also precludes any realistic challenge to the judgment that is made by the prosecutor. Secondly, material is disclosable if it

12   *Ibid*, Ch 6, paras 56–73.
13   Ch 4, para 19, relying on data from the Crown Court survey.
14   Page 222, para 8, relying on Levi, *The Investigation, Prosecution and Trial of Serious Fraud* (Royal Commission on Criminal Justice Research Study No 14, HMSO, 1993).
15   Under Part II of the Criminal Procedure and Investigations Act 1996.

"undermines the case for the defence". The fact that the prosecutor will not necessarily know what that case is has already been noted. It is also narrower than the Keane test at common law, and is vague. It is designed to ensure that there is disclosure, at this stage, of material which has adverse effect on the strength of the prosecution case. Thus, statements by witnesses who contradict the testimony of those who will be called to testify for the prosecution, inconsistent forensic evidence, the previous convictions of prosecution witnesses, matters that relate to the credibility of prosecution witnesses, and inconsistent versions of statements are all examples of material which would have this effect. Many of these matters would, in any event, have been disclosable by the prosecutor at common law. The significance of the change made by the new Act is that the prosecutor focuses on what may weaken the prosecution case, not on the possible avenues of defence which might later be raised.

The third issue that arises in respect of primary prosecution disclosure is in relation to sensitive material. This is dealt with later.

The Act makes a significant change by requiring defence disclosure following primary prosecution disclosure. By section 5, once the prosecutor has complied or purported to comply, with the duty of primary prosecution disclosure, the accused is under a duty to serve on the prosecutor a defence statement. A defence statement is a written statement:

(a) setting out in general terms the nature of the accused's defence;
(b) indicating the matters on which he takes issue with the prosecution;
(c) setting out, in the case of each such matter, the reason why he takes issue with the prosecution.

The purpose of this scheme is to avoid so called "trial by ambush", with the accused coming up with a defence at a late stage.[16] It also is intended to permit a prosecutor to re-assess what has been disclosed, and what further needs to be disclosed, in the light of positive knowledge as to what the defence actually is. Similar provisions apply specifically in the context of alibi evidence.[17]

If an accused does not issue a defence statement, or if the defence statement issued is inadequate, then the sanctions contained in section 11 of the 1996 Act apply. By section 11(3) in these circumstances:

(a) with leave of the court, any other party may make such comment as appears appropriate;
(b) the court or jury may draw such influences as appear proper in deciding whether the accused is guilty of the offence concerned.

This power to draw influences is in similar terms to that contained in the 1987 Act concerning cases of serious or complex fraud,[18] and to the provisions in sections 34, 36 and 37 governing silence at or before trial.[19]

The third stage of the disclosure scheme is secondary prosecution disclosure. Once the defence has engaged in defence disclosure, it is the duty of the prosecutor to engage in secondary prosecution disclosure. By section 7(2) the prosecutor must:

(a) disclose to the accused any prosecution material which has not been previously disclosed to the accused;

16   See p 500, *ante*.
17   Section 11 of the Criminal Justice Act 1967 is repealed.
18   See Criminal Justice Act 1987, s 10.
19   See p 318, *ante*.

(b) give to the accused a written statement that there is no material of that type.

Unlike the duty of primary prosecution disclosure, this is objective in nature ie it is open to a court to review the judgment made and its reasonableness. It is at this stage, therefore, that a court will be able most effectively to intervene, and that will often be done in the context of a preparatory hearing or pre-trial review.

Sensitive material

We have already seen[20] that a court has the power to refuse to disclose certain types of information in the public interest. The 1996 Act leaves the substantive rules governing disclosure of sensitive material unchanged, but changes the procedure to be followed. Provisions in the 1996 Act[1] permit such material to be withheld where disclosure would be contrary to the public interest. Disclosure in such circumstances is governed by the pre-existing common law rules. As before, decisions as to whether or not material is to be withheld, and to what extent, are matters for the court, not for the prosecutor. What is, or is not sensitive material, will initially be determined by the disclosure officer, but subject to the ultimate decision of the court. Examples of such material given by the Code of Practice include the following:

(a) material relating to national security;

(b) material received from the intelligence and security agencies;

(c) material relating to intelligence from foreign sources which reveals intelligence gathering methods which are sensitive;

(d) material such as telephone subscriber cheques and itemised billing which is supplied to an investigator for intelligence purposes only;

(e) material given in confidence;

(f) material relating to the identity or activities of informants, or undercover police officers, or other persons supplying information to the police who may be in danger if their identities are revealed;

(g) material revealing the location of premises or other places used for police surveillance or the identity of any person allowing a police officer to use them for surveillance;

(h) material revealing, either directly or indirectly, techniques and methods relied on by a police officer in the course of a criminal investigation, for example covert surveillance techniques, or other methods of detecting crime;

(i) material whose disclosure might facilitate the commission of other offences or hinder the prevention and detection of crime;

(j) internal police communications such as management minutes;

(k) material on the strength of which search warrants were obtained;

(l) material containing details of persons taking part in identification parades;

(m) material supplied to an investigator during a criminal investigation which has been generated by an official other body concerned with the regulation or supervision of bodies corporate or of persons engaged in financial activities;

(n) material supplied to an investigator during a criminal investigation which relates to a child witness and which has been generated by a local authority social services department or other party contacted by the investigator during the investigation.

20 See p 498, *ante.*
1   See ss 3(6), 7(5), 8(5), 9(8).

The disclosure officer will, in the first instance, compile a list of sensitive material, which will be supplied to the prosecutor. It will be for the prosecutor to decide whether or not a claim to withhold relevant material is to be made. Clearly, if a document is not relevant and material, it need not be disclosed, and issues of public interest immunity do not arise. Where a claim of immunity is made in respect of documents that are relevant, the court has to balance the respective public interest in maintaining the sensitivity of the document, on the one hand, and in ensuring a fair trial of an accused, on the other. This balancing function, in a criminal case, is not at all easy, and, although the case law[3] suggests that relevant material can be withheld in a criminal case, it is unlikely to be withheld where material may assist the defence. The Scott Report observed that there was no reported case:

"in which the judge has concluded that documents would be of assistance to the defendant that is none the less declined on public interest immunity grounds to order them to be disclosed. The firm conclusion is, in my opinion justified, that in criminal cases the only question should be whether the documents might be of assistance to the defendant".[4]

The law relating to public interest immunity, and the withholding of documents, is currently under review by the Government. It remains to be seen as to what changes in the substantive law are in fact made.

E THE INDICTMENT

I Introduction

A bill of indictment is a written or printed accusation of crime made at the suit of the Crown against one or more persons. A bill of indictment may be preferred by any person[5] against any other person before the Crown Court, generally within 28 days of committal or notice of transfer, or within a period to be specified following a person being sent for trial under Schedule 3 of the 1998 Act.[6] However, a bill of indictment is of no legal validity in itself. It only becomes a legal document when it is turned into an indictment proper by being signed by the appropriate officer of the court, who in turn can only sign the draft bill if he is satisfied that the accused is validly before the court.[7] The judge of the court may direct the appropriate officer to sign the bill, either on his own motion or on the application of the prosecution. After it has been signed, the proper officer must on request supply to the defendant a copy free of charge.[8]

Where the bill is preferred on the authority of a committal for trial it may charge any offence which appears on the depositions, or statements, in addition to or in place of the offence or offences for which he was committed, subject to the normal rules as

---

2   See *R v Chief Constable of the West Midlands Police, ex parte Wiley* [1995] 1 AC 274; [1994] 3 All ER 420.

3   *R v Governor of Brixton Prison, ex parte Osman* [1992] 1 All ER 108; [1991] 1 WLR 281; *R v Clowes* [1992] 3 All ER 440.

4   *Op cit*, Vol, III, paras 6.18–79.

5   Except in those cases where a private person has no right to institute proceedings: see p 460, *ante*.

6   See p 485, *ante*.

7   Through committal proceedings, notice of transfer, voluntary bill, or by direction of the Court of Appeal. An alternative procedure under the Perjury Act 1911, s 9, existed until abolished by the Prosecution of Offences Act 1985, s 28.

8   Indictment Rules 1971, r 10(1).

to joinder of offences.[9] It is immaterial that the "added" offences involve a higher penalty than the original charge or charges. Although the accused will necessarily have knowledge of the facts alleged to constitute the offence, if not of the precise charge based on those facts, there are obvious possibilities of injustice, and the Court of Appeal has said[10] that whenever it is decided to bring such "fresh" charges, the police ought to see the defendant and warn him of the charges under caution, so that he may make a statement in answer if he wishes.

The whole of the indictment may consist of such "substitute" charge or charges. If the defendant considers that one or more of such charges does not fairly arise out of the facts in the depositions he may move to quash the indictment. It is then for the trial judge to rule on the sufficiency of the indictment. Where however the defendant was committed for trial in respect of two offences which had been repealed by statute, it was held that he was never lawfully committed at all, and it was immaterial that the third count of the indictment was in respect of an offence which both existed and was disclosed by the depositions.[11]

Clearly, there is a certain risk of hardship to the defendant in this procedure, since he may successfully resist a particular charge at the stage of committal proceedings, only to find (on the assumption that he is committed for trial in respect of other matters) that the same charge appears in the indictment:

"We think it right to say that it is an undesirable practice and can easily in some cases work hardship on defendants, and the right to prefer in the indictment charges which the magistrate has rejected is one which ought to be very carefully regarded."[12]

2   Form and contents

The rules as to the form of indictments are now contained in the Indictments Act 1915 and the Indictment Rules 1971. The drafting of the indictment is the responsibility of counsel for the prosecution,[13] whose duty it is to ensure that it is in proper form for the particular case. In most cases, other than those of complexity or difficulty, the actual drafting is undertaken by, or on behalf of, the Crown Prosecution Service.

An indictment is in three parts; introductory matters, statement of offence and particulars of offence. The introductory matters are twofold, first the court of trial and secondly the name of the defendant, appearing in the form:

THE QUEEN v [Defendant] charged as follows:

As regards the statement of offence and particulars of offence, the rules provide[14] that every indictment must contain, and need not contain more than, a statement of the specific offence with which the defendant is charged, describing the offence shortly, together with such particulars as are necessary to give reasonable information as to the nature of the charge. Where, however, the offence is created by statute, there must

9   See p 505, *post.*
10   In *R v Dickson* [1969] 1 All ER 729; [1969] 1 WLR 405, where the defendant's solicitors had six days' notice of "fresh" charges.
11   *R v Lamb* [1969] 1 All ER 45; [1968] 1 WLR 1946.
12   Per Finnemore J in *R v Dawson*; *R v Wenlock* [1960] 1 All ER 558 at 562; [1960] 1 WLR 163 at 168.
13   *R v Newland* [1988] QB 402; [1988] 2 All ER 891.
14   Indictment Rules 1971, r 5(1). Cf the rules for the content of an information: see p 563, *post.* There may also be approved forms of indictment for individual offences: *ibid.*

be a reference to the statute and to the relevant section, and all the essential elements of the offence must be disclosed in the particulars, unless the defendant is not prejudiced or embarrassed by failure to describe any such element.[15] The fact that an indictment is defective does not render the trial a nullity. Whether a conviction obtained on an indictment that is deficient can stand will turn, ultimately, upon whether injustice or unfairness has been caused to the defendant.

Whether these provisions are effective is open to doubt. The Royal Commission on Criminal Justice observed[16] that indictments were largely formal in nature, giving little information. It found widespread evidence of a failure to comply with the duty to give reasonable information as to the nature of the charge, and agreed with the Law Commission when that body observed:

"There are strong reasons of justice and efficiency why the particulars in each count in an indictment should contain sufficiently clear factual allegations to inform the jury of the issues it will have to decide, and more generally, to enable the indictment to operate as a practical agenda for the trial."[17]

3 Joinder; separate trials

Hitherto we have considered an indictment charging one offence only. However, within certain limits, a single indictment may charge more than one offence, or be drawn in respect of more than one defendant, or both. This is known as joinder.

a Joinder of offenders

The basic rule is that where two or more persons join in the commission of an offence, all or any number of them may be jointly indicted for that offence, or each may be indicted separately. If they are in fact indicted separately there would be no power in any court to order "consolidation" of the indictments, however desirable this might seem from the point of view of saving time and expense,[18] but, of course, the same result could be achieved through the use of the voluntary bill procedure[19] to supersede existing indictments. However, joinder is now very common. The matter is one of judicial discretion, and what is in the interests of justice. Where the individual offences of the different accused are related to each other by virtue of time or some other link, then it may well be appropriate for them to be tried together.[20] The fact that evidence against one accused is inadmissible against another will be a relevant factor, though not necessarily decisive. Another consideration will be the length of the trial that will ensue should they be tried together. This is returned to later.[1]

b Joinder of offences

The basic rule is to be found in rule 9 of the 1971 Rules:

15 *Ibid*, r 6. It is not necessary for the indictment to specify or negative any exception, exemption, excuse, proviso or qualification. There is, again, an analogy with the rules for the content of an information.
16 Ch 8, para 5.
17 *Counts in an Indictment* (Law Commission, 1992).
18 *Crane v Director of Public Prosecutions* [1921] 2 AC 299.
19 See p 492, *ante*.
20 *R v Assim* [1966] 2 QB 249; [1966] 2 All ER 881.
1   See p 507, *post*.

"Charges for any offences may be joined in the same indictment if those charges are found on the same facts or form or are a part of a series of offences of the same or a similar character."

It should also be noted that in some limited circumstances summary offences may be tried with offences that are to be tried on indictment.[2]

It is a matter of fact and degree in each case as to whether this rule is satisfied, in accordance with principles set out in the cases. In *Ludlow v Metropolitan Police Commissioner*[3] the House of Lords indicated that in deciding whether offences were of a similar character, regard should be had both to their legal and factual characteristics. To show a "series of offences" the prosecution must be able to show some nexus between them, a "feature of similarity which in all the circumstances of the case enables the offences to be tried together". It is not necessary that the evidence in respect of one charge should be admissible on another. Clearly, if that is the case joinder will be appropriate. In *Director of Public Prosecutions v P*[4] the House of Lords reviewed the tests for similar fact evidence that govern such admissibility. Prior to that decision it had been thought that there needed to be a "striking similarity"[5] between the facts of the different charges, or between the charges and previous convictions, for admissibility of evidence of one offence to be admissible on another.[6] That was rejected by the House of Lords in *P*, where the court indicated that what was required was positive probative value,[7] which could arise from striking similarity but did not inevitably have to do so. The repetition, without collusion,[8] of allegations could of itself have strong probative force. However, although the approach of the law to similar fact evidence was modified, the position in respect of joinder was left ambiguous and unclear.

The application of the principle in a non-sexual case was seen in *R v Cannan*[9] where the Court of Appeal held that a trial judge was entitled in his discretion to order the trial together of six offences involving three separate women. Three counts involved abduction, rape and buggery against one woman, another alleged attempted kidnapping against a second, and two more counts of alleged abduction and murder of a third. Sexual cases, by contrast, are particularly difficult because of the prejudice that may arise. In *Director of Public Prosecutions v Boardman*[10] Lord Cross seemed to equate the test for joinder of offences with their admissibility as evidence under the similar fact evidence rule. He stated that if each count was inadmissible in respect of the other offences then they ought to be tried separately. It is, he said, asking too much of any jury to disregard the other charges when considering each individual charge.

This approach is contrary to the wording of rule 9 itself. Despite the House of Lords not putting the matter beyond doubt in *DPP v P*, the wording of rule 9 is clear. In *R v*

---

2   Criminal Justice Act 1988, s 40. The charge must be founded on the same facts or evidence, or be part of a series of offences.
3   [1971] AC 29; [1970] 1 All ER 567. The House was considering the appropriate provision of the 1915 Rules, which were materially the same as r 9. See also: *R v Kray* [1970] 1 QB 125; [1969] 3 All ER 941.
4   [1991] 2 AC 447; *sub nom R v P* [1991] 3 All ER 337. See *R v Tickner* [1992] Crim LR 44.
5   A phrase coined by Lord Goddard CJ in *R v Sims* [1946] KB 531, [1946] 1 All ER 697.
6   Under the so-called similar fact evidence rule.
7   Although in *DPP v Boardman* [1975] AC 421 the House of Lords has appeared to adopt this statement, subsequent cases had stressed that "striking similarity" was not the universal test: positive probative value was what the law required: see *R v Rance and Herron* (1975) 62 Cr App R 118, *R v Scarrott* [1978] QB 1016.
8   For the position in cases where identity is in issue, see *R v McGranaghan* [1992] *R v Barnes*; *R v Downey*.
9   (1990) 92 Cr App Rep 16.
10   [1975] AC 421; *sub nom Boardman v Director of Public Prosecutions* [1974] 3 All ER 887.

Christou[11] the House of Lords held that where an accused person was charged with sexual offences against more than one person, where the evidence of one complainant was not admissible on charges concerning other complainants, the trial judge had a discretion to order that the charges be tried together. The judge is not obliged to exercise that discretion in favour of the accused simply because the evidence is not admissible on more than one count of the indictment. The key issue is simply: can the issues be resolved fairly? In that case the appellant was charged with sexual offences against his two young female cousins, C and M, with whom he had been living at the time of the alleged offences. The House of Lords concluded that the trial judge had acted properly in requiring that they be tried together, notwithstanding the fact that the evidence of C was not admissible on the counts that related solely to M. Further, in the case of *R v West*[12], the court had to consider the same issue in the context of a non-sexual offence. The appellant had been tried and convicted of ten counts of murder. The evidence on many of these counts was admissible on other counts, under the so-called similar fact evidence rule. The Court of Appeal held, however, that the trial judge had acted properly in declining to sever the indictment and order separate trials in respect of three counts which were unaffected by similar fact evidence. This was a matter for the judge's discretion, which he had not exercised improperly.[13]

4   Long trials: the number of counts and accused

It has already been seen that the joinder of offenders, and of charges, is permissible. The danger exists that an indictment may become so overloaded that, as a result, the trial becomes too complex in terms of the issues the jury has to comprehend and decide, or unmanageable in terms of time. On many occasions the courts have complained of indictments which are overloaded.

In *R v Novac*[14] where a large number of counts of sexual offences were laid against four defendants, Bridge LJ observed:

"whatever advantages were expected to accrue from one long trial they were heavily outweighed by the disadvantages. A trial of such dimensions puts an immense burden on both judge and jury. In the course of a four or five day summing up the most careful and conscientious judge may so easily overlook some essential matter. Even if the summing up is faultless, it is by no means cynical to doubt whether the average juror can be expected to take it all in and apply all the directions given. Some criminal prosecutions involve considerations of matters so plainly inextricable and indivisible that a long and complex trial is an ineluctable necessity. But we are convinced that nothing short of the criterion of absolute necessity can justify the imposition of the burden of a very long trial on the court."

The problem has arisen particularly in two different situations. The first concerns the use of conspiracy charges. There may be both evidential and tactical reasons why prosecutors may wish to lay a count of conspiracy in addition to counts alleging specific offences. This practice was disapproved in a *Practice Note* in 1977.[15] The onus is on

11   [1997] AC 117
12   [1996] 2 Cr App Rep 375.
13   *R v Trew* (1996).
14   (1976) 65 Cr App Rep 107.
15   [1977] 2 All ER 540; *sub nom Practice Direction* [1977] 1 WLR 537.

the prosecution to justify a joinder of a conspiracy charge with other substantive offences. If it cannot, it must elect to proceed either upon the conspiracy charge or the substantive offences. Justification might exist where the substantive offences which the prosecution is in a position to prove do not adequately reflect the extent and persistence of the defendants' criminality. Thus, for example, there might be evidence to show that a person had been engaged for some time in the importation of drugs of various kinds, although the prosecution might only be able to prove one specific importation.

Secondly, a number of long complex fraud cases has placed great strain upon the jury trial system.[16] In *R v Cohen*[17] the trial was so long that the judge's summing-up (itself of considerable length) dealt only with one of the issues before the court. In passing sentence following convictions, later quashed on appeal, McKinnon J observed:

"All involved in this case have been called upon to achieve what no-one in our courts should be asked to achieve. That applies to the defendants, to the jury and to me."

The solution to the problem has not proved easy. The Roskill Report on Fraud Trials[18] advocated the abolition of jury trial in complex fraud cases, to be replaced by trial by judge and two specialist assessors. Such recommendations are a response to a recognition that such trials are inevitably long, causing unacceptable disruption to the lives of jurors, and unduly complex, the evidence often being beyond the comprehension of jurors. Such claims are, of course, difficult to gauge in the light of the prohibition on study of how in fact juries reach their verdicts, and upon what evidence.[19]

By contrast, others argue for the simplification of such cases. In its evidence to the Royal Commission, the Law Society[20] argued that such trials should be simplified by not including superfluous counts, and by keeping prosecution evidence within strict limits, principally by limiting the number of accused in the indictment. The Royal Commission itself considered the restriction of jury trial to be beyond its scope, but echoed the calls set out above for the number of counts or particulars on an indictment to be kept to a minimum.[1] In that regard, its recommendation for a review of the relationship between the criminal law and non-criminal action by financial regulators may be important in reducing the scope of criminal trials in such cases.[2]

5 Duplicity

Where two or more offences are joined in one indictment each one must be alleged in a separate count or paragraph of the indictment.[3] If an indictment in fact charges more than one offence in a single count then it is bad for duplicity. This must be distinguished from the analogous situation which, more accurately, may be described as uncertainty.

16   See, generally, the Roskill Committee, *op cit*, and Royal Commission on Criminal Justice Report, Ch 7, paras 59–67.
17   [1992] NLJR 1267. The jury retired on the 184th day of the trial.
18   See n 16, *ante*.
19   Contempt of Court Act 1981, s 8. For discussion of jury trial generally, see p 230, *ante*.
20   Evidence of the Law Society to the Royal Commission on Criminal Justice (1992).
1   Ch 8, para 79.
2   Ch 7, para 64.
3   Indictment Rules 1971, r 4(2). Each count is equivalent to a separate indictment. Counts must be numbered consecutively: r 4(2).

This arises where a statutory provision contains one offence, which may be committed by a variety of means, or by virtue of different states of mind. Whether a count in an indictment may charge simply by reference to the statutory provision, or must allege the specific ingredients in each count, charging more than one count if necessary, is a question of construction of the relevant statute.[4]

In deciding into which category the statutory provision falls regard should be had to the question of whether different maximum punishments exist according to the presence or absence of specific factual ingredients.[5] Where that is so, it is likely that a court will consider the statute to create separate offences, which should therefore be indicated separately.

6 Objecting to the indictment: amendment

If the defendant desires to object to the validity of the indictment he should do so before he is arraigned. The grounds of objection have already been explained,[6] though the power of the court to quash an indictment to prevent abuse of the process of the court should also be noted.

The Court of Appeal does not readily hear objections to the validity of an indictment where the objection was not taken at the trial, although failure to take it is not insuperable. When objection is taken the court may (unless it rules against the objection altogether) either quash the indictment or amend it. The Indictments Act 1915 permits a court to make such order of amendment as it thinks necessary to meet the circumstances of the case, unless amendment cannot be made without injustice.[7]

A new count may be added before the defendant is arraigned, and even after arraignment a count can be added charging a completely new offence;[8] the question is one of degree depending on the facts of the particular case.[9]

Application for amendment may be made by either side and at any time. Since counsel for the prosecution has general responsibility for the correctness of the indictment he should not open his case without being satisfied on the point and should make any necessary application for amendment before the defendant is arraigned, having inspected the indictment for the purpose. Defending counsel should also inspect, in his own client's interests.

Amendment may be made by the judge of his own motion, but before doing so he should give both sides the opportunity of commenting on the proposed amendment.[10]

F PRE-TRIAL REVIEW

No formal system for pre-trial review by the court of trial existed until 1996, although informal arrangements operate. Pre-trial reviews in fact operated in Crown Courts across the country, providing a basis for voluntary discussion of matters affecting a forthcoming trial, such as the plea to be entered, length of trial, points of law or

---

4 See p 563, *post*, for similar issues in respect of duplicity of charges of summary offences.
5 *R v Courtie* [1984] AC 463; [1984] 1 All ER 740.
6 See p 508, *ante*.
7 Section 5(1).
8 *R v Radley* (1973) 58 Cr App Rep 394, where the amendment was made at the conclusion of the prosecution opening; cf *R v Tirado* (1974) 59 Cr App Rep 80.
9 It seems that an amendment on immaterial matter may be made at or after verdict: *R v Dossi* (1918) 87 LJKB 1024.
10 *R v West* [1948] 1 KB 709; [1948] 1 All ER 718.

admissibility of evidence.[11] Such reviews appear to have occurred in approximately 25% of cases.[12]

The one exception to this arrangement were cases involving serious fraud. Under the Criminal Justice Act 1987,[13] a trial judge may order a preparatory hearing if the case is of such seriousness and complexity that substantial benefits are likely to accrue from it. The purposes of the hearing are:

(a) to identify material issues to be decided at the trial;
(b) to consider how the juries' comprehension of the issues can be assisted;
(c) to expedite such proceedings;
(d) to assist the judge's management of such issues. This power remains unaffected by the changes described below.

Unlike the informal preparatory hearings in ordinary cases, which can only deal with matters relating to the indictment, these hearings in serious fraud cases can deal with questions both of law and of admissibility of evidence. The judge may make orders concerning the form of presentation of the prosecution case, can require the defence to set out in writing, and in general terms, the nature of the defence relied upon, and deal with various matters relating to the agreement of documents. An appeal lies against such decisions.[14]

The Royal Commission considered one trial project that had involved all cases being listed for a "pleas and directions" hearing.[15] The majority of the Commission considered such a scheme to be both unnecessary and impracticable. Instead it proposed a scheme based on the automatic completion of forms with details of plea. The disclosure obligations recommended by the Commission[16] would then have occured, and both prosecution and defence would then indicate whether a preparatory hearing was needed and for what purpose.[17] Such hearings would occur in a minority of cases, usually those anticipated to last at least five days, although it would be open to the parties to require a hearing in shorter cases.[18] Such hearings would deal with plea, matters of evidence (including issues of admissibility) and expert opinion, matters generally relating to the trial. Such decisions would be binding on the trial judge and counsel. For this reason the Royal Commission was concerned that the practice of returned briefs be minimised as much as possible.[19]

Pleas and directions hearings ("PDH") in Crown Court cases have become in effect mandatory. The advantages of the hearing lie in the ability of the court to engage in effective case-management, to the benefit not only of the workload of the court in general but also to the effective handling of individual cases. However, the Narey Report[20] did accept that there may be some merit in the claim that PDH should not be mandatory in all cases since in straightforward ones they may involve an additional and unnecessary burden. The matter is one which be the subject of further consideration.

---

11   The Royal Commission on Criminal Justice (at Ch 7, para 10) identified also a scheme based on the exchange of forms, recommended by a Working Party chaired by Watkins LJ. The results obtained in a pilot scheme were disappointing.
12   *Ibid*, para 11, relying on the Crown Court Survey.
13   Section 7(1).
14   *Ibid*, s 9(10).
15   Working Group on Pre-trial Issues: Recommendation 92 (cited by RCCJ, Ch 7, para 12).
16   See p 495, *ante*.
17   RCCJ, para 20.
18   *Ibid*, para 17.
19   *Ibid*, para 36.
20   See p 493, *ante*.

Following the recommendations of the Royal Commission, the Government published in 1995 a consultation paper.[1] This paper recognised the desirability of achieving the objectives identified by the Royal Commission, namely the achievement of shorter and more efficient trials. However, it did not adopt the Royal Commission's proposals for pre-trial exchange of papers in less complex cases, and considered that the way forward was creation of a system based on a mixture of binding rulings at pleas and directions hearings, coupled with preparatory hearings to be held in complex or potentially lengthy cases. The Government's approach was given statutory effect by Parts III and IV of the Criminal Procedure and Investigations Act of 1996.

By section 40 of the 1996 Act, a judge may, at a pre-trial hearing make a binding ruling as to:

(a)   any question as to the admissibility of evidence;
(b)   any other question of law relating to the case concerned.

A "pre-trial hearing" can be held after committal for trial and before the commencement of the trial itself, and thus permits not simply questions of law to be determined, but also whether material should be disclosed, whether counts on an indictment should be quashed, and whether or not orders should be made, for example, under section 4 of the Contempt of Court Act 1981.

In addition, by section 29(1) of the 1996 Act, where it appears to a Crown Court judge that an indictment reveals a case of such complexity, or a case whose trial is likely to be of such length, that substantial benefits are likely to accrue from a preparatory hearing, such a hearing may be held. The purpose of the preparatory hearing is defined by section 29(2) as:

(a)   identifying issues which are likely to be material to the verdict of the jury;
(b)   assisting the comprehension of any such issues;
(c)   expediting the proceedings before the jury;
(d)   assisting the judge's management of the trial.

These provisions are not, in principle, new, and are similar to those found in section 7 of the Criminal Justice Act of 1987, dealing with cases of serious or complex fraud. The significance of a preparatory hearing is made clear by section 31(4). Under that sub-section, a judge at a preparatory hearing may order the prosecutor:

(1)   to give to the court and the accused a written statement of certain matters which include the principal facts of the case for the prosecution, the witnesses who will speak to them, any exhibits relevant to those facts, any proposition of law on which the prosecutor proposes to rely, and the consequences that flow from any of those matters.
(2)   to prepare the prosecution evidence and any explanatory material in such a form as required by the court;
(3)   to give to the court and the accused written notice of documents the truth of contents of which ought in the prosecutor's view to be admitted, and of any such matters which in his view ought to be agreed;
(4)   to make any amendments of any case statement given as appear to the judge to be appropriate.

---

1   *Improving the effectiveness of pre-trial hearings in the Crown Court* (HMSO, 1995, Cm 2924).

G   ARRAIGNMENT AND PLEAS

1   Attendance of the accused

On the day fixed the accused will, if he has been detained in custody, be brought from the prison or remand centre where he has been detained and lodged in the cells. If he has been on bail he must surrender to his bail and will then be placed in the cells to await his trial. It may be that the defendant has been on bail and does not appear, in which case the court of trial may issue a warrant, called a "bench warrant" for the arrest of the defendant; this is a summary procedure and will not normally be used unless the arrest of the defendant is a matter of urgency.

Still further powers are provided by section 7(3) of the Bail Act 1976 by which a constable may arrest without a warrant any person who has been released on bail in criminal proceedings if, inter alia, he has reasonable grounds for believing that the person is unlikely to appear at the time and place required.

2   Arraignment

Assuming that the defendant has appeared at, or has been brought to, the court, the first formal step in his trial will be the arraignment, which is the process of calling an accused forward to answer an indictment. The defendant will be brought from the cells into the dock[2] and the proper officer will first ask him his name. Assuming that he is the person named in the indictment he will then be asked to plead. The indictment will be read to him (omitting only the introductory matters) and he will be asked to plead to it; further, where the indictment contains more than one count, each should be put to the defendant separately and he should be asked to plead separately, for each count is equivalent to a separate indictment.[3]

On arraignment the defendant may, of course, simply say nothing. If this occurs, the first question is whether the defendant is mute of malice, that is to say, able to speak but refusing to do so, or whether he is mute by visitation of God, that is to say, temporarily or permanently unable to speak. If there is any doubt a jury must be sworn to try the issue. Witnesses may be called on either side and counsel may address the jury; the judge will then sum up the case to the jury, who will retire if necessary and then give a verdict.[4] If the finding is that the defendant is mute of malice the court may then order the proper officer of the court to enter a plea of not guilty on behalf of the defendant (assuming that he still declines to speak);[5] the trial will then proceed as if the defendant had himself pleaded not guilty. If, however, the finding is that the defendant is mute by visitation of God, the defendant may yet be perfectly well able to defend himself, and a plea of not guilty should be entered by the court and the trial should proceed in the ordinary way.

However there may well be some questions of whether the defendant is fit to plead, the test for which is whether he is fit to challenge jurors, instruct counsel, understand the evidence and give evidence himself.[6] The procedure to be followed is contained

---

2   The Royal Commission did not recommend that docks be abolished. It considered that they should be situated as near as possible to the accused's legal representatives: Ch 8, para 109.

3   *R v Boyle* [1954] 2 QB 292; [1954] 2 All ER 721.

4   This may in some circumstances be by a majority: see p 529, *post*.

5   Criminal Law Act 1967, s 6(1)(c).

6   *R v Berry* (1977) 66 Cr App Rep 156; not whether he is able to defend himself properly or well: *R v Robertson* [1968] 3 All ER 557; [1968] 1 WLR 1767.

in the Criminal Procedure (Insanity) Act 1964.[7] A jury must be sworn to try the issue. Again, evidence may be called by either side and speeches will be made; the judge will direct the jury, who will return a verdict. If the finding is that the defendant is unfit to plead, the trial does not proceed, but the defendant is not free to go; he is liable to be detained in hospital or made subject to various orders.[8] The court has power, in the interests of the accused, to postpone trial of the issue of fitness to plead until any time up to the opening of the case for the defence. If, before such time, the defendant is acquitted (on a submission of no case to answer) his fitness or otherwise will not be determined.[9] This is to ensure that the case against the person being detained is in fact tested, and to ensure that an innocent person is not subject to detention. If the finding is one of fitness to plead, the defendant will then be called upon to plead to the indictment; if he still declines to answer, a plea of not guilty will be entered on his behalf.

3   Pleas

Assuming that all questions of fitness to plead have been disposed of adversely to the defendant, in the sense that the trial on the substantive issues must go on, various pleas are open to the defendant. In the vast majority of cases the alternatives are pleas of guilty or not guilty.

The decision to accept a plea to a lesser charge is that of the prosecutor, and does not require the consent of the court unless the decision arises after the prosecution has called its evidence and a case to answer has been found.[10] Such decisions may often assist in avoiding the time and expense of a trial, and are one explanation for the problem of "cracked trials". These are cases that are listed for trial but where on the day of trial the defendant pleads guilty.[11]

By contrast, the holding of discussions informally with the trial judge to ascertain attitudes to likely sentence is a practice that has been heavily criticised by the Court of Appeal.[12] Out-of-court discussions with the trial judge should not occur unless absolutely essential, and then subject to various conditions. The Royal Commission proposed[13] a modification to this rule, so that judges may indicate the highest sentence that they would impose at that point on the basis of the facts put to them.[14] This might occur at pre-hearing, and encourage an accused to plead guilty. There is, of course, a danger that some defendants might plead guilty when they were, in fact, innocent.[15] The Crown Court Survey[16] found some evidence of this, but the significance of the data obtained is open to doubt.[17]

7   As amended by the Criminal Procedure (Insanity and Unfitness to Plead) Act 1991. See ss 4, 4a and 5 of the 1964 Act.
8   *Ibid*, s 5.
9   *Ibid*, s 4; see, for such a case, *R v Burles* [1970] 2 QB 191; [1970] 1 All ER 642.
10   *R v Grafton* [1993] QB 101; [1992] 4 All ER 609. The position is different if counsel expressly asks for the approval of the judge: *R v Broad* (1978) 68 Cr App Rep 281. See, generally, Farquharson Committee Report (1986) LS Gaz 3599.
11   RCCJ, Ch 7, para 13. The Crown Court Study showed that "cracked" trials were 26% of all cases, creating serious problems (para 45).
12   *R v Turner* [1970] 2 QB 321; [1970] 2 All ER 281; *R v Coward* (1979) 70 Cr App Rep 70.
13   *Op cit.*
14   Report, Ch 7, para 50.
15   It is for this reason that an accused must plead personally, not through counsel.
16   See generally Ashworth, "Plea, Venue and Discontinuance" [1993] Crim LR 830.
17   RCCJ, Ch 7, para 45.

In fact the majority of accused persons at Crown Court plead guilty.[18] Therefore they obtain a "discount" on the otherwise justified sentence.[19] The Royal Commission proposed a formalised system, of graduated discounts, to encourage early pleas of guilty.[20] On the other hand, the research shows that approximately 50% of those pleading not guilty are in fact acquitted,[1] with a significant number of "non-jury" acquittals. These non-jury acquittals merit further mention: the statistical evidence suggests that discharge, usually where the prosecution offers no evidence, is far more common than judges directing a jury to enter a "not guilty" verdict because of the inadequacy of the evidence before the court.[2]

a   Plea of guilty

On the assumption that the plea covers the whole indictment, counsel briefed for the prosecution will give a brief outline of the facts and then call a police officer to give the antecedent history of the defendant, in the form of a sheet setting out the defendant's home and educational background, previous jobs, criminal record and anything else thought to be relevant. He may be cross-examined by defending counsel. The court will then usually consider a pre-sentence report,[3] presented usually on behalf of a probation officer. There is then a plea in mitigation made by counsel for the defence, sometimes supported by witnesses (very rarely the defendant). The defendant will then usually be given the opportunity of saying something himself to the court, after which sentence will be passed. If there are two defendants, one of whom is pleading guilty and the other not guilty, the one pleading guilty will not normally be sentenced until the trial of the other defendant is concluded.[4]

It is customary for the normal rules of evidence to be relaxed at proceedings following a plea of guilty. The rules of evidence do not apply to "antecedent evidence", which is invariably given by a single police officer on the basis of files concerning the defendant which the officer has in court. Nevertheless the officer should not make allegations against the defendant which he has reason to think that the latter would deny and which he cannot properly prove.[5] Of course, if matters of importance are disputed, then the court may require them to be formally proved. In addition, where despite the plea of guilty there is a factual dispute that will affect the basis upon which the court will sentence the accused, the trial judge will hear evidence to determine that question, a so called "Newton" hearing.[6]

If the defendant pleads guilty to some, but not all, counts or pleads guilty to a lesser offence, the prosecution must decide whether to proceed on the remaining counts or "accept" the defendant's pleas, in which event the counts to which he has not pleaded guilty will be left "on the file". Although the defendant will never have been in peril of conviction on those counts, so that he could theoretically be tried on them, in practice this would not be permitted without leave of the court and, indeed, the counts on the

18   *Op cit*, Ch 6.
19   See, eg, *R v Hollington and Emmens* (1985) 82 Cr App Rep 281.
20   *Ibid*, para 47.
1   Vennard, "The Outcome of Contested Trials" in Moxon (ed) *Managing Criminal Justice*.
2   *Ordered and Directed Acquittals in the Crown Court*, RCCJ Research Study No 15 (HMSO, 1993).
3   Criminal Justice Act 1991, s 3. These were formerly known as Social Inquiry Reports. See further, p 534, *post*.
4   *R v Weekes* (1982) 74 Cr App Rep 161. The position may be different if the accused is going to give evidence for the prosecution against his co-accused.
5   Cf *R v Robinson* (1969) 53 Cr App Rep 314, where the officer described the defendant as "the principal drug pusher" in the Midlands, evidence the reception of which the Court of Appeal described as a "clear and obvious injustice". See also *R v Wilkins* (1977) 66 Cr App Rep 49.
6   *R v Newton* (1982) 77 Cr App Rep 13.

file are sometimes ordered to be marked with words such as "not to be proceeded with without the leave of this court or of the Court of Appeal". However, even if the prosecution is content to adopt this course, the judge must, if asked, consent to it and, if he does not, he may order the trial to proceed.[7]

b Plea of not guilty

It should be noted that this is not necessarily a positive assertion that the defendant is innocent but merely a request or a challenge to the prosecution to prove the case against him.

A defendant may plead guilty to one count in the indictment but not guilty to another, or even admit part of an offence contained in a single count but not the rest of the offence.[8] He may also plead not guilty to the offence charged but guilty to some other offence of which he may lawfully be convicted by way of alternative verdict; thus he may plead not guilty to murder but guilty to manslaughter. The whole question of alternative verdicts is now regulated by section 6(3) of the Criminal Law Act 1967. This enables the jury to acquit of the offence charged, but to convict of another offence which the court has jurisdiction to try and which is expressly or by implication alleged in the indictment.[9]

The point arises, often acutely, when the judge comes to sum up the case to the jury. Where nothing appears on the depositions which can be said to reduce the crime charged to the lesser offence of which the defendant wishes to plead guilty, it is the duty of counsel for the Crown to present the offence charged in the indictment, leaving it to the jury "in the exercise of their undoubted prerogative" to return a verdict of guilty of the lesser offence.[10] Even where there is material on the depositions capable of sustaining a lesser charge, the prosecution is entitled to formulate its charges as it thinks fit. However, it is for the discretion of the trial judge whether to direct the jury as to the potential for an alternative verdict.

Secondly, the defendant may change his plea once the trial has started but in this case the appropriate verdict must be returned by the jury which will have been sworn to try the case;[11] it may seem a formality that if the defendant changes his plea, for example, from "not guilty" to "guilty", the foreman of the jury should be required to stand up and say that the defendant is guilty, but:

"once a prisoner is in charge of a jury he can only be either convicted or discharged by the verdict of the jury".[12]

c Autrefois acquit *and* autrefois convict

These are by far the most important of a number of so-called "special pleas in bar" which can be raised by the defendant when the indictment is put to him.[13] The substance

---

7   *R v Broad* (1978) 68 Cr App Rep 281.
8   *Machent v Quinn* [1970] 2 All ER 255.
9   What is included " by implication" is often difficult to decide. The test is whether the allegations in the indictment are capable of including the elements of the alternative offence: *Metropolitan Police Commissioner v Wilson* [1984] AC 242; *sub nom R v Wilson* [1983] 3 All ER 448.
10   *R v Soanes* [1948] 1 All ER 289.
11   *R v Heyes* [1951] 1 KB 29; [1950] 2 All ER 587.
12   *Ibid* per Lord Goddard CJ [1951] 1 KB at 30; [1950] 2 All ER at 588.
13   Others are demurrer (that the facts alleged do not constitute the offence charged); plea to the jurisdiction (that the court has no jurisdiction to try); pardon (that a pardon has been granted). These are extremely rare.

of the pleas in bar is that there is some reason why the court should not proceed to try the defendant, which should be made the subject of immediate inquiry, so that if the reason is found to be a valid one the defendant should be released and further proceedings stayed.[14] The general principle of the two pleas of *autrefois acquit* and *autrefois convict* is that the same person should not be put in jeopardy twice for the same offence founded on the same facts, not merely for the same facts. The two pleas were extensively considered by the House of Lords in *Connelly v Director of Public Prosecutions*.[15] The following principles emerge from that and subsequent cases.

(1) A man cannot be tried for a crime in respect of which he has previously been convicted or acquitted. The reason for this is that an accused should not be put in peril twice. It is for this reason that the doctrine does not apply where the accused was never in fact in jeopardy. In *R v Dabhade*[16] a charge was formally dismissed, because in law it was defective. The accused was committed for trial on a substituted charge of theft. In dismissing an appeal against conviction, based upon the principle of *autrefois acquit*, the Court of Appeal indicated that where a charge was dismissed because it was defective, or because the evidence was insufficient to sustain a conviction, or because of a rationalisation of the prosecution case, the appellant was never in fact in jeopardy.

(2) The same rule applies where a person could have been convicted of the alleged offence on a previous indictment. In this context the rule as to alternative verdict offences is of importance. As has already been seen,[17] a defendant on being charged with certain crimes may plead, or be found, guilty of certain other crimes and not guilty of the offence charged, without the need for a fresh indictment. Thus on a charge of murder the accused may be convicted of manslaughter. The doctrines of *autrefois acquit* and *autrefois convict* apply to any offence which was an alternative verdict offence to the original offence, and of which the accused was acquitted or convicted. Thus if the defendant is acquitted of murder, the defence of *autrefois acquit* will be open to him if charged with manslaughter or attempted murder arising out of the death of the same person.

(3) The rule applies if the crime in respect of which he is charged is in effect, or substantially the same as, the crime of which he was earlier acquitted or could have been (or was) convicted. This is in reality a matter for the common sense of the court.

(4) One test of when the rule applies is to ask whether the evidence necessary to support the second indictment, or whether the facts which constitute the second offence, would have been sufficient to procure a legal conviction on the first indictment either as to the offence charged or of an offence of which the accused could have been found guilty.

(5) The matter is not decided simply by comparing indictments, but on the overall facts. The accused may adduce evidence as to the identity of the persons involved, and as to dates and other facts necessary to show that the doctrine applies.

(6) It is not within the doctrine that the facts under examination, or the witnesses being called in the later proceedings, are the same as those in the earlier proceedings.

(7) Irrespective of the above, a person may be able to show that a matter has in fact been decided already by a court competent to decide it, in the sense of a finding

---

14   See the remarks of Lord Goddard CJ in *R v County of London Quarter Sessions, ex parte Downes* [1954] 1 QB 1 at 5–6; [1953] 2 All ER at 750.
15   [1964] AC 1254; [1964] 2 All ER 401.
16   [1993] QB 329; [1992] 4 All ER 796.
17   See p 515, *ante*.

or plea of guilty and a sentence passed pursuant to that finding or plea. The matter must, though, in fact have been decided. In *Richards v R*[18] the accused pleaded guilty to manslaughter, but had not been sentenced. At a resumed hearing the prosecution was halted, and the appellant subsequently tried and convicted and sentenced to death[19] for murder. In dismissing the appeal against conviction the Privy Council was of the view that the plea of *autrefois convict* did not assist the accused, because the adjudication was not in fact complete.

4 Motion to quash the indictment

Instead of entering any plea, general or special, the defendant may move to quash the indictment. This may be done on several grounds. If any of the rules, already described,[20] as to the framing of the indictment have not been followed this may be made the ground for a motion to quash; however it has already been seen that the court possesses ample power to amend the indictment and it will only be rarely that a motion to quash on this ground will succeed. It could only do so on the ground of some grave defect of substance, such as the insufficiency of the particulars of offence, or duplicity. An indictment may also be quashed on the ground that the offence charged in it is not one known to the law. Yet another ground is that the appropriate officer did not have jurisdiction to sign it; as has already been seen he can sign it only if certain conditions are satisfied. An indictment can also be quashed if it amounts to an abuse of the process of the court.[1]

5 Preliminary points of law

It sometimes happens that there is a point of law involved in a case the decision of which may effectively dispose of the whole case. Thus, for example, the basic facts alleged by the prosecution may be admitted by the defence, the sole issue being whether those admitted facts amount to the offence charged. In cases of this sort it is obviously a sterile exercise to go through the motions of trial by jury when the outcome of the case will depend entirely upon the judge's decision as to the law. The judge hears argument upon the law (before empanelling a jury); if a ruling is given which, in the view of the accused and his advisers, is fatal to the defence, the accused can then change his plea.[2] The point may, in fact, be dealt with at a preliminary hearing, or through a pre-trial ruling.[3] However it is necessary for a plea of not guilty to be taken before the point of law is argued.

---

18 [1993] AC 217; [1992] 4 All ER 807.
19 It was a Privy Council appeal from Jamaica, where the death penalty still exists.
20 See p 503, *ante*.
1 See p 464, *ante*.
2 See, eg, *Director of Public Prosecutions v Doot* [1973] AC 807; [1973] 1 All ER 940. An accused who has pleaded guilty in such circumstances can appeal against his conviction on the ground that the preliminary point of law was wrongly decided against him.
3 See p 510, *ante*.

6 Empanelling the jury: challenges

Assuming that there is a plea of not guilty to some part of the indictment the next stage of the trial will be the swearing of the jury. The Juries Act confers on the Lord Chancellor general responsibility for the summoning of jurors,[4] a function in reality performed locally. From all the jurors summoned, twelve will be chosen by ballot; a jury should be randomly selected[5] and a court has no power to interfere with the selection of a jury except in the rarest of cases, and for cause, for example relating to the physical or mental fitness of the proposed juror.[6] The selected jurors will take their places in the jury box. Before the jury is sworn the defendant is given the opportunity to challenge members of the jury for cause, either to the whole panel summoned or to an individual juror. The burden is on the party making the challenge to show such a cause, the issue being tried by the trial judge. Prior to 1988 an accused had a right of peremptory challenge of up to three jurors, which meant that, unlike for cause, the defendant did not have to state any reason for challenge. This right was abolished by the Criminal Justice Act 1988. By contrast the right of the Crown to require jurors to "stand by" still exists.[7] By this procedure, the juror is asked to stand down, but consideration of the cause of challenge (since a challenge by the Crown must be for cause) is postponed. It will usually then happen that there are enough "spare" jurors for a whole jury to be assembled, however many more challenges are made, so that the trial can proceed and the cause of the Crown's challenge is never made the subject of enquiry. The Crown will usually act on the basis of knowledge of a potential juror's criminal record[8] or, in exceptional cases of other matters disclosed on an authorised check of police records.[9]

Each member of the jury having been sworn individually, the appropriate officer of the court then tells the jury of the terms of the offences to which the defendant has pleaded not guilty and informs them that it is their duty, having heard the evidence, to say whether he is guilty or not. The trial judge may also explain certain features about a criminal trial to the jury.[10]

H COURSE OF THE TRIAL

I Publicity

English law regards "open justice" as a fundamental principle,[11] which therefore means that the trial, including the process of arraignment described above, should be open to the public, and may be reported. Despite this, the principle is not unlimited, and may be departed from where necessary where openness or publicity would harm the interests of justice.[12] Powers exist to postpone the reporting of all or part of a trial,[13] to prevent

---

4　Juries Act 1974, s 2.
5　See RCCJ, Ch 8, paras 52–64.
6　See p 234, *ante*.
7　See *Attorney General's Guidelines* (1989).
8　These may disqualify a juror from service: see p 224, *ante*.
9　*Attorney General's Guidelines on Jury Checks* [1988] 3 All ER 1086, and p 225, *ante*.
10　Royal Commission on Criminal Procedure, Cmnd 8092 (HMSO, 1981), para 67.
11　*Scott v Scott* [1913] AC 417; [1911–13] All ER Rep 1.
12　See p 151, *ante*.
13　Contempt of Court Act 1981, s 4(2). A right of appeal against such an order exists: Criminal Justice Act 1988, s 159.

reporting,[14] or in some situations to sit in camera. In addition, a variety of statutory powers exist that limit the principle.[15]

2   Procedure at the hearing

Prosecuting counsel starts by making an opening speech. This will be an outline of the allegations against the defendant and of the evidence which it is proposed to call in support of the allegations. No reference should be made to any item of evidence if counsel has been informed that there is going to be an objection to the admissibility of that evidence. The fact that evidence is relevant[16] is not sufficient: for it to be considered at a trial it must also be admissible, and there are a number of rules of evidence which exclude evidence that might be thought to be relevant. Examples of these include evidence of the character of the accused unless it is directly relevant to the issue before the court[17] and evidence of out-of-court statements.[18] A judge may also exclude from evidence relevant material where the fairness of the trial demands that that be done.[19] Therefore, in opening the case prosecuting counsel must take care not to refer to evidence that is not admissible, or which is likely to be excluded. Objections to the admissibility of evidence, or for the exclusion of evidence will be tried by the judge, usually (although not always) in the absence of the jury, at the time in the trial when the evidence would otherwise have been called. This procedure is known as a "voir dire", taking its name from the name of the oath taken by witnesses during that hearing.

The institution of the opening speech has been criticised on the ground that counsel may make allegations which are not borne out by the evidence of his witnesses (even before they are the subject of cross-examination) yet the jury may recollect only the statements of counsel, since they came first.[20] It is a strict rule that prosecuting counsel should limit his observations to what appears in the depositions, or witness statements. The only exception arises in the case of those witnesses in respect of whom a notice of additional evidence has been served. Even this practice is not strictly required by law, but the court has an inherent discretion to prevent oppressive conduct towards the defendant[1] and it is most unlikely that a judge would allow additional evidence to be called unless a notice of additional evidence, setting out a summary of that witness's evidence, had been served on the defendant.

---

14   Contempt of Court Act 1981, s 11.
15   See generally p 151, *ante*.
16   "Relevance" was defined in Stephen's Digest as meaning that "… any two facts to which it is applied are so related to each other that according to the common course of events one either taken by itself or in connection with other facts proves or renders probable the past, present or future existence or non existence of the other." For the difficulties in determining whether evidence is sufficiently relevant, see *R v Blastland* [1986] AC 41; [1985] 2 All ER 1095; *R v Kearley* [1992] 2 AC 228; [1992] 2 All ER 345.
17   Usually under the so-called similar fact evidence rule. For the broad thrust of that rule, see p 506, *ante*.
18   In *R v Sharp* [1988] 1 All ER 65; [1988] 1 WLR 7, the House of Lords approved the definition of hearsay in *Cross on Evidence*, 6th ed: "An assertion other than one made by a person while giving oral evidence in the proceedings is inadmissible as evidence of any fact asserted".
19   See PACE, s 78, discussed at p 317, *ante*.
20   The Royal Commission recommended that opening speeches should not contain such statements: whether matters are proved will be decided during the trial. The RCCJ suggested opening speeches should be restricted to explanation of the issues (Ch 8, para 9), and that such speeches should be limited in length to fifteen minutes.
1   See the remarks of Lord Devlin in *Connolly v Director of Public Prosecutions* [1964] AC 1254 at 1346 *et seq*; [1964] 2 All ER 401 at 438 *et seq*.

Prosecution witnesses will then be called[2] and will be subject to examination-in-chief by prosecuting counsel, cross-examination by defending counsel and re-examination by prosecuting counsel. Examination-in-chief is the first stage in the examination of a witness, and is carried out by the party calling the witness. The purpose of examination in chief is to elicit the testimony the witness has to give on the relevant matters. An advocate cannot ask the witness leading questions. A leading question is one which suggests to the witness the answer that is expected or which assumes a fact still to be proved. It is sometimes said that any question that can be answered with a simple "Yes" or "No" is a leading question. This is often, although not invariably, true. Leading questions are often permitted on formal matters, such as name, address and occupation, and it is permissible for a party to lead a witness with the concurrence of the other parties and the court. Nor can an advocate cross-examine his or her own witness by putting previous inconsistent statements to the witness, unless the court rules that that witness is "hostile". A witness is hostile if that witness is "not desirous of telling the truth at the instance of the party calling him".[3] Some hostility or animosity is called for: it is not enough that the evidence is unfavourable to the party calling him. If the witness is hostile, then, at common law, he may be asked leading questions by the party calling him, and, under section 3 of the Criminal Procedure Act 1865, previous inconsistent statements may be put to him, which will affect the "credit" of the witness in the eyes of the jury. More usually, a witness will ask, or be invited, to refresh his memory from an out-of-court statement made when the events were still fresh in the mind.[4] The answers of a witness must be accepted by the advocate calling that witness, even if the witness has "not come up to proof" (ie not testified as anticipated).

Following examination-in-chief, a witness will be cross-examined by the advocate for the party not calling that witness. The purpose of cross-examination is to weaken the testimony of the witness, either by casting doubt about his testimony, or by eliciting facts favourable to the cross-examiner, or by discrediting the credit of the witness in the eyes of the jury. An advocate may, for this purpose, ask leading questions and, indeed, there are few limits on what may be asked in cross-examination: normally, any question relevant to the issues in the case will be allowed.[5] Exceptions to this general rule exist in respect of questions relating to the interception of communications[6] and in respect of matters for which a claim of public interest immunity is successfully made.[7] By contrast, the law imposes limits on questions that may be asked and which affect the credit or credibility of the witness. The basic rule is that the question must,

2   It is the duty of the prosecution to take all reasonable steps to secure the attendance at the trial of all witnesses (other than those subject to a conditional witness order) named on the back of the indictment (*R v Cavanagh* [1972] 2 All ER 704; [1972] 1 WLR 676). However the prosecution has a discretion whether to call a particular witness and, having called him, whether to adduce his evidence-in-chief or merely to tender him for cross-examination. Where the witness's evidence is capable of belief the prosecution should call him even though his evidence is unfavourable to the prosecution case and if they do not do so, the judge may intervene and direct that he be called; on the other hand if the witness's evidence does not appear to be capable of belief the prosecution need not call him and it will then be for the defence to call him if they wish to do so; *R v Oliva* [1965] 3 All ER 116; [1965] 1 WLR 1028.

3   *Ewer v Ambrose* (1825) 3 B & C 746

4   *R v Da Silva* [1990] 1 All ER 29; [1990] 1 WLR 31. If the witness wishes to refresh his memory, and have the document with him, actually whilst testifying, it must be contemporaneous, ie made whilst the events were still fresh in the mind of the maker of the statement: *R v Richardson* [1971] 2 QB 484. See also *A-G's Reference (No 3 of 1979)* (1979) 69 Cr App Rep 411 and cf *R v Chisnell* [1992] Crim LR 507 (police officers allowed to refresh memory from notes transcribed many months earlier, but at a time when the events were still fresh in the mind).

5   *CT Hobbs v Tinling & Co* [1929] 2 KB 1; [1929] All ER Rep 33; *R v Funderburk* [1990] 2 All ER 482; [1990] 1 WLR 587.

6   Interception of Communications Act 1985, s 9.

7   See p 498, *ante*

if asked, relate to the likely standing of the witness in the eyes of the court.[8] In sexual cases, there may be specific limits imposed on what questions may be asked, and by whom. Thus, changes are proposed so that an unrepresented defendant may not cross-examine the complainant of a sexual offence,[9] and in cases involving a "rape offence",[10] the leave of the court will be required before an accused may cross-examine a complainant of a sexual offence about sexual experience with a person other than the accused.[11]

Even where questions relating to credit are permitted, the law imposes strict limits as to how far the cross-examiner may adduce other evidence to contradict (i.e. rebut) the testimony of that witness. The reason for this is that there is a need to keep the trial to the issues at hand, and to prevent the trial from becoming an exploration of a multiplicity of other matters. This is known as the collateral evidence rule: the answers of a witness in cross-examination to matters that relate to credit are regarded as final, and can only be rebutted if one of the exceptions to the rule exists.[12] There are four such exceptions that potentially arise. The first is if the witness denies a previous conviction: the denial may be rebutted.[13] Secondly, if the witness denies making a previous inconsistent statement, that denial may be rebutted.[14] Thirdly, the cross-examiner may rebut a denial of bias.[15] Finally, if the witness denies having a general reputation for untruthfulness, that denial may be rebutted.[16]

Cross-examination is followed, sometimes, by re-examination by the advocate for the party calling the witness. The purpose of re-examination is limited to clarifying matters that have arisen out of the testimony the witness has given to the court, usually in the hope of bolstering testimony which has been shaken under cross-examination. As in examination-in-chief, leading questions may not be asked. Furthermore, a party cannot use re-examination as an opportunity for raising matters which he omitted to raise in examination-in-chief unless the form of the cross-examination justifies this.

When all the witnesses for the prosecution have been examined, prosecuting counsel will close his case by saying "that is the case for the prosecution" or words to that effect. There may then be a submission by defending counsel that there is no case to answer as regards the whole or some part of the indictment. This may be put in two ways: first that there is no evidence that the crime alleged against the accused was committed by him; secondly that the evidence, taken at its highest, is so tenuous that a jury could not properly convict on it.[17] This is a matter for the judge to determine and, although there is no set rule, it is usually regarded as desirable that the argument on the submission should take place in the absence of the jury. Prosecuting counsel has, of course, a right to reply to defending counsel's submission. If the submission is upheld the trial will end as regards that part of the indictment at least, although the jury should be instructed to return a formal verdict of not guilty; this is analogous to the case where the defendant changes his plea to guilty in the course of the trial.[18] Even

---

8   See *Hobbs v Tinling, supra,* n 5.
9   Although not yet in force.
10 Sexual Offences (Amendment) Act 1976.
11 See *R v Viola* [1982] 3 All ER 73; [1982] 1 WLR 1138. Leave may also be granted in respect of matters that affect the witnesses' credit. What is not permissible is to ask questions designed to create the inference: "well, members of the jury, that's the sort of girl she is": per May J in *R v Lawrence* [1977] Crim LR 492. See generally, Temkin, "Sexual History Evidence – The Ravishment of Section 2" [1993] Crim LR 3.
12 *Harris v Tippett* (1811) 2 Camp 637.
13 Criminal Procedure Act 1865, s 6.
14 *Ibid,* s 4.
15 *A-G v Hitchcock* (1847) 1 Exch 91.
16 (1977) 66 Cr App R 6.
17 *R v Galbraith* [1981] 2 All ER 1060; [1981] 1 WLR 1039.
18 See p 513, *ante.*

if no formal verdict is taken, the case, once withdrawn from the jury, is completely "dead" and cannot be revived by the defendant's own evidence or evidence given by a prosecution witness who is allowed to be recalled.[19] Similarly where two men are jointly charged, and a successful submission is made on behalf of one of them, he is to be regarded as no longer charged during what remains of the trial.[20]

The role of the judge at this stage is crucial. If the prosecution evidence is such that no properly directed jury could convict upon it then it is the duty of the judge to stop the case.[1] This is particularly so where the prosecution rely wholly on the confession of a person who suffers a significant degree of mental handicap, the confession itself being unconvincing. Such a case should be withdrawn from the jury.[2] By contrast, if the case is one where the strengths or weaknesses of the case depend upon the view to be taken as to the reliability of a witness or other matters properly within the remit of the jury, then the case should be left to the jury to decide.[3]

If the submission is simply rejected, the trial will proceed. Even if no submission is made the judge may at any time after the close of the prosecution's case ask the jury whether they think that the prosecution case has been proved and invite them to return a verdict of not guilty if they think that it has not;[4] the more desirable practice is for the judge to take the initiative and direct the jury to return a verdict of not guilty.

The defence case will then open, assuming that the trial is proceeding as to part or all of the indictment. Defence counsel has no right to make an opening speech to the jury unless he is calling witnesses as to fact other than the defendant (whether or not he is also calling the defendant); even then the matter is in his discretion.[5] Witnesses for the defence are then called. If the defendant is giving evidence it is the general rule that he must give evidence before other witnesses; he must be in court, and if he heard the evidence of other witnesses before him,[6] he might be tempted to "trim" his own evidence. A witness about whose evidence there could be no controversy may of course be taken before the defendant. What evidence is called for the defence depends on the nature of the case. An accused person is not a compellable witness in his own defence.[7] However, if he fails to testify in his own defence without good cause, or refuses without good cause to answer any question, the court may draw such inference as it thinks proper.[8] An exception to this is where it appears to the court that the physical or mental condition of the accused makes it undesirable for him to give evidence.

Whether an inference is in fact drawn is a matter for the jury, based on their own perception of common-sense.[9] If good cause is argued by the accused, an evidential basis to establish it must exist: it is not enough for the accused simply to assert.[10] Age is not a barrier.[11] Until 1998, no inference could be drawn in respect of an accused

19   *R v Plain* [1967] 1 All ER 614; [1967] 1 WLR 565. The corollary of this is that if the submission is wrongly rejected the accused is entitled to have his subsequent conviction quashed by the Court of Appeal, even though evidence subsequently given would support that conviction; *R v Cockley* [1984] Crim LR 429.
20   *R v Meek* (1966) 110 Sol Jo 867.
1   *R v Galbraith* [1981] 2 All ER 1060; [1981] 1 WLR 1039.
2   *R v McKenzie* [1993] 1 WLR 453.
3   *R v Galbraith*, n 1, supra.
4   *R v Young* [1964] 2 All ER 480; [1964] 1 WLR 717.
5   The Royal Commission recommended that the right of the defence to make a speech at the commencement of the case should be extended to all cases, in substitution for the right here described.
6   Police and Criminal Evidence Act 1984, s 79.
7   Criminal Evidence Act 1898, s 1(a).
8   Criminal Justice and Public Order Act 1994, s 35.
9   *R v Cowan* [1996] QB 373; *Murray v DPP* [1994] 1 WLR 1.
10   See *Practice Direction: Crown Court (Defendants's Evidence)* [1995] 2 Cr App Rep 192.
11   See *R v Friend* [1997] 2 All ER 1011.

aged under 14. This was considered illogical by the Government, in the light of the fact that an inference can be drawn from the silence of a suspect aged under 14 at the investigatory stage, and the Crime and Disorder Act 1998 removed the age limitation.

All defence witnesses are subject to examination-in-chief, cross-examination and re-examination in the normal way.[12] Where there is more than one defendant, cross-examination of prosecution witnesses and speeches will normally be taken in the order in which the defendants' names appear on the indictment, although there is no fixed rule on the matter. Once the case for the defence has been closed the prosecution may be allowed to call rebutting evidence, in the discretion of the judge. The general rule is that rebutting evidence should be allowed only where evidence has been called on behalf of the defendant which could not fairly have been foreseen by the prosecution.[13] In determining this it should be borne in mind that in most cases the defence will have given a defence statement pursuant to section 5 of the Criminal Procedure and Investigations Act 1996.[14] Rebutting evidence may be called at any time up to the conclusion of the summing-up and retirement of the jury and defending counsel has a right to cross-examine the witnesses called in rebuttal. Further, if evidence is called after the conclusion of the speeches, counsel may deliver supplemental speeches dealing with the new evidence.

The judge has a right to recall witnesses himself or even call witnesses whom neither side has called; he may also question witnesses to clarify matters of doubt or to probe further into matters which he thinks have not been sufficiently investigated. However, a judge must be careful not to overstep the mark. In *R v Grafton*[15] prosecuting counsel decided during his case to offer no further evidence. The trial judge disagreed with that decision, and called the one remaining prosecution witness. In quashing the resulting conviction, the Court of Appeal stressed that the judge's power to call witnesses should be used sparingly, and only to advance the ends of fairness and justice. Until the case for the Crown is complete it is the Crown's decision as to whether or not the prosecution should proceed. However, the Royal Commission recommended that trial judges be more questioning of counsel (in the absence of the jury) as to why witnesses who are believed to have evidence of relevance have not been called.[16]

Closing speeches and the summing-up then follow. These are dealt with later.[17]

3   Witnesses

The procedure to be followed in the calling of evidence has been noted above. The general rule is that any person who is capable of giving intelligible testimony is a competent witness then follow. A person who is incapable of such testimony because of mental capacity, whether of a permanent or temporary nature,[18] will not be competent and thus will not be heard. Until recently, it was thought that special rules applied to young children,[19] but widespread criticism led to changes in the law. These have the effect of applying the same test of competence to a child as to an adult.[20] Special rules

12   For the limits to cross-examination, see p 521, *ante*.
13   *R v Pilcher* (1974) 60 Cr App Rep 1.
14   See p 501, *ante*.
15   [1993] QB 101; [1992] 4 All ER 609.
16   Report, Ch 8, para 18.
17   See p 528, *post*.
18   *R v Baines* [1987] Crim LR 508.
19   *R v Hayes* (1976) 64 Cr App Rep 82; *R v Wallwork* (1958) 42 Cr App Rep 153.
20   *DPP v M* [1997] 2 All ER 749; *G v DPP* [1997] 2 All ER 755.

continue to apply to accused persons: an accused is not a competent witness for the prosecution, although he is competent in his own defence.[1]

A witness who is competent is usually compellable. In other words, the witness can be required to attend court to testify, on pain of being punished for contempt of court. The attendance of a witness at the Crown Court is compelled by the issue of a witness order or witness summons, issued by the Crown Court.[2] A witness can resist the granting of a witness summons only if he or she has no relevant evidence to give, or if the witness is entitled to claim public interest immunity to resist the claim that he or she should testify or produce relevant documents.[3] To the general rule that a witness is compellable there are certain exceptions. An accused person is never compellable in his own defence. The spouse of the accused is only compellable in certain limited situations, contained in section 80(3) of the Police and Criminal Evidence Act 1984. These situations are as follows:

(1) where the offence charged involves an assault on, or injury or threat of injury to, the spouse or a person at the time of the offence under the age of 16 years;
(2) a sexual offence alleged to have been committed against a person under the age of 16 years;
(3) an offence of attempting, conspiring, aiding or abetting, counselling or inciting such an offence.

Where the spouse is competent but not compellable the trial judge is under a duty to inform the witness of that witness' right not to testify.[4] If the witness then decides to give evidence, that witness can then be treated in the normal way, for example, he/she may be declared hostile.

Various other persons are not compellable witnesses. This includes the sovereign, as well as foreign sovereigns, ambassadors, High Commissioners and various grades of diplomatic staff. In any legal proceedings to which a bank is not a party, a bank or bank officer cannot be compelled to produce any banker's book the contents of which can be proved by secondary evidence, eg by the production of documentary evidence.[5]

Where a witness testifies he or she usually does so orally. The general rule is that all witnesses must give evidence on oath, but a child under the age of 14 always gives unsworn evidence.[6] Any person having authority to hear evidence has the power to administer an oath,[7] but it is usually administered by the clerk to the court. The usual form of oath runs as follows:

"I swear by Almighty God that the evidence I shall give shall be the truth, the whole truth and nothing but the truth."

The witness holds the New Testament, or in the case of Jews the Old Testament, in his uplifted hand.[8] This form of oath is only appropriate to members of the Christian and Jewish faiths. Any person who objects to taking the usual oath may take any other form of oath, according to his religious beliefs, which he declares to be binding on his conscience. As an alternative, a person who objects to being sworn is permitted to

1   See Criminal Evidence Act 1898, s 1(a).
2   Criminal Procedure (Attendance of Witnesses) Act 1965, s 2.
3   See p 498, *ante*.
4   *R v Thompson* (1976) 64 Cr App Rep 96.
5   Bankers' Books Evidence Act 1879, s 3.
6   Criminal Justice Act 1991, s 52.
7   Evidence Act 1851, s 16.
8   Oaths Act 1978, s 1.

"make his solemn affirmation" instead of taking the oath. This substitutes the words "I (name) do solemnly sincerely and truly declare and affirm" for "I swear by Almighty God ...".[9] A witness is also permitted to affirm if it is not reasonably practicable without inconvenience or delay to administer the form of oath appropriate to the witness' beliefs (for example, because the book on which the witness wishes to swear is not available).[10] An affirmation is not unsworn testimony: it is equivalent to an oath and a false statement on affirmation amounts to perjury.[11]

Once sworn, or having affirmed, a witness gives evidence orally, usually in open court. Exceptions to this are permitted where it is essential for the administration of justice, or where statute specifically authorises. In some circumstances, for example, a witness may give evidence from behind a screen,[12] so that the witness does not have to face the alleged perpetrator of the offence, or through a live TV link.[13] The use of video links is particularly important in cases involving children's evidence, especially where it is alleged that the child is the victim of abuse. In such cases the law is increasingly concerned to ensure that the child does not have the damage of the alleged offence compounded by the experience of having to face the alleged perpetrator in open court. This power to take evidence through a live TV link also extends to cases where an adult witness is outside the United Kingdom.[14] In addition, a video recorded interview with a child may sometimes be admissible as the evidence in chief of that child. This is dealt with below.

Documentary evidence

Normally, the evidence given by a witness is oral in nature. A technical rule of evidence, the hearsay rule, prevents the out-of-court statements of a person being adduced to prove the truth of the assertions contained in those statements.[15] The reasons for this general rule reflect the oral nature of the criminal trial: an out-of-court statement may, if it is made orally, be prone to distortion or inaccuracy. If the maker of the statement is available to testify, his out-of-court statement is self serving and adds nothing to what he can tell the court. If, by contrast, the maker of the statement is unavailable to testify, the witness cannot be cross-examined on what is alleged to have been said in that statement.[16]

Yet it can clearly be seen that the out-of-court statements of an individual may be both relevant and reliable, often made at a time when the events or matters in issue were fresh in the mind of that person. For that reason the hearsay rule has been severely criticised, and is subject to a wide range of exceptions.[17] Firstly, an out-of-court statement is admissible in evidence of the fact that it is made is itself relevant. Thus,

9   Children and Young Persons Act 1963, s 28.
10   Oaths Act 1978, s 5(2).
11   *Ibid*, s 5(4).
12   *R v X, Y & Z* (1989) 91 Cr App R 36.
13   Criminal Justice Act 1988, s 32A.
14   *Ibid*, s 32A(2).
15   See p 519, *ante*.
16   *Teper v R* [1952] AC 480, [1952] 2 All ER 447.
17   No new common law exceptions can be created: *Myers v DPP* [1965] AC 1001, [1964] 2 All ER 881. For this reason the courts often seem to classify as non-hearsay evidence that might logically be classified as hearsay: see eg, *R v Cook* [1987] QB 417; [1987] 1 All ER 1049. See, generally, Birch, "Hearsay Logic and Hearsay Fiddles", in *Essays in Honour of J C Smith*, Butterworths, 1987.

in *R v Lydon*[18] pieces of paper inscribed "Sean rules" and "Sean rules 85" were relevant and admissible in order to draw the circumstantial inference that the accused (known as Sean) was associated with the gun near which the pieces of paper were found. Secondly, an out-of-court statement can be used by a witness to refresh his memory, provided certain pre-conditions are satisfied.[19] Thirdly, certain out-of-court statements may be admissible because they comprise part of the events in issue. This is known as the *res gestae* rule. A witness may testify as to statements made by another person where those statements were so bound up with the events in question as to dominate the mind of the individual and eliminate the risk of concoction.[20] Fourthly, certain statutory exceptions exist to the general rule. One set of provisions of this type are the provisions in sections 5A to 5F of the Magistrates' Courts Act 1980[1] which permit statements used for committal proceedings to be adduced in evidence. Another set are the provisions of sections 23 to 26 of the Criminal Justice Act 1988, which permit documentary evidence to be adduced in certain circumstances where the witness is unavailable to testify, subject to a power in the hands of the court to exclude, or to decline to admit, such evidence where it would not be in the interests of justice to do so. Thus, section 23 of the 1988 Act permits an out-of-court statement to be adduced if the maker of the statement is dead, unfit to give evidence, or fails to give evidence through fear. Section 24 permits certain business documents to be adduced in evidence. The court has a discretion to exclude a document where to admit it would be unfair, and, in respect of documents prepared for the purposes of pending or contemplated criminal proceedings, similar considerations are additional pre-conditions to admissibility.[2]

One particular exception to the rule, mentioned above, is the power to consider a video recording of an interview with a child. In cases involving offences of violence, or sexual offences, the video recording of the interview with a child may, with leave of the court be adduced.[3] If such a video is shown, what the child says is evidence and can be used to prove the truth of the matters to which the child speaks. Leave will be granted unless:

(a) it appears to the court that the child will not be available for cross examination;
(b) rules of court governing disclosure of the circumstances in which the recording was made have not been complied with;
(c) the court is of the opinion that, in the interests of justice, the recording ought not to be admitted. In considering whether or not leave should be granted, the court must consider whether any prejudice to the accused which might result is outweighed by the desirability of showing the whole, or substantially the whole, of the video.[4] A *Memorandum of Good Practice*,[5] has been adopted intended to govern how such video recorded interviews should be conducted so as to ensure that the interview can safely be relied on.

---

18 (1987) 85 Cr App R 221. See also *Woodhouse v Hall* (1980) 72 Cr App Rep 39, where the fact that the masseuses at a massage parlour offered sexual services was a fact from which a circumstantial inference could be drawn that the premises were being used as a brothel. Thus no hearsay problem arose, and the police officers were entitled to give evidence of those conversations. Cf *R v Rice* [1963] 1 QB 857; [1963] 1 All ER 832, itself doubted in *Myers v DPP*, *supra*.
19 See generally p 520, *ante*.
20 *R v Andrews* [1987] AC 281; [1987] 1 All ER 513.
1   See p 488, *ante*.
2   For the relevant principles see *R v Cole* [1990] 2 All ER 108, [1990] 1 WLR 866.
3   Criminal Justice Act 1991, s 54, incorporating a new s 32A into the Criminal Justice Act 1988.
4   *Ibid*, s 32A(3).
5   Home Office, HMSO, 1992.

4   The burden of proof and the right of silence

The burden of proof in a criminal case is on the prosecution. The prosecution must prove each element of the crime charged. This includes, subject to certain limited exceptions,[6] disproving any defence that is raised. This fundamental principle was well demonstrated in *Woolmington v Director of Public Prosecutions*[7] where the accused, charged with murdering his wife, claimed that the killing was an accident. The trial judge in his summing up directed the jury that if the Crown proved that the accused killed the deceased the burden rested on the accused to prove provocation or accident. The conviction was quashed in the House of Lords because of this misdirection. In the famous words of Lord Sankey LC:

> "…throughout the web of the English criminal law one golden thread is always to be seen, that is the duty of the prosecution to prove the prisoner's guilt, subject to …. The defence of insanity and subject also to any statutory exception."[8]

The circumstances in which the law departs from the principle are limited. The burden of proving a special plea in bar is on the accused. Thus, if it is claimed that the accused has been previously acquitted on the same charge, then the doctrine of *autrefois acquit* will apply.[9] The burden of proof on this point will be on the accused. Another example is the defence of insanity: the burden of proving insanity is on the defence where this issue is raised by the defence, as is the burden of proving diminished responsibility or unfitness to plead.[10] Certain statutory exceptions also exist.[11] Whenever a burden of proof is placed on the accused, the standard of proof is not that normally imposed on the prosecution ("beyond reasonable doubt") but the lesser, civil, standard of the balance of probabilities.[12]

The fact that the burden of proof is on the prosecution is crucially connected with the basic principle that an accused person has the right not to self-incriminate. As already noted,[13] this is a right recognised both by English law and by the European Convention of Human Rights. It is for this reason that an accused person cannot, generally, be required to self-incriminate or required to testify in his own defence. An accused is a competent, but not compellable, witness in his own defence. Further, if self incriminatory statements are obtained from an accused person unfairly, or by a trick, or in circumstances where they should not be relied on because safeguards created by the law have been evaded or ignored,[14] they will be excluded for evidence. Inroads into these principles have in recent years been made by Parliament. The fact that

---

6   These include the burden of proving a plea in bar (eg *autrefois acquit*, see p 515), insanity, diminished responsibility, unfitness to plead as well as under specific statutory exceptions.

7   [1935] AC 462. Cf *R v Bone* [1968] 2 All ER 644; [1968] 1 WLR 983 in which the defendant's conviction was quashed because of the trial judge's failure to direct that, in relation to the defence of duress, it was for the prosecution to disprove the defence rather than for the defendant to prove it.

8   *Ibid*, at p 481.

9   See p 515, *ante*.

10   Homicide Act 1957, s 2(2); *R v Dunbar* [1958] 1 QB 1; [1957] 2 All ER 737.

11   See, eg Road Traffic Act 1988, s 5(2).; Prevention of Crime Act 1953, s 1. For a general, and important statutory exception, see Magistrates Courts' Act 1980, s 101 which provides that, on summary trial, where an enactment makes the commission of a particular act an offence subject to a proviso, exception, excuse or qualification, the burden of proving that falls on the accused. For the application of s 101, see *R v Hunt* [1987] AC 352; [1987] 1 All ER 1.

12   *R v Carr-Briant* [1943] KB 607; [1943] 2 All ER 156.

13   See p 126, *ante*.

14   *R v Mason* [1987] 3 All ER 481; [1988] 1 WLR 139. For some of the authorities in terms of PACE, s 78, see p 317, *ante*.

inferences may now be drawn from a failure to mention facts at the investigatory stage,[15] or from a failure to disclose the nature of the defence later relied on,[16] has already been seen. As already noted, section 35 of the Criminal Justice and Public Order Act 1994 now permits a court to draw such inference as it thinks proper from a failure of an accused to give evidence or his refusal, without good cause, to answer any question. Whether an inference is in fact drawn will depend on all the circumstances, and whether an evidential basis has been established to explain the failure to testify or to answer the relevant question.[17]

If an accused decides to testify in his own defence, he is given protections not available to other witnesses. Although he is subject to cross-examination in the normal way, the effect of s 1(f) of the Criminal Evidence Act 1898 is that an accused has a "shield": he may not be cross-examined about previous convictions or bad character unless such matters are relevant to the issue (ie admissible under the similar fact evidence rule)[18] or unless the accused has lost his shield. The shield may be lost if, under s 1(f)(ii) of the 1898 Act, he has asserted his own good character or cast an imputation on the character of the prosecutor, a prosecution witness or the deceased victim of the crime of murder.[19] Further, he loses his shield if he gives evidence against a co-accused.[20]

5   Conclusion of the case

Each side may address the jury, except that where a defendant is unrepresented and either gives no evidence at all or only gives evidence himself the prosecution have no right to sum up their case.[1] In all cases the rule is that prosecuting counsel speaks first and is then followed by counsel for the defendant.[2] The judge will then sum up.

The purpose of the summing-up is to instruct the jury as to the burden and standard of proof,[3] the role of judge and jury, and to give directions on points of law where it is necessary to do so. The Judicial Studies Board[4] has prepared model directions on common issues and points of law for the benefit of judges. The judge will also usually give a summary of the facts: indeed, in *R v Gregory*[5] the Court of Appeal suggested that there must be a reminder of the facts in all cases. However, in *R v Wilson*[6] the Court of Appeal upheld a conviction in a case where a judge considered the trial so short that a summary of the facts was unnecessary.

Criticism of this part of the judicial function has from time to time been made,[7] that summings-up can unwittingly, and occasionally deliberately, influence the juries'

15   See pp 317–318, *ante.*
16   See pp 499–500, *ante.*
17   See *R v Cowan*, p 522, *ante.*
18   See p 506, *ante.*
19   See *Selvey v DPP* [1970] AC 304; [1968] 2 All ER 497; *R v Tanner* (1977) 66 Cr App Rep 56. For the relevant principles see *R v Britzman* [1983] 1 All ER 369, [1983] 1 WLR 350.
20   Criminal Evidence Act 1898, s 1(f)(iii).
1   *R v Harrison* (1923) 17 Cr App Rep 156. Where the defendant is represented but calls no evidence, counsel for the prosecution has a right to make a closing speech but the Court of Appeal has stated that it is a right which it should rarely be necessary to exercise save in long and complex cases: *R v Bryant* [1979] QB 108; [1978] 2 All ER 689, an instructive case on the history of the procedure relating to speeches in criminal trials.
2   Criminal Procedure (Right of Reply) Act 1964.
3   See p 527, *ante.*
4   Responsible for the training of the judiciary. Such model directions must be adapted to the needs of the particular case.
5   [1993] Crim LR 623.
6   [1991] Crim LR 838.
7   See RCCJ, Ch 8, para 20.

view of the facts. Some suggested to the Royal Commission that, as in the United States, no summing-up of the facts should be given. This was rejected, but the Commission did disagree with the approach taken in *R v Gregory*, and indicated that it is in each case a question of fairness and balance.[8]

6   Verdict

No pressure should be placed on a jury to reach a verdict.[9] The jury generally retire to the jury room to consider their verdict. They are put in charge of officers of the court called jury bailiffs who must take an oath not, without the leave of the court, to allow any person to speak to the jury or to speak to them themselves without such leave, except only to ask them if they are agreed upon their verdict. Once they have retired to consider their verdict, the jury can separate only with leave of the court, which in turn can be given only in cases of "evident necessity"[10] such as a juror being taken ill in the course of the jury's deliberations. They do not have to stay in the same jury room until they have reached a conclusion, but they must not separate, subject to the very limited exception noted above, and it is desirable if not essential for them always to be in the custody of one of the court bailiffs while, for example, staying at a hotel overnight.[11] The jury may, of course, ask for further guidance from the judge upon any point of law or evidence arising in the case, but both the request for information and the answer to it must be given in open court; if the jury have asked for guidance in the form of a note sent to the judge, this note should be read out verbatim and then the answer given.[12]

When the jury have concluded their deliberations they will return to court and one of their number, whom they have appointed foreman, will stand up and, subject to the possibility of a majority verdict, in answer to questions put by the appropriate officer of the court, deliver the verdict of the jury.[13] The Criminal Justice Act 1967[14] introduced into English law the majority verdict. A verdict need not be unanimous if when there are not less than eleven jurors, ten agree on the verdict, and when there are ten, if nine agree.[15] The law cannot accept any majority verdict unless the jury have had not less than two hours of deliberation, or such longer period as the court thinks reasonable having regard to the nature and complexity of the case,[16] nor can the court accept a majority verdict of guilty unless the foreman of the jury states in open court the number

---

8   *Ibid*, para 22.
9   *R v McKenna* [1960] 1 QB 411; [1960] 1 All ER 326: judge told jury that they would be kept overnight if they failed to agree a verdict within 10 minutes. A guilty verdict was returned after 6 minutes. The resulting conviction was quashed on appeal. See also: *Bushell's case* (1670) Vaugh 135, 124 ER 1006.
10   *R v Neal* [1949] 2 KB 590; [1949] 2 All ER 438. Breach of this rule will almost invariably amount to a material irregularity resulting in a subsequent conviction being quashed; *R v Goodson* [1975] 1 All ER 760; [1975] 1 WLR 549 (where a juror, after retirement, was permitted by the jury bailiff to leave the jury room, following which he was seen making a telephone call); but compare *R v Alexander* [1974] 1 All ER 539; [1974] 1 WLR 422 in which the irregularity was a trifling one (juror returned to court simply to collect one or more of the exhibits and was observed throughout) and was held to be of insufficient gravity to justify quashing the conviction.
11   It may be necessary to restrict their reading or television viewing: see *Re Central Independent Television* [1991] 1 All ER 347; [1991] 1 WLR 4.
12   *R v Green* [1950] 1 All ER 38.
13   Once a verdict is given in the presence and hearing of all the jury, their assent to it is conclusively presumed: *R v Roads* [1967] 2 QB 108; [1967] 2 All ER 84.
14   Section 13 (now Juries Act 1974, s 17).
15   Majority verdicts are not considered desirable in re-trials; cf *R v Mansfield* [1978] 1 All ER 134; [1977] 1 WLR 1102.
16   Juries Act 1974, s 17(4).

of jurors who agreed on, and dissented from, the verdict.[17] A Practice Direction[18] contains procedure whereby it is hoped to conceal the fact that an acquittal was by a majority. In *R v Pigg*[19] the House of Lords held that the words "ten agreed" (in answer to the question how many agreed and how many dissented) was sufficient compliance with the statute. If after such discussion as is practicable in the circumstances the jury still cannot reach the necessary measure of agreement the judge has no option but to discharge them. The defendant will then be remanded in custody or on bail to be tried afresh. Theoretically this could happen several times, but if successive juries disagree the practice is for the prosecution to offer no evidence at a third trial. On a re-trial, the fact that there has been a previous trial is usually irrelevant and inadmissible, but it may become necessary to refer to it, for example for the purpose of proving that the defendant or a witness made some particular statement or admission. Thus in *R v McGregor*[20] the defendant was charged with receiving. At an earlier, abortive, trial he had admitted possession. A police officer was allowed to give evidence of this admission.

Other circumstances in which the jury may be discharged are:[1]

(1) illness. If during the course of a criminal trial a juror falls ill he may be discharged by the judge from further service, and depending on the facts, normally will be so discharged. The judge may then discharge the whole jury, but does not have to do so; neither is discharge of the single juror fatal to the continuance of the trial, since statute now provides that when, in the course of a trial, any member of the jury dies or is discharged the trial may nevertheless continue provided that the number of jurors does not fall below nine. If, however, the charge is murder or any offence punishable by death the prosecution and every accused must consent in writing to the trial continuing, even if only one juror is discharged or dies;
(2) misconduct of a juror, such as holding improper conversations with a member of the public about the case or absenting himself from his colleagues at the time when the jury were in the course of retiring to consider their verdict; and
(3) improper revelation to the jury of the defendant's past criminal record. In such a case the jury is frequently discharged in the defendant's own interest, although every case depends on its own facts.

17   *Ibid*, s 17(3). The requirement of this subsection is mandatory so that if, for whatever reason, the foreman does not so state the conviction will inevitably be quashed: *R v Barry* [1975] 2 All ER 760; [1975] 1 WLR 1190.
18   *Practice Direction* [1967] 3 All ER 137; [1967] 1 WLR 1198. Errors in the summing-up should be corrected by counsel before the jury retire: *R v Southgate* [1963] 2 All ER 833; [1963] 1 WLR 809n.
19   [1983] 1 All ER 56; [1983] 1 WLR 6.
20   [1968] 1 QB 371; [1967] 2 All ER 267.
1   Juries Act 1974, s 16. The judge may discharge a juror whether as being through illness incapable of continuing to act or for any other reason" (s 16(1)). This is a matter left to the discretion of the trial judge, although the Court of Appeal will interfere if injustice has resulted. In *R v Hambery* [1977] QB 924; [1977] 3 All ER 561 the trial judge discharged a lady juror in order to permit her to go away on holiday, a course which the Court of Appeal saw no reason to criticise.

CHAPTER 23

Sentences

A INTRODUCTION

The law governing the sentencing of offenders has undergone frequent changes in recent years, often of a radical nature. In part these changes have been a response to the stated desire of political parties to reduce the incidence of crime, and in part due to the often competing philosophies as to the purpose of custodial sentences. There has also been a need to keep the size of the prison population in check, although, paradoxically, some changes have had the potential to significantly increase the prison population.[1] The result has been a plethora of statutes making new provision, or amending existing provision, or even substituting new changes for those that reached the statute book but which never were fully implemented.[2] The position in respect of sentencing legislation reached such a level of complexity that the Lord Bingham CJ in *R v Governor of Brockhill Prison, ex parte Evans*[3] was moved to observe (in the context of the date of release of prisoners) as follows:

> "The Law Commission has described it as an important feature of any criminal justice system that sentencing provisions should be accessible and comprehensible and has recommended the enactment of a comprehensive statutory consolidation of such provisions ... We hope that this may be seen as a task commanding a high degree of priority ...".

The Crime and Disorder Act 1998 is the precursor to such consolidation, containing a large number of pre-consolidation amendments.[4]

---

1   It is estimated the mandatory and minimum sentence provisions of the Crime (Sentences) Act 1997 would, if fully implemented increase the prison population by some 11,000 prisoners: Lord McIntosh, HL 2nd Reading, HL Deb 577, col. 982.
2   See, eg Crime and Disorder Act 1998, ss 69–74, which introduced the new detention and training orders (as to which see p 576, *post*) for the never, implemented secure training order provisions in Criminal Justice and Public Order Act 1994, ss 1–18.
3   [1997] QB 443; [1997] 1 All ER 439.
4   See s 97 and Sch 7. For the position regarding consolidation procedures, see Chapter 2, *ante*.

The sentencing powers available to a magistrates' court following conviction on summary trial are more limited than those available to the Crown Court. These specific rules are dealt with separately,[5] but complex rules exist to enable a magistrates' court which considers its sentencing powers to be inadequate to commit the offender to the Crown Court for sentence.[6] In addition, special rules, orders and procedures apply to children and young persons, and have recently been significantly modified as part of a general review of the youth justice system. These are also dealt with separately.[7]

1   Consistency of sentencing and appropriate sentences

It is of considerable importance that different courts sentence consistently for the same type of offence, and impose a penalty appropriate to the level of seriousness of the offence of which the offender is convicted. On the other hand, the fact that a sentencing court has, or should have, a discretion to sentence in accordance with the circumstances of the particular offence is equally important and, to some, a basic constitutional principle. It was well explained as follows:

> "Attempts by the executive arm of government to influence sentencing are unconstitutional, attempts by the legislature to interfere with the discretion of the courts are, even if not strictly unconstitutional, bound to result in potential confusion and injustice to defendants, the sentencing powers of the courts should therefore be left to the wisdom of the courts under the guidance of the Court of Appeal."[8]

It was this last concern that led to trenchant opposition to the introduction in the Crime (Sentences) Act 1997 of mandatory and minimum sentences.[9] Certain offences carry a mandatory sentence. Others carry a minimum sentence.[10] Consistency is also achieved through the Attorney-General's power to make a reference to the Court of Appeal in a case where the sentence imposed is considered to be unduly lenient,[11] and through the practice of the Court of Appeal of issuing guideline judgments setting out the appropriate approach to offences of similar types.[12] In respect of summary offences the Magistrates' Association has issued Guidelines in respect of a wide range of offences.[13]

---

5   See p 571, *post.*
6   See p 572, *post.*
7   See p 576, *post.*
8   Ashworth *Sentencing and Penal Policy* (Wiedenfeld and Nicholson, 1983) at p 54. See also *Sentencing and Criminal Justice* (2nd ed, Butterworths, 1995) at pp 40–51; cf Walker and Padfield *Sentencing Theory, Law and Practice* (Butterworths, 1996) at p 380, who see no constitutional principle which forbids or even discourages Parliament from limiting the discretion of sentences if that has advantages.
9   See, eg Lord Woolf CJ, in the Second Reading, Debate of Crime (Sentences) Act 1997, *op cit*, col 997 where he complained of "the legislature taking over what has been accepted to be the proper role of the judiciary".
10   See p 538, *post.*
11   See p 534, *post.*
12   See p 533, *post.*
13   See p 571, *post.*

2   Sentencing Advisory Panel and the role of the Court of Appeal

Existing mechanisms to ensure sentencing consistency have proved inadequate. For that reason the Crime and Disorder Act 1998 creates a new Sentencing Advisory Panel.[14] It also imposes a new duty on the Court of Appeal to issue guidance on appropriate sentences for specific types of offence.[15] The Sentencing Advisory Panel will have the power to propose to the Court of Appeal (Criminal Division) that guidelines for sentencing in particular categories of indictable offence be framed or revised. It must so propose if directed to do so by the Home Secretary. This power, or duty, only extends to indictable offences. The Panel will be under a duty to consult, to formulate its own views and communicate them to the Court of Appeal and to furnish information to the Court of Appeal about the sentences imposed by courts in England and Wales for offences of the relevant category, the cost of different sentences and their relative effectiveness in preventing re-offending.[16] The recommendations of the Panel will not in any way bind the Court of Appeal but will clearly have a highly persuasive effect.

Section 75 of the 1998 Act imposes a duty on the Court of Appeal (Criminal Division) to consider whether to frame guidelines as to the sentencing of offences of particular categories. That Court must also consider whether it is appropriate to review existing sentencing guidelines. The duty arises where the Court:

(a)   is seized of an appeal against the sentence passed for an offence; or
(b)   receives a proposal under from the Sentencing Advisory Panel in respect of a particular category of offence.

"The relevant category" means any category within which the offence falls or to which the proposal relates.[17]

Guidelines shall have regard to the need to promote consistency in sentencing; the sentences imposed by courts in England and Wales for offences of the relevant category; the cost of different sentences and their relative effectiveness in preventing re-offending; the need to promote public confidence in the criminal justice system; and the views communicated to the court by the Sentencing Advisory Panel.[18] The guidelines framed or revised by the Court shall include criteria for determining the seriousness of offences, including (where appropriate) criteria for determining the weight to be given to any previous convictions of offenders or any failures of theirs to respond to previous sentences.

These provisions are to be welcomed, although it should be remembered that hitherto there has been no obstacle to the court setting out sentencing principles for particular offences if it had wanted to do so. Guideline judgments already exist in respect of a wide range offences.[19] Some commentators think these provisions do not go far enough. During the passage of the Crime and Disorder Act 1998, an unsuccessful attempt was made to create a body with wider advisory powers, a Standing Advisory Council on Criminal Justice and the Penal System. Such a body would have had a research and advisory function enabling it to be pro-active in examining the operation of the criminal justice system and to make recommendations. By contrast, the Government considered

---

14   Crime and Disorder Act 1998, s 81.
15   *Ibid*, s 80.
16   *Ibid*, s 81.
17   *Ibid*, s 80.
18   *Ibid*, s 80.
19   See, eg *R v Billham; R v Bibi* (1980) 71 Cr App Rep 360; *R v Willis* (1974) 60 Cr App Rep 146; *R v Taylor, Roberts and Simons* (1977) 64 Cr App Rep 182.

such a body to be an additional and unnecessary bureaucratic burden, which would not add to the plethora of advice on offer.[20] There is no likelihood of achieving the Sentencing Council for which some have argued.[1]

3   The role of the Attorney-General

The prosecution has a limited role in the sentencing process. It is under a duty to bring to the attention of the sentencing court matters relating to the power of the court, and has the right to correct misstatements of fact that may be made by an accused during the sentencing process. However, the prosecution has no specific right of appeal in an individual case against a sentence perceived as being unduly lenient. It was to permit some higher court review of such sentences that the Criminal Justice Act 1988 introduced powers which entitle the Attorney-General to refer to the Court of Appeal cases in which he considers an over-lenient sentence to have been imposed. Where such a reference is made the Court of Appeal may quash any sentence imposed and, in its place, impose such sentence as it thinks appropriate, within the powers that were available to the sentencing court. The Court of Appeal will not intervene unless the sentencing judge's sentence was wrong in principle, so that public confidence would be damaged if the sentence were not altered.[2]

4   The sentencing process

A judge will sentence on the basis of the guilty plea or verdict of the jury. If there is a significant dispute about what factually occurred, then, following a plea of guilty, unless the prosecution accepts the defence version, a hearing is held to decide any dispute.[3] However, if there is a verdict (as opposed to a plea) of guilty, the judge sentences on the basis of the facts as they appear to him.

a   Passing sentence

If the defendant has been found guilty on any part of the indictment the court will then proceed to sentence, in a similar manner to that following a plea of guilty.[4] There is first an inquiry into the defendant's antecedents. A pre-sentence report is then considered.[5] The defendant is then customarily given an opportunity of making such observations as he wishes, in addition to his counsel's speech in mitigation. It should always be made clear whether separate sentences are intended to be consecutive or concurrent.[6] In the course of this part of the trial it not infrequently happens that the defendant asks for other offences to be taken into consideration. This practice is based on convention and has no statutory foundation; yet at the same time it is extremely convenient both from the point of view of the police and of the defendant. If there are other offences which the defendant has committed but which are still untried (or

---

20   For such bodies, see, eg, Criminal Justice Consultative Council; Trial Issues Group; HM Inspectors of Prisons and Probation; The Law Commission; National Audit Office; Select Committee on Home Affairs.

1   See, especially, Ashworth *Sentencing and Criminal Justice* (Butterworths, 1995) at Ch 13.

2   *Attorney-General's Reference (No 5 of 1989) (R v Hill-Trevor)* (1989) 90 Cr App R 358.

3   Known as a *Newton* hearing: *R v Newton* (1982) 77 Cr App Rep 13.

4   See p 514, *ante.*

5   See p 536, *post.*

6   *Practice Direction* [1962] 1 All ER 417; [1962] 1 WLR 191.

unknown), then the defendant may admit them to the court of trial and ask the judge to take them into consideration when sentencing him for the offence of which he has just been convicted. In practice he will probably tell the police well before the hearing that he wishes certain offences to be taken into consideration or the police may suggest the matter to him and he will then be supplied with an appropriate form of admission; however there seems to be nothing to prevent a court taking an offence into consideration even if the defendant does not either admit it or ask for it to be taken into consideration until the actual trial. However:

> "If justice is to be done it is essential that the practice should not be followed except with the express and unequivocal assent of the offender himself. Accordingly, he should be informed explicitly of each offence which the judge proposes to take into consideration; and should explicitly admit that he committed them and should state his desire that they should be taken into consideration in determining the sentence to be passed on him."[7]

Once the defendant has served his sentence he will not, by long established custom, be prosecuted in respect of any of the offences which have been taken into consideration, although if he were prosecuted the defence of *autrefois convict* would not be open to him, there having been no trial, let alone conviction, in respect of those offences.[8] If, however, his conviction were quashed, a prosecution might be brought. The mere fact that the defendant asks for the offence to be taken into consideration does not, of course, compel the court to do so. Certain limitations have been laid down in the cases. Broadly, the offence to be taken into consideration should be of the same character as the offence of which the defendant has been convicted; if the defendant has already been separately committed for trial in respect of the offence to be taken into consideration the judge should obtain the consent of the prosecution before doing so.[9] Even if the prosecution does consent, the judge ought to consider whether the public interest requires a separate inquiry. Neither ought the court to take into consideration an offence carrying disqualification from driving.[10] The reason is that in very many cases it will be desirable if not obligatory to disqualify the defendant, yet there can only be a disqualification on conviction, and taking other offences into consideration does not amount to a conviction in respect of them. A sentence takes effect from the beginning of the day on which it is imposed, unless the court otherwise directs. Any sentence imposed, or other order made, by the Crown Court may, under section 47(2) of the Supreme Court Act 1981, be varied or rescinded by the Crown Court within the period of 28 days from the date of such sentence or order.

b Deferment of sentence

As an alternative to passing sentence immediately upon an offender, the judge has power to defer sentence for the purpose of enabling the court or any other court to which it falls to deal with him to have regard, in dealing with him to his conduct after conviction (including, where appropriate, the making by him of reparation for his offence) or to any change in his circumstances.[11] The deferment can only be made if

---

7   *Anderson v Director of Public Prosecutions* [1978] AC 964 at 977; *sub nom Director of Public Prosecutions v Anderson* [1978] 2 All ER 512, at 515–516, per Lord Diplock.
8   *R v Nicholson* [1947] 2 All ER 535.
9   *R v McLean* [1911] 1 KB 332.
10   *R v Williams* [1962] 3 All ER 639; [1962] 1 WLR 1268.
11   Powers of Criminal Courts Act 1973, s 1. For the principles governing the exercise of such power, see *R v George* [1984] 3 All ER 13, [1984] 1 WLR 1082.

the offender consents and the court is satisfied, having regard to the nature of the offence and the character and circumstances of the offender, that it would be in the interests of justice to do so. The power to defer sentence is intended for cases such as those in which a persistent offender has at last shown an inclination to settle down and work or those in which persons have, under domestic or financial pressure, stolen from their employers sums which they say they propose to repay. Accordingly it will not be appropriate to defer sentence where the offence is so minor that it would not merit a sentence of imprisonment in any event. Nor is it appropriate to do so where the offence is so serious that it must inevitably result in a substantial custodial sentence. This is because it would not be appropriate to impose a custodial sentence if the information before the court about the offender's conduct during the period of deferment is favourable to him.[12]

The period of deferment may be anything up to six months and there must not be a further deferment on the specified date.[13] Furthermore, where sentence is deferred, all aspects of the sentence should be deferred; the sentence must not be "split" by, for example, imposing an immediate disqualification from driving, but deferring the remainder of the sentence.

c Pre-sentence reports and other reports

A court must generally consider a pre-sentence report ("PSR") before sentencing an offender to a custodial sentence. Such a report will also be a pre-condition to the imposition of certain community orders.[14] A PSR is a written report usually prepared by the probation service, although it may well be prepared by a social worker if the offender is under the age of 18.[15] Failure to consider such a report does not invalidate a sentence passed, but in the event of an appeal the court must obtain one.[16] The report, prepared in accordance with National Standards, will contain an assessment of the offence and its seriousness, of any factors that relate to the offender which may affect the assessment of seriousness, of the attitudes of the offender and other matters which may be relevant to the sentence ultimately imposed. It is not the practice of probation to prepare PSR in respect of those accused who indicate an intention to deny the offence. In such a case there will need to be an adjournment in order for a report to be prepared, causing delay. It was for this reason that the requirement to obtain a PSR was modified in 1994,[17] to permit a court to sentence without one where such a report is considered unnecessary. This exception does not apply in respect of offenders aged under 18, unless the offence for which the offender is being sentenced is triable only on indictment, and it is considered that sufficient information is available.

In addition to a PSR a court may wish, or be required, to consider other reports. Thus, a court may require a specialist report indicating the risk to the community that a sex offender poses. Other orders may require a report from a doctor or psychologist

---

12 Powers of Criminal Courts Act 1973, s 1(2).
13 *R v Fairhead* [1975] 2 All ER 737. However, a restitution order may be made under the Theft Act 1968, even if the passing of the sentence is in other respects deferred: Theft Act 1968, s 28(1) (as amended by the Criminal Law Act 1977, Sch 12).
14 See Criminal Justice Act 1991, s 6(3), as amended by Crime and Disorder Act 1998, Sch 8. The relevant orders are a probation order which includes additional requirements under Sch 1A to Powers of Criminal Courts Act 1973, community service order, combination order, supervision order containing requirements, and a drug treatment and testing order.
15 Under the new youth justice provisions, a report will be prepared by an appropriate member of the team. That may be a probation officer, even in the case of a 13- or 14-year-old: see, generally p 577, *post*.
16 1991 Act, s 3(4), 6(4).
17 Criminal Justice and Public Order Act 1994, Sch 9, paras 40–42.

setting out details of a particular condition or addiction as a pre-requisite to the making of a particular order. Thus, for example, before a court can impose a probation order with a requirement for medical treatment, it must first consider a report from a qualified medical practitioner.[18]

Where a PSR has been obtained a copy is given to the offender or his solicitor. Until recently, it was not the practice to give a copy to the prosecutor. That has now changed. The Crime (Sentences) Act 1997 imposed such a requirement,[19] so as to ensure that the prosecutor is in possession of all relevant material governing sentence. The lack of a PSR has, in the past potentially hampered the ability of the prosecution to assist the court by providing an informed response where conflicting information is received by the court from the defence and from the probation service. The Act limits the use to which the prosecution may put information contained in a PSR.

B SENTENCES AND ORDERS

I Death

The death penalty was abolished for murder in 1965[20] and is now being abolished for all civilian offences, including treason and piracy with violence.[1]

2 Imprisonment and other custodial sentences

In cases of murder, a sentence of life imprisonment is mandatory. The trial judge may in open court declare the period[2] which in his view should elapse before the release of the accused on licence.[3] That recommendation is not binding on the Home Secretary, who, in consultation with the trial judge and Lord Chief Justice, will set the "tariff". This tariff determines when the defendant's continued imprisonment will be reviewed by the Parole Board, but the fact that there is executive determination as to what the appropriate tariff is has caused considerable debate and controversy, and it is far from clear that the current position in fact complies with the European Convention on Human Rights.[4] The question of release on licence is for the Home Secretary, after a recommendation for release by the Parole Board.[5]

---

18   See Powers of Criminal Courts Act 1973, Sch 1A (inserted therein by Criminal Justice Act 1991), para 5.
19   Crime (Sentences) Act 1997, s 50.
20   Murder (Abolition of Death Penalty) Act 1965. The provisions of that Act were expressed to be temporary, but Parliament decided in 1969 that abolition was to be permanent.
1   See Crime and Disorder Act 1998, s 36. The death penalty for arson of Her Majesty's ships and dockyards was abolished by s 11(2) of the Criminal Damage Act 1971.
2   This can include a recommendation that a defendant never be released: *R v Skingle and Sparrow* (1971) Times, 16 October (reported, but not on that point, at [1973] 2 All ER 129; [1973] 1 WLR 488, *sub nom R v Sparrow*).
3   This power only applies in mandatory life sentence cases, but in any event in all life imprisonment cases judges give recommendations of the necessary period of detention to meet the requirements of retribution and deterrence. See p 544, *post*.
4   See the judgment of the Court of Human Rights in *Thynne, Wilson and Gunnell v United Kingdom* (1990) 13 EHRR 666; *Hussain v United Kingdom* (1996) 22 EHRR 1; *R v Secretary of State for the Home Department, ex parte Furber* [1998] 1 All ER 23; [1998] 1 Cr App Rep (S) 208.
5   See p 545, *post*.

Apart from these cases, sentences of imprisonment, which may for some offences include life imprisonment,[6] may only be imposed if the criteria prescribed by law are satisfied. In some certain limited situations a court is obliged to impose a mandatory term or a minimum term. These provisions were introduced by the Crime (Sentences) Act 1997 despite the fact that they remove the ability of the court to have regard to the facts of the individual case. By section 2 of the 1997 Act, where an offender is convicted of a serious offence, having at the date of commission already been convicted of one other such offence, he must (if he was at least 18 at the time of the commission of the second offence) be sentenced to a term of life imprisonment unless exceptional circumstances exist to justify the court not doing so. The term "serious offence" includes a range of serious violent or sexual offences.[7] The rationale for this provision is that repeat offenders are considered to constitute an on-going risk: a life term permits the Parole Board to recommend the release of the offender only where there is not an unacceptable level risk to the community. However, this blanket, mandatory approach pays no regard to the levels of risk that in fact exist in any individual case, and is, arguably, unnecessary given that it is open to a court in respect of a majority of the types of offence that fall within this provision to impose a discretionary life sentence.

Further, the 1997 Act introduces minimum sentences in respect of repeat drug trafficking[8] and repeat burglary offences,[9] although the provisions relating to burglary have not been implemented, and may not ever be so. Where an offender aged 18 or over commits a drug trafficking offence, having at that date already two separate and consecutive convictions for such offences, a court must impose a minimum term of seven years' imprisonment unless there are specific circumstances relating to the offence or the offender which justify it not so doing. Again, the rationale for the provision is open to doubt: the majority of such offences will in any event attract a long sentence.

Apart from cases which fall within these specific provisions, the general rules governing the imposition of terms of imprisonment were recast by the Criminal Justice Act 1991. By section 1(2) of the 1991 Act, a court can only impose a custodial sentence if:

(1) the offence[10] is so serious that only such a sentence can be justified; or
(2) the offence is a violent or sexual offence,[11] and only such a sentence would be adequate to protect the public from serious harm from the offender.

The intent is that imprisonment should not be used as a punishment unless the seriousness of the offence, or the risk to the public, warrants it. Nevertheless, difficulties quickly arose with the detailed rules governing offence seriousness, which had to be amended in key respects. Offence seriousness is to be assessed in the light of the offence

---

6   Known as discretionary life sentences. For the principles to be applied see *R v Hodgson* (1968) 52 Cr App Rep 113 where the following criteria for the imposition of such a sentence were set out: the offence must in itself be grave enough to require a very long sentence; it must appear from the nature of the offence or from the accused's history that he is a person of unstable character likely to commit such offences in the future; if he commits such offences the consequences to others may be specially injurious. A discretionary sentence is to be regarded as exceptional, needed where it is important to monitor the prisoner's progress so that release will only occur when public safety will not be jeopardised.
7   Defined by Crime (Sentences) Act 1997, s 2(5)-2(7).
8   See 1997 Act, s 3.
9   *Ibid*, s 4.
10 And any associated offences.
11 These terms are defined by Criminal Justice Act 1991, s 31(2). See also *R v Robinson* [1993] 2 All ER 1; [1993] 1 WLR 168. 1 S 1(2), as amended by Criminal Justice Act 1993, s 66.

for which the sentence is being passed, together with any associated offences.[12] This is a change from the law as originally conceived, which restricted the court to considering only one associated offence. An "associated offence" is an offence for which the offender is being dealt with on the same sentencing occasion, or which the offender is asking to be taken into consideration on that occasion.[13] Particular problems also arose in respect of whether an offence is aggravated by the fact that the offender has previous convictions. As originally enacted, section 29 of the Criminal Justice Act 1991 required a court to disregard previous convictions unless they demonstrated aggravating features of the offence for which sentence was being passed.[14] This led to difficulties in both interpretation and application.[15] As a result, changes were made which allow a court to take into account previous convictions.[16] A court may also treat the commission of an offence whilst on bail as an aggravating factor.[17] In deciding offence seriousness, the courts have adopted an approach based upon whether "right thinking members of the public, knowing all the facts, feel that justice had not been done by passing of a sentence other than a custodial one."[18] Offences can be regarded as serious enough to warrant custody in the light of a person's previous convictions,[19] or in the light of the fact that the offence was committed whilst the offender was on bail.[20] The imposition of a term of imprisonment does not mean that the term specified is that which the offender actually serves. The length of time that a prisoner actually serves is dealt with later.[1]

A sentence of imprisonment may be imposed but suspended, i.e. ordered not to take effect immediately.[2] The sentence must not be for more than two years and the period of suspension must be between one and two years.[3] The effect of a suspended sentence is that so far as that sentence is concerned, the defendant is not liable to be imprisoned unless (1) during the period of suspension he commits another offence punishable with imprisonment, and thereafter (2) a court order that the sentence shall take effect.[4] When suspended sentences were first introduced there was a tendency for courts to impose a suspended sentence upon persons who, but for the existence of the power to impose suspended sentences, would not have received a sentence of imprisonment at all. However, suspended sentences are custodial sentences,[5] and therefore the criteria for the imposition of a custodial sentence (*supra*) must be satisfied before the decision whether it should be suspended is taken.[6] In addition the Criminal Justice Act 1991

---

12   Section 1(2), as amended by Criminal Justice Act 1993, s 66.
13   *Ibid*, s 31.
14   Section 29(1).
15   For a summary of the problems, see *R v Bexley* [1993] 2 All ER 23; [1993] 1 WLR 192.
16   Criminal Justice Act 1993, s 66(6).
17   Section 29(2) (as amended).
18   *R v Bradbourn* (1985) 7 Cr App R (S) 180, dealing with the wording of Criminal Justice Act 1982, s 1(4A)(c) relating to the imprisonment of persons under 21 years of age. See *R v Cox (David)* [1993] 2 All ER 19; [1993] 1 WLR 188; *R v Cunningham* [1993] 2 All ER 15; [1993] 1 WLR 183; *R v Lewis (John)* (1993) Times, 29 March.
19   See n 17, *ante*.
20   Section 29(2).
1   Powers of Criminal Courts Act 1973, ss 22–25.
2   See Power of Criminal Courts Act 1973, s 22.
3   Where the court passes a suspended sentence for a term of more than six months, it has power under section 26 to make a "suspended sentence supervision order" which places the offender under the supervision of a probation officer during the period of the suspended sentence. There is no power to make such an order when only a part of the sentence is suspended under the Criminal Law Act 1977, s 47 (*infra*).
4   Powers of Criminal Courts Act 1973, s 22(1)
5   *Ibid*, s 23.
6   See s 1(2).

has made it harder for a court to impose a suspended sentence. Under the revised terms of section 22 of the Powers of Criminal Courts Act 1973[7] the power to suspend a sentence of imprisonment should only be used where the exceptional circumstances of the case justify it. The Act provides no guidance at to what might amount to exceptional circumstances for this purpose. It has been noted earlier that whether a custodial sentence can be imposed depends upon offence seriousness. So too with the imposition of community sentences.[8] In either instance, offence seriousness is to be assessed in the light of the offence for which the sentence is being passed, together with any associated offences.[9] This is a change from the law as originally conceived, which restricted the court to considering only one associated offence.[10]

The length of any custodial sentence imposed will be such as is commensurate with the offence, in the light of any associated offences.[11] Alternatively, if the basis of a custodial sentence for a violent or sexual offence is a necessity to protect the public, the length may be such as is necessary for that purpose.[12] Regard should also be had to the fact that the offender has pleaded guilty, if that is in fact the case. Section 48 of the Criminal Justice and Public Order Act 1994 requires a sentencing court to take into account (a) the stage in the proceedings for the offence at which the offender indicated his intention to plead guilty; and (b) the circumstances in which this indication was given. The provision was introduced to give effect to a recommendation of the Royal Commission on Criminal Justice, so that court time, and anxiety for the victim, are reduced. It should be noted that "discount" can be lost if a long sentence is necessary for public protection, or if a version of events is proffered by the offender which is rejected by the court. An early indication of a guilty plea is not relevant to the question of the level of offence seriousness.

3   Young offenders

Generally, although not always, young offenders are dealt with in the youth court. However, for the most serious crimes they will be tried on indictment and, if found guilty, sentenced by that court. The general considerations that apply to young offenders are dealt with in due course.[13] Irrespective of whether an offender is a young offender (ie under 18) there are restrictions on the power of a court to impose a custodial sentence on a person aged under 21. Where an offender is not less than 18 but under 21, and a custodial sentence is justified, he may be sentenced to detention in a young offenders' institution.[14] Generally, such a detention cannot be ordered unless he has been legally represented at the time of sentencing extremely limited.[15] Where an offender is aged between 12 and 18, he may be sentenced to a detention and training order, which couples a period in custody in secure accommodation amounting to one-half of the length of the order, with an equivalent period of supervision. This order, introduced by the Crime and Disorder Act 1998,[16] is discussed in more detail in due course.[17] The

---

7   Criminal Justice Act 1991, s 22(2), inserted by the Criminal Justice Act 1993, s 5(1).
8   See *infra*.
9   Criminal Justice Act 1991, s 1(2) as amended by the Criminal Justice Act 1993, s 66(1).
10   See p 539, *ante*.
11   Criminal Justice Act 1991, s 2(1)(a).
12   *Ibid*, s 2(1)(b).
13   See p 576, *post*.
14   Criminal Justice Act 1982, s 1A.
15   *Ibid*, s 3.
16   Section 73.

1998 Act confers the power to extend the operation to 10- and 11-year-olds, but such powers have not been brought into effect.

Two other provisions should be noted. Section 53 of the Children and Young Persons Act 1933 provides that a person convicted of an offence who appears to the court to have been under the age of eighteen years at the time the offence was committed shall not, if he is convicted of murder, be sentenced to imprisonment for life, but instead the court must sentence him to be detained during Her Majesty's Pleasure. If he is sentenced in that way, he is detained in such place and under such conditions as the Home Secretary directs. Section 53(2) provides that where:

(a) a young person is convicted on indictment of any offence punishable in the case of an adult with imprisonment for fourteen years or more, not being an offence the sentence for which is fixed by law; or

(b) a child is convicted of manslaughter, and the court is of opinion that none of the other methods in which the case may legally be dealt with is suitable,

the court may sentence the offender to be detained for such period (not exceeding the maximum term of imprisonment with which the offence is punishable in the case of an adult) as may be specified in the sentence. Where such a sentence has been passed, the child or young person will be liable to be detained in such place and on such conditions as the Home Secretary directs.

The second special provision is that contained in section 8(2) of the Criminal Justice Act 1982. This provides that where a person aged 18 or over but under the age of 21 years is convicted of any offence other than murder for which a person aged 21 years or over would be liable to imprisonment for life, the court shall, if it considers that a custodial sentence for life would be appropriate, sentence him to custody for life.

4 Community sentences

If an offence is serious enough to warrant the passing of a community sentence, but not so serious so as to require a custodial sentence, the court may make one or more community orders These are as follows:

(1) *Probation:* where an offender, aged not less than 16 years, is placed under the supervision of a probation officer for a period not exceeding three years.[18] A probation order may contain requirements to keep in touch with a supervising officer, for the general purpose of securing the rehabilitation of the offence and for the protection of the public from him. These can include requirements as to residence (including in a probation hostel), as to participation in particular activities or relate to medical treatment or treatment for addiction to drugs or alcohol.

(2) *Community service orders:* where an offender, aged not less than 16 years, is required to perform work in the community for periods not less than 40 hours or not more than 240 hours;[19]

(3) *Combination orders:* these are a combination of probation and community service orders, which may be imposed on a person aged at least 16 years.[20] A combination order is an order which requires the offender:

17   See p 578, *post.*
18   See Powers of Criminal Courts Act 1973, s 2(1).
19   *Ibid*, s 14.
20   *Ibid*, s 11.

    (a) to be under the supervision of a probation officer for a period not less than 12 months or more than three years, and

    (b) to perform unpaid work for a specified number of hours, not less than 40 or more than 100.

(4) *Curfew orders:* where the power to make a curfew order exists a court may impose on an offender aged 16 or over requirements to remain at a particular place specified in the order for specified periods. The period of restriction must not be less than two hours nor more than 12 hours in any one day, and an order cannot extend beyond a period of six months. An order can include provisions relating to electronic monitoring.

(5) *Supervision orders:* used for the supervision of offenders under 18 years of age.[1]

(6) *Attendance centre orders:* where an offender aged at least 10 but under 21 years is required to attend an attendance centre for a specified number of hours. The number of hours that may be imposed varies according to the age of the offender.

(7) *Drug treatment and testing orders.*[2] Where a court considers that a person, aged not less than 16 at the date of conviction for an offence, is dependent on or has a propensity to misuse drugs, and his dependency is such as requires and may be susceptible to treatment, the court may make a drug treatment and testing order. Such an order may include requirements that the offender submit to treatment, with a view to reduce or eliminate the dependency or propensity.

The idea behind these orders is that offenders should be both punished and rehabilitated within the community. The particular order or orders forming part of the sentence must be commensurate with the seriousness of the offence and other offences associated with it, and be the most suitable for the offender, although the scope of such orders has been extended to include the use of community service and attendance centre orders for fine default, despite the fact that the normal threshold for the imposition of a community order has not been reached. Further, a community service order or a curfew order may be made in respect of persistent petty offenders. There are certain limits as to which community orders can be combined. Such orders have historically been viewed as being dependent on the offender being willing to consent to the making of such an order. That, generally, has changed. Although certain requirements still require the consent of the offender, changes made by the Crime (Sentences) Act 1997 have resulted in the current position being that consent to the making of a probation order or community service or supervision order is no longer required.

Failure to comply with the requirements of a community order can result in the offender being punished, or being re-sentenced for the original offence.[3]

5   Fines

A Crown Court may impose a fine in lieu of, or in addition to, dealing with him in any other way. Unless a limit is fixed by the statute prescribing the offence, there is no limit to the amount of the fine. The court is obliged to fix a period of imprisonment or detention in default of payment.

---

1   See Children and Young Persons Act 1969, ss 11–12D.
2   See Crime and Disorder Act 1998, ss 61–64.
3   See Criminal Justice Act 1991, Sch 2, Crime and Disorder Act 1998, Sch 4, 5.

6 Absolute and conditional discharges

Where a court thinks it inappropriate to pass any sentence, or make a probation order, it may discharge the offender either absolutely, without any condition, or subject to the condition that he does not commit any further offence for a period fixed by the court, not exceeding three years.[4] If he commits another offence in that period he is liable to be sentenced for his original offence.

7 Compensation and restitution

a Compensation

A court by or before which a person is convicted of an offence may, instead of or in addition to dealing with him in any other way, make an order requiring him to pay compensation for any personal injury, loss or damage resulting from that offence (or any other offence which is taken into consideration). However, no compensation order may be made in favour of the dependants of a deceased person in consequence of his death, nor in respect of injury, loss or damage due to a road accident. In determining whether to make an order and the amount of such order the court must have regard to the offender's means. In practice the power to make compensation orders has been exercised somewhat sparingly. In particular, the Court of Appeal has repeatedly stated that no order should be made where it might result in the accused committing further offences in order to discharge his obligations; for this reason a substantial compensation order will not usually be appropriate where the offender is imprisoned since the need to discharge the order may hinder his rehabilitation on his release.[5]

If there are subsequent civil proceedings, the damages are assessed without reference to the order, but the order is taken into account when enforcing the judgment.[6] Compensation is of such amount as the court considers appropriate, having regard to any evidence and to any representations made by or on behalf of the accused or the prosecutor.[7]

b Restitution

Where goods have been stolen and either a person is convicted of any offence with reference to the theft or such offence is taken into consideration on conviction of any other offence, the court may order anyone in possession of the goods to restore them to any person entitled to recover them from him, or may order the restoration of any goods directly or indirectly representing the stolen goods (eg the proceeds of sale), or may order a sum not exceeding the value of the goods to be paid out of any money of the person convicted that was taken out of his possession on his apprehension.[8] However, it should be borne in mind that this provision does not give the police power to seize money or other property when apprehending someone, in anticipation of a compensation or restitution order being made in due course. The police may, however, justifiably take possession of money or other property which they reasonably believe

---

4   Powers of Criminal Courts Act 1973, s 1A.
5   See *R v Oddy* [1974] 2 All ER 666; [1974] 1 WLR 1212 and the cases therein cited.
6   See s 38 of the 1973 Act. Where the offender is a child or young person the court should normally order payment by his parent or guardian: Children and Young Persons Act 1969, s 3(6).
7   1973 Act, s 35(1A).
8   Theft Act 1968, s 28 (as amended by Criminal Justice Act 1972).

to be material evidence in relation to crime.[9] A restitution order, under the above provisions, should only be made in clear and obvious cases. If there is any serious dispute concerning the ownership of the goods in question, this should be left to be determined by a civil court in the normal way and no order should be made.[10]

8　Miscellaneous orders

The principal sentences and orders the court has power to make have been considered above. There are, in addition, various other forms of order which may be made, detailed consideration of which is beyond the scope of this work. However, it may be noted that the Crown Court has, in addition to the powers detailed above, power to make orders for costs either out of central funds or *inter partes*,[11] orders depriving offenders of property used, or intended for use, for the purpose of crime,[12] orders disqualifying an offender from holding or obtaining a licence to drive a motor vehicle,[13] orders authorising the admission to and detention in specified hospitals of offenders suffering from mental illness, psychopathic disorder, subnormality or severe subnormality[14] and recommendations for deportation.[15] Significant powers of confiscation and forfeiture also exist under the Drug Trafficking Offences Act 1986.

Where the Crown Court imposes a fine, forfeits a recognisance or makes an order for costs, it may order the person concerned to be searched and any money found on him to be applied towards payment of the fine or other sum.[16]

9　Imprisonment – the period served

The present arrangements for early release are governed by provisions in Part II of the Criminal Justice Act 1991. Provisions in the Crime (Sentences) Act 1997 dealing with sentence length have not been implemented and are repealed by the Crime and Disorder Act 1998, a step which reflects the constant change, often contradictory, that characterises sentencing law and policy.

With regard to discretionary life prisoners, the 1991 Act created new procedures governing early release.[17] A court may indicate the period that must expire before the offender may have his case considered by the Parole Board. If the Parole Board recommends release, then the Home Secretary is duty bound to release him. In other cases of imprisonment, the 1991 Act created a complicated system, which has been amended by the 1998 Act. Those provisions differ according to whether the prisoner is a short-term or long-term prisoner. A "short-term prisoner" is a person serving a

---

9　Police and Criminal Evidence Act 1984, s 19. This power is subject to some limitation: see s 19(2)–(6).

10　*R v Ferguson* [1970] 2 All ER 820; [1970] 1 WLR 1246.

11　Costs in Criminal Cases Act 1973, ss 3, 4.

12　Powers of Criminal Courts Act 1973, s 43. The power is limited to personal property and so cannot extend to the defendant's house: *R v Khan* [1982] 3 All ER 969; [1982] 1 WLR 1405, one of several unsuccessful attempts by the courts to relieve drug dealers of their ill-gotten gains. See Criminal Justice Act (Commencement No 3) Order 1992 (SI 1992/333).

13　Road Traffic Offenders Act 1988, s 37.

14　Mental Health Act 1983, s 37.

15　Immigration Act 1971, s 6.

16　Powers of Criminal Courts Act 1973, s 34A.

17　Criminal Justice Act 1991, s 34, following a finding by the European Court of Human Rights that the pre-existing law did not comply with art 5(2) of the Convention.

term of imprisonment for a term of less than four years.[18] A "long-term prisoner" is a person serving a term of imprisonment of four years or more.[19] The length of the sentence is calculated by aggregating consecutive terms of imprisonment, the overall term being regarded as a single term.[20] In summary, the effect of what amounts to an extremely complicated scheme of legislation is a follows:

(a) a short-term prisoner serving less than three months, serves one half of that sentence before being released unconditionally.[1]

(b) for a short-term prisoner, he serves a minimum of 30 days (if his sentence is for three months or more), one-quarter of the term of imprisonment (if the sentence was four or months or more but less than eight) or a minimum of half-sentence less 60 days (if his term is more than eight months but less than four years).[2] His release shall include curfew conditions, which require the released person to remain, for specified periods, at a specified place.

(c) in respect of long-term prisoners, discretionary conditional release on licence can occur at half-sentence, on the recommendation of the Parole Board.[3] If granted the licence continues until the three-quarters sentence point. If refused, automatic conditional release occurs at the two-thirds sentence point with the licence continuing until the three-quarters point.

Even when an offender is released, ongoing obligations may arise. In respect of life prisoners, their release is on licence which continues without time limitation, and they may be subject to recall to prison.[4] In addition, offenders who were convicted of, or cautioned for, or under statutory supervision in respect of, a specified sexual offence on or after 1 September 1997 are under an obligation to notify the police of their names and addresses, and subsequent changes to those names and addresses.[5]

18 1991 Act, s 33(5).
19 *Ibid.*
20 *Ibid*, s 51(2).
1   1991 Act, s 33(1)(A).
2   1991 Act, s 3(1); Crime and Disorder Act 1998, s 91.
3   1991 Act, s 35.
4   1991 Act, s 39.
5   Sex Offenders Act 1997, ss 1, 2.

CHAPTER 24

Appeal Following Trial on Indictment

A INTRODUCTION

If a defendant is convicted on indictment at the Crown Court his appeal lies, if at all, to the Court of Appeal (Criminal Division). Appeals from the decisions of the magistrates' court acting summarily, and from the Crown Court acting in its appellate capacity, lie to the Divisional Court of the Queen's Bench Division, and will be dealt with later.

The role and powers of the Court of Appeal (Criminal Division) have been the subject of a great deal of debate in recent years,[1] largely generated by a series of cases where convictions have had to be overturned, often some years after conviction and subsequent appeal.[2] In particular, the question of when the court should be able to overturn a conviction, how it should treat fresh evidence, and whether it should have greater powers to order re-trials, have each been raised, and the subject of consideration by the Royal Commission on Criminal Justice.[3] However, it is important to remember that controversy about the criminal appellate system is not new.

I The development of the Court of Appeal (Criminal Division)

Until 1907 there was, in fact, no right of appeal at all. Where points of law arose on trial on indictment the trial judge could, but was not obliged to, refer such points for consideration by a court known as the Court for Crown Cases Reserved. Not until the passage of the Criminal Appeal Act 1907 was a formal appellate system introduced, and that Act was passed largely in response to a miscarriage of justice caused by the mistaken identification of an accused.[4] The 1907 Act created the Court of Criminal Appeal, which was given powers to allow appeals against conviction if that conviction

---

1 See O'Connor "The Court of Appeal: Re-Trials & Tribulations" [1990] Crim LR 615; JUSTICE *Report on Miscarriages of Justice* (1989).
2 See eg *R v Maguire* [1992] QB 936; [1992] 2 All ER 433; *R v McIlkenny* [1992] 2 All ER 417.
3 Cm 2263 (1993, HMSO).
4 The *Adolph Beck* case.

was unreasonable or could not be supported having regard to the evidence, or if there was a wrong decision on a question of law. No power to order a re-trial existed at that time. The Criminal Appeal Act 1964 created a power to order a new trial, although only on the ground of "fresh evidence",[5] a restriction that was not removed until the passing of the Criminal Justice Act 1988.[6] By the Criminal Appeal Act 1966, the jurisdiction of the Court of Criminal Appeal was transferred to the Court of Appeal (Criminal Division).[7]

The whole of the pre-existing legislation was consolidated in the Criminal Appeal Act 1968. However, the powers of, and the use of such powers by, the Court of Appeal attracted considerable attention, and concern, as miscarriages of justice came to light. The Royal Commission on Criminal Justice therefore considered the powers and functions of the Court of Appeal (Criminal Division). The result was a government consultation paper, followed by the passage of the Criminal Appeal Act 1995. That Act, based on the recommendations of the Royal Commission, significantly amends the existing legislation.

Before looking at the substance of the powers themselves, three general points need to be remembered:

(a) The right of appeal is that of the accused, except in cases referred to the court by the Home Secretary.[8] The prosecution has no right of appeal against acquittal, although there is a limited power for points of law, and lenient sentences to be referred to the Court of Appeal by the Attorney-General.[9]

(b) The court's powers derive solely from statute. The court has no inherent or residual power which entitle it to fill gaps in the statutory provisions. Criticism can fairly be made of the statutory provisions, not only in the obvious cases where the court's role has been limited, but also in other areas where gaps in the appellate system exist.

(c) The recent controversies about the actions of the court must be viewed in the light of the overall function and role of the court. This is dealt with below.

2   The role of the Court of Appeal

The court has been at pains to stress the limits of its powers. In *R v McIlkenny*[10] Lloyd, Mustill and Farquharson LJJ in a joint judgment observed:

"Under jury trial juries not only find the facts; they also apply the law. Since they are not experts in the law, they are directed as to the relevant law by the judge. But the task of applying the law to the facts, and so reaching a verdict, belongs to the jury and the jury alone. The primacy of the jury in the English criminal justice system explains why, historically, the Court of Appeal had so limited a function Since justice is as much concerned with the conviction of the guilty as the acquittal of the innocent, and the task of convicting the guilty belongs constitutionally to the jury, not to us, the role [of the court] is necessarily limited. Hence it is true to say that whereas the Civil Division of the Court of Appeal

5   Section 1, re-enacted in Criminal Appeal Act 1968, s 7.
6   See *post*.
7   Being one of two divisions of the Court of Appeal: Supreme Court Act 1981, s 3(1). For the Civil Division, see p 439, *ante*.
8   See p 551, *post*.
9   See p 534, *ante*.
10   [1992] 2 All ER 417.

has appellate jurisdiction in the full sense, the Criminal Division is perhaps more accurately described as a court of review."

The point has also cogently been made that not only is the court subordinate to the jury; also the jury's role is itself limited.[11] It is not the task of the jury within the adversarial system to pronounce innocence or guilt, but rather whether it has been proved, according to law, that the accused is guilty as charged. For these reasons the Court of Appeal has considered itself constrained in dealing with appeals, particularly those based upon new evidence. The extent to which these constraints are justifiable, or in the public interest, is a matter for debate. The Royal Commission on Criminal Justice concluded that such considerations as to the role of the jury have too heavily influenced the court, and that the Court of Appeal should be "readier to overturn jury verdicts than it has shown itself in the past".[12] In particular it should be more prepared to consider arguments that a jury has made a mistake, and to admit evidence that might favour a defendant even if it was, or could have been, available at the trial. It is debatable as to how far the various legislative changes will, in fact, result in a greater willingness by the Court of Appeal to follow a more liberal approach.

B   THE GROUNDS OF APPEAL

I   Appeal against conviction

By section 1 of the Criminal Appeal Act 1968, a person convicted on indictment may appeal to the Court of Appeal:

(a)   against his conviction, on any ground which involves a question of law alone;
(b)   with the leave of the Court of Appeal, against his conviction on any ground which involves a question of fact alone, or a question of mixed law and fact, or any other ground which appears to the court to be a sufficient ground of appeal.

Where leave to appeal is required, it may be granted in the first instance by a single judge of the court; if he refuses, the applicant may have his case considered by the court itself.[13] This process excludes a large proportion of cases. In 1992, of 1,552 applicants for leave to appeal, 33% had leave granted, the percentage rising to 36% on application to the full court. Of those granted leave to appeal, 45 per cent succeeded.[14] The Royal Commission found that the chances of success are distinctly higher where the defendant is represented. In this regard the Commission found uneven and unsatisfactory provision for the giving of legal advice on appeal, which is part of the professional duty of solicitor and counsel. Initial advice after the case on appeal is within the scope of criminal legal aid (99% of cases within the Crown Court). The research also found misunderstandings about the powers of the court regarding length of sentence. The Commission concluded that interpreter facilities should be made available by the Prison Service to facilitate the giving of advice to those who do not understand English. The present requirement to obtain leave should be kept, and legal aid extended to cover advice as to whether an application should be renewed.

The trial judge may also grant a certificate that the case is fit for appeal, on a question of fact or mixed law and fact. This should only be done where the trial judge is satisfied

11   See p 465, *ante*.
12   Report, Ch 10.
13   Criminal Appeal Act 1968, s 31(3).
14   See Royal Commission on Criminal Justice, Report, Ch 10, paras 1-26.

that there is a substantial point, and one worthy of consideration by the Court of Appeal.[15]

Nothing in the Act prevents an appeal against conviction in a case where the accused in fact pleaded guilty at his trial. However, an appeal in such circumstances will only succeed if: (i) the defendant did not appreciate the nature of the charge; or (ii) he did not intend to admit that he was guilty of it; or (iii) on the admitted facts, he could not in law have been guilty of the offence to which he pleaded guilty. Such cases are rare, but not unknown.[16] In *R v Boal*[17] the court was prepared to entertain an appeal where the defendant had pleaded guilty as a result of advice based upon a misunderstanding of the law by his barrister.

2   Appeal against sentence

The defendant may appeal against the sentence passed on him after conviction unless the sentence is one fixed by law. Such an appeal requires the leave of a single judge, or, if refused, of the full court.[18] The appeal can be not only against the sentence, but also against any order that forms part of the sentence, such as a compensation order,[19] disqualification from driving, a binding over order[20] or recommendation for deportation.[1] There is no right of appeal against a recommendation that a defendant convicted of murder should serve a certain number of years, because this is not a recommendation binding on the Home Secretary.[2] By contrast, if a judge makes an order, in respect of a discretionary life sentence, specifying what part of the sentence must expire before the offender is able to have his case referred to the Parole Board, this has legal consequences and would appear to be a matter which can be subject to an appeal.[3]

The prosecution also has the right to have the sentence of a court reviewed. By section 36 of the Criminal Justice Act 1988, if it appears to the Attorney-General that the sentencing of a person in a proceeding in the Crown Court has been unduly lenient, in respect of an offence triable only on indictment (or such other offence as the Secretary of State may order) then, with leave of the Court of Appeal, the case may be referred to them for the sentence to be reviewed. The application must be made within 28 days of the sentence being passed.[4]

Concern was expressed at the time this power was introduced that a defendant is in jeopardy twice.[5] The power to review granted by the Act is in respect of a sentence perceived to be unduly lenient, not simply in respect of a sentence with which the court disagrees. The power is used where the judge has erred as a matter of sentencing principle, and thus is a means of achieving consistent application of sentencing policy.[6]

---

15   *R v Eyles* (1963) 47 Cr App Rep 260; cf *R v Smith* [1974] QB 354; [1974] 1 All ER 632.
16   *R v Forde* [1923] 2 KB 400, at 403; *R v Gould* [1968] 2 QB 65; [1968] 1 All ER 849; cf *R v Vickers* [1975] 2 All ER 945; [1975] 1 WLR 811.
17   [1992] QB 591; [1992] 3 All ER 177.
18   Criminal Appeal Act 1968, s 11.
19   Powers of Criminal Courts Act 1973, s 36(3)(b).
20   *R v Williams* [1982] 3 All ER 1092; [1982] 1 WLR 1398.
1   See the Criminal Appeal Act 1968, s 50(1), defining sentence to include "any order made by a court when dealing with an offender".
2   *R v Aitken* [1966] 2 All ER 453n; [1966] 1 WLR 1076.
3   See the terms of Criminal Justice Act 1991, s 34(2).
4   Criminal Justice Act 1988, Sch 3.
5   See [1988] Crim LR at p 103.
6   Through guideline judgments. See p 533, *ante*.

3   Criminal Cases Review Commission

Once the avenues of appeal outlined above have been exhausted then, unless a final appeal to the House of Lords is permitted,[7] the one remaining formal option open to an accused is the making of an application to the Criminal Cases Review Commission. The Commission was established by the 1995 Act following consistent, and justified, criticism of the pre-existing system under s 17 of the 1968 Act whereby a convicted person might apply to the Home Secretary for his case to be referred back to the Court of Appeal, or whereby the Home Secretary might of his own motion refer back a case, or point arising in a case.[8] This is what occurred in *R v Berry (No 2)*[9] where a finding on a point of law by the Court of Appeal led to that court quashing a conviction, the court not determining another ground of appeal that was before the court. On appeal to the House of Lords by the prosecution, the decision of the Court of Appeal was reversed. The Court of Appeal now being without jurisdiction to deal with this further point, the only way in which it could now be dealt with by the court was for the Home Secretary to make a reference under section 17, which is in fact what occurred.

The operation of section 17, and, generally the role of the Home Office, was considered by the Royal Commission on Criminal Justice.[10] It noted that the Royal Prerogative of mercy in respect of trials on indictment was "seldom exercised",[11] and it noted also that section 17 references were made in only a small proportion of the cases of those brought to the attention of the Home Office by the parties, or by campaigning groups such as JUSTICE.[12] The restrictive nature of the test[13] used by the Home Secretary to decide whether a reference should be made had been identified by the May Committee,[14] which also criticised the Home Office for not being pro-active in miscarriage cases. References back were only made in cases where fresh evidence had emerged since the trial and appeal. The view of the May Committee that there was a need for change was supported by the Royal Commission. It recommended that the Home Secretary's power to make references under section 17 should be abolished. Instead, the role now performed by the Home Office should be given to an independent body, a new Criminal Cases Review Authority. This authority, to comprise both lawyers and lay persons, would oversee any further investigations needed into cases referred to it by complainants, although it would not appear to have powers to instigate investigations on its own motion.

This recommendation was accepted in principle. The result was the creation, by the 1995 Act, of the Criminal Cases Review Commission. At least one-third of the members of the Commission must be lawyers,[16] and two-thirds persons who have knowledge or expertise of any part of the criminal justice system.[17] Members are appointed by the Crown on the advice of the Prime Minister,[18] and hold office for an

---

7   See p 558, *post*.
8   1968 Act, s 17(1)(a).
9   [1991] 2 All ER 789; [1991] 1 WLR 125; for the resulting decision, see *R v Berry* (3 April 1992, unreported).
10   *Op cit*, Ch 11.
11   *Ibid*, para 3.
12   A campaigning organisation with a primary aim of investigation of, and campaigning against, miscarriages of justice. See, in particular, JUSTICE, *Miscarriages of Justice*, 1989.
13   Royal Commission Report, *op cit*, Ch 11.
14   Established to report on the miscarriage of justice in the Guildford and Woolwich pub bombings cases.
15   Royal Commission Report, *op cit*, Ch 11, para 1.
16   1995 Act, s 8(5).
17   *Ibid*, s 8(6).
18   *Ibid*, s 8(4).

initial terms of five years, renewable only once. The Commissioners are aided by caseworkers, and have a general power to undertake, or to arrange the undertaking by others, of inquiries.[19] The number, and type of cases dealt with remains to be seen as the Commission develops its work and procedures. It should be noted that legal aid is not available to lawyers pursuing miscarriage cases, a significant gap, convicted persons therefore being highly dependent on the public spiritedness of lawyers undertaking what amounts to *pro bono* work (ie without payment).

Although the Commission has the power to undertake inquiries, this is likely to be exceptional. Rather, the intention is that inquiries be carried out by the police under the supervision and instruction of the Commission, a position regarded as inevitable by the Royal Commission on Criminal Justice. The Review Commission has the power to require the original investigatory body to appoint an investigating officer to report back to the Commission,[20] or to appoint an investigator from another police force.[1]

The Commission takes over the powers formerly exercised by the Home Secretary under s 17 of the 1968 Act. The powers to refer cases (which now include convictions on summary trial) are contained in s 13 of the 1995 Act. Firstly, there must be a real possibility that a conviction would not be upheld if a reference were made. Secondly, the reason for this must be that an argument or evidence was not raised at trial or on appeal. Finally, an appeal must have been heard or leave to appeal refused. The second and third criteria are not absolutes: the Commission can, despite them, refer a case where exceptional circumstances exist.[2]

If the Commission decides to make a reference, then the case returns to the Court of Appeal to be dealt with in the normal way, although the court has the power itself to refer a case to the Commission for investigation and report.[3] For that reason, the changes made by the 1995 Act to the powers of the court are just as important as the creation of the Commission itself. If the Commission decides not to make a reference, it is required to state the reasons why it has so decided.[4]

4 Reference following acquittal

The prosecution does not have any right to appeal against acquittal, unlike the position in cases of summary trial. However, the Criminal Justice Act 1972[5] gives to the prosecution a limited right to have points of law which arose during a trial resulting in an acquittal reconsidered by the Court of Appeal. The nature of the procedure is that of a reference of a point of law, rather than an appeal, for the outcome of the reference has no effect on the acquittal in the case.

The Act and the rules made thereunder go to great length to protect the acquitted person. Not only is his acquittal unaffected, he may appear to present argument in the Court of Appeal, is entitled to be represented by counsel and have his costs paid out of central funds. His identity must not be disclosed during the proceedings in the Court of Appeal except by his consent.

---

19   *Ibid*, s 21.
20   *Ibid*, s 19.
1   *Ibid*, s 2.
2   *Ibid*, s 13(2).
3   *Ibid*, s 15.
4   *Ibid*, s 14(6). See, generally, *R v Secretary of State for the Home Department, ex parte Hickey (No 2)* [1995] 1 All ER 90; [1995] 1 WLR 734.
5   Section 36(1); this provision came into operation on 1 October 1973 and the first reference under it was *Re A-G's Reference (No 1 of 1974)* [1974] QB 744; [1974] 2 All ER 899.

The purpose of the power is to enable clarification of points of law which are important, and before wrong interpretations of law become entrenched at trial court level. The court may, of its own motion or on application, refer the point to the House of Lords.

C   POWERS OF THE COURT

I   Power to quash a conviction

The powers to quash a conviction are contained in section 2 of the 1968 Act. In its original form, section 2 set out three grounds, which were not mutually exclusive. These were as follows:

(a)   under all the circumstances of the case the conviction[6] is unsafe and unsatisfactory;
(b)   there was a wrong decision on a point of law;
(c)   there was a material irregularity in the course of the trial.

In addition, section 2 contained a proviso. The Court of Appeal might, on an appeal against conviction, dismiss the appeal, even though of the opinion that the point raised might be decided in favour of the appellant, if it is considered that no miscarriage of justice has actually occurred. The test is whether a reasonable jury, after a proper summing-up, could have failed to convict the appellant:[7] in other words, the court was putting itself in the place of the jury. It was often applied where there has been a misdirection on a matter of law.

The relationship between the proviso and the powers contained in section 2(1) of the 1968 Act discussed was complex. If the conviction is found to be unsafe or unsatisfactory under section 2(1)(c) there was no room for the exercise of the proviso. In relation to the other grounds, the Court of Appeal in *R v Maguire*[8] equated the "no miscarriage of justice" test in the proviso with whether the conviction could be regarded as safe or satisfactory.

"If the court is unable to hold that 'no miscarriage of justice has actually occurred' in a case of irregularity then the conviction is not safe. If it does so hold then the court is effectively saying that the conviction is safe and satisfactory."

For this reason it has been argued that there was really only one test that the court should apply in deciding the use of section 2(1): has there been a miscarriage of justice?[9] The majority of the Royal Commission took the view:[10]

---

6   "Conviction" was substituted for "verdict of the jury" by the Criminal Law Act 1977, s 44. The previous wording appeared to preclude an appeal if the accused pleaded guilty, unless the count to which the accused pleaded guilty disclosed no offence known to the law or (perhaps) on the admitted facts he could not in point of law have been guilty of the offence; this, presumably erroneous, drafting in the 1968 Act went judicially unnoticed until *Director of Public Prosecutions v Shannon* [1975] AC 717; *sub nom R v Shannon* [1974] 2 All ER 1009, in which case Lord Salmon drew attention to the need for some amendment to s 2(1) of the 1968 Act.

7   *Stirland v Director of Public Prosecutions* [1944] AC 315; [1944] 2 All ER 13; see also (among many cases) *R v Haddy* [1944] KB 442; [1944] 1 All ER 319. For the proper attitude to application of the proviso in a murder case, see *Anderson v R* [1972] AC 100; [1971] 3 All ER 768.

8   [1992] QB 936; [1992] 2 All ER 433.

9   See O'Connor, *op cit* at [1990] Crim LR 615.

10   Report, *op cit*, Ch 10, para 38.

(1) if a conviction was safe despite an error, then the appeal should be dismissed;
(2) if an error was made that rendered the conviction unsafe, then the conviction should be quashed;
(3) if an error may render a conviction unsafe, then the conviction should be quashed and a re-trial ordered. This would render the proviso redundant.

The majority took the view that this should be the case even where appeals are based upon pre-trial malpractice or procedural irregularity. It is not the purpose of the appellate process to discipline the police or prosecution – the judge will have excluded tainted evidence anyway.

These arguments have not entirely disappeared as a result of the changes in the law made by the 1995 Act. That Act introduces a new section 2, containing a single test. The proviso is abolished. Henceforth, the test is this: the court shall allow an appeal against conviction if they think that the conviction is unsafe. This formulation should be compared with the recommendation of the Royal Commission that the single ground be "the conviction is or may be unsafe".[11] The difference in wording may in fact be of little consequence, in the light of the tests adopted by the courts to the question as to whether a conviction is unsafe, and in the light of parliamentary intent. The wording of the original section 2 ("unsafe or unsatisfactory") was considered by the House of Lords in *Stafford v Director of Public Prosecutions*,[12] where Viscount Dilhorne cited with approval a passage from the judgment of the court in *R v Cooper*:[13]

> "The court must in the end ask itself a subjective question, whether we are content to let the matter stand as it is, or whether there is not some lurking doubt in our minds which makes us wonder whether an injustice has been done. This is a reaction which may not be based strictly on the evidence as such; it is a reaction that can be produced by the general feeling of the case as the court experiences it to be."

The Royal Commission received conflicting evidence about the application of this "lurking doubt" approach. Research indicated that between 1968–89 only six cases applied the test, and in 1989 one out of 114 appeals. Yet the more recent research for the years 1991–1992 showed a greater use of this power (14 out of 102).[14] However the language of lurking doubt was not always used by the court. For the court to conclude that a verdict was unsatisfactory because of an injustice in the case and in the verdict was no different from an application of the "lurking doubt" test. Nevertheless, the court in *R v Maguire*[15] stressed that it is the words of the Act that have to be applied, not some other reformulation of the question. Despite the fact that the word "or" was used, the weight of authority suggests that "unsafe" and "unsatisfactory" in fact were regarded as bearing the same meaning.[16] This was a view supported by the Royal Commission. On this basis, the change in wording in section 2 does not change or limit the scope of the role of the court.[17] Not only will the court be able to interfere where the verdict of the jury is unsatisfactory on the evidence, but

---

11   *Ibid*, para 46.
12   [1974] AC 878; [1973] 3 All ER 762.
13   [1969] 1 QB 267, at 271; [1969] 1 All ER 32, at 34, per Widgery LJ (as he then was).
14   Report, Ch 10 para 43.
15   *R v Maguire* [1992] QB 936; [1992] 2 All ER 433.
16   See O'Connor, *op cit*, n 1, p 546, *ante*; cf J C Smith, "The Criminal Appeal Act 1995" [1995] Crim LR 920.
17   See Smith, *op cit*, at p 924, as to parliamentary intent.

also on the various other grounds relating to errors of law, misdirections and the like which underpinned the majority of successful appeals. Errors in summing up, misdirection on matters of law, a failure in appropriate cases to withdraw the case from the jury are all instances where section 2(1)(a) operate and will continue to do so. The unsafeness of the conviction may have arisen because of the way the case was conducted. In respect of appeals based upon error by lawyers, the test identified in *R v Ensor*[18] was whether injustice had been suffered as a result of flagrantly incompetent advocacy. This was, in the view of the Royal Commission,[19] too narrow:

> "It cannot possibly be right that there should be defendants serving prison sentences for no other reason than that their lawyers made a decision which later turns out to have been mistaken. What matters is not the degree to which the lawyers were at fault, but whether the particular decision, whether reasonable or unreasonable, caused a miscarriage of justice."

A wide variety of errors, usually of a procedural nature, may cause a conviction to be unsafe. These might include unfair conduct or undue interruption by the judge, improper disclosure to the jury of the defendant's character, tampering with a juror, misconduct on the part of a juror and failure to inform an undefended person of his right to call witnesses. In *R v Maguire*[20] it was held that a failure to comply with the requirements concerning disclosure of unused material amounted to a "material irregularity".

One area of uncertainty that remains are cases where a conviction for an offence, other than that for which the accused was tried, is upheld on appeal by virtue of the proviso. One such case was *R v Pickford*,[1] where the accused had pleaded guilty to an offence that, in law, he could not have committed as charged. The Court of Appeal upheld the conviction, applying the proviso, on the grounds that although the appellant had not in law committed the offence charged (incitement of a boy to commit incest with the boy's mother) he had in fact incited the mother to commit the incest (which was in law an offence). It is unclear as to whether this type of case is no longer good law on the grounds that the proviso has been abolished, or whether such a conviction would be regarded as "safe". The fact that the court felt constrained to use the proviso provides clear evidence that such a conviction cannot be regarded as "safe".

2   Power to substitute an alternative verdict

Where the defendant has been convicted of an offence and (1) the jury could on the same indictment have found him guilty of some other offence; and (2) it appears to the Court of Appeal that the jury must have been satisfied of the facts proving him guilty of that other offence, the court may, instead of allowing or dismissing the appeal against conviction, substitute a verdict of guilty of that other offence and pass sentence on the defendant for it.[2] The sentence must not be greater than that passed on the defendant at the trial, and must not, of course, exceed the maximum permitted by law for the substituted offence.[3] The court exercises this power with care, particularly in the light of (2) above, which involves some consideration of a verdict of a jury for

---

18   [1989] 2 All ER 586; [1989] 1 WLR 497.
19   Report, para 59.
20   [1992] QB 936; [1992] 2 All ER 433.
1   [1995] 1 Cr App Rep 420. For other authorities in similar vein, see *R v Boal* [1992] QB 591; *R v Ayres* (1984) 78 Cr App Rep 232; *R v McHugh* (1976) 64 Cr App Rep 92.
2   Criminal Appeal Act 1968, s 3(1).
3   *Ibid*, s 3(2).

which no reasons are given. Further, it is a material, though not decisive, point against exercising the power if the jury were not given any direction as to the alternative offence.[4] Where the indictment contains counts for two offences (such as theft and handling) which are in the circumstances alternative to each other, and the jury convict of one but acquit of the other, the court cannot substitute a verdict of guilty of the latter, even if that seems the correct verdict, since the jury expressly acquitted. The proper course, if there is a conviction on one, is for the jury to be discharged from giving a verdict on the other whereupon the Court of Appeal may substitute a verdict of guilty.[5] This may also be important from the point of view of a re-trial.

3 Power to receive fresh evidence and to order a new trial

The power to receive fresh evidence was contained in the 1907 Act, and is now to be found in section 23 of the 1968 Act, as now amended by the 1995 Act. This section contains both a duty and a discretion. Until being amended by the 1995 Act, section 23(2) imposed a duty to receive fresh evidence if:

(a) the evidence is likely to be credible, and would have been admissible at the trial; and

(b) there is a reasonable explanation for the evidence not being adduced at trial.

The Royal Commission considered that the test for admissibility of fresh evidence ("likely to be credible") was too high a threshold, and the 1995 Act amends section 23 by substituting the phrase "capable of belief" for "likely to be credible". Thus the intent of the change is that the court now has to consider whether such evidence is capable of being believed without having to take a view as to whether, on the facts, it is likely to be so.[6]

The court may decline to receive such evidence if it is satisfied that the evidence, if received, would not afford any ground for allowing the appeal.[7] In addition, under section 23(1) the court has a discretion to admit the evidence of any witness or document if it thinks it necessary or expedient in the interests of justice to do so. In this situation the evidence does not have to satisfy the criteria in section 23(2) of not being tendered at the trial. Thus, in *R v Lattimore*[8] some of the evidence was in fact given at the trial, and all of it was in fact available. It was allowed to be heard because it cast doubt upon the confession evidence upon which the prosecution case largely depended. The court will only exceptionally allow the discretion to be used as a means of different defences being put forward at the appellate stage. In *R v Ahluwalia*[9] the court, exceptionally, allowed fresh medical evidence to be adduced to support a defence of diminished responsibility to the charge of murder of the appellant's husband, a defence which had not been raised at trial.

Appeals on the grounds of fresh evidence are rare. The Royal Commission considered the powers contained in section 23 to be adequate, although it considered the court should take a broad view as to whether evidence was available at the time of

4 See, generally, *R v Caslin* [1961] 1 All ER 246; [1961] 1 WLR 59. This case was decided under the corresponding provisions of the Criminal Appeal Act 1907, but appears still to be good law.

5 *R v Melvin and Eden* [1953] 1 QB 481; [1953] 1 All ER 294.

6 A contrary view is taken by J C Smith at [1995] Crim LR at 928, but it is submitted the amendment makes no sense at all unless construed in the way suggested above.

7 Criminal Appeal Act 1968, s 23(2).

8 (1975) 62 Cr App Rep 53.

9 [1992] 4 All ER 889.

trial, and, if so, if there was a reasonable explanation for it not being adduced at the time. In respect of changes of evidence by a witness, if there is some reasonable explanation why a witness wishes to depart from previous evidence the court should receive it, if capable of belief.

Complementary to the power to receive fresh evidence is the power to order a new trial, first introduced in 1964.[10] If the court is satisfied that the evidence would have created a reasonable doubt in the minds of the jury, it must allow the appeal and quash the conviction, but may order a new trial if it considers that the interests of justice so require.[11] This power to order re-trial is not now confined to fresh evidence cases.[12] The power to order re-trials is at the heart of the debate as to how cases where fresh evidence comes to light should be dealt with. It has been argued by Lord Devlin[13] that a conviction should always be quashed where fresh evidence has been received, since a conviction is bound to be unsafe or unsatisfactory if not based on all the evidence. That, though, is not the approach of the courts. In *Stafford v Director of Public Prosecutions*[14] the House of Lords considered that the verdict should be quashed if the court itself considers the verdict to be unsafe or unsatisfactory, thus requiring the court to take a view of the effect of the fresh evidence tendered. This approach has been criticised as restricting the use of the re-trial powers.[15] During the period 1966–68 re-trials were ordered in only 9 out of 45 fresh evidence cases. During 1981–86 only 14 retrials were ordered.

In *R v McIlkenny*[16] the Court of Appeal described its approach as follows:

"Nor is there any difficulty in fresh evidence cases, where the fresh evidence is discovered soon after the trial. If the evidence is incredible, or inadmissible, or would not afford a ground for allowing the appeal, we decline to receive it. If the fresh evidence surmounts that preliminary hurdle, we first quash the conviction, if we think it unsafe or unsatisfactory, and then order a retrial if the interests of justice so require. Where new evidence is conclusive, we quash the conviction without ordering a retrial. The difficulty becomes acute when there is no contest. For then we have to make up our minds whether the convictions are unsafe or unsatisfactory without having the benefit of having the evidence tested by cross-examination. Where a retrial is still possible, the quashing of the conviction is only the first half of a two stage process. Where a retrial is no longer possible, it is the end of the road."

The position is regarded by many as unsatisfactory, bearing in mind that any of these cases will involve complex and disputed questions of fact. The question remains as to whether these are matters best dealt with by the appellate courts or by some other means.

What should the court do? The criticism, notably by Lord Devlin, accepted by the Royal Commission, which concluded[17] that once the court has received evidence that is relevant and capable of belief it should quash the conviction and order a re-trial unless that is not practicable or desirable. The Court of Appeal has not seen or heard the other witnesses, and is not the appropriate tribunal to assess the ultimate credibility and effect

---

10   Criminal Appeal Act 1964, s 1.
11   Criminal Appeal Act 1968, ss 7 and 8.
12   See amendments to s 7 by Criminal Justice Act 1988.
13   Royal Commission on Criminal Justice, Report, *op cit*, Ch 10, para 62.
14   [1974] AC 878; [1973] 3 All ER 762.
15   Royal Commission, Report, para 66.
16   [1992] 2 All ER 417.
17   Report, para 63.

on a jury of the fresh evidence. It should not normally decide the question of weight unless it is satisfied that the fresh evidence causes the verdict to be unsafe.

4   Venire de novo

The appeal court has always had the power to order a *venire de novo* where proceedings in the court of trial were so defective as to amount to a nullity. To the defendant this no doubt seems very like ordering a new trial, but strictly the court is ordering not a new trial but a proper one. It has not, unfortunately, been established what degree of irregularity suffices to render proceedings a nullity; there are only particular examples in the cases of proceedings which have been held to be a nullity. This has been held to be so where the judge at the trial was not properly qualified,[18] where the defendant specifically asked for but was denied his right of peremptory challenges,[19] or where a plea of not guilty was misheard and dealt with as a plea of guilty.[20]

5   Hospital orders

The court has certain powers to consider whether a hospital order was rightly made, and in some circumstances can substitute a verdict of guilty for an offence which was charged at the trial, of which the defendant could have been convicted, for the special verdict of not guilty by reason of insanity or against a finding of unfitness to plead reached at the trial.[1]

D   APPEALS AGAINST SENTENCE

On an appeal against sentence the court may reduce the sentence, or may vary it, by substituting one form of detention for another. The court will interfere with a sentence where it is "wrong in principle", an approach that applies also to references made by the Attorney-General. Where the sentence is against conviction only there is no power to interfere with the sentence in any way. Nor, except on an Attorney-General's reference, has the court the power to increase sentence, a power that once existed but was rarely used.[2]

E   PROCEDURE

Under section 9(d) and (e) of the Criminal Appeal Act 1907 the court had the power to appoint a special commissioner to conduct an inquiry into documents and to appoint assessors where their special expert knowledge was likely to be required for the determination of a case. These powers were little, if ever used, and not re-enacted by the 1968 Act. The Royal Commission considered that the Court of Appeal is not well

---

18   *R v Cronin* [1940] 1 All ER 618.
19   *R v Williams* (1925) 19 Cr App Rep 67. Such right no longer exists; see p 518, *ante*.
20   *R v Scothern* [1961] Crim LR 326.
1   See p 513, *ante*.
2   Abolished by Criminal Appeal Act 1966, s 4(2).

constituted to supervise or direct police or other investigations. Nor should the same body exercise judicial and investigatory functions.[3]

As noted above, some appeals to the court may be brought without leave, but in most cases there must be an application to the court itself for leave. The time limit for giving notice of appeal, or application for leave to appeal, is 28 days from the date of conviction or sentence. This time may be extended by the court. Such application is made in the first instance to a single judge of the court, who considers it in private. A single judge has most of the powers of a court of three judges (besides, of course, the power to grant leave); exceptionally he does not have any of the powers relating to fresh evidence. An application may of course be abandoned, and notice of abandonment cannot be withdrawn although it may be treated as a nullity if the abandonment was not the result of a deliberate and informed decision in the sense that "the mind of the appellant did not go with his act of abandonment."[4] For example, where an application for leave to appeal was granted but, because of a postal strike, was not communicated to the applicant before he gave notice of abandonment, he was permitted to withdraw his notice.[5] If the single judge refuses leave to appeal (or to exercise any other of his powers) the applicant may be considered by a court of two judges.[6] Both the single judge and the court may grant legal aid and bail. Bail, for obvious reasons, is very rarely granted;[7] indeed almost the only cases where it will be granted are where the defendant has obtained (or does not need) leave to appeal and has a very good chance of succeeding on appeal, or where the defendant has been given a comparatively short sentence after a long and complex trial.[8] In the latter case he might otherwise have served much of his sentence before the appeal was heard.

Time spent on bail does not, of course, count as part of the sentence.[9] Conversely, time spent in custody pending the determination of the appeal now counts as part of the defendant's sentence, subject to any direction to the contrary (for which reasons must be given). No such direction may be given where the defendant obtained leave to appeal, from the Court of Appeal or the trial court.[10]

Once an appeal has been heard and dismissed, or a notice of appeal abandoned, it cannot be re-opened.

F   APPEAL TO THE HOUSE OF LORDS

A further appeal lies by either prosecution or defence from the Court of Appeal (Criminal Division) to the House of Lords if:

---

3   Report, Ch 11, para 11.
4   *R v Medway* [1976] QB 779; [1976] 1 All ER 527.
5   *R v Noble* [1971] 3 All ER 361; [1971] 1 WLR 1772.
6   Criminal Appeal Act 1968, s 31(2); Supreme Court Act 1981, s 55(4). The application must normally be made to the court within 14 days of communication of the notice of refusal by the single judge, but the court has jurisdiction to extend the time even though the further application is not made until after the 14 days have expired: *R v Ward* [1971] 3 All ER 619; [1971] 1 WLR 1450; *R v Doherty* [1971] 3 All ER 622n; [1971] 1 WLR 1454n.
7   If the appeal is dismissed, it may embarrass the court to order the defendant's return to prison. "The court is always anxious in such a case, because although a man may have been on bail, he will have had the appeal hanging over him for all this time": Lord Parker CJ in *R v Cavendish* [1961] 2 All ER 856, at 858; [1961] 1 WLR 1083, at 1085.
8   *R v Walton* (1978) 68 Cr App Rep 293.
9   Criminal Appeal Act 1968, s 29.
10   See p 548, *ante*.

(1) the Court of Appeal certifies that a point of law of general public importance is involved in the decision; and

(2) either the Court of Appeal or the House of Lords gives leave to appeal on the ground that the point is one which ought to be considered by the House.

The certificate was considered a necessary condition, to avoid the House of Lords being inundated with hopeless applications. This justification was not accepted by the Royal Commission, which recommended its abolition.[11] If the Court of Appeal is satisfied that there is a point of law of general public importance involved it will give the certificate, as it were, automatically. There will always, nevertheless, be an element of discretion as to whether an appeal is allowed to proceed, since even if the point were of general public importance it might still not be worthy of consideration by the House of Lords in the particular case; for example it might already be the subject of clear and satisfactory decisions of lower courts. This element of discretion is preserved by the requirement that there can be no further proceedings. On the other hand, the Court of Appeal may give a certificate and yet refuse leave, in which case a petition may be made to the House of Lords for leave to appeal, the petition being heard by the Appeals Committee of the House.

It is proper and convenient that the certificate should state what the point of law of general public importance is;[12] however, it seems likely that other points may be raised by either side once the case is before the House of Lords on the point certified.[13] However, the grant of a certificate on some point affecting the validity of the conviction does not enable the appellant to argue that the sentence is invalid.[14] The House of Lords may exercise similar powers to those of the court below.

The procedure described above does not apply following the hearing of an Attorney-General's reference after acquittal.[15] In these cases the Court of Appeal may of its own motion or in pursuance of an application refer the point of law in the case to the House of Lords "if they appear to the court that the point ought to be considered by that House"[16] and there is, accordingly, no need for a certificate that a point of law of general public importance is involved. Indeed the point of law need not be a point of general public importance, although no doubt the Court of Appeal would only refer such a point to the House as a matter of practice.

---

11 Report, *op cit*, Ch 10, para 79.
12 *Jones v Director of Public Prosecutions* [1962] AC 635; [1962] 1 All ER 569.
13 *A-G for Northern Ireland v Gallagher* [1963] AC 349; [1961] 3 All ER 299.
14 See p 553, *ante*.
15 Under the Criminal Justice Act 1972, s 36; see p 551, *ante*.
16 Criminal Justice Act 1972, s 36(3).

CHAPTER 25

Summary Procedure and Appeals

The often forgotten,[1] central role of the magistrates' courts[2] in dealing with criminal cases has already been noted.[3] In excess of 93% of criminal business is dealt with summarily,[4] including virtually all cases involving children and young persons which are dealt with in the youth court. This level of work is increasing in the light of recent legislation and practice changes.[5] The issues raised by this, in terms of the composition of the court and the choice of mode of trial have already been noted.[6] In this chapter, the procedural differences between trial on indictment and summary trial are discussed. For this purpose, summary trial refers to trial irrespective of whether it is the trial of a summary-only offence or of an either-way offence in fact being tried summarily. It also refers to trial in the youth court.

A PROCESS

Summary procedure is commenced by process. The way an accused person may be brought before a court has already been discussed.[7] As the result of the laying of an information, either a summons to appear in court or a warrant to arrest the accused is obtained. Alternatively, the criminal proceedings can be commenced by bringing the offender to court following arrest, assuming the power of arrest to be available. A warrant cannot be issued in any case where a summons has already been issued. In any event, as has already been noted, a warrant cannot be issued for the arrest of an adult in the case of a summary offence, unless the offence is punishable with imprisonment or the defendant's address is "not sufficiently established" for a summons to be served on him. Even where a warrant may lawfully be issued, it is rarely thought

---

1 See the admonition of Darbyshire "An Essay on the Importance and Neglect of the Magistracy" [1997] Crim LR 639
2 For this purpose we can include the youth courts.
3 See Chapter 3, *ante*.
4 Royal Commission on Criminal Justice, *op cit*, p 2.
5 See p 476, *ante*.
6 See pp 475-476, *ante*.
7 See p 464, *ante*.

necessary in the case of any summary offence. The position therefore is that a summons or a warrant may be issued if:

(a) the summary offence was committed or is suspected to have been committed within the area; or

(b) it appears to the magistrate issuing process necessary or expedient, with a view to the better administration of justice, that the person charged should be tried jointly with or in the same place as some other person who is charged with an offence and who is in custody or is to be proceeded against within the area; or

(c) the person charged resides, or is believed to reside or be within the area; or

(d) under any enactment the magistrates' court has jurisdiction to try the offence. In this context, there should be noted section 2(6) of the Magistrates' Courts Act 1980, permitting a magistrates' court to try a number of offences provided that it has jurisdiction to try any one of them; or

(e) the offence was committed outside England and Wales and, where it is an offence exclusively punishable on summary conviction, if a magistrates' court for the area would have jurisdiction to try the offence if the offender were before it.[8]

B JURISDICTION

A magistrates' court for an area[9] has jurisdiction to try summary offences committed within that area. It also has jurisdiction as a court of trial in the following circumstances:

(1) where a person is brought before the court on a summons or warrant issued under section 1(2)(b) of the Act (to be tried jointly with another person over whom the court has jurisdiction);[10]

(2) in relation to either way offences, in any case where it has jurisdiction to conduct committal proceedings;[11]

(3) in relation to the trial of juveniles for indictable offences, in any case where it has jurisdiction to conduct committal proceedings;

(4) where it has jurisdiction to try an offender for a summary offence, it can also try him for any other summary offence.

C THE COURSE OF THE TRIAL

I Time-limit

Unless expressly provided to the contrary a magistrates' court cannot try an information charging a summary offence unless the information was laid[12] within six months from

---

8 Magistrates' Courts Act 1980, s 1(2); see the rules as to offences committed on boundaries etc which also apply here, p 467, *ante*.

9 Viz county, a London commission area or the City of London (Magistrates' Courts Act 1980, s 2(1)). The provisions as to offences committed on boundaries, etc (p 467, *ante*) also apply here.

10 See p 467, *ante*.

11 See p 486, *ante*.

12 See *R v Kennet JJ, ex parte Humphrey* [1993] Crim LR 787 (letter stating intention to charge sufficient); *R v Pontypridd Juvenile Court, ex parte B* [1988] Crim LR 842 (feeding of an information into a computer link to magistrates' court sufficient, irrespective of receipt).

the time when the offence was committed.[13] However, it may try summarily an either-way offence outside that period, since this statutory time-limit is confined to summary offences.[14] Time runs from the time of commission of the offence, not from the time of its discovery; however, it is sufficient if the information is laid within the six months, even if the trial takes place outside that time. It is in each case a question of construction of the statute whether the offence in question is a continuing offence, that is, committed each day that the act or state of affairs in question continues, or whether it is a "once and for all" offence in that it is committed on one day and one day only. Thus in *R v Wimbledon Justices, ex parte Derwent*[15] a statute made it an offence to let or offer to let a house in excess of a certain rent. The divisional court held that a person lets a house once and for all when he demises it by means of a lease and that an information laid six months after the date of the demise was out of time. Proceedings could therefore be restrained by prohibition since:

"If in a case brought before justices it can be seen on the face of the proceedings that the offence is alleged to have been committed more than six months before the information was laid, justices have no power to enter upon the case at all, because they have no jurisdiction to sit on a court of summary jurisdiction in the case of an offence alleged to have been committed more than six months before the proceedings were instituted."[16]

Even where the offence is continuing it seems that the time-limit runs from each day, so that the magistrates cannot hear any information that charges the offence as occurring more than six months before the date of the information;[17] in other words the matter is to be regarded as if the defendant committed the offence once every day. Where an information is laid in time it may be amended to charge a different offence, after the expiry of six months from the commission of that offence, provided that this does not cause injustice.[18]

The general need to avoid delay in criminal proceedings has already been noted.[19] So, too, has the doctrine of abuse of process.[20] This doctrine applies to summary proceedings equally as to proceedings on indictment. In *R v Willesden Justices, ex parte Clemmings*[1], Lord Bingham CJ indicated that magistrates had the power to stop a prosecution where there was an abuse of process, because:

(a) the prosecution have manipulated or misused the process of the court so as to deprive the accused of a protection provided by law or to take unfair advantage of a technicality; or

(b) the accused has been, or would be, prejudiced in the preparation or conduct of his defence by delay on the part of the prosecution, which was unjustifiable.

---

13   Magistrates' Courts Act 1980, s 127(1).
14   *Ibid*, s 127(2); see also *Kemp v Liebherr (Great Britain) Ltd* [1987] 1 All ER 885; [1987] 1 WLR 607.
15   [1953] 1 QB 380; [1953] 1 All ER 390.
16   [1953] 1 QB 380, at 385; [1953] 1 All ER 390, at 391, per Lord Goddard CJ.
17   *R v Chertsey Justices, ex parte Franks* [1961] 2 QB 152; [1961] 1 All ER 825.
18   *R v Newcastle-upon-Tyne Justices, ex parte John Bryce (Contractors) Ltd* [1976] 2 All ER 611; [1976] 1 WLR 517.
19   See p 493, *ante*.
20   See p 464, *ante*.
1   (1987) 87 Cr App R 280

The principles on which these rules will be exercised are broadly those as apply more generally.[2] The court will consider whether the wrongdoing is deliberate, whether prejudice has been caused or the potential for it arises.[3]

2 Number of offences

A magistrates' court must not proceed to the trial of an information which charges more than one offence.[4] This is a natural rule, since the information fulfils the same function in summary trial as the indictment in the case of trial at the Crown Court; the same considerations of, inter alia, fairness to the defendant, which prohibit duplicity in an indictment, also prohibit an information charging more than one offence. Thus in *Ware v Fox*[5] an information charged the defendant with being concerned in the management of premises which were used for the purpose of smoking cannabis or cannabis resin or dealing in cannabis or cannabis resin. The Queen's Bench divisional court held that on the proper construction of the relevant statute[6] the information alleged two offences, namely managing premises used for smoking and managing premises used for dealing and was bad for duplicity. By contrast, section 5 of the Public Order Act 1936 created[7] the offence of using "threatening, abusive or insulting words or behaviour with intent to provoke a breach of the peace or whereby a breach of the peace is likely to be occasioned". It was held in *Vernon v Paddon*[8] that the section created one offence, the essential feature of which is conduct intended to provoke a breach of the peace or whereby such a breach was likely to be occasioned.

The issue as to whether an information is bad for duplicity is not always easy to decide. In *R v Courtie*[9] Lord Diplock suggested that where one provision involved the imposition of different penalties depending on whether the prosecution established particular factual ingredients then Parliament had created two separate offences, and these should be the subject of separate informations. Applying this principle a divisional court in *Director of Public Prosecutions v Corcoran*[10] held that an information charging an offence of failure, without reasonable excuse, to provide a specimen of breath, blood or urine, contrary to section 7(6) of the Road Traffic Act 1988, was bad for duplicity, because the maximum punishment for this offence depended on the purpose for which the specimen was being sought. However, a short time later a differently constituted divisional court, in dismissing appeals in several cases,[11] overruled the earlier ruling and distinguished *R v Courtie*. On a construction of the statutory provisions, this was one offence; the question of punishment was relevant to sentence only.

Where an information is found to charge more than one offence the prosecutor should be called on to elect before the trial begins on which offence to proceed; if he

---

2 See p 464, *ante*.
3 See generally, *R v Brentford JJ, ex parte Wong* [1981] QB 445; *R v Oxford City Justices, ex parte Smith* (1987) 75 Cr App Rep 200; *R v Canterbury and St Augustine Justices, ex parte Turner* (1983) 147 JP 193.
4 Magistrates' Courts Rules 1981, r 12(1). However, two or more informations may be set out in a single document (*ibid*, r 12(2)); see *Shah v Swallow* [1984] 2 All ER 528; *sub nom Director of Public Prosecutions v Shah* [1984] 1 WLR 886.
5 [1967] 1 All ER 100; [1967] 1 WLR 379.
6 Dangerous Drugs Act 1965, s 5.
7 Now repealed and replaced by Public Order Act 1986, s 5.
8 [1973] 3 All ER 302; [1973] 1 WLR 663.
9 [1984] AC 463; [1984] 1 All ER 740.
10 [1993] 1 All ER 912.
11 *Shaw v Director of Public Prosecutions (and other cases)* [1993] 1 All ER 918.

declines to make his election the information should be dismissed.[12] It is important that the matter should be put right at the outset, since, as will be noted below, the magistrates must state the substance of the information to the defendant and ask him to plead to it. However, even after a trial has started an information bad for duplicity can be cured, by the court requiring the prosecutor to elect, just as it can prior to the trial itself.[13] The prosecutor will elect as to which offence he wishes to proceed on, the remainder will be struck out and the trial begun afresh. Again, if the prosecutor declines to elect, the information as a whole will be struck out.

To avoid difficulty the information itself should always be in court from the beginning of proceedings.[14] It is however quite permissible, and indeed common, for two informations against the same defendant, or (where the cases are related) against different defendants, to be tried together. It was formerly thought that this could only be done by consent but the House of Lords in *Chief Constable of Norfolk v Clayton*[15] held that, although magistrates should first seek consent to such a course, they could nevertheless in the exercise of their discretion order a joint trial even without the consent of the parties, although they should not do so where it would not be fair and just to a defendant.[16]

Where there are informations charging an offence and an attempt to commit that offence, these may be ordered to be tried together without the consent of the defendant[17] and this will usually be done.

3   Pre-trial procedures

a   Administrative hearings

The general approach now being pursued in respect of the criminal justice process is the need to ensure that delay is reduced and kept to a minimum. It was with this aim that the Narey Report[18] recommended a wide range of structural and procedural reforms, including reforms to summary process. In particular, it recommended the establishment of procedures that will permit administrative hearings, giving case-management powers to justices' clerks in much the same way as, on indictment, the court may engage in pleas and directions hearings and preparatory hearings. Clearly such hearings could deal with a variety of administrative matters, thus saving court time, and reducing its waste through unnecessary adjournments. Although experiments along these lines have from time to time occurred,[19] the basis on which they have been conducted is open to some doubt, and necessary changes are now being introduced by the Crime and Disorder Act 1998. This it does in two ways.

The first is by early administrative hearings. Section 47 of the 1998 Act provides that the first hearing before a magistrates' court following the charging of a person

---

12   *Edwards v Jones* [1947] KB 659; [1947] 1 All ER 830.
13   Magistrates' Courts Rules 1981, *op cit*, r 12(3)-(5).
14   Per Lord Parker CJ and Salmon J (as he then was) in *Hargreaves v Alderson* [1964] 2 QB 159; [1962] 3 All ER 1019; see also *Garman v Plaice* [1969] 1 All ER 62; [1969] 1 WLR 19.
15   [1983] 2 AC 473; *sub nom Clayton v Chief Constable of Norfolk* [1983] 1 All ER 984. This does not, however, enable a summons and cross-summons to be tried together; this cannot be done *semble* even by consent: *R v Epsom Justices, ex parte Gibbons* [1984] QB 574; [1983] 3 All ER 523.
16   The wishes of the parties should not lightly be overruled: *R v Highbury Corner M.C., ex parte McGinley* (1986) 150 JP 257.
17   Criminal Attempts Act 1981, s 4(2).
18   *Review of Delay in the Criminal Justice System*, 27 February 1997.
19   Although with no clear basis in law.

with an offence at a police station may be conducted by a single justice.[20] At such a hearing the accused must be asked whether he wishes to receive legal aid, if he does his eligibility is to be determined and, if he is in fact eligible, the necessary arrangement must be put in hand for him to obtain it. The single justice may also exercise any other power exercisable by a single justice (see below).

The second is the extension of the powers which may be exercised by a single justice. By section 49 of the Crime and Disorder Act 1998, a range of powers is conferred on a single justice, or, where rules provide,[1] on a justices' clerk. These powers comprise authority:

(a) to extend bail or to impose or vary conditions of bail;
(b) to mark an information as withdrawn;
(c) to dismiss an information or discharge an accused where no evidence is offered by the prosecution;
(d) to make an order for the payment of the accused's costs out of central funds;
(e) to request a pre-sentence report[2] following a guilty plea, and, for that purpose, to give an indication of the seriousness of the offence;
(f) to request a medical report and, for that purpose to remand the accused in custody or on bail;
(g) to remit an offender to another court for sentence;
(h) to determine mode of trial on an amended charge;
(i) to vary the time for appearance at court specified by police bail;
(j) to extend, with the consent of the accused, a custody or other time limit;
(k) to grant representation for the Crown Court under the Legal Aid Act 1988;
(l) to order production of a driving licence;
(m) to give a direction prohibiting the publication or disclosure of certain matters;
(n) to give, vary or revoke directions, which may include directions as to a timetable for the proceedings, the attendance of the parties, the service of documents and the manner in which evidence is to be given.

These changes individually focus on matters of considerable detail. Together, they provide a means whereby summary cases are not subject to continual or unnecessary adjournments, or unnecessary hearings on what are important, but often administrative or preparatory, matters. However, it remains to be seen the extent to which collectively this greater administrative management by justices, or, often, justices' clerks, will reduce significantly delays in the magistrates' courts.

b   Disclosure

The new regime for the disclosure of unused material by the prosecution and for defence disclosure, both contained in the Criminal Procedure and Investigations Act 1996, has already been discussed.[3] Until the passage of that Act the position regarding prosecution disclosure in summary proceedings had been unclear. In one case[4] a divisional court decided that the interests of justice required that decisions as to whether material should be disclosed should be restricted to the Crown Courts and were not matters for consideration by magistrates. However, that was a case concerned with committal

20 Powers to extend this jurisdiction to justices' clerks are conferred by s 48(2). See further, p 567, *post*.
1   See *supra*, n 15C.
2   Where required by Criminal Justice Act 1991, s 3. See, further, p 536, *ante*.
3   See pp 494–496, *ante*.
4   *R v South Worcestershire Magistrates, ex parte Lilley* [1995] 4 All ER 186; (1995) 159 JP 598.

proceedings, and did not address the more general question of disclosure on summary trial. Logically, there should be no fundamental difference between trial on indictment and summary trial in this respect, although various practical issues arise, and the position was clarified by another divisional court in *R v Bromley Magistrates' Court, ex parte Smithy and Wilkins*,[5] where Simon Brown LJH observed that an accused in a summary case is as much entitled to the safeguard designed to secure a fair trial in a magistrates' court as in the Crown Court.

Section 1 of the 1996 Act applies the disclosure provisions of that Act (ie prosecution and defence disclosure) to cases where a person is charged with a summary offence in which a court proceeds to summary trial and the accused pleads not guilty, and to cases where a magistrates' court proceeds to summary trial on an either-way offence to which the accused pleads not guilty. It also applies to the trial in the youth court of an indictable offence in respect of a person under the age of 18. The effect of this is that the duty of primary and secondary prosecution disclosure arises.[6] A court will also have powers to determine questions as to whether material should be withheld in the public interest.[7] In respect of defence disclosure, the position is slightly different. There is no obligation on the defence to disclose the nature of the defence. However, section 6 of the 1996 Act creates a power for voluntary defence disclosure in summary cases, with the potential for an inference to be drawn[8] for inadequate or incomplete disclosure. The advantage for the accused in engaging in voluntary defence disclosure is that only if he does so will the prosecutor be under an obligation to engage in secondary prosecution disclosure.[9]

One further change made by the 1996 Act should be noted. In cases of trial on indictment the law requires advance notice to be given of expert evidence which is to be called. No such obligation has existed hitherto in summary cases. There can be no real justification for this distinction, and the 1996 Act rectifies the omission by authorising the making of rules which will extend to summary cases.[10] No such rules have yet been made.

4   Hearing

If the defendant appears at the hearing, the court must state to him the substance of the information and ask him whether he pleads guilty or not guilty. In spite of these words, the same pleas as are open to a defendant charged with an indictable offence may be raised by a defendant charged with a summary offence. If the plea is one of not guilty the prosecutor may make an opening speech, and will then call his evidence. Where the prosecutor is unrepresented, it is open to the magistrates, in their discretion, to permit their clerk to examine prosecution witnesses.[11] Section 97 of the Magistrates' Courts Act 1980 will apply, and the witnesses will be subject to cross-examination and re-examination according to the circumstances of the case, and in accordance with the procedures and rules of evidence already noted.[12] If necessary, a witness can be summonsed to the court to give evidence by witness summons issued under section

5   [1995] 4 All ER 146; (1994) 159 JP 251.
6   See p 495, *ante.*
7   Criminal Procedure and Investigations Act 1996, s 3(6) and s 14. See, further, p 495, *ante.*
8   See 1996 Act, s 11. The inference will be of the same type as may be drawn under Criminal Justice and Public Order Act 1994, ss 34–38, as to which see p 318, *ante.*
9   Under 1996 Act, s 7. See p 495, *ante.*
10   1996 Act, s 19(1).
11   *Simms v Moore* [1970] 2 QB 327; [1970] 3 All ER 1.
12   See p 520, *ante.*

97 of the 1980 Act. Alternatively, in some circumstances the written statement of the witness may be considered by the court.[13] Clearly, such out-of-court statements infringe the rule of evidence relating to hearsay[14] but, nevertheless, Parliament has created, for good reason, a range of statutory exceptions that apply in summary proceedings, and which add to the limited common law exceptions to the hearsay rule already noted.[15]

The procedure followed during the examination and cross-examination of witnesses mirrors that in trial on indictment, although rules of evidence may sometimes be applied less strictly here are, of course, important differences. Since there is no jury, the magistrates are both the tribunal of law and tribunal of fact: in other words, all decisions are for them irrespective of whether they are matters of fact or law. Thus the magistrates will decide questions of admissibility of evidence, although the procedures for doing so (which are quite clear in trial on indictment) are less clear on summary trial. It has been noted[16] that a Crown Court may hold a hearing (known as a *voir dire*, after the name of the oath taken by witnesses who testify at such a hearing) in order to decide questions of admissibility of evidence. Such a hearing is held in the absence of the jury, so that the jury does not hear evidence which may later be ruled inadmissible. The concept of a *voir dire* in magistrates' courts is wholly artificial, and the cases leave unclear the extent to which a magistrates' court, on summary trial, must conduct a "trial within a trial" in order to decide whether evidence is admissible.[17]

It is also pertinent to consider the role of the justices' clerk. The functions of justices' clerks are considered elsewhere.[18] The clerk will generally advise on matters of law and procedure, and ensure that the trial is conducted properly, but must take great care to ensure that he plays no part in decisions on matters of fact, which are for the justices themselves.[19] The clerk may assist a party to present his case.[20] Care should be taken to avoid influencing the decisions of the justices on matters of fact or sentence, or to avoid giving the appearance of doing so.

At the conclusion of the evidence for the prosecution the defendant may address the court, whether or not he calls evidence; if he is calling evidence it will follow at once. The defendant may then address the court a second time but only if he himself has given evidence, another witness has been called on his behalf, and the court gives leave.[1] If the defendant addresses the court twice the prosecutor has a right to address the court a second time immediately before the defendant's second speech. The court will then retire if necessary and convict the defendant or dismiss the charge. If on the other hand the defendant pleads guilty the court may convict him without hearing evidence.[2] The wording of the subsection shows that it is often desirable to hear some evidence, particularly where it is part of the prosecution's case that the offence was committed in circumstances of aggravation, or perhaps if a committal for sentence to

---

13 Under Criminal Justice Act 1988, ss 23–26; see also Magistrates' Courts Act 1980, s 102; Criminal Justice Act 1967, s 9

14 Hearsay evidence can be defined as any statement containing an assertion, express or implied, made by a person otherwise than while giving evidence and tendered to prove the truth of that assertion: *R v Sharp* [1988] 1 All ER 65, [1988] 1 WLR 7, approving the definition in *Cross on Evidence*, (6th Edn, Butterworths).

15 See p 525, *ante*.

16 See p 519, *ante*.

17 See, in particular, *R v Liverpool Juvenile Court, ex parte R* [1988] QB 1, which provides that *a voir dire* should be held in respect of confession evidence.

18 See Chapter 12, *ante*

19 *R v Sussex JJ, ex parte MacCarthy* [1924] 1 KB 256.

20 See *ante*.

1 Magistrates' Courts Rules 1981, r 14.

2 Magistrates' Courts Act 1980, s 9(3).

the Crown Court is contemplated or if the plea of guilty tendered may be "equivocal".[3] In any event the court retains full power over the case until sentence is passed and has discretion to allow a change of plea until that time if justice so requires.[4] Whether there is a plea of guilty or finding of guilt, there will normally be such an inquiry into the past record of the defendant as follows conviction of an indictable offence; the court may then adjourn, for not more than four weeks at a time, for inquiries to be made or for the purpose of determining the best way to deal with the case.[5] When the court resumes it need not be composed of the same magistrates; if, however, there are any newcomers the court which sentences or deals with the offender must make such inquiry into the facts and circumstances of the case as are necessary to acquaint the newcomers fully with those facts and circumstances.[6] This must be done even though the court will "ex hypothesi" have held some such inquiry before; the use of the words "the court" seems to prohibit the newcomers being given information privately before the court sits.[7]

Finally, note should be taken of the power which magistrates have under the Justices of the Peace Act 1361 to bind over a defendant to keep the peace or be of good behaviour even where he is acquitted.[8]

D   ABSENCES

I   General effects of absence[9]

It sometimes happens that one or both of the parties fails to appear at the trial or adjourned trial of the information. If the defendant does not appear the court may hear the case in his absence provided that, where a summons was issued, either the court is satisfied that the summons was served on the defendant within what appears to be a reasonable time before the hearing, or the defendant appeared on a previous occasion to answer the information.[10] Alternatively the court may adjourn the hearing, with or without issuing a warrant for the arrest of the defendant; but a warrant can only be issued if the court is satisfied as to the matters stated above, and if the information is substantiated on oath. There is a further restriction on the issue of a warrant; if the court adjourns the trial after hearing evidence, or convicting the defendant without hearing evidence on a plea of guilty, the court must not issue a warrant unless it thinks it undesirable, by reason of the gravity of the offence, to continue the hearing in his absence. In any event, a warrant cannot be issued unless the offence is punishable by

---

3   See p 515, *ante*.
4   *S (An Infant) v Manchester City Recorder* [1971] AC 481; [1969] 3 All ER 1230.
5   Magistrates' Courts Act 1980, s 10(3); the period is three weeks if the defendant is in custody.
6   Magistrates' Courts Act 1980, s 98(7). This is perhaps the nearest that English law comes to allowing special "sentencing tribunals".
7   In the event of a question arising which might require reference to the European Court for a preliminary ruling the justices may, on application or otherwise, order the question to be referred and the hearing will then be adjourned pending receipt of the European Court's ruling; for a case in which this was done, and observations as to the approach which magistrates should adopt to this problem, see *R v Plymouth Justices, ex parte Rogers* [1982] QB 863; [1982] 2 All ER 175.
8   See *Veater v G* [1981] 2 All ER 304; [1981] 1 WLR 567; *Hughes v Holley* (1986) 86 Cr App Rep 130.
9   Magistrates' Courts Act 1980, ss 11–16. As to absence during the initial procedure on information for an offence triable either way, see p 465, *ante*. See now Magistrates' Courts (Procedure) Act 1998.
10   The mode of service is prescribed by the Magistrates' Courts Rules 1981, r 99. If the court proceeds in the absence of the defendant in a case where he has not been duly served in accordance with this rule, the "hearing" is a complete nullity: *R v Seisdon Justices, ex parte Dougan* [1983] 1 All ER 6; [1982] 1 WLR 1476.

imprisonment or unless the court, having convicted the defendant, proposes to disqualify him.

The accused may be represented at the hearing by solicitor or counsel,[11] in such circumstances the accused being deemed to be present even if not physically in court. If the accused in fact is present he may be assisted by another person,[12] although the court may decline this if the level or nature of the assistance is unreasonable.

If the prosecutor fails to appear the court may dismiss the information or, if evidence has been received on a previous occasion, continue the hearing.[13] This is one example of the importance of the stage of the trial at which the justices begin to hear evidence. Alternatively the court may adjourn the trial, or may in an appropriate case dismiss the information for want of prosecution under section 15(1) of the Magistrates' Courts Act 1980. However, this power should not be used for this purpose save in exceptional cases. In *R v Hendon Justices, ex parte Director of Public Prosecutions*[14] a magistrates' court dismissed an information for want of prosecution when the defendants, their advocates and the prosecution witnesses were all at court, but the prosecuting solicitor was not. This absence occurred because of an error in court administration, and the court was aware that a solicitor was on his way to rectify the position. In quashing the order of the justices the divisional court stressed that the duty of the magistrates' court is to hear informations properly brought before it. The prosecution had a right to be heard; the proper course was to adjourn until the hearing could proceed.

If neither side appears, the court may again dismiss the information or, if evidence has been received on a previous occasion, continue the hearing;[15] alternatively the hearing may simply be adjourned.

2   Pleading guilty by post

The Magistrates' Courts Act 1957 provided a new and convenient procedure whereby the defendant can plead guilty in cases where his appearance at court would be no more than a formality, if not a serious waste of time and money. It is now governed by section 12 of the 1980 Act. The procedure laid down by the Act is generally acknowledged to have worked well and is extensively used, particularly in motoring cases; however, it has no application at all to: (1) youth court proceedings in respect of persons under 16 years; (2) offences triable either way; or (3) offences for which the accused is liable to be sentenced to imprisonment for a term exceeding three months. Where the Act does apply, the procedure is as follows. The prosecutor will serve with the summons a notice in prescribed terms as to the effect of section 12 of the Act and a concise statement of such facts as he will place before the court if the defendant does decide to plead guilty by post. Although the Act is silent on the point it seems that it is entirely within the discretion of the prosecutor as to whether he will make use of the Act and serve the above documents with the summons, even on the assumption that the Act applies to the offence charged. Where, however, the prosecutor does elect to use the procedure, he must serve the documents and then inform the clerk to the justices that he has done so. It is then for the defendant or his solicitor to inform the clerk that he desires to plead guilty without appearing, if that is so, by sending, appropriately completed, the part of the notice described above. He does not, of course, have to use

11   Magistrates' Courts Act 1980, s 12.
12   *R v Leicester City Justices, ex parte Barow* [1991] 2 QB 60; [1991] 3 All ER 935.
13   Magistrates' Courts Act 1980, s 15.
14   [1994] QB 167; [1993] 1 All ER 411.
15   Magistrates' Courts Act 1980, s 16.

the procedure, and even if he does at first give notification that he is not going to appear he may change his mind and appear.

If, however, he does not appear the court may proceed to hear the case in his absence (whether or not the prosecutor is also absent) provided that it is satisfied that the notice and statement of facts were served on the defendant with the summons. Before accepting the plea of guilty and convicting the defendant in his absence the court must cause to be read out aloud the defendant's notification that he is going to plead guilty, the statement of facts served on the defendant and any statement by way of mitigation which the defendant himself may have submitted. The statement of facts read out must be precisely the same as that served upon the defendant. These rules must be meticulously observed, and breach of them may be a ground for quashing the conviction by means of certiorari:

"we all know that these matters have to be dealt with expeditiously.[16] It seems to me, however, to be quite clear that, before the magistrates can exercise jurisdiction in a case of this sort, they must strictly observe the conditions of the statute. Mere knowledge of the contents of the accused's submission, the mere reading of it themselves, is not sufficient; the submission must be read in open court."[17]

The rule that the precise statement of facts must be read out is also important, because after hearing it the magistrates may decide that the case is too grave to be dealt with in the way contemplated by the parties and may adjourn the case for the defendant to be present.

Assuming that, after hearing the notification of intention to plead guilty, the statement of facts and the submissions in mitigation, the magistrates accept the plea, they will record a conviction and (in the majority of cases to which the Act applies) impose a fine. Where they think it desirable to imprison the defendant or to impose any disqualification on him they must adjourn the hearing[18] without imposing any penalty whatever. There must then be sent to the defendant a notice stating the time and place of the adjourned hearing and the reason for the present adjournment (that is that the court is considering imprisonment or disqualification). If he chooses not to appear after receiving notice of what the court has in mind the court can proceed to disqualify him in his absence;[19] they cannot however sentence him to imprisonment or detention in his absence.[20] In such a case the proper course is to issue a warrant for the defendant's arrest.[1] Thus a person can never be sentenced to imprisonment in his absence and can only be disqualified in his absence following an adjournment for the purpose of giving him an opportunity to appear. However, a person may be committed to prison, for default in payment of a fine, in his absence.[2]

16   Section 12, as amended by the Criminal Justice Act 1991, s 69.
17   *R v Oldham Justices, ex parte Morrissey* [1958] 3 All ER 559n, at 560; [1959] 1 WLR 58, at 59, per Lord Parker CJ.
18   Under the Magistrates' Courts Act 1980, s 10(3): see p 568, *ante*. This applies even if disqualification is mandatory under the "totting-up" provisions; further there may even in this case be grounds for mitigating the normal consequences of conviction, which the defendant should have the chance to state: *R v Llandrindod Wells Justices, ex parte Gibson* [1968] 2 All ER 20; [1968] 1 WLR 598.
19   *Ibid*, s 11(4). But, now, see Magistrates Courts (Procedure) Act 1998.
20   *Ibid*, s 11(3).
1   *Ibid*, s 13(3).
2   *Ibid*, s 82(5); *R v Dudley Magistrates' Court, ex parte Payne* [1979] 2 All ER 1089; [1979] 1 WLR 891.

E   SENTENCE

The types of sentence imposable by magistrates are basically similar to those available to the Crown Court, although the extent of magistrates' powers in relation to severity of sentence is more limited. They can normally only sentence to imprisonment for up to six months in respect of any one offence[3] (or 12 months in the case of consecutive sentences).[4]

Their powers relating to the imposition of fines and the making of compensation orders are restricted. Since all summary jurisdiction derives from statute the amount of the maximum fine for any offence is prescribed by statute. However where a statute provides for imprisonment or other detention but makes no express provision for a fine, there is a general power to fine instead of imposing a custodial sentence.[5]

As a result of inflation statutory fines may quickly become too low and, to combat this phenomenon, the Criminal Justice Act 1982, section 37 introduced "the standard scale" of fines for summary offences. This scale consists of 5 levels and the ensuing sections of the 1982 Act provided for the substitution of a level on the standard scale for the figures prescribed by existing statutory provisions. Thus, for example, a summary offence formerly punishable with a fine of £100 became punishable with a fine up to level 3. To keep pace with inflation these levels may be increased by order of the Secretary of State,[6] although it should be remembered that the fine that may be imposed in respect of an either way offence will be determined by the terms of the specific statutory provision. The maximum compensation that magistrates can order under a compensation order is similarly limited.[7]

The position regarding the appropriate level of fines for summary offences has proved somewhat controversial. In an attempt to create some equal impact of fines upon those of different incomes, the Criminal Justice Act 1991 introduced[8] a system of "unit fines", whereby the actual amount of a fine depended upon a complex formula that sought to multiply an amount related to the seriousness of the offence with a multiple reflecting the level of disposable income of the defendant. After widespread public concern, the scheme was abandoned. The position is now governed by a revised section 18 of the Criminal Justice Act 1991,[9] which requires the sentencing court to take in to account both the seriousness of the offence and the ability of the defendant to pay [10]

Finally, reference should be made to the provisions, now contained in section 39 of the 1980 Act, whereby a person aged 17 or over who has been convicted before different magistrates' courts of two or more offences punishable with imprisonment or disqualification from driving, may be remitted to be dealt with by one of the courts concerned.

A wide range of special rules govern the sentencing and treatment of young offenders by the youth court. These are dealt with later.[11]

---

3   Magistrates' Courts Act 1980, s 31(1); they can, of course, commit to the Crown Court for sentence in the circumstances noted at pp 572–574, *post.*
4   *Ibid*, s 133.
5   Magistrates' Courts Act 1980, s 34(3).
6   Magistrates' Courts Act 1980, s 143 (as amended by the Criminal Justice Act 1982, s 48). They were increased by the Criminal Justice Act 1991, s 17, under which the maximum fine for a level 5 offence is £5,000.
7   *Ibid*, s 40(1); s 143 applies to s 40(1).
8   Criminal Justice Act 1991, ss 18 19.
9   As substituted by Criminal Justice Act 1993, s 65(1).
10   1991 Act, s 18(2). For discussion of offence seriousness under the 1991 Act, see p 538, *ante.*
11   See p 576, *post.*

F   COMMITTALS FOR SENTENCE

In some instances a defendant who has been tried in the magistrates' court may be committed to the Crown Court to be sentenced or otherwise dealt with. The case then becomes:

> "a sort of composite case in which power is given to one court to convict and to another to give judgment; and until the judgment is given the hearing of the case is not complete.[12]

Although these instances vary in detail, there are basically three objects of committal for sentence, namely to ensure that:

(a) a defendant receives greater punishment than a magistrates' court has power to inflict, if thought to deserve it,
(b) the same court which made an order should deal with its breach, and
(c) generally, that there should be uniformity in sentencing. It may be noted at this stage that where the magistrates exercise their power under section 1(1) of the Powers of Criminal Courts Act 1973[13] to defer sentence, it is usually wrong when the defendant comes before them again to be dealt with to commit him for sentence.[14] Furthermore, if the justices do decide to commit the defendant for sentence they must be scrupulously careful to leave all questions associated with sentence to the Crown Court. They cannot therefore impose any order such as a compensation order and all matters relating to sentence are out of the justices' hands.[15]

I   Summary trial of an adult for an either-way offence

If a magistrates' court tries an adult for an either-way offence and convicts him, but considers:

(a) that the offence, or the combination of the offence and other offences associated with it,[16] is so serious that greater punishment should be inflicted than the magistrates' court has power to impose; or
(b) in the case of a violent or sexual offence[17] committed by a person not less than 21 years of age, that a term of imprisonment longer than the magistrates' court has power to impose is necessary to protect the public from serious harm from him;

it may commit the defendant to the Crown Court for sentence.

This power is contained in section 38 of the Magistrates' Courts Act 1980.[18] Although the power to commit extends to all either-way offences tried summarily, it

---

12   Lord Goddard CJ in *R v Norfolk Justices, ex parte Director of Public Prosecutions* [1950] 2 KB 558, at 568; *sub nom R v Greenhoe Justices, ex parte Director of Public Prosecutions* [1950] 2 All ER 42, at 46.
13   See p 535, *ante*.
14   *R v Gilby* [1975] 2 All ER 743; [1975] 1 WLR 924; cf *R v Harling* (1977) 65 Cr App Rep 320.
15   *R v Brogan* [1975] 1 All ER 879; [1975] 1 WLR 393.
16   See p 538, *ante*.
17   Defined in the Criminal Justice Act 1991, s 31(1); see *R v Robinson* [1993] 2 All ER 1; [1993] 1 WLR 168.
18   As substituted by Criminal Justice Act 1991, s 25.

does not apply to cases under the Criminal Damage Act 1971 where the magistrates proceed to summary trial on the basis that the value involved does not exceed the relevant sum.[19]

Committal will normally be to the most convenient location of the Crown Court. In selecting this the justices may have regard to directions given by the presiding judge or judges of the circuit.[20] Committal may be in custody or on bail, but the Court of Appeal has indicated that:

> "the cases must be rare when magistrates' courts can properly commit for [sentence] on bail because the whole purpose of the committal is to have the man sent to prison, and have him sent to prison for a longer period than the magistrates' court could impose."[1]

However, the defendant may give notice of appeal against conviction and may then, *qua* appellant, be released on bail, although, where a possibly severe sentence awaits him, bail will only be granted "with extreme care, and only in really exceptional cases".[2] There is no appeal against the order of committal as such;[3] if the defendant thinks that the committal was bad in law, for example because he was not warned that he might be committed, he should apply to a divisional court of the Queen's Bench Division for an order of certiorari or prohibition; the Crown Court will not, of course, sentence him until the result of his application is known, since the order of committal may be held to be a nullity. On such an application the divisional court can only hear argument as to the legality of the committal and cannot entertain any suggestion that the committal was too harsh a step to take having regard to the facts; this is an argument to be addressed (although not in so many words) to the Crown Court when the defendant appears there for sentence.

On such appearance, procedure is as if the defendant had been committed for trial to the Crown Court and had pleaded guilty to the charge. No actual plea will be taken, since that stage of the trial is concluded, but otherwise the position is as if the defendant had pleaded guilty at the Crown Court itself. Thus notices required to be served "three days before the trial" may be served three days before the hearing at the Crown Court,[4] and, if the defendant has been granted bail, but fails to surrender, the Crown Court may issue a bench warrant.[5] It might then be thought that the Crown Court could allow the defendant to withdraw his plea of guilty (if such was tendered) in the magistrates' court, before he was sentenced, and it is now clear from *R v Mutford and Lothingland Justices, ex parte Harber*[6] following the decision of the House of Lords in *S (An Infant) v Manchester City Recorder*[7] that this is permissible. The Crown Court certainly has such a power when trying a case on indictment.[8]

At the hearing there should be formal identification by the police of the defendant as the person who appeared at the magistrates' court and was committed; if there is no police officer present who can give this information, the defendant may, it seems, be

19   Magistrates' Courts Act 1980, s 33(1)(b); see p 469, *ante*.
20   See *Practice Direction (Crown Court Business: Classification)* [1987] 3 All ER 1064; [1987] 1 WLR 1671.
1   *R v Coe* [1969] 1 All ER 65, at 68; [1968] 1 WLR 1950, at 1954.
2   *Re Whitehouse* [1951] 1 KB 673, at 675; [1951] 1 All ER 353, at 354.
3   *R v London Sessions Appeal Committee, ex parte Rogers* [1951] 2 KB 74; [1951] 1 All ER 343.
4   *R v Grant* [1951] 1 KB 500; [1951] 1 All ER 28.
5   Bail Act 1976, s 7.
6   [1971] 2 QB 291; [1971] 1 All ER 81. The Crown Court can only take into consideration what took place in the magistrates' court: *R v Marylebone Justices, ex parte Westminster City Council* [1971] 1 All ER 1025; [1971] 1 WLR 567.
7   [1971] AC 481; [1969] 3 All ER 1230.
8   See p 513, *ante*.

asked whether he was the person who appeared and was committed. The Crown Court will inquire into the circumstances of the case as it would following a plea of guilty before itself; prosecuting counsel will give the court an outline of the facts. It should be noted that if there is a dispute as to the facts of the offence upon which the defendant has been committed for sentence, the Crown Court can either resolve that matter itself, if necessary by hearing evidence, or can remit the case to the magistrates' court for such dispute to be resolved.[9] The court will then consider the defendant's antecedents, and usually a pre-sentence report;[10] defending counsel (or solicitor) will then address the court in mitigation. The Crown Court can then pass any sentence up to the maximum which the particular indictable offence carries and can deal with the defendant in any manner in which it could deal with him if he had just been convicted of the offence on indictment before the court.[11] The position as to appeal itself against this sentence has already been considered.[12]

If the defendant appeals against conviction, as well as being committed for sentence, the Crown Court will of course hear his appeal first, since, if this succeeds, there will be no cause to sentence him.

2 Offences under the Bail Act 1976

The Bail Act 1976 created three new summary offences: the first two consist of failure of a person released on bail in criminal proceedings, without reasonable cause, to surrender to custody, or, having reasonable cause, to surrender at the appointed place as soon after the appointed time as reasonably practicable;[13] the third offence is that of agreeing to indemnify sureties in criminal proceedings.[14] Each of these offences is a summary offence (and therefore triable only summarily);[15] in each case the magistrates have power to impose imprisonment for up to three months or a fine of up to level 5 or both. However, exceptionally, the Act provides that in each case if the court thinks:

(a) that the circumstances of the offence are such that greater punishment should be inflicted for that offence than the court has power to inflict, or

(b) in a case where it commits that person for trial to the Crown Court for another offence, that it would be appropriate for him to be dealt with by that court for the bail offence,

it may commit him in custody or on bail to the Crown Court for sentence. In the Crown Court the convicted person is liable to imprisonment for up to 12 months or a fine or both.[16]

This form of statutory provision, namely one that provides for committal for sentence in the case of a purely summary offence, is wholly exceptional.

---

9   *Munroe v Crown Prosecution Service* [1988] Crim LR 823.
10   See p 536, *ante*.
11   Powers of Criminal Courts Act 1973, s 42.
12   See p 549, *ante*.
13   Bail Act 1976, s 6(1); the marginal note refers to the offence as "absconding" although that word does not appear in the body of the section.
14   *Ibid*, s 9(1).
15   Although the offences under s 6 may alternatively be punished as contempts of court (s 6(5)).
16   Bail Act 1976, ss 6(7), 9(4).

3 Committal under the Powers of Criminal Courts Act 1973[17]

Various powers exist to commit for sentence under the 1973 Act. An offender may be committed where his conviction puts him in breach of a Crown Court community order,[18] Crown Court conditional discharge[19] or Crown Court suspended sentence.[20]

4 Committal under the Criminal Justice Act 1991;[1] prisoners on licence

Where a person released on licence is convicted by a magistrates' court of an offence punishable on indictment with imprisonment, the court may commit him for sentence to the Crown Court, in custody or on bail. That court may revoke the licence.[2]

5 Committal under the Mental Health Act 1983[3]

A magistrates' court may make an order under the Mental Health Act 1983 committing the defendant, if he is fourteen or over, to a hospital, but it cannot at the same time make an order restricting the defendant's discharge for a fixed number of years. If, therefore, the court considers that a hospital order is appropriate but that it must in the particular case be accompanied by restrictions on release, the magistrates' court may, instead of making a hospital or any other order, commit the defendant to the Crown Court to be dealt with. Committal must be in custody; if, however, the magistrates' court is satisfied that arrangements have been made by a hospital to receive the defendant in the event of the Crown Court making a hospital order, the court may itself direct the defendant to be admitted to that hospital and to be detained there, pending determination of the case by the Crown Court. The Crown Court may make a hospital order, with or without restrictions, or it may deal with the defendant in any way in which the magistrates' court could have done.

6 Incorrigible rogues

A person deemed to be an "incorrigible rogue", within the meaning of section 5 of the Vagrancy Act 1824, for one of the various causes there specified, may be committed to the "house of correction" that is, in custody or on bail to the Crown Court for sentence. The Crown Court may impose up to a year's imprisonment. A person is deemed to be a rogue within section 5 if, inter alia, he breaks or escapes out of a place of legal confinement before the expiry of his sentence or if he is apprehended as a rogue and vagabond and violently resists the constable "or other peace officer" so arresting him.

It is not of course for every offence that the defendant can be committed for sentence. Thus the defendant may be convicted of two or more offences, and prima facie liable to be committed in respect of only one. Now, however, for the sake of uniformity,

---

17   As amended by the Criminal Justice Act 1991.
18   Criminal Justice Act 1991, Sch 2, para 7(2)(b).
19   Powers of Criminal Courts Act 1973, s 1B(5).
20   *Ibid*, s 24(2).
1   Section 40(3).
2   See further, Criminal Justice Act 1991, s 40, and p 544, *ante*.
3   Section 43.

where a defendant is committed for sentence under any of the above cases, except section 43 of the Mental Health Act 1983, in respect of an offence, he may also be committed in respect of other offences.[4] If the offence in respect of which the committal is being made (the "relevant offence") is an offence triable either way, then the other offence may be any other offences whatsoever in respect of which the committing court has power to deal with him (being an offence of which he has been convicted by that or any other court).[5] If, on the other hand, the relevant offence is a summary offence, then the other offences are limited to offences of which the committing court has convicted the defendant, being offences punishable with imprisonment or disqualification from driving, or in respect of which there is in existence a suspended sentence which the committing court has power to implement.[6] Where there is a committal in respect of the "second offence", the Crown Court can only deal with the defendant as the magistrates could have done; subject to this, they have all duties and powers of sentence transferred to them, except that the magistrates' court may impose an order of interim disqualification from driving, pending the defendant's appearance at the higher court.

G   YOUTH JUSTICE

Procedures in the youth court mirror those that apply on summary trial in the magistrates' court, although a clear division between the two courts exists,[7] those who sit in the youth court are members of a youth court panel,[8] and special restrictions apply on the reporting of proceedings.[9] The child or young person will be accompanied by parent, guardian or social worker, and the proceedings will be very much more informal than those in the magistrates' court, clearly essential because of the age of the person before the court.

I   Aims and provision of youth justice

Although no fundamental differences exist in terms of procedure, youth justice raises very distinct issues which are reflected in the powers, and objectives of the youth court (and of the Crown Court when dealing with children and young persons). Section 44 of the Children and Young Persons Act 1933 requires any court, in fulfilling its duties, to take account of the welfare of the child or young person before it. More recently considerable debate has occurred as to the role and functions of the youth justice system. In a Consultation Paper,[10] the Government stated its belief that action was needed to bring about greater consistency in the approach to work with young offenders in the community and to ensure that all the relevant local agencies play a full part. It also

---

4   Criminal Justice Act 1967, s 56(1) (as substituted by the Criminal Law Act 1977, s 46). This has, of course, no application to a committal of someone in respect of a community order since such a committal does not arise out of a subsequent conviction but simply out of failure to comply with the terms of the original order.

5   This could arise where the offender (if an adult) had been convicted of offences by other magistrates' courts and those courts had remitted him to the committing court to be dealt with for those offences under s 39 of the Magistrates' Courts Act.

6   Under s 24(1) of the Powers of Criminal Courts Act 1973.

7   See generally Chapter 8.

8   *Ibid.*

9   See p 182, *ante.*

10   *No More Excuses – A New Approach to Tackling Youth Crime in England and Wales*, Cm 3809 (1997).

believed that the youth justice system should seek to prevent crime. For that reason, section 37 of the Crime and Disorder Act 1998 states that:

"It shall be the principal aim of the youth justice system to prevent offending by children and young persons."

By section 37(2) it shall be the duty of all persons and bodies carrying out functions in relation to the youth justice system to have regard to that aim. This is a broad statement of an overall duty that will apply not only to local authorities, health authorities, probation services, voluntary agencies, the police, but also to the courts in dealing with young offenders after conviction.

The role of local authorities in establishing youth offending teams and creating youth justice strategies should be noted. Each local authority is under a duty to secure that, to such extent as is appropriate for their area, all youth justice services are available there,[11] performed in partnership with other agencies such as the police. Local Authorities will operate within the overall guidance given by a new Youth Justice Board.[12] This will comprise 10, 11 or 12 members, appointed by the Home Secretary, and who will include persons with extensive recent experience of the youth justice system. Its functions are set out by section 42(5) of the Crime and Disorder Act, and include:

(a) the monitoring of the operation of the youth justice and the provision of youth justice services;
(b) advising the Home Secretary on the operation of that system and the provision of such services; how the principal aim of that system might most effectively be pursued; the content of any national standards he may see fit to set with respect to the provision of such services, or the accommodation in which children and young persons are kept in custody; and the steps that might be taken to prevent offending by children and young persons;
(c) the monitoring and collection of information about the youth justice system and the provision of services by local authorities;
(d) the identification and promotion of good practice in the context of the operation of the youth justice system and the provision of youth justice services, the prevention of offending by children and young persons; and in respect of working with children and young persons who are or are at risk of becoming offenders.

The new youth justice teams, which will be introduced following pilot studies, are intended to be an important element in the strategy to deal with youth offending introduced by the Crime and Disorder Act 1998. At least one team will be established in each local authority area, and will include at least one probation officer, local authority social worker, police officer, nominee of a health authority and of the local education authority. These youth justice teams will be under a duty to co-ordinate the provision of youth justice services within the local authority area, and to carry out such functions as are assigned to the team in the local authority's youth justice plan made under section 41.[13] Not only is it intended that youth offending teams should co-ordinate local provision relating to work with young offenders, but they also play a key role in the reprimand and caution system introduced by the 1998 Act, and in respect of various of the orders that may be made by a court when dealing with young offenders. Their

11   1998 Acts, s 38.
12   *Ibid*, s 41.
13   *Supra*.

primary functions are likely to include report-writing for courts, the preparation of reparation or action plans, and the supervision of young offenders within the community, based upon an inter-agency partnership philosophy.[14]

2   Imprisonment

The powers of a youth court to sentence a young person to detention are limited. The Crown Court, following trial on indictment, has various powers. Section 53 of the Children and Young Persons Act 1933 prescribes a mandatory detention during Her Majesty's Pleasure for conviction for murder committed by an offender under 18 at the time of the offence, and a term of imprisonment for certain specified offences of seriousness, where the court is satisfied that no other method of dealing with the case is appropriate. However, the powers of the youth court have been limited to detention in a young offenders' institution: by section 1A of the Criminal Justice Act 1982, the sentence that a court shall pass (apart from where section 8 of the 1982 Act or section 53 of the 1933 Act apply) is a term of detention in a young offenders' institution. The maximum period of such detention that a youth court has power to impose corresponds with its maximum power of imprisonment for an adult, viz. six months or twelve months for consecutive sentences.[15] It is for this reason that section 37(1) of the Magistrates' Courts Act 1980 provides:

"where a person who is not less than 15 nor more than 17 years old is convicted by a magistrates' court[16] of an offence punishable on conviction on indictment with a term of imprisonment exceeding six months, then if the court is of opinion that he should be sentenced to a greater term of detention in a young offender institution than it has power to impose the court may commit him in custody or on bail to the Crown Court for sentence."

Because an offender aged less than 18 could not be sentenced to a term of detention exceeding 12 months in any event,[17] this power of committal has been of limited application.

In respect of offenders aged under 15, no power of detention has existed, other than to require detention in secure accommodation under a supervision order.[18] However, the availability of local authority secure accommodation has been limited. The Crime (Sentences) Act 1997 introduced a new custodial sentence for 12- to 14-year-old offenders, namely the secure training order.[19] This provision was severely criticised, and never brought into effect. It has now been repealed and replaced with a new order, the detention and training order. Section 60 of the Crime and Disorder Act 1998 allows a court to sentence a young offender to a detention and training order requiring the offender to be subject to a period of detention and training, followed by a period of supervision. Where a child or young person is convicted of an offence which is punishable with imprisonment in the case of a person aged 21 or over, and the court is satisfied that a custodial sentence is justified by the seriousness of the offence or the

---

14   Consultation Paper, *op cit*; see also Morgan Report *Safer Communities: the Local Delivery of Crime Prevention through the Partnership Approach* (1991)

15   Magistrates' Courts Act 1980, s 133 (as amended).

16   But an adult magistrates' court must remit the case to the youth court for sentence: Children and Young Persons Act 1969, s 7(8).

17   Magistrates' Courts Act 1980, s 24(3).

18   Children and Young Persons Act 1969, s 12D.

19   1997 Act, ss 1–4.

need to protect the public,[20] the sentence that the court is to pass is a detention and training order. This replaces the order of detention in a young offenders' institution and applies to those aged 12 to 17. The Act in fact grants power to extend the order to cover 10- and 11-year olds, but this provision is not, for the moment, to be implemented.[1] There are also pre-conditions on the imposition of the order on certain offenders: in the case of an offender under the age of 15 at the time of the conviction, the court must be of the opinion that he is a persistent offender; in the case of an offender under the age of 12 at that time, the court must consider that only a custodial sentence would be adequate to protect the public from further offending by him; and the offence was committed on or after such date as the Home Secretary may appoint.

A detention and training order is an order that the offender in respect of whom it is made shall be subject, for the term specified in the order, to a period of detention and training followed by a period of supervision. The term of a detention and training order shall be 4, 6, 8, 10, 12, 18, or 24 months. Thus the length of sentence that a youth court may impose has been increased. The order will be served in such secure accommodation as may be determined by the Secretary of State or by such other person as may be authorised by him for that purpose. That could be a young offenders' institution, a secure training centre,[2] or in local authority secure accommodation. The period of detention is half the length of the order.[3] The other half of the order is a period of supervision by a probation officer, local authority social worker or member of a youth offending team.[4] By section 73(1) where a detention and training order is in force in respect of an offender and it appears on information to a justice of the peace acting for a relevant petty sessions area that the offender is in breach of the order, a summons may be issued, and the youth court may order the offender to be detained, in such secure accommodation as the Home Secretary may determine, for such period, not exceeding the shorter of three months or the remainder of the term of the detention and training order, as the court may specify; or impose on the offender a fine not exceeding level 3 on the standard scale.

3   Punishment or supervision in the community

A range of community or other orders exists and is available in respect of young offenders. These include probation orders (in respect of offenders aged 16 or over), community service orders (in respect of offenders aged 16 or over), combination orders, supervision orders and attendance sentence orders.[5] To these existing orders must be added new orders introduced by the Crime and Disorder Act 1998. These include a reparation order, a sentence requiring a young offender to make reparation to the victim of the offence or a person otherwise affected by it, or to the community at large.[6] The order is intended to help show young offenders the harm which they have done to the community and to their victims, and enable the courts to impose punishments which make some amends to the victim, or to the community generally. Another new order is the action plan order.[7] This requires a young offender to comply with an action plan intended to address his offending behaviour. The intention is that the action plan order

---

20   See p 538, *ante*.
1   See s 60(1), (4).
2   See 1997 Act, ss 5–12.
3   1998 Act, s 73.
4   As to which, see p 577, *ante*.
5   Criminal Justice Act 1982, s 1.
6   Crime and Disorder Act 1998, s 67.
7   See 1998 Act, s 69.

should be a new kind of community penalty – one which provides the opportunity for a short but intensive programme of work with the young offender constructed by or on behalf of the youth offending team, in consultation with the offender's parents, to tackle the causes of offending at an early stage.

4   Other orders

A youth court may fine a young offender an amount not exceeding £1,000, and may order the fine to be paid by a parent or guardian.[8] It may impose absolute or conditional discharges,[9] make compensation orders[10] or impose disqualifications.[11]

H   APPEALS FOLLOWING SUMMARY TRIAL

A defendant convicted by a magistrates' court may appeal either:

(1) to the Crown Court, and thence by way of case stated to the Queen's Bench Division of the High Court; or
(2) by case stated to the Queen's Bench Division of the High Court;
(3) from the Queen's Bench Divisional Court to the House of Lords, in certain circumstances.

In addition to those rights of appeal there is the possibility of applying for judicial review. Each of these will be considered in turn.

I   Appeal to the Crown Court

Where the defendant has been convicted in the magistrates' court of either a summary offence or an either way offence tried summarily he may appeal to the Crown Court, if he pleaded guilty against his sentence only, or if he pleaded not guilty against both conviction and sentence.[12] It will be seen that there is an express statutory prohibition against an appeal against conviction if the defendant pleaded guilty. This may be contrasted with the position following trial on indictment, where, as already noted,[13] there is nothing in the Criminal Appeal Act to prevent an appeal against conviction to the Court of Appeal even if the defendant pleaded guilty. It has been observed that the judges have laid down that appeals against conviction following a plea of guilty will only be entertained by the Court of Appeal in certain exceptional circumstances; so in the case of appeals to the Crown Court also, the judges have given a construction to the statute which evades the effect of the exact words used by Parliament, but on this occasion in favour of the defendant. It has been held that to make a plea of guilty binding and effective it must be unambiguous;[14] if therefore the defendant says the actual word "guilty" but adds to it a statement which, if true, amounts to a defence to the charge,

---

8   Children and Young Person Act 1933, s 55, as amended by Criminal Justice Act 1991, s 57.
9   See p 554, *ante*.
10   See p 554, *ante*.
11   See p 554, *ante*.
12   Magistrates' Courts Act 1980, s 108(1).
13   See p 548, *ante*.
14   *R v Durham Quarter Sessions, ex parte Virgo* [1952] 2 QB 1; [1952] 1 All ER 466.

or if from the circumstances it is clear that he is denying the charge but has pleaded guilty through ignorance of the law, a plea of guilty accepted in these circumstances is a nullity.[15] The Crown Court can, therefore, hear an appeal against the "conviction" which is equally a nullity, and under powers presently to be considered can remit the case to the magistrates with an expression of opinion that a plea of not guilty ought to be entered. Where on the other hand there has been a deliberate and unequivocal plea of guilty, no appeal against conviction can be entertained.[16]

The expression "sentence" includes any order made on conviction by a magistrates' court, with an exception in respect of an order for absolute or conditional discharge, although if on a later date sentence is passed in respect of the offence for which the order for conditional discharge was made, that is following "breach" of the order, there may be:

(1) an appeal against that later sentence;
(2) an order for the payment of costs;
(3) an order for the destruction of an animal, made under the Protection of Animals Act 1911; and
(4) any order, if the court has no discretion as to the making of the order or its terms, for example if the court is bound to order endorsement of a driving licence.[17] It has already been noted that there is no appeal against a committal for sentence, in the cases already discussed in which there may be such a committal, although there may be an appeal against the conviction on which the committal is based.

There is a right of appeal against an order to enter into recognisances to keep the peace or be of good behaviour,[18] and this right exists where such an order has been made following acquittal.[19]

With limited exceptions only the defendant may appeal. The procedure is that an appeal must be commenced by giving notice of appeal, to the clerk of the magistrates court, and to the other party, within 21 days after the day on which the decision of the magistrates' court was given (meaning the day on which sentence is passed if there is an adjournment of the case after conviction). The Crown Court may extend the time, either in relation to a notice not yet given or to a notice already given but out of time.

Proceedings before the Crown Court on an appeal against conviction take the form of a complete rehearing of the case;[20] the prosecution must open the case and call its witnesses afresh and either side may introduce fresh evidence without any leave. This is of course in sharp contrast to proceedings in the Court of Appeal. The Crown Court may confirm, reverse or vary the decision of the magistrates' court,[1] or remit the case with an expression of their opinion;[2] as already seen this latter procedure will be appropriate where an "equivocal" plea of guilty has been entered, which in all the circumstances the Crown Court considers should have been treated as a plea of not guilty. As regards appeals against sentence, the Crown Court may impose any sentence which the magistrates' court could have passed, whether more or less severe than that which they actually passed. The court may also do this if the appeal is against conviction

15   *R v Blandford Justices, ex parte G* [1967] 1 QB 82; [1966] 1 All ER 1021.
16   *P Foster (Haulage) Ltd v Roberts* [1978] 2 All ER 751.
17   Magistrates' Courts Act 1980, s 108(3).
18   Magistrates' Courts (Appeals from Binding Over Orders) Act 1956.
19   *Shaw v Hamilton* [1982] 2 All ER 718; [1982] 1 WLR 1308.
20   Supreme Court Act 1981, s 48. Although the prosecution cannot alter the case by amending the information (*Garfield v Maddocks* [1974] QB 7; [1973] 2 All ER 303).
1   Supreme Court Act 1981, s 48(2)(a).
2   *Ibid*, s 48(2)(b).

only.[3] Again, there is a sharp contrast between appeals to the Crown Court and appeals to the Court of Appeal following trial on indictment, since the Court of Appeal never has had the power to interfere with the sentence in any way if the appeal is against conviction only and, in addition, cannot now increase sentence;[4] the Crown Court can do both. Finally, the Crown Court may:

> "make such other order in the matter as the court thinks just, and by such order exercise any power which the said authority might have exercised."[5]

The wording is liberal, but it was held[6] on an almost identical provision in the previous legislation, that quarter sessions had no power to vary the sentence by quashing the sentence passed at the magistrates' court and committing to itself for sentence. The reason lies in the point already noted[7] that committal for sentence is not itself a sentence; if therefore magistrates elect to sit as a sentencing court instead of as a committing court quarter sessions could not go behind that election. Their power was to interfere with a sentence, not a decision as to whether the defendant should be committed or sentenced. This is presumably still true for the Crown Court.

If the appeal is against sentence only it may proceed on the basis of the facts relevant to sentence produced before the magistrates, if counsel for the appellant agrees to that course; there will then be no need for any evidence whatever to be called before the Crown Court. The same strictness of proof is not demanded in matters relevant to sentence as in matters relevant to conviction. In fact proceedings on an appeal against sentence normally take the same course as if the defendant had just been convicted, or had pleaded guilty, before the court.[8]

From the Crown Court a further appeal lies by way of case stated to the Queen's Bench Division of the High Court; this will be considered below.

2   Appeal by case stated to the Queen's Bench Division from magistrates' courts and the Crown Court

a   Magistrates' courts and youth courts

Any person who was a party to proceedings before a magistrates' court (or youth court) or (although not a party) is aggrieved by the conviction, order, determination or other proceeding may appeal against the proceeding on the ground that it is wrong in law or in excess of jurisdiction by applying to the magistrates' court to state a case for the opinion of a divisional court of the Queen's Bench Division of the High Court.[9] The power to appeal by way of case stated is not normally a proper way of challenging a

---

3   *Ibid,* s 9(4). However the Crown Court cannot impose a sentence which the magistrates could not have imposed. Thus an unrepresented defendant who has not previously been sentenced to imprisonment cannot (subject to minor exceptions) be sentenced to imprisonment (Powers of Criminal Courts Act 1973, s 21(1)). Accordingly, on appeal in such a case, the Crown Court cannot impose a sentence of imprisonment even though the accused is legally represented on his appeal: *R v Birmingham Justices, ex parte Wyatt* [1975] 3 All ER 897; [1976] 1 WLR 260.
4   See p 557, *ante.*
5   Supreme Court Act 1981, s 48(2)(c). Note, in addition, the provisions as to ordering questions to be referred to the European Court for preliminary ruling (Crown Court (References to the European Court) Rules 1972); see p 117, *ante.*
6   In *R v Bullock* [1964] 1 QB 481; [1963] 3 All ER 506.
7   See p 572, *ante.*
8   See p 552, *ante.*
9   Magistrates' Courts Act 1980, s 111(1).

sentence that has been imposed, the proper procedure for which is appeal to the Crown Court.[10] Only where the sentence is, by any acceptable standard "astonishing" will proceedings by way of case stated be entertained.[11]

Thus, either the defendant or the prosecutor in a criminal case may make application for a case to be stated. Application may also be made by a person aggrieved, but:

"the words 'person aggrieved' do not really mean a man who is disappointed of a benefit which he might have received if some other order had been made (still less does it mean someone having a merely sympathetic interest in the proceedings). A 'person aggrieved' must be a man who has suffered a legal grievance, a man against whom a decision has been pronounced which has wrongfully deprived him of something, or wrongfully refused him something, or wrongfully affected his title to something."[12]

A party to proceedings who has succeeded in part only may appeal against the incompleteness of his success. Executors of a person who has died since the hearing of the case in the magistrates' court are "interested", at any rate if a fine has been imposed, since the money to pay this would come out of the estate of the deceased; they may accordingly bring an appeal by way of case stated.[13] If the deceased had been sentenced to imprisonment the executors appear not to be "interested".[14]

Application must be made in writing, within 21 days after the day on which the decision of the magistrates' court was given,[15] again, if the magistrates adjourn after conviction, the day on which sentence is actually passed is the first day on which time begins to run.[16] The application should be delivered to the clerk of the magistrates' court whose decision is being questioned or sent to him by post; the names of the magistrates constituting the court do not have to be given and it is therefore immaterial that there is an error in their names.[17]

The application must identify the point of law on which the opinion of the High Court is sought.[18]

The magistrates may refuse to state a case only on the ground that the application is in their opinion frivolous, and may not refuse to state a case if the application is made by or under the direction of the Attorney-General, even in the unlikely event of such an application being considered frivolous.[19] On refusal the magistrates must give the applicant a certificate of refusal if he so requires; he may then apply to the High Court for an order of mandamus directing the justices to state a case.[20] On the making of the application, whether granted or refused, the applicant loses his right to appeal to the Crown Court.[1]

---

10 *Tucker v Director of Public Prosecutions* [1992] 4 All ER 901.
11 *Ibid*, per Pill J.
12 *Ex parte Sidebotham* (1880) 14 Ch D 458, at 465, per James LJ, described as "the best definition of the expression 'aggrieved'" in *R v London Sessions, ex parte Westminster Corporation* [1951] 2 KB 508, at 511; [1951] 1 All ER 1032, at 1033, per Lord Goddard CJ.
13 *Hodgson v Lakeman* [1943] 1 KB 15. *Aliter* in an appeal following trial on indictment: *R v Jefferies* [1969] 1 QB 120; [1968] 3 All ER 238.
14 *R v Rowe* [1955] 1 QB 573; [1955] 2 All ER 234.
15 Magistrates' Courts Act 1980, s 111(2), (3).
16 *Ibid.*
17 *R v Oxford (Bullingdon) Justices, ex parte Bird* [1948] 1 KB 100.
18 Magistrates' Courts Rules 1981, r 76(1).
19 Magistrates' Courts Act 1980, s 111(5).
20 Magistrates' Courts Act 1980, s 111(6).
1   *Ibid*, s 111(4).

A "case" will normally contain a statement of the information as laid, the facts found, the contentions of the parties, the cases cited, the decision and the question or questions for the decision of the High Court. If one or other of the parties is contending that there was no evidence on which the magistrates could come to their decision, a statement of the evidence should be included. This form, originally settled by Lord Goddard CJ, should always be used. The case may be stated by all the justices whose decision is questioned or by any two of them[2] and may be stated in relation to a number of different prosecutions, even against different defendants on different days, provided that they raise precisely the same point. Under no circumstances should the case state that the decision was that of a majority, if that was the position.[3] The case should in any event be submitted to both parties for their consideration and in the event of any difficulty it should be left to the parties themselves to produce a draft and submit it to the magistrates for their consideration.[4] If, in spite of this, a party to an appeal considers that the facts have been improperly stated in the case he may apply to the Queen's Bench Division for the case to be remitted to the justices for restatement of the facts, the application being accompanied by an affidavit setting out the facts which it is alleged should go in the case.[5] Periods of 21 days are allowed for delivering the draft case to the parties, for the parties to make representations and for the justices to prepare the final case.[6] These time-limits are not inflexible and may be extended, but in such event a written statement of the reasons for the delay must accompany the final case.[7]

On the hearing the court will hear and determine the questions of law arising, after argument by counsel for the parties. The court may allow argument on a point not raised in the court below or even take such a point itself,[8] provided that in each case the point is one of pure law, not requiring any evidence. The magistrates themselves may file an affidavit, setting out the grounds of the decision and any facts which they may consider to have a bearing on the issues;[9] in view of the existence of the case this procedure will rarely be appropriate. Unless misconduct is alleged there is no need for the justices to be represented by counsel. The court may reverse, affirm or amend the decision in respect of which the case has been stated, or may remit the matter to the magistrates with its opinion, or make such other order as it sees fit.[10]

b   The Crown Court

The Crown Court may also state a case for the opinion of the High Court. Either party to any order, judgment or other decision of the Crown Court, other than one relating solely to trial on indictment, may apply for a case to be stated on the ground that the decision is wrong in law or in excess of jurisdiction.[11] Thus, either party to an appeal

2   Magistrates' Courts Rules 1981, r 78(2).
3   *More O'Ferrall Ltd v Harrow Urban District Council* [1947] KB 66, at 70; [1946] 2 All ER 489, at 491.
4   *Cowlishaw v Chalkley* [1955] 1 All ER 367n, [1955] 119 JP 171.
5   *Spicer v Warbey* [1953] 1 All ER 284; [1953] 1 WLR 334.
6   Magistrates' Courts Rules 1981, rr 77, 78.
7   *Ibid*, r 79.
8   *Whitehead v Haines* [1965] 1 QB 200; [1964] 2 All ER 530.
9   Review of Justices Decisions Act 1872.
10   Summary Jurisdiction Act 1857, s 6. If a question arises which is appropriate to be referred to the European Court for a preliminary ruling (as to which, see p 117, *ante*) the court may, of its own motion or on application, make an order whereupon proceedings will be stayed pending receipt of the ruling, unless the divisional court otherwise orders: RSC, Ord 114. A rehearing is only appropriate where a fair trial is still possible; cf *Griffith v Jenkins* [1992] 2 AC 76; [1992] 1 All ER 65 in which case the House of Lords laid down guidelines as to the circumstances in which the power to order a rehearing should be exercised.
11   Supreme Court Act 1981, s 28. Certain decisions of the Crown Court are made final; see s 28(2)(b).

from the magistrates' court, against conviction or sentence may apply, as (apparently) may a person sentenced at the Crown Court after committal for sentence from a magistrates' court. These provisions are in several respects an extension of the old law; however, a person aggrieved by the Crown Court's decision, but not a party, still has no right of appeal. Application should be made in writing to the appropriate officer of the Crown Court within 21 days after the decision; again, the Crown Court may only refuse to state a case if the application is considered frivolous.[12] The powers of the Queen's Bench Division appear to be the same as those exercisable on an appeal from the magistrates.[13]

3   Appeal to the House of Lords

Finally it should be noted that an appeal to the House of Lords may be made from the divisional court of the Queen's Bench Division, subject to the same conditions as those governing appeals from the Court of Appeal in the case of trial on indictment.[14] Thus there must be a certificate from the divisional court that a point of law of general public importance is involved in its decision and either the divisional court or the House of Lords must give leave to appeal on the ground that the point is one which ought to be considered by the House of Lords. In this way a summary offence may be considered by four courts; the magistrates' court, the Crown Court, the divisional court of the Queen's Bench Division and the House of Lords.[15]

I   JUDICIAL REVIEW

Magistrates' courts and the Crown Court, in the exercise of their jurisdiction over summary offences, are inferior courts and therefore their proceedings are amenable to judicial review by the High Court.[16] This procedure may be appropriate where there is no right of appeal. Thus, for example, it has been noted[17] that there is no right of appeal from an order for the payment of costs; nevertheless the High Court has on *Wednesbury* principles[18] been prepared to quash an order for costs which was so far outside the normal sum imposed as to involve an error of law.[19] Similarly, following an appeal against sentence from a magistrates' court to the Crown Court, there is no further appeal (except by way of case stated if a point of law is involved); nevertheless

---

12   Crown Court Rules 1982, r 26.
13   The case of *Harris, Simon & Co Ltd v Manchester City Council* [1975] 1 All ER 412; [1975] 1 WLR 100 demonstrated a little known legal oddity whereby under the Manchester General Improvement Act 1851 an objection to the Manchester City Council's resolution to stop up two streets was made by way of appeal to the Crown Court (as successor to the jurisdiction of quarter sessions) where the objection is heard as an appeal by judge and jury. Since juries do not make detailed findings of fact, the divisional court on an appeal by way of case stated approached the case on the basis that the appeal could succeed only if the judge had misdirected the jury or if their conclusion was perverse, in the sense of being a conclusion which no reasonable jury could have reached. This instance of an appeal by way of case stated of the verdict of a jury appears to be unique.
14   Administration of Justice Act 1960, s 1.
15   *Spicer v Holt* [1977] AC 987; [1976] 3 All ER 71 is a case in which this happened. It might, in addition, be considered by the European Court, to the extent that a question arising in the proceedings was referred to that court for a preliminary ruling; see p 112, *ante*.
16   See p 145, *ante* for details of this jurisdiction and procedure.
17   See p 145, *ante*.
18   As to which see p 146, *ante*.
19   *R v Tottenham Justices, ex parte Joshi* [1982] 2 All ER 507; [1982] 1 WLR 631.

in *R v St Albans Crown Court, ex parte Cinnamond*[20] a disqualification of 18 months for careless driving, although within the jurisdiction of the court, was quashed as being so far outside the normal sentence imposed by courts for this offence as to enable the divisional court to hold that it must have involved an error of law.

20   [1981] QB 480; [1981] 1 All ER 802.

Index